Blackstone's

Police Investigators' Manual

Blackstone's
Police Investigators' Manual

2022

Paul Connor
Glenn Hutton
David Johnston
Elliot Gold

OXFORD
UNIVERSITY PRESS

OXFORD
UNIVERSITY PRESS

Great Clarendon Street, Oxford, OX2 6DP,
United Kingdom

Oxford University Press is a department of the University of Oxford.
It furthers the University's objective of excellence in research, scholarship,
and education by publishing worldwide. Oxford is a registered trade mark of
Oxford University Press in the UK and in certain other countries

© Oxford University Press 2021

The moral rights of the authors have been asserted

First Edition published in 1998
Twenty-third Edition published in 2020
Twenty-fourth Edition published in 2021

Impression: 2

Public sector information reproduced under Open Government Licence v3.0
(http://www.nationalarchives.gov.uk/doc/open-government-licence/open-government-licence.htm)

Published in the United States of America by Oxford University Press
198 Madison Avenue, New York, NY 10016, United States of America

British Library Cataloguing in Publication Data
Data available

Library of Congress Control Number
Data available

ISBN 978–0–19–284813–0

DOI: 10.1093/law/9780192848130.001.0001

Printed and bound by CPI Group (UK) Ltd, Croydon, CR0 4YY

Contents

PART 1   General Principles, Police Powers and Procedures

How to Use *Blackstone's Police Investigators' Manual 2022*

The National Investigators' Examination (NIE) contains questions based solely on the material within Parts One to Four of the *Blackstone's Police Investigators' Manual*. Part Five contains material for Immigration Enforcement Investigators and National Crime Agency (NCA) Investigators, whilst Part Six is for National Crime Agency (NCA) Investigators only. Please see below for further information on the different candidate groups.

Any feedback regarding content or editorial matters in this Manual can be emailed to police.uk@oup.com.

Police Investigators

All police candidates taking the NIE exam in 2022 are required to study the material contained in Parts One, Two, Three and Four of the Manual only. This includes all the PACE and Disclosure Codes of Practice extracts contained in Part One—see further information on grey lined material below.

Police NIE examinations taking place in 2022 will be based solely on the material contained in Parts One to Four.

National Crime Agency (NCA) Investigators

All NCA candidates taking the NIE are required to study the material contained in Parts One, Two, Three and Four of the Manual. NCA candidates taking the NCA Specific Powers Examination are required to study the material contained within Parts Five and Six. These Parts cover immigration, customs and cross-border offences.

Immigration Enforcement (IE) Investigators

All IE candidates taking the Immigration Enforcement Investigators' Examination are required to study the selected paragraphs contained in Parts One, Two, Three and Five of the manual as laid out in the Immigration Enforcement Investigators' Examination Rules and Syllabus.

Use of a Grey Line to Denote Legislation

Codes of Practice, specifically PACE and the Disclosure Code of Practice issued under the Criminal Procedure and Investigations Act 1996, are now incorporated within chapters in the main body of the Manual. A thick grey line down the margin is used to denote text that is an extract of the Code itself (i.e. the actual wording of the legislation) and does not form part of the general commentary of the chapter.

Table of Cases

Table of Legislation

Table of Statutory Instruments

Table of Codes of Practice

Table of European Legislation

Table of International Treaties and Conventions

General Principles, Police Powers and Procedures

1.1 | *Mens Rea* (State of Mind)

1.1.1 Introduction

Any analysis of law begins with an examination of *mens rea* (state of mind) and *actus reus* (criminal conduct). These concepts are fundamental to understanding all offences and the idea of criminal liability generally

Mens rea alone will not amount to an offence; thinking about committing a crime is not committing a crime. In fact, the default position is that the application of the mind is essential for liability to exist as acts (or omissions) alone cannot amount to a crime unless they are accompanied by '*mens rea*' at the time of the act (or omission).

It is therefore vital to consider, among others, what is meant by terms such as 'intent' and 'recklessness'.

1.1.2 Intent

'Intent' is a word often used in relation to consequences. If a defendant intends something to happen, he/she wishes to bring about a consequence. In some offences, say burglary under s. 9(1)(a) of the Theft Act 1968, the defendant's *intention* may be very clear; he/she may enter a house as a trespasser *intending* to steal property inside.

However, there will often be consequences following a defendant's actions that he/she did not *intend* to happen. What if, in the above burglary, the householder came across the burglar and suffered a heart attack? It might be reasonable to suggest that it was the defendant's behaviour that had brought about the situation (**see chapter 1.2**). The defendant, however, may argue that, although he/she intended to break in and steal, there had never been any *intention* of harming the occupant. At this point, you might say that the defendant should have thought about that before breaking into someone else's house. This brings in the concept of *foresight*, a concept that has caused the courts some difficulty over the years—for several reasons.

First, there is the Criminal Justice Act 1967 which says (under s. 8) that a court/jury, in determining whether a person has committed an offence:

- shall not be bound in law to infer that he intended or foresaw a result of his actions by reason only of its being a natural and probable consequence of those actions; but
- shall decide whether he did intend or foresee that result by reference to all the evidence, drawing such inferences from the evidence as appear proper in the circumstances.

Secondly, there is the body of case law which has developed around the area of 'probability', culminating in two cases in the House of Lords (*R* v *Moloney* [1985] AC 905 and *R* v *Hancock* [1986] AC 455). Following those cases, it is settled that foresight of the probability of a consequence does not amount to an intention to bring that consequence about, *but may be evidence of it.*

So you cannot claim that a defendant *intended* a consequence of his/her behaviour simply because it was virtually certain to occur. What you can do is to put evidence of the defendant's foresight of that probability before a court, which may infer an intention from it. Such an argument would go like this:

- at the time of the criminal act there was a *probability* of a consequence;

- the greater the probability of a consequence, the more likely it is that the defendant *foresaw* that consequence;
- if the defendant foresaw that consequence, the more likely it is that the defendant *intended* it to happen.

Whether or not a defendant intended a particular consequence will be a question of fact left to the jury (or magistrate(s) where appropriate). In murder cases (**see chapter 2.1**), where death or serious bodily harm was a *virtual certainty* from the defendant's actions and he/she had appreciated that to be the case, the jury *may* infer that the defendant intended to bring about such consequences (*R v Nedrick* [1986] 1 WLR 1025). Therefore, where the defendant threw a three-month-old baby down onto a hard surface in a fit of rage, the jury *might* have inferred both that death/serious bodily harm was a virtual certainty from the defendant's actions and that he must have appreciated that to be the case; they should therefore have been directed by the trial judge accordingly (*R v Woollin* [1999] 1 AC 82).

Finally, the relevant intent may have been formed, not of the defendant's own volition, but influenced in some way by other external factors. An example is where the defendant's thinking is affected by duress (as to which, **see para. 1.4.3**).

1.1.2.1 Offences of 'Specific' and 'Basic' Intent

Crimes of 'specific' intent are only committed where the defendant is shown to have had a particular intention to bring about a specific consequence at the time of the criminal act. Murder is such a crime as is burglary with intent (Theft Act 1968, s. 9(1)(a)). The common feature with these offences is that the *intention* of the offender is critical—without that intent, the offence does not exist.

Other criminal offences require no further proof of anything other than the 'basic' intention to bring about the given circumstances. For example, the offence of maliciously wounding or inflicting grievous bodily harm (Offences Against the Person Act 1861, s. 20) or taking a conveyance (Theft Act 1968, s. 12(1)).

The important difference between offences of specific and basic intent is that, in the case of the latter, *recklessness* will often be enough to satisfy the mental element.

Whether an offence is one of 'specific' or 'basic' intent connects to the issues around voluntary or involuntary intoxication.

1.1.2.2 Intoxication: Voluntary or Involuntary

Intoxication potentially removes the necessary *mens rea* required for a defendant to commit an offence (intoxication is not a defence—if it were, a significant proportion of criminal behaviour would go unpunished).

Intoxication can be divided into two categories; voluntary intoxication (you got yourself in that condition) and involuntary intoxication (you are not responsible for getting in that condition). The distinction is important when considering whether the offence alleged is one of 'specific' or 'basic' intent.

Where an offence is a specific intent offence, such as murder, defendants who were voluntarily intoxicated at the time the offence was committed may be able to show they were so intoxicated that they were incapable of forming the *mens rea* required for the offence. An individual who is voluntarily intoxicated *would not* be able to say this if accused of an offence of basic intent as the courts have accepted that a defendant is still capable of forming basic intent even when completely inebriated (*DPP v Majewski* [1977] AC 443).

Where the offence is a basic intent offence, such as s. 47 assault, defendants who were involuntarily intoxicated (perhaps because their drink had been spiked) at the time of the offence may be able to say that they lacked the *mens rea* for that basic intent offence.

If defendants simply misjudge the amount or strength of intoxicants which they take, this will not be regarded as involuntary intoxication (*R* v *Allen* [1988] Crim LR 698). So if a defendant knowingly drinks beer but is unaware that the beer has been laced with vodka, this will still be 'voluntary' intoxication. Similarly, if defendants can be shown to have actually formed the required *mens rea* necessary for the offence, intoxication (voluntary or involuntary) will not be available as a drunken intent is still an 'intent' (*R* v *Kingston* [1995] 2 AC 355).

The source of the intoxication can be drink or drugs. In the latter case, however, the courts will consider the known effects of the drug in deciding whether or not defendants had formed the required degree of *mens rea*; the characteristics of the drugs will be relevant in determining whether defendants behaved recklessly in taking them.

Where the defendant forms a 'mistaken belief' based on the fact that he/she is intoxicated, that belief may sometimes be raised as a defence. In cases of criminal damage where a defendant has mistakenly believed that the property being damaged is his/her own property, and that mistaken belief has arisen from the defendant's intoxicated state, the courts have accepted the defence under s. 5 of the Criminal Damage Act 1971 (*Jaggard* v *Dickinson* [1981] QB 527) (see chapter 3.10). However, this appears to be confined to the wording of that particular statute and the courts have refused to accept similar defences of mistaken, drunken belief (e.g. in *R* v *O'Grady* [1987] QB 995, where a defendant charged with murder could not rely on a mistake induced by his own voluntary intoxication and claim 'self-defence'), or where the defendant mistakenly believed that the victim of a rape was consenting to sexual intercourse. The Court of Appeal has confirmed that the decision in *O'Grady* also applies to manslaughter (*R* v *Hatton* [2005] EWCA Crim 2951).

If defendants become intoxicated in order to gain false courage to go and commit a crime, they will not be able to claim a defence of intoxication *even if the crime is one of specific intent*. This is because they have already formed the intent required and the intoxication is merely a means of plucking up 'Dutch' courage to carry it out (*Attorney-General for Northern Ireland* v *Gallagher* [1963] AC 349).

1.1.3 Recklessness

Recklessness is a state of mind that is relevant to a large number of crimes and is essentially concerned with unjustified risk-taking. Following the case of *R* v *G and R* [2003] UKHL 50, the approach taken to the interpretation of the word 'reckless' is that it will be 'subjective'.

The requirements of subjective recklessness can be found in the case of *R* v *Cunningham* [1957] 2 QB 396 and are satisfied in situations where *the defendant* foresees the consequences of his/her actions as being probable or even possible. In *G*, the House of Lords held that a person acts recklessly with respect to:

- a circumstance when he/she is *aware* of a risk that it exists or will exist;
- a result when he/she is *aware* of the risk that it will occur;

and it is, in the circumstances known to him/her, *unreasonable* to take that risk.

To establish recklessness, therefore, requires consideration of the degree of risk that is actually foreseen by the defendant of which he/she is aware and whether it was reasonable.

1.1.3.1 Awareness

Here we are concerned with what was going on in the mind of the defendant—were they aware of the risk? For example, in *G* the defendants were two children (aged 11 and 12) who set fire to some newspapers in the rear yard of a shop premises whilst camping out. The children put the burning papers under a wheelie bin and left them, expecting the small fire to burn itself out on the concrete floor of the yard. In fact, the fire spread causing around £1,000,000 of damage. The children were convicted of criminal damage under the former law ('objective' recklessness) on the basis that the fire would have been obvious to any reasonable bystander. The convictions were quashed by the House of Lords who reinstated the general subjective element described above. A reasonable bystander might well have been aware of the risk of such activity—the children were not.

1.1.3.2 Reasonableness

The risk a defendant is aware of may be small but that does not automatically mean that it is reasonable to take that risk. Each situation will be decided on its own merits, but whether the risk is reasonable or not will be decided by the court—not the defendant. What this does is to introduce an objective element into the recklessness equation but, even though that is the case, it must be stressed that recklessness is still subjective—the key question is whether the defendant was aware of the risk.

1.1.3.3 Different Crime = Different Risk

Depending on the crime, the nature of the risk the defendant needs to be aware of will change. For example, to commit an offence under s. 20 of the Offences Against the Person Act 1861 (wounding or inflicting grievous bodily harm (**see chapter 2.7**)), the defendant must unlawfully and recklessly wound or inflict grievous bodily harm on the victim. Here 'recklessness' means that the defendant was aware of the risk that *some harm* would befall the victim. If we consider simple criminal damage under s. 1(1) of the Criminal Damage Act 1971 (**see chapter 3.10**), then the risk the defendant would need to be aware of to be reckless is that property belonging to another would be damaged or destroyed.

1.1.4 Malice

The term 'malice' is particularly relevant to ss. 18, 20, 23 and 24 of the Offences Against the Person Act 1861 (offences relating to grievous bodily harm/wounding and poisoning). It *should not* be considered as one relating to ill will, spite or wickedness. 'Malice' requires either the actual intention to cause the relevant harm or at least foresight of the risk of causing *some harm* (though not the extent of the harm) to a person.

....

EXAMPLE

D throws a coin at V thinking that this will result in a small cut to V's forehead (so D has foresight that *some harm*, albeit minor, will befall V as a result of D's actions). The coin actually strikes V in the eye, causing V serious injury and the loss of sight in the eye.

It does not matter that the harm that D foresaw was minor compared to the resultant harm caused to V. D has committed a s. 20 grievous bodily harm offence because D has behaved 'maliciously'—D saw the risk of *some harm* befalling V but went on to take the risk anyway.

....

1.1.5 Wilfully

'Wilfully' is mentioned in offences such as child cruelty (s. 1 of the Children and Young Persons Act 1933). The term 'wilfully' should not be understood in a literal sense as meaning 'deliberate' or 'voluntary'. It is taken to mean intentionally or recklessly (subjective) (*Attorney-General's Reference (No. 3 of 2003)* [2005] QB 73).

1.1.6 Dishonestly

The expression 'dishonesty' is defined for certain purposes in s. 2 of the Theft Act 1968. However, it has also been extended by common law decisions of the courts (as per the decision in *Barlow Clowes* and *Royal Brunei Airlines*) and it is critical, in dealing with offences requiring proof of dishonesty (such as theft or fraud), that you identify the nature of the state of mind required and the ways in which it can be proved/disproved. For a full discussion of this concept, **see chapter 3.1**.

1.1.7 Knowing

The term 'knowing' is relevant to several offences such as s. 22 of the Theft Act 1968 (handling stolen goods). One *knows* something if one is absolutely sure that it is so. Since it is difficult to be absolutely sure of anything, it has to be accepted that a person who feels 'virtually certain' about something can equally be regarded as 'knowing' it (*R v Dunne* (1998) 162 JP 399).

1.1.8 Belief

The degree of certainty required to be experienced by an accused to create a 'belief' would appear to be the same for 'knowing'—the difference is that knowing something implies correctness of belief whereas a 'belief' could turn out to be mistaken. This is how 'belief' has been interpreted by the courts for the purposes of handling stolen goods (s. 22 of the Theft Act 1968) where it has been stressed that there is a need to distinguish belief from recklessness or suspicion and that it is not sufficient that an accused believed it to be more probable than not that the goods were stolen.

1.1.9 Negligence

Negligence is generally concerned with the defendant's compliance with the standards of reasonableness of ordinary people. The concept of negligence focuses on the consequences of the defendant's conduct rather than demanding proof of a particular state of mind at the time and ascribes some notion of 'fault' or 'blame' to the defendant who must be shown to have acted in a way that runs contrary to the expectations of the reasonable person.

The most important common law criminal offence that can be committed by negligence is manslaughter (manslaughter by gross negligence). Other offences that can be committed by negligence do not usually contain the word itself but attract that test in relation to the mental element (for example, offences involving standards of driving).

1.1.10 Strict Liability

Some offences are said to be offences of 'strict liability'. This expression generally means that there is little to prove beyond the act itself; however, in most cases it is more accurate to say that there is no need to prove *mens rea* in relation to one particular aspect of the behaviour. There have been isolated instances in which the courts have held that an offence does not require any *mens rea* to be proved. For example, in *DPP* v *H* [1997] 1 WLR 1406 it was stated that the offence of driving with excess alcohol, contrary to the Road Traffic Act 1988, s. 5 did not require proof of any *mens rea*.

Situations where strict liability is imposed are usually to enforce statutory regulation (e.g. road traffic offences), particularly where there is some social danger or concern presented by the proscribed behaviour.

As a general rule, however, there is a presumption that *mens rea* is required for a criminal offence unless Parliament clearly indicates otherwise (*B (A Minor)* v *DPP* [2000] 2 AC 428). This rule should be borne in mind, not only when approaching the rest of the material in this Manual, but also when considering criminal law in general.

1.1.11 Transferred *Mens Rea*

The state of mind required for one offence can, on occasions, be 'transferred' from the original target or victim to another. *This only operates if the crime remains the same.* In other words, a defendant cannot be convicted if he/she acted with the *mens rea* for one offence but commits the *actus reus* of another offence. In *R* v *Latimer* (1886) 17 QBD 359, the defendant lashed out with his belt at one person but missed, striking a third party instead. As it was proved that the defendant had the required *mens rea* when he swung the belt, the court held that the same *mens rea* could support a charge of wounding against any other victim injured by the same act. If the *nature of the offence* changes, then this approach will not operate. Therefore if a defendant is shown to have thrown a rock at a crowd of people intending to injure one of them, the *mens rea* required for that offence cannot be 'transferred' to an offence of criminal damage if the rock misses that person and breaks a window instead (*R* v *Pembliton* (1874) LR 2 CCR 119).

The issue of transferred *mens rea* can be important in relation to the liability of accessories (as to which, **see chapter 1.2**). If the principal's intentions are to be extended to an accessory, it must be shown that those intentions were either contemplated and accepted by that person at the time of the offence or that they were 'transferred'.

....

EXAMPLE

A person (X) encourages another (Y) to assault Z. Y decides to attack a different person instead. X will not be liable for that assault because it was not contemplated or agreed by X. If, however, in trying to assault Z, Y happens to injure a third person inadvertently, then 'transferred *mens rea*' may result in X being liable for those injuries even though X had no wish for that person to be so injured.

....

Actus Reus (Criminal Conduct)

1.2.1 Introduction

Having considered *mens rea* (state of mind), the next key element is that of the *actus reus* (criminal conduct). Many statutory offences describe the sort of behaviour that will attract liability, but there are some important general rules that also need to be considered.

For a person to be found guilty of a criminal offence you must show that he/she:

- acted in a particular way;
- failed to act in a particular way (omissions); or
- brought about a state of affairs.

This is the *actus reus* of an offence, i.e. the behavioural element of an offence.

When proving the required *actus reus*, you must show:

- that the defendant's conduct was voluntary; and
- that it occurred while the defendant still had the requisite *mens rea*.

1.2.2 Voluntary Act

This can best be understood by considering that a voluntary act is something *done* by the defendant, whereas an involuntary act is something that *happens* to a defendant. You must show that a defendant acted or omitted to act 'voluntarily'; that is, by the operation of free will.

If a person is shoved into a shop window, he/she cannot be said to be guilty of criminal damage even though he/she was the immediate physical cause of the damage. Similarly, if a person was standing in front of a window waiting to break it and someone came up and pushed that person into the window, the presence of the requisite *mens rea* would still not be enough to attract criminal liability for the damage. In each case, the person being pushed could not be said to be acting of his/her own volition in breaking the window and therefore could not perform the required *actus reus*.

This aspect of voluntariness is also important when defendants have lost control of their own physical actions. Reflexive actions are generally not classed as being willed or voluntary, hence the (limited) availability of the 'defence' of automatism (**see para. 1.2.3**).

Likewise, the *unexpected* onset of a sudden physical impairment (such as severe cramp when driving, actions when sleepwalking) can also render any linked actions 'involuntary'. If the onset of the impairment could reasonably have been foreseen (e.g. where someone is prone to blackouts), the defendant's actions may be said to have been willed in that he/she could have prevented the loss of control or at least avoided the situation (e.g. driving) which allowed the consequences to occur.

1.2.3 Automatism

Strictly speaking, automatism is not a 'defence'; it is an absence of a fundamental requirement for any criminal offence; namely, the 'criminal conduct' (*actus reus*). Criminal conduct must be voluntary and willed; it follows that if defendants have *total* loss of control over their actions, they cannot be held liable for those actions and there may be grounds to claim a defence of automatism. This view was confirmed in *R v Coley* [2013] EWCA Crim 223, where it was said that the question is not whether the accused is acting consciously or not but whether there is a 'complete destruction of voluntary control'. The best example of this defence is one where a swarm of bees flies into a car causing a reflex action by the driver resulting in an accident (an example given in *Hill v Baxter* [1958] 1 QB 277). As the driver's actions are involuntary and not sufficient to support a criminal charge, the defence of automatism would be available. Other examples might include a person inadvertently dropping and damaging property when suddenly seized by cramp or discharging a firearm as a result of an irresistible bout of sneezing.

If the loss of control is brought about by voluntary intoxication or by insanity, the defence becomes narrower.

1.2.4 Coincidence with *Mens Rea*

It must be shown that the defendant had the requisite *mens rea* at the time of carrying out the *actus reus*. However, there is no need for that 'state of mind' to remain unchanged throughout the entire commission of the offence. If a person (X) poisons another (Y) intending to kill Y at the time, it will not alter X's criminal liability if X changes his mind immediately after giving the poison or even if X does everything he can to halt its effects (*R v Jakeman* (1983) 76 Cr App R 223).

Conversely, if the *actus reus* is a continuing act, as 'appropriation' is (**see chapter 3.1**), it may begin without any particular *mens rea* but the required 'state of mind' may come later while the *actus reus* is still continuing. If this happens, whereby the *mens rea* 'catches up' with the *actus reus*, the offence is complete at the first moment that the two elements (*actus reus* and *mens rea*) unite.

For example, in a case where a motorist was directed to pull his car over to the kerb by a police officer and drove it onto the officer's foot, there was no proof that he did so deliberately. However, it was clear that he deliberately left it there after the officer told him what he had done. His conviction for assaulting the officer was upheld by the Divisional Court on the basis that there was an ongoing act, which became a criminal assault once the motorist became aware of it (*Fagan v Metropolitan Police Commissioner* [1969] 1 QB 439).

1.2.5 Omissions

Most criminal offences require a defendant to carry out some positive act before liability can be imposed. Ordinarily, there is no liability for a failure (or omission) to act unless the law specifically imposes such a DUTY on a person.

....

EXAMPLE

A sees B drowning and is able to save him by holding out his hand. A abstains from doing so in order that B may be drowned, and B is drowned. A has committed no offence.

....

Although A may have failed to save B, he did no positive act to cause B's death and, under English law, A has done nothing wrong.

However, although criminal conduct is most often associated with *actions*, occasionally liability is brought about by a failure to act. Most of the occasions where failure or omission will attract liability are where a **DUTY** *to act* has been created. Such a **DUTY** can arise from a number of circumstances, the main ones being:

D Dangerous situation created by the defendant. For example, in *R v Miller* [1983] 2 AC 161 the defendant was 'sleeping rough' and entered a building and fell asleep on a mattress while smoking a cigarette. When he awoke, he saw the mattress was smouldering but instead of calling for help or doing anything about the smouldering mattress, he simply moved into another room in the building and fell asleep. The mattress caught fire and the fire spread to the rest of the building. The defendant was convicted of arson, not for starting the fire but for failing to do anything about it.

U Under statute, contract or a person's public 'office'. Examples would include:
- Statute—a driver who is involved in a damage or injury accident fails to stop at the scene of the accident (s. 170 of the Road Traffic Act 1988), a driver who fails to cooperate with a preliminary test procedure (s. 6(6) of the Road Traffic Act 1988) or a person who does not disclose information in relation to terrorism (s. 19 of the Terrorism Act 2000).
- Contract—a crossing keeper omitted to close the gates (a job that was part of his contractual obligations) at a level crossing and a person was subsequently killed by a passing train (*R v Pittwood* (1902) 19 TLR 37).
- Public office—whilst on duty, a police officer stood aside and watched as a man was beaten to death outside a nightclub. The officer then left the scene, without calling for assistance or summoning an ambulance. For this, the officer was convicted of the common law offence of misconduct in a public office (*R v Dytham* [1979] QB 722).

T Taken it upon him/herself—the defendant voluntarily undertakes to care for another who is unable to care for him/herself as a result of age, illness or infirmity and then fails to care for that person. For example, in *R v Stone* [1977] QB 354 the defendant accepted a duty to care for her partner's mentally ill sister who subsequently died from neglect.

Y Young person—in circumstances where the defendant is in a parental relationship with a child or a young person, i.e. an obligation exists for the parent to look after the health and welfare of the child and he/she does not do so.

Whether or not there is a sufficient proximity between the defendant and the victim brought about by a duty to act will be a question of law (*R v Singh* [1999] Crim LR 582 and *R v Khan* [1998] Crim LR 830).

Having established such a duty, you must also show that the defendant has *voluntarily* omitted to act as required or that he/she has not done enough to discharge that duty. If a defendant is unable to act (e.g. because someone else has stopped him/her) or is incapable of doing more because of his/her own personal limitations (e.g. a child is drowning in a river but the parent is unable to save the child because of an inability to swim), the *actus reus* will *not* have been made out (*R v Reid* [1992] 1 WLR 793).

Some statutory offences are specifically worded to remove any doubt as to whether they can be committed by omission as well as by a positive act (e.g. torture under the Criminal Justice Act 1988, s. 134). Other offences have been held by the courts to be capable of commission by both positive acts and by omission (e.g. false accounting under the Theft Act 1968, s. 17, **see chapter 3.1**).

1.2.6 Causal Link or Chain of Causation

Once the *actus reus* has been proved, you must then show a *causal link* between it and the relevant consequences. That is, you must prove that the consequences would not have happened 'but for' the defendant's act or omission.

In a case of simple criminal damage, it may be relatively straightforward to prove this causal link: a defendant throws a brick at a window and the window is broken by the brick hitting it; the window would not have broken 'but for' the defendant's conduct. Where the link becomes more difficult to prove is when the defendant's behaviour triggers other events or aggravates existing circumstances. For example, in *R v McKechnie* [1992] Crim LR 194 the defendant attacked the victim, who was already suffering from a serious ulcer, causing him brain damage. The brain damage (caused by the assault) prevented doctors from operating on the ulcer which eventually ruptured, killing the victim. The Court of Appeal, upholding the conviction for manslaughter, held that the defendant's criminal conduct (the assault) had made a significant contribution to the victim's death even though the untreated ulcer was the actual cause of death.

In some cases, a significant delay can occur between the acts which put in train the criminal consequences. An example is where a defendant transported an accomplice to a place near to the victim's house some 13 hours before the accomplice shot and killed the victim. Despite the delay and despite the fact the accomplice had not fully made up his mind about the proposed shooting at the time he was dropped off by the defendant, there was no intervening event that diverted or hindered the planned murder (*R v Bryce* [2004] EWCA Crim 1231).

In a case which had similar facts to our 'simple damage' example above, the defendant entered a house after throwing a brick through a window. Although the defendant did not attack the occupant, an 87-year-old who died of a heart attack some hours later, the Court of Appeal accepted that there could have been a causal link between the defendant's behaviour and the death of the victim. If so, a charge of manslaughter would be appropriate (*R v Watson* [1989] 1 WLR 684).

1.2.7 Intervening Act

The causal link can be broken by a new intervening act provided that the 'new' act is 'free, deliberate and informed' (*R v Latif* [1996] 1 WLR 104).

If a drug dealer supplies drugs to another person who then kills him/herself by taking an overdose, the dealer cannot, without more, be said to have *caused* the death. Death would have been brought about by the deliberate exercise of free will by the user (*R v Kennedy* [2007] UKHL 38 (**see para. 2.1.4.1**)). The supplier is unlikely to be held liable for *causing* death in such a case unless he/she actually takes a more active part in the administering of the drug (*R v Dias* [2001] EWCA Crim 2986).

It is foreseeable that the victim of an attack or accident may require medical treatment, but it is also foreseeable that his/her injuries may be misdiagnosed or that treatment may not be carried out correctly. This is one reason why incorrect medical treatment is hardly ever categorised by the courts as amounting to an intervening act. For example, in *R v Smith* [1959] 2 QB 35 two soldiers were fighting each other when one stabbed the other with a bayonet. Other soldiers carried the injured man to a medical centre, dropping him twice on the way. An overworked doctor failed to notice that one of the injured man's lungs had been pierced and the treatment the soldier received 'might well have affected his chances of recovery'. This did not, however, break the chain of causation as the original injury was still the operating and substantial cause of death. An *exceptional* case is *R v Jordan* (1956) 40 Cr App R 152, where the defendant had stabbed the deceased, who was taken to hospital for treatment. The deceased received treatment for the injuries and recovered so that the original injury brought about by the stabbing had almost totally healed. At this time, there was a mix-up resulting in the administration of a drug (terra-mycin) after the deceased had shown he was intolerant to it (treatment described as 'palpably wrong' by the court). The court concluded that it was the medical treatment that had caused the death and not the stab wound. *R v Jordan* has been described as a very particular case, depending on its exact facts. In *Smith*, the death could still be attributed to the wound inflicted by being stabbed with a bayonet, whereas in *Jordan* the wound had largely healed and the mistreatment of the deceased was the sole cause of death. Furthermore, the mistreatment was so bizarre as to be unforeseeable. Had the victim in *Jordan* died from the first dose of antibiotics, a conviction for murder would almost certainly be upheld. This is apparent from the case of *R v Cheshire* [1991] 3 All ER 670, in which the victim was shot with a shotgun causing injury to his hip. As part of his emergency treatment, a tracheotomy was carried out. Whilst the gunshot wounds healed, there were complications regarding the tracheotomy which caused the victim to die. The defendant was convicted regarding the death as the complications were still a natural consequence of his original act (the shooting). The basic rule is that an intervening act will not generally break the causal link/chain of causation.

There is also a rule which says defendants must 'take their victims as they find them'. This means that if victims have a particular characteristic, such as a very thin skull or a very nervous disposition, which makes the consequences of an act against them much more acute, that is the defendant's bad luck. An example of this principle can be seen in *R v Harvey* [2010] EWCA Crim 1317 where, during a 'domestic tiff', the offender threw a television remote control at his wife, which hit her behind the ear. Unknown to anyone, she had an unusual weakness of the vertebral artery, which ruptured and caused her death. Save for the death, the offence charged would have been one of battery. Such characteristics (e.g. where an assault victim died after refusing a blood transfusion on religious grounds (*R v Blaue* [1975] 1 WLR 1411)) will not break the causal link.

Actions by the victim will sometimes be significant in the chain of causation, such as where a victim of a sexual assault was injured when jumping from her assailant's car in an attempt to escape (*R v Roberts* (1971) 56 Cr App R 95). Where such actions take place, the victim's behaviour will not necessarily be regarded as introducing a new intervening act. If the victim's actions are those which might reasonably be anticipated from any victim in such a situation, there will be no new and intervening act and the defendant will be responsible for the consequences flowing from them. So, in *R v Corbett* [1996] Crim LR 594, the defendant was convicted of manslaughter when a man he was assaulting was struck and killed by a car as he attempted to escape. If, however, the victim's actions are done entirely of his/her own volition or where those actions are, in the words of Stuart-Smith LJ, 'daft' (*R v Williams* [1992] 1 WLR 380), they will amount to a new intervening act and the defendant cannot be held responsible for them.

An 'act of God' or other exceptional natural event may break the chain of causation leading from the defendant's initial act, if it was the sole immediate cause of the consequences in question. Such an event must be 'of so powerful a nature that the conduct of the defendant was not a cause at all, but was merely a part of the surrounding circumstances' (*Southern Water Authority v Pegrum* [1989] Crim LR 442). If the defendant attacks his/her victim and leaves him slowly dying of his injuries, then the chain of causation may be broken if the victim is ultimately killed by a lightning bolt or a falling tree, rather than the original injuries. In contrast, routine hazards, such as seasonal rain or cold winter nights, would not have such an effect (*Alphacell Ltd v Woodward* [1972] AC 824).

1.2.8 Principals and Accessories

Once you have established the criminal conduct and the required state of mind, you must identify what degree of involvement the defendant had.

There are two ways of attracting criminal liability for an offence: either as a *principal* or an *accessory* (accessories can also be referred to as *secondary parties*).

A principal offender is one whose conduct has met all the requirements of the particular offence. An accessory is someone who helped in or brought about the commission of the offence. If an accessory 'aids, abets, counsels or procures' the commission of an offence, he/she will be treated by a court in the same way as a principal offender for an indictable offence (Accessories and Abettors Act 1861, s. 8) or for a summary offence (Magistrates' Courts Act 1980, s. 44). The expression 'aid, abet, counsel and procure' is generally used in its entirety when charging a defendant, without separating out the particular element that applies. Generally speaking, the expressions mean as follows:

- aiding = giving help, support or assistance;
- abetting = inciting, instigating or encouraging.

Each of these would usually involve the presence of the secondary party at the scene (unless, for example, part of some pre-arranged plan):

- counselling = advising or instructing;
- procuring = bringing about.

These last two activities would generally be expected to take place before the commission of the offence. These are purely guides by which to separate the elements of this concept and will not necessarily apply in all cases.

If an accessory is present at the scene of a crime when it is committed, his/her presence may amount to encouragement which would support a charge of aiding or abetting if he/she was there as part of an agreement in respect of the principal offence. This would not be the case if a person was simply passing by and watched the offence. It is not an offence to do so, as the ordinary citizen is not under a duty to prevent an offence occurring and failing to do so will not create liability as an accomplice (*R v Coney* (1882) 8 QBD 534).

What of the situation where the accessory is not present during the substantive offence? The position can be summarised as follows:

Where the principal (P) relies on acts of the accessory (D) which assist in the preliminary stages of a crime later committed in D's absence, it is necessary to prove *intentional assistance by D* in acts which D knew were steps taken by P towards the commission of the crime. Therefore the prosecution must prove:

- an act done by D;
- which *in fact* assisted the later commission of the offence;
- that D did the act deliberately realising that it was capable of assisting the offence;
- that D, at the time of doing the act, contemplated the commission of the offence by P; and
- that, when doing the act, D intended to assist P.

(*R v Bryce* [2004] EWCA Crim 1231.)

'Counselling' an offence requires no causal link (*R v Calhaem* [1985] QB 808). As long as the principal offender is aware of the 'counsellor's' advice or encouragement, the latter will be guilty as an accessory, even if the principal would have committed the offence anyway (*Attorney-General* v *Able* [1984] QB 795).

However, if you are trying to show that a defendant *procured* an offence, you must show a causal link between his/her conduct and the offence (*Attorney-General's Reference (No. 1 of 1975)* [1975] QB 773).

If the principal cannot be traced or identified, the accessory may still be liable (*Hui Chi-ming* v *The Queen* [1992] 1 AC 34). Similarly, an accessory may be convicted of procuring an offence even though the principal is acquitted or has a defence for his/her actions. This is because the principal often supplies the *actus reus* for the accessory's offence. If the accessory also has the required *mens rea*, the offence will be complete and should not be affected by the fact that there is some circumstance or characteristic preventing the principal from being prosecuted.

Additionally, if the accessory had some responsibility and the actual ability to control the actions of the principal, his/her failure to do so may attract liability (e.g. a driving instructor who fails to prevent a learner driver from driving without due care and attention (*Rubie* v *Faulkner* [1940] 1 KB 571)).

It is possible for an accomplice to change his/her mind before the criminal act is carried out. However, the exact requirements for making an effective 'withdrawal' before any liability is incurred are unclear. Evidence such as how far the proposed plan had proceeded before the withdrawal, and the amount/nature of any help or encouragement already given by the accessory, will be relevant. Simply fleeing at the last moment because someone was approaching would generally not be enough. In the absence of some overwhelming supervening event, an accessory can only avoid liability for assistance rendered to the principal offender towards the commission of the crime by acting in a way that amounts to the *countermanding* of any earlier assistance, such as a withdrawal from the common purpose. Repentance alone will not be enough (*R* v *Becerra* (1976) 62 Cr App R 212 and *R* v *Mitchell* (1999) 163 JP 75).

A person whom the law is intended to protect from certain types of offence cannot be an accessory to such offences committed against them. For example, a girl under 16 years of age is protected (by the Sexual Offences Act 2003 (**see chapter 4.4**)) from people having sexual intercourse with her. If a 15-year-old girl allows someone to have sexual intercourse with her, she cannot be charged as an accessory to the offence (*R* v *Tyrrell* [1894] 1 QB 710).

1.2.8.1 State of Mind for Accessories

Generally, the state of mind (*mens rea*) which is needed to convict an accessory is: 'proof of intention to aid as well as of knowledge of the circumstances' (*National Coal Board* v *Gamble* [1959] 1 QB 11 at p. 20). Whether there was such an intention to aid the principal is a question of fact to be decided in the particular circumstances of each case. The requirement for proof of intention to aid means that the wider notions of recklessness and negligence are not enough to convict an accessory.

The *minimum* state of mind required of an accessory to an offence is set out in *Johnson* v *Youden* [1950] 1 KB 544. In that case, the court held that before anyone can be convicted of aiding and abetting an offence, he/she must at least know the essential matters that constitute that offence. Therefore the accessory to an offence of drink/driving must at least have been aware that the 'principal' (the driver) had been drinking (*Smith* v *Mellors and Soar* (1987) 84 Cr App R 279).

Occasionally statutes will make specific provision for the state of mind and/or the conduct of accessories and principals. An example can be found in s. 7 of the Protection from Harassment Act 1997 (**see chapter 2.8**).

1.2.8.2 Joint Enterprise and 'Parasitic Accessory Liability'

A joint criminal enterprise exists where two (or more) people embark on the commission of an offence by one or both (or all) of them. It is a joint enterprise because all the parties have a common goal—that an offence will be committed.

KEYNOTE

As the parties to a joint enterprise share a combined purpose, each would be liable for the consequences of the actions of the other in the pursuit of their joint enterprise (but see below for such liability when the nature of the offence changes). This is the case even if the consequences of the joint enterprise are a result of a mistake. For example, two offenders (A and B) agree to carry out a burglary on a particular house. Offender A leads the way but makes an error and mistakenly breaks into the wrong house. This error by offender A will not prevent offender B being guilty as an accomplice to the burglary offence.

Parasitic Accessory Liability

What happens when one party goes beyond that which was agreed or contemplated by the other? This particular narrower area of secondary responsibility is described as 'parasitic accessory liability'.

EXAMPLE

Two men (A and B) agree to carry out an offence of theft. During the course of the offence, the owner of the property subject of the offence appears and tries to prevent the offence taking place. Offender A produces a flick-knife and stabs the victim, causing grievous bodily harm. Offender B had no idea that offender A had a flick-knife and had never contemplated the use of violence during the theft offence.

The actions of offender A are a departure from the nature and type of crime that was envisaged by offender B who did not know that A possessed a flick-knife; it is an act so fundamentally different from that originally contemplated by B that B is most unlikely to be liable for the injuries caused to the victim (*R* v *Anderson* [1966] 2 QB 110).

The situation would alter if offender B knew that offender A possessed the flick-knife and encouraged A to use the flick-knife. Here, offender B could be convicted of a wounding offence if it can be proved that he had *intended* to assist or encourage the wounding offence. *Foresight* that the wounding might occur is simply evidence (albeit sometimes strong evidence) of intent to assist or encourage. It is a question for the jury in every case whether the intention to assist or encourage is shown—a person is not to be taken to have had an intention merely because of foreseeability. This was the ruling in *R* v *Jogee* [2016] UKSC 8 and *Ruddock* v *The Queen* [2016] UKPC 7. In *Jogee* and *Ruddock*, the court made it clear that the ruling:

- did not affect the law that a person who joins in a crime which any reasonable person would realise involves a risk of harm, and death results, is at least guilty of manslaughter. Manslaughter cases can vary in their gravity, but may be very serious and the maximum sentence is life imprisonment (**see para. 2.1.4**);
- does not affect the rule that a person who intentionally encourages or assists in the commission of a crime is as guilty as the person who physically commits it;
- did not alter the fact that it is open to a jury to infer intentional encouragement or assistance, for example from weight of numbers in a combined attack, whether more or less spontaneous or planned, or from knowledge that weapons are being carried. It is commonplace for juries to have to decide what inferences they can properly draw about intention from an accused person's behaviour and what he/she knew.

1.2.9 Corporate Liability

Companies which are 'legally incorporated' have a legal personality of their own and they can commit offences. There are difficulties associated with proving and punishing criminal conduct by companies. However, companies have been prosecuted for offences of strict liability (*Alphacell Ltd* v *Woodward* [1972] AC 824), offences requiring *mens rea* (*Tesco Supermarkets Ltd* v *Nattrass* [1972] AC 153) and offences of being an 'accessory' (*R* v *Robert Millar (Contractors) Ltd* [1970] 2 QB 54). There are occasions where the courts will accept that the knowledge of certain employees will be extended to the company (*Tesco Stores Ltd* v *Brent London Borough Council* [1993] 1 WLR 1037).

Clearly, there are some offences that would be conceptually impossible for a legal corporation to commit (e.g. some sexual offences) but, given that companies can be guilty as accessories (*Robert Miliar*), they may well be capable of aiding and abetting such offences even though they could not commit the offence as a principal.

A company (CLL Ltd) has also been convicted, along with its managing director, of manslaughter (*R v Kite* [1996] 2 Cr App R (S) 295). Companies can be prosecuted for such offences under the terms of the Corporate Manslaughter and Corporate Homicide Act 2007.

1.2.10   Vicarious Liability

The general principle in criminal law is that liability is *personal*. There are, however, occasions where liability can be transmitted *vicariously* to another.

The most frequent occasions are cases where a statutory duty is breached by employees in the course of their employment (*National Rivers Authority* v *Alfred McAlpine Homes (East) Ltd* [1994] 4 All ER 286), or where a duty is placed upon a particular individual, such as a licensee, who delegates some of his/her functions to another. The purpose behind this concept is generally to prevent individuals or organisations from evading liability by getting others to carry out unlawful activities on their behalf.

1.3 | Incomplete Offences

1.3.1 Introduction

There are circumstances where defendants are interrupted or frustrated in their efforts to commit an offence, perhaps as a result of police intervention or as a result of things not going as the defendants had hoped. In these cases, the defendant's conduct may be dealt with using incomplete offences.

It should be noted that most incomplete offences *cannot* be mixed, and that most *cannot* be attempted. For instance, you *cannot* conspire to aid and abet, neither can you attempt to conspire. There are, as ever, limited exceptions to this rule.

1.3.2 Encouraging or Assisting Crime

The common law offence of inciting an offence was abolished by the Serious Crime Act 2007. Incitement was replaced by the offences under ss. 44, 45 and 46 of the Act.

KEYNOTE

Note that any references in existing legislation to the common law offence of incitement are to be read as references to the offences in ss. 44, 45 and 46, i.e. to be read as 'encouraging or assisting an offence'.

OFFENCE: **Intentionally Encouraging or Assisting an Offence—*Serious Crime Act 2007, s. 44***
> • Triable in the same way as the anticipated offence • Where the anticipated offence is murder, the offence is punishable by life imprisonment • In any other case, a person is liable to any penalty for which he/she would be liable on conviction of the anticipated offence

The Serious Crime Act 2007, s. 44 states:

(1) A person commits an offence if—
    (a) he does an act capable of encouraging or assisting in the commission of an offence; and
    (b) he intends to encourage or assist its commission.
(2) But he is not to be taken to have intended to encourage or assist the commission of an offence merely because such encouragement or assistance was a foreseeable consequence of his act.

KEYNOTE

Section 44 involves the defendant intentionally encouraging or assisting an offence. To commit the offence, the defendant must actually do an act capable of encouraging or assisting the commission of an offence and intend to encourage or assist in its commission.

....

EXAMPLE

D might supply P with a weapon with the intent that P will use it to kill or seriously injure another person. Alternatively, D might simply offer verbal encouragement to P to commit the offence.

The defendant must intend to encourage or assist in the commission of the 'anticipated' offence.

EXAMPLE

D gives P a baseball bat and intends P to use it to inflict a minor injury on V. However, P uses the baseball bat to attack V and intentionally kills V—D would not be liable for encouraging or assisting murder, unless he also believes or is reckless as to whether V will be killed.

OFFENCE: **Encouraging or Assisting an Offence Believing it will be Committed— *Serious Crime Act 2007, s. 45***

> • Triable in the same way as the anticipated offence • Where the anticipated offence is murder, the offence is punishable by life imprisonment • In any other case, a person is liable to any penalty for which he/she would be liable on conviction of the anticipated offence

The Serious Crime Act 2007, s. 45 states:

> A person commits an offence if—
> (a) he does an act capable of encouraging or assisting in the commission of an offence; and
> (b) he believes—
>   (i) that the offence will be committed; and
>   (ii) that his act will encourage or assist its commission.

KEYNOTE

This covers the situation where the defendant may not intend that a particular offence is committed, but he/she believes both that it will be committed and that his/her act will encourage its commission. For example, D supplies a weapon to P believing P is going to commit murder with the weapon but being quite indifferent as to whether or not P will do so as it is D's sole concern to make a profit from the sale of the weapon.

OFFENCE: **Encouraging or Assisting Offences Believing One or More will be Committed—*Serious Crime Act 2007, s. 46***

> • Triable on indictment • Where the reference offence is murder, the offence is punishable with life imprisonment • In any other case, a person is liable to any penalty for which he he/she would be liable on conviction of the reference offence

The Serious Crime Act 2007, s. 46 states:

> (1) A person commits an offence if—
> (a) he does an act capable of encouraging or assisting the commission of one or more of a number of offences: and
> (b) he believes—
>   (i) that one or more of those offences will be committed (but has no belief as to which); and
>   (ii) that his act will encourage or assist the commission of one or more of them.
> (2) It is immaterial for the purposes of subsection (1)(b)(ii) whether a person has any belief as to which offence will be encouraged or assisted.

KEYNOTE

This covers a situation where D may not intend that a particular offence is committed but believes that one or more offences will be committed and that his/her act will encourage or assist the commission of one or more of those offences.

D drives P to the home of V knowing that P is going to harm V but not knowing whether this will take the form of an assault on V or the murder of V.

In respect of each offence (ss. 44, 45 and 46), D must merely do an act that is capable of encouraging or assisting the commission of an offence(s). Section 49(1) of the Act states that offences can be committed regardless of whether or not the encouragement or assistance has the effect which the defendant intended or believed it would have.

D, a surgeon, wishes to sexually assault his patients whilst they are unconscious under anaesthetic. To do so, D will need the cooperation of his assistant, V. D puts his idea to V while they are having a drink in a pub, intending to encourage V to take part in the offences. V is outraged and wants nothing to do with D's plan. The fact that V is not remotely interested in D's plan and is not encouraged to take part in it will not alter the fact that D has committed an offence under s. 44 of the Act.

An 'act' may take a number of different forms, including a course of conduct or a failure to discharge a duty. It includes threatening another person or putting pressure on another person to commit the offence (s. 65).

What of the situation where, rather than approaching others, an undercover police officer is approached to take part in a proposed offence?

In relation to this activity, s. 49(1) would still apply as there is no need for the person encouraged to have any intention of going on to commit the offence. In a case involving incitement (the predecessor of these offences), the Divisional Court held that there is no requirement for 'parity of *mens rea*' between the parties (*DPP* v *Armstrong* [2000] Crim LR 379). In that case, the defendant had approached an undercover police officer asking him to supply child pornography. At his trial, the defendant argued that as the officer in reality had no intention of supplying the pornography, there was no offence of incitement. On appeal by the prosecutor, the Divisional Court held that incitement, like conspiracies and attempts, was an auxiliary offence where criminal liability was attributed to the defendant where the full offence had not been committed. Consequently, the intent of the person incited (in this case, an undercover police officer) was irrelevant.

A person can be convicted of more than one of these offences (s. 44, 45 or 46) in relation to the same act (s. 49(3)).

Section 50 of the Act sets out that it will be a defence to the offences under ss. 44, 45 and 46 if the person charged acted reasonably; that is, in the circumstances he/she was aware of, or in the circumstances he/she reasonably believed existed, it was reasonable to act as he/she did.

Section 51 limits liability by setting out in statute the common law exception established in *R* v *Tyrrell* [1894] 1 QB 710. A person cannot be guilty of the offences in ss. 44, 45 and 46 if, in relation to an offence that is a 'protective' offence, the person who does the act capable of encouraging or assisting that offence falls within the category of persons that offence was designed to protect and would be considered as the victim.

D is a 12-year-old girl and encourages P, a 40-year-old man, to have sex with her. P is not interested and does not attempt to have sex with D. D cannot be liable of encouraging or assisting child rape despite the fact that it is her intent that P has sexual intercourse with a child under 13 (child rape) because she would be considered the 'victim' of that offence had it taken place, and the offence of child rape was enacted to protect children under the age of 13.

The offences under ss. 44, 45 and 46 do not apply to the offence of corporate manslaughter.

1.3.3 Conspiracy

Conspiracies can be divided into statutory and common law conspiracies.

1.3.3.1 Statutory Conspiracy

OFFENCE: **Statutory Conspiracy—*Criminal Law Act 1977, s. 1***
  • Triable on indictment • Where conspiracy is to commit murder, an offence punishable by life imprisonment or any indictable offence punishable with imprisonment where no maximum term is specified—life imprisonment • In other cases, sentence is the same as for completed offence

The Criminal Law Act 1977, s. 1 states:

(1) Subject to the following provisions of this Part of this Act, if a person agrees with any other person or persons that a course of conduct shall be pursued which, if the agreement is carried out in accordance with their intentions, either—
  (a) will necessarily amount to or involve the commission of any offence or offences by one or more of the parties to the agreement; or
  (b) would do so but for the existence of facts which render the commission of the offence or any of the offences impossible,
  he is guilty of conspiracy to commit the offence or offences in question.

KEYNOTE

A charge of conspiracy can be brought in respect of an agreement to commit indictable or summary offences. Conspiracy is triable only on indictment even if it relates to a summary offence (in which case the consent of the DPP will be required). Offences of conspiracy are committed at the time of the agreement; it is immaterial whether or not the substantive offence is ever carried out.

Agreeing with Another

For there to be a conspiracy, there must be an agreement—a 'meeting of minds'. Therefore there must be at least two people (two minds) involved. Consequently, A cannot be guilty of a conspiracy with B (if B is the only other party to the agreement) if B intends to frustrate or sabotage it; there would not be a 'meeting of minds' in terms of an agreement to carry out an offence.

Each conspirator must be aware of the overall common purpose to which they all attach themselves. If one conspirator enters into *separate* agreements with different people, each agreement is a separate conspiracy (*R v Griffiths* [1966] 1 QB 589).

A person can be convicted of conspiracy even if the actual identity of the other conspirators is unknown (as to the affect of the acquittal of one party to a conspiracy on the other parties, see the Criminal Law Act 1977, s. 5(8)).

A defendant *cannot* be convicted of a statutory conspiracy if the only other party to the agreement is:

• his/her spouse or civil partner;
• a person under 10 years of age;
• the intended victim (Criminal Law Act 1977, s. 2(2)).

A husband and wife can both be convicted of a statutory conspiracy if they conspire with a third party (not falling into the above categories) (*R v Chrastny* [1991] 1 WLR 1381).

A person is not guilty of statutory conspiracy if the only other person with whom he/she agrees is their civil partner. A civil partnership is a legally recognised union available to both same-sex couples and opposite-sex couples (under the Civil Partnership Act 2004 and the Civil Partnerships, Marriages and Deaths (Registration etc.) Act 2019).

A corporation may be a party to a conspiracy (*R* v *ICR Haulage Ltd* [1944] KB 551), but a company and one of its directors cannot be the only parties to a conspiracy because there can be no 'meeting of minds' (*R* v *McDonnell* [1966] 1 QB 233).

The 'end product' of the agreement must be the commission of an offence by *one or more of the parties to the agreement*. Once agreed upon, any failure to bring about the end result or an abandoning of the agreement altogether will not prevent the statutory conspiracy being committed. An agreement to aid and abet an offence of conspiracy is not, in law, capable of constituting a statutory conspiracy under s. 1(1) of the Criminal Law Act 1977 (*R* v *Kenning* [2008] EWCA Crim 1534).

What if a defendant enters into an agreement with another person to commit an offence but that other person is in fact a police officer? Under normal circumstances, forming an agreement with another person to carry out an offence is a conspiracy. If, however, one of only two conspirators is an undercover officer who has no intention of going through with the agreement, there is a strong argument that there can be no 'true' conspiracy as the only other person had no intention of going through with the plan (*Yip Chiu-Cheung* v *The Queen* [1995] 1 AC 111). In conspiracies, the intention of at least two parties *is* the basis of the whole offence. So, in cases where the only other 'conspirator' is a police officer, encouraging an offence may be a more appropriate charge.

1.3.3.2 Common Law Conspiracies

OFFENCE: **Conspiracy to Defraud—*Common Law***

> • Triable on indictment • 10 years' imprisonment and/or a fine

Conspiracy to defraud involves:

> ... an agreement by two or more [persons] by dishonesty to deprive a person of something which is his or to which he is or would or might be entitled [or] an agreement by two or more by dishonesty to injure some proprietary right [of the victim] ...
>
> (*Scott* v *Metropolitan Police Commissioner* [1975] AC 819)

KEYNOTE

This offence has been endorsed by senior judges as representing an effective means of dealing with multiple defendants engaged in a fraudulent course of conduct.

The common law offence of conspiracy to defraud can be divided into two main types. The first is contained in the case of *Scott*, the second involves a dishonest agreement to deceive another into acting in a way that is contrary to his/her duty (*Wai Yu-Tsang* v *The Queen* [1992] 1 AC 269).

Although the requirement for an agreement between at least two people is the same, this offence is broader than statutory conspiracy. There is no requirement to prove that the end result would amount to the commission of an *offence*, simply that it would result in depriving a person of something under the specified conditions or in injuring his/her proprietary right.

You must show *intent* to defraud a victim (*R* v *Hollinshead* [1985] AC 975).

You must also show that a defendant was dishonest as set out in *Barlow Clowes* and *Royal Brunei Airlines* (see para. 3.1.4).

Clearly there will be circumstances where the defendant's behaviour will amount to both a statutory conspiracy and a conspiracy to defraud. The Criminal Justice Act 1987, s. 12 makes provision for such circumstances and allows the prosecution to choose which charge to prefer.

Examples of common law conspiracies to defraud include:

- Buffet car staff selling their own home-made sandwiches on British Rail trains thereby depriving the company of the opportunity to sell their own products (*R* v *Cooke* [1986] AC 909).
- Directors agreeing to conceal details of a bank's trading losses from its shareholders (*Wai Yu-Tsang*).

1.3.4 Attempts

The Criminal Attempts Act 1981, s. 1 states:

(1) If, with intent to commit an offence to which this section applies, a person does an act which is more than merely preparatory to the commission of the offence, he is guilty of attempting to commit the offence.

...

(2) A person may be guilty of attempting to commit an offence to which this section applies even though the facts are such that the commission of the offence is impossible.

(3) In any case where—

(a) apart from this subsection a person's intention would not be regarded as having amounted to an intent to commit an offence; but

(b) if the facts of the case had been as he believed them to be, his intention would be so regarded,

then, for the purposes of subsection (1) above, he shall be regarded as having had an intent to commit that offence.

(4) This section applies to any offence which, if it were completed, would be triable in England and Wales as an indictable offence, other than—

(a) conspiracy (at common law or under section 1 of the Criminal Law Act 1977 or any other enactment);

(b) aiding, abetting, counselling, procuring or suborning the commission of an offence;

(c) an offence under section 2(1) of the Suicide Act 1961 (c 60) (encouraging or assisting suicide);

(d) offences under section 4(1) (assisting offenders) or 5(1) (accepting or agreeing to accept consideration for not disclosing information about a relevant offence) of the Criminal Law Act 1967.

KEYNOTE

Most attempts at committing criminal offences will be governed by s. 1. Although some statutory exceptions apply, the sentence generally for such attempts will be:

- for murder—life imprisonment;
- for indictable offences—the same maximum penalty as the substantive offence;
- for either way offences—the same maximum penalty as the substantive offence when tried *summarily*.

If the attempted offence is triable summarily only, it cannot be an offence under s. 1. However, if the only reason the substantive offence is triable summarily is because of a statutory limit imposed in some cases (e.g. in cases of low-value shoplifting (see chapter 3.1) or criminal damage to property of a low value (see chapter 3.10)), the offence can be attempted.

If the offence attempted is triable only on indictment, the attempt will be triable only on indictment. Similarly, if the offence attempted is an 'either way' offence, so too will the attempt be triable either way (s. 4(1)).

Many other statutory offences contain references to 'attempts', including:

- Theft Act 1968, s. 9(1)(b) (burglary);
- Firearms Act 1968, s. 17 (using firearm to resist arrest).

Section 3 of the Criminal Attempts Act 1981 deals with such statutory provisions and they will generally be governed by the same principles as those set out here.

An Act which is More than Merely Preparatory

An attempt requires an act—an omission to act would not create liability for an attempt (e.g. a refusal to call an ambulance for a person who is gravely ill cannot amount to attempted murder).

A defendant's actions must be shown to have gone beyond mere preparation towards the commission of the substantive offence. Whether the defendant did or did not go beyond that point will be a question of fact for the jury/magistrate(s). There is no formula used by the courts in interpreting this requirement so it is useful to examine several cases where the courts have considered what this element of the offence means.

An example of where the defendant was held to have done no more than merely preparatory acts was *R v Campbell* [1991] Crim LR 268, where the appellant armed himself with an imitation gun, approached to within a yard of a post office which he intended to rob, but never drew his weapon; it was held that there was no evidence on which a jury could properly have concluded that his acts went beyond mere preparation. In *R v Bowles* [2004] EWCA Crim 1608, the defendant had been convicted of several offences involving dishonesty against an elderly neighbour. The neighbour's long-standing will left her estate to charity but, following his arrest, police officers searched the defendant's premises and found a new will, fully complete except for the signature. The defendant and his wife were named as the main beneficiaries and were to inherit the neighbour's house. Although the defendant's son was said to have been heard making reference to the fact that he was going to inherit the house, the 'new' will had been drafted over six months earlier and there was no evidence of any steps to have it executed, or any evidence of it being used. The Court of Appeal held that the making of the will was no more than merely preparatory and the defendant's conviction for attempting to make a false instrument was quashed.

In *R v Geddes* [1996] Crim LR 894, the defendant was found trespassing in the lavatory block of a school, armed with a knife, lengths of rope and tape. It appears he intended to kidnap a child; his conviction for attempted false imprisonment was quashed on appeal. Citing *Campbell* with approval, Lord Bingham CJ held that no jury could have concluded that the defendant's acts had gone beyond mere preparation. He may have equipped himself, and put himself in a position to commit the crime, but it could not be said that he had actually tried or started to commit it.

Courts have accepted an approach of questioning whether the defendant had 'embarked on the crime proper' (*R v Gullefer* [1990] 1 WLR 1063) but there is no requirement to have passed a point of no return leading to the commission of the substantive offence.

Mens Rea for Attempt

To prove an 'attempt' you must show an *intention* on the part of the defendant to commit the substantive offence.

This requirement means a higher level or degree of *mens rea* may be required to prove an attempt than for the substantive offence. For instance, the *mens rea* required to prove an offence of murder is the intention to kill *or* cause grievous bodily harm, whereas the *mens rea* for attempted murder is nothing less than an *intent* to kill (*R v Whybrow* (1951) 35 Cr App R 141). In *R v Jones* [1990] 1 WLR 1057, the defendant was charged with attempted murder. He climbed into the car of the victim and drew a loaded gun with the intention of killing him, but was disarmed in a struggle that followed. The Court of Appeal held that it was open to a jury to regard this as attempted murder.

A defendant's intention may be *conditional*; that is, he/she may only intend to steal from a house if something worth stealing is later found inside. The conditional nature of this intention will not generally prevent the charge of attempt being brought and the defendant's intentions will, in accordance with s. 1(3), be judged *on the facts as he/she believed them to be*.

Although 'intent to commit' the offence is required under s. 1(1), there are occasions where a state of mind that falls short of such a precise intention may suffice. For instance, in cases of attempted rape (**see chapter 4.2**) the courts have accepted that recklessness as to whether the victim is consenting was (under the earlier sexual offences legislation) sufficient *mens rea* for attempted rape because it is sufficient for the substantive offence (*R v Khan* [1990] 1 WLR 813).

In proving an 'attempt' it is enough to show that defendants were in one of the states of mind required for the substantive offence and that they did their best, so far as they were able, to do what was necessary for the commission of the full offence (*Attorney-General's Reference (No. 3 of 1992)* [1994] 1 WLR 409).

1.3.5 Impossibility

Difficulties have arisen where, despite the efforts of the defendant, his/her ultimate intention has been impossible (such as trying to extract cocaine from a powder which is, unknown to the defendant, only talc). Impossibility is dealt with by s. 1(3) of the Criminal Attempts Act 1981 and its interpretation through the courts. It differs, however, in some incomplete offences.

EXAMPLE

If a person tries to handle goods which are not in fact stolen, the following rules would apply:

- A defendant could *not* be guilty of encouraging another or of common law conspiracy to defraud in these circumstances. The *physical* impossibility (the goods are not actually stolen) of what the defendant sought to do would preclude such a charge.
- A defendant *could* be guilty of a statutory conspiracy with another to handle 'stolen' goods and also of attempting to handle 'stolen' goods under these circumstances. The physical impossibility would not preclude such charges as a result of the Criminal Attempts Act 1981 and the House of Lords' decision in *R v Shivpuri* [1987] AC 1 (you can conspire and/or attempt to commit the impossible). The only form of impossibility which would preclude liability under the Criminal Attempts Act 1981 or for a statutory conspiracy would be the *legal* impossibility.

1.4 General Defences

1.4.1 Introduction

There are various defences available to a person charged with an offence. Some defences are specific to certain offences (e.g. criminal damage and murder), whereas others can be used to answer a wider range of charges and are often referred to as 'general defences'. This chapter examines several of these 'general defences'.

1.4.2 Inadvertence and Mistake

There are occasions where a defendant makes a mistake about some circumstance or consequence; however, claims that a defendant 'made a mistake' or did something 'inadvertently' will only be an effective defence if they negate the *mens rea* for that offence. Therefore, if someone wanders out of a shop with something that has not yet been paid for, that mistake or inadvertence might negative any *mens rea* of 'dishonesty'. As the requirement for the *mens rea* in such a case is *subjective*, then the defendant's mistake or inadvertence will be judged subjectively. The same will generally be true for offences requiring subjective recklessness. It does not matter whether the mistake was 'reasonable' (*DPP* v *Morgan* [1976] AC 182). The appropriate test is whether the defendant's mistaken belief was an honest and genuine one.

There are occasions where a genuine mistake on the part of the defendant may amount to a defence. In *R* v *Lee* [2001] 1 Cr App R 19, a case arising from an assault on two arresting police officers, the Court of Appeal reviewed the law in this area, reaffirming the following points:

- A genuine or honest mistake could provide a defence to many criminal offences requiring a particular state of mind, including assault with intent to resist arrest (*R* v *Brightling* [1991] Crim LR 364).
- A defence of mistake has to involve a mistake of fact not a mistake of law (see below).
- People under arrest are not entitled to form their own view as to the lawfulness of that arrest. They have a duty to comply with the police and hear the details of the charge against them (*R* v *Bentley* (1850) 4 Cox CC 406).
- Belief in one's own innocence, however genuine or honestly held, cannot afford a defence to a charge of assault with intent to resist arrest under s. 38 of the Offences Against the Person Act 1861.

A defendant attempted to argue that his honest and reasonable mistake as to the *facts* of his arrest (as opposed to the law), after he was lawfully arrested for a public order offence, was different from the decision in *Lee*. The Divisional Court did not agree (*Hewitt* v *DPP* [2002] EWHC 2801 (QB)).

Generally, it is no defence to claim a mistake as to the law because all people are presumed to know the law once it is made. With statutory instruments, a defendant can show that the instrument in question was not in force at the time of the offence or that the behaviour that it sought to control was beyond the powers (*ultra vires*) of that instrument.

There is one particular example, however, where a mistaken belief in the legal position is specifically provided for in a criminal offence. This is where a person appropriates property in the belief that he/she has a legal right to deprive another person of it under s. 2 of the Theft Act 1968 (**see chapter 3.1**).

In relation to offences involving negligence, inadvertence would clearly not amount to a defence and any 'mistake' would generally need to be shown to be a reasonable one.

1.4.3   Duress

Where a person is threatened with death or serious physical injury unless he/she carries out a criminal act, he/she may have a defence of duress (*R v Graham* [1982] 1 WLR 294). The threat of serious physical injury does not appear to include serious *psychological* injury (*R v Baker* [1997] Crim LR 497). Where relevant intent is an ingredient of the offence, defendants might claim that they only formed that intent as a result of duress. However, unless it is shown that the intent had or could have been formed *only* by reason of that duress (e.g. the duress was the only thing causing the defendant to form that intent), the defence will fail (*R v Fisher* [2004] EWCA Crim 1190).

It would seem that the threat need not be made solely to the person who goes on to commit the relevant offence; there are authorities to suggest that threats of death/serious harm to loved ones may allow a defence of duress.

> **KEYNOTE**
>
> The defence is not available in respect of an offence of murder (*R v Howe* [1987] AC 417) or attempted murder (*R v Gotts* [1992] 2 AC 412), as a principal or secondary offender. It is, however, *available in other offences even in offences of strict liability* (*Eden District Council v Braid* [1998] COD 259—taxi driver threatened and forced to carry excessive number of people in breach of his licensing conditions).

There are several key elements to this defence:

- the threat must have driven the defendant to commit the offence;
- the defendant must have acted as a sober and reasonable person sharing the defendant's characteristics would have done;
- the threatened death/injury must be anticipated at or near the time of the offence—not some time in the distant future.

Duress is not available as a defence if it is proved that the defendant failed to take advantage of an opportunity to neutralise the effects of the threat (perhaps by escaping from it), which a reasonable person of a similar sort to the defendant would have taken in the same position. An example of this approach is the case of *R v Heath* [2000] Crim LR 109, where the defendant alleged that he had been pressurised into transporting drugs. Because the defendant had more than one safe avenue of escape (going to the police, which he did not do because he was scared and because he was a drug addict, and going to his parents in Scotland, which he did not do because he did not want them to know about the position he was in) the defence failed. Whether a defendant could be expected to take such an opportunity of rendering the threat ineffective, e.g. by seeking police protection, will be a matter for the jury. Therefore, a defendant who is ordered to steal from a shop in 24 hours' time, or suffer a serious physical injury for failing to do so, might be unable to utilise the defence as a jury may consider that the defendant had ample opportunity to take evasive action and avoid the threat.

If defendants knowingly expose themselves to a risk of such a threat of death or serious physical injury, they cannot claim duress as a defence. So if a person joins a violent gang or an active terrorist organisation, he/she cannot claim duress as a defence to any crimes he/she may go on to commit under threat of death or serious injury from another member or rival of that organisation (*R v Sharp* [1987] QB 853). However, if the purpose of the organisation or gang is not predominantly violent or dangerous (e.g. a gang of shoplifters), the defence of duress *may* be available in relation to offences committed while under threat of death or serious physical injury from other gang members (*R v Shepherd* (1987) 86 Cr App R 47).

1.4.4 Duress of Circumstances

There may be times when circumstances leave the defendant no alternative but to commit an offence. In *R v Martin* [1989] 1 All ER 652, the defendant had driven whilst disqualified from driving. He claimed he did so because his wife had threatened to commit suicide if he did not drive their son to work. His wife had attempted suicide on previous occasions and the son was late for work and she feared he would lose his job if her husband did not get him to work. The Court of Appeal stated that, in these circumstances, the defence of duress of circumstances was *available* to the defendant. In such cases, the court will consider the reasonableness of the defendant's behaviour in the light of the prevailing circumstances. If the defendant commits a very serious offence in order to avoid very minor or trivial consequences, this defence is unlikely to be available.

This type of duress should be distinguished from that at **para. 1.4.5.** There the duress comes from a threat which compels a person to commit an offence: a 'gun to the head' type of situation where one person says to another *'Do this or else …'*. With duress of circumstances, there is no such threat being made. Rather, there is a threatening situation or set of circumstances from which the defendant wishes to escape and, in so doing, feels impelled to commit an offence as the lesser of two present evils. Here the threat is 'situational' and the defendant feels *'If I don't do this, then the consequence will be death or serious physical injury …'*.

This defence was examined by the Court of Appeal in a case where someone jumped onto the bonnet of the car that the appellant was driving. The appellant drove for some distance with the man on the bonnet of the car, braking after a short time to go over a speed ramp. The man fell from the bonnet and the appellant drove on, running the man over and causing him grievous bodily harm (as to which, **see chapter 2.7**). In determining whether or not the defence of 'duress of circumstances' was available, the court held that the jury must ask two questions in relation to the appellant:

- Was he (or might he have been) impelled to act as he did because, as a result of what he reasonably believed to be the situation, he had good cause to fear he would suffer death or serious injury if he did not do so?
- If so, would a sober person of reasonable firmness and sharing the same characteristics have responded to the situation in the way that he did?

If each question were answered 'yes', the defence would be made out (*R v Cairns* [1999] 2 Cr App R 137).

The important aspect to this defence, then, is that it will only be available to defendants as long as they are acting under compulsion of the prevailing circumstances when committing the offence. It appears that defendants need only hold an *honest* belief that those circumstances exist without necessarily having *reasonable grounds* for that belief (*DPP v Rogers* [1998] Crim LR 202) and there is no need for the threat to be 'real'. There is certainly no need for the threat (perceived threat) to amount to a criminal offence. The Court of Appeal has accepted the possibility of a 'duress of circumstances' defence being applicable where a defendant acted in fear of the consequences of war being declared on Iraq (*R v Jones (Margaret)* [2004] EWCA Crim 1981). However, the defendant's actions in order to avoid that perceived threatening situation must be reasonable and proportionate to the threat presented. Therefore defendants in situations like *Willer* and *Cairns* would not be able to claim duress of circumstances if they drove at their victims repeatedly until all had been injured to a point where they no longer posed a threat.

An attempt to extend the defence was made in *R v Altham* [2006] EWCA Crim 7, where the defendant had been charged with possessing a controlled drug (cannabis). The defendant appealed against his conviction, arguing that he needed to smoke cannabis to ease the pain he suffered from injuries received in a car accident. It was argued that the defence of duress of circumstances should be open to the defendant on the basis that he was suffering serious physical harm. The prosecution countered that pain can never amount to serious physical harm. The appeal was dismissed and the court stated that the defence could not be available in this type of circumstance because it would allow unlawful activity to be undertaken and would conflict with the purpose and effect of the intention of the Misuse of Drugs Act 1971.

The defence is not available in relation to offences of murder, attempted murder, treason and offences under the Misuse of Drugs Act 1971. The defence is available against any other charge (including hijacking (*R v Abdul-Hussain* [1999] Crim LR 570)).

1.4.5 Defence of Self, Others or Property

Where the common law defences of self-defence, defence of property or the Criminal Law Act 1967 defence of lawful arrest are raised in relation to taking someone's life, the provisions of Article 2 of the European Convention on Human Rights will apply. As Article 2 is relevant to such defences, it is appropriate to consider its provisions.

1.4.5.1 Human Rights—The Right to Life

Article 2 of the Convention states:

1. Everyone's right to life shall be protected by law. No one shall be deprived of his life intentionally save in the execution of a sentence of a court following his conviction of a crime for which this penalty is provided by law.
2. Deprivation of life shall not be regarded as inflicted in contravention of this Article when it results from the use of force which is no more than absolutely necessary:
   (a) in defence of any person from unlawful violence;
   (b) in order to effect a lawful arrest or to prevent the escape of a person lawfully detained;
   (c) in action lawfully taken for the purpose of quelling a riot or insurrection.

KEYNOTE

Taking Life

It can be seen that the Article allows for a number of limited exceptions when the taking of life by the State may not be a violation of this Convention right. All of the situations covered are generally concerned with protecting life, preventing crime and preserving order. The exceptions include actions taken in defending another person (*not property*) from unlawful violence and effecting a lawful arrest. Therefore the Convention acknowledges that there will be occasions when the State is compelled to take the life of an individual, such as where a police officer has to use lethal force to protect the life of another.

However, while limited in themselves, these exceptions will also be subject to very restrictive interpretation by the courts.

When a life is taken under any of the three situations set out at para. 2(a)–(c), the force used must be shown to have been *no more than absolutely necessary* (a more stringent test than the general test imposed in our domestic criminal law by s. 3 of the Criminal Law Act 1967 (as to which, **see para. 1.4.5.3**)). This test was examined by the European Commission on Human Rights in *Stewart* v *United Kingdom* (1985) 7 EHRR CD

---

453. There the Commission held that force will be absolutely necessary only if it is strictly proportionate to the legitimate purpose being pursued. In order to meet those criteria, regard must be had to:

- the nature of the aim being pursued;
- the inherent dangers to life and limb from the situation; and
- the degree of risk to life presented by the amount of force employed.

This test applies not only to cases where there has been an intentional taking of life, but also where there has been a permitted use of force that has led to the death of another. The test has been held to be a stricter one than even the general requirement of 'proportionality' that runs throughout the Convention (*McCann* v *United Kingdom* (1996) 21 EHRR 97).

This area is of importance because not only are the courts concerned with any individual actions that directly lead to the death of another, but also because they will take into account 'other factors' surrounding and leading up to the incident that caused the loss of life.

Such other factors are likely to include:

- the planning and control of the operation;
- the training given to the officers concerned; and
- the briefing/instructions that they received.

Where the use of force by the police results in the deprivation of life, the training, briefing, deployment and overall competence of everyone involved in the relevant operation will potentially come under the scrutiny of the court. These considerations, which were made clear by the European Court of Human Rights in the *McCann* case (involving the shooting of three terrorists by the SAS in Gibraltar in 1988), were applied by the Court to an incident when police officers shot and killed a gunman and his hostage (*Andronicou* v *Cyprus* (1998) 25 EHRR 491). In that case, the Court found that the police operation had been planned and managed in a way that was intended to minimise the risk to life, even though the officers ultimately made a mistake as to the extent of the gunman's weapons and ammunition when they took the decision to open fire. The Court found that the exceptional requirements of Article 2(2) had been made out and that there had been no violation of Article 2 by the police.

Protecting Life

A further area of importance lies in the second arm of Article 2—that of protecting the lives of others. This area was considered in the case of *Osman* v *United Kingdom* (2000) 29 EHRR 245. In *Osman*, the European Commission said that Article 2 must be interpreted as requiring preventive steps to be taken to protect life from '*known and avoidable dangers*' (emphasis added). The Commission went on to say that the extent of this obligation (which is clearly of the first importance to those tasked with investigating and preventing crime) will vary 'having regard to the source and degree of danger and the means available to combat it'. The European Court of Human Rights said in *Osman* that it will be enough for an applicant to show that the authorities did not do all that could reasonably be expected of them to avoid a '*real and immediate risk to life*' (emphasis added) of which they have or ought to have knowledge. As such, whether a police officer or police force has failed in this positive obligation to protect life will only be answerable in the light of all the circumstances of a particular case. This requirement is, therefore, very similar to the test for negligence in civil law in England and Wales.

1.4.5.2 **Use of Force in Defence, Prevention of Crime and Lawful Arrest**

Considered against the backdrop of Article 2 of the European Convention on Human Rights, there are circumstances where the use of force against a person or property will be permissible. This aspect of criminal law is dealt with by s. 76 of the Criminal Justice and Immigration Act 2008. Section 76 provides a gloss on the common law of self-defence and the defences provided by s. 3(1) of the Criminal Law Act 1967, which relate to the use of force in the prevention of crime or making an arrest. Section 76 aims to improve understanding of the practical application of these areas of law using elements of case law to illustrate how the defence operates. It does not change the current test that allows the use of reasonable force.

KEYNOTE

The law can be formulated quite simply along the following lines:

A person may use such force as is reasonable in the circumstances as he/she believes them to be for the purpose of:

(a) self-defence; or
(b) defence of another; or
(c) defence of property; or
(d) prevention of crime; or
(e) lawful arrest.

1.4.5.3 Criminal Law Act 1967

A defendant charged with an offence may seek to rely on the common law defence of self-defence or the defence provided by s. 3(1) of the Criminal Law Act 1967.

The Criminal Law Act 1967, s. 3(1) states:

> A person may use such force as is reasonable in the circumstances in the prevention of crime or in effecting or assisting in the lawful arrest of offenders or suspected offenders or of persons unlawfully at large.

It is to these potential defences that s. 76 of the Criminal Justice and Immigration Act 2008 applies, particularly to the question of whether the degree of force used was reasonable in the circumstances. The 'degree of force' means the type and amount of force used. Section 76(10)(b) states that reasonable force in self-defence includes acting in the defence of another person.

The question whether the degree of force used by the defendant was reasonable in the circumstances is to be decided by reference to the circumstances *as the defendant believed them to be* (s. 76(3)). If the defendant claims to have held a particular belief as to the existence of any circumstances, the reasonableness or otherwise of that belief is relevant to the question whether the defendant genuinely held it. If it is determined that the defendant did genuinely hold the belief, then the defendant is entitled to rely on it even if the belief was mistaken or, if it was mistaken, the mistake was a reasonable one to have made.

....

EXAMPLE

X has a long and violent history and has been convicted of several wounding offences involving the use of a knife. In an unprovoked attack, X attacks Y in a pub by punching Y in the face. Y is aware of X's violent past and, after being punched, Y sees X's hand move towards the inside of his jacket. Y genuinely believes that X is going to stab him and so grabs hold of a chair and smashes it against X's arm, breaking X's arm in the process. X was not going to stab Y as he did not have a knife.

....

Y reacted to the circumstances as he believed them to be. The reasonableness of Y's belief is relevant in deciding whether or not Y actually held the belief. If the court accepted that Y held the belief, the fact that X did not have a knife and was not going to stab Y (a mistake by Y) will not affect Y's ability to utilise the defence.

The situation would be different if Y had been drunk and, simply seeing X walk into the pub, mistakenly thought X was going to stab him. This is because s. 76(5) would not enable Y to rely on any mistaken belief due to intoxication that was voluntarily induced.

Section 76(6) adds that the degree of force used by the defendant is not to be regarded as reasonable in the circumstances as the defendant believed them to be if it was disproportionate in those circumstances.

In deciding whether or not the degree of force used was reasonable in the circumstances, s. 76(7) requires certain considerations to be taken into account:

- that a person acting for a legitimate purpose (the purposes of the defences to which s. 76 applies) may not be able to weigh to a nicety the exact measure of any necessary action; and
- that evidence of a person having only done what the person honestly and instinctively thought was necessary for a legitimate purpose constitutes strong evidence that only reasonable action was taken by that person for that purpose.

This does not prevent other matters from being taken into account where they are relevant in deciding whether the degree of force used was reasonable in the circumstances.

KEYNOTE

Section 76 retains a single test for self-defence and the prevention of crime (or the making of an arrest). The law has been developed in line with case law regarding self-defence and the use of force, most notably *Palmer* v *The Queen* [1971] AC 814. The defence will be available if a person honestly believed it was necessary to use force and if the degree of force used was not disproportionate in the circumstances as he/she viewed them. The person who uses force is to be judged on the basis of the circumstances as he/she perceived them. In the heat of the moment, he/she will not be expected to have judged exactly what action was called for, and a degree of latitude may be given to a person who only did what he/she honestly and instinctively thought was necessary. Defendants are entitled to have their actions judged on the basis of their view of the facts as they honestly believed them to be.

1.4.5.4 'Householder' Cases

Section 43 of the Crime and Courts Act 2013 amends s. 76 of the Criminal Justice and Immigration Act 2008 so that the use of *disproportionate* force can be regarded as reasonable in the circumstances as the accused believed them to be when householders are acting to protect themselves or others from trespassers in their homes (self-defence). The use of *grossly* disproportionate force would still not be permitted. The provisions also extend to people who live and work in the same premises and armed forces personnel who may live and work in buildings such as barracks for periods of time. The provisions *will not* cover other scenarios where the use of force might be required, for example when people are defending themselves from attack on the street, preventing crime or protecting property; the current law on the use of reasonable force will apply in these situations.

1.4.5.5 Defence of Property

Section 76(2)(aa) of the Criminal Justice and Immigration Act 2008 makes it clear that the 'common law defence of defence of property' is governed by s. 76 (as well as self-defence, the prevention of crime and making an arrest).

In addition, s. 3(1) of the Criminal Law Act 1967 states that reasonable force may be used in the prevention of crime. Therefore, if a person is acting in order to prevent a crime against his/her property, it follows that force can be used to protect property.

Whether or not such force is reasonable will be subject to the requirements of s. 76 of the Criminal Justice and Immigration Act 2008. However, it might be somewhat problematic (if not impossible) to reconcile reasonable force to protect property with the taking of a person's life. It may be that such lethal force would fall foul of s. 76(6) which states that if the force used is disproportionate then it will not be regarded as being reasonable in the circumstances. Allied to this, is the fact that Article 2 of the European Convention on Human Rights does not support the taking of life in the defence of property and it can be seen that such a defence may well fail.

1.4.6 Police Officers

When using force against others, police officers will be criminally liable for any assaults they commit, in the same way as any other person.

However, just as the same offences and sentences will apply, similarly the same general defences will potentially be available to the officer. One specific issue that can often arise where force is used by a police officer is the technique employed by the officer in applying force or striking someone. This may consist of a particular technique that the officer has been trained to use—either with or without some form of weapon. The issue of whether a particular technique is a 'proper' or 'recognised' one, is not the same as the question of the *lawfulness* of any force used on that occasion. Clearly, the controlled use of a technique in which an officer has been trained may help a court in determining the issue of the lawfulness or otherwise of the use of force. So, too, will any training that the officer has (or has not) received in relation to the use of force and personal protection. However, there are times when using an 'authorised technique' will nevertheless be unlawful; conversely, there will be circumstances in which the use of an improvised strike or use of an object may be lawful. All will turn on the circumstances of the case.

1.4.7 Infancy

Children under the age of 10 are *irrebuttably* presumed to be incapable of criminal responsibility (*doli incapax*) by virtue of s. 50 of the Children and Young Persons Act 1933.

1.5 Issues in Evidence

1.5.1 Introduction

Evidence can be described as information that may be presented to a court so that it may decide on the probability of some facts asserted before it, that is information by which facts in issue tend to be proved or disproved. There are several types of evidence by which facts are open to proof—or disproof—and these are discussed below.

1.5.2 Weight and Admissibility of Evidence

The two questions that need to be applied to any evidence are:

- admissibility; and
- weight.

The question of admissibility, to be decided by the judge in all cases, is whether the evidence is relevant to a fact in issue. All evidence of facts in issue and all evidence which is sufficiently relevant to prove (or disprove) facts in issue are potentially admissible.

The admissibility of evidence is very important to the outcome of any trial as it is from this that a person's guilt is decided. When collecting evidence in a case it should always be a consideration whether the evidence being collected is the best available and whether it will be admissible.

Once it is established that the evidence is admissible, it is put before the court to determine what weight it will attach to the evidence, that is, how much effect does it have on proving or disproving the case.

1.5.2.1 Evidence Gathering

The word evidence must not be confused with information. In relation to preparing an offence file, the investigation of the offence will result in the collection of information. What is and what is not evidence can be decided at a later stage with the help of the CPS. The importance of this distinction is that rules of evidence should not restrict the initial collection of information, otherwise a fact vital to the outcome of the case may be disregarded as irrelevant and/or inadmissible.

1.5.2.2 Reasons for Excluding Admissible Evidence

Even though evidence may be admissible in criminal cases, at common law, the trial judge has a general discretion to exclude legally admissible evidence tendered by the prosecution. This can be seen in *R* v *Sang* [1980] AC 402, where it was held that:

- A trial judge, as part of his/her duty to ensure that an accused receives a fair trial, always has a discretion to exclude evidence tendered by the prosecution if in his/her opinion its prejudicial effect outweighs its probative value. In deciding if the evidence should be admitted, the question the judge asks him/herself is whether it is fair to allow the evidence, not whether it is obtained fairly or by unfair means.
- With the exception of admissions and confessions (here s. 76 of the Police and Criminal Evidence Act 1984 applies) and generally with regard to evidence obtained from the

accused after the commission of the offence, the judge generally has no discretion whether to exclude relevant admissible evidence on the ground that this was obtained by improper or unfair means.

If the evidence is relevant to the matters in issue then it is admissible and the court is not concerned with how the evidence was obtained (*Kuruma, Son of Kaniu* v *The Queen* [1955] AC 197). This proposition was upheld in *Jeffrey* v *Black* [1978] QB 490 where evidence was admissible concerning the unlawful search of premises.

Evidence may also be excluded for the following reasons:

- the incompetence of the witness;
- it relates to previous convictions, the character or disposition of the accused;
- it falls under hearsay;
- it is non-expert opinion evidence;
- it is privileged information;
- it is withheld as a matter of public policy.

There are also powers to exclude evidence under ss. 76 and 78 of the Police and Criminal Evidence Act 1984.

1.5.3 Facts in Issue

In a criminal case, facts in issue are those facts which must be proved by the prosecution in order to establish the defendant's guilt, or in exceptional cases those facts which are the essential elements of a defence, where the burden of proof is on the defendant to prove the defence.

Such facts will include:

- the identity of the defendant;
- the *actus reus*;
- the *mens rea*.

The relevant criminal conduct (*actus reus*) and state of mind (*mens rea*) will always be facts in issue, and it is therefore essential that these features are understood, both as general concepts and also in relation to the particular offence being investigated.

1.5.4 Burden of Proof

In *Re B (Children)* [2008] UKHL 35 Lord Hoffmann commented:

> If a legal rule requires a fact to be proved (a 'fact in issue'), a judge or jury must decide whether or not it happened. There is no room for a finding that it might have happened. The law operates a binary system in which the only values are 0 and 1. The fact either happened or it did not. If the tribunal is left in doubt, the doubt is resolved by a rule that one party or the other carries the burden of proof. If the party who bears the burden of proof fails to discharge it, a value of 0 is returned and the fact is treated as not having happened. If he does discharge it, a value of 1 is returned and the fact is treated as having happened.

The facts in issue fall into two distinct categories:

- the facts that the *prosecution* bear the burden of proving or disproving in order to establish the defendant's guilt;
- the facts which, in exceptional circumstances, the *defence* need to prove to show that the defendant is not guilty.

1.5.4.1 Duty of the Prosecution

'Throughout the web of the English criminal law one golden thread is always to be seen; that is the duty of the prosecution to prove the prisoner's guilt.' This famous passage is taken from the House of Lords' decision in *Woolmington* v *DPP* [1935] AC 462. The underlying principle was perhaps best explained by Geoffrey Lawrence QC in an address to the jury in a murder trial:

> The possibility of guilt is not enough, suspicion is not enough, probability is not enough, likelihood is not. A criminal matter is not a question of balancing probabilities and deciding in favour of probability.
>
> If the accusation is not proved beyond reasonable doubt against the man accused in the dock, then by the law he is entitled to be acquitted, because that is the way our rules work. It is no concession to give him the benefit of the doubt. He is entitled by law to a verdict of not guilty.

(See Brian Harris, *The Literature of the Law,* Blackstone Press, 1998.)

Therefore the general rule is that the prosecution have the legal (or persuasive) burden of proving all the elements of the offence in order to prove guilt.

In *Evans* v *DPP* [2001] EWHC Admin 369, it was held that the justices had wrongly applied *the balance of probabilities* in finding the defendant guilty rather than the full criminal standard of proof.

Where the defendant enters a plea of not guilty to the charge, the onus is on the prosecution to prove the whole of their case. This includes the 'identity of the accused, the nature of the act and the existence of any necessary knowledge or intent' (*R* v *Sims* [1946] KB 531).

Generally the onus is on the prosecution in the first instance to establish particular facts to prove the accused's guilt beyond all reasonable doubt. However, once a *prima facie* case is made out, the defence have to establish particular facts in order to rebut the prosecution evidence. Here there is a shift of the onus to establish particular facts.

1.5.4.2 Duty of the Defence

Exceptionally, the defence may have the burden of proof. In such circumstances the standard of proof for the defence is less rigorous than for the prosecution when establishing guilt (beyond all reasonable doubt). The defence will succeed if the court or jury are satisfied that the defence evidence is more probably true than false. This standard of proof is referred to as *the balance of probabilities,* the same standard of proof as operates in a civil trial.

Generally the prosecution bear the duty of proving or disproving certain facts and, if they fail to do so, the defence need say nothing; the prosecution fails and the defendant is acquitted.

Exceptionally, the common law (e.g. the defence of insanity), or a statute (e.g. diminished responsibility (s. 2 of the Homicide Act 1957)), may impose a burden on the defence to prove the defence.

The law relating to the carrying of weapons is a good illustration of where the defence may have a burden of proof. Once the prosecution have proved (beyond a reasonable doubt) that a defendant was carrying an offensive weapon, the burden then shifts to the defence to prove (on the balance of probabilities) that the defendant had lawful authority or reasonable excuse.

There will also be occasions where the defence have what is called an *evidential burden* in relation to certain specific defences they intend to rely on. Common examples of defences that only place an evidential burden on the defence are defences relating to alibis, self-defence, accident and provocation. In contrast to the evidential burden borne by the prosecution (to show that there is a case to answer by the end of the prosecution evidence), the defence's evidential burden arises somewhat differently. Unlike those defences that place a full legal burden of proof on the defence, the defence do not have to satisfy the judge of anything as such. All that the defence have to do is to ensure that there is enough evidence relating to the defence that is to be raised to enable the judge to direct the jury upon that defence as a live issue.

Section 101 of the Magistrates' Courts Act 1980 places a legal burden of proof on the accused either expressly or by implication. The section provides that where the accused relies for his/her defence on any *exemption, proviso, excuse* or *qualification*, the burden of proving this is on the accused.

KEYNOTE

An example of a summary offence where the burden of proof is on the defence is driving without insurance where the accused is required to prove he/she is insured (*Williams* v *Russell* (1933) 149 LT 190). An example of an indictable offence is where the accused was convicted on indictment of selling intoxicating liquor without a licence and the Court of Appeal held that it was for the accused to prove that he was the holder of a licence (*R* v *Edwards* [1975] QB 27).

1.6 | Entry, Search and Seizure

PACE Code of Practice for Searches of Premises by Police Officers and the Seizure of Property found by Police Officers on Persons or Premises (Code B)

A thick grey line down the margin denotes text that is an extract of the PACE Code itself (i.e. the actual wording of the legislation).

1.6.1 Introduction to Code B

The main police powers dealing with entry to premises, searching them and seizing evidence from them, are contained within the Police and Criminal Evidence Act 1984; Code B of the Codes of Practice provides detailed guidance in relation to these features.

There are many other statutes that allow such processes to take place. However, only one common law power of entry without warrant exists—to deal with a breach of the peace.

A general point worth remembering is that where police officers enter premises *lawfully* (including where they are there by invitation), they are on the premises for *all* lawful purposes (*Foster* v *Attard* [1986] Crim LR 627). This means that they can carry out any lawful functions while on the premises, even if that was not the original purpose for entry. For instance, if officers entered under a lawful power provided by the Misuse of Drugs Act 1971, they may carry out other lawful functions such as enforcing the provisions of the Gaming Act 1968. If officers are invited onto premises by someone entitled to do so, they are lawfully there unless and until that invitation is withdrawn. Once the invitation is withdrawn, the officers will become trespassers unless they have a power to be there, and the person may remove them by force (*Robson* v *Hallett* [1967] 2 QB 939). If that invitation is terminated, the person needs to communicate that clearly to the officer; merely telling officers to 'fuck off' is not necessarily sufficient (*Snook* v *Mannion* [1982] RTR 321).

The above issues are of significance to police officers but the features of the Police and Criminal Evidence Act 1984 and Code B remain the most important for the purposes of operational policing and that is the focus of this chapter.

PACE Code of Practice for Searches of Premises by Police Officers and the Seizure of Property found by Police Officers on Persons or Premises (Code B)

This Code applies to applications for warrants made after midnight 6 March 2011 and to searches and seizures taking place after midnight on 27 October 2013.

1 Introduction

1.1 This Code of Practice deals with police powers to:
- search premises
- seize and retain property found on premises and persons

1.1A These powers may be used to find:
- property and material relating to a crime
- wanted persons
- children who abscond from local authority accommodation where they have been remanded or committed by a court

1.2 A justice of the peace may issue a search warrant granting powers of entry, search and seizure, e.g. warrants to search for stolen property, drugs, firearms and evidence of serious offences. Police also have powers without a search warrant. The main ones provided by the Police and Criminal Evidence Act 1984 (PACE) include powers to search premises:
- to make an arrest
- after an arrest

1.3 The right to privacy and respect for personal property are key principles of the Human Rights Act 1998. Powers of entry, search and seizure should be fully and clearly justified before use because they may significantly interfere with the occupier's privacy. Officers should consider if the necessary objectives can be met by less intrusive means.

1.3A Powers to search and seize must be used fairly, responsibly, with respect for people who occupy premises being searched or are in charge of property being seized and without unlawful discrimination. Under the Equality Act 2010, section 149, when police officers are carrying out their functions, they also have a duty to have due regard to the need to eliminate unlawful discrimination, harassment and victimisation, to advance equality of opportunity between people who share a relevant protected characteristic and people who do not share it, and to take steps to foster good relations.

1.4 In all cases, police should therefore:
- exercise their powers courteously and with respect for persons and property
- only use reasonable force when this is considered necessary and proportionate to the circumstances.

1.5 If the provisions of PACE and this Code are not observed, evidence obtained from a search may be open to question.

KEYNOTE

In para. 1.3A, 'relevant protected characteristic' includes: age, disability, gender reassignment, pregnancy and maternity, race, religion or belief, sex and sexual orientation.

---

2 General

2.1 This Code must be readily available at all police stations for consultation by:
- police officers
- police staff
- detained persons
- members of the public

2.2 The *Notes for Guidance* [incorporated within Keynotes of this Manual] are not provisions of this Code.

2.3 This Code applies to searches of premises:
(a) by police for the purposes of an investigation into an alleged offence, with the occupier's consent, other than:

- routine scene of crime searches;
- calls to a fire or burglary made by or on behalf of an occupier or searches following the activation of fire or burglar alarms or discovery of insecure premises;
- searches when *paragraph 5.4* applies;
- bomb threat calls;

(b) under powers conferred on police officers by PACE, sections 17, 18 and 32;

(c) undertaken in pursuance of search warrants issued to and executed by constables in accordance with PACE, sections 15 and 16;

(d) subject to *paragraph 2.6*, under any other power given to police to enter premises with or without a search warrant for any purpose connected with the investigation into an alleged or suspected offence.

For the purposes of this Code, 'premises' as defined in PACE, section 23, includes any place, vehicle, vessel, aircraft, hovercraft, tent or movable structure and any offshore installation as defined in the Mineral Workings (Offshore Installations) Act 1971, section 1.

2.4 A person who has not been arrested but is searched during a search of premises should be searched in accordance with Code A.

2.5 This Code does not apply to the exercise of a statutory power to enter premises or to inspect goods, equipment or procedures if the exercise of that power is not dependent on the existence of grounds for suspecting that an offence may have been committed and the person exercising the power has no reasonable grounds for such suspicion.

2.6 This Code does not affect any directions or requirements of a search warrant, order or other power to search and seize lawfully exercised in England or Wales that any item or evidence seized under that warrant, order or power be handed over to a police force, court, tribunal, or other authority outside England or Wales. For example, warrants and orders issued in Scotland or Northern Ireland, and search warrants and powers provided for in sections 14 to 17 of the Crime (International Co-operation) Act 2003.

2.7 When this Code requires the prior authority or agreement of an officer of at least inspector or superintendent rank, that authority may be given by a sergeant or chief inspector authorised to perform the functions of the higher rank under PACE, section 107.

2.8 Written records required under this Code not made in the search record shall, unless otherwise specified, be made:
- in the recording officer's pocket book ('pocket book' includes any official report book issued to police officers) or
- on forms provided for the purpose.

2.9 Nothing in this Code requires the identity of officers, or anyone accompanying them during a search of premises, to be recorded or disclosed:
(a) in the case of enquiries linked to the investigation of terrorism; or
(b) if officers reasonably believe recording or disclosing their names might put them in danger.

In these cases officers should use warrant or other identification numbers and the name of their police station. Police staff should use any identification number provided to them by the police force.

2.10 The 'officer in charge of the search' means the officer assigned specific duties and responsibilities under this Code. Whenever there is a search of premises to which this Code applies one officer must act as the officer in charge of the search.

2.11 In this Code:
(a) 'designated person' means a person other than a police officer, designated under the Police Reform Act 2002, Part 4 who has specified powers and duties of police officers conferred or imposed on them;
(b) any reference to a police officer includes a designated person acting in the exercise or performance of the powers and duties conferred or imposed on them by their designation;
(c) a person authorised to accompany police officers or designated persons in the execution of a warrant has the same powers as a constable in the execution of the warrant and the

search and seizure of anything related to the warrant. These powers must be exercised in the company and under the supervision of a police officer.

2.12 If a power conferred on a designated person:

  (a) allows reasonable force to be used when exercised by a police officer, a designated person exercising that power has the same entitlement to use force;

  (b) includes power to use force to enter any premises, that power is not exercisable by that designated person except:

   (i) in the company and under the supervision of a police officer; or

   (ii) for the purpose of:

    • saving life or limb; or

    • preventing serious damage to property.

2.13 Designated persons must have regard to any relevant provisions of the Codes of Practice.

1.6.3.1

KEYNOTE

The purpose of para. 2.9(b) of Code B is to protect those involved in serious organised crime investigations or arrests of particularly violent suspects when there is reliable information that those arrested or their associates may threaten or cause harm to the officers or anyone accompanying them during a search of premises. In cases of doubt, an officer of inspector rank or above should be consulted.

For the purposes of para. 2.10, the officer in charge of the search should normally be the most senior officer present. Some exceptions are:

(a) a supervising officer who attends or assists at the scene of a premises search may appoint an officer of lower rank as officer in charge of the search if that officer is:

  • more conversant with the facts;

  • a more appropriate officer to be in charge of the search;

(b) when all officers in a premises search are the same rank. The supervising officer if available must make sure one of them is appointed officer in charge of the search, otherwise the officers themselves must nominate one of their number as the officer in charge;

(c) a senior officer assisting in a specialist role. This officer need not be regarded as having a general supervisory role over the conduct of the search or be appointed or expected to act as the officer in charge of the search.

Except in (c), nothing in this keynote diminishes the role and responsibilities of a supervisory officer who is present at the search or knows of a search taking place.

An officer of the rank of inspector or above may direct a designated investigating officer not to wear a uniform for the purposes of a specific operation.

1.6.3.2

KEYNOTE

Application for Warrant—s. 15 PACE

The Police and Criminal Evidence Act 1984, s. 15 states:

(1) This section and section 16 below have effect in relation to the issue to constables under any enactment, including an enactment contained in an Act passed after this Act, of warrants to enter and search premises; and an entry on or search of premises under a warrant is unlawful unless it complies with this section and section 16 below.

(2) Where a constable applies for any such warrant, it shall be his duty—

  (a) to state—

   (i) the ground on which he makes the application;

   (ii) the enactment under which the warrant would be issued; and

   (iii) if the application is for a warrant authorising entry and search on more than one occasion, the ground on which he applies for such a warrant, and whether he seeks a warrant authorising an unlimited number of entries, or (if not) the maximum number of entries desired;

  (b) to specify the matters set out in subsection (2A) below; and

  (c) to identify, so far as is practicable, the articles or persons to be sought.

(2A) The matters which must be specified pursuant to subsection (2)(b) above are—

  (a) if the application relates to one or more sets of premises specified in the application each set of premises which it is desired to enter and search; and

(b) if the application relates to any premises occupied or controlled by a person specified in the application—

    (i) as many sets of premises which it is desired to enter and search as it is reasonably practicable to specify;

    (ii) the person who is in occupation or control of those premises and any others which it is desired to enter and search;

    (iii) why it is necessary to search more premises than those specified under sub-paragraph (i); and

    (iv) why it is not reasonably practicable to specify all the premises which it is desired to enter and search.

(3) An application for such a warrant shall be made ex parte and supported by information in writing.

(4) The constable shall answer on oath any question that the justice of the peace or judge hearing the application asks him.

(5) A warrant shall authorise an entry on one occasion only unless it specifies that it authorises multiple entries.

(5A) If it specifies that it authorises multiple entries, it must also specify whether the number of entries authorised is unlimited, or limited to a specified maximum.

(6) A warrant—

(a) shall specify—

    (i) the name of the person who applies for it;

    (ii) the date on which it is issued;

    (iii) the enactment under which it is issued;

    (iv) each set of premises to be searched, or (in the case of an all premises warrant) the person who is in occupation or control of premises to be searched, together with any premises under his occupation or control which can be specified and which are to be searched; and

(b) shall identify, so far as is practicable, the articles or persons to be sought.

(7) Two copies shall be made of a warrant (see section 8(1A)(a) above) which specifies only one set of premises and does not authorise multiple entries; and as many copies as are reasonably required may be made of any other kind of warrant.

(8) The copies shall be clearly certified as copies.

<hr>

1.6.3.3   KEYNOTE

Execution of a Warrant—s. 16 PACE

The Police and Criminal Evidence Act 1984, s. 16 states:

(1) A warrant to enter and search premises may be executed by any constable.

(2) Such a warrant may authorise persons to accompany any constable who is executing it.

(2A) A person so authorised has the same powers as the constable whom he accompanies in respect of—

(a) the execution of the warrant, and

(b) the seizure of anything to which the warrant relates.

(2B) But he may exercise those powers only in the company, and under the supervision, of a constable.

(3) Entry and search under a warrant must be within three months from the date of its issue.

(3A) If the warrant is an all premises warrant, no premises which are not specified in it may be entered or searched unless a police officer of at least the rank of inspector has in writing authorised them to be entered.

(3B) No premises may be entered or searched for the second or any subsequent time under a warrant which authorises multiple entries unless a police officer of at least the rank of inspector has in writing authorised that entry to those premises.

(4) Entry and search under a warrant must be at a reasonable hour unless it appears to the constable executing it that the purpose of a search may be frustrated on an entry at a reasonable hour.

(5) Where the occupier of premises which are to be entered and searched is present at the time when a constable seeks to execute a warrant to enter and search them, the constable—

(a) shall identify himself to the occupier and, if not in uniform, shall produce to him documentary evidence that he is a constable;

(b) shall produce the warrant to him; and

(c) shall supply him with a copy of it.

(6) Where—

(a) the occupier of such premises is not present at the time when a constable seeks to execute such a warrant; but

(b) some other person who appears to the constable to be in charge of the premises is present, Subsection (5) above shall have effect as if any reference to the occupier were a reference to that other person.

(7) If there is no person present who appears to the constable to be in charge of the premises, he shall leave a copy of the warrant in a prominent place on the premises.

(8) A search under a warrant may only be a search to the extent required for the purpose for which the warrant was issued.

(9) A constable executing the warrant shall make an endorsement on it stating—

    (a) whether the articles or persons sought were found; and

    (b) whether any articles were seized, other than articles which were sought; and

    unless the warrant is a warrant specifying one set of premises only, he shall do so separately in respect of each set of premises entered and searched, which he shall in each case state in the endorsement.

(10) A warrant shall be returned to the appropriate person mentioned in subsection (10A) below—

    (a) when it has been executed; or

    (b) in the case of a specific premises warrant which has not been executed, or an all premises warrant, or any warrant authorising multiple entries, upon the expiry of the period of three months referred to in subsection (3) above or sooner.

(10A) The appropriate person is—

    (a) if the warrant was issued by a justice of the peace, the designated officer for the local justice area in which the justice was acting when he issued the warrant;

    (b) if it was issued by a judge, the appropriate officer of the court from which he issued it.

(11) A warrant which is returned under subsection (10) above shall be retained for 12 months from its return—

    (a) by the designated officer for the local justice area, if it was returned under paragraph (i) of that subsection; and

    (b) by the appropriate officer, if it was returned under paragraph (ii).

(12) If during the period for which a warrant is to be retained the occupier of premises to which it relates asks to inspect it, he shall be allowed to do so.

1.6.3.4   KEYNOTE

General Points

If an application for a warrant is refused, no further application can be made unless it is supported by additional grounds.

'Premises' include any place, and in particular, (a) any vehicle, vessel, aircraft or hovercraft; (b) any offshore installation; (c) any renewable energy installation; (d) any tent or moveable structure (s. 23 of the 1984 Act).

The details of the extent of the proposed search should be made clear in the application and the officer swearing the warrant out must be prepared to answer *any* questions put to him/her on oath under s. 15(4). Courts will go into background detail about the particular premises, or part of the premises, and who is likely to be present on the premises at the time the warrant is executed (e.g. children).

1.6.3.5   KEYNOTE

Examples

Sections 15 and 16 of the 1984 Act apply to all search warrants issued to and executed by constables under any enactment, e.g. search warrants issued by:

(a) a justice of the peace under:

- Theft Act 1968, s. 26—stolen property;
- Misuse of Drugs Act 1971, s. 23—controlled drugs;
- PACE, s. 8—evidence of an indictable offence;
- Terrorism Act 2000, sch. 5, para. 1;
- Terrorism Prevention and Investigation Measures Act 2011, sch. 5, para. 8(2)(b)—search of premises for compliance purposes.

(b) a Circuit judge under:

- PACE, sch. 1;
- Terrorism Act 2000, sch. 5, para. 11.

Examples of the other powers in para. 2.3(d) include:

(a) Road Traffic Act 1988, s. 6E(1) giving police power to enter premises under s. 6E(1) to:

- require a person to provide a specimen of breath; or
- arrest a person following
  - ◊ a positive breath test;
  - ◊ failure to provide a specimen of breath;

(b) Transport and Works Act 1992, s. 30(4) giving police powers to enter premises mirroring the powers in (a) in relation to specified persons working on transport systems to which the Act applies;

(c) Criminal Justice Act 1988, s. 139B giving police power to enter and search school premises for offensive weapons, bladed or pointed articles;

(d) Terrorism Act 2000, sch. 5, paras 3 and 15 empowering a superintendent in urgent cases to give written authority for police to enter and search premises for the purposes of a terrorist investigation;

(e) Explosives Act 1875, s. 73(b) empowering a superintendent to give written authority for police to enter premises, examine and search them for explosives;

(f) search warrants and production orders or the equivalent issued in Scotland or Northern Ireland endorsed under the Summary Jurisdiction (Process) Act 1881 or the Petty Sessions (Ireland) Act 1851 respectively for execution in England and Wales.

(g) Terrorism Prevention and Investigation Measures Act 2011, sch. 5, paras 5(1), 6(2)(b) and 7(2), searches relating to TPIM notices (see para. 10.1).

Searching Persons

The Criminal Justice Act 1988, s. 139B provides that a constable who has reasonable grounds for suspecting that an offence under the Criminal Justice Act 1988, s. 139A or 139AA has been or is being committed may enter school premises and search the premises and any persons on the premises for any bladed or pointed article or offensive weapon. Persons may be searched under a warrant issued under the Misuse of Drugs Act 1971, s. 23(3) to search premises for drugs or documents only if the warrant specifically authorises the search of persons on the premises. Powers to search premises under certain terrorism provisions also authorise the search of persons on the premises, e.g. under paras 1, 2, 11 and 15 of sch. 5 to the Terrorism Act 2000 and s. 52 of the Anti-terrorism, Crime and Security Act 2001.

Immigration Act 1971

The Immigration Act 1971, part III and sch. 2 gives immigration officers powers to enter and search premises, seize and retain property, with and without a search warrant. These are similar to the powers available to police under search warrants issued by a justice of the peace and without a warrant under ss. 17, 18, 19 and 32 of the 1984 Act except they only apply to specified offences under the Immigration Act 1971 and immigration control powers. For certain types of investigations and enquiries these powers avoid the need for the Immigration Service to rely on police officers becoming directly involved. When exercising these powers, immigration officers are required by the Immigration and Asylum Act 1999, s. 145 to have regard to this Code's corresponding provisions. When immigration officers are dealing with persons or property at police stations, police officers should give appropriate assistance to help them discharge their specific duties and responsibilities.

1.6.3.6   **KEYNOTE**

Exclusion of Evidence

If the provisions of these sections are not fully complied with, any entry and search made under a warrant will be unlawful. Although the officers executing the warrant may have some protection from personal liability where there has been a defect in the *procedure* by which the warrant was issued, failure to follow the requirements of ss. 15 and 16 may result in the exclusion of any evidence obtained under the warrant. Therefore, where officers failed to provide the occupier of the searched premises with a copy of the warrant (under s.16(5)(c)), they were obliged to return the property seized during the search (*R* v *Chief Constable of Lancashire, ex parte Parker* [1993] QB 577).

If a warrant itself is invalid for some reason, any entry and subsequent seizure made under it are unlawful (*R* v *Central Criminal Court and British Railways Board, ex parte AJD Holdings Ltd* [1992] Crim LR 669).

Very minor departures from the letter of the warrant, however, will not render any search unlawful (*Attorney-General of Jamaica* v *Williams* [1998] AC 351).

KEYNOTE

Search Warrants for Indictable Offences—s. 8 PACE

The Police and Criminal Evidence Act 1984, s. 8 states:

(1) If on an application made by a constable a justice of the peace is satisfied that there are reasonable grounds for believing—

    (a) that an indictable offence has been committed; and

    (b) that there is material on premises mentioned in subsection (1A) below which is likely to be of substantial value (whether by itself or together with other material) to the investigation of the offence; and

    (c) that the material is likely to be relevant evidence; and

    (d) that it does not consist of or include items subject to legal privilege, excluded material or special procedure material; and

    (e) that any of the conditions specified in subsection (3) below applies in relation to each set of premises specified in the application

    he may issue a warrant authorising a constable to enter and search the premises.

(1A) The premises referred to in subsection (1)(b) above are—

    (a) one or more sets of premises specified in the application (in which case the application is for a 'specific premises warrant'); or

    (b) any premises occupied or controlled by a person specified in the application, including such sets of premises as are so specified (in which case the application is for an 'all premises warrant').

(1B) If the application is for an all premises warrant, the justice of the peace must also be satisfied—

    (a) that because of the particulars of the offence referred to in paragraph (a) of subsection (1) above, there are reasonable grounds for believing that it is necessary to search premises occupied or controlled by the person in question which are not specified in the application in order to find the material referred to in paragraph (b) of that subsection; and

    (b) that it is not reasonably practicable to specify in the application all the premises which he occupies or controls and which might need to be searched.

(1C) The warrant may authorise entry to and search of premises on more than one occasion if, on the application, the justice of the peace is satisfied that it is necessary to authorise multiple entries in order to achieve the purpose for which he issues the warrant.

(1D) If it authorises multiple entries, the number of entries authorised may be unlimited, or limited to a maximum.

(2) A constable may seize and retain anything for which a search has been authorised under subsection (1) above.

(3) The conditions mentioned in subsection (1)(e) above are—

    (a) that it is not practicable to communicate with any person entitled to grant entry to the premises;

    (b) that it is practicable to communicate with a person entitled to grant entry to the premises but it is not practicable to communicate with any person entitled to grant access to the evidence;

    (c) that entry to the premises will not be granted unless a warrant is produced;

    (d) that the purpose of a search may be frustrated or seriously prejudiced unless a constable arriving at the premises can secure immediate entry to them.

(4) In this Act 'relevant evidence', in relation to an offence, means anything that would be admissible in evidence at a trial for the offence.

(5) The power to issue a warrant conferred by this section is in addition to any such power otherwise conferred.

This section provides that a constable can apply for two different types of search warrant: a 'specific premises warrant' for the search of one set of premises; and an 'all premises warrant' when it is necessary to search all premises occupied or controlled by an individual, but where it is not reasonably practicable to specify all such premises at the time of applying for the warrant. The warrant allows access to all premises occupied or controlled by that person, both those which are specified on the application, and those which are not. Note that s. 8(1C) and (1D) provide that a warrant (either an 'all premises warrant' or a 'specific premises warrant') may authorise access on more than one occasion, and if multiple entries are authorised these may be unlimited or limited to a maximum.

The officer applying for a warrant under s. 8 must have reasonable grounds for believing that material which is likely *to be of substantial value to the investigation of the offence* is on the premises specified. Therefore, when executing such a warrant, the officer must be able to show that any material seized thereunder fell within that description (*R* v *Chief Constable of the Warwickshire Constabulary, ex parte Fitzpatrick* [1999] 1 WLR 564). Possession of a warrant under s. 8 does not authorise police officers to seize all material found on the relevant premises to be taken away and 'sifted' somewhere else (*R* v *Chesterfield Justices, ex parte Bramley* [2000] QB 576) (see s. 50 of the Criminal Justice and Police Act 2001 for the power to 'seize and sift').

This means that material which is solely of value for *intelligence* purposes may not be seized under a s. 8 warrant.

The power to apply for and execute a warrant under s. 8 and to carry out the actions under s. 8(2) are among those powers that can be conferred on a person designated as an Investigating Officer under sch. 4 to the Police Reform Act 2002.

The conditions set out under s. 8(1)(e) are part of the *application* process, not part of the general execution process (which is set out at s. 16 above). Therefore the officer swearing out a s. 8 warrant will have to satisfy the court that any of those conditions apply.

1.6.3.8 KEYNOTE

Legally Privileged Material

Material which falls within the definition in s. 10 of the 1984 Act is subject to legal privilege which means that it cannot be searched for or seized.

The Police and Criminal Evidence Act 1984, s. 10 states:

(1) Subject to subsection (2) below, in this Act 'items subject to legal privilege' means—
  (a) communications between a professional legal adviser and his client or any person representing his client made in connection with the giving of legal advice to the client;
  (b) communications between a professional legal adviser and his client or any person representing his client or between such an adviser or his client or any such representative and any other person made in connection with or in contemplation of legal proceedings and for the purposes of such proceedings; and
  (c) items enclosed with or referred to in such communications and made—
    (i) in connection with the giving of legal advice; or
    (ii) in connection with or in contemplation of legal proceedings and for the purposes of such proceedings,
  when they are in the possession of a person who is entitled to possession of them.

Items held with the intention of furthering a criminal purpose are not subject to this privilege (s. 10(2)). When making an application for a warrant to search for and seize such material the procedure under sch. 1 should be used. Occasions where this will happen are rare and would include instances where a solicitor's firm is the subject of a criminal investigation (*R v Leeds Crown Court, ex parte Switalski* [1991] Crim LR 559). However, it may be possible during a search to ascertain which material is subject to legal privilege and which might be lawfully seized under the warrant being executed. Therefore, although a warrant cannot authorise a search for legally privileged material, the fact that such material is inadvertently seized in the course of a search authorised by a proper warrant does not render the search unlawful (*R v HM Customs and Excise, ex parte Popely* [2000] Crim LR 388).

1.6.3.9 KEYNOTE

Excluded Material

Access to 'excluded material' can generally only be gained by applying to a judge for a production order under the procedure set out in s. 9 of, and sch. 1 to, the 1984 Act and PACE Code B. That strict statutory procedure also applies to the application for and execution of warrants by Investigating Officers designated under sch. 4 to the Police Reform Act 2002.

The Police and Criminal Evidence Act 1984, s. 11 states:

(1) Subject to the following provisions of this section, in this Act 'excluded material' means—
  (a) personal records which a person has acquired or created in the course of any trade, business, profession or other occupation or for the purposes of any paid or unpaid office and which he holds in confidence;
  (b) human tissue or tissue fluid which has been taken for the purposes of diagnosis or medical treatment and which a person holds in confidence;
  (c) journalistic material which a person holds in confidence and which consists—

            (i)   of documents; or

            (ii) of records other than documents.

    (2) A person holds material other than journalistic material in confidence for the purposes of this section if he holds it subject—

            (a) to an express or implied undertaking to hold it in confidence; or

            (b) to a restriction on disclosure or an obligation of secrecy contained in any enactment, including an enactment contained in an Act passed after this Act.

    (3) A person holds journalistic material in confidence for the purposes of this section if—

            (a) he holds it subject to such an undertaking, restriction or obligation; and

            (b) it has been continuously held (by one or more persons) subject to such an undertaking, restriction or obligation since it was first acquired or created for the purposes of journalism.

Medical records and dental records would fall into this category, as might records made by priests or religious advisers.

'Personal records' are defined under s. 12 of the 1984 Act and include records relating to the physical or mental health, counselling or assistance given to an individual who can be identified by those records.

'Journalistic material' is defined under s. 13 as material acquired or created for the purposes of journalism.

1.6.3.10

KEYNOTE

Special Procedure Material

Special procedure material can be gained by applying for a search warrant or a production order under sch. 1 to the 1984 Act.

The Police and Criminal Evidence Act 1984, s. 14 states:

    (1) In this Act 'special procedure material' means—

            (a) material to which subsection (2) below applies; and

            (b) journalistic material, other than excluded material.

    (2) Subject to the following provisions of this section, this subsection applies to material, other than items subject to legal privilege and excluded material, in the possession of a person who—

            (a) acquired or created it in the course of any trade, business, profession or other occupation or for the purpose of any paid or unpaid office; and

            (b) holds it subject—

                (i)   to an express or implied undertaking to hold it in confidence; or

                (ii) to a restriction or obligation such as is mentioned in section 11(2)(b) above.

For items subject to 'legal privilege' and 'excluded material', see paras 1.6.3.8 and 1.6.3.9.

The person believed to be in possession of the material must have come by it under the circumstances set out at s. 14(2)(a) *and* must hold it under the undertakings or obligations set out at s. 14(2)(b).

1.6.4

3 Search warrants and production orders

(a) Before making an application

3.1   When information appears to justify an application, the officer must take reasonable steps to check the information is accurate, recent and not provided maliciously or irresponsibly. An application may not be made on the basis of information from an anonymous source if corroboration has not been sought.

3.2   The officer shall ascertain as specifically as possible the nature of the articles concerned and their location.

3.3   The officer shall make reasonable enquiries to:

    (i)   establish if:

- anything is known about the likely occupier of the premises and the nature of the premises themselves;
- the premises have been searched previously and how recently;

(ii) obtain any other relevant information.

3.4 An application:

    (a) to a justice of the peace for a search warrant or to a Circuit judge for a search warrant or production order under PACE, Schedule 1 must be supported by a signed written authority from an officer of inspector rank or above:

Note: If the case is an urgent application to a justice of the peace and an inspector or above is not readily available, the next most senior officer on duty can give the written authority.

    (b) to a circuit judge under the Terrorism Act 2000, Schedule 5 for
- a production order;
- search warrant; or
- an order requiring an explanation of material seized or produced under such a warrant or production order

must be supported by a signed written authority from an officer of superintendent rank or above.

3.5 Except in a case of urgency, if there is reason to believe a search might have an adverse effect on relations between the police and the community, the officer in charge shall consult the local police/community liaison officer:
- before the search; or
- in urgent cases, as soon as practicable after the search.

(b) Making an application

3.6 A search warrant application must be supported in writing, specifying:

    (a) the enactment under which the application is made;

    (b)

        (i) whether the warrant is to authorise entry and search of:
- one set of premises; or
- if the application is under PACE section 8, or Schedule 1, paragraph 12, more than one set of specified premises or all premises occupied or controlled by a specified person; and

        (ii) the premises to be searched;

    (c) the object of the search;

    (d) the grounds for the application, including, when the purpose of the proposed search is to find evidence of an alleged offence, an indication of how the evidence relates to the investigation;

    (da) where the application is under PACE section 8, or Schedule 1, paragraph 12 for a single warrant to enter and search:

        (i) more than one set of specified premises, the officer must specify each set of premises which it is desired to enter and search

        (ii) all premises occupied or controlled by a specified person, the officer must specify:
- as many sets of premises which it is desired to enter and search as it is reasonably practicable to specify;
- the person who is in occupation or control of those premises and any others which it is desired to search;
- why it is necessary to search more premises than those which can be specified;
- why it is not reasonably practicable to specify all the premises which it is desired to enter and search;

    (db) whether an application under PACE section 8 is for a warrant authorising entry and search on more than one occasion, and if so, the officer must state the grounds for this and whether the desired number of entries authorised is unlimited or a specified maximum;

(e) there are no reasonable grounds to believe the material to be sought, when making application to a:
  (i) justice of the peace or a Circuit Judge consists of or includes items subject to legal privilege;
  (ii) justice of the peace, consists of or includes excluded material or special procedure material;
Note: this does not affect the additional powers of seizure in the Criminal Justice and Police Act 2001, Part 2 covered in paragraph 7.7;
(f) if applicable, a request for the warrant to authorise a person or persons to accompany the officer who executes the warrant.

3.7 A search warrant application under PACE, Schedule 1, paragraph 12(a), shall if appropriate indicate why it is believed service of notice of an application for a production order may seriously prejudice the investigation. Applications for search warrants under the Terrorism Act 2000, Schedule 5, paragraph 11 must indicate why a production order would not be appropriate.

3.8 If a search warrant application is refused, a further application may not be made for those premises unless supported by additional grounds.

1.6.4.1

KEYNOTE

The identity of an informant need not be disclosed when making an application, but the officer should be prepared to answer any questions the magistrate or judge may have about:

- the accuracy of previous information from that source
- any other related matters.

Under s. 16(2) of the 1984 Act, a search warrant may authorise persons other than police officers to accompany the constable who executes the warrant. This includes, for example, any suitably qualified or skilled person or an expert in a particular field whose presence is needed to help accurately identify the material sought or to advise where certain evidence is most likely to be found and how it should be dealt with. It does not give them any right to force entry, but it gives them the right to be on the premises during the search and to search for or seize property without the occupier's permission.

The information supporting a search warrant application should be as specific as possible, particularly in relation to the articles or persons being sought and where in the premises it is suspected they may be found.

1.6.5

4 Entry without warrant—particular powers

(a) Making an arrest etc.

4.1 The conditions under which an officer may enter and search premises without a warrant are set out in PACE, section 17. It should be noted that this section does not create or confer any powers of arrest.

1.6.5.1

KEYNOTE

Power of Entry—s.17 PACE

The Police and Criminal Evidence Act 1984, s. 17 states:

(1) Subject to the following provisions of this section, and without prejudice to any other enactment, a constable may enter and search any premises for the purpose—

    (a)   of executing—

        (i) a warrant of arrest issued in connection with or arising out of criminal proceedings; or

        (ii) a warrant of commitment issued under section 76 of the Magistrates' Courts Act 1980;

    (b)   of arresting a person for an indictable offence;

    (c)   of arresting a person for an offence under—

        (i) section 1 (prohibition of uniforms in connection with political objectives) of the Public Order Act 1936;

        (ii) any enactment contained in sections 6 to 8 or 10 of the Criminal Law Act 1977 (offences relating to entering and remaining on property);

        (iii) section 4 of the Public Order Act 1986 (fear or provocation of violence);

        (iiia) section 4 (driving etc. when under influence of drink or drugs) or 163 (failure to stop when required to do so by constable in uniform) of the Road Traffic Act 1988;

        (iiib) section 27 of the Transport and Works Act 1992 (which relates to offences involving drink or drugs);

        (iv) section 76 of the Criminal Justice and Public Order Act 1994 (failure to comply with interim possession order);

        (v) any of sections 4, 5, 6(1) and (2), 7 and 8(1) and (2) of the Animal Welfare Act 2006 (offences relating to the prevention of harm to animals);

        (vi) section 144 of the Legal Aid, Sentencing and Punishment of Offenders Act 2012 (squatting in a residential building);

    (ca) of arresting, in pursuance of section 32(1A) of the Children and Young Persons Act 1969, any child or young person who has been remanded or committed to local authority accommodation or youth detention accommodation under section 91 of the Legal Aid, Sentencing and Punishment of Offenders Act 2012;

    (caa) of arresting a person for an offence to which section 61 of the Animal Health Act 1981 applies;

    (cab) of arresting a person under any of the following provisions—

        (i) section 30D(1) or (2A);

        (ii) section 46A(1) or (1A);

        (iii) section 5B(7) of the Bail Act 1976 (arrest where a person fails to surrender to custody in accordance with a court order);

        (iv) section 7(3) of the Bail Act 1976 (arrest where a person is not likely to surrender to custody etc.);

        (v) section 97(1) of the Legal Aid, Sentencing and Punishment of Offenders Act 2012 (arrest where a child is suspected of breaking conditions of remand);

    (cb) of recapturing any person who is, or is deemed for any purpose to be, unlawfully at large while liable to be detained—

        (i) in a prison, remand centre, young offender institution or secure training centre, or

        (ii) in pursuance of section 92 of the Powers of Criminal Courts (Sentencing) Act 2000 (dealing with children and young persons guilty of grave crimes), in any other place;

    (d)   of recapturing any person whatever who is unlawfully at large and whom he is pursuing; or

    (e)   of saving life or limb or preventing serious damage to property.

(2) Except for the purpose specified in paragraph (e) of subsection (1) above, the powers of entry and search conferred by this section—

    (a)   are only exercisable if the constable has reasonable grounds for believing that the person whom he is seeking is on the premises; and

    (b)   are limited, in relation to premises consisting of two or more separate dwellings, to powers to enter and search—

        (i) any parts of the premises which the occupiers of any dwelling comprised in the premises use in common with the occupiers of any other such dwelling; and

        (ii) any such dwelling in which the constable has reasonable grounds for believing that the person whom he is seeking may be.

(3) The powers of entry and search conferred by this section are only exercisable for the purposes specified in subsection (1)(c)(ii) or (iv) above by a constable in uniform.

(4) The power of search conferred by this section is only a power to search to the extent that is reasonably required for the purpose for which the power of entry is exercised.

(5) Subject to subsection (6) below, all the rules of common law under which a constable has power to enter premises without a warrant are hereby abolished.

(6) Nothing in subsection (5) above affects any power of entry to deal with or prevent a breach of the peace.

Force may be used in exercising the power of entry where it is necessary to do so. Generally, the officer should first attempt to communicate with the occupier of the premises, explaining by what authority and for what purpose entry is to be made, before making a forcible entry. Clearly though, there will be occasions where such communication is impossible, impracticable or unnecessary; in those cases there is no need for the officer to enter into such an explanation (*O'Loughlin* v *Chief Constable of Essex* [1998] 1 WLR 374).

In a case where police had been called to an address by an abandoned 999 call, the officers had to move a man away from the front door in order to gain entry under s. 17. It was held that the officers had the power to use reasonable force in order to do so under s. 117 of the Police and Criminal Evidence Act 1984 (*Smith (Peter John)* v *DPP* [2001] EWHC Admin 55).

'Unlawfully at large' does not have a particular statutory meaning and can apply to someone who is subject to an order under the Mental Health Act 1983 or someone who has escaped from custody. The pursuit of the person who is unlawfully at large must be 'fresh', that is, the power will only be available while the officer is actually 'pursuing' the person concerned (*D'Souza* v *DPP* [1992] 1 WLR 1073).

The power of a constable under s. 17(1)(d) to enter and search premises to recapture a person who is unlawfully at large and whom he/she is pursuing extends to entry to retake a mentally ill patient unlawfully at large provided that such a patient is liable to be retaken and returned to hospital and provided that the pursuit of such a person is almost contemporaneous with the entry to the premises, a term which is somewhat wider than 'hot pursuit'.

The officer must have reasonable grounds to *believe* that the person is on the premises in all cases except saving life and limb at s. 17(1)(e).

The power to enter and search any premises in the relevant police area for the purpose of saving life or limb or preventing serious damage to property above is among those that can be conferred on a designated person under sch. 4 to the Police Reform Act 2002.

(b) Search of premises where arrest takes place or the arrested person was immediately before arrest

4.2   When a person has been arrested for an indictable offence, a police officer has power under PACE, section 32 to search the premises where the person was arrested or where the person was immediately before being arrested.

1.6.5.2

KEYNOTE

Power to Search after Arrest—s. 32 PACE

The Police and Criminal Evidence Act 1984, s. 32 states:

(1)   A constable may search an arrested person, in any case where the person to be searched has been arrested at a place other than a police station, if the constable has reasonable grounds for believing that the arrested person may present a danger to himself or others.

(2)   Subject to subsections (3) to (5) below, a constable shall also have power in any such case—
   (a)   to search the arrested person for anything—
      (i)   which he might use to assist him to escape from lawful custody; or
      (ii)   which might be evidence relating to an offence; and
   (b)   if the offence for which he has been arrested is an indictable offence, to enter and search any premises in which he was when arrested or immediately before he was arrested for evidence relating to the offence.

(3)   The power to search conferred by subsection (2) above is only a power to search to the extent that is reasonably required for the purpose of discovering any such thing or any such evidence.

(4)   The powers conferred by this section to search a person are not to be construed as authorising a constable to require a person to remove any of his clothing in public other than an outer coat, jacket or gloves but they do authorise a search of a person's mouth.

(5)   A constable may not search a person in the exercise of the power conferred by subsection (2)(a) above unless he has reasonable grounds for believing that the person to be searched may have concealed on him anything for which a search is permitted under that paragraph.

The power to search the arrested person under s. 32(1) is a general one relating to safety.

The House of Lords have confirmed that the police have a common law power to search for and seize property after a lawful arrest (*R* v *Governor of Pentonville Prison, ex parte Osman* [1990] 1 WLR 277). This decision was confirmed by the House of Lords in *R (On the Application of Rottman)* v *Commissioner of Police of the*

Metropolis [2002] UKHL 20. In *Rottman* it was held that it was a well-established principle of the common law that an arresting officer had the power to search a room in which a person had been arrested (per *Ghani v Jones* [1970] 1 QB 693). This extended power is not limited to purely 'domestic' offences, but also applies to cases involving extradition offences.

Section 32 also states:

(6) A constable may not search premises in the exercise of the power conferred by subsection (2)(b) above unless he has reasonable grounds for believing that there is evidence for which a search is permitted under that paragraph on the premises.

(7) In so far as the power of search conferred by subsection (2)(b) above relates to premises consisting of two or more separate dwellings, it is limited to a power to search—

(a) any dwelling in which the arrest took place or in which the person arrested was immediately before his arrest; and

(b) any parts of the premises which the occupier of any such dwelling uses in common with the occupiers of any other dwellings comprised in the premises.

(8) A constable searching a person in the exercise of the power conferred by subsection (1) above may seize and retain anything he finds, if he has reasonable grounds for believing that the person searched might use it to cause physical injury to himself or to any other person.

(9) A constable searching a person in the exercise of the power conferred by subsection (2)(a) above may seize and retain anything he finds, other than an item subject to legal privilege, if he has reasonable grounds for believing—

(a) that he might use it to assist him to escape from lawful custody; or

(b) that it is evidence of an offence or has been obtained in consequence of the commission of an offence.

(10) Nothing in this section shall be taken to affect the power conferred by section 43 of the Terrorism Act 2000.

Both 'reasonable grounds' and 'immediately' are questions of fact for a court to determine. It has been held that the power under s. 32(2)(b) is one for use at the time of arrest and should not be used to return to the relevant premises some time after the arrest in the way that s. 18 of the 1984 Act may be used (*R v Badham* [1987] Crim LR 202).

Officers exercising their power to enter and search under s. 32 must have a *genuine belief* that there is evidence on the premises; it is not a licence for a general fishing expedition (*R v Beckford* [1992] 94 Cr App R 43).

The Divisional Court has refused to allow s. 32 to be used in a situation where the arrested person had not been in the relevant premises (where he did not live) for a period of over two hours preceding his arrest and where there were no reasonable grounds for believing that he presented a danger to himself or others (*Hewitson v Chief Constable of Dorset Police* [2003] EWHC 3296 (QB)).

(c) Search of premises occupied or controlled by the arrested person

4.3 The specific powers to search premises which <u>are</u> occupied or controlled by a person arrested for an indictable offence are set out in PACE, section 18. They may not be exercised, except if section 18(5) applies, unless an officer of inspector rank or above has given written authority. That authority should only be given when the authorising officer is satisfied that the premises <u>are</u> occupied or controlled by the arrested person and that the necessary grounds exist. If possible the authorising officer should record the authority on the Notice of Powers and Rights and, subject to *paragraph 2.9*, sign the Notice. The record of the grounds for the search and the nature of the evidence sought as required by section 18(7) of the Act should be made in:

- the custody record if there is one, otherwise
- the officer's pocket book, or
- the search record.

KEYNOTE

Power to Search after Arrest for Indictable Offence—s. 18 PACE

The Police and Criminal Evidence Act 1984, s. 18 states:

(1) Subject to the following provisions of this section, a constable may enter and search any premises occupied or controlled by a person who is under arrest for an indictable offence, if he has reasonable grounds for suspecting that there is on the premises evidence, other than items subject to legal privilege, that relates—

(a) to that offence; or

(b) to some other indictable offence which is connected with or similar to that offence.

(2) A constable may seize and retain anything for which he may search under subsection (1) above.

(3) The power to search conferred by subsection (1) above is only a power to search to the extent that is reasonably required for the purpose of discovering such evidence.

(4) Subject to subsection (5) below, the powers conferred by this section may not be exercised unless an officer of the rank of inspector or above has authorised them in writing.

(5) A constable may conduct a search under subsection (1)—

(a) before the person is taken to a police station or released on bail under section 30A; and

(b) without obtaining an authorisation under subsection (4), if the condition in subsection (5A) is satisfied.

(5A) The condition is that the presence of the person at a place (other than a police station) is necessary for the effective investigation of the offence.

(6) If a constable conducts a search by virtue of subsection (5) above, he shall inform an officer of the rank of inspector or above that he has made the search as soon as practicable after he has made it.

(7) An officer who—

(a) authorises a search; or

(b) is informed of a search under subsection (6) above, shall make a record in writing—

(i) of the grounds for the search; and

(ii) of the nature of the evidence that was sought.

(8) If the person who was in occupation or control of the premises at the time of the search is in police detention at the time the record is to be made, the officer shall make the record as part of his custody record.

The power under s. 18 only applies to premises which *are* occupied and controlled by a person under arrest for an indictable offence; reasonable *suspicion* that the person occupies or controls the premises *is not sufficient*. A short stay may be sufficient to amount to 'occupation', but it must be such as to support the belief that it will have caused or contributed to the evidence sought being on the premises (*R (AB and CD)* v *Huddersfield Magistrates' Court and Chief Constable of West Yorkshire Police* [2014] 2 Cr App R 409 (25)).

The search is limited to evidence relating to the indictable offence for which the person has been arrested or another indictable offence which is similar or connected; it does not authorise a general search for anything that might be of use for other purposes (e.g. for intelligence reports). The extent of the search is limited by s. 18(3). If you are looking for a stolen fridge-freezer, you would not be empowered to search through drawers or small cupboards. You would be able to, however, if you were looking for packaging, receipts or other documents relating to the fridge-freezer.

That authority is for a search which is lawful *in all other respects*, that is, the other conditions imposed by s. 18 must be met. An inspector cannot make an otherwise unlawful entry and search lawful simply by authorising it (*Krohn* v *DPP* [1997] COD 345).

Where officers carry out a search under s. 18 they must, so far as is possible in the circumstances, explain to the occupier(s) the reason for it. If officers attempt to carry out an authorised search under s. 18 without attempting to explain to an occupier the reason, it may mean that the officers are not acting in the execution of their duty and their entry may be lawfully resisted (*Lineham* v *DPP* [2000] Crim LR 861).

The provision under s. 18(5) relates to cases where the presence of the person *is in fact necessary* for the effective investigation of the offence. If such a search is made, the searching officer must inform an inspector (or above) as soon as practicable after the search.

If the person is in police detention after the arrest, the facts concerning the search must be recorded in the custody record. Where a person is re-arrested under s. 31 of the 1984 Act for an indictable offence, the powers to search under s. 18 begin again, that is, a new power to search is created in respect of each indictable offence.

5 Search with consent

5.1 Subject to *paragraph 5.4*, if it is proposed to search premises with the consent of a person entitled to grant entry the consent must, if practicable, be given in writing on the Notice of Powers and Rights before the search. The officer must make any necessary enquiries to be satisfied the person is in a position to give such consent.

5.2 Before seeking consent the officer in charge of the search shall state the purpose of the proposed search and its extent. This information must be as specific as possible, particularly regarding the articles or persons being sought and the parts of the premises to be searched. The person concerned must be clearly informed they are not obliged to consent, that any consent can be withdrawn at any time, including before the search starts or while it is under-way and anything seized may be produced in evidence. If at the time the person is not suspected of an offence, the officer shall say this when stating the purpose of the search.

5.3 An officer cannot enter and search or continue to search premises under *paragraph 5.1* if consent is given under duress or withdrawn before the search is completed.

5.4 It is unnecessary to seek consent under *paragraphs 5.1* and *5.2* if this would cause disproportionate inconvenience to the person concerned.

KEYNOTE

In a lodging house or similar accommodation, every reasonable effort should be made to obtain the consent of the tenant, lodger or occupier. A search should not be made solely on the basis of the landlord's consent.

If the intention is to search premises under the authority of a warrant or a power of entry and search without warrant, and the occupier of the premises cooperates in accordance with para. 6.4, there is no need to obtain written consent.

Paragraph 5.4 is intended to apply when it is reasonable to assume innocent occupiers would agree to, and expect, police to take the proposed action, e.g. if:

- a suspect has fled the scene of a crime or to evade arrest and it is necessary quickly to check surrounding gardens and readily accessible places to see if the suspect is hiding or;
- police have arrested someone in the night after a pursuit and it is necessary to make a brief check of gardens along the pursuit route to see if stolen or incriminating articles have been discarded.

6 Searching premises—general considerations

(a) Time of searches

6.1 Searches made under warrant must be made within three calendar months of the date of the warrant is issued or within the period specified in the enactment under which the warrant is issued if this is shorter.

6.2 Searches must be made at a reasonable hour unless this might frustrate the purpose of the search.

6.3 When the extent or complexity of a search mean it is likely to take a long time, the officer in charge of the search may consider using the seize and sift powers referred to in *section 7*.

6.3A A warrant under PACE, section 8 may authorise entry to and search of premises on more than one occasion if, on the application, the justice of the peace is satisfied that it is necessary to authorise multiple entries in order to achieve the purpose for which the warrant is issued. No premises may be entered or searched on any subsequent occasions without the prior written authority of an officer of the rank of inspector who is not involved in the investigation. All other warrants authorise entry on one occasion only.

6.3B Where a warrant under PACE section 8, or Schedule 1, paragraph 12 authorises entry to and search of all premises occupied or controlled by a specified person, no premises which are not specified in the warrant may be entered and searched without the prior written authority of an officer of the rank of inspector who is not involved in the investigation.

(b) Entry other than with consent

6.4 The officer in charge of the search shall first try to communicate with the occupier, or any other person entitled to grant access to the premises, explain the authority under which entry is sought and ask the occupier to allow entry, unless:

(i) the search premises are unoccupied;

(ii) the occupier and any other person entitled to grant access are absent;

(iii) there are reasonable grounds for believing that alerting the occupier or any other person entitled to grant access would frustrate the object of the search or endanger officers or other people.

6.5 Unless *sub-paragraph 6.4(iii)* applies, if the premises are occupied the officer, subject to *paragraph 2.9*, shall, before the search begins:

(i) identify him or herself, show their warrant card (if not in uniform) and state the purpose of, and grounds for, the search, and

(ii) identify and introduce any person accompanying the officer on the search (such persons should carry identification for production on request) and briefly describe that person's role in the process.

6.6 Reasonable and proportionate force may be used if necessary to enter premises if the officer in charge of the search is satisfied the premises are those specified in any warrant, or in exercise of the powers described in *paragraphs 4.1 to 4.3*, and if:

(i) the occupier or any other person entitled to grant access has refused entry;

(ii) it is impossible to communicate with the occupier or any other person entitled to grant access; or

(iii) any of the provisions of *paragraph 6.4* apply.

(c) Notice of Powers and Rights

6.7 If an officer conducts a search to which this Code applies the officer shall, unless it is impracticable to do so, provide the occupier with a copy of a Notice in a standard format:

(i) specifying if the search is made under warrant, with consent, or in the exercise of the powers described in *paragraphs 4.1 to 4.3*. Note: the notice format shall provide for authority or consent to be indicated, see *paragraphs 4.3 and 5.1*;

(ii) summarising the extent of the powers of search and seizure conferred by PACE and other relevant legislation as appropriate;

(iii) explaining the rights of the occupier, and the owner of the property seized;

(iv) explaining compensation may be payable in appropriate cases for damages caused entering and searching premises, and giving the address to send a compensation application, and

(v) stating this Code is available at any police station.

6.8 If the occupier is:

• present, copies of the Notice and warrant shall, if practicable, be given to them before the search begins, unless the officer in charge of the search reasonably believes this would frustrate the object of the search or endanger officers or other people

• not present, copies of the Notice and warrant shall be left in a prominent place on the premises or appropriate part of the premises and endorsed, subject to *paragraph 2.9* with the name of the officer in charge of the search, the date and time of the search

the warrant shall be endorsed to show this has been done.

(d) Conduct of searches

6.9 Premises may be searched only to the extent necessary to achieve the object of the search, having regard to the size and nature of whatever is sought.

6.9A A search may not continue under:
- a warrant's authority once all the things specified in that warrant have been found
- any other power once the object of that search has been achieved.

6.9B No search may continue once the officer in charge of the search is satisfied whatever is being sought is not on the premises. This does not prevent a further search of the same premises if additional grounds come to light supporting a further application for a search warrant or exercise or further exercise of another power. For example, when, as a result of new information, it is believed articles previously not found or additional articles are on the premises.

6.10 Searches must be conducted with due consideration for the property and privacy of the occupier and with no more disturbance than necessary. Reasonable force may be used only when necessary and proportionate because the cooperation of the occupier cannot be obtained or is insufficient for the purpose.

6.11 A friend, neighbour or other person must be allowed to witness the search if the occupier wishes unless the officer in charge of the search has reasonable grounds for believing the presence of the person asked for would seriously hinder the investigation or endanger officers or other people. A search need not be unreasonably delayed for this purpose. A record of the action taken should be made on the premises search record including the grounds for refusing the occupier's request.

6.12 A person is not required to be cautioned prior to being asked questions that are solely necessary for the purpose of furthering the proper and effective conduct of a search, see Code C, *paragraph 10.1(c)*. For example, questions to discover the occupier of specified premises, to find a key to open a locked drawer or cupboard or to otherwise seek cooperation during the search or to determine if a particular item is liable to be seized.

6.12A If questioning goes beyond what is necessary for the purpose of the exemption in Code C, the exchange is likely to constitute an interview as defined by Code C, *paragraph 11.1A* and would require the associated safeguards included in Code C, *section 10*.

(e) Leaving premises

6.13 If premises have been entered by force, before leaving the officer in charge of the search must make sure they are secure by:
- arranging for the occupier or their agent to be present
- any other appropriate means.

(f) Searches under PACE Schedule 1 or the Terrorism Act 2000, Schedule 5

6.14 An officer shall be appointed as the officer in charge of the search, see *paragraph 2.10*, in respect of any search made under a warrant issued under PACE Act 1984, Schedule 1 or the Terrorism Act 2000, Schedule 5. They are responsible for making sure the search is conducted with discretion and in a manner that causes the least possible disruption to any business or other activities carried out on the premises.

6.15 Once the officer in charge of the search is satisfied material may not be taken from the premises without their knowledge, they shall ask for the documents or other records concerned. The officer in charge of the search may also ask to see the index to files held on the premises, and the officers conducting the search may inspect any files which, according to the index, appear to contain the material sought. A more extensive search of the premises may be made only if:

- the person responsible for them refuses to:
  - produce the material sought, or
  - allow access to the index
- it appears the index is:
  - inaccurate, or
  - incomplete
  - for any other reason the officer in charge of the search has reasonable grounds for believing such a search is necessary in order to find the material sought.

1.6.7.1

KEYNOTE

Whether compensation is appropriate depends on the circumstances in each case. Compensation for damage caused when effecting entry is unlikely to be appropriate if the search was lawful, and the force used can be shown to be reasonable, proportionate and necessary to effect entry. If the wrong premises are searched by mistake everything possible should be done at the earliest opportunity to allay any sense of grievance and there should normally be a strong presumption in favour of paying compensation.

It is important that, when possible, all those involved in a search are fully briefed about any powers to be exercised and the extent and limits within which it should be conducted.

In all cases the number of officers and other persons involved in executing the warrant should be determined by what is reasonable and necessary according to the particular circumstances.

1.6.8

7 Seizure and retention of property

(a) Seizure

7.1 Subject to *paragraph 7.2*, an officer who is searching any person or premises under any statutory power or with the consent of the occupier may seize anything:
   (a) covered by a warrant
   (b) the officer has reasonable grounds for believing is evidence of an offence or has been obtained in consequence of the commission of an offence but only if seizure is necessary to prevent the items being concealed, lost, disposed of, altered, damaged, destroyed or tampered with
   (c) covered by the powers in the Criminal Justice and Police Act 2001, Part 2 allowing an officer to seize property from persons or premises and retain it for sifting or examination elsewhere.

7.2 No item may be seized which an officer has reasonable grounds for believing to be subject to legal privilege, as defined in PACE, section 10, other than under the Criminal Justice and Police Act 2001, Part 2.

7.3 Officers must be aware of the provisions in the Criminal Justice and Police Act 2001, section 59, allowing for applications to a judicial authority for the return of property seized and the subsequent duty to secure in section 60, see *paragraph 7.12(iii)*.

7.4 An officer may decide it is not appropriate to seize property because of an explanation from the person holding it but may nevertheless have reasonable grounds for believing it was obtained in consequence of an offence by some person. In these circumstances, the officer should identify the property to the holder, inform the holder of their suspicions and explain the holder may be liable to civil or criminal proceedings if they dispose of, alter or destroy the property.

7.5 An officer may arrange to photograph, image or copy, any document or other article they have the power to seize in accordance with *paragraph 7.1*. This is subject to specific restrictions on the examination, imaging or copying of certain property seized under the Criminal Justice and Police Act 2001, Part 2. An officer must have regard to their statutory obligation to retain an original document or other article only when a photograph or copy is not sufficient.

7.6 If an officer considers information stored in any electronic form and accessible from the premises could be used in evidence, they may require the information to be produced in a form:
- which can be taken away and in which it is visible and legible; or
- from which it can readily be produced in a visible and legible form.

1.6.8.1

KEYNOTE

General Powers of Seizure—s. 19 PACE

The Police and Criminal Evidence Act 1984, s. 19 states:

(1) The powers conferred by subsections (2), (3) and (4) below are exercisable by a constable who is lawfully on any premises.

(2) The constable may seize anything which is on the premises if he has reasonable grounds for believing—
   (a) that it has been obtained in consequence of the commission of an offence; and
   (b) that it is necessary to seize it in order to prevent it being concealed, lost, damaged, altered or destroyed.

(3) The constable may seize anything which is on the premises if he has reasonable grounds for believing—
   (a) that it is evidence in relation to an offence which he is investigating or any other offence; and
   (b) that it is necessary to seize it in order to prevent the evidence being concealed, lost, altered or destroyed.

(4) The constable may require any information which is stored in any electronic form and is accessible from the premises to be produced in a form in which it can be taken away and in which it is visible and legible or from which it can readily be produced in a visible and legible form if he has reasonable grounds for believing—
   (a) that—
      (i) it is evidence in relation to an offence which he is investigating or any other offence; or
      (ii) it has been obtained in consequence of the commission of an offence; and
   (b) that it is necessary to do so in order to prevent it being concealed, lost, or destroyed.

(5) The powers conferred by this section are in addition to any power otherwise conferred.

(6) No power of seizure conferred on a constable under any enactment (including an enactment contained in an Act passed after this Act) is to be taken to authorise the seizure of an item which the constable exercising the power has reasonable grounds for believing to be subject to legal privilege.

For this power to apply, the officers concerned must be on the premises lawfully. If the officers are on the premises only with the consent of the occupier, they become trespassers once that consent has been withdrawn. Once the officers are told to leave, they are no longer 'lawfully' on the premises. They must be given a reasonable opportunity to leave and cannot then seize any property that they may find. For this reason, it is far safer to exercise a power where one exists, albeit that the *cooperation* of the relevant person should be sought.

Where the 'premises' searched is a vehicle (s. 23), the vehicle (the 'premises') can itself be seized (*Cowan* v *Commissioner of Police for the Metropolis* [2000] 1 WLR 254). In *Cowan* it was held that the power to seize 'premises', where it was appropriate and practical to do so, was embodied in both ss. 18 and 19 and also at common law. Therefore, the powers of seizure conferred by ss. 18(2) and 19(3) of the Police and Criminal Evidence Act 1984 extend to the seizure of the whole premises when it is physically possible to seize and retain the premises in their totality and practical considerations make seizure desirable. The police may remove premises such as tents, vehicles or caravans to a police station for the purpose of preserving evidence. However, it does not extend to seizing things that are not on the premises, such as a car parked in a car park adjacent to the premises (*Wood* v *North Avon Magistrates' Court* [2009] EWHC 3614 (Admin)).

Unless the elements above are satisfied, the power under s. 19 will not apply. Therefore, the power does not authorise the seizure of property purely for intelligence purposes.

Section 19(5) expressly preserves any common law power of search and seizure; however, in *R (On the Application of Rottman)* v *Commissioner of Police for the Metropolis* [2002] UKHL 20, it was held that s. 19 was confined to 'domestic' offences (and did not extend to extradition offences). The same applies to powers under s. 18 of the Police and Criminal Evidence Act 1984.

If the warrant under which entry or seizure was made is invalid, the officers will not be on the premises lawfully.

The power of seizure under s. 19(1), along with the power to require information stored in any electronic form to be made accessible under s. 19(4), are among those that can be conferred on an Investigating Officer designated under sch. 4 to the Police Reform Act 2002. The safeguards provided by s. 19(6) in relation to privileged material also apply to the exercise of these powers by designated Investigating Officers.

1.6.8.2

KEYNOTE

Powers of Seizure and Information in Electronic Form

The Police and Criminal Evidence Act 1984, s. 20 states:

(1) Every power of seizure which is conferred by an enactment to which this section applies on a constable who has entered premises in the exercise of a power conferred by an enactment shall be construed as including a power to require any information stored in any electronic form and accessible from the premises to be produced in a form in which it can be taken away and in which it is visible and legible or from which it can readily be produced in a visible and legible form.

(2) This section applies—

(a) to any enactment contained in an Act passed before this Act;

(b) to sections 8 and 18 above;

(c) to paragraph 13 of Schedule 1 to this Act; and

(d) to any enactment contained in an Act passed after this Act.

This provision applies to:

- powers conferred under pre-PACE statutes;
- powers exercised under a s. 8 warrant (for 'indictable offences');
- powers exercised under s. 18 (following arrest for an indictable offence);
- powers under sch. 1 ('excluded' or 'special procedure material');
- powers exercised under s. 19 (officers lawfully on premises);
- powers of seizure exercised by Investigating Officers designated under sch. 4 to the Police Reform Act 2002.

1.6.8.3

KEYNOTE

Supply of Copies of Seized Material

Section 21 of the 1984 Act makes provision for the supplying of copies of records of seizure to certain people after property has been seized. If requested by the person who had custody or control of the seized property immediately before it was seized, the officer in charge of the investigation must allow that person access to it under police supervision. The officer must also make provisions to allow for the property to be photographed or copied by that person or to supply the person with photographs/copies of it within a reasonable time. Such a request need not be complied with if there are reasonable grounds to believe that to do so would prejudice any related investigation or criminal proceedings (s. 21(8)).

1.6.8.4

KEYNOTE

Retention of Seized Material

The provisions for accessing and copying of seized material as set out in ss. 21 and 22 of the Police and Criminal Evidence Act 1984 also apply to powers of seizure exercised by Investigating Officers designated under sch. 4 to the Police Reform Act 2002.

Section 22 of the 1984 Act makes provision for the retention of seized property. Section 22(1) provides that anything seized may be retained for as long as necessary in all the circumstances. However, s. 22(2) allows for property to be retained for use as evidence in a trial, forensic examination or further investigation *unless a photograph or copy would suffice*. Seized property may be retained in order to establish its lawful owner (s. 22(2)(b)). Once this power to retain property is exhausted, a person claiming it can rely on his/her right to possession at the time the property was seized as giving sufficient title to recover the property from the police.

This situation was confirmed by the Court of Appeal in a case where the purchaser of a stolen car was allowed to rely upon his possession of the car at the time it was seized. As it could not be established that anyone else was entitled to the vehicle, the court allowed the claimant's action for return of the car to him (*Costello* v *Chief Constable of Derbyshire Constabulary* [2001] EWCA Civ 381). Clearly any claim based on previous possession where it would be unlawful for the police to return the property (e.g. a controlled drug) could not be enforced. There is no specific provision under s. 22 for the retention of property for purely intelligence purposes.

The importance of police officers being able to point clearly to the need for retaining property either in order to establish its owner or as a necessary part of the investigative or law enforcement process when relying on the above powers, was highlighted by the Court of Appeal in *Gough* v *Chief Constable of the West Midlands Police* [2004] EWCA Civ 206. In that case it was clear that neither of these purposes was being served and therefore the officers could not rely on the statutory power for retaining the property.

Property seized simply to prevent an arrested person from using it to escape or to cause injury, damage etc. cannot be retained for those purposes once the person has been released (s. 22(3)). This includes car keys belonging to someone who is released from police detention having been detained under the relevant drink driving legislation.

1.6.8.5   **KEYNOTE**

Prohibitions on Re-use of Information Seized

Information gained as a result of a lawful search may be passed on to other individuals and organisations for purposes of investigation and prosecution. It must not be used for private purposes (*Marcel* v *Commissioner of Police for the Metropolis* [1992] Ch 225).

1.6.8.6   **KEYNOTE**

Disposal of Property in Police Possession

Any person claiming property seized by the police may apply to a magistrates' court under the Police (Property) Act 1897 for its possession and should, if appropriate, be advised of this procedure.

(b) Criminal Justice and Police Act 2001: Specific procedures for seize and sift powers

7.7   The Criminal Justice and Police Act 2001, Part 2 gives officers limited powers to seize property from premises or persons so they can sift or examine it elsewhere. Officers must be careful they only exercise these powers when it is essential and they do not remove any more material than necessary. The removal of large volumes of material, much of which may not ultimately be retainable, may have serious implications for the owners, particularly when they are involved in business or activities such as journalism or the provision of medical services. Officers must carefully consider if removing copies or images of relevant material or data would be a satisfactory alternative to removing originals. When originals are taken, officers must be prepared to facilitate the provision of copies or images for the owners when reasonably practicable.

7.8   Property seized under the Criminal Justice and Police Act 2001, sections 50 or 51 must be kept securely and separately from any material seized under other powers. An examination under section 53 to determine which elements may be retained must be carried out at the earliest practicable time, having due regard to the desirability of allowing the person from whom the property was seized, or a person with an interest in the property, an opportunity of being present or represented at the examination.

7.8A All reasonable steps should be taken to accommodate an interested person's request to be present, provided the request is reasonable and subject to the need to prevent harm to, interference with, or unreasonable delay to the investigatory process. If an examination proceeds in the absence of an interested person who asked to attend or their representative, the officer who exercised the relevant seizure power must give that person a written notice of why the examination was carried out in those circumstances. If it is necessary for security reasons or to maintain confidentiality officers may exclude interested persons from decryption or other processes which facilitate the examination but do not form part of it.

7.9 It is the responsibility of the officer in charge of the investigation to make sure property is returned in accordance with sections 53 to 55. Material which there is no power to retain must be:
- separated from the rest of the seized property
- returned as soon as reasonably practicable after examination of all the seized property.

7.9A Delay is only warranted if very clear and compelling reasons exist, e.g. the:
- unavailability of the person to whom the material is to be returned
- need to agree a convenient time to return a large volume of material.

7.9B Legally privileged, excluded or special procedure material which cannot be retained must be returned:
- as soon as reasonably practicable
- without waiting for the whole examination.

7.9C As set out in section 58, material must be returned to the person from whom it was seized, except when it is clear some other person has a better right to it.

7.10 When an officer involved in the investigation has reasonable grounds to believe a person with a relevant interest in property seized under section 50 or 51 intends to make an application under section 59 for the return of any legally privileged, special procedure or excluded material, the officer in charge of the investigation should be informed as soon as practicable and the material seized should be kept secure in accordance with section 61.

7.11 The officer in charge of the investigation is responsible for making sure property is properly secured. Securing involves making sure the property is not examined, copied, imaged or put to any other use except at the request, or with the consent, of the applicant or in accordance with the directions of the appropriate judicial authority. Any request, consent or directions must be recorded in writing and signed by both the initiator and the officer in charge of the investigation.

7.12 When an officer exercises a power of seizure conferred by sections 50 or 51 they shall provide the occupier of the premises or the person from whom the property is being seized with a written notice:
(i) specifying what has been seized under the powers conferred by that section;
(ii) specifying the grounds for those powers;
(iii) setting out the effect of sections 59 to 61 covering the grounds for a person with a relevant interest in seized property to apply to a judicial authority for its return and the duty of officers to secure property in certain circumstances when an application is made;
(iv) specifying the name and address of the person to whom:
- notice of an application to the appropriate judicial authority in respect of any of the seized property must be given;
- an application may be made to allow attendance at the initial examination of the property.

7.13 If the occupier is not present but there is someone in charge of the premises, the notice shall be given to them. If no suitable person is available, so the notice will easily be found it should either be:
- left in a prominent place on the premises
- attached to the exterior of the premises.

KEYNOTE

Seize and Sift Powers

The Criminal Justice and Police Act 2001 powers allow officers to remove materials from the premises being searched where there are real practical difficulties in not doing so.

These seize and sift powers only extend the scope of *some other existing power*. They do not provide free-standing powers to seize property—rather, they supplement other powers of search and seizure where the relevant conditions and circumstances apply. The full list of these powers is set out in sch. 1 to the Act and includes all the relevant powers under the Police and Criminal Evidence Act 1984, along with those under other key statutes such as the Firearms Act 1968 and the Misuse of Drugs Act 1971. If there is no existing power of seizure other than the Criminal Justice and Police Act 2001, then there is no power.

Section 50 of the 2001 Act provides the extended powers to seize material where it is not reasonably practicable to sort through it at the scene of the search. The factors that can be taken into account in considering whether or not it is reasonably practicable for something to be determined, or for relevant material to be separated from other materials, are set out in s. 50(3); these include the length of time and number of people that would be required to carry out the determination or separation on those premises within a reasonable period, whether that would involve damage to property, any apparatus or equipment that would be needed and (in the case of separation of materials) whether the separation would be likely to prejudice the use of some or all of the separated seizable property. Section 50 also allows for the seizure of material that is reasonably believed to be legally privileged where it is not reasonably practicable to separate it. In some cases, the power to 'seize' will be read as a power to take copies (s. 63).

Section 51 provides for extended seizure of materials in the same vein as above but where the material is found on people who are being lawfully searched.

Initial Examination

Where any property has been seized under s. 50 or 51, the officer in possession of it is under a duty to make sure that a number of things are done (s. 53). These include ensuring that an initial examination of the property is carried out *as soon as reasonably practicable* after the seizure. In determining the earliest practicable time to carry out an initial examination of the seized property, due regard must be had to the desirability of allowing the person from whom it was seized (or a person with an interest in it) an opportunity of being present, or of being represented, at the examination (s. 53(4)). Officers should consider reaching agreement with owners and/or other interested parties on the procedures for examining a specific set of property, rather than awaiting the judicial authority's determination. Agreement can sometimes give a quicker and more satisfactory route for all concerned and minimise costs and legal complexities. What constitutes a relevant interest in specific material may depend on the nature of that material and the circumstances in which it is seized. Anyone with a reasonable claim to ownership of the material and anyone entrusted with its safe keeping by the owner should be considered.

The officer must also ensure that any such examination is confined to whatever is *necessary* for determining how much of the property:

- is property for which the person seizing it had power to search when making the seizure but is not property that has to be returned (by s. 54—see Protected Material, below);
- is property authorised to be retained (by s. 56—**see para. 1.6.8.9**); or
- is something which, in all the circumstances, it will not be reasonably practicable, following the examination, to separate from the property above (see generally s. 53(3)).

The officer must ensure that anything found not to fall within the categories above is separated from the rest of the seized property and *is returned as soon as reasonably practicable* after the examination of all the seized property. That officer is also under a duty to ensure that, until the initial examination of all the seized property has been completed and anything which does not fall within the categories above has been returned, the seized property is kept separate from anything seized under any other power.

Protected Material

If, at any time, after a seizure of anything has been made in exercise of *any statutory power of seizure*, it appears that the property is subject to legal privilege (or it has such an item comprised in it), s. 54 imposes a general duty on the officer in possession of the property to ensure that the item is returned as soon as reasonably practicable after the seizure. This general duty is subject to some exceptions (e.g. where in all the circumstances it is not reasonably practicable for that item to be separated from the rest of that property without prejudicing the use of the rest of that property—see s. 54(2)) but is otherwise very wide-ranging and absolutely clear. A similar duty is generally imposed in relation to property that appears to be excluded material or special procedure material (s. 55).

1.6.8.8

(c) Retention

7.14 Subject to *paragraph 7.15*, anything seized in accordance with the above provisions may be retained only for as long as is necessary. It may be retained, among other purposes:

 (i) for use as evidence at a trial for an offence;

 (ii) to facilitate the use in any investigation or proceedings of anything to which it is inextricably linked;

 (iii) for forensic examination or other investigation in connection with an offence;

 (iv) in order to establish its lawful owner when there are reasonable grounds for believing it has been stolen or obtained by the commission of an offence.

7.15 Property shall not be retained under *paragraph 7.14(i), (ii)* or *(iii)* if a copy or image would be sufficient.

1.6.8.9

KEYNOTE

Retention of Property

The Act authorises the retention of certain seized property by the police. In order to be retained, the property must have been seized on any premises by a constable who was lawfully on the premises, by a person authorised under a relevant statute (s. 56(5)) who was on the premises accompanied by a constable, or by a constable carrying out a lawful search of any person (s. 56). Generally property so seized will fall within these categories if there are reasonable grounds for believing:

- that it is property obtained in consequence of the commission of an offence; or
- that it is evidence in relation to any offence; *and* (in either case)
- that it is necessary for it to be retained in order to prevent its being concealed, lost, altered or destroyed

(for full details see s. 56(2) and (3)). Note, so far as s. 56(2) is concerned, property may be retained if it is necessary to prevent it being 'damaged', in addition to the other factors listed.

These are fairly wide provisions and, if the property fits the above description, it may be retained even if it was not being searched for. Section 57 goes on to make certain provisions for the retention of property under other statutes such as s. 5(4) of the Knives Act 1997, para. 7(2) of sch. 9 to the Data Protection Act 1998, and sch. 5 to the Human Tissue Act 2004.

Inextricably Linked Material

Paragraph 7.14(i) applies if inextricably linked material is seized under the Criminal Justice and Police Act 2001, s. 50 or 51. Inextricably linked material is material it is not reasonably practicable to separate from other linked material without prejudicing the use of that other material in any investigation or proceedings. For example, it may not be possible to separate items of data held on computer disk without damaging their evidential integrity. There are very strict limits on what use can be made of this material—it must not be examined, imaged, copied or used for any purpose other than for proving the source and/or integrity of the linked material (s. 62).

(d) Rights of owners etc.

7.16 If property is retained, the person who had custody or control of it immediately before seizure must, on request, be provided with a list or description of the property within a reasonable time.

7.17 That person or their representative must be allowed supervised access to the property to examine it or have it photographed or copied, or must be provided with a photograph or copy, in either case within a reasonable time of any request and at their own expense, unless the officer in charge of an investigation has reasonable grounds for believing this would:

(i) prejudice the investigation of any offence or criminal proceedings; or

(ii) lead to the commission of an offence by providing access to unlawful material such as pornography.

A record of the grounds shall be made when access is denied.

KEYNOTE

Notice

Where a person exercises a power of seizure conferred by s. 50 or 51, that person will be under a duty, on doing so, to give the occupier or person from whom property is seized a written notice (s. 52). That notice will specify:

- what has been seized and the grounds on which the powers have been exercised;
- the effect of the safeguards and rights to apply to a judicial authority for the return of the property (see Return of Property Seized, below);
- the name and address of the person to whom notice of an application to a judge and an application to be allowed to attend the initial examination should be sent.

Where it appears to the officer exercising a power of seizure under s. 50 that the occupier of the premises is not present at the time of the exercise of the power, but there is some other person present who is in charge of the premises, the officer may give the notice to that other person (s. 52(2)). Where it appears that there is no one present on the premises to whom a notice can be given, the officer must, before leaving the premises, attach a notice in a prominent place to the premises (s. 52(3)).

Return of Property Seized

There are specific obligations on the police to return property seized under these powers—particularly where the property includes legally privileged, excluded or special procedure material. The general rule is that any extraneous property initially seized under these provisions must be returned—usually—to the person from whom it was seized unless the investigating officer considers that someone else has a better claim to it (ss. 53 to 58).

Any person with a relevant interest in the seized property may apply to the appropriate judicial authority, on one or more of the grounds in s. 59(3) for the return of the whole or a part of the seized property. Generally those grounds are that there was no power to make the seizure or that the seized property did not fall into one of the permitted categories (s. 59). Where a person makes such an application, the police must secure the property in accordance with s. 61 (e.g. in a way that prevents investigators from looking at or copying it until the matter has been considered by a judge). There are other occasions where protected material is involved that will also give rise to the duty to secure the property under s. 61. The mechanics of securing property vary according to the circumstances; 'bagging up', i.e. placing material in sealed bags or containers and strict subsequent control of access, is the appropriate procedure in many cases. The 'judicial authority' (at least a Crown Court judge) will be able to make a number of wide-ranging orders in relation to the treatment of the seized property, including its return or examination by a third party. Failure to comply with any such order will amount to a contempt of court (s. 59(9)). Requirements to secure and return property apply equally to all copies, images or other material created because of seizure of the original property.

When material is seized under the powers of seizure conferred by the Police and Criminal Evidence Act 1984, the duty to retain it under the Code of Practice issued under the Criminal Procedure and Investigations Act 1996 is subject to the provisions on retention of seized material in s. 22 of the 1984 Act.

8 Action after searches

8.1 If premises are searched in circumstances where this Code applies, unless the exceptions in *paragraph 2.3(a)* apply, on arrival at a police station the officer in charge of the search shall make or have made a record of the search, to include:

   (i) the address of the searched premises;

   (ii) the date, time and duration of the search;

   (iii) the authority used for the search:

- if the search was made in exercise of a statutory power to search premises without warrant, the power which was used for the search:
- if the search was made under a warrant or with written consent;
  - a copy of the warrant and the written authority to apply for it, see paragraph 3.4; or
  - the written consent;

shall be appended to the record or the record shall show the location of the copy warrant or consent.

   (iv) subject to paragraph 2.9, the names of:

- the officer(s) in charge of the search;
- all other officers and any authorised persons who conducted the search;

   (v) the names of any people on the premises if they are known;

   (vi) any grounds for refusing the occupier's request to have someone present during the search, see *paragraph 6.11*;

   (vii) a list of any articles seized or the location of a list and, if not covered by a warrant, the grounds for their seizure;

   (viii) whether force was used, and the reason;

   (ix) details of any damage caused during the search, and the circumstances;

   (x) if applicable, the reason it was not practicable;

     (a) to give the occupier a copy of the Notice of Powers and Rights, see *paragraph 6.7*;

     (b) before the search to give the occupier a copy of the Notice, see *paragraph 6.8*;

   (xi) when the occupier was not present, the place where copies of the Notice of Powers and Rights and search warrant were left on the premises, *see paragraph 6.8.*

8.2 On each occasion when premises are searched under warrant, the warrant authorising the search on that occasion shall be endorsed to show:

   (i) if any articles specified in the warrant were found and the address where found;

   (ii) if any other articles were seized;

   (iii) the date and time it was executed and if present, the name of the occupier or if the occupier is not present the name of the person in charge of the premises;

   (iv) subject to paragraph 2.9 the names of the officers who executed it and any authorised persons who accompanied them;

   (v) if a copy, together with a copy of the Notice of Powers and Rights was:

- handed to the occupier; or
- endorsed as required by paragraph 6.8; and left on the premises and where.

8.3 Any warrant shall be returned within three calendar months of its issue or sooner on completion of the search(es) authorised by that warrant, if it was issued by a:

- justice of the peace, to the designated officer for the local justice area in which the justice was acting when issuing the warrant; or
- judge, to the appropriate officer of the court concerned.

9 Search registers

9.1 A search register will be maintained at each sub-divisional or equivalent police station. All search records required under *paragraph 8.1* shall be made, copied, or referred to in the register.

1.6.11

10 Searches under Schedule 5 to the Terrorism Prevention and Investigation Measures Act 2011

10.1 This Code applies to the powers of constables under Schedule 5 to the Terrorism Prevention and Investigation Measures Act 2011 relating to TPIM notices to enter and search premises subject to the modifications in the following paragraphs.

10.2 In paragraph 2.3(d), the reference to the investigation into an alleged or suspected offence include the enforcement of terrorism prevention and investigation measures which may be imposed on an individual by a TPIM notice in accordance with the Terrorism Prevention and Investigation Measures Act 2011.

10.3 References to the purpose and object of the entry and search of premises, the nature of articles sought and what may be seized and retained include (as appropriate):

(a) in relation to the power to search *without a search warrant in paragraph 5* (for purposes of serving TPIM notice), finding the individual on whom the notice is to be served.

(b) in relation to the power to search *without a search warrant in paragraph 6* (at time of serving TPIM notice), ascertaining whether there is anything in the premises, that contravenes measures specified in the notice.

(c) in relation to the power to search *without a search warrant under paragraph 7* (suspected absconding), ascertaining whether a person has absconded or if there is anything on the premises which will assist in the pursuit or arrest of an individual in respect of whom a TPIM notice is in force who is reasonably suspected of having absconded.

(d) in relation to the power to search *under a search warrant* issued under *paragraph 8* (for compliance purposes), determining whether an individual in respect of whom a TPIM notice is in force is complying with measures specified in the notice.

KEYNOTE

Searches of individuals under sch. 5, paras 6(2)(a) (at time of serving TPIM notice) and 8(2)(a) (for compliance purposes) must be conducted and recorded in accordance with Code A. See Code A, para. 2.18A for details.

1.7 Detention and Treatment of Persons by Police Officers

PACE Code of Practice for the Detention, Treatment and Questioning of Persons by Police Officers (Code C)

A thick grey line down the margin denotes text that is an extract of the PACE Code itself (i.e. the actual wording of the legislation).

1.7.1 Introduction

The powers to detain people who have been arrested and the manner in which they must be dealt with are primarily contained in the Police and Criminal Evidence Act 1984 and the PACE Codes of Practice. These Codes are intended to protect the basic rights of detained people. If these Codes are followed, it is more likely that evidence obtained while people are in custody will be admissible; the provisions of the 1984 Act give guidance in numerous areas. The Human Rights Act 1998 makes it even more important to comply with the 1984 Act and its associated Codes of Practice. This can be seen from the case of *R v Chief Constable of Kent Constabulary, ex parte Kent Police Federation Joint Branch Board* [2000] 2 Cr App R 196, where the court stated that the 1984 Act and the Codes of Practice represented the balance between the important duty of the police to investigate crime and apprehend criminals and the rights of the private citizen. A breach of Code C is fundamental in affecting the fairness of the evidence (*R v Aspinall* [1999] 2 Cr App R 115).

This chapter examines the treatment of persons who have been detained by police. The majority of this is contained within PACE Code C. Some sections of Code C deal with the interviewing of suspects and as such are included in **chapter 1.9**. Code H is the corresponding Code which applies to persons detained for the purposes of a terrorist investigation; the two Codes are similar and provide further clarity on their application. They also reflect changes to legislation that apply to both these Codes. These include consequential changes to custody records as a result of the reduced stop and search recording requirements in s. 3 of the Police and Criminal Evidence Act 1984, introduced in March 2011. References to terrorism matters, where appropriate, are included in the keynotes to this chapter.

The main responsibility for a detained person lies with the custody officer; however, it is important that all staff, including supervisors involved in investigations or those dealing with detained persons, are aware of the provisions of the Act and the Codes.

As the key reference point for the treatment of detained persons lies in the PACE Codes, this chapter and the subsequent chapters that deal with those in police detention are based around the Codes of Practice with the keynotes combining the Notes for Guidance to the legislation, and case law that support the Codes.

As Code C uses terms such as 'custody officer' and 'designated person' (amongst others), it is useful to examine briefly what they mean before examining Code C in detail.

1.7.2 Custody Officers

Custody officers are responsible for the reception and treatment of prisoners detained at the police station.

The role of the custody officer is to act independently of those conducting the investigation, thereby ensuring the welfare and rights of the detained person (this requirement is contained in s. 36(5) of the 1984 Act). Section 36 requires that one or more custody officers must be appointed for each designated police station. However, in *Vince v Chief Constable of Dorset* [1993] 1 WLR 415, it was held that a chief constable was under a duty to appoint one custody officer for each designated police station and had a discretionary power to appoint more than one, but this duty did not go so far as to require a sufficient number to ensure that the functions of custody officer were always performed by them. The provision of the facility of a custody officer must be reasonable. Section 36(3) states that a custody officer must be an officer of at least the rank of sergeant. However, s. 36(4) allows officers of any rank to perform the functions of custody officer at a designated police station if a custody officer is not readily available to perform them. The effect of s. 36(3) and (4) is that the practice of allowing officers of any other rank to perform the role of custody officer where a sergeant (*who has no other role to perform*) is in the police station must therefore be unlawful. Should a decision be made to use acting sergeants or untrained custody officers, this may lead to a claim in negligence by the officer or the detained person where there is a breach of the Codes or someone is injured as a result of the failure to manage the custody suite effectively. It could also lead to a prosecution under health and safety legislation.

For cases where arrested people are taken to a non-designated police station, s. 36(7) states that an officer of any rank not involved in the investigation should perform the role of custody officer. If no such person is at the station, the arresting officer (or any other officer involved in the investigation) or the officer that released him/her under s. 30A of the 1984 Act (bail prior to being taken to a police station) should perform the role. In these cases, an officer of at least the rank of inspector at a designated police station must be informed. It is suggested that once informed, that officer should consider the circumstances of the detained person.

Where a custody officer feels that he/she is unable to comply with the minimum standards of detention as required by the 1984 Act, it is suggested that he/she should draw this to the attention of the line manager and/or the superintendent responsible for the custody suite. Custody officers should be mindful of Article 5 of the European Convention on Human Rights in considering whether they are able to manage the number of detained persons in their custody to ensure that their detention is not longer than needed.

1.7.3 Designated Support Staff

Sections 38 and 39 of the Police Reform Act 2002, as amended by the Policing and Crime Act 2017, allow the chief officer of police of any police force to designate a relevant employee as either or both of the following:

- a community support officer;
- a policing support officer.

Previously designated officers fell under four headings, these being community support officer, investigating officer, detention officer and escort officer. It is suggested that policing support officers will still perform these roles.

Designated officers are given powers to carry out certain functions that would up to this time have been carried out by police officers only. Before a person can be given the powers of a designated officer, the chief officer of police must be satisfied that the person is a suitable person to carry out the functions for which he/she is designated, is capable of effectively carrying out those functions, and has received adequate training in the carrying out of those functions and in the exercise and performance of the powers and duties of a designated officer.

The powers and duties that may be conferred or imposed on a community support officer or a policing support officer include any power or duty of a constable, except the following powers and functions:

- any power or duty of a constable to make an arrest;
- any power or duty of a constable to stop and search an individual or a vehicle or other thing;
- the power of a constable, under s. 36(4) of PACE, to perform the functions of a custody officer at a designated police station if a custody officer is not readily available to perform them;
- any power that is exercisable only by a constable of a particular rank.

Where these powers have been given to a community support officer or police support officer they can be used within their police force area or in such areas outside their police area as set out by the chief officer of the force. It should be noted that not all designated officers will be designated with the same range of powers and it will be important to know what powers a particular designated officer has been given and therefore what his/her role will be. Although the titles of investigating officer, detention officer and escort officer no longer exist, it is suggested that the functions will still be performed by policing support officers and therefore the roles are set out below.

1.7.3.1 Investigating Officers

- To act as the supervisor of any access to seized material to which a person is entitled, to supervise the taking of a photograph of seized material or to photograph it him/herself.
- There is no power for a community support officer or policing support officer to arrest a detainee for further offences.
- Power for the custody officer to transfer to a designated officer responsibility for a detainee. This power includes a duty for the person investigating the offence, once the detainee is returned to the custody of the custody officer, to report back to the custody officer on how the Codes were complied with.
- To question an arrested person under ss. 36 and 37 of the Criminal Justice and Public Order Act 1994 about facts which may be attributable to the person's participation in an offence. The designated person may also give the suspect the necessary warning about the capacity of a court to draw inferences from a failure to give a satisfactory account in response to questioning.

1.7.3.2 Detention Officers

- Powers to search detained persons, to take fingerprints and certain samples without consent and to take photographs.

- To require certain defined categories of persons who have been convicted, cautioned, reprimanded or warned in relation to recordable offences to attend a police station to have their fingerprints taken.
- To carry out non-intimate searches of persons detained at police stations or elsewhere and to seize items found during such searches.
- To carry out searches and examinations in order to determine the identity of persons detained at police stations. Identifying marks found during such processes may be photographed.
- To carry out intimate searches in the same very limited circumstances that are applicable to constables.
- To take fingerprints without consent in the same circumstances that a constable can.
- To take non-intimate samples without consent and to inform the person from whom the sample is to be taken of any necessary authorisation by a senior officer and of the grounds for that authorisation.
- To require certain defined categories of persons who have been charged with or convicted of recordable offences to attend a police station to have a sample taken.
- To inform a person that intimate samples taken from him/her may be the subject of a speculative search (i.e. this will satisfy the requirement that the person must be informed that the sample will be the subject of a speculative search).
- To photograph detained persons in the same way that constables can.

1.7.3.3 Escort Officers

- To transport arrested persons to police stations and escort detained persons from one police station to another or between police stations and other locations specified by the custody officer.
- To carry out the duty of taking a person arrested by a constable to a police station as soon as practicable.
- With the authority of the custody officer, to escort detainees between police stations or between police stations and other specified locations.
- To conduct non-intimate searches of the detainee; and to seize or retain, or cause to be seized or retained, anything found on such a search (restrictions on power to seize personal effects are the same as for police officers, as is the requirement that the search be carried out by a member of the same sex).

Where any of the powers allow for the use of reasonable force when exercised by a police constable, a designated person has the same entitlement to use reasonable force as a constable.

It is important to note that not all support staff will be designated for the purposes of the Police Reform Act 2002 and non-designated staff will not have the additional powers as outlined above.

1.7.4 Designated Police Stations

Section 30 of the Police and Criminal Evidence Act 1984 requires that a person who has been arrested must be taken to a police station *as soon as practicable* after arrest, unless the arrested person has been released prior to arrival at the police station. Section 30A of the 1984 Act allows a constable to release a person who is under arrest. However, not all police stations have charge rooms or facilities for dealing with prisoners, so the 1984 Act requires that prisoners who will be detained (or who are likely to be detained) for more than six hours must go to a 'designated' police station. A designated police station is one that has enough facilities for the purpose of detaining arrested people. Section 35 requires the chief officer of police to designate sufficient police stations to deal with prisoners. It is for the chief officer to decide which stations are to be designated stations and these details are then published. Police stations can be designated permanently or for any specified periods provided that they are not designated for part of a day.

1.7.5   PACE Code of Practice for the Detention, Treatment and Questioning of Persons by Police Officers (Code C)

This Code applies to people in police detention after 00.00 on 21 August 2019, notwithstanding that their period of detention may have commenced before that time.

1 General

1.0   The powers and procedures in this Code must be used fairly, responsibly, with respect for the people to whom they apply and without unlawful discrimination. Under the Equality Act 2010, section 149 (Public sector Equality Duty), police forces must, in carrying out their functions, have due regard to the need to eliminate unlawful discrimination, harassment, victimisation and any other conduct which is prohibited by that Act, to advance equality of opportunity between people who share a relevant protected characteristic and people who do not share it, and to foster good relations between those persons. The Equality Act also makes it unlawful for police officers to discriminate against, harass or victimise any person on the grounds of the 'protected characteristics' of age, disability, gender reassignment, race, religion or belief, sex and sexual orientation, marriage and civil partnership, pregnancy and maternity, when using their powers.

1.1   All persons in custody must be dealt with expeditiously, and released as soon as the need for detention no longer applies.

1.1A   A custody officer must perform the functions in this Code as soon as practicable. A custody officer will not be in breach of this Code if delay is justifiable and reasonable steps are taken to prevent unnecessary delay. The custody record shall show when a delay has occurred and the reason.

1.2   This Code of Practice must be readily available at all police stations for consultation by:
- police officers;
- police staff;
- detained persons;
- members of the public.

1.3   The provisions of this Code:
- include the *Annexes*
- do not include the *Notes for Guidance* which form guidance to police officers and others about its application and interpretation.

1.4   If at any time an officer has any reason to suspect that a person of any age may be vulnerable (see *paragraph 1.13(d)*), in the absence of clear evidence to dispel that suspicion, that person shall be treated as such for the purposes of this Code and to establish whether any such reason may exist in relation to a person suspected of committing an offence (see *paragraph 10.1*), the custody officer in the case of a detained person, or the officer investigating the offence in the case of a person who has not been arrested or detained, shall take, or cause to be taken, (see *paragraph 3.5*) the following action:

(a) reasonable enquiries shall be made to ascertain what information is available that is relevant to any of the factors described in *paragraph 1.13(d)* as indicating that the person may be vulnerable might apply;

(b) a record shall be made describing whether any of those factors appear to apply and provide any reason to suspect that the person may be vulnerable or (as the case may be) may not be vulnerable; and

(c) the record mentioned in sub-paragraph (b) shall be made available to be taken into account by police officers, police staff and any others who, in accordance with the provisions of this or any other Code, are required or entitled to communicate with the person in question. This would include any solicitor, appropriate adult and health care professional and is particularly relevant to communication by telephone or by means of a live link (see *paragraphs 12.9A* (interviews), *13.12* (interpretation), and *15.3C, 15.11A, 15.11B, 15.11C* and *15.11D* (reviews and extension of detention)).

1.5 Anyone who appears to be under 18, shall, in the absence of clear evidence that they are older and subject to *paragraph 1.5A*, be treated as a juvenile for the purposes of this Code and any other Code.

1.5A *Not used.*

1.6 If a person appears to be blind, seriously visually impaired, deaf, unable to read or speak or has difficulty orally because of a speech impediment, they shall be treated as such for the purposes of this Code in the absence of clear evidence to the contrary.

1.7 The appropriate adult' means, in the case of a:

(a) juvenile:

(i) the parent, guardian or, if the juvenile is in the care of a local authority or voluntary organisation, a person representing that authority or organisation,

(ii) a social worker of a local authority;

(iii) failing these, some other responsible adult aged 18 or over who is *not*:
~ a police officer;
~ employed by the police;
~ under the direction or control of the chief officer of a police force; or
~ a person who provides services under contractual arrangements (but without being employed by the chief officer of a police force), to assist that force in relation to the discharge of its chief officer's functions, whether or not they are on duty at the time.

(b) a person who is vulnerable (see *paragraph 1.4*):

(i) a relative, guardian or other person responsible for their care or custody;

(ii) someone experienced in dealing with vulnerable people but who is not:
~ a police officer;
~ employed by the police;
~ under the direction or control of the chief officer of a police force; or
~ a person who provides services under contractual arrangements (but without being employed by the chief officer of a police force), to assist that force in relation to the discharge of its chief officer's functions, whether or not they are on duty at the time;

(iii) failing these, some other responsible adult aged 18 or over other than a person described in the bullet points in *sub-paragraph (b)(ii)* above.

1.7A The role of the appropriate adult is to safeguard the rights, entitlements and welfare of juveniles and vulnerable persons (see *paragraphs 1.4* and *1.5*) to whom the provisions of this and any other Code of Practice apply. For this reason, the appropriate adult is expected, amongst other things, to:

• support, advise and assist them when, in accordance with this Code or any other Code of Practice, they are given or asked to provide information or participate in any procedure;

• observe whether the police are acting properly and fairly to respect their rights and entitlements, and inform an officer of the rank of inspector or above if they consider that they are not;

• assist them to communicate with the police whilst respecting their right to say nothing unless they want to as set out in the terms of the caution (see *paragraphs 10.5* and *10.6*);

help them to understand their rights and ensure that those rights are protected and respected (see *paragraphs 3.15, 3.17, 6.5A* and *11.17*).

1.8   If this Code requires a person be given certain information, they do not have to be given it if at the time they are incapable of understanding what is said, are violent or may become violent or in urgent need of medical attention, but they must be given it as soon as practicable.

1.9   References to a custody officer include any police officer who, for the time being, is performing the functions of a custody officer.

1.9A   When this Code requires the prior authority or agreement of an officer of at least inspector or superintendent rank, that authority may be given by a sergeant or chief inspector authorised to perform the functions of the higher rank under the Police and Criminal Evidence Act 1984 (PACE), section 107.

1.10   Subject to *paragraph 1.12*, this Code applies to people in custody at police stations in England and Wales, whether or not they have been arrested, and to those removed to a police station as a place of safety under the Mental Health Act 1983, sections 135 and 136, as amended by the Policing and Crime Act 2017 (see *paragraph 3.16*). Section 15 applies solely to people in police detention, e.g. those brought to a police station under arrest or arrested at a police station for an offence after going there voluntarily.

1.11   No part of this Code applies to a detained person:

(a) to whom PACE Code H applies because:

- they are detained following arrest under section 41 of the Terrorism Act 2000 (TACT) and not charged; or

- an authorisation has been given under section 22 of the Counter-Terrorism Act 2008 (CTACT) (post-charge questioning of terrorist suspects) to interview them.

(b) to whom the Code of Practice issued under paragraph 6 of Schedule 14 to TACT applies because they are detained for examination under Schedule 7 to TACT.

1.12   This Code does not apply to people in custody:

(i) arrested by officers under the Criminal Justice and Public Order Act 1994, section 136(2) on warrants issued in Scotland, or arrested or detained without warrant under section 137(2) by officers from a police force in Scotland. In these cases, police powers and duties and the person's rights and entitlements whilst at a police station in England or Wales are the same as those in Scotland;

(ii) arrested under the Immigration and Asylum Act 1999, section 142(3) in order to have their fingerprints taken;

(iii) whose detention has been authorised under Schedules 2 or 3 to the Immigration Act 1971 or section 62 of the Nationality, Immigration and Asylum Act 2002;

(iv) who are convicted or remanded prisoners held in police cells on behalf of the Prison Service under the Imprisonment (Temporary Provisions) Act 1980;

(v) Not used.

(vi) detained for searches under stop and search powers except as required by Code A.

The provisions on conditions of detention and treatment in *sections 8* and *9* must be considered as the minimum standards of treatment for such detainees.

1.13   In this Code:

(a) 'designated person' means a person other than a police officer, who has specified powers and duties conferred or imposed on them by designation under section 38 or 39 of the Police Reform Act 2002;

(b) reference to a police officer includes a designated person acting in the exercise or performance of the powers and duties conferred or imposed on them by their designation;

(c) if there is doubt as to whether the person should be treated, or continue to be treated, as being male or female in the case of:

(i) a search or other procedure to which this Code applies which may only be carried out or observed by a person of the same sex as the detainee; or

(ii) any other procedure which requires action to be taken or information to be given that depends on whether the person is to be treated as being male or female;

then the gender of the detainee and other parties concerned should be established and recorded in line with Annex L of this Code.

(d) 'vulnerable' applies to any person who, because of a mental health condition or mental disorder:

(i) may have difficulty understanding or communicating effectively about the full implications for them of any procedures and processes connected with:

- their arrest and detention; or (as the case may be)
- their voluntary attendance at a police station or their presence elsewhere (see *paragraph 3.21*), for the purpose of a voluntary interview; and
- the exercise of their rights and entitlements

(ii) does not appear to understand the significance of what they are told, of questions they are asked or of their replies:

(iii) appears to be particularly prone to:

- becoming confused and unclear about their position;
- providing unreliable, misleading or incriminating information without knowing or wishing to do so;
- accepting or acting on suggestions from others without consciously knowing or wishing to do so; or
- readily agreeing to suggestions or proposals without any protest or question.

(e) 'Live link' means

(i) for the purpose of *paragraph 12.9A*; an arrangement by means of which the *interviewing officer* who is not present at the police station where the detainee is held, is able to see and hear, and to be seen and heard by, the detainee concerned, the detainee's solicitor, appropriate adult and interpreter (as applicable) and the officer who has custody of that detainee.

(ii) for the purpose of *paragraph 15.9A*; an arrangement by means of which the *review officer* who is not present at the police station where the detainee is held, is able to see and hear, and to be seen and heard by, the detainee concerned and the detainee's solicitor, appropriate adult and interpreter (as applicable). The use of live link for decisions about detention under *section 45A of PACE* is subject to regulations made by the Secretary of State being in force.

(iii) for the purpose of *paragraph 15.11A*; an arrangement by means of which the *authorising officer* who is not present at the police station where the detainee is held, is able to see and hear, and to be seen and heard by, the detainee concerned and the detainee's solicitor, appropriate adult and interpreter (as applicable).

(iv) for the purpose of *paragraph 15.11C*; an arrangement by means of which the *detainee* when not present in the court where the hearing is being held, is able to see and hear, and to be seen and heard by, the court during the hearing.

Note: Chief officers must be satisfied that live link used in their force area for the above purposes provides for accurate and secure communication between the detainee, the detainee's solicitor, appropriate adult and interpreter (as applicable). This includes ensuring that at any time during which the live link is being used: a person cannot see, hear or otherwise obtain access to any such communications unless so authorised or allowed by the custody officer or, in the case of an interview, the interviewer and that as applicable, the confidentiality of any private consultation between a suspect and their solicitor and appropriate adult is maintained.

1.14 Designated persons are entitled to use reasonable force as follows:

(a) when exercising a power conferred on them which allows a police officer exercising that power to use reasonable force, a designated person has the same entitlement to use force; and

(b) at other times when carrying out duties conferred or imposed on them that also entitle them to use reasonable force, for example:

- when at a police station carrying out the duty to keep detainees for whom they are responsible under control and to assist any police officer or designated person to keep any detainee under control and to prevent their escape;
- when securing, or assisting any police officer or designated person in securing, the detention of a person at a police station;
- when escorting, or assisting any police officer or designated person in escorting, a detainee within a police station;
- for the purpose of saving life or limb;
- or preventing serious damage to property.

1.15 Nothing in this Code prevents the custody officer, or other police officer or designated person (see *paragraph 1.13(a)*) given custody of the detainee by the custody officer, from allowing another person (see *(a)* and *(b)* below) to carry out individual procedures or tasks at the police station if the law allows. However, the officer or designated person given custody remains responsible for making sure the procedures and tasks are carried out correctly in accordance with the Codes of Practice (see *paragraph 3.5* and *Note 3F*). The other person who is allowed to carry out the procedures or tasks must be someone who *at that time*, is:

(a) under the direction and control of the chief officer of the force responsible for the police station in question; or

(b) providing services under contractual arrangements (but without being employed by the chief officer the police force), to assist a police force in relation to the discharge of its chief officer's functions.

1.16 Designated persons and others mentioned in *sub-paragraphs (a)* and *(b)* of *paragraph 1.15*, must have regard to any relevant provisions of the Codes of Practice.

1.17 In any provision of this or any other Code which allows or requires police officers or police staff to make a record in their report book, the reference to report book shall include any official report book or electronic recording device issued to them that enables the record in question to be made and dealt with in accordance with that provision. References in this and any other Code to written records, forms and signatures include electronic records and forms and electronic confirmation that identifies the person making the record or completing the form.

Chief officers must be satisfied as to the integrity and security of the devices, records and forms to which this *paragraph* applies and that use of those devices, records and forms satisfies relevant data protection legislation.

1.7.5.1

KEYNOTE

Code C recognises that detained persons are treated in accordance with the Equality Act 2010; for these Codes 'relevant protected characteristic' includes age, disability, gender reassignment, pregnancy and maternity, race, religion or belief, sex and sexual orientation. For further detailed guidance and advice on the Equality Act, see <https://www.gov.uk/guidance/equality-act-2010-guidance>. Code C does not affect the principle that all citizens have a duty to help police officers to prevent crime and discover offenders. This is a civic rather than a legal duty; but when a police officer is trying to discover whether, or by whom, an offence has been committed, he/she is entitled to question any person from whom he/she thinks useful information can be obtained, subject to the restrictions imposed by this Code. A person's declaration that he/she is unwilling to reply does not alter this entitlement.

Paragraph 1.1A is intended to cover delays which may occur in processing detainees, e.g. if a large number of suspects are brought into the station simultaneously to be placed in custody, or interview rooms are all being used, or perhaps there are difficulties contacting an appropriate adult, solicitor or interpreter. However, if that delay was not 'justified', it could lead to actions for unlawful detention and false imprisonment, and any evidence obtained as a result may be held to be inadmissible (*Roberts v Chief Constable of Cheshire Constabulary* [1999] 1 WLR 662).

Although certain sections of this Code apply specifically to people in custody at police stations, a person who attends a police station or other location voluntarily to assist with an investigation should be treated with no less consideration, e.g. offered or allowed refreshments at appropriate times, and enjoy an absolute right to obtain legal advice or communicate with anyone outside the police station or other location (see paras 3.21 and 3.22).

1.7.5.2

KEYNOTE

Meaning of Police Detention

Police detention is defined by s. 118 of the Police and Criminal Evidence Act 1984 which states:

(2) Subject to subsection (2A) a person is in police detention for the purposes of this Act if—
  (a) he has been taken to a police station after being arrested for an offence or after being arrested under section 41 of the Terrorism Act 2000, or
  (b) he is arrested at a police station after attending voluntarily at the station or accompanying a constable to it, and is detained there or is detained elsewhere in the charge of a constable, except that a person who is at a court after being charged is not in police detention for those purposes.
(2A) Where a person is in another's lawful custody by virtue of paragraph 22, 34(1) or 35(3) of Schedule 4 to the Police Reform Act 2002, he shall be treated as in police detention.

Paragraph 22 of sch. 4 to the Police Reform Act 2002 refers to the power to transfer persons into the custody of investigating officers, para. 34(1) relates to designated escort officers taking an arrested person to a police station and para. 35(3) deals with a designated escort officer transferring a detainee from one police station to another. Code C, para. 2.1A states that a person is at a police station when they are in the boundary of any building or enclosed yard which forms part of that police station. Therefore they are in police detention when they are within that boundary/yard.

1.7.5.3

KEYNOTE

Vulnerable Person as a Result of Mental Health Condition or Mental Disorder

A person may be vulnerable as a result of having a mental health condition or mental disorder. Similarly, simply because an individual does not have, or is not known to have, any such condition or disorder, does not mean that they are not vulnerable for the purposes of this Code. It is therefore important that the custody officer in the case of a detained person or the officer investigating the offence in the case of a person who has not been arrested or detained, as appropriate, considers on a case-by-case basis, whether any of the factors described in para. 1.13(d) might apply to the person in question. In doing so, the officer must take into account the particular circumstances of the individual and how the nature of the investigation might affect them and bear in mind that juveniles, by virtue of their age, will always require an appropriate adult.

In relation to the reasonable inquiries to ascertain what information is available that is relevant to any of the factors described in para. 1.13(d), indicating that the person may be vulnerable, examples of relevant information that may be available include:

- the behaviour of the adult or juvenile;
- the mental health and capacity of the adult or juvenile;
- what the adult or juvenile says about themselves;
- information from relatives and friends of the adult or juvenile;
- information from police officers and staff and from police records;
- information from health and social care (including liaison and diversion services) and other professionals who know, or have had previous contact with, the individual and may be able to contribute to assessing their need for help and support from an appropriate adult. This includes contacts and assessments arranged by the police or at the request of the individual or (as applicable) their appropriate adult or solicitor.

The Mental Health Act 1983 Code of Practice at page 26 describes the range of clinically recognised conditions which can fall with the meaning of mental disorder for the purpose of para. 1.13(d). The Code is published here: <https://www.gov.uk/government/publications/code-of-practice-mental-health-act-1983>.

When a person is under the influence of drink and/or drugs, it is not intended that they are to be treated as vulnerable and requiring an appropriate adult for the purpose of para. 1 unless other information indicates that any of the factors described in para. 1.13(d) may apply to that person. When the person has recovered from the effects of drink and/or drugs, they should be reassessed in accordance with para. 1.4. See para. 15.4A for application to live link.

1.7.5.4 KEYNOTE

Appropriate Adults

In *R* v *Aspinall* [1999] 2 Cr App R 115, the Court of Appeal emphasised the importance of appropriate adults. There it was held that an appropriate adult played a significant role in respect of a vulnerable person whose condition rendered him/her liable to provide information which was unreliable, misleading or self-incriminating.

A person, including a parent or guardian, should not be an appropriate adult if he/she is:

* suspected of involvement in the offence;
* the victim;
* a witness;
* involved in the investigation; or
* has received admissions prior to attending to act as the appropriate adult.

If a juvenile's parent is estranged from the juvenile, he/she should not be asked to act as the appropriate adult if the juvenile expressly and specifically objects to his/her presence.

Paragraph 1.5 reflects the statutory definition of 'arrested juvenile' in s. 37(15) of PACE. This section was amended by s. 42 of the Criminal Justice and Courts Act 2015 with effect from 26 October 2015, and includes anyone who appears to be under the age of 18. This definition applies for the purposes of the detention and bail provisions in ss. 34 to 51 of PACE. With effect from 3 April 2017, amendments made by the Policing and Crime Act 2017 require persons under the age of 18 to be treated as juveniles for the purposes of all other provisions of PACE and the Codes.

If a juvenile (see Code C, para. 1.5) admits an offence to, or in the presence of, a social worker or member of a youth offending team other than during the time that person is acting as the juvenile's appropriate adult, another appropriate adult should be appointed in the interest of fairness.

In the case of someone who is vulnerable, it may be more satisfactory if the appropriate adult is someone experienced or trained in their care rather than a relative lacking such qualifications. But if the person prefers a relative to a better qualified stranger or objects to a particular person their wishes should, if practicable, be respected.

A detainee should always be given an opportunity, when an appropriate adult is called to the police station, to consult privately with a solicitor in the appropriate adult's absence if he/she wants. An appropriate adult is not subject to legal privilege.

An appropriate adult who is not a parent or guardian in the case of a juvenile, or a relative, guardian or carer in the case of a vulnerable person, must be independent of the police as their role is to safeguard the person's rights and entitlements. Additionally, a solicitor or independent custody visitor who is present at the police station and acting in that capacity may not be the appropriate adult. The custody officer must remind the appropriate adult and detainee about the right to legal advice and record any reasons for waiving it in accordance with s. 6.

While an appropriate adult should be given access to a juvenile in police detention, this does not mean that he/she has free access to the custody area. In *Butcher* v *DPP* [2003] EWHC 580 (Admin), the custody officer physically escorted the detainee's appropriate adult from the custody suite as she had entered it without being invited and had been verbally abusive and aggressive. The court held that the custody sergeant had not detained the appropriate adult, but had merely used reasonable force to remove her in order to maintain the operational effectiveness of the custody suite. The court held that the custody sergeant was entitled to ask her to leave and to use reasonable force when she failed to comply with that request.

It is also important to consider the welfare of the appropriate adult. This is demonstrated by the case of *Leach* v *Chief Constable of Gloucestershire Constabulary* [1999] 1 WLR 1421. Here L was asked by a police officer to attend police interviews of a murder suspect who was also thought to be mentally disordered, as an 'appropriate adult' per the requirement of the Codes. She was told only that the suspect was a 52-year-old male, and was not informed of the nature of the case. The suspect was in fact Frederick West, who was being questioned in connection with murders committed in particularly harrowing and traumatic circumstances. For many weeks L acted as an appropriate adult, accompanying the officer and suspect to murder scenes, and on many occasions being left alone in a locked cell with the suspect. She claimed to be suffering from post-traumatic stress and psychological injury as well as a stroke as a result of her experiences. The Court of Appeal said that the Fred West case was notorious among modern crimes and it was foreseeable that psychiatric harm might arise. While there was no requirement to, in such cases counselling or trained help should be offered.

1.7.5.5

KEYNOTE

Using Live Link for a Detained Person with Eyesight or Hearing Impairment

For the purpose of the provisions of PACE that allow a live link to be used, any impairment of the detainee's eyesight or hearing is to be disregarded. This means that if a detainee's eyesight or hearing is impaired, the arrangements which would be needed to ensure effective communication if all parties were physically present in the same location, for example using sign language, would apply to the live link arrangements.

1.7.6

Code C—2 Custody Records

2.1A When a person:
- is brought to a police station under arrest
- is arrested at the police station having attended there voluntarily or
- attends a police station to answer bail

they must be brought before the custody officer as soon as practicable after their arrival at the station or if applicable, following their arrest after attending the police station voluntarily.

This applies to both designated and non-designated police stations. A person is deemed to be 'at a police station' for these purposes if they are within the boundary of any building or enclosed yard which forms part of that police station.

2.1 A separate custody record must be opened as soon as practicable for each person brought to a police station under arrest or arrested at the station having gone there voluntarily or attending a police station in answer to street bail. All information recorded under this Code must be recorded as soon as practicable in the custody record unless otherwise specified. Any audio or video recording made in the custody area is not part of the custody record.

2.2 If any action requires the authority of an officer of a specified rank, subject to *paragraph 2.6A*, their name and rank must be noted in the custody record.

2.3 The custody officer is responsible for the custody record's accuracy and completeness and for making sure the record or copy of the record accompanies a detainee if they are transferred to another police station. The record shall show the:
- time and reason for transfer;
- time a person is released from detention.

2.3A If a person is arrested and taken to a police station as a result of a search in the exercise of any stop and search power to which PACE Code A (Stop and search) or the 'search powers code' issued under TACT applies, the officer carrying out the search is responsible for ensuring that the record of that stop and search is made as part of the person's custody record. The custody officer must then ensure that the person is asked if they want a copy of the search record and if they do, that they are given a copy as soon as practicable. The person's entitlement to a copy of the search record which is made as part of their custody record is in addition to, and does not affect, their entitlement to a copy of their custody record or any other provisions of *section 2* (Custody records) of this Code. (See Code A, *paragraph 4.2B* and the TACT search powers code *paragraph 5.3.5*).

2.4 The detainee's solicitor and appropriate adult must be permitted to inspect the whole of the detainee's custody record as soon as practicable after their arrival at the station and at any other time on request, whilst the person is detained. This includes the following specific records relating to the reasons for the detainee's arrest and detention and the offence concerned, to which *paragraph 3.1(b)* refers:

(a) The information about the circumstances and reasons for the detainee's arrest as recorded in the custody record in accordance with *paragraph 4.3* of Code G. This applies to any further offences for which the detainee is arrested whilst in custody;

(b) The record of the grounds for each authorisation to keep the person in custody. The authorisations to which this applies are the same as those described at items (i)(a) to (d) in the table in *paragraph 2* of *Annex M* of this Code.

Access to the records in sub-paragraphs (a) and (b) is in addition to the requirements in *paragraphs 3.4(b)*, *11.1A*, *15.0*, *15.7A(c)* and *16.7A* to make certain documents and materials available and to provide information about the offence and the reasons for arrest and detention.

Access to the custody record for the purposes of this paragraph must be arranged and agreed with the custody officer and may not unreasonably interfere with the custody officer's duties. A record shall be made when access is allowed and whether it includes the records described in sub-paragraphs (a) and (b) above.

2.4A When a detainee leaves police detention or is taken before a court they, their legal representative or appropriate adult shall be given, on request, a copy of the custody record as soon as practicable. This entitlement lasts for 12 months after release.

2.5 The detainee, appropriate adult or legal representative shall be permitted to inspect the original custody record after the detainee has left police detention provided they give reasonable notice of their request. Any such inspection shall be noted in the custody record.

2.6 Subject to *paragraph 2.6A*, all entries in custody records must be timed and signed by the maker. Records entered on computer shall be timed and contain the operator's identification.

2.6A Nothing in this Code requires the identity of officers or other police staff to be recorded or disclosed:

(a) *Not used.*

(b) if the officer or police staff reasonably believe recording or disclosing their name might put them in danger.

In these cases, they shall use their warrant or other identification numbers and the name of their police station.

2.7 The fact and time of any detainee's refusal to sign a custody record, when asked in accordance with this Code, must be recorded.

1.7.6.1   **KEYNOTE**

The purpose of using warrant or identification numbers instead of names referred to in Code C, para. 2.6A is to protect those involved in serious organised crime investigations or arrests of particularly violent suspects when there is reliable information that those arrested or their associates may threaten or cause harm to those involved. In cases of doubt, an officer of inspector rank or above should be consulted.

Code C—3 Initial Action

(a) Detained persons—normal procedure

3.1 When a person is brought to a police station under arrest or arrested at the station having gone there voluntarily, the custody officer must make sure the person is told clearly about:

(a) the following continuing rights, which may be exercised at any stage during the period in custody:

(i) their right to consult privately with a solicitor and that free independent legal advice is available as in *section 6*;

(ii) their right to have someone informed of their arrest as in *section 5*;

(iii) their right to consult the Codes of Practice; and

(iv) if applicable, their right to interpretation and translation (see *paragraph 3.12*) and their right to communicate with their High Commission, Embassy or Consulate (see *paragraph 3.12A*).

(b) their right to be informed about the offence and (as the case may be) any further offences for which they are arrested whilst in custody and why they have been arrested and detained in accordance with *paragraphs 2.4, 3.4(a)* and *11.1A* of this Code and *paragraph 3.3* of Code G.

3.2 The detainee must also be given a written notice, which contains information:

(a) to allow them to exercise their rights by setting out:

(i) their rights under *paragraph 3.1, paragraph 3.12* and *3.12A*;

(ii) the arrangements for obtaining legal advice, see *section 6*;

(iii) their right to a copy of the custody record as in *paragraph 2.4A*;

(iv) their right to remain silent as set out in the caution in the terms prescribed in *section 10*;

(v) their right to have access to materials and documents which are essential to effectively challenging the lawfulness of their arrest and detention for any offence and (as the case may be) any further offences for which they are arrested whilst in custody, in accordance with *paragraphs 3.4(b), 15.0, 15.7A(c)* and *16.7A* of this Code;

(vi) the maximum period for which they may be kept in police detention without being charged, when detention must be reviewed and when release is required;

(vii) their right to medical assistance in accordance with *section 9* of this Code;

(viii) their right, if they are prosecuted, to have access to the evidence in the case before their trial in accordance with the Criminal Procedure and Investigations Act 1996, the Attorney General's Guidelines on Disclosure, the common law and the Criminal Procedure Rules; and

(b) briefly setting out their other entitlements while in custody, by:

(i) mentioning:

~ the provisions relating to the conduct of interviews;

~ the circumstances in which an appropriate adult should be available to assist the detainee and their statutory rights to make representations whenever the need for their detention is reviewed;

(ii) listing the entitlements in this Code, concerning;

~ reasonable standards of physical comfort;

~ adequate food and drink;

~ access to toilets and washing facilities, clothing, medical attention, and exercise when practicable.

~ personal needs relating to health, hygiene and welfare concerning the provision of menstrual and any other health, hygiene and welfare products needed by the detainee in question and speaking about these in private to a member of the custody staff (see *paragraphs 9.3A* and *9.3B*).

3.2A The detainee must be given an opportunity to read the notice and shall be asked to sign the custody record to acknowledge receipt of the notice. Any refusal to sign must be recorded on the custody record.

3.3 *Not used.*

3.3A An 'easy read' illustrated version should also be provided if available.

3.4 (a) The custody officer shall:

- record the offence(s) that the detainee has been arrested for and the reason(s) for the arrest on the custody record. See *paragraph 10.3 and Code G paragraphs 2.2 and 4.3*;

- note on the custody record any comment the detainee makes in relation to the arresting officer's account but shall not invite comment. If the arresting officer is not physically present when the detainee is brought to a police station, the arresting officer's account must be made available to the custody officer remotely or by a third party on the arresting officer's behalf. If the custody officer authorises a person's detention, subject to *paragraph 1.8*, that officer must record the grounds for detention in the detainee's presence and at the same time, inform them of the grounds. The detainee must be informed of the grounds for their detention before they are questioned about any offence;

- note any comment the detainee makes in respect of the decision to detain them but shall not invite comment;

- not put specific questions to the detainee regarding their involvement in any offence, nor in respect of any comments they may make in response to the arresting officer's account or the decision to place them in detention. Such an exchange is likely to constitute an interview as in *paragraph 11.1A* and require the associated safeguards in *section 11.*

Note: This *sub-paragraph* also applies to any further offences and grounds for detention which come to light whilst the person is detained.

See *paragraph 11.13* in respect of unsolicited comments.

(b) Documents and materials which are essential to effectively challenging the lawfulness of the detainee's arrest and detention must be made available to the detainee or their solicitor. Documents and materials will be 'essential' for this purpose if they are capable of undermining the reasons and grounds which make the detainee's arrest and detention necessary. The decision about whether particular documents or materials must be made available for the purpose of this requirement therefore rests with the custody officer who determines whether detention is necessary, in consultation with the investigating officer who has the knowledge of the documents and materials in a particular case necessary to inform that decision. A note should be made in the detainee's custody record of the *fact* that documents or materials have been made available under this sub-paragraph and when. The investigating officer should make a separate note of what is made available and how it is made available in a particular case. This sub-paragraph also applies (with modifications) for the purposes of *sections 15 (Reviews and extensions of detention)* and *16 (Charging detained persons).* See *paragraphs 15.0 and 16.7A.*

3.5 The custody officer or other custody staff as directed by the custody officer shall:

(a) ask the detainee whether at this time, they:

(i) would like legal advice, see *paragraph 6.5*;

(ii) want someone informed of their detention, see *section 5*;

(b) ask the detainee to sign the custody record to confirm their decisions in respect of (*a*);

(c) determine whether the detainee:

(i) is, or might be, in need of medical treatment or attention, see *section 9*;

(ii) is a juvenile and/or vulnerable and therefore requires an appropriate adult (see *paragraphs 1.4, 1.5, and 3.15*);

(iia) wishes to speak in private with a member of the custody staff who may be of the same sex about any matter concerning their personal needs relating to health, hygiene and welfare (see *paragraph 9.3A*);

(iii) requires:
- help to check documentation (see *paragraphs 3.20*);
- an interpreter (see *paragraph 3.12*).

(ca) if the detainee is a female aged 18 or over, ask if they require or are likely to require any menstrual products whilst they are in custody (see *paragraph 9.3B*). For girls under 18, see *paragraph 3.20A*;

(d) record the decision and actions taken as applicable in respect of (c) and (ca).

Where any duties under this paragraph have been carried out by custody staff at the direction of the custody officer, the outcomes shall, as soon as practicable, be reported to the custody officer who retains overall responsibility for the detainee's care and treatment and ensuring that it complies with this Code.

3.6 When the needs mentioned in *paragraph 3.5(c)* are being determined, the custody officer is responsible for initiating an assessment to consider whether the detainee is likely to present specific risks to custody staff, any individual who may have contact with detainee (e.g. legal advisers, medical staff) or themselves. This risk assessment must include the taking of reasonable steps to establish the detainee's identity and to obtain information about the detainee that is relevant to their safe custody, security and welfare and risks to others. Such assessments should therefore always include a check on the Police National Computer (PNC), to be carried out as soon as practicable, to identify any risks that have been highlighted in relation to the detainee. Although such assessments are primarily the custody officer's responsibility, it may be necessary for them to consult and involve others, e.g. the arresting officer or an appropriate healthcare professional, see *paragraph 9.13*. Other records held by or on behalf of the police and other UK law enforcement authorities that might provide information relevant to the detainee's safe custody, security and welfare and risk to others and to confirming their identity should also be checked. Reasons for delaying the initiation or completion of the assessment must be recorded.

3.7 Chief officers should ensure that arrangements for proper and effective risk assessments required by *paragraph 3.6* are implemented in respect of all detainees at police stations in their area.

3.8 Risk assessments must follow a structured process which clearly defines the categories of risk to be considered and the results must be incorporated in the detainee's custody record. The custody officer is responsible for making sure those responsible for the detainee's custody are appropriately briefed about the risks. If no specific risks are identified by the assessment, that should be noted in the custody record. See *paragraph 9.14*.

3.8A The content of any risk assessment and any analysis of the level of risk relating to the person's detention is not required to be shown or provided to the detainee or any person acting on behalf of the detainee. But information should not be withheld from any person acting on the detainee's behalf, for example, an appropriate adult, solicitor or interpreter, if to do so might put that person at risk.

3.9 The custody officer is responsible for implementing the response to any specific risk assessment, e.g.:
- reducing opportunities for self harm;
- calling an appropriate healthcare professional;
- increasing levels of monitoring or observation;
- reducing the risk to those who come into contact with the detainee.

3.10 Risk assessment is an ongoing process and assessments must always be subject to review if circumstances change.

3.11 If video cameras are installed in the custody area, notices shall be prominently displayed showing cameras are in use. Any request to have video cameras switched off shall be refused.

(b) Detained persons—special groups

3.12 If the detainee appears to be someone who does not speak or understand English or who has a hearing or speech impediment, the custody officer must ensure:

(a) that without delay, arrangements (*see paragraph 13.1ZA*) are made for the detainee to have the assistance of an interpreter in the action under *paragraphs 3.1 to 3.5*. If the person appears to have a hearing or speech impediment, the reference to 'interpreter' includes appropriate assistance necessary to comply with *paragraphs 3.1 to 3.5*. See *paragraph 13.1C* if the detainee is in Wales. See *section 13*;

(b) that in addition to the continuing rights set out in *paragraph 3.1(a)(i)* to *(iv)*, the detainee is told clearly about their right to interpretation and translation;

(c) that the written notice given to the detainee in accordance with *paragraph 3.2* is in a language the detainee understands and includes the right to interpretation and translation together with information about the provisions in *section 13* and *Annex M*, which explain how the right applies; and

(d) that if the translation of the notice is not available, the information in the notice is given through an interpreter and a written translation provided without undue delay.

3.12A If the detainee is a citizen of an independent Commonwealth country or a national of a foreign country, including the Republic of Ireland, the custody officer must ensure that in addition to the continuing rights set out in *paragraph 3.1(a)(i)* to *(iv)*, they are informed as soon as practicable about their rights of communication with their High Commission, Embassy or Consulate set out in *section 7*. This right must be included in the written notice given to the detainee in accordance with *paragraph 3.2*.

3.13 If the detainee is a juvenile, the custody officer must, if it is practicable, ascertain the identity of a person responsible for their welfare. That person:

- may be:
  - ~ the parent or guardian;
  - ~ if the juvenile is in local authority or voluntary organisation care, or is otherwise being looked after under the Children Act 1989, a person appointed by that authority or organisation to have responsibility for the juvenile's welfare;
  - ~ any other person who has, for the time being, assumed responsibility for the juvenile's welfare.
- must be informed as soon as practicable that the juvenile has been arrested, why they have been arrested and where they are detained. This right is in addition to the juvenile's right in *section 5* not to be held incommunicado.

3.14 If a juvenile is known to be subject to a court order under which a person or organisation is given any degree of statutory responsibility to supervise or otherwise monitor them, reasonable steps must also be taken to notify that person or organisation (the 'responsible officer'). The responsible officer will normally be a member of a Youth Offending Team, except for a curfew order which involves electronic monitoring when the contractor providing the monitoring will normally be the responsible officer.

3.15 If the detainee is a juvenile or a vulnerable person, the custody officer must, as soon as practicable, ensure that:

- the detainee is informed of the decision that an appropriate adult is required and the reason for that decision (see *paragraph 3.5(c)(ii)* and; the detainee is advised:
  - ~ of the duties of the appropriate adult as described in *paragraph 1.7A*; and
  - ~ that they can consult privately with the appropriate adult at any time.
- the appropriate adult, who in the case of a juvenile may or may not be a person responsible for their welfare, as in *paragraph 3.13*, is informed of:
  - ~ the grounds for their detention;
  - ~ their whereabouts; and
- the attendance of the appropriate adult at the police station to see the detainee is secured.

3.16 It is imperative that a person detained under the Mental Health Act 1983, section 135 or 136, be assessed as soon as possible within the permitted period of detention specified in that Act. A police station may only be used as a place of safety in accordance with The Mental Health Act 1983 (Places of Safety) Regulations 2017. If that assessment is to take place at the police station, an approved mental health professional and a registered medical practitioner shall be called to the station as soon as possible to carry it out. The appropriate adult has no role in the assessment process and their presence is not required. Once the detainee has been assessed and suitable arrangements made for their treatment or care, they can no longer be detained under section 135 or 136. A detainee must be immediately discharged from detention if a registered medical practitioner, having examined them, concludes they are not mentally disordered within the meaning of the Act.

3.17 If the appropriate adult is:

- already at the police station, the provisions of *paragraphs 3.1 to 3.5* must be complied with in the appropriate adult's presence;
- not at the station when these provisions are complied with, they must be complied with again in the presence of the appropriate adult when they arrive,

and a copy of the notice given to the detainee in accordance with *paragraph 3.2*, shall also be given to the appropriate adult.

3.17A The custody officer must ensure that at the time the copy of the notice is given to the appropriate adult, or as soon as practicable thereafter, the appropriate adult is advised of the duties of the appropriate adult as described in *paragraph 1.7A*.

3.18 *Not used.*

3.19 If the detainee, or appropriate adult on the detainee's behalf, asks for a solicitor to be called to give legal advice, the provisions of *section 6* apply (see *paragraph 6.5A*).

3.20 If the detainee is blind, seriously visually impaired or unable to read, the custody officer shall make sure their solicitor, relative, appropriate adult or some other person likely to take an interest in them and not involved in the investigation is available to help check any documentation. When this Code requires written consent or signing the person assisting may be asked to sign instead, if the detainee prefers. This paragraph does not require an appropriate adult to be called solely to assist in checking and signing documentation for a person who is not a juvenile, or is not vulnerable (see *paragraph 3.15*).

3.20A The Children and Young Persons Act 1933, section 31, requires that arrangements must be made for ensuring that a girl under the age of 18, while detained in a police station, is under the care of a woman. The custody officer must ensure that the woman under whose care the girl is, makes the enquiries and provides the information concerning personal needs relating to their health, hygiene and welfare described in *paragraph 9.3A* and menstrual products described in *paragraph 9.3B*. The section also requires that arrangements must be made for preventing any person under 18, while being detained in a police station, from associating with an adult charged with any offence, unless that adult is a relative or the adult is jointly charged with the same offence as the person under 18.

(c) Detained persons—Documentation

3.20B The grounds for a person's detention shall be recorded, in the person's presence if practicable. See *paragraph 1.8*.

3.20C Action taken under *paragraphs 3.12 to 3.20A* shall be recorded.

(d) Persons attending a police station or elsewhere voluntarily

3.21 Anybody attending a police station or other location (see *paragraph 3.22*) voluntarily to assist police with the investigation of an offence may leave at will unless arrested. The person may only be prevented from leaving at will if their arrest on suspicion of committing the offence is necessary in accordance with Code G. See *Code G Note 2G*.

Action if arrest becomes necessary

(a) If during a person's voluntary attendance at a police station or other location it is decided for any reason that their arrest is necessary, they must:

- be informed at once that they are under arrest and of the grounds and reasons as required by *Code G*, and
- be brought before the custody officer at the police station where they are arrested or (as the case may be) at the police station to which they are taken after being arrested elsewhere. The custody officer is then responsible for making sure that a custody record is opened and that they are notified of their rights in the same way as other detainees as required by this Code.

Information to be given when arranging a voluntary interview:

(b) If the suspect's arrest is not necessary but they are cautioned as required in *section 10*, the person who, after describing the nature and circumstances of the suspected offence, gives the caution must at the same time, inform them that they are not under arrest and that they are not obliged to remain at the station or other location (see *paragraph 3.22*). The rights, entitlements and safeguards that apply to the conduct and recording of interviews with suspects are not diminished simply because the interview is arranged on a voluntary basis. For the purpose of arranging a voluntary interview (see *Code G Note 2F*), the duty of the interviewer reflects that of the custody officer with regard to detained suspects. As a result:

  (i) the requirement in *paragraph 3.5(c)(ii)* to determine whether a detained suspect requires an appropriate adult, help to check documentation or an interpreter shall apply equally to a suspect who has not been arrested; and

  (ii) the suspect must not be asked to give their informed consent to be interviewed until *after* they have been informed of the rights, entitlements and safeguards that apply to voluntary interviews. These are set out in *paragraph 3.21A* and the interviewer is responsible for ensuring that the suspect is so informed and for explaining these rights, entitlements and safeguards.

3.21A The interviewer must inform the suspect that the purpose of the voluntary interview is to question them to obtain evidence about their involvement or suspected involvement in the offence(s) described when they were cautioned and told that they were not under arrest. The interviewer shall then inform the suspect that the following matters will apply if they agree to the voluntary interview proceeding:

(a) Their right to information about the offence(s) in question by providing sufficient information to enable them to understand the nature of any such offence(s) and why they are suspected of committing it. This is in order to allow for the effective exercise of the rights of the defence as required by *paragraph 11.1A*. It applies whether or not they ask for legal advice and includes any further offences that come to light and are pointed out during the voluntary interview and for which they are cautioned.

(b) Their right to free legal advice by:

  (i) explaining that they may obtain free and independent legal advice if they want it, and that this includes the right to speak with a solicitor on the telephone and to have the solicitor present during the interview;

  (ii) asking if they want legal advice and recording their reply; and

  (iii) if the person requests advice, securing its provision before the interview by contacting the Defence Solicitor Call Centre and explaining that the time and place of the interview will be arranged to enable them to obtain advice and that the interview will be delayed until they have received the advice unless, in accordance with *paragraph 6.6(c)* (Nominated solicitor not available and duty solicitor declined) or *paragraph 6.6(d)* (Change of mind), an officer of the rank of inspector or above agrees to the interview proceeding; or

  (iv) if the person declines to exercise the right, asking them why and recording any reasons given.

Note: When explaining the right to legal advice and the arrangements, the interviewer must take care not to indicate, except to answer a direct question, that the time taken to arrange and complete the voluntary interview might be reduced if:

- the suspect does not ask for legal advice or does not want a solicitor present when they are interviewed; or
- the suspect asks for legal advice or (as the case may be) asks for a solicitor to be present when they are interviewed, but changes their mind and agrees to be interviewed without waiting for a solicitor.

(c) Their right, if in accordance with *paragraph 3.5(c)(ii)* the interviewer determines:

    (i) that they are a juvenile or are vulnerable; or

    (ii) that they need help to check documentation (see *paragraph 3.20*), to have the appropriate adult present or (as the case may be) to have the necessary help to check documentation; and that the interview will be delayed until the presence of the appropriate adult or the necessary help, is secured.

(d) If they are a juvenile or vulnerable and do not want legal advice, their appropriate adult has the right to ask for a solicitor to attend if this would be in their best interests and the appropriate adult must be so informed. In this case, action to secure the provision of advice if so requested by their appropriate adult will be taken without delay in the same way as if requested by the person (see *sub-paragraph (b)(iii)*). However, they cannot be forced to see the solicitor if they are adamant that they do not wish to do so (see *paragraphs 3.19* and *6.5A*).

(e) Their right to an interpreter, if in accordance with, *paragraphs 3.5(c)(ii)* and *3.12*, the interviewer determines that they require an interpreter and that if they require an interpreter, making the necessary arrangements in accordance with *paragraph 13.1ZA* and that the interview will be delayed to make the arrangements.

(f) That interview will be arranged for a time and location (see *paragraph 3.22*) that enables:

    (i) the suspect's rights described above to be fully respected; and

    (ii) the whole of the interview to be recorded using an authorised recording device in accordance with Code E (Code of Practice on Audio recording of interviews with suspects) or (as the case may be) Code F (Code of Practice on visual recording with sound of interviews with suspects); and

(g) That their agreement to take part in the interview also signifies their agreement for that interview to be audio-recorded or (as the case may be) visually recorded with sound.

3.21B The provision by the interviewer of factual information described in *paragraph 3.21A* and, if asked by the suspect, further such information, does not constitute an interview for the purpose of this Code and *when that information is provided*:

(a) the interviewer must remind the suspect about the caution as required in *section 10* but must not *invite* comment about the offence or put specific questions to the suspect regarding their involvement in any offence, nor in respect of any comments they may make when given the information. Such an exchange is itself likely to constitute an interview as in *paragraph 11.1A* and require the associated interview safeguards in *section 11*.

(b) Any comment the suspect makes when the information is given which might be relevant to the offence, must be recorded and dealt with in accordance with *paragraph 11.13*.

(c) The suspect must be given a notice summarising the matters described in *paragraph 3.21A* and which includes the arrangements for obtaining legal advice. If a specific notice is not available, the notice given to detained suspects with references to detention-specific requirements and information redacted, may be used.

(d) For juvenile and vulnerable suspects (see *paragraphs 1.4* and *1.5*):

    (i) the information must be provided or (as the case may be) provided again, together with the notice, in the presence of the appropriate adult;

      (ii) if cautioned in the absence of the appropriate adult, the caution must be repeated in the appropriate adult's presence (see *paragraph 10.12*);

      (iii) the suspect must be informed of the decision that an appropriate is required and the reason (see *paragraph 3.5(c)(ii)*;

      (iv) the suspect *and* the appropriate adult shall be advised:

- that the duties of the appropriate adult include giving advice and assistance in accordance with *paragraphs 1.7A* and *11.17*;
- and that they can consult privately at any time.

      (v) their informed agreement to be interviewed voluntarily must be sought and given in the *presence* of the appropriate adult and for a juvenile, the agreement of a parent or guardian of the juvenile is also required.

3.22 If the other location mentioned in *paragraph 3.21* is any place or premises for which the interviewer requires the person's informed consent to remain, for example, the person's home, then the references that the person is 'not obliged to remain' and that they 'may leave at will' mean that the person may also withdraw their consent and require the interviewer to leave.

Commencement of voluntary interview—general

3.22A Before asking the suspect any questions about their involvement in the offence they are suspected of committing, the interviewing officer must ask them to confirm that they agree to the interview proceeding. This confirmation shall be recorded in the interview record made in accordance with section 11 of this Code (written record) or Code E or Code F.

Documentation

3.22B Action taken under *paragraphs 3.21A to 3.21B* shall be recorded. The record shall include the date time and place the action was taken, who was present and anything said to or by the suspect and to or by those present.

3.22 *Not used.*

3.23 *Not used.*

(e) Persons answering street bail

3.25 When a person is answering street bail, the custody officer should link any documentation held in relation to arrest with the custody record. Any further action shall be recorded on the custody record in accordance with *paragraphs 3.20B* and *3.20C* above.

(f) Requirements for suspects to be informed of certain rights

3.26 The provisions of this section identify the information which must be given to suspects who have been cautioned in accordance with *section 10 of this Code* according to whether or not they have been arrested and detained. It includes information required by *EU Directive 2012/13* on the right to information in criminal proceedings. If a complaint is made by or on behalf of such a suspect that the information and (as the case may be) access to records and documents has not been provided as required, the matter shall be reported to an inspector to deal with as a complaint for the purposes of *paragraph 9.2*, or *paragraph 12.9* if the challenge is made during an interview. This would include, for example:

(a) in the case of a detained suspect:

- not informing them of their rights (see paragraph 3.1);
- not giving them a copy of the Notice (see paragraph 3.2(a));
- not providing an opportunity to read the notice (see paragraph 3.2A);
- not providing the required information (see paragraphs 3.2(a), 3.12(b) and, 3.12A;
- not allowing access to the custody record (see paragraph 2.4);
- not providing a translation of the Notice (see *paragraph 3.12(c)* and *(d)*); and

(b) in the case of a suspect who is not detained:

- not informing them of their rights or providing the required information (see *paragraph 3.21(b) to 3.21B*).

KEYNOTE

Detention of People under Arrest

Section 37 of the 1984 Act states:

> (1) Where—
>> (a) a person is arrested for an offence—
>>> (i) without a warrant; or
>>> (ii) under a warrant not endorsed for bail,
>> (b) [repealed],
>> the custody officer at each police station where he is detained after his arrest shall determine whether he has before him sufficient evidence to charge that person with the offence for which he was arrested and may detain him at the police station for such period as is necessary to enable him to do so.
> (2) If the custody officer determines that he does not have such evidence before him, the person arrested shall be released
>> (a) without bail unless the pre-conditions for bail are satisfied, or
>> (b) on bail if those pre-conditions are satisfied, (subject to subsection (3)),
> (3) If the custody officer has reasonable grounds for believing that the person's detention without being charged is necessary to secure or preserve evidence relating to an offence for which the person is under arrest or to obtain such evidence by questioning the person he may authorise the person arrested to be kept in police detention.
> (4) Where a custody officer authorises a person who has not been charged to be kept in police detention, he shall, as soon as is practicable, make a written record of the grounds for the detention.
> (5) Subject to subsection (6) below, the written record shall be made in the presence of the person arrested who shall at that time be informed by the custody officer of the grounds for his detention.

It is suggested that the custody officer record all the reasons for authorising the person's detention as it may be necessary in any criminal or civil proceedings. Indeed, it will be difficult for the custody officer to explain his/her decision without such information.

Section 37(6) states that subs. (5) above shall not apply where the person arrested is, at the time when the written record is made: incapable of understanding what is said to him; violent or likely to become violent; or in urgent need of medical attention.

People who have been arrested, returned on bail or have voluntarily given themselves up at a police station, which includes a person who has attended the police station after having been given street bail, will be brought before a custody officer who must decide whether the person should be detained at the police station or released. People who attend police stations voluntarily to assist the police with their investigations are not subject to this procedure; their treatment is dealt with by s. 29 of the 1984 Act. However, if an officer forms a view that the person should be arrested at the police station for the purpose of interview and informs the custody officer of this view, the custody officer can authorise detention for the interview and is entitled to assume that the arrest by the officer is lawful (*Al-Fayed* v *Metropolitan Police Commissioner* [2004] EWCA Civ 1579).

If the grounds were not given at the time of arrest (on justifiable grounds) the custody officer should consider whether the arrested person is now in a position to be given the grounds for the arrest (as being the first practicable opportunity (s. 28(3) of the 1984 Act)). If the grounds for arrest were not given when they should have been, the arrest is unlawful regardless of what information is given later (*Wilson* v *Chief Constable of Lancashire* [2000] Po LR 367).

Having heard the details of and grounds for the arrest, the custody officer must decide whether or not there are reasons which justify authorising that person's detention (s. 37 of the 1984 Act deals with the procedures to be followed before a person is charged). Some commentators have suggested that it is also the role of the custody officer to establish that the arrest itself was lawful. While good practice, the custody officer's duty is confined to acting in accordance with the requirements set out in s. 37 of the 1984 Act. These duties do not appear to include considering whether the arrest was lawful unless this is relevant to the main question of whether there is sufficient evidence to charge the suspect. The view is supported by the decision of the Divisional Court in *DPP* v *L* [1999] Crim LR 752, where the court held that there was no express or implied requirement imposing a duty on a custody officer to inquire into the legality of an arrest and in that case the custody officer was therefore entitled to assume that it was lawful. A subsequent finding that the arrest was unlawful did not invalidate the decision of the custody officer to hold the person in custody. However, where the custody officer is aware that the arrest is unlawful, he/she will need to consider whether continued detention is justifiable, particularly in light of the Human Rights Act 1998. The Codes allow for the custody officer to delegate actions to other members of staff; a custody officer or other officer who, in accordance with this Code, allows or directs the carrying out of any task or action relating to a detainee's care, treatment, rights and entitlements to another officer or any police staff must be satisfied that the officer or police staff concerned is suitable, trained and competent to carry out the task or action in question.

Paragraphs 3.2, 3.4 and 3.12 set out the minimum of what should be included in the notice of entitlement, which should be available in Welsh, the main minority ethnic languages and the principal European languages, wherever they are likely to be helpful.

Access to 'easy read' illustrated versions should also be provided if they are available. For access to currently available notices see <https://www.gov.uk/notice-of-rights-and-entitlements-a-persons-rights-in-police-detention>.

The need for detained persons to understand their rights is fundamental to their fair treatment. A procedure for determining whether a person needs an interpreter might involve a telephone interpreter service or using cue cards or similar visual aids which enable detainees to indicate their ability to speak and understand English and their preferred language. This could be confirmed through an interpreter who could also assess the extent to which the person can speak and understand English.

Paragraph 3.21 sets out what information should be given to a person voluntarily attending a police station or other location; it should be noted that it does not include any requirement to provide a written notice other than the detail concerning the arrangements for obtaining legal advice.

If the person is arrested on a warrant, any directions given by the court in the warrant must be followed. Consideration can always be given to contacting the court to get a variation on the conditions of the warrant. (If the warrant was issued for the arrest of a person who has not yet been charged or summonsed for an offence, he/she should be dealt with as any other person arrested for an offence without warrant unless there are any additional directions on the warrant that must be followed.)

Where a person who has been bailed under s. 37(7)(a) in order that the DPP can make a case disposal decision answers his/her bail or is arrested for failing to return on bail, detention can only be authorised to allow him/her to be further bailed under s. 37D of the 1984 Act or in order that he/she can be charged or cautioned for offences connected with the original bail. If the person is not in a fit state to be dealt with he/she may be kept in police detention until he/she is (s. 37D of the 1984 Act).

1.7.7.2

KEYNOTE

Authorising a Person's Detention

A custody officer can authorise the detention of a person when there is sufficient evidence to charge and, more commonly, when there is *not* sufficient evidence to charge the suspect. If there is insufficient evidence to charge, the custody officer must decide if the detention is necessary to secure or preserve evidence relating to an offence for which the person is under arrest or to obtain such evidence by questioning him/her.

If a person representing the detained person does not consider that the detention is lawful he/she can apply to the court for the detainee's release (*habeas corpus*). A detainee may also be able to make an application for release or damages following the incorporation of the European Convention on Human Rights (Article 5(4)).

Where a detained person wishes to consult the Codes of Practice, this does not entitle the person concerned to delay unreasonably any necessary investigative or administrative action whilst he/she does so. Examples of action which need not be delayed unreasonably include: procedures requiring the provision of breath, blood or urine specimens under the Road Traffic Act 1988 or the Transport and Works Act 1992; searching detainees at the police station, taking fingerprints, footwear impressions or non-intimate samples without consent for evidential purposes.

1.7.7.3

KEYNOTE

Risk Assessments

The custody officer is responsible for initiating a risk assessment to consider whether detainees are likely to present specific risks to custody staff or themselves (Code C, para. 3.6). The risk assessment must follow a structured process which clearly defines the categories of risk to be considered (the Detention and Custody Authorised Professional Practice (APP) produced by the College of Policing (see <https://www.app.college.police.uk/app-content/detention-and-custody-2/>) provides more detailed guidance on risk assessments). For this reason it is suggested that the risk assessment should be completed prior to the detainee being placed in a cell or detention room.

In addition to considering risk assessments for detained persons, the custody officer also needs to consider the safety of others who are in the custody area. Home Office Circular 34/2007 provides guidance on the arrangements for the safety and security of the custody suite, in particular in respect of solicitors and accredited and probationary representatives working in custody suites. The guidance has been issued following a number of incidents having been brought to the attention of the Home Office and the Health and Safety Executive (HSE), highlighting the actual and potential risks faced by solicitors, particularly when carrying out private consultations with their clients in the custody area, and the Authorised Professional Practice (APP) on Detention and Custody provides more detailed guidance on risk assessments and identifies key risk areas which should always be considered.

1.7.7.4

KEYNOTE

Documents or Material that Undermine the Need to Keep a Suspect in Custody

For the purposes of para. 3.4(b) and Code C, s. 15: investigating officers are responsible for bringing to the attention of the officer who is responsible for authorising the suspect's detention, or (as the case may be) continued detention (before or after charge), any documents and materials in their possession or control which appear to undermine the need to keep the suspect in custody. In accordance with part IV of PACE, this officer will be either the custody officer, the officer reviewing the need for detention before or after charge (PACE, s. 40), or the officer considering the need to extend detention without charge from 24 to 36 hours (PACE, s. 42). The authorising officer is then responsible for determining, which, if any, of those documents and materials are capable of undermining the need to detain the suspect and must therefore be made available to the suspect or their solicitor. It is not the case that documents need to be copied and provided to the suspect or their solicitor; the way in which documents and materials are 'made available' is a matter for the investigating officer to determine on a case-by-case basis and having regard to the nature and volume of the documents and materials involved. For example, they may be made available by supplying a copy or allowing supervised access to view. However, for view-only access it will be necessary to demonstrate that sufficient time is allowed for the suspect and solicitor to view and consider the documents and materials in question. It is suggested that a record should be made of what material was provided.

1.7.7.5

KEYNOTE

Detained Persons—Special Groups

The Children and Young Persons Act 1933, s. 31, requires that arrangements must be made for ensuring that a girl under the age of 18, while detained in a police station, is under the care of a woman. Guidance for police officers and police staff on the operational application of s. 31 of the Children and Young Persons Act 1933 has been published by the College of Policing and is available at: <https://www.app.college.police.uk/detention-and-custody-index/#children-and-young-persons>.

In cases where a juvenile is in police detention it may be necessary to inform more than one person. For instance, if the juvenile is in local authority or voluntary organisation care but living with his/her parents or other adults responsible for his/her welfare, although there is no legal obligation to inform them, they should normally be contacted, as well as the authority or organisation, unless suspected of involvement in the offence concerned. Even if the juvenile is not living with his/her parents, consideration should be given to informing them.

The purpose of the provisions at paras 3.19 and 6.5A is to protect the rights of juvenile and vulnerable persons who may not understand the significance of what is said to them. They should always be given an opportunity, when an appropriate adult is called to the police station, to consult privately with a solicitor in the absence of the appropriate adult if they want.

1.7.7.6

KEYNOTE

Interviews Elsewhere than a Police Station

An interviewer who is not sure, or has any doubt, about whether a place or location elsewhere than a police station is suitable for carrying out a voluntary interview, particularly in the case of a juvenile or vulnerable person, should consult an officer of the rank of sergeant or above for advice. Detailed guidance for police officers and staff concerning the conduct and recording of voluntary interviews has been published by the College of Policing (Investigative Interviewing App) It follows a review of operational issues arising when voluntary interviews need to be arranged. The aim is to ensure the effective implementation of the safeguards in paras 3.21 to 3.223 particularly concerning the rights of suspects, the location for the interview and supervision. For voluntary interviews conducted by non-police investigators, the provision of legal advice is set out by the Legal Aid Agency at para. 9.54 of the 2017 Standard Crime Contract Specification. This is published at <https://www.gov.uk/government/publications/standard-crime-contract-2017> and the rules mean that a non-police interviewer who does not have their own statutory power of arrest would have to inform the suspect that they have a right to seek legal advice if they wish, but payment would be a matter for them to arrange with the solicitor.

1.7.8

Code C—4 Detainee's Property

(a) Action

4.1 The custody officer is responsible for:
   (a) ascertaining what property a detainee:
       (i) has with them when they come to the police station, whether on:
           • arrest or re-detention on answering to bail;
           • commitment to prison custody on the order or sentence of a court;
           • lodgement at the police station with a view to their production in court from prison custody;
           • transfer from detention at another station or hospital;
           • detention under the Mental Health Act 1983, section 135 or 136;
           • remand into police custody on the authority of a court.
       (ii) might have acquired for an unlawful or harmful purpose while in custody;
   (b) the safekeeping of any property taken from a detainee which remains at the police station. The custody officer may search the detainee or authorise their being searched to the extent they consider necessary, provided a search of intimate parts of the body or involving the removal of more than outer clothing is only made as in *Annex A*. A search may only be carried out by an officer of the same sex as the detainee. See *Annex L*.

4.2 Subject to *paragraph 4.3A*, detainees may retain clothing and personal effects at their own risk unless the custody officer considers they may use them to cause harm to themselves or others, interfere with evidence, damage property, effect an escape or they are needed as evidence. In this event the custody officer may withhold such articles as they consider necessary and must tell the detainee why.

4.3 Personal effects are those items a detainee may lawfully need, use or refer to while in detention but do not include cash and other items of value.

4.3A For the purposes of *paragraph 4.2*, the reference to clothing and personal effects shall be treated as including menstrual and any other health, hygiene and welfare products needed by the detainee in question (see *paragraphs 9.3A* and *9.3B*) and a decision to withhold any such products must be subject to a further specific risk assessment.

(b) Documentation

4.4 It is a matter for the custody officer to determine whether a record should be made of the property a detained person has with him or had taken from him on arrest. Any record made is not required to be kept as part of the custody record but the custody record should be noted as to where such a record exists and that record shall be treated as being part of the custody record for the purpose of this and any other Code of Practice (see *paragraphs 2.4, 2.4A* and *2.5*). Whenever a record is made the detainee shall be allowed to check and sign the record of property as correct. Any refusal to sign shall be recorded.

4.5 If a detainee is not allowed to keep any article of clothing or personal effects, the reason must be recorded.

1.7.8.1

KEYNOTE

Section 54 of the 1984 Act states:

(1) The custody officer at a police station shall ascertain everything which a person has with him when he is—
   (a) brought to the station after being arrested elsewhere or after being committed to custody by an order or sentence of a court; or
   (b) arrested at the station or detained there, as a person falling within section 34(7), under section 37 above.

(2) The custody officer may record or cause to be recorded all or any of the things which he ascertains under subsection (1).

(2A) In the case of an arrested person, any such record may be made as part of his custody record.

(3) Subject to subsection (4) below, a custody officer may seize and retain any such thing or cause any such thing to be seized and retained.

(4) Clothes and personal effects may only be seized if the custody officer—
   (a) believes that the person from whom they are seized may use them—
      (i) to cause physical injury to himself or any other person;
      (ii) to damage property;
      (iii) to interfere with evidence; or
      (iv) to assist him to escape; or
   (b) has reasonable grounds for believing that they may be evidence relating to an offence.

(5) Where anything is seized, the person from whom it is seized shall be told the reason for the seizure unless he is—
   (a) violent or likely to become violent; or
   (b) incapable of understanding what is said to him.

(6) Subject to subsection (7) below, a person may be searched if the custody officer considers it necessary to enable him to carry out his duty under subsection (1) above and to the extent that the custody officer considers necessary for that purpose.

(6A) A person who is in custody at a police station or is in police detention otherwise than at a police station may at any time be searched in order to ascertain whether he has with him anything which he could use for any of the purposes specified in subsection (4) (a) above.

(6B) Subject to subsection (6C) below, a constable may seize and retain, or cause to be seized and retained, anything found on such a search.

(6C) A constable may only seize clothes and personal effects in the circumstances specified in subsection (4) above.

(7) An intimate search may not be conducted under this section.

(8) A search under this section shall be carried out by a constable.

(9) The constable carrying out a search shall be of the same sex as the person searched.

The custody officer must also consider what property the detained person might have in his/her possession for an unlawful or harmful purpose while in custody. The safekeeping of any property taken from the detained person and kept at the police station is the responsibility of the custody officer.

The custody officer does not need to record everything a detained person has with him/her. The custody officer will have a discretion as to the nature and detail of any recording and there is no requirement for this to be recorded in the custody record. However, custody officers should be mindful of any force instructions as to what will need to be recorded and where. It is suggested that it will still be necessary to make records, not least to ensure against claims that property has been mishandled or removed. The custody officer will have to make judgements about how to balance the need for recording against the amount of administrative work involved.

A not uncommon situation is where a detained person, possibly drunk, vomits on their clothes. *Pile* v *Chief Constable of Merseyside Police* [2020] EWHC 2472 (QB) was such a case. Ms Pile brought a case against the force to establish the liberty of inebriated English subjects to be allowed to lie, undisturbed, overnight in their own vomit-soaked clothing. At the time, she was at a police station in Liverpool, having been arrested for the offence of being drunk and disorderly. She had vomited over her own clothing and did not know where she was due to her intoxication. Four female police officers removed her outer clothing and provided her with a clean, dry outfit to wear. The court determined that in this situation the removal of Ms Pile's clothes had nothing to do with a search under s. 54 nor did this breach a detainee's rights under Article 8 of the European Convention on Human Rights. The Court of Appeal found it to be entirely justified that four members of staff were sent in to remove Ms Pile's clothing, due to her earlier aggressive behaviour when brought into custody. The court stated that if fewer than four attended the cell, there may well have been a greater risk that one of them would be injured because the claimant could not otherwise be adequately restrained.

1.7.8.2 KEYNOTE

The Search

While the custody officer has a duty to ascertain what property a person has with him/her (often by means of searching the person), there is also a need to consider the rights of the detained person. The custody officer may authorise a constable to search a detained person, or may search the detained person him/herself in order to ascertain what property the detained person has with him/her (s. 54(6)). It should be noted that the custody officer must first authorise any search and the extent of the search; officers should not search a person until this authority has been given. Therefore the custody officer may only authorise a search to the extent that he/she considers necessary to comply with this duty. In order to safeguard the rights of the detained person, there are three levels to which searches can be conducted:

- searches that do not involve the removal of more than the detained person's outer clothing (this includes shoes and socks);
- strip searches;
- intimate searches.

Each of these is examined below.

The extent of the search is determined by the custody officer on the basis of what he/she honestly believes is necessary in order to comply with the above duties. Both the decision to search the detained person and the extent of the search must be decided on the facts of the case in question. It may be important to consider cultural issues that might affect the detained person; for instance, would it be necessary and justifiable to search a Sikh's turban? Force standing orders are not an automatic right to search all detained persons (*Brazil* v *Chief Constable of Surrey* [1983] 1 WLR 1155). A custody officer can authorise a strip search but an intimate search can only be authorised by an officer of the rank of inspector or above.

1.7.8.3 KEYNOTE

Searches that Do Not Involve the Removal of More than the Detained Person's Outer Clothing

In effect, this is any search that does not become a strip search or an intimate search. This type of search applies to almost every person coming before the custody officer. Typically this will involve emptying out all items that are in the person's pockets, removing jewellery and the searching of other areas that can be conducted without the need to remove more than outer garments, such as coats and possibly items such as jumpers. This type of authorisation would also lend itself to a 'pat down' of the detained person. If there is any doubt as to whether the search goes beyond one that falls into this category, it is suggested that it should be treated as a strip search. Where metal detectors are used in custody suites, an indication from the device may give the grounds for authorising a strip search.

Not all detained persons need to be searched; s. 54(1) and para. 4.1 require a detainee to be searched when it is clear the custody officer will have continuing duties in relation to that detainee or when that detainee's behaviour or offence makes an inventory appropriate. They do not require every detainee to be searched, e.g. if it is clear that a person will only be detained for a short period and is not to be placed in a cell, the custody officer may decide not to search him/her. In such a case the custody record will be endorsed 'not searched', para. 4.4 will not apply, and the detainee will be invited to sign the entry. If the detainee refuses, the custody officer will be obliged to ascertain what property he/she has in accordance with para. 4.1.

1.7.8.4

KEYNOTE

Strip Searches

Strip searches are dealt with in Code C, Annex A, paras 9 to 12.

1.7.8.5

KEYNOTE

Intimate Searches

Intimate searches are dealt with in Code C, Annex A. An intimate search is a search which consists of the physical examination of a person's body orifices other than the mouth.

1.7.8.6

KEYNOTE

Drug Search—X-rays and Ultrasound Scans

Section 55A of the 1984 Act allows detained persons to have an X-ray taken of them or an ultrasound scan to be carried out on them (or both). This is dealt with in Code C, Annex K.

1.7.8.7

KEYNOTE

Conduct of a Search

- Reasonable force may be used (s. 117 of the 1984 Act).
- The custody officer should specify the level of the search to be conducted and this must be recorded in the person's record.
- Reference to Code A, para. 3.1 may be useful when considering how to conduct the search: 'Every reasonable effort must be made to minimise the embarrassment that a person being searched may experience.'
- Annex L should be referred to for guidance when establishing the gender of persons for the purpose of searching.

1.7.8.8

KEYNOTE

What Property Can Be Retained?

Once a person has been searched and the custody officer has ascertained what property the detained person has with him/her, a decision must be made as to what property will be returned to the detained person and what property will be retained by the police.

It is suggested that the custody officer may authorise the seizure of an article of clothing under s. 54(4)(b) of the 1984 Act, where he/she has reasonable grounds for believing that such clothing may be evidence relating to an offence. For instance, if the detained person is wearing a pair of trainers of the same type as those which are reasonably believed to have made impressions at the scene of a recent burglary and the detained person has a burglary record then, unless the custody officer knows of other facts clearly putting the suspect at some other place at the time of the offence, he/she is plainly justified in having those shoes forensically examined. However, it is submitted that this does not authorise the custody officer to seize footwear on the off-chance that some officer or some other police force may have obtained impressions at a burglary site which might match the trainers of the detained person.

Where property by virtue of its nature, quantity or size in the detainee's possession at the time of arrest has not been brought to the police station the custody officer is not required to record this on the custody record. Only items of clothing worn by the detained person which have been withheld need to be recorded on the custody record.

Unless the property has been seized and retained as evidence under s. 22 of the 1984 Act, it must be returned to the detained person on his/her release. If property has been seized from a third party in the course of the investigation the property can only be retained for so long as is necessary in accordance with s. 22(1) of the 1984 Act; even if it might be needed for another matter it should be returned to the third party unless there was an additional power to seize the item (*Settelen* v *Metropolitan Police Commissioner* [2004] EWHC 2171 (Ch)). If property is rightfully seized but retained unnecessarily this would be unlawful and could lead to a claim for damages (*Martin* v *Chief Constable of Nottinghamshire* [2003] EWCA Civ 398). The seizure of a person's property is also protected by the European Convention on Human Rights, First Protocol, Article 1.

1.7.9

Code C—5 Right not to be Held Incommunicado

(a) Action

5.1   Subject to paragraph 5.7B, any person arrested and held in custody at a police station or other premises may, on request, have one person known to them or likely to take an interest in their welfare informed at public expense of their whereabouts as soon as practicable. If the person cannot be contacted the detainee may choose up to two alternatives. If they cannot be contacted, the person in charge of detention or the investigation has discretion to allow further attempts until the information has been conveyed.

5.2   The exercise of the above right in respect of each person nominated may be delayed only in accordance with *Annex B*.

5.3   The above right may be exercised each time a detainee is taken to another police station.

5.4   If the detainee agrees, they may at the custody officer's discretion, receive visits from friends, family or others likely to take an interest in their welfare, or in whose welfare the detainee has an interest.

5.5   If a friend, relative or person with an interest in the detainee's welfare enquires about their whereabouts, this information shall be given if the suspect agrees and *Annex B* does not apply.

5.6 The detainee shall be given writing materials, on request, and allowed to telephone one person for a reasonable time. Either or both of these privileges may be denied or delayed if an officer of inspector rank or above considers sending a letter or making a telephone call may result in any of the consequences in:

    (a) *Annex B paragraphs 1* and *2* and the person is detained in connection with an indictable offence;

    (b) *Not used.*

Nothing in this paragraph permits the restriction or denial of the rights in *paragraphs 5.1* and *6.1.*

5.7 Before any letter or message is sent, or telephone call made, the detainee shall be informed that what they say in any letter, call or message (other than in a communication to a solicitor) may be read or listened to and may be given in evidence. A telephone call may be terminated if it is being abused. The costs can be at public expense at the custody officer's discretion.

5.7A Any delay or denial of the rights in this section should be proportionate and should last no longer than necessary.

5.7B In the case of a person in police custody for specific purposes and periods in accordance with a direction under the Crime (Sentences) Act 1997, Schedule 1 (productions from prison etc.), the exercise of the rights in this section shall be subject to any additional conditions specified in the direction for the purpose of regulating the detainee's contact and communication with others whilst in police custody.

(b) Documentation

5.8 A record must be kept of any:

    (a) request made under this section and the action taken;

    (b) letters, messages or telephone calls made or received or visit received;

    (c) refusal by the detainee to have information about them given to an outside enquirer.

The detainee must be asked to countersign the record accordingly and any refusal recorded.

1.7.9.1

KEYNOTE

Right to Have Someone Informed

A person may request an interpreter to interpret a telephone call or translate a letter. In addition to Code C, this right can be denied or delayed where a person is detained under s. 41 of or sch. 7 to the Terrorism Act 2000 by an officer of the rank of inspector or above (Code H, s. 5). The grounds are the same as those regulating the holding of people *incommunicado*. Should there be any delay in complying with a request by a detained person to have someone informed of his/her detention or to communicate with someone, the detained person should be informed of this and told the reason for it and a record kept (s. 56(6) of the 1984 Act). Subject to having sufficient personnel to supervise a visit and any possible hindrance to the investigation, the custody officer also has a discretion to allow visits to the detained person at the police station.

It is suggested that with the Codes of Practice outlining the limited rights for the detained person to make telephone calls and the right to restrict these calls, if the person has a mobile telephone it can be seized for the period of his/her detention. There is no case law on this point and any force policy should be followed. If the detainee does not know anyone to contact for advice or support or cannot contact a friend or relative, the custody officer should bear in mind any local voluntary bodies or other organisations which might be able to help. Paragraph 6.1 applies if legal advice is required.

The additional conditions mentioned in para. 5.7B are contained in Prison Service Instruction 26/2012 (Production of Prisoners at the Request of Warranted Law Enforcement Agencies), which provides detailed guidance and instructions for police officers and Governors and Directors of Prisons regarding applications for prisoners to be transferred to police custody and their safe custody and treatment while in police custody.

Code C—6 Right to Legal Advice

(a) Action

6.1 Unless *Annex B* applies, all detainees must be informed that they may at any time consult and communicate privately with a solicitor, whether in person, in writing or by telephone, and that free independent legal advice is available. See *paragraph 3.1, Notes 1I, 6B and 6J*.

6.2 *Not used.*

6.3 A poster advertising the right to legal advice must be prominently displayed in the charging area of every police station.

6.4 No police officer should, at any time, do or say anything with the intention of dissuading any person who is entitled to legal advice in accordance with this Code, whether or not they have been arrested and are detained, from obtaining legal advice.

6.5 The exercise of the right of access to legal advice may be delayed only as in *Annex B*. Whenever legal advice is requested, and unless *Annex B* applies, the custody officer must act without delay to secure the provision of such advice. If the detainee has the right to speak to a solicitor in person but declines to exercise the right the officer should point out that the right includes the right to speak with a solicitor on the telephone. If the detainee continues to waive this right, or a detainee whose right to free legal advice is limited to telephone advice from the Criminal Defence Service (CDS) Direct declines to exercise that right, the officer should ask them why and any reasons should be recorded on the custody record or the interview record as appropriate. Reminders of the right to legal advice must be given as in *paragraphs 3.5, 11.2, 15.4, 16.4, 16.5, 2B of Annex A, 3 of Annex K and 5 of Annex M* of this Code and Code D, *paragraphs 3.17(ii)* and *6.3*. Once it is clear a detainee does not want to speak to a solicitor in person or by telephone they should cease to be asked their reasons.

6.5A In the case of a person who is a juvenile or is vulnerable, an appropriate adult should consider whether legal advice from a solicitor is required. If such a detained person wants to exercise the right to legal advice, the appropriate action should be taken and should not be delayed until the appropriate adult arrives. If the person indicates that they do not want legal advice, the appropriate adult has the right to ask for a solicitor to attend if this would be in the best interests of the person and must be so informed. In this case, action to secure the provision of advice if so requested by the appropriate adult shall be taken without delay in the same way as when requested by the person. However, the person cannot be forced to see the solicitor if they are adamant that they do not wish to do so.

6.6 A detainee who wants legal advice may not be interviewed or continue to be interviewed until they have received such advice unless:

(a) *Annex B* applies, when the restriction on drawing adverse inferences from silence in *Annex C* will apply because the detainee is not allowed an opportunity to consult a solicitor; or

(b) an officer of superintendent rank or above has reasonable grounds for believing that:

   (i) the consequent delay might:
   - lead to interference with, or harm to, evidence connected with an offence;
   - lead to interference with, or physical harm to, other people;
   - lead to serious loss of, or damage to, property;
   - lead to alerting other people suspected of having committed an offence but not yet arrested for it;
   - hinder the recovery of property obtained in consequence of the commission of an offence.

   (ii) when a solicitor, including a duty solicitor, has been contacted and has agreed to attend, awaiting their arrival would cause unreasonable delay to the process of investigation.

Note: In these cases the restriction on drawing adverse inferences from silence in *Annex C* will apply because the detainee is not allowed an opportunity to consult a solicitor.

(c) the solicitor the detainee has nominated or selected from a list:
  (i) cannot be contacted;
  (ii) has previously indicated they do not wish to be contacted; or
  (iii) having been contacted, has declined to attend; and
    - the detainee has been advised of the Duty Solicitor Scheme but has declined to ask for the duty solicitor;
    - in these circumstances the interview may be started or continued without further delay provided an officer of inspector rank or above has agreed to the interview proceeding.

Note: The restriction on drawing adverse inferences from silence in *Annex C* will not apply because the detainee is allowed an opportunity to consult the duty solicitor;

(d) the detainee changes their mind about wanting legal advice or (as the case may be) about wanting a solicitor present at the interview and states that they no longer wish to speak to a solicitor. In these circumstances, the interview may be started or continued without delay provided that:
  (i) an officer of inspector rank or above:
    - speaks to the detainee to enquire about the reasons for their change of mind, and
    - makes, or directs the making of, reasonable efforts to ascertain the solicitor's expected time of arrival and to inform the solicitor that the suspect has stated that they wish to change their mind and the reason (if given);
  (ii) the detainee's reason for their change of mind (if given) and the outcome of the action in (i) are recorded in the custody record;
  (iii) the detainee, after being informed of the outcome of the action in (i) above, confirms in writing that they want the interview to proceed without speaking or further speaking to a solicitor or (as the case may be) without a solicitor being present and do not wish to wait for a solicitor by signing an entry to this effect in the custody record;
  (iv) an officer of inspector rank or above is satisfied that it is proper for the interview to proceed in these circumstances and:
    - gives authority in writing for the interview to proceed and, if the authority is not recorded in the custody record, the officer must ensure that the custody record shows the date and time of the authority and where it is recorded, and
    - takes, or directs the taking of, reasonable steps to inform the solicitor that the authority has been given and the time when the interview is expected to commence and records or causes to be recorded, the outcome of this action in the custody record.
  (v) When the interview starts and the interviewer reminds the suspect of their right to legal advice (see *paragraph 11.2*, Code E *paragraph 4.5* and Code F *paragraph 4.5*), the interviewer shall then ensure that the following is recorded in the written interview record or the interview record made in accordance with Code E or F:
    - confirmation that the detainee has changed their mind about wanting legal advice or (as the case may be) about wanting a solicitor present and the reasons for it if given;
    - the fact that authority for the interview to proceed has been given and, subject to *paragraph 2.6A*, the name of the authorising officer;
    - that if the solicitor arrives at the station before the interview is completed, the detainee will be so informed without delay and a break will be taken to allow them to speak to the solicitor if they wish, unless *paragraph 6.6(a)* applies, and
    - that at any time during the interview, the detainee may again ask for legal advice and that if they do, a break will be taken to allow them to speak to the solicitor, unless *paragraph 6.6(a), (b)*, or *(c)* applies.

Note: In these circumstances, the restriction on drawing adverse inferences from silence in *Annex C* will not apply because the detainee is allowed an opportunity to consult a solicitor if they wish.

6.7   If *paragraph 6.6(a)* applies, where the reason for authorising the delay ceases to apply, there may be no further delay in permitting the exercise of the right in the absence of a further authorisation unless *paragraph 6.6(b), (c)* or *(d)* applies. If *paragraph 6.6(b)(i)* applies, once sufficient information has been obtained to avert the risk, questioning must cease until the detainee has received legal advice unless *paragraph 6.6(a), (b)(ii), (c)* or *(d)* applies.

6.8   A detainee who has been permitted to consult a solicitor shall be entitled on request to have the solicitor present when they are interviewed unless one of the exceptions in *paragraph 6.6* applies.

6.9   The solicitor may only be required to leave the interview if their conduct is such that the interviewer is unable properly to put questions to the suspect.

6.10   If the interviewer considers a solicitor is acting in such a way, they will stop the interview and consult an officer not below superintendent rank, if one is readily available, and otherwise an officer not below inspector rank not connected with the investigation. After speaking to the solicitor, the officer consulted will decide if the interview should continue in the presence of that solicitor. If they decide it should not, the suspect will be given the opportunity to consult another solicitor before the interview continues and that solicitor given an opportunity to be present at the interview.

6.11   The removal of a solicitor from an interview is a serious step and, if it occurs, the officer of superintendent rank or above who took the decision will consider if the incident should be reported to the Solicitors Regulatory Authority. If the decision to remove the solicitor has been taken by an officer below superintendent rank, the facts must be reported to an officer of superintendent rank or above, who will similarly consider whether a report to the Solicitors Regulatory Authority would be appropriate. When the solicitor concerned is a duty solicitor, the report should be both to the Solicitors Regulatory Authority and to the Legal Aid Agency.

6.12   'Solicitor' in this Code means:

- a solicitor who holds a current practising certificate;
- an accredited or probationary representative included on the register of representatives maintained by the Legal Aid Agency.

6.12A An accredited or probationary representative sent to provide advice by, and on behalf of, a solicitor shall be admitted to the police station for this purpose unless an officer of inspector rank or above considers such a visit will hinder the investigation and directs otherwise. Hindering the investigation does not include giving proper legal advice to a detainee. Once admitted to the police station, *paragraphs 6.6* to *6.10* apply.

6.13   In exercising their discretion under *paragraph 6.12A*, the officer should take into account in particular:

- whether:
  - ~ the identity and status of an accredited or probationary representative have been satisfactorily established;
  - ~ they are of suitable character to provide legal advice, e.g. a person with a criminal record is unlikely to be suitable unless the conviction was for a minor offence and not recent.
- any other matters in any written letter of authorisation provided by the solicitor on whose behalf the person is attending the police station.

6.14   If the inspector refuses access to an accredited or probationary representative or a decision is taken that such a person should not be permitted to remain at an interview, the inspector must notify the solicitor on whose behalf the representative was acting and give them an opportunity to make alternative arrangements. The detainee must be informed and the custody record noted.

6.15   If a solicitor arrives at the station to see a particular person, that person must, unless *Annex B* applies, be so informed whether or not they are being interviewed and asked if they would like to see the solicitor. This applies even if the detainee has declined legal advice or, having requested it, subsequently agreed to be interviewed without receiving advice. The solicitor's attendance and the detainee's decision must be noted in the custody record.

(b) Documentation

6.16 Any request for legal advice and the action taken shall be recorded.

6.17 A record shall be made in the interview record if a detainee asks for legal advice and an interview is begun either in the absence of a solicitor or their representative, or they have been required to leave an interview.

1.7.10.1 **KEYNOTE**

Right to Legal Advice

A poster or posters of the right to legal advice containing translations into Welsh, the main minority ethnic languages and the principal European languages should be displayed wherever they are likely to be helpful and it is practicable to do so.

Section 58 of the Police and Criminal Evidence Act 1984 provides an almost inalienable right for a person arrested and held in custody at a police station or other premises to consult privately with a solicitor free of charge at any time if he/she requests it. In R v Alladice (1988) 87 Cr App R 380 the Court of Appeal made it clear that:

> … no matter how strongly and however justifiably the police may feel that their investigation and detection of crime is being hindered by the presence of a solicitor … they are nevertheless confined to the narrow limits imposed by section 58.

A detainee has a right to free legal advice and to be represented by a solicitor. Note for Guidance 6B explains the arrangements which enable detainees to obtain legal advice. An outline of these arrangements is also included in the Notice of Rights and Entitlements given to detainees in accordance with para. 3.2. The arrangements also apply, with appropriate modifications, to persons attending a police station or other location (see para. 3.22) voluntarily who are cautioned prior to being interviewed. See para. 3.21. When a detainee asks for free legal advice, the Defence Solicitor Call Centre (DSCC) must be informed of the request. Free legal advice will be limited to telephone advice provided by the Criminal Defence Service Direct (CDS Direct) if a detainee is:

- detained for a non-imprisonable offence;
- arrested on a bench warrant for failing to appear and being held for production at court (except where the solicitor has clear documentary evidence available that would result in the client being released from custody);
- arrested for drink driving (driving/in charge with excess alcohol, failing to provide a specimen, driving/in charge whilst unfit through drink); or
- detained in relation to breach of police or court bail conditions

unless one or more exceptions apply, in which case the DSCC should arrange for advice to be given by a solicitor at the police station, for example:

- the police want to interview the detainee or carry out an eye-witness identification procedure;
- the detainee needs an appropriate adult;
- the detainee is unable to communicate over the telephone;
- the detainee alleges serious misconduct by the police;
- the investigation includes another offence not included in the list;
- the solicitor to be assigned is already at the police station.

When free advice is not limited to telephone advice, detainees can ask for free advice from a solicitor they know or if they do not know a solicitor or the solicitor they know cannot be contacted, from the duty solicitor.

To arrange free legal advice, the police should telephone the DSCC. The call centre will decide whether legal advice should be limited to telephone advice from CDS Direct, or whether a solicitor known to the detainee or the duty solicitor should speak to the detainee.

When detainees want to pay for legal advice themselves:

- the DSCC will contact a solicitor of their choice on their behalf;
- they may, when free advice is only available by telephone from CDS Direct, still speak to a solicitor of their choice on the telephone for advice, but the solicitor would not be paid by legal aid and may ask the person to pay for the advice;

- they should be given an opportunity to consult a specific solicitor or another solicitor from that solicitor's firm. If this solicitor is not available, they may choose up to two alternatives. If these alternatives are not available, the custody officer has discretion to allow further attempts until a solicitor has been contacted and agreed to provide advice;
- they are entitled to a private consultation with their chosen solicitor on the telephone or the solicitor may decide to come to the police station;
- If their chosen solicitor cannot be contacted, the DSCC may still be called to arrange free legal advice.

Apart from carrying out duties necessary to implement these arrangements, an officer must not advise the suspect about any particular firm of solicitors.

No police officer or police staff shall indicate to any suspect, except to answer a direct question, that the period for which he/she is liable to be detained, or if not detained, the time taken to complete the interview, might be reduced: if the suspect does not ask for legal advice or does not want a solicitor present when he/she is interviewed; or if he/she has asked for legal advice or (as the case may be) asked for a solicitor to be present when he/she is interviewed but changes his/her mind and agrees to be interviewed without waiting for a solicitor.

A detainee has a right to free legal advice and to be represented by a solicitor. A detainee is not obliged to give reasons for declining legal advice and should not be pressed to do so. The solicitor's only role in the police station is to protect and advance the legal rights of his/her client. On occasions, this may require the solicitor to give advice which has the effect of the client avoiding giving evidence which strengthens a prosecution case. The solicitor may intervene in order to seek clarification, challenge an improper question to the client or the manner in which it is put, advise the client not to reply to particular questions or if he/she wishes to give the client further legal advice.

An officer who takes the decision to exclude a solicitor must be in a position to satisfy the court that the decision was properly made. In order to do this he/she may need to witness what is happening. Paragraph 6.9 only applies if the solicitor's approach or conduct prevents or unreasonably obstructs proper questions being put to the suspect or the suspect's response being recorded. Examples of unacceptable conduct include answering questions on a suspect's behalf or providing written replies for the suspect to quote.

If an officer of at least inspector rank considers that a particular solicitor or firm of solicitors is persistently sending probationary representatives who are unsuited to provide legal advice, he/she should inform an officer of at least superintendent rank, who may wish to take the matter up with the Solicitors Regulation Authority.

Whenever a detainee exercises his/her right to legal advice by consulting or communicating with a solicitor, he/she must be allowed to do so in private. This right to consult or communicate in private is fundamental. If the requirement for privacy is compromised because what is said or written by the detainee or solicitor for the purpose of giving and receiving legal advice is overheard, listened to or read by others without the informed consent of the detainee, the right will effectively have been denied. When a detainee chooses to speak to a solicitor on the telephone, he/she should be allowed to do so in private unless this is impractical because of the design and layout of the custody area or the location of telephones. However, the normal expectation should be that facilities will be available, unless they are being used, at all police stations to enable detainees to speak in private to a solicitor either face to face or over the telephone.

This right to have a private consultation also applies to juveniles who, should they wish to have a private consultation without the appropriate adult being present, must be permitted to do so. This point was considered in *R (On the Application of M (A Child)) v Commissioner of the Police of the Metropolis* [2001] EWHC 533 (Admin), where the court said that ideally there ought be a consultation room at every police station and facilities for private telephone calls to be made for legal consultations. However, there was no breach of Article 6(3) of the European Convention on Human Rights where it could not be shown that a detainee had been denied adequate facilities for the preparation of his defence.

Once a person has indicated a wish to have a solicitor, and has not yet been advised by a solicitor, he/she can only be interviewed in limited circumstances as set out in Code C, para. 6.6. In considering whether a detainee can be interviewed or continue to be interviewed under para. 6.6 without having received legal advice which he/she has requested, the officer making this decision should, if practicable, ask the solicitor for an estimate of how long it will take to come to the station and relate this to the time that detention is permitted, the time of day (i.e. whether the rest period under para. 12.2 is imminent) and the requirements of other investigations. Subject to the constraints of Annex B, a solicitor may advise more than one client in an investigation if he/she wishes. Any question of a conflict of interest is for the solicitor under his/her professional code of conduct. If, however, waiting for a solicitor to give advice to one client may lead to unreasonable delay to the interview with another, the provisions of para. 6.6(b) may apply.

Where the solicitor is on the way or is to set off immediately, it will not normally be appropriate to begin an interview before he/she arrives. If it appears necessary to begin an interview before the solicitor's arrival, he/she should be given an indication of how long the police would be able to wait before starting the interview so that there is an opportunity to make arrangements for someone else to provide legal advice.

Code C, Annex B provides an exception to this right to legal advice. The same exception also applies where the person is held under prevention of terrorism legislation (Terrorism Act 2000, s. 41 or sch. 8) and the conditions in Code H, Annex B apply. In addition, a uniformed officer of at least the rank of inspector not connected with the case may be present if authorised by an Assistant Chief Constable or Commander (Terrorism Act 2000, sch. 8, para. 9 and Code H, paras 6.4, 6.5). The delay can only be for a maximum of 36 hours (48 hours from the time of arrest in terrorism cases) or until the time the person will first appear at court, whichever is the sooner (see below). The 36-hour period is calculated from the 'relevant time'.

Another exception is in relation to the drink-drive procedure for s. 7 of the Road Traffic Act 1988. In *DPP v Noe* [2000] RTR 351 a request to see a solicitor or alternatively to consult a law book to verify the legality of the police request for a specimen of breath was not a reasonable excuse under s. 7. This is confirmed by *Campbell* v *DPP* [2002] EWHC 1314 (Admin), in which it was held that it was entirely proportionate to allow a police officer to require a member of the community to provide a specimen, albeit that legal advice had not been obtained.

Where Code C, para. 6.6 is used it will have to be justified at court if the interview is to be admissible. This power might prove useful in circumstances where there are 'delaying tactics' by legal representatives, particularly where they are aware that the detained person's relevant time is due to expire within a short period.

When detainees who wanted legal advice change their mind, an officer of inspector rank or above must authorise the continuation of the interview. It is permissible for such authorisation to be given over the telephone, if the authorising officer is able to satisfy him/herself about the reason for the detainee's change of mind and is satisfied that it is proper to continue the interview in those circumstances.

In terrorism cases a direction may be given by an officer of at least the rank of Commander or Assistant Chief Constable which may provide that a detained person who wishes to exercise the right to consult a solicitor may do so only in the sight and hearing of a qualified officer, this person being a uniformed officer of at least the rank of inspector not connected with the investigation from the authorising officer's force (Code H, para. 6.5).

1.7.11 Code C—7 Citizens of Independent Commonwealth Countries or Foreign Nationals

(a) Action

7.1 A detainee who is a citizen of an independent Commonwealth country or a national of a foreign country, including the Republic of Ireland, has the right, upon request, to communicate at any time with the appropriate High Commission, Embassy or Consulate. That detainee must be informed as soon as practicable of this right and asked if they want to have their High Commission, Embassy or Consulate told of their whereabouts and the grounds for their detention. Such a request should be acted upon as soon as practicable.

7.2 A detainee who is a citizen of a country with which a bilateral consular convention or agreement is in force requiring notification of arrest must also be informed that subject to *paragraph 7.4*, notification of their arrest will be sent to the appropriate High Commission,

Embassy or Consulate as soon as practicable, whether or not they request it. A list of the countries to which this requirement currently applies and contact details for the relevant High Commissions, Embassies and Consulates can be obtained from the Consular Directorate of the Foreign and Commonwealth Office (FCO) as follows:

- from the FCO web pages:
  - ~ https://gov.uk/government/publications/table-of-consular-conventions-and-mandatory-notification-obligations, and
  - ~ https://www.gov.uk/government/publications/foreign-embassies-in-the-uk
- by telephone to 020 7008 3100,
- by email to fcocorrespondence@fco.gov.uk.
- by letter to the Foreign and Commonwealth Office, King Charles Street, London, SW1A 2AH.

7.3 Consular officers may, if the detainee agrees, visit one of their nationals in police detention to talk to them and, if required, to arrange for legal advice. Such visits shall take place out of the hearing of a police officer.

7.4 Notwithstanding the provisions of consular conventions, if the detainee claims that they are a refugee or have applied or intend to apply for asylum, the custody officer must ensure that UK Visas and Immigration (UKVI) (formerly the UK Border Agency) is informed as soon as practicable of the claim. UKVI will then determine whether compliance with relevant international obligations requires notification of the arrest to be sent and will inform the custody officer as to what action police need to take.

(b) Documentation

7.5 A record shall be made:
- when a detainee is informed of their rights under this section and of any requirement in *paragraph 7.2*;
- of any communications with a High Commission, Embassy or Consulate, and
- of any communications with UKVI about a detainee's claim to be a refugee or to be seeking asylum and the resulting action taken by police.

1.7.11.1

KEYNOTE

The exercise of the rights in this section may not be interfered with even where Code C, Annex B applies.

1.7.12

Code C—8 Conditions of Detention

(a) Action

8.1 So far as it is practicable, not more than one detainee should be detained in each cell.

8.2 Cells in use must be adequately heated, cleaned and ventilated. They must be adequately lit, subject to such dimming as is compatible with safety and security to allow people detained overnight to sleep. No additional restraints shall be used within a locked cell unless absolutely necessary and then only restraint equipment, approved for use in that force by the chief officer, which is reasonable and necessary in the circumstances having regard to the detainee's demeanour and with a view to ensuring their safety and the safety of others. If a detainee is deaf or a vulnerable person, particular care must be taken when deciding whether to use any form of approved restraints.

8.3 Blankets, mattresses, pillows and other bedding supplied shall be of a reasonable standard and in a clean and sanitary condition.

8.4 Access to toilet and washing facilities must be provided. This must take account of the dignity of the detainee.

8.5 If it is necessary to remove a detainee's clothes for the purposes of investigation, for hygiene, health reasons or cleaning, removal shall be conducted with proper regard to the dignity, sensitivity and vulnerability of the detainee and replacement clothing of a reasonable standard of comfort and cleanliness shall be provided. A detainee may not be interviewed unless adequate clothing has been offered.

8.6 At least two light meals and one main meal should be offered in any 24-hour period. Drinks should be provided at meal times and upon reasonable request between meals. Whenever necessary, advice shall be sought from the appropriate healthcare professional, on medical and dietary matters. As far as practicable, meals provided shall offer a varied diet and meet any specific dietary needs or religious beliefs the detainee may have. The detainee may, at the custody officer's discretion, have meals supplied by their family or friends at their expense.

8.7 Brief outdoor exercise shall be offered daily if practicable.

8.8 A juvenile shall not be placed in a police cell unless no other secure accommodation is available and the custody officer considers it is not practicable to supervise them if they are not placed in a cell or that a cell provides more comfortable accommodation than other secure accommodation in the station. A juvenile may not be placed in a cell with a detained adult.

(b) Documentation

8.9 A record must be kept of replacement clothing and meals offered.

8.10 If a juvenile is placed in a cell, the reason must be recorded.

8.11 The use of any restraints on a detainee whilst in a cell, the reasons for it and, if appropriate, the arrangements for enhanced supervision of the detainee whilst so restrained, shall be recorded. See *paragraph 3.9*.

1.7.12.1 **KEYNOTE**

The provision of bedding, medical and dietary matters are of particular importance in the case of a person likely to be detained for an extended period. In deciding whether to allow meals to be supplied by family or friends, the custody officer is entitled to take account of the risk of items being concealed in any food or package and the officer's duties and responsibilities under food handling legislation. Meals should, so far as practicable, be offered at recognised meal times, or at other times that take account of when the detainee last had a meal.

In cells subject to CCTV monitoring, privacy in the toilet area should be ensured by any appropriate means and detainees should be made aware of this when they are placed in the cell. If a detainee or appropriate adult on their behalf, expresses doubts about the effectiveness of the means used, reasonable steps should be taken to allay those doubts, for example, by explaining or demonstrating the means used.

It is suggested that the custody officer should undertake a further risk assessment which should be recorded in the custody record before more than one person is placed in a cell. Any steps taken to minimise the risk should also be included in the custody record. (Paragraph 2.3 requires the time of release to be recorded; this is relevant in calculating any period of detention which may still be remaining if the person has been bailed, and periods in police detention also count towards the period a person serves in custody.)

Section 117 of the 1984 Act provides that where any provision of the Act confers a power on a constable and does not provide that the power may only be exercised with the consent of some person, other than a police officer, the officer may use reasonable force, if necessary, in the exercise of the power.

This is not a blanket power to use force. In *R v Jones* (1999) *The Times*, 21 April, the court said that s. 117 should not be interpreted as giving a right to police to exercise force whenever the consent of a suspect was not required.

The Detention and Custody Authorised Professional Practice (APP) produced by the College of Policing (see <https://www.app.college.police.uk>) provides more detailed guidance on matters concerning detainee health care and treatment and associated forensic issues which should be read in conjunction with ss. 8 and 9 of this Code.

Code C—9 Care and Treatment of Detained Persons

(a) General

9.1 Nothing in this section prevents the police from calling an appropriate healthcare professional to examine a detainee for the purposes of obtaining evidence relating to any offence in which the detainee is suspected of being involved.

9.2 If a complaint is made by, or on behalf of, a detainee about their treatment since their arrest, or it comes to notice that a detainee may have been treated improperly, a report must be made as soon as practicable to an officer of inspector rank or above not connected with the investigation. If the matter concerns a possible assault or the possibility of the unnecessary or unreasonable use of force, an appropriate healthcare professional must also be called as soon as practicable.

9.3 Subject to *paragraph 9.6* in the case of a person to whom The Mental Health Act 1983 (Places of Safety) Regulations 2017 apply, detainees should be visited at least every hour.

 If no reasonably foreseeable risk was identified in a risk assessment, see *paragraphs 3.6 to 3.10*, there is no need to wake a sleeping detainee. Those suspected of being under the influence of drink or drugs or both or of having swallowed drugs, or whose level of consciousness causes concern must, subject to any clinical directions given by the appropriate healthcare professional, see *paragraph 9.13*:
 - be visited and roused at least every half hour;
 - have their condition assessed as in *Annex H*;
 - and clinical treatment arranged if appropriate.

9.3A As soon as practicable after arrival at the police station, each detainee must be given an opportunity to speak in private with a member of the custody staff who if they wish, may be of the same sex as the detainee (see *paragraph 1.13(c)*), about any matter concerning the detainee's personal needs relating to their health, hygiene and welfare that might affect or concern them whilst in custody. If the detainee wishes to take this opportunity, the necessary arrangements shall be made as soon as practicable. In the case of a juvenile or vulnerable person, the appropriate adult must be involved in accordance with *paragraph 3.17* and in the case of a girl under 18, see *paragraph 3.20A*.

9.3B Each female detainee aged 18 or over shall be asked in private if possible and at the earliest opportunity, if they require or are likely to require any menstrual products whilst they are in custody. They must also be told that they will be provided free of charge and that replacement products are available. At the custody officer's discretion, detainees may have menstrual products supplied by their family or friends at their expense. For girls under 18, see *paragraph 3.20A*.

9.4 When arrangements are made to secure clinical attention for a detainee, the custody officer must make sure all relevant information which might assist in the treatment of the detainee's condition is made available to the responsible healthcare professional. This applies whether or not the healthcare professional asks for such information. Any officer or police staff with relevant information must inform the custody officer as soon as practicable.

(b) Clinical treatment and attention

9.5 The custody officer must make sure a detainee receives appropriate clinical attention as soon as reasonably practicable if the person:
 (a) appears to be suffering from physical illness; or
 (b) is injured; or
 (c) appears to be suffering from a mental disorder; or
 (d) appears to need clinical attention.

9.5A This applies even if the detainee makes no request for clinical attention and whether or not they have already received clinical attention elsewhere. If the need for attention appears urgent, e.g. when indicated as in Annex H, the nearest available healthcare professional or an ambulance must be called immediately.

9.5B The custody officer must also consider the need for clinical attention in relation to those suffering the effects of alcohol or drugs.

9.6 *Paragraph 9.5* is not meant to prevent or delay the transfer to a hospital if necessary of a person detained under the Mental Health Act 1983, sections 135 and 136, as amended by the Policing and Crime Act 2017. When an assessment under that Act is to take place at a police station (see *paragraph 3.16*) the custody officer must also ensure that in accordance with The Mental Health Act 1983 (Places of Safety) Regulations 2017, a health professional is present and available to the person throughout the period they are detained at the police station and that at the welfare of the detainee is checked by the health professional at least once every thirty minutes and any appropriate action for the care and treatment of the detainee taken.

9.7 If it appears to the custody officer, or they are told, that a person brought to a station under arrest may be suffering from an infectious disease or condition, the custody officer must take reasonable steps to safeguard the health of the detainee and others at the station. In deciding what action to take, advice must be sought from an appropriate healthcare professional. The custody officer has discretion to isolate the person and their property until clinical directions have been obtained.

9.8 If a detainee requests a clinical examination, an appropriate healthcare professional must be called as soon as practicable to assess the detainee's clinical needs. If a safe and appropriate care plan cannot be provided, the appropriate healthcare professional's advice must be sought. The detainee may also be examined by a medical practitioner of their choice at their expense.

9.9 If a detainee is required to take or apply any medication in compliance with clinical directions prescribed before their detention, the custody officer must consult the appropriate healthcare professional before the use of the medication. Subject to the restrictions in *paragraph 9.10*, the custody officer is responsible for the safekeeping of any medication and for making sure the detainee is given the opportunity to take or apply prescribed or approved medication. Any such consultation and its outcome shall be noted in the custody record.

9.10 No police officer may administer or supervise the self-administration of medically prescribed controlled drugs of the types and forms listed in the Misuse of Drugs Regulations 2001, Schedule 2 or 3. A detainee may only self-administer such drugs under the personal supervision of the registered medical practitioner authorising their use or other appropriate healthcare professional. The custody officer may supervise the self-administration of, or authorise other custody staff to supervise the self-administration of, drugs listed in Schedule 4 or 5 if the officer has consulted the appropriate healthcare professional authorising their use and both are satisfied self-administration will not expose the detainee, police officers or anyone else to the risk of harm or injury.

9.11 When appropriate healthcare professionals administer drugs or authorise the use of other medications, supervise their self-administration or consult with the custody officer about allowing self-administration of drugs listed in Schedule 4 or 5, it must be within current medicines legislation and the scope of practice as determined by their relevant statutory regulatory body.

9.12 If a detainee has in their possession, or claims to need, medication relating to a heart condition, diabetes, epilepsy or a condition of comparable potential seriousness then, even though *paragraph 9.5* may not apply, the advice of the appropriate healthcare professional must be obtained.

9.13 Whenever the appropriate healthcare professional is called in accordance with this section to examine or treat a detainee, the custody officer shall ask for their opinion about:
- any risks or problems which police need to take into account when making decisions about the detainee's continued detention;
- when to carry out an interview if applicable; and
- the need for safeguards.

9.14 When clinical directions are given by the appropriate healthcare professional, whether orally or in writing, and the custody officer has any doubts or is in any way uncertain about any aspect of the directions, the custody officer shall ask for clarification. It is particularly important that directions concerning the frequency of visits are clear, precise and capable of being implemented.

(c) Documentation

9.15 A record must be made in the custody record of:

(a) the arrangements made for an examination by an appropriate healthcare professional under *paragraph 9.2* and of any complaint reported under that paragraph together with any relevant remarks by the custody officer;

(b) any arrangements made in accordance with *paragraph 9.5*;

(c) any request for a clinical examination under *paragraph 9.8* and any arrangements made in response;

(d) the injury, ailment, condition or other reason which made it necessary to make the arrangements in (a) to (c);

(e) any clinical directions and advice, including any further clarifications, given to police by a healthcare professional concerning the care and treatment of the detainee in connection with any of the arrangements made in (a) to (c);

(f) if applicable, the responses received when attempting to rouse a person using the procedure in *Annex H*.

9.16 If a healthcare professional does not record their clinical findings in the custody record, the record must show where they are recorded. However, information which is necessary to custody staff to ensure the effective ongoing care and well being of the detainee must be recorded openly in the custody record, see *paragraph 3.8* and *Annex G, paragraph 7*.

9.17 Subject to the requirements of *Section 4*, the custody record shall include:

- a record of all medication a detainee has in their possession on arrival at the police station;
- a note of any such medication they claim to need but do not have with them.

1.7.13.1

KEYNOTE

A 'health care professional' means a clinically qualified person working within the scope of practice as determined by his/her relevant professional body. Whether a health care professional is 'appropriate' depends on the circumstances of the duties he/she carries out at the time.

Paragraph 9.3 also applies to a person in police custody by order of a magistrates' court under the Criminal Justice Act 1988, s. 152 (as amended by the Drugs Act 2005, s. 8) to facilitate the recovery of evidence after being charged with drug possession or drug trafficking and suspected of having swallowed drugs. In the case of the health care needs of a person who has swallowed drugs, the custody officer, subject to any clinical directions, should consider the necessity for rousing every half hour. This does not negate the need for regular visiting of the suspect in the cell. Whenever possible, juveniles (which includes 17-year-olds) and vulnerable detainees should be visited more frequently. The purpose of recording a person's responses when attempting to rouse them using the procedure in Annex H is to enable any change in the individual's consciousness level to be noted and clinical treatment arranged if appropriate.

Paragraph 9.5 does not apply to minor ailments or injuries which do not need attention. However, all such ailments or injuries must be recorded in the custody record and any doubt must be resolved in favour of calling the appropriate health care professional. The custody officer should always seek to clarify directions that the detainee requires constant observation or supervision and should ask the appropriate health care professional to explain precisely what action needs to be taken to implement such directions.

A detainee who appears drunk or behaves abnormally may be suffering from illness, the effects of drugs or may have sustained injury, particularly a head injury which is not apparent. A detainee needing or dependent on certain drugs, including alcohol, may experience harmful effects within a short time of being deprived of his/her supply. In these circumstances, when there is any doubt, police should always act urgently to call an appropriate health care professional or an ambulance, see Annex H for observation list for a detained person. *Watling* v *The Chief Constable of Suffolk Constabulary & Anor* [2019] EWHC 2342 (QB) highlights the responsibility to care for a detainee and the link to Article 3 of the Human Rights Act 1998. The claimant was driving his car when he suddenly felt dizzy. He was stopped by police and the officer formed the suspicion that the claimant was driving under the influence of drugs and arrested him. He was taken into custody and 3 hours later he was seen by a forensic medical examiner who concluded that he had suffered a stroke and he was taken to hospital. Due to the stroke, the claimant was left with 'Rankin scale 3' moderate disability. The claimant brought a claim, amongst other things, for damages for breach of Article 3 of the European Convention on Human Rights (ECHR). To engage Article 3 (torture or inhuman or degrading treatment or punishment), all behaviour alleged to constitute the inhuman or degrading treatment must attain a minimum level of severity and go beyond that which is considered reasonably coincidental to the fact of detention. The test as to whether the threshold of severity has been reached is objective and to be determined after consideration of all circumstances, including the gravity of the consequences or potential consequences of the alleged ill-treatment on a person with the attributes of the victim. In the present case, those attributes included: the fact that the claimant was a detainee and therefore vulnerable, as well as the particularly grave potential damage that could be caused to him as a stroke victim in the event that he did not receive appropriate treatment in a reasonable time frame. In this case, the claim failed; however, the court did make the observation that there will be cases where the difference in approach is capable of producing a different result to that arrived at under Article 3.

Any information that is available about the detained person should be considered in deciding whether to request a medical examination. In *R* v *HM Coroner for Coventry, ex parte Chief Constable of Staffordshire Police* (2000) 164 JP 665 the detained person had been drunk on arrest and was detained to be interviewed. The detained person made no complaint of his condition but his sister called the police to advise them that he would get the shakes. It was clear at interview and the following morning that he did have the shakes but no complaint was made and no doctor was called. A verdict of accidental death aggravated by neglect was an option in the case as the deceased had died while in police custody. The court considered the facts, such as the deceased's withdrawal and the warning as to his condition, from which a properly directed jury could have concluded that had certain steps been taken it was at least possible that the deceased would not have died. In this case, a verdict of accidental death aggravated by neglect was left open to the jury, even though a doctor at the inquest gave evidence that he doubted whether calling a doctor would have made any difference to the eventual outcome. In addition, such a failure to act could lead to disciplinary action.

Except as allowed for under the Mental Health Act 1983 (Places of Safety) Regulations 2017, a police station must not be used as a place of safety for persons detained under s. 135 or 136 of that Act. Chapter 16 of the Mental Health Act 1983 Code of Practice (as revised), provides more detailed guidance about arranging assessments under the Mental Health Act and transferring detainees from police stations to other places of safety. Additional guidance in relation to amendments made to the Mental Health Act in 2017 are published at <https://www.gov.uk/government/publications/mental-health-act-1983-implementing-changes-to-police-powers>.

Matters concerning personal needs to which para. 9.3A applies include any requirement for menstrual products, incontinence products and colostomy appliances, where these needs have not previously been identified (see para. 3.5(c)). It also enables adult women to speak in private to a female officer about their requirements for menstrual products if they decline to respond to the more direct enquiry envisaged under para. 9.3B. This contact should be facilitated at any time, where possible. Detailed guidance for police officers and staff concerning menstruating female detainees in police custody is included in the College of Policing Authorised Professional Practice (APP).

1.7.13.2   **KEYNOTE**

Medical Record Forming Part of the Custody Record

It is important to respect a person's right to privacy, and information about his/her health must be kept confidential and only disclosed with his/her consent or in accordance with clinical advice when it is necessary to protect the detainee's health or that of others who come into contact with him/her.

A solicitor or appropriate adult must be permitted to consult a detainee's custody record as soon as practicable after his/her arrival at the station and at any other time while the person is detained (Code C, para. 2.4). Therefore details required to be included in the custody record concerning the detainee's injuries and ailments will be accessible to both the solicitor and appropriate adult. However, paras 9.15 and 9.16 do not require any information about the cause of any injury, ailment or condition to be recorded on the custody record if it appears capable of providing evidence of an offence.

As the Codes (paras 9.15 to 9.17) specify matters which must be included within the custody record, it is suggested that all other matters recorded by the appropriate health care professional do not form part of the custody record and therefore do not need to be made available to the solicitor or appropriate adult under Code C, para. 2.4, i.e. the notes made by the health care professional.

1.7.13.3 KEYNOTE

Independent Custody Visiting (Lay Visitors)

Section 51 of the Police Reform Act 2002 introduced independent custody visitors on a statutory basis. The arrangements may confer on independent custody visitors such powers as the police authority considers necessary to enable them to carry out their functions under the arrangements and may, in particular, confer on them powers to:

- require access to be given to each police station;
- examine records relating to the detention of persons;
- meet detainees for the purposes of a discussion about their treatment and conditions while detained; and
- inspect the facilities including, in particular, cell accommodation, washing and toilet facilities and the facilities for the provision of food.

A Code of Practice on Independent Custody Visiting has been published outlining the role of the independent visitor (this can be found at <https://www.icva.org.uk>).

Code C—10 Cautions [see chapter 1.9]

Code C—11 Interviews—General [see chapter 1.9]

Code C—12 Interviews in Police Stations [see chapter 1.9]

1.7.14 Code C—13 Interpreters

(a) General

13.1 Chief officers are responsible for making arrangements (see *paragraph 13.1ZA*) to provide appropriately qualified independent persons to act as interpreters and to provide translations of essential documents for:

(a) detained suspects who, in accordance with *paragraph 3.5(c)(ii)*, the custody officer has determined require an interpreter, and

(b) suspects who are not under arrest but are cautioned as in *section 10* who, in accordance with *paragraph 3.21(b)*, the interviewer has determined require an interpreter. In these cases, the responsibilities of the custody officer are, if appropriate, assigned to the interviewer. An interviewer who has any doubts about whether and what arrangements for an interpreter must be made or about how the provisions of this section should be applied to a suspect who is not under arrest should seek advice from an officer of the rank of sergeant or above.

If the suspect has a hearing or speech impediment, references to 'interpreter' and 'interpretation' in this Code include arrangements for appropriate assistance necessary to establish effective communication with that person. See *paragraph 13.1C* below if the person is in Wales.

13.1ZA References in *paragraph 13.1* above and elsewhere in this Code (see *paragraphs 3.12(a)*, *13.2, 13.2A, 13.5, 13.6, 13.9, 13.10, 13.10A, 13.10D* and *13.11 below* and in any other Code, to making arrangements for an interpreter to assist a suspect, mean making arrangements for the interpreter to be *physically* present in the same location as the suspect *unless* the provisions in *paragraph 13.12* below, and Part 1 of *Annex N*, allow live-link interpretation to be used.

13.1A The arrangements *must* comply with the minimum requirements set out in *Directive 2010/ 64/EU* of the European Parliament and of the Council of 20 October 2010 on the right to interpretation and translation in criminal proceedings. The provisions *of this* Code implement the requirements for those to whom this Code applies. These requirements include the following:

- That the arrangements made and the quality of interpretation and translation provided shall be sufficient to 'safeguard the fairness of the proceedings, in particular by ensuring that suspected or accused persons have knowledge of the cases against them and are able to exercise their right of defence'. This term which is used by the Directive means that the suspect must be able to understand their position and be able to communicate effectively with police officers, interviewers, solicitors and appropriate adults as provided for by this and any other Code in the same way as a suspect who can speak and understand English and who does not have a hearing or speech impediment and who would therefore not require an interpreter. See paragraphs 13.12 to 13.14 and Annex N for application to live-link interpretation.
- The provision of a written translation of all documents considered essential for the person to exercise their right of defence and to '*safeguard the fairness of the proceedings*' as described above. For the purposes of this Code, this includes any decision to authorise a person to be detained and details of any offence(s) with which the person has been charged or for which they have been told they may be prosecuted, see *Annex M*.
- Procedures to help determine:
  - ~ whether a suspect can speak and understand English and needs the assistance of an interpreter, see *paragraph 13.1*; and
  - ~ whether another interpreter should be arranged or another translation should be provided when a suspect complains about the quality of either or both, see *paragraphs 13.10A* and *13.10C*.

13.1B All reasonable attempts should be made to make the suspect understand that interpretation and translation will be provided at public expense.

13.1C With regard to persons in Wales, nothing in this or any other Code affects the application of the Welsh Language Schemes produced by police and crime commissioners in Wales in accordance with the Welsh Language Act 1993. See *paragraphs 3.12* and *13.1*.

(b) Interviewing suspects—foreign languages

13.2 Unless *paragraphs 11.1* or *11.18(c)* apply, a suspect who for the purposes of this Code requires an interpreter because they do not appear to speak or understand English (see *paragraphs 3.5(c)(ii)* and *3.12*) must not be interviewed unless arrangements are made for a person capable of interpreting to assist the suspect to understand and communicate.

13.2A If a person who is a juvenile or a vulnerable person is interviewed and the person acting as the appropriate adult does not appear to speak or understand English, arrangements must be made for an interpreter to assist communication between the person, the appropriate adult and the interviewer, unless the interview is urgent and *paragraphs 11.1 or 11.18(c)* apply.

13.3　When a written record of the interview is made (see *paragraph 11.7*), the interviewer shall make sure the interpreter makes a note of the interview at the time in the person's language for use in the event of the interpreter being called to give evidence, and certifies its accuracy. The interviewer should allow sufficient time for the interpreter to note each question and answer after each is put, given and interpreted. The person should be allowed to read the record or have it read to them and sign it as correct or indicate the respects in which they consider it inaccurate. If an audio or visual record of the interview is made, the arrangements in Code E or F shall apply. See *paragraphs 13.12* to *13.14* and Annex N for application to live-link interpretation.

13.4　In the case of a person making a statement under caution (see *Annex D*) to a police officer or other police staff in a language other than English:

(a) the interpreter shall record the statement in the language it is made;

(b) the person shall be invited to sign it;

(c) an official English translation shall be made in due course. See *paragraphs 13.12* to *13.14* and Annex N for application to live-link interpretation.

(c) Interviewing suspects who have a hearing or speech impediment

13.5　Unless *paragraphs 11.1 or 11.18(c)* (urgent interviews) apply, a suspect who for the purposes of this Code requires an interpreter or other appropriate assistance to enable effective communication with them because they appear to have a hearing or speech impediment (see *paragraphs 3.5(c)(ii)* and *3.12*) must not be interviewed without arrangements having been made to provide an independent person capable of interpreting or of providing other appropriate assistance.

13.6　An interpreter should also be arranged if a person who is a juvenile or who is mentally disordered or mentally vulnerable is interviewed and the person who is present as the appropriate adult, appears to have a hearing or speech impediment, unless the interview is urgent and *paragraphs 11.1 or 11.18(c)* apply.

13.7　If a written record of the interview is made, the interviewer shall make sure the interpreter is allowed to read the record and certify its accuracy in the event of the interpreter being called to give evidence. If an audio or visual recording is made, the arrangements in Code E or F apply. See *paragraphs 13.12* to *13.14* and Annex N for application to live-link interpretation.

(d) Additional rules for detained persons

13.8　*Not used.*

13.9　If *paragraph 6.1* applies and the detainee cannot communicate with the solicitor because of language, hearing or speech difficulties, arrangements must be made for an interpreter to enable communication. A police officer or any other police staff may not be used for this purpose.

13.10　After the custody officer has determined that a detainee requires an interpreter (see *paragraph 3.5(c)(ii)*) and following the initial action in *paragraphs 3.1* to *3.5*, arrangements must also be made for an interpreter to:

- explain the grounds and reasons for any authorisation for their continued detention, before or after charge and any information about the authorisation given to them by the authorising officer and which is recorded in the custody record. See *paragraphs 15.3, 15.4* and *15.16(a)* and *(b)*;

- to provide interpretation at the magistrates' court for the hearing of an application for a warrant of further detention or any extension or further extension of such warrant to explain any grounds and reasons for the application and any information about the authorisation of their further detention given to them by the court (see PACE, sections 43 and 44 and *paragraphs 15.2* and *15.16(c)*); and

- explain any offence with which the detainee is charged or for which they are informed they may be prosecuted and any other information about the offence given to them by or on behalf of the custody officer, see *paragraphs 16.1* and *16.3*.

13.10A If a detainee complains that they are not satisfied with the quality of interpretation, the custody officer or (as the case may be) the interviewer, is responsible for deciding whether to make arrangements for a different interpreter in accordance with the procedures set out in the arrangements made by the chief officer, *see paragraph 13.1A.*

(e) Translations of essential documents

13.10B Written translations, oral translations and oral summaries of essential documents in a language the detainee understands shall be provided in accordance with *Annex M* (Translations of documents and records).

13.10C If a detainee complains that they are not satisfied with the quality of the translation, the custody officer or (as the case may be) the interviewer, is responsible for deciding whether a further translation should be provided in accordance with the procedures set out in the arrangements made by the chief officer, see *paragraph 13.1A.*

(f) Decisions not to provide interpretation and translation

13.10D If a suspect challenges a decision:
- made by the custody officer or (as the case may be) by the interviewer, in accordance with this Code (see *paragraphs 3.5(c)(ii)* and *3.21(b))* that they do not require an interpreter, or
- made in accordance with *paragraphs 13.10A, 13.10B* or *13.10C* not to make arrangements to provide a different interpreter or another translation or not to translate a requested document,

the matter shall be reported to an inspector to deal with as a complaint for the purposes of *paragraph 9.2* or *paragraph 12.9* if the challenge is made during an interview.

(g) Documentation

13.11 The following must be recorded in the custody record or, as applicable, the interview record:
- (a) Action taken to arrange for an interpreter, including the live-link requirements in Annex N as applicable;
- (b) Action taken when a detainee is not satisfied about the standard of interpretation or translation provided, see *paragraphs 13.10A* and *13.10C;*
- (c) When an urgent interview is carried out in accordance with *paragraph 13.2* or *13.5* in the absence of an interpreter;
- (d) When a detainee has been assisted by an interpreter for the purpose of providing or being given information or being interviewed;
- (e) Action taken in accordance with *Annex M* when:
  - a written translation of an essential document is provided;
  - an oral translation or oral summary of an essential document is provided instead of a written translation and the authorising officer's reason(s) why this would not prejudice the fairness of the proceedings (see *Annex M, paragraph 3);*
  - a suspect waives their right to a translation of an essential document (see *Annex M, paragraph 4);*
  - when representations that a document which is not included in the table is essential and that a translation should be provided are refused and the reason for the refusal (see *Annex M, paragraph 8).*

(h) Live-link interpretation

13.12 In this section and in *Annex N, 'live-link* interpretation' means an arrangement to enable communication between the suspect and an interpreter who is not *physically* present with the suspect. The arrangement must ensure that anything said by any person in the suspect's presence and hearing can be interpreted in the same way as if the interpreter was physically present at that time. The communication must be by audio *and* visual means for the purpose of an interview, and for all other purposes it may be *either*, by audio and visual means, or by audio means *only*, as follows:

(a) Audio and visual communication

This applies for the purposes of an interview conducted and recorded in accordance with Code E (Audio recording) or Code F (Visual recording) and during that interview, live link interpretation must *enable*:

(i) the suspect, the interviewer, solicitor, appropriate adult and any other person *physically* present with the suspect at any time during the interview and an interpreter who is not *physically* present, to *see* and *hear* each other; and

(ii) the interview to be conducted and recorded in accordance with the provisions of Codes C, E and F, subject to the modifications in Part 2 of Annex N.

(b) Audio and visual or audio without visual communication.

This applies to communication for the purposes of any provision of this or any other Code except as described in (a), which requires or permits information to be given to, sought from, or provided by a suspect, whether orally or in writing, which would include communication between the suspect and their solicitor and/or appropriate adult, and for these cases, live link interpretation must:

(i) *enable* the suspect, the person giving or seeking that information, any other person *physically* present with the suspect at that time and an interpreter who is not so present, to either *see* and *hear* each other, or to *hear without seeing* each other (for example by using a telephone); and

(ii) enable that information to be given to, sought from, or provided by, the suspect in accordance with the provisions of this or any other Code that apply to that information, as modified for the purposes of the live-link, by Part 2 of Annex N.

13.12A The requirement in *sub-paragraphs 13.12(a)(ii) and (b)(ii)*, that live-link interpretation must enable compliance with the relevant provisions of the Codes C, E and F, means that the arrangements must provide for any written or electronic record of what the suspect says in their own language which is made by the interpreter, to be securely transmitted without delay so that the suspect can be invited to read, check and if appropriate, sign or otherwise confirm that the record is correct or make corrections to the record.

13.13   Chief officers must be satisfied that live-link interpretation used in their force area for the purposes of *paragraphs 3.12(a) and (b)*, provides for accurate and secure communication with the suspect. This includes ensuring that at any time during which live link interpretation is being used: a person cannot see, hear or otherwise obtain access to any communications between the suspect and interpreter or communicate with the suspect or interpreter unless so authorised or allowed by the custody officer or, in the case of an interview, the interviewer and that as applicable, the confidentiality of any private consultation between a suspect and their solicitor and appropriate adult (see *paragraphs 13.2A, 13.6 and 13.9*) is maintained. See *Annex N paragraph 4.*

1.7.14.1 **KEYNOTE**

Where the detained person is unable to speak effectively in English, an interpreter must be called to safeguard the rights of the person and to allow him/her to communicate. A procedure for determining whether a person needs an interpreter might involve a telephone interpreter service or using cue cards or similar visual aids which enable detainees to indicate their ability to speak and understand English and their preferred language. This could be confirmed through an interpreter who could also assess the extent to which the person can speak and understand English. There should also be a procedure for determining whether suspects who require an interpreter require assistance in accordance with para. 3.20 to help them check and if applicable sign any documentation. Chief officers have discretion when determining the individuals or organisations they use to provide interpretation and translation services for their forces provided that these services are compatible with the requirements of the Directive.

The importance of the role of the interpreter in proceedings can be seen in *Bielecki* v *DPP* [2011] EWHC 2245 (Admin). This was a drink-drive case where the defendant, who was Polish, had been required to provide breath specimens for analysis under the Road Traffic Act; this had been communicated through a Polish-speaking interpreter, who was present to translate at the police station. The defendant failed to provide the breath specimens and his defence was that he did not understand the requirement. The court held that it was a legitimate inference for the magistrates to draw that the words had been translated accurately. There was no evidence that the interpreter suggested to the officers that the defendant had not understood what was being said. A court could draw the inference, if the evidence supported it, that someone being asked to do something in a police station by a police officer with the assistance of an accredited interpreter of the relevant language had been asked the correct question and understood it and also the consequences of not responding to it (*Bielecki* v *DPP* [2011] EWHC 2245 (Admin)).

The interpreter is there for the benefit of the detained person and should not be considered to be part of the prosecution team. The case of *R (On the Application of Bozkurt)* v *Thames Magistrates' Court* [2001] EWHC Admin 400 demonstrates the importance of the interpreter's independence in proceedings. In *Bozkurt*, the police arranged for an interpreter to attend the custody suite and interpret for the drink-drive procedure at the police station. The police then arranged for the interpreter to attend court. The interpreter translated for the defendant while he took advice from the duty solicitor at court. The interpreter failed to inform the solicitor that he had translated for the drink-drive procedure at the police station. The court held that an interpreter was under an equal duty to that of the solicitor to keep confidential what he might hear during a conference. In these circumstances, it would have been preferable for a different interpreter to be used, or at least for the interpreter to have obtained the permission of the solicitor to interpret for the conference.

The Codes provide consistency with paras 3.5(c)(ii) and 3.12 where the need for an interpreter is determined according to a person's ability to speak and understand English. The EU Directive requires interpreters to be independent. It is important to note that police officers acting as interpreters is not allowed as this causes a conflict with the requirement for interpreters to be independent. The revised Codes enable the use of live-link electronic communication systems to provide interpretation services for suspects while not requiring the interpreter to be physically present at the police station. The revisions incorporate detailed conditions and safeguards to ensure that live-link interpretation does not adversely impact on the suspect.

Where live-link interpretation has been authorised some changes need to be made to s. 13 of Code C. For the third sentence of para. 13.3, *substitute*: 'A clear legible copy of the complete record shall be sent without delay via the live-link to the interviewer. The interviewer, after confirming with the suspect that the copy is legible and complete, shall allow the suspect to read the record, or have the record read to them by the interpreter and to sign the copy as correct or indicate the respects in which they consider it inaccurate. The interviewer is responsible for ensuring that that the signed copy and the original record made by the interpreter are retained with the case papers for use in evidence if required and must advise the interpreter of their obligation to keep the original record securely for that purpose.' See Code C, Annex N.

For para. 13.4(b), *substitute*: 'A clear legible copy of the complete statement shall be sent without delay via the live-link to the interviewer. The interviewer, after confirming with the suspect that the copy is legible and complete, shall invite the suspect to sign it. The interviewer is responsible for ensuring that the signed copy and the original record made by the interpreter are retained with the case papers for use in evidence if required and must advise the interpreter of their obligation to keep the original record securely for that purpose.' See Code C, Annex N.

Finally for para. 13.7 after the first sentence, *insert*: 'A clear legible copy of the certified record must be sent without delay via the live-link to the interviewer. The interviewer is responsible for ensuring that the original certified record and the copy are retained with the case papers for use as evidence if required and must advise the interpreter of their obligation to keep the original record securely for that purpose.'

Code C—14 Questioning—Special Restrictions

14.1 If a person is arrested by one police force on behalf of another and the lawful period of detention in respect of that offence has not yet commenced in accordance with PACE, section 41 no questions may be put to them about the offence while they are in transit between the forces except to clarify any voluntary statement they make.

14.2 If a person is in police detention at a hospital they may not be questioned without the agreement of a responsible doctor.

KEYNOTE

If questioning takes place at a hospital under para. 14.2, or on the way to or from a hospital, the period of questioning concerned counts towards the total period of detention permitted.

Code C—15 Reviews and Extensions of Detention

(a) Persons detained under PACE

15.0 The requirement in *paragraph 3.4(b)* that documents and materials essential to challenging the lawfulness of the detainee's arrest and detention must be made available to the detainee or their solicitor, applies for the purposes of this section as follows:

(a) The officer reviewing the need for detention without charge (*PACE, section 40*), or (as the case may be) the officer considering the need to extend detention without charge from 24 to 36 hours (*PACE, section 42*), is responsible, in consultation with the investigating officer, for deciding which documents and materials are essential and must be made available.

(b) When *paragraph 15.7A* applies (application for a warrant of further detention or extension of such a warrant), the officer making the application is responsible for deciding which documents and materials are essential and must be made available before the hearing.

15.1 The review officer is responsible under PACE, section 40 for periodically determining if a person's detention, before or after charge, continues to be necessary. This requirement continues throughout the detention period and, except when a telephone or a live link is used in accordance with *paragraphs 15.9 to 15.11C*, the review officer must be present at the police station holding the detainee.

15.2 Under PACE, section 42, an officer of superintendent rank or above who is responsible for the station holding the detainee may give authority any time after the second review to extend the maximum period the person may be detained without charge by up to 12 hours. Except when a live link is used as in *paragraph 15.11A*, the superintendent must be present at the station holding the detainee. Further detention without charge may be authorised only by a magistrates' court in accordance with PACE, sections 43 and 44 and unless the court has given a live link direction as in *paragraph 15.11B*, the detainee must be brought before the court for the hearing.

15.2A An authorisation under section 42(1) of PACE extends the maximum period of detention permitted before charge for indictable offences from 24 hours to 36 hours. Detaining a juvenile or vulnerable person for longer than 24 hours will be dependent on the circumstances of the case and with regard to the person's:

(a) special vulnerability;

(b) the legal obligation to provide an opportunity for representations to be made prior to a decision about extending detention;

(c) the need to consult and consider the views of any appropriate adult; and

(d) any alternatives to police custody.

15.3 Before deciding whether to authorise continued detention the officer responsible under *paragraph 15.1* or *15.2* shall give an opportunity to make representations about the detention to:

(a) the detainee, unless in the case of a review as in *paragraph 15.1*, the detainee is asleep;

(b) the detainee's solicitor if available at the time; and

(c) the appropriate adult if available at the time.

15.3A Other people having an interest in the detainee's welfare may also make representations at the authorising officer's discretion.

15.3B Subject to *paragraph 15.10*, the representations may be made orally in person or by telephone or in writing. The authorising officer may, however, refuse to hear oral representations from the detainee if the officer considers them unfit to make representations because of their condition or behaviour.

15.3C The decision on whether the review takes place in person or by telephone or by video conferencing is a matter for the review officer. In determining the form the review may take, the review officer must always take full account of the needs of the person in custody. The benefits of carrying out a review in person should always be considered, based on the individual circumstances of each case with specific additional consideration if the person is:

(a) a juvenile (and the age of the juvenile); or

(b) a vulnerable person; or

(c) in need of medical attention for other than routine minor ailments; or

(d) subject to presentational or community issues around their detention. See *paragraph 1.4(c)*.

15.4 Before conducting a review or determining whether to extend the maximum period of detention without charge, the officer responsible must make sure the detainee is reminded of their entitlement to free legal advice, see paragraph 6.5, unless in the case of a review the person is asleep. When determining whether to extend the maximum period of detention without charge, it should also be pointed out that for the purposes of *paragraph 15.2*, the superintendent or (as the case may be) the court, responsible for authorising any such extension, will not be able to use a live link unless the detainee has received legal advice on the use of the live link (see *paragraphs 15.11A(ii)* and *15.11C(ii))* and given consent to its use (see *paragraphs 15.11A(iii)* and *15.11C(iii)*. The detainee must also be given information about how the live link is used.

15.4A Following sections 45ZA and 45ZB of PACE, when the reminder and information concerning legal advice and about the use of the live link is given and the detainee's consent is sought, the presence of an appropriate adult is required if the detainee in question is a juvenile (see *paragraph 1.5*) or is a *vulnerable adult* by virtue of being a person aged 18 or over who, because of a mental disorder established in accordance *paragraphs 1.4* and *1.13(d)* or for *any other reason* (see *paragraph 15.4B*), may have difficulty understanding the purpose of:

(a) an authorisation under section 42 of PACE or anything that occurs in connection with a decision whether to give it (see *paragraphs 15.2* and *15.2A*); or

(b) a court hearing under section 43 or 44 of PACE or what occurs at the hearing it (see *paragraphs 15.2* and *15.7A*).

15.4B For the purpose of using a live link in accordance with sections 45ZA and 45ZB of PACE to authorise detention without charge (see *paragraphs 15.11A* and *15.11C*), the reference to 'any other reason' would extend to difficulties in understanding the purposes mentioned in paragraph 15.4A that might arise if the person happened to be under the influence of drink or drugs at the time the live link is to be used. This does not however apply for the purposes of *paragraphs 1.4* and *1.13(d)*.

15.5 If, after considering any representations, the review officer under *paragraph 15.1* decides to keep the detainee in detention or the superintendent under *paragraph 15.2* extends the maximum period for which they may be detained without charge, then any comment made by the detainee shall be recorded. If applicable, the officer shall be informed of the comment as soon as practicable. See also *paragraphs 11.4* and *11.13*.

15.6   No officer shall put specific questions to the detainee:
- regarding their involvement in any offence;
- or in respect of any comment they may make:
  - ~ when given the opportunity to make representations; or
  - ~ in response to a decision to keep them in detention or extend the maximum period of detention.

Such an exchange could constitute an interview as in *paragraph 11.1A* and would be subject to the associated safeguards in *section 11* and, in respect of a person who has been charged, *paragraph 16.5*. See also *paragraph 11.13*.

15.7   A detainee who is asleep at a review, see *paragraph 15.1*, and whose continued detention is authorised must be informed about the decision and reason as soon as practicable after waking.

15.7A   When an application is made to a magistrates' court under PACE, section 43 for a warrant of further detention to extend detention without charge of a person arrested for an indictable offence, or under section 44, to extend or further extend that warrant, the detainee:

(a) must, unless the court has given a live link direction as in *paragraph 15.11C*, be brought to court for the hearing of the application;

(b) is entitled to be legally represented if they wish, in which case, *Annex B* cannot apply; and

(c) must be given a copy of the information which supports the application and states:

(i) the nature of the offence for which the person to whom the application relates has been arrested;

(ii) the general nature of the evidence on which the person was arrested;

(iii) what inquiries about the offence have been made and what further inquiries are proposed;

(iv) the reasons for believing continued detention is necessary for the purposes of the further inquiries;

Note: A warrant of further detention can only be issued or extended if the court has reasonable grounds for believing that the person's further detention is necessary for the purpose of obtaining evidence of an indictable offence for which the person has been arrested and that the investigation is being conducted diligently and expeditiously.
See *paragraph 15.0(b)*.

15.8   *Not used.*

(b) Review of detention by telephone and live link facilities

15.9   PACE, section 40A provides that the officer responsible under section 40 for reviewing the detention of a person who has not been charged, need not attend the police station holding the detainee and may carry out the review by telephone.

15.9A   PACE, section 45A(2) provides that the officer responsible under section 40 for reviewing the detention of a person who has not been charged, need not attend the police station holding the detainee and may carry out the review using a live link. See *paragraph 1.13(e)(ii)*.

15.9B   A telephone review is not permitted where facilities for review by live link exist and it is practicable to use them.

15.9C   The review officer can decide at any stage that a telephone review or review by live link should be terminated and that the review will be conducted in person. The reasons for doing so should be noted in the custody record.

15.10   When a review is carried out by telephone or by live link facilities, an officer at the station holding the detainee shall be required by the review officer to fulfil that officer's obligations under PACE section 40 and this Code by:

(a) making any record connected with the review in the detainee's custody record;

(b) if applicable, making the record in (a) in the presence of the detainee; and

(c) for a review by telephone, giving the detainee information about the review.

15.11 When a review is carried out by telephone or by live link facilities, the requirement in *paragraph 15.3* will be satisfied:

(a) if facilities exist for the immediate transmission of written representations to the review officer, e.g. fax or email message, by allowing those who are given the opportunity to make representations, to make their representations:

    (i) orally by telephone or (as the case may be) by means of the live link; or

    (ii) in writing using the facilities for the immediate transmission of written representations; and

(b) (a) in all other cases, by allowing those who are given the opportunity to make representations, to make their representations orally by telephone or by means of the live link.

(c) Authorisation to extend detention using live link (sections 45ZA and 45ZB)

15.11A For the purpose of *paragraphs 15.2* and *15.2A*, a superintendent who is not present at the police station where the detainee is being held but who has access to the use of a live link (see *paragraph 1.13(e)(iii)*) may, using that live link, give authority to extend the maximum period of detention permitted before charge, if, and only if, the following conditions are satisfied:

    (i) the custody officer considers that the use of the live link is appropriate;

    (ii) the detainee in question has requested and received legal advice on the use of the live link (see *paragraph 15.4*).

    (iii) the detainee has given their consent to the live link being used (see *paragraph 15.11D*)

15.11B When a live link is used:

(a) the authorising superintendent shall, with regard to any record connected with the authorisation which PACE, section 42 and this Code require to be made by the authorising officer, require an officer at the station holding the detainee to make that record in the detainee's custody record;

(b) the requirement in *paragraph 15.3* (allowing opportunity to make representations) will be satisfied:

    (i) if facilities exist for the immediate transmission of written representations to the authorising officer, e.g. fax or email message, by allowing those who are given the opportunity to make representations, to make their representations:

      • in writing by means of those facilities or

      • orally by means of the live link; or

    (ii) in all other cases, by allowing those who are given the opportunity to make representations, to make their representations orally by means of the live link.

(c) The authorising officer can decide at any stage to terminate the live link and attend the police station where the detainee is held to carry out the procedure in person. The reasons for doing so should be noted in the custody record.

15.11C For the purpose of *paragraph 15.7A* and the hearing of an application to a magistrates' court under PACE, section 43 for a warrant of further detention to extend detention without charge of a person arrested for an *indictable offence*, or under PACE, section 44, to extend or further extend that warrant, the magistrates' court may give a direction that a live link (see *paragraph 1.13(e)(iv)*) be used for the purposes of the hearing if, and only if, the following conditions are satisfied:

    (i) the custody officer considers that the use of the live link for the purpose of the hearing is appropriate;

    (ii) the detainee in question has requested and received legal advice on the use of the live link (see *paragraph 15.4*);

(iii) the detainee has given their consent to the live link being used (see *paragraph 15.11D*); and

(iv) it is not contrary to the interests of justice to give the direction.

15.11D References in *paragraphs 15.11A(iii)* and *15.11C(iii)* to the consent of the detainee mean:

    (a) if detainee is aged 18 or over, the consent of that detainee;

    (b) if the detainee is aged 14 and under 18, the consent of the detainee *and* their parent or guardian; and

    (c) if the detainee is aged under 14, the consent of their parent or guardian.

15.11E The consent described in *paragraph 15.11D* will only be valid if:

    (i) in the case of a detainee aged 18 or over *who is a vulnerable adult* as described in *paragraph 15.4A)*, information about how the live link is used *and* the reminder about their right to legal advice mentioned in *paragraph 15.4* and their consent, are given in the *presence of the appropriate adult*; and

    (ii) in the case of a *juvenile*:

- if information about how the live link is used and the reminder about their right to legal advice mentioned in *paragraph 15.4* are given in the *presence of the appropriate adult* (who may or may not be their parent or guardian); and

- if the juvenile is <u>aged 14 or over</u>, their consent is given in the *presence of the appropriate adult* (who may or may not be their parent or guardian).

Note: If the juvenile is <u>aged under 14</u>, the consent of their parent or guardian is sufficient in its own right

(d) Documentation

15.12 It is the officer's responsibility to make sure all reminders given under *paragraph 15.4* are noted in the custody record.

15.13 The grounds for, and extent of, any delay in conducting a review shall be recorded.

15.14 When a review is carried out by telephone or video conferencing facilities, a record shall be made of:

    (a) the reason the review officer did not attend the station holding the detainee;

    (b) the place the review officer was;

    (c) the method representations, oral or written, were made to the review officer, see *paragraph 15.11*.

15.15 Any written representations shall be retained.

15.16 A record shall be made as soon as practicable of:

    (a) the outcome of each review of detention before or after charge, and if *paragraph 15.7* applies, of when the person was informed and by whom;

    (b) the outcome of any determination under PACE, section 42 by a superintendent whether to extend the maximum period of detention without charge beyond 24 hours from the relevant time. If an authorisation is given, the record shall state the number of hours and minutes by which the detention period is extended or further extended.

    (c) the outcome of each application under PACE, section 43, for a warrant of further detention or under section 44, for an extension or further extension of that warrant. If a warrant for further detention is granted under section 43 or extended or further extended under 44, the record shall state the detention period authorised by the warrant and the date and time it was granted or (as the case may be) the period by which the warrant is extended or further extended.

Note: Any period during which a person is released on bail does not count towards the maximum period of detention without charge allowed under PACE, sections 41 to 44.

KEYNOTE

Relevant Time

There are limits on how long a person can be detained. The Police and Criminal Evidence Act 1984 and the Codes of Practice talk of the 'relevant time'. This is the time from which the limits of detention are calculated. The relevant time of a person's detention starts in accordance with s. 41(2)–(5) of the 1984 Act. Section 41 states:

(2) The time from which the period of detention of a person is to be calculated (in this Act referred to as 'the relevant time')—

    (a) in the case of a person to whom this paragraph applies, shall be—

        (i) the time at which that person arrives at the relevant police station; or

        (ii) the time 24 hours after the time of that person's arrest,

        whichever is the earlier;

    (b) in the case of a person arrested outside England and Wales, shall be—

        (i) the time at which that person arrives at the first police station to which he is taken in the police area in England or Wales in which the offence for which he was arrested is being investigated; or

        (ii) the time 24 hours after the time of that person's entry into England and Wales,

        whichever is the earlier;

    (c) in the case of a person who—

        (i) attends voluntarily at a police station; or

        (ii) accompanies a constable to a police station without having been arrested, and is arrested at the police station, the time of his arrest;

    (ca) in the case of a person who attends a police station to answer to bail granted under section 30A, the time he arrives at the police station;

    (d) in any other case, except where subsection (5) below applies, shall be the time at which the person arrested arrives at the first police station to which he is taken after his arrest.

(3) Subsection (2)(a) above applies to a person if—

    (a) his arrest is sought in one police area in England and Wales;

    (b) he is arrested in another police area; and

    (c) he is not questioned in the area in which he is arrested in order to obtain evidence in relation to an offence for which he is arrested;

    and in sub-paragraph (i) of that paragraph 'the relevant police station' means the first police station to which he is taken in the police area in which his arrest was sought.

(4) Subsection (2) above shall have effect in relation to a person arrested under section 31 above as if every reference in it to his arrest or his being arrested were a reference to his arrest or his being arrested for the offence for which he was originally arrested.

(5) If—

    (a) a person is in police detention in a police area in England and Wales ('the first area'); and

    (b) his arrest for an offence is sought in some other police area in England and Wales ('the second area'); and

    (c) he is taken to the second area for the purposes of investigating that offence, without being questioned in the first area in order to obtain evidence in relation to it,

    the relevant time shall be—

        (i) the time 24 hours after he leaves the place where he is detained in the first area; or

        (ii) the time at which he arrives at the first police station to which he is taken in the second area, whichever is the earlier.

Note that under s. 41(5) the relevant time may vary, depending on whether the detainee is interviewed in relation to the offence while still in the first police area.

For those detained under the Terrorism Act 2000 the detention clock starts from the time the person is arrested, not the time he/she arrives at the police station.

The Criminal Justice Act 2003 inserted s. 41(2)(ca) into the Police and Criminal Evidence Act 1984. This allows for a person who has been arrested to be released before being taken to a police station. When the person attends the police station to which he/she has been bailed the relevant time starts when he/she arrives at the police station.

Some situations occur where a person is arrested at one police station and has been circulated as wanted by another police station in the same force area. In these cases, where the person is not wanted on warrant, the detention clock for the second offence starts at the same time as for the original offence for which he/she was arrested. Consideration will need to be given as to how to protect the detention period for the second of-fence while officers are dealing with the first matter. Options that might be considered would include bailing the person for one of the offences or conducting both investigations at the same station. Here there may be a risk of 'confusing' the suspect, which may allow him/her to retract or qualify any confession he/she might make.

In *Henderson* v *Chief Constable of Cleveland* [2001] EWCA Civ 335 the court considered the policy of not executing a court warrant until after other matters for which the person had been detained were com-pleted. The court held that, once a warrant was executed. there was a requirement to follow the directions of the warrant. The police, however, had a discretion as to *when* to execute the warrant. This may be relevant where a person has been arrested for one offence and it is discovered that he/she is also wanted for another offence or where there are warrants in existence for that person at more than one court. In such cases, if the warrant is executed immediately, the direction on the warrant tells officers to take the person before the next available court, an action which could interfere with the investigation. If *Henderson* is followed there is no requirement to execute the warrant straight away and the other matters can be dealt with before the requirement to produce the person at court under the warrant applies.

1.7.16.2   KEYNOTE

Limits on Detention and Review

Once detention has been authorised this does not mean that a person can be detained indefinitely. Section 34 of the Police and Criminal Evidence Act 1984 requires the custody officer to release a person if he/she becomes aware that the grounds for detention no longer apply and that no other grounds exist for the continuing deten-tion (unless the person appears to have been unlawfully at large when he/she was arrested). Failure to comply with this could also lead to a breach of Article 5 of the European Convention on Human Rights. If there are additional grounds, these should be recorded in the custody record and the person informed of these additional grounds in the same way as when a person is first detained. For example, this could be for new offences or it could be that it becomes necessary to preserve evidence by questioning the detained person.

It is only the *custody officer* who can authorise the release of a detained person (s. 34(3)). In addition to the requirement to release a person should the grounds for detention no longer exist, there are also max-imum time limits for which a person can be detained without charge. Once this limit has been reached any prosecution will need to proceed by summons or by warrant.

1.7.16.3   KEYNOTE

Time Limits: Without Charge

While a person is in police detention there is a requirement that his/her continuing detention is reviewed. There are minimum time requirements for when these reviews must be conducted, with the timing of the first review being calculated from the time detention is authorised. This time can be considered as the 'review time'. The question of whether a person should be kept in custody is a continuous one and the review process is intended as an added protection to the detained person.

The maximum period that a person can be detained without charge is 96 hours (with the exception of sus-pected acts of terrorism, in which case it is 14 days). The necessity for the continued detention of the person must be reviewed throughout this time. The period of detention is calculated from the 'relevant time' which can be calculated from Table A below (do not confuse the relevant time with the time from which reviews are due). The relevant time 'clock' will always start before, or at the same time as, the review 'clock'. This is because the review clock does not start until detention has been authorised, which clearly cannot happen until the person is brought before the custody officer which, as can be seen from the table below, is at the very latest the time the prisoner walks into the custody suite (with the exception of where the person has been under arrest for 24 hours but has not yet been taken to a police station).

This relevant time period (that is, the maximum period a person can be detained for) relates to the actual time spent in custody and not a 24-hour period in time. This means that every time the person is bailed the clock stops and usually continues from the time that the person returns to custody for the offence(s) for which he/she was bailed. Any time during which a person is on bail does not count when calculating how long a detained person has been in police detention (amendments to the 1984 Act made by the Police (Detention and Bail) Act 2011). This legislation applies retrospectively and therefore the changes to ss. 34 and 47 brought about by this Act are deemed always to have had effect.

Where a person has been released and re-arrested for an offence, it is possible that the relevant time will start again. This is covered by s. 47 of the 1984 Act:

(2) Where a person who was released on bail under this Part subject to a duty to attend at a police station is re-arrested, the provisions of this Part of this Act shall apply to him/her as they apply to a person arrested for the first time but this subsection does not apply to a person who is arrested under section 46A above or has attended a police station in accordance with the grant of bail (and who accordingly is deemed by section 34(7) above to have been arrested for an offence).

In cases where this subsection applies, the relevant time starts again and a fresh clock starts. This will apply where the person has been re-arrested for the same offence because of some new evidence (except at such time as when he/she is returning on bail at the appointed time) under ss. 30C(4), 41(9) or 47(2).

Section 41 states:

(9) A person released under subsection (7) [i.e. where his/her relevant time period had expired] above shall not be re-arrested without a warrant for the offence for which he was previously arrested unless new evidence justifying a further arrest has come to light since his release; but this subsection does not prevent an arrest under section 46A below.

Section 47 states:

(4) Nothing in the Bail Act 1976 shall prevent the re-arrest without warrant of a person released on bail subject to a duty to attend at a police station if new evidence justifying a further arrest has come to light since his release.

Section 30C states:

(5) Nothing in section 30A or 30B or in this section prevents the re-arrest without warrant of a person released on bail under section 30A (Release of a person arrested by a constable elsewhere than a police station) if new evidence justifying a further arrest has come to light since his release.

The issue will be whether new evidence has come to light since the grant of bail and it will be a question of fact as to what the new evidence is. It is suggested that this must be evidence which was not available at the time the person was last in detention or which would not have been available even if all reasonable inquiries had been conducted.

It will always be important to check how much time is left on the person's 'relevant time' and when his/her next review is due.

For the purposes of Code C, paras 3.4(b) and 15.0, investigating officers are responsible for bringing to the attention of the officer who is responsible for authorising the suspect's continued detention (before or after charge), any documents and materials in their possession or control which appear to undermine the need to keep the suspect in custody. In accordance with part IV of PACE, this officer will be either the custody officer, the officer reviewing the need for detention before or after charge (PACE, s. 40), or the officer considering the need to extend detention without charge from 24 to 36 hours (PACE, s. 42). The authorising officer is then responsible for determining, which, if any, of those documents and materials are capable of undermining the need to detain the suspect and must therefore be made available to the suspect or their solicitor. It is not the case that documents need to be copied and provided to the suspect or their solicitor; the way in which documents and materials are 'made available' is a matter for the investigating officer to determine on a case-by-case basis and having regard to the nature and volume of the documents and materials involved. For example, they may be made available by supplying a copy or allowing supervised access to view. However, for view-only access, it will be necessary to demonstrate that sufficient time is allowed for the suspect and solicitor to view and consider the documents and materials in question.

1.7.16.4

KEYNOTE

The Three Stages of Pre-charge Detention

After the custody officer has authorised detention but before a person has been charged there are three distinct stages of detention. These are distinguished by the level at which authorisation for continuing detention is required. The three stages of detention under the 1984 Act are:

- the basic period of detention, which is the period of detention up to 24 hours, as first authorised by the custody officer;
- those authorised by an officer of the rank of superintendent or above (s. 42) up to 36 hours (indictable offences only);
- those authorised by a magistrates' court (ss. 43 and 44) up to a maximum of 96 hours.

Each of these is examined in detail below.

1.7.16.5

KEYNOTE

The Basic Period of Detention

The majority of people detained by the police are detained for less than six hours; most other cases are dealt with within 24 hours. If a person's continued detention is not authorised beyond 24 hours and the person is not charged with an offence, he/she *must* be released (with or without bail) and cannot be re-arrested for the offence unless new evidence comes to light (s. 41(7) and (9) of the 1984 Act).

If a detained person is taken to hospital for medical treatment, the time at hospital and the period spent travelling to and from the hospital does not count towards the relevant time unless the person is asked questions for the purpose of obtaining evidence about an offence. Where questioning takes place, this period would count towards the relevant time and therefore the custody officer must be informed of it (s. 41(6)).

1.7.16.6

KEYNOTE

Detention Authorised by an Officer of the Rank of Superintendent or Above

Under s. 42(1) of the Police and Criminal Evidence Act 1984, detention can only be authorised beyond 24 hours and up to a maximum of 36 hours from the relevant time if:

- an offence being investigated is an 'indictable offence'; and
- an officer of the rank of superintendent or above is responsible for the station at which the person is detained (referred to here as the authorising officer); and
- that senior officer is satisfied that:
  - there is not sufficient evidence to charge; and
  - the investigation is being conducted diligently and expeditiously; and
  - the person's detention is necessary to secure or preserve evidence relating to the offence or to obtain such evidence by questioning that person.

The procedure under PACE, s. 42 can be conducted in person or by live link.

If the authorising officer considers that there is sufficient evidence to charge, he/she cannot authorise further detention beyond 24 hours unless the detained person is in custody for another indictable offence for which further detention can be authorised (*R v Samuel* [1988] QB 615 and Code H, para. 14.3). It is suggested that in considering the strength of evidence the authorising officer may wish to consult with any readily accessible CPS representative.

The grounds for this continuing detention are the same as those when the custody officer made the initial decision to detain, with the additional requirements that the case has been conducted diligently and expeditiously. To be able to satisfy the senior officer of this, it will be necessary for the custody record to be available for inspection and also details of what inquiries have been made and evidence that the investigation has been moving at a pace that will satisfy the senior officer that the inquiries should not already have been completed.

Although the authorising officer can authorise detention up to a maximum of 36 hours from the 'relevant time' of detention, the period can be shorter than this. It can then be further authorised by that officer or any other officer of the rank of superintendent or above who is responsible for the station at which the person is detained to allow the period to be further extended up to the maximum 36-hour period (s. 42(2)). The officer responsible for the station holding the detainee includes a superintendent or above who, in accordance with their force operational policy or police regulations, is given that responsibility on a temporary basis whilst the appointed long-term holder is off duty or otherwise unavailable.

Section 42(5)–(8) mirrors the responsibility on the authorising officer at this stage with those of the review officer (see para. 1.7.16.13) during the 'general period' of detention with regard to allowing representations, informing the detained person of the decision to authorise further detention and the need to record the decision. The main difference here is that the authorising officer must look into how the case is being investigated and whether this is being done diligently and expeditiously. Consequently, the authorising officer must also consider any representations on these points and these points should also be covered in any record as to whether detention should continue. When considering whether to authorise further detention the authorising officer must check whether the detained person has exercised his/her right to have someone informed and to consult with a legal representative.

If it is proposed to transfer a detained person from one police area to another for the purpose of investigating the offences for which he/she is detained, the authorising officer may take into consideration the period it will take to get to the other police area when deciding whether detention can go beyond 24 hours (s. 42(3)).

Where a person has been arrested under s. 41 of the Terrorism Act 2000 he/she can be kept in police detention (in this case, this is generally from the time of the arrest) up to 48 hours without the court authorising an extension of time.

1.7.16.7   **KEYNOTE**

Warrants of Further Detention

Once the 36-hour limit has been reached, a person's detention can only continue with the authority of the courts through the issuing of a warrant of further detention.

Applications for warrants of further detention are made at the magistrates' court. Initially, the magistrates can issue a warrant for further detention for a period of up to 36 hours. This can be extended by the courts on further applications by police up to a maximum total period of detention of 96 hours. The warrant will specify what period of further detention the court has authorised.

The grounds on which the court must decide whether to grant a warrant authorising further detention are the same as those that must be considered by a 'superintendent's review'.

Should it be necessary to apply for a warrant, it is important that the time restraints are kept in mind at all times and the application procedure followed closely.

1.7.16.8   **KEYNOTE**

Warrants of Further Detention: Procedure

The application is made in the magistrates' court and both the detained person and the police must be in attendance (s. 43(1) and (2) of the Police and Criminal Evidence Act 1984). The application is made by laying an information before the court. The officer making the application does so on oath and is subject to cross-examination. Under s. 43(14) the information must set out:

- the nature of the offence (this must be an indictable offence);
- the general nature of the evidence on which the person was arrested;
- what inquiries have been made;
- what further inquiries are proposed; and
- the reasons for believing that continuing detention is necessary for such further inquiries.

It will be important to be able to demonstrate why the person needs to remain in detention while additional inquiries are made, for instance that further facts need to be verified before further questioning of the suspect can continue and that this cannot be done effectively if the person is released. The detained person must be provided with a copy of the information before the matter can be heard (s. 43(2)). He/she is also entitled to be legally represented. If the person is not legally represented but then requests legal representation at court, the case must be adjourned to allow representation (s. 43(3)). In cases where the person is not represented it may be prudent to remind the person of his/her right to legal representation prior to the court hearing and to make a record of this in the custody record. Should the detained person choose to be legally represented at court, and thereby try to delay the police investigation, s. 43(3)(b) allows the person to be taken back into police detention during the adjournment.

1.7.16.9

KEYNOTE

Warrants of Further Detention: Timing of the Application

Officers should be mindful of whether a warrant for further detention may be required. If it appears likely that the investigation of the indictable offence requires the person's detention to go beyond 36 hours, then thought must be given as to when to make the application to the magistrates' court, and whether a court will be available to hear the application. If a court will not be available, then consideration should be given to making an earlier application. An application to a magistrates' court should be made between 10 am and 9 pm, and if possible during normal court hours. It will not usually be practicable to arrange for a court to sit specially outside the hours of 10 am to 9 pm. If it appears that a special sitting may be needed outside normal court hours but between 10 am and 9 pm, the clerk to the justices should be given notice and informed of this possibility, while the court is sitting if possible.

Section 43(5) allows the application to be made *before* the expiry of the 36-hour period (calculated from the relevant time) or, where it has not been practicable for the court to sit within the 36-hour period, the application can be made within the next six hours. There are dangers in applying outside the 36-hour period as if the court feels that it would have been reasonable to make the application within the 36-hour period it must refuse the application for the warrant regardless of the merits of the case (s. 43(7)). In R v *Slough Justices, ex parte Stirling* [1987] Crim LR 576, the 36-hour period expired at 12.53 pm. The case was not heard by the justices until 2.45 pm. The Divisional Court held that the police should have made their application between 10.30 am and 11.30 am, even though this was before the 36-hour time limit had been reached.

If the court is not satisfied that there are reasonable grounds for believing that further detention is justified, the court may either refuse the application or adjourn the hearing until such time as it specifies up to the end of the 36-hour period of detention (s. 43(8)). If the application is refused, the person must be charged or released with or without bail at the expiry of the current permissible period of detention (s. 43(15)).

The application for the warrant can be made at any time, *even before a superintendent's review has been carried out*. If the application is made within the 36-hour period and it is refused, it does not mean that the person must be released straight away. Section 43(16) allows the person to be detained until the end of the current detention period (24 hours or 36 hours). The benefit of an early application has to be set against the risk that, once the court has refused an application, it is not allowed to hear any further applications for a warrant of further detention unless new evidence has come to light since the application was refused (s. 43(17)).

1.7.16.10

KEYNOTE

Applying to Extend Warrants of Further Detention

Under s. 44 of the 1984 Act, the process for applying to extend the warrant follows the same procedure as for the initial warrant, with the exception that the application *must be* made before the expiry of the extension given in the previous warrant. Once the period of detention that has been authorised has expired, and no other applications have been made, the detained person must be charged or released with or without bail.

1.7.16.11

1.7.16.12

Detention for the purpose of re-arrest

(1) A person arrested under section 137A in respect of a specified offence may be detained but only for the purpose of—

(a) enabling a warrant for the person's arrest in respect of the offence to be obtained and then executed under section 136, or

(b) enabling the person to be re-arrested under section 137.

(2) The person may be detained for that purpose—

(a) for an initial period of 3 hours beginning with the time of the arrest;

(b) for a second period of no more than 21 hours beginning with the end of the initial period, but only if detention for that period is authorised by both an officer of at least the rank of inspector in the arresting force and an officer of at least the rank of inspector in the investigating force;

(c) for a third period of no more than 12 hours beginning with the end of the second period, but only if detention for that period is authorised by both an officer of a rank above that of inspector in the arresting force and an officer of a rank above that of inspector in the investigating force.

(3) An officer of the arresting force may give an authorisation for the purpose of subsection (2)(b) or (c) only if satisfied that it is in the interests of justice to do so.

(4) An officer of the investigating force may give an authorisation for the purpose of subsection (2)(b) only if satisfied that—

(a) there are reasonable grounds to suspect that the person has committed the specified offence,

(b) a constable intends that the person be arrested as soon as is reasonably practicable (whether by the obtaining and execution of a warrant under section 136 or under section 137) and is acting expeditiously for that purpose, and

(c) it is in the interests of justice to give the authorisation.

(5) An officer of the investigating force may give an authorisation for the purpose of subsection (2)(c) only if satisfied that—

(a) there continue to be reasonable grounds to suspect that the person has committed the specified offence,

(b) a constable intends that the person be arrested as soon as is reasonably practicable (whether by the obtaining and execution of a warrant under section 136 or under section 137) and is acting expeditiously for that purpose, and

(c) it is in the interests of justice to give the authorisation.

(6) If, at any time while the person is detained, an appropriate officer in the investigating force is satisfied that it is no longer in the interests of justice for the person to be detained—

(a) the officer must notify the arresting force, and

(b) the person must be released immediately.

(7) In subsection (6), 'appropriate officer' means—

(a) in relation to the person's detention for the initial period, any constable;

(b) in relation to the person's detention for the second period, an officer of at least the rank of inspector;

(c) in relation to the person's detention for the third period, an officer of a rank above that of inspector.

1.7.16.13 **KEYNOTE**

The Review

This review acts as another safeguard to protect the detained person's right to be detained for only such periods as are necessary. Reviews of police detention are covered by s. 40 of the Police and Criminal Evidence Act 1984.

The Review Officer

The 'review officer' for the purposes of ss. 40, 40A and 45A of the 1984 Act means, in the case of a person arrested but not charged, an officer of at least *inspector* rank not directly involved in the investigation and, if a person has been arrested and charged, the *custody officer*.

It is important to understand the difference between the action of authorising an extension to the 'detention clock' and the role of the review officer. These are two distinct roles and both need to be carried out. When an officer of the rank of superintendent or above extends the 'relevant time' period, this is not automatically a review (although there is nothing to stop that officer from conducting the review). This means that the 'reviewing' officer may still have to conduct a review even though the relevant time has only recently been extended, unless the officer of the rank of superintendent or above extending the relevant time has shown the review as having been conducted in the custody record.

Timing of the Review

Section 40 sets out the times when reviews must be conducted:

(3) Subject to subsection (4) ...
    (a) the first review shall be not later than six hours after the detention was first authorised;
    (b) the second review shall be not later than nine hours after the first;
    (c) subsequent reviews shall be at intervals of not more than nine hours.

The periods set out in s. 40(3) are the *maximum* periods that a review can be left; should the review officer wish to review before this time for operational reasons, etc. the review could be brought forward. The first review must be made within six hours of the custody officer authorising detention (this, it must be remembered, is not the time from which the 24-hour clock starts, i.e. the time the detainee came into the station, but the time at which the custody officer authorised detention). Thereafter, each review must be made within nine hours of the last review.

Method of the Review

Section 40 reviews can be conducted in person, by live link or on the telephone where live link is not available. The provisions of PACE, s. 40A allowing telephone reviews or live link do not apply to reviews of detention after charge by the custody officer.

In considering whether the use of the live link is appropriate in the case of a juvenile or vulnerable person, the custody officer and the superintendent should have regard to the detainee's ability to understand the purpose of the authorisation or (as the case may be) the court hearing, and be satisfied that the suspect is able to take part effectively in the process (see para. 1.4(c)). The appropriate adult should always be involved. For the purpose of paras 15.11D and 15.11E, the consent required from a parent or guardian may, for a juvenile in the care of a local authority or voluntary organisation, be given by that authority or organisation. In the case of a juvenile, nothing in paras 15.11D and 15.11E require the parent, guardian or representative of a local authority or voluntary organisation to be present with the juvenile to give their consent, unless they are acting as the appropriate adult. However, it is important that the parent, guardian or representative of a local authority or voluntary organisation who is not present is fully informed before being asked to consent. They must be given the same information as that given to the juvenile and the appropriate adult in accordance with para. 15.11E. They must also be allowed to speak to the juvenile and the appropriate adult if they wish. Provided the consent is fully informed and is not withdrawn, it may be obtained at any time before the live link is used.

Review Considerations

When reviewing the detention of a person the review officer goes through the same process as the custody officer did when detention was first authorised (ss. 40(8) and 37(1)–(6)), namely by asking:

- Is there sufficient evidence to charge? If 'yes', charge or release the person with or without bail. If 'no', then:
- Is detention necessary in order to secure or preserve evidence or is it necessary to detain the person in order to obtain such evidence by questioning him/her? If 'yes', authorise continued detention. If 'no', release the person with or without bail.

It is suggested that in order to consider whether there is sufficient evidence to charge, the review officer should have consideration for the Code for Crown Prosecutors and the Threshold Test. The situation may arise where the review officer considers that there is sufficient evidence to charge and only authorises continued detention to charge even though the custody officer disagrees. In this case, it is suggested that the custody officer must either charge or release the person with or without bail in line with s. 37B of the Police and Criminal Evidence Act 1984. Where bailed this may be in order to submit papers to the CPS in order for a decision to be made as to whether to charge and for what offence. There may also be situations where the custody officer has concluded that there is sufficient evidence to charge but the review officer disagrees; in these cases the review officer cannot overrule the custody officer's decision under s. 37(7). In any case where the decision has been made that there is sufficient evidence to charge, the review officer should confirm that the referral has been made, note the custody record to this effect and, thereafter, check to ensure that the decision is made within a *reasonable time*.

It is also suggested that the reviewing officer (or any other officer other than a superintendent or above) cannot tell the custody officer what he/she must do. The reviewing officer may wish to give advice but it will be for the custody officer to decide whether to take that advice. Clearly failure to do so could lead to internal criticism, but legally there is no requirement to follow that advice.

If there is not sufficient evidence to charge, the review officer may want to consider the question: 'If this person is released what evidence will be lost?' If the answer is none, continued detention would seem unlawful.

In cases where it has been decided that a person should be charged but he/she has been detained because he/she is not in a fit state to be charged (s. 37(9)), the review officer must determine whether the person is yet in a fit state. If the detainee is in a fit state, the custody officer should be informed that the person should be charged or released. If the detainee is not in a fit state, detention can be authorised for a further period (s. 40(9)). In such cases, if the person is still unfit, it may be prudent to consider his/her welfare.

The detainee need not be woken for the review. However, if the detainee is likely to be asleep, e.g. during a period of rest, at the latest time a review or authorisation to extend detention may take place, the officer should, if the legal obligations and time constraints permit, bring forward the procedure to allow the detainee to make representations. A detainee not asleep during the review must be present when the grounds for his/her continued detention are recorded and must at the same time be informed of those grounds unless the review officer considers that the person is incapable of understanding what is said, is violent or likely to become violent or is in urgent need of medical attention. In relation to the detainee's solicitor or appropriate adult being 'available' to make representations, this includes being contactable in time to enable him/her to make representations remotely by telephone or other electronic means or in person by attending the station. Reasonable efforts should therefore be made to give the solicitor and appropriate adult sufficient notice of the time the decision is expected to be made so that they can make themselves available.

Delaying the Review

Section 40(4)(b) does allow reviews to be delayed if it is not practicable to carry out the review. Conducting late reviews should be avoided where at all possible. In *Roberts* v *Chief Constable of Cheshire Constabulary* [1999] 1 WLR 662, the defendant had his first review conducted 8 hours 20 minutes after his detention had been authorised. The Court of Appeal held that under s. 40(1)(b) of the 1984 Act a review of his detention should have been carried out by an officer of the rank of inspector or above six hours after detention was first authorised. Section 34(1) was mandatory and provided that a person must not be kept in police detention except in accordance with the relevant provisions of the Act. Therefore, the respondent's detention had been unlawful unless some event occurred to have made it lawful. The court made it clear that the 1984 Act existed in order to ensure that members of the public were not detained except in certain defined circumstances. In the absence of a review, the time spent in detention between 5.25 am and 7.45 am, meant that for that period the defendant's detention was unlawful and amounted to a false imprisonment.

Section 40(4) provides two other occasions where it may be justified to delay the review if at that time:

- the person in detention is being questioned by a police officer and the review officer is satisfied that an interruption of the questioning for the purpose of carrying out the review would prejudice the investigation in connection with which he/she is being questioned (s. 40(4)(b)(i));
- no review officer is readily available (s. 40(4)(b)(ii)).

It is likely that it will be necessary to justify why no review officer was available and that where it is known that a review may fall during an interview, the review is conducted prior to the interview where appropriate. With the ability to undertake reviews by telephone (or video link when regulations allow), a delay to a review is likely to need greater justification.

If the review is delayed, then it must still be conducted as soon as practicable and the reason for the delay must be recorded in the custody record by the review officer. In these circumstances the nine-hour period until the next review is calculated from the latest time the review should have been carried out and not from the time it was actually carried out. For instance, if the review was due at 3.15 pm and was delayed until 4 pm, the next review would have to be conducted no later than 12.15 am and not 1 am. When the review is conducted the review officer does not have to authorise detention for the full nine-hour period; he/she could decide that the case should be reviewed again within a shorter period and the review decision would reflect this.

Non-statutory Reviews

The detention of persons in police custody not subject to the statutory review requirement in para. 15.1 should still be reviewed periodically as a matter of good practice. The purpose of such reviews is to check that the particular power under which a detainee is held continues to apply, any associated conditions are complied with, and to make sure that appropriate action is taken to deal with any changes. This includes the detainee's prompt release when the power no longer applies, or his/her transfer if the power requires the detainee be taken elsewhere as soon as the necessary arrangements are made. Examples include persons: arrested on warrant because they failed to answer bail to appear at court; arrested under the Bail Act 1976, s. 7(3) for breaching a condition of bail granted after charge and in police custody for specific purposes and periods under the Crime (Sentences) Act 1997, sch. 1; convicted or remand prisoners, held in police stations on behalf of the Prison Service under the Imprisonment (Temporary Provisions) Act 1980, s. 6; being detained to prevent them causing a breach of the peace; detained at police stations on behalf of Immigration Enforcement (formerly the UK Immigration Service); or detained by order of a magistrates' court under the Criminal Justice Act 1988, s. 152 (as amended by the Drugs Act 2005, s. 8) to facilitate the recovery of evidence after being charged with drug possession or drug trafficking and suspected of having swallowed drugs.

The detention of persons remanded into police detention by order of a court under the Magistrates' Courts Act 1980, s. 128 is subject to a statutory requirement to review that detention. This is to make sure that the detainee is taken back to court no later than the end of the period authorised by the court or when the need for his/her detention by police ceases, whichever is the sooner.

1.7.16.14

KEYNOTE

Terrorism Act Reviews

In cases where the person has been detained under the Terrorism Act 2000, the first review should be conducted as soon as reasonably practicable after his/her arrest and then at least every 12 hours; after 24 hours it must be conducted by an officer of the rank of superintendent or above. Once a warrant of further detention has been obtained there is no requirement to conduct further reviews. If an officer of higher rank than the review officer gives directions relating to the detained person, and those directions are at variance with the performance by the review officer of a duty imposed on him/her, then he/she must refer the matter at once to an officer of at least the rank of superintendent.

A review officer may authorise a person's continued detention if satisfied that detention is necessary:

(a) to obtain relevant evidence whether by questioning the person or otherwise;

(b) to preserve relevant evidence;

(c) while awaiting the result of an examination or analysis of relevant evidence;

(d) for the examination or analysis of anything with a view to obtaining relevant evidence;

(e) pending a decision to apply to the Secretary of State for a deportation notice to be served on the detainee, the making of any such application, or the consideration of any such application by the Secretary of State;

(f) pending a decision to charge the detainee with an offence.

Section 14 of Code H provides guidance on terrorism reviews and extensions of detention. In all cases the review officer must be satisfied that the matter is being dealt with diligently and expeditiously. Where the detained person's rights to a solicitor have been withheld or he/she is being held *incommunicado* at the time of the review, the review officer must consider whether the reason or reasons for which the delay was authorised continue to exist. If in his/her opinion the reason or reasons no longer exist, he/she must inform the officer who authorised the delay of his/her opinion. When recording the grounds for the review the officer must also include his/her conclusion on whether there is a continuing need to withhold the detained person's rights.

In cases where the person is detained under the Terrorism Act 2000 and the review officer does not authorise continued detention, the person does not have to be released if an application for a warrant for further detention is going to be applied for or if an application has been made and the result is pending (s. 41 and sch. 8).

1.7.17   Code C—16 Charging Detained Persons

(a) Action

16.1   When the officer in charge of the investigation reasonably believes there is sufficient evidence to provide a realistic prospect of conviction for the offence (see *paragraph 11.6*), they shall without delay, and subject to the following qualification, inform the custody officer who will be responsible for considering whether the detainee should be charged. When a person is detained in respect of more than one offence it is permissible to delay informing the custody officer until the above conditions are satisfied in respect of all the offences, but see *paragraph 11.6*. If the detainee is a juvenile or a vulnerable person, any resulting action shall be taken in the presence of the appropriate adult if they are present at the time.

16.1A   Where guidance issued by the Director of Public Prosecutions under PACE, section 37A is in force the custody officer must comply with that Guidance in deciding how to act in dealing with the detainee.

16.1B   Where in compliance with the DPP's Guidance the custody officer decides that the case should be immediately referred to the CPS to make the charging decision, consultation should take place with a Crown Prosecutor as soon as is reasonably practicable. Where the Crown Prosecutor is unable to make the charging decision on the information available at that time, the detainee may be released without charge and on bail (with conditions if necessary) under section 37(7)(a). In such circumstances, the detainee should be informed that they are being released to enable the Director of Public Prosecutions to make a decision under section 37B.

16.2   When a detainee is charged with or informed they may be prosecuted for an offence, they shall, unless the restriction on drawing adverse inferences from silence applies, see *Annex C*, be cautioned as follows:

> '*You do not have to say anything. But it may harm your defence if you do not mention now something which you later rely on in court. Anything you do say may be given in evidence.*'

Where the use of the Welsh Language is appropriate, a constable may provide the caution directly in Welsh in the following terms:

> '*Does dim rhaid i chi ddweud dim byd. Ond gall niweidio eich amddiffyniad os na fyddwch chi'n sôn, yn awr, am rywbeth y byddwch chi'n dibynnu arno nes ymlaen yn y llys. Gall unrhyw beth yr ydych yn ei ddweud gael ei roi fel tystiolaeth.*'

Annex C, paragraph 2 sets out the alternative terms of the caution to be used when the restriction on drawing adverse inferences from silence applies.

16.3 When a detainee is charged they shall be given a written notice showing particulars of the offence and, subject to *paragraph 2.6A*, the officer's name and the case reference number. As far as possible the particulars of the charge shall be stated in simple terms, but they shall also show the precise offence in law with which the detainee is charged. The notice shall begin:

'You are charged with the offence(s) shown below.' Followed by the caution.

If the detainee is a juvenile, mentally disordered or otherwise mentally vulnerable, a copy of the notice should also be given to the appropriate adult.

16.4 If, after a detainee has been charged with or informed they may be prosecuted for an offence, an officer wants to tell them about any written statement or interview with another person relating to such an offence, the detainee shall either be handed a true copy of the written statement or the content of the interview record brought to their attention. Nothing shall be done to invite any reply or comment except to:

(a) caution the detainee, *'You do not have to say anything, but anything you do say may be given in evidence.'*;

Where the use of the Welsh Language is appropriate, caution the detainee in the following terms:

'Does dim rhaid i chi ddweud dim byd, ond gall unrhyw beth yr ydych yn ei ddweud gael ei roi fel tystiolaeth.'

and

(b) remind the detainee about their right to legal advice.

16.4A If the detainee:
- cannot read, the document may be read to them;
- is a juvenile, mentally disordered or otherwise mentally vulnerable, the appropriate adult shall also be given a copy, or the interview record shall be brought to their attention.

16.5 A detainee may not be interviewed about an offence after they have been charged with, or informed they may be prosecuted for it, unless the interview is necessary:
- to prevent or minimise harm or loss to some other person, or the public
- to clear up an ambiguity in a previous answer or statement
- in the interests of justice for the detainee to have put to them, and have an opportunity to comment on, information concerning the offence which has come to light since they were charged or informed they might be prosecuted.

Before any such interview, the interviewer shall:

(a) caution the detainee, *'You do not have to say anything, but anything you do say may be given in evidence.'*

Where the use of the Welsh Language is appropriate, the interviewer shall caution the detainee: *'Does dim rhaid i chi ddweud dim byd, ond gall unrhyw beth yr ydych yn ei ddweud gael ei roi fel tystiolaeth.'*

(b) remind the detainee about their right to legal advice.

16.6 The provisions of *paragraphs 16.2* to *16.5* must be complied with in the appropriate adult's presence if they are already at the police station. If they are not at the police station then these provisions must be complied with again in their presence when they arrive unless the detainee has been released.

16.7 When a juvenile is charged with an offence and the custody officer authorises their continued detention after charge, the custody officer must make arrangements for the juvenile to be taken into the care of a local authority to be detained pending appearance in court unless the custody officer certifies in accordance with PACE, section 38(6), that:

(a) for any juvenile; it is impracticable to do so and the reasons why it is impracticable must be set out in the certificate that must be produced to the court; or,

(b) in the case of a juvenile of at least 12 years old, no secure accommodation is available and other accommodation would not be adequate to protect the public from serious harm from that juvenile. See *Note 16D.*

Note: Chief officers should ensure that the operation of these provisions at police stations in their areas is subject to supervision and monitoring by an officer of the rank of inspector or above.

16.7A The requirement in *paragraph 3.4(b)* that documents and materials essential to effectively challenging the lawfulness of the detainee's arrest and detention must be made available to the detainee and, if they are represented, their solicitor, applies for the purposes of this section and a person's detention after charge. This means that the custody officer making the bail decision (PACE, section 38) or reviewing the need for detention after charge (PACE, section 40), is responsible for determining what, if any, documents or materials are essential and must be made available to the detainee or their solicitor.

(b) Documentation

16.8 A record shall be made of anything a detainee says when charged.

16.9 Any questions put in an interview after charge and answers given relating to the offence shall be recorded in full during the interview on forms for that purpose and the record signed by the detainee or, if they refuse, by the interviewer and any third parties present. If the questions are audibly recorded or visually recorded the arrangements in Code E or F apply.

16.10 If arrangements for a juvenile's transfer into local authority care as in *paragraph 16.7* are not made, the custody officer must record the reasons in a certificate which must be produced before the court with the juvenile.

1.7.17.1

KEYNOTE

Juveniles and Appropriate Adults

There is no power under PACE to detain a person and delay action under paras 16.2 to 16.5 solely to await the arrival of the appropriate adult. Reasonable efforts should therefore be made to give the appropriate adult sufficient notice of the time the decision (charge etc.) is to be implemented so that he/she can be present. If the appropriate adult is not, or cannot be, present at that time, the detainee should be released on bail to return for the decision to be implemented when the adult is present, unless the custody officer determines that the absence of the appropriate adult makes the detainee unsuitable for bail for this purpose. After charge, bail cannot be refused, or release on bail delayed, simply because an appropriate adult is not available, unless the absence of that adult provides the custody officer with the necessary grounds to authorise detention after charge under s. 38 of the 1984 Act

Except as in para. 16.7, neither a juvenile's behaviour nor the nature of the offence provides grounds for the custody officer to decide it is impracticable to arrange the juvenile's transfer to local authority care. Impracticability concerns the transport and travel requirements and the lack of secure accommodation which is provided for the purposes of restricting liberty does not make it impracticable to transfer the juvenile. Rather, 'impracticable' should be taken to mean that exceptional circumstances render movement of the child impossible or that the juvenile is due at court in such a short space of time that transfer would deprive them of rest or cause them to miss a court appearance. When the reason for not transferring the juvenile is an imminent court appearance, details of the travelling and court appearance times which justify the decision should be included in the certificate. The availability of secure accommodation is only a factor in relation to a juvenile aged 12 or over when other local authority accommodation would not be adequate to protect the public from serious harm from them. The obligation to transfer a juvenile to local authority accommodation applies as much to a juvenile charged during the daytime as to a juvenile to be held overnight, subject to a requirement to bring the juvenile before a court under PACE, s. 46.

The Concordat on Children in Custody published by the Home Office in 2017 provides detailed guidance with the aim of preventing the detention of children in police stations following charge. It is available here: <https://www.gov.uk/government/publications/concordat-on-children-in-custody>.

1.7.17.2 KEYNOTE

The Decision Whether or Not to Charge

Section 37 of the Police and Criminal Evidence Act 1984 states:

(7) Subject to section 41(7) below [expiry of 24 hours after the relevant time], if the custody officer determines that he has before him sufficient evidence to charge the person arrested with the offence for which he was arrested, the person arrested—

    (a) shall be—

        (i) released without charge and on bail, or

        (ii) kept in police detention,

    for the purpose of enabling the Director of Public Prosecutions to make a decision under section 37B below,

    (b) shall be released without charge and without bail unless the pre-conditions for bail are satisfied,

    (c) shall be released without charge and on bail if those pre-conditions are satisfied but not for the purpose mentioned in paragraph (a), or

    (d) shall be charged.

(7A) The decision as to how a person is to be dealt with under subsection (7) above shall be that of the custody officer.

(7B) Where a person is released under subsection (7)(a) above, it shall be the duty of the custody officer to inform him that he is being released or (as the case may be) detained, to enable the Director of Public Prosecutions to make a decision under section 37B below.

(8) Where—

    (a) a person is released under subsection (7)(b) or (c) above; and

    (b) at the time of his release a decision whether he should be prosecuted for the offence for which he was arrested has not been taken,

    it shall be the duty of the custody officer so to inform him/her.

Section 37A of the Police and Criminal Evidence Act 1984 states:

(1) The Director of Public Prosecutions may issue guidance—

    (a) for the purpose of enabling custody officers to decide how persons should be dealt with under section 37(7) above or 37(C) or 37CA(2) below, and

    (b) as to the information to be sent to the Director of Public Prosecutions under section 37B(1) below.

    …

(3) Custody officers are to have regard to guidance under this section in deciding how persons should be dealt with under section 37(7) above or 37C(2) or 37CA(2) below.

Unless officers are still investigating other offences for which the person has been arrested and is in police detention, s. 37(7) requires the custody officer to review the evidence in order to determine whether there is sufficient evidence to charge the detained person. If the custody officer decides that there is sufficient evidence to charge the detained person that person must be charged or, if not charged, released in relation to that matter, as set out in s. 37(7) above. The pre-conditions mentioned in s. 37(7)(b) are set out in s. 50A of the Police and Criminal Evidence Act 1984:

50A Interpretation of references to pre-conditions for bail

For the purposes of this Part the following are the pre-conditions for bail in relation to the release of a person by a custody officer—

(a) that the custody officer is satisfied that releasing the person on bail is necessary and proportionate in all the circumstances (having regard, in particular, to any conditions of bail which would be imposed), and

(b) that an officer of the rank of inspector or above authorises the release on bail (having considered any representations made by the person or the person's legal representative).

Under s. 37A(1) guidance has been issued to enable custody officers to decide whether there is sufficient evidence to charge and for which offences the police may charge without reference to the CPS. Where in accordance with the guidance the case is referred to the CPS for decision, the custody officer should ensure that an officer involved in the investigation sends to the CPS such information as is specified in the guidance. A detained person should not be kept in custody just for the sole purpose of seeking advice from the CPS as to what offences the offender should be charged with (*R (On the Application of G) v Chief Constable of West Yorkshire Police and DPP* [2008] EWCA Civ 28).

Charging decisions in cases will be made following a review of evidence and in accordance with the Code for Crown Prosecutors. This requires that the custody officer or Crown Prosecutor making the decision is satisfied that there is enough evidence for there to be a realistic prospect of conviction and that it is in the public interest to prosecute (Full Code Test). In order to allow the matter to have full consideration, often the time needed to consider the matter will require the detained person to be bailed. However, there will clearly be occasions when it will not be desirable to bail the detained person but the evidence required to permit the Full Code Test to be applied is not available. In such a case the Threshold Test should be applied; this requires there to be reasonable suspicion that the suspect has committed an offence and it is in the public interest to charge that suspect. The evidential considerations include

- there is insufficient evidence currently available to apply the evidential stage of the Full Code Test; and
- there are reasonable grounds for believing that further evidence will become available within a reasonable period; and
- the seriousness or the circumstances of the case justifies the making of an immediate charging decision; and
- there are continuing substantial grounds to object to bail in accordance with the Bail Act 1976 and in all the circumstances of the case it is proper to do so.

The Code for Crown Prosecutors advises that a prosecution will automatically take place once the evidential stage is met. A prosecution will usually take place unless the prosecutor is satisfied that there are public interest factors tending against prosecution which outweigh those tending in favour.

The public interest factors to be considered are:

- How serious is the offence committed?
- What is the level of culpability of the suspect?
- What are the circumstances of and the harm caused to the victim?
- Was the suspect under the age of 18 at the time of the offence?
- What is the impact on the community?
- Is prosecution a proportionate response?
- Do sources of information require protecting?

It is quite possible that one public interest factor alone may outweigh a number of other factors.

When a person is arrested under the provisions of the Criminal Justice Act 2003 which allow a person to be retried after being acquitted of a serious offence, provided a further prosecution has not been precluded by the Court of Appeal, an officer of the rank of superintendent or above who has not been directly involved in the investigation is responsible for determining whether the evidence is sufficient to charge.

1.7.17.3

KEYNOTE

Sufficient Evidence to Charge

Here the custody officer is looking at the evidence in order to satisfy him/herself that no further investigation is needed before the person can be charged. If this is the case, detention may be authorised for the purpose of charging the detained person. Where the custody officer is considering bail as in para. 16.1B, see para. 1.7.17.5.

Where Guidance issued by the DPP under s. 37A is in force, a custody officer who determines in accordance with that Guidance that there is sufficient evidence to charge the detainee may detain that person for no longer than is reasonably necessary to decide how that person is to be dealt with under PACE, s. 37(7) (a)–(d), including, where appropriate, consultation with the Duty Prosecutor. The period is subject to the maximum period of detention before charge determined by PACE, ss. 41 to 44. Where in accordance with the Guidance the case is referred to the CPS for decision, the custody officer should ensure that an officer involved in the investigation sends to the CPS such information as is specified in the Guidance. The DPP has published the sixth edition of Charging (The Director's Guidance), which is effective from 31 December 2020.

Where there is sufficient evidence to charge, a delay in bringing charges may be seen to be unreasonable under Article 6 of the European Convention on Human Rights (*D v HM Advocate* [2000] HRLR 389). In deciding whether there is sufficient evidence to charge for the purposes of authorising detention or when a person's detention is reviewed, where there is a conflict between the detained person's account and victims' or witnesses' accounts it is reasonable to be in possession of at least one witness statement in the English language before preferring charges (*R (On the Application of Wiles) v Chief Constable of Hertfordshire* [2002] EWHC 387 (Admin)). There is no breach of PACE in keeping the detained person in police detention while a statement is translated. It is suggested that the translation needs to be completed expeditiously.

Under s. 37(9) of the 1984 Act release can be delayed if the person is not in a fit state to be released (e.g. he/she is drunk) until he/she is fit.

1.7.17.4 KEYNOTE

Insufficient Evidence to Charge

This creates two separate criteria for detention, that is to say, where detention is necessary to:

- secure and preserve evidence relating to an offence for which the person is arrested; or
- obtain such evidence by questioning the detained person.

If the custody officer has determined that there is not sufficient evidence to charge the person, the person must be released unless the custody officer has *reasonable grounds for believing* that the person's detention is necessary to preserve or obtain such evidence by questioning the person and the custody officer must be able to justify any decision not to release a person from detention.

When deciding if detention should be authorised in order to obtain evidence by questioning, the case of *R v McGuinness* [1999] Crim LR 318 should be considered. There the court held that the words 'sufficient evidence to prosecute' and 'sufficient evidence for a prosecution to succeed', in Code C, para. 16.1 (this was the wording under the previous PACE Code of Practice), had to involve some consideration of any explanation, or lack of one, from the suspect. While an interview may not be needed in all cases, questioning of detained people before they are charged may be necessary, particularly where intention or dishonesty is involved or where there may be a defence. It may also be important to put questions to the person about the offence or his/her explanation, as this may be important to negate any defence the person raises at court (see s. 34 of the Criminal Justice and Public Order Act 1994) **(see para. 1.9.2.3)**.

Where initial suspicion rests on several people, it may be appropriate to hold all suspects until they all are interviewed before deciding whether there is enough evidence to warrant a charge against any of them. Detention for questioning where there are reasonable grounds for suspecting that an offence has been committed is lawful so long as the suspicion has not been dispelled in the interim and the questioning is not unnecessarily delayed (*Clarke v Chief Constable of North Wales* [2000] All ER (D) 477).

The mere fact that a person needs to be interviewed about the offence is not of itself justification for authorising detention. The question that has to be asked is whether the person can be bailed prior to the interview or even bailed before being taken to the police station (s. 30A of the 1984 Act). Factors which might be relevant in making this decision include:

- whether the person may interfere with witnesses;
- whether he/she is likely to return if bailed;
- where there is more than one suspect, that they would have an opportunity to confer before their interviews;
- whether there is outstanding property;
- whether the person's name and address are verified.

The fact that the officers and any legal representative will be ready to start the interview shortly may also be relevant when making this decision.

1.7.17.5

KEYNOTE

Cases where the Detained Person is Bailed to Allow Consultation with the CPS

Section 37B of the Police and Criminal Evidence Act 1984 states:

(1) Where a person is dealt with under section 37(7)(a) above, an officer involved in the investigation of the offence shall, as soon as is practicable, send to the Director of Public Prosecutions such information as may be specified in guidance under section 37A above.

(2) The Director of Public Prosecutions shall decide whether there is sufficient evidence to charge the person with an offence.

(3) If he decides that there is sufficient evidence to charge the person with an offence, he shall decide—

  (a) whether or not the person should be charged and, if so, the offence with which he should be charged, and

  (b) whether or not the person should be given a caution and, if so, the offence in respect of which he should be given a caution.

(4) The Director of Public Prosecutions shall give notice of his decision to an officer involved in the investigation of the offence.

(4A) Notice under subsection (4) above shall be in writing but in the case of a person kept in police detention under section 37(7)(a) above it may be given orally in the first instance and confirmed in writing subsequently.

(5) If his decision is—

  (a) that there is not sufficient evidence to charge the person with an offence, or

  (b) that there is sufficient evidence to charge the person with an offence but that the person should not be charged with an offence or given a caution in respect of an offence,

  a custody officer shall give the person notice in writing that he is not to be prosecuted.

Where a person has been bailed under s. 37(7)(a) with or without bail conditions, the CPS must be consulted in order to determine what case disposal decision will be made (this may itself require further inquiries to gather further evidence). This referral should be made using forms MG3 (Report to Crown Prosecutor for a Charging Decision), and MG3A (Further Report to Crown Prosecutor for a Charging Decision). The pre-charge advice file can be a pre-charge expedited report (straightforward and guilty plea cases) or a pre-charge evidential report (contested/Crown Court cases) and must also include other relevant information, including:

Pre-charge Expedited Report

- MG3;
- MG11(s)—Witness statement or Index notes (if offence is witnessed by more than one officer and up to four, use the statement of one officer and summarise the others);
- MG15—Record of interview;
- Phoenix print of suspect(s)' previous convictions/cautions/reprimands/final warnings. If there is any other information that may be relevant, include it on form MG6—Case File Information.

Pre-charge Evidential Report

- MG3;
- MG5—Case summary (unless the statements cover all elements of the case);
- MG6—Case file information;
- MG11—Key witness statement(s), or Index notes (if offence is witnessed by police use the statement of one officer and summarise the others);
- MG12—Exhibit list;
- MG15—Interview record;
- Crime report and incident log;
- Unused material likely to undermine the case;
- Copies of key documentary exhibits;
- Phoenix print of suspect(s)' pre-cons/cautions/reprimands/final warnings.

The prosecutor will decide whether there is sufficient evidence to charge or caution the person and shall give written notice of the decision to an officer involved in the investigation of the details of the offence. This decision must be followed (s. 37B(6)) if the decision was for the person to be cautioned (this includes conditional cautions), and if the person refuses, or for some other reason a caution cannot be given, he/she must be charged with the offence (s. 37B(7)).

In cases where the prosecutor decides that there is not sufficient evidence to charge the person with an offence, or that there is sufficient evidence to charge the person with an offence but that the person should not be charged with an offence or given a caution in respect of an offence, the custody officer must inform the person in writing of the decision. Similarly the person must be informed of those cases where there is insufficient evidence to charge him/her, but if further evidence or information comes to light in the future the case may be reconsidered under the Code for Crown Prosecutors.

In cases where further time is needed to obtain evidence or for the prosecutor to make a case disposal decision, the person can be further bailed. In these cases the custody officer must give the person notice in writing. This does not affect any bail conditions that were included when the detained person was bailed (s. 37D(1)–(3)).

1.7.17.6

KEYNOTE

Bail to Allow Referral to the CPS

Section 47 of the Police and Criminal Evidence Act 1984 states:

> (1A) The normal powers to impose conditions of bail shall be available to him where a custody officer releases a person on bail under this Part [sections 34–52] (except sections 37C(2)(b) and 37CA(2)(b)).

In this subsection, 'the normal powers to impose conditions of bail' has the meaning given in s. 3(6) of the Bail Act 1976.

Where the person is bailed after charge or bailed without charge and on bail for the purpose of enabling the CPS to make a decision regarding case disposal, the custody officer may impose conditions on that bail (see para. 1.10.7). In cases where a person is released without being charged under s. 37(7)(b) or (c), that is to say bail is not given for the purposes of a CPS referral, the custody officer cannot impose new conditions on that bail (s. 47(1A)).

1.7.17.7

KEYNOTE

Alternatives to Prosecution

The custody officer must take into account alternatives to prosecution under the Crime and Disorder Act 1998 applicable to persons under 18, and in national guidance on the cautioning of offenders applicable to persons aged 18 and over.

1.7.17.8

KEYNOTE

Simple Caution

There are occasions where a person for whom there is sufficient evidence to charge may be cautioned as an alternative method of disposing with the case. A simple caution (once known as a formal or police caution) is a formal warning that may be given by the police to persons aged 18 or over who admit to committing an offence ('offenders'). The simple caution scheme is designed to provide a means of dealing with low-level, mainly first-time, offending without a prosecution. A simple caution may only be given where specified criteria are met.

Guidance as to the use of cautioning is provided by the Ministry of Justice's *Simple cautions: guidance for police and prosecutors* (MoJ Guidance): see <https://www.gov.uk/government/publications/simple-cautions-guidance-for-police-and-prosecutors>. The MoJ Guidance applies to all decisions relating to simple cautions from the commencement date, regardless of when the offence was committed.

Section 17(3) of the Criminal Justice and Courts Act 2015 prohibits a constable from giving a simple caution if the offence is an either-way offence specified by order made by the Secretary of State, except in exceptional circumstances relating to the person or the offence. An either-way offence is an offence which, if committed by an adult, is triable either on indictment or summarily.

The offences specified by the Secretary of State are set out in Annex B of the MoJ guidance; it should be noted that some of these offences have been repealed but they may still be cautionable where the offence was committed before the date of repeal.

R v *Chief Constable of Lancashire Constabulary, ex parte Atkinson* (1998) 162 JP 275 is a case which considered the level of evidence required before a caution can be considered. There the court said that, provided it was clear that there had been an admission of guilt, it was not necessary, for the purposes of administering a caution, to show that the admission had been obtained in circumstances which satisfied the Codes of Practice. However, police officers would be well advised to take precautions that would satisfy Code C. It would be both fairer and more reliable for a formal interview to take place.

Before making a case disposal decision it is essential that the matter has been fully investigated in order to reach an informed decision. In *Omar* v *Chief Constable of Bedfordshire Constabulary* [2002] EWHC 3060 (Admin), the Divisional Court quashed a caution that had been administered in order to allow a prosecution to be pursued. The court held that a number of reasonable lines of inquiry had not been made; for instance, the police had failed to take a statement from the victim's friend or obtain CCTV footage that was available or fully investigate the victim's injuries. Further, the length of time in custody (17 hours) should not have been a relevant consideration and also the suspect's admission was ambiguous. Therefore, it was in the public interest that a decision to caution rather than to charge should not prevent the subsequent pursuit of the prosecution of the offender.

The MoJ Guidance states that 'simple cautions are generally intended for low level, mainly first time offending. An assessment of the seriousness of the offence is the starting point for considering whether a simple caution may be appropriate.' Officers are referred to the National Decision Model and the Association of Chief Police Officers (ACPO) *Gravity Factors Matrix* to assist them in reaching this decision. The guidelines should be considered carefully in all cases as any decision can be challenged by judicial review. It is important that the full implications of accepting a caution are made clear to suspects so that they are able to give informed consent or there is a risk that the courts may overturn the caution (*R (On the Application of Stratton)* v *Chief Constable of Thames Valley* [2013] EWHC 1561 (Admin)).

While there is no general obligation on the police to disclose material prior to charge, there may be a need to make some disclosure to a suspect's legal representative in order that he/she can advise on whether a caution should be accepted (*DPP* v *Ara* [2001] EWHC Admin 493). In *Ara*, the suspect had been interviewed without a legal representative being present but the officers refused to disclose the terms of the interview.

In cases where the case has been referred to the CPS under s. 37B of the 1984 Act and a decision has been made that the suspect should receive a caution, an officer involved in the investigation of the offence will be informed in writing. The notification will include the offence in respect of which a caution should be administered. If it is not possible to give the suspect such a caution then he/she must be charged with the offence (s. 37B(7)).

1.7.17.9

KEYNOTE

Young Offenders, Youth Cautions

Sections 66A to 66G, 66ZA and 66ZB of the Crime and Disorder Act 1998 make provisions for youth cautions and youth conditional cautions, which replace reprimands and warnings for children and young persons. A reprimand or warning of a person under s. 65 of the Crime and Disorder Act 1998 is to be treated as a youth caution given to that person under s. 66ZA(1) of the 1998 Act.

1.7.17.10

KEYNOTE

Conditional Cautioning

Sections 22 to 27 of the Criminal Justice Act 2003 introduced conditional cautioning, the aim being to deal with offenders without the involvement of the usual court processes. A conditional caution allows an authorised person (usually a police officer) or a relevant prosecutor (usually the CPS) to decide to give a caution to an offender aged 18 or over with one or more conditions attached. When an offender is given a conditional caution for an offence, criminal proceedings for that offence are halted while the offender is given an opportunity to comply with the conditions. Where the conditions are complied with, the prosecution is not normally commenced. However, where there is no reasonable excuse for non-compliance, criminal proceedings may be commenced for the original offence and the conditional caution will cease to have effect. A conditional caution can be given for one or more offences.

Section 24A of the Criminal Justice Act 2003 allows a constable to arrest without warrant any person whom the officer has reasonable grounds for believing has failed, without reasonable excuse, to comply with any of the conditions attached to the conditional caution. Certain provisions of the Police and Criminal Evidence Act 1984 relating to detention, reviews, searches, and searches and examinations to ascertain identity apply, with modifications, to a person arrested under s. 24A of the Criminal Justice Act 2003.

Guidance on conditional cautioning to police officers and Crown prosecutors issued by the DPP under s. 37A of the Police and Criminal Evidence Act 1984 is set out below.

1. Introduction
   1.1 In determining whether to offer a Conditional Caution in any case authorised persons and relevant prosecutors must follow the Code of Practice for Adult Conditional Cautions 2013 and comply with this Guidance.
   1.2 This Guidance assists Authorised Persons and Relevant Prosecutors (the decision makers) to apply the Code of Practice on Adult Conditional Cautions in deciding how an offender should be dealt with when it is determined that:
      • there is sufficient evidence to charge an offender with an offence; and
      • the public interest in the case may be met by a caution with suitable conditions providing reparation to the victim or community; which may modify offending behaviour; ensure the departure and non return of a foreign offender from the UK; or provide an appropriate penalty; and
      • In all the circumstances of the case a Conditional Caution appears appropriate.
   1.3 This Guidance specifies:
      • the offences and circumstances when a Conditional Caution may be considered and whether the decision to offer one may be made by a police officer or is to be referred to a prosecutor.
      • the practical arrangements for recording decisions in cases, consulting with the UK Border Agency, making referrals to prosecutors and for dealing with non-compliance with any conditions.

2. Authorised persons
   2.1 An authorised person (for the purpose of administering a Conditional Caution) is a police officer not below the rank of Sergeant or any person specifically authorised to do so by the Director of Public Prosecutions.

3. Excluded Offences—for which a Conditional Caution may not be offered
   3.1 A Conditional Caution may not be offered for any offence classified as Hate Crime or Domestic Violence, otherwise it may be considered in any case in the circumstances set out below.
   3.2 If a Conditional Caution is being considered in an offence involving domestic abuse or hate crime then the prosecutor must refer a domestic abuse case to the HQ Violence Against Women Strategy Manager and a hate crime case to HQ Hate Crime team for advice. Otherwise a Conditional Caution may be considered in any case in the circumstances set out below.

4. Summary offences and either way cases
   4.1 An authorised person may offer a Conditional Caution for any summary only offence and any either way offence. For serious either way offences, a Conditional Caution may only be offered if the Foreign National Offender provisions apply or in exceptional circumstances as set out below. The decision that exceptional circumstances exist in any case may only be made by a police officer not below the rank of Inspector.

5. Offences committed by Relevant Foreign Offenders
   5.1 The Code of Practice makes specific provision for offences committed by Foreign Offenders where a Conditional Caution is proposed to facilitate the removal of the offender from the jurisdiction and ensure non return. In such cases the greater public interest is in removal from the jurisdiction and

the Code permits consideration in any case where the decision maker considers that the sentence likely to be imposed by the court for the offence concerned will not exceed 2 years' imprisonment. Further guidance is provided below on how to assess that. The authorised person or prosecutor must record the reasons for reaching this conclusion in any case.

6. Indictable only offences to be referred to prosecutors

6.1 As such offences will generally attract significant custodial sentences on conviction the maintenance of public confidence in the Justice System will ordinarily require such cases to be dealt with at court. Any indictable only case considered by the police as suitable for a Conditional Caution must be referred to a prosecutor.

6.2 Unless the foreign offender conditions are to be offered only in the most exceptional circumstances will a Conditional Caution be an appropriate way of dealing with such a case. The decision to authorise a Conditional Caution in any Indictable Only case must be approved by a Deputy Chief Crown Prosecutor.

6.3 Before considering referring any indictable only offence to a prosecutor, authorised persons must first determine that exceptional circumstances as set out below are present in the case or that the foreign offender conditions are appropriate.

7. Identification of cases in which a Conditional Caution is permissible

7.1 Police and prosecutors should ensure that a Conditional Caution is considered in any case for which it is permitted and provides an appropriate outcome for the victim, community and offender.

7.2 Where a Conditional Caution with suitable conditions may provide reparation to the victim or community; be effective in modifying offending behaviour; facilitate removal from the jurisdiction and ensure non return; or provide an appropriate penalty, the offender should not be charged unless it is determined that the case is too serious for a conditional caution to be appropriate.

8. Making prompt decisions

8.1 Wherever possible, the decision to administer a Conditional Caution should be made as early as possible and while the offender is still in custody. If, for any reason, this is not possible, the offender (including a foreign national) may be released on bail, with or without conditions (under section 37(7) PACE) for a short period unless there are operational reasons or other circumstances relating to the victim or offender justifying a longer period, or where further information is required relating to the consideration of any specific condition.

9. Prosecutor's post charge review—cases that should have been considered for a Conditional Caution

9.1 Where an offender is charged with an offence, but it appears upon review by a prosecutor that a Conditional Caution is more appropriate, the reviewing prosecutor should direct an authorised person to offer a Conditional Caution. This includes any case where authorised persons ordinarily make that decision. The current prosecution should be adjourned whilst this action is taken. The authorised person shall then offer a caution with conditions as specified by the prosecutor. If it proves then not to be possible to administer the caution an alternative out of court disposal may not be offered and the prosecution must continue.

9.2 In the case of foreign offenders this may include cases where an asylum or human rights claim has been withdrawn or resolved after charge.

10. Deciding whether a Conditional Caution is a suitable response—Requirement for sufficient evidence to charge the offender

10.1 Before a Conditional Caution can be considered, there must be sufficient evidence available to provide a realistic prospect of conviction in accordance with the Full Code Test set out in the Code for Crown Prosecutors.

10.2 In making this assessment, an authorised person may offer a Conditional Caution where;

- The suspect has made a clear and reliable admission to the offence and has said nothing that could be used as a defence, or
- The suspect has made no admission but has not denied the offence or otherwise indicated it will be contested and the commission of the offence and the identification of the offender can be established by reliable evidence or the suspect can be seen clearly committing the offence on a good quality visual recording.

11. Deciding whether a Conditional Caution is a suitable response—Assessing the Public Interest

11.1 Once the evidential test is met, the decision maker must then be satisfied that the public interest can best be served by the offender complying with suitable conditions aimed at reparation; rehabilitation; removal from the UK and ensuring no return for a period; or punishment, taking into account the interests of the victim, the community, and/or needs of the offender. They must also be satisfied that a prosecution will continue to be necessary, and could go ahead, should the offer of a Conditional Caution be declined or the offender does not complete the conditions.

11.2 In determining whether a Conditional Caution is appropriate to the circumstances of an offence decision makers must assess the seriousness of the case to ensure that this out of court disposal provides an appropriate and proportionate response to the offending behaviour and meets the justice of the case.

12. Assessing Seriousness

12.1 An assessment of the seriousness of the offence is the starting point for considering whether a Conditional Caution may be appropriate. The more serious the offence, the less likely a Conditional Caution will be appropriate. Wherever the circumstances of an offence indicate that an immediate custodial sentence or high level community order is the appropriate sentence, a Conditional Caution should not be offered unless the specific provisions concerning foreign nationals apply or the exceptional circumstances set out below are met. The Magistrates' Court Sentencing Guidelines provides a sentencing starting point for a range of offences at high level community order or period of imprisonment. Those specific either way offences are set out in Annex A.

12.2 The seriousness of the offence and the range of penalties likely to be imposed must be carefully considered in every case taking into account the Magistrates' Court Sentencing Guidelines. Cases routinely dealt with at the Crown court (specified in the Guidelines and set out in Annex A) or likely to be considered for a high level community order or period of imprisonment should generally proceed to court.

12.3 Indictable only offences must be referred to prosecutors to determine whether a Conditional Caution is appropriate, including where foreign offender conditions may be suitable. A Conditional Caution will only be appropriate for an indictable only offence in the most exceptional circumstances. In considering such cases prosecutors will assess the factors referred to below and make a review record of the exceptional circumstances found.

12.4 Police decision makers will also need to consider and apply the ACPO gravity factors matrix when considering whether to issue a Conditional Caution.

13. Considering the totality of offending and history of offending

13.1 In assessing the seriousness of the offence under consideration and determining whether the case should proceed to court or is suitable for a Conditional Caution the decision maker should also take into account the totality of any current offending and any history of previous convictions and cautions particularly any which are recent or of a similar nature. However a record of previous offending should not rule out the possibility of a Conditional Caution especially where there have been no similar offences during the last two years or where it appears that the Conditional Caution is likely to change the pattern of offending behaviour.

13.2 It is unlikely that domestic abuse in intimate (whether current or previous) partner cases would ever be appropriate for conditional caution. This is because of the repetitive pattern of domestic abuse and the risk experienced by victims. However, where there are no elements of controlling and coercive behaviour, and where there is no pattern of abuse or repetitive behaviour there may be rare occasions in domestic abuse cases not involving intimate partners where a conditional caution could be considered. The specific Domestic Abuse Guidelines for Prosecutors may be helpful when considering whether this is an exceptional case.

13.3 It is unlikely that hate crime offences would be appropriate for conditional cautions. This is because of the serious nature of these offences and the targeting of an individual because of their personal characteristics, or perceived personal characteristics. The devastating impact of hate crimes on, not only the individual but also cn communities and wider society demands a robust response and the opportunity to apply for a sentence uplift to send the clear message that those who target people because of their race, religion, sexual orientation, transgender identity or disability should expect to receive a higher sentence. However there may be rare occasions, for example a young person of good character, which may merit the consideration of a conditional caution. The legal guidance on Hate Crime Prosecutions may be helpful when considering whether this is an exceptional case.

13.4 In such cases prosecutors should ensure that they have fully considered the risk assessment provided by the police, the history of the relationship and the circumstances of the offence before seeking additional advice from the HQ Violence Against Women Strategy Manager or HQ Hate Crime team.

14. Exceptional circumstances where a Conditional Caution may be appropriate for an offence likely to attract a high level community order or a custodial sentence

14.1 The decision to offer a Conditional Caution for an indictable only offence, an either way offence routinely dealt with at the Crown court or likely to attract a high level community order or sentence of imprisonment, may only be taken in exceptional circumstances where the decision maker is able to conclude that the public interest does not require the immediate prosecution of the offender and that if it took place a court would not impose a period of imprisonment or high level community order.

14.2 In reaching that conclusion, the decision maker must carefully assess the public interest in the case and the likely sentence informed by the appropriate sentencing guidelines and authorities. The decision maker must record (on an MG6) the reason for concluding that exceptional circumstances are met in the case. Authorised persons should only refer indictable only cases to prosecutors where they are able to clearly specify the exceptional circumstances present in the case in accordance with this guidance.

14.3 In assessing whether exceptional circumstances exist in a case, the following factors must be taken into account:

- The extent of culpability and/or harm caused
- The degree of intention or the foreseeability of any resultant harm
- Any significant aggravating factors
- Any significant mitigating factors
- The lack of any recent similar previous convictions or cautions
- Any other factors relating the offender or commission of the offence likely to have a significant impact on sentence
- The overall justice of the case and whether the circumstances require it to be dealt with in open court
- The range of sentences appropriate to the circumstances of the case.

14.4 Any aggravating circumstances, including the methodology employed by the offender (for example, any breach of trust or advantage taken of the vulnerable or young) may all increase the seriousness of the offence to the point where the case should proceed to court.

15. The decision to offer a Conditional Caution

15.1 The decision makers' review

15.1.1 A Conditional Caution may be appropriate where the decision maker believes that while the public interest requires a prosecution in the first instance the interests of the victim, community or offender are better served by the offender complying with suitable conditions aimed at reparation, rehabilitation, punishment or in the case of a foreign national offender removal from the jurisdiction.

15.1.2 It must be determined that a Conditional Caution is likely to be effective and should be offered. Where the offender shows genuine remorse, indicates a willingness to be cautioned and comply with the proposed conditions a Conditional Caution may be considered. A Conditional Caution will not be appropriate for an offender who fails to accept responsibility at the time the caution is administered.

15.1.3 Where the offender indicates that they do not wish to accept the caution or any of the conditions at that stage, the case will be considered again by the decision maker who will determine whether alternative conditions are appropriate or whether the case should proceed to prosecution. Where it proves not to be possible to give the caution because it is not accepted or reasonable conditions are declined the offender should be charged with the offence. In such circumstances an alternative out of court disposal may not be offered.

15.2 Foreign Offender Conditions

15.2.1 Such conditions may only be offered to a foreign offender having no leave to enter or remain in the UK and in respect of whom there is power to enforce departure. They cannot be offered where the offender makes or has an outstanding asylum or Human rights claim to remain in the UK or where the offender admits to committing a document or identity fraud offence in order to make a claim for asylum or where the offender may be a trafficked victim. This does not, however, prevent foreign offender conditions from being offered where the asylum or human rights claim has been refused (and any appeal against that refusal has been finally determined), where the relevant foreign offender voluntarily withdraws the claim, or where the relevant foreign offender's grant of asylum has been revoked or not renewed by virtue of paragraph 339A of the Immigration Rules. The police must consult the UK Border Agency who will confirm the offender's status and that of any dependents and whether the individual can be removed from the UK. This information must be available to the decision maker at the time the Conditional Caution is offered.

15.2.2 Foreign offender conditions may be offered in a case that would ordinarily result in the imposition of imprisonment following conviction. However it may only be offered where, in all the circumstances of the case, the decision maker assesses that the sentence likely to be imposed for the offence under consideration would be less than two years' imprisonment. The decision maker must make a record of the reason for reaching that conclusion.

15.2.3 The purpose of the Conditional Caution will be to bring about the departure of the offender from the UK and to ensure that return does not occur for a specified period of time. Both of these objects should be set as conditions in every case. They should only be used where it will be practicable to remove the person within a reasonable period of time. The offender may be required to:
- Report regularly to an immigration office, reporting centre, police station or other similar place, pending removal
- Obtain or assist authorities in obtaining a valid national travel document, or
- Comply with removal directions and any lawful directions given to effect departure
- Not to return to the UK within a specified period of time, normally 5 years as set out in the Immigration Rules

15.2.4 Priority should be given to conditions to facilitate the early removal of the offender from the UK; however any other rehabilitative, reparative, or punitive conditions appropriate to the circumstances of the case may also be included provided the circumstances of the offender and any detention under immigration powers permit completion. Other conditions should not be included if they are likely to delay the removal or may not be completed prior to the likely removal date.

15.2.5 The normal period not to return should be 5 years. However there may be indictable only cases involving a foreign offender where a prosecutor considers that exceptional circumstances exist permitting the offer of a Conditional Caution including a condition preventing return for a period of 10 years instead.

15.3 Offering a financial penalty condition

15.3.1 A financial penalty can only be offered in accordance with the scales set out in Annex B to this Guidance but only for those offences contained in an Order made under section

23A of the Act. Ordinarily the standard penalty should be offered. Where, however, there is substantial mitigation for the commission of the offence or the offender is in receipt of state benefit (such as income support or job seeker's allowance) as their main or only source of income, a penalty within the mitigated range may be offered instead.

15.3.2 When attaching a financial penalty condition, the amount of the penalty, the designated officer for the local justice area to whom the penalty must be paid, and the address of that officer for payment must be set out in the documentation to be handed to the offender at the time of the administration of the Conditional Caution.

16. Practical arrangements for the referral of cases

16.1 Consultation with UK Border Agency

16.1.1 As soon as it appears that a foreign offender has been detained the custody officer should contact UKBA to establish whether the individual is classified as a relevant foreign offender. Once confirmed UKBA will provide any immigration papers required and will liaise over the appropriate conditions to be offered.

16.2 Referral of cases to prosecutors

16.2.1 Where an authorised person considers that, exceptionally, an indictable only offence may be appropriate for a condition [sic] caution the case must be referred to a prosecutor. This will be done by submitting the case to the Head of the Crown Court Unit for the relevant CPS Area. The CPS Area will provide a response within 7 days. If, for any reason, it proves not to be possible to administer the caution the offender should be charged with the offence and may not be offered any other out of court disposal.

16.3 Requirements for an MG5

16.3.1 In any case which is to be referred to a Crown Prosecutor the police will prepare an MG5 report and will attach to it the victim or losers witness statement and any other evidential material necessary to establish whether the Full Code Test is met. An MG6 must be provided setting out the views of any victim and (where appropriate) the Inspectors assessment of the exceptional circumstances considered by the police to be present in the case justifying the offer of a Conditional Caution. Confirmation by the UKBA as to the status and ability to remove from the UK of any foreign offender will also be required where the removal and non return conditions are to be considered.

16.4 Contents of the MG5 Report

16.4.1 The MG5 report should set out the circumstances of the offence, summarising any admissions in interview, providing the details of any victims and any previous convictions or cautions applicable to the offender. An MG6 should set out any views of the victim as to any restorative or reparative conditions and details of any compensation to be considered. The report should set out the proposed conditions to be included and confirm that the offender is willing to admit the offence and be cautioned.

16.5 Police decision making—recording the decision

16.5.1 The authorised person must make a brief record of the reasons why a Conditional Caution was or was not considered appropriate in any case and why any particular conditions were selected. The reasons should specify whether reparative, rehabilitative or punitive objectives were sought to be achieved. This may be recorded on an MG6 or a case review document.

16.5.2 As any refusal to be conditionally cautioned or failure to complete conditions may lead to subsequent prosecution authorised persons should ensure that details of the evidential basis for the decision are recorded including sufficient witnesses details to enable an appropriate file to be provided to the prosecutor. This may be done by completion of an MG5 or a case review document.

16.6 Authorising the Conditional Caution

16.6.1 Once satisfied that the Conditional Caution and the proposed conditions are an appropriate and proportionate response to the offending behaviour, the decision maker will complete the Authority to Give a Conditional Caution which will be retained with the MG5 or case review document. A copy of the Authority to Give a Conditional Caution is attached at Annex C.

16.7 Dealing with non-compliance with Conditions

16.7.1 If following administration of the caution it becomes clear that the offender is not complying with any conditions the decision maker must determine whether there is any reasonable excuse for that non-compliance and if not what action is to be taken. In determining what action to take at that stage the decision maker may deem the caution as completed, vary conditions or prosecute for the original offence. An alternative form of out of court disposal may not be offered.

16.7.2 Where the original decision to offer the caution was made by an authorised person the authorised person may make that decision but if it is considered that charging is appropriate and the offence is one that cannot be charged by the police the case must be referred to a prosecutor to decide whether to charge. Where the decision to offer the Conditional Caution was made by a prosecutor the case must be referred back to a prosecutor.

16.7.3 Once a decision is made as to how the non compliance is to be dealt with the police with ensure that PNC is updated to record that.

16.8 Retention of papers to prosecute following non-compliance

16.8.1 Once a Conditional Caution has been authorised in any case, the MG5 (or any other record of the decision), the Inspectors finding as to any exceptional circumstances, the Authority to give a Conditional Caution and confirmed MG14 will be retained by the police pending completion of the conditions. This material will be used in the event of a prosecution resulting from any non-compliance. Any information concerning the personal details of victims and their views must not be included in any information provided to the offender or their legal representative. In the event of a prosecution for non-compliance the police will only be requested to provide witness statements following a not guilty plea and case management hearing where the issues in dispute in the case have been identified.

17. Commencement

17.1 This Guidance will come into effect in England and Wales on 8th April 2013.

Annex A: Either Way offences

Either Way offences having a sentencing starting point in a magistrates' court at custody or high level community order

Assault occasioning actual bodily harm—S.47 OAPA 1861

Wounding or causing grievous bodily harm—S.20 OAPA 1861

Possession of an offensive weapon—S.1 Prevention of Crime Act 1953

Possession of a bladed article—S.139 Criminal Justice Act 1988

Harassment—putting people in fear of violence—S.4 Protection from Harassment Act 1977

Stalking—involving violence or serious alarm or distress—S.4A Protection from Harassment Act 1977

Violent Disorder—S.2 Public Order Act 1986

Affray—S.3 POA 1986

Cruelty to a child—S.1 Children and Young Persons Act 1933

Sexual Assault—S.3 & S.7 Sexual Offences Act 2003

Witness Intimidation—S.51 Criminal Justice and Public Order Act 1994

Either Way offences routinely dealt with at the Crown Court

Arson—S.1 and S.4 Criminal Damage Act 1971

Assault occasioning actual bodily harm (including Racial or religiously aggravated)—S.47 OAPA 1863

Assault W/I to resist arrest—S.38 OAPA 1861

Bladed article/offensive weapon, possession of—S.139 Criminal Justice Act 1988

Burglary (dwelling)—S.9 Theft Act 1968

Burglary (non dwelling)—S.9 Theft Act 1968

Child prostitution and pornography—Sexual Offences Act 2003

Criminal damage (including Racial or religiously aggravated) over £5,000—Criminal Damage Act 1971

Cruelty to a child—S.1 Children and Young Persons Act 1933

Drugs—Class A—Possession—Misuse of Drugs Act 1971

Drugs—Class A Produce—Supply—Misuse of Drugs Act 1971

Drugs—Class B & C—supply posses w/I to supply Misuse of Drugs Act 1971

Drugs—Cultivation of cannabis—Misuse of Drugs Act 1971

Exploitation of prostitution—S.33A, S.52–53 Sexual Offences Act 2003

Firearm, carrying in a public place—S.19 Firearms Act 1968

Fraud (banking & insurance)—Fraud Act 2006

Fraud (confidence)—Fraud Act 2006

Fraud (possessing, making or supplying articles for use)—Fraud Act 2006

Grievous bodily harm/unlawful wounding (including Racial or religiously aggravated) S.20 OAPA 1861

Handling Stolen Goods S.22—Theft Act 1968

Harassment (including Racial or religiously aggravated)—Protection from Harassment Act 1977

Human Trafficking Offences—S.57–59 Sexual Offences Act 2003, S.4 Asylum and Immigration Act 2004, S.71 Coroners and Justice Act 2009

Identity documents—possess—Part 1 S.1–5 Forgery Act 1861, Identity Cards Act 2006, Identity Documents Act 2010

Indecent Photographs of children—Protection of Children Act 1978

Keeping a brothel used for prostitution—Sexual Offences Act 1956

Protective Order—Breach of Public order Act s.2 violent disorder

Sexual Assault—S.3 & S.7 Sexual Offences Act 2003

Theft—Theft Act 1968

Threats to Kill—S.16 OAPA 1861

Voyeurism—S.67 Sexual Offences Act 2003

Witness intimidation—S.51 Criminal Justice and Public Order Act 1994

Cause death by Careless driving—S.2B Road Traffic Act 1988

Cause death by driving unlicensed/disqualified—S.3ZB Road Traffic Act 1988

Dangerous Driving—S.2A Road Traffic Act 1988

1.7.18   Code C—17 Testing Persons for the Presence of Specified Class A Drugs

(a) Action

17.1 This section of Code C applies only in selected police stations in police areas where the provisions for drug testing under section 63B of PACE (as amended by section 5 of the Criminal Justice Act 2003 and section 7 of the Drugs Act 2005) are in force and in respect of which the Secretary of State has given a notification to the relevant chief officer of police that arrangements for the taking of samples have been made. Such a notification will cover either a police area as a whole or particular stations within a police area. The notification indicates whether the testing applies to those arrested or charged or under the age of 18 as the case may be and testing can only take place in respect of the persons so indicated in the notification. Testing cannot be carried out unless the relevant notification has been given and has not been withdrawn. See *Note 17F*

17.2 A sample of urine or a non-intimate sample may be taken from a person in police detention for the purpose of ascertaining whether they have any specified Class A drug in their body only where they have been brought before the custody officer and:

(a) either the arrest condition, see *paragraph 17.3*, or the charge condition, see *paragraph 17.4* is met;

(b) the age condition see *paragraph 17.5*, is met;

(c) the notification condition is met in relation to the arrest condition, the charge condition, or the age condition, as the case may be. (Testing on charge and/or arrest must be specifically provided for in the notification for the power to apply. In addition, the fact that testing of under 18s is authorised must be expressly provided for in the notification before the power to test such persons applies.). See *paragraph 17.1*; and

(d) a police officer has requested the person concerned to give the sample (the request condition).

17.3 The arrest condition is met where the detainee:

(a) has been arrested for a trigger offence, but not charged with that offence; or

(b) has been arrested for any other offence but not charged with that offence and a police officer of inspector rank or above, who has reasonable grounds for suspecting that their misuse of any specified Class A drug caused or contributed to the offence, has authorised the sample to be taken.

17.4 The charge condition is met where the detainee:

(a) has been charged with a trigger offence, or

(b) has been charged with any other offence and a police officer of inspector rank or above, who has reasonable grounds for suspecting that the detainee's misuse of any specified Class A drug caused or contributed to the offence, has authorised the sample to be taken.

17.5 The age condition is met where:

(a) in the case of a detainee who has been arrested but not charged as in *paragraph 17.3*, they are aged 18 or over;

(b) in the case of a detainee who has been charged as in *paragraph 17.4*, they are aged 14 or over.

17.6 Before requesting a sample from the person concerned, an officer must:

(a) inform them that the purpose of taking the sample is for drug testing under PACE. This is to ascertain whether they have a specified Class A drug present in their body;

(b) warn them that if, when so requested, they fail without good cause to provide a sample they may be liable to prosecution;

(c) where the taking of the sample has been authorised by an inspector or above in accordance with *paragraph 17.3(b)* or *17.4(b)* above, inform them that the authorisation has been given and the grounds for giving it;

(d) remind them of the following rights, which may be exercised at any stage during the period in custody:

(i) the right to have someone informed of their arrest [see *section 5*];

(ii) the right to consult privately with a solicitor and that free independent legal advice is available [see *section 6*]; and

(iii) the right to consult these Codes of Practice [see *section 3*].

17.7 In the case of a person who has not attained the age specified in section 63B(5A) of PACE—

(a) the making of the request for a sample under *paragraph 17.2(d)* above;

(b) the giving of the warning and the information under *paragraph 17.6* above; and

(c) the taking of the sample may not take place except in the presence of an appropriate adult.

17.8 Authorisation by an officer of the rank of inspector or above within *paragraph 17.3(b)* or *17.4(b)* may be given orally or in writing but, if it is given orally, it must be confirmed in writing as soon as practicable.

17.9 If a sample is taken from a detainee who has been arrested for an offence but not charged with that offence as in *paragraph 17.3*, no further sample may be taken during the same continuous period of detention. If during that same period the charge condition is also met in respect of that detainee, the sample which has been taken shall be treated as being taken by virtue of the charge condition, see *paragraph 17.4*, being met.

17.10 A detainee from whom a sample may be taken may be detained for up to six hours from the time of charge if the custody officer reasonably believes the detention is necessary to enable a sample to be taken. Where the arrest condition is met, a detainee whom the custody officer has decided to release on bail without charge may continue to be detained, but not beyond 24 hours from the relevant time (as defined in section 41(2) of PACE), to enable a sample to be taken.

17.11 A detainee in respect of whom the arrest condition is met, but not the charge condition, see *paragraphs 17.3* and *17.4*, and whose release would be required before a sample can be taken had they not continued to be detained as a result of being arrested for a further offence which does not satisfy the arrest condition, may have a sample taken at any time within 24 hours after the arrest for the offence that satisfies the arrest condition.

(b) Documentation

17.12 The following must be recorded in the custody record:
   (a) if a sample is taken following authorisation by an officer of the rank of inspector or above, the authorisation and the grounds for suspicion;
   (b) the giving of a warning of the consequences of failure to provide a sample;
   (c) the time at which the sample was given; and
   (d) the time of charge or, where the arrest condition is being relied upon, the time of arrest and, where applicable, the fact that a sample taken after arrest but before charge is to be treated as being taken by virtue of the charge condition, where that is met in the same period of continuous detention. See *paragraph 17.9*.

(c) General

17.13 A sample may only be taken by a prescribed person.

17.14 Force may not be used to take any sample for the purpose of drug testing.

17.15 The terms 'Class A drug' and 'misuse' have the same meanings as in the Misuse of Drugs Act 1971. 'Specified' (in relation to a Class A drug) and 'trigger offence' have the same meanings as in Part III of the Criminal Justice and Court Services Act 2000.

17.16 Any sample taken:
   (a) may not be used for any purpose other than to ascertain whether the person concerned has a specified Class A drug present in his body; and
   (b) can be disposed of as clinical waste unless it is to be sent for further analysis in cases where the test result is disputed at the point when the result is known, including on the basis that medication has been taken, or for quality assurance purposes.

(d) Assessment of misuse of drugs

17.17 Under the provisions of Part 3 of the Drugs Act 2005, where a detainee has tested positive for a specified Class A drug under section 63B of PACE a police officer may, at any time before the person's release from the police station, impose a requirement on the detainee to attend an initial assessment of their drug misuse by a suitably qualified person and to remain for its duration. Where such a requirement is imposed, the officer must, at the same time, impose a second requirement on the detainee to attend and remain for a follow-up assessment. The officer must inform the detainee that the second requirement will cease to have effect if, at the initial assessment they are informed that a follow-up assessment is not necessary These requirements may only be imposed on a person if:

(a) they have reached the age of 18

(b) notification has been given by the Secretary of State to the relevant chief officer of police that arrangements for conducting initial and follow-up assessments have been made for those from whom samples for testing have been taken at the police station where the detainee is in custody.

17.18 When imposing a requirement to attend an initial assessment and a follow-up assessment the police officer must:

(a) inform the person of the time and place at which the initial assessment is to take place;

(b) explain that this information will be confirmed in writing; and

(c) warn the person that they may be liable to prosecution if they fail without good cause to attend the initial assessment and remain for its duration and if they fail to attend the follow-up assessment and remain for its duration (if so required).

17.19 Where a police officer has imposed a requirement to attend an initial assessment and a follow-up assessment in accordance with *paragraph 17.17*, he must, before the person is released from detention, give the person notice in writing which:

(a) confirms their requirement to attend and remain for the duration of the assessments; and

(b) confirms the information and repeats the warning referred to in *paragraph 17.18*.

17.20 The following must be recorded in the custody record:

(a) that the requirement to attend an initial assessment and a follow-up assessment has been imposed; and

(b) the information, explanation, warning and notice given in accordance with *paragraphs 17.17* and *17.19*.

17.21 Where a notice is given in accordance with *paragraph 17.19*, a police officer can give the person a further notice in writing which informs the person of any change to the time or place at which the initial assessment is to take place and which repeats the warning referred to in *paragraph 17.18(c)*.

17.22 Part 3 of the Drugs Act 2005 also requires police officers to have regard to any guidance issued by the Secretary of State in respect of the assessment provisions.

1.7.18.1

KEYNOTE

The power to take samples is subject to notification by the Secretary of State that appropriate arrangements for the taking of samples have been made for the police area as a whole or for the particular police station concerned for whichever of the following is specified in the notification: persons in respect of whom the arrest condition is met; persons in respect of whom the charge condition is met; and/or persons who have not attained the age of 18.

A sample has to be sufficient and suitable. A sufficient sample is sufficient in quantity and quality to enable drug-testing analysis to take place. A suitable sample is one which by its nature is suitable for a particular form of drug analysis. It can only be taken by a prescribed person as defined in regulations made by the Secretary of State under s. 63B(6) of the Police and Criminal Evidence Act 1984. The regulations are currently contained in the Police and Criminal Evidence Act 1984 (Drug Testing Persons in Police Detention) (Prescribed Persons) Regulations 2001 (SI 2001/2645). Samples, and the information derived from them, may not subsequently be used in the investigation of any offence or in evidence against the persons from whom they were taken.

When warning a person who is asked to provide a urine or non-intimate sample in accordance with para. 17.6(b), the following form of words may be used:

You do not have to provide a sample, but I must warn you that if you fail or refuse without good cause to do so, you will commit an offence for which you may be imprisoned, or fined, or both.

Where the Welsh language is appropriate, the following form of words may be used:

Does dim rhaid i chi roi sampl, ond mae'n rhaid i mi eich rhybuddio y byddwch chi'n cyflawni trosedd os byddwch chi'n methu neu yn gwrthod gwneud hynny heb reswm da, ac y gellir, oherwydd hynny, eich carcharu, eich dirwyo, neu'r ddau.

The trigger offences referred to in the section are:

1. Offences under the following provisions of the Theft Act 1968:

    section 1   (theft)
    section 8   (robbery)
    section 9   (burglary)
    section 10   (aggravated burglary)
    section 12   (taking a motor vehicle or other conveyance without authority)
    section 12A   (aggravated vehicle-taking)
    section 22   (handling stolen goods)
    section 25   (going equipped for stealing, etc.)

2. Offences under the following provisions of the Misuse of Drugs Act 1971, if committed in respect of a specified Class A drug:

    section 4   (restriction on production and supply of controlled drugs)
    section 5(2)   (possession of a controlled drug)
    section 5(3)   (possession of a controlled drug with intent to supply)

3. Offences under the following provisions of the Fraud Act 2006:

    section 1   (fraud)
    section 6   (possession, etc. of articles for use in frauds)
    section 7   (making or supplying articles for use in frauds)

3A. An offence under s. 1(1) of the Criminal Attempts Act 1981 if committed in respect of an offence under:
    (a) any of the following provisions of the Theft Act 1968:

    section 1   (theft)
    section 8   (robbery)
    section 9   (burglary)
    section 22   (handling stolen goods)

    (b) section 1 of the Fraud Act 2006 (fraud)

4. Offences under the following provisions of the Vagrancy Act 1824:

    section 3   (begging)
    section 4   (persistent begging)

For the purposes of needing the presence of an appropriate adult for Code C, para. 17.7, an appropriate adult means the person's:

(a) parent or guardian or, if they are in the care of a local authority or voluntary organisation, a person representing that authority or organisation; or

(b) a social worker of a local authority; or

(c) if no person falling within (a) or (b) above is available, any responsible person aged 18 or over who is not:
  • employed by the police;
  • under the direction or control of the chief officer of police force;
  • or a person who provides services under contractual arrangements (but without being employed by the chief officer of a police force), to assist that force in relation to the discharge of its chief officer's functions whether or not they are on duty at the time.

If the person wishing to act as appropriate adult appears to be under 17 they should be treated as that age and not be allowed to act as an appropriate adult unless they can show themselves to be over 18.

Code C—Annex A: Intimate and Strip Searches

A Intimate search

1. An intimate search consists of the physical examination of a person's body orifices other than the mouth. The intrusive nature of such searches means the actual and potential risks associated with intimate searches must never be underestimated.

(a) Action

2. Body orifices other than the mouth may be searched only:
   (a) if authorised by an officer of inspector rank or above who has reasonable grounds for believing that the person may have concealed on themselves:
       (i) anything which they could and might use to cause physical injury to themselves or others at the station; or
       (ii) a Class A drug which they intended to supply to another or to export;
       (iii) and the officer has reasonable grounds for believing that an intimate search is the only means of removing those items; and
   (b) if the search is under *paragraph 2(a)(ii)* (a drug offence search), the detainee's appropriate consent has been given in writing.

2A. Before the search begins, a police officer or designated detention officer, must tell the detainee:—
   (a) that the authority to carry out the search has been given;
   (b) the grounds for giving the authorisation and for believing that the article cannot be removed without an intimate search.

2B. Before a detainee is asked to give appropriate consent to a search under *paragraph 2(a)(ii)* (a drug offence search) they must be warned that if they refuse without good cause their refusal may harm their case if it comes to trial. This warning may be given by a police officer or member of police staff. In the case of juveniles, or vulnerable suspects, the seeking and giving of consent must take place in the presence of the appropriate adult. A juvenile's consent is only valid if their parent's or guardian's consent is also obtained unless the juvenile is under 14, when their parent's or guardian's consent is sufficient in its own right. A detainee who is not legally represented must be reminded of their entitlement to have free legal advice, see Code C, *paragraph 6.5*, and the reminder noted in the custody record.

3. An intimate search may only be carried out by a registered medical practitioner or registered nurse, unless an officer of at least inspector rank considers this is not practicable and the search is to take place under *paragraph 2(a)(i)*, in which case a police officer may carry out the search.

3A. Any proposal for a search under *paragraph 2(a)(i)* to be carried out by someone other than a registered medical practitioner or registered nurse must only be considered as a last resort and when the authorising officer is satisfied the risks associated with allowing the item to remain with the detainee outweigh the risks associated with removing it.

4. An intimate search under:
   • *paragraph 2(a)(i)* may take place only at a hospital, surgery, other medical premises or police station;
   • *paragraph 2(a)(ii)* may take place only at a hospital, surgery or other medical premises and must be carried out by a registered medical practitioner or a registered nurse.

5. An intimate search at a police station of a juvenile or vulnerable person may take place only in the presence of an appropriate adult of the same sex (see *Annex L*), unless the detainee specifically requests a particular adult of the opposite sex who is readily available. In the case of a juvenile, the search may take place in the absence of the appropriate adult only if the juvenile signifies in the presence of the appropriate adult they do not want the adult present during

the search and the adult agrees. A record shall be made of the juvenile's decision and signed by the appropriate adult.

6. When an intimate search under *paragraph 2(a)(i)* is carried out by a police officer, the officer must be of the same sex as the detainee (see *Annex L*). A minimum of two people, other than the detainee, must be present during the search. Subject to *paragraph 5*, no person of the opposite sex who is not a medical practitioner or nurse shall be present, nor shall anyone whose presence is unnecessary. The search shall be conducted with proper regard to the dignity, sensitivity and vulnerability of the detainee including in particular, their health, hygiene and welfare needs to which *paragraphs 9.3A* and *9.3B* apply.

(b) Documentation

7. In the case of an intimate search, the following shall be recorded as soon as practicable in the detainee's custody record:
   (a) for searches under *paragraphs 2(a)(i)* and *(ii)*;
      • the authorisation to carry out the search;
      • the grounds for giving the authorisation;
      • the grounds for believing the article could not be removed without an intimate search;
      • which parts of the detainee's body were searched;
      • who carried out the search;
      • who was present;
      • the result.
   (b) for searches under *paragraph 2(a)(ii)*:
      • the giving of the warning required by *paragraph 2B*;
      • the fact that the appropriate consent was given or (as the case may be) refused, and if refused, the reason given for the refusal (if any).

8. If an intimate search is carried out by a police officer, the reason why it was impracticable for a registered medical practitioner or registered nurse to conduct it must be recorded.

1.7.19.1

KEYNOTE

An intimate search can only be authorised in relation to a person who has been arrested and is in police detention (s. 55(1)) (**see para. 1.7.5.2**). An officer may give an authorisation under subsection (1) orally or in writing but, if he/she gives it orally, he/she shall confirm it in writing as soon as practicable (s. 55(3)).

Before authorising any intimate search, the authorising officer must make every reasonable effort to persuade the detainee to hand the article over without a search. If the detainee agrees, a registered medical practitioner or registered nurse should whenever possible be asked to assess the risks involved and, if necessary, attend to assist the detainee.

If the detainee does not agree to hand the article over without a search, the authorising officer must carefully review all the relevant factors before authorising an intimate search. In particular, the officer must consider whether the grounds for believing that an article may be concealed are reasonable.

If authority is given for a search for anything which the detained person could and might use to cause physical injury to him/herself or others at the station, a registered medical practitioner or registered nurse shall be consulted whenever possible. The presumption should be that the search will be conducted by the registered medical practitioner or registered nurse and the authorising officer must make every reasonable effort to persuade the detainee to allow the medical practitioner or nurse to conduct the search. A constable should only be authorised to carry out a search as a last resort and when all other approaches have failed. In these circumstances, the authorising officer must be satisfied that the detainee might use the article to cause physical injury to him/herself and/or others at the station and the physical injury likely to be caused is sufficiently severe to justify authorising a constable to carry out the search. If an officer has any doubts whether to authorise an intimate search by a constable, the officer should seek advice from an officer of superintendent rank or above. Annex L should be referred to for guidance when establishing the gender of persons for the purpose of searching.

The following form of words should be used when asking a detained person to consent to an intimate drug offence search:

You do not have to allow yourself to be searched, but I must warn you that if you refuse without good cause, your refusal may harm your case if it comes to trial.

Where the use of the Welsh language is appropriate, the following form of words may be used:

Nid oes rhaid i chi roi caniatâd i gael eich archwilio, ond mae'n rhaid i mi eich rhybuddio os gwrthodwch heb reswm da, y gallai eich penderfyniad i wrthod wneud niwed i'ch achos pe bai'n dod gerbron llys.

1.7.19.2

B Strip search

9. A strip search is a search involving the removal of more than outer clothing. In this Code, outer clothing includes shoes and socks.

(a) Action

10. A strip search may take place only if it is considered necessary to remove an article which a detainee would not be allowed to keep and the officer reasonably considers the detainee might have concealed such an article. Strip searches shall not be routinely carried out if there is no reason to consider that articles are concealed.

The conduct of strip searches

11. When strip searches are conducted:
    (a) a police officer carrying out a strip search must be the same sex as the detainee (see *Annex L*);
    (b) the search shall take place in an area where the detainee cannot be seen by anyone who does not need to be present, nor by a member of the opposite sex (see *Annex L*) except an appropriate adult who has been specifically requested by the detainee;
    (c) except in cases of urgency, where there is risk of serious harm to the detainee or to others, whenever a strip search involves exposure of intimate body parts, there must be at least two people present other than the detainee, and if the search is of a juvenile or vulnerable person, one of the people must be the appropriate adult. Except in urgent cases as above, a search of a juvenile may take place in the absence of the appropriate adult only if the juvenile signifies in the presence of the appropriate adult that they do not want the appropriate adult to be present during the search and the appropriate adult agrees. A record shall be made of the juvenile's decision and signed by the appropriate adult. The presence of more than two people, other than an appropriate adult, shall be permitted only in the most exceptional circumstances;
    (d) the search shall be conducted with proper regard to the dignity, sensitivity and vulnerability of the detainee in these circumstances, including in particular, their health, hygiene and welfare needs to which *paragraphs 9.3A* and *9.3B* apply. Every reasonable effort shall be made to secure the detainee's co-operation, maintain their dignity and minimise embarrassment. Detainees who are searched shall not normally be required to remove all their clothes at the same time, e.g. a person should be allowed to remove clothing above the waist and redress before removing further clothing;
    (e) if necessary to assist the search, the detainee may be required to hold their arms in the air or to stand with their legs apart and bend forward so a visual examination may be made of the genital and anal areas provided no physical contact is made with any body orifice;
    (f) if articles are found, the detainee shall be asked to hand them over. If articles are found within any body orifice other than the mouth, and the detainee refuses to hand them over, their removal would constitute an intimate search, which must be carried out as in *Part A*;

(g) a strip search shall be conducted as quickly as possible, and the detainee allowed to dress as soon as the procedure is complete.

(b) Documentation

12. A record shall be made on the custody record of a strip search including the reason it was considered necessary, those present and any result.

KEYNOTE

Annex A, para. 11 applies to all the powers given to custody officers under s. 54 of the 1984 Act, including the power to remove and seize clothing under s. 54(4). In *Davies v Chief Constable of Merseyside* [2015] EWCA Civ 114 the court held that Annex A, para. 11 applied to any strip search, not just those strip searches carried out in compliance with para. 10. For example it would apply where the custody officer determines that a detained person is a suicide risk and orders the removal of their clothing under s. 54 so they can be dressed in a safety gown.

The Codes do not preclude officers of the opposite sex being indirectly involved in the strip search process. In the case of *PD (by her mother and litigation friend ZD) v Chief Constable of Merseyside Police* [2015] EWCA Civ 114 a 14-year-old, female detainee was flagged as a suicide risk by the custody officer; as a result of this she was ordered to have her clothing removed, as part of a safety procedure to reduce risk factors. Two female officers, and two male officers, took the claimant into a private room. The court found that para 11(b) of Annex A allows a male officer to be involved in the management of the detained person. The essential requirement was that the removal should take place in an area where no one who was not immediately involved, and no male officer, could observe the detainee. In this case the two male officers left the cell and stayed in the corridor outside while the 14-year-old was undressed. The cell door was left ajar for security reasons but a safety blanket was used to protect the detainee's dignity.

Code C—Annex B: Delay in Notifying Arrest or Allowing Access to Legal Advice

A Persons detained under PACE

1. The exercise of the rights in *Section 5* or *Section 6*, or both, may be delayed if the person is in police detention, as in PACE, section 118(2), in connection with an indictable offence, has not yet been charged with an offence and an officer of superintendent rank or above, or inspector rank or above only for the rights in *Section 5*, has reasonable grounds for believing their exercise will:
   (i) lead to:
      • interference with, or harm to, evidence connected with an indictable offence; or
      • interference with, or physical harm to, other people; or
   (ii) lead to alerting other people suspected of having committed an indictable offence but not yet arrested for it; or
   (iii) hinder the recovery of property obtained in consequence of the commission of such an offence.
2. These rights may also be delayed if the officer has reasonable grounds to believe that:
   (i) the person detained for an indictable offence has benefited from their criminal conduct (decided in accordance with Part 2 of the Proceeds of Crime Act 2002); and
   (ii) the recovery of the value of the property constituting that benefit will be hindered by the exercise of either right.
3. Authority to delay a detainee's right to consult privately with a solicitor may be given only if the authorising officer has reasonable grounds to believe the solicitor the detainee wants to consult will, inadvertently or otherwise, pass on a message from the detainee or act in some

other way which will have any of the consequences specified under *paragraphs 1* or *2*. In these circumstances, the detainee must be allowed to choose another solicitor.

4. If the detainee wishes to see a solicitor, access to that solicitor may not be delayed on the grounds they might advise the detainee not to answer questions or the solicitor was initially asked to attend the police station by someone else. In the latter case, the detainee must be told the solicitor has come to the police station at another person's request, and must be asked to sign the custody record to signify whether they want to see the solicitor.

5. The fact the grounds for delaying notification of arrest may be satisfied does not automatically mean the grounds for delaying access to legal advice will also be satisfied.

6. These rights may be delayed only for as long as grounds exist and in no case beyond 36 hours after the relevant time as in PACE, section 41. If the grounds cease to apply within this time, the detainee must, as soon as practicable, be asked if they want to exercise either right, the custody record must be noted accordingly, and action taken in accordance with the relevant section of the Code.

7. A detained person must be permitted to consult a solicitor for a reasonable time before any court hearing.

B Not used

C Documentation

13. The grounds for action under this Annex shall be recorded and the detainee informed of them as soon as practicable.

14. Any reply given by a detainee under *paragraphs 6* or *11* must be recorded and the detainee asked to endorse the record in relation to whether they want to receive legal advice at this point.

D Cautions and special warnings

15. When a suspect detained at a police station is interviewed during any period for which access to legal advice has been delayed under this Annex, the court or jury may not draw adverse inferences from their silence.

1.7.20.1

KEYNOTE

Even if Annex B applies in the case of a juvenile, or a vulnerable person, action to inform the appropriate adult and the person responsible for a juvenile's welfare, if that is a different person, must nevertheless be taken as in paras 3.13 and 3.15. Similarly, for detained persons who are citizens of independent Commonwealth countries or foreign nationals the exercise of the rights in Code C, s. 7 may not be interfered with.

In cases where the person is detained under the Terrorism Act 2000 an officer of the rank of superintendent or above may delay the exercise of either right or both if he/she has reasonable grounds for believing that the exercise of the right will lead to any of the consequences of:

- interference with or harm to evidence of a serious offence;
- interference with or physical injury to any person;
- the alerting of persons who are suspected of having committed a serious offence but who have not been arrested for it;
- the hindering of the recovery of property obtained as a result of a serious offence or in respect of which a forfeiture order could be made under s. 23;
- interference with the gathering of information about the commission, preparation or instigation of acts of terrorism;
- the alerting of a person and thereby making it more difficult to prevent an act of terrorism;

- the alerting of a person and thereby making it more difficult to secure a person's apprehension, prosecution or conviction in connection with the commission, preparation or instigation of an act of terrorism;
- the detained person having benefited from his/her criminal conduct, and the recovery of the value of the property constituting the benefit will be hindered by informing the named person of the detained person's detention or access to legal advice. For these purposes whether a person has benefited from his/her criminal conduct is to be decided in accordance with part 2 of the Proceeds of Crime Act 2002. Briefly, criminal conduct is conduct which constitutes an offence in England and Wales, or would constitute such an offence if it occurred in England and Wales. A person benefits from conduct if he/she obtains property as a result of or in connection with the conduct (Code H, Annex B, paras 1 and 2).

When considering the delay of access to a solicitor the authorising officer must bear in mind that access to a solicitor is 'a fundamental right of a citizen' (*R* v *Samuel* [1988] QB 615). The authorising officer must actually believe that by allowing access to the solicitor he/she will intentionally or inadvertently alert other suspects.

Occasions where delay will be authorised in such circumstances will be rare and only when it can be shown that the suspect is capable of misleading that particular solicitor and there is more than a substantial risk that the suspect will succeed in causing information to be conveyed which will lead to one or more of the specified consequences. In deciding whether such an interview will be admissible the court will consider how reliable it is and will consider how the refusal to allow that particular detained person access to a solicitor affected his/her decision to make a confession. One such case where the confession was excluded is *R* v *Sanusi* [1992] Crim LR 43, where a person from another country was denied access to a solicitor and the court held that his right to advice was particularly significant due to his lack of familiarity with police procedures.

Code C—Annex C: Restriction on Drawing Adverse Inferences from Silence and Terms of the Caution when the Restriction Applies [see chapter 1.9]

Code C—Annex D: Written Statements Under Caution [see chapter 1.9]

1.7.21 Code C—Annex E: Summary of Provisions Relating to Vulnerable Persons

1. If at any time, an officer has reason to suspect that a person of any age may be vulnerable (see *paragraph 1.13(d)*), in the absence of clear evidence to dispel that suspicion that person shall be treated as such for the purposes of this Code and to establish whether any such reason may exist in relation to a person suspected of committing an offence (see *paragraph 10.1*), the custody officer.

   In the case of a detained person, or the officer investigating the offence in the case of a person who has not been arrested or detained, shall take, or cause to be taken, (see *paragraph 3.5*) the following action:

   (a) reasonable enquiries shall be made to ascertain what information is available that is relevant to any of the factors described in *paragraph 1.13(d)* as indicating that the person may be vulnerable might apply;

   (b) a record shall be made describing whether any of those factors appear to apply and provide any reason to suspect that the person may be vulnerable or (as the case may be) may not be vulnerable; and

   (c) the record mentioned in sub-paragraph (b) shall be made available to be taken into account by police officers, police staff and any others who, in accordance with the provisions of this or any other Code, are entitled to communicate with the person in question. This would include any solicitor, appropriate adult and health care professional and is particularly relevant to communication by telephone or by means of a live link (see *paragraphs 12.9A (interviews), 13.12 (interpretation), and 15.3C, 15.11A, 15.11B, 15.11C and 15.11D (reviews and extension of detention)).*

2. In the case of a person who is vulnerable, 'the appropriate adult' means:

   (i) a relative, guardian or other person responsible for their care or custody;

   (ii) someone experienced in dealing with vulnerable persons but who is not:

   ~ a police officer;

   ~ employed by the police;

   ~ under the direction or control of the chief officer of a police force;

   ~ a person who provides services under contractual arrangements (but without being employed by the chief officer of a police force), to assist that force in relation to the discharge of its chief officer's functions, whether or not they are on duty at the time.

   (iii) failing these, some other responsible adult aged 18 or over who is other than a person described in the bullet points in *sub-paragraph (ii)* above.

   See *paragraph 1.7(b)*.

2A The role of the appropriate adult is to safeguard the rights, entitlements and welfare of 'vulnerable persons' (see *paragraph 1*) to whom the provisions of this and any other Code of Practice apply. For this reason, the appropriate adult is expected, amongst other things, to:

   • support, advise and assist them when, in accordance with this Code or any other Code of Practice, they are given or asked to provide information or participate in any procedure;

   • observe whether the police are acting properly and fairly to respect their rights and entitlements, and inform an officer of the rank of inspector or above if they consider that they are not;

   • assist them to communicate with the police whilst respecting their right to say nothing unless they want to as set out in the terms of the caution (see *paragraphs 10.5* and *10.6*); and

   • help them understand their rights and ensure that those rights are protected and respected (see *paragraphs 3.15, 3.17, 6.5A* and *11.17*).

   See *paragraph 1.7A*.

3. If the custody officer authorises the detention of a vulnerable person, the custody officer must as soon as practicable inform the appropriate adult of the grounds for detention and the person's whereabouts, and ask the adult to come to the police station to see them. If the appropriate adult:

   • is already at the station when information is given as in *paragraphs 3.1* to *3.5* the information must be given in their presence;

   • is not at the station when the provisions of *paragraph 3.1* to *3.5* are complied with these provisions must be complied with again in their presence once they arrive.

   See *paragraphs 3.15* to *3.17*.

4. If the appropriate adult, having been informed of the right to legal advice, considers legal advice should be taken, the provisions of *section 6* apply as if the vulnerable person had requested access to legal advice. See *paragraphs 3.19, 6.5A*.

5. The custody officer must make sure a person receives appropriate clinical attention as soon as reasonably practicable if the person appears to be suffering from a mental disorder or in urgent cases immediately call the nearest appropriate healthcare professional or an ambulance. See Code C *paragraphs 3.16, 9.5* and *9.6* which apply when a person is detained under the Mental Health Act 1983, sections 135 and 136, as amended by the Policing and Crime Act 2017.

6. Not used.

7. If a vulnerable person is cautioned in the absence of the appropriate adult, the caution must be repeated in the appropriate adult's presence. See *paragraph 10.12*.

8. A vulnerable person must not be interviewed or asked to provide or sign a written statement in the absence of the appropriate adult unless the provisions of *paragraphs 11.1* or *11.18* to *11.20* apply. Questioning in these circumstances may not continue in the absence of the appropriate adult once sufficient information to avert the risk has been obtained. A record shall

be made of the grounds for any decision to begin an interview in these circumstances. See *paragraphs 11.1, 11.15* and *11.18* to *11.20*.

9. If the appropriate adult is present at an interview, they shall be informed they are not expected to act simply as an observer and the purposes of their presence are to:
   - advise the interviewee;
   - observe whether or not the interview is being conducted properly and fairly;
   - facilitate communication with the interviewee.

   See *paragraph 11.17*.

10. If the detention of a vulnerable person is reviewed by a review officer or a superintendent, the appropriate adult must, if available at the time, be given an opportunity to make representations to the officer about the need for continuing detention. See *paragraph 15.3*.

11. If the custody officer charges a vulnerable person with an offence or takes such other action as is appropriate when there is sufficient evidence for a prosecution this must be carried out in the presence of the appropriate adult if they are at the police station. A copy of the written notice embodying any charge must also be given to the appropriate adult. See *paragraphs 16.1* to *16.4A*.

12. An intimate or strip search of a vulnerable person may take place only in the presence of the appropriate adult of the same sex, unless the detainee specifically requests the presence of a particular adult of the opposite sex. A strip search may take place in the absence of an appropriate adult only in cases of urgency when there is a risk of serious harm to the detainee or others. See *Annex A, paragraphs 5* and *11(c)*.

13. Particular care must be taken when deciding whether to use any form of approved restraints on a mentally disordered or otherwise mentally vulnerable person in a locked cell. See *paragraph 8.2*.

1.7.21.1

KEYNOTE

The purpose of the provisions at paras 3.19 and 6.5A (access to legal advice) is to protect the rights of a vulnerable person who does not understand the significance of what is said to them. A vulnerable person should always be given an opportunity, when an appropriate adult is called to the police station, to consult privately with a solicitor in the absence of the appropriate adult if they want.

Although vulnerable persons are often capable of providing reliable evidence, they may, without knowing or wanting to do so, be particularly prone in certain circumstances to provide information that may be unreliable, misleading or self-incriminating. Special care should always be taken when questioning such a person, and the appropriate adult should be involved if there is any doubt about a person's mental state or capacity. Because of the risk of unreliable evidence, it is important to obtain corroboration of any facts admitted whenever possible. Because of the risks referred to above, which the presence of the appropriate adult is intended to minimise, officers of superintendent rank or above should exercise their discretion to authorise the commencement of an interview in the appropriate adult's absence only in exceptional cases, if it is necessary to avert one or more of the specified risks in para. 11.1. See paras 11.1 and 11.18 to 11.20. There is no requirement for an appropriate adult to be present if a person is detained under s. 136 of the Mental Health Act 1983 for assessment.

For the purposes of inquiries as to whether a suspect may be vulnerable, examples of relevant information that may be available include:

- the behaviour of the adult or juvenile;
- the mental health and capacity of the adult or juvenile;
- what the adult or juvenile says about themselves;
- information from relatives and friends of the adult or juvenile;
- information from police officers and staff and from police records;
- information from health and social care (including liaison and diversion services) and other professionals who know, or have had previous contact with, the individual and may be able to contribute to assessing

their need for help and support from an appropriate adult. This includes contacts and assessments arranged by the police or at the request of the individual or (as applicable) their appropriate adult or solicitor.

The Mental Health Act 1983 Code of Practice at page 26 describes the range of clinically recognised conditions which can fall with the meaning of mental disorder for the purpose of para. 1.13(d). The Code is published at: <https://www.gov.uk/government/publications/code-of-practice-mental-health-act-1983>.

When a person is under the influence of drink and/or drugs, it is not intended that they are to be treated as vulnerable and requiring an appropriate adult for the purpose of Annex E, para. 1 unless other information indicates that any of the factors described in para. 1.13(d) may apply to that person. When the person has recovered from the effects of drink and/or drugs, they should be reassessed in accordance with Annex E, para. 1. See para. 15.4A for application to live link.

1.7.22 | **Code C—Annex F: *Not used* [see Code C, section 7]**

1.7.23 | **Code C—Annex G: Fitness to be Interviewed**

1. This Annex contains general guidance to help police officers and healthcare professionals assess whether a detainee might be at risk in an interview.
2. A detainee may be at risk in a interview if it is considered that:
   (a) conducting the interview could significantly harm the detainee's physical or mental state;
   (b) anything the detainee says in the interview about their involvement or suspected involvement in the offence about which they are being interviewed **might** be considered unreliable in subsequent court proceedings because of their physical or mental state.
3. In assessing whether the detainee should be interviewed, the following must be considered:
   (a) how the detainee's physical or mental state might affect their ability to understand the nature and purpose of the interview, to comprehend what is being asked and to appreciate the significance of any answers given and make rational decisions about whether they want to say anything;
   (b) the extent to which the detainee's replies may be affected by their physical or mental condition rather than representing a rational and accurate explanation of their involvement in the offence;
   (c) how the nature of the interview, which could include particularly probing questions, might affect the detainee.
4. It is essential healthcare professionals who are consulted consider the functional ability of the detainee rather than simply relying on a medical diagnosis, e.g. it is possible for a person with severe mental illness to be fit for interview.
5. Healthcare professionals should advise on the need for an appropriate adult to be present, whether reassessment of the person's fitness for interview may be necessary if the interview lasts beyond a specified time, and whether a further specialist opinion may be required.
6. When healthcare professionals identify risks they should be asked to quantify the risks. They should inform the custody officer:
   • whether the person's condition:
     ~ is likely to improve;
     ~ will require or be amenable to treatment; and
   • indicate how long it may take for such improvement to take effect.
7. The role of the healthcare professional is to consider the risks and advise the custody officer of the outcome of that consideration. The healthcare professional's determination and any advice or recommendations should be made in writing and form part of the custody record.
8. Once the healthcare professional has provided that information, it is a matter for the custody officer to decide whether or not to allow the interview to go ahead and if the interview is to proceed, to determine what safeguards are needed. Nothing prevents safeguards being provided in addition to those required under the Code. An example might be to have an appropriate

healthcare professional present during the interview, in addition to an appropriate adult, in order constantly to monitor the person's condition and how it is being affected by the interview.

1.7.24 Code C—Annex H: Detained Person: Observation List

1. If any detainee fails to meet any of the following criteria, an appropriate healthcare professional or an ambulance must be called.
2. When assessing the level of rousability, consider:

    Rousability—can they be woken?
    - go into the cell
    - call their name
    - shake gently

    Response to questions—can they give appropriate answers to questions such as:
    - What's your name?
    - Where do you live?
    - Where do you think you are?

    Response to commands—can they respond appropriately to commands such as:
    - Open your eyes!
    - Lift one arm, now the other arm!
3. Remember to take into account the possibility or presence of other illnesses, injury, or mental condition; a person who is drowsy and smells of alcohol may also have the following:
    - Diabetes
    - Epilepsy
    - Head injury
    - Drug intoxication or overdose
    - Stroke

Code C—Annex I: *Not used*

Code C—Annex J: *Not used*

1.7.25 Code C—Annex K: X-rays and Ultrasound Scans

(a) Action

1. PACE, section 55A allows a person who has been arrested and is in police detention to have an X-ray taken of them or an ultrasound scan to be carried out on them (or both) if:
    (a) authorised by an officer of inspector rank or above who has reasonable grounds for believing that the detainee:
        (i) may have swallowed a Class A drug; and
        (ii) was in possession of that Class A drug with the intention of supplying it to another or to export; and
    (b) the detainee's appropriate consent has been given in writing.
2. Before an x-ray is taken or an ultrasound scan carried out, a police officer or designated detention officer must tell the detainee:—
    (a) that the authority has been given; and
    (b) the grounds for giving the authorisation.
3. Before a detainee is asked to give appropriate consent to an x-ray or an ultrasound scan, they must be warned that if they refuse without good cause their refusal may harm their case if it comes to trial, This warning may be given by a police officer or member of police staff. In the case of juveniles and vulnerable persons, the seeking and giving of consent must take place in the presence of the appropriate adult. A juvenile's consent is only valid if their parent's or guardian's consent is also obtained unless the juvenile is under 14, when their parent's or guardian's consent is sufficient in its own right. A detainee who is not legally represented must

be reminded of their entitlement to have free legal advice, see Code C, *paragraph 6.5*, and the reminder noted in the custody record.

4. An x-ray may be taken, or an ultrasound scan may be carried out, only by a registered medical practitioner or registered nurse, and only at a hospital, surgery or other medical premises.

(b) Documentation

5. The following shall be recorded as soon as practicable in the detainee's custody record:
    (a) the authorisation to take the x-ray or carry out the ultrasound scan (or both);
    (b) the grounds for giving the authorisation;
    (c) the giving of the warning required by *paragraph 3*; and
    (d) the fact that the appropriate consent was given or (as the case may be) refused, and if refused, the reason given for the refusal (if any); and
    (e) if an x-ray is taken or an ultrasound scan carried out:
        • where it was taken or carried out;
        • who took it or carried it out;
        • who was present;
        • the result.

6. *Not used.*

1.7.25.1

KEYNOTE

If authority is given for an x-ray to be taken or an ultrasound scan to be carried out (or both), consideration should be given to asking a registered medical practitioner or registered nurse to explain to the detainee what is involved and to allay any concerns that the detainee might have about the effect on him/her of taking an x-ray or carrying out an ultrasound scan. If appropriate consent is not given, evidence of the explanation may, if the case comes to trial, be relevant to determining whether the detainee had a good cause for refusing.

The following form of words may be used to warn a detainee who is asked to consent to an x-ray being taken or an ultrasound scan being carried out (or both):

You do not have to allow an x-ray of you to be taken or an ultrasound scan to be carried out on you, but I must warn you that if you refuse without good cause, your refusal may harm your case if it comes to trial.

Where the use of the Welsh language is appropriate, the following form of words may be provided in Welsh:

Does dim rhaid i chi ganiatáu cymryd sgan uwchsain neu belydr-x (neu'r ddau) arnoch, ond mae'n rhaid i mi eich rhybuddio os byddwch chi'n gwrthod gwneud hynny heb reswm da, fe allai hynny niweidio eich achos pe bai'n dod gerbron llys.

1.7.26

Code C—Annex L: Establishing Gender of Persons for the Purpose of Searching and Certain Other Procedures

1. Certain provisions of this and other PACE Codes explicitly state that searches and other procedures may only be carried out by, or in the presence of, persons of the same sex as the person subject to the search or other procedure or require action to be taken or information to be given which depends on whether the detainee is treated as being male or female.

2. All searches and procedures must be carried out with courtesy, consideration and respect for the person concerned. Police officers should show particular sensitivity when dealing with transgender individuals (including transsexual persons) and transvestite persons.

(a) Consideration

3. In law, the gender (and accordingly the sex) of an individual is their gender as registered at birth unless they have been issued with a Gender Recognition Certificate (GRC) under the Gender Recognition Act 2004 (GRA), in which case the person's gender is their acquired gender. This means that if the acquired gender is the male gender, the person's sex becomes that of a man

and, if it is the female gender, the person's sex becomes that of a woman and they must be treated as their acquired gender.

4. When establishing whether the person concerned should be treated as being male or female for the purposes of these searches, procedures and requirements, the following approach which is designed to maintain his dignity, minimise embarrassment and secure the person's co-operation should be followed:

(a) The person must not be asked whether they have a GRC (see *paragraph 8*);

(b) If there is no doubt as to as to whether the person concerned should be treated as being male or female, they should be dealt with as being of that sex.

(c) If at any time (including during the search or carrying out the procedure or requirement) there is doubt as to whether the person should be treated, or continue to be treated, as being male or female:

(i) the person should be asked what gender they consider themselves to be. If they express a preference to be dealt with as a particular gender, they should be asked to indicate and confirm their preference by signing the custody record or, if a custody record has not been opened, the search record or the officer's notebook. Subject to (ii) below, the person should be treated according to their preference except with regard to the requirements to provide that person with information concerning menstrual products and their personal needs relating to health, hygiene and welfare described in *paragraph 3.20A* (if aged under 18) and *paragraphs 9.3A* and *9.3B* (if aged 18 or over). In these cases, a person whose confirmed preference is to be dealt with as being male should be asked in private whether they wish to speak in private with a member of the custody staff of a gender of their choosing about the provision of menstrual products and their personal needs, notwithstanding their confirmed preference;

(ii) if there are grounds to doubt that the preference in (i) accurately reflects the person's predominant lifestyle, for example, if they ask to be treated as a woman but documents and other information make it clear that they live predominantly as a man, or vice versa, they should be treated according to what appears to be their predominant lifestyle and not their stated preference;

(iii) If the person is unwilling to express a preference as in (i) above, efforts should be made to determine their predominant lifestyle and they should be treated as such. For example, if they appear to live predominantly as a woman, they should be treated as being female; except with regard to the requirements to provide that person with information concerning menstrual products and their personal needs relating to health, hygiene and welfare described in *paragraph 3.21A* (if aged under 18) and *paragraphs 9.4A* and *9.4B* (if aged 18 or over). In these cases, a person whose predominant lifestyle has been determined to be male should be asked in private whether they wish to speak in private with a member of the custody staff of a gender of their choosing about the provision of menstrual products and their personal needs, notwithstanding their determined predominant lifestyle; or

(iv) if none of the above apply, the person should be dealt with according to what reasonably appears to have been their sex as registered at birth.

5. Once a decision has been made about which gender an individual is to be treated as, each officer responsible for the search, procedure or requirement should where possible be advised before the search or procedure starts of any doubts as to the person's gender and the person informed that the doubts have been disclosed. This is important so as to maintain the dignity of the person and any officers concerned.

(b) Documentation

6. The person's gender as established under *paragraph 4(c)(i)* to *(iv)* above must be recorded in the person's custody record or, if a custody record has not been opened, on the search record or in the officer's notebook.

7. Where the person elects which gender they consider themselves to be under *paragraph 4(b)(i)* but, following *4(b)(ii)* is not treated in accordance with their preference, the reason must be recorded in the search record, in the officer's notebook or, if applicable, in the person's custody record.

(c) Disclosure of information

8. Section 22 of the GRA defines any information relating to a person's application for a GRC or to a successful applicant's gender before it became their acquired gender as 'protected information'. Nothing in this Annex is to be read as authorising or permitting any police officer or any police staff who has acquired such information when acting in their official capacity to disclose that information to any other person in contravention of the GRA. Disclosure includes making a record of 'protected information' which is read by others.

1.7.26.1

KEYNOTE

Provisions to which para. 1 applies include:

- in Code C: paras 3.20A, 4.1 and Annex A, paras 5, 6 and 11 (searches, strip and intimate searches of detainees under ss. 54 and 55 of the 1984 Act);
- in Code A: paras 2.7 and 3.6 and Note 4;
- in Code D: para. 5.5 and Note 5F (searches, examinations and photographing of detainees under s. 54A of the 1984 Act) and para. 6.9 (taking samples);
- in Code H: paras 3.21A, 4.1 and Annex A, paras 6, 7 and 12 (searches, strip and intimate searches under ss. 54 and 55 of the 1984 Act of persons arrested under s. 41 of the Terrorism Act 2000) and para. 9.4B.

While there is no agreed definition of transgender (or trans), it is generally used as an umbrella term to describe people whose gender identity (self-identification as being a woman, man, neither or both) differs from the sex they were registered as at birth. The term includes, but is not limited to, transsexual people. Transsexual means a person who is proposing to undergo, is undergoing or has undergone a process (or part of a process) for the purpose of gender reassignment which is a protected characteristic under the Equality Act 2010 by changing physiological or other attributes of their sex. This includes aspects of gender such as dress and title. It would apply to a woman making the transition to being a man and a man making the transition to being a woman, as well as to a person who has only just started out on the process of gender reassignment and to a person who has completed the process. Both would share the characteristic of gender reassignment with each having the characteristics of one sex, but with certain characteristics of the other sex. Transvestite means a person of one gender who dresses in the clothes of a person of the opposite gender. However, transvestites do not live permanently in the gender opposite to their birth sex.

It is important to check the force guidance and instructions for the deployment of transgender officers and staff under their direction and control to duties which involve carrying out, or being present at, any of the searches and procedures described in para. 1. Force guidance which must be provided by each force's chief officer must comply with the Equality Act 2010.

The reason for the exception in relation to paras 3.21A, 9.4A and 9.4B is to modify the same sex/gender approach for searching, procedures or requirements to acknowledge the possible needs of transgender individuals in respect of menstrual products and other personal needs relating to health, hygiene and welfare and ensure that these are not overlooked as a result of their expressed preference or predominant lifestyle.

1.7.27

Code C—Annex M: Documents and Records to be Translated

1. For the purposes of Directive 2010/64/EU of the European Parliament and of the Council of 20 October 2010 and this Code, essential documents comprise records required to be made in accordance with this Code which are relevant to decisions to deprive a person of their liberty, to

any charge and to any record considered necessary to enable a detainee to defend themselves in criminal proceedings and to safeguard the fairness of the proceedings. Passages of essential documents which are not relevant need not be translated.

2. The table below lists the documents considered essential for the purposes of this Code and when (subject to *paragraphs 3 to 7*) written translations must be created and provided. See *paragraphs 13.12* to *13.14* and *Annex N* for application to live-link interpretation.

Table of essential documents:

	Essential documents for the purposes of this Code	When translation to be created	When translation to be provided.
(i)	The grounds for each of the following authorisations to keep the person in custody as they are described and referred to in the custody record: (a) Authorisation for detention before and after charge given by the custody officer and by the review officer, see Code C paragraphs 3.4 and 15.16(a). (b) Authorisation to extend detention without charge beyond 24 hours given by a superintendent, see Code C paragraph 15.16(b). (c) A warrant of further detention issued by a magistrates' court and any extension(s) of the warrant, see Code C paragraph 15.16(c). (d) An authority to detain in accordance with the directions in a warrant of arrest issued in connection with criminal proceedings including the court issuing the warrant.	As soon as practicable after each authorisation has been recorded in the custody record.	As soon as practicable after the translation has been created, whilst the person is detained or after they have been released.
(ii)	Written notice showing particulars of the offence charged required by Code C paragraph 16.3 or the offence for which the suspect has been told they may be prosecuted.	As soon as practicable after the person has been charged or reported.	
(iii)	Written interview records: Code C11.11, 13.3, 13.4 & Code E4.7 Written statement under caution: Code C Annex D.	To be created contemporaneously by the interpreter for the person to check and sign.	As soon as practicable after the person has been charged or told they may be prosecuted.

3. The custody officer may authorise an oral translation or oral summary of documents (i) to (ii) in the table (but not (iii)) to be provided (through an interpreter) instead of a written translation. Such an oral translation or summary may only be provided if it would not prejudice the fairness of the proceedings by in any way adversely affecting or otherwise undermining or limiting the ability of the suspect in question to understand their position and to communicate effectively with police officers, interviewers, solicitors and appropriate adults with regard to their detention and the investigation of the offence in question and to defend themselves in the event of criminal proceedings. The quantity and complexity of the information in the document should always be considered and specific additional consideration given if the suspect is vulnerable or is a juvenile (see *Code C paragraph 1.5*). The reason for the decision must be recorded (see *paragraph 13.11(e)*).

4. Subject to *paragraphs 5* to *7* below, a suspect may waive their right to a written translation of the essential documents described in the table but only if they do so voluntarily after receiving legal advice or having full knowledge of the consequences and give their unconditional and fully informed consent in writing (see *paragraph 9*).

5. The suspect may be asked if they wish to waive their right to a written translation and before giving their consent, they must be reminded of their right to legal advice and asked whether they wish to speak to a solicitor.

6. No police officer or police staff should do or say anything with the intention of persuading a suspect who is entitled to a written translation of an essential document to waive that right.

7. For the purpose of the waiver:

    (a) the consent of a vulnerable person is only valid if the information about the circumstances under which they can waive the right and the reminder about their right to legal advice mentioned in *paragraphs 3* to *5* and their consent is given in the presence of the appropriate adult.

    (b) the consent of a juvenile is only valid if their parent's or guardian's consent is also obtained unless the juvenile is under 14, when their parent's or guardian's consent is sufficient in its own right and the information and reminder mentioned in *subparagraph (a)* above and their consent is also given in the presence of the appropriate adult (who may or may not be a parent or guardian).

8. The detainee, their solicitor or appropriate adult may make representations to the custody officer that a document which is not included in the table is essential and that a translation should be provided. The request may be refused if the officer is satisfied that the translation requested is not essential for the purposes described in *paragraph 1* above.

9. If the custody officer has any doubts about

    • providing an oral translation or summary of an essential document instead of a written translation (see paragraph 3);
    • whether the suspect fully understands the consequences of waiving their right to a written translation of an essential document (see paragraph 4), or
    • about refusing to provide a translation of a requested document (see *paragraph 7*),
    • the officer should seek advice from an inspector or above.

Documentation

10. Action taken in accordance with this Annex shall be recorded in the detainee's custody record or interview record as appropriate (see *Code C paragraph 13.11(e)*).

1.7.27.1

KEYNOTE

This Annex lists the essential documents and the requirements to provide translations to reflect the terms of EU Directive 2010/64. It is not necessary to disclose information in any translation which is capable of undermining or otherwise adversely affecting any investigative processes, for example, by enabling the suspect to fabricate an innocent explanation or to conceal lies from the interviewer. No police officer or police staff shall indicate to any suspect, except to answer a direct question, whether the period for which they are liable to be detained or if not detained, the time taken to complete the interview, might be reduced:

• if they do not ask for legal advice before deciding whether they wish to waive their right to a written translation of an essential document; or
• if they decide to waive their right to a written translation of an essential document.

There is no power under PACE to detain a person or to delay their release solely to create and provide a written translation of any essential document.

Code C—Annex N: Live-link Interpretation (para. 13.12)

Part 1: When the physical presence of the interpreter is not required.

1. EU Directive 2010/64 (see *paragraph 13.1*), Article 2(6) provides 'Where appropriate, communication technology such as videoconferencing, telephone or the Internet may be used, unless the physical presence of the interpreter is required in order to safeguard the fairness of the proceedings.' This Article permits, but does not require the use of a live-link, and the following provisions of this Annex determine whether the use of a live-link is appropriate in any particular case.

2. Decisions in accordance with this Annex that the physical presence of the interpreter is not required and to permit live-link interpretation, must be made on a case by case basis. Each decision must take account of the age, gender and vulnerability of the suspect, the nature and circumstances of the offence and the investigation and the impact on the suspect according to the particular purpose(s) for which the suspect requires the assistance of an interpreter and the time(s) when that assistance is required. For this reason, the custody officer in the case of a detained suspect, or in the case of a suspect who has not been arrested, the interviewer (subject to *paragraph 13.1(b)*), must consider whether the ability of the particular suspect, to communicate confidently and effectively for the purpose in question (see *paragraph 3*) is likely to be adversely affected or otherwise undermined or limited if the interpreter is not physically present and live-link interpretation is used. Although a suspect for whom an appropriate adult is required may be more likely to be adversely affected as described, it is important to note that a person who does not require an appropriate adult may also be adversely impacted by the use of live-link interpretation.

3. Examples of purposes referred to in *paragraph 2* include:
   (a) understanding and appreciating their position having regard to any information given to them, or sought from them, in accordance with this or any other Code of Practice which, in particular, include:
   - the caution (see *paragraphs C10.1* and *10.12*).
   - the special warning (see *paragraphs 10.10* to *10.12*).
   - information about the offence (see *paragraphs 10.3, 11.1A*).
   - the grounds and reasons for detention (see *paragraphs 13.10* and *13.10A*).
   - the translation of essential documents (see *paragraph 13.10B* and *Annex M*).
   - their rights and entitlements (see *paragraph 3.12* and *C3.21(b)*).
   - intimate and non-intimate searches of detained persons at police stations.
   - provisions and procedures to which Code D (Identification) applies concerning, for example, eye-witness identification, taking fingerprints, samples and photographs.
   (b) understanding and seeking clarification from the interviewer of questions asked during an interview conducted and recorded in accordance with Code E or Code F and of anything else that is said by the interviewer and answering the questions.
   (c) consulting privately with their solicitor and (if applicable) the appropriate adult (see *paragraphs 3.18, 13.2A, 13.6* and *13.9*):
   (i) to help decide whether to answer questions put to them during interview; and
   (ii) about any other matter concerning their detention and treatment whilst in custody.
   (d) communicating with practitioners and others who have some formal responsibility for, or an interest in, the health and welfare of the suspect. Particular examples include appropriate healthcare professionals (see *section 9* of this Code), Independent Custody Visitors and drug arrest referral workers.

4. If the custody officer or the interviewer (subject to *paragraph 13.1(b)*) is satisfied that for a particular purpose as described in *paragraphs 2 and 3 above*, the live-link interpretation *would not* adversely affect or otherwise undermine or limit the suspect's ability to communicate

confidently and effectively for *that* purpose, they must so inform the suspect, their solicitor and (if applicable) the appropriate adult. At the same time, the operation of live-link interpretation must be explained and demonstrated to them, they must be advised of the chief officer's obligations concerning the security of live-link communications under *paragraph 13.13* and they must be asked if they wish to make representations that live-link interpretation should not be used or if they require more information about the operation of the arrangements. They must also be told that at any time live-link interpretation is in use, they may make representations to the custody officer or the interviewer that its operation should cease and that the physical presence of an interpreter should be arranged.

When the authority of an inspector is required

5. If:
   (i) representations are made that live-link interpretation should not be used, or that at any time live-link interpretation is in use, its operation should cease and the physical presence of an interpreter arranged; and
   (ii) the custody officer or interviewer (subject to *paragraph 13.1(b)*) is unable to allay the concerns raised; then live-link interpretation may not be used, or (as the case may be) continue to be used, unless authorised in writing by an officer of the rank of inspector or above, in accordance with paragraph 6.

6. Authority may be given if the officer is satisfied that for the purpose(s) in question at the time an interpreter is required, live-link interpretation is necessary and justified. In making this decision, the officer must have regard to:
   (a) the circumstances of the suspect;
   (b) the nature and seriousness of the offence;
   (c) the requirements of the investigation, including its likely impact on both the suspect and any victim(s);
   (d) the representations made by the suspect, their solicitor and (if applicable) the appropriate adult that live-link interpretation should not be used (see *paragraph 5*)
   (e) the availability of a suitable interpreter to be *physically* present compared with the availability of a suitable interpreter for live-link interpretation; and
   (f) the risk if the interpreter is not *physically* present, evidence obtained using link interpretation might be excluded in subsequent criminal proceedings; and
   (g) the likely impact on the suspect and the investigation of any consequential delay to arrange for the interpreter to be *physically* present with the suspect.

7. For the purposes of Code E and live-link interpretation, there is no requirement to make a visual recording which shows the interpreter as viewed by the suspect and others present at the interview. The audio recording required by that Code is sufficient. However, the authorising officer, in consultation with the officer in charge of the investigation, may direct that the interview is conducted and recorded in accordance with Code F. This will require the visual record to show the live-link interpretation arrangements and the interpreter as seen and experienced by the suspect during the interview. This should be considered if it appears that the admissibility of interview evidence might be challenged because the interpreter was not *physically* present or if the suspect, solicitor or appropriate adult make representations that Code F should be applied.

Documentation

8. A record must be made of the actions, decisions, authorisations and outcomes arising from the requirements of this Annex. This includes representations made in accordance with *paragraphs 4* and *7*.

Part 2: Modifications for live-link interpretation

9. The following modification shall apply for the purposes of live-link interpretation:

   (a) Code C paragraph 13.3:

   For the third sentence, *substitute:* 'A clear legible copy of the complete record shall be sent without delay via the live-link to the interviewer. The interviewer, after confirming with the suspect that the copy is legible and complete, shall allow the suspect to read the record, or have the record read to them by the interpreter and to sign the copy as correct or indicate the respects in which they consider it inaccurate. The interviewer is responsible for ensuring that that the signed copy and the original record made by the interpreter are retained with the case papers for use in evidence if required and must advise the interpreter of their obligation to keep the original record securely for that purpose.';

   (b) Code C paragraph 13.4:

   For sub-paragraph (b), *substitute*: 'A clear legible copy of the complete statement shall be sent without delay via the live-link to the interviewer. The interviewer, after confirming with the suspect that the copy is legible and complete, shall invite the suspect to sign it. The interviewer is responsible for ensuring that that the signed copy and the original record made by the interpreter are retained with the case papers for use in evidence if required and must advise the interpreter of their obligation to keep the original record securely for that purpose.';

   (c) Code C paragraph 13.7:

   After the first sentence, *insert*: 'A clear legible copy of the certified record must be sent without delay via the live-link to the interviewer. The interviewer is responsible for ensuring that the original certified record and the copy are retained with the case papers for use as evidence if required and must advise the interpreter of their obligation to keep the original record securely for that purpose.'

   (d) Code C paragraph 11.2, Code E paragraphs 3.4 and 4.3 and Code F paragraph 2.5.- interviews
   At the beginning of each paragraph, *insert*: 'Before the interview commences, the operation of live-link interpretation shall be explained and demonstrated to the suspect, their solicitor and appropriate adult, unless it has been previously explained and demonstrated (see Code C Annex N *paragraph 4*).'

   (e) Code E, paragraph 3.20 (signing master recording label)
   After the *third sentence*, insert, 'If live-link interpretation has been used, the interviewer should ask the interpreter to observe the removal and sealing of the master recording and to confirm in writing that they have seen it sealed and signed by the interviewer. A clear legible copy of the confirmation signed by the interpreter must be sent via the live-link to the interviewer. The interviewer is responsible for ensuring that the original confirmation and the copy are retained with the case papers for use in evidence if required and must advise the interpreter of their obligation to keep the original confirmation securely for that purpose.'
   Note: By virtue of *paragraphs 2.1* and *2.3 of Code F*, this applies when a visually recording to which Code F applies is made.

1.7.28.1   **KEYNOTE**

For purposes other than an interview, audio-only live-link interpretation, for example by telephone (see Code C, para. 13.12(b)) may provide an appropriate option until an interpreter is physically present or audio-visual live-link interpretation becomes available. A particular example would be the initial action required when a detained suspect arrives at a police station to inform them of, and to explain, the reasons for their arrest and detention and their various rights and entitlements. Another example would be to inform the suspect by telephone, that an interpreter they will be able to see and hear is being arranged. In these circumstances, telephone live-link interpretation may help to allay the suspect's concerns and contribute to the completion of the risk assessment (see Code C, para. 3.6). In deciding whether to give authority for the use of live link the authorising officer may take account of the availability of a suitable interpreter in relation to the location of the police station and the language and type of interpretation (oral or sign language) required. The explanation and demonstration of live-link interpretation to the suspect prior to its use is intended to help the suspect, solicitor and appropriate adult make an informed decision and to allay any concerns they may have.

1.8 | Identification

PACE Code of Practice for the Identification of Persons by Police Officers (Code D)

> A thick grey line down the margin denotes text that is an extract of the PACE Code itself (i.e. the actual wording of the legislation)

1.8.1 Introduction

A critical issue in the investigation and prosecution of offences is the identification of the offender. Many different methods of identification exist but the main feature which must be considered in relation to each is its *reliability*.

The visual identification of suspects by witnesses is one of the most common forms of identification; it is also one of the most unreliable. Even under research conditions, the recall of eye witnesses is inconsistent; where the witness sees or experiences the spontaneous commission of a crime, that reliability is reduced even further.

It was for these reasons that the *Turnbull* guidelines were set out, together with the provisions of Code D. In response to widespread concern over the problems posed by cases of mistaken identification, the Court of Appeal in *Turnbull* [1977] QB 224 laid down important guidelines for judges in trials that involve disputed identification evidence. The guidelines provide that where the case against an accused depends wholly or substantially on the correctness of one or more identifications of the accused—which the defence alleges to be mistaken—the judge should warn the jury of the special need for caution before convicting the accused in reliance on the correctness of the identification(s). The judge should tell the jury that:

- caution is required to avoid the risk of injustice;
- a witness who is honest may be wrong even if they are convinced they are right;
- a witness who is convincing may still be wrong;
- more than one witness may be wrong;
- a witness who recognises the defendant, even when the witness knows the defendant very well, may be wrong.

The judge should direct the jury to examine the circumstances in which the identification by each witness can be made. Some of these circumstances may include:

- the length of time the accused was observed by the witness;
- the distance the witness was from the accused;
- the state of the light;
- the length of time elapsed between the original observation and the subsequent identification to the police.

This also applies to recognition cases. It is commonly accepted that recognition is more reliable than identification of a stranger; however, even when the witness appears to recognise someone he/she knows, the jury should be reminded that mistakes in recognition of close relatives and friends are sometimes made

If there is no identification evidence, the *Turnbull* guidelines will not apply. Identification evidence relates to identifying the person and not necessarily the actions of that person, for instance evidence that a person was present at a scene is identification, evidence that the person identified stabbed someone is not identification evidence and does not need a *Turnbull* warning (*R v Nawaz* [2020] EWCA Crim 893). It should be remembered that a witness who does not identify the suspect may still be able to provide other valuable evidence to the case, for instance a description of the person who committed the offence, or a description of what he/she was wearing. Again it is not uncommon for witnesses to qualify their identification of the suspect by indicating that they 'cannot be quite certain'. While a defendant cannot be convicted on such a qualified identification alone, it may be admissible to support the case where other evidence is also available (*R v George* [2002] EWCA Crim 1923).

A lot will depend on the individual circumstances of each case, but it is essential that these issues are covered in any interview or other evidence-gathering process.

'Dock identifications', where the witness's first identification of the accused involves pointing out the person in the dock, are often dramatised by filmmakers but, in practice, are generally disallowed as being unreliable and unfair.

The Police and Criminal Evidence Act 1984 Code of Practice, Code D provides guidance for the identification of persons by police officers. This chapter sets out the actual Codes of Practice with keynotes which incorporate the notes of guidance to the Code.

Generally, the methods of identification covered by Code D can be divided into two:

- occasions where the identity of the suspect is known; and
- occasions where the identity of the suspect is not known.

Where the identity of the suspect is known this can be further divided into those cases where the suspect is available and those where he/she is not available.

Although a breach of Code D (or any of the other Codes of Practice) will not automatically result in the evidence being excluded (*R v Khan* (1999) 19 July, CA, unreported), the judge or magistrate(s) will consider the effects of any breach on the fairness of any subsequent proceedings. The Codes are intended to provide protection to suspects and, if it is felt that the breach of Code D has resulted in unfairness or other prejudicial effect on the defendant, the court may exclude the related evidence under s. 78 of the Police and Criminal Evidence Act 1984.

New Codes were introduced in 2017, eye-witness and witness identification procedures are updated to take account of changes and developments in case law and police practice and to address operational concerns raised by the police. In respect of the video identification procedure, these support and extend the identification officer's discretion concerning the selection and use of 'historic' images, the presence of solicitors at witness viewings and to direct other police officers and police staff to implement any arrangements for any identification procedures. The role and responsibility of the investigating officer is clarified in relation to viewing of CCTV and similar images by someone who is not an eye-witness. The revisions to the 2017 Code also reflect amendments to the Police and Criminal Evidence Act 1984 concerning the retention of fingerprints, footwear impressions and DNA profiles and samples, made by the Anti-social Behaviour, Crime and Policing Act 2014.

The Police Reform Act 2002 has introduced designated support staff who have some of the powers that police officers have (**see chapter 1.7**).

PACE Code of Practice for the Identification of Persons by Police Officers (Code D)

This code has effect in relation to any identification procedure carried out after midnight on 23 February 2017.

1 Introduction

1.1 This Code of Practice concerns the principal methods used by police to identify people in connection with the investigation of offences and the keeping of accurate and reliable criminal records. The powers and procedures in this code must be used fairly, responsibly, with respect for the people to whom they apply and without unlawful discrimination. Under the Equality Act 2010, section 149 (Public sector Equality Duty), police forces must, in carrying out their functions, have due regard to the need to eliminate unlawful discrimination, harassment, victimisation and any other conduct which is prohibited by that Act, to advance equality of opportunity between people who share a relevant protected characteristic and people who do not share it, and to foster good relations between those persons. The Equality Act also makes it unlawful for police officers to discriminate against, harass or victimise any person on the grounds of the 'protected characteristics' of age, disability, gender reassignment, race, religion or belief, sex and sexual orientation, marriage and civil partnership, pregnancy and maternity when using their powers.

1.2 In this Code, identification by an eye-witness arises when a witness who has seen the offender committing the crime and is given an opportunity to identify a person suspected of involvement in the offence in a video identification, identification parade or similar procedure. These eye-witness identification procedures which are in Part A of section 3 below, are designed to:

- test the eye-witness' ability to identify the suspect as the person they saw on a previous occasion
- provide safeguards against mistaken identification.

While this Code concentrates on visual identification procedures, it does not prevent the police making use of aural identification procedures such as a 'voice identification parade', where they judge that appropriate.

1.2A In this Code, separate provisions in Part B of section 3 below, apply when any person, including a police officer, is asked if they recognise anyone they see in an image as being someone who is known to them and to test their claim that they recognise that person. These separate provisions are not subject to the eye-witnesses identification procedures described in *paragraph 1.2*.

1.2B Part C applies when a film, photograph or image relating to the offence or any description of the suspect is broadcast or published in any national or local media or on any social networking site or on any local or national police communication systems.

1.3 Identification by fingerprints applies when a person's fingerprints are taken to:

- compare with fingerprints found at the scene of a crime
- check and prove convictions
- help to ascertain a persons identity.

1.3A Identification using footwear impressions applies when a person's footwear impressions are taken to compare with impressions found at the scene of a crime.

1.4 Identification by body samples and impressions includes taking samples such as a cheek swab, hair or blood to generate a DNA profile for comparison with material obtained from the scene of a crime, or a victim.

1.5 Taking photographs of arrested people applies to recording and checking identity and locating and tracing persons who:

- are wanted for offences
- fail to answer their bail.

1.6 Another method of identification involves searching and examining detained suspects to find, e.g., marks such as tattoos or scars which may help establish their identity or whether they have been involved in committing an offence.

1.7 The provisions of the Police and Criminal Evidence Act 1984 (PACE) and this Code are designed to make sure fingerprints, samples, impressions and photographs are taken, used and retained, and identification procedures carried out, only when justified and necessary for preventing, detecting or investigating crime. If these provisions are not observed, the application of the relevant procedures in particular cases may be open to question.

1.8 The provisions of this Code do not authorise, or otherwise permit, fingerprints or samples to be taken from a person detained solely for the purposes of assessment under section 136 of the Mental Health Act 1983.

1.8.2.1

KEYNOTE

In para. 1.1, under the Equality Act 2010, s. 149, the 'relevant protected characteristics' are: age, disability, gender reassignment, pregnancy and maternity, race, religion/belief, sex and sexual orientation. For further detailed guidance and advice on the Equality Act, see <https://www.gov.uk/guidance/equality-act-2010-guidance>. For advice on the use of voice identification parades, see Home Office Circular 57/2003.

1.8.3

Code D—2 General

2.1 This Code must be readily available at all police stations for consultation by:
- police officers and police staff
- detained persons
- members of the public

2.2 The provisions of this Code:
- include the *Annexes*
- do not include the *Notes for guidance*.

2.3 Code C, *paragraph 1.4* and the *Notes for guidance* applicable to those provisions apply to this Code with regard to a suspected person who may be mentally disordered or otherwise mentally vulnerable.

2.4 Code C, *paragraphs 1.5* and *1.5A* and the *Notes for guidance* applicable to those provisions apply to this Code with regard to a suspected person who appears to be under the age of 18.

2.5 Code C, *paragraph 1.6* applies to this Code with regard to a suspected person who appears to be blind, seriously visually impaired, deaf, unable to read or speak or has difficulty communicating orally because of a speech impediment.

2.6 In this Code:
- 'appropriate adult' means the same as in Code C, *paragraph 1.7*
- 'solicitor' means the same as in Code C, *paragraph 6.12*

and the *Notes for guidance* applicable to those provisions apply to this Code.
- *where* a search or other procedure under this Code may only be carried out or observed by a person of the same sex as the person to whom the search or procedure applies, the gender of the detainee and other persons present should be established and recorded in line with Annex L of Code C.

2.7 References to a custody officer include any police officer who, for the time being, is performing the functions of a custody officer, see *paragraph 1.9* of Code C.

2.8 When a record of any action requiring the authority of an officer of a specified rank is made under this Code, subject to *paragraph 2.18*, the officer's name and rank must be recorded.

2.9 When this Code requires the prior authority or agreement of an officer of at least inspector or superintendent rank, that authority may be given by a sergeant or chief inspector who has been authorised to perform the functions of the higher rank under PACE, section 107.

2.10 Subject to *paragraph 2.18*, all records must be timed and signed by the maker.

2.11 Records must be made in the custody record, unless otherwise specified. In any provision of this Code which allows or requires police officers or police staff to make a record in their report book, the reference to 'report book' shall include any official report book or electronic recording device issued to them that enables the record in question to be made and dealt with in accordance with that provision. References in this Code to written records, forms and signatures include electronic records and forms and electronic confirmation that identifies the person completing the record or form.

Chief officers must be satisfied as to the integrity and security of the devices, records and forms to which this *paragraph* applies and that use of those devices, records and forms satisfies relevant data protection legislation.

(taken from *Code C paragraph 1.17*).

2.12 If any procedure in this Code requires a person's consent, the consent of a:
- mentally disordered or otherwise mentally vulnerable person is only valid if given in the presence of the appropriate adult
- juvenile is only valid if their parent's or guardian's consent is also obtained unless the juvenile is under 14, when their parent's or guardian's consent is sufficient in its own right. If the only obstacle to an identification procedure in *section 3* is that a juvenile's parent or guardian refuses consent or reasonable efforts to obtain it have failed, the identification officer may apply the provisions of *paragraph 3.21* (suspect known but not available).

2.13 If a person is blind, seriously visually impaired or unable to read, the custody officer or identification officer shall make sure their solicitor, relative, appropriate adult or some other person likely to take an interest in them and not involved in the investigation is available to help check any documentation. When this Code requires written consent or signing, the person assisting may be asked to sign instead, if the detainee prefers. This paragraph does not require an appropriate adult to be called solely to assist in checking and signing documentation for a person who is not a juvenile, or mentally disordered or otherwise mentally vulnerable (see Code C *paragraph 3.15*).

2.14 If any procedure in this Code requires information to be given to or sought from a suspect, it must be given or sought in the appropriate adult's presence if the suspect is mentally disordered, otherwise mentally vulnerable or a juvenile. If the appropriate adult is not present when the information is first given or sought, the procedure must be repeated in the presence of the appropriate adult when they arrive. If the suspect appears deaf or there is doubt about their hearing or speaking ability or ability to understand English, the custody officer or identification officer must ensure that the necessary arrangements in accordance with Code C are made for an interpreter to assist the suspect.

2.15 Any procedure in this Code involving the participation of a suspect who is mentally disordered, otherwise mentally vulnerable or a juvenile must take place in the presence of the appropriate adult. See Code C *paragraph 1.4*.

2.15A Any procedure in this Code involving the participation of a witness who is or appears to be mentally disordered, otherwise mentally vulnerable or a juvenile should take place in the presence of a pre-trial support person unless the witness states that they do not want a support person to be present. A support person must not be allowed to prompt any identification of a suspect by a witness.

2.16 References to:
- 'taking a photograph', include the use of any process to produce a single, still or moving, visual image
- 'photographing a person', should be construed accordingly
- 'photographs', 'films', 'negatives' and 'copies' include relevant visual images recorded, stored, or reproduced through any medium
- 'destruction' includes the deletion of computer data relating to such images or making access to that data impossible

2.17 This Code does not affect or apply to, the powers and procedures:

    (i) for requiring and taking samples of breath, blood and urine in relation to driving offences, etc., when under the influence of drink, drugs or excess alcohol under the:

- Road Traffic Act 1988, sections 4 to 11
- Road Traffic Offenders Act 1988, sections 15 and 16
- Transport and Works Act 1992, sections 26 to 38;

    (ii) under the Immigration Act 1971, Schedule 2, paragraph 18, for taking photographs, measuring and identifying and taking biometric information (not including DNA) from persons detained or liable to be detained under that Act, Schedule 2, paragraph 16 (Administrative Provisions as to Control on Entry etc.); or for taking fingerprints in accordance with the Immigration and Asylum Act 1999, sections 141 and 142(4), or other methods for collecting information about a person's external physical characteristics provided for by regulations made under that Act, section 144;

    (iii) under the Terrorism Act 2000, Schedule 8, for taking photographs, fingerprints, skin impressions, body samples or impressions from people:

- arrested under that Act, section 41,
- detained for the purposes of examination under that Act, Schedule 7, and to whom the Code of Practice issued under that Act, Schedule 14, paragraph 6, applies ('the terrorism provisions')

    (iv) for taking photographs, fingerprints, skin impressions, body samples or impressions from people who have been:

- arrested on warrants issued in Scotland, by officers exercising powers mentioned in Part X of the Criminal Justice and Public Order Act 1994;
- arrested or detained without warrant by officers from a police force in Scotland exercising their powers of arrest or detention mentioned in Part X of the Criminal Justice and Public Order Act 1994.

Note: In these cases, police powers and duties and the person's rights and entitlements whilst at a police station in England and Wales are the same as if the person had been arrested in Scotland by a Scottish police officer.

2.18 Nothing in this Code requires the identity of officers or police staff to be recorded or disclosed:

    (a) in the case of enquiries linked to the investigation of terrorism;

    (b) if the officers or police staff reasonably believe recording or disclosing their names might put them in danger.

In these cases, they shall use their warrant or other identification numbers and the name of their police station.

2.19 In this Code:

    (a) 'designated person' means a person other than a police officer, who has specified powers and duties conferred or imposed on them by designation under section 38 or 39 of the Police Reform Act 2002;

    (b) any reference to a police officer includes a designated person acting in the exercise or performance of the powers and duties conferred or imposed on them by their designation.

2.20 If a power conferred on a designated person:

    (a) allows reasonable force to be used when exercised by a police officer, a designated person exercising that power has the same entitlement to use force;

    (b) includes power to use force to enter any premises, that power is not exercisable by that designated person except:

      (i) in the company, and under the supervision, of a police officer; or

      (ii) for the purpose of:

- saving life or limb; or
- preventing serious damage to property.

2.21 In the case of a detained person, nothing in this Code prevents the custody officer, or other police officer or designated person given custody of the detainee by the custody officer for the purposes of the investigation of an offence for which the person is detained, from allowing another person (see (a) and (b) below) to carry out individual procedures or tasks at the police station if the law allows. However, the officer or designated person given custody remains responsible for making sure the procedures and tasks are carried out correctly in accordance with the Codes of Practice. The other person who is allowed to carry out the procedures or tasks must be *someone who at that time* is:

(a) under the direction and control of the chief officer of the force responsible for the police station in question; or

(b) providing services under contractual arrangements (but without being employed by the chief officer the police force), to assist a police force in relation to the discharge of its chief officer's functions.

2.22 Designated persons and others mentioned in *sub-paragraphs (a)* and *(b)* of *paragraph 2.21* must have regard to any relevant provisions of the Codes of Practice.

1.8.3.1 KEYNOTE

People who are seriously visually impaired or unable to read may be unwilling to sign police documents. The alternative, i.e. the representative signing on his/her behalf, seeks to protect the interests of both police and suspects.

For the purposes of any procedures within this Code which require an appropriate adult's consent, where a juvenile is in the care of a local authority or voluntary organisation the consent may be given by that authority or organisation. Where a parent, guardian or representative of a local authority or voluntary organisation is not acting as the appropriate adult under para. 2.14 or 2.15 he/she does not have to be present to give consent. However, it is important that a parent or guardian not present is fully informed before being asked to consent. He/she must be given the same information about the procedure and the juvenile's suspected involvement in the offence as the juvenile and appropriate adult. The parent or guardian must also be allowed to speak to the juvenile and the appropriate adult if he/she wishes. Provided the consent is fully informed and is not withdrawn, it may be obtained at any time before the procedure takes place.

The Youth Justice and Criminal Evidence Act 1999 guidance 'Achieving Best Evidence in Criminal Proceedings: Guidance on interviewing victims and witnesses, and guidance on using special measures' indicates that a pre-trial support person should accompany a vulnerable witness during any identification procedure. It states that this support person should not be (or not be likely to be) a witness in the investigation.

The purpose of using warrant or identification numbers instead of names referred to in Code D, para. 2.18(b) is to protect those involved in serious organised crime investigations or arrest of particularly violent suspects when there is reliable information that those arrested or their associates may threaten or cause harm to those involved. In cases of doubt, an officer of inspector rank or above should be consulted.

1.8.4 ▎ Code D—3 Identification by Witnesses

1.8.4.1 KEYNOTE

Visual Identification

Section 3 of Code D is split into Parts A and B, thereby distinguishing eye-witness identification procedures such as video identification from procedures for obtaining recognition evidence by viewing CCTV or similar images.

3 Identification and recognition of suspects

Part (A) Identification of a suspect by an eye-witness

3.0 This part applies when an eye-witness has seen a person committing a crime or in any other circumstances which tend to prove or disprove the involvement of the person they saw in a crime, for example, close to the scene of the crime, immediately before or immediately after it was committed. It sets out the procedures to be used to test the ability of that eye-witness to identify a person suspected of involvement in the offence ('the suspect') as the person they saw on the previous occasion. This part does not apply to the procedure described in Part B which is used to test the ability of someone who is not an eye-witness, to recognise anyone whose image they see.

3.1 A record shall be made of the description of the suspect as first given by the eye-witness. This record must:

(a) be made and kept in a form which enables details of that description to be accurately produced from it, in a visible and legible form, which can be given to the suspect or the suspect's solicitor in accordance with this Code; and

(b) unless otherwise specified, be made before the eye-witness takes part in any identification procedures under *paragraphs 3.5 to 3.10, 3.21, 3.23* or Annex E (Showing Photographs to Eye-Witnesses).

A copy of the record shall where practicable, be given to the suspect or their solicitor before any procedures under *paragraphs 3.5 to 3.10, 3.21* or *3.23* are carried out.

3.1A References in this Part:

(a) to the identity of the suspect being 'known' mean that there is sufficient information known to the police to establish, in accordance with Code G (Arrest), that there are reasonable grounds to suspect a particular person of involvement in the offence;

(b) to the suspect being 'available' mean that the suspect is immediately available, or will be available within a reasonably short time, in order that they can be invited to take part in at least one of the eye-witness identification procedures under *paragraphs 3.5 to 3.10* and it is practicable to arrange an effective procedure under *paragraphs 3.5 to 3.10*; and

(c) to the eye-witness identification procedures under *paragraphs 3.5 to 3.10* mean:

- Video identification (*paragraphs 3.5 and 3.6*);
- Identification parade (*paragraphs 3.7 and 3.8*); and
- Group identification (*paragraphs 3.9 and 3.10*).

(a) Cases when the suspect's identity is not known

3.2 In cases when the suspect's identity is not known, an eye-witness may be taken to a particular neighbourhood or place to see whether they can identify the person they saw on a previous occasion. Although the number, age, sex, race, general description and style of clothing of other people present at the location and the way in which any identification is made cannot be controlled, the principles applicable to the formal procedures under *paragraphs 3.5 to 3.10* shall be followed as far as practicable. For example:

(a) where it is practicable to do so, a record should be made of the eye-witness' description of the person they saw on the previous occasion, as in *paragraph 3.1(a)*, before asking the eye-witness to make an identification;

(b) Care must be taken not provide the eye-witness with any information concerning the description of the suspect (if such information is available) and not to direct the eyewitness' attention to any individual unless, taking into account all the circumstances, this cannot be avoided. However, this does not prevent an eye-witness being asked to look carefully at the people around at the time or to look towards a group or in a particular direction, if this appears necessary to make sure that the witness does not overlook a possible suspect simply because the eye-witness is looking in the opposite direction and also to enable the eye-witness to make comparisons between any suspect and others who are in the area;

(c) where there is more than one eye-witness, every effort should be made to keep them separate and eye-witnesses should be taken to see whether they can identify a person independently;

(d) once there is sufficient information to establish, in accordance with *paragraph 3.1A(a)*, that the suspect is 'known', e.g. after the eye-witness makes an identification, the provisions set out from *paragraph 3.4* onwards shall apply for that and any other eyewitnesses in relation to that individual;

(e) the officer or police staff accompanying the eye-witness must record, in their report book, the action taken as soon as practicable and in as much detail, as possible. The record should include:

(i) the date, time and place of the relevant occasion when the eye-witness claims to have previously seen the person committing the offence in question or in any other circumstances which tend to prove or disprove the involvement of the person they saw in a crime (see *paragraph 3.0*); and

(ii) where any identification was made:

- how it was made and the conditions at the time (e.g., the distance the eyewitness was from the suspect, the weather and light);
- if the eye-witness's attention was drawn to the suspect; the reason for this; and
- anything said by the eye-witness or the suspect about the identification or the conduct of the procedure.

3.3 An eye-witness must not be shown photographs, computerised or artist's composite likenesses or similar likenesses or pictures (including 'E-fit' images) if in accordance with *paragraph 3.1A*, the identity of the suspect is known and they are available to take part in one of the procedures under *paragraphs 3.5 to 3.10*. If the suspect's identity is not known, the showing of any such images to an eye-witness to see if they can identify a person whose image they are shown as the person they saw on a previous occasion must be done in accordance with *Annex E*.

1.8.4.3

KEYNOTE

Identification at the Scene

The need for 'scene identifications' was recognised by Lord Lane CJ in *R v Oscar* [1991] Crim LR 778 and by the Court of Appeal in *R v Rogers* [1993] Crim LR 386.

In *Oscar*, the court held that there had been no requirement for an identity parade in that case and Lord Lane pointed out that, in any case, a later parade where the suspect was dressed differently would be of no value at all. In *Rogers*, the suspect was found near a crime scene and was confronted by a witness who positively identified him. The court held that the identification in that case was necessary for an arrest to be made, although the court considered that a later parade could have been carried out.

The admissibility and value of identification evidence obtained when carrying out the procedure under para. 3.2 (taking an eye-witness to see whether they can identify the person they saw on a previous occasion) may be compromised if before a person is identified, the eye-witness' attention is specifically drawn to that person; or if the suspect's identity becomes known before the procedure.

Careful consideration must be given before a decision to identify a suspect in this manner is used. If there is sufficient evidence to arrest the suspect without using a witness's identification, then it is likely that the courts will find that one of the three identification methods outlined at Code D, para. 3.4 should have been used and the evidence may be excluded. Confrontations between witnesses and suspects on the street can be useful at times, but where this takes place it defeats the formal identification process and needs to be carefully considered. The reason for this is that, even if the suspect is picked out on the identification parade by that witness, the defence will be able to argue that the identification was from the confrontation after the incident and not at the time of the commission of the offence. If there is more than one witness available and a decision is taken to use a witness to try to identify a suspect at the scene, other witnesses should be moved away, so as to reduce the possibility of a chance encounter with the suspect. Where possible, these witnesses should be kept apart until the identification parade and ideally should not discuss the matter between themselves.

An example where a street identification was appropriate is *R* v *El-Hinnachi* [1998] 2 Cr App R 226. Here an affray took place in the car park of a public house. A witness had seen the man earlier in the pub and she'd had an unobstructed view in good light before the attack. The witness described the attacker's clothing to the police and then identified a group of men who had been stopped by other officers a short distance away. The court accepted that due to the fast-moving incident, this correct approach should, however, be avoided where possible. The defendants were not known suspects when they were stopped by the police prior to the witness's identification. The court also accepted that it had not been practicable for a record to have been made of the witness's description, as required by Code D, para. 3.1, prior to the identification.

A not uncommon situation is where police officers chase a suspect who is arrested by other officers on the description circulated by the chasing officer, who then attends the scene to confirm the person's identity. The case of *R* v *Nunes* [2001] EWCA Crim 2283, covers this point and points out the dangers of this practice. The facts of the case were that a police officer saw a man inside a house and circulated a description on his radio. A person fitting the description was seen and arrested. The first officer arrived on the scene and identified the arrested person as the man he had earlier seen in the house. The Court of Appeal held that on the particular facts of this case the identification amounted to a breach of the Code. By the time of the identification, the man had been arrested for suspected involvement in the offence and, on his arrest, the identity of the suspect was known to the police. Therefore, by the time the witnessing officer arrived on the scene, the case involved 'disputed identification evidence' because the suspect had said that he had not done anything while the police had told him he matched the description of a suspected burglar. That said, the court did go on to hold that the judge had the discretion to allow the identification evidence to be adduced notwithstanding the breach of the Codes, but a full and careful direction regarding the breaches, together with a warning about the shortcomings in the procedure, would have been necessary.

Where a suspect is identified by witnesses, other evidence should still be sought to strengthen the case (or to prove the person's innocence) as identification evidence is often challenged at court. Such supporting evidence may include admissions by the suspect that links him/her to the identification evidence; e.g. that he/she owns the vehicle that was driven at the time of the offence (*R* v *Ward* [2001] Crim LR 316).

1.8.4.4 (b) Cases when the suspect is known and available

3.4 If the suspect's identity is known to the police (see *paragraph 3.1A(a)*) and they are available (see *paragraph 3.1A(b)*), the identification procedures that may be used are set out in *paragraphs 3.5* to *3.10* below as follows:
- video identification;
- identification parade; or
- group identification.

(i) Video identification

3.5 A 'video identification' is when the eye-witness is shown images of a known suspect, together with similar images of others who resemble the suspect. *Moving* images must be used unless the conditions in sub-paragraph (a) or (b) below apply:
   (a) this sub-paragraph applies if:
      (i) the identification officer, in consultation with the officer in charge of the investigation, is satisfied that because of aging, or other physical changes or differences, the appearance of the suspect has significantly changed since the previous occasion when the eye-witness claims to have seen the suspect (see *paragraph 3.0*);

(ii) an image (moving or still) is available which the identification officer and the officer in charge of the investigation reasonably believe shows the appearance of the suspect as it was at the t me the suspect was seen by the eye-witness; and

(iii) having regard to the extent of change and the purpose of eye-witness identification procedures (see *paragraph 3.0*), the identification officer believes that that such an image should be shown to the eye-witness.

In such a case, the identificat on officer may arrange a video identification procedure using the image described in (ii). In accordance with the 'Notice to suspect' (see paragraph 3.17(vi)), the suspect must first be given an opportunity to provide their own image(s) for use in the procedure but it is for the identification officer and officer in charge of the investigation to decide whether, following (ii) and (iii), any image(s) provided by the suspect should be used.

A video identification using an image described above may, at the discretion of the identification officer be arranged in addition to, or as an alternative to, a video identification using *moving* images taken after the suspect has been given the information and notice described in *paragraphs 3.17* and *3.18*.

See paragraph 3.21 in any case where the suspect deliberately takes steps to frustrate the eye-witness identification arrangements and procedures.

(b) this sub-paragraph applies if, in accordance with *paragraph 2A* of *Annex A* of this Code, the identification officer does not consider that replication of a physical feature or concealment of the location of the feature can be achieved using a moving image. In these cases, still images may be used.

3.6 Video identifications must be carried out in accordance with *Annex A*.

(ii) Identification parade

3.7 An 'identification parade' is when the eye-witness sees the suspect in a line of others who resemble the suspect.

3.8 Identification parades must be carried out in accordance with *Annex B*.

(iii) Group identification

3.9 A 'group identification' is when the eye-witness sees the suspect in an informal group of people.

3.10 Group identifications must be carried out in accordance with *Annex C*.

Arranging eye-witness identification procedures—duties of identification officer

3.11 Except as provided for in *paragraph 3.13*, the arrangements for, and conduct of, the eye-witness identification procedures in *paragraphs 3.5* to *3.10* and circumstances in which any such identification procedure must be held shall be the responsibility of an officer not below inspector rank who is not involved with the investigation ('the identification officer'). The identification officer may direct another officer or police staff, see *paragraph 2.21*, to make arrangements for, and to conduct, any of these identification procedures and except as provided for in *paragraph 7* of *Annex A*, any reference in this section to the identification officer includes the officer or police staff to whom the arrangements for, and/or conduct of, any of these procedure has been delegated. In de egating these arrangements and procedures, the identification officer must be able to supervise effectively and either intervene or be contacted for advice. Where any action referred to in this paragraph is taken by another officer or police staff at the direction of the identification officer, the outcome shall, as soon as practicable, be reported to the identification officer. For the purpose of these procedures, the identification officer retains overall responsibility for ensuring that the procedure complies with this Code and in add tion, in the case of detained suspect, their care and treatment until returned to the custody officer. Except as permitted by this Code, no officer or any other person involved with the investigation of the case against the suspect may take any part in these procedures or act as the identification officer.

This paragraph does not prevent the identification officer from consulting the officer in charge of the investigation to determine which procedure to use. When an identification procedure is required, in the interest of fairness to suspects and eye-witnesses, it must be held as soon as practicable.

Circumstances in which an eye-witness identification procedure must be held

3.12 If, before any identification procedure set out in *paragraphs 3.5 to 3.10* has been held
(a) an eye-witness has identified a suspect or purported to have identified them; or
(b) there is an eye-witness available who expresses an ability to identify the suspect; or
(c) there is a reasonable chance of an eye-witness being able to identify the suspect,
and the eye-witness in (a) to (c) has not been given an opportunity to identify the suspect in any of the procedures set out in *paragraphs 3.5 to 3.10*, then an identification procedure shall be held if the suspect disputes being the person the eye-witness claims to have seen on a previous occasion (see *paragraph 3.0*), unless:
(i) it is not practicable to hold any such procedure; or
(ii) any such procedure would serve no useful purpose in proving or disproving whether the suspect was involved in committing the offence, for example
   • where the suspect admits being at the scene of the crime and gives an account of what took place and the eye-witness does not see anything which contradicts that; or
   • when it is not disputed that the suspect is already known to the eye-witness who claims to have recognised them when seeing them commit the crime.
3.13 An eye-witness identification procedure may also be held if the officer in charge of the investigation, after consultation with the identification officer, considers it would be useful.

1.8.4.5 **KEYNOTE**

When Must an Identification Procedure be Held?

Identification procedures should be held for the benefit of the defence as well as the prosecution (*R* v *Wait* [1998] Crim LR 68). The key factor to consider when deciding whether to hold an identification parade is whether *a failure to hold a parade could be a matter of genuine potential prejudice to the suspect*. In *R* v *SBC (A Juvenile)* [2001] EWCA Crim 885 the defence was one of duress but the appeal was based on the failure of the police to hold identification parades. The Court of Appeal stated that this was not a case about identification, as none of the defendants denied their presence at the scene. What they denied was their criminal participation in the activities that took place. It followed, therefore, that Code D did not apply. Other examples would be where it is not in dispute that the suspect is already well known to the witness who claims to have seen the suspect commit the crime or where there is no reasonable possibility that a witness would be able to make an identification.

Any decision to proceed without an identification parade must be capable of justification later to the relevant court. The courts have taken different approaches to justification based on practical difficulties. In an early case, the submissions of the identification officer that it was impracticable to find enough people who sufficiently resembled the defendant were treated fairly dismissively by the trial judge (*R* v *Gaynor* [1988] Crim LR 242). In other cases, however, the courts have been more lenient, accepting that the timescales involved in arranging identification parades may render them 'impracticable' (see *R* v *Jamel* [1993] Crim LR 52, where the court refused an objection by the defence to a group identification). A group identification was used in *Jamel* because a parade using mixed-race volunteers would have taken too long to arrange. All reasonable steps must be taken to investigate the possibility of one identification option before moving on to an alternative, and an offer from a suspect's solicitor to find volunteers to stand on a parade is such a 'reasonable' step (*R* v *Britton & Richards* [1989] Crim LR 144).

There have been a number of Court of Appeal cases concerning the requirement to hold identification parades. It is suggested that these should be applied to the Code regardless of which form of identification procedure is used. The leading case is *R v Forbes* [2001] 1 AC 473, which was based on earlier versions of the Code of Practice. The House of Lords held that if the police are in possession of sufficient evidence to justify the arrest of a suspect, and that suspect's identification depends on eye-witness identification evidence, even in part, then if the identification is disputed, the Code requires that an identification parade should be held with the suspect's consent, unless one of the exceptions applies.

The House of Lords went on to say that this mandatory obligation to hold an identification procedure applies even if there has been a 'fully satisfactory', 'actual and complete' or 'unequivocal' identification of the suspect.

Despite the wording of Code D, it has been held that a suspect's right to have an identification [procedure] is not confined to cases where a dispute over identity has already arisen; that right also applies where such a dispute might reasonably be anticipated (*R v Rutherford and Palmer* (1994) 98 Cr App R 191). Similarly, a suspect's failure to request an identification [procedure] does not mean that the police may proceed without one (*R v Graham* [1994] Crim LR 212).

It is important to consider the distinction between identification of a suspect and the suspect's clothing or other features. In *D v DPP* (1998) *The Times*, 7 August, a witness had observed two youths for a continuous period of five to six minutes and then informed the police of what he had seen, describing the age of the youths and the clothes that they were wearing. The court held that there had not been an identification within the terms of the Codes of Practice because the witness had at no stage identified the defendant or the co-accused. He had described only their clothing and their approximate ages, and the police, acting on that information, had made the arrests. An identification parade could have served no useful purpose, since the clothing would have been changed and those persons used for the parade would have been the same approximate age. This point was further supported in *R v Haynes* [2004] EWCA Crim 390, where the Court of Appeal held that as a practical point the identification parade, whether or not the suspect was regarded as a known or unknown suspect, was of little value where the witness identified the suspect by clothing and not by recognition of the suspect's features. An identification parade would have provided little assistance.

The question for the court will be whether it is fair to admit the identification evidence. When looking at this issue the court will consider how reliable that identification evidence is.

In para. 3.5(a)(i), examples of physical changes or differences that the identification officer may wish to consider include hair style and colour, weight, facial hair, wearing or removal of spectacles and tinted contact lenses, facial injuries, tattoos and make-up.

1.8.4.6   Selecting an eye-witness identification procedure

3.14 If, because of *paragraph 3.12*, an identification procedure is to be held, the suspect shall initially be invited to take part in a video identification unless:

(a) a video identification is not practicable; or

(b) an identification parade is both practicable and more suitable than a video identification; or

(c) *paragraph 3.16* applies.

The identification officer and the officer in charge of the investigation shall consult each other to determine which option is to be offered. An identification parade may not be practicable because of factors relating to the witnesses, such as their number, state of health, availability and travelling requirements. A video identification would normally be more suitable if it could be arranged and completed sooner than an identification parade. Before an option is offered the suspect must also be reminded of their entitlement to have free legal advice, see Code C, *paragraph 6.5*.

3.15 A suspect who refuses the identification procedure in which the suspect is first invited to take part shall be asked to state their reason for refusing and may get advice from their solicitor and/or if present, their appropriate adult. The suspect, solicitor and/or appropriate adult shall be allowed to make representations about why another procedure should be used. A record should be made of the reasons for refusal and any representations made. After considering any reasons given, and representations made, the identification officer shall, if appropriate, arrange for the suspect to be invited to take part in an alternative which the officer considers suitable and practicable. If the officer decides it is not suitable and practicable to invite the suspect to take part in an alternative identification procedure, the reasons for that decision shall be recorded.

3.16 A suspect may initially be invited to take part in a group identification if the officer in charge of the investigation considers it is more suitable than a video identification or an identification parade and the identification officer considers it practicable to arrange.

Notice to suspect

3.17 Unless *paragraph 3.20* applies, before any eye-witness identification procedure set out in *paragraphs 3.5* to *3.10* is arranged, the following shall be explained to the suspect:

(i) the purpose of the procedure (see *paragraph 3.0*);

(ii) their entitlement to free legal advice; see Code C, *paragraph 6.5*;

(iii) the procedures for holding it, including their right, subject to *Annex A, paragraph 9*, to have a solicitor or friend present;

(iv) that they do not have to consent to or co-operate in the procedure;

(v) that if they do not consent to, and co-operate in, a procedure, their refusal may be given in evidence in any subsequent trial and police may proceed covertly without their consent or make other arrangements to test whether an eye-witness can identify them, see *paragraph 3.21*;

(vi) whether, for the purposes of a video identification procedure, images of them have previously been obtained either:
   • in accordance with *paragraph 3.20*, and if so, that they may co-operate in providing further, suitable images to be used instead; or
   • in accordance with *paragraph 3.5(a)*, and if so, that they may provide their own images for the identification officer to consider using.

(vii) if appropriate, the special arrangements for juveniles;

(viii) if appropriate, the special arrangements for mentally disordered or otherwise mentally vulnerable people;

(ix) that if they significantly alter their appearance between being offered an identification procedure and any attempt to hold an identification procedure, this may be given in evidence if the case comes to trial, and the identification officer may then consider other forms of identification, see *paragraph 3.21*;

(x) that a moving image or photograph may be taken of them when they attend for any identification procedure;

(xi) whether, before their identity became known, the eye-witness was shown photographs, a computerised or artist's composite likeness or similar likeness or image by the police,

(xii) that if they change their appearance before an identification parade, it may not be practicable to arrange one on the day or subsequently and, because of the appearance change, the identification officer may consider alternative methods of identification,

(xiii) that they or their solicitor will be provided with details of the description of the suspect as first given by any eye-witnesses who are to attend the procedure or confrontation, see *paragraph 3.1*.

3.18 This information must also be recorded in a written notice handed to the suspect. The suspect must be given a reasonable opportunity to read the notice, after which, they should be asked to sign a copy of the notice to indicate if they are willing to co-operate with the making of a video or take part in the identification parade or group identification. The signed copy shall be retained by the identification officer.

3.19 In the case of a detained suspect, the duties under *paragraphs 3.17* and *3.18* may be performed by the custody officer or by another officer or police staff not involved in the investigation as directed by the custody officer, if:

(a) it is proposed to release the suspect in order that an identification procedure can be arranged and carried out and an inspector is not available to act as the identification officer, see *paragraph 3.11*, before the suspect leaves the station; or

(b) it is proposed to keep the suspect in police detention whilst the procedure is arranged and carried out and waiting for an inspector to act as the identification officer, see *paragraph 3.11*, would cause unreasonable delay to the investigation.

The officer concerned shall inform the identification officer of the action taken and give them the signed copy of the notice.

3.20 If the identification officer and officer in charge of the investigation suspect, on reasonable grounds that if the suspect was given the information and notice as in *paragraphs 3.17* and *3.18*, they would then take steps to avoid being seen by a witness in any identification procedure, the identification officer may arrange for images of the suspect suitable for use in a video identification procedure to be obtained before giving the information and notice. If suspect's images are obtained in these circumstances, the suspect may, for the purposes of a video identification procedure, co-operate in providing new images which if suitable, would be used instead. see *paragraph 3.17(vi)*.

1.8.4.7 **KEYNOTE**

When an eye-witness attending an identification procedure has previously been shown photographs, or been shown or provided with computerised or artist's composite likenesses, or similar likenesses or pictures, it is the officer in charge of the investigation's responsibility to make the identification officer aware of this. The purpose of allowing the custody officer or other officer not involved in the investigation to undertake the role of the identification officer at Code D, paras 3.17 and 3.18 is to avoid or reduce delays in arranging identification procedures by enabling the required information and warning to be given at the earliest opportunity.

1.8.4.8 **(c) Cases when the suspect is known but not available**

3.21 When a known suspect is not available or has ceased to be available, see *paragraph 3.1A*, the identification officer may make arrangements for a video identification (see paragraph 3.5 and *Annex A*). If necessary, the identification officer may follow the video identification procedures using any suitable moving or still images and these may be obtained covertly if necessary. Alternatively, the identification officer may make arrangements for a group identification without the suspect's consent (see Annex C *paragraph 34*). These provisions may also be applied to juveniles where the consent of their parent or guardian is either refused or reasonable efforts to obtain that consent have failed (see *paragraph 2.12*).

3.22 Any covert activity should be strictly limited to that necessary to test the ability of the eye-witness to identify the suspect as the person they saw on the relevant previous occasion.

3.23 The identification officer may arrange for the suspect to be confronted by the eye-witness if none of the options referred to in *paragraphs 3.5* to *3.10* or *3.21* are practicable. A 'confrontation' is when the suspect is directly confronted by the eye-witness. A confrontation does not require the suspect's consent. Confrontations must be carried out in accordance with Annex D.

3.24 Requirements for information to be given to, or sought from, a suspect or for the suspect to be given an opportunity to view images before they are shown to an eye-witness, do not apply if the suspect's lack of co-operation prevents the necessary action.

KEYNOTE

Which Identification Procedure should be Used?

Code D, para. 3.21 also apples where a suspect refuses or fails to take part in a video identification, an iden-tification parade or a group identification, or refuses or fails to take part in the only practicable options from that list. It enables any suitable images of the suspect, moving or still, which are available or can be obtained, to be used in an identification procedure. Examples include images from custody and other CCTV systems and from visually recorded interview records.

It is only if none of the other options are practicable that the identification officer may arrange for the suspect to be confronted by the witness. A confrontation does not require the suspect's consent. In *R* v *McCulloch, Smith & Wheeler* (1999) 6 May, unreported, the Court of Appeal made it clear that confrontations between suspects and witnesses should only be carried out if no other identification procedure is practicable.

1.8.4.10 (d) Documentation

3.25 A record shall be made of the video identification, identification parade, group identification or confrontation on forms provided for the purpose.

3.26 If the identification officer considers it is not practicable to hold a video identification or identification parade requested by the suspect, the reasons shall be recorded and explained to the suspect.

3.27 A record shall be made of a person's failure or refusal to co-operate in a video identification, identification parade or group identification and, if applicable, of the grounds for obtaining images in accordance with *paragraph 3.20*.

(e) Not used

3.28 *Not used.*

3.29 *Not used.*

(f) Destruction and retention of photographs taken or used in eye-witness identification procedures

3.30 PACE, section 64A, see *paragraph 5.12*, provides powers to take photographs of suspects and allows these photographs to be used or disclosed only for purposes related to the prevention or detection of crime, the investigation of offences or the conduct of prosecutions by, or on behalf of, police or other law enforcement and prosecuting authorities inside and outside the United Kingdom or the enforcement of a sentence. After being so used or disclosed, they may be retained but can only be used or disclosed for the same purposes.

3.31 Subject to *paragraph 3.33*, the photographs (and all negatives and copies), of suspects *not* taken in accordance with the provisions in *paragraph 5.12* which are taken for the purposes of, or in connection with, the identification procedures in *paragraphs 3.5* to *3.10, 3.21 or 3.23* must be destroyed unless the suspect:

(a) is charged with, or informed they may be prosecuted for, a recordable offence;

(b) is prosecuted for a recordable offence;

(c) is cautioned for a recordable offence or given a warning or reprimand in accordance with the Crime and Disorder Act 1998 for a recordable offence; or

(d) gives informed consent, in writing, for the photograph or images to be retained for pur-poses described in *paragraph 3.30*.

3.32 When *paragraph 3.31* requires the destruction of any photograph, the person must be given an opportunity to witness the destruction or to have a certificate confirming the destruction if they request one within five days of being informed that the destruction is required.

3.33 Nothing in *paragraph 3.31* affects any separate requirement under the Criminal Procedure and Investigations Act 1996 to retain material in connection with criminal investigations.

1.8.4.11 Part (B) Recognition by *controlled* showing of films, photographs and images

3.34 This Part of this section applies when, for the purposes of obtaining evidence of recognition, arrangements are made for a person, including a police officer, who is *not* an eye-witness

(a) to view a film, photograph or any other visual medium; and

(b) on the occasion of the viewing, to be asked whether they recognise anyone whose image is shown in the material as someone who is known to them.

The arrangements for such viewings may be made by the officer in charge of the relevant investigation. Although there is no requirement for the identification officer to make the arrangements or to be consulted about the arrangements, nothing prevents this.

3.35 To provide safeguards against mistaken recognition and to avoid any possibility of collusion, on the occasion of the viewing, the arrangements should ensure:

(a) that the films, photographs and other images are shown on an individual basis;

(b) that any person who views the material;

　(i) is unable to communicate with any other individual to whom the material has been, or is to be, shown;

　(ii) is not reminded of any photograph or description of any individual whose image is shown or given any other indication as to the identity of any such individual;

　(iii) is not be told whether a previous witness has recognised any one;

(c) that immediately before a person views the material, they are told that:

　(i) an individual who is known to them may, or may not, appear in the material they are shown and that if they do not recognise anyone, they should say so;

　(ii) at any point, they may ask to see a particular part of the material frozen for them to study and there is no limit on how many times they can view the whole or any part or parts of the material; and

(d) that the person who views the material is not asked to make any decision as to whether they recognise anyone whose image they have seen as someone known to them until they have seen the whole of the material at least twice, unless the officer in charge of the viewing decides that because of the number of images the person has been invited to view, it would not be reasonable to ask them to view the whole of the material for a second time. A record of this decision must be included in the record that is made in accordance with *paragraph 3.36*.

3.36 A record of the circumstances and conditions under which the person is given an opportunity to recognise an individual must be made and the record must include:

(a) whether the person knew or was given information concerning the name or identity of any suspect;

(b) what the person has been told *before* the viewing about the offence, the person(s) depicted in the images or the offender and by whom;

(c) how and by whom the witness was asked to view the image or look at the individual;

(d) whether the viewing was alone or with others and if with others, the reason for it;

(e) the arrangements under which the person viewed the film or saw the individual and by whom those arrangements were made;

(f) subject to *paragraph 2.18*, the name and rank of the officer responsible for deciding that the viewing arrangements should be made in accordance with this Part;

(g) the date time and place images were viewed or further viewed or the individual was seen;

(h) the times between which the images were viewed or the individual was seen;

(i) how the viewing of images or sighting of the individual was controlled and by whom;

(j) whether the person was familiar with the location shown in any images or the place where they saw the individual and if so, why;

(k) whether or not, on this occasion, the person claims to recognise any image shown, or any individual seen, as being someone known to them, and if they do:

    (i) the reason;

    (ii) the words of recognition;

    (iii) any expressions of doubt; and

    (iv) what features of the image or the individual triggered the recognition.

3.37 The record required under *paragraph 3.36* may be made by the person who views the image or sees the individual and makes the recognition; and if applicable, by the officer or police staff in charge of showing the images to that person or in charge of the conditions under which that person sees the individual. The person must be asked to read and check the completed record and as applicable, confirm that it is correctly and accurately reflects the part they played in the viewing.

1.8.4.12

KEYNOTE

Photographs, Image and Sound Reproduction Generally

The use of photographic and computer-generated images (such as E-Fit) to identify suspects has increased considerably over the past few years. Although the courts will exercise considerable caution when admitting such evidence (*R v Blenkinsop* [1995] 1 Cr App R 7), these methods of identification are particularly useful. Expert evidence may be admitted to interpret images on film (see e.g. *R v Stockwell* (1993) 97 Cr App R 260) and police officers who are very familiar with a particular film clip (e.g. of crowd violence at a football match) may be allowed to assist the court in interpreting and explaining events shown within it (*R v Clare* [1995] 2 Cr App R 333).

Logically E-Fit and other witness-generated images would be treated as 'visual statements', in that they represent the witness's recollection of what he/she saw. However, the Court of Appeal has decided that they are not to be so treated (*R v Cook* [1987] QB 417) and therefore the restrictions imposed by the rule against hearsay will not apply (see also *R v Constantinou* (1990) 91 Cr App R 74, where this ruling was followed in relation to a photofit image).

1.8.4.13

KEYNOTE

Recognition Cases

Recognition cases, that is to say, those cases where the witness states that he/she knows the person who committed the offence as opposed to only being able to give a description, need to be carefully considered and Part B of section 3 of this Code adhered to. The eye-witness identification procedures in Part A should not be used to test whether a witness can recognise a person as someone he/she knows and would be able to give evidence of recognition along the lines of 'On (describe date, time, location) I saw an image of an individual who I recognised as XY'. In these cases, the procedures in Part B of section 3 of this Code shall apply. The admissibility and value of evidence of recognition obtained when carrying out the procedures in Part B may be compromised if before the person is recognised, the witness who has claimed to know him/her is given or is made, or becomes, aware of, information about the person which was not previously known to the witness personally but which he/she has purported to rely on to support his/her claim that the person is in fact known to him/her.

In *R v Ridley* (1999) *The Times*, 13 October, the Court of Appeal stated that there has never been a rule that an identification parade had to be held in all recognition cases and that it will be a question of fact in each case whether or not there is a need to do so. The view that an identification procedure is not required in these cases is supported by para. 3.12(ii).

The facts in *Ridley*, which it is suggested are not uncommon among patrolling officers, were that two police officers in a marked police vehicle noticed a car, which had been stolen earlier that day, drive past them. Both officers said that they recognised the defendant driving the car. The officers gave chase and gave evidence that the car was speeding and being driven dangerously. They decided that it was unsafe to continue pursuit, but arrested the suspect six days later. One of the officers claimed to have recognised the suspect because she had interviewed him for some 20 minutes five months previously and had seen him about town. She gave evidence that she had a view of the suspect in the car for about nine seconds. The other officer said that he recognised the suspect from a photograph but could not say when he had seen that photograph. He said that he had seen the suspect in the car for about two seconds. The court found that the female police officer's identification had been complete and there was no requirement for her to have further identified the suspect.

Ridley can be contrasted with *R v Conway* (1990) 91 Cr App R 143, where the witnesses' evidence was not as strong. There the witnesses stated that they recognised the accused simply because they knew him. The defence argument was that the witnesses did not actually know the accused and so could not have recognised him at the time of the offence. His conviction was quashed because of the prejudice caused by the absence of a parade. In *R v Davies* [2004] EWCA Crim 2521 a witness identified a masked attacker from his voice and eyes. The court in this case held that this identification evidence coupled with other circumstantial evidence was sufficient for a conviction.

A case can still amount to one of recognition, even where the witness does not know the name of the suspect but later obtained those details from a third party, for example where the witness and the suspect went to the same school and the witness became aware of the suspect's full names from other pupils at the school (*R v C; R v B* [2003] EWCA Crim 718).

In *R (On the Application of H) v DPP* [2003] EWHC 133 (Admin), the court accepted that it was reasonable for the police not to undertake an identification procedure. In the circumstances of the case the police had every reason to believe that the claimant and the victim were well known to each other. The claimant had accepted that the victim knew her. There was no question of doubt as to the victim's ability to recognise the claimant and as such this was a case of pure recognition where it was futile to hold an identification parade.

Care must be taken in cases where it is believed that the case is one of recognition not requiring an identification procedure. In *R v Harris* [2003] EWCA Crim 174 the witness stated that he recognised the suspect as being someone he went to school with. The suspect gave a prepared statement in which he disputed the suggestion that he was well known to the witness. Here the court held that an identification procedure should have been undertaken, as the circumstances of the case did not fall within the general exception of the Code, i.e. that an identification procedure would serve no useful purpose in proving or disproving whether the suspect had been involved in committing the offence. It is suggested therefore that where a suspect disputes that a witness knows him/her, an identification procedure should be considered.

When a suspect is filmed committing an offence, it may be admissible to give evidence of identification by way of recognition from a witness not present at the scene. In *Attorney-General's Ref (No. 2 of 2002)* [2002] EWCA Crim 2373 the Court reviewed the previous case law and concluded that there are at least four circumstances in which a jury could be invited to conclude that a defendant committed an offence on the basis of photographic evidence from the scene

- where the photographic image was sufficiently clear the jury could compare it with the defendant sitting in the dock;
- where a witness knew the defendant sufficiently well to recognise him or her as the offender depicted in the photographic image;
- where a witness who did not know the defendant spent substantial time viewing and analysing photographic images from the scene, thereby acquiring special knowledge which the jury did not have, evidence of identification based on comparison between them and a reasonably contemporary photo of the defendant could be given so long as the image and photograph were available to the jury. Further, in *R v Savalia* [2011] EWCA Crim 1334 the court held that this did not just apply to facial features but could properly be extended to apply to identification of a defendant from closed-circuit television footage based on a combination of factors, including build and gait;

- a suitably qualified expert with facial mapping skills giving opinion evidence of identification based on a comparison between images from the scene and a reasonably contemporary photograph of the defendant could be given so long as the image and photograph were available to the jury.

In *R* v *Purlis* [2017] EWCA Crim 1134, a dashboard camera captured a robber departing the scene in the car. The court allowed a facial mapping expert to give evidence that by comparing images from the dashcam with photographs of the suspect he could identify features which taken together lent powerful support to the contention that the images were of the same man. This followed the case of *R* v *Atkins* [2010] 1 Cr App R 8 where the court held that it is important to approach the evidence of facial mapping with caution. That does not mean that you cannot rely on the expert evidence. Simply that it needs to be considered with care. The court went on to say that an expert who spends many years studying this kind of evidence can properly form an opinion as to the significance of what he/she has found.

CCTV

The case of *R* v *Lariba* [2015] EWCA Crim 478 involved police officers while off duty recognising a suspect for a local 'gang' murder from CCTV pictures that had been circulated on the internet by their own police force. The officers were local officers who regularly came into contact with gang members; although the suspect's face was partially covered the officers recognised him from his general demeanour, skin tone, hairline, eyebrows and clothing. At the time of the recognition the officers did not make any notes.

The Court of Appeal considered that the strength of the connection between the witnesses and the appellant was relevant to the issue whether a partial facial view of the suspect would be sufficient to permit recognition, noting that the witnesses were police officers who saw and spoke to Lariba on many occasions. The Court of Appeal stated that the more familiar in face, head, build and manner the person is to the witness the more likely it is that the witness can make a reliable identification of that person from a CCTV recording providing a similarly incomplete view of his face. In relation to formal identification procedures the Court of Appeal stated that Code D, para. 3.28 permits viewing of images with a view to recognition by a witness or police officer and tracing a suspect. Code D applies to any occasion when, for the purpose of obtaining evidence of recognition, any person including a police officer views a photographic or other recording (para. 3.34). The context of paras 3.35 and 3.36 was said to demonstrate that the procedure can in practice only apply to arrangements made by the police for specific viewing. They cannot practicably apply to invitations to the public in general to view scenes of crime or other images of suspects via television or internet outlets with a request that recognition is reported to the investigation team.

It is important that where pictures or film are shown to specific police officers to try to identify suspects, this must be done in a controlled way. In *R* v *Smith (Dean) and others* [2008] EWCA Crim 1342, the court held that a police officer who was asked to view a CCTV recording to see if he could recognise any suspects involved in a robbery was not in the same shoes as a witness asked to identify someone he/she had seen committing a crime. However, safeguards that Code D was designed to put in place were equally important in cases where a police officer was asked to see whether he/she could recognise anyone in a CCTV recording. Whether or not Code D applied, there had to be in place some record that assisted in gauging the reliability of the assertion that the police officer recognised an individual. It was important that a police officer's initial reactions to viewing a CCTV recording were set out and available for scrutiny. Thus, if the police officer failed to recognise anyone on first viewing but did so subsequently, those circumstances ought to be noted. If a police officer failed to pick anybody else out, that also should be recorded, as should any words of doubt. Furthermore, it was necessary that if recognition took place a record was made of what it was about the image that was said to have triggered the recognition. The case of *R* v *JD* [2012] EWCA Crim 2637 further highlights the need to keep records and comply with the Codes. As there was no record of how the police officer in this case viewed the CCTV, the court held that the defence could not test the officer's account that he watched the footage alone and no records had been made as to what features of the image triggered the recognition and other aspects of the recognition. It had been highly suggestive of the investigating constable to tell C that she believed D to feature in the CCTV footage rather than simply asking him to watch it and waiting to see if he recognised anybody. Another case is *R* v *McCook* [2012] EWCA Crim 2817, where the court commented on some of the processes required by Code D, for example the witness's statement did not reveal the nature of the viewing equipment, the number of times the footage was played, how the viewing arrangements were made, what the witness had been told prior to the viewing and whether or not he/she was alone.

If a film which has been shown to a witness is later lost or unavailable, the witness may give evidence of what he/she saw on that film but the court will have to consider all the relevant circumstances in deciding whether to admit that evidence and what weight to attach to it (*Taylor* v *Chief Constable of Cheshire* [1986] 1 WLR 1479).

In cases where officers view many hours of CCTV which results in them identifying suspects from these viewings, it is important that they provide an objective means of testing the accuracy of their recognition identification. This may include any initial reactions to seeing the CCTV images if the officer fails to recognise anyone on the initial viewing but does so at a later date; where there is recognition, any factors relating to the image that caused that recognition to occur (*R* v *Yaryare, Hassan and Oman* [2020] EWCA Crim 1314). In this case, the trial judge emphasised that from a practical point of view it may be unrealistic to expect an officer to note all of his or her passing thoughts whilst watching CCTV footage time and again. Any conclusions in a case such as the present are likely to emerge incrementally, and the fine detail of an improving or changing recognition may be difficult to record in a log. However, that said, the officer should record, in accordance with the approach established in Code D, at the least, the 'Red Letter' events—the moments, for instance, when they first begin to note similarities with a particular individual, along with any significant features that occur to them during the process of viewing. They should also note any factors that tend to indicate the suspect does not match a particular individual who is being considered.

Social Media Identifications

Other types of identification are also coming before the courts which have been seen on social media platforms. In *R* v *Crampton* [2020] EWCA Crim 1334, the victim, when aged between 4 and 6, was left at home by her parents with a man called Mark who sexually assaulted her. The family did not report the matter to police out of concern that this might further traumatise the child. They took the view that it was best to forget about the incident. The victim did not, however, forget and eventually, in 2018 aged 25, she reported the matter to police naming the perpetrator as Mark Crampton, having identified him as the offender after she found a photograph of him on Facebook. The complainant accurately recollected that the man who had abused her had blonde curly hair and this was not something that was evident from the Facebook image. Crampton was interviewed and charged with sexual offences; no formal identification procedure was held. The judgment was that this was a breach of Code D and a formal identification procedure should be held. The court commented that

> The danger of course with these identifications is that they do not take place under the controlled conditions of an identification procedure, which of course these days 99 times out of 100 is a VIPER procedure. But as the CPS makes clear on their website Facebook identifications are increasingly common and are admissible in evidence and frankly if the position was the other way, then it would be a very strange state of affairs because it is the natural reaction of anybody seeking to identify the suspect of having committed a crime against them or somebody else to look on Facebook in order to identify who they are. So, the courts will have to wrestle with Facebook identifications for a considerable time into the future.

R v *McCullough* [2011] EWCA Crim 1413 was a case where the victim of a robbery identified the suspect from a photograph on Facebook and then later identified the suspect on a video identification parade. The Court of Appeal found that the Facebook identification was far from ideal and it was capable of having a substantial effect on the weight of the witness's subsequent identification of the defendant in the formal identification procedure. The key here is that the formal identification procedure is still required.

In *R* v *Alexander and McGill* [2012] EWCA Crim 2768 the victim identified the suspects through their Facebook account pictures. The court observed that it was therefore incumbent upon investigators to take steps to obtain, in as much detail as possible, evidence in relation to the initial identification. In this case, before trial, requests were made by the defence for photographs of the other Facebook pages that had been considered by victim and his sister so that the defendants could consider how their identifications might have been made.

1.8.4.14

KEYNOTE

Voice Identification

The Codes do not preclude the police making use of aural identification procedures such as a 'voice identification parade', where they judge that appropriate.

Generally, a witness may give evidence identifying the defendant's voice (*R* v *Robb* (1991) 93 Cr App R 161), while expert testimony may be admitted in relation to tape recordings of a voice which is alleged to belong to the defendant. In the latter case, the jury should be allowed to hear the recording(s) so that they can draw their own conclusions (*R* v *Bentum* (1989) 153 JP 538).

In *R* v *Flynn*; *R* v *St John* [2008] EWCA Crim 970 the Court of Appeal held that where the voice identification is from a recording a prerequisite for making a speaker identification was that there should be a sample of an adequate size from the disputed recording that could confidently be attributed to a single speaker. The court also recognised that expert evidence showed that lay listeners with considerable familiarity with a voice and listening to a clear recording could still make mistakes. It is therefore suggested that other supporting evidence will be needed for a conviction to succeed.

Home Office Circular 57/2003, *Advice on the Use of Voice Identification Parades*, provides guidance on the use of voice identification parades.

1.8.4.15

KEYNOTE

Identification of Disqualified Drivers

Another common identification problem is that of disqualified drivers and being able to satisfy the court that the person charged with disqualified driving is the same person who was disqualified by the court. This is because s. 73 of the Police and Criminal Evidence Act 1984 requires proof that the person named in a certificate of conviction as having been convicted is the person whose conviction is to be proved. There has been some guidance from the courts as to how this can be achieved. In *R* v *Derwentside Justices, ex parte Heaviside* [1996] RTR 384, the court stated that this could be done by:

- fingerprints under s. 39 of the Criminal Justice Act 1948;
- the evidence of a person who was present in court when the disqualification order was made;
- admission of the defendant (preferably in interview) (*DPP* v *Mooney* (1997) RTR 434);
- requiring the suspect's solicitor who was present when he/she was disqualified on the earlier occasion to give evidence (such a summons is a last resort when there was no other means of identifying whether an individual had been disqualified from driving) (*R (On the Application of Howe) and Law Society (Interested Party)* v *South Durham Magistrates' Court and CPS (Interested Party)* [2004] EWHC 362 (Admin)).

The methods outlined in *Heaviside* are not exhaustive, but just suggested methods (*DPP* v *Mansfield* [1997] RTR 96).

1.8.4.16

Part (C) Recognition by *uncontrolled* viewing of films, photographs and images

3.38 This Part applies when, for the purpose of identifying and tracing suspects, films and photographs of incidents or other images are:

    (a) shown to the public (which may include police officers and police staff as well as members of the public) through the national or local media or any social media networking site; or

    (b) circulated through local or national police communication systems for viewing by police officers and police staff; and

   the viewing is not formally controlled and supervised as set out in Part B.

3.39 A copy of the relevant material released to the national or local media for showing as described in sub-paragraph 3.38(a), shall be kept. The suspect or their solicitor shall be allowed to view such material before any eye-witness identification procedure under *paragraphs 3.5 to 3.10, 3.21 or 3.23* of Part A are carried out, provided it is practicable and would not unreasonably delay the investigation. This paragraph does not affect any separate requirement under the Criminal Procedure and Investigations Act 1996 to retain material in connection with criminal investigations that might apply to *sub-paragraphs 3.38(a) and (b)*.

3.40 Each eye-witness involved in any eye-witness identification procedure under *paragraphs 3.5 to 3.10, 3.21 or 3.23* shall be asked, *after they have taken part*, whether they have seen any film, photograph or image relating to the offence or any description of the suspect which has been broadcast or published as described in *paragraph 3.38(a)* and their reply recorded. If they have, they should be asked to give details of the circumstances and subject to the eyewitness's recollection, the record described in *paragraph 3.41* should be completed.

3.41 As soon as practicable after an individual (member of the public, police officer or police staff) indicates in response to a viewing that they may have information relating to the identity and whereabouts of anyone they have seen in that viewing, arrangements should be made to ensure that they are asked to give details of the circumstances and, subject to the individual's recollection, a record of the circumstances and conditions under which the viewing took place is made. This record shall be made in accordance with the provisions of *paragraph 3.36* insofar as they can be applied to the viewing in question.

1.8.4.17

KEYNOTE

It is important that the record referred to in paras 3.36 and 3.41 is made as soon as practicable after the viewing and whilst it is fresh in the mind of the individual who makes the recognition.

1.8.5

Code D—4 Identification by Fingerprints and Footwear Impressions

(A) Taking fingerprints in connection with a criminal investigation

(a) General

4.1 References to 'fingerprints' means any record, produced by any method, of the skin pattern and other physical characteristics or features of a person's:
   (i) fingers; or
   (ii) palms.

(b) Action

4.2 A person's fingerprints may be taken in connection with the investigation of an offence only with their consent or if *paragraph 4.3* applies. If the person is at a police station consent must be in writing.

4.3 PACE, section 61, provides powers to take fingerprints without consent from any person aged ten or over as follows:
   (a) under section 61(3), from a person detained at a police station in consequence of being arrested for a recordable offence, if they have not had their fingerprints taken in the course of the investigation of the offence unless those previously taken fingerprints are not a complete set or some or all of those fingerprints are not of sufficient quality to allow satisfactory analysis, comparison or matching;

(b) under section 61(4), from a person detained at a police station who has been charged with a recordable offence, or informed they will be reported for such an offence if they have not had their fingerprints taken in the course of the investigation of the offence unless those previously taken fingerprints are not a complete set or some or all of those fingerprints are not of sufficient quality to allow satisfactory analysis, comparison or matching.

(c) under section 61(4A), from a person who has been bailed to appear at a court or police station if the person:

   (i) has answered to bail for a person whose fingerprints were taken previously and there are reasonable grounds for believing they are not the same person; or

   (ii) who has answered to bail claims to be a different person from a person whose fingerprints were previously taken;

and in either case, the court or an officer of inspector rank or above, authorises the fingerprints to be taken at the court or police station (an inspector's authority may be given in writing or orally and confirmed in writing as soon as practicable);

(ca) under section 61(5A) from a person who has been arrested for a recordable offence and released if the person:

   (i) is on bail and has not had their fingerprints taken in the course of the investigation of the offence, or;

   (ii) has had their fingerprints taken in the course of the investigation of the offence, but they do not constitute a complete set or some, or all, of the fingerprints are not of sufficient quality to allow satisfactory analysis, comparison or matching;

(cb) under section 61(5B) from a person not detained at a police station who has been charged with a recordable offence or informed they will be reported for such an offence if:

   (i) they have not had their fingerprints taken in the course of the investigation; or

   (ii) their fingerprints have been taken in the course of the investigation of the offence but either:

     • they do not constitute a complete set or some, or all, of the fingerprints are not of sufficient quality to allow satisfactory analysis, comparison or matching; or

     • the investigation was discontinued but subsequently resumed and, before the resumption, their fingerprints were destroyed pursuant to section 63D(3).

(d) under section 61(6), from a person who has been:

   (i) convicted of a recordable offence; or

   (ii) given a caution in respect of a recordable offence which, at the time of the caution, the person admitted;

if, since being convicted or cautioned:

     • their fingerprints have not been taken; or

     • their fingerprints which have been taken do not constitute a complete set or some, or all, of the fingerprints are not of sufficient quality to allow satisfactory analysis, comparison or matching;

and in either case, an officer of inspector rank or above, is satisfied that taking the fingerprints is necessary to assist in the prevention or detection of crime and authorises the taking;

(e) under section 61(6A) from a person a constable reasonably suspects is committing or attempting to commit, or has committed or attempted to commit, any offence if either:

   (i) the person's name is unknown to, and cannot be readily ascertained by, the constable; or

   (ii) the constable has reasonable grounds for doubting whether a name given by the person is their real name.

Note: fingerprints taken under this power are not regarded as having been taken in the course of the investigation of an offence.

(f) under section 61(6D) from a person who has been convicted outside England and Wales of an offence which if committed in England and Wales would be a qualifying offence as defined by PACE, section 65A if:

   (i) the person's fingerprints have not been taken previously under this power or their fingerprints have been so taken on a previous occasion but they do not constitute a complete set or some, or all, of the fingerprints are not of sufficient quality to allow satisfactory analysis, comparison or matching; and

   (ii) a police officer of inspector rank or above is satisfied that taking fingerprints is necessary to assist in the prevention or detection of crime and authorises them to be taken.

4.4 PACE, section 63A(4) and Schedule 2A provide powers to:

(a) make a requirement (in accordance with *Annex G*) for a person to attend a police station to have their fingerprints taken in the exercise of one of the following powers (described in *paragraph 4.3* above) within certain periods as follows:

   (i) *section 61(5A)*—Persons arrested for a recordable offence and released, see *paragraph 4.3(ca)*: In the case of a person whose fingerprints were taken in the course of the investigation but those fingerprints do not constitute a complete set or some, or all of the fingerprints are not of sufficient quality, the requirement may not be made more than six months from the day the investigating officer was informed that the fingerprints previously taken were incomplete or below standard. In the case of a person whose fingerprints were destroyed prior to the resumption of the investigation, the requirement may not be made more than six months from the day on which the investigation resumed.

   (ii) *section 61(5B)*—Persons not detained at a police station charged etc. with a recordable offence, see *paragraph 4.3(cb)*: The requirement may not be made more than six months from:

      • the day the person was charged or informed that they would be reported, if fingerprints have not been taken in the course of the investigation of the offence; or

      • the day the investigating officer was informed that the fingerprints previously taken were incomplete or below standard, if fingerprints have been taken in the course of the investigation but those fingerprints do not constitute a complete set or some, or all, of the fingerprints are not of sufficient quality; or

      • the day on which the investigation was resumed, in the case of a person whose fingerprints were destroyed prior to the resumption of the investigation.

   (iii) *section 61(6)*—Person convicted or cautioned for a recordable offence in England and Wales, see *paragraph 4.3(d)*: Where the offence for which the person was convicted or cautioned is a qualifying offence, there is no time limit for the exercise of this power. Where the conviction or caution is for a recordable offence which is not a qualifying offence, the requirement may not be made more than two years from:

      • in the case of a person who has not had their fingerprints taken since the conviction or caution, the day on which the person was convicted or cautioned, or, if later, the day on which Schedule 2A came into force (March 7, 2011); or

      • in the case of a person whose fingerprints have been taken in the course of the investigation but those fingerprints do not constitute a complete set or some, or all, of the fingerprints are not of sufficient quality, the day on which an officer from the force investigating the offence was informed that the fingerprints previously taken were incomplete or below standard, or, if later, the day on which Schedule 2A came into force (March 7, 2011).

   (iv) *section 61(6D)*—A person who has been convicted of a qualifying offence outside England and Wales, see *paragraph 4.3(g)*: There is no time limit for making the requirement.

Note: A person who has had their fingerprints taken under any of the powers in section 61 mentioned in *paragraph 4.3* on two occasions in relation to any offence may not be required under Schedule 2A to attend a police station for their fingerprints to be taken again under section 61 in relation to that offence, unless authorised by an officer of inspector rank or above. The fact of the authorisation and the reasons for giving it must be recorded as soon as practicable.

(b) arrest, without warrant, a person who fails to comply with the requirement.

4.5 A person's fingerprints may be taken, as above, electronically.

4.6 Reasonable force may be used, if necessary, to take a person's fingerprints without their consent under the powers as in *paragraphs 4.3* and *4.4*.

4.7 Before any fingerprints are taken:

(a) without consent under any power mentioned in *paragraphs 4.3* and *4.4* above, the person must be informed of:

(i) the reason their fingerprints are to be taken;

(ii) the power under which they are to be taken; and

(iii) the fact that the relevant authority has been given if any power mentioned in *paragraph 4.3(c)*, *(d)* or *(f)* applies

(b) with or without consent at a police station or elsewhere, the person must be informed:

(i) that their fingerprints may be subject of a speculative search against other fingerprints, and

(ii) that their fingerprints may be retained in accordance with *Annex F, Part (a)* unless they were taken under the power mentioned in *paragraph 4.3(e)* when they must be destroyed after they have being checked.

(c) Documentation

4.8A A record must be made as soon as practicable after the fingerprints are taken, of:

- the matters in *paragraph 4.7(a)(i)* to *(iii)* and the fact that the person has been informed of those matters; and
- the fact that the person has been informed of the matters in *paragraph 4.7(b)(i)* and *(ii)*.

The record must be made in the person's custody record if they are detained at a police station when the fingerprints are taken.

4.8 If force is used, a record shall be made of the circumstances and those present.

4.9 *Not used*

1.8.5.1

KEYNOTE

The power under s. 61(6A) of the 1984 Act described in para. 4.3(e) allows fingerprints of a suspect who has not been arrested to be taken in connection with any offence (whether recordable or not) using a mobile device and then checked on the street against the database containing the national fingerprint collection. Fingerprints taken under this power cannot be retained after they have been checked. The results may make an arrest for the suspected offence based on the name condition unnecessary (see Code G, para. 2.9(a)) and enable the offence to be disposed of without arrest, e.g. by summons/charging by post, penalty notice or words of advice. If arrest for a non-recordable offence is necessary for any other reasons, this power may also be exercised at the station. Before the power is exercised, the officer should:

- inform the person of the nature of the suspected offence and why he/she is suspected of committing it;
- give the person a reasonable opportunity to establish his/her real name before deciding that his/her name is unknown and cannot be readily ascertained or that there are reasonable grounds to doubt that a name that he/she has given is his/her real name;
- as applicable, inform the person of the reason why his/her name is not known and cannot be readily ascertained or of the grounds for doubting that a name he/she has given is his/her real name, including, for example, the reason why a particular document the person has produced to verify his/her real name is not sufficient.

Speculative Search

Paragraph 4.7(b) makes reference to a 'speculative search'. Fingerprints, footwear impressions or a DNA sample (and the information derived from it) taken from a person arrested on suspicion of being involved in a recordable offence, or charged with such an offence, or informed they will be reported for such an offence, may be the subject of a speculative search. This means that the fingerprints, footwear impressions or DNA sample may be checked against other fingerprints, footwear impressions and DNA records held by, or on behalf of, the police and other law enforcement authorities in, or outside, the United Kingdom, or held in connection with, or as a result of, an investigation of an offence inside or outside the United Kingdom. Fingerprints, footwear impressions and samples taken from a person suspected of committing a recordable offence but not arrested, charged or informed that he/she will be reported for it, may be subject to a speculative search only if the person consents in writing. The following is an example of a basic form of words:

I consent to my fingerprints/DNA sample and information derived from it being retained and used only for purposes related to the prevention and detection of a crime, the investigation of an offence or the conduct of a prosecution either nationally or internationally.

I understand that this sample may be checked against other fingerprint/DNA records held by or on behalf of relevant law enforcement authorities, either nationally or internationally

I understand that once I have given my consent for the sample to be retained and used I cannot withdraw this consent.

1.8.5.2

4.10   *Not used*

4.11   *Not used*

4.12   *Not used*

4.13   *Not used*

4.14   *Not used*

4.15   *Not used*

1.8.5.3

(C) Taking footwear impressions in connection with a criminal investigation

(a) Action

4.16 Impressions of a person's footwear may be taken in connection with the investigation of an offence only with their consent or if *paragraph 4.17* applies. If the person is at a police station consent must be in writing.

4.17 PACE, section 61A, provides power for a police officer to take footwear impressions without consent from any person over the age of ten years who is detained at a police station:

(a) in consequence of being arrested for a recordable offence; or if the detainee has been charged with a recordable offence, or informed they will be reported for such an offence; and

(b) the detainee has not had an impression of their footwear taken in the course of the investigation of the offence unless the previously taken impression is not complete or is not of sufficient quality to allow satisfactory analysis, comparison or matching (whether in the case in question or generally).

4.18 Reasonable force may be used, if necessary, to take a footwear impression from a detainee without consent under the power in *paragraph 4.17*.

4.19 Before any footwear impression is taken with, or without, consent as above, the person must be informed:

(a) of the reason the impression is to be taken;

(b) that the impression may be retained and may be subject of a speculative search against other impressions, unless destruction of the impression is required in accordance with *Annex F, Part B.*

(b) Documentation

4.20 A record must be made as soon as possible, of the reason for taking a person's footwear impressions without consent. If force is used, a record shall be made of the circumstances and those present.

4.21 A record shall be made when a person has been informed under the terms of *paragraph 4.19(b),* of the possibility that their footwear impressions may be subject of a speculative search.

1.8.5.4

KEYNOTE

Recordable Offences

References to 'recordable offences' in this Code relate to those offences for which convictions, cautions, reprimands and warnings may be recorded in national police records. See the Police and Criminal Evidence Act 1984, s. 27(4). The recordable offences current at the time when this Code was prepared are any offences which carry a sentence of imprisonment on conviction (irrespective of the period, or the age of the offender or actual sentence passed) as well as the non-imprisonable offences under the Vagrancy Act 1824, ss. 3 and 4 (begging and persistent begging), the Street Offences Act 1959, s. 1 (loitering or soliciting for purposes of prostitution), the Road Traffic Act 1988, s. 25 (tampering with motor vehicles), the Criminal Justice and Public Order Act 1994, s. 167 (touting for hire car services) and others listed in the National Police Records (Recordable Offences) Regulations 2000 (SI 2000/1139), as amended.

Qualifying Offences

A qualifying offence is one of the offences specified in PACE, s. 65A. These include offences which involve the use or threat of violence or unlawful force against persons, sexual offences, offences against children and other offences, for example:

- murder, false imprisonment, kidnapping contrary to common law;
- manslaughter, conspiracy to murder, threats to kill, wounding with intent to cause grievous bodily harm (GBH), causing GBH and assault occasioning actual bodily harm contrary to the Offences Against the Person Act 1861;
- criminal possession or use of firearms contrary to ss. 16 to 18 of the Firearms Act 1968;
- robbery, burglary and aggravated burglary contrary to ss. 8, 9 or 10 of the Theft Act 1968 or an offence under s. 12A of that Act involving an accident which caused a person's death;
- criminal damage required to be charged as arson contrary to s. 1 of the Criminal Damage Act 1971;
- taking, possessing and showing indecent photographs of children contrary to s. 1 of the Protection of Children Act 1978;
- rape, sexual assault, child sex offences, exposure and other offences contrary to the Sexual Offences Act 2003.

It should be noted that this list is not exhaustive.

Whether fingerprint evidence is admissible as evidence tending to prove guilt, depends on:

- the experience and expertise of the witness: this requires at least three years' experience;
- the number of similar ridge characteristics (if there are fewer than eight ridge characteristics matching the fingerprints of the accused with those found by the police, it is unlikely that a judge would exercise his/her discretion to admit such evidence);
- whether there are dissimilar characteristics;
- the size of print relied on; and
- the quality and clarity of print relied on.

The jury should be warned that expert evidence is not conclusive in itself and that guilt has to be proved in the light of all evidence (*R* v *Buckley* [1999] EWCA Crim 1191).

1.8.5.5

1.8.5.6

KEYNOTE

Retention of Fingerprints

Code D, Annex F deals with the destruction and the speculative searches of fingerprints and samples and speculative searches of footwear impressions, see para. 1.8.13.

1.8.5.7

KEYNOTE

Criminal Record and Conviction Certificates

Under s. 118 of the Police Act 1997, in certain circumstances the Secretary of State issues certificates concerning an individual's previous convictions. In some cases the Secretary of State will not do this until it has been possible to verify the person's identity, which can be done through the taking of his/her fingerprints. Where this is the case, the Secretary of State may require the police officer in charge of the specified police station, or any other police station the Secretary of State reasonably determines, to take the applicant's fingerprints at the specified station at such reasonable time as the officer may direct and notify the applicant.

If fingerprints are taken in these circumstances they must be destroyed as soon as is practicable after the identity of the applicant is established to the satisfaction of the Secretary of State. The destruction can be witnessed by the person giving the fingerprints if he/she requests and/or the person can ask for a certificate stating that the fingerprints have been destroyed. The certificate must be issued within three months of the request.

In the case of an individual under the age of 18 years the consent of the applicant's parent or guardian to the taking of the applicant's fingerprints is also required.

1.8.5.8

KEYNOTE

Other Body Prints

While the more established and convincing body marks are fingerprints it is possible for other body prints to be used as evidence to identify a suspect. In *R v Kempster* [2008] EWCA Crim 975 the police recovered an ear print from the fixed window pane to the side of the window that had been forced in order to gain entry to the property. In this case the conviction was not successful, but it was recognised that an ear print comparison was capable of providing information that could identify a person who had left an ear print on a surface. This would only be achieved with certainty where the minutiae of the ear structure could be identified and matched.

The Judicial College publication *The Crown Court Compendium* states that ear print comparison suffers a disadvantage in common with facial mapping. While there is general agreement among experts that no two ears are the same, it is virtually impossible to obtain an ear impression which contains all relevant features of the ear. The crime scene impression is also likely to have been subject to variations in pressure and to at least minute movement, either of which will affect the reliability of the detail left. The scope for a significant number of reliable features for comparison is therefore limited and even if there is a match between them, there is no means of assessing the statistical probability that the crime scene impression was left by someone other than the defendant.

Fingerprints etc. and non-intimate samples may be taken from an arrested or detained person with the authority of an officer of a rank no lower than inspector.

Code D—5 Examinations to Establish Identity and the Taking of Photographs

(A) Detainees at police stations

(a) Searching or examination of detainees at police stations

5.1 PACE, section 54A(1), allows a detainee at a police station to be searched or examined or both, to establish:

(a) whether they have any marks, features or injuries that would tend to identify them as a person involved in the commission of an offence and to photograph any identifying marks, see *paragraph 5.5*; or

(b) their identity.

A person detained at a police station to be searched under a stop and search power, see Code A, is not a detainee for the purposes of these powers.

5.2 A search and/or examination to find marks under section 54A(1)(a) may be carried out without the detainee's consent, see *paragraph 2.12*, only if authorised by an officer of at least inspector rank when consent has been withheld or it is not practicable to obtain consent.

5.3 A search or examination to establish a suspect's identity under section 54A(1)(b) may be carried out without the detainee's consent, see *paragraph 2.12*, only if authorised by an officer of at least inspector rank when the detainee has refused to identify themselves or the authorising officer has reasonable grounds for suspecting the person is not who they claim to be.

5.4 Any marks that assist in establishing the detainee's identity, or their identification as a person involved in the commission of an offence, are identifying marks. Such marks may be photographed with the detainee's consent, see *paragraph 2.12*; or without their consent if it is withheld or it is not practicable to obtain it.

5.5 A detainee may only be searched, examined and photographed under section 54A, by a police officer of the same sex.

5.6 Any photographs of identifying marks, taken under section 54A, may be used or disclosed only for purposes related to the prevention or detection of crime, the investigation of offences or the conduct of prosecutions by, or on behalf of, police or other law enforcement and prosecuting authorities inside, and outside, the UK. After being so used or disclosed, the photograph may be retained but must not be used or disclosed except for these purposes.

5.7 The powers, as in *paragraph 5.1*, do not affect any separate requirement under the Criminal Procedure and Investigations Act 1996 to retain material in connection with criminal investigations.

5.8 Authority for the search and/or examination for the purposes of *paragraphs 5.2* and *5.3* may be given orally or in writing. If given orally, the authorising officer must confirm it in writing as soon as practicable. A separate authority is required for each purpose which applies.

5.9 If it is established a person is unwilling to co-operate sufficiently to enable a search and/or examination to take place or a suitable photograph to be taken, an officer may use reasonable force to:

(a) search and/or examine a detainee without their consent; and

(b) photograph any identifying marks without their consent.

5.10 The thoroughness and extent of any search or examination carried out in accordance with the powers in section 54A must be no more than the officer considers necessary to achieve the required purpose. Any search or examination which involves the removal of more than the person's outer clothing shall be conducted in accordance with Code C, Annex A, paragraph 11.

5.11 An intimate search may not be carried out under the powers in section 54A.

(b) Photographing detainees at police stations and other persons elsewhere than at a police station

5.12 Under PACE, section 64A, an officer may photograph:

(a) any person whilst they are detained at a police station; and

(b) any person who is elsewhere than at a police station and who has been:

    (i) arrested by a constable for an offence;

    (ii) taken into custody by a constable after being arrested for an offence by a person other than a constable;

    (iii) made subject to a requirement to wait with a community support officer under paragraph 2(3) or (3B) of Schedule 4 to the Police Reform Act 2002;

    (iiia) given a direction by a constable under section 27 of the Violent Crime Reduction Act 2006.

    (iv) given a penalty notice by a constable in uniform under Chapter 1 of Part 1 of the Criminal Justice and Police Act 2001, a penalty notice by a constable under section 444A of the Education Act 1996, or a fixed penalty notice by a constable in uniform under section 54 of the Road Traffic Offenders Act 1988;

    (v) given a notice in relation to a relevant fixed penalty offence (within the meaning of paragraph 1 of Schedule 4 to the Police Reform Act 2002) by a community support officer by virtue of a designation applying that paragraph to him;

    (vi) given a notice in relation to a relevant fixed penalty offence (within the meaning of paragraph 1 of Schedule 5 to the Police Reform Act 2002) by an accredited person by virtue of accreditation specifying that that paragraph applies to him; or

    (vii) given a direction to leave and not return to a specified location for up to 48 hours by a police constable (under section 27 of the Violent Crime Reduction Act 2006).

5.12A Photographs taken under PACE, section 64A:

(a) may be taken with the person's consent, or without their consent if consent is withheld or it is not practicable to obtain their consent, and

(b) may be used or disclosed only for purposes related to the prevention or detection of crime, the investigation of offences or the conduct of prosecutions by, or on behalf of, police or other law enforcement and prosecuting authorities inside and outside the United Kingdom or the enforcement of any sentence or order made by a court when dealing with an offence. After being so used or disclosed, they may be retained but can only be used or disclosed for the same purposes.

5.13 The officer proposing to take a detainee's photograph may, for this purpose, require the person to remove any item or substance worn on, or over, all, or any part of, their head or face. If they do not comply with such a requirement, the officer may remove the item or substance.

5.14 If it is established the detainee is unwilling to co-operate sufficiently to enable a suitable photograph to be taken and it is not reasonably practicable to take the photograph covertly, an officer may use reasonable force.

(a) to take their photograph without their consent; and

(b) for the purpose of taking the photograph, remove any item or substance worn on, or over, all, or any part of, the person's head or face which they have failed to remove when asked.

5.15 For the purposes of this Code, a photograph may be obtained without the person's consent by making a copy of an image of them taken at any time on a camera system installed anywhere in the police station.

(c) Information to be given

5.16 When a person is searched, examined or photographed under the provisions as in *paragraph 5.1* and *5.12*, or their photograph obtained as in *paragraph 5.15*, they must be informed of the:

(a) purpose of the search, examination or photograph;

(b) grounds on which the relevant authority, if applicable, has been given; and

(c) purposes for which the photograph may be used, disclosed or retained.

This information must be given before the search or examination commences or the photograph is taken, except if the photograph is:

    (i) to be taken covertly;

    (ii) obtained as in *paragraph 5.15*, in which case the person must be informed as soon as practicable after the photograph is taken or obtained.

(d) Documentation

5.17 A record must be made when a detainee is searched, examined, or a photograph of the person, or any identifying marks found on them, are taken. The record must include the:

    (a) identity, subject to *paragraph 2.18*, of the officer carrying out the search, examination or taking the photograph;

    (b) purpose of the search, examination or photograph and the outcome;

    (c) detainee's consent to the search, examination or photograph, or the reason the person was searched, examined or photographed without consent;

    (d) giving of any authority as in *paragraphs 5.2* and *5.3*, the grounds for giving it and the authorising officer.

5.18 If force is used when searching, examining or taking a photograph in accordance with this section, a record shall be made of the circumstances and those present.

(B) Persons at police stations not detained

5.19 When there are reasonable grounds for suspecting the involvement of a person in a criminal offence, but that person is at a police station **voluntarily** and not detained, the provisions of *paragraphs 5.1* to *5.18* should apply, subject to the modifications in the following paragraphs.

5.20 References to the 'person being detained' and to the powers mentioned in *paragraph 5.1* which apply only to detainees at police stations shall be omitted.

5.21 Force may not be used to:

    (a) search and/or examine the person to:

        (i) discover whether they have any marks that would tend to identify them as a person involved in the commission of an offence; or

        (ii) establish their identity,

    (b) take photographs of any identifying marks, see *paragraph 5.4*; or

    (c) take a photograph of the person.

5.22 Subject to *paragraph 5.24*, the photographs of persons or of their identifying marks which are not taken in accordance with the provisions mentioned in *paragraphs 5.1* or *5.12*, must be destroyed (together with any negatives and copies) unless the person:

    (a) is charged with, or informed they may be prosecuted for, a recordable offence;

    (b) is prosecuted for a recordable offence;

    (c) is cautioned for a recordable offence or given a warning or reprimand in accordance with the Crime and Disorder Act 1998 for a recordable offence; or

    (d) gives informed consent, in writing, for the photograph or image to be retained as in *paragraph 5.6*.

5.23 When *paragraph 5.22* requires the destruction of any photograph, the person must be given an opportunity to witness the destruction or to have a certificate confirming the destruction provided they so request the certificate within five days of being informed the destruction is required.

5.24 Nothing in *paragraph 5.22* affects any separate requirement under the Criminal Procedure and Investigations Act 1996 to retain material in connection with criminal investigations.

1.8.6.1

KEYNOTE

The conditions under which fingerprints may be taken to assist in establishing a person's identity, are described in s. 4.

A photograph taken under s. 54A of the Police and Criminal Evidence Act 1984 may be used by, or disclosed to, any person for any purpose related to the prevention or detection of crime, the investigation of an offence or the conduct of a prosecution. The use of the photograph is for any conduct which constitutes a criminal offence (whether under UK law or in another country). Examples of purposes related to the prevention or detection of crime, the investigation of offences or the conduct of prosecutions include:

- checking the photograph against other photographs held in records or in connection with, or as a result of, an investigation of an offence to establish whether the person is liable to arrest for other offences;
- when the person is arrested at the same time as other people, or at a time when it is likely that other people will be arrested, using the photograph to help establish who was arrested, at what time and where;
- when the real identity of the person is not known and cannot be readily ascertained or there are reasonable grounds for doubting that a name and other personal details given by the person are his/her real name and personal details. In these circumstances, using or disclosing the photograph to help to establish or verify the person's real identity or determine whether he/she is liable to arrest for some other offence, e.g. by checking it against other photographs held in records or in connection with, or as a result of, an investigation of an offence;
- when it appears that any identification procedure in s. 3 may need to be arranged for which the person's photograph would assist;
- when the person's release without charge may be required, and if the release is:
  - (i) on bail to appear at a police station, using the photograph to help verify the person's identity when he/she answers bail and if the person does not answer bail, to assist in arresting him/her; or
  - (ii) without bail, using the photograph to help verify the person's identity or assist in locating him/her for the purposes of serving him/her with a summons to appear at court in criminal proceedings;
- when the person has answered to bail at a police station and there are reasonable grounds for doubting that he/she is the person who was previously granted bail, using the photograph to help establish or verify his/her identity;
- when the person has been charged with, reported for, or convicted of, a recordable offence and his/her photograph is not already on record as a result of any of the circumstances set out in the bullet points above or his/her photograph is on record but his/her appearance has changed since it was taken and the person has not yet been released or brought before a court;
- when the person arrested on a warrant claims to be a different person from the person named on the warrant and a photograph would help to confirm or disprove this claim.

Looking at paras 5.2 and 5.4, examples of when it would not be practicable to obtain a detainee's consent for the examination of, or the taking of a photograph of an identifying mark include:

- when the person is drunk or otherwise unfit to give consent;
- when there are reasonable grounds to suspect that if the person became aware that a search or examination was to take place or an identifying mark was to be photographed, he/she would take steps to prevent this happening, e.g. by violently resisting, covering or concealing the mark, etc. and it would not otherwise be possible to carry out the search or examination or to photograph any identifying mark;
- in the case of a juvenile, if the parent or guardian cannot be contacted in sufficient time to allow the search or examination to be carried out or the photograph to be taken.

Looking at para. 5.12A, examples of when it would not be practicable to obtain the person's consent to a photograph being taken include:

- when the person is drunk or otherwise unfit to give consent;
- when there are reasonable grounds to suspect that if the person became aware that a photograph suitable to be used or disclosed for the use and disclosure described in para. 5.6 was to be taken, he/she would take steps to prevent it being taken, e.g. by violently resisting, covering or distorting his/her face, etc., and it would not otherwise be possible to take a suitable photograph;

- when, in order to obtain a suitable photograph, it is necessary to take it covertly; and
- in the case of a juvenile, if the parent or guardian cannot be contacted in sufficient time to allow the photograph to be taken.

There is no power to arrest a person convicted of a recordable offence solely to take his/her photograph. The power to take photographs in this section applies only where the person is in custody as a result of the exercise of another power, e.g. arrest for fingerprinting under PACE, sch. 2A, para. 17

The use of reasonable force to take the photograph of a suspect elsewhere than at a police station must be carefully considered. In order to obtain a suspect's consent and co-operation to remove an item of religious headwear to take his/her photograph, a constable should consider whether in the circumstances of the situation the removal of the headwear and the taking of the photograph should be by an officer of the same sex as the person. It would be appropriate for these actions to be conducted out of public view.

1.8.7 Code D—6 Identification by Body Samples and Impressions

(A) General

6.1 References to:
  (a) an 'intimate sample' mean a dental impression or sample of blood, semen or any other tissue fluid, urine, or pubic hair, or a swab taken from any part of a person's genitals or from a person's body orifice other than the mouth;
  (b) a 'non-intimate sample' means:
   (i) a sample of hair, other than pubic hair, which includes hair plucked with the root;
   (ii) a sample taken from a nail or from under a nail;
   (iii) a swab taken from any part of a person's body other than a part from which a swab taken would be an intimate sample;
   (iv) saliva;
   (v) a skin impression which means any record, other than a fingerprint, which is a record, in any form and produced by any method, of the skin pattern and other physical characteristics or features of the whole, or any part of, a person's foot or of any other part of their body.

1.8.7.1 KEYNOTE

Intimate and Non-intimate Samples—General

The analysis of intimate and non-intimate samples may provide essential evidence in showing or refuting a person's involvement in an offence. However, the courts have made it clear that DNA evidence alone will not be sufficient for a conviction and that there needs to be supporting evidence to link the suspect to the crime.

The purpose behind the taking of many samples is to enable the process of DNA profiling. Very basically, this involves an analysis of the sample taken from the suspect (the first sample), an analysis of samples taken from the crime scene or victim (the second sample) and then a comparison of the two. Both the process and the conclusions which might be drawn from the results are set out by Lord Taylor CJ in *R* v *Deen* (1994) *The Times*, 10 January.

The matching process involves creating 'bands' from each sample and then comparing the number of those bands which the two samples share. The more 'matches' that exist between the first and second samples, the less probability there is of that happening by pure chance. A 'good match' between the two samples does not of itself prove that the second sample came from the defendant. In using such samples to prove identification the prosecution will give evidence of:

- the probability of such a match happening by chance; and
- the likelihood that the person responsible was in fact the defendant.

While DNA evidence is often portrayed in the media as conclusive evidence of guilt, the question for the courts remains 'How reliable is this piece of evidence in proving or disproving the person's involvement in the offence?'

In most cases there will be other evidence against the defendant which clearly increases the likelihood of his/her having committed the offence. Such evidence may include confessions, or may show that the suspect was near the crime scene at the time of the offence or that the suspect lived in the locality or had connections in the area.

It will be for the prosecution to produce other facts to the court which reduce the 'chance' of the DNA sample belonging to someone other than the defendant. This may require further inquiries linking the suspect to the area or circumstances of the crime or may come from questions put to the suspect during interview. In *R* v *Lashley* (2000) 25 February, unreported, the sole evidence against the defendant for a robbery was DNA evidence from a half-smoked cigarette found behind the counter of the post office. The DNA matched a sample obtained from the suspect and would have matched the profile of seven to 10 other males in the United Kingdom. The court held that the significance of DNA evidence depended critically upon what else was known about the suspect. Had there been evidence that the suspect was in the area, or normally lived there, or had connections there, at the material time, then the jury could have found that the case was compelling. This, the court said, would be because it may have been almost incredible that two out of seven men in the United Kingdom were in the vicinity at the relevant time. The courts are willing to allow the jury to consider partial or incomplete DNA profiles in some circumstances. In *R* v *Bates* [2006] EWCA Crim 1395, DNA evidence at the scene produced a partial profile that was interpreted as providing a 1 in 610,000 probability that Bates was the killer. The Court of Appeal held that there was no reason why partial-profile DNA evidence should not be admissible provided that the jury were made aware of its inherent limitations and were given a sufficient explanation to enable them to evaluate it.

If there is a decision to charge on a partial DNA profile basis of such a match, the supporting evidence needs to be all the stronger. The amount of supporting evidence required will depend on the value of the DNA evidence in the context of the case. A scientist should be consulted where the value of the DNA evidence requires clarification.

While it is still the case that other evidence to support a DNA profile should be found, the case of *R* v *FNC* [2015] EWCA Crim 1732 held that where DNA is directly deposited in the course of the commission of a crime by the offender, a very high DNA match with the defendant is sufficient to raise a case for the defendant to answer. There was a clear distinction between DNA deposited on an article left at the scene and a case where there could be no doubt that the DNA was deposited in the course of the commission of the offence by the person who committed it. In this case the allegation was that the semen on the back of the complainant's trousers was consistent with the defendant ejaculating on to the complainant's trousers as alleged.

R v *Tsekiri* [2017] EWCA Crim 40 was a case where the DNA of a suspect of a robbery was found on the external door handle of the car belonging to the victim. The suspect gave a no comment interview, the DNA therefore being the main evidence in the case. The court identified relevant matters when deciding if the DNA was sufficient evidence to convict on. These matters being:

- Is there any evidence of some other explanation for the presence of the defendant's DNA on the item other than involvement in the crime?
- Was the article apparently associated with the offence itself? The position could be different if the article was not necessarily so connected with the offence, e.g. if a DNA profile were to be found on a cigarette stub discarded at the scene of a street robbery.
- How readily movable is the article in question? A DNA profile on a small article of clothing or something such as a cigarette end at the scene of a crime might be of less probative force than the same profile on a vehicle.
- Is there evidence of some geographical association between the offence and the offender?
- In the case of a mixed profile, is the DNA profile which matches the defendant the major contributor to the overall DNA profile?
- Is it more or less likely that the DNA profile attributable to the defendant was deposited by primary or secondary transfer?

This is not an exhaustive list and each case will depend on its own facts.

These points may need to be considered when preparing questions for an interview with the suspect.

It is also important to ensure that there is no cross-contamination of DNA evidence between crime scenes, victims and suspects, as was seen in the infamous American case of OJ Simpson's murder trial. It will be important to ensure that any allegations that officers may have contaminated evidence through handling/being present at several crime scenes can be successfully challenged. It is suggested that the best evidence here will be through records of crime scene logs and, where suspects have been or are being held in custody, records of who visited the custody suite. It will also be important that suspects and victims are kept apart. The integrity and continuity of DNA samples will be important evidence and likely to be challenged by the defence if not managed properly.

Speculative searches may be carried out of the National DNA Database and a suspect may now be charged on the basis of a match between a profile from DNA from the scene of the crime and a profile on the National DNA Database from an individual, so long as there is further supporting evidence (Home Office Circular 58/2004, *Charges on Basis of Speculative Search Match on the National DNA Database*).

It should also be noted that the databases can also now be used for the purpose of identifying a deceased person or a person from whom a body part came (Serious Organised Crime and Police Act 2005, s. 117(7) amending s. 64 of the 1984 Act).

An insufficient sample is one which is not sufficient either in quantity or quality to provide information for a particular form of analysis, such as DNA analysis. A sample may also be insufficient if enough information cannot be obtained from it by analysis because of loss, destruction, damage or contamination of the sample or as a result of an earlier, unsuccessful attempt at analysis. An unsuitable sample is one which, by its nature, is not suitable for a particular form of analysis.

1.8.7.2 (B) Action

(a) Intimate samples

6.2 PACE, section 62, provides that intimate samples may be taken under:
   (a) section 62(1), from a person in police detention only:
      (i) if a police officer of inspector rank or above has reasonable grounds to believe such an impression or sample will tend to confirm or disprove the suspect's involvement in a recordable offence, and gives authorisation for a sample to be taken; and
      (ii) with the suspect's written consent;
   (b) section 62(1A), from a person not in police detention but from whom two or more non-intimate samples have been taken in the course of an investigation of an offence and the samples, though suitable, have proved insufficient if:
      (i) a police officer of inspector rank or above authorises it to be taken; and
      (ii) the person concerned gives their written consent.
   (c) section 62(2A), from a person convicted outside England and Wales of an offence which if committed in England and Wales would be qualifying offence as defined by PACE, section 65A from whom two or more non-intimate samples taken under section 63(3E) (see *paragraph 6.6(h)* have proved insufficient if:
      (i) a police officer of inspector rank or above is satisfied that taking the sample is necessary to assist in the prevention or detection of crime and authorises it to be taken; and
      (ii) the person concerned gives their written consent.
6.2A PACE, section 63A(4) and Schedule 2A provide powers to:
   (a) make a requirement (in accordance with Annex G) for a person to attend a police station to have an intimate sample taken in the exercise of one of the following powers (see *paragraph 6.2*):
      (i) section 62(1A)—Persons from whom two or more non-intimate samples have been taken and proved to be insufficient, see *paragraph 6.2(b)*: There is no time limit for making the requirement.

(ii) section 62(2A)—Persons convicted outside England and Wales from whom two or more non-intimate samples taken under section 63(3E) (see *paragraph 6.6(g)* have proved insufficient, see *paragraph 6.2(c)*: There is no time limit for making the requirement.

(b) arrest without warrant a person who fails to comply with the requirement

6.3 Before a suspect is asked to provide an intimate sample, they must be:

(a) informed:

(i) of the reason, including the nature of the suspected offence (except if taken under *paragraph 6.2(c)* from a person convicted outside England and Wales.

(ii) that authorisation has been given and the provisions under which given;

(iii) that a sample taken at a police station may be subject of a speculative search;

(b) warned that if they refuse without good cause their refusal may harm their case if it comes to trial. If the suspect is in police detention and not legally represented, they must also be reminded of their entitlement to have free legal advice, see Code C, *paragraph 6.5*, and the reminder noted in the custody record. If *paragraph 6.2(b)* applies and the person is attending a station voluntarily, their entitlement to free legal advice as in Code C, *paragraph 3.21* shall be explained to them.

6.4 Dental impressions may only be taken by a registered dentist. Other intimate samples, except for samples of urine, may only be taken by a registered medical practitioner or registered nurse or registered paramedic.

1.8.7.3

KEYNOTE

Intimate Samples

Taking a sample without the relevant authority may amount to inhuman or degrading treatment under Article 3 of the European Convention on Human Rights. It may also amount to a criminal offence of assault (see chapter 2.7) and give rise to liability at civil law.

For recordable offences and qualifying offences, see para. 1.8.5.4, Keynote.

Nothing in para. 6.2 prevents intimate samples being taken for elimination purposes with the consent of the person concerned, but the provisions of para. 2.12, relating to the role of the appropriate adult, should be applied. Paragraph 6.2(b) does not, however, apply where the non-intimate samples were previously taken under the Terrorism Act 2000, sch. 8, para. 10.

In warning a person who is asked to provide an intimate sample, the following form of words may be used:

You do not have to provide this sample/allow this swab or impression to be taken, but I must warn you that if you refuse without good cause, your refusal may harm your case if it comes to trial.

1.8.7.4

(b) Non-intimate samples

6.5 A non-intimate sample may be taken from a detainee only with their written consent or if *paragraph 6.6* applies.

6.6 A non-intimate sample may be taken from a person without the appropriate consent in the following circumstances:

(a) under *section 63(2A)* from a person who is in police detention as a consequence of being arrested for a recordable offence and who has not had a non-intimate sample of the same type and from the same part of the body taken in the course of the investigation of the offence by the police or they have had such a sample taken but it proved insufficient.

(b) Under *section 63(3)* from a person who is being held in custody by the police on the authority of a court if an officer of at least the rank of inspector authorises it to be taken. An authorisation may be given:

(i) if the authorising officer has reasonable grounds for suspecting the person of involvement in a recordable offence and for believing that the sample will tend to confirm or disprove that involvement, and

(ii) in writing or orally and confirmed in writing, as soon as practicable; but an authorisation may not be given to take from the same part of the body a further non-intimate sample consisting of a skin impression unless the previously taken impression proved insufficient

(c) under *section 63(3ZA)* from a person who has been arrested for a recordable offence and released if:

(i) [in the case of a person who is on bail,] they have not had a sample of the same type and from the same part of the body taken in the course of the investigation of the offence, or;

(ii) [in any case,] the person has had such a sample taken in the course of the investigation of the offence, but either:

- it was not suitable or proved insufficient; or
- the investigation was discontinued but subsequently resumed and before the resumption, any DNA profile derived from the sample was destroyed and the sample itself was destroyed pursuant to section 63R(4), (5) or (12).

(d) under *section 63(3A)*, from a person (whether or not in police detention or held in custody by the police on the authority of a court) who has been charged with a recordable offence or informed they will be reported for such an offence if the person:

(i) has not had a non-intimate sample taken from them in the course of the investigation of the offence; or

(ii) has had a sample so taken, but it was not suitable or proved insufficient, or

(iii) has had a sample taken in the course of the investigation of the offence and the sample has been destroyed and in proceedings relating to that offence there is a dispute as to whether a DNA profile relevant to the proceedings was derived from the destroyed sample.

(e) under *section 63(3B)*, from a person who has been:

(i) convicted of a recordable offence; or

(ii) given a caution in respect of a recordable offence which, at the time of the caution, the person admitted;

if, since their conviction or caution a non-intimate sample has not been taken from them or a sample which has been taken since then was not suitable or proved insufficient and in either case, an officer of inspector rank or above, is satisfied that taking the fingerprints is necessary to assist in the prevention or detection of crime and authorises the taking;

(f) under *section 63(3C)* from a person to whom section 2 of the Criminal Evidence (Amendment) Act 1997 applies (persons detained following acquittal on grounds of insanity or finding of unfitness to plead).

(g) under *section 63(3E)* from a person who has been convicted outside England and Wales of an offence which if committed in England and Wales would be a qualifying offence as defined by PACE, section 65A if:

(i) a non-intimate sample has not been taken previously under this power or unless a sample was so taken but was not suitable or proved insufficient; and

(ii) a police officer of inspector rank or above is satisfied that taking a sample is necessary to assist in the prevention or detection of crime and authorises it to be taken.

6.6A PACE, *section 63A(4)* and *Schedule 2A* provide powers to:

(a) make a requirement (in accordance with Annex G) for a person to attend a police station to have a non-intimate sample taken in the exercise of one of the following powers (see *paragraph 6.6* above) within certain time limits as follows:

(i) *section 63(3ZA)*—Persons arrested for a recordable offence and released, see paragraph 6.6(c): In the case of a person from whom a non-intimate sample was taken in the course of the investigation but that sample was not suitable or proved insufficient, the requirement may not be made more than six months from the day the investigating officer was informed that the sample previously taken was not suitable or proved insufficient. In the case of a person whose DNA profile and sample was destroyed prior to the resumption of the investigation, the requirement may not be made more than six months from the day on which the investigation resumed.

    (ii) *section 63(3A)*—Persons charged etc. with a recordable offence, see *paragraph 6.6(d)*: The requirement may not be made more than six months from:

- the day the person was charged or informed that they would be reported, if a sample has not been taken in the course of the investigation;
- the day the investigating officer was informed that the sample previously taken was not suitable or proved insufficient, if a sample has been taken in the course of the investigation but the sample was not suitable or proved insufficient; or
- the day on which the investigation was resumed, in the case of a person whose DNA profile and sample were destroyed prior to the resumption of the investigation.

    (iii) *section 63(3B)*—Person convicted or cautioned for a recordable offence in England and Wales, see *paragraph 6.6(e)*: Where the offence for which the person was convicted etc. is also a qualifying offence, there is no time limit for the exercise of this power. Where the conviction etc. was for a recordable offence that is *not* a qualifying offence, the requirement may not be made more than two years from:

- in the case of a person whose sample has not been taken since they were convicted or cautioned, the day the person was convicted or cautioned, , or, if later. the day Schedule 2A came into force (March 7 2011); or
- in the case of a person whose sample has been taken but was not suitable or proved insufficient, the day an officer from the force investigating the offence was informed that the sample previously taken was not suitable or proved insufficient or, if later, the day Schedule 2A came into force (March 7 2011).

    (iv) *section 63(3E)*—A person who has been convicted of qualifying offence outside England and Wales, see *paragraph 6.6(h)*: There is no time limit for making the requirement.

Note: A person who has had a non-intimate sample taken under any of the powers in section 63 mentioned in *paragraph 6.6* on two occasions in relation to any offence may not be required under Schedule 2A to attend a police station for a sample to be taken again under section 63 in relation to that offence, unless authorised by an officer of inspector rank or above. The fact of the authorisation and the reasons for giving it must be recorded as soon as practicable.

    (b) arrest, without warrant, a person who fails to comply with the requirement.

6.7 Reasonable force may be used, if necessary, to take a non-intimate sample from a person without their consent under the powers mentioned in *paragraph 6.6*.

6.8 Before any non-intimate sample is taken:

    (a) without consent under any power mentioned in *paragraphs 6.6* and *6.6A*, the person must be informed of:

        (i) the reason for taking the sample;

        (ii) the power under which the sample is to be taken;

        (iii) the fact that the relevant authority has been given if any power mentioned in *paragraph 6.6(b)*, *(e)* or *(g)* applies, including the nature of the suspected offence (except if taken under *paragraph 6.6(e)* from a person convicted or cautioned, or under *paragraph 6.6(g)* if taken from a person convicted outside England and Wales;

    (b) with or without consent at a police station or elsewhere, the person must be informed:

        (i) that their sample or information derived from it may be subject of a speculative search against other samples and information derived from them and

        (ii) that their sample and the information derived from it may be retained in accordance with Annex F, Part (a).

(c) Removal of clothing

6.9 When clothing needs to be removed in circumstances likely to cause embarrassment to the person, no person of the opposite sex who is not a registered medical practitioner or registered health care professional shall be present, (unless in the case of a juvenile, mentally disordered or mentally vulnerable person, that person specifically requests the presence of an appropriate adult of the opposite sex who is readily available) nor shall anyone whose presence is unnecessary. However, in the case of a juvenile, this is subject to the overriding proviso that such a removal of clothing may take place in the absence of the appropriate adult only if the juvenile signifies in their presence, that they prefer the adult's absence and they agree.

(c) Documentation

6.10 A record must be made as soon as practicable after the sample is taken of:
- The matters in *paragraph 6.8(a)(i)* to *(iii)* and the fact that the person has been informed of those matters; and
- The fact that the person has been informed of the matters in paragraph 6.8(b)(i) and (ii).

6.10A If force is used, a record shall be made of the circumstances and those present.

6.11 A record must be made of a warning given as required by *paragraph 6.3*.

6.12 *Not used.*

1.8.7.5

KEYNOTE

Taking a Non-intimate Sample

Where a non-intimate sample consisting of a skin impression is taken electronically from a person, it must be taken only in such manner, and using such devices, as the Secretary of State has approved for the purpose of the electronic taking of such an impression (s. 63(9A) of PACE). No such devices are currently approved.

When hair samples are taken for the purpose of DNA analysis (rather than for other purposes, such as making a visual match), the suspect should be permitted a reasonable choice as to what part of the body the hairs are taken from. When hairs are plucked, they should be plucked individually, unless the suspect prefers otherwise and no more should be plucked than the person taking them reasonably considers necessary for a sufficient sample.

Fingerprints, footwear impressions or a DNA sample (and the information derived from it) taken from a person arrested on suspicion of being involved in a recordable offence, or charged with such an offence, or informed they will be reported for such an offence, may be the subject of a speculative search. This means the fingerprints, footwear impressions or DNA sample may be checked against other fingerprints, footwear impressions and DNA records held by, or on behalf of, the police and other law enforcement authorities in, or outside, the United Kingdom, or held in connection with, or as a result of, an investigation of an offence inside or outside the United Kingdom. See Annex F regarding the retention and use of fingerprints and samples taken with consent for elimination purposes.

Urine and non-intimate samples and the information derived from testing detained persons for the presence of specified Class A drugs, may not be subsequently used in the investigation of any offence or in evidence against the persons from whom they were taken.

1.8.7.6

KEYNOTE

Power to Require Persons to Attend a Police Station to Provide Samples

Code D, Annex G deals with the requirement for a person to attend a police station for fingerprints and samples.

KEYNOTE

Destruction of Samples

Code D, Annex F deals with the destruction and the speculative searches of fingerprints and samples and speculative searches of footwear impressions. It is important that the Annex is followed, particularly in relation to obtaining consent and explaining to volunteers what they are consenting to.

Code D—Annex A: Video Identification

(a) General

1. The arrangements for obtaining and ensuring the availability of a suitable set of images to be used in a video identification must be the responsibility of an identification officer (see *paragraph 3.11* of this Code) who has no direct involvement with the case.

2. The set of images must include the suspect and at least eight other people who, so far as possible, and subject to *paragraph 7*, resemble the suspect in age, general appearance and position in life. Only one suspect shall appear in any set unless there are two suspects of roughly similar appearance, in which case they may be shown together with at least twelve other people.

2A. If the suspect has an unusual physical feature, e.g., a facial scar, tattoo or distinctive hairstyle or hair colour which does not appear on the images of the other people that are available to be used, steps may be taken to:

   (a) conceal the location of the feature on the images of the suspect and the other people; or

   (b) replicate that feature on the images of the other people.

   For these purposes, the feature may be concealed or replicated electronically or by any other method which it is practicable to use to ensure that the images of the suspect and other people resemble each other. The identification officer has discretion to choose whether to conceal or replicate the feature and the method to be used.

2B. If the identification officer decides that a feature should be concealed or replicated, the reason for the decision and whether the feature was concealed or replicated in the images shown to any eye-witness shall be recorded.

2C. If the eye-witness requests to view any image where an unusual physical feature has been concealed or replicated without the feature being concealed or replicated, the identification officer has discretion to allow the eye-witness to view such image(s) if they are available.

3. The images used to conduct a video identification shall, as far as possible, show the suspect and other people in the same positions or carrying out the same sequence of movements. They shall also show the suspect and other people under identical conditions unless the identification officer reasonably believes:

   (a) because of the suspect's failure or refusal to co-operate or other reasons, it is not practicable for the conditions to be identical; and

   (b) any difference in the conditions would not direct an eye-witness' attention to any individual image.

4. The reasons identical conditions are not practicable shall be recorded on forms provided for the purpose.

5. Provision must be made for each person shown to be identified by number.

6. If police officers are shown, any numerals or other identifying badges must be concealed. If a prison inmate is shown, either as a suspect or not, then either all, or none of, the people shown should be in prison clothing.

7. The suspect or their solicitor, friend, or appropriate adult must be given a reasonable opportunity to see the complete set of images before it is shown to any eye-witness. If the suspect has a reasonable objection to the set of images or any of the participants, the suspect shall

be asked to state the reasons for the objection. Steps shall, if practicable, be taken to remove the grounds for objection. If this is not practicable, the suspect and/or their representative shall be told why their objections cannot be met and the objection, the reason given for it and why it cannot be met shall be recorded on forms provided for the purpose. The requirement in *paragraph 2* that the images of the other people 'resemble' the suspect does not require the images to be identical or extremely similar.

8. Before the images are shown in accordance with *paragraph 7*, the suspect or their solicitor shall be provided with details of the first description of the suspect by any eye-witnesses who are to attend the video identification. When a broadcast or publication is made, as in *paragraph 3.38(a)*, the suspect or their solicitor must also be allowed to view any material released to the media by the police for the purpose of recognising or tracing the suspect, provided it is practicable and would not unreasonably delay the investigation.

9. No unauthorised people may be present when the video identification is conducted. The suspect's solicitor, if practicable, shall be given reasonable notification of the time and place the video identification is to be conducted. The suspect's solicitor may only be present at the video identification on request and with the prior agreement of the identification officer, if the officer is satisfied that the solicitor's presence will not deter or distract any eye-witness from viewing the images and making an identification. If the identification officer is not satisfied and does not agree to the request, the reason must be recorded. The solicitor must be informed of the decision and the reason for it. and that they may then make representations about why they should be allowed to be present. The representations may be made orally or in writing, in person or remotely by electronic communication and must be recorded. These representations must be considered by an officer of at least the rank of inspector who is not involved with the investigation and responsibility for this may not be delegated under *paragraph 3.11*. If, after considering the representations, the officer is satisfied that the solicitor's presence will deter or distract the eye-witness, the officer shall inform the solicitor of the decision and reason for it and ensure that any response by the solicitor is also recorded. If allowed to be present, the solicitor is not entitled to communicate in any way with an eye-witness during the procedure but this does not prevent the solicitor from communicating with the identification officer. The suspect may not be present when the images are shown to any eye-witness and is not entitled to be informed of the time and place the video identification procedure is to be conducted. The video identification procedure itself shall be recorded on video with sound. The recording must show all persons present within the sight or hearing of the eye-witness whilst the images are being viewed and must include what the eye-witness says and what is said to them by the identification officer and by any other person present at the video identification procedure. A supervised viewing of the recording of the video identification procedure by the suspect and/or their solicitor may be arranged on request, at the discretion of the investigating officer. Where the recording of the video identification procedure is to be shown to the suspect and/or their solicitor, the investigating officer may arrange for anything in the recording that might allow the eye-witness to be identified to be concealed if the investigating officer considers that this is justified. In accordance with *paragraph 2.18*, the investigating officer may also arrange for anything in that recording that might allow any police officers or police staff to be identified to be concealed.

(b) Conducting the video identification

10. The identification officer is responsible for making the appropriate arrangements to make sure, before they see the set of images, eye-witnesses are not able to communicate with each other about the case, see any of the images which are to be shown, see, or be reminded of, any photograph or description of the suspect or be given any other indication as to the suspect's identity, or overhear an eye-witness who has already seen the material. There must be no discussion with the eye-witness about the composition of the set of images and they must not be told whether a previous eye-witness has made any identification.

11. Only one eye-witness may see the set of images at a time. Immediately before the images are shown, the eye-witness shall be told that the person they saw on a specified earlier occasion may, or may not, appear in the images they are shown and that if they cannot make an identification, they should say so. The eye-witness shall be advised that at any point, they may ask to see a particular part of the set of images or to have a particular image frozen for them to study. Furthermore, it should be pointed out to the eye-witness that there is no limit on how many times they can view the whole set of images or any part of them. However, they should be asked not to make any decision as to whether the person they saw is on the set of images until they have seen the whole set at least twice.

12. Once the eye-witness has seen the whole set of images at least twice and has indicated that they do not want to view the images, or any part of them, again, the eye-witness shall be asked to say whether the individual they saw in person on a specified earlier occasion has been shown and, if so, to identify them by number of the image. The eye-witness will then be shown that image to confirm the identification, see *paragraph 17*.

13. Care must be taken not to direct the eye-witness' attention to any one individual image or give any indication of the suspect's identity. Where an eye-witness has previously made an identification by photographs, or a computerised or artist's composite or similar likeness, they must not be reminded of such a photograph or composite likeness once a suspect is available for identification by other means in accordance with this Code. Nor must the eye-witness be reminded of any description of the suspect.

13A. If after the video identification procedure has ended, the eye-witness informs any police officer or police staff involved in the post-viewing arrangements that they wish to change their decision about their identification, or they have not made an identification when in fact they could have made one, an accurate record of the words used by the eye-witness and of the circumstances immediately after the procedure ended, shall be made. If the eyewitness has not had an opportunity to communicate with other people about the procedure, the identification officer has the discretion to allow the eye-witness a second opportunity to make an identification by repeating the video identification procedure using the same images but in different positions.

14. After the procedure, action required in accordance with *paragraph 3.40* applies.

(c) Image security and destruction

15. Arrangements shall be made for all relevant material containing sets of images used for specific identification procedures to be kept securely and their movements accounted for. In particular, no-one involved in the investigation shall be permitted to view the material prior to it being shown to any witness.

16. As appropriate, *paragraph 3.30* or *3.31* applies to the destruction or retention of relevant sets of images.

(d) Documentation

17. A record must be made of all those participating in, or seeing, the set of images whose names are known to the police.

18. A record of the conduct of the video identification must be made on forms provided for the purpose. This shall include anything said by the witness about any identifications or the conduct of the procedure and any reasons it was not practicable to comply with any of the provisions of this Code governing the conduct of video identifications. This record is in addition to any statement that is taken from any eye-witness after the procedure.

KEYNOTE

Annex A Video Identification

The purpose of the video identification is to test the eye-witness's ability to distinguish the suspect from others and it would not be a fair test if all the images shown were identical or extremely similar to each other. The identification officer is responsible for ensuring that the images shown are suitable for the purpose of this test. *R v Day* [2019] EWCA Crim 935 provides an example of this responsibility. In this case, the victim was attacked by a man whom she did not know as she was crossing an isolated footbridge between two villages. She described her attacker to police as being aged in his mid-40s, 5ft 10ins tall, of medium build, with a bald head and a scab above his right eye. She said that she would remember him again due to his scab and also due to the impact the incident had had upon her. A video identification procedure was held. The suspect was wearing spectacles when he attended the police station. Video clips of the suspect were of him both with and without spectacles, and had used the clip in which he was not wearing spectacles. The reason for this was that it would have been virtually impossible to find in the database images of a sufficient number of men wearing glasses who sufficiently resembled the appellant. Neither the suspect nor anyone else whose image was used in the procedure was bald, the images chosen were as close as possible a match to the appearance of the suspect. The defence appealed against the video identification. The court held that the Code of Practice in relation to video identification requires that the images chosen to be shown with the image of the suspect must, so far as possible, resemble the suspect in age, general appearance and position in life. The first responsibility of the identification officer is to assemble images which as closely as possible resemble the suspect. Provided this is done, it is then permissible for the identification officer to arrange for the imagery either to include or not to include some non-permanent feature of clothing or accessories in order as closely as possible to match the description of the offender. Given that the victim described her attacker as not wearing glasses, it was correct to use images which showed the appellant and others not wearing glasses.

The purpose of allowing the identity of the eye-witness to be concealed is to protect them in cases when there is information that suspects or their associates may threaten the witness or cause them harm or when the investigating officer considers that special measures may be required to protect their identity during the criminal process.

1.8.9 Code D—Annex B: Identification Parades

(a) General

1. A suspect must be given a reasonable opportunity to have a solicitor or friend present, and the suspect shall be asked to indicate on a second copy of the notice whether or not they wish to do so.

2. An identification parade may take place either in a normal room or one equipped with a screen permitting witnesses to see members of the identification parade without being seen. The procedures for the composition and conduct of the identification parade are the same in both cases, subject to *paragraph 8* (except that an identification parade involving a screen may take place only when the suspect's solicitor, friend or appropriate adult is present or the identification parade is recorded on video).

3. Before the identification parade takes place, the suspect or their solicitor shall be provided with details of the first description of the suspect by any witnesses who are attending the identification parade. When a broadcast or publication is made as in *paragraph 3.38(a)*, the suspect or their solicitor should also be allowed to view any material released to the media by the police for the purpose of identifying and tracing the suspect, provided it is practicable to do so and would not unreasonably delay the investigation.

(b) Identification parades involving prison inmates

4. If a prison inmate is required for identification, and there are no security problems about the person leaving the establishment, they may be asked to participate in an identification parade or video identification.

5. An identification parade may be held in a Prison Department establishment but shall be conducted, as far as practicable under normal identification parade rules. Members of the public shall make up the identification parade unless there are serious security, or control, objections to their admission to the establishment. In such cases, or if a group or video identification is arranged within the establishment, other inmates may participate. If an inmate is the suspect, they are not required to wear prison clothing for the identification parade unless the other people taking part are other inmates in similar clothing, or are members of the public who are prepared to wear prison clothing for the occasion.

(c) Conduct of the identification parade

6. Immediately before the identification parade, the suspect must be reminded of the procedures governing its conduct and cautioned in the terms of Code C, paragraphs 10.5 or 10.6, as appropriate.

7. All unauthorised people must be excluded from the place where the identification parade is held.

8. Once the identification parade has been formed, everything afterwards, in respect of it, shall take place in the presence and hearing of the suspect and any interpreter, solicitor, friend or appropriate adult who is present (unless the identification parade involves a screen, in which case everything said to, or by, any witness at the place where the identification parade is held, must be said in the hearing and presence of the suspect's solicitor, friend or appropriate adult or be recorded on video).

9. The identification parade shall consist of at least eight people (in addition to the suspect) who, so far as possible, resemble the suspect in age, height, general appearance and position in life. Only one suspect shall be included in an identification parade unless there are two suspects of roughly similar appearance, in which case they may be paraded together with at least twelve other people. In no circumstances shall more than two suspects be included in one identification parade and where there are separate identification parades, they shall be made up of different people.

10. If the suspect has an unusual physical feature, e.g., a facial scar, tattoo or distinctive hairstyle or hair colour which cannot be replicated on other members of the identification parade, steps may be taken to conceal the location of that feature on the suspect and the other members of the identification parade if the suspect and their solicitor, or appropriate adult, agree. For example, by use of a plaster or a hat, so that all members of the identification parade resemble each other in general appearance.

11. When all members of a similar group are possible suspects, separate identification parades shall be held for each unless there are two suspects of similar appearance when they may appear on the same identification parade with at least twelve other members of the group who are not suspects. When police officers in uniform form an identification parade any numerals or other identifying badges shall be concealed.

12. When the suspect is brought to the place where the identification parade is to be held, they shall be asked if they have any objection to the arrangements for the identification parade or to any of the other participants in it and to state the reasons for the objection. The suspect may obtain advice from their solicitor or friend, if present, before the identification parade proceeds. If the suspect has a reasonable objection to the arrangements or any of the participants, steps shall, if practicable, be taken to remove the grounds for objection. When it is

not practicable to do so, the suspect shall be told why their objections cannot be met and the objection, the reason given for it and why it cannot be met, shall be recorded on forms provided for the purpose.

13. The suspect may select their own position in the line, but may not otherwise interfere with the order of the people forming the line. When there is more than one witness, the suspect must be told, after each witness has left the room, that they can, if they wish, change position in the line. Each position in the line must be clearly numbered, whether by means of a number laid on the floor in front of each identification parade member or by other means.

14. Appropriate arrangements must be made to make sure, before witnesses attend the identification parade, they are not able to:
    (i) communicate with each other about the case or overhear a witness who has already seen the identification parade;
    (ii) see any member of the identification parade;
    (iii) see, or be reminded of, any photograph or description of the suspect or be given any other indication as to the suspect's identity; or
    (iv) see the suspect before or after the identification parade.

15. The person conducting a witness to an identification parade must not discuss with them the composition of the identification parade and, in particular, must not disclose whether a previous witness has made any identification.

16. Witnesses shall be brought in one at a time. Immediately before the witness inspects the identification parade, they shall be told the person they saw on a specified earlier occasion may, or may not, be present and if they cannot make an identification, they should say so. The witness must also be told they should not make any decision about whether the person they saw is on the identification parade until they have looked at each member at least twice.

17. When the officer or police staff (see *paragraph 3.11*) conducting the identification procedure is satisfied the witness has properly looked at each member of the identification parade, they shall ask the witness whether the person they saw on a specified earlier occasion is on the identification parade and, if so, to indicate the number of the person concerned, see *paragraph 28*.

18. If the witness wishes to hear any identification parade member speak, adopt any specified posture or move, they shall first be asked whether they can identify any person(s) on the identification parade on the basis of appearance only. When the request is to hear members of the identification parade speak, the witness shall be reminded that the participants in the identification parade have been chosen on the basis of physical appearance only. Members of the identification parade may then be asked to comply with the witness' request to hear them speak, see them move or adopt any specified posture.

19. If the witness requests that the person they have indicated remove anything used for the purposes of *paragraph 10* to conceal the location of an unusual physical feature, that person may be asked to remove it.

20. If the witness makes an identification after the identification parade has ended, the suspect and, if present, their solicitor, interpreter or friend shall be informed. When this occurs, consideration should be given to allowing the witness a second opportunity to identify the suspect.

21. After the procedure, action required in accordance with *paragraph 3.40* applies.

22. When the last witness has left, the suspect shall be asked whether they wish to make any comments on the conduct of the identification parade.

(d) Documentation

23. A video recording must normally be taken of the identification parade. If that is impracticable, a colour photograph must be taken. A copy of the video recording or photograph shall be supplied, on request, to the suspect or their solicitor within a reasonable time.

24. As appropriate, paragraph *3.30* or *3.31*, should apply to any photograph or video taken as in paragraph *23*.

25. If any person is asked to leave an identification parade because they are interfering with its conduct, the circumstances shall be recorded.

26. A record must be made of all those present at an identification parade whose names are known to the police.

27. If prison inmates make up an identification parade, the circumstances must be recorded.

28. A record of the conduct of any identification parade must be made on forms provided for the purpose. This shall include anything said by the witness or the suspect about any identifications or the conduct of the procedure, and any reasons it was not practicable to comply with any of this Code's provisions.

1.8.9.1

KEYNOTE

Conduct of Identification Parades

Identification evidence can be crucial to the success of a prosecution. There are clear guidelines that must be followed. Where such guidelines are not followed it is likely that the defence will argue strongly to have the identification evidence excluded. In *R v Jones* (1999) *The Times*, 21 April, identification evidence was excluded as the officers told the suspect that if he did not comply with the procedure, force would be used against him.

Annexes A to F of Code D set out in detail the procedures and requirements which must be followed in conducting identification procedures.

Although the courts are aware of the many practical difficulties involved in organising and running identification procedures (see e.g. *R v Jamel* [1993] Crim LR 52), any flaws in the procedure will be considered in the light of their potential impact on the defendant's trial. Serious or deliberate breaches (such as the showing of photographs to witnesses before the parade), will invariably lead to any evidence so gained being excluded (*R v Finley* [1993] Crim LR 50). The key question for the court will be whether the breach of the Codes is likely to have made the identification less reliable. Things may not always go according to plan, for instance in *Abdullah, Pululu v R* [2019] EWCA Crim 1137, two victims were attacked and robbed by a group of men. One of the victims attended an identification procedure and, although he was aware that only one suspect was on the procedure, he in fact picked out two men. Even though the victim had been told he could only pick out one person, he picked out two because they looked like each other. Whilst this is not ideal, the Court of Appeal held that the victim's video identification evidence was correctly admitted as potentially probative and its weaknesses were properly identified in the *Turnbull* direction.

Breaches which appear to impact on the safeguards imposed by Annexes A–F to separate the functions of investigation and identification (e.g. where the investigating officer becomes involved with the running of the parade in a way which allows him/her to talk to the witnesses (*R v Gall* (1990) 90 Cr App R 64)) will also be treated seriously by the court.

The case of *R v Marrin* [2002] EWCA Crim 251, provides some guidance as to methods that could be used to get a suitable pool of participants for an identification parade. The court held that there was nothing inherently unfair or objectionable in some colouring or dye being used on the facial stubble of some volunteers to make them look more like the suspect. However, care needed to be taken with such measures because the procedure would be undermined if it was obvious to the witness that make-up had been used. Another point raised was that it may sometimes be appropriate for those on parade to wear hats, but if possible the wearing of hats should be avoided if hats had not been worn during the offence because this would make it more difficult for a witness to make an identification. However, there could be circumstances where the wearing of hats could help to achieve a resemblance and might be desirable to minimise differences. Finally, an identification of a suspect was not invalidated by the witness's request for the removal of a hat. There was nothing unfair in that taking place and there was no breach of any Code either.

It is important to follow the guidance in the Codes regardless of what agreement is obtained from the suspect or his/her solicitor. In *R v Hutton* [1999] Crim LR 74, at the suggestion of the suspect's solicitor, all the participants in the identification parade wore back-to-front baseball caps and had the lower part of their faces obscured by material. That identification was the only evidence against the defendant on that count. The court excluded the evidence and did not accept the fact that the decision had been agreed by the defence.

It will be essential that any photographs, photofits or other such material is stored securely in a manner that restricts access so as to be able to demonstrate to the court that the material cannot have been viewed by any of the witnesses and that copies have not been made that have not been accounted for. Where a witness attending an identification procedure has previously been shown photographs, or been shown or provided with computerised or artist's composite likenesses, or similar likenesses or pictures, it is the officer in charge of the investigation's responsibility to make the identification officer aware of this.

1.8.10 Code D—Annex C: Group Identification

(a) General

1. The purpose of this Annex is to make sure, as far as possible, group identifications follow the principles and procedures for identification parades so the conditions are fair to the suspect in the way they test the witness' ability to make an identification.

2. Group identifications may take place either with the suspect's consent and co-operation or covertly without their consent.

3. The location of the group identification is a matter for the identification officer, although the officer may take into account any representations made by the suspect, appropriate adult, their solicitor or friend.

4. The place where the group identification is held should be one where other people are either passing by or waiting around informally, in groups such that the suspect is able to join them and be capable of being seen by the witness at the same time as others in the group. For example people leaving an escalator, pedestrians walking through a shopping centre, passengers on railway and bus stations, waiting in queues or groups or where people are standing or sitting in groups in other public places.

5. If the group identification is to be held covertly, the choice of locations will be limited by the places where the suspect can be found and the number of other people present at that time. In these cases, suitable locations might be along regular routes travelled by the suspect, including buses or trains or public places frequented by the suspect.

6. Although the number, age, sex, race and general description and style of clothing of other people present at the location cannot be controlled by the identification officer, in selecting the location the officer must consider the general appearance and numbers of people likely to be present. In particular, the officer must reasonably expect that over the period the witness observes the group, they will be able to see, from time to time, a number of others whose appearance is broadly similar to that of the suspect.

7. A group identification need not be held if the identification officer believes, because of the unusual appearance of the suspect, none of the locations it would be practicable to use, satisfy the requirements of paragraph 6 necessary to make the identification fair.

8. Immediately after a group identification procedure has taken place (with or without the suspect's consent), a colour photograph or video should be taken of the general scene, if practicable, to give a general impression of the scene and the number of people present. Alternatively, if it is practicable, the group identification may be video recorded.

9. If it is not practicable to take the photograph or video in accordance with paragraph 8, a photograph or film of the scene should be taken later at a time determined by the identification officer if the officer considers it practicable to do so.

10. An identification carried out in accordance with this Code remains a group identification even though, at the time of being seen by the witness, the suspect was on their own rather than in a group.

11. Before the group identification takes place, the suspect or their solicitor shall be provided with details of the first description of the suspect by any witnesses who are to attend the identification. When a broadcast or publication is made, as in *paragraph 3.38(a)*, the suspect or their solicitor should also be allowed to view any material released by the police to the media for the purposes of identifying and tracing the suspect, provided that it is practicable and would not unreasonably delay the investigation.

12. After the procedure, action required in accordance with *paragraph 3.40* applies.

(b) Identification with the consent of the suspect

13. A suspect must be given a reasonable opportunity to have a solicitor or friend present. They shall be asked to indicate on a second copy of the notice whether or not they wish to do so.

14. The witness, the person carrying out the procedure and the suspect's solicitor, appropriate adult, friend or any interpreter for the witness, may be concealed from the sight of the individuals in the group they are observing, if the person carrying out the procedure considers this assists the conduct of the identification.

15. The person conducting a witness to a group identification must not discuss with them the forthcoming group identification and, in particular, must not disclose whether a previous witness has made any identification.

16. Anything said to, or by, the witness during the procedure about the identification should be said in the presence and hearing of those present at the procedure.

17. Appropriate arrangements must be made to make sure, before witnesses attend the group identification, they are not able to:
    (i) communicate with each other about the case or overhear a witness who has already been given an opportunity to see the suspect in the group;
    (ii) see the suspect; or
    (iii) see, or be reminded of, any photographs or description of the suspect or be given any other indication of the suspect's identity.

18. Witnesses shall be brought one at a time to the place where they are to observe the group. Immediately before the witness is asked to look at the group, the person conducting the procedure shall tell them that the person they saw on a specified earlier occasion may, or may not, be in the group and that if they cannot make an identification, they should say so. The witness shall be asked to observe the group in which the suspect is to appear. The way in which the witness should do this will depend on whether the group is moving or stationary.

Moving group

19. When the group in which the suspect is to appear is moving, e.g. leaving an escalator, the provisions of *paragraphs 20 to 24* should be followed.

20. If two or more suspects consent to a group identification, each should be the subject of separate identification procedures. These may be conducted consecutively on the same occasion.

21. The person conducting the procedure shall tell the witness to observe the group and ask them to point out any person they think they saw on the specified earlier occasion.

22. Once the witness has been informed as in *paragraph 21* the suspect should be allowed to take whatever position in the group they wish.

23. When the witness points out a person as in *paragraph 21* they shall, if practicable, be asked to take a closer look at the person to confirm the identification. If this is not practicable, or they cannot confirm the identification, they shall be asked how sure they are that the person they have indicated is the relevant person.

24. The witness should continue to observe the group for the period which the person conducting the procedure reasonably believes is necessary in the circumstances for them to be able to

make comparisons between the suspect and other individuals of broadly similar appearance to the suspect as in *paragraph 6*.

Stationary groups

25. When the group in which the suspect is to appear is stationary, e.g. people waiting in a queue, the provisions of *paragraphs 26* to *29* should be followed.

26. If two or more suspects consent to a group identification, each should be subject to separate identification procedures unless they are of broadly similar appearance when they may appear in the same group. When separate group identifications are held, the groups must be made up of different people.

27. The suspect may take whatever position in the group they wish. If there is more than one witness, the suspect must be told, out of the sight and hearing of any witness, that they can, if they wish, change their position in the group.

28. The witness shall be asked to pass along, or amongst, the group and to look at each person in the group at least twice, taking as much care and time as possible according to the circumstances, before making an identification. Once the witness has done this, they shall be asked whether the person they saw on the specified earlier occasion is in the group and to indicate any such person by whatever means the person conducting the procedure considers appropriate in the circumstances. If this is not practicable, the witness shall be asked to point out any person they think they saw on the earlier occasion.

29. When the witness makes an indication as in *paragraph 28*, arrangements shall be made, if practicable, for the witness to take a closer look at the person to confirm the identification. If this is not practicable, or the witness is unable to confirm the identification, they shall be asked how sure they are that the person they have indicated is the relevant person.

All cases

30. If the suspect unreasonably delays joining the group, or having joined the group, deliberately conceals themselves from the sight of the witness, this may be treated as a refusal to co-operate in a group identification.

31. If the witness identifies a person other than the suspect, that person should be informed what has happened and asked if they are prepared to give their name and address. There is no obligation upon any member of the public to give these details. There shall be no duty to record any details of any other member of the public present in the group or at the place where the procedure is conducted.

32. When the group identification has been completed, the suspect shall be asked whether they wish to make any comments on the conduct of the procedure.

33. If the suspect has not been previously informed, they shall be told of any identifications made by the witnesses.

(c) Group Identification without the suspect's consent

34. Group identifications held covertly without the suspect's consent should, as far as practicable, follow the rules for conduct of group identification by consent.

35. A suspect has no right to have a solicitor, appropriate adult or friend present as the identification will take place without the knowledge of the suspect.

36. Any number of suspects may be identified at the same time.

(d) Identifications in police stations

37. Group identifications should only take place in police stations for reasons of safety, security or because it is not practicable to hold them elsewhere.

38. The group identification may take place either in a room equipped with a screen permitting witnesses to see members of the group without being seen, or anywhere else in the police station that the identification officer considers appropriate.

39. Any of the additional safeguards applicable to identification parades should be followed if the identification officer considers it is practicable to do so in the circumstances.

(e) Identifications involving prison inmates

40. A group identification involving a prison inmate may only be arranged in the prison or at a police station.

41. When a group identification takes place involving a prison inmate, whether in a prison or in a police station, the arrangements should follow those in *paragraphs 37 to 39*. If a group identification takes place within a prison, other inmates may participate. If an inmate is the suspect, they do not have to wear prison clothing for the group identification unless the other participants are wearing the same clothing.

(f) Documentation

42. When a photograph or video is taken as in *paragraph 8* or *9*, a copy of the photograph or video shall be supplied on request to the suspect or their solicitor within a reasonable time.

43. *Paragraph 3.30* or *3.31*, as appropriate, shall apply when the photograph or film taken in accordance with *paragraph 8* or *9* includes the suspect.

44. A record of the conduct of any group identification must be made on forms provided for the purpose. This shall include anything said by the witness or suspect about any identifications or the conduct of the procedure and any reasons why it was not practicable to comply with any of the provisions of this Code governing the conduct of group identifications.

1.8.11   Code D—Annex D: Confrontation by an Eye-witness

1. Before the confrontation takes place, the eye-witness must be told that the person they saw on a specified earlier occasion may, or may not, be the person they are to confront and that if they are not that person, then the witness should say so.

2. Before the confrontation takes place the suspect or their solicitor shall be provided with details of the first description of the suspect given by any eye-witness who is to attend. When a broadcast or publication is made, as in *paragraph 3.38(a)*, the suspect or their solicitor should also be allowed to view any material released to the media for the purposes of recognising or tracing the suspect, provided it is practicable to do so and would not unreasonably delay the investigation.

3. Force may not be used to make the suspect's face visible to the eye-witness.

4. Confrontation must take place in the presence of the suspect's solicitor, interpreter or friend unless this would cause unreasonable delay.

5. The suspect shall be confronted independently by each eye-witness, who shall be asked 'Is this the person?'. If the eye-witness identifies the person but is unable to confirm the identification, they shall be asked how sure they are that the person is the one they saw on the earlier occasion.

6. The confrontation should normally take place in the police station, either in a normal room or one equipped with a screen permitting the eye-witness to see the suspect without being seen. In both cases, the procedures are the same except that a room equipped with a screen may be used only when the suspect's solicitor, friend or appropriate adult is present or the confrontation is recorded on video.

7. After the procedure, action required in accordance with *paragraph 3.40* applies.

Code D—Annex E: Showing Photographs to Eye-witnesses

(a) Action

1. An officer of sergeant rank or above shall be responsible for supervising and directing the showing of photographs. The actual showing may be done by another officer or police staff, see *paragraph 3.11*.

2. The supervising officer must confirm the first description of the suspect given by the eye-witness has been recorded before they are shown the photographs. If the supervising officer is unable to confirm the description has been recorded they shall postpone showing the photographs.

3. Only one eye-witness shall be shown photographs at any one time. Each witness shall be given as much privacy as practicable and shall not be allowed to communicate with any other eye-witness in the case.

4. The eye-witness shall be shown not less than twelve photographs at a time, which shall, as far as possible, all be of a similar type.

5. When the eye-witness is shown the photographs, they shall be told the photograph of the person they saw on a specified earlier occasion may, or may not, be amongst them and if they cannot make an identification, they should say so. The eye-witness shall also be told they should not make a decision until they have viewed at least twelve photographs. The eye-witness shall not be prompted or guided in any way but shall be left to make any selection without help.

6. If an eye-witness makes an identification from photographs, unless the person identified is otherwise eliminated from enquiries or is not available, other eye-witnesses shall not be shown photographs. But both they, and the eye-witness who has made the identification, shall be asked to attend a video identification, an identification parade or group identification unless there is no dispute about the suspect's identification.

7. If the eye-witness makes a selection but is unable to confirm the identification, the person showing the photographs shall ask them how sure they are that the photograph they have indicated is the person they saw on the specified earlier occasion.

8. When the use of a computerised or artist's composite or similar likeness has led to there being a known suspect who can be asked to participate in a video identification, appear on an identification parade or participate in a group identification, that likeness shall not be shown to other potential eye-witnesses.

9. When an eye-witness attending a video identification, an identification parade or group identification has previously been shown photographs or computerised or artist's composite or similar likeness (and it is the responsibility of the officer in charge of the investigation to make the identification officer aware that this is the case), the suspect and their solicitor must be informed of this fact before the identification procedure takes place.

10. None of the photographs shown shall be destroyed, whether or not an identification is made, since they may be required for production in court. The photographs shall be numbered and a separate photograph taken of the frame or part of the album from which the eye-witness made an identification as an aid to reconstituting it.

(b) Documentation

11. Whether or not an identification is made, a record shall be kept of the showing of photographs on forms provided for the purpose. This shall include anything said by the eye-witness about any identification or the conduct of the procedure, any reasons it was not practicable to comply with any of the provisions of this Code governing the showing of photographs and the name and rank of the supervising officer.

12. The supervising officer shall inspect and sign the record as soon as practicable.

KEYNOTE

Identification Where There Is No Suspect

Where the police have no suspect, Code D provides for witnesses (including police officers) to be shown photographs. If photographs are to be shown, the procedure set out at Annex E must be followed. When it is proposed to show photographs to a witness in accordance with Annex E, it is the responsibility of the officer in charge of the investigation to confirm to the officer responsible for supervising and directing the showing, that the first description of the suspect given by that witness has been recorded. If this description has not been recorded, the procedure under Annex E must be postponed. Except for the provisions of Annex E, para. 1, a police officer who is a witness for the purposes of this part of the Code is subject to the same principles and procedures as a civilian witness.

Using photographs from police criminal records can affect the judgment of a jury and nothing should be done to draw their attention to the fact that the defendant's photograph was already held by the police (*R v Lamb* (1980) 71 Cr App R 198). This rule does not apply if the jury are already aware of the defendant's previous convictions (*R v Allen* [1996] Crim LR 426).

Code D—Annex F: Fingerprints, Samples and Footwear Impressions—Destruction and Speculative Searches

Part A: Fingerprints and samples

Paragraphs 1 to 12 summarise and update information which is available at:

https://www.gov.uk/government/publications/protection-of-freedoms-act-2012-dna-and-fingerprintprovisions/protection-of-freedoms-act-2012-how-dna-and-fingerprint-evidence-is-protected-in-law

DNA samples

1. A DNA sample is an individual's biological material, containing all of their genetic information. The Act requires all DNA samples to be destroyed within 6 months of being taken. This allows sufficient time for the sample to be analysed and a DNA profile to be produced for use on the database.

2. The only exception to this is if the sample is or may be required for disclosure as evidence, in which case it may be retained for as long as this need exists under the Criminal Procedure and Investigations Act 1996.

DNA profiles and fingerprints

3. A DNA profile consists of a string of 16 pairs of numbers and 2 letters (XX for women, XY for men) to indicate gender. This number string is stored on the National DNA Database (NDNAD). It allows the person to be identified if they leave their DNA at a crime scene.

4. Fingerprints are usually scanned electronically from the individual in custody and the images stored on IDENT1, the national fingerprint database.

Retention Periods: Fingerprints and DNA profiles

5. The retention period depends on the outcome of the investigation of the recordable offence in connection with which the fingerprints and DNA samples was taken, the age of the person at the time the offence was committed and whether the *recordable* offence is a qualifying offence and whether it is an excluded offence (See Table *Notes (a)* to *(c)*), as follows:

Table—Retention periods

(a) Convictions

Age when offence committed	Outcome	Retention Period
Any age	Convicted or given a caution or youth caution for a recordable offence which is also a qualifying offence.	INDEFINITE
18 or over	Convicted or given a caution for a recordable offence which is NOT a qualifying offence.	INDEFINITE
Under 18	Convicted or given a youth caution for a recordable offence which is NOT a qualifying offence.	1st conviction or youth caution—5 years plus length of any prison sentence. Indefinite if prison sentence 5 years or more 2nd conviction or youth caution: Indefinite

(b) Non-Convictions

Age when offence committed	Outcome	Retention Period
Any age	Charged but not convicted of a recordable qualifying offence.	3 years plus a 2 year extension if granted by a District Judge (or indefinite if the individual has a previous conviction for a recordable offence which is not excluded)
Any age	Arrested for, but not charged with, a recordable qualifying offence	3 years if granted by the Biometrics Commissioner plus a 2 year extension if granted by a District Judge (or indefinite if the individual has a previous conviction for a recordable offence which is not excluded)
Any age	Arrested for or charged with a recordable offence which is not a qualifying offence.	Indefinite if the person has a previous conviction for a recordable offence which is not excluded otherwise NO RETENTION)
18 or over	Given Penalty Notice for Disorder for recordable offence	2 years

Table Notes:
(a) A 'recordable' offence is one for which the police are required to keep a record. Generally speaking, these are imprisonable offences; however, it also includes a number of non-imprisonable offences such as begging and taxi touting. The police are not able to take or retain the DNA or fingerprints of an individual who is arrested for an offence which is not recordable.
(b) A 'qualifying' offence is one listed under section 65A of the Police and Criminal Evidence Act 1984 (the list comprises sexual, violent, terrorism and burglary offences).
(c) An 'excluded' offence is a recordable offence which is not a qualifying offence, was committed when the individual was under 18, for which they received a sentence of fewer than 5 years' imprisonment and is the only recordable offence for which the person has been convicted

Speculative searches

6. Where the retention framework above requires the deletion of a person's DNA profile and fingerprints, the Act first allows a *speculative search* of their DNA and fingerprints against DNA and fingerprints obtained from crime scenes which are stored on NDNAD and IDENT1. Once the speculative search has been completed, the profile and fingerprints are deleted unless there is

a match, in which case they will be retained for the duration of any investigation and thereafter in accordance with the retention framework (e.g. if that investigation led to a conviction for a qualifying offence, they would be retained indefinitely).

Extensions of retention period

7. For qualifying offences, PACE allows chief constables to apply for extensions to the given retention periods for DNA profiles and fingerprints if considered necessary for prevention or detection of crime.

8. Section 20 of the Protection of Freedoms Act 2012 established the independent office of Commissioner for the Retention and Use of Biometric Material (the 'Biometrics Commissioner'). For details, see https://www.gov.uk/government/organisations/biometricscommissioner.

9. Where an individual is arrested for, but not charged with, a qualifying offence, their DNA profile and fingerprint record will normally be deleted. However, the police can apply to the Biometrics Commissioner for permission to retain their DNA profile and fingerprint record for a period of 3 years. The application must be made within 28 days of the decision not to proceed with a prosecution.

10. If the police make such an application, the Biometrics Commissioner would first give both them and the arrested individual an opportunity to make written representations and then, taking into account factors including the age and vulnerability of the victim(s) of the alleged offences, and their relationship to the suspect, make a decision on whether or not retention is appropriate.

11. If after considering the application, the Biometrics Commissioner decides that retention is not appropriate, the DNA profile and fingerprint record in question must be destroyed.

12. If the Biometrics Commissioner agrees to allow retention, the police will be able to retain that individual's DNA profile and fingerprint record for a period of 3 years from the date the samples were taken. At the end of that period, the police will be able to apply to a District Judge (Magistrates' Courts) for a single 2 year extension to the retention period. If the application is rejected, the force must then destroy the DNA profile and fingerprint record.

Part B: Footwear impressions

13. Footwear impressions taken in accordance with section 61A of PACE (see *paragraphs 4.16* to *4.21*) may be retained for as long as is necessary for purposes related to the prevention or detection of crime, the investigation of an offence or the conduct of a prosecution.

Part C: Fingerprints, samples and footwear impressions taken in connection with a criminal investigation from a person not suspected of committing the offence under investigation for elimination purposes.

14. When fingerprints, footwear impressions or DNA samples are taken from a person in connection with an investigation and the person is *not suspected of having committed the offence*, they must be destroyed as soon as they have fulfilled the purpose for which they were taken unless:
   (a) they were taken for the purposes of an investigation of an offence for which a person has been convicted; and
   (b) fingerprints, footwear impressions or samples were also taken from the convicted person for the purposes of that investigation.
   However, subject to *paragraph 14*, the fingerprints, footwear impressions and samples, and the information derived from samples, may not be used in the investigation of any offence or in evidence against the person who is, or would be, entitled to the destruction of the fingerprints, footwear impressions and samples.

15. The requirement to destroy fingerprints, footwear impressions and DNA samples, and information derived from samples and restrictions on their retention and use in *paragraph 14* do

not apply if the person gives their written consent for their fingerprints, footwear impressions or sample to be retained and used after they have fulfilled the purpose for which they were taken. This consent can be withdrawn at any time.

16. When a person's fingerprints, footwear impressions or sample are to be destroyed:
    (a) any copies of the fingerprints and footwear impressions must also be destroyed; and
    (b) neither the fingerprints, footwear impressions, the sample, or any information derived from the sample, may be used in the investigation of any offence or in evidence against the person who is, or would be, entitled to its destruction.

1.8.13.1 **KEYNOTE**

Fingerprints, footwear impressions and samples given voluntarily for the purposes of elimination play an important part in many police investigations. It is, therefore, important to make sure innocent volunteers are not deterred from participating and their consent to their fingerprints, footwear impressions and DNA being used for the purposes of a specific investigation is fully informed and voluntary. If the police or volunteer seek to have the fingerprints, footwear impressions or samples retained for use after the specific investigation ends, it is important the volunteer's consent to this is also fully informed and voluntary. The volunteer must be told that they may withdraw their consent at any time.

The consent must be obtained in writing using current nationally agreed forms provided for police use according to the purpose for which the consent is given. This purpose may be either:

- DNA/fingerprints/footwear impressions—to be used only for the purposes of a specific investigation; or
- DNA/fingerprints/footwear impressions—to be used in the specific investigation and retained by the police for future use.

To minimise the risk of confusion:

- if a police officer or member of police staff has any doubt about:
  - how the consent forms should be completed and signed, or
  - whether a consent form they propose to use and refer to is fully compliant with the current nationally agreed form,
  the relevant national police helpdesk (for DNA or fingerprints) should be contacted.
- in each case, the meaning of consent should be explained orally and care taken to ensure the oral explanation accurately reflects the contents of the written form the person is to be asked to sign.

The provisions for the retention of fingerprints, footwear impressions and samples in para. 15 allow for all fingerprints, footwear impressions and samples in a case to be available for any subsequent miscarriage of justice investigation.

1.8.14 **Code D—Annex G: Requirement for a Person to Attend a Police Station for Fingerprints and Samples**

1. A requirement under Schedule 2A for a person to attend a police station to have fingerprints or samples taken:
   (a) must give the person a period of at least seven days within which to attend the police station; and
   (b) may direct them to attend at a specified time of day or between specified times of day.
2. When specifying the period and times of attendance, the officer making the requirements must consider whether the fingerprints or samples could reasonably be taken at a time when the person is required to attend the police station for any other reason.
3. An officer of the rank of inspector or above may authorise a period shorter than 7 days if there is an urgent need for person's fingerprints or sample for the purposes of the investigation of an offence. The fact of the authorisation and the reasons for giving it must be recorded as soon as practicable.

4. The constable making a requirement and the person to whom it applies may agree to vary it so as to specify any period within which, or date or time at which, the person is to attend. However, variation shall not have effect for the purposes of enforcement, unless it is confirmed by the constable in writing.

1.8.14.1

KEYNOTE

The specified period within which the person is to attend need not fall within the period allowed (if applicable) for making the requirement.

To justify the arrest without warrant of a person who fails to comply with a requirement (see paras 4.4(b) and 6.7(b) above), the officer making the requirement, or confirming a variation, should be prepared to explain how, when and where the requirement was made or the variation was confirmed and what steps were taken to ensure the person understood what to do and the consequences of not complying with the requirement.

Following the correct procedure for requesting samples is crucial. In *R (On the Application of R) v A Chief Constable* [2013] EWHC 2864 (Admin), R had been convicted of unlawful act manslaughter in 1984. Twenty years after a kidnap conviction in 1993, R was asked to provide a non-intimate sample to be placed on the police national DNA database. R refused to provide a sample and was handed a letter informing him that he had seven days to attend the police station to provide the sample, and if he failed to do so he would be arrested and a sample would be forcibly taken from him pursuant to the Police and Criminal Evidence Act 1984, s. 63(3B)(a). When the letter was served authority had not been given by an inspector. The court held that a requirement to attend a police station to provide a non-intimate sample under the 1984 Act could not be made to a person who did not consent to providing a sample unless an officer of the rank of inspector or above had first given authorisation for the taking of the sample under s. 63(3B)(b). The letter handed to R constituted a demand that he attend a police station to provide a sample within seven days. That demand was unlawful because it was made without prior authorisation by an inspector or an officer of higher rank.

The second point in this case related to the authority that was eventually given by the inspector and the historic nature of the conviction; the court held that the inspector was fully justified in concluding that the public interest in the detection of crime outweighed the limited interference with R's private life. The absence of specific grounds for suspicion of R did not render the requirement to provide a sample disproportionate. The conclusion that R might have committed other offences during the period of his admitted offending and after 1995 was justified. While there was a theoretical deterrent effect in the knowledge by R that police were in possession of his DNA profile, it was the objective of solving crime which provided the legitimate justification for the requirement in the instant case. The requirement that R attend the police station to give a sample was proportionate.

Interviews

PACE Code of Practice for the Detention, Treatment and Questioning of Persons by Police Officers (Code C)

PACE Code of Practice on Audio Recording Interviews with Suspects (Code E)

PACE Code of Practice on Visual Recording with Sound of Interviews with Suspects (Code F)

A thick grey line down the margin denotes text that is an extract of the PACE Code itself (i.e. the actual wording of the legislation).

1.9.1 Introduction

The PACE Codes of Practice C, E and F are intended to provide protection to people being interviewed by the police and lay down guidelines as to how interviews should be conducted. This chapter examines the treatment of suspects when they are interviewed. The chapter includes the relevant sections of Code C and all of Code E and F. The chapter sets out the actual Codes of Practice with keynotes, which incorporate the notes of guidance to the Code, relevant legislation and case law.

See chapter 1.7 regarding designated officers carrying out some functions of police officers.

Code C was amended on 23 February 2017. Code H applies to persons detained for the purposes of a terrorist investigation; references to terrorism matters, where appropriate, are included in the keynotes to this chapter.

1.9.2 PACE Code of Practice for the Detention, Treatment and Questioning of Persons by Police Officers (Code C)

10 Cautions

(a) When a caution must be given

10.1 A person whom there are grounds to suspect of an offence, must be cautioned before any questions about an offence, or further questions if the answers provide the grounds for suspicion, are put to them if either the suspect's answers or silence, (i.e. failure or refusal to *answer* or *answer* satisfactorily) may be given in evidence to a court in a prosecution. A person need not be cautioned if questions are for other necessary purposes, e.g.:

(a) solely to establish their identity or ownership of any vehicle;

(b) to obtain information in accordance with any relevant statutory requirement, see *paragraph 10.9*;

(c) in furtherance of the proper and effective conduct of a search, e.g. to determine the need to search in the exercise of powers of stop and search or to seek co-operation while carrying out a search; or

(d) to seek verification of a written record as in *paragraph 11.13*.

(e) *Not used.*

10.2 Whenever a person not under arrest is initially cautioned, or reminded that they are under caution, that person must at the same time be told they are not under arrest and must be informed of the provisions of *paragraph 3.21* which explain that they need to agree to be interviewed, how they may obtain legal advice according to whether they are at a police station or elsewhere and the other rights and entitlements that apply to a voluntary interview.

10.3 A person who is arrested, or further arrested, must be informed at the time if practicable or, if not, as soon as it becomes practicable thereafter, that they are under arrest and of the grounds and reasons for their arrest, see paragraph 3.4 and *Code G, paragraphs 2.2 and 4.3*.

10.4 As required by *Code G, section 3*, a person who is arrested, or further arrested, must also be cautioned unless:

(a) it is impracticable to do so by reason of their condition or behaviour at the time;

(b) they have already been cautioned immediately prior to arrest as in *paragraph 10.1*.

1.9.2.1

KEYNOTE

In considering whether there are grounds to suspect a person of committing an offence there must be some reasonable, objective grounds for the suspicion, based on known facts or information which are/ is relevant to the likelihood that the offence has been committed and that the person to be questioned committed it.

An arrested person must be given sufficient information to enable him/her to understand that he/she has been deprived of his/her liberty and the reason for the arrest, e.g. when a person is arrested on suspicion of committing an offence he/she must be informed of the suspected offence's nature, and when and where it was committed. The suspect must also be informed of the reason or reasons why the arrest is considered necessary. Vague or technical language should be avoided. If it appears that a person does not understand the caution, the person giving it should explain it in his/her own words.

Ibrahim v *the United Kingdom* (Application nos 50541/08, 50571/08, 50573/08 and 40351/09) was a case in the European Court of Human Rights against the United Kingdom. The applicants alleged a violation of Article 6 in that they had been interviewed by the police without access to a lawyer and that statements made in those interviews had been used at their trials. The case stemmed from the investigation of the four bombs that were detonated on the London transport system in July 2005 but failed to explode. The perpetrators fled the scene. One person who was not suspected of having detonated a bomb was initially interviewed by the police as a witness. He started to incriminate himself by explaining his encounter with a suspected bomber shortly after the attacks and the assistance he had provided to that suspect. According to the applicable Code of Practice, he should have been cautioned and offered legal advice at that point. However, after taking instructions from a senior officer, the police continued to question him as a witness and took a written statement from him. The court held that there had been no compelling reasons for restricting his access to legal advice and for failing to inform him of his right to remain silent. It was significant that there was no basis in domestic law for the police to choose not to caution him at the point at which he had started to incriminate himself. Indeed, the Court stated that the decision had been contrary to the applicable Code of Practice. As a result, the applicant had been misled as to his procedural rights.

(b) Terms of the cautions

10.5 The caution which must be given on:

(a) arrest; or

(b) all other occasions before a person is charged or informed they may be prosecuted; see *section 16*,

should, unless the restriction on drawing adverse inferences from silence applies, see *Annex C*, be in the following terms:

'You do not have to say anything. But it may harm your defence if you do not mention when questioned something which you later rely on in Court. Anything you do say may be given in evidence.'

Where the use of the Welsh Language is appropriate, a constable may provide the caution directly in Welsh in the following terms:

'Does dim rhaid i chi ddweud dim byd. Ond gall niweidio eich amddiffyniad os na fyddwch chi'n sôn, wrth gael eich holi, am rywbeth y byddwch chi'n dibynnu arno nes ymlaen yn y Llys. Gall unrhyw beth yr ydych yn ei ddweud gael ei roi fel tystiolaeth.'

10.6 *Annex C, paragraph 2* sets out the alternative terms of the caution to be used when the restriction on drawing adverse inferences from silence applies.

10.7 Minor deviations from the words of any caution given in accordance with this Code do not constitute a breach of this Code, provided the sense of the relevant caution is preserved.

10.8 After any break in questioning under caution, the person being questioned must be made aware they remain under caution. If there is any doubt the relevant caution should be given again in full when the interview resumes.

10.9 When, despite being cautioned, a person fails to co-operate or to answer particular questions which may affect their immediate treatment, the person should be informed of any relevant consequences and that those consequences are not affected by the caution. Examples are when a person's refusal to provide:

- their name and address when charged may make them liable to detention;
- particulars and information in accordance with a statutory requirement, e.g. under the Road Traffic Act 1988, may amount to an offence or may make the person liable to a further arrest.

KEYNOTE

As well as considering whether to administer the caution again after a break in questioning or at the beginning of a subsequent interview, the interviewing officer should summarise the reason for the break and confirm this with the suspect. This may help to show to the court that nothing occurred during an interview break or between interviews which influenced the suspect's recorded evidence.

Nothing in this Code requires a caution to be given or repeated when informing a person not under arrest that he/she may be prosecuted for an offence. However, a court will not be able to draw any inferences under the Criminal Justice and Public Order Act 1994, s. 34, if the person was not cautioned.

The giving of a warning or the service of the Notice of Intended Prosecution required by the Road Traffic Offenders Act 1988, s. 1 does not amount to informing a detainee that he/she may be prosecuted for an offence and so does not preclude further questioning in relation to that offence.

Section 34 of the Criminal Justice and Public Order Act 1994

Section 34 of the Criminal Justice and Public Order Act 1994 provides that inferences can be drawn if, when questioned by the police under caution, charged or officially informed that he/she may be prosecuted, the accused fails to mention a fact on which he/she later relies in his/her defence, and which he/she could reasonably have been expected to mention at the time.

Section 34 states:

(1) Where, in any proceedings against a person for an offence, evidence is given that the accused—
  (a) at any time before he was charged with the offence, on being questioned under caution by a constable trying to discover whether or by whom the offence had been committed, failed to mention any fact relied on in his defence in those proceedings; or
  (b) on being charged with the offence or officially informed that he might be prosecuted for it, failed to mention any such fact, or
  (c) at any time after being charged with the offence, on being questioned under section 22 of the Counter-Terrorism Act 2008 (post-charge questioning), failed to mention any such fact,
  being a fact which in the circumstances existing at the time the accused could reasonably have been expected to mention when so questioned, charged or informed, as the case may be, subsection (2) below applies.
(2) Where this subsection applies—
  (a) ...
  (b) a judge, in deciding whether to grant an application made by the accused under paragraph 2 of Schedule 3 to the Crime and Disorder Act 1998;
  (c) the court, in determining whether there is a case to answer; and
  (d) the court or jury, in determining whether the accused is guilty of the offence charged,
  may draw such inferences from the failure as appear proper.
(2A) Where the accused was at an authorised place of detention at the time of the failure, subsections (1) and (2) above do not apply if he had not been allowed an opportunity to consult a solicitor prior to being questioned, charged or informed as mentioned in subsection (1) above.
(3) Subject to any directions by the court, evidence tending to establish the failure may be given before or after evidence tending to establish the fact which the accused is alleged to have failed to mention.
(4) This section applies in relation to questioning by persons (other than constables) charged with the duty of investigating offences or charging offenders as it applies in relation to questioning by constables; and in subsection (1) above 'officially informed' means informed by a constable or any such person.
(5) This section does not—
  (a) prejudice the admissibility in evidence of the silence or other reaction of the accused in the face of anything said in his presence relating to the conduct in respect of which he is charged, in so far as evidence thereof would be admissible apart from this section; or
  (b) preclude the drawing of any inference from any such silence or other reaction of the accused which could properly be drawn apart from this section.

Section 34 deals with the 'failure to mention any fact' and the word 'fact' is given its normal dictionary definition of 'something that is actually the case' (*R v Milford* [2001] Crim LR 330). Where an accused alleges that he/she did mention the relevant fact when being questioned, it is for the prosecution to prove the contrary before any adverse inference can be drawn. The court have said that the object of s. 34 is to deter late fabrication and to encourage early disclosure of genuine defences (*Brizzalari* [2004] EWCA Crim 310).

There have been numerous domestic and European case decisions about failure to advance facts following legal advice to remain silent, and more recent cases have attempted to unravel the difficulties experienced in this area. These cases have accepted that a genuine reliance by a defendant on his/her solicitor's advice to remain silent is not in itself enough to preclude adverse comment. The real question to be answered is whether the defendant remained silent, not because of legal advice, but because there was no satisfactory explanation to give (*R v Beckles* [2004] EWCA Crim 2766, *R v Bresa* [2005] EWCA Crim 1414 and *R v Loizou* [2006] EWCA Crim 1719). In *R v Ahmed, Mohamed, Bahdon, R and G* [2019] EWCA Crim 1085, the victim was robbed by a group of youths and then assaulted with an iron bar. R was seen on CCTV footage holding something and it was the prosecution case that it was a metal pole. R gave a no comment interview; however, at trial he said he was carrying a piece of bendable plastic tubing (as opposed to an iron bar) and he explained why he was carrying it. R stated that he did not mention those things in interview because he was aged 16 and was acting on his solicitor's advice to say no comment during the interview. On appeal, the court held that the judge was right to direct the jury that they could draw a s. 34 adverse inference if they concluded that, in the context of him being just 16 and having been advised to make no comment at an early stage of the investigation when there had not been lengthy consideration of it, he could reasonably have been expected to have mentioned those matters at the interview, and the only sensible reason that he did not do so was that he had not yet thought of them or did not think that they would withstand scrutiny.

In assessing whether to draw an inference from a failure to mention facts later relied on as part of the defence, the court may look at the validity of the waiver to legal advice. In *R* v *Saunders* [2012] EWCA Crim 1380, the suspect declined the offer of legal representation, and in interview she either made no comment or denied the allegations put to her. At trial she blamed her cousin who she said had been staying at her flat at the time. The prosecution sought to rely on her interview to show that she had made no mention of her cousin at that stage. In accepting the prosecution's submission the court considered the extent of her knowledge and the extent to which her decision caused her disadvantage. As to the first factor, the defendant had particular experience and understanding of the interview procedure having experienced it before and was well fitted to decide whether she wanted legal advice. She was neither unintelligent nor vulnerable and could be expected to be well aware of the benefit of legal advice.

In relation to s. 34, the accused cannot be convicted solely on an inference drawn from silence. The European Court of Human Rights, although accepting that there are cases which clearly call for an accused to provide an explanation, stated that the court is required to apply 'particular caution' before invoking the accused's silence against him (*Condron* v *United Kingdom* (2001) 31 EHRR 1). In *R* v *Condron* [1997] 1 WLR 827, the court held that the jury must be satisfied that the prosecution has established a case to answer before drawing any inferences from silence. In *R* v *Miah* [2009] EWCA Crim 2368, Hughes LJ said: 'Section 34 bites not on silence in interview but upon the late advancing of a case which could have been made earlier. What it does is to permit the jury to ask why, if there is an explanation for the evidence, or a defence to the accusation, the defendant did not advance it when he could have done, providing only that it was reasonable to expect him to have done so then.'

In *R* v *Argent* [1997] 2 Cr App R 27, the court stated that personal factors which might be relevant to an assessment of what an individual could reasonably have been expected to mention were age, experience, mental capacity, state of health, sobriety, tiredness, personality, knowledge and legal advice.

In *R* v *Flynn* [2001] EWCA Crim 1633, the court held that the police are entitled to conduct a second interview with a suspect, having obtained evidence from their witnesses which was not available in the first interview, and adverse inference could be drawn from the suspect's silence.

Where an accused, following legal advice, fails to answer questions during interview but presents a prepared statement, no adverse inference can be drawn where the accused's defence does not rely on any facts not mentioned in the interview (*R* v *Knight* [2003] EWCA Crim 1977). However, this would not be the case when evidence of facts relied on during the trial was not contained within the pre-prepared statement (*R* v *Turner* [2003] EWCA Crim 3108). If the prepared statement is very bland compared with any detailed defence given at trial, a jury may be directed to consider why a more detailed statement was not provided earlier (*R* v *Cross* [2017] EWCA Crim 1036).

Section 34 differs from the other 'inference' sections in that the questioning need not occur at a police station and therefore the presence of a legal representative is not required. However, it appears clear that, should the prosecution seek to draw any inferences of an accused's silence where such questioning has occurred, the questions would need to be asked of the suspect again once he/she had access to legal advice.

A requirement to caution the person is contained in s. 34(1)(a) in order to make clear the risks connected with a failure to mention facts which later form part of the defence.

Section 22(9) of the Counter-Terrorism Act 2008 adds s. 34(1)(c) to the Criminal Justice and Public Order Act 1994, which extends inferences from silence to post-charge questioning which has been authorised by a judge of the Crown Court if the offence is a terrorism offence or it appears to the judge that the offence has a terrorist connection. The post-charge questioning provisions of the 2008 Act require the issue of a mandatory Code for the video recording with sound of such questioning (**see appendix** of this manual).

(c) Special warnings under the Criminal Justice and Public Order Act 1994, sections 36 and 37

10.10   When a suspect interviewed at a police station or authorised place of detention after arrest fails or refuses to answer certain questions, or to answer satisfactorily, after due warning, a court or jury may draw such inferences as appear proper under the Criminal Justice and Public Order Act 1994, sections 36 and 37. Such inferences may only be drawn when:

(a) the restriction on drawing adverse inferences from silence, see *Annex C*, does not apply; and

(b) the suspect is arrested by a constable and fails or refuses to account for any objects, marks or substances, or marks on such objects found:

- on their person;
- in or on their clothing or footwear;
- otherwise in their possession; or
- in the place they were arrested;

(c) the arrested suspect was found by a constable at a place at or about the time the offence for which that officer has arrested them is alleged to have been committed, and the suspect fails or refuses to account for their presence there.

When the restriction on drawing adverse inferences from silence applies, the suspect may still be asked to account for any of the matters in (*b*) or (*c*) but the special warning described in *paragraph 10.11* will not apply and must not be given.

10.11   For an inference to be drawn when a suspect fails or refuses to answer a question about one of these matters or to answer it satisfactorily, the suspect must first be told in ordinary language:

(a) what offence is being investigated;

(b) what fact they are being asked to account for;

(c) this fact may be due to them taking part in the commission of the offence;

(d) a court may draw a proper inference if they fail or refuse to account for this fact; and

(e) a record is being made of the interview and it may be given in evidence if they are brought to trial.

(d) Juveniles and vulnerable persons

10.11A   The information required in *paragraph 10.11* must not be given to a suspect who is a juvenile or a vulnerable person unless the appropriate adult is present.

10.12   If a juvenile or a vulnerable person is cautioned in the absence of the appropriate adult, the caution must be repeated in the appropriate adult's presence.

10.12A   *Not used.*

(e) Documentation

10.13   A record shall be made when a caution is given under this section, either in the interviewer's report book or in the interview record.

KEYNOTE

Sections 36 and 37 of the Criminal Justice and Public Order Act 1994

The Criminal Justice and Public Order Act 1994, ss. 36 and 37 apply only to suspects who have been arrested by a constable or an officer of Revenue and Customs and are given the relevant warning by the police or customs officer who made the arrest or who is investigating the offence. They do not apply to any interviews with suspects who have not been arrested. The suspect must also be at a police station or other authorised detention place.

Inferences from Silence: Failure to Account for Objects, Substances and Marks

Section 36 of the Criminal Justice and Public Order Act 1994 provides that inferences can be drawn from an accused's failure to give evidence or refusal to answer any question about any object, substance or mark which may be attributable to the accused in the commission of an offence.

Section 36 states:

(1) Where—
    (a) a person is arrested by a constable, and there is—
        (i) on his person; or
        (ii) in or on his clothing or footwear; or
        (iii) otherwise in his possession; or
        (iv) in any place in which he is at the time of his arrest,
    (b) any object, substance or mark, or there is any mark on any such object; and
    (c) that or another constable investigating the case reasonably believes that the presence of the object, substance or mark may be attributable to the participation of the person arrested in the commission of an offence specified by the constable; and
    (d) the constable informs the person arrested that he so believes, and requests him to account for the presence of the object, substance or mark; and
    (e) the person fails or refuses to do so,
    then if, in any proceedings against the person for the offence so specified, evidence of those matters is given, subsection (2) below applies.

(2) Where this subsection applies—
    (a) a magistrates' court inquiring into the offence as examining justices; in deciding whether to grant an application for dismissal made by the accused under section 6 of the Magistrates' Courts Act 1980 (application for dismissal of charge in course of proceedings with a view to transfer for trial);
    (b) a judge, in deciding whether to grant an application made by the accused under—
        (i) section 6 of the Criminal Justice Act 1987 (application for dismissal of charge of serious fraud in respect of which notice of transfer has been given under section 4 of that Act); or
        (ii) paragraph 5 of schedule 6 to the Criminal Justice Act 1991 (application for dismissal of charge of violent or sexual offence involving a child in respect of which notice of transfer has been given under section 53 of that Act);
    (c) the court, in determining whether there is a case to answer; and
    (d) the court or jury, in determining whether the accused is guilty of the offence charged, may draw such inferences from the failure or refusal as appear proper.

(3) Subsections (1) and (2) above apply to the condition of clothing or footwear as they apply to a substance or mark thereon.

(4) Subsections (1) and (2) above do not apply unless the accused was told in ordinary language by the constable when making the request mentioned in subsection (1)(c) above what the effect of this section would be if he failed or refused to comply with the request.

(4A) Where the accused was at an authorised place of detention at the time of the failure or refusal, subsections (1) and (2) do not apply if he had not been allowed an opportunity to consult a solicitor prior to the request being made.

(5) This section applies in relation to officers of customs and excise as it applies in relation to constables.

(6) This section does not preclude the drawing of any inference from a failure or refusal of the accused to account for the presence of an object, substance or mark or from the condition of clothing or footwear which could properly be drawn apart from this section.

As with s. 37 below, an inference may only be drawn where four conditions are satisfied:

- the accused has been arrested;
- a constable reasonably believes that the object, substance or mark (or the presence of the accused (s. 37)) may be attributable to the accused's participation in a crime (s. 36 (an offence 'specified by the constable') or s. 37 (the offence for which he/she was arrested));
- the constable informs the accused of his/her belief and requests an explanation (by giving a special warning (see below));
- the constable tells the suspect (in ordinary language) the effect of a failure or refusal to comply with the request.

The request for information under both s. 36 and s. 37 is a form of questioning and should be undertaken during the interview at the police station. The request for such information prior to this would be an exception to the rule.

The interviewing officer is required to give the accused a 'special warning' for an inference to be drawn from a suspect's failure or refusal to answer a question about one of these matters or to answer it satisfactorily. This 'special warning' is provided by PACE Code C, para. 10.11, which states that the interviewing officer must first tell the suspect *in ordinary language*:

- what offence is being investigated;
- what fact the suspect is being asked to account for;
- that the interviewing officer believes this fact may be due to the suspect's taking part in the commission of the offence in question;
- that a court may draw a proper inference if the suspect fails or refuses to account for the fact about which he/she is being questioned;
- that a record is being made of the interview and that it may be given in evidence at any subsequent trial.

Section 36 considers the circumstances of the suspect at the time of arrest; it is suggested therefore that in relation to items that are *otherwise in the possession of the suspect* under s. 36(1)(a) there must be some link to the suspect at the time of arrest and this would not for instance include items found sometime later at a search of the suspect's home address some distance away.

As with s. 34, in relation to s. 36 the accused cannot be convicted solely on an inference drawn from a failure or refusal (s. 38(3))

Inferences from Silence: Failure to Account for Presence

Section 37 of the Criminal Justice and Public Order Act 1994 provides that inferences can be drawn from an accused's failure to give evidence or refusal to answer any question about his/her presence at a place or time when the offence for which he/she was arrested was committed.

Section 37 states:

(1) Where—
   (a) a person arrested by a constable was found by him at a place at or about the time the offence for which he was arrested is alleged to have been committed; and
   (b) that or another constable investigating the offence reasonably believes that the presence of the person at that place and at that time may be attributable to his participation in the commission of the offence; and
   (c) the constable informs the person that he so believes, and requests him to account for that presence; and
   (d) the person fails or refuses to do so.
   then if, in any proceedings against the person for the offence, evidence of those matters is given, subsection (2) below applies.

(2) Where this subsection applies—
   (a) a magistrates' court inquiring into the offence as examining justices; in deciding whether to grant an application for dismissal made by the accused under section 6 of the Magistrates' Courts Act 1980 (application for dismissal of charge in course of proceedings with a view to transfer for trial);
   (b) a judge, in deciding whether to grant an application made by the accused under—
      (i) section 6 of the Criminal Justice Act 1987 (application for dismissal of charge of serious fraud in respect of which notice of transfer has been given under section 4 of that Act); or
      (ii) paragraph 5 of schedule 6 to the Criminal Justice Act 1991 (application for dismissal of charge of violent or sexual offence involving child in respect of which notice of transfer has been given under section 53 of that Act);
   (c) the court, in determining whether there is a case to answer; and
   (d) the court or jury, in determining whether the accused is guilty of the offence charged,
   may draw such inferences from the failure or refusal as appear proper.

(3) Subsections (1) and (2) do not apply unless the accused was told in ordinary language by the constable when making the request mentioned in subsection (1)(c) above what the effect of this section would be if he failed or refused to comply with the request.

(3A) Where the accused was at an authorised place of detention at the time of the failure or refusal, subsections (1) and (2) do not apply if he had not been allowed an opportunity to consult a solicitor prior to the request being made.

(4) This section applies in relation to officers of customs and excise as it applies in relation to constables.

(5) This section does not preclude the drawing of any inference from a failure or refusal of the accused to account for his presence at a place which could properly be drawn apart from this section.

Section 37 appears somewhat restrictive in that it is only concerned with the suspect's location at the time of arrest and applies only when he/she was found at that location at or about the time of the offence. It would not apply where the suspect has been seen near the scene of a crime but is arrested elsewhere.

In these circumstances the provisions for mentioning relevant facts in s. 34 of the Act are likely to be appropriate.

PACE Code C also applies to s. 37 in relation to the 'special warning' required to be given by the interviewing officer.

Unlike s. 36, here the officer that sees the person at or near the scene of the alleged offence must be the arresting officer.

As with ss. 34 and 36, in relation to s. 37 the accused cannot be convicted solely on an inference drawn from a failure or refusal (s. 38(3)).

1.9.2.6

KEYNOTE

Inferences from Silence at Trial

Section 35 of the Criminal Justice and Public Order Act 1994 provides that inferences can be drawn from an accused's failure to give evidence or refusal to answer any question, without good cause, where the person has been sworn. Section 35 states:

(1) At the trial of any person for an offence, subsections (2) and (3) below apply unless—
   (a) the accused's guilt is not in issue; or
   (b) it appears to the court that the physical or mental condition of the accused makes it undesirable for him to give evidence;
   but subsection (2) below does not apply if, at the conclusion of the evidence for the prosecution, his legal representative informs the court that the accused will give evidence or, where he is unrepresented, the court ascertains from him that he will give evidence.
(2) Where this subsection applies, the court shall, at the conclusion of the evidence for the prosecution, satisfy itself (in the case of proceedings on indictment with a jury, in the presence of the jury) that the accused is aware that the stage has been reached at which evidence can be given for the defence and that he can, if he wishes, give evidence and that, if he chooses not to give evidence, or having been sworn, without good cause refuses to answer any question, it will be permissible for the court or jury to draw such inferences as appear proper from his failure to give evidence or his refusal, without good cause, to answer any question.
(3) Where this subsection applies, the court or jury, in determining whether the accused is guilty of the offence charged, may draw such inferences as appear proper from the failure of the accused to give evidence or his refusal, without good cause, to answer any question.
(4) This section does not render the accused compellable to give evidence on his own behalf, and he shall accordingly not be guilty of contempt of court by reason of a failure to do so.
(5) For the purposes of this section a person who, having been sworn, refuses to answer any question shall be taken to do so without good cause unless—
   (a) he is entitled to refuse to answer the question by virtue of any enactment, whenever passed or made, or on the ground of privilege; or
   (b) the court in the exercise of its general discretion excuses him from answering it.
(6) [repealed]

In *R* v *Friend* [1997] 1 WLR 1433 (in considering s. 35(1)(b) of the Act), the accused was aged 15 with a mental age of nine and an IQ of 63. It was held that the accused's mental condition did not make it 'undesirable' for him to give evidence and it was right that inferences be drawn under s. 35(3).

As with s. 34, in relation to s. 35 the accused cannot be convicted solely on an inference drawn from a failure or refusal (s. 38(3)).

It must be made clear to the accused that when the prosecution case has finished he/she may give evidence if he/she so wishes. The court must inform the accused that if he/she fails to give evidence or, being sworn, refuses to answer any question without good cause, then the jury may infer such inferences that appear proper from such a failure to give evidence or a refusal to answer any question. In *R* v *Gough* [2001] EWCA Crim 2545, it was held that it is mandatory for the court to inform the accused of his/her right to give or not to give evidence even where the accused has absconded.

In *Murray* v *United Kingdom* (1996) 22 EHRR 29 it was held that it would be incompatible with the rights of an accused to base a conviction 'solely or mainly' on their silence, or on their refusal to answer questions or give evidence in person. The Court of Appeal also held that in cases involving directions under s. 34, the burden of proof remained on the Crown despite the fact that the accused chose to make no comment (*R v Gowland-Wynn* [2001] EWCA Crim 2715). In *Compton* [2002] EWCA Crim 2835, the court stated that the jury must be told that they can only hold against a defendant a failure to give an explanation if they are sure the defendant had no acceptable explanation to offer.

Code C—11 Interviews—General

(a) Action

11.1A An interview is the questioning of a person regarding their involvement or suspected involvement in a criminal offence or offences which, under paragraph 10.1, must be carried out under caution. Before a person is interviewed, they and, if they are represented, their solicitor must be given sufficient information to enable them to understand the nature of any such offence, and why they are suspected of committing it (see *paragraphs 3.4(a)* and *10.3*), in order to allow for the effective exercise of the rights of the defence. However, whilst the information must always be sufficient for the person to understand the nature of any offence, this does not require the disclosure of details at a time which might prejudice the criminal investigation. The decision about what needs to be disclosed for the purpose of this requirement therefore rests with the investigating officer who has sufficient knowledge of the case to make that decision. The officer who discloses the information shall make a record of the information disclosed and when it was disclosed. This record may be made in the interview record, in the officer's report book or other form provided for this purpose. Procedures under the Road Traffic Act 1988, section 7 or the Transport and Works Act 1992, section 31 do not constitute interviewing for the purpose of this Code.

11.1 Following a decision to arrest a suspect, they must not be interviewed about the relevant offence except at a police station or other authorised place of detention, unless the consequent delay would be likely to:

(a) lead to:

- interference with, or harm to, evidence connected with an offence;
- interference with, or physical harm to, other people; or
- serious loss of, or damage to, property;

(b) lead to alerting other people suspected of committing an offence but not yet arrested for it; or

(c) hinder the recovery of property obtained in consequence of the commission of an offence.

Interviewing in any of these circumstances shall cease once the relevant risk has been averted or the necessary questions have been put in order to attempt to avert that risk.

11.2 Immediately prior to the commencement or re-commencement of any interview at a police station or other authorised place of detention, the interviewer should remind the suspect of their entitlement to free legal advice and that the interview can be delayed for legal advice to be obtained, unless one of the exceptions in *paragraph 6.6* applies. It is the interviewer's responsibility to make sure all reminders are recorded in the interview record.

11.3 *Not used.*

11.4 At the beginning of an interview the interviewer, after cautioning the suspect, see *section 10*, shall put to them any significant statement or silence which occurred in the presence and hearing of a police officer or other police staff before the start of the interview and which have not been put to the suspect in the course of a previous interview. The interviewer shall ask the suspect whether they confirm or deny that earlier statement or silence and if they want to add anything.

11.4A A significant statement is one which appears capable of being used in evidence against the suspect, in particular a direct admission of guilt. A significant silence is a failure or refusal to answer a question or answer satisfactorily when under caution, which might, allowing for the restriction on drawing adverse inferences from silence, see *Annex C*, give rise to an inference under the Criminal Justice and Public Order Act 1994, Part III.

11.5 No interviewer may try to obtain answers or elicit a statement by the use of oppression. Except as in *paragraph 10.9*, no interviewer shall indicate, except to answer a direct question, what action will be taken by the police if the person being questioned answers questions, makes a statement or refuses to do either. If the person asks directly what action will be taken if they answer questions, make a statement or refuse to do either, the interviewer may inform them what action the police propose to take provided that action is itself proper and warranted.

11.6 The interview or further interview of a person about an offence with which that person has not been charged or for which they have not been informed they may be prosecuted, must cease when:

(a) the officer in charge of the investigation is satisfied all the questions they consider relevant to obtaining accurate and reliable information about the offence have been put to the suspect, this includes allowing the suspect an opportunity to give an innocent explanation and asking questions to test if the explanation is accurate and reliable, e.g. to clear up ambiguities or clarify what the suspect said;

(b) the officer in charge of the investigation has taken account of any other available evidence; and

(c) the officer in charge of the investigation, or in the case of a detained suspect, the custody officer, see *paragraph 16.1*, reasonably believes there is sufficient evidence to provide a realistic prospect of conviction for that offence.

This paragraph does not prevent officers in revenue cases or acting under the confiscation provisions of the Criminal Justice Act 1988 or the Drug Trafficking Act 1994 from inviting suspects to complete a formal question and answer record after the interview is concluded.

1.9.3.1

KEYNOTE

Code C, para. 11.1 deals with when an interview should be held. By itself this might suggest that an interview is not needed when there is other strong evidence. However, the Criminal Procedure and Investigations Act 1996 Code of Practice, para. 3.4 states: 'In conducting an investigation, the investigator should pursue all reasonable lines of enquiry, whether these point towards or away from the suspect. What is reasonable will depend on the particular circumstances.' Interviewers should keep this in mind when deciding what questions to ask in an interview. Although juveniles or vulnerable persons are often capable of providing reliable evidence, they may, without knowing or wishing to do so, be particularly prone in certain circumstances to providing information that may be unreliable, misleading or self incriminating. Special care should always be taken when questioning such a person, and the appropriate adult should be involved if there is any doubt about a person's age, mental state or capacity. Because of the risk of unreliable evidence it is also important to obtain corroboration of any facts admitted whenever possible. Because of the risks, which the presence of the appropriate adult is intended to minimise, officers of superintendent rank or above should exercise their discretion under para. 11.18(a) to authorise the commencement of an interview in the appropriate adult's absence only in exceptional cases, if it is necessary to avert one or more of the specified risks in para. 11.1.

Whether an interaction between a police officer and a member of the public is defined as an interview by the court can be crucial as to whether it will be admissible in evidence. It is therefore essential to understand the definition of an interview for the purposes of the Police and Criminal Evidence Act 1984 and when a caution must be given and which caution must be given.

If a person is asked questions for reasons *other than obtaining evidence about his/her involvement or suspected involvement in an offence,* this is not an interview (and a caution need not be given). This point is confirmed in the case of *R* v *McGuinness* [1999] Crim LR 318, where the court confirmed that it was only when a person was suspected of an offence that the caution must be administered before questioning. Consequently, in *R* v *Miller* [1998] Crim LR 209 the court held that asking a person the single question, 'Are these ecstasy tablets?' criminally implicated the person and therefore the conversation was an interview (i.e. it would not be necessary to ask such a question if there were no suspicion that the tablets were a controlled substance).

Guidance on when questions do not amount to an interview is given by Code C, para. 10.1. This is not an exhaustive list, and officers may have other valid reasons to speak to a person before it becomes an interview.

Before a person can be interviewed about his/her involvement in an offence, that person must be cautioned. So it might be said that an interview is any questioning of a person after such time as a caution has been or should have been administered. Where a person is arrested for an offence, he/she must also be cautioned, as any questioning will amount to an interview.

The requirement in para. 11.1A for a suspect to be given sufficient information about the offence applies prior to the interview and whether or not they are legally represented. What is sufficient will depend on the circumstances of the case, but it should normally include, as a minimum, a description of the facts relating to the suspected offence that are known to the officer, including the time and place in question. This aims to avoid suspects being confused or unclear about what they are supposed to have done and to help an innocent suspect to clear the matter up more quickly.

If a person has not been arrested then he/she can be interviewed almost anywhere (but an officer intending to interview a person on private property must consider whether he/she is trespassing). If the interview with a person not under arrest takes place in a police station, Code C, para. 3.21 must be followed. Juveniles should not be arrested at their place of education unless this is unavoidable. When a juvenile is arrested at his/her place of education, the principal or his/her nominee must be informed; this also applies to 17-year-olds.

Significant Statement/Silence

At the start of the interview the investigating officer should put to the suspect any significant statement or silence which occurred before his/her arrival at the police station.

Significant statements/silence described in paras 11.4 and 11.4A will always be relevant to the offence and must be recorded. When a suspect agrees to read records of interviews and other comments and sign them as correct, he/she should be asked to endorse the record with, for example, 'I agree that this is a correct record of what was said' and add his/her signature. If the suspect does not agree with the record, the interviewer should record the details of any disagreement and ask the suspect to read these details and sign them to the effect that they accurately reflect his/her disagreement. Any refusal to sign should be recorded. Even where, as required by para. 11.4, at the beginning of an interview the interviewer puts to the detainee any significant statement or silence which occurred in the presence and hearing of a police officer or other police staff, this does not prevent the interviewer from putting significant statements and silences to a suspect again at a later stage or a further interview as the interviewer may wish to go through any significant statement or silence again if during earlier interviews adverse inferences could not be drawn.

This aspect of the interview is very important in terms of establishing whether the facts are disputed. If they are not disputed at this stage, it is unlikely that they will be challenged at any later court hearing and, if challenged, the defence will have to explain why this was not done at the time of the interview.

The courts may view a failure to put the statement to the suspect in a sinister light. In R v Allen [2001] EWCA Crim 1607, the court was concerned that the police failed to put the admission to the suspect in interview, despite thorough questioning, which it felt clearly placed a question mark over the admission's reliability.

If the suspect remains silent in relation to a 'significant silence', that silence may give rise to an adverse inference being drawn under s. 34 of the Criminal Justice and Public Order Act 1994 if the person raises it in his/her defence at court (as this is a very important issue, it may be necessary to delay the interview until the arrest notes are completed or the officers witnessing the offence/arrest have been consulted to ensure that all matters are put to the suspect at this stage). Consideration should be given to putting questions to a suspect who makes no comment, or even where the legal representative has stated that the suspect will make no comment, as this may allow the court to draw inferences against a defence that the suspect raises at court (see para. 1.9.2.3).

Where live-link interpretation has been authorised Code C, para. 11.2 should be read with the following inserted at the start of the paragraph:

> Before the interview commences, the operation of live-link interpretation shall be explained and demonstrated to the suspect, their solicitor and appropriate adult, unless it has been previously explained and demonstrated (see Code C Annex N paragraph 4).

The Policing and Crime Act 2017 has amended s. 39 of the 1984 Act to allow interviews to be conducted by live link. 'Live link' is defined by the Act as an arrangement by which the officer who is not at the police station is able to see and hear, and to be seen and heard by, the person in police detention, any legal representative of that person and the officer who has custody of that person at the police station if the custody officer, in accordance with any code of practice issued under this Act, transfers or permits the transfer of a person in police detention to an officer for the purpose of an interview that is to be conducted to any extent by means of a live link by another police officer who is investigating the offence but is not at the police station where the person in police detention is held at the time of the interview, then the officer who is not at the police station has the same duty to ensure that the person is treated in accordance with the provisions of the 1984 Act and the Codes of Practice.

1.9.3.2

(b) Interview records

11.7

    (a) An accurate record must be made of each interview, whether or not the interview takes place at a police station.

    (b) The record must state the place of interview, the time it begins and ends, any interview breaks and, subject to *paragraph 2.6A*, the names of all those present; and must be made on the forms provided for this purpose or in the interviewer's report book or in accordance with Codes of Practice E or F.

    (c) Any written record must be made and completed during the interview, unless this would not be practicable or would interfere with the conduct of the interview, and must constitute either a verbatim record of what has been said or, failing this, an account of the interview which adequately and accurately summarises it.

11.8 If a written record is not made during the interview it must be made as soon as practicable after its completion.

11.9 Written interview records must be timed and signed by the maker.

11.10 If a written record is not completed during the interview the reason must be recorded in the interview record.

11.11 Unless it is impracticable, the person interviewed shall be given the opportunity to read the interview record and to sign it as correct or to indicate how they consider it inaccurate. If the person interviewed cannot read or refuses to read the record or sign it, the senior interviewer present shall read it to them and ask whether they would like to sign it as correct or make their mark or to indicate how they consider it inaccurate. The interviewer shall certify on the interview record itself what has occurred.

11.12 If the appropriate adult or the person's solicitor is present during the interview, they should also be given an opportunity to read and sign the interview record or any written statement taken down during the interview.

11.13 A record shall be made of any comments made by a suspect, including unsolicited comments, which are outside the context of an interview but which might be relevant to the offence. Any such record must be timed and signed by the maker. When practicable the suspect shall be given the opportunity to read that record and to sign it as correct or to indicate how they consider it inaccurate.

11.14 Any refusal by a person to sign an interview record when asked in accordance with this Code must itself be recorded.

(c) Juveniles and vulnerable persons

11.15 A juvenile or vulnerable person must not be interviewed regarding their involvement or suspected involvement in a criminal offence or offences, or asked to provide or sign a written statement under caution or record of interview, in the absence of the appropriate adult unless *paragraphs 11.1* or *11.18* to *11.20* apply.

11.16 Juveniles may only be interviewed at their place of education in exceptional circumstances and only when the principal or their nominee agrees. Every effort should be made to notify the parent(s) or other person responsible for the juvenile's welfare and the appropriate adult, if this is a different person, that the police want to interview the juvenile and reasonable time should be allowed to enable the appropriate adult to be present at the interview. If awaiting the appropriate adult would cause unreasonable delay, and unless the juvenile is suspected of an offence against the educational establishment, the principal or their nominee can act as the appropriate adult for the purposes of the interview.

11.17 If an appropriate adult is present at an interview, they shall be informed:
- that they are not expected to act simply as an observer; and
- that the purpose of their presence is to:
  ~ advise the person being interviewed;
  ~ observe whether the interview is being conducted properly and fairly; and
  ~ facilitate communication with the person being interviewed. See *paragraph 1.7A*.

11.17A The appropriate adult may be required to leave the interview if their conduct is such that the interviewer is unable properly to put questions to the suspect. This will include situations where the appropriate adult's approach or conduct prevents or unreasonably obstructs proper questions being put to the suspect or the suspect's responses being recorded. If the interviewer considers an appropriate adult is acting in such a way, they will stop the interview and consult an officer not below superintendent rank, if one is readily available, and otherwise an officer not below inspector rank not connected with the investigation. After speaking to the appropriate adult, the officer consulted must remind the adult that their role under *paragraph 11.17* does not allow them to obstruct proper questioning and give the adult an opportunity to respond. The officer consulted will then decide if the interview should continue without the attendance of that appropriate adult. If they decide it should, another appropriate adult must be obtained before the interview continues, unless the provisions of *paragraph 11.18* below apply.

(d) Vulnerable suspects—urgent interviews at police stations

11.18 The following interviews may take place only if an officer of superintendent rank or above considers delaying the interview will lead to the consequences in *paragraph 11.1(a)* to *(c)*, and is satisfied the interview would not significantly harm the person's physical or mental state (see *Annex G*):
(a) an interview of a detained juvenile or person who is vulnerable without the appropriate adult being present;
(b) an interview of anyone detained other than in (a) who appears unable to:
- appreciate the significance of questions and their answers; or
- understand what is happening because of the effects of drink, drugs or any illness, ailment or condition;
(c) an interview, without an interpreter having been arranged, of a detained person whom the custody officer has determined requires an interpreter (see *paragraphs 3.5(c)(ii)* and *3.12*) which is carried out by an interviewer speaking the suspect's own language or (as the case may be) otherwise establishing effective communication which is sufficient to enable the necessary questions to be asked and answered in order to avert the consequences. See *paragraphs 13.2* and *13.5*.

11.19 These interviews may not continue once sufficient information has been obtained to avert the consequences in *paragraph 11.1(a)* to *(c)*.

11.20 A record shall be made of the grounds for any decision to interview a person under *paragraph 11.18*.

(e) Conduct and recording of Interviews at police stations—use of live link

11.21 When a suspect in police detention is interviewed using a live link by a police officer who is not at the police station where the detainee is held, the provisions of this section that govern the conduct and making a written record of that interview, shall be subject to *paragraph 12.9B* of this Code.

(f) Witnesses

11.22 The provisions of this Code and Codes E and F which govern the conduct and recording of interviews do not apply to interviews with, or taking statements from, witnesses.

1.9.3.3

KEYNOTE

Paragraph 17A makes provision for requiring the appropriate adult to leave the interview if their conduct is such that the interviewer is unable properly to put questions to the suspect. It must be noted that the appropriate adult may intervene if they consider it is necessary to help the suspect understand any question asked and to help the suspect to answer any question. Paragraph 11.17A only applies if the appropriate adult's approach or conduct prevents or unreasonably obstructs proper questions being put to the suspect or the suspect's response being recorded. Examples of unacceptable conduct include answering questions on a suspect's behalf or providing written replies for the suspect to quote. An officer who takes the decision to exclude an appropriate adult must be in a position to satisfy the court the decision was properly made. In order to do this, they may need to witness what is happening and give the suspect's solicitor (if they have one) who witnessed what happened, an opportunity to comment.

Paragraph 11.18(c) is worthy of note; this requires urgent interviews authorised by a superintendent under para. 11.18 which would have had an interpreter to be carried out by an interviewer who can speak the suspect's own language or in some other way establish effective communication to allow the questions to be asked and answered.

1.9.3.4

KEYNOTE

Statements from Suspects

Statements made by an accused under caution to the police, whether in writing or verbally are confidential in the sense that they may be used against the suspect in proceedings, not that they could be used for any purpose of the police. It is clearly implicit in the relationship between the police and the accused that the information, before being used in open court, is used only for the purposes for which it is provided and not for extraneous purposes, such as the media. However, the obligation of confidentiality (which is now included in the Police Standards of Professional Behaviour) in respect of such a statement will be brought to an end where the contents of the statement are already in the public domain (*Bunn* v *British Broadcasting Corporation* [1998] 3 All ER 552).

1.9.4

Code C—12 Interviews in Police Stations

(a) Action

When the interviewer and suspect are present in the same police station

12.1 If a police officer wants to interview or conduct enquiries which require the presence of a detainee, the custody officer is responsible for deciding whether to deliver the detainee into the officer's custody. An investigating officer who is given custody of a detainee takes over responsibility for the detainee's care and safe custody for the purposes of this Code until they return the detainee to the custody officer when they must report the manner in which they complied with the Code whilst having custody of the detainee.

12.2 Except as below, in any period of 24 hours a detainee must be allowed a continuous period of at least 8 hours for rest, free from questioning, travel or any interruption in connection with the investigation concerned. This period should normally be at night or other appropriate time which takes account of when the detainee last slept or rested. If a detainee is arrested at a police station after going there voluntarily, the period of 24 hours runs from the time of their arrest and not the time of arrival at the police station. The period may not be interrupted or delayed, except:

   (a) when there are reasonable grounds for believing not delaying or interrupting the period would:

   (i) involve a risk of harm to people or serious loss of, or damage to, property;

   (ii) delay unnecessarily the person's release from custody; or

   (iii) otherwise prejudice the outcome of the investigation;

   (b) at the request of the detainee, their appropriate adult or legal representative;

   (c) when a delay or interruption is necessary in order to:

   (i) comply with the legal obligations and duties arising under section 15; or

   (ii) to take action required under *section 9* or in accordance with medical advice.

   If the period is interrupted in accordance with *(a)*, a fresh period must be allowed. Interruptions under *(b)* and *(c)* do not require a fresh period to be allowed.

12.3 Before a detainee is interviewed, the custody officer, in consultation with the officer in charge of the investigation and appropriate healthcare professionals as necessary, shall assess whether the detainee is fit enough to be interviewed. This means determining and considering the risks to the detainee's physical and mental state if the interview took place and determining what safeguards are needed to allow the interview to take place. See *Annex G*. The custody officer shall not allow a detainee to be interviewed if the custody officer considers it would cause significant harm to the detainee's physical or mental state. Vulnerable suspects listed at *paragraph 11.18* shall be treated as always being at some risk during an interview and these persons may not be interviewed except in accordance with *paragraphs 11.18* to *11.20*.

12.4 As far as practicable interviews shall take place in interview rooms which are adequately heated, lit and ventilated.

12.5 A suspect whose detention without charge has been authorised under PACE because the detention is necessary for an interview to obtain evidence of the offence for which they have been arrested may choose not to answer questions but police do not require the suspect's consent or agreement to interview them for this purpose. If a suspect takes steps to prevent themselves being questioned or further questioned, e.g. by refusing to leave their cell to go to a suitable interview room or by trying to leave the interview room, they shall be advised their consent or agreement to interview is not required. The suspect shall be cautioned as in *section 10*, and informed if they fail or refuse to co-operate, the interview may take place in the cell and that their failure or refusal to co-operate may be given in evidence. The suspect shall then be invited to co-operate and go into the interview room. If they refuse and the custody officer considers, on reasonable grounds, that the interview should not be delayed, the custody officer has discretion to direct that the interview be conducted in a cell.

12.6 People being questioned or making statements shall not be required to stand.

12.7 Before the interview commences each interviewer shall, subject to *paragraph 2.6A*, identify themselves and any other persons present to the interviewee.

12.8 Breaks from interviewing should be made at recognised meal times or at other times that take account of when an interviewee last had a meal. Short refreshment breaks shall be provided at approximately two hour intervals, subject to the interviewer's discretion to delay a break if there are reasonable grounds for believing it would:

  (i) involve a:

    • risk of harm to people;

    • serious loss of, or damage to, property;

  (ii) unnecessarily delay the detainee's release; or

  (iii) otherwise prejudice the outcome of the investigation.

12.9   If during the interview a complaint is made by or on behalf of the interviewee concerning the provisions of any of the Codes, or it comes to the interviewer's notice that the interviewee may have been treated improperly, the interviewer should:

  (i) record the matter in the interview record; and

  (ii) inform the custody officer, who is then responsible for dealing with it as in *section 9*.

Interviewer not present at the same station as the detainee—use of live link

12.9A Amendments to PACE, section 39, allow a person in police detention to be interviewed using a live link (see *paragraph 1.13(e)(i)*) by a police officer who is not at the police station where the detainee is held. Subject to *sub-paragraphs (a)* to *(f)* below, the custody officer is responsible for deciding on a case by case basis whether a detainee is fit to be interviewed (see *paragraph 12.3*) and should be delivered into the physical custody of an officer who is not involved in the investigation, for the purpose of enabling another officer who is investigating the offence for which the person is detained and who is not at the police station where the person is detained, to interview the detainee by means of a live link.

(a) The custody officer must be satisfied that the live link to be used provides for accurate and secure communication with the suspect. The provisions of *paragraph 13.13* shall apply to communications between the interviewing officer, the suspect and anyone else whose presence at the interview or, (as the case may be) whose access to any communications between the suspect and the interviewer, has been authorised by the custody officer or the interviewing officer.

(b) Each decision must take account of the age, gender and vulnerability of the suspect, the nature and circumstances of the offence and the investigation and the impact on the suspect of carrying out the interview by means of a live link. For this reason, the custody officer must consider whether the ability of the particular suspect, to communicate confidently and effectively for the purpose of the interview is likely to be adversely affected or otherwise undermined or limited if the interviewing officer is not physically present and a live-link is used. Although a suspect for whom an appropriate adult is required may be more likely to be adversely affected as described, it is important to note that a person who does not require an appropriate adult may also be adversely impacted if interviewed by means of a live link.

(c) If the custody officer is satisfied that interviewing the detainee by means of a live link *would not* adversely affect or otherwise undermine or limit the suspect's ability to communicate confidently and effectively for the purpose of the *interview*, the officer must so inform the suspect, their solicitor and (if applicable) the appropriate adult. At the same time, the operation of the live-link must be explained and demonstrated to them, they must be advised of the chief officer's obligations concerning the security of live-link communications under *paragraph 13.13* and they must be asked if they wish to make representations that the live-link should not be used or if they require more information about the operation of the arrangements. They must also be told that at any time live-link is in use, they may make representations to the custody officer or the interviewer that its operation should cease and that the physical presence of the interviewer should be arranged.

When the authority of an inspector is required

(d) If:

   (i) representations are made that a live-link should not be used to carry out the interview, or that at any time it is in use, its operation should cease and the physical presence of the interviewer arranged; and

   (ii) the custody officer in consultation with the interviewer is unable to allay the concerns raised;

   then live-link may not be used, or (as the case may be) continue to be used, unless authorised in writing by an officer of the rank of inspector or above in accordance with *sub-paragraph (e)*.

(e) Authority may be given if the officer is satisfied that interviewing the detainee by means of a live link is necessary and justified. In making this decision, the officer must have regard to:

   (i) the circumstances of the suspect;

   (ii) the nature and seriousness of the offence;

   (iii) the requirements of the investigation, including its likely impact on both the suspect and any victim(s);

   (iv) the representations made by the suspect, their solicitor and (if applicable) the appropriate adult that a live-link should not be used (see *sub-paragraph (b)*;

   (v) the impact on the investigation of making arrangements for the physical presence of the interviewer; and

   (vi) the risk if the interpreter is not *physically* present, evidence obtained using link interpretation might be excluded in subsequent criminal proceedings; and

   (vii) the likely impact on the suspect and the investigation of any consequential delay to arrange for the interpreter to be *physically* present with the suspect.

(f) The officer given custody of the detainee *and* the interviewer take over responsibility for the detainee's care, treatment and safe custody for the purposes of this Code until the detainee is returned to the custody officer. On that return, both must report the manner in which they complied with the Code during period in question.

12.9B When a suspect detained at a police station is interviewed using a live link in accordance with *paragraph 12.9A*, the officer given custody of the detainee at the police station *and* the interviewer who is not present at the police station, take over responsibility for ensuring compliance with the provisions of *sections 11* and *12* of this Code, or *Code E* (Audio recording) or *Code F* (Audio visual recording) that govern the conduct and recording of that interview. In these circumstances:

(a) *the interviewer who is not at the police station where the detainee is held* must direct the officer having physical custody of the suspect at the police station, to take the action required by those provisions and which the interviewer would be required to take if they were present at the police station.

(b) *the officer having physical custody of the suspect at the police station* must take the action required by those provisions and which would otherwise be required to be taken by the interviewer if they were present at the police station. This applies whether or not the officer has been so directed by the interviewer but in such a case, the officer must inform the interviewer of the action taken.

(c) *during the course of the interview*, the officers in (a) and (b) may consult each other as necessary to clarify any action to be taken and to avoid any misunderstanding. Such consultations must, if in the hearing of the suspect and any other person present with the suspect (for example, a solicitor, appropriate adult or interpreter) be recorded in the interview record.

(b) Documentation

12.10 A record must be made of the:
- time a detainee is not in the custody of the custody officer, and why reason
- for any refusal to deliver the detainee out of that custody.

12.11 A record shall be made of the following:
  (a) the reasons it was not practicable to use an interview room;
  (b) any action taken as in *paragraph 12.5*; and
  (c) the actions, decisions, authorisations, representations and outcomes arising from the requirements of *paragraphs 12.9A* and *12.9B*.

The record shall be made on the custody record or in the interview record for action taken whilst an interview record is being kept, with a brief reference to this effect in the custody record.

12.12 Any decision to delay a break in an interview must be recorded, with reasons, in the interview record.

12.13 All written statements made at police stations under caution shall be written on forms provided for the purpose.

12.14 All written statements made under caution shall be taken in accordance with *Annex D*. Before a person makes a written statement under caution at a police station, they shall be reminded about the right to legal advice.

1.9.4.1

KEYNOTE

Meal breaks should normally last at least 45 minutes and shorter breaks after two hours should last at least 15 minutes. If the interviewer prolongs the interview to avoid the risk of harm to people, serious loss of, or damage to, property, to delay the detainee's release or otherwise prejudice the outcome of the investigation, a longer break should be provided. If there is a short interview, and another short interview is contemplated, the length of the break may be reduced if there are reasonable grounds to believe that this is necessary to avoid any of the consequences in para. 12.8(i)–(iii).

When deciding whether to hand over a detained person to the interviewing officer under para. 12.1 the custody officer should be mindful of whether there is sufficient relevant time remaining for the detained person to be interviewed (see Code C, para. 15).

Statements under caution, particularly of a detained person, are less common than interviews. If a person has been interviewed and it has been audio or visually recorded or an interview has been recorded contemporaneously in writing, statements under caution should normally be taken in these circumstances only at the person's express wish. See Code C, Annex C for restrictions on drawing inferences and Annex D for the variable declarations the person must include in his/her statements. A person may however be asked if they want to make such a statement.

1.9.4.2

KEYNOTE

Solicitors and Legal Advice

Code C, s. 6 provides guidance with regard to legal advice and access to solicitors during interview. Where a solicitor is available at the time the interview begins or while it is in progress, the solicitor must be allowed to be present while the person is interviewed (Code C, para. 6.8).

If the investigating officer considers that a solicitor is acting in such a way that he/she is unable properly to put questions to the suspect, he/she will stop the interview and consult an officer not below the rank of superintendent, if one is readily available, otherwise an officer not below the rank of inspector who is not connected with the investigation, to decide whether that solicitor should be excluded from the interview. The interview may also have to be stopped in order to allow another solicitor to be instructed (Code C, para. 6.10).

If a request for legal advice is made during an interview, the interviewing officer must stop the interview immediately and arrange for legal advice to be provided. If the suspect changes his/her mind again, the interview can continue provided Code C, para. 6.6 is complied with.

KEYNOTE

What Should Be Disclosed to the Solicitor Before Interview?

It is important not to confuse the duty of disclosure to a person once charged with the need to disclose evidence to suspects before interviewing them. After a person has been charged, and before trial, the rules of disclosure are clear (**see chapter 1.11**) and almost all material must be disclosed to the defence.

Prior to charge, Code C, para. 11.1A provides that some disclosure must be given before a person is interviewed in order to allow for the effective exercise of the rights of the defence. What is sufficient will depend on the circumstances of the case, but it should normally include, as a minimum, a description of the facts relating to the suspected offence that are known to the officer, including the time and place in question; additionally, the custody record must be provided. In respect of the provision of a copy of the 'first description' of a suspect, it should be noted that Code D (para. 3.1) states that a copy of the 'first description' shall, where practicable, be given to the suspect or his/her solicitor before any procedures under paras 3.5 to 3.10, 3.21 or 3.23 are carried out. In other words, the disclosure requirement is that a copy of the 'first description' shall, where practicable, be given to the suspect or his/her solicitor before a video identification, an identification parade, a group identification or confrontation takes place. Therefore, an officer disclosing information to a solicitor at the interview stage (which is taking place in advance of any identification procedures) need not provide the 'first description' of a suspect at that time.

Further, there is nothing within the Criminal Justice and Public Order Act 1994 that states that information must be disclosed before an inference from silence can be made. Indeed, in *R v Imran* [1997] Crim LR 754, the court held that it is totally wrong to submit that a defendant should be prevented from lying by being presented with the whole of the evidence against him/her prior to the interview.

In *R v Argent* [1997] Crim LR 346, the court dismissed the argument that an inference could not be drawn under s. 34 of the Criminal Justice and Public Order Act 1994 because there had not been full disclosure at the interview. However, the court did recognise that it may be a factor to take into account for the jury to decide whether the failure to answer questions was reasonable (**see para. 1.9.2.3** regarding s. 34 of the Criminal Justice and Public Order Act 1994).

In *Black v R* [2020] EWCA Crim 915, the court confirmed 'that an inference should only be drawn under section 34 of the CJPOA 1994 if the prosecution case at the time of the interview is so strong as to justify an answer. ... [I]f nothing has been said or shown to the defendant at the police interview to call for an answer from the defendant, it would be wrong to draw an inference against the defendant for a failure to provide such an answer. It is also established that the strength or weakness of the prosecution case at interview may be a relevant circumstance for the jury to consider under section 34 of the CJPOA 1994.'

In *R v Roble* [1997] Crim LR 449, the court suggested that an inference would not be drawn where a solicitor gave advice to remain silent where, for example, the interviewing officer had disclosed too little of the case for the solicitor usefully to advise his/her client, or where the nature of the offence, or the material in the hands of the police, was so complex or related to matters so long ago that no sensible immediate response was feasible.

It was not uncommon in the past for solicitors to advise on no comment interviews and this has been relied on by defendants to avoid adverse inferences being drawn from their silence. In *R v Morgan* [2001] EWCA Crim 445, the Court of Appeal stated that a court was entitled to assume that a solicitor would advise his/her client about the adverse inferences rule. In *R v Ali* [2001] EWCA Crim 683, the court stated that the question was not whether the advice to remain silent was good advice but whether it provided an adequate reason for failing to answer questions.

In *R v Hoare* [2004] EWCA Crim 784, the Court of Appeal held that the purpose of s. 34 was to qualify a defendant's right to silence, rather than to exclude a jury from drawing an adverse inference against a defendant merely because he/she had been advised by his/her solicitor to remain silent, whether or not he/she genuinely or reasonably relied on that advice. Where a defendant had an explanation to give that was consistent with his/her innocence it was not 'reasonable', within the meaning of s. 34(1), for him/her to fail to give that explanation in interview even where he/she had been advised by his/her solicitor to remain silent. Legal advice by itself could not preclude the drawing of an adverse inference.

There is a balance to be struck between providing the solicitor with enough information to understand the nature of the case against his/her client and keeping back material which, if disclosed, may allow the suspect the opportunity to avoid implicating him/herself. For instance in *R v Thirlwell* [2002] EWCA Crim 286, the Court of Appeal agreed that the solicitor had not been entitled to provisional medical evidence as to possible causes of death in a murder case.

Useful guidance is provided in the College of Policing Investigative Interviewing APP; this can be found at <https://www.app.college.police.uk/app-content/investigations/investigative-interviewing/#pre-interview- briefings>.

1.9.4.4   **KEYNOTE**

'Live link' means an arrangement by means of which the interviewing officer who is not at the police station is able to see and hear, and to be seen and heard by, the detainee concerned, the detainee's so-licitor, any appropriate adult present and the officer who has custody of that detainee. See paras 13.12 to 13.14 and Annex N for application to live-link interpretation. In considering whether the use of the live link is appropriate in a particular case, the custody officer, in consultation with the interviewer, should make an assessment of the detainee's ability to understand and take part in the interviewing process and make a record of the outcome. If the suspect has asked for legal advice, their solicitor should be involved in the assessment and in the case of a juvenile or vulnerable person, the appropriate adult should be involved.

The explanation and demonstration of live-link interpretation is intended to help the suspect, solicitor and appropriate adult make an informed decision and to allay any concerns they may have. Factors affecting the arrangements for the interviewer to be physically present will include the location of the police station where the interview would take place and the availability of an interviewer with sufficient knowledge of the investigation who can attend that station and carry out the interview.

1.9.5   **Code C—Annex C: Restriction on Drawing Adverse Inferences from Silence and Terms of the Caution when the Restriction Applies**

(a) The restriction on drawing adverse inferences from silence

1. The Criminal Justice and Public Order Act 1994, sections 34, 36 and 37 as amended by the Youth Justice and Criminal Evidence Act 1999, section 58 describe the conditions under which adverse inferences may be drawn from a person's failure or refusal to say anything about their involvement in the offence when interviewed, after being charged or informed they may be prosecuted. These provisions are subject to an overriding restriction on the ability of a court or jury to draw adverse inferences from a person's silence. This restriction applies:

    (a) to any detainee at a police station, who, before being interviewed, see *section 11* or being charged or informed they may be prosecuted, see *section 16*, has:

      (i) asked for legal advice, see *section 6, paragraph 6.1*;

      (ii) not been allowed an opportunity to consult a solicitor, including the duty solicitor, as in this Code; and

      (iii) not changed their mind about wanting legal advice, see *section 6, paragraph 6.6(d)*.
      Note the condition in (ii) will:

        ~ apply when a detainee who has asked for legal advice is interviewed before speaking to a solicitor as in *section 6, paragraph 6.6(a)* or *(b)*;

        ~ not apply if the detained person declines to ask for the duty solicitor, see *section 6, paragraphs 6.6(c)* and *(d)*.

(b) to any person charged with, or informed they may be prosecuted for, an offence who:

    (i) has had brought to their notice a written statement made by another person or the content of an interview with another person which relates to that offence, see *section 15, paragraph 16.4*;

    (ii) is interviewed about that offence, see *section 16, paragraph 16.5*; or

    (iii) makes a written statement about that offence, see *Annex D, paragraphs 4 and 9*.

(b) Terms of the caution when the restriction applies

2. When a requirement to caution arises at a time when the restriction on drawing adverse inferences from silence applies, the caution shall be:

'You do not have to say anything, but anything you do say may be given in evidence.'

Where the use of the Welsh Language is appropriate, the caution may be used directly in Welsh in the following terms:

'Does dim rhaid i chi ddweud dim byd, ond gall unrhyw beth yr ydych chi'n ei ddweud gael ei roi fel tystiolaeth.'

3. Whenever the restriction either begins to apply or ceases to apply after a caution has already been given, the person shall be re-cautioned in the appropriate terms. The changed position on drawing inferences and that the previous caution no longer applies shall also be explained to the detainee in ordinary language.

1.9.5.1

KEYNOTE

The restriction on drawing inferences from silence does not apply to a person who has not been detained and who therefore cannot be prevented from seeking legal advice if he/she wants to (see Code C, paras 10.2 and 3.15).

The following is suggested as a framework to help explain changes in the position on drawing adverse inferences if the restriction on drawing adverse inferences from silence applies. Annex C, para. 2 sets out the alternative terms of the caution to be used when the restriction on drawing adverse inferences from silence applies. The situation is likely to occur during a detainee's detention where it will be necessary to administer both of these cautions at various times during his/her detention. As there is a significant difference between them in relation to the right to silence, it will be important to make it clear which caution applies to the detainee during any interview or charge procedure. Guidance as to what the detainee should be told is provided by Code C, Annex C, Note C2; this paragraph gives sample explanations that need to be explained to the detainee before the change in caution is given.

Full caution already given (in most cases given when arrested)	→ Detainee's access to legal advice restricted as per Code C, Annex C, para. 1. Need to give alternative caution.	→ Explain change in caution as set out at Code C, Annex C, Note C2(a)(i).	→ Give caution as set out at Annex C, para. 2.
Full caution already given	→ Detainee has been charged but is further interviewed (Code C, Annex C, para. 1). Need to give alternative caution.	→ Explain change in caution as set out at Code C, Annex C, Note C2(a)(ii).	→ Give caution as set out at Annex C, para. 2.
Caution as set out at Annex C, para. 2, given	→ Detainee has now had access to a solicitor or changed his/her mind. Need to give alternative caution.	→ Explain change in caution as set out at Code C, Annex C, Note C2(b).	→ Give caution as set out at Code C, para. 10.5.

Where Code C, Annex C, para. 1 applies (i.e. the detainee has not been given access to a solicitor) and the detainee is charged with an offence or informed that he/she may be prosecuted, the caution at Annex C, para. 2 should be used; on all other occasions the caution at Code C, para. 16.2 should be used.

When the circumstances of the detained person change and restrictions on drawing adverse inferences now apply, the following form of words, where applicable, can be used:

The caution you were previously given no longer applies. This is because after that caution:

(i) you asked to speak to a solicitor but have not yet been allowed an opportunity to speak to a solicitor; or

(ii) you have been charged with/informed you may be prosecuted.

See para. 1(b).

Followed by:

This means that from now on, adverse inferences cannot be drawn at court and your defence will not be harmed just because you choose to say nothing. Please listen carefully to the caution I am about to give you because it will apply from now on. You will see that it does not say anything about your defence being harmed.

The following form of words should be used where the circumstances set out in Annex C, para. 1(a) that a restriction on drawing adverse inferences ceases to apply before or at the time the person is charged or informed that he/she may be prosecuted apply:

The caution you were previously given no longer applies. This is because after that caution you have been allowed an opportunity to speak to a solicitor. Please listen carefully to the caution I am about to give you because it will apply from now on. It explains how your defence at court may be affected if you choose to say nothing.

1.9.6   Code C—Annex D: Written Statements under Caution

(a) Written by a person under caution

1. A person shall always be invited to write down what they want to say.

2. A person who has not been charged with, or informed they may be prosecuted for, any offence to which the statement they want to write relates, shall:

   (a) unless the statement is made at a time when the restriction on drawing adverse inferences from silence applies, see *Annex C*, be asked to write out and sign the following before writing what they want to say:

   'I make this statement of my own free will. I understand that I do not have to say anything but that it may harm my defence if I do not mention when questioned something which I later rely on in court. This statement may be given in evidence.';

   (b) if the statement is made at a time when the restriction on drawing adverse inferences from silence applies, be asked to write out and sign the following before writing what they want to say;

   'I make this statement of my own free will. I understand that I do not have to say anything. This statement may be given in evidence.'

3. When a person, on the occasion of being charged with or informed they may be prosecuted for any offence, asks to make a statement which relates to any such offence and wants to write it they shall:

   (a) unless the restriction on drawing adverse inferences from silence, see *Annex C*, applied when they were so charged or informed they may be prosecuted, be asked to write out and sign the following before writing what they want to say:

   'I make this statement of my own free will. I understand that I do not have to say anything but that it may harm my defence if I do not mention when questioned something which I later rely on in court. This statement may be given in evidence.';

(b) if the restriction on drawing adverse inferences from silence applied when they were so charged or informed they may be prosecuted, be asked to write out and sign the following before writing what they want to say:

'I make this statement of my own free will. I understand that I do not have to say anything. This statement may be given in evidence.'

4. When a person who has already been charged with or informed they may be prosecuted for any offence asks to make a statement which relates to any such offence and wants to write it, they shall be asked to write out and sign the following before writing what they want to say:

'I make this statement of my own free will. I understand that I do not have to say anything. This statement may be given in evidence.';

5. Any person writing their own statement shall be allowed to do so without any prompting except a police officer or other police staff may indicate to them which matters are material or question any ambiguity in the statement.

(b) Written by a police officer or other police staff

6. If a person says they would like someone to write the statement for them, a police officer, or other police staff shall write the statement.

7. If the person has not been charged with, or informed they may be prosecuted for, any offence to which the statement they want to make relates they shall, before starting, be asked to sign, or make their mark, to the following:

(a) unless the statement is made at a time when the restriction on drawing adverse inferences from silence applies, see *Annex C*:

'I, ..., wish to make a statement. I want someone to write down what I say. I understand that I do not have to say anything but that it may harm my defence if I do not mention when questioned something which I later rely on in court. This statement may be given in evidence.';

(b) if the statement is made at a time when the restriction on drawing adverse inferences from silence applies:

'I, ..., wish to make a statement. I want someone to write down what I say. I understand that I do not have to say anything. This statement may be given in evidence.'

8. If, on the occasion of being charged with or informed they may be prosecuted for any offence, the person asks to make a statement which relates to any such offence they shall before starting be asked to sign, or make their mark to, the following:

(a) unless the restriction on drawing adverse inferences from silence applied, see *Annex C*, when they were so charged or informed they may be prosecuted:

'I, ..., wish to make a statement. I want someone to write down what I say. I understand that I do not have to say anything but that it may harm my defence if I do not mention when questioned something which I later rely on in court. This statement may be given in evidence.';

(b) if the restriction on drawing adverse inferences from silence applied when they were so charged or informed they may be prosecuted:

'I, ..., wish to make a statement. I want someone to write down what I say. I understand that I do not have to say anything. This statement may be given in evidence.'

9. If, having already been charged with or informed they may be prosecuted for any offence, a person asks to make a statement which relates to any such offence they shall before starting, be asked to sign, or make their mark to:

'I, ..., wish to make a statement. I want someone to write down what I say. I understand that I do not have to say anything. This statement may be given in evidence.'

10. The person writing the statement must take down the exact words spoken by the person making it and must not edit or paraphrase it. Any questions that are necessary, e.g. to make it more intelligible, and the answers given must be recorded at the same time on the statement form.

11. When the writing of a statement is finished the person making it shall be asked to read it and to make any corrections, alterations or additions they want. When they have finished reading they shall be asked to write and sign or make their mark on the following certificate at the end of the statement:

'I have read the above statement, and I have been able to correct, alter or add anything I wish. This statement is true. I have made it of my own free will.'

12. If the person making the statement cannot read, or refuses to read it, or to write the above mentioned certificate at the end of it or to sign it, the person taking the statement shall read it to them and ask them if they would like to correct, alter or add anything and to put their signature or make their mark at the end. The person taking the statement shall certify on the statement itself what has occurred.

1.9.6.1   **KEYNOTE**

The sections of Code C above need to be read in conjunction with Code E where the interview of a suspect is to be audio recorded.

1.9.7   **PACE Code of Practice on Audio Recording Interviews with Suspects (Code E)**

This Code applies to interviews carried out after 00.00 on 31st July 2018, notwithstanding that the interview may have commenced before that time.

1 General

1.0 The procedures in this Code must be used fairly, responsibly, with respect for the people to whom they apply and without unlawful discrimination. Under the Equality Act 2010, section 149 (Public Sector Equality Duty), police forces must, in carrying out their functions, have due regard to the need to eliminate unlawful discrimination, harassment, victimisation and any other conduct which is prohibited by that Act, to advance equality of opportunity between people who share a relevant protected characteristic and people who do not share it, and to foster good relations between those persons. The Equality Act *also* makes it unlawful for police officers to discriminate against, harass or victimise any person on the grounds of the `protected characteristics' of age, disability, gender reassignment, race, religion or belief, sex and sexual orientation, marriage and civil partnership, pregnancy and maternity, when using their powers.

1.1 This Code of Practice must be readily available for consultation by:

- police officers
- police staff
- detained persons
- members of the public.

1.2 The *Notes for Guidance* included are not provisions of this Code. They form guidance to police officers and others about its application and interpretation.

1.3 Nothing in this Code shall detract from the requirements of Code C, the Code of Practice for the detention, treatment and questioning of persons by police officers.

1.4 The interviews and other matters to which this Code applies are described in section 2. This Code does not apply to the conduct and recording in England and Wales, of:

- interviews of persons detained under section 41 of, or Schedule 7 to, the Terrorism Act 2000, and
- post-charge questioning of persons authorised under section 22 of the Counter Terrorism Act 2008.

These must be video recorded with sound in accordance with the provisions of the separate Code of Practice issued under *paragraph 3 of Schedule 8 to the Terrorism Act 2000* and under *section 25 of the Counter-Terrorism Act 2008*. If, during the course of an interview or questioning under this Code, it becomes apparent that the interview or questioning should be conducted under that separate Code, the interview should only continue in accordance with that Code.

Note: The provisions of this Code and Code F which govern the conduct and recording of interviews *do not apply* to interviews with, or taking statements from, witnesses.

1.5 In this Code:

- 'appropriate adult' has the same meaning as in Code C, *paragraph 1.7*.
- 'vulnerable person' has the same meaning as described in Code C *paragraph 1.13(d)*.
- 'solicitor' has the same meaning as in Code C, *paragraph 6.12*.
- 'interview' has the same meaning as in *Code C, paragraph 11.1A*.

1.5A The provisions of this Code which require interviews with suspects to be audio recorded and the provisions of Code F which permit simultaneous visual recording provide safeguards:

- for suspects against inaccurate recording of the words used in questioning them and of their demeanour during the interview; and;
- for police interviewers against unfounded allegations made by, or on behalf of, suspects about the conduct of the interview and what took place during the interview which might otherwise appear credible.

Recording of interviews must therefore be carried out openly to instil confidence in its reliability as an impartial and accurate record of the interview.

1.5B The provisions of Code C:

- *sections 10 and 11*, and the applicable *Notes for Guidance* apply to the conduct of interviews to which this Code applies.
- *paragraphs 11.7 to 11.14* apply only when a written record is needed.

1.5C Code C, *paragraphs 10.10, 10.11* and *Annex C* describe the restriction on drawing adverse inferences from an arrested suspect's failure or refusal to say anything about their involvement in the offence when interviewed or after being charged or informed they may be prosecuted, and how it affects the terms of the caution and determines if and by whom a special warning under sections 36 and 37 of the Criminal Justice and Public Order Act 1994 can be given.

1.6 In this Code:

(a) in relation to the place where an interview of a suspect to which this Code or (as the case may be) Code F, applies, is conducted and recorded:

(i) '*authorised*' in relation to the recording devices described in (ii) and (iii), means any such device that the chief officer has authorised interviewers under their direction and control to use to record the interview in question at the place in question, provided that the interviewer in question has been trained to set up and operate the device, in compliance with the manufacturer's instructions and subject to the operating procedures required by the chief officer;

(ii) '*removable recording media device*' means a recording device which, when set up and operated in accordance with the manufacturer's instructions and the operating procedures required by the chief officers, uses removable, physical recording media (such as magnetic tape, optical disc or solid state memory card) for the purpose of making a clear and accurate, audio recording or (as the case may be) audio-visual recording, of the interview in question which can then be played back and copied using that device or any other device. A sign or indicator on the device which is visible to the suspect must show when the device is recording;

(iii) '*secure digital recording network device*' means a recording device which, when set up and operated in accordance with the manufacturer's instructions and the operating procedures required by the chief officers, enables a clear and accurate original audio recording or (as the case may be) audio-visual recording, of the interview in question, to be made and stored using non-removable storage, as a digital file or a series of such files that can be securely transferred by a wired or wireless connection to a remote secure network file server system (which may have cloud based storage) which ensures that access to interview recordings for all purposes is strictly controlled and is restricted to those whose access, either generally or in specific cases, is necessary. Examples of access include playing back the whole or part of any original recording and making one or more copies of, the whole or part of that original recording. A sign or indicator on the device which is visible to the suspect must show when the device is recording.

(b) 'designated person' means a person other than a police officer, who has specified powers and duties conferred or imposed on them by designation under section 38 or 39 of the Police Reform Act 2002.

(c) any reference to a police officer includes a designated person acting in the exercise or performance of the powers and duties conferred or imposed on them by their designation.

1.7 Section 2 of this Code sets out the requirement that an authorised recording device, if available, must be used to record a suspect interview and when such a device cannot be used, it allows a 'relevant officer' (see *paragraph 2.3(c)*) to decide that the interview is to be recorded in writing in accordance with Code C. For detained suspects, the 'relevant officer' is the custody officer and for voluntary interviews, the officer is determined according to the type of offence (indictable or summary only) and where the interview takes place (police station or elsewhere). Provisions in sections 3 and 4 deal with the conduct and recording of interviews according to the type of authorised recording device used. Section 3 applies to *removable recording media devices* (see *paragraph 1.6(a)(i)*) and section 4 applies to *secure digital recording network devices* (see *paragraph 1.6(a)(ii)*). The Annex applies when a voluntary interview is conducted elsewhere than at a police station about one of the four offence types specified in the Annex. For such interviews, the relevant officer is the interviewer.

1.8 Nothing in this Code prevents the custody officer, or other officer given custody of the detainee, from allowing police staff who are not designated persons to carry out individual procedures or tasks at the police station if the law allows. However, the officer remains responsible for making sure the procedures and tasks are carried out correctly in accordance with this Code. Any such police staff must be:

(a) a person employed by a police force and under the control and direction of the chief officer of that force; or

(b) employed by a person with whom a police force has a contract for the provision of services relating to persons arrested or otherwise in custody.

1.9 Designated persons and other police staff must have regard to any relevant provisions of the Codes of Practice.

1.10 References to pocket book shall include any official report book or electronic recording device issued to police officers or police staff that enables a record required to be made by any provision of this Code (but which is not an audio record to which *paragraph 2.1* applies) to be made and dealt with in accordance with that provision. References in this Code to written records, forms and signatures include electronic records and forms and electronic confirmation that identifies the person making the record or completing the form.

Chief officers must be satisfied as to the integrity and security of the devices, records and forms to which this paragraph applies and that use of those devices, records and forms satisfies relevant data protection legislation.

1.11 References to a custody officer include those performing the functions of a custody officer as in *paragraph 1.9* of Code C.

1.12 *Not used.*

1.13 Nothing in this Code requires the identity of officers or police staff conducting interviews to be recorded or disclosed if the interviewer reasonably believes recording or disclosing their name might put them in danger. In these cases, the officers and staff should use warrant or other identification numbers and the name of their police station. Such instances and the reasons for them shall be recorded in the custody record or the interviewer's pocket book.

1.9.7.1 **KEYNOTE**

The Codes recognise the importance that detained persons are treated in accordance with the Equality Act 2010; section 149, the 'relevant protected characteristics' are: age, disability, gender reassignment, pregnancy and maternity, race, religion/belief, and sex and sexual orientation. For further detailed guidance and advice on the Equality Act, see: <https://www.gov.uk/guidance/equality-act-2010-guidance>.

It is important to ensure interviews are conducted at appropriate locations; an interviewer who is not sure, or has any doubt, about whether a place or location elsewhere than a police station is suitable for carrying out an interview of a juvenile or vulnerable person, using a particular recording device, should consult an officer of the rank of sergeant or above for advice. See Code C, paras 3.21 and 3.22.

Attention is drawn to the provisions set out in Code C about the matters to be considered when deciding whether a detained person is fit to be interviewed. Anyone who appears to be under 18, shall, in the absence of clear evidence that they are older and subject to Code C, para. 1.5A, be treated as a juvenile for the purposes of this Code.

The reason for the interviewer using his/her warrant number or other identification numbers and the name of his/her police station is to protect those involved in serious organised crime investigations or arrests of particularly violent suspects when there is reliable information that those arrested or their associates may threaten or cause harm to those involved. In cases of doubt, an officer of the rank of inspector or above should be consulted.

1.9.8 **Code E—2 Interviews and other matters to be audio recorded under this Code**

(a) Requirement to use authorised audio-recording device when available

2.1 Subject to *paragraph 2.3*, if an authorised recording device (see *paragraph 1.6(a)*) in working order *and* an interview room or other location suitable for that device to be used, are available, then that device shall be used to record the following matters:

(a) any interview with a person cautioned in accordance with Code C, *section 10* in respect of any *summary* offence or any *indictable* offence, which includes any offence triable either way, when:

(i) that person (the suspect) is questioned about their involvement or suspected involvement in that offence and they have not been charged or informed they may be prosecuted for that offence; and

(ii) exceptionally, further questions are put to a person about any offence *after* they have been charged with, or told they may be prosecuted for, that offence (see Code C, *paragraph 16.5*).

(b) when a person who has been charged with, or informed they may be prosecuted for, any offence, is told about any written statement or interview with another person and they are handed a true copy of the written statement or the content of the interview record is brought to their attention in accordance with Code C, *paragraph 16.4.*

2.2 The whole of each of the matters described in *paragraph 2.1* shall be audio-recorded, including the taking and reading back of any statement as applicable.

2.3 A written record of the matters described in *paragraph 2.1(a)* and *(b)* shall be made in accordance with Code C, *section 11*, only if,

(a) an authorised recording device (see *paragraph 1.6(a)*) in working order is *not available;* or

(b) such a device is available but a location suitable for using that device to make the audio recording of the matter in question is not available; and

(c) the 'relevant officer' described in *paragraph 2.4* considers on reasonable grounds, that the proposed interview or (as the case may be) continuation of the interview or other action, should not be delayed until an authorised recording device in working order *and* a suitable interview room or other location become available and decides that a written record shall be made;

(d) if in accordance with *paragraph 3.9*, the suspect or the appropriate adult on their behalf, objects to the interview being audibly recorded and the 'relevant officer' described in *paragraph 2.4*, after having regard to the nature and circumstances of the objections, decides that a written record shall be made;

(e) in the case of a detainee who refuses to go into or remain in a suitable interview room and in accordance with Code C *paragraphs 12.5* and *12.11*, the custody officer directs that interview be conducted in a cell and considers that an authorised recording device cannot be safely used in the cell.

Note: When the suspect appears to have a hearing impediment, this paragraph does not affect the separate requirement in *paragraphs 3.7* and *4.4* for the interviewer to make a written note of the interview at the same time as the audio recording.

(b) Meaning of 'relevant officer'

2.4 In *paragraph 2.3(c)*:

(a) if the person to be interviewed is arrested elsewhere than at a police station for an offence and before they arrive at a police station, an urgent interview in accordance with *Code C paragraph 11.1* is necessary to avert one or more of the risks mentioned in *sub-paragraphs (a)* to *(c)* of that paragraph, the 'relevant officer' means the *interviewer*, who may or may not be the arresting officer, who must have regard to the time, place and urgency of the proposed interview.

(b) if the person in question has been taken to a police station after being arrested elsewhere for an offence or is arrested for an offence whilst at a police station after attending voluntarily and is detained at that police station or elsewhere in the charge of a constable, the 'relevant officer' means the *custody officer at the station where the person's detention was last authorised*. The custody officer must have regard to the nature of the investigation and in accordance with *Code C paragraph 1.1*, ensure that the detainee is dealt with expeditiously, and released as soon as the need for their detention no longer applies.

(c) In the case of a voluntary interview (see *Code C paragraph 3.21* to *3.22*) which takes place:

(i) at a police station and the offence in question is an indictable offence, the 'relevant officer' means *an officer of the rank of sergeant or above*, in consultation with the investigating officer;

(ii) at a police station and the offence in question is a summary offence, the 'relevant officer' means *the interviewer* in consultation with the investigating officer if different,

(iii) elsewhere than at a police station and the offence is one of the four indictable offence types which satisfy the conditions in Part 1 of the Annex to this Code, the 'relevant officer' means *the interviewer* in consultation with the investigating officer, if different.

(iv) elsewhere than at a police station and the offence in question is an indictable offence which is not one of the four indictable offence types which satisfy the conditions in Part 1 of the Annex to this Code, the 'relevant officer' means an *officer of the rank of sergeant or above*, in consultation with the investigating officer.

(v) elsewhere than at a police station and the offence in question is a summary only offence, the 'relevant officer' means *the interviewer* in consultation with the investigating officer, if different.

(c) Duties of the 'relevant officer' and the interviewer

2.5 When, in accordance with *paragraph 2.3*, a written record is made:
(a) the relevant officer must:
(i) record the reasons for not making an audio recording and the date and time the decision in *paragraph 2.3(c)* or (as applicable) *paragraph 2.3(d)* was made; and
(ii) ensure that the suspect is informed that a written record will be made; (b) the interviewer must ensure that the written record includes:
(i) the date and time the decision in *paragraph 2.3(c)* or (as applicable) *paragraph 2.3(d)* was made, who made it and where the decision is recorded, and (ii) the fact that the suspect was informed.
(c) the written record shall be made in accordance with Code C, *section 11*.

(d) Remote monitoring of interviews

2.6 If the interview room or other location where the interview takes place is equipped with facilities that enable audio recorded interviews to be remotely monitored as they take place, the interviewer must ensure that suspects, their legal representatives and any appropriate adults are fully aware of what this means and that there is no possibility of privileged conversations being listened to. With this in mind, the following safeguards should be applied:
(a) The remote monitoring system should only be able to operate when the audio recording device has been turned on.
(b) The equipment should incorporate a light, clearly visible to all in the interview room, which is automatically illuminated as soon as remote monitoring is activated.
(c) Interview rooms and other locations fitted with remote monitoring equipment must contain a notice, prominently displayed, referring to the capacity for remote monitoring and to the fact that the warning light will illuminate whenever monitoring is taking place.
(d) At the beginning of the interview, the interviewer must explain the contents of the notice to the suspect and if present, to the solicitor and appropriate adult and that explanation should itself be audio recorded.
(e) The fact that an interview, or part of an interview, was remotely monitored should be recorded in the suspect's custody record or, if the suspect is not in detention, the interviewer's pocket book. That record should include the names of the officers doing the monitoring and the purpose of the monitoring (e.g. for training, to assist with the investigation, etc.)

(e) Use of live link—Interviewer not present at the same station as the detainee

2.7 Code C *paragraphs 12.9A* and *12.9B* set out the conditions which, if satisfied allow a suspect in police detention to be interviewed using a live link by a police officer who is not present at the police station where the detainee is held. These provisions also set out the duties and responsibilities of the custody officer, the officer having physical custody of the suspect and the interviewer and the modifications that apply to ensure that any such interview is conducted and audio recorded in accordance with this Code or (as the case may be) visually recorded in accordance with Code F.

KEYNOTE

Code C sets out the circumstances in which a suspect may be questioned about an offence after being charged with it. The requirements of Code E do not preclude audio-recording at police discretion at police stations or elsewhere when persons are charged with, or told they may be prosecuted for, an offence or they respond after being so charged or informed. If, during the course of an interview under this Code, it becomes apparent that the interview should be conducted under one of the terrorism Codes for video recording of interviews, the interview should only continue in accordance with the relevant Code.

A decision not to audio-record an interview for any reason may be the subject of comment in court. The 'relevant officer' responsible should be prepared to justify that decision.

Code C sets out the procedures to be followed when a person's attention is drawn after charge, to a statement made by another person. One method of bringing the content of an interview with another person to the notice of a suspect may be to play them a recording of that interview. The person may not be questioned about the statement or interview record unless this is allowed in accordance with para. 16.5 of Code C.

A voluntary interview should be arranged for a time and place when it can be audio recorded and enable the safeguards and requirements set out in Code C, paras 3.21 to 3.22B to be implemented. It would normally be reasonable to delay the interview to enable audio recording unless the delay to do so would be likely to compromise the outcome of the interview or investigation, for example if there are grounds to suspect that the suspect would use the delay to fabricate an innocent explanation, influence witnesses or tamper with other material evidence.

Objections by the suspect or appropriate adult to the interview being audibly recorded are meant to apply to objections based on the suspect's genuine and honestly held beliefs and to allow officers to exercise their discretion to decide that a written interview record is to be made according to the circumstances surrounding the suspect and the investigation. Objections that appear to be frivolous with the intentions of frustrating or delaying the investigation would not be relevant.

1.9.9 Code E—3 Interview recording using *removable recording media* device

(a) Recording and sealing master recordings—general

3.1 When using an authorised *removable recording media* device (see *paragraph 1.6(a)(i)*), one recording, the master recording, will be sealed in the suspect's presence. A second recording will be used as a working copy. The master recording is any of the recordings made by a multi-deck/drive machine or the only recording made by a single deck/drive machine. The working copy is one of the other recordings made by a multi-deck/drive machine or a copy of the master recording made by a single deck/drive machine.

3.2 The purpose of sealing the master recording before it leaves the suspect's presence is to establish their confidence that the integrity of the recording is preserved. If a single deck/drive machine is used the working copy of the master recording must be made in the suspect's presence and without the master recording leaving their sight. The working copy shall be used for making further copies if needed.

(b) Commencement of interviews

3.3 When the suspect is brought into the interview room or arrives at the location where the interview is to take place, the interviewer shall, without delay but in the suspect's sight, unwrap or open the new recording media, load the recording device with new recording media and set it to record.

3.4 The interviewer must point out the sign or indicator which shows that the recording equipment is activated and is recording (see *paragraph 1.6(a)(i)*) and shall then:

(a) tell the suspect that the interview is being audibly recorded using an authorised *removable recording media* device and outline the recording process;

(b) subject to *paragraph 1.13*, give their name and rank and that of any other interviewer present;

(c) ask the suspect and any other party present, e.g. the appropriate adult, a solicitor or interpreter, to identify themselves;

(d) state the date, time of commencement and place of the interview;

(e) tell the suspect that:

- they will be given a copy of the recording of the interview in the event that they are charged or informed that they will be prosecuted but if they are not charged or informed that they will be prosecuted they will only be given a copy as agreed with the police or on the order of a court; and

- they will be given a written notice at the end of the interview setting out their right to a copy of the recording and what will happen to the recording and;

(f) if equipment for remote monitoring of interviews as described in *paragraph 2.6* is installed, explain the contents of the notice to the suspect, solicitor and appropriate adult as required by *paragraph 2.6(d)* and point out the light that illuminates automatically as soon as remote monitoring is activated.

3.5 Any person entering the interview room after the interview has commenced shall be invited by the interviewer to identify themselves for the purpose of the audio recording and state the reason why they have entered the interview room.

3.6 The interviewer shall:

- caution the suspect, see Code C, *section 10*; and

- if they are detained, remind them of their entitlement to free legal advice, see Code C, *paragraph 11.2*; or

- if they are not detained under arrest, explain this and their entitlement to free legal advice (see Code C, *paragraph 3.21*) and ask the suspect to confirm that they agree to the voluntary interview proceeding (see *Code C, paragraph 3.22A*).

3.7 The interviewer shall put to the suspect any significant statement or silence, see Code C, *paragraph 11.4*.

(c) Interviews with suspects who appear to have a hearing impediment

3.8 If the suspect appears to have a hearing impediment, the interviewer shall make a written note of the interview in accordance with Code C, at the same time as audio recording it in accordance with this Code.

(d) Objections and complaints by the suspect

3.9 If the suspect or an appropriate adult on their behalf, objects to the interview being audibly recorded either at the outset, during the interview or during a break, the interviewer shall explain that the interview is being audibly recorded and that this Code requires the objections to be recorded on the audio recording. When any objections have been audibly recorded or the suspect or appropriate adult have refused to have their objections recorded, the relevant officer shall decide in accordance with *paragraph 2.3(d)* (which requires the officer to have regard to the nature and circumstances of the objections) whether a written record of the interview or its continuation, is to be made and that audio recording should be turned off. Following a decision that a written record is to be made, the interviewer shall say they are turning off the recorder and shall then make a written record of the interview as in Code C, *section 11*. If, however, following a decision that a written record is not to be made, the interviewer may proceed to question the suspect with the audio recording still on. This procedure also applies in cases where the suspect has previously objected to the interview being visually recorded, see Code F, *paragraph 2.7*, and the investigating officer has decided to audibly record the interview.

3.10 If in the course of an interview a complaint is made by or on behalf of the person being questioned concerning the provisions of this or any other Codes, or it comes to the interviewer's notice that the person may have been treated improperly, the interviewer shall act as in Code C, *paragraph 12.9*.

3.11 If the suspect indicates they want to tell the interviewer about matters not directly connected with the offence of which they are suspected and they are unwilling for these matters to be audio recorded, the suspect should be given the opportunity to tell the interviewer about these matters after the conclusion of the formal interview.

(e) Changing recording media

3.12 When the recorder shows the recording media only has a short time left to run, the interviewer shall so inform the person being interviewed and round off that part of the interview. If the interviewer leaves the room for a second set of recording media, the suspect shall not be left unattended. The interviewer will remove the recording media from the recorder and insert the new recording media which shall be unwrapped or opened in the suspect's presence. The recorder should be set to record on the new media. To avoid confusion between the recording media, the interviewer shall mark the media with an identification number immediately after it is removed from the recorder.

(f) Taking a break during interview

3.13 When a break is taken, the fact that a break is to be taken, the reason for it and the time shall be recorded on the audio recording.

3.14 When the break is taken and the interview room vacated by the suspect, the recording media shall be removed from the recorder and the procedures for the conclusion of an interview followed, see *paragraph 3.19*.

3.15 When a break is a short one and both the suspect and an interviewer remain in the interview room, the recording may be stopped. There is no need to remove the recording media and when the interview recommences the recording should continue on the same recording media. The time the interview recommences shall be recorded on the audio recording.

3.16 After any break in the interview the interviewer must, before resuming the interview, remind the person being questioned of their right to legal advice if they have not exercised it and that they remain under caution or, if there is any doubt, give the caution in full again.

(g) Failure of recording equipment

3.17 If there is an equipment failure which can be rectified quickly, e.g. by inserting new recording media, the interviewer shall follow the appropriate procedures as in *paragraph 3.12*. When the recording is resumed the interviewer shall explain what happened and record the time the interview recommences. However, if it is not possible to continue recording using the same recording device or by using a replacement device, the interview should be audio-recorded using a secure digital recording network device as in *paragraph 4.1*, if the necessary equipment is available. If it is not available, the interview may continue and be recorded in writing in accordance with *paragraph 2.3* as directed by the 'relevant officer'.

(h) Removing recording media from the recorder

3.18 Recording media which is removed from the recorder during the interview shall be retained and the procedures in *paragraph 3.12* followed.

(i) Conclusion of interview

3.19 At the conclusion of the interview, the suspect shall be offered the opportunity to clarify anything they have said and asked if there is anything they want to add.

3.20 At the conclusion of the interview, including the taking and reading back of any written statement, the time shall be recorded and the recording shall be stopped. The interviewer shall seal the master recording with a master recording label and treat it as an exhibit in accordance with force standing orders. The interviewer shall sign the label and ask the suspect and any third party present during the interview to sign it. If the suspect or third party refuse to sign the label an officer of at least the rank of inspector, or if not available the custody officer, or if the suspect has not been arrested, a sergeant, shall be called into the interview room and asked, subject to *paragraph 1.13*, to sign it.

3.21 The suspect shall be handed a notice which explains:

- how the audio recording will be used;
- the arrangements for access to it;
- that if they are charged or informed they will be prosecuted, a copy of the audio recording will be supplied as soon as practicable or as otherwise agreed between the suspect and the police or on the order of a court.

(j) After the interview

3.22 The interviewer shall make a note in their pocket book that the interview has taken place and that it was audibly recorded, the time it commenced, its duration and date and identification number of the master recording.

3.23 If no proceedings follow in respect of the person whose interview was recorded, the recording media must be kept securely as in *paragraph 3.22*.

(k) Master Recording security

(i) General

3.24 The officer in charge of each police station at which interviews with suspects are recorded or as the case may be, where recordings of interviews carried out elsewhere than at a police station are held, shall make arrangements for master recordings to be kept securely and their movements accounted for on the same basis as material which may be used for evidential purposes, in accordance with force standing orders.

(ii) Breaking master recording seal for criminal proceedings

3.25 A police officer has no authority to break the seal on a master recording which is required for criminal trial or appeal proceedings. If it is necessary to gain access to the master recording, the police officer shall arrange for its seal to be broken in the presence of a representative of the Crown Prosecution Service. The defendant or their legal adviser should be informed and given a reasonable opportunity to be present. If the defendant or their legal representative is present they shall be invited to re-seal and sign the master recording. If either refuses or neither is present this should be done by the representative of the Crown Prosecution Service.

(iii) Breaking master recording seal: other cases

3.26 The chief officer of police is responsible for establishing arrangements for breaking the seal of the master copy where no criminal proceedings result, or the criminal proceedings to which the interview relates, have been concluded and it becomes necessary to break the seal. These arrangements should be those which the chief officer considers are reasonably necessary to demonstrate to the person interviewed and any other party who may wish to use or refer to the interview record that the master copy has not been tampered with and that the interview record remains accurate.

3.27 Subject to *paragraph 3.29*, a representative of each party must be given a reasonable opportunity to be present when the seal is broken and the master recording copied and resealed.

3.28 If one or more of the parties is not present when the master copy seal is broken because they cannot be contacted or refuse to attend or *paragraph 3.29* applies, arrangements should be made for an independent person such as a custody visitor, to be present. Alternatively, or as an additional safeguard, arrangements should be made to visually record the procedure.

3.29 *Paragraph 3.28* does not require a person to be given an opportunity to be present when;

(a) it is necessary to break the master copy seal for the proper and effective further investigation of the original offence or the investigation of some other offence; and

(b) the officer in charge of the investigation has reasonable grounds to suspect that allowing an opportunity might prejudice such an investigation or criminal proceedings which may be brought as a result or endanger any person.

(iv) Documentation

3.30 When the master recording seal is broken, a record must be made of the procedure followed, including the date, time, place and persons present.

1.9.9.1 **KEYNOTE**

Preparation before Interview at Police Station

Preparation is essential before any interview (indeed it is the first step in the PEACE interviewing model). This preparation should include the following points:

- Decide where the interview will be conducted. Consider the availability of a room and the timing of the interview.
- The location must have a seat for the person being interviewed (Code C, para. 12.6) and should be adequately lit, heated and ventilated (Code C, para. 12.4). The detained person must also have clothing of a reasonable standard of comfort and cleanliness (Code C, para. 8.5). (It will be a question of fact as to what amounts to adequate clothing and it is suggested that if the clothing is such as to degrade the detained person or make him/her uncomfortable, it may lead to the confession being held to be unreliable.)
- In deciding the timing of the interview, consideration must be given to the detainee's rest period, which should not be interrupted or delayed unless Code C, para. 12.2 applies. Where the interview goes ahead during the rest period under Code C, para. 12.2(a), a fresh rest period must be allowed. Before a detainee is interviewed, the custody officer, in consultation with the officer in charge of the investigation and appropriate health care professionals as necessary, shall assess whether the detainee is fit enough to be interviewed (Code C, para. 12.3 and Annex G).
- If legal advice has been requested you must arrange for the legal representative to be present at the interview unless Code C, para. 6.6 applies.
- If a person has asked for legal advice and an interview is initiated in the absence of a legal adviser (e.g. where the person has agreed to be interviewed without his/her legal adviser being present or because of the urgent need to interview under Code C, para. 11.1), a record must be made in the interview record (Code C, para. 6.17).
- If an appropriate adult should be present, arrange for his/her attendance. (For the definition of appropriate adult, see Code C, para. 1.7.)
- If an interpreter is needed for the interview, arrange for his/her attendance. The provisions of Code C, s. 13 on interpreters for hearing impaired persons or for interviews with suspects who have difficulty understanding English apply to these interviews.
- The reason for the interviewer making a written note of the interview where a person is deaf or has impaired hearing is to give the equivalent rights of access to the full interview record as far as this is possible using audio recording. The interview notes must be in accordance with Code C.
- It is also important to draw up an interview plan and to include any relevant areas that may provide a general or specific defence.
- Look at the evidence available and identify any significant statement or silence by the suspect in order that it can be put to him/her in interview (Code C, para. 11.4).

- In planning for the interview officers should be mindful that a confession can be very damning evidence against a defendant, it is important to provide safeguards that give all suspects the same level of protection. The PACE Codes of Practice recognise certain groups as being in need of additional protection. These groups include juveniles, under 18-year-olds, people who do not speak English, those who are vulnerable and those who are deaf or have a hearing impediment. Such suspects must not be interviewed without the relevant person being present. See Code C, s. 13.

1.9.9.2 KEYNOTE

Commencement of interviews

When outlining the recording process, the interviewer should refer to Code E, para. 1.6(a)(ii) and (iii) and briefly describe how the recording device being used is operated and how recordings are made. For the purpose of voice identification, the interviewer should ask the suspect and any other people present to identify themselves.

In considering whether to caution again after a break, the interviewer should bear in mind that they may have to satisfy a court that the person understood that they were still under caution when the interview resumed. The interviewer should also remember that it may be necessary to show to the court that nothing occurred during a break or between interviews which influenced the suspect's recorded evidence. After a break or at the beginning of a subsequent interview, the interviewer should consider summarising on the record the reason for the break and confirming this with the suspect. Failure of recording equipment (para. 3.17).

1.9.9.3 KEYNOTE

Objections and Complaints by the Suspect

The relevant officer should be aware that a decision to continue recording against the wishes of the suspect may be the subject of comment in court. If the custody officer, or in the case of a person who has not been arrested, a sergeant, is called to deal with the complaint, the recorder should, if possible, be left on until the officer has entered the room and spoken to the person being interviewed. Continuation or termination of the interview should be at the interviewer's discretion pending action by an inspector under Code C, para. 9.2.

If the complaint is about a matter not connected with this Code or Code C, the decision to continue is at the interviewer's discretion. When the interviewer decides to continue the interview, they shall tell the suspect that at the conclusion of the interview, the complaint will be brought to the attention of the custody officer, or in the case of a person who has not been arrested, a sergeant. When the interview is concluded the interviewer must, as soon as practicable, inform the custody officer or, as the case may be, the sergeant, about the existence and nature of the complaint made.

1.9.9.4 KEYNOTE

Failure of Recording Equipment

Where the interview is being recorded and the media or the recording equipment fails the interviewer should stop the interview immediately. Where part of the interview is unaffected by the error and is still accessible on the media, that part shall be copied and sealed in the suspect's presence as a master copy and the interview recommenced using new equipment/media as required. Where the content of the interview has been lost in its entirety, the media should be sealed in the suspect's presence and the interview begun again. If the recording equipment cannot be fixed and no replacement is immediately available, subject to para. 2.3, the interview should be recorded in accordance with Code C, s. 11. Any written record of an audio recorded interview should be made in accordance with current national guidelines for police officers, police staff and CPS prosecutors concerned with the preparation, processing and submission of prosecution files. Master Recording security (paras 3.24 to 3.30).

KEYNOTE

Master Recording

The master recording must be sealed at the conclusion of the interview. Care must be taken of working copy recordings because their loss or destruction may lead unnecessarily to the need to access master recordings. Breaking master recording seal for criminal proceedings (para. 3.25).

The most common reasons for needing access to master copies that are not required for criminal proceedings arise from civil actions and complaints against police and civil actions between individuals arising out of allegations of crime investigated by police.

Examples of outcomes or likely outcomes of the investigation that might help the officer in charge of the investigation to decide whether a representative of each party needs to be present when the seal is broken and the master recording copied and re-sealed might be: (i) the prosecution of one or more of the original suspects; (ii) the prosecution of someone previously not suspected, including someone who was originally a witness, and (iii) any original suspect being treated as a prosecution witness and when premature disclosure of any police action, particularly through contact with any parties involved, could lead to a real risk of compromising the investigation and endangering witnesses.

If the master recording has been delivered to the Crown Court for their keeping after committal for trial the Crown prosecutor will apply to the chief clerk of the Crown Court centre for the release of the recording for unsealing by the Crown prosecutor. Reference to the CPS or to the Crown prosecutor in this part of the Code should be taken to include any other body or person with a statutory responsibility for the proceedings for which the police-recorded interview is required. Breaking master recording seal: other cases (paras 3.26 to 3.29).

1.9.10 Code E—4 Interview recording using secure digital recording network device

(a) General

4.1 An authorised secure digital recording network device (see *paragraph 1.6(a)(iii)* does not use removable media and this section specifies the provisions which will apply when such a device is used. For ease of reference, it repeats in full some of the provisions of section 3 that apply to both types of recording device.

(b) Commencement of interviews

4.2 When the suspect is brought into the interview room or arrives at the location where the interview is to take place, the interviewer shall without delay and in the sight of the suspect, switch on the recording equipment and in accordance with the manufacturer's instructions start recording.

4.3 The interviewer must point out the sign or indicator which shows that the recording equipment is activated and is recording (see *paragraph 1.6(a)(iii)*) and shall then:

(a) tell the suspect that the interview is being audibly recorded using an authorised *secure digital recording network device* and outline the recording process;

(b) subject to *paragraph 1.13*, give their name and rank and that of any other interviewer present;

(c) ask the suspect and any other party present, e.g. the appropriate adult, a solicitor or interpreter, to identify themselves;

(d) state the date, time of commencement and place of the interview; and

(e) inform the person that:

• they will be given access to the recording of the interview in the event that they are charged or informed that they will be prosecuted but if they are not charged or informed that they will be prosecuted they will only be given access as agreed with the police or on the order of a court; and

- they will be given a written notice at the end of the interview setting out their rights to access the recording and what will happen to the recording.

(f) If equipment for remote monitoring of interviews as described in *paragraph 2.6* is installed, explain the contents of the notice to the suspect, solicitor and appropriate adult as required by *paragraph 2.6(d)* and point out the light that illuminates automatically as soon as remote monitoring is activated.

4.4 *Paragraphs 3.5* to *3.7* apply.

(c) Interviews with suspects who appear to have a hearing impediment

4.5 *Paragraph 3.8* applies.

(d) Objections and complaints by the suspect

4.6 *Paragraphs 3.9, 3.10* and *3.11* apply.

(e) Taking a break during interview

4.7 When a break is taken, the fact that a break is to be taken, the reason for it and the time shall be recorded on the audio recording. The recording shall be stopped and the procedures in *paragraphs 4.11* and *4.12* for the conclusion of interview followed.

4.8 When the interview recommences the procedures in *paragraphs 4.2* to *4.3* for commencing an interview shall be followed to create a new file to record the continuation of the interview. The time the interview recommences shall be recorded on the audio recording.

4.9 After any break in the interview the interviewer must, before resuming the interview, remind the person being questioned of their right to legal advice if they have not exercised it and that they remain under caution or, if there is any doubt, give the caution in full again.

(f) Failure of recording equipment

4.10 If there is an equipment failure which can be rectified quickly, e.g. by commencing a new secure digital network recording using the same device or a replacement device, the interviewer shall follow the appropriate procedures as in *paragraphs 4.7 to 4.9 (Taking a break during interview)*. When the recording is resumed, the interviewer shall explain what happened and record the time the interview recommences. However, if it is not possible to continue recording on the same device or by using a replacement device, the interview should be audio-recorded on removable media as in *paragraph 3.3*, if the necessary equipment is available. If it is not available, the interview may continue and be recorded in writing in accordance with *paragraph 2.3* as directed by the 'relevant officer'.

(g) Conclusion of interview

4.11 At the conclusion of the interview, the suspect shall be offered the opportunity to clarify anything he or she has said and asked if there is anything they want to add.

4.12 At the conclusion of the interview, including the taking and reading back of any written statement:

(a) the time shall be orally recorded.

(b) the suspect shall be handed a notice which explains:
- how the audio recording will be used
- the arrangements for access to it

- that if they are charged or informed that they will be prosecuted, they will be given access to the recording of the interview either electronically or by being given a copy on removable recording media, but if they are not charged or informed that they will prosecuted, they will only be given access as agreed with the police or on the order of a court.

(c) the suspect must be asked to confirm that he or she has received a copy of the notice at *sub-paragraph (b)* above. If the suspect fails to accept or to acknowledge receipt of the notice, the interviewer will state for the recording that a copy of the notice has been provided to the suspect and that he or she has refused to take a copy of the notice or has refused to acknowledge receipt.

(d) the time shall be recorded and the interviewer shall ensure that the interview record is saved to the device in the presence of the suspect and any third party present during the interview and notify them accordingly. The interviewer must then explain that the record will be transferred securely to the remote secure network file server (see *paragraph 4.15*). If the equipment is available to enable the record to be transferred there and then in the suspect's presence, then it should be so transferred. If it is transferred at a later time, the time and place of the transfer must be recorded. The suspect should then be informed that the interview is terminated.

(h) After the interview

4.13 The interviewer shall make a note in their pocket book that the interview has taken place and that it was audibly recorded, time it commenced, its duration and date and the identification number, filename or other reference for the recording.

4.14 If no proceedings follow in respect of the person whose interview was recorded, the recordings must be kept securely as in *paragraphs 4.14* and *4.15*.

(i) Security of secure digital network interview records

4.15 The recordings are first saved locally on the device before being transferred to the remote network file server system (see *paragraph 1.6(a)(iii)*). The recording remains on the local device until the transfer is complete. If for any reason the network connection fails, the recording will be transferred when the network connection is restored (see *paragraph 4.12(d)*). The interview record files are stored in read only form on non-removable storage devices, for example, hard disk drives, to ensure their integrity.

4.16 Access to interview recordings, including copying to removable media, must be strictly controlled and monitored to ensure that access is restricted to those who have been given specific permission to access for specified purposes when this is necessary. For example, police officers and CPS lawyers involved in the preparation of any prosecution case, persons interviewed if they have been charged or informed they may be prosecuted and their legal representatives.

1.9.10.1

KEYNOTE

The notice given to the suspect at the conclusion of the interview (see Code E, para. 4.12(b)) should provide a brief explanation of the secure digital network and how access to the recording is strictly limited. The notice should also explain the access rights of the suspect, their legal representative, the police and the prosecutor to the recording of the interview. Space should be provided on the form to insert the date, the identification number, filename or other reference for the interview recording.

Code E—Annex: Paragraph 2.4(C)(iii)—Four Indictable Offence Types for which the interviewer may Decide to make a written record of a Voluntary Interview elsewhere than at a Police Station when an Authorised Audio Recording Device cannot be used.

Part 1: Four specified indictable offence types—two conditions

1. The first condition is that the *indictable* offence in respect of which the person has been cautioned is *one* of the following:

   (a) Possession of a controlled drug contrary to section 5(2) of the Misuse of Drugs Act 1971 if the drug is cannabis as defined by that Act and in a form commonly known as herbal cannabis or cannabis resin;

   (b) Possession of a controlled drug contrary to section 5(2) of the Misuse of Drugs Act 1971 if the drug is khat as defined by that Act.

   (c) Retail theft (shoplifting) contrary to section 1 of the Theft Act 1968; and

   (d) Criminal damage to property contrary to section 1(1) of the Criminal Damage Act 1971, and in this paragraph, the reference to each of the above offences applies to an attempt to commit that offence as defined by section 1 of the Criminal Attempts Act 1981.

2. The **second** condition is that:

   (a) where the person has been cautioned in respect of an offence described in *paragraph 1(a)* (Possession of herbal cannabis or cannabis resin) or *paragraph 1(b)* (Possession of khat), the requirements of *paragraphs 3* and *4* are satisfied; or

   (b) where the person has been cautioned in respect of an offence described in *paragraph 1(c)* (Retail theft), the requirements of *paragraphs 3* and *5* are satisfied; or

   (c) where the person has been cautioned in respect of an offence described in *paragraph 1(d)* (criminal damage), the requirements of *paragraphs 3* and *6* are satisfied.

3. The requirements of this paragraph that apply to all four offences described in *paragraph 1* are that:

   (i) with regard to the person suspected of committing the offence:
   - they appear to be aged 18 or over;
   - there is no reason to suspect that they are a vulnerable person for whom an appropriate adult is required (see *paragraph 1.5* of this Code);
   - they do *not* appear to be unable to understand what is happening because of the effects of drink, drugs or illness, ailment or condition;
   - they do *not* require an interpreter in accordance with Code C section 13; and
   - in accordance with Code G (Arrest), their arrest is *not* necessary in order to investigate the offence;

   (ii) it appears that the commission of the offence:
   - has *not* resulted in any injury to any person;
   - has *not* involved any realistic threat or risk of injury to any person; and
   - has *not* caused any *substantial* financial or material loss to the private property of any individual; and

   (iii) the person is not being interviewed about any other offence.

4. The requirements of this paragraph that apply to the offences described in *paragraph 1(a)* (possession of herbal cannabis or cannabis resin) and *paragraph 1(b)* (possession of khat) are that a police officer who is experienced in the recognition of the physical appearance, texture and smell of herbal cannabis, cannabis resin or (as the case may be) khat, is able to say that the substance which has been found in the suspect's possession by that officer or, as the case may be, by any other officer not so experienced and trained:

   (i) is a controlled drug being either herbal cannabis, cannabis resin or khat; and

(ii) the quantity of the substance found is consistent with personal use by the suspect and does not provide any grounds to suspect an intention to supply others.

5. The requirements of this paragraph that apply to the offence described in *paragraph 1(c)* (retail theft), are that it appears to the officer:

(i) that the value of the property stolen does not exceed £100 inclusive of VAT;

(ii) that the stolen property has been recovered and remains fit for sale unless the items stolen comprised drink or food and have been consumed; and

(iii) that the person suspected of stealing the property is not employed (whether paid or not) by the person, company or organisation to which the property belongs.

6. The requirements of this paragraph that apply to the offence described in *paragraph 1(d)* (Criminal damage), are that it appears to the officer:

(i) that the value of the criminal damage does *not exceed* £300; and

(ii) that the person suspected of damaging the property is not employed (whether paid or not) by the person, company or organisation to which the property belongs.

Part 2: Other provisions applicable to all interviews to which this Annex applies

7. *Paragraphs 3.21* to *3.22B* of Code C set out the responsibilities of the interviewing officer for ensuring compliance with the provisions of Code C that apply to the conduct and recording of voluntary interviews to which this Annex applies.

8. If it appears to the interviewing officer that before the conclusion of an interview, any of the requirements in *paragraphs 3 to 6* of *Part 1* that apply to the offence in question described in *paragraph 1* of Part 1 have ceased to apply; this Annex shall cease to apply. The person being interviewed must be so informed and a break in the interview must be taken. The reason must be recorded in the written interview record and the continuation of the interview shall be audio recorded in accordance with section 2 of this Code. For the purpose of the continuation, the provisions of *paragraphs 3.3* and *4.2* (Commencement of interviews) shall apply.

1.9.11.1

KEYNOTE

The purpose of allowing the interviewer to decide that a written record is to be made is to support the policy which gives police in England and Wales options for dealing with low level offences quickly and non-bureaucratically in a proportionate manner. Guidance for police about these options is available at: <https://www.app.college.police.uk/app-content/prosecution-and-case-management/justice-outcomes/>.

A decision in relation to a particular indictable offence that the conditions and requirements in this Annex are satisfied is an operational matter for the interviewing officer according to all the particular circumstances of the case. These circumstances include the outcome of the officer's investigation at that time and any other matters that are relevant to the officer's consideration as to how to deal with the matter. Under the Misuse of Drugs Act 1971 cannabis includes any part of the cannabis plant but not mature stalks and seeds separated from the plant, cannabis resin and cannabis oil, but para. 1(a) applies only to the possession of herbal cannabis and cannabis resin. Khat includes the leaves, stems and shoots of the plant.

The power to issue a Penalty Notice for Disorder (PND) for an offence contrary to s. 1 of the Theft Act 1968 applies when the value of the goods stolen does not exceed £100 inclusive of VAT. The power to issue a PND for an offence contrary to s. 1(1) of the Criminal Damage Act 1971 applies when the value of the damage does not exceed £300.

The provisions of Code C that apply to the conduct and recording of voluntary interviews to which this Annex applies are described in paras 3.21 to 3.22B of Code C. They include the suspect's right to free legal advice, the provision of information about the offence before the interview (see Code C, para. 11.1A) and the right to interpretation and translation (see Code C, s. 13). These and other rights and entitlements are summarised in the notice that must be given to the suspect.

The requirements in para. 3 will cease to apply if, for example during the course of an interview, as a result of what the suspect says or other information which comes to the interviewing officer's notice:

- it appears that the suspect:
  - ~ is aged under 18;
  - ~ does require an appropriate adult;
  - ~ is unable to appreciate the significance of questions and their answers;
  - ~ is unable to understand what is happening because of the effects of drink, drugs or illness, ailment or condition; or
  - ~ requires an interpreter; or
- the police officer decides that the suspect's arrest is now necessary (see Code G).

1.9.12   ## PACE Code of Practice on Visual Recording with Sound of Interviews with Suspects (Code F)

Fet

This contents of this Code should be considered if an interviewer proposes to make a visual recording with sound of an interview with a suspect after 00.00 on 31 July 2018.

There is no statutory requirement under PACE to visually record interviews.

1 General

1.0   The procedures in this Code must be used fairly, responsibly, with respect for the people to whom they apply and without unlawful discrimination. Under the Equality Act 2010, section 149 (Public Sector Equality Duty), police forces must, in carrying out their functions, have due regard to the need to eliminate unlawful discrimination, harassment, victimisation and any other conduct which is prohibited by that Act, to advance equality of opportunity between people who share a relevant protected characteristic and people who do not share it, and to foster good relations between those persons. The Equality Act *also* makes it unlawful for police officers to discriminate against, harass or victimise any person on the grounds of the 'protected characteristics' of age, disability, gender reassignment, race, religion or belief, sex and sexual orientation, marriage and civil partnership, pregnancy and maternity, when using their powers.

1.1   This Code of Practice must be readily available for consultation by police officers and other police staff, detained persons and members of the public.

1.2   The *Notes for Guidance* included are not provisions of this code. They form guidance to police officers and others about its application and interpretation.

1.3   Nothing in this Code shall detract from the requirements of Code C, the Code of Practice for the detention, treatment and questioning of persons by police officers.

1.4   The interviews and matters to which this Code applies and provisions that govern the conduct and recording of those interviews and other matters are described in section 2.
Note: The provisions of this Code and Code E which govern the conduct and recording of interviews *do not apply* to interviews with, or taking statements from, witnesses.

1.5   *Not used.*

1.5A   The provisions of Code E which require interviews with suspects to be audio recorded and the provisions of this Code which permit simultaneous visual recording provide safeguards:
- for suspects against inaccurate recording of the words used in questioning them and of their demeanour during the interview; and
- for police interviewers against unfounded allegations made by, or on behalf of, suspects about the conduct of the interview and what took place during the interview which might otherwise appear credible.

The visual recording of interviews must therefore be carried out openly to instil confidence in its reliability as an impartial and accurate record of the interview.

1.6   *Not used.*

1.6A   *Not used.*

1.7   *Not used.*

1.8   *Not used.*

1.9.12.1

KEYNOTE

Under the Equality Act 2010, s. 149, the 'relevant protected characteristics' are: age, disability, gender re-assignment, pregnancy and maternity, race, religion/belief, and sex and sexual orientation. For further detailed guidance and advice on the Equality Act, see: <http://www.gov.uk/guidance/equality-act-2010-guidance>.

1.9.13

Code F—2 When interviews and matters to which Code F applies may be visually recorded with sound and provisions for their conduct and recording.

(a) General

2.1 For the purpose of this Code, a visual recording with sound means an audio recording of an interview or other matter made in accordance with the requirement in *paragraph 2.1* of the Code of Practice on audio recording interviews with suspects (Code E) during which a *simultaneous* visual recording is made which shows the suspect, the interviewer and those in whose presence and hearing the audio recording was made.

2.2 There is no statutory requirement to make a visual recording, however, the provisions of this Code shall be followed on any occasion that the 'relevant officer' described in *Code E paragraph 2.4* considers that a visual recording of any matters mentioned in *paragraph 2.1* should be made. Having regard to the safeguards described in *paragraph 1.5A*, examples of occasions when the relevant officer is likely to consider that a visual recording should be made include when:

  (a) the suspect (whether or not detained) requires an appropriate adult;

  (b) the suspect or their solicitor or appropriate adult requests that the interview be recorded visually;

  (c) the suspect or other person whose presence is necessary is deaf or deaf/blind or speech impaired and uses sign language to communicate;

  (d) the interviewer anticipates that when asking the suspect about their involvement in the offence concerned, they will invite the suspect to demonstrate their actions or behaviour at the time or to examine a particular item or object which is handed to them;

  (e) the officer in charge of the investigation believes that a visual recording with sound will assist in the conduct of the investigation, for example, when briefing other officers about the suspect or matters coming to light during the course of the interview; and

  (f) the authorised recording device that would be used in accordance with *paragraph 2.1 of Code E* incorporates a camera and creates a combined audio and visual recording and does not allow the visual recording function to operate independently of the audio recording function.

2.3 For the purpose of making such a visual recording, the provisions of Code E and the relevant *Notes for Guidance* shall apply equally to visual recordings with sound as they do to audio-only recordings, subject to the additional provisions in *paragraphs 2.5* to *2.12* below which apply exclusively to visual recordings.

2.4 This Code does not apply to the conduct and recording in England and Wales, of:

  • interviews of persons detained under section 41 of, or Schedule 7 to, the Terrorism Act 2000, and

  • post-charge questioning of persons authorised under section 22 of the Counter Terrorism Act 2008. These must be video recorded with sound in accordance with the provisions of the separate Code of Practice issued under paragraph 3 of Schedule 8 to the Terrorism Act 2000 and under section 25 of the Counter-Terrorism Act 2008. If, during the course of an interview or questioning being visually recorded under this Code, it becomes apparent that the interview or questioning should be conducted under that separate Code, the interview should only continue in accordance with that Code (see *Code E paragraph 1.4*).

(b) Application of Code E—additional provisions that apply to visual recording with sound.

(i) General

2.5 Before visual recording commences, the interviewer must inform the suspect that in accordance with *paragraph 2.2*, a visual recording is being made and explain the visual and audio recording arrangements. If the suspect is a juvenile or a vulnerable person (see Code C, *paragraphs 1.4, 1.5* and *1.13(d)*), the information and explanation must be provided or (as the case may be) provided again, in the presence of the appropriate adult.

2.6 The device used to make the visual recording at the same time as the audio recording (see *paragraph 2.1*) must ensure coverage of as much of the room or location where the interview takes place as it is practically possible to achieve whilst the interview takes place.

2.7 In cases to which *paragraph 1.13* of Code E (disclosure of identity of officers or police staff conducting interviews) applies:
   (a) the officers and staff may have their backs to the visual recording device; and
   (b) when in accordance with Code E *paragraph 3.21* or *4.12* as they apply to this Code, arrangements are made for the suspect to have access to the visual recording, the investigating officer may arrange for anything in the recording that might allow the officers or police staff to be identified to be concealed.

2.8 Following a decision made by the relevant officer in accordance with *paragraph 2.2* that an interview or other matter mentioned in *paragraph 2.1* above should be *visually recorded*, the relevant officer may decide that the interview is not to be visually recorded if it no longer appears that a visual recording should be made or because of a fault in the recording device. However, a decision not to make a *visual recording* does not detract in any way from the requirement for the interview to be *audio recorded* in accordance with *paragraph 2.1 of Code E*.

2.9 The provisions in *Code E paragraph 2.6* for remote monitoring of interviews shall apply to visually recorded interviews.

(ii) Objections and complaints by the suspect about visual recording

2.10 If the suspect or an appropriate adult on their behalf objects to the interview being *visually* recorded either at the outset or during the interview or during a break in the interview, the interviewer shall explain that the visual recording is being made in accordance with *paragraph 2.2* and that this Code requires the objections to be recorded on the *visual* recording. When any objections have been recorded or the suspect or the appropriate adult have refused to have their objections recorded visually, the relevant officer shall decide in accordance with *paragraph 2.8* and having regard to the nature and circumstances of the objections, whether visual recording should be turned off. Following a decision that visual recording should be turned off, the interviewer shall say that they are turning off the *visual* recording. The audio recording required to be maintained in accordance with Code E shall continue and the interviewer shall ask the person to record their objections to the interview being *visually* recorded on the audio recording. If the relevant officer considers that visual recording should not be turned off, the interviewer may proceed to question the suspect with the visual recording still on. If the suspect also objects to the interview being audio recorded, *paragraph 3.9* of Code E will apply if a removable recording media device (see Code

E *paragraph 1.6(a)(ii)*) is being used) and *paragraph 4.6* of Code E will apply if a secure digital recording device (see Code E *paragraph 1.6(a)(iii)*) is being used.

2.11 If the suspect indicates that they wish to tell the interviewer about matters not directly connected with the offence of which they are suspected and that they are unwilling for these matters to be visually recorded, the suspect should be given the opportunity to tell the interviewer about these matters after the conclusion of the formal interview.

(iii) Failure of visual recording device

2.12 If there is a failure of equipment and it is not possible to continue visual recording using the same type of recording device (i.e. a removable recording media device as in Code E *paragraph 1.6(a)(ii)* or a secure digital recording network device as in Code E *paragraph 1.6(a)(iii)*) or by using a replacement device of either type, the relevant officer may decide that the interview is to continue without being visually recorded. In these circumstances, the continuation of the interview must be conducted and recorded in accordance with the provisions of Code E.

1.9.13.1

KEYNOTE

Paragraph 2.1 of Code E which is referred to in Code F, para. 2.1 above describes the requirement that authorised audio-recording devices are to be used for recording interviews and other matters.

Interviewers will wish to arrange that, as far as possible, visual recording arrangements are unobtrusive. It must be clear to the suspect, however, that there is no opportunity to interfere with the recording equipment or the recording media. A decision made in accordance with para. 2.8 not to record an interview visually for any reason may be the subject of comment in court. The 'relevant officer' responsible should therefore be prepared to justify that decision.

Objections by the suspect or appropriate adult on their behalf to the interview being visually recorded are meant to apply to objections based on the suspect's genuine and honestly held beliefs and to allow officers to exercise their discretion to decide whether a visual recording is to be made according to the circumstances surrounding the suspect and the investigation. Objections that appear to be frivolous with the intentions of frustrating or delaying the investigation would not be relevant. The relevant officer should be aware that a decision to continue visual recording against the wishes of the suspect may be the subject of comment in court.

Where the interview is being visually recorded and the media or the recording device fails, the interviewer should stop the interview immediately. Where part of the interview is unaffected by the error and is still accessible on the media or on the network device, that part shall be copied and sealed in the suspect's presence as a master copy or saved as a new secure digital network recording as appropriate. The interview should then be recommenced using a functioning recording device and new recording media as appropriate. Where the media content of the interview has been lost in its entirety, the media should be sealed in the suspect's presence and the interview begun again. If the visual recording equipment cannot be fixed and a replacement device is not immediately available, the interview should be audio recorded in accordance with Code E. The visual recording made in accordance with this Code may be used for eye-witness identification procedures to which para. 3.21 and Annex E of Code D apply.

1.9.14 Interviews on Behalf of Scottish Forces and Vice Versa

The CPS, in consultation with the Scottish Crown Office, has produced guidelines in relation to the potential admissibility of interview evidence when officers from England and Wales conduct interviews on behalf of Scottish forces and vice versa. These interviews relate to people subject to cross-border arrest as provided by ss. 136 to 140 of the Criminal Justice and Public Order Act 1994.

KEYNOTE

Suspects in England and Wales: Interview Evidence Required for Prosecutions in Scotland or Northern Ireland

Section 137A provides additional cross-border powers of arrest in urgent cases, this section states:

(1) A constable of a police force in England and Wales may arrest a person in England and Wales without a warrant if—

    (a) the constable has reasonable grounds for suspecting that the person has committed a specified offence in Scotland or in Northern Ireland, and

    (b) the constable also has reasonable grounds for believing that it is necessary to arrest the person—

        (i) to allow the prompt and effective investigation of the offence, or

        (ii) to prevent any prosecution for the offence from being hindered by the disappearance of the person.

For detention of a person arrested under this power, **see para. 1.7.16.12.** Where the arrest is in England and Wales under this subsection or in Northern Ireland under s. 137(4), the constable has the powers of entry and search conferred by s. 137E.

The specified offences committed in England and Wales to which this power of arrest applies include:

(a) an offence (including an offence under the common law) that is punishable by virtue of any statutory provision with imprisonment or another form of detention for a term of 10 years or with a greater punishment,

(b) any of the following offences:

    1 Any of the following offences at common law—

        (a) false imprisonment;

        (b) kidnapping;

        (c) indecent exposure;

        (d) cheating in relation to the public revenue.

    2 An offence under any of the following provisions of the Offences against the Person Act 1861—

        (a) section 20 (inflicting bodily injury);

        (b) section 24 (administering poison etc with intent);

        (c) section 27 (exposing child whereby life is endangered etc);

        (d) section 31 (setting spring-guns etc with intent);

        (e) section 37 (assaulting an officer etc on account of his preserving wreck);

        (f) section 47 (assault occasioning actual bodily harm).

    3 (1) An offence under any of the following provisions of the Sexual Offences Act 1956—

        (a) section 10 (incest by a man);

        (b) section 11 (incest by a woman);

        (c) section 30 (man living on the earnings of prostitution);

        (d) section 31 (woman exercising control over a prostitute);

        (e) section 33A (keeping a brothel used for prostitution).

      (2) An offence under section 12 of that Act (buggery), other than an offence committed by a person where the other person involved in the conduct constituting the offence consented to it and was aged 16 or over.

      (3) An offence under section 13 of that Act (indecency between men), where the offence was committed by a man aged 21 or over and the other person involved in the conduct constituting the offence was under the age of 16.

    4 An offence under section 4 of the Criminal Law Act 1967 (assisting offenders).

    5 An offence under section 5 of the Sexual Offences Act 1967 (living on the earnings of male prostitution).

    6 An offence under any of the following provisions of the Firearms Act 1968—

        (a) section 1(1) (possession etc of firearms or ammunition without certificate);

        (b) section 2(1) (possession etc of shot gun without certificate);

        (c) section 3(1) (manufacturing, selling etc firearms or ammunition by way of trade or business without being registered as a firearms dealer).

7 An offence under section 106A of the Taxes Management Act 1970 (fraudulent evasion of income tax).

8 (1) An offence under section 50(2) or (3) of the Customs and Excise Management Act 1979 (improper importation of goods), other than an offence mentioned in subsection (5B) of that section.

(2) An offence under section 68(2) of that Act (exportation of prohibited or restricted goods).

(3) An offence under section 170 of that Act (fraudulent evasion of duty etc), other than an offence mentioned in subsection (4B) of that section.

9 An offence under section 4 of the Aviation Security Act 1982 (offences in relation to certain dangerous articles).

10 An offence under section 127 of the Mental Health Act 1983 (ill-treatment of patients).

11 An offence under either of the following provisions of the Child Abduction Act 1984—

(a) section 1 (abduction of child by parent etc);

(b) section 2 (abduction of child by other persons).

12 An offence under section 1 of the Prohibition of Female Circumcision Act 1985 (prohibition of female circumcision).

13 An offence under either of the following provisions of the Public Order Act 1986—

(a) section 2 (violent disorder);

(b) section 3 (affray).

14 An offence under section 160 of the Criminal Justice Act 1988 (possession of indecent photograph of a child).

15 An offence under section 2 of the Computer Misuse Act 1990 (unauthorised access with intent to commit or facilitate commission of further offences).

16 An offence under section 72(1), (3) or (8) of the Value Added Tax Act 1994 (fraudulent evasion of VAT etc).

17 An offence under either of the following provisions of the Protection from Harassment Act 1997—

(a) section 4 (putting people in fear of violence);

(b) section 4A (stalking involving fear of violence or serious alarm or distress).

18 An offence under section 29(1)(a) or (b) of the Crime and Disorder Act 1998 (certain racially or religiously aggravated assaults).

19 An offence under section 38B of the Terrorism Act 2000 (information about acts of terrorism).

20 An offence under section 3 of the Sexual Offences (Amendment) Act 2000 (sexual activity with a person aged under 18 in abuse of a position of trust).

21 An offence under section 35 of the Tax Credits Act 2002 (tax credit fraud).

22 (1) An offence under any of the following provisions of the Sexual Offences Act 2003—

(a) section 13 (child sex offences committed by children or young persons);

(b) section 16 (abuse of position of trust: sexual activity with a child);

(c) section 17 (abuse of position of trust: causing or inciting a child to engage in sexual activity);

(d) section 18 (abuse of position of trust: sexual activity in the presence of a child);

(e) section 19 (abuse of position of trust: causing a child to watch a sexual act);

(f) section 40 (care workers: sexual activity in the presence of a person with a mental disorder);

(g) section 41 (care workers: causing a person with a mental disorder to watch a sexual act);

(h) section 52 (causing or inciting prostitution for gain);

(i) section 53 (controlling prostitution for gain).

(2) An offence under section 25 or 26 of that Act (family child sex offences) where the offence is committed by a person under the age of 18.

(3) An offence under section 47 of that Act (paying for sexual services of a child), where the offence is committed against a person aged 16 or over.

23 An offence under either of the following provisions of the Terrorism Act 2006—

(a) section 1 (encouragement of terrorism);

(b) section 2 (dissemination of terrorist publications).

24 An offence under section 45 of the Serious Crime Act 2015 (participating in activities of organised crime group).

25 An offence under section 68 of the Policing and Crime Act 2017 (breach of pre-charge bail conditions relating to travel), or

(c) an offence of attempting or conspiring to commit, or of inciting the commission of, an offence mentioned in paragraph (a) or (b), or

(d) an offence under Part 2 of the Serious Crime Act 2007 (encouraging or assisting crime) in relation to an offence mentioned in paragraph (a) or (b).

- Where English officers do not have any statutory or common law powers to detain or arrest a suspect without warrant who is believed to have committed an offence in Scotland and there is insufficient evidence for the issue of a warrant, and the case is not sufficiently serious to justify officers travelling to England or Wales to exercise their cross-border powers under the Act, English or Welsh officers can be requested to invite the suspect to attend an interview on a voluntary basis for interview under caution.

- Where a Scottish officer has attended to interview the suspect, the Scottish form of caution should be given (similarly any variations from Northern Ireland should also be applied).

- English and Welsh constables interviewing suspects in England/Wales when they are aware that the interview is required for a prosecution in Scotland, should comply with the PACE Codes of Practice, save that a Scottish caution should be used in the following terms:

You are not obliged to say anything but anything you do say will be noted and may be used in evidence.

The use of an English/Welsh caution may render the interview inadmissible in Scotland.

Scottish officers should assist the interviewing officers by providing a schedule of points to be covered in an interview and a possible list of appropriate questions.

In all circumstances, officers should ensure that suspects fully understand the significance of a caution or warning.

1.9.14.2

KEYNOTE

Suspects in Scotland or Northern Ireland: Interview Evidence Required for Prosecutions in England and Wales

Suspects are not warned that a failure to answer questions may harm their defence. Failure to answer questions cannot harm their defence. Interviews under caution are, however, subject to guidelines which incorporate judicial precedent fairness to the accused.

In investigations of any great seriousness, English/Welsh constables should attend in Scotland, arrest the suspect and bring him/her back to their jurisdiction for interview. If such an arrest is made, the arrested person must be taken either to the nearest designated police station in England or a designated police station in a police area in England and Wales in which the offence is being investigated (s. 137(1) and (7)(a) of the Criminal Justice and Public Order Act 1994).

Under s 137A:

(2) a constable of a police force in Scotland may arrest a person in Scotland without a warrant if—

(a) the constable has reasonable grounds for suspecting that the person has committed a specified offence in England and Wales or in Northern Ireland, and

(b) the constable is satisfied that it would not be in the interests of justice to delay the arrest either to enable a warrant for the person's arrest to be obtained and then executed under section 136 or to enable a power of arrest under section 137 to be exercised.

(3) Without prejudice to the generality of subsection (2)(b), it would not be in the interests of justice to delay an arrest for a purpose mentioned in that subsection if the constable reasonably believes that, unless the person is arrested without delay, the person will obstruct the course of justice in any way, including by seeking to avoid arrest or interfering with witnesses or evidence.

There is a similar power for a constable of a police force in Northern Ireland who has reasonable grounds for suspecting that the person has committed a specified offence in England and Wales or in Scotland (s. 137(4)).

Where the arrest is in Scotland under subs. (2), the constable has the same powers of entry and search for the purpose of the arrest as a constable of a police force in Scotland would have if there were reasonable grounds for suspecting that the offence had been committed in Scotland.

The specified offences committed in Scotland to which this power of arrest applies include:

(a) an offence (including an offence under the common law) that is punishable by virtue of any statutory provision with imprisonment or another form of detention for a term of 10 years or with a greater punishment,

(b) any of the following offences:

1 Any of the following offences at common law—

  (a) culpable homicide;

  (b) treason;

  (c) rape;

  (d) assault, where the assault results in serious injury or endangers life;

  (e) assault with intent to rape or ravish;

  (f) indecent assault;

  (g) abduction with intent to rape;

  (h) public indecency;

  (i) clandestine injury to women;

  (j) lewd, indecent or libidinous behaviour or practices;

  (k) sodomy, other than an offence committed by a person where the other person involved in the conduct constituting the offence consented to it and was aged 16 or over;

  (l) abduction;

  (m) mobbing;

  (n) fire-raising;

  (o) robbery;

  (p) fraud;

  (q) extortion;

  (r) embezzlement;

  (s) theft;

  (t) threats;

  (u) attempting to pervert the course of justice.

2 An offence under any of the following provisions of the Firearms Act 1968—

  (a) section 1(1) (possession etc of firearms or ammunition without certificate);

  (b) section 2(1) (possession etc of shot gun without certificate);

  (c) section 3(1) (manufacturing, selling etc firearms or ammunition by way of trade or business without being registered as a firearms dealer).

3 An offence under section 106A of the Taxes Management Act 1970 (fraudulent evasion of income tax).

4 (1) An offence under section 50(2) or (3) of the Customs and Excise Management Act 1979 (improper importation of goods), other than an offence mentioned in subsection (5B) of that section.

  (2) An offence under section 68(2) of that Act (exportation of prohibited or restricted goods).

  (3) An offence under section 170 of that Act (fraudulent evasion of duty etc), other than an offence mentioned in subsection (4B) of that section.

5 An offence under section 4 of the Aviation Security Act 1982 (offences in relation to certain dangerous articles).

6 An offence under either of the following provisions of the Civic Government (Scotland) Act 1982—

  (a) section 51(2) (publication etc of obscene material);

  (b) section 52 (taking, distributing etc indecent photographs of children).

7 An offence under section 6 of the Child Abduction Act 1984 (parent etc. taking or sending a child out of the United Kingdom).

8 An offence under section 1 of the Prohibition of Female Circumcision Act 1985 (prohibition of female circumcision).

9 An offence under section 2 of the Computer Misuse Act 1990 (unauthorised access with intent to commit or facilitate commission of further offences).

10 An offence under section 72(1), (3) or (8) of the Value Added Tax Act 1994 (fraudulent evasion of VAT etc).

11 An offence under any of the following provisions of the Criminal Law (Consolidation) (Scotland) Act 1995—

    (a) section 7 (procuring prostitution etc);

    (b) section 8(3) (unlawful detention of women and girls);

    (c) section 10 (parents etc encouraging girls under 16 to engage in prostitution etc);

    (d) section 11(1)(b) (males soliciting etc for immoral purposes).

12 An offence under section 38B of the Terrorism Act 2000 (information about acts of terrorism).

13 An offence under section 35 of the Tax Credits Act 2002 (tax credit fraud).

14 An offence under section 313 of the Mental Health (Care and Treatment) (Scotland) Act 2003 (persons providing care services: sexual offences).

15 An offence under either of the following provisions of the Terrorism Act 2006—

    (a) section 1 (encouragement of terrorism);

    (b) section 2 (dissemination of terrorist publications).

16 Any of the following offences under the Sexual Offences (Scotland) Act 2009—

    (a) section 8 (sexual exposure);

    (b) section 9 (voyeurism);

    (c) section 11 (administering a substance for sexual purposes);

    (d) section 32 (causing an older child to be present during a sexual activity);

    (e) section 33 (causing an older child to look at a sexual image);

    (f) section 34(1) (communicating indecently with an older child);

    (g) section 34(2) (causing an older child to see or hear an indecent communication);

    (h) section 35 (sexual exposure to an older child);

    (i) section 36 (voyeurism towards an older child);

    (j) section 42 (sexual abuse of trust);

    (k) section 46 (sexual abuse of trust of a mentally disordered person).

17 An offence under either of the following provisions of the Criminal Justice and Licensing (Scotland) Act 2010—

    (a) section 38 (threatening or abusive behaviour);

    (b) section 39 (stalking).

18 An offence under section 2 of the Abusive Behaviour and Sexual Harm (Scotland) Act 2016 (disclosing etc an intimate photograph or film), or

(c) an offence of attempting or conspiring to commit, or of inciting the commission of, an offence mentioned in paragraph (a) or (b).

The specified offences committed in Northern Ireland to which this power of arrest applies include:

(a) an offence (including an offence under the common law) that is punishable by virtue of any statutory provision with imprisonment or another form of detention for a term of 10 years or with a greater punishment,

(b) any of the following offences:

    1 Any of the following offences at common law—

        (a) false imprisonment;

        (b) kidnapping;

        (c) riot;

        (d) affray;

        (e) indecent exposure;

        (f) cheating in relation to the public revenue.

    2 An offence under any of the following provisions of the Offences against the Person Act 1861—

        (a) section 20 (inflicting bodily injury);

(b) section 24 (administering poison etc with intent);

(c) section 27 (exposing child whereby life is endangered etc);

(d) section 31 (setting spring-guns etc with intent);

(e) section 37 (assaulting an officer etc on account of his preserving wreck);

(f) section 47 (assault occasioning actual bodily harm).

3 An offence under section 11 of the Criminal Law Amendment Act 1885 (indecency between men), where the offence was committed by a man aged 21 or over and the other person involved in the conduct constituting the offence was under the age of 16.

4 An offence under either of the following provisions of the Punishment of Incest Act 1908—

(a) section 1 (incest by a man);

(b) section 2 (incest by a woman).

5 An offence under section 4 of the Criminal Law Act (Northern Ireland) 1967 (assisting offenders).

6 An offence under section 106A of the Taxes Management Act 1970 (fraudulent evasion of income tax).

7 (1) An offence under section 50(2) or (3) of the Customs and Excise Management Act 1979 (improper importation of goods), other than an offence mentioned in subsection (5B) of that section.

(2) An offence under section 68(2) of that Act (exportation of prohibited or restricted goods).

(3) An offence under section 170 of that Act (fraudulent evasion of duty etc), other than an offence mentioned in subsection (4B) of that section.

8 An offence under section 4 of the Aviation Security Act 1982 (offences in relation to certain dangerous articles).

9 An offence under Article 8 of the Homosexual Offences (Northern Ireland) Order 1982 (SI 1982/1536 (N.I. 19)) (living on the earnings of male prostitution).

10 An offence under section 1 of the Prohibition of Female Circumcision Act 1985 (prohibition of female circumcision).

11 An offence under either of the following provisions of the Child Abduction (Northern Ireland) Order 1985 (SI 1985/1638 (N.I. 17))—

(a) Article 3 (abduction of child by parent etc);

(b) Article 4 (abduction of child by other persons).

12 An offence under Article 121 of the Mental Health (Northern Ireland) Order 1986 (SI 1986/595 (N.I. 4)) (ill-treatment of patients).

13 An offence under Article 15 of the Criminal Justice (Evidence, Etc.) (Northern Ireland) Order 1988 (SI 1988/1847 (N.I. 17)) (possession of indecent photograph of a child).

14 An offence under section 2 of the Computer Misuse Act 1990 (unauthorised access with intent to commit or facilitate commission of further offences).

15 An offence under section 72(1), (3) or (8) of the Value Added Tax Act 1994 (fraudulent evasion of VAT etc).

16 An offence under Article 6 of the Protection from Harassment (Northern Ireland) Order 1997 (SI 1997/1180 (N.I. 9)) (putting people in fear of violence).

17 An offence under section 38B of the Terrorism Act 2000 (information about acts of terrorism).

18 An offence under section 3 of the Sexual Offences (Amendment) Act 2000 (sexual activity with a person aged under 18 in abuse of a position of trust).

19 An offence under section 35 of the Tax Credits Act 2002 (tax credit fraud).

20 An offence under section 53 of the Sexual Offences Act 2003 (controlling prostitution for gain).

21 An offence under any of the following provisions of the Firearms (Northern Ireland) Order 2004 (SI 2004/702 (N.I. 3))—

(a) Article 3(1)(b) (possession etc of firearms other than handguns without certificate);

(b) Article 3(2) (possession etc of ammunition without certificate);

(c) Article 24(1) (manufacturing, selling etc firearms or ammunition by way of trade or business without being registered as a firearms dealer).

22 An offence under either of the following provisions of the Terrorism Act 2006—

    (a) section 1 (encouragement of terrorism);

    (b) section 2 (dissemination of terrorist publications).

23 (1) An offence under any of the following provisions of the Sexual Offences (Northern Ireland) Order 2008 (SI 2008/1769 (N.I. 2))—

      (a) Article 20 (child sex offences committed by children or young persons);

      (b) Article 23 (abuse of position of trust: sexual activity with a child);

      (c) Article 24 (abuse of position of trust: causing or inciting a child to engage in sexual activity);

      (d) Article 25 (abuse of position of trust: sexual activity in the presence of a child);

      (e) Article 51 (care workers: sexual activity with a person with a mental disorder);

      (f) Article 53 (care workers: sexual activity in the presence of a person with a mental disorder);

      (g) Article 62 (causing or inciting prostitution for gain);

      (h) Article 63 (controlling prostitution for gain);

      (i) Article 64 (keeping a brothel used for prostitution).

    (2) An offence under Article 32 or 33 of that Order (family child sex offences) where the offence is committed by a person under the age of 18.

    (3) An offence under Article 37 of that Order (paying for sexual services of a child), where the offence is committed against a person aged 16 or over.

24 An offence under section 68 of the Policing and Crime Act 2017 (breach of pre-charge bail conditions relating to travel), or

(c) an offence of attempting or conspiring to commit, or of inciting the commission of, an offence mentioned in paragraph (a) or (b), or

(d) an offence under Part 2 of the Serious Crime Act 2007 (encouraging or assisting crime) in relation to an offence mentioned in paragraph (a) or (b).

Where Scottish officers do not have any statutory or common law powers to detain or arrest a suspect without warrant who is believed to have committed an offence in England and Wales, if there is insufficient evidence for the issue of a warrant, and the case is not sufficiently serious to justify officers travelling to Scotland, Scottish officers can be requested to invite the suspect to attend a police station on a voluntary basis for interview under caution.

When it has not been practicable for an English/Welsh constable to make an arrest, but a constable has gone to Scotland to interview a suspect following arrest or detention by a Scottish constable for Scottish offences, or a person has voluntarily agreed to be interviewed, the English/Welsh constable should comply, insofar as it is practical, with the PACE Codes of Practice, in particular:

- A suspect not under arrest or detention should be told that he/she is not under arrest or detention and that he/she is free to leave.
- A suspect should be told that he/she may seek legal advice and that arrangements are made for legal representation when required. An appropriate adult should also be present when interviewing a youth or a mentally disordered or mentally handicapped person.
- An English/Welsh law caution should be administered. When appropriate, officers should warn arrested suspects of the consequences of failure or refusal to account for objects, substances or marks (s. 36 of the 1994 Act) and the failure or refusal to account for their presence in a particular place (s. 37).
- The interview should be audio recorded if possible.
- If it is not possible to audio record the interview, a contemporaneous written record of the interview should be made. The suspect must be given the opportunity to read the record and to sign it.

Scottish constables interviewing suspects in Scotland when they are aware that the interview is required for a prosecution in England and Wales, should comply with Scottish law. In addition, insofar as it is practical:

- A suspect should be told that he/she may seek legal advice and that arrangements are made for legal representation when required. A solicitor may be present during any subsequent interview if the suspect requires. An appropriate adult should also be present when interviewing a youth or a mentally disordered or mentally vulnerable person.

- When it is certain that the interview evidence will only be used in English/Welsh courts, the appropriate English/Welsh caution should be used.
- The interview should be audio recorded if possible.
- If it is not possible to audio record the interview, a written contemporaneous record of the interview should be made. The suspect must be given the opportunity to read the record and to sign it.

English/Welsh officers should assist interviewing Scottish or Northern Irish officers by providing a schedule of points to be covered in an interview. This could include a list of appropriate questions.

1.10 Release of Person Arrested

1.10.1 Introduction

The release of persons arrested is regulated by the Bail Act 1976, the Police and Criminal Evidence Act 1984 and the Criminal Justice and Public Order Act 1994.

Significant changes to the existing legislation have been made by the Policing and Crime Act 2017 providing for a presumption in favour of releasing a suspect without bail, with bail only being imposed when it is both necessary and proportionate. It also sets out a clear expectation that pre-charge bail should not last longer than 28 days and should only be extendable in complex cases or exceptional circumstances.

1.10.2 Person Arrested Elsewhere than at a Police Station

Where a person is arrested at any place other than a police station, or taken into custody by a constable following an arrest made by a civilian, the constable is normally obliged to take that person to a designated police station (Police and Criminal Evidence Act 1984, s. 30(1), (1A), (1B) and (2)), or in certain circumstances to a non-designated police station ((s. 30(3) to (6)).

An arrested person may, instead of being taken to a police station, be released with bail (known as 'street bail') or without bail to attend at a police station at a later date. The provisions of the 1984 Act in relation to this are detailed below.

1.10.2.1 Release of Arrested Person and Street Bail

The Police and Criminal Evidence Act 1984, s. 30A provides for persons arrested elsewhere than at a police station to be released with or without bail without being required to attend a police station.

Section 30A(1) A constable may release a person who is arrested or taken into custody in the circumstances mentioned in s. 30(1)—
(a) without bail unless subs. (1A) applies, or
(b) on bail if subs. (1A) applies.

Section 30A(1A) This subsection applies if—
(a) the constable is satisfied that releasing the person on bail is necessary and proportionate in all the circumstances (having regard, in particular, to any conditions of bail which would be imposed), and
(b) a police officer of the rank of inspector or above authorises the release on bail having considered any representations made by the person.

Section 30A(2) A person may be released under subs. (1) at any time before he arrives at a police station.

Section 30A(3) A person released on bail under subs. (1) must be required to attend a police station.

Section 30A(3A) Where a constable releases a person on bail under subs. (1)—
(a) no recognizance for the person's surrender to custody shall be taken from the person,
(b) no security for the person's surrender to custody shall be taken from the person or from anyone else on the person's behalf,

(c) the person shall not be required to provide a surety or sureties for his surrender to custody, and

(d) no requirement to reside in a bail hostel may be imposed as a condition of bail.

Section 30A(3B)   Subject to subs. (3A), where a constable releases a person on bail under subs. (1) the constable may impose, as conditions of the bail, such requirements as appear to the constable to be necessary—

(a) to secure that the person surrenders to custody,

(b) to secure that the person does not commit an offence while on bail,

(c) to secure that the person does not interfere with witnesses or otherwise obstruct the course of justice, whether in relation to him or any other person, or

(d) for the person's own protection or, if the person is under the age of 18, for the person's own welfare or in the person's own interests.

Section 30A(4)   Where a person is released on bail under subs. (1), a requirement may be imposed on the person as a condition of bail only under the preceding provisions of this section.

Section 30A(5)   The police station which the person is required to attend may be any police station.

KEYNOTE

Section 30A(3B) enables the officer granting bail to consider attaching conditions relevant and proportionate to the suspect and the offence. The conditions that may be considered are the same as those available to a custody officer as contained in s. 3A(5) of the 1976 Act, except for those specified in s. 30A(3A).

A constable who is satisfied that there are no grounds for keeping the arrested person under arrest or releasing him or her on bail under s. 30A must release that person (s. 30(7) and (7A)).

1.10.2.2   Notice in Writing

Section 30B(1)   Where a constable releases a person under s. 30A, he must give that person a notice in writing before he is released.

Section 30B(2)   The notice must state—

(a) the offence for which he was arrested,

(b) the grounds on which he was arrested, and

(c) whether the person is being released without bail or on bail.

Section 30B(3)   A notice given to a person released on bail must inform him that he is required to attend a police station.

Section 30B(4)   The notice must also specify—

(a) the police station which the person is required to attend, and

(b) the time on the bail end date when the person is required to attend the police station.

Section 30B(4A)   If the person is granted bail subject to conditions under s. 30A(3B), the notice also—

(a) must specify the requirements imposed by those conditions,

(b) must explain the opportunities under ss. 30CA(1) and 30CB(1) for variation of those conditions.

Section 30B(6)   The person may be required to attend a different police station from that specified in the notice under subs. (1) or to attend at a different time or an additional time.

Section 30B(6A)   A person may not be required under subs. (6) to attend at a police station at a time which is after the bail end date in relation to the person.

Section 30B(7)   He must be given notice in writing of any such change as is mentioned in subs. (6) but more than one such notice may be given to him.

Section 30B(8)   In this section 'bail end date', in relation to a person, means the last day of the period of 28 days beginning with the day after the day on which the person was arrested for the offence in relation to which bail is granted under section 30A.

1.10.2.3 Release, Attendance and Re-arrest

Section 30C(1)   A person who has been required to attend a police station is not required to do so if he is given notice in writing that his attendance is no longer required.

Section 30C(2)   If a person is required to attend a police station which is not a designated police station he must be—
(a) released, or
(b) taken to a designated police station, not more than six hours after his arrival.

Section 30C(3)   Nothing in the Bail Act 1976 applies in relation to bail under s. 30A.

Section 30C(4)   Nothing in s. 30A or 30B or in this section prevents the re-arrest without warrant of a person released under s. 30A if, since the person's release, new evidence has come to light or an examination or analysis of existing evidence has been made which could not reasonably have been made before the person's release.

1.10.2.4 Variation of Bail Conditions: Police

Section 30CA(1)   Where a person released on bail under s. 30A(1) is on bail subject to conditions—
(a) a relevant officer at the police station at which the person is required to attend, may, at the request of the person but subject to subs. (2), vary the conditions.

Section 30CA(2)   On any subsequent request made in respect of the same grant of bail, subs. (1) confers power to vary the conditions of the bail only if the request is based on information that, in the case of the previous request or each previous request, was not available to the relevant officer considering that previous request when he/she was considering it.

Section 30CA(3)   Where conditions of bail granted to a person under s. 30A(1) are varied under subs. (1)—
(a) paras (a) to (d) of s. 30A(3A) apply,
(b) requirements imposed by the conditions as so varied must be requirements that appear to the relevant officer varying the conditions to be necessary for any of the purposes mentioned in paras (a) to (d) of s. 30A(3B), and
(c) the relevant officer who varies the conditions must give the person notice in writing of the variation.

Section 30CA(4)   Power under subs. (1) to vary conditions is, subject to subs. (3)(a) and (b), power—
(a) to vary or rescind any of the conditions, and
(b) to impose further conditions.

1.10.2.5 Variation of Bail Conditions: Court

Section 30CB(1) Where a person released on bail under s. 30A(1) is on bail subject to conditions, a magistrates' court may, on an application by or on behalf of the person, vary the conditions if—

(a) the conditions have been varied under s. 30CA(1) since being imposed under s. 30A(3B),

(b) a request for variation under s. 30CA(1) of the conditions has been made and refused, or

(c) a request for variation under s. 30CA(1) of the conditions has been made and the period of 48 hours beginning with the day when the request was made has expired without the request having been withdrawn or the conditions having been varied in response to the request.

> **KEYNOTE**
>
> Where the court varies the conditions they must be seen as necessary for any of the purposes mentioned in s. 30A(3B)(a)–(d), and bail continues subject to the varied conditions (s. 30CB(3)(b) and (c)). It was held in *R (On the Application of Ajaib)* v *Birmingham Magistrates' Court* [2009] EWHC 2127 (Admin) that in deciding to vary bail conditions, the court was entitled to rely on a police officer's evidence whilst allowing him to withhold specific information. In this case the police asserted that they held material disclosure of which would prejudice their inquiries, suggesting that the suspect was liquidating his assets to travel abroad.

1.10.2.6 Power of Arrest for Non-attendance and Breach of Bail Conditions

Section 30D(1) A constable may arrest without warrant a person who—

(a) has been released on bail under s. 30A subject to a requirement to attend a specified police station, but

(b) fails to attend the police station at the specified time.

Section 30D(2) A person arrested under subs. (1) must be taken to a police station (which may be the specified police station or any other police station) as soon as practicable after the arrest.

Section 30D(2A) A person who has been released on bail under s. 30A may be arrested without a warrant by a constable if the constable has reasonable grounds for suspecting that the person has broken any of the conditions of bail.

Section 30D(2B) A person arrested under subs. (2A) must be taken to a police station (which may be the specified police station mentioned in subs. (1) or any other police station) as soon as practicable after the arrest.

Section 30D(3) In subs. (1), 'specified' means specified in a notice under subs. (1) of s. 30B or, if notice of change has been given under subs. (7) of that section, in that notice.

> **KEYNOTE**
>
> Section 30D(1) and (2) relate to a person's failure to answer his/her bail at the specified time and place. Section 30D(2A) and (2B) provide a power of arrest where a constable has reasonable grounds to suspect that a person has broken any of the conditions of bail.

1.10.3 Pre-charge Release of Person Arrested and Bail

The Police and Criminal Evidence Act 1984 provides for the following pre-charge scenarios:

- the custody officer determines that there is sufficient evidence to charge that person with the offence for which he or she was arrested and may detain him or her at the police station for such period as is necessary to enable him or her to do so (s. 37(1));

- the custody officer determines that there is insufficient evidence to charge that person with the offence for which he or she has been arrested, the person shall be released pending the obtaining of further evidence with bail where the pre-conditions for bail are satisfied or without bail (release under investigation) where the pre-conditions for bail are not met (s. 37(2));
- the custody officer has reasonable grounds for believing that the person's detention without being charged is necessary to secure or preserve evidence, then the person may be kept in police detention (s. 37(3));
- subject to s. 41(7) (below), if there is sufficient evidence to charge the person the custody officer shall release the person without charge and on bail or keep the person in police detention, for the purpose of enabling the DPP to make a decision under s. 37B (s. 37(7)(a));
- there is sufficient evidence to charge and the custody officer releases the person without charge and without bail unless the pre-conditions for bail are satisfied (s. 37(7)(b));
- there is sufficient evidence to charge and the custody officer releases the person without charge and on bail if those pre-conditions are satisfied but not for the purpose under s. 37B (s. 37(7)(c));
- there is sufficient evidence and the person is charged (s. 37(7)(d));
- a review officer concludes that the detention of a person without charge can no longer be justified and the custody officer releases the person without bail unless the pre-conditions for bail are satisfied (s. 40(8));
- a person, who at the expiry of 24 hours after the relevant time is in police detention and has not been charged, shall be released at that time without bail unless the pre-conditions for bail are satisfied, or on bail if those pre-conditions are satisfied (s. 41(7)). This subsection does not apply to a person whose detention for more than 24 hours has been authorised or otherwise permitted (s. 41(8)).

KEYNOTE

The decision as to how a person is to be dealt with under subs. (7) above shall be that of the custody officer (s. 37(7A)).

In relation to s. 37(2), the *National Police Chiefs Council's Operational guidance for pre-charge bail and released under investigation* (January 2019) sets out the test for continued investigation in cases where a suspect has been released under investigation (RUI). The RUI process must be capable of withstanding scrutiny, having due regard to proportionality and necessity. Where suspects are subject to RUI, investigations must be conducted expeditiously. Suggested good practice is that investigations must have a documented supervisory review at least every 30 days. Where high priority and safeguarding is an issue, reviews should be every 10 days. Subsequent reviews will be conducted by an inspector at three months and a superintendent at six months.

In relation to s. 37(7)(a) and (c), s. 37B provides for occasions where it is considered necessary to refer the case to the DPP for a decision as to whether there is sufficient evidence to charge the person.

The release on bail of a person under this part of the Act shall be a release on bail granted in accordance with ss. 3, 3A, 5 and 5A of the Bail Act 1976 as they apply to bail granted by a constable (s. 47(1)).

Where a person has been granted bail to attend at a police station (s. 47(3)(b)), a custody officer may subsequently appoint a different time, or an additional time for attendance to answer bail and must give the person notice in writing of any changes (s. 47(4A) and (4B)). A custody officer may not appoint a time for a person's attendance under subs. (4A) which is after the end of the applicable bail period in relation to the person (s. 47(4E)).

If bail conditions have been imposed by the custody officer these may be varied by a magistrates' court on the application of the suspect (s. 47(1E)). The magistrates may confirm or remove the existing conditions or impose other conditions (Criminal Procedure Rules 2020, r. 14.6). Irrespective of the outcome it continues to be police bail.

> A person released on bail under ss. 37(7)(a) and 37(7)(c) who breaches that bail and is arrested under s. 46A (**see para. 1.10.3.3**) shall be charged or released without bail unless the pre-conditions for bail are satisfied, or on bail if those pre-conditions are satisfied (ss. 37C and 37CA).
>
> Nothing prevents the re-arrest without warrant of a person released on bail subject to a duty to attend at a police station if new evidence justifying a further arrest has come to light since his/her release (s. 47(2)).
>
> Where a person is released under s. 41(7) (expiry of 24 hours' detention), s. 42(10) (expiry of authority of continued detention) or s. 43(18) (expiry of warrant of further detention), he or she shall not be re-arrested without a warrant for the offence for which he or she was previously arrested unless, since the person's release, new evidence has come to light or an examination or analysis of existing evidence has been made which could not reasonably have been made before their release.

1.10.3.1 Pre-conditions for Bail

The meaning of 'pre-conditions for bail' (introduced by the Policing and Crime Act 2017) is contained in the Police and Criminal Evidence Act 1984, s. 50A which states:

Interpretation of references to pre-conditions for bail

For the purposes of this Part the following are the pre-conditions for bail in relation to the release of a person by a custody officer—

(a) that the custody officer is satisfied that releasing the person on bail is necessary and proportionate in all the circumstances (having regard, in particular, to any conditions of bail which would be imposed), and

(b) that an officer of the rank of inspector or above authorises the release on bail (having considered any representations made by the person or the person's legal representative).

1.10.3.2 Period of Bail and Extensions

The Police and Criminal Evidence Act 1984 provides a regime of time limits and extensions introduced in respect of pre-charge bail. The following is an overview of these changes.

Applicable Bail Period: Initial Limit

When the custody officer is releasing a person on bail to attend at a police station under s. 47(3)(c), he or she must appoint a time on the day on which the 'applicable bail period' in relation to the person ends (s. 47ZA(1) and (2)).

The 'applicable bail period', in relation to a person, means in a Serious Fraud Office (SFO) case, the period of three months beginning with the person's bail start date, or in a Financial Conduct Authority (FCA) case or any other case, the period of 28 days beginning with the person's bail start date. A person's bail start date is the day after the day on which the person was arrested for the relevant offence (s. 47ZB).

The applicable bail period may be changed by the custody officer where the person is on bail in relation to one or more offences other than the relevant offence and it is appropriate to align the person's attendance in relation to the relevant offence with the person's attendance in relation to one or more other offences (s. 47ZA(3)). This subsection applies where the custody officer believes that a decision as to whether to charge the person with the relevant offence would be made before the end of the applicable bail period in relation to the person (s. 47ZA(4)). Where subs. (3) or (4) applies, the power may be exercised so as to appoint a time on a day falling before the end of the applicable bail period in relation to the person (s. 47ZA(5)).

Applicable Bail Period: Extension of Initial Limit in Standard Cases

Section 47ZD allows a senior police officer (an officer of superintendent rank or above (s. 47ZB(4)(d)) to extend bail from 28 days to three months where the conditions A to D set out in s. 47ZC are met. The senior officer must arrange for the suspect or their legal representative to be invited to make representations, and must consider any that are made before making a decision. The suspect (or their representative) must be informed of the outcome. The four conditions outlined in s. 47ZC are:

Condition A—the officer has reasonable grounds for suspecting the person in question to be guilty of the relevant offence.

Condition B—the officer has reasonable grounds for believing:

(a) in a case where the person in question is or is to be released on bail under s. 37(7)(c) or 37CA(2)(b), that further time is needed for making a decision as to whether to charge the person with the relevant offence, or

(b) otherwise, that further investigation is needed of any matter in connection with the relevant offence.

Condition C—the officer has reasonable grounds for believing:

(a) in a case where the person in question is or is to be released on bail under s. 37(7)(c) or 37CA(2)(b), that the decision as to whether to charge the person with the relevant offence is being made diligently and expeditiously, or

(b) otherwise, that the investigation is being conducted diligently and expeditiously.

Condition D—the decision-maker has reasonable grounds for believing that the release on bail of the person in question is necessary and proportionate in all the circumstances (having regard, in particular, to any conditions of bail which are, or are to be, imposed).

Applicable Bail Period: Extension of Initial Limit in Designated Cases

Pre-charge bail may be extended to a point six months after arrest if the conditions A to D of s. 47ZC are met where a case has been designated as 'exceptionally complex' by a senior prosecutor designated for the purpose by the Director of the SFO, the Chief Executive of the FCA or the DPP. Where so designated by the DPP, a police officer of at least the rank of assistant chief constable (Commander in the Metropolitan or City of London forces), may authorise the applicable bail period in relation to the person to be extended so that it ends at the end of the period of six months beginning with the person's bail start date (s. 47ZE).

Applicable Bail Period: Extensions by Magistrates' Court

Apart from the exception provided by s. 47ZE, pre-charge bail beyond the point three months after arrest must be authorised by a magistrates' court. An application must be made before the previous bail period expires and the court may only authorise an extension of bail where satisfied that conditions B to D as set out in s. 47ZC are met (s. 47ZF). The court may extend the bail period by three months, or where investigations to be made are likely to take more than three to conclude, extend the bail by a further six months. Further extensions of the bail period for periods of three months and six months may be authorised by the court (s. 47ZG).

Withholding Sensitive Information

Section 47ZH provides that the police or prosecutors may apply to the court to withhold certain information relevant to the application to extend bail from the person on bail and their legal representatives. The court may only allow information to be withheld for the four grounds set out in subs. (4)—essentially: that there are reasonable grounds to believe that disclosing that information would lead to evidence being interfered with; a person coming to harm; another suspect escaping arrest for an indictable offence; the recovery of property obtained as a result of an indictable offence being hindered.

Applicable Bail Period: Cases Referred to the DPP

Bail time limits do not apply in cases where an individual is bailed under s. 37(7)(a) or 37C(2)(b) while waiting for a charging decision to be made by the DPP. However, where a charging decision has been requested from the DPP, but the DPP requests further information from the police before reaching that decision, bail time limits will re-apply during the period that the police are gathering that information and, accordingly, the police must set a new bail return date that is not after the end of the person's applicable bail period. If, at the point that the DPP makes the request for further information, the person's applicable bail period would end within seven days of the DPP's request, the person's applicable bail period is extended to seven days from that request in order to give the police time to gather the information, seek a bail extension or release the suspect from bail. Where the information requested by the DPP is provided, the bail time limit is again suspended (s. 47ZL).

1.10.3.3 Power of Arrest for Failure to Answer to Police Bail

The Police and Criminal Evidence Act 1984, s. 46A states:

(1)   A constable may arrest without a warrant any person who, having been released on bail under this Part of this Act subject to a duty to attend at a police station, fails to attend at that police station at the time appointed for him to do so.

(1ZA) The reference in subsection (1) to a person who fails to attend at a police station at the time appointed for him to do so includes a reference to a person who—
    (a) attends at a police station to answer to bail granted subject to the duty mentioned in section 47(3)(b), but
    (b) leaves the police station at any time before the beginning of proceedings in relation to a live link direction under section 57C of the Crime and Disorder Act 1998 in relation to him without informing a constable that he does not intend to give his consent to the direction.

(1ZB) The reference in subsection (1) to a person who fails to attend at a police station at the time appointed for the person to do so includes a reference to a person who—
    (a) attends at a police station to answer to bail granted subject to the duty mentioned in section 47(3)(b), but
    (b) refuses to be searched under section 54B.

(1A)   A person who has been released on bail under this Part may be arrested without warrant by a constable if the constable has reasonable grounds for suspecting that the person has broken any of the conditions of bail.

(2)   A person who is arrested under this section shall be taken to the police station appointed as the place at which he is to surrender to custody as soon as practicable after the arrest.

(3)   For the purposes of—
    (a) section 30 above (subject to the obligation in subsection (2) above), and
    (b) section 31 above,
    an arrest under this section shall be treated as an arrest for an offence.

KEYNOTE

In subs. (1ZB)(a) the reference to s. 47(3)(b) relates to 'live link bail'.

The offence for which a person is arrested under subs. (1) is the offence for which he or she was granted bail (s. 34(7)).

Section 46A(1) provides a power of arrest only where a person *fails to attend at that police station at the time appointed.* This should be contrasted with s. 46A(1A) where a person released on bail under s. 47 may be arrested if there are *reasonable grounds for suspecting that the person has broken any of the conditions of bail.*

1.10.3.4 Breach of Pre-charge Bail Conditions Relating to Travel

OFFENCE: **Breach of Pre-charge Bail Conditions Relating to Travel—*Policing and Crime Act 2017, s. 68***

    • 12 months' imprisonment and/or a fine on indictment • Six months' imprisonment and/or a fine summarily

The Policing and Crime Act 2017, s. 68 states:

(3) The person commits an offence if—

    (a) the person's release on bail is subject to the travel restriction condition mentioned in subsection (2)(a) and he or she fails to comply with the condition, or

    (b) the person's release on bail is subject to a travel restriction condition mentioned in subsection (2)(b) to (f) and he or she fails, without reasonable excuse, to comply with the condition.

KEYNOTE

This offence relates to a person who breaches certain travel-related conditions of pre-charge bail for those arrested on suspicion of committing a terrorist offence.

Each of the following is a travel restriction condition contained in s. 68(2)(a):

(a) the person must not leave the United Kingdom,

(b) the person must not enter any port, or one or more particular ports, in the United Kingdom,

(c) the person must not go to a place in Northern Ireland that is within one mile of the border between Northern Ireland and the Republic of Ireland,

(d) the person must surrender all of his or her travel documents or all of his or her travel documents that are of a particular kind,

(e) the person must not have any travel documents, or travel documents of a particular kind, in his or her possession (whether the documents relate to that person or to another person),

(f) the person must not obtain, or seek to obtain, any travel documents (whether relating to that person or to another person) or travel documents of a particular kind (e.g. passports, travel tickets or other documents that would enable a person to leave the United Kingdom).

The offence would apply where a person has been arrested under s. 24 of PACE or art. 26 of the Police and Criminal Evidence (Northern Ireland) Order 1989 on suspicion of committing a terrorist offence, as listed in s. 41 of the Counter-Terrorism Act 2008, has been released on pre-charge bail subject to a travel restriction condition and subsequently breaches, without reasonable excuse, any of those conditions. The offences listed in s. 41 of the Counter-Terrorism Act 2008 cover a range of offences including membership of a proscribed organisation, fundraising in support of terrorism, and encouraging terrorist acts.

This section provides another tool for the police to tackle terrorism by deterring those arrested on suspicion of a terrorist offence from breaching a travel restriction condition imposed under the terms of their pre-charge bail, and by adding to the range of offences which might be prosecuted in cases where such a person has returned to the United Kingdom.

A 'travel document' means anything that is or appears to be a passport, or a ticket or other document that permits a person to make a journey by any means from a place in the United Kingdom to a place outside the United Kingdom (s. 69(2)). 'Passport' means a UK passport, a passport issued by or on behalf of the authorities of a country or territory outside the United Kingdom (or by or on behalf of an international organisation) or a document that can be used (in some or all circumstances) instead of a passport (s. 69(3)).

The offence can be tried on indictment in the Crown Court, which means that the Criminal Attempts Act 1981 applies so as to make it an offence to attempt to breach a travel restriction condition.

1.10.3.5 Notification of Decision not to Prosecute

The custody officer is under a duty to notify a person released under s. 34, 37 or 37CA if a decision is made not to prosecute that person, either due to there being insufficient evidence, or where there is sufficient evidence but a decision is made that the person should not be charged or cautioned (s. 34(5B)). A notice in writing that the person is not to be prosecuted must be given to the person (s. 34(5C)). However, this does not prevent the prosecution of the person for an offence if new evidence comes to light after the notice was given (s. 34(5D)). These provisions also apply to a person released after the expiry of 24 hours' detention under s. 41(7) (s. 41(10) to (12)).

1.10.4 Police Bail After Charge

Where a person is charged at the police station (otherwise than a warrant backed for bail) the custody officer must make a decision to keep the person in custody until they can be brought before a magistrates' court, or to release the person either on bail or without bail, unless one or more conditions in the Police and Criminal Evidence Act 1984, s. 38, are satisfied (s. 38(1)).

Where the custody officer decides to bail a person who has been charged, s. 47(3) of the 1984 Act provides they may do so:

(a) to appear before a magistrates' court at such time and such place as the custody officer may appoint;

(b) to attend at such police station as the custody officer may appoint at such time as he may appoint for the purposes of—

    (i) proceedings in relation to a live link direction under section 57C of the Crime and Disorder Act 1998 (use of live link direction at preliminary hearings where accused is at police station); and

    (ii) any preliminary hearing in relation to which such a direction is given; or

(c) to attend at such police station as the custody officer may appoint at such time as he may appoint for purposes other than those mentioned in paragraph (b).

KEYNOTE

Where a custody officer grants bail to a person to appear before a magistrates' court, he must appoint for the appearance a date which is not later than the first sitting of the court after the person is charged with the offence. If informed by the court that the appearance cannot be accommodated until a later date, that later date. For a person subject to a duty to appear at a police station, the custody officer may give notice in writing to that person that his/her attendance at the police station is not required (s. 47(3A)).

In *Williamson* v *Chief Constable of West Midlands* [2003] EWCA Civ 337, it was clarified that the Bail Act 1976 does not apply to 'breach of the peace' as it is not a criminal offence.

1.10.5 Bail Restrictions

The Criminal Justice and Public Order Act 1994 provides for those occasions when bail may only be granted in *exceptional circumstances* where a person is charged with certain specified offences. Section 25 of the 1994 Act states:

(1) A person who in any proceedings has been charged with or convicted of an offence to which this section applies in circumstances to which it applies shall be granted bail in those proceedings only if the court or, as the case may be, the constable considering the grant of bail is of the opinion that there are exceptional circumstances which justify it.

(2) This section applies, subject to subsection (3) below, to the following offences, that is to say—

    (a) murder;

    (b) attempted murder;

    (c) manslaughter;

    (d) rape under the law of Scotland;

    (e) an offence under section 1 of the Sexual Offences Act 1956 (rape);

    (f) an offence under section 1 of the Sexual Offences Act 2003 (rape);

    (g) an offence under section 2 of that Act (assault by penetration);

    (h) an offence under section 4 of that Act (causing a person to engage in sexual activity without consent) where the activity caused involved penetration within subsection (4)(a) to (d) of that section;

    (i) an offence under section 5 of that Act (rape of a child under 13);

    (j) an offence under section 6 of that Act (assault of a child under 13 by penetration);

    (k) an offence under section 8 of that Act (causing or inciting a child under 13 to engage in sexual activity), where an activity involving penetration within subsection (3)(a) to (d) of that section was caused;

(l) an offence under section 30 of that Act (sexual activity with a person with a mental disorder impeding choice), where the touching involved penetration within subsection (3)(a) to (d) of that section;

(m) an offence under section 31 of that Act (causing or inciting a person, with a mental disorder impeding choice, to engage in sexual activity), where an activity involving penetration within subsection (3)(a) to (d) of that section was caused;

(n) an attempt to commit an offence within any of paragraphs (d) to (m).

(3) This section applies in the circumstances described in subsection (3A) or (3B) only.

(3A) This section applies where—

(a) the person has been previously convicted by or before a court in any part of the United Kingdom of any offence within subsection (2) or of culpable homicide, and

(b) if that previous conviction is one of manslaughter or culpable homicide—

(i) the person was then a child or young person, and was sentenced to long-term detention under any of the relevant enactments, or

(ii) the person was not then a child or young person, and was sentenced to imprisonment or detention.

(3B) This section applies where—

(a) the person has been previously convicted by or before a court in another member State of any relevant foreign offence corresponding to an offence within subsection (2) or to culpable homicide, and

(b) if the previous conviction is of a relevant foreign offence corresponding to the offence of manslaughter or culpable homicide—

(i) the person was then a child or young person, and was sentenced to detention for a period in excess of 2 years, or

(ii) the person was not then a child or young person, and was sentenced to detention.

(4) This section applies whether or not an appeal is pending against conviction or sentence.

(5) In this section—

'conviction' includes—

(a) a finding that a person is not guilty by reason of insanity;

(b) a finding under section 4A(3) of the Criminal Procedure (Insanity) Act 1964 (cases of unfitness to plead) that a person did the act or made the omission charged against him; and

(c) a conviction of an offence for which an order is made discharging the offender absolutely or conditionally;

and 'convicted' shall be construed accordingly;

'relevant foreign offence', in relation to a member State other than the United Kingdom, means an offence under the law in force in that member State;

'the relevant enactments' means—

(a) as respects England and Wales, section 91 of the Powers of Criminal Courts (Sentencing) Act 2000;

(b) . . .

(c) . . .

(5A) For the purposes of subsection (3B), a relevant foreign offence corresponds to another offence if the relevant foreign offence would have constituted that other offence if it had been done in any part of the United Kingdom at the time when the relevant foreign offence was committed.

KEYNOTE

Section 25 provides that bail may not be granted where a person is charged with murder, attempted murder, manslaughter, rape or attempted rape if he/she has been previously convicted of any of these offences unless there are exceptional circumstances. A person charged with murder may not be granted bail except by order of a Crown Court judge (s. 115 of the Coroners and Justice Act 2009). This does not apply to attempted murder or conspiracy to murder.

Even where a person's custody time limit had expired, s. 25 could still be applied and the evidential burden was on the defence to demonstrate that exceptional circumstances existed. Also, in the case of *Hurnam* v *State of Mauritius* [2005] UKPC 49, the Privy Council stated that the seriousness of the offence is not a conclusive reason for refusing bail and the court must consider whether or not the accused is likely to abscond if released on bail.

In all other cases the custody officer must consider the issue of bail and s. 38(1) of the 1984 Act sets out the occasions where bail can be refused.

1.10.6 Grounds for Refusing Bail

The Police and Criminal Evidence Act 1984, s. 38(1) provides that where an arrested person is charged with an offence, the custody officer, subject to s. 25 of the Criminal Justice and Public Order Act 1994, need not grant bail if the person arrested *is not an arrested juvenile* and one or more of the following grounds apply:

- the person's name or address cannot be ascertained or the custody officer has reasonable grounds for doubting whether a name or address furnished is his/her real name or address;
- the custody officer has reasonable grounds for believing that the person arrested will fail to appear in court to answer to bail;
- in the case of a person arrested for an imprisonable offence, the custody officer has reasonable grounds for believing that the detention of the person arrested is necessary to prevent him/her from committing an offence;
- in a case of a person aged 18 or over, where a sample may be taken from the person under s. 63B (where there is a provision for drug testing in force for that police area and station), the custody officer has reasonable grounds for believing that the detention of the person is necessary to enable the sample to be taken;
- in the case of a person arrested for an offence which is not an imprisonable offence, the custody officer has reasonable grounds for believing that the detention of the person arrested is necessary to prevent him/her from causing physical injury to any other person or from causing loss of or damage to property;
- the custody officer has reasonable grounds for believing that the detention of the person arrested is necessary to prevent him/her from interfering with the administration of justice or with the investigation of offences or of a particular offence;
- the custody officer has reasonable grounds for believing that the detention of the person arrested is necessary for his/her own protection; or
- the person is charged with murder.

If the person arrested is *an arrested juvenile* and one or more of the following grounds apply:

- any of the requirements of paras (a) to (h) above, but in the case of para. (d) only if the arrested juvenile has attained the minimum age;
- the custody officer has reasonable grounds for believing that the arrested juvenile ought to be detained in his/her own interests.

KEYNOTE

Juveniles being detained 'in their own interests' means for their own welfare. The expression 'welfare' has a wider meaning than just 'protection' and might apply to juveniles who, if released, might be homeless or become involved in prostitution or vagrancy (Bail Act 1976, sch. 1, part I, para. (3)).

In taking the decisions required by s. 38(1), except where a defendant's name and address cannot be ascertained, detention is necessary for the person's own protection, or a juvenile is detained in his/her own interests, the custody officer is required to have regard to the same considerations as those which a court is required to have regard to in taking corresponding decisions under the Bail Act 1976, sch. 1, part I, para. 2(1) (s. 38(2A)).

Schedule 1, part I, para. 2(1) provides that the defendant need not be granted bail if the court (custody officer) is satisfied that there are substantial grounds for believing that the defendant, if released on bail (whether subject to conditions or not) would:

- fail to surrender to custody, or
- commit an offence while on bail, or
- interfere with witnesses or otherwise obstruct the course of justice, whether in relation to him/herself or any other person.

In *R (On the Application of Ajaib)* v *Birmingham Magistrates' Court* [2009] EWHC 2127 (Admin), it was held that a police officer's opinion that the accused is a 'flight risk' was sufficient even though the source of information giving rise to the officer's opinion was not disclosed.

Schedule 1, part I, para 9 provides that in taking the decisions required by para. 2(1), the court (custody officer) will have regard to such of the following considerations as appear to be relevant:

(a) the nature and seriousness of the offence or default (and the probable method of dealing with the defendant for it);
(b) the character, antecedents, associations and community ties of the defendant;
(c) the defendant's record as respects the fulfilment of his/her obligations under previous grants of bail in criminal proceedings;
(d) except in the case of a defendant whose case is adjourned for inquiries or a report, the strength of the evidence of his/her having committed the offence or having defaulted;
(e) if the court is satisfied that there are substantial grounds for believing that the defendant, if released on bail (whether subject to conditions or not), would commit an offence while on bail, the risk that the defendant may do so by engaging in conduct that would, or would be likely to, cause physical or mental injury to any person other than the defendant, as well as to any others which appear to be relevant. This includes domestic violence where a person is associated with the accused within the meaning of the Family Law Act 1996, s. 62.

Where bail is refused, the custody officer must inform the detained person of the reasons why and make an entry as to these reasons in the custody record (s. 38(3) and (4)). This must be done as soon as the decision to refuse bail is made unless the conditions set out in PACE, Code C, para. 1.8. apply, i.e. the person is incapable of understanding, is violent or is in urgent need of medical attention. In such cases, the person must be informed as soon as practicable.

The decision regarding bail is part of the process of investigation of crime with a view to prosecution and so the police enjoy immunity in respect of decisions to refuse bail (*Gizzonio* v *Chief Constable of Derbyshire* (1998) *The Times*, 29 April).

In relation to the detention of juveniles where bail has been refused, see para. 1.7.17, Charging Detained Persons and para. 1.7.17.1, Juveniles and Appropriate Adults.

1.10.7   Bail Consideration by the Custody Officer

The granting of bail in criminal proceedings is provided by s. 3 of the Bail Act 1976 and this section examines the general provisions in relation to bail granted by a custody officer, the conditions that may be attached and applications to vary or remove those conditions.

1.10.7.1   General Provisions

Section 3 states:

(1) A person granted bail in criminal proceedings shall be under a duty to surrender to custody, and that duty is enforceable in accordance with section 6 of this Act.
(2) No recognizance for his surrender to custody shall be taken from him.
(3) Except as provided by this section—
    (a) no security for his surrender to custody shall be taken from him,
    (b) he shall not be required to provide a surety or sureties for his surrender to custody, and
    (c) no other requirement shall be imposed on him as a condition of bail.
(4) He may be required, before release on bail, to provide a surety or sureties to secure his surrender to custody.
(5) He may be required, before release on bail, to give security for his surrender to custody. The security may be given by him or on his behalf.
(6) He may be required to comply, before release on bail or later, with such requirements as appear to the court to be necessary—
    (a) to secure that he surrenders to custody,
    (b) to secure that he does not commit an offence while on bail,

(c) to secure that he does not interfere with witnesses or otherwise obstruct the course of justice whether in relation to himself or any other person,

(ca) for his own protection or, if he is a child or young person, for his own welfare or in his own interests.

KEYNOTE

Guidance to courts, applicable also to a custody officer, when approaching the decision to grant bail was given in *R v Mansfield Justices, ex parte Sharkey* [1985] QB 613, where it was held that any relevant risk, for example, absconding, must be a 'real' risk, not just a fanciful one.

Where a custody officer grants bail there is a requirement for a record to be made of the decision in the prescribed manner and containing the prescribed particulars. If requested, a copy of the record of the decision must, as soon as practicable, be given to the person in relation to whom the decision was taken (s. 5(1)).

1.10.7.2 Custody Officer: Conditions of Bail

The power of a custody officer to impose bail conditions is provided by s. 3A of the 1976 Act, which states:

(5) Where a constable grants bail to a person no conditions shall be imposed under subsections (4), (5), (6) or (7) of section 3 of this Act unless it appears to the constable that it is necessary to do so—

   (a) for the purpose of preventing that person from failing to surrender to custody, or

   (b) for the purpose of preventing that person from committing an offence while on bail, or

   (c) for the purpose of preventing that person from interfering with witnesses or otherwise obstructing the course of justice, whether in relation to himself or any other person, or

   (d) for that person's own protection, or if he is a child or young person, for his own welfare or in his own interests.

KEYNOTE

Subsection 3(7) relates to a parent/guardian standing surety for a person under the age of seventeen (see para. 1.10.7.4).

Where a custody officer decides to grant bail and considers one or more of the requirements in s. 3A(5)(a)–(d) apply, one or more of the following conditions can be imposed:

- the accused is to live and sleep at a specified address;
- the accused is to notify any changes of address;
- the accused is to report periodically (daily, weekly or at other intervals) to his/her local police station;
- the accused is restricted from entering a certain area or building or to go within a specified distance of a specified address;
- the accused is not to contact (whether directly or indirectly) the victim of the alleged offence and/or any other probable prosecution witness;
- the accused is to surrender his/her passport;
- the accused's movements are restricted by an imposed curfew between set times (i.e. when it is thought the accused might commit offences or come into contact with witnesses);
- the accused is required to provide a surety or security.

In *McDonald v Dickson* [2003] SLT 476, it was held that a condition for an accused to remain in his dwelling at all times except between 10 am and 12 noon did not amount to detention or deprivation of his liberty and did not constitute an infringement of his right to liberty under the European Convention on Human Rights, Article 5.

A bail condition prohibiting a person from residing at their home address was held to be disproportionate even where the police were investigating a serious offence of racially aggravated harassment against neighbours (*R (On the Application of Carson) v Ealing Magistrates' Court* [2012] EWHC 1456 (Admin)).

In relation to non-imprisonable offences it has been held that a hunt protester who was arrested for an offence under s. 5 of the Public Order Act 1986 was rightly required as a condition of his bail not to attend another hunt meeting before his next court appearance (*R v Bournemouth Magistrates' Court, ex parte Cross* [1989] Crim LR 207).

1.10.7.3 Applications to Vary or Remove Bail Conditions

The power to vary or remove conditions is provided by s. 3A of the Bail Act 1976. Section 3A(4) substitutes s. 3(8) and states:

> Where a custody officer has granted bail in criminal proceedings he or another custody officer serving at the same police station may, at the request of the person to whom it was granted, vary the conditions of bail and in doing so he may impose conditions or more onerous conditions.

KEYNOTE

Section 3A(5) (see para. 1.2.7.2) also applies on any request to a custody officer to vary or remove conditions of bail.

There is a requirement that a custody officer either imposing or varying the conditions of bail must include a note of the reasons in the custody record and give a copy of that note to the person in relation to whom the decision was taken (s. 5A(3)).

An accused may also apply to the magistrates' court under s. 43B(1) of the Magistrates' Courts Act 1980, to vary conditions of police bail. The prosecution may apply to the magistrates' court to reconsider bail and vary the conditions of bail, impose conditions in respect of bail that has been granted unconditionally, or withhold bail (s. 5B(1)). This only applies to bail granted by the magistrates' court or a constable and only in relation to offences triable on indictment or either way (s. 5B(2)). The application can only be on the basis of information that was not available to the court or constable when the original decision was taken (s. 5B(3)).

1.10.7.4 Police Bail: Surety

The Bail Act 1976, s. 8 states:

(1) This section applies where a person is granted bail in criminal proceedings on condition that he provides one or more surety or sureties for the purpose of securing that he surrenders to custody.

(2) In considering the suitability for that purpose of a proposed surety, regard may be had (amongst other things) to—

    (a) the surety's financial resources;

    (b) his character and any previous convictions of his; and

    (c) his proximity (whether in point of kinship, place of residence or otherwise) to the person for whom he is to be surety.

KEYNOTE

The question as to whether or not sureties are necessary is at the discretion of the custody officer (or court). A person cannot stand as his/her own surety (s. 3(2)).

There is no power to grant conditional bail with a surety to ensure no further offending; a surety can be sought only for the purpose of securing surrender to custody and not for any other purpose (*R (On the Application of Shea) v Winchester Crown Court* [2013] EWHC 1050 (Admin)).

The decision as to the suitability of individual sureties is a matter for the custody officer. Where no surety, or suitable surety, is available, the custody officer can fix the amount of cash or security in which the surety is to be bound for the purpose of enabling the recognizance of the surety to be entered into subsequently (s. 8(3)).

Where a court grants bail but is unable to release the person where no surety or no suitable surety is available, the court may fix the amount in which the surety is to be bound, and the recognizance of the surety may later be entered into before a police officer who is either of the rank of inspector or above or who is in charge of a police station, or other person as specified in s. 8(4) in conjunction with the Criminal Procedure Rules 2020, r. 14.14.

The normal consequence for a surety, where an accused fails to answer bail, is that he/she is required to forfeit the entire cash or security in which he/she stood surety. The power to forfeit recognizances is a matter for a court (Magistrates' Courts Act 1980, s. 120).

It is not necessary to prove that the surety had any involvement in the accused's non-appearance (*R* v *Warwick Crown Court, ex parte Smalley* [1987] 1 WLR 237). However, in *R* v *York Crown Court, ex parte Coleman* (1988) 86 Cr App R 151, it was held that where a surety had taken all reasonable steps to ensure the accused's appearance the recognizance ought not to be forfeited.

The Bail Act 1976 provides that a surety may notify a constable *in writing* that the accused is unlikely to surrender to custody and for that reason he/she wishes to be relieved of his/her obligations as surety. This written notification provides a constable with the power to arrest the accused without warrant (s. 7(3)).

Where a parent or guardian of a person under the age of 17 consents to be surety, they may be required to secure that the person complies with any requirement imposed by virtue of s. 3(6) (**see para. 1.10.7.1**). No requirement shall be imposed on the parent or guardian where it appears that the person will attain the age of 17 before the time to be appointed for their surrender to custody (s. 3(7)).

1.10.7.5 Security

A person granted bail may be required to give security for his/her surrender to custody (Bail Act 1976, s. 3(5)). The security can be money or some other valuable item which will be liable to forfeiture in the event of non-attendance in answer to bail.

A security may be required as a condition of bail but only if it is considered necessary to prevent the person absconding.

A third party may make an asset available to an accused to enable him/her to provide it as security for his/her release on bail (*R (On the Application of Stevens)* v *Truro Magistrates' Court* [2001] EWHC Admin 558).

1.10.7.6 Acknowledging Bail

OFFENCE: **Acknowledging Bail in the Name of Another—*Forgery Act 1861, s. 34***
   • Triable on indictment • Seven years' imprisonment

The Forgery Act 1861, s. 34 states:

> Whosoever, without lawful authority or excuse (the proof whereof shall lie on the party accused), shall in the name of any other person acknowledge any recognizance or bail, ... or judgment or any deed or other instrument, before any court, judge, or other person lawfully authorised in that behalf, shall be guilty of felony ...

KEYNOTE

This offence occurs where a person impersonates another person for the purpose of acting as a surety.

Provided the bail or recognizance is valid, this offence would appear to apply equally to bail granted by a court or the police.

1.10.8 Live Link Bail

The use of a live link at preliminary hearings where the accused is at a police station is provided by the Crime and Disorder Act 1998. Section 57C of the Act states:

(1)   This section applies in relation to a preliminary hearing in a magistrates' court.

(2)   Where subsection (3) or (4) applies to the accused, the court may give a live link direction in relation to his attendance at the preliminary hearing.

(3)   This subsection applies to the accused if—
   (a)   he is in police detention at a police station in connection with the offence; and

(b) it appears to the court that he is likely to remain at that station in police detention until the beginning of the preliminary hearing.

(4) This subsection applies to the accused if he is at a police station in answer to live link bail in connection with the offence.

(5) A live link direction under this section is a direction requiring the accused to attend the preliminary hearing through a live link from the police station.

(6) But a direction given in relation to an accused to whom subsection (3) applies has no effect if he does not remain in police detention at the police station until the beginning of the preliminary hearing.

(6A) A live link direction under this section may not be given unless the court is satisfied that it is not contrary to the interests of justice to give the direction.

KEYNOTE

A magistrates' court may rescind a live link direction under this section at any time during a hearing to which it relates (s. 57C(8)).

Where a live link direction is given to an accused who is answering to live link bail he/she is to be treated as having surrendered to the custody of the court (as from the time when the direction is given) (s. 57C(10)).

The accused is to be treated as present in court when he/she attends via a live link and he/she must be able to see and hear, and to be seen and heard by, the court during the hearing (s. 57A(2)).

In this section, 'live link bail' means bail granted under part 4 of the Police and Criminal Evidence Act 1984 subject to the duty mentioned in s. 47(3)(b) of that Act (s. 57C(11)).

A person who fails to answer to live link bail or leaves the police station at any time before the beginning of proceedings in relation to a live link direction may be arrested (for s. 46A of the Police and Criminal Evidence Act 1984, see para. 1.10.3.3).

1.10.8.1 Searches of Persons Answering to Live Link Bail

The Police and Criminal Evidence Act 1984, s. 54B states:

(1) A constable may search at any time—
   (a) any person who is at a police station to answer to live link bail; and
   (b) any article in the possession of such a person.

(2) If the constable reasonably believes a thing in the possession of the person ought to be seized on any of the grounds mentioned in subsection (3) the constable may seize and retain it or cause it to be seized and retained.

(3) The grounds are that the thing—
   (a) may jeopardise the maintenance of order in the police station;
   (b) may put the safety of any person in the police station at risk; or
   (c) may be evidence of, or in relation to, an offence.

(4) The constable may record or cause to be recorded all or any of the things seized and retained pursuant to subsection (2).

(5) An intimate search may not be carried out under this section.

(6) The constable carrying out a search under subsection (1) must be of the same sex as the person being searched.

KEYNOTE

A constable may retain a thing seized under s. 54B in order to establish its lawful owner where there are reasonable grounds for believing that it has been obtained in consequence of the commission of an offence (s. 54C(2)).

If a thing seized under s. 54B may be evidence of, or in relation to, an offence, a constable may retain it for use as evidence at a trial for an offence, or for forensic examination or for investigation in connection with an offence (s. 54C(3)).

Nothing may be retained for either of the purposes mentioned in subs. (3) if a photograph or copy would be sufficient for that purpose (s. 54C(4)).

Designated detention officers, as well as constables, can use the powers in ss. 54B and 54C to search and seize. Anything seized by a designated detention officer must be delivered to a constable as soon as practicable and in any case before the person from whom the thing was seized leaves the police station (Police Reform Act 2002, sch. 4, part 3, para. 27A).

Section 46A(1ZB) (see para. 1.10.3.3) provides a constable with a power of arrest for defendants who attend the police station to answer live link bail but refuse to be searched under s. 54B.

1.10.9   Liability to Arrest for Absconding or Breaking Bail Conditions

The Bail Act 1976, s. 7 states:

(1)   If a person who has been released on bail in criminal proceedings and is under a duty to surrender into the custody of a court fails to surrender to custody at the time appointed for him to do so the court may issue a warrant for his arrest.

(1A)   Subsection (1B) applies if—
(a)   a person has been released on bail in connection with extradition proceedings;
(b)   the person is under a duty to surrender into the custody of a constable; and
(c)   the person fails to surrender to custody at the time appointed for him to do so.

(1B)   A magistrates' court may issue a warrant for the person's arrest.

(2)   If a person who has been released on bail in criminal proceedings absents himself from the court at any time after he has surrendered into the custody of the court and before the court is ready to begin or to resume the hearing of the proceedings, the court may issue a warrant for his arrest but no warrant shall be issued under this subsection where that person is absent in accordance with leave given to him by or on behalf of the court.

(3)   A person who has been released on bail in criminal proceedings and is under a duty to surrender into the custody of a court may be arrested without warrant by a constable—
(a)   if the constable has reasonable grounds for believing that person is not likely to surrender to custody;
(b)   if the constable has reasonable grounds for believing that that person is likely to break any of the conditions of his bail or has reasonable grounds for suspecting that that person has broken any of those conditions; or
(c)   in a case where that person was released on bail with one or more surety or sureties, if a surety notifies a constable in writing that that person is unlikely to surrender to custody and that for that reason the surety wishes to be relieved of his obligations as a surety.

KEYNOTE

Breach of conditions of bail is not a Bail Act offence, nor is it a contempt of court unless there is some additional feature (*R* v *Ashley* [2003] EWCA Crim 2571).

Where a person is arrested under s. 7 he/she shall be brought before a magistrate as soon as practicable and in any event within 24 hours (s. 7(4)(a)). However, in the case of a person charged with murder, or with murder and one or more other offences, he/she must be brought before a judge of the Crown Court (s. 7(8)).

This section requires that a detainee not merely be brought to the court precincts or cells but actually be dealt with by a justice within 24 hours of being arrested (*R (On the Application of Culley)* v *Dorchester Crown Court* [2007] EWHC 109 (Admin)).

In *R* v *Evans* [2011] EWCA Crim 2842, the Court of Appeal stated:

The general practice of accepting surrender by way of entry into the dock accords not only with common experience and general practice but also with principle ... Crown Court surrender may also be accomplished by the commencement of any hearing before the judge where the defendant is formally identified and whether he enters the dock or not.

The word 'court' includes a judge of the court or a justice of the peace. Also a bail notice stating a particular time of attendance is a notice that may happen at any time from 9.30 am onwards. Mere arrival at the Crown Court building does not constitute surrender, neither does reporting to an advocate. Surrender has to be accomplished personally by the defendant.

Section 7 does not create an offence, it merely confers a power of arrest (*R* v *Gangar* [2008] EWCA Crim 2987).

1.10.10   Offence of Absconding by Person Released on Bail

The Bail Act 1976 s. 6 creates two offences in relation to absconding and states:

(1) If a person who has been released on bail in criminal proceedings fails without reasonable cause to surrender to custody he shall be guilty of an offence.
(2) If a person who—
   (a) has been released on bail in criminal proceedings, and
   (b) having reasonable cause therefor, has failed to surrender to custody, fails to surrender to custody at the appointed place as soon after the appointed time as is reasonably practicable he shall be guilty of an offence.

KEYNOTE

Section 6 applies where:

- the police grant bail to a suspect to appear at the police station;
- the police grant bail to a defendant to appear at court on the first appearance;
- the court grants bail to the defendant to return to court at a later date.

The burden of proof in relation to showing 'reasonable cause' (s. 6(1)) is a matter for the accused (s. 6(3)).

A person who has 'reasonable cause' still commits the offence if he/she fails to surrender 'as soon after the appointed time as is reasonably practicable'. Where an accused was half an hour late in appearing at court it was held that he/she had absconded (*R* v *Scott* [2007] EWCA Crim 2757). In *Laidlaw* v *Atkinson* (1986) *The Times*, 2 August, it was held that being mistaken about the day on which one should have appeared was not a reasonable excuse. Also, there is no requirement on the court to inquire as to whether a person arrested for failing to comply with bail conditions had any reasonable excuse for breaching bail (*R (On the Application of Vickers)* v *West London Magistrates' Court* (2003) EWHC 1809 (Admin)).

Failure to give to a person granted bail in criminal proceedings a copy of the record of the decision does not constitute reasonable cause for that person's failure to surrender to custody (s. 6(4)).

Failing to answer bail granted by a police officer is a summary offence and the decision to initiate proceedings is for the police/prosecutor using the written charge and requisition procedure. Such an offence may not be tried unless proceedings are commenced either within six months of the commission of the offence, or within three months: (a) after the person surrenders to custody at the appointed place; (b) is arrested, or attends at a police station, in connection with the bail offence or the offence for which he/she was granted bail; or (c) the person appears or is brought before a court in connection with the bail offence or the offence for which he/she was granted bail (s. 6(12)–(14)).

1.10.11   Remands in Police Custody

Where a person is remanded in custody it normally means detention in prison. However, s. 128 of the Magistrates' Courts Act 1980 provides that a magistrates' court may remand a person to police custody:

- for a period not exceeding three clear days (24 hours for persons under 18 (s. 91(5) of the Legal Aid, Sentencing and Punishment of Offenders Act 2012) (s. 128(7));
- for the purpose of inquiries into offences (other than the offence for which he/she appears before the court) (s. 128(8)(a));
- as soon as the need ceases he/she must be brought back before the magistrates (s. 128(8)(b));
- the conditions of detention and periodic review apply as if the person was arrested without warrant on suspicion of having committed an offence (s. 128(8)(c) and (d)).

1.11 Disclosure of Evidence
Criminal Procedure and Investigations Act 1996 and Code of Practice

A thick grey line down the margin denotes text that is an extract of the Code itself (i.e. the actual wording of the legislation).

1.11.1 Introduction

During 2017 there were a number of high-profile cases that collapsed due to failures in the management of the disclosure of material by the police, attracting considerable adverse comment and risking public confidence. Also during 2017 Her Majesty's Inspectorate of Constabulary (HMIC), in collaboration with Her Majesty's Crown Prosecution Service Inspectorate (HMCPSI) published their report: 'Making it fair—a joint inspection of the disclosure of unused material in volume Crown Court cases'. This inspection identified a number of issues which are contributing to widespread failures across the board by both police and prosecutors. Additionally, in November 2018 the Attorney General's Review of the efficiency and effectiveness of disclosure in the criminal justice system highlighted significant concerns with the culture around disclosure, engagement between prosecutors, investigators and defence practitioners, and the challenge of the exponential increase in digital data. The A-G's Review made a series of practical recommendations, which included earlier engagement between the prosecution and defence, harnessing the use of technology and culture change.

Disclosure can be grouped under two main areas: the material the prosecution will use in court to prove the case against the defendant, and all other material not forming part of the prosecution case which might have a bearing on the decision the court makes.

The Criminal Procedure and Investigations Act 1996 (the 1996 Act) is made up of seven parts. It is the first two parts which are of interest to the police:

- part I sets out the procedures for disclosure and the effects of failing to comply with the Act; and
- part II sets out the duties of police officers in relation to the disclosure provisions.

The 1996 Act introduced a Code of Practice which sets out the manner in which police officers are to record, retain and reveal to the prosecutor material obtained in a criminal investigation and which may be relevant to the investigation, and related matters. The Code assumes that the defence have already been informed of the details of the prosecution case and is included within this chapter. In addition to the Code of Practice this chapter also makes reference to the Attorney-General's Guidelines on Disclosure for Investigators, Prosecutors and Defence Practitioners (referred to in this chapter as the A-G's Guidelines); as well as the CPS Disclosure Manual. The Codes of Practice and the A-G's Guidelines have both been updated as of December 2020. *R v Gohil and Preko* [2018] EWCA Crim 140 highlighted the importance of the essential need for coordination between investigators, prosecutors and independent counsel with their separate roles.

1.11.2 Failure to Comply

Compliance with the rules of disclosure, by both the defence and prosecution, is essential if the 1996 Act is to have any real value. First, in cases where the defence are obliged to make disclosure to the prosecution, failure to do so may lead to the court or jury drawing such inferences as appear proper in deciding the guilt or innocence of the accused (s. 11(5) of the 1996 Act). Should the prosecution fail to comply with their obligations then an accused does not have to make defence disclosure and no such inference can be made. Secondly, failure by the prosecution to comply with the rules could lead to the court staying the proceedings on the grounds that there has been an abuse of process (s. 10). It could also lead to an action for damages or such other relief as the court sees fit under the Human Rights Act 1998, particularly in relation to Article 6 of the European Convention on Human Rights and the right to a fair trial. Additionally, where the prosecution have not made disclosure on time or fully, a stay on the proceedings or a further adjournment is possible. Even if there has been a failure to comply with disclosure the case will not automatically be stayed and therefore any failings should be brought to the attention of the CPS so that the matter can be considered. In *R (On the Application of Ebrahim)* v *Feltham Magistrates' Court* [2001] EWHC Admin 130 the court stated that:

> It must be remembered that it is commonplace in a criminal trial for the defendant to rely on holes in the prosecution case. If in such a case, there is sufficient credible evidence, apart from the missing evidence, which, if believed, would justify safe conviction then the trial should proceed, leaving the defendant to seek to persuade the jury or magistrates not to convict because evidence that might otherwise have been available was not before the court through no fault of the defendant.

Further guidance was provided in *R* v *Brooks* [2004] EWCA Crim 3537, a case where the prosecution failed to comply with the disclosure requirements. The Court of Appeal held that if the court was satisfied that the prosecution had deliberately withheld evidence from the court or frustrated the defence, the court did have the power to stay the prosecution. If the court was not so satisfied it would consider whether, despite all that had gone wrong, a fair trial was possible.

Failure to disclose may result in convictions being overturned; for instance in *R* v *Poole* [2003] EWCA Crim 1753, the Court of Appeal overturned convictions for murder because the non-disclosure of prosecution evidence influenced the jury's assessment of the reliability of the evidence of a key eye-witness. In this case the witness gave an account that was false in a material particular. However, the police did not follow up those inconsistencies and they failed to inform the CPS that his evidence was unreliable.

The level of disclosure that is required will be a question of fact in each case. In *Filmer* v *DPP* [2006] EWHC 3450 (Admin) the court held that the extent of disclosure required from the prosecution depends on the evidence and issue in a particular case. The prosecution are required to provide sufficient disclosure to enable a defendant to present his/her case. The court went on to say that this has to be the approach otherwise the prosecution would have to second guess every question the defence may want to ask (this is where the defence disclosure becomes relevant, **see para. 1.11.11.1**).

1.11.3 Disclosing Initial Details of the Prosecution Case

This refers to the material that the defence are entitled to have in order to consider whether to plead guilty or not guilty. In some cases, it is not a question of whether the defendant committed the crime but whether the prosecution are in a position to prove the offence and, in order to consider this, the defence are unlikely to agree to plead or decide on the mode of trial without knowing the strength of the prosecution case. It is clearly in the public interest that guilty pleas are entered or indicated as soon as possible (*R* v *Calderdale*

Magistrates' Court, ex parte Donahue [2001] Crim LR 141) and often this cannot be achieved unless advanced information has been provided. The need to know as early as possible whether a defendant is going to plead not guilty can be particularly important as there are time limits by which the courts have to set trials and committals. Often these can be delayed because the prosecution have not complied with their disclosure duties.

Ensuring that all defendants receive copies of any initial details of the prosecution case (or any later disclosure) is also important. In *R v Tompkins* [2005] EWCA Crim 3035 the court held that where there has been non-disclosure at the time a plea had been entered, a defendant who had pleaded guilty should not in any way be in a worse position than a defendant who had pleaded not guilty.

1.11.3.1 Obligations on Prosecution Regarding Disclosing the Initial Details of the Prosecution Case

In the magistrates' court, Part 8 of the Criminal Procedure Rules 2020 provides that where the offence is one that can be tried in a magistrates' court the prosecutor must provide initial details of the prosecution case to the court and the defendant as soon as practicable, and in any event no later than the beginning of the day of the first hearing. These initial details must include (r. 8.3):

(a) where, immediately before the first hearing in the magistrates' court, the defendant was in police custody for the offence charged—
  (i) a summary of the circumstances of the offence, and
  (ii) the defendant's criminal record, if any;
(b) where paragraph (a) does not apply—
  (i) a summary of the circumstances of the offence,
  (ii) any account given by the defendant in interview, whether contained in that summary or in another document,
  (iii) any written witness statement or exhibit that the prosecutor then has available and considers material to plea, or to the allocation of the case for trial, or to sentence,
  (iv) the defendant's criminal record, if any, and
  (v) any available statement of the effect of the offence on a victim, a victim's family or others.

For trials at the Crown Court, the defence will receive the majority of the prosecution case through the disclosure of witness statements or depositions. If the prosecution wish to use any additional evidence after committal they must serve this on the defence.

It is suggested that Article 6 of the European Convention on Human Rights supports the need to provide initial details of the prosecution case to the defence in all cases and that this should be done as soon as possible. Article 6(3)(a) states that a person is:

… to be informed promptly … and in detail, of the nature and cause of the accusation against him;

Article 6(3)(b) states that an accused is entitled to:

… have adequate time … for the preparation of his defence.

However, the point concerning initial information in summary cases was considered in *R v Stratford Justices, ex parte Imbert* [1999] 2 Cr App R 276, where the court gave its opinion that Article 6 does not give an absolute right to pre-trial disclosure; it will be a question of whether the defendant can have a fair trial. Clearly, it will be easier to satisfy this test where initial information has been provided to the defence. This information might also include the following and so consideration should be had to providing this material to the prosecutor so that he/she can forward it to the defence where appropriate (ensuring that the addresses and other details of witnesses and victims are protected):

- a copy of the custody record;
- copies of any interview tape(s);
- a copy of any first descriptions where relevant;

- significant information that might affect a bail decision or enable the defence to contest the allocation hearing (A-G's Guidelines, para. 78 and CPIA Code, para. 6.5);
- any material which is relevant to sentence (e.g. information which might mitigate the seriousness of the offence or assist the accused to lay blame in whole or in part upon a co-accused or another person);
- statements and/or a summary of the prosecution cases;
- a copy of any video evidence.

(For the actual disclosure that must be provided to the prosecutor in order to allow the defence to prepare their case, **see para. 1.11.9.**)

Where a person has made several statements but all the relevant evidence for the prosecution case is contained in one statement, it is only that one statement which needs to be disclosed. In order to comply with disclosing the initial details of the prosecution case the defence need to be either given a copy of the document or allowed to inspect the document (or a copy of it). In *R* v *Lane and Lane* [2011] EWCA Crim 2745 one of the witnesses refused to put incriminating evidence into his statement due to fear of repercussions. The police had notified the prosecution of the witness's increased knowledge, but the prosecution failed to notify the defence that the statement had been a partial account. The Court of Appeal held that the statement was untruthful as it did not disclose all the information that it should have done. The witness should have been told to make a full statement or he should have been abandoned as a witness, but he should never have been allowed to make a partial statement.

The following sections set out the Disclosure Code of Practice issued under the Criminal Procedure and Investigations Act 1996; the latest Code came into effect on 31 December 2020.

1.11.4 | Disclosure Code of Practice—1 Introduction

1.1 This Code of Practice applies in respect of criminal investigations conducted by police officers which begin on or after the day on which this Code comes into effect. Persons other than police officers who are charged with the duty of conducting an investigation as defined in the Act are to have regard to the relevant provisions of the Code, and should take these into account in applying their own operating procedures.

1.2 This Code does not apply to persons who are not charged with the duty of conducting an investigation as defined in the Act.

1.3 Nothing in this Code applies to material intercepted in obedience to a warrant issued under section 2 of the Interception of Communications Act 1985 or section 5 of the Regulation of Investigatory Powers Act 2000, or to any copy of that material as defined in section 10 of the 1985 Act or section 15 of the 2000 Act and by sections of the Investigatory Powers Act 2016.

1.4 This Code extends only to England and Wales.

1.11.4.1 KEYNOTE

Aims of the 1996 Act

The aim of the disclosure rules within the Criminal Procedure and Investigations Act 1996 is to make sure that a defendant gets a fair trial and speeds up the whole trial process. This was confirmed by *R* v *Stratford Justices, ex parte Imbert* [1999] 2 Cr App R 276, where the court said that the legislation was to try to ensure that nothing which might assist the defence was kept from the accused.

The Act creates an initial duty on the prosecution to disclose with a continuing duty to disclose until the accused is acquitted or convicted or the prosecutor decides not to proceed with the case.

The following diagram, which is taken from para. 16 of the A-G's Guidelines, illustrates how material that forms part of an investigation may be categorised and consequently treated.

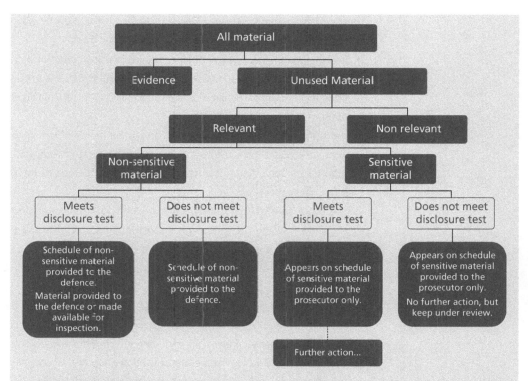

The prosecution must, from the start, consider any material that might undermine the prosecution case or assist the defence (s. 3 of the 1996 Act). It is submitted that this requires the prosecution to consider in more detail the types of defence that might be used at trial. Once the prosecution have provided their initial disclosure the defence in some cases are obliged to provide a defence statement and in other cases this is optional (see para. 1.11.11.1). Once the defence have provided their defence statement it may provide greater focus to the prosecution as to what other unused material may need to be disclosed.

While the duty of disclosure is placed on the prosecutor, the police have a responsibility to assist in this process. It is therefore vital that police officers understand, not only the statutory requirements made of them, but also the extent of their role within the whole disclosure process.

The HMIC report found that police are routinely failing to comply with guidance and requirements when completing and recording data, such as the non-sensitive disclosure schedule (known as MG6C). Many officers submitted schedules that had missing or deficient data and were often ignorant of processes behind sensitive material, such as information for warrants. The inspection found that in 33% of cases the disclosure officer's report, the MG6E, was either not supplied at all or was wholly inadequate. It is the responsibility of the disclosure officer to comply with the disclosure rules, but it is suggested there is also a supervisory responsibility as well.

1.11.5 Disclosure Code of Practice—2 Definitions

2.1 In this Code:

- *a criminal investigation* is an investigation conducted by police officers with a view to it being ascertained whether a person should be charged with an offence, or whether a person charged with an offence is guilty of it. This will include:
  - investigations into crimes that have been committed;
  - investigations whose purpose is to ascertain whether a crime has been committed, with a view to the possible institution of criminal proceedings; and
  - investigations which begin in the belief that a crime may be committed, for example when the police keep premises or individuals under observation for a period of time, with a view to the possible institution of criminal proceedings;

- charging a person with an offence includes prosecution by way of summons or postal requisition;
- *an investigator* is any police officer involved in the conduct of a criminal investigation. All investigators have a responsibility for carrying out the duties imposed on them under this Code, including in particular recording information, and retaining records of information and other material;
- the *officer in charge of an investigation* is the police officer responsible for directing a criminal investigation. They are also responsible for ensuring that proper procedures are in place for recording information, and retaining records of information and other material, in the investigation;
- the *disclosure officer* is the person responsible for examining material retained by the police during the investigation; revealing material to the prosecutor during the investigation and any criminal proceedings resulting from it, and certifying that they have done this; and disclosing material to the accused at the request of the prosecutor;
- the *prosecutor* is the authority responsible for the conduct, on behalf of the Crown, of criminal proceedings resulting from a specific criminal investigation;
- *material* is material of any kind, including information and objects, which is obtained or inspected in the course of a criminal investigation and which may be relevant to the investigation. This includes not only material coming into the possession of the investigator (such as documents seized in the course of searching premises) but also material generated by them (such as interview records);
- *sensitive material* is material, the disclosure of which, the disclosure officer believes, would give rise to a real risk of serious prejudice to an important public interest;
- references to *prosecution disclosure* are to the duty of the prosecutor under sections 3 and 7A of the Act to disclose material which is in their possession or which they have inspected in pursuance of this Code, and which might reasonably be considered capable of undermining the case against the accused, or of assisting the case for the accused;
- references to the disclosure of material to a person accused of an offence include references to the disclosure of material to his legal representative;
- references to police officers and to the chief officer of police include those employed in a police force as defined in section 3(3) of the Prosecution of Offences Act 1985.

1.11.5.1   **KEYNOTE**

Criminal Investigation

Section 1 of the Criminal Procedure and Investigations Act 1996 defines in which type of cases the disclosure provisions apply. In reality, this applies to all cases other than those where the defendant pleads guilty at the magistrates' court. These rules only apply where no criminal investigation into the alleged offence took place before 1 April 1997. If an investigation began before 1 April 1997, then it will be necessary to refer to the common law rules; however, NPCC has stated that the 1996 Act should be followed in all cases when considering disclosure. For those investigations that started after 4 April 2005, the amendments introduced by the Criminal Justice Act 2003 will apply.

Some guidance is given by the case of *R v Uxbridge Magistrates' Court, ex parte Patel* (2000) 164 JP 209, as to the time an investigation begins. There it was said that the phrase 'criminal investigation' in s. 1(3) of the 1996 Act means that a criminal investigation could begin into an offence before it was committed. This could be so in a surveillance case or where a series of offences was committed, some before and some after the appointed day. Whether in any given case that was the correct view would be a question of fact for the court to determine.

Section 1 also defines a criminal investigation and states:

(4) For the purposes of this section a criminal investigation is an investigation which police officers or other persons have a duty to conduct with a view to it being ascertained—
   (a) whether a person should be charged with an offence, or
   (b) whether a person charged with an offence is guilty of it.

Consequently, this part of the Act also applies to other people, besides the police, who carry out investigations where they have a duty to ascertain whether criminal offences have been committed (e.g. National Crime Agency, HM Revenue and Customs, Department of Work and Pensions investigators). It does not apply to those whose primary responsibility does not relate to criminal offences (e.g. local authorities and schools).

1.11.5.2

KEYNOTE

Disclosure Officer

A disclosure officer can be a police officer or civilian. If not appointed at the start of an investigation, a disclosure officer must be appointed in sufficient time to be able to prepare the unused material schedules for inclusion in the full file submitted to the CPS (CPS Disclosure Manual, chapter 3).

1.11.5.3

KEYNOTE

Prosecutor

This role is defined by s. 2(3) of the 1996 Act as being 'any person acting as prosecutor whether an individual or a body'. In other words, the person who will be taking the case to court. On most occasions, this will be the CPS. It would also apply to the Serious Fraud Office or the Data Protection Registrar. In the case of private prosecutions, the prosecutor is obliged to comply with the disclosure provisions of the 1996 Act but does not have to comply with the Code of Practice. The prosecutor is responsible for ensuring that initial disclosure is made to the defence as well as any further disclosure as required under the continuing duty to disclose. The prosecutor should also be available to advise the OIC, disclosure officer and investigators on matters relating to the relevance of material recorded and retained by police, sensitive material and any other disclosure issues that might arise.

   Should there need to be an application to the court to withhold material because of public interest (**see para. 1.11.9.3**), this will be done through the prosecutor.

   A more detailed explanation of the roles and responsibilities of the prosecutor are set out in the CPS Disclosure Manual.

1.11.5.4

KEYNOTE

Relevant Material

The material will be *relevant* whether or not it is beneficial to the prosecution case, weakens the prosecution case or assists the defence case. It is not only material that will become 'evidence' in the case that should be considered; any information, record or thing which may have a bearing on the case can be material for the purposes of disclosure. The way in which evidence has been obtained may in itself be relevant.

   As restated in the 2017 HMIC inspection, disclosure of unused material is a key component of the investigative and prosecution process. It should be considered at the point where a criminal investigation commences, continue at the point of charge, and be at the forefront as the case progresses and at every subsequent court hearing. Every unused item that is retained by police and considered relevant to an investigation should be reviewed to ascertain whether its existence is capable of undermining the prosecution or assisting the defence case. If either factor applies, unless certain restrictions apply, it must be disclosed to the defence.

   What is relevant to the offence is once again a question of fact, and will not include everything. In *DPP* v *Metten* (1999) 22 January, unreported, it was claimed that the constables who had arrested the defendant had known the identities of potential witnesses to the arrest and these had not been disclosed. The court said that this was not relevant to the case as it did not fall within the definition of an investigation in s. 2(1) of the 1996 Act in that it concerned the time of arrest, and not what happened at the time the *offence* was committed. Paragraphs 5.4 and 5.5 of the Code give guidance on items that might be considered to be relevant material in a case.

Relevant material may relate to the credibility of witnesses, such as previous convictions, the fact that they have a grudge against the defendant, or where a witness is subsequently shown to be unreliable (*R* v *Dunn* [2016] EWCA Crim 1392). It might even include the weather conditions for the day if relevant to the issue of identification. It may include information that house-to-house inquiries were made and that no one witnessed anything.

Particularly at the early stages of an investigation (sometimes not until the defence statement is provided outlining the defence case), it may not be possible to know whether material is relevant. If in doubt, it should be recorded and placed on the appropriate schedule of unused material. Throughout the case, investigators and all others involved should continually review the material in the light of the investigation.

Material includes information given orally. Where relevant material is not recorded in any way, it will need to be reduced into a suitable form (CPS Disclosure Manual, chapter 4).

1.11.6 Disclosure Code of Practice—3 General Responsibilities

3.1 The functions of the investigator, the officer in charge of an investigation and the disclosure officer are separate. Whether they are undertaken by one, two or more persons will depend on the complexity of the case and the administrative arrangements within each police force. Where they are undertaken by more than one person, close consultation between them is essential to the effective performance of the duties imposed by this code.

3.2 In any criminal investigation, one or more deputy disclosure officers may be appointed to assist the disclosure officer, and a deputy disclosure officer may perform any function of a disclosure officer as defined in paragraph 2.1.

3.3 The chief officer of police for each police force is responsible for putting in place arrangements to ensure that in every investigation the identity of the officer in charge of an investigation and the disclosure officer is recorded. The chief officer of police for each police force shall ensure that disclosure officers and deputy disclosure officers have sufficient skills and authority, commensurate with the complexity of the investigation, to discharge their functions effectively. An individual must not be appointed as disclosure officer, or continue in that role, if that is likely to result in a conflict of interest, for instance, if the disclosure officer is the victim of the alleged crime which is the subject of the investigation. The advice of a more senior officer must always be sought if there is doubt as to whether a conflict of interest precludes an individual acting as disclosure officer. If thereafter the doubt remains, the advice of a prosecutor should be sought.

3.4 The officer in charge of an investigation may delegate tasks to another investigator, to civilians employed by the police force, or to other persons participating in the investigation under arrangements for joint investigations, but they remain responsible for ensuring that these have been carried out and for accounting for any general policies followed in the investigation. In particular, it is an essential part of their duties to ensure that all material which may be relevant to an investigation is retained, and either made available to the disclosure officer or (in exceptional circumstances) revealed directly to the prosecutor.

3.5 In conducting an investigation, the investigator should pursue all reasonable lines of inquiry, whether these point towards or away from the suspect. What is reasonable in each case will depend on the particular circumstances. It is a matter for the investigator, with the assistance of the prosecutor if required, to decide what constitutes a reasonable line of inquiry in each case.

3.6 If the officer in charge of an investigation believes that other persons may be in possession of material that may be relevant to the investigation, and if this has not been obtained under paragraph 3.5 above, they should ask the disclosure officer to inform them of the existence of the investigation and to invite them to retain the material in case they receive a request for its disclosure. The disclosure officer should inform the prosecutor that they may have such material. However, the officer in charge of an investigation is not required to make speculative enquiries of other persons; there must be some reason to believe that they may have relevant material. That reason may come from information provided to the police by the accused or from other inquiries made or from some other source.

3.7 If, during a criminal investigation, the officer in charge of an investigation or disclosure officer for any reason no longer has responsibility for the functions falling to them, either their supervisor or the police officer in charge of criminal investigations for the police force concerned must assign someone else to assume that responsibility. That person's identity must be recorded, as with those initially responsible for these functions in each investigation.

1.11.6.1

KEYNOTE

General Responsibility of the Disclosure Officer

The disclosure officer creates the link between the investigation team and the prosecutor (CPS) and is therefore very important to the disclosure process. For investigations carried out by the police, generally speaking there is no restriction on who performs this role; however, they must be suitably trained and experienced. The role and responsibility of the disclosure officer is set out in the CPS Disclosure Manual, chapter 3:

- examine, inspect, view or listen to all relevant material that has been retained by the investigator and that does not form part of the prosecution case;
- create schedules that fully describe the material;
- identify all material which satisfies the disclosure test using the MG6E;
- submit the schedules and copies of disclosable material to the prosecutor;
- at the same time, supply to the prosecutor a copy of material falling into any of the categories described in para. 7.3 of the Code and copies of all documents required to be routinely revealed and which have not previously been revealed to the prosecutor;
- consult with and allow the prosecutor to inspect the retained material;
- review the schedules and the retained material continually, particularly after the defence statement has been received, identify to the prosecutor material that satisfies the disclosure test using the MG6E and supply a copy of any such material not already provided;
- schedule and reveal to the prosecutor any relevant additional unused material pursuant to the continuing duty of disclosure;
- certify that all retained material has been revealed to the prosecutor in accordance with the Code;
- where the prosecutor requests the disclosure officer to disclose any material to the accused, give the accused a copy of the material or allow the accused to inspect it.

As stated at the start of this keynote the disclosure officer has a responsibility to communicate effectively with the prosecutor ensuring that all the schedules are completed properly and all material is examined to satisfy themselves that there is no further material that should be brought to the attention of the prosecutor.

1.11.6.2

KEYNOTE

Reasonable Lines of Inquiry

An officer who is classed as an investigator must pursue all reasonable lines of inquiry (Code, para. 3.5) and having done so retain all material which is relevant to the case (**see para. 1.11.8.1**), whether or not it is helpful to the prosecution (Code, para. 5.1). Failure to do so could lead to a miscarriage of justice. In *R v Poole* [2003] EWCA Crim 1753, Y provided a statement to police in a murder case. It transpired that N had been with Y at the relevant time and this cast doubt over Y's evidence. The police did not follow up the inconsistencies. The Court of Appeal held that the failure to disclose N's evidence was a material irregularity which in part led to a successful appeal by the defendant. The investigator also has a responsibility to identify material that could be sensitive and bring this to the attention of the CPS. This need to be proactive was reinforced in *R v Joof* [2012] EWCA

Crim 1475 where the court held that the responsibilities imposed by the Criminal Procedure and Investigations Act 1996 and the A-G's Guidelines could not be circumvented by not making inquiries. An officer who believed that a person might have information which might undermine the prosecution case or assist the defence could not decline to make inquiries in order to avoid the need to disclose what might be said. Where material is identified steps must be taken to record and retain the material. For information recorded on computers, see 'Digital Guidance', chapter 30 of the CPS Disclosure Manual and Annex A to the A-G's Guidelines.

1.11.6.3 **KEYNOTE**

Pre-charge Engagement with Suspects or their Legal Advisors

In some investigations it may be appropriate for the officer in charge of the investigation to seek engagement with the defence at the pre-charge stage. This is likely to be where it is possible that such engagement will lead to the defence volunteering additional information which may assist in identifying new lines of inquiry. Pre-charge engagement in these circumstances refers to voluntary engagement between the parties to an investigation after the first PACE interview, and before any suspect has been formally charged. Pre-charge engagement is a voluntary process and it may be terminated at any time. It does not refer to engagement between the parties to an investigation by way of further PACE interviews (A-G's Guidelines, paras 26 and B3). Annex B of the A-G's Guideline sets out the process for any such pre-charge engagement.

Pre-charge engagement may take place whenever it is agreed between the parties that it may assist the investigation. The engagement should not, however, be considered a replacement to a further interview with a suspect. Investigators and prosecutors should be conscious that adverse inferences under s. 34 of the Criminal Justice and Public Order Act 1994 are not available at trial where a suspect failed to mention a fact when asked about a matter in pre-charge engagement.

This engagement may, among other things, involve:

a. Giving the suspect the opportunity to comment on any proposed further lines of inquiry.
b. Ascertaining whether the suspect can identify any other lines of inquiry.
c. Asking whether the suspect is aware of, or can provide access to, digital material that has a bearing on the allegation.
d. Discussing ways to overcome barriers to obtaining potential evidence, such as revealing encryption keys.
e. Agreeing any key word searches of digital material that the suspect would like carried out.
f. Obtaining a suspect's consent to access medical records.
g. The suspect identifying and providing contact details of any potential witnesses.
h. Clarifying whether any expert or forensic evidence is agreed and, if not, whether the suspect's representatives intend to instruct their own expert, including timescales for this.

Depending on the circumstances, it may be appropriate for an investigator, the prosecutor, the suspect's representative or an unrepresented suspect to initiate pre-charge engagement. Where a suspect is not yet represented, an investigator should take care to ensure that the suspect understands their right to legal advice before the pre-charge engagement process commences. Sufficient time should be given to enable a suspect to access this advice if they wish to do so.

When referring a case to a prosecutor, the investigator should inform the prosecutor if any pre-charge engagement has already taken place and should indicate if they believe pre-charge engagement would benefit the case. It should also be noted that the prosecutor may advise the investigator to initiate and carry out pre-charge engagement, or do so themselves (A-G's Guidelines, Appendix B).

1.11.6.4 **KEYNOTE**

Material that Undermines the Prosecution Case

Material that undermines the prosecution test will consist mainly of material which raises question marks over the strength of the prosecution case, the value of evidence given by witnesses and issues relating to identification. If officers feel that the material is not relevant to the prosecution case but may be useful to the defence in cross-examination, it may well come within the category of material which undermines the prosecution case. In *Tucker* v *CPS* [2008] EWCA Crim 3063, the prosecution did not reveal to the defence a record containing important information as to a possible motive for a witness lying about the defendant's involvement in the offence. This led to the conviction being overturned. It was clearly material that undermined the prosecution case as it raised questions over the value of the witness's evidence.

Disclosure of previous convictions and other matters that might affect the credibility of a witness may 'undermine the prosecution case' as it may limit the value of the witness's testimony. This factor may not be apparent at the time but may come to light after the initial disclosure, such as where it becomes known that the witness has a grudge against the defendant. This is one reason why the 1996 Act requires the decision as to whether material undermines the prosecution case to be continuously monitored throughout the case.

In *R (On the Application of Ebrahim,* v *Feltham Magistrates' Court* [2001] EWHC Admin 130 the court stated that the extent of the investigation should be proportionate to the seriousness of the matter being investigated. What is reasonable in a case may well depend on such factors as the staff and resources available, the seriousness of the case, the strength of evidence against the suspect and the nature of the line of inquiry to be pursued. If in doubt it is suggested that the CPS is contacted for guidance.

Paragraph 5.16 of the CPS Disclosure Manual makes important observations concerning negative results: when making inquiries, 'negative results can sometimes be as significant to an investigation as positive ones'. It is impossible to define precisely when a negative result may be significant, as every case is different. However, it will include the result of any inquiry that differs from what might be expected, given the prevailing circumstances. Not only must material or information which points towards a fact or an individual be retained, but also that which casts doubt on the suspect's guilt, or implicates another person. Examples of negative information include:

- a CCTV camera that did not record the crime/location/suspect in a manner which is consistent with the prosecution case (the fact that a CCTV camera did not function or have videotape loaded will not usually be considered relevant negative information);
- where a number of people present at a particular location at the particular time that an offence is alleged to have taken place state that they saw nothing unusual;
- where a finger-mark from a crime scene cannot be identified as belonging to a known suspect;
- any other failure to match a crime scene sample with one taken from the accused.

1.11.6.5

KEYNOTE

Complaints against Police Officers Involved in a Case

Not only might the credibility of witnesses undermine the prosecution case, but so too might complaints against officers involved in the case, together with any occasions where officers have not been believed in court in the past. In these cases, it will be necessary to decide whether this information should be disclosed to the defence and, if disclosed, in how much detail. This question is probably best answered by the following extract from advice given to prosecutors by the DPP:

It is, of course, necessary in the first instance for the police to bring such matters to the notice of the prosecutor, but it is submitted that the prosecutor should have a greater element of discretion than with the disclosure of previous convictions. With convictions against prosecution witnesses, disclosure normally follows, whereas in relation to disciplinary findings regard should be had to the nature of the finding and its likely relevance to the matters in issue. Findings which involve some element of dishonesty should invariably be disclosed, while matters such as disobedience to orders, neglect of duty and discreditable conduct will often have no relevance to the officer's veracity or the guilt or otherwise of a defendant. Certainly, there should be no duty on the prosecution to disclose details of unsubstantiated complaints even though this is a popular type of inquiry from some defence representatives. The imposition of such a duty would only encourage the making of false complaints in the hope that they might be used to discredit an officer in the future.

Professional Standards Departments (PSDs) have final responsibility for the value judgement on whether information relating to misconduct of police officers should be revealed to the prosecutor. This decision must be made on a case-by-case basis; guidance may be sought from the prosecutor. Responsibility to reveal relevant misconduct findings, or criminal convictions or cautions, rests with the police officer concerned. The officer, assisted by the PSD, should ensure that there is a sufficient level of detail on the MG6B to enable the CPS to make an informed decision about disclosure of the information in the proceedings in question (CPS Disclosure Manual, chapter 18).

Some guidance is given by the courts. In *R* v *Edwards* [1991] 1 WLR 207 the court held that a disciplinary finding and reprimand of a DCI for countersigning interview notes which had been wrongly re-written in another case should have been disclosed to the defence. *R* v *Guney* [1998] 2 Cr App R 242 followed *Edwards*. In *Guney* six police officers went to the defendant's home with a warrant to search for drugs. Three of the officers had formerly been members of a squad which had been subject to 'considerable internal police interest'. The court held that the defence were not entitled to be informed of every occasion when any officer had given evidence 'unsuccessfully' or whenever allegations were made against him/her. In this case, the information should have been disclosed. The court went on to say that the records available to the CPS should include transcripts of any decisions of the Court of Appeal Criminal Division where convictions were quashed because of the misconduct or lack of veracity of identified police officers as well as cases stopped by the trial judge or discontinued on the same basis. The systematic collection of such material was preferable to the existing haphazard arrangement.

If in doubt advice should be sought from the CPS.

1.11.6.6

KEYNOTE

Third Party Material

Third party material can be considered in two categories:

(a) that which is or has been in the possession of the police or which has been inspected by the police;
(b) all other material not falling under (a).

Material which falls into the first category is covered by the same rules of disclosure as any other material the police have. Where police do not have material that they believe may be relevant to the case, para. 3.6 of the Code provides direction.

In the vast majority of cases the third party will make the material available to the investigating officer. However, there may be occasions where the third party refuses to hand over the material and/or allow it to be examined.

If the OIC, the investigator or the disclosure officer believes that a third party holds material that may be relevant to the investigation, that person or body should be told of the investigation. They should be alerted to the need to preserve relevant material. Consideration should be given as to whether it is appropriate to seek access to the material and, if so, steps should be taken to obtain such material. It will be important to do so if the material or information is likely to undermine the prosecution case, or to assist a known defence. A letter should be sent to the third party together with the explanatory leaflet provided in the CPS Disclosure Manual at Annex B.

Where access to the material is declined or refused by the third party and it is believed that it is reasonable to seek production of the material before a suspect is charged, the investigator should consider making an application under sch. 1 to the Police and Criminal Evidence Act 1984 (special procedure material) (CPS Disclosure Manual, chapter 5).

Where the suspect has been charged and the third party refuses to produce the material, application will have to be made to the court for a witness summons. In the magistrates' court this is covered by s. 97 of the Magistrates' Courts Act 1980 and in the Crown Court it is covered by ss. 2(2) and 2A to 2D of the Criminal Procedure (Attendance of Witnesses) Act 1965. The third party may still wish to resist the requirement to produce the material and the point was considered in *R* v *Brushett* [2001] Crim LR 471 (this was a case that concerned Social Services Department files relating to a children's home). The court considered a number of earlier cases and established some central principles as follows:

• To be material evidence documents must be not only relevant to the issues arising in the criminal proceedings, but also documents admissible as such in evidence.
• Documents which are desired merely for the purpose of possible cross-examination are not admissible in evidence and, thus, are not material for the purposes of s. 97.

- Whoever seeks production of documents must satisfy the justices with some evidence that the documents are 'likely to be material' in the sense indicated, likelihood for this purpose involving a real possibility, although not necessarily a probability.
- It is not sufficient that the applicant merely wants to find out whether or not the third party has such material documents. This procedure must not be used as a disguised attempt to obtain discovery.
- Where social services documents are supplied to the prosecution, the prosecution should retain control of such material as part of the disclosure regime. That is envisaged by the rules. It cannot be acceptable to return material to social services to avoid the obligations arising under the rules. In any event, the obligation would arise in relation to the notes taken and retained.
- The obligation laid on the prosecution by statute and rules cannot be avoided by a third party making an agreement with the prosecution that the prosecution will abrogate any duties laid upon it by either common law or statute.
- If circumstances arise where it would be unjust not to allow disclosure of certain other material, so a defendant would not receive a fair trial in the sense that he/she could not establish his innocence where he/she might otherwise do so, then that material must be disclosed.
- The fact that the prosecution have knowledge of the third party material may be a relevant factor to allow the defence access.
- Material concerning false allegations in the past may be relevant material (*R* v *Bourimech* [2002] EWCA Crim 2089).
- If the disputed material might prove the defendant's innocence or avoid a miscarriage of justice, the weight came down resoundingly in favour of disclosing it (*R* v *Reading Justices, ex parte Berkshire County Council* (1996) 1 Cr App R 239).

In *R* v *Alibhai* [2004] EWCA Crim 681 the Court of Appeal held that under the Criminal Procedure and Investigations Act 1996 the prosecutor was only under a duty to disclose material in the hands of third parties if that material had come into the prosecutor's hands and the prosecutor was of the opinion that such material undermined the case. However, the A-G's Guidelines went further by requiring a prosecutor to take steps pursuing third party disclosure if there was a suspicion that documents would be detrimental to the prosecution or of assistance to the defence. However, in such circumstances, the prosecutor enjoyed a margin of consideration as to what steps were appropriate. The provisions for disclosure are not intended to create duties for third parties to follow. The disclosure duties under the 1996 Act were created in respect of material that the prosecution or the police had and which the prosecution had inspected. Material was not prosecution material unless it was held by the investigator or by the disclosure officer (*DPP* v *Wood and McGillicuddy* [2006] EWHC 32 (Admin)).

The A-G's Guidelines also deal with materials held by third parties (including government agencies) in paras 26–53.

The CPIA Code and A-G's Guidelines make clear the obligation on the investigator to pursue all reasonable lines of inquiry in relation to material held by third parties within the UK. Paragraphs 31–33 deal with cases where a government department or another Crown body has material that may be relevant to an issue in the case. Paragraphs 38–44 deal with other domestic bodies that have material or information which might be relevant to the case, such as a local authority, social services department, hospital, doctor, school, provider of forensic services or CCTV operator.

Crown servants have a duty to support the administration of justice and should take reasonable steps to identify and consider such material. If access is denied to relevant material, the investigator or prosecutor should consider the reasons given by the government department or Crown body and what, if any, further steps might be taken to obtain the material. The final decision on further steps rests with the prosecutor. However, other third parties have no obligation under the CPIA 1996 to reveal material to investigators or prosecutors. There is also no duty on the third party to retain material which may be relevant to the investigation and, in some circumstances, the third party may not be aware of the investigation or prosecution. If access to the material is refused and, despite the reasons given for refusal of access, it is still believed that it is reasonable to seek production of the material or information and that the requirements of a witness summons are satisfied (or any other relevant power), then the prosecutor or investigator should apply for the summons causing a representative of the third party to produce the material to court (A-G's Guidelines, paras 40 and 41).

The obligations under the CPIA Code to pursue all reasonable lines of inquiry apply to material held overseas. Where it appears that there is relevant material, the prosecutor must take reasonable steps to obtain it, either informally or making use of the powers contained in the Crime (International Co-operation) Act 2003 and any international conventions. There is no absolute duty on the prosecutor to disclose relevant material held overseas by entities not subject to the jurisdiction of the courts in England and Wales. However, consideration should be given to whether the type of material believed to be held can be provided to the defence (A-G's Guidelines, paras 45–53).

In all cases of material held by third parties, where appropriate the defence should be informed of the steps taken to obtain material and the results of the line of inquiry (A-G's Guidelines, paras 37, 44 and 53).

1.11.7 Disclosure Code of Practice—4 Recording of Information

4.1 If material which may be relevant to the investigation consists of information which is not recorded in any form, the officer in charge of an investigation must ensure that it is recorded in a durable or retrievable form.

4.2 Where it is not practicable to retain the initial record of information because it forms part of a larger record which is to be destroyed, its contents should be transferred as a true record to a durable and more easily-stored form before that happens.

4.3 Negative information is often relevant to an investigation. If it may be relevant it must be recorded. An example might be a number of people present in a particular place at a particular time who state that they saw nothing unusual.

4.4 Where information which may be relevant is obtained, it must be recorded at the time it is obtained or as soon as practicable after that time. This includes, for example, information obtained in house-to-house enquiries, although the requirement to record information promptly does not require an investigator to take a statement from a potential witness where it would not otherwise be taken.

1.11.7.1 KEYNOTE

Contemporaneous Records

The need for contemporaneous records is also required under the Police and Criminal Evidence Act 1984 and if not complied with could affect the admissibility of important evidence (s. 78 of the 1984 Act).

1.11.8 Disclosure Code of Practice—5 Retention of Material

(a) Duty to retain material

5.1 The investigator must retain material obtained in a criminal investigation which may be relevant to the investigation. Material may be photographed, video-recorded, captured digitally or otherwise retained in the form of a copy rather than the original at any time, if the original is perishable; the original was supplied to the investigator rather than generated by them and is to be returned to its owner; or the retention of a copy rather than the original is reasonable in all the circumstances.

5.2 Where material has been seized in the exercise of the powers of seizure conferred by the Police and Criminal Evidence Act 1984, the duty to retain it under this Code is subject to the provisions on the retention of seized material in section 22 of that Act.

5.3 If the officer in charge of an investigation becomes aware as a result of developments in the case that material previously examined but not retained (because it was not thought to be relevant) may now be relevant to the investigation, they should, wherever practicable, take steps to obtain it or ensure that it is retained for further inspection or for production in court if required.

5.4 The duty to retain material includes in particular the duty to retain material falling into the following categories:

- Records which are derived from tapes or recordings of telephone messages (for example, 999 calls) containing descriptions of an alleged offence or offender;
- Any incident logs relating to the allegation;
- Contemporaneous records of the incident, such as:
  - crime reports and crime report forms;
  - an investigation log;
  - any record or note made by an investigator (including police notebook entries and other handwritten notes) on which they later make a statement or which relates to contact with suspects, victims or witnesses;
  - an account of an incident or information relevant to an incident noted by an investigator in manuscript or electronically;
  - records of actions carried out by officers (such as house-to-house interviews, CCTV or forensic enquiries) noted by a police officer in manuscript or electronically;
  - CCTV footage, or other imagery, of the incident in action;
- The defendant's custody record or voluntary attendance record;
- Any previous accounts made by a complainant or any other witnesses;
- Interview records (written records, or audio or video tapes, of interviews with actual or potential witnesses or suspects);
- Any material casting doubt on the reliability of a witness e.g. relevant previous convictions and relevant cautions of any prosecution witnesses and any co accused;
- Final versions of witness statements (and draft versions where their content differs from the final version), including any exhibits mentioned (unless these have been returned to their owner on the understanding that they will be produced in court if required);
- Material relating to other suspects in the investigation;
- Communications between the police and experts such as forensic scientists, reports of work carried out by experts, and schedules of scientific material prepared by the expert for the investigator, for the purposes of criminal proceedings;
- Records of the first description of a suspect by each potential witness who purports to identify or describe the suspect, whether or not the description differs from that of subsequent descriptions by that or other witnesses.

5.5 The duty to retain material, where it may be relevant to the investigation, also includes in particular the duty to retain any material which may satisfy the test for prosecution disclosure in the Act, such as:

- information provided by an accused person which indicates an explanation for the offence with which they have been charged;
- any material casting doubt on the reliability of a confession;
- any material casting doubt on the reliability of a prosecution witness.

5.6 The duty to retain material falling into these categories does not extend to items which are purely ancillary to such material and possess no independent significance (for example, duplicate copies of records or reports).

(b) Length of time for which material is to be retained

5.7 All material which may be relevant to the investigation must be retained until a decision is taken whether to institute proceedings against a person for an offence.

5.8 If a criminal investigation results in proceedings being instituted, all material which may be relevant must be retained at least until the accused is acquitted or convicted or the prosecutor decides not to proceed with the case.

5.9 Where the accused is convicted, all material which may be relevant must be retained at least until:

- the convicted person is released from custody, or discharged from hospital, in cases where the court imposes a custodial sentence or a hospital order;
- six months from the date of conviction, in all other cases.

If the court imposes a custodial sentence or hospital order and the convicted person is released from custody or discharged from hospital earlier than six months from the date of conviction, all material which may be relevant must be retained at least until six months from the date of conviction.

5.10 If an appeal against conviction is in progress when the release or discharge occurs, or at the end of the period of six months specified in paragraph 5.9, all material which may be relevant must be retained until the appeal is determined. Similarly, if the Criminal Cases Review Commission is considering an application at that point in time, all material which may be relevant must be retained at least until the Commission decides not to refer the case to the Court.

1.11.8.1

KEYNOTE

Retention of Material

In order to disclose material to the defence, there is a need first to find it and secondly to retain it. Retention of material applies to documents and other evidence, including digital media. Failure to retain material could lead to the prosecution losing the case, particularly where the court considers that its absence will lead to the defendant not being able to receive a fair trial (Article 6 of the European Convention on Human Rights). In *Mouat* v *DPP* [2001] EWHC Admin 130 the defendant had been charged with speeding. Police officers had recorded a video of the defendant driving at speed and had shown the video to the defendant prior to charge but had later recorded over it. The defendant contended that he had been intimidated by the unmarked police car being driven only inches from his rear bumper. The policy of the force was to keep videos for 28 days, unless they recorded an offence, in which case they were kept for 12 months. The court held that the police were under a duty to retain the video tapes at least until the end of the suspended enforcement period, during which time the defendant was entitled to consider whether he wished to contest his liability in court.

In deciding what material should be retained in an investigation, consideration should be given to any force orders, what powers there are to seize and retain the said material, as well as the Disclosure Code and the A-G's Guidelines. Where an investigator discovers material that is relevant to the case, he/she must record that information or retain the material (Code, para. 5.1).

When deciding if the material should be retained the A-G's Guidelines provide that:

> The investigator should also exercise considerable caution in reaching that conclusion. The investigator should be particularly mindful of the fact that some investigations continue over some time. Material that is incapable of impact may change over time and it may not be possible to foresee what the issues in the case will be.
>
> (A-G's Guidelines, para. 23)

It is important to note that the material itself does not have to be admissible in court for it to undermine the prosecution case. This point was made in *R* v *Preston* [1994] 2 AC 130, where it was said that:

> In the first place, the fact that an item of information cannot be put in evidence by a party does not mean that it is worthless. Often, the train of inquiry which leads to the discovery of evidence which is admissible at a trial may include an item which is not admissible, and this may apply, although less frequently, to the defence as well as the prosecution.

If, during the lifetime of a case, the OIC becomes aware that material which has been examined during the course of an investigation, but not retained, becomes relevant as a result of new developments, para. 5.3 of the Code will apply. That officer should take steps to recover the material wherever practicable, or ensure that it is preserved by the person in possession of it (CPS Disclosure Manual, chapter 5).

In some of these cases the investigation may well have started some time before the defendant became a suspect. In such cases all the material from the investigation/operation would have to be reviewed to see if it is relevant to the defence case. In cases where there is a surveillance operation or observation point, it may be that the details of the observation point and the surveillance techniques would not be revealed but it would be necessary to retain material generating from it (see para. 1.11.9.3).

KEYNOTE

CCTV

The likelihood of an incident being caught on CCTV can be quite strong, which raises the question as to the responsibility of the police to investigate the possibility of there being a recording and retaining the recording tape. This point was considered in *R (On the Application of Ebrahim) v Feltham Magistrates' Court* [2001] EWHC Admin 130. These cases related to the obliteration of video evidence. In coming to its judgment, the court considered a number of previous decisions where the police were not required to retain CCTV evidence. The general question for the court was whether the prosecution had been under a duty to obtain or retain video evidence. If there was no such duty, the prosecution could not have abused the process of the court simply because the material was no longer available, i.e. it was a reasonable line of inquiry (as to whether they were under a duty to obtain the evidence, **see para. 1.11.6.2**). *Ebrahim* shows that CCTV footage does not necessarily have to be retained in all cases. *R v Dobson* [2001] EWCA Crim 1606 followed *Ebrahim*. Dobson had been convicted of arson with intent to endanger life, his defence being that he was elsewhere at the time. There had been a strong possibility that the route that Dobson claimed to have taken would have been covered by CCTV but it would have depended on which side of the road he had been using and which way the cameras were pointing at the time. Dobson's solicitors had not asked for the tapes to be preserved at interview and the police confirmed that the possibility of investigating the tapes had been overlooked. The tapes had been overwritten after 31 days. In following the principles set down in *Ebrahim*, the police, by their own admissions, had failed in their duty to obtain and retain the relevant footage. While there was plainly a degree of prejudice in Dobson being deprived of the opportunity of checking the footage in the hope that it supported his case, that prejudice was held not to have seriously prejudiced his case given the uncertainty of the likelihood that it would assist and the fact that Dobson had equally been in a position to appreciate the possible existence and significance of the tapes. The fact that there was no suggestion of malice or intentional omission by the police was also an important consideration for the court.

1.11.9 Disclosure Code of Practice—6 Preparation of Material for Prosecutor

(a) Schedules of unused material

6.1 The officer in charge of the investigation, the disclosure officer or an investigator may seek advice from the prosecutor about whether any particular item of material may be relevant to the investigation.

6.2 Material which may be relevant to an investigation and has been retained in accordance with this code, and which the disclosure officer believes will not form part of the prosecution case, must be listed on the appropriate schedule of unused material.

6.3 The disclosure officer must ensure that the appropriate schedule of unused material is prepared in the following circumstances:
- the accused is charged with an offence which is triable only on indictment;
- the accused is charged with an offence which is triable either way, and it is considered that the case is likely to be tried on indictment;
- the accused is charged with an either-way offence that is likely to remain in the magistrates' court, and it is considered that they are likely to plead not guilty;
- the accused is charged with a summary offence and it is considered that they are likely to plead not guilty.

6.4 Where, however, the accused is charged with a summary offence or an either-way offence, and it is considered that they are likely to plead guilty (e.g. because they have admitted the offence), a schedule is not required unless a not guilty plea is subsequently entered or indicated.

6.5 Irrespective of the anticipated plea, the Common Law test for disclosure requires material to be disclosed if there is material known to the disclosure officer that might assist the defence with the early preparation of their case or at a bail hearing (for example, a key prosecution witness has relevant previous convictions or a witness has withdrawn their statement). A note must be made on the case summary for the prosecutor of any such material, which must be revealed to the prosecutor who will review it and consider whether it is disclosable. Where there is no such material, a certificate to that effect must be completed.

6.6 Material in the following list (which where it exists will have been retained or recorded in accordance with paragraph 5.4) is likely to include information which meets the test for prosecution disclosure. This material must therefore, subject to the exception at 6.4 above, be scheduled and provided to the prosecutor. In reviewing this material, disclosure officers and prosecutors are to start with a presumption that it is likely to meet the disclosure test, although the material will need to be carefully considered and the disclosure test applied before a decision is made:

a) records which are derived from tapes or recordings of telephone messages (for example 999 calls) containing descriptions of an alleged offence or offender;

b) any incident logs relating to the allegation;

c) contemporaneous records of the incident, such as:
   - crime reports and crime report forms;
   - an investigation log;
   - any record or note made by an investigator (including police notebook entries and other handwritten notes) on which they later make a statement or which relates to contact with suspects, victims or witnesses;
   - an account of an incident or information relevant to an incident noted by an investigator in manuscript or electronically;
   - records of actions carried out by officers (such as house-to-house interviews, CCTV or forensic enquiries) noted by a police officer in manuscript or electronically;
   - CCTV footage, or other imagery, of the incident in action;

d) the defendant's custody record or voluntary attendance record;

e) any previous accounts made by a complainant or by any other witnesses;

f) interview records (written records, or audio or video tapes, of interviews with actual or potential witnesses or suspects);

g) any material casting doubt on the reliability of a witness e. g. relevant previous convictions and relevant cautions of any prosecution witnesses and any co-accused.

This material must be listed on the schedule by the disclosure officer in addition to all other material which may be relevant to an investigation; it is likely that some of this material will need to be redacted (see 6.12).

(b) Way in which material is to be listed on schedule

6.7 Material which the disclosure officer does not believe is sensitive must be listed on a schedule of non-sensitive material, which must include a statement that the disclosure officer does not believe the material is sensitive. Where there is sensitive unused material, see para 6.13 below.

6.8 The disclosure officer should ensure, subject to paras 6.10–6.11 below, that each item of material is listed separately on the schedule, and is numbered consecutively (which may include numbering by volume and sub-volume).

6.9 The description of each item should make clear the nature of the item and should contain sufficient detail to enable the prosecutor to decide whether they need to inspect the material before deciding whether or not it should be disclosed.

6.10 In some investigations it may be disproportionate to list each item of material separately. These may be listed in a block or blocks and described by quantity and generic title.

6.11 Even if some material is listed in a block, the disclosure officer must ensure that any items among that material which might satisfy the test for prosecution disclosure are listed and described individually.

(c) Redaction of sensitive material

6.12 The disclosure officer should redact any sensitive information contained in material that is likely to satisfy the test for prosecution disclosure. The disclosure officer should also redact any personal, confidential information in material that is to be disclosed. Such could include a person's date of birth, address, email address and phone number.

6.13 Any material which is believed to be sensitive must be listed on a schedule of sensitive material. If there is no sensitive material, the disclosure officer must record this fact on a schedule of sensitive material, or otherwise so indicate.

6.14 Subject to paragraph 6.15 below, the disclosure officer must list on a sensitive schedule any material the disclosure of which they believe would give rise to a real risk of serious prejudice to an important public interest, and the reason for that belief. The schedule must include a statement that the disclosure officer believes the material is sensitive. Depending on the circumstances, examples of such material may include the following among others:
- material relating to national security;
- material received from the intelligence and security agencies;
- material relating to intelligence from foreign sources which reveals sensitive intelligence gathering methods;
- material given in confidence;
- material relating to the identity or activities of informants, or undercover police officers, or witnesses, or other persons supplying information to the police who may be in danger if their identities are revealed;
- material revealing the location of any premises or other place used for police surveillance, or the identity of any person allowing a police officer to use them for surveillance;
- material revealing, either directly or indirectly, techniques and methods relied upon by a police officer in the course of a criminal investigation, for example covert surveillance techniques, or other methods of detecting crime;
- material whose disclosure might facilitate the commission of other offences or hinder the prevention and detection of crime;
- material upon the strength of which search warrants were obtained;
- material containing details of persons taking part in identification parades;
- material supplied to an investigator during a criminal investigation which has been generated by an official of a body concerned with the regulation or supervision of bodies corporate or of persons engaged in financial activities, or which has been generated by a person retained by such a body;
- material supplied to an investigator during a criminal investigation which relates to a child or young person and which has been generated by a local authority social services department, an Area Child Protection Committee or other party contacted by an investigator during the investigation;
- material relating to the private life of a witness.

6.15 In exceptional circumstances, where an investigator considers that material is so sensitive that its revelation to the prosecutor by means of an entry on the sensitive schedule is inappropriate, the existence of the material must be revealed to the prosecutor separately. This will apply only where compromising the material would be likely to lead directly to the loss of life, or directly threaten national security.

6.16 In such circumstances, the responsibility for informing the prosecutor lies with the investigator who knows the detail of the sensitive material. The investigator should act as soon as is reasonably practicable after the file containing the prosecution case is sent to the prosecutor. The investigator must also ensure that the prosecutor is able to inspect the material so that they can assess whether it is disclosable and, if so, whether it needs to be brought before a court for a ruling or disclosure.

1.11.9.1

KEYNOTE

Initial Disclosure

Under s. 3 of the 1996 Act, all previously undisclosed material that might undermine the prosecution case must be disclosed to the defence. If there is no such material, then the accused must be given a written statement to that effect. This applies to all material in possession of the police or that has been inspected under the provisions of the Disclosure Code of Practice. This therefore requires the disclosure officer to know what material exists and what material has already been made available to the defence. The court in *Grant* [2015] EWCA Crim 1815 stated that there is corporate knowledge implied by the possession of the relevant information that falls to be disclosed by any arm of the prosecution; the courts will expect the disclosure officer to be aware of any material held or inspected by other officers in the case.

In magistrates' courts there is now a streamlined procedure in summary cases that are expected to end in a guilty plea, so that a schedule of unused material need not be served in such cases, but that the prosecution should perform its obligations at common law (as set out in *R v DPP, ex parte Lee*, **see para. 1.11.10.2**) and provide written confirmation that it has been done.

The prosecution only have to disclose material relevant to the prosecution in question. For instance, surveillance logs concerning another matter would not need to be disclosed (*R v Dennis* (2000) 13 April, unreported). It is up to the prosecutor to decide on the format in which material is disclosed to the accused. If material is to be copied, s. 3(3) of the 1996 Act leaves open the question of whether this should be done by the prosecutor or by the police. The prosecutor must also provide the defence with a schedule of all non-sensitive material (s. 4(2) of the 1996 Act). This includes all other information in police possession, or material that has been examined by the police other than 'sensitive material' (this is disclosed to the prosecutor separately). 'Sensitive material' is material which it is not in the public interest to disclose. At this stage, the defence are not entitled to inspect items on the schedule that have not been disclosed (s. 3(6) and (7)).

Material must not be disclosed to the extent that the court concludes that it is not in the public interest to disclose it and orders accordingly or it is material whose disclosure is prohibited by s. 17 of the Regulation of Investigatory Powers Act 2000 unless it falls within the exception provided by s. 18 of the Act.

1.11.9.2

KEYNOTE

Completing the Schedules

It is important that the schedules themselves are completed fully. Guidance is given by paras 6.8 to 6.11 of the Code and in detail in the CPS Disclosure Manual, chapters 6 to 8. Where appropriate, use should be made of the block listing provisions in para. 6.10 of the Code. It may not be practicable to list each item of material separately. If so, these may be listed in a block and described by quantity and generic title (A-G's Guidelines, para. A50). The disclosure officer should keep a copy of the schedules sent to the prosecutor, in case there are any queries that need to be resolved and to assist in keeping track of the items listed should the schedules need to be updated (CPS Disclosure Manual, chapter 6).

The following items should also be considered when deciding on initial disclosure in cases where the disclosure is in the public interest (that is where they are not *'sensitive material'*):

* records of previous convictions and cautions for prosecution witnesses;
* any other information which casts doubt on the reliability of a prosecution witness or on the accuracy of any prosecution evidence;
* any motives for the making of false allegations by a prosecution witness;
* any material which may have a bearing on the admissibility of any prosecution evidence;
* the fact that a witness has sought, been offered or received a reward;
* any material that might go to the credibility of a prosecution witness;
* any information which may cast doubt on the reliability of a confession. Any item which relates to the accused's mental or physical health, his intellectual capacity, or to any ill-treatment which the accused

may have suffered when in the investigator's custody is likely to have the potential for casting doubt on the reliability of a purported confession;

- information that a person other than the accused was or might have been responsible or which points to another person whether charged or not (including a co-accused) having involvement in the commission of the offence (CPS Disclosure Manual, chapter 10).

The disclosure officer should be mindful of the need to demonstrate that he/she has taken all reasonable steps should it transpire that full disclosure had not been made.

The prosecutor is required to advise the disclosure officer of any items on the MG6C that should properly be on the MG6D and vice versa; any apparent omissions or amendments required; insufficient or unclear descriptions of items or where there is a failure to provide schedules at all. In circumstances where the schedules are inadequate, the prosecutor will return them with a target date for resubmission. The disclosure officer must take all necessary remedial action and provide properly completed schedules to the prosecutor. Failure to do so may result in the matter being raised with a senior officer. There may be occasions where schedules need to be edited; the Codes place responsibility for keeping them accurate and up to date on the disclosure officer. The disclosure officer must provide different certifications in the course of the disclosure process, to cover:

- revelation of all relevant retained material;
- whether material satisfies the disclosure test; and
- whether material satisfies the disclosure test following a defence statement as part of the continuing duty.

The case against each accused must be considered and certified separately (CPS Disclosure Manual, chapter 10).

1.11.9.3

KEYNOTE

Sensitive Material

This is material which the disclosure officer believes it is not in the public interest to disclose. While the general principle that governs the 1996 Act and Article 6 of the European Convention is that material should not be withheld from the defence, sensitive material is an exception to this. In *Van Mechelen* v *Netherlands* (1998) 25 EHRR 647, the court stated that in some cases it may be necessary to withhold certain evidence from the defence so as to preserve the fundamental rights of another individual or to safeguard an important public interest. However, only such measures restricting the rights of the defence which are strictly necessary are permissible under Article 6. It should be noted that the court did recognise that the entitlement of disclosure of relevant evidence was not an absolute right but could only be restricted as was strictly necessary. In *R* v *Keane* [1994] 1 WLR 746 Lord Taylor CJ stated that 'the judge should carry out a balancing exercise, having regard both to the weight of the public interest in non-disclosure and to the importance of the documents to the issues of interest, present and potential, to the defence, and if the disputed material might prove a defendant's innocence or avoid a miscarriage of justice, the balance came down resoundingly in favour of disclosure'.

Decisions as to what should be withheld from the defence are a matter for the court and, where necessary, an application to withhold the material must be made to the court (*R* v *Ward* [1993] 1 WLR 619). The application of public interest immunity was considered by the House of Lords in *R* v *H* [2004] UKHL 3. In this case, the defendants were charged with conspiracy to supply a Class A drug following a covert police investigation, and sought disclosure of material held by the prosecution relating to the investigation. The prosecution resisted the disclosure on grounds of public interest immunity. The court held that if the material did not weaken the prosecution case or strengthen the defence, there would be no requirement to disclose it. Once material is considered to be sensitive then it should be disclosed only if the public interest application fails (unless abandoning the case is considered more appropriate); before such action is taken there must be consultation between the CPS (Unit Head or above) and police (ACC or above). Such material is not as wide as it seems; for instance it does not mean evidence which might harm the prosecution case. This category is limited and the Code of Practice, at para. 6.12, gives a number of examples of such material. It will be for the disclosure officer to decide what material, if any, falls into this category; guidance is provided in chapters 13 and 34 of the CPS Disclosure Manual.

Paragraph 6.14 of the Code provides examples of sensitive material. Many of these items are included within the common law principles of public interest immunity. The case law in this area will still apply to decisions regarding the disclosure of such material. These groups are not exclusive and the areas most likely to apply will be those concerning the protection of intelligence and intelligence methods. In any consideration as to what should be withheld, the provisions of part II of the Regulation of Investigatory Powers Act 2000 should be referred to. Part II of the Act will make provision, not only for the gathering and recording of intelligence, but also disclosure of any material gained and methods used. Claims to withhold material may be made by parties other than the prosecutor (who would do so on behalf of the police). In some cases, the relevant minister or the Attorney-General may intervene to claim immunity. Alternatively, the claim to immunity may be made by the party seeking to withhold the evidence, either on its own initiative or at the request of the relevant government department.

Guidance is also provided in para. 115 of the A-G's Guidelines: even where an application is made to the court to withhold material a prosecutor should aim to disclose as much of the material as he/she properly can (by giving the defence redacted or edited copies of summaries).

In deciding whether material attracts public interest immunity the court will have to be satisfied that the material in no way helps the defence or undermines the prosecution case. Where the material related to secret or confidential systems it should not be revealed as this would aid serious criminal enterprise in the future (*R* v *Templar* [2003] EWCA Crim 3186).

Where police consider that material should not be disclosed due to its sensitive nature, the CPS Disclosure Manual, chapter 10 should be followed. This states that in order to assist the prosecutor to decide how to deal with sensitive material which the investigator believes may meet the disclosure test, he/she should provide detailed information dealing with the following issues:

- the reasons why the material is said to be sensitive;
- the degree of sensitivity said to attach to the material, i.e. why it is considered that disclosure will create a real risk of serious prejudice to an important public interest;
- the consequences of revealing to the defence:
  - the material itself,
  - the category of the material,
  - the fact that an application is being made;
- the apparent significance of the material to the issues in the trial;
- the involvement of any third parties in bringing the material to the attention of the police;
- where the material is likely to be the subject of an order for disclosure, what police views are regarding continuance of the prosecution;
- whether it is possible to disclose the material without compromising its sensitivity.

In applications for public interest immunity, the CPS has an obligation to ensure that all such material is in its possession and the police have a duty to pass the material on (*R* v *Menga and Marshalleck* [1998] Crim LR 58).

Care must be taken to safeguard material that is sensitive and keep it separate from other material because if the material subject to a public interest immunity order for non-disclosure is inadvertently disclosed by the prosecution to lawyers for the defendants, those lawyers cannot be ordered not to further disseminate that material to any third party, including their own clients (*R* v *G* [2004] EWCA Crim 1368).

The investigator also has a responsibility to identify material that could be sensitive and bring this to the attention of the CPS. Where material is identified steps must be taken to record and retain the material. For information recorded on computers, see 'Digital guidance', chapter 30 of the CPS Disclosure Manual and Annex A to the A-G's Guidelines.

1.11.9.4

KEYNOTE

Informants

The courts recognise the need to protect the identity of informants to ensure that the supply of information about criminal activities does not dry up and to ensure the informants' own safety. However, there may be occasions where if the case is to continue the identity of an informant will have to be disclosed.

This is particularly so where there is a suggestion that an informant has participated in the events constituting, surrounding or following the crime; the judge must consider whether this role so impinges on an issue of interest to the defence, present or potential, as to make disclosure necessary (*R v Turner* [1995] 1 WLR 264).

The need to disclose details of informants has been considered by the Court of Appeal in two cases. The first case, *R v Denton* [2002] EWCA Crim 272, concerned a defendant who was a police informer. The defendant was charged with murder and alleged that he had been told by his police handlers not to tell his lawyers about his status. The court held that there was no duty for the Crown to disclose to the defence, or to seek a ruling from the judge, as to any information regarding an accused being a police informer. On any common sense view, the material had already been disclosed to the defendant, and the Crown had no duty to supply the defendant with information with which he was already familiar. This last point may also be relevant to other situations. The second case, *R v Dervish* [2001] EWCA Crim 2789, concerned an undercover operation that was commenced after an informant gave information. The court held in this case that the public interest in protecting the identification of an informant had to be balanced against the right of the defendant to a fair trial; if there was material that might assist the defence, the necessity for the defendant to have a fair trial would outweigh the other interests in the case and the material would have to be disclosed or the prosecution discontinued. There had been no such material in this case. In *R v Edwards (formerly Steadman)* [2012] EWCA Crim 5, a murder case, the prosecution failed to disclose the fact that they were seeking one of the witness's registration as an informant, and that this witness was willing to give information if he did not receive any additional custodial sentence in respect of the offences with which he had been charged. The court stated that these were factors which should have been made available to the jury in deciding the credibility of the witness. However, in the circumstances of the case, even with full and proper disclosure, the task of assessing this witness's reliability would have changed neither the landscape of the trial nor the jury's deliberations upon the evidence. The circumstantial case was compelling, and the verdict was safe.

Where an informant who has participated in the crime is called to give evidence at the trial there would have to be very strong reasons for this fact not to be disclosed (*R v Patel* [2001] EWCA Crim 2505).

There are strong links between the principles of informants and undercover police officers. In *R v Barkshire* [2011] EWCA Crim 1885, the Court of Appeal, upholding the appeal, held that recordings and the statement of an undercover police officer contained information which assisted the defence. They showed that the undercover officer had been involved in activities which went much further than the authorisation that he had been given. They appeared to show him as an enthusiastic supporter of criminal activity, arguably, as an *agent provocateur*. Further, the recordings supported the defendant's contentions that their intended activities were directed to the saving of life and avoidance of injury, and that they proposed to conduct the occupation in a careful and proportionate manner. This material was pertinent to a potential submission of abuse of process by way of entrapment and in any event had the capacity to support B's defence.

1.11.9.5

KEYNOTE

Observation Points and the *Johnson* Ruling

R v Rankine [1986] 2 WLR 1075, considering previous cases, stated that it was the rule that police officers should not be required to disclose sources of their information, whether those sources were paid informers or public-spirited citizens, subject to a discretion to admit to avoid a miscarriage of justice and that observation posts were included in this rule.

In *R* v *Johnson* [1988] 1 WLR 1377, the appellant was convicted of supplying drugs. The only evidence against him was given by police officers, who testified that, while stationed in private premises in a known drug-dealing locality, they had observed him selling drugs. The defence applied to cross-examine the officers on the exact location of the observation posts, in order to test what they could see, having regard to the layout of the street and the objects in it. In the jury's absence, the prosecution called evidence as to the difficulty of obtaining assistance from the public, and the desire of the occupiers, who were also occupiers at the time of the offence, that their names and addresses should not be disclosed because they feared for their safety.

The judge ruled that the exact location of the premises need not be revealed. The appeal was dismissed; although the conduct of the defence was to some extent affected by the restraints placed on it, this led to no injustice. The jury were well aware of the restraints, and were most carefully directed about the very special care they had to give to any disadvantage they may have brought to the defence. *Johnson* was applied and approved in *R* v *Hewitt* (1992) 95 Cr App R 81 (see also *R* v *Grimes* [1994] Crim LR 213).

In *Johnson*, Watkins LJ at pp. 1385–6 gave the following guidance as to the minimum evidential requirements needed if disclosure is to be protected:

a) The police officer in charge of the observations to be conducted, no one of lower rank than a sergeant should usually be acceptable for this purpose, must be able to testify that beforehand he visited all observation places to be used and ascertained the attitude of occupiers of premises, not only to the use to be made of them, but to the possible disclosure thereafter of the use made and facts which could lead to the identification of the premises thereafter and of the occupiers. He may of course in addition inform the court of difficulties, if any, usually encountered in the particular locality of obtaining assistance from the public.

b) A police officer of no lower rank than a chief inspector must be able to testify that immediately prior to the trial he visited the places used for observations, the results of which it is proposed to give in evidence, and ascertained whether the occupiers are the same as when the observations took place and whether they are or are not, what the attitude of those occupiers is to the possible disclosure of the use previously made of the premises and of facts which could lead at the trial to identification of premises and occupiers.

Such evidence will of course be given in the absence of the jury when the application to exclude the material evidence is made. The judge should explain to the jury, as this judge did, when summing up or at some appropriate time before that, the effect of his ruling to exclude, if he so rules.

The guidelines in *Johnson* do not require a threat of violence before protection can be afforded to the occupier of an observation post; it suffices that the occupier is in fear of harassment (*Blake* v *DPP* (1993) 97 Cr App R 169).

This extended the rules established in *R* v *Rankine* [1986] QB 861 and is based on the protection of the owner or occupier of the premises, and not on the identity of the observation post. Thus, where officers have witnessed the commission of an offence as part of a surveillance operation conducted from an unmarked police vehicle, information relating to the surveillance and the colour, make and model of the vehicle should not be withheld (*R* v *Brown and Daley* (1988) 87 Cr App R 52).

1.11.10 | Disclosure Code of Practice—7 Revelation of Material to Prosecutor

7.1 Where cases have been charged on the Full Code Test and it is anticipated that the defendant will plead not guilty, the disclosure officer should provide the schedules concerning unused material to the prosecutor at the point of charge (for police charged cases) or prior to charge (for CPS charged cases).

7.2 In all other cases the disclosure officer must provide the schedules as soon as possible after a not guilty plea has been either indicated or entered.

7.3 The disclosure officer should draw the attention of the prosecutor to any material an investigator has retained (including material to which paragraph 6.15 applies) which it is considered may satisfy the test for prosecution disclosure in the Act, explaining the reasons for coming to that view.

7.4 The disclosure officer must give the prosecutor a copy of any such material (unless it has already been supplied as part of the file containing the material for the prosecution case), together with any material which falls into the following categories:
- information provided by an accused person which indicates an explanation for the offence with which they have been charged;
- any material casting doubt on the reliability of a confession;
- any material casting doubt on the reliability of a prosecution witness

7.5 The disclosure officer must give the prosecutor a copy of any material which has been scheduled in accordance with paragraph 6.6, indicating whether it is, or is not, considered to satisfy the test for prosecution disclosure, and in either case explaining the reasons for coming to that view.

7.6 The disclosure officer must comply with a request from the prosecutor to be allowed to inspect material which has not already been copied to them. If the prosecutor asks to be provided with a copy of such material it should be provided, except where (having consulted the officer in charge of the investigation) the disclosure officer believes that the material is too sensitive to be copied and can only be inspected.

7.7 If material consists of information which is recorded other than in writing, whether it should be given to the prosecutor in its original form as a whole, or by way of relevant extracts recorded in the same form, or in the form of a transcript, is a matter for agreement between the disclosure officer and the prosecutor.

1.11.10.1   **KEYNOTE**

What Satisfies the Test for Prosecution Disclosure

Paragraphs 7.3 to 7.4 of the Code create a catch-all provision and presumably require the disclosure officer to make inquiries of the other investigating officers who have been involved in the case to ensure that all material is included.

However, what needs to be disclosed should be balanced by the A-G's Guidelines:

The statutory disclosure regime does not require the prosecutor to make available to the accused either neutral material or material which is adverse to the accused. ... [P]rosecutors should not disclose material which they are not required to, as this would overburden the participants in the trial process, divert attention away from the relevant issues and may lead to unjustifiable delays. Disclosure should be completed in a thinking manner, in light of the issues in the case, and not simply as a schedule completing exercise.

Defence statements are an integral part of the statutory disclosure regime. A defence statement should help to focus the attention of the prosecutor, court and co-defendants on the relevant issues in order to identify material which may meet the test for disclosure.

(A-G's Guidelines, paras 3, 4 and 121)

There will occasionally be cases where the police investigation has been intelligence-led; there may be a deputy disclosure officer appointed just to deal with intelligence material which, by its very nature, is likely to be sensitive (see para. 1.11.9.3). Where there are a number of disclosure officers assigned to a case, there should be a lead disclosure officer who is the focus for inquiries and whose responsibility it is to ensure that the investigator's disclosure obligations are complied with. Where appropriate, regular case conferences and other meetings should be held to ensure prosecutors are apprised of all relevant developments in investigations. Full records should be kept of such meetings (A-G's Guidelines, para. 10).

It should be noted that where material is available to police from a particular source, e.g. local authority records, a decision that some of the material is relevant does not mean that it all has to be disclosed. This point was reinforced by the case of *R v Abbott* [2003] EWCA Crim 350, where the Court of Appeal held that the defendant was not entitled to blanket disclosure of all the files.

1.11.10.2

KEYNOTE

Time Period for Initial Disclosure

While there are provisions to set specific time periods by which initial disclosure must be met, none currently exist. Until such time, disclosure at this stage must be made as soon as practicable after the duty arises.

In *R* v *Bourimech* [2002] EWCA Crim 2089, the defendant sought disclosure following the service of his defence statement of a previous crime report made by the victim. One day before the trial was scheduled to begin, the crime report relating to that incident was served among other papers on the defence. This report escaped the notice of the defence until the final day of the trial. The court held that the defect in disclosure amounted to unfairness in the proceedings and the court could not be confident that if the victim had been cross-examined in relation to the previous allegation the jury might have been influenced by the credit and credibility of the witness.

In most cases prosecution disclosure can wait until after this time without jeopardising the defendant's right to a fair trial. However, the prosecutor must always be alive to the need to make disclosure of material that should be disclosed at an earlier stage (*R* v *DPP, ex parte Lee* [1999] 1 WLR 1950). Examples include:

- previous convictions of a complainant or a deceased if that information could reasonably be expected to assist the defence when applying for bail;
- material that might enable a defendant to make an application to stay the proceedings as an abuse of process;
- material that might enable a defendant to submit that he/she should only be sent for trial on a lesser charge, or perhaps that he/she should not be sent for trial at all;
- depending on what the defendant chooses to reveal about his/her case at this early stage, material that would enable the defendant and his/her legal advisers to make preparations for trial that would be significantly less effective if disclosure were delayed; for example, names of eye-witnesses whom the prosecution did not intend to use.

It should be noted that any disclosure by the prosecution prior to the application hearing would not normally exceed that required by s. 3 of the 1996 Act.

1.11.11   Disclosure Code of Practice—8 Subsequent Action by Disclosure Officer

8.1 At the time when a schedule of non-sensitive material is prepared, the disclosure officer may not know exactly what material will form the case against the accused. In addition, the prosecutor may not have given advice about the likely relevance of particular items of material. Once these matters have been determined, the disclosure officer must give the prosecutor, where necessary, an amended schedule listing any additional material:
- which may be relevant to the investigation,
- which does not form part of the case against the accused,
- which is not already listed on the schedule, and
- which they believe is not sensitive,

unless they are informed in writing by the prosecutor that the prosecutor intends to disclose the material to the defence.

8.2 Section 7A of the Act imposes a continuing duty on the prosecutor, for the duration of criminal proceedings against the accused, to disclose material which satisfies the test for disclosure (subject to public interest considerations). To enable this to be done, any new material coming to light should be treated in the same way as the earlier material.

8.3 In particular, after a defence statement has been given, or details of the issues in dispute have been recorded on the Preparation for Effective Trial form or the Plea and Trial Preparation Hearing form, the disclosure officer must look again at the material which has been retained and must draw the attention of the prosecutor to any material which might reasonably be considered capable of undermining the case for the prosecution against the accused or of assisting the case for the accused; and must reveal it to them in accordance with paragraphs 7.4 and 7.5 above.

1.11.11.1

Disclosure by the Defence

The duty on the defence to make disclosure only arises *after* the prosecution has made the initial disclosure (s. 5(1) of the 1996 Act). This duty falls into two categories: compulsory and voluntary. The disclosure required by the defence is limited to material that they intend to use at trial.

The defence statement should set out the nature of the defendant's defence, including any particular defences on which he/she intends to rely and particulars of the matters of fact on which the defendant intends to rely; this means the defence will need to disclose a factual narrative of their case. In addition, those issues, relevant to the case, which the accused disputes with the prosecution must be set out with reasons. The defence statement must indicate any point of law (including any point as to the admissibility of evidence or an abuse of process) which the defendant wishes to raise, and any authority on which he/she intends to rely for that purpose (s. 6A of the 1996 Act). This requirement to give reasons is intended to stop the defence going on a 'fishing expedition' to speculatively look at material in order to find some kind of defence.

Where the defence case involves an alibi, the statement must give details of the alibi, including the name and address of any alibi witness. In cases where there are co-accused, there is no duty to disclose this information to the other defendants, although this could be done voluntarily.

An alibi for the purposes of the defence statement is defined as evidence tending to show that by reason of the presence of the accused at a particular place or in a particular area at a particular time, he/she was not, or was unlikely to have been, at the place where the offence is alleged to have been committed at the time of its alleged commission. Where this applies, the defence must provide details including the name, address and date of birth of any witness the accused believes is able to give evidence in support of the alibi, or as many of those details as are known to the accused when the statement is given. Where such details are not known, the statement must include any information in the accused's possession which might be of material assistance in identifying or finding any such witness (s. 6A(2) of the 1996 Act).

The defence must also give to the court and the prosecutor notice of any other witnesses other than the defendant who will be called to give evidence. If any other witness is to be called then the name, address and date of birth of each such proposed witness, or as many of those details as are known to the accused must be provided. If any of this information is not available the defence must provide any information in their possession which might be of material assistance in identifying or finding any such proposed witness (s. 6C of the 1996 Act), see para. 1.11.11.7.

There may be occasions where the defence statement is allowed to be used in cross-examination when it is alleged that the defendant has changed his/her defence or in re-examination to rebut a suggestion of recent invention (*R* v *Lowe* [2003] EWCA Crim 3182).

1.11.11.2

Compulsory Disclosure by Defence (s. 5)

In proceedings before the Crown Court, where the prosecutor has provided initial disclosure, or purported to, the accused must serve a defence statement on the prosecutor and the court. The accused must also provide details of any witnesses he/she intends to call at the trial. Where there are other accused in the proceedings and the court so orders, the accused must also give a defence statement to each of the other accused specified by the court, and a request for a copy of the defence statement may be made by any co-accused.

Once a defence statement has been provided (whether compulsorily or voluntarily), the prosecution must disclose any prosecution material that:

- might be reasonably expected to assist the accused's defence; and
- has not already been disclosed.

It will be a question of fact whether material in police possession might be reasonably expected to assist the defence case. If the court feels that material that was not disclosed would to any reasonable person have been expected to help the defence case, the case may fail.

The defence statement is likely to point the prosecution to other lines of inquiry. The disclosure officer should share the information with any deputy disclosure officer and the officer in charge of the investigation. Further investigation in these circumstances should be considered and reasonable lines of inquiry followed (CPS Disclosure Manual, chapter 15).

If there is no additional material to be disclosed then the prosecutor must give a written statement to this effect. It is not the responsibility of the prosecutor or the police to examine material held by third parties which the defence have stated they wish to examine (the defence can request this from the third party or apply for a witness summons). However, there may be occasions where matters disclosed in the defence statement lead investigators to look at material held by third parties as it might impact on the prosecution case. This stage of the disclosure process may require further inquiries prompted by the defence statement. The result of those inquiries may then have to be disclosed because it either undermines the prosecution case or it assists the accused's defence.

1.11.11.3

KEYNOTE

Voluntary Disclosure by Accused (s. 6)

In the magistrates' court, the accused is not obliged to serve a defence statement but may choose to do so, in which case the statutory provisions apply. However, it is a mandatory requirement for the accused to provide details of his or her witnesses. The purpose of s. 6 of the 1996 Act is to allow the defence, in cases where the case is being tried summarily as a not guilty plea, to obtain further disclosure from the prosecution after the initial disclosure. This is only likely to happen where:

- the defence are not satisfied with the material disclosed at the initial disclosure stage or where they wish to examine items listed in the schedule of non-sensitive material;
- the defence wish to show the strength of their case in order to persuade the prosecution not to proceed.

If the defence decide to make a defence statement they must comply with the same conditions imposed on compulsory defence disclosure.

1.11.11.4

KEYNOTE

Time Period for the Defence Statement

Once the prosecution provides the initial disclosure, the defence have 14 days in respect of summary proceedings, or 28 days in respect of Crown Court proceedings within which the accused in criminal proceedings must give: a compulsory defence statement under s. 5 of the Act; a voluntary defence statement under s. 6 of the Act; or a notice of his/her intention to call any person, other than him/herself, as a witness at trial under s. 6C of the Act (Alibi witness). The court can only grant an extension if satisfied that the accused could not reasonably have given a defence statement or given notification within the relevant period. There is no limit on the number of days by which the relevant period may be extended or the number of applications for extensions that may be made (Criminal Procedure and Investigations Act 1996 (Defence Disclosure Time Limits) Regulations 2011 (SI 2011/209)).

1.11.11.5

KEYNOTE

Effect of Failure in Defence Disclosure

If the defence fail to give a defence statement under s. 5 or, where a defence statement is provided, they:

- are outside the time limits;
- set out inconsistent defences in a defence statement or at trial put forward a different defence; or

- at trial adduce evidence in support of an alibi without having given particulars of the alibi in a defence statement, or call a witness in support of an alibi without providing details of the witness or information that might help trace the witness;

then the following sanctions may apply:

- the court or, with the leave of the court, any other party may make such comment as appears appropriate;
- the court or jury may draw such inferences as appear proper in deciding whether the accused is guilty of the offence concerned (but there must also be other evidence to convict the defendant);
- even if the defence serve the defence statement outside the time limits, the prosecution must still consider the impact of the statement in terms of the need for any further disclosure (*Murphy* v *DPP* [2006] EWHC 1753 (Admin)).

1.11.11.6

KEYNOTE

Continuing Duty of Prosecutor to Disclose (s. 7A)

Section 7A places a continuing duty on the prosecutor at any time between the initial disclosure and the accused being acquitted or convicted or the prosecutor deciding not to proceed with the case concerned, to keep under review the question of further disclosure. In considering the need for further disclosure the prosecutor must consider whether material might reasonably be considered capable of undermining the case for the prosecution against the accused or of assisting the case for the accused. If there is any such material, it must be disclosed to the accused as soon as is reasonably practicable. Consideration of what might need to be disclosed could change depending on the state of affairs at that time (including the case for the prosecution as it then stands) and so should be reviewed on a continuing basis (s. 7A(4)).

In *R* v *Tyrell* [2004] EWCA Crim 3279 this responsibility was clearly outlined. The court held that there was an obligation to consider whether there was any material in the hands of the prosecution which might undermine the case against the applicants or might reasonably be expected to assist the disclosed defences. In addition, the Crown had to consider whether there was any material which might be relevant to an issue which might feature in the trial; this clearly required a continuing duty. In this case, the court found that disclosure had been considered many times as the case progressed in relation to a variety of issues as they arose and ensured a fair trial.

Material must not be disclosed to the extent that the court concludes that it is not in the public interest to disclose it and orders accordingly or it is material whose disclosure is prohibited by s. 17 of the Regulation of Investigatory Powers Act 2000.

There is a duty on the prosecution to continue to review the disclosure of prosecution material right up until the case is completed (acquittal, conviction or discontinuance of the case).

In *R (Nunn)* v *CC of Suffolk Police* [2015] AC 225 the court stated that there can be no doubt that if the police or prosecution come into possession, after the appellate process is exhausted, of something new which might afford arguable grounds for contending that the conviction was unsafe, it is their duty to disclose it to the convicted defendant. Simple examples might include a new (and credible) confession by someone else, or the discovery, incidentally to a different investigation, of a pattern, or of evidence, which throws doubt on the original conviction. Sometimes such material may appear unexpectedly and adventitiously; in other cases it may be the result of a re-opening by the police of the inquiry. In either case, the new material is likely to be unknown to the convicted defendant unless disclosed to him. In all such cases, there is a clear obligation to disclose it (para. 138 of the A-G's Guidelines). The court also considered the A-G's Guidelines at para. 137 that prosecutors must consider disclosing in the interests of justice any material relevant to sentence, such as information not known to the defendant which might assist him in placing his role in the offence in the correct context vis-à-vis other offenders. There is also a common law duty post-conviction and pending appeal '... to disclose to the defendant any material which comes to light and might cast doubt on the safety of the conviction' (*R* v *Gohil and Preko* [2018] EWCA Crim 140).

If the defence are not satisfied that the prosecution have disclosed all they should have, s. 8 of the 1996 Act allows for the defence to apply to the court for further disclosure.

1.11.11.7

KEYNOTE

Interviewing Defence Witnesses or Alibi Witnesses

Section 21A of the Criminal Procedure and Investigations Act 1996 introduced a Code of Practice for Arranging and Conducting Interviews of Witnesses Notified by the Accused. The Code sets out guidance that police officers and other persons charged with investigating offences must follow if they arrange or conduct interviews of proposed witnesses whose details are disclosed to the prosecution under the 1996 Act. These are set out below:

Arrangement of the interview

Information to be provided to the witness before any interview may take place

3.1 If an investigator wishes to interview a witness, the witness must be asked whether he consents to being interviewed and informed that:
- an interview is being requested following his identification by the accused as a proposed witness under section 6A(2) or section 6C of the Act,
- he is not obliged to attend the proposed interview,
- he is entitled to be accompanied by a solicitor at the interview (but nothing in this Code of Practice creates any duty on the part of the Legal Services Commission to provide funding for any such attendance), and
- a record will be made of the interview and he will subsequently be sent a copy of the record.

3.2 If the witness consents to being interviewed, the witness must be asked:
- whether he wishes to have a solicitor present at the interview,
- whether he consents to a solicitor attending the interview on behalf of the accused, as an observer, and
- whether he consents to a copy of the record being sent to the accused. If he does not consent, the witness must be informed that the effect of disclosure requirements in criminal proceedings may nevertheless require the prosecution to disclose the record to the accused (and any co-accused) in the course of the proceedings.

Information to be provided to the accused before any interview may take place

4.1 The investigator must notify the accused or, if the accused is legally represented in the proceedings, the accused's representatives:
- that the investigator requested an interview with the witness,
- whether the witness consented to the interview, and
- if the witness consented to the interview, whether the witness also consented to a solicitor attending the interview on behalf of the accused, as an observer.

4.2 If the accused is not legally represented in the proceedings, and if the witness consents to a solicitor attending the interview on behalf of the accused, the accused must be offered the opportunity, a reasonable time before the interview is held, to appoint a solicitor to attend it.

Identification of the date, time and venue for the interview

5 The investigator must nominate a reasonable date, time and venue for the interview and notify the witness of them and any subsequent changes to them.

Notification to the accused's solicitor of the date, time and venue of the interview

6 If the witness has consented to the presence of the accused's solicitor, the accused's solicitor must be notified that the interview is taking place, invited to observe, and provided with reasonable notice of the date, time and venue of the interview and any subsequent changes.

Conduct of the interview

The investigator conducting the interview

7 The identity of the investigator conducting the interview must be recorded. That person must have sufficient skills and authority, commensurate with the complexity of the investigation, to discharge his functions effectively. That person must not conduct the interview if that is likely to result in a conflict of interest, for instance, if that person is the victim of the alleged crime which is the subject of the

proceedings. The advice of a more senior officer must always be sought if there is doubt as to whether a conflict of interest precludes an ndividual conducting the interview. If thereafter the doubt remains, the advice of a prosecutor must be sought.

Attendance of the accused's solicitor

8.1   The accused's solicitor may only attend the interview if the witness has consented to his presence as an observer. Provided that the accused's solicitor was g ven reasonable notice of the date, time and place of the interview, the fact that the accused's sol citor is not present will not prevent the interview from being conducted. If the witness at any time withdraws consent to the accused's solicitor being present at the interview, the interview may continue without the presence of the accused's solicitor.

8.2   The accused's solicitor may attend only as an observer.

Attendance of the witness's solicitor

9   Where a witness has indicated that he wishes to appoint a solicitor to be present, that solicitor must be permitted to attend the interview.

Attendance of any other appropriate person

10   A witness under the age of 18 or a witness who is mentally disordered or otherwise mentally vulnerable must be interviewed in the presence of an appropriate person.

Recording of the interview

11.1   An accurate record must be made of the interview, whether it takes place at a police station or elsewhere. The record must be made, where practicable, by audio recording or by visual recording with sound, or otherwise in writing. Any written record must be made and completed during the interview, unless this would not be practicable or would interfere with the conduct of the interview, and must constitute either a verbatim record of what has been said or, failing this, an account of the interview which adequately and accurately summarises it. If a written record is not made during the interview it must be made as soon as practicable after its completion. Written interview records must be timed and signed by the maker.

11.2   A copy of the record must be given, within a reasonable time of the interview, to:
(a)   the witness, and
(b)   if the witness consents, to the accused or the accused's solicitor.

1.11.12   Disclosure Code of Practice—9 Certification by Disclosure Officer

9.1   The disclosure officer must certify to the prosecutor that to the best of their knowledge and belief, all relevant material which has been retained and made available to them has been revealed to the prosecutor in accordance with this Code. They must sign and date the disclosure officer certificate. It will be necessary to certify not only at the time when the schedule and accompanying material is submitted to the prosecutor, and when relevant material which has been retained is reconsidered after the accused has given a defence statement, but also whenever a schedule is otherwise given or material is otherwise revealed to the prosecutor.

1.11.13   Disclosure Code of Practice—10 Disclosure of Material to Accused

10.1   A prosecutor must review the schedules of unused material provided by the disclosure officer and endorse the schedule to indicate whether each item of material does or does not meet the test for disclosure. If any of the material does meet the test for disclosure, the prosecutor should record the reason for this decision.

10.2   A prosecutor must additionally review any material provided by the disclosure officer under paragraph 6.6 (material likely to meet the test for disclosure). The prosecutor must endorse the schedule to indicate whether the material does or does not meet the test for disclosure, and must record the reason for the decision.

10.3 When a prosecutor provides material to the defence in accordance with the obligation under section 3 or section 7A of the Criminal Procedure and Investigations Act 1996, the prosecutor must at the same time provide the schedule of non-sensitive material to the defence.

10.4 Other than early disclosure under Common Law, in the magistrates' court the schedule (and any relevant unused material to be disclosed under it) must be disclosed to the accused either:

- at the hearing where a not guilty plea is entered, or
- as soon as possible following a formal indication from the accused or representative that a not guilty plea will be entered at the hearing.

In the Crown Court, initial disclosure should if possible be served prior to the Plea and Trial Preparation Hearing (PTPH). Where this has not been done, it should be served as soon as possible after that hearing and in accordance with any direction made by the Court.

10.5 If material has been copied to the prosecutor, and it is to be disclosed, whether it is disclosed by the prosecutor or the disclosure officer is a matter of agreement between the two of them.

10.6 If material has not already been copied to the prosecutor, and they request its disclosure to the accused on the ground that:

- it satisfies the test for prosecution disclosure, or
- the court has ordered its disclosure after considering an application from the accused,

the disclosure officer must disclose it to the accused.

10.7 The disclosure officer must disclose material to the accused either by giving them a copy or by allowing them to inspect it. If the accused person asks for a copy of any material which they have been allowed to inspect, the disclosure officer must supply it, unless in the opinion of the disclosure officer that is either not practicable (for example because the material consists of an object which cannot be copied, or because the volume of material is so great), or not desirable (for example because the material is a statement by a child witness in relation to a sexual offence).

10.8 If material which the accused has been allowed to inspect consists of information which is recorded other than in writing, whether it should be given to the accused in its original form or in the form of a transcript is a matter for the discretion of the disclosure officer. If the material is transcribed, the disclosure officer must ensure that the transcript is certified to the accused as a true record of the material which has been transcribed.

10.9 If a court concludes that an item of sensitive material satisfies the prosecution disclosure test and that the interests of the defence outweigh the public interest in withholding disclosure, it will be necessary to disclose the material if the case is to proceed. This does not mean that sensitive documents must always be disclosed in their original form: for example, the court may agree that sensitive details still requiring protection should be blocked out, or that documents may be summarised, or that the prosecutor may make an admission about the substance of the material under section 10 of the Criminal Justice Act 1967.

1.11.13.1   **KEYNOTE**

Disclosing Material to the Defence

The court can order disclosure of material which the prosecution contend is sensitive. In such cases it may be appropriate to seek guidance on whether to disclose the material or offer no evidence, thereby protecting the sensitive material or the source of that material (e.g. where informants or surveillance techniques are involved).

Forces may have instructions as to providing further copies when requested by the defence in relation to procedures and costs. It is suggested that where copies are provided, some proof of delivery should be obtained.

1.11.13.2   **KEYNOTE**

Disclosure of Statements in Cases of Complaints against the Police

Statements made by witnesses during an investigation of a complaint against a police officer are disclosable; however, the timing of the disclosure may be controlled. In *R v Police Complaints Authority, ex parte Green* [2002] EWCA Civ 389, the Court of Appeal stated that there is no requirement to disclose witness statements to eye-witness complainants during the course of an investigation. The evidence of such complainants could be contaminated and, therefore, disclosure would risk hindering or frustrating the very purpose of the investigation. A complainant's legitimate interests were appropriately and adequately safeguarded by his/her right to a thorough and independent investigation, to contribute to the evidence, to be kept informed of the progress of the investigation and to be given reasoned conclusions on completion of the investigation. However, a complainant had no right to participate in the investigation as though he/she were supervising it. The general rule was that complainants, whether victims or next of kin, were not entitled to the disclosure of witness statements used in the course of a police investigation until its conclusion at the earliest.

Police complaints and disciplinary files may also fall within sensitive material that does not have to be disclosed (*Halford v Sharples* [1992] 1 WLR 736). This would not apply to written complaints against the police prompting investigations or the actual statements obtained during the investigations, although immunity may be claimed in the case of a particular document by reason of its contents (*R v Chief Constable of the West Midlands Police, ex parte Wiley* [1995] 1 AC 274). However, the working papers and reports prepared by the investigating officers do form a class which is entitled to immunity and therefore production of such material should be ordered only where the public interest in disclosure of their contents outweighs the public interest in preserving confidentiality (*Taylor v Anderton* [1995] 1 WLR 447).

1.11.13.3   **KEYNOTE**

Confidentiality

The defence may only use material disclosed to them under the 1996 Act for purposes related to the defence case; any other use will be a contempt of court. Once evidence has been given in open court, however, the material is available for other purposes.

1.12 | The Regulation of Investigatory Powers Act 2000

1.12.1 Introduction

The Regulation of Investigatory Powers Act 2000 (RIPA) is the Act governing the law in relation to the use of covert techniques by *public authorities* regarding the use of human intelligence sources and surveillance. It requires that when the police or other law enforcement bodies (e.g. the Serious Fraud Office or the National Crime Agency (NCA)), the security and intelligence services (MI5, MI6 and GCHQ), as well as a large number of other public bodies, including local government, need to use these covert techniques to obtain private information about a person, they do so in a way that is necessary, proportionate, and compatible with human rights. Surveillance measures necessarily involve some interference with private life but have the legitimate aim of protecting national security and economic well-being (*Kennedy* v *United Kingdom* (2011) 52 EHRR 4).

In a policing context, any breach of the Act's provisions, or the provisions contained in the Codes of Practice, issued by the Secretary of State under s. 71, can have three main consequences:

- any evidence obtained may be excluded by a court or tribunal as being unfair;
- proceedings may be taken under the relevant police conduct regulations; or
- a person may make a claim before the Investigatory Powers Tribunal.

1.12.2 Surveillance and Covert Human Intelligence Sources

Part II of the Regulation of Investigatory Powers Act 2000, s. 26 provides:

(1) This Part applies to the following conduct—
    (a) directed surveillance;
    (b) intrusive surveillance; and
    (c) the conduct and use of covert human intelligence sources.

KEYNOTE

Although only s. 26(1)(c) expressly uses the word 'covert' for the nature of the activity, it is relevant to *all three* of these areas. Part II is concerned with *covert* activity and so, as a general rule, if it is not covert, it is not covered.

Some law enforcement activities fall outside the scope of the Act, e.g. 'property interference' which is a very intrusive form of intelligence gathering such as attaching listening devices within people's homes. This type of activity is covered by part III of the Police Act 1997 and is beyond the scope of this Manual.

1.12.3 Covert Human Intelligence Sources (CHIS): Definition

The following, which relates to s. 26, is an extract from the Covert Human Intelligence Sources Revised Code of Practice (August 2018), Chapter 2, which states:

Definition of a covert human intelligence source (CHIS)
    2.1 Under the 2000 Act, a person is a CHIS if:
        • they establish or maintain a personal or other relationship with a person for the covert purpose of facilitating the doing of anything falling within paragraph 26(8)(b) or (c);

- they covertly use such a relationship to obtain information or to provide access to any information to another person; or
- they covertly disclose information obtained by the use of such a relationship or as a consequence of the existence of such a relationship.

    See section 26(8) of the 2000 Act.

2.2 A relationship is established or maintained for a covert purpose if and only if it is conducted in a manner that is calculated to ensure that one of the parties to the relationship is unaware of the purpose.

    See section 26(9)(b) of the 2000 Act for full definition.

2.3 A relationship is used covertly, and information obtained is disclosed covertly, if and only if the relationship is used or the information is disclosed in a manner that is calculated to ensure that one of the parties to the relationship is unaware of the use or disclosure in question.

    See section 26(9)(c) of the 2000 Act for full definition.

2.4 The Regulation of Investigatory Powers (Covert Human Intelligence Sources: Relevant Source) Order 2013 ('the 2013 Relevant Sources Order') further defines a particular type of CHIS as a 'relevant source'. This is a source holding an office, rank or position with the public authorities listed in the Order and Annex B to this code. Enhanced authorisation arrangements are in place for this type of CHIS as detailed in this code. Such sources will be referred to as a 'relevant source' throughout this code.

2.5 Any police officer deployed as a 'relevant source' in England and Wales will be required to comply with and uphold the principles and standards of professional behaviour set out in the College of Policing Code of Ethics.

KEYNOTE

Covert

A purpose is 'covert' here only if the relationship (and the subsequent disclosure of information) is conducted in a manner that is calculated to ensure that one of the parties is unaware of that purpose. Therefore the definition would not usually apply to members of the public generally supplying information to the police. Similarly, people who have come across information in the ordinary course of their jobs who suspect criminal activity (such as bank staff, local authority employees etc.) do not have a covert relationship with the police simply by passing on information.

Great care will be needed, however, if the person supplying the information is asked by the police to do something further in order to develop or enhance it. Any form of direction or tasking by the police in this way could make the person a CHIS and thereby attract all the statutory provisions and safeguards.

Use and Conduct

There are two areas to be considered when considering covert human intelligence sources: the 'use' of a CHIS and 'conduct' as a CHIS. Both areas are strictly controlled by the legislation and require the relevant authorisation if they are to be lawful.

The 'use' of a CHIS involves any action on behalf of a public authority to induce, ask or assist a person to engage in the conduct of a CHIS, or to obtain information by means of the conduct of a CHIS (s. 26(7)(b)).

The conduct of a CHIS is any conduct of a CHIS which falls within para. 2.1 above, that is, steps taken by the CHIS on behalf, or at the request, of a public authority (s. 26(7)(a)). Most CHIS authorisations will be for both use and conduct as public authorities usually task the CHIS to undertake covert action, and because the CHIS will be expected to take action in relation to the public authority, such as responding to particular tasking.

Generally, covertly recording conversations and other personal information about a particular person will amount to some form of 'surveillance' (and therefore will be governed by the strict rules regulating such operations). However, such use of a CHIS will not amount to 'surveillance' (s. 48(3)).

Note that, apart from the many other considerations of using a CHIS, the police owe a duty to take reasonable care to avoid unnecessary disclosure to the general public of information provided by a CHIS (*Swinney* v *Chief Constable of Northumbria (No. 2)* (1999) 11 Admin LR 811).

1.12.3.1 CHIS: General Rules on Authorisations

In relation to the authorisation of a CHIS by the police the Regulation of Investigatory Powers Act 2000, s. 29 states:

(1) Subject to the following provisions of this Part, the persons designated for the purposes of this section shall each have power to grant authorisations for the conduct or the use of a covert human intelligence source.

(2) A person shall not grant an authorisation for the conduct or the use of a covert human intelligence source unless he believes—

    (a) that the authorisation is necessary on grounds falling within subsection (3);

    (b) that the authorised conduct or use is proportionate to what is sought to be achieved by that conduct or use; and

    (c) that arrangements exist for the source's case that satisfy—

        (i) the requirements of subsection (4A), in the case of a source of a relevant collaborative unit;

        (ii) ...

        (iii) the requirements of subsection (5), in the case of any other source;

        and that satisfy such other requirements as may be imposed by order made by the Secretary of State.

(2A) For the meaning of 'relevant collaborative unit' in subsection (2)(c)(i), see section 29A.

(3) An authorisation is necessary on grounds falling within this subsection if it is necessary—

    (a) in the interests of national security;

    (b) for the purpose of preventing or detecting crime or of preventing disorder;

    (c) in the interests of the economic well-being of the United Kingdom;

    (d) in the interests of public safety;

    (e) for the purpose of protecting public health;

    (f) for the purpose of assessing or collecting any tax, duty, levy or other imposition, contribution or charge payable to a government department; or

    (g) for any purpose (not falling within paragraphs (a) to (f)) which is specified for the purposes of this subsection by an order made by the Secretary of State.

KEYNOTE

Note that in relation to s. 29(3)(b), preventing and detecting crime is defined in s. 81(5) and goes beyond the prosecution of offenders and includes actions taken to avert, end or disrupt the commission of criminal offences.

An authorisation under this section may not have the effect of authorising a covert human intelligence resource who is a person designated under s. 38 of the Police Reform Act 2002 to establish contact in person with another person (subs. (6A)). However, although a designated staff member or volunteer would not be able to work undercover face-to-face, they could do so online, for example as part of an online child sexual abuse investigation.

For the purposes of section 29(2)(c)(i), a 'relevant collaborative unit' is a unit that either consists of two or more police forces whose chief officers of police have made an agreement under s. 22A of the Police Act 1996 (s. 29A(2)) or it consists of one or more police forces and the National Crime Agency by virtue of an agreement made under s. 22A (s. 29A(3)).

The following extract from the Covert Human Intelligence Sources Code of Practice, Chapter 3, explains the terms 'necessary' and 'proportionate' contained within s. 29(2) and details the extent of authorisations:

Necessity and Proportionality

3.2 The 2000 Act stipulates that the authorising officer must believe that an authorisation for the use or conduct of a CHIS is necessary in the circumstances of the particular case for one or more of the statutory grounds listed in section 29(3) of the 2000 Act.

3.3 If the use or conduct of the CHIS is deemed necessary on one or more of the statutory grounds, the person granting the authorisation must also believe that it is proportionate to what is sought to be achieved by carrying it out. The degree of intrusiveness of the actions tasked on or undertaken by an authorised CHIS will vary from case to case, and therefore proportionality must be assessed on an individual basis. This involves balancing the seriousness of the intrusion into the private or family life of the subject of the operation (or any other person who may be affected) against the need for the activity in investigative and operational terms.

3.4 The authorisation will not be proportionate if it is excessive in the overall circumstances of the case. Each action authorised should bring an expected benefit to the investigation or operation and should not be disproportionate or arbitrary. The fact that a suspected offence may be serious will not alone render the use or conduct of a CHIS proportionate. Similarly, an offence may be so minor that any deployment of a CHIS would be disproportionate. No activity should be considered proportionate if the information, which is sought, could reasonably be obtained by other less intrusive means.

3.5 The following elements of proportionality should therefore be considered:
- balancing the size and scope of the proposed activity against the gravity and extent of the perceived crime or harm;
- explaining how and why the methods to be adopted will cause the least possible intrusion on the subject and others;
- whether the conduct to be authorised will have any implications for the privacy of others, and an explanation of why (if relevant) it is nevertheless proportionate to proceed with the operation;
- evidencing, as far as reasonably practicable, what other methods had been considered and why they were not implemented, or have been implemented unsuccessfully;
- considering whether the activity is an appropriate use of the legislation and a reasonable way, having considered all reasonable alternatives, of obtaining the information sought.

Extent of authorisations

3.7 An authorisation under Part II of the 2000 Act for the use or conduct of a CHIS will provide lawful authority for any such activity that:
- involves the use or conduct of a CHIS as is specified or described in the authorisation;
- is carried out by or in relation to the person to whose actions as a CHIS the authorisation relates; and
- is carried out for the purposes of, or in connection with, the investigation or operation so described

3.8 In the above context, it is important that the CHIS is fully aware of the extent and limits of any conduct authorised, and that those involved in the use of a CHIS are fully aware of the extent and limits of the authorisation in question.

Authorising officers are also required to take into account collateral intrusion, namely, the risk of interference with the private and family life of persons who are not the intended subjects of the CHIS activity (Code of Practice, para. 3.9). They will also need to be aware of any particular sensitivities in the local community. Consideration should also be given to any adverse impact on community confidence or safety that may result from the use or conduct of a CHIS or use of information obtained from that CHIS (para. 3.17).

1.12.3.2 CHIS: Authorisation Procedures

The following extract from the Covert Human Intelligence Sources Code of Practice, Chapter 5, outlines authorisation procedures for the use or conduct of a CHIS:

Authorisation Procedures

5.4 Responsibility for authorising the use or conduct of a CHIS rests with the authorising officer and all authorisations require the personal authority of the authorising officer. The 2010 CHIS Order as amended by the 2013 Relevant Sources Order designates the authorising officer for each different public authority and the officers entitled to act only in urgent cases. In certain circumstances the Secretary of State will be the authorising officer (see section 30(2) of the 2000 Act).

5.5 The authorising officer must give authorisations in writing, except in urgent cases, where they may be given orally. In such cases, a statement that the authorising officer has expressly authorised the action should be recorded in writing by the applicant (or the person with whom the authorising officer spoke) as a priority. This statement need not contain the full detail of the application, which should however subsequently be recorded in writing when reasonably practicable (generally the next working day).

5.6 Other officers entitled to act in urgent cases may only give authorisation in writing e.g. written authorisation for directed surveillance given by a Superintendent.

5.7 A case is not normally to be regarded as urgent unless the time that would elapse before the authorising officer was available to grant the authorisation would, in the judgment of the person giving the authorisation, be likely to endanger life or jeopardise the operation or investigation for which the authorisation was being given. An authorisation is not to be regarded as urgent where the need for an authorisation has been neglected or the urgency is of the applicant's or authorising officer's own making.

KEYNOTE

Authorising CHIS

Authorising officers should, where possible, be independent of the investigation. However, it is recognised that this is not always possible, especially in the cases of small organisations, or where it is necessary to act urgently or for security reasons.

The Regulation of Investigatory Powers (Directed Surveillance and Covert Human Intelligence Sources) Order 2010 (SI 2010/521, as amended by SI 2013/2788), prescribes the ranks of those within the police service in England and Wales who can authorise a CHIS. The ranks, mode of authorisation and associated time frames are summarised below:

Type of Authorisation	→	Ordinary CHIS	Urgent CHIS
		↓	↓
Minimum Rank	→	Superintendent or above	Inspector or above
		↓	↓
Form	→	In Writing	Inspector—In Writing Superintendent—In Writing or Oral
		↓	↓
Time Frame	→	12 months beginning on the day the authorisation is granted	72 hours beginning from the time authorisation is granted

The relevant rank of an authorising officer for a CHIS is a superintendent and above. However, in urgent cases, where it is not reasonably practicable to have the application considered by someone of that rank in the same organisation, an inspector may generally give the relevant authorisation (sch. 1, part 1 of the 2010 Order). Unless it is renewed, the authorisation given by a superintendent will ordinarily cease to have effect after 12 months beginning on the day it was granted (s. 43(3)(b)). If that authorisation was given orally by a superintendent in an urgent case, it will only last for 72 hours unless renewed, and where the case is urgent and the authority was given by an inspector, it will cease to have effect 72 hours later unless renewed (s. 43(3)(a)).

Authorisations may also be made on an application made by a member of another police force where such a police force is party to a collaborative agreement that provides for this (s. 33(3ZA)–(3ZC)).

Long-term authorisations (those exceeding 12 months) can only be given by a chief constable/commissioner and are subject to approval by a Judicial Commissioner.

A single authorisation can combine two or more different authorisations (e.g. the use of surveillance and the use of a CHIS) but they operate independently of each other (s. 43(2)). This means that when one authorisation lapses, any other authorisations made at the same time do not necessarily end as well.

Authorising 'Relevant Sources'

The ranks, mode of authorisation and associated time frames are summarised below:

Type of Authorisation	→	Ordinary 'Relevant Source'	Urgent 'Relevant Source'
		↓	↓
Minimum Rank	→	ACC/Commander or above	Superintendent or above
		↓	↓
Form	→	In Writing	In Writing
		↓	↓
Time Frame	→	12 months beginning on the day the authorisation is granted	72 hours beginning from the time authorisation is granted

---

All deployments of undercover officers (referred to in the Order and Code as 'relevant sources') must be authorised by an assistant chief constable/commander or in urgent cases by a superintendent.

Authorisations lasting more than 12 months must be approved by a chief constable/commissioner and the Office of Surveillance Commissioners must give prior approval (sch. 1, part 1A to the 2010 Order). The CHIS Code of Practice states that all police officers deployed as a relevant source must comply with the College of Policing Code of Ethics.

Authorising Juvenile/Vulnerable CHIS

Type of Authorisation	→	Juvenile/Vulnerable CHIS
		↓
Minimum Rank	→	ACC/Commander
		↓
Form	→	In Writing
		↓
Time Frame	→	Four months beginning on the day the authorisation is granted

The ranks, mode of authorisation and associated time frames are summarised below:

Special safeguards apply in relation to juveniles and vulnerable individuals. Juveniles are those under 18 years of age. On no occasion should the use or conduct of a CHIS under 16 years of age be authorised to give information against his parents or any person who has parental responsibility for him. In other cases, authorisations should not be granted unless the special provisions contained within the Regulation of Investigatory Powers (Juveniles) (Amendment) Order 2018 (SI 2018/715) are satisfied.

A vulnerable individual is a person who is or may be in need of community care services by reason of mental or other disability, age or illness and who is or may be unable to take care of him/herself, or unable to protect him/herself against significant harm or exploitation.

The authorisation levels for juveniles and vulnerable individuals are assistant chief constable/commander where they are to be used as sources. Regular reviews of authorisations are required to assess whether it remains necessary and proportionate to use a CHIS and whether the authorisation remains justified. An authorisation must be cancelled if the use or conduct of the CHIS no longer satisfies the criteria for authorisation.

In *R (On the Application of Just for Kids Law) v Secretary of State for the Home Department* [2019] EWHC 1772 (Admin) the court held that the scheme relating to the use of a juvenile CHIS adequately protects children's welfare and their Article 8 rights.

An enhanced authorisation regime exists when, through the use or conduct of a CHIS, it is likely that knowledge of legally privileged material or other confidential information will be required (the Regulation of Investigatory Powers (Covert Human Intelligence Sources: Matters Subject to Legal Privilege) Order 2010 (SI 2010/521, as amended by SI 2013/2788)).

1.12.4 Covert Surveillance

The Covert Surveillance and Property Interference Revised Code of Practice (August 2018) provides:

2 Activity by public authorities to which this code applies

2.1 Part II of the 2000 Act provides for the *authorisation* of covert surveillance by *public authorities* listed at Schedule 1 of the 2000 Act where that surveillance is likely to result in the obtaining of *private information* about a person.

2.2 Surveillance, for the purpose of the 2000 Act, includes monitoring, observing or listening to persons, their movements, conversations or other activities and communications. It may be conducted with or without the assistance of a surveillance device and includes the recording of any information obtained.

(See section 48(2) of the 2000 Act)

2.3 Surveillance is covert if, and only if, it is carried out in a manner calculated to ensure that any persons who are subject to the surveillance are unaware that it is or may be taking place.
(As defined in section 26(9)(a) of the 2000 Act)

2.4 Specifically, covert surveillance may be authorised under the 2000 Act if it is either intrusive or directed:

- Directed surveillance is covert surveillance that is not intrusive but is carried out in relation to a specific investigation or operation in such a manner as is likely to result in the obtaining of *private information* about any person (other than by way of an immediate response to events or circumstances such that it is not reasonably practicable to seek *authorisation* under the 2000 Act);
- Intrusive surveillance is covert surveillance that is carried out in relation to anything taking place on residential premises or in any private vehicle (and that involves the presence of an individual on the premises or in the vehicle or is carried out by a means of a surveillance device).

KEYNOTE

Private Information

Private information includes any information relating to a person's private or family life (s. 26(10)). It should be taken generally to include any aspect of a person's private or personal relationship with others, including family. Family should be treated as extending beyond the formal relationships created by marriage or civil partnership and may include professional or business relationships. Private information may include personal data, such as names, telephone numbers and address details.

What DOES NOT Constitute Surveillance

Some surveillance activity does not constitute intrusive or directed surveillance for the purposes of part II of the 2000 Act and includes:

- covert surveillance by way of an immediate response to events, e.g. where police officers conceal themselves to observe suspicious persons that they come across in the course of a routine patrol;
- covert surveillance as part of general observation activities, e.g. where plain clothes police officers are on patrol to monitor a high street crime hot-spot or prevent and detect shoplifting;
- covert surveillance not relating to specified grounds, e.g. where a specific investigation or operation does not relate to the grounds specified at s. 28(3) of the 2000 Act;
- overt use of CCTV and ANPR systems, e.g. members of the public will be aware that such systems are in use, and their operation is covered by the Surveillance Camera Code of Practice issued under the Protection of Freedoms Act 2012 that sets out a framework of good practice that includes existing legal obligations, including the processing of personal data under the Data Protection Act 2018 and a public authority's duty to adhere to the Human Rights Act 1998. The overt use of ANPR systems to monitor traffic flows or detect motoring offences does not require an authorisation under the 2000 Act;
- certain other specific situations, e.g. the use of a recording device by a CHIS in respect of whom an appropriate use or conduct authorisation has been granted permitting him to record any information obtained in his presence (s. 48(3));
- the recording, whether overt or covert, of an interview with a member of the public where it is made clear that the interview is entirely voluntary and that the interviewer is a member of a public authority.

1.12.4.1 Directed and Intrusive Surveillance

Chapter 3 of the Code of Practice provides guidance on directed surveillance and states:

Directed surveillance

3.1 Surveillance is directed surveillance if the following are all true:

- it is covert, but not intrusive surveillance;
- it is conducted for the purposes of a specific investigation or operation;
- it is likely to result in the obtaining of *private information* about a person (whether or not one specifically identified for the purposes of the investigation or operation);
- it is conducted otherwise than by way of an immediate response to events or circumstances the nature of which is such that it would not be reasonably practicable for an *authorisation* under Part II of the 2000 Act to be sought.

3.2 Thus, the planned covert surveillance of a specific person, where not intrusive, would constitute directed surveillance if such surveillance is likely to result in the obtaining of *private information* about that, or any other person.

KEYNOTE

Where private information is acquired by means of covert surveillance of a person having a reasonable expectation of privacy, a directed surveillance authorisation is appropriate. The fact that a directed surveillance authorisation is available does not mean it is required. There may be other lawful means of obtaining personal data that do not involve directed surveillance.

While a person may have a reduced expectation of privacy when in a public place, covert surveillance of that person's activities in public may still result in the obtaining of private information. This is likely to be the case where that person has a reasonable expectation of privacy even though acting in public and where a record is being made by a public authority of that person's activities for future consideration or analysis. Note also that a person in police custody will have certain expectations of privacy.

Authorising of Directed Surveillance

An authorisation for directed surveillance should not be granted unless it is believed to be proportionate to what is sought to be achieved and necessary on the specified grounds **(see para. 1.12.3.1** in relation to 'necessary' and 'proportionate'). The specified grounds, contained in s. 28(3), are:

- in the interests of national security;
- for the purpose of preventing or detecting crime or of preventing disorder;
- in the interests of the economic well-being of the United Kingdom;
- in the interests of public safety;
- for the purpose of protecting public health;
- for the purpose of assessing or collecting any tax, duty, levy or other imposition, contribution or charge payable to a government department; or
- for any purpose (not falling within paras (a) to (f)) which is specified for the purposes of this subsection by an order made by the Secretary of State.

The Regulation of Investigatory Powers (Directed Surveillance and Covert Human Intelligence Sources) Order 2003 (SI 2003/3171), as amended, sets out the relevant roles and ranks for those who can authorise directed surveillance. The ranks, mode of authorisation and associated time frames are summarised below:

Type of Authorisation	→	Ordinary Directed Surveillance	Urgent Directed Surveillance
		↓	↓
Minimum Rank	→	Superintendent or above	Inspector or above
		↓	↓
Form	→	In Writing	Inspector—In Writing Superintendent—In Writing or Oral
		↓	↓
Time Frame	→	Three months beginning on the day the authorisation is granted	72 hours beginning from the time authorisation is granted

In the case of the police the relevant rank will generally be at superintendent level and above, and the authorisation must be in writing except in urgent cases where oral authorisation may be given (s. 43(1)(a)). A written authorisation ceases to have effect after three months beginning on the day it was granted, and if given orally will only last 72 hours unless renewed (s. 43(3)). Where it is not reasonably practicable to have the application considered by a superintendent or above, having regard to the urgency of the case, then an inspector may give the relevant authorisation which will only last 72 hours unless renewed by a superintendent. For the NCA the authorising officer is a Senior Manager (Grade 2) and for urgent cases a Principal Officer (Grade 3).

In *Davies* v *British Transport Police* (2018) IPT/17/93/H it was held that an authorisation should have been obtained where a police officer covertly observed a man on a train suspected of sexual assaults and also took photographs of the suspect.

Authorisations may also be made on an application made by a member of another police force where such police forces are party to a collaborative agreement that provides for them (s. 33(3ZA)–(3ZC)).

As with a CHIS, the Codes of Practice provide additional procedural safeguards regarding where the material sought by the surveillance is subject to legal privilege, is confidential personal information or some journalistic material. It is of interest to note that the House of Lords has held that the 2000 Act permits covert surveillance of communications between lawyers and their clients even though these may be subject to legal professional privilege (*Re McE (Northern Ireland)* [2009] UKHL 15).

1.12.4.2 Intrusive Surveillance

Chapter 3 of the Code of Practice also provides guidance on intrusive surveillance and states:

Intrusive Surveillance

3.19 Intrusive surveillance is covert surveillance that is:
- carried out in relation to anything taking place on residential premises, or
- in any private vehicle, and
- involves the presence of an individual on the premises or in the vehicle, or
- is carried out by a means of a surveillance device.

3.21 The definition of surveillance as intrusive relates to the location of the surveillance, and not any other consideration of the nature of the information that is expected to be obtained, as it is assumed that intrusive surveillance will always be likely to result in the obtaining of private information. Accordingly, it is not necessary to consider whether or not intrusive surveillance is likely to result in the obtaining of private information.

KEYNOTE

Residential Premises

'Residential premises' are considered to be so much of any premises as is for the time being occupied or used by any person, however temporarily, for residential purposes or otherwise as living accommodation. This specifically includes hotel or prison accommodation that is so occupied or used (s. 48(1)). However, common areas (such as hotel dining areas) to which a person has access in connection with their use or occupation of accommodation are specifically excluded (s. 48(7)). The Act further states that the concept of premises should be taken to include any place whatsoever, including any vehicle or movable structure, whether or not occupied as land (s. 48(8)).

Private Vehicle

A 'private vehicle' is defined as any vehicle, including vessels, aircraft or hovercraft, which is used primarily for the private purposes of the person who owns it or a person otherwise having the right to use it. This would include, for example, a company car, owned by a leasing company and used for business and pleasure by the employee of a company (s. 48(1) and (7)).

In *R* v *Plunkett* [2013] EWCA Crim 261, in admitting evidence of statements and admissions by the accused in a police van which were covertly recorded, it was held that a police van is not a private vehicle for the purposes of s. 26(3) and that the authorisation given by a superintendent under s. 28 for directed surveillance was appropriate.

Surveillance is not intrusive if it is carried out by means only of a surveillance device designed or adapted principally for the purpose of providing information about the location of a vehicle (s. 25(4)(a)).

Consistent Quality

If the surveillance is carried out by means of a surveillance device in relation to anything taking place on the premises or private vehicle, but is carried out without that device being present on the premises or in the vehicle, it is not intrusive unless the device is such that it consistently provides information of the same quality and detail as might be expected to be obtained from a device actually present on the premises or in the vehicle (s. 25(5)).

Legal Consultations

The Regulation of Investigatory Powers (Extension of Authorisation Provisions: Legal Consultations) Order 2010 (SI 2010/461) provides that directed surveillance carried out in relation to anything taking place on any premises specified in the Order that are being used for the purpose of legal consultations shall be treated as 'intrusive surveillance'. The 'any premises' includes prisons, police stations, high security psychiatric hospitals, the place of business of any professional legal adviser; and any place used for the sittings and business of any court, tribunal, inquest or inquiry.

Authorising Intrusive Surveillance

As with the other authorisations under the Act, the authorising officer shall not grant an authorisation for the carrying out of intrusive surveillance unless he/she believes that the authorisation is necessary on the specified grounds and that the authorised surveillance is proportionate to what is sought to be achieved by carrying it out (s. 32(2)). The specified grounds, contained in s. 32(3) are:

- in the interests of national security;
- for the purpose of preventing or detecting serious crime;
- in the interests of the economic well-being of the United Kingdom.

In relation to 'national security' a senior authorising officer or designated deputy of a law enforcement agency shall not issue an authorisation for intrusive surveillance where the investigation or operation is within the responsibilities of one of the intelligence services and properly falls to be authorised by warrant issued by the Secretary of State.

'Serious crime' is defined in s. 81(2) and (3) as crime that comprises an offence for which a person who has attained the age of 21 and has no previous convictions could reasonably be expected to be sentenced to imprisonment for a term of three years or more, or which involves the use of violence, results in substantial financial gain or is conducted by a large number of persons in pursuit of a common purpose.

The ranks, mode of authorisation and associated time frames are summarised below:

Type of Authorisation	→	Ordinary Intrusive Surveillance	Urgent Intrusive Surveillance
		↓	↓
Minimum Rank	→	Chief Constable/Commissioner (or designated deputy)	Chief Constable/Commissioner (or designated deputy)
		↓	↓
Form	→	In Writing	In Writing or Oral
		↓	↓
Time Frame	→	Three months beginning when the Surveillance Commissioner approves the authorisation	72 hours beginning from the time authorised (provided notice is given to the Surveillance Commissioner)

Authorisations for intrusive surveillance will generally be granted by chief constables/commissioners and the Director General of the NCA (s. 32), or in some cases designated deputies.

A written authorisation will cease to have effect (unless renewed) at the end of a period of three months. Oral authorisations given in urgent cases will cease to have effect (unless renewed) at the end of the period of 72 hours beginning with the time when they took effect.

Except in urgent cases, authorisation granted for intrusive surveillance will not take effect until a Surveillance Commissioner has approved it and written notice of the Commissioner's decision has been given to the person who granted the authorisation. This means that the approval will not take effect until the notice has been received in the office of the person who granted the authorisation within the relevant force or organisation (s. 35(3)(a)). When the authorisation is urgent it will take effect from the time it is granted provided notice is given to the Surveillance Commissioner (s. 35(3)(b)).

Authorisations may also be made on an application made by a member of another police force where such police forces are party to a collaborative agreement that provides for them (s. 33(3ZA)–(3ZC)).

Serious Crime and Other Offences

2.1 Homicide

2.1.1 Introduction

Homicide covers offences of murder, manslaughter and other occasions where a person causes, or is involved in, the death of another. The common law in relation to homicide is important, not only because of the gravity of the offences themselves, but also because the cases have defined a number of key issues in criminal law applicable to many other offences.

In all cases of homicide, the general criminal conduct (*actus reus*) is the same—the killing of another person.

2.1.2 Murder

OFFENCE: **Murder—*Common Law***

- Life imprisonment (mandatory)

Murder is committed when a person unlawfully kills another human being under the Queen's Peace, with malice aforethought.

KEYNOTE

A conviction for murder carries a mandatory sentence of life imprisonment (if the offence is committed by a person aged 18 but under 21, the sentence is 'custody for life' (also mandatory) and in the case of a defendant who is under 18, 'detention at Her Majesty's pleasure': Powers of Criminal Courts (Sentencing) Act 2000, s. 90).

'Unlawful killing' means actively causing the death of another without justification. 'Unlawfully' can be taken to exclude killings for which the accused has a complete and valid justification, such as killing (reasonably) in self-defence. It also includes occasions where someone fails to act after creating a situation of danger (see chapter 1.2).

'Another human being' includes a baby who has been born alive and has an existence independent of its mother. 'Existence independent of its mother' means that the child is fully expelled from the womb; the umbilical cord need not be cut. If a defendant intended to kill or cause serious injury to the mother, that intention cannot support a charge of murder in respect of the baby if it goes on to die after being born alive. It may, however, support a charge of manslaughter (*Attorney-General's Reference (No. 3 of 1994)* [1998] AC 245). It would certainly be appropriate to charge a person with the murder of the child if he/she intended the child to die after having been born alive.

'Under the Queen's Peace' appears to exclude deaths caused during the legitimate prosecution of warfare (War Crimes Act 1991).

Under the provisions of the Offences Against the Person Act 1861 (s. 9), any British citizen who commits a murder anywhere in the world may be tried in England or Wales. It does not matter what nationality the victim was or where in the world the act took place—all that matters is that at the time the offence was committed, the defendant was a British citizen.

It should be noted that the only state of mind or *mens rea* that will support a charge of attempted murder is an *intention to kill*. Nothing less will suffice.

2.1.2.1 Malice Aforethought

The cases of *R* v *Moloney* [1985] AC 905 and *R* v *Hancock* [1986] AC 455 identify the *mens rea* required for murder as an intention:

- to kill; or
- to cause grievous bodily harm.

Murder is therefore a crime of 'specific intent'.

The term 'malice aforethought' is often associated with some form of premeditation; this is not required.

2.1.2.2 Year and a Day

Section 1 of the Law Reform (Year and a Day Rule) Act 1996 abolished the limitation that death had to occur within a year and a day of the infliction of injury.

However, by s. 2 of the Act, the consent of the Attorney-General is required before proceedings can be instituted for a 'fatal offence' where either:

(a) the injury alleged to have caused the death was sustained more than three years before death occurred; or

(b) the person has previously been convicted of an offence committed in circumstances alleged to be connected to the death.

2.1.3 Voluntary Manslaughter and 'Special Defences'

As a conviction for murder leaves a judge no discretion in sentencing a defendant, a number of 'special defences' have developed around the offence (diminished responsibility, loss of control and suicide pact). Rather than securing an acquittal, they allow for a conviction of 'voluntary manslaughter' instead of murder (hence, they are also termed 'partial' defences to murder). Consequently, voluntary manslaughter is more a finding by a court than an offence with which a person can be charged. It should be noted that these 'special defences' are only available to a defendant who is charged with an offence of murder—they cannot be used in answer to any other charge, e.g. attempted murder.

2.1.3.1 Diminished Responsibility

The Homicide Act 1957, s. 2 states:

> (1) A person ('D') who kills or is a party to a killing of another is not to be convicted of murder if D was suffering from an abnormality of mental functioning which—
>   (a) arose from a recognised medical condition,
>   (b) substantially impaired D's ability to do one or more of the things mentioned in subsection (1A), and
>   (c) provides an explanation for D's acts and omissions in doing or being party to the killing.
> (1A) Those things are—
>   (a) to understand the nature of D's conduct;
>   (b) to form a rational judgment;
>   (c) to exercise self-control.
> (1B) For the purposes of subsection (1)(c), an abnormality of mental functioning provides an explanation for D's conduct if it causes, or is a significant contributory factor in causing, D to carry out that conduct.
> (2) On a charge of murder, it shall be for the defence to prove that the person charged is by virtue of this section not liable to be convicted of murder.

(3) A person who but for this section would be liable, whether as principal or as accessory, to be convicted of murder shall be liable instead to be convicted of manslaughter.

(4) The fact that one party to a killing is by virtue of this section not liable to be convicted of murder shall not affect the question whether the killing amounted to murder in the case of any other party to it.

KEYNOTE

The definition requires that the abnormality *substantially* impaired the defendant's ability to do one (or more) of three things and also provides that the defendant's abnormality of mental functioning should be at least a significant contributory factor in causing the defendant's acts or omissions. Whether the 'impairment of mental responsibility' is 'substantial' or not will be a question of fact for the jury to decide. Minor lapses of lucidity will not be enough.

The abnormality must arise from a *recognised medical condition*. 'Abnormality of mind' has been held to be 'a state of mind so different from that of ordinary human beings that the reasonable man would term it abnormal' (*R* v *Byrne* [1960] 2 QB 396). This includes the mental inability to exert control over one's behaviour and to form a rational judgement.

There may be any number of causes of the 'abnormality' of the mind. Examples include post-natal depression and pre-menstrual symptoms (*R* v *Reynolds* [1988] Crim LR 679) and 'battered wives' syndrome' (*R* v *Hobson* [1998] 1 Cr App R 31). In *R* v *Dietschmann* [2003] UKHL 10, the House of Lords accepted that a mental abnormality caused by a grief reaction to the recent death of an aunt with whom the defendant had had a physical relationship could suffice. In that case, their lordships went on to hold that there is no requirement to show that the 'abnormality of mind' was the *sole* cause of the defendant's acts in committing the killing.

The burden of proving these features lies with the defence and the standard required is one of a balance of probabilities.

2.1.3.2 Loss of Control

The Coroners and Justice Act 2009, s. 54 states:

(1) Where a person ('D') kills or is a party to the killing of another ('V'), D is not to be convicted of murder if—
   (a) D's acts and omissions in doing or being a party to the killing resulted from D's loss of self-control,
   (b) the loss of self-control had a qualifying trigger, and
   (c) a person of D's sex and age, with a normal degree of tolerance and self-restraint and in the circumstances of D, might have reacted in the same or in a similar way to D.

(2) For the purposes of subsection (1)(a), it does not matter whether or not the loss of control was sudden.

(3) In subsection (1)(c) the reference to 'the circumstances of D' is a reference to all of D's circumstances other than those whose only relevance to D's conduct is that they bear on D's general capacity for tolerance or self-restraint.

(4) Subsection (1) does not apply if, in doing or being a party to the killing, D acted in a considered desire for revenge.

(5) On a charge of murder, if sufficient evidence is adduced to raise an issue with respect to the defence under subsection (1), the jury must assume that the defence is satisfied unless the prosecution proves beyond reasonable doubt that it is not.

(6) For the purposes of subsection (5), sufficient evidence is adduced to raise an issue with respect to the defence if evidence is adduced on which, in the opinion of the trial judge, a jury, properly directed, could reasonably conclude that the defence might apply.

(7) A person who, but for this section, would be liable to be convicted of murder is liable instead to be convicted of manslaughter.

(8) The fact that one party to a killing is by virtue of this section not liable to be convicted of murder does not affect the question whether the killing amounted to murder in the case of any other party to it.

KEYNOTE

In *R v Asmelash* [2013] EWCA Crim 157, the Court of Appeal confirmed that in considering the question under s. 54(1)(c) of whether 'a person of D's sex and age, with a normal degree of tolerance and self-restraint and in the circumstances of D, might have reacted in the same or similar way to D', the fact that the accused had voluntarily consumed alcohol was *not* to be included in D's circumstances.

The loss of control *need not be sudden* (s. 54(2)). Although subs. (2) in the partial defence states that *it is not a requirement* for the partial defence that the loss of self-control be sudden, it will remain open for the judge (in deciding whether to leave the defence to the jury) and the jury (in determining whether the killing did in fact result from a loss of self-control and whether the other aspects of the partial defence are satisfied) to take into account any delay between a relevant incident and the killing.

Section 54(3) supplements s. 54(1)(c) by clarifying that the reference to the defendant's circumstances in that subsection means all of those circumstances except those whose only relevance to the defendant's conduct is that they impact upon the defendant's general level of tolerance and self-restraint. Thus, a defendant's history of abuse at the hands of the victim could be taken into account in deciding whether an ordinary person might have acted as the defendant did, whereas the defendant's generally short temper could not. Consequently, when applying the test in s. 54(1)(c) the jury will consider whether a person of the defendant's sex and age with an ordinary level of tolerance and self-restraint and in the defendant's specific circumstances (in the sense described earlier in this paragraph) might have acted as the defendant did.

Those acting in a considered desire for revenge cannot rely on the partial defence, even if they lose self-control as a result of a qualifying trigger.

Qualifying Trigger

Section 55 of the Coroners and Justice Act 2009, explains the phrase 'qualifying trigger' mentioned in s. 54(1)(b). The loss of self-control must be attributable to:

- *The defendant's fear of serious violence from the victim against the defendant or another identified person.* This will be a subjective test and the defendant will need to show that he/she lost self-control because of a genuine fear of serious violence, whether or not the fear was in fact reasonable. The fear of serious violence needs to be in respect of violence against the defendant or against another identified person. For example, the fear of serious violence could be in respect of a child of the defendant, but it could not be a fear that the victim would in the future use serious violence against people generally.
- *To a thing or things done or said (or both) which constituted circumstances of an extremely grave character and caused the defendant to have a justifiable sense of being seriously wronged.* Whether a defendant's sense of being seriously wronged is justifiable will be an objective question for a jury to determine. This sets a high threshold for the circumstances in which a partial defence is available where a person loses self-control in response to words or actions. It effectively restricts the potential availability of a partial defence in cases where a loss of control is attributable to things done or said.
- *A combination of the above two factors.*

Section 55(6) states that in determining whether a loss of self-control had a qualifying trigger:

- the defendant's fear of serious violence is to be disregarded to the extent that it was caused by a thing which the defendant incited to be done or said for the purpose of providing an excuse to use violence;
- a sense of being seriously wronged by a thing done or said is not justifiable if the defendant incited the thing to be done or said for the purpose of providing an excuse to use violence;
- the fact that a thing done or said constituted sexual infidelity is to be disregarded.

2.1.3.3 Suicide Pact

The Homicide Act 1957, s. 4 states:

(1) It shall be manslaughter, and shall not be murder, for a person acting in pursuance of a suicide pact between him and another to kill the other or be a party to the other being killed by a third person.

2.1.4 Involuntary Manslaughter

Involuntary manslaughter occurs where the defendant causes the death of another but is not shown to have had the required *mens rea* for murder.

OFFENCE: **Manslaughter—*Common Law***
- Triable on indictment • Life imprisonment

Involuntary manslaughter—that is, those cases which do not involve the 'special defences' under the Homicide Act 1957 or Coroners and Justice Act 2009—can be separated into occasions where a defendant:

- kills another by an *unlawful* act which was *likely to cause bodily harm*; or
- kills another by *gross negligence*.

2.1.4.1 Manslaughter by Unlawful Act

There are three elements to the offence of manslaughter by an unlawful act (also called constructive manslaughter). You must prove:

(1) an unlawful act;
(2) that the unlawful act is likely to cause bodily harm; and
(3) the defendant had the *mens rea* for the unlawful act.

An Unlawful Act

The accused's act must be inherently unlawful, in that it constitutes *a criminal offence in its own right*, irrespective of the fact that it ultimately results in someone's death. An act that only becomes unlawful by virtue of the way in which it is carried out will not be enough. For instance, 'driving' is clearly not an inherently unlawful act but becomes so if done dangerously or carelessly on a road or public place. If someone drives dangerously and thereby causes the death of another, the act of driving, albeit carried out in a way that attracts criminal liability, is *not* an 'unlawful act' for the purposes of unlawful act manslaughter (*Andrews* v *DPP* [1937] AC 576). Hence, the existence of statutory offences addressing most instances of death that are caused by poor standards of driving. If a defendant uses a motor vehicle as a means to commit an 'unlawful act' (e.g. an assault), he/she can be charged with manslaughter as long as the 'act' goes beyond poor driving. The CPS has published a policy document which sets out the way in which it will deal with cases of bad driving. Unlawful act manslaughter will be considered the most appropriate charge when there is evidence to prove that the vehicle was used as an instrument of attack (but where the necessary intent for murder was absent), or to cause fright, and death resulted. There are, however, reasons of policy (*R* v *Lawrence* [1982] AC 510) why, in all but the most deliberate of cases, the offences under the Road Traffic Act 1988 should be used. The inherently unlawful act need not be directed or aimed at anyone and can include acts committed against or to-wards property, such as criminal damage or arson (*R* v *Goodfellow* (1986) 83 Cr App R 23). Generally, if the actions of the victim break the chain of causation between the defendant's unlawful act and the cause of death, the defendant will not be responsible for the death of that victim (**see chapter 1.2**). This is why drug dealers who supply controlled drugs cannot generally be held liable for the ultimate deaths of their 'victims' unless they have done far more than just supply a drug (*R* v *Dalby* [1982] 1 WLR 425 and *R* v *Armstrong* [1989] Crim LR 149). This view was affirmed in the case of *R* v *Kennedy* [2007] UKHL 38. The circum-stances were that the defendant had prepared a dose of heroin for the deceased and had given the syringe to the deceased before leaving the room they were both in. The deceased injected the drug and as a result died. The House of Lords ruled that a supplier of a drug is not guilty of manslaughter where the deceased freely and voluntarily self-administered the drug. An *omission* to do something will not suffice as manslaughter by unlawful act requires *an act*.

The Unlawful Act is Likely to Cause Bodily Harm

The unlawful act must involve a risk of some bodily harm (albeit not serious harm). That risk will be judged *objectively*; that is, would the risk of harm be foreseen by a reasonable and sober person watching the act (*R* v *Church* [1966] 1 QB 59)? Such acts might include dropping a paving stone off a bridge into the path of a train (*DPP* v *Newbury* [1977] AC 500), setting fire to your house (*Goodfellow*) or firing a gun at police officers and then holding someone else in front of you when the officers return fire (*R* v *Pagett* (1983) 76 Cr App R 279).

The 'harm' likely to result from the act must be physical; the risk of emotional or psy-chological harm does not appear to be enough (*R* v *Dawson* (1985) 81 Cr App R 150). In *R* v *Carey* [2006] EWCA Crim 17, the Court of Appeal observed that the law of unlawful act manslaughter required the commission of an unlawful act which was recognised, by a sober and reasonable person, as being *dangerous* and likely to subject the victim to the risk of some physical harm *which in turn* caused the victim's death.

The Defendant had the *Mens Rea* for the Unlawful Act

The defendant must possess the *mens rea* for the unlawful act which led to the death of a victim. If he/she did not have that *mens rea*, the offence of manslaughter by unlawful act will not be made out. For example, in *R* v *Lamb* [1967] 2 QB 981 the defendant pretended to fire a revolver at his friend. Although the defendant believed that the weapon would not fire, the chamber containing a bullet moved round to the firing pin and the defendant's friend was killed. Lamb was charged with manslaughter by unlawful act (the unlawful act being assault) but it could not be proved that Lamb had the *mens rea* required (an intent or recklessness to cause a person to apprehend immediate unlawful violence) for an assault (**see chapter 2.7**) and his conviction for manslaughter was quashed.

The accused cannot rely on his/her lack of *mens rea* induced by voluntary intoxication as manslaughter is a crime of basic intent (*R* v *Lipman* [1970] 1 QB 152). This was an extreme case in many ways, in which the accused killed his girlfriend while suffering LSD-induced hallucinations that he was at the centre of the earth being attacked by snakes. If the unlawful act alleged were to be a crime of specific intent, then the accused's intoxication should be relevant.

2.1.4.2 Manslaughter by Gross Negligence

Manslaughter is the only criminal offence at common law capable of being committed by negligence.

A charge of manslaughter may be brought where a person, by an instance of *gross negligence*, has brought about the death of another. The ingredients of this offence essentially consist of death resulting from a negligent breach of a duty of care owed by the defendant to the victim in circumstances so reprehensible as to amount to gross negligence (*R v Misra and Srivastava* [2004] EWCA Crim 2375). The most difficult task in defining the degree of negligence that will qualify as 'gross' falls to the trial judge when addressing the jury. Whether a defendant's conduct will amount to gross negligence is a question of fact for the jury to decide in the light of all the evidence (*R v Bateman* (1925) 19 Cr App R 8).

What is clear from the decided cases is that civil liability, although a starting point for establishing the breach of a duty of care, is not enough to amount to 'gross negligence' (*R v Adomako* [1995] 1 AC 171). The test in *Adomako* as summarised by Lord Mackay seems to provide the leading authority on the area—that test for the jury being: '... whether, having regard to the risk of death involved, the conduct of the defendant was so bad in all the circumstances as to amount in their judgment to a criminal act or omission'.

It is not possible to bring proceedings for gross negligence manslaughter against a company or other organisation to which the offence under the Corporate Manslaughter and Corporate Homicide Act 2007 applies (s. 20 of the Corporate Manslaughter and Corporate Homicide Act 2007).

2.1.5 Causing or Allowing a Child or Vulnerable Adult to Die or Suffer Serious Physical Harm

This offence deals with the situation where a child or other vulnerable person dies or suffers serious physical harm as a result of an unlawful act (or omission) of one of several people but it cannot be shown which of them actually caused the death or allowed it to occur.

> OFFENCE: **Causing or Allowing a Child or Vulnerable Adult to Die or Suffer Serious Harm—*Domestic Violence, Crime and Victims Act 2004, s. 5***
> • Triable on indictment • Where the child or vulnerable adult dies, 14 years' imprisonment or a fine or both • Where the child or vulnerable adult suffers serious physical harm, 10 years' imprisonment or a fine or both

The Domestic Violence, Crime and Victims Act 2004, s. 5 states:

(1) A person ('D') is guilty of an offence if—
    (a) a child or vulnerable adult ('V') dies or suffers serious physical harm as a result of the unlawful act of a person who—
        (i) was a member of the same household as V, and
        (ii) had frequent contact with him,
    (b) D was such a person at the time of that act,

(c) at that time there was a significant risk of serious physical harm being caused to V by the unlawful act of such a person, and

(d) either D was the person whose act caused the death or serious physical harm—

    (i)   D was, or ought to have been, aware of the risk mentioned in paragraph (c),

    (ii) D failed to take such steps as he could reasonably have been expected to take to protect V from the risk, and

    (iii) the act occurred in circumstances of the kind that D foresaw or ought to have foreseen.

KEYNOTE

'Child' means a person under the age of 16 and 'vulnerable adult' means a person aged 16 or over whose ability to protect him/herself from violence, abuse or neglect is significantly impaired through physical or mental disability or illness, through old age or otherwise (s. 5(6)).

It is necessary to prove that the victim died or suffered serious physical harm *as a result of the unlawful act* of a person who fits a number of criteria. For these purposes, 'act' includes 'omissions' and an act or omission will generally only be 'unlawful' if it would have amounted to an offence (s. 5(5) and (6)). It must be shown that the defendant was, *at the time of the act*, a member of the same household as the victim *and* had frequent contact with the victim. For these purposes, people will be a member of a particular household if they visit it so often and for such periods of time that it is reasonable to regard them as a member of it *even if they do not actually live there* (s. 5(4)(a)). Where, as often happens, the victim lived in different households at different times, the 'same household' criterion will mean the household in which the victim was living at the time of the act that caused the death or serious physical harm (s. 5(4)(b)).

Unless the defendant is the mother or father of the victim: (a) he/she cannot be charged with an offence under this section if aged under 16 at the time of the act; and (b) restrictions will be made on what steps would have been reasonable for a defendant to have taken while under that age (see s. 5(3)).

2.2 Misuse of Drugs

2.2.1 Introduction

This chapter deals, in the main, with offences created by the Misuse of Drugs Act 1971. As some of the concepts associated with drug offences, e.g. 'possession' and 'supply', are important to assist in understanding the legislation, they are dealt with before any offences associated with them. A methodical approach is then taken by dealing with drug offences in the order of possession, supply and production, finishing with an examination of other drug-related offences and police powers.

2.2.2 Classification

Drugs that are subject to the provisions of the Misuse of Drugs Act 1971 are listed in parts I, II and III of sch. 2 to the Act.

The divisions are made largely on the basis of each substance's potential effects on both the person taking it and society in general. The list of controlled drugs is large, and for full details reference should be made to sch. 2 to the Misuse of Drugs Act 1971. Examples of some of the more commonly encountered drugs include:

- **Class A**—this class includes heroin (diamorphine), methadone, cocaine, LSD, 'Ecstasy' (MDMA) and 'crystal meth' (methylamphetamine). It also includes fungus (of any kind) which contains psilocin (such as 'magic mushrooms').
- **Class B**—this class includes cannabis, cannabis resin, codeine, ketamine and ritalin (methylphenidate).
- **Class C**—this class includes valium (diazepam), khat (the leaves, stems or shoots of the plant of the species *Catha edulis*) and GHB (gamma hydroxybutyrate).

If the charge alleges possession of one particular drug, then that drug must be identified.

Note that although a substance may appear in sch. 2 to the Act, there may be restrictions on the occasions where possession is treated as an offence (**see para. 2.2.3.7**).

It is not necessary, when prosecuting an offence, to distinguish between the various chemical forms in which a drug exists (i.e. as a salt, ester or other form) (*R* v *Greensmith* [1983] 1 WLR 1124).

A defendant's admission may, in some cases, be relied upon to prove his/her knowledge as to what a particular substance is (*R* v *Chatwood* [1980] 1 WLR 874).

2.2.2.1 Temporary Class Drug Orders

The Home Secretary has the power, under the Misuse of Drugs Act 1971, to make any drug subject to temporary control.

Temporary class drug orders can be made if the following two conditions are met:

(1) the drug is not already controlled under the Act as a Class A, B or C drug;
(2) the ACMD (Advisory Council on the Misuse of Drugs) has been consulted and determined that the order should be made, or the Home Secretary has received a recommendation

from the Advisory Council that the order should be made, on the basis that it appears to the Home Secretary that:

(a) the drug is being, or is likely to be, misused; and

(b) the misuse is having, or is capable of having, harmful effects.

The order will come into immediate effect and will last for up to 12 months, subject to Parliament agreeing to it within 40 sitting days of the order being made. The order enables the government to act to protect the public against harmful new psychoactive substances while expert advice is being prepared.

Such a drug will be referred to as a 'temporary class drug' and will be a 'controlled drug' for the purposes of the Misuse of Drugs Act 1971, and other legislation such as the Proceeds of Crime Act 2002, unless otherwise stated. With the *exception of the possession* offence, all the offences under the Misuse of Drugs Act will apply including possession in connection with an offence or prohibition, under ss. 3, 4 and 5(3) of the Act, i.e. possession with intent to supply. Offences committed under the Act in relation to a temporary class drug are subject to the following maximum penalties:

- 14 years' imprisonment and an unlimited fine on indictment; and
- six months' imprisonment and a £5,000 fine on summary conviction.

Simple possession of a temporary class drug is not an offence under the 1971 Act; however, law enforcement officers have been given the following powers to enable them to take action to prevent possible harm to the individual:

- Search and detain a person (or vehicle etc.) where there are reasonable grounds to suspect that the person is in possession of a temporary class drug.
- Seize, detain and dispose of a suspected temporary class drug.
- Arrest or charge a person who commits the offence of intentionally obstructing an enforcement officer in the exercise of their powers.

2.2.2.2 Cannabis

The Misuse of Drugs Act 1971, s. 37 states:

> 'cannabis' (except in the expression 'cannabis resin') means any plant of the genus *Cannabis* or any part of any such plant (by whatever name designated) except that it does not include cannabis resin or any of the following products after separation from the rest of the plant, namely—
> (a) mature stalk of any such plant,
> (b) fibre produced from mature stalk of any such plant, and
> (c) seed of any such plant,
> 'cannabis resin' means the separated resin, whether crude or purified, obtained from any plant of the genus *Cannabis*.

KEYNOTE

Cannabis is a Class B drug. Therefore cannabis, cannabis resin, cannabis oil, cannabinol and its derivatives, any preparations or other product containing these substances and any substance which is an ester or ether either of cannabinol or of a cannabinol derivative are also Class B drugs. As cannabis and cannabis resin are both in the same class for the purposes of the 1971 Act, there would be no duplicity if a person is charged with possessing either one or the other in the same charge (*R* v *Best* (1980) 70 Cr App R 21).

2.2.3 Possession

'Possession' is a neutral concept, not implying any kind of fault, blame or guilt. This is the key feature to recognise before considering specific offences under *any* legislation. There are two elements to possession; the physical element and the mental element (*R* v *Lambert* [2002] 2 AC 545).

2.2.3.1 Custody or Control

The physical element involves proof that the thing is in the custody of the defendant or subject to his/her control. For example, if X has a wrap of cocaine in his jacket pocket, X has control of the wrap of cocaine (although *mere custody* does not mean that X is in 'possession' at this stage).

This approach is enlarged by s. 37(3) of the Misuse of Drugs Act 1971 which states that: 'For the purposes of this Act the things which a person has in his possession shall be taken to include anything subject to his control which is in the custody of another'.

EXAMPLE

X buys a controlled drug via the internet, directing that it be sent by post to his home address. X is in possession of that drug from the time it arrives through his letterbox (*R* v *Peaston* (1979) 69 Cr App R 203).

2.2.3.2 Knowledge of Possession

The second element involves that the defendant knows that the thing in question is under his/her control. He/she need not know what its nature is, but as long as he/she knows that the thing, whatever it is, is under his/her control, it is in his/her possession.

EXAMPLE

X and Y are walking along a street. X is going through his pockets looking for his wallet and, as he is searching for the wallet, he hands Y several tablets of Ecstasy and asks him to hold onto them while he continues searching. Y has no idea that the tablets he takes hold of are a controlled drug.

- Y has control of the Ecstasy tablets (they are in his hand);
- Y has knowledge of the presence of the Ecstasy tablets in his hand;
- *therefore Y has possession of the Ecstasy tablets.*

Nobody is suggesting, at this stage, that Y is guilty of an offence. Of course, Y could rightly be arrested on *suspicion* of possessing a controlled drug but arresting on suspicion that a person has committed an offence and *proving* guilt in relation to it are two different things. Indeed, Y's lack of knowledge about what the tablets are may afford him a defence (**see para. 2.2.9**). But the fact remains that ignorance of, or mistake as to the quality of, the thing in question does not prevent the accused being in possession of it.

What if the thing is inside a container, e.g. a box, a bag or a cigarette packet, and the person claims not to have known the thing was inside the container? In such cases, the common law makes the same requirements; you need to show that the person had custody of the container together with a knowledge that it (the container) contained *something*.

EXAMPLE

X is given a packet of cigarettes by Y. X believes the packet contains cigarettes only. The packet does contain several cigarettes but also contains a wrap of cocaine. X does not know about the wrap of cocaine and puts the pack of cigarettes into his pocket.

- X has custody of the pack of cigarettes (they are in his pocket);

- X has knowledge of the presence of the pack of cigarettes (X put them there);
- X knows that the pack of cigarettes contains *something*;
- *therefore X has possession of the wrap of cocaine.*

....

Nobody is suggesting X is guilty of an offence but he is in 'possession' of the wrap of cocaine.

In *R v Forsyth* [2001] EWCA Crim 2926, the defendant argued that there was a distinction between a person carrying something *in* a container and a person carrying *something inside something else* in a container. In that particular case, the defendant was found in possession of a box which contained a safe; inside the safe was a significant quantity of a controlled drug. The defendant argued that this type of possession should be differentiated from the situation where someone simply had possession of a box with drugs in it. The Court of Appeal ruled that there was no difference and the issues of proof were the same.

A person does not possess something of which he/she is completely unaware as there would be no knowledge of possession. If a drug is put into someone's pocket without his/her knowledge, he/she is not in possession of it (*Warner* v *Metropolitan Police Commissioner* [1969] 2 AC 256).

2.2.3.3 Joint Possession

To show that two or more persons are in possession of a controlled drug requires more than a mere ability to control it (*R v Kousar* [2009] EWCA Crim 139). Mere knowledge of the presence of a drug in the hands of a confederate is not enough; joint possession must be established (*R v Searle* [1971] Crim LR 592). In *Searle*, it was stated that this could be established by asking the question 'do the drugs form part of a common pool from which all had the right to draw?' In *R v Strong* (1989) *The Times*, 26 January 1990, the prosecution put the case on the basis that there was joint possession; that is, each of the co-accused had control of one or more of the packages of cannabis. The Court of Appeal followed *Searle*, and said that what was being looked for was whether each person had the right to say what should be done with the cannabis. Mere presence in the same vehicle as the drugs, and knowing they were there, was not sufficient.

Further issues that can arise from this view of 'possession' were highlighted in *Adams* v *DPP* [2002] EWHC 438 (Admin), where a small quantity of controlled drugs were found in the defendant's home during the execution of a search warrant. There was no proof that the drugs were owned by the defendant or that she was specifically aware of their presence but she *did* know that her home was used by various people who were highly likely to bring controlled drugs into it. She was convicted of possession. In hearing her appeal, the Administrative Court held that where knowledge of possession of drugs was limited to the fact that a visitor had brought drugs into the defendant's home intending to take them, that was not sufficient evidence from which it was appropriate to infer that she had control over the drugs.

The court also held that giving consent (explicitly or impliedly) for the use of a controlled drug did not of itself constitute possession. Similarly, an inference that the defendant knew whose drugs had been found in her home did not amount to evidence of control over the drug itself even though she may well have been able to exercise control over what actually took place in her home.

2.2.3.4 Points to Prove

Once 'possession' has been proved, it is then necessary to prove that what the defendant possesses is, in fact, a controlled drug. If this is established, then the defendant has a case to answer in relation to the offence of possession of a controlled drug.

EXAMPLE

X is subject to a stop and search procedure under s. 23 of the Misuse of Drugs Act 1971 (**see para. 2.2.17.1**). During the search, several packets containing cannabis resin are found in X's coat pocket.

In order to prove 'possession' of the cannabis for the purpose of the possession of a controlled drug offence, you must show:

- that X possessed the cannabis (X has custody/control of it and he knows it is in his possession); and
- that the contents of the packets are a controlled drug.

....

2.2.3.5   Quality

In the above example, *you would not have to show that X knew what the resin was*. That is, you do not need to show that X knew the *quality* of what he possessed to prove that X 'possessed' it.

If the defendant admits to knowing that the cannabis resin was there but thought it was chocolate, he is in possession of it (*R v Marriott* [1971] 1 WLR 187).

Therefore, if a defendant had a packet of cigarettes with him and admitted to knowing that he had them, he would be in possession of a controlled drug if one cigarette was shown to have contained cannabis. The fact that the defendant thought they contained tobacco would be irrelevant to the 'possession' concept (*R v Searle* [1971] Crim LR 592) (although he may have a defence under s. 28: **see para. 2.2.9**).

2.2.3.6   Quantity

The *quantity* of a controlled drug, however, may be so small that the defendant could not possibly have known about it; therefore it could not be 'possessed'.

The House of Lords suggested that if something is 'visible, tangible and measurable' that may be sufficient (*R v Boyesen* [1982] AC 768). If the amount recovered is too small to support a charge of possession, it might be used to prove earlier possession of the drug (*R v Graham* [1970] 1 WLR 113 and *Hambleton* v *Callinan* [1968] 2 QB 427 where traces of a controlled drug in a urine sample were held to be possible evidence of earlier possession of that drug).

Quantity is not only relevant to the fact of possession, it is also relevant to the intention of the person in whose possession the drug is found. Larger quantities (particularly if they are also divided into smaller amounts) may indicate an intention to supply and may be proof of that intention in some circumstances.

2.2.3.7   Possession of a Controlled Drug

OFFENCE: **Possession of Controlled Drug—*Misuse of Drugs Act 1971, s. 5***

> • Triable either way • Class A (seven years' imprisonment and/or a fine on indictment; six months' imprisonment and/or prescribed sum summarily) • Class B (five years' imprisonment and/or a fine on indictment; three months' imprisonment and/or a fine summarily) • Class C (two years' imprisonment and/or a fine on indictment; three months' imprisonment and/or a fine summarily) • See Keynote for possession of cannabis or cannabis resin

The Misuse of Drugs Act 1971, s. 5 states:

> (2) Subject to section 28 of this Act and to subsection (4) below, it is an offence for a person to have a controlled drug in his possession in contravention of subsection (1) ...

2.2.3.8 Section 5—The Defence to Unlawful Possession

Section 5 provides a defence to an offence of unlawful possession:

(4) In any proceedings for an offence under subsection (2) above in which it is proved that the accused had a controlled drug in his possession, it shall be a defence for him to prove—

(a) that, knowing or suspecting it to be a controlled drug, he took possession of it for the purpose of preventing another from committing or continuing to commit an offence in connection with that drug and that as soon as possible after taking possession of it he took all such steps as were reasonably open to him to destroy the drug or to deliver it into the custody of a person lawfully entitled to take custody of it; or

(b) that, knowing or suspecting it to be a controlled drug, he took possession of it for the purpose of delivering it into the custody of a person lawfully entitled to take custody of it and that as soon as possible after taking possession of it he took all such steps as were reasonably open to him to deliver it into the custody of such a person.

take custody of it. The defendant must prove that this was his/her intention at the time of taking possession (*R* v *Dempsey* (1986) 82 Cr App R 291).

Section 5(4) will not provide a defence to any other offence connected with the controlled drug (e.g. supplying or offering to supply).

Duress of circumstances is not a defence to this, or any other, offence under the Misuse of Drugs Act 1971 (see para. 1.4.4).

2.2.4 Supplying

In *R* v *Maginnis* [1987] AC 303, the House of Lords held that 'supply' involves more than a mere transfer of physical control of the item from one person to another but includes a further concept; namely, that of 'enabling the recipient to apply the thing handed over to purposes for which he desires or has a duty to apply it'. In other words, *the person to whom the drug is given must derive some benefit from being given the drug.*

Supplying Explained

So the key to working out if there has been a 'supply' is to ask 'Does being given the drug benefit the person to whom the drug has been given?' If the answer is 'yes', then the person *giving the drug* is 'supplying' it.

KEYNOTE

In *R* v *Dempsey* (1986) 82 Cr App R 291, a registered drug addict (A) was in lawful possession of a drug. A asked his partner (B) to hold on to some of that drug while he went to administer the remainder of it to himself in a gents' toilet. Both A and B were arrested, A being subsequently charged with 'supplying' B with the drug.

There is no 'supply' from A to B as when A gives the drug to B, B *does not benefit from* the action; B is simply holding on to the drug (although, of course, B would be in unlawful possession of the drug at that stage). If A had given the drug to B for B to use, there would be a 'supply' by A to B as B *is benefiting* from the action; B gets to use the drug. If B intends to give back the drug to A, then B would commit the offence of possession with intent to supply.

In *R* v *Maginnis* [1987] AC 303, a drug trafficker (A) temporarily left drugs with (B); B expected A to pick up the drugs the following day and was charged and convicted of possession with intent to supply. The same approach taken with *Dempsey* applies. In *Maginnis*, when A gives the drugs to B, B does not benefit from it and there is no 'supply' from A to B; if B returns the drugs to A, there is a 'supply' from B to A as A benefits from being given the drug (to sell or use). As B intends to return the drug to A, B is in possession with intent to supply.

If the drug trafficker in *Maginnis* had given the custodian of the drug £50 as a reward for holding the drug, then there would have been a 'supply' from A to B as B would benefit from holding the drug (he has been paid £50, benefiting financially from being given the drug).

The issue has been further explored in a case involving a person who claimed that he had been coerced into holding controlled drugs for unnamed dealers. When found in possession of the drugs, the defendant claimed the defence of duress (as to which, **see chapter 1.4**) and said that he had only been an 'involuntary custodian' of them, intending to return them at a later date. The Court of Appeal decided that it was irrelevant whether a person was a voluntary or involuntary custodian of the drugs and that an intention to return them to their depositor amounted to an 'intention to supply' (*R* v *Panton* [2001] EWCA Crim 611).

Dividing up controlled drugs which have been jointly purchased and then handing them out so that persons may use the drug will amount to 'supplying' (*R* v *Buckley* (1979) 69 Cr App R 371).

If a police informer provides a controlled drug to another in order that the other be arrested, there will still be a 'supplying' of the drug (*R* v *X* [1994] Crim LR 827).

Injecting Others

Injecting another with that person's own controlled drug has been held *not to amount* to 'supplying' in a case where the defendant assisted in pushing down the plunger of a syringe that the other person was already using (*R* v *Harris* [1968] 1 WLR 769). It may amount to an offence of 'poisoning' under s. 23 of the Offences Against the Person Act 1861. The problem with charging the supplier of drugs for self-injection by someone who then dies as a result lies in the issues of causation. The general view is that the supplier is unlikely to be held liable for *causing* death in such a case (*R* v *Dias* [2001] EWCA Crim 2986). Where the defendant *actually carries out* the injection, liability for causing the death of another in this way can be made out even if the drug injected is not a controlled drug (*R* v *Andrews* [2002] EWCA Crim 3021, involving an injection of insulin with consent).

2.2.4.1 **Supplying a Controlled Drug**

OFFENCE: **Supplying Controlled Drug—*Misuse of Drugs Act 1971, s. 4(3)***
> • Triable either way • Class A (life imprisonment and/or a fine on indictment; six months' imprisonment and/or prescribed sum summarily) • Class B (14 years' imprisonment and/or a fine on indictment; six months' imprisonment and/or prescribed sum summarily) • Class C (14 years' imprisonment and/or a fine on indictment; three months' imprisonment and/or a fine summarily)

The Misuse of Drugs Act 1971, s. 4 states:

(3) Subject to section 28 of this Act, it is an offence for a person—
    (a) to supply or offer to supply a controlled drug to another in contravention of subsection (1) above; or
    (b) to be concerned in the supplying of such a drug to another in contravention of that subsection; or
    (c) to be concerned in the making to another in contravention of that subsection of an offer to supply such a drug.

KEYNOTE

The three ingredients of this offence were set out in *R* v *Hughes* (1985) 81 Cr App R 344:
(a) the supply of a drug to another, or as the case may be, the making of an offer to supply the drug to another in contravention of s. 4(1) of the Misuse of Drugs Act 1971;
(b) participation by the accused in an enterprise involving such supply or, as the case may be, such an offer to supply; and
(c) knowledge by the accused of the nature of the enterprise, i.e. that it involved supply of a drug or, as the case may be, offering to supply a drug.

Proof of actual supply is a prerequisite for an offence charged under s. 4(3)(b).
  'Supplying' includes distributing (s. 37(1)).

Offering to Supply

An offer may be by words or conduct. If by words, it must be ascertained whether an offer to supply a controlled drug was made. If words are used, the defence under s. 28 (**see para. 2.2.9**) does not appear to apply (*R* v *Mitchell* [1992] Crim LR 723).

Whether the accused had a controlled drug in his/her possession, had access to controlled drugs or whether the substance in his/her possession was a controlled drug at all is immaterial (*R* v *Goodward* [1992] Crim LR 588). The offence is committed whether or not the offer is genuine and once an offer is made the offence is complete; it cannot be withdrawn. If the offer is made to an undercover police officer, the offence is still committed and the defendant cannot claim that such an offer was not a 'real' offer (*R* v *Kray* [1998] EWCA Crim 3211).

If the object of a conspiracy (see **chapter 1.3**) is to supply a controlled drug to a co-conspirator, any subsequent charge must make that clear; stating that the defendants conspired to supply the drug to 'another' implies that the supply was to be made to someone *other than any of the conspirators* (*R* v *Jackson* [2000] 1 Cr App R 97).

2.2.4.2 Specific Situations

Section 4A of the Misuse of Drugs Act 1971 requires courts to treat certain conditions as 'aggravating' factors when considering the seriousness of the offence under s. 4(3) if committed by a person aged 18 or over.

The conditions are either:

(1) that the offence was committed on or in the vicinity of school premises at a relevant time. 'Vicinity' is not defined and will be left to each court relying on its local knowledge. Other buildings and premises (e.g. cafes and shopping centres) can fall within this description and courts may decide that a route used to get to or from a school or a place where schoolchildren gather (even if trespassing) may be in the 'vicinity'. School premises are land used for the purposes of a school but *excluding* any land occupied solely as a dwelling *by a person employed at the school* (s. 4A(8)). A 'relevant time' is any time when the school premises are in use by people under the age of 18 (and one hour before the start/after the end of any such time) (s. 4A(5)); or

(2) that in connection with the commission of the offence, the offender used a 'courier' who, at the time the offence was committed, was under the age of 18. A person uses a courier if he/she causes or permits another person (the courier):

  (a) to deliver a controlled drug to a third person, or

  (b) to deliver a 'drug related consideration' (basically any money, goods etc. obtained or intended to be used in connection with the supply of a controlled drug) to him/herself or a third person (s. 4A(6) and (7)).

2.2.5 Possession with Intent to Supply

This is an offence that brings the concepts of 'possession' and 'supply' together.

OFFENCE: **Possession with Intent to Supply—*Misuse of Drugs Act 1971, s. 5(3)***
  • Triable either way • Class A (life imprisonment and/or a fine on indictment; six months' imprisonment and/or a prescribed sum summarily) • Class B (14 years' imprisonment and/or a fine on indictment; six months' imprisonment and/or prescribed sum summarily) • Class C (14 years' imprisonment and/or a fine on indictment; three months imprisonment and/or a fine summarily)

The Misuse of Drugs Act 1971, s. 5 states:

(3) Subject to section 28 of this Act, it is an offence for a person to have a controlled drug in his possession, whether lawfully or not, with intent to supply it to another in contravention of section 4(1) of this Act.

The lawfulness or otherwise of the *possession* is irrelevant; what matters is the lawfulness of the intended supply. If a police officer is in lawful possession of a controlled drug but intends to supply it unlawfully to another, the offence is committed.

You must show that the intention was that the *person in possession of the controlled drug* (rather than some third party) would supply it at some point in the future (*R* v *Greenfield* (1984) 78 Cr App R 179).

If more than one person has possession of the relevant controlled drug, you must show an individual intention to supply it by each person charged; it is not enough to show a joint venture whereby one or more parties simply knew of another's intent (*R* v *Downes* [1984] Crim LR 552). Given the decision of the Court of Appeal in *R* v *Kray* [1998] EWCA Crim 3211, possession with intent to supply a controlled drug to a person who is in fact an undercover police officer would appear to amount to an offence under this section.

All that is necessary in proving the offence under s. 5(3) is to show that the defendant had a controlled drug in his/her possession and intended to supply that substance to another. If the substance in the defendant's possession is a Class A drug and he/she intended to supply it to another person, the fact that he/she thought the drug was some other type of drug does not matter (*R* v *Leeson* [2000] 1 Cr App R 233).

Possession of drugs paraphernalia (e.g. clingfilm, contact details, etc.) will be relevant evidence to show that a defendant was an active dealer in drugs but it does not prove the intention to supply and the trial judge will give a jury careful directions as to the probative value of such items found in the defendant's possession (*R* v *Haye* [2002] EWCA Crim 2476).

Where a Rastafarian was prosecuted for possessing cannabis with intent to supply others as part of their religious worship, he claimed that his rights under Articles 8 and 9 of the European Convention on Human Rights had been unnecessarily and disproportionately interfered with. The Court of Appeal, while reducing the sentence, held that such a prosecution had been properly brought (*R* v *Taylor* [2001] EWCA Crim 2263).

In proving an intention to supply, you may be able to adduce evidence of the defendant's unexplained wealth (*R* v *Smith (Ivor)* [1995] Crim LR 940) or the presence of large sums of money with the drugs seized (*R* v *Wright* [1994] Crim LR 55).

For the purposes of the offence under s. 4 (supplying a controlled drug) and this offence, the 'another' cannot be someone charged in the same count, but can be someone charged in other counts in the same indictment.

2.2.6 Supply of Articles

OFFENCE: **Supplying Articles for Administering or Preparing Controlled Drugs— *Misuse of Drugs Act 1971, s. 9A***

- Triable summarily • Six months' imprisonment and/or a fine

The Misuse of Drugs Act 1971, s. 9A states:

(1) A person who supplies or offers to supply any article which may be used or adapted to be used (whether by itself or in combination with another article or other articles) in the administration by any person of a controlled drug to himself or another, believing that the article (or the article as adapted) is to be so used in circumstances where the administration is unlawful, is guilty of an offence.

(2) It is not an offence under subsection (1) above to supply or offer to supply a hypodermic syringe, or any part of one.

(3) A person who supplies or offers to supply any article which may be used to prepare a controlled drug for administration by any person to himself or another believing that the article is to be so used in circumstances where the administration is unlawful is guilty of an offence.

2.2.7 Production of a Controlled Drug

OFFENCE: **Producing Controlled Drug—*Misuse of Drugs Act 1971, s. 4(2)***
   • Triable either way • Class A (life imprisonment and/or a fine on indictment; six months' imprisonment and/or prescribed sum summarily) • Class B (14 years' imprisonment and/or a fine on indictment; six months' imprisonment and/or prescribed sum summarily) • Class C (five years' imprisonment and/or a fine on indictment; three months' imprisonment and/or a fine summarily)

The Misuse of Drugs Act 1971, s. 4 states:

(2) Subject to section 28 of this Act, it is an offence for a person—
   (a) to produce a controlled drug in contravention of subsection (1) ... ; or
   (b) to be concerned in the production of such a drug in contravention of that subsection by another.

2.2.8 Cultivation of Cannabis

OFFENCE: **Cultivation of Cannabis—Misuse *of Drugs Act 1971, s. 6***
   • Triable either way • 14 years' imprisonment and/or a fine on indictment
   • Six months' imprisonment and/or prescribed sum summarily

The Misuse of Drugs Act 1971, s. 6 states:

(1) Subject to any regulations under section 7 of this Act for the time being in force, it shall not be lawful for a person to cultivate any plant of the genus *Cannabis*.
(2) Subject to section 28 of this Act, it is an offence to cultivate any such plant in contravention of subsection (1) above.

2.2.9 General Defence under Section 28

There is a general defence (available under s. 28 of the Misuse of Drugs Act 1971) to a defendant charged with certain drugs offences. Section 28 applies to offences of:

- unlawful production (s. 4(2));
- unlawful supply (s. 4(3));
- unlawful possession (s. 5(2));
- possession with intent to supply (s. 5(3));
- unlawful cultivation of cannabis (s. 6(2));
- offences connected with opium (s. 9) (not covered in the NPPF Step 2 Exam syllabus).

The defences under s. 28 are *not* available in cases of conspiracy as conspiracy is not an offence under the 1971 Act (*R v McGowan* [1990] Crim LR 399).

The Misuse of Drugs Act 1971, s. 28 states:

(2) Subject to subsection (3) below, in any proceedings for an offence to which this section applies it shall be a defence for the accused to prove that he neither knew of nor suspected nor had reason to suspect the existence of some fact alleged by the prosecution which it is necessary for the prosecution to prove if he is to be convicted of the offence charged.

(3) Where in any proceedings for an offence to which this section applies it is necessary, if the accused is to be convicted of the offence charged, for the prosecution to prove that some substance or product involved in the alleged offence was the controlled drug which the prosecution alleges it to have been, and it is proved that the substance or product in question was that controlled drug, the accused—

   (a) shall not be acquitted of the offence charged by reason only of proving that he neither knew nor suspected nor had reason to suspect that the substance or product in question was the particular controlled drug alleged; but

   (b) shall be acquitted thereof—

      (i) if he proves that he neither believed nor suspected nor had reason to suspect that the substance or product in question was a controlled drug; or

      (ii) if he proves that he believed the substance or product in question to be a controlled drug, or a controlled drug of a description, such that, if it had in fact been that controlled drug, or a controlled drug of that description, he would not at the material time have been committing any offence to which this section applies.

2.2.9.1 Lack of Knowledge of Some Alleged Fact

Section 28(2) allows a defence where the defendant did not *know, suspect* or *have reason to suspect* the existence of some fact which is essential to proving the case.

EXAMPLE

X is stopped in the street by Y who asks him to drop off a letter in an envelope at a nearby address in exchange for £10. As X approaches the address, he is arrested for possessing a controlled drug (which is inside the envelope), with intent to supply.

X is in 'possession' of the drug as he has custody of it and knows that the envelope contains *something*; what s. 28(2) does is to allow X a defence. X can discharge the evidential burden by showing that he neither knew nor suspected that the envelope contained a controlled drug, and that he neither knew nor suspected that he was supplying it to another. Both of these elements would be facts which the prosecution would have to allege to prove the offence.

If X knew the person to be a local drug dealer, or the reward for his errand was disproportionately large, say £1,000, then he may not be able to discharge this evidential burden.

The test for 'reason to suspect' is an *objective* one (*R v Young* [1984] 1 WLR 654). Consequently, where a 'reason to suspect' was not apparent to a defendant because he/she was too intoxicated to see it, the defence will not apply.

2.2.9.2 General Lack of Knowledge about Drug in Question

The wording of s. 28(3)(a) prevents defendants from claiming a 'defence' when what they thought was one type of controlled drug was in fact another different controlled drug.

Section 28(3)(b), however, has two strands, one concerned with the defendant's general lack of knowledge about the drug in question and the other (**see para. 2.2.9.3**) concerning the defendant's conditional belief.

Section 28(3)(b)(i) will allow defendants to prove that they did not believe or suspect the substance in question to be a controlled drug and that they had no reason so to suspect.

This clearly overlaps with s. 28(2), and X in the above example would also be able to claim this lack of knowledge. However, if he believed the envelope to contain amphetamine when it turned out to contain heroin, this lack of knowledge would not be permitted as a defence under s. 28(3).

2.2.9.3 Conditional Belief about Drug in Question

In contrast to s. 28(3)(a), the second strand of s. 28(3)(b)(ii) allows defendants to discharge the evidential burden by showing that they *did* believe the drug in question to be a particular controlled drug. It is then open to defendants to claim that, had the drug in question actually been the drug which they believed it to be, then they would not have committed any offences in relation to that drug.

EXAMPLE

A registered heroin addict is prescribed methadone. She collects her prescription from a chemist but is mistakenly given pethidine instead. She may be able to discharge the evidential burden by showing that she *believed* the drug in question to be methadone *and* that, if it had been, she would not have committed an offence by possessing it.

2.2.10 Regulated Possession and Supply of Controlled Drugs

The statutory framework governing controlled drugs does not simply ban substances and their possession outright. People working at various levels within the system need to be able to access, analyse and prescribe substances that are controlled by the 1971 Act. To that end, the framework takes account of the differing legitimate activities that may be relevant to individual people or particular circumstances. The majority of the exceptions and conditions imposed on this lawful possession and use can be found in the Misuse of Drugs Regulations 2001 and also in the Misuse of Drugs and Misuse of Drugs (Safe Custody) (Amendment) Regulations 2007 (SI 2007/2154).

The importance of the 2001 Regulations lies in the fact that they exempt certain drugs and certain people (pharmacists, laboratory workers and police officers etc.) from the main offences of possession, supply and importation *as long as they are acting lawfully within the parameters set out by those regulations*. A person in such an occupation who possesses, supplies or imports a controlled drug outside the terms of the exemptions will commit an offence.

Among the key regulations (SI 2001/3998) are:

- Regulation 4—which sets out those controlled drugs which will be exempted from the main offences of importation/exportation when they are contained in medicinal products.
- Regulation 5—allowing people holding a licence issued by the Secretary of State to produce, supply, offer to supply or have in their possession a controlled drug.
- Regulation 6—this allows anyone who is *lawfully* in possession of a controlled drug to give the drug back to the person from whom he/she obtained it and would cover registered heroin addicts properly returning methadone to a chemist. Regulation 6 also allows others to possess and supply certain controlled drugs under strict conditions. Regulation 6 allows police constables to have any controlled drug in their possession, or to supply such a drug to anyone who is lawfully allowed to have it (reg. 6(5)–(7)). These exemptions only apply where constables are *acting in the course of their duty as such*.

Other people who are given the same protection are Customs and Excise officers, postal workers and people engaged in conveying the drug to someone who may lawfully possess it. This last category would include civilian support staff, exhibits officers and others who, although not police constables, are nevertheless properly engaged in conveying controlled drugs to others.

The Misuse of Drugs (Amendments) (Cannabis and Licence Fees) (England, Wales and Scotland) Regulations 2018 (SI 2018/1055), in force as of 1 November 2018, amend the Misuse of Drugs Regulations 2001 to allow the wider use of cannabis-based products for medicinal use in humans, essentially for medical purposes. Additional controls, beyond those generally provided for in relation to drugs specified in sch. 2 to the 2001 Regulations, are imposed for cannabis-based products for medicinal use in humans. The law does not limit the types of conditions that can be considered for treatment and doctors will no longer need to seek approval from an expert panel in order for patients to access the medicines. The decision to prescribe these unlicensed medicines must be made by a specialist doctor—not a GP. These doctors focus on one field of medicine, such as neurology or paediatrics, and are listed on the General Medical Council's specialist register. They must make decisions on prescribing cannabis-based products for medicinal use on a case-by-case basis, and only when the patient has an unmet special clinical need that cannot be met by licensed products.

2.2.11 Occupiers, etc.

OFFENCE: **Occupier or Manager of Premises Permitting Drug Misuse—*Misuse of Drugs Act 1971, s. 8***

> • Triable either way • Class A or B (14 years' imprisonment and/or a fine on indictment; six months' imprisonment and/or prescribed sum summarily) • Class C (14 years' imprisonment and/or a fine on indictment; three months' imprisonment and/or a fine summarily)

The Misuse of Drugs Act 1971, s. 8 states:

> A person commits an offence if, being the occupier or concerned in the management of any premises, he knowingly permits or suffers any of the following activities to take place on those premises, that is to say—
>
> (a) producing or attempting to produce a controlled drug in contravention of section 4(1) of this Act;
>
> (b) supplying or attempting to supply a controlled drug to another in contravention of section 4(1) of this Act, or offering to supply a controlled drug to another in contravention of section 4(1);
>
> (c) preparing opium for smoking;
>
> (d) smoking cannabis, cannabis resin or prepared opium.

KEYNOTE

Occupier

A person does not have to be a tenant, or to have estate in land, in order to be an 'occupier'. The term 'occupier' should be given a 'common sense' interpretation (*R* v *Tao* [1977] QB 141). For the purposes of s. 8, a person is in occupation of premises, whatever his/her legal status, if the prosecution can show that the accused exercised control, or had the authority of another, to exclude persons from the premises or to prohibit any of the activities referred to in s. 8 (*R* v *Coid* [1998] Crim LR 199).

Concerned in the Management

To be a manager, the accused must run, organise and plan the use of the premises (*R* v *Josephs* (1977) 65 Cr App R 253) and so must be involved in more than menial or routine duties.

'Premises' is not defined.

The permitting or suffering of these activities requires a degree of *mens rea* (*Sweet* v *Parsley* [1970] AC 132) even if that degree is little more than wilful blindness (*R* v *Thomas* (1976) 63 Cr App R 65). For the purposes of s. 8(b), and therefore presumably s. 8(a), it is not necessary to show that the defendant knew exactly which drugs were being produced, supplied etc.; only that they were 'controlled drugs' (*R* v *Bett* [1999] 1 WLR 2109).

However, the precise activities that are described under s. 8 will need to be proved. So, for instance, if the offence charged is one of knowingly permitting the smoking of cannabis (under subs. (d)), it must be shown that this actually took place; it is not enough that the owner/occupier had given permission for this to happen (*R* v *Auguste* [2003] EWCA Crim 3929). This is also the case when the offence charged is one of supplying or attempting to supply a controlled drug to another (under s. 8(b)), i.e. it must be shown that the supply or attempted supply actually took place (*R* v *McGee* [2012] EWCA Crim 613).

An occupier who permits the growing of cannabis plants commits this offence (*Taylor* v *Chief Constable of Kent* [1981] 1 WLR 606).

2.2.12 Community Protection Notices

Community Protection Notices (under part 4 of the Anti-social Behaviour, Crime and Policing Act 2014) provide powers allowing the police to close premises where drugs offences (amongst other things) take place.

2.2.13 Assisting or Inducing Offence Outside United Kingdom

OFFENCE: **Assisting or Inducing Misuse of Drugs Offence Outside UK—*Misuse of Drugs Act 1971, s. 20***

- Triable either way • 14 years' imprisonment and/or a fine on indictment
- Six months' imprisonment and/or a fine summarily

The Misuse of Drugs Act 1971, s. 20 states:

A person commits an offence if in the United Kingdom he assists in or induces the commission in any place outside the United Kingdom of an offence punishable under the provisions of a corresponding law in force in that place.

KEYNOTE

In order to prove this offence, you must show that the offence outside the United Kingdom actually took place. This offence may overlap with the offences of importation/exportation.

'Assisting' includes taking containers to another country in the knowledge that they will later be filled with a controlled drug and sent on to a third country (*R* v *Evans* (1977) 64 Cr App R 237). For an offence to amount to one under 'corresponding law' for these purposes, a certificate relating to the domestic law concerned with the misuse of drugs must be obtained from the government of the relevant country (s. 36).

2.2.14 Incitement

OFFENCE: **Incitement—*Misuse of Drugs Act 1971, s. 19***

- Triable and punishable as for substantive offence incited

The Misuse of Drugs Act 1971, s. 19 states:

It is an offence for a person to incite another to commit an offence under any other provision of this Act.

KEYNOTE

A person inciting an undercover police officer may commit an offence under s. 19, even though there was no possibility of the officer actually being induced to commit the offence (*DPP* v *Armstrong* [2000] Crim LR 379).

2.2.15 Importation of Controlled Drugs

Section 3 of the Misuse of Drugs Act 1971 prohibits the import or export of a controlled drug unless authorised by the regulations made under the Act. The relevant offences and respective penalties are contained in the Customs and Excise Management Act 1979 which provides the following penalties for the improper importation or exportation of controlled drugs:

- Class A—life imprisonment;
- Class B—14 years' imprisonment;
- Class C—14 years' imprisonment.

2.2.16 Travel Restriction Orders

The Criminal Justice and Police Act 2001 allows courts (in practice, the Crown Court) to impose travel restrictions on offenders convicted of drug trafficking offences. Travel restriction orders prohibit offenders from leaving the United Kingdom at any time during the period beginning from their release from custody (other than on bail or temporary release for a fixed period) and up to the end of the order. The minimum period for such an order is two years (s. 33(3)); there is no maximum period prescribed in the legislation.

Where a court:

- has convicted a person of a drug trafficking offence; and
- it has determined that a sentence of four years or more is appropriate;

it is under a *duty* to consider whether or not a travel restriction order would be appropriate (s. 33). If the court decides not to impose an order, it must give its reasons for not doing so.

A 'drug trafficking offence' is defined by s. 34 of the Act and includes the production of a controlled drug (s. 4(2)), the supply of a controlled drug (s. 4(3)) and the importation/exportation offences under s. 3 along with inciting a person to commit these offences under s. 19 of the Misuse of Drugs Act 1971. It also includes aiding, abetting, counselling or procuring these offences.

The sentence of four years or more must be a single sentence of over four years (not an aggregate) in order to impose a travel restriction order.

Offenders may also be required to surrender their UK passport as part of the order.

An offender may apply to the court that made a restriction order to have it revoked or suspended (s. 35) and the court must consider the strict criteria set out in s. 35 when considering any such suspension or revocation. If an order is suspended, the offender has a legal obligation to be back in the United Kingdom when the period of suspension ends (s. 35(5)(a)).

OFFENCE: **Contravening a Travel Restriction Order—*Criminal Justice and Police Act 2001, s. 36***
- Triable either way • Five years' imprisonment and/or a fine on indictment
- Six months' imprisonment and/or a fine summarily

The Criminal Justice and Police Act 2001, s. 36 states:

(1) A person who leaves the United Kingdom at a time when he is prohibited from leaving it by a travel restriction order is guilty of an offence …

(2) A person who is not in the United Kingdom at the end of a period during which a prohibition imposed on him by a travel restriction order has been suspended shall be guilty of an offence …

KEYNOTE

These offences do not require a particular state of mind.

The first offence requires proof of two things: (a) that there was an order in existence in respect of the offender; and (b) that he/she left the United Kingdom during the time it was in force. There is no requirement that the person leave the United Kingdom *voluntarily* in order to be guilty (although he/she would have a good argument if he/she were taken out of the jurisdiction against his/her will or without his/her knowledge).

Travel restriction orders do not prevent the proper exercise of any prescribed power to remove a person from the United Kingdom (s. 37). So if the Secretary of State deports someone who is under a travel restriction order, that person would not commit the above offence.

The second offence requires proof that there was a suspended order in existence in respect of the offender and that, at the end of the suspension period, the offender was not in the United Kingdom.

Failing to deliver up a passport when required by an order is a summary offence (six months' imprisonment and/or a fine (s. 36(3)).

2.2.17 Police Powers

The 1971 Act provides a number of specific enforcement powers.

2.2.17.1 Powers of Entry, Search and Seizure

The Misuse of Drugs Act 1971, s. 23 states:

(1) A constable or other person authorised in that behalf by a general or special order of the Secretary of State (or in Northern Ireland either of the Secretary of State or the Ministry of Home Affairs for Northern Ireland) shall, for the purposes of the execution of this Act, have power to enter the premises of a person carrying on business as a producer or supplier of any controlled drugs and to demand the production of, and to inspect, any books or documents relating to dealings in any such drugs and to inspect any stocks of any such drugs.

(2) If a constable has reasonable grounds to suspect that any person is in possession of a controlled drug in contravention of this Act or of any regulations or orders made thereunder, the constable may—
   (a) search that person, and detain him for the purpose of searching him;
   (b) search any vehicle or vessel in which the constable suspects that the drug may be found, and for that purpose require the person in control of the vehicle or vessel to stop it;
   (c) seize and detain, for the purposes of proceedings under this Act, anything found in the course of the search which appears to the constable to be evidence of an offence under this Act.

   In this subsection 'vessel' includes a hovercraft within the meaning of the Hovercraft Act 1968; and nothing in this subsection shall prejudice any power of search or any power to seize or detain property which is exercisable by a constable apart from this subsection.

(3) If a justice of the peace (or in Scotland a justice of the peace, a magistrate or a sheriff) is satisfied by information on oath that there is reasonable ground for suspecting—
   (a) that any controlled drugs are, in contravention of this Act or of any regulations or orders made thereunder, in the possession of a person on any premises; or
   (b) that a document directly or indirectly relating to, or connected with, a transaction or dealing which was, or an intended transaction or dealing which would if carried out be, an offence under this Act, or in the case of a transaction or dealing carried out or intended to be carried out in a place outside the United Kingdom, an offence against the provisions of a corresponding law in force in that place, is in the possession of a person on any premises,

   he may grant a warrant authorising any constable at any time or times within one month from the date of the warrant, to enter, if need be by force, the premises named in the warrant, and to search the premises and any persons found therein and, if there is reasonable ground for suspecting that an offence under this Act has been committed in relation to any controlled drugs found on the premises or in the possession of any such persons, or that a document so found is such a document as is mentioned in paragraph (b) above, to seize and detain those drugs or that document, as the case may be.

KEYNOTE

If a warrant obtained under s. 23 authorises the search of *premises only*, that in itself will not give the officers authority to search people found on those premises unless the officer can point to some other power authorising the search (*Hepburn* v *Chief Constable of Thames Valley* [2002] EWCA Civ 1841).

However, where the warrant authorises the search of premises *and* people, the Divisional Court has held that it is reasonable to restrict the movement of people within the premises to allow the search to be conducted properly (*DPP* v *Meaden* [2003] EWHC 3005 (Admin)).

PACE Code A applies to the exercise of any power to search people for controlled drugs specifically included in a warrant issued under s. 23.

A warrant issued under s. 23 of the Act lasts for a period of *one month* from the date of issue.

2.2.17.2 Obstruction

OFFENCE: **Obstruction—*Misuse of Drugs Act 1971, s. 23(4)***
- Triable either way • Two years' imprisonment and/or a fine on indictment
- Six months' imprisonment and/or a fine summarily

The Misuse of Drugs Act 1971, s. 23 states:

(4) A person commits an offence if he—
- (a) intentionally obstructs a person in the exercise of his powers under this section; or
- (b) conceals from a person acting in the exercise of his powers under subsection (1) above any such books, documents, stocks or drugs as are mentioned in that subsection; or
- (c) without reasonable excuse (proof of which shall lie on him) fails to produce any such books or documents as are so mentioned where their production is demanded by a person in the exercise of his powers under that subsection.

KEYNOTE

The offence of obstructing a person in the exercise of his/her powers is only committed if the obstruction was intentional (*R* v *Forde* (1985) 81 Cr App R 19).

2.2.18 Psychoactive and Intoxicating Substances

The Psychoactive Substances Act 2016 creates a number of offences and powers in relation to 'psychoactive substances', including the offence of supplying, or offering to supply, a psychoactive substance.

OFFENCE: **Supplying, or Offering to Supply, a Psychoactive Substance— *Psychoactive Substances Act 2016, s. 5***

- Triable either way • Seven years' imprisonment and/or fine on indictment
- Six months' imprisonment and/or a fine

The Psychoactive Substances Act 2016, s. 5 states:

(1) A person commits an offence if—
- (a) the person intentionally supplies a substance to another person,
- (b) the substance is a psychoactive substance,
- (c) the person knows or suspects, or ought to know or suspect, that the substance is a psychoactive substance, and
- (d) the person knows, or is reckless as to whether, the psychoactive substance is likely to be consumed by the person to whom it is supplied, or by some other person, for its psychoactive effects.
(2) A person ('P') commits an offence if—
- (a) P offers to supply a psychoactive substance to another person ('R'), and
- (b) P knows or is reckless as to whether R, or some other person, would, if P supplied a substance to R in accordance with the offer, be likely to consume the substance for its psychoactive effects.
(3) For the purposes of subsection 2(b), the reference to a substance's psychoactive effects includes a reference to the psychoactive effects which the substance would have if it were the substance which P had offered to supply to R.
(4) ...

KEYNOTE

'Psychoactive Substance' and 'Psychoactive Effect'

Section 2 of the Act defines a 'psychoactive substance' as any substance which is capable of producing a psychoactive effect in a person who consumes it.

A substance produces a psychoactive effect in a person if, by stimulating or depressing the person's central nervous system, it affects the person's mental functioning or emotional state. The main effect of psychoactive substances is on a person's brain, the major part of the central nervous system. By speeding up or slowing down activity on the central nervous system, psychoactive substances cause an alteration in the individual's state of consciousness by producing a range of effects including, but not limited to: hallucinations; change in alertness, perception of time and space, mood or empathy with others; and drowsiness (s. 2(2)).

An individual consumes a substance if the individual causes or allows the substance, or fumes given off by the substance, to enter the individual's body in any way. For example, this includes injecting, eating or drinking, snorting, inhaling and smoking (s. 2(3)).

For the supply offence, the conduct element is satisfied if a person supplies a substance to another person and that substance is a psychoactive substance. By virtue of s. 59(2)(b), supplying for these purposes covers distribution. The transaction does not need to result in payment or reward and would include social supply between friends.

There are three mental elements of the supply offence.

- First, the prosecution must show that the supplying of the substance is intentional.
- Second, the defendant must have known or suspected, or ought to have known or suspected, that the substance is a psychoactive substance.
- Third, the defendant must know, or be reckless as to whether, the psychoactive substance is likely to be consumed by the person to whom it is supplied or another person for its psychoactive effects.

The recklessness test would prevent a *head* shop proprietor escaping liability by arguing that because the psychoactive substances sold in his/her shop were labelled as 'plant food', 'research chemicals' or 'not for human consumption', he/she did not know that the substances were likely to be consumed.

The conduct element of the offering to supply offence is that the defendant offers to supply a psychoactive substance to another person. Such an offer could take the form of an advertisement, including a catalogue of psychoactive substances on display on a website with the facility to purchase online.

There is one mental element to the offer to supply offence, namely that the defendant knows, or is reckless as to whether, the substance that is being offered is likely to be consumed by the person to whom it is supplied or by another person for its psychoactive effects. This element of the offence is constructed in such a way that it would capture circumstances where a person purports to offer to supply a psychoactive substance to another person but, in fact, either has no intention of fulfilling his/her side of the deal or intends to pass off some other substance as a psychoactive substance. Subsection (3) ensures that such conduct would still be caught by the offering to supply offence.

It is worth noting that this offence covers the supply/offer to supply of a psychoactive substance to a person of *any age*.

OFFENCE: **Supply of Butane Lighter Refill to Person under 18—*Cigarette Lighter Refill (Safety) Regulations 1999, reg. 2***
- Triable summarily • Six months' imprisonment and/or a fine

The Cigarette Lighter Refill (Safety) Regulations 1999 (SI 1999/1844), reg. 2 states:

No person shall supply any cigarette lighter refill canister containing butane or a substance with butane as a constituent part to any person under the age of eighteen years.

KEYNOTE

There is no requirement that the person believed or even suspected the person to be under 18. The 1999 Regulations are made under the Consumer Protection Act 1987, s. 11.

2.3 Firearms and Gun Crime

2.3.1 Introduction

The key piece of legislation governing firearms is the Firearms Act 1968. The Act covers numerous activities involving firearms and also deals with serious offences involving the criminal use of firearms.

2.3.2 Definitions—Firearm, Ammunition and Imitation Firearm

Before examining any offences relating to firearms, it is useful to begin with some definitions.

2.3.2.1 Firearms

The Firearms Act 1968, s. 57 states:

(1) In this Act, the expression 'firearm' means—
   (a) a lethal barrelled weapon (see subsection (1B));
   (b) a prohibited weapon;
   (c) a relevant component part in relation to a lethal barrelled weapon or a prohibited weapon (see subsection (1D));
   (d) an accessory to a lethal barrelled weapon or a prohibited weapon where the accessory is designed or adapted to diminish the noise or flash caused by firing the weapon.

KEYNOTE

Lethal Barrelled Weapon

A 'lethal barrelled weapon' means a barrelled weapon of any description from which a shot, bullet or other missile, with kinetic energy of more than one joule at the muzzle of the weapon, can be discharged (s. 57(1B)).

An item which could only discharge a missile in combination with other tools extraneous to it would not be a lethal barrelled weapon. Section 57(1) refers to the capacity of an item and not to its capacity in combination with other equipment. Thus, an old and damaged starting pistol with a partially drilled barrel could not be regarded as a 'prohibited weapon', and thus a firearm within s. 57, merely because it could be made to discharge a pellet with the aid of a vice-clamp, a mallet and a metal punch (R v Bewley [2012] EWCA Crim 1457).

Air pistols (R v Thorpe [1987] 1 WLR 383) and imitation revolvers (Cafferata v Wilson [1936] 3 All ER 149) have been held to be lethal barrelled weapons. A signalling pistol which fired explosive magnesium and phosphorous flares capable of killing at short range has been held to be lethal (Read v Donovan [1947] KB 326). That is not to say, however, that they will always be so; each case must be determined in the light of the evidence available.

Prohibited Weapon

The effect of s. 57(1)(b) is to make a prohibited weapon a firearm whether it is lethal barrelled or not. It follows that *all prohibited weapons are firearms* although not all firearms will be prohibited weapons (prohibited weapons are discussed at **para. 2.3.8**).

Relevant Component Part

For the purpose of s. 57(1)(c), each of the following items is a relevant component part in relation to a lethal barrelled weapon or a prohibited weapon—

- the barrel, chamber or cylinder;
- frame, body or receiver;
- a breech, block, bolt or other mechanism for containing the pressure of discharge at the rear of the chamber, but only where the item is capable of being used as a part of a lethal barrelled weapon or a prohibited weapon (s. 57(1D)).

Magazines, sights and furniture are not considered 'component parts'.

Accessory

While silencers and flash eliminators are accessories, a silencer or a flash eliminator *on its own* is not a firearm. However, if a defendant is found in possession of a silencer or flash eliminator which has been manufactured for a weapon *that is also in the defendant's possession*, that will be enough to bring the silencer or flash eliminator under s. 57(1). If the silencer is made for a different weapon, it may still come under the s. 57 definition but the prosecution will have to show that it could be used with the defendant's weapon and that he/she had it for that purpose (*R v Buckfield* [1998] Crim LR 673). Section 57(1) does not include telescopic sights or magazines.

Exception for Airsoft Guns

Airsoft is a skirmishing game in which players shoot small spherical plastic missiles at opponents from imitation firearms using compressed air.

An 'airsoft gun' is not to be regarded as a firearm for the purposes of this Act (s. 57A).

Section 57A(2) states that an 'airsoft gun' is a barrelled weapon of any description which—

- is designed to discharge only a small plastic missile (whether or not it is also capable of discharging any other kind of missile); and
- is not capable of discharging a missile (of any kind) with kinetic energy at the muzzle of the weapon that exceeds the permitted level.

A 'small plastic missile' is a missile made wholly or partly from plastics, is spherical and does not exceed 8 millimetres in diameter (s. 57A(3)).

The exemption is not absolute—if the kinetic energy at the muzzle exceeds the permitted level, then it will be a firearm. The 'permitted kinetic energy level' is:

- in the case of a weapon which is capable of discharging two or more missiles successively without repeated pressure on the trigger (an automatic weapon), 1.3 joules;
- in any other case (a single shot variant), 2.5 joules.

2.3.2.2 Deactivation of Firearms

A weapon ceases to be a firearm if it is deactivated in line with the provisions of the Firearms (Amendment) Act 1988, s. 8 which states:

> For the purposes of the principal Act and this Act it shall be presumed, unless the contrary is shown, that a firearm has been rendered incapable of discharging any shot, bullet or other missile, and has consequently ceased to be a firearm within the meaning of those Acts, if—
> (a) it bears a mark which has been approved by the Secretary of State for denoting that fact and which has been made either by one of the two companies mentioned in section 58(1) of the principal Act or by such other person as may be approved by the Secretary of State for the purposes of this section; and
> (b) that company or person has certified in writing that work has been carried out on the firearm in a manner approved by the Secretary of State for rendering it incapable of discharging any shot, bullet or other missile.

2.3.2.3 Ammunition

Ammunition is defined by s. 57 of the Firearms Act 1968 which states:

(2) In this Act, the expression 'ammunition' means any ammunition for any firearm and includes grenades, bombs and other like missiles, whether capable of use with a firearm or not, and also includes prohibited ammunition.

2.3.2.4 Imitation Firearm

Some, though not all, offences which regulate the use of firearms will also apply to *imitation* firearms. Whether they do so can be found either in the specific wording of the offence or by virtue of the Firearms Act 1982.

There are two types of imitation firearms:

- general imitations—those which have the appearance of firearms (which are covered by s. 57 of the Firearms Act 1968); and
- imitations of section 1 firearms—those which both have the appearance of a section 1 firearm and which can be readily converted into such a firearm (which are covered by ss. 1 and 2 of the Firearms Act 1982).

It has been held that the definition in s. 57 requires the defendant to be carrying a 'thing' which is separate and distinct from the person and therefore capable of being possessed (*R* v *Bentham* [2005] UKHL 18). Holding your fingers under your coat and pretending that it is a firearm (*Bentham*) will not therefore amount to an imitation firearm for the relevant offences, as an unsevered hand or finger was part of oneself and therefore could not be 'possessed' in the way envisaged by the Act. The 'imitation' must have the appearance of a firearm and it is not necessary for any object to have been constructed, adapted or altered so as to resemble a firearm (*R* v *Williams* [2006] EWCA Crim 1650). In *K* v *DPP* [2006] EWHC 2183 (Admin), it was held that in some circumstances a realistic toy gun, in this case a plastic ball-bearing gun, could become an imitation firearm. This category does not include anything which resembles a prohibited weapon that is designed or adapted to discharge noxious liquid etc.

Whether or not something has the appearance of being a firearm will be a question of fact for the jury/magistrate(s) to decide in each case.

2.3.3 Categories of Firearms and Related Offences

The law regulating firearms classifies weapons into several categories, each of which is specifically defined. These definitions have associated offences dealing with activities such as their possession etc. Alongside these offences are exemptions which allow those activities to be lawful.

2.3.4 Section 1 Firearm

There is a group of firearms which, although not a category defined in the 1968 Act, is subject to a number of offences including s. 1 (see below). Firearms which fall into this group are often referred to as 'section 1 firearms' and include all firearms except shotguns (**see para. 2.3.5**) and conventional air weapons. However, shotguns which have been 'sawn off' (i.e. had their barrels shortened) are section 1 firearms, as are air weapons declared to be 'specially dangerous'.

Section 1 ammunition includes any ammunition for a firearm except:

- cartridges containing five or more shot, none of which is bigger than 0.36 inches in diameter;
- ammunition for an airgun, air rifle or air pistol; and
- blank cartridges not more than one inch in diameter (s. 1(4)).

2.3.4.1 Conversion

Some weapons which began their life as section 1 firearms or prohibited weapons will remain so even after their conversion to a shotgun, air weapon or other type of firearm (s. 7 of the Firearms (Amendment) Act 1988).

2.3.4.2 Possessing etc. Firearm or Ammunition without Certificate

OFFENCE: **Possessing etc. Firearm or Ammunition without Certificate—*Firearms Act 1968, s. 1***
- Triable either way • Five years' imprisonment and/or a fine on indictment
- Six months' imprisonment and/or a fine summarily

The Firearms Act 1968, s. 1 states:

(1) Subject to any exemption under this Act, it is an offence for a person—
  (a) to have in his possession, or to purchase or acquire, a firearm to which this section applies without holding a firearm certificate in force at the time, or otherwise than as authorised by such a certificate;

(b) to have in his possession or to purchase or acquire, any ammunition to which this section applies without holding a firearm certificate in force at the time, or otherwise than as authorised by such a certificate, or in quantities in excess of those so authorised.

KEYNOTE

This offence relates to those firearms described above (see para. 2.3.4) as section 1 firearms.

If the firearm involved is a sawn-off shotgun, the offence becomes 'aggravated' (under s. 4(4)) and attracts a maximum penalty of seven years' imprisonment.

The Firearms Act 1982 applies to this section and so the 'general definition' of an imitation firearm *does not* apply. For this offence, the definition of an imitation firearm is one 'that has the appearance of a section 1 firearm and which can be readily converted into such a firearm' (which is covered by ss. 1 and 2 of the Firearms Act 1982).

The certificate referred to is issued by the chief officer of police under s. 26A. Such certificates may carry significant restrictions on the types of firearms which the holder is allowed, together with the circumstances under which he/she may have them (s. 44(1) of the Firearms (Amendment) Act 1997).

The issue of whether a certificate covers a particular category of weapon is a matter of law for the judge to decide and cannot be affected by the intentions or misunderstanding of the defendant (*R* v *Paul (Benjamin)* [1999] Crim LR 79).

A person may hold a European firearms pass or similar document, in which case he/she will be governed by the provisions of ss. 32A to 32C of the Firearms Act 1968.

If a person has such a certificate which allows the possession etc. of the firearm in question and under the particular circumstances encountered, no offence is committed.

Acquire will include hiring, accepting as a gift and borrowing, and 'acquisition' is to be construed accordingly (s. 57(4) of the Firearms Act 1968).

2.3.4.3 Shortening Section 1 Firearm

OFFENCE: **Shortening Barrel of Smooth-bore Section 1 Firearm to Less Than 24 Inches—*Firearms (Amendment) Act 1988, s. 6(1)***

- Triable either way • Five years' imprisonment and/or a fine on indictment
- Six months' imprisonment and/or a fine summarily

The Firearms (Amendment) Act 1988, s. 6 states:

(1) Subject to subsection (2) below, it is an offence to shorten to a length less than 24 inches the barrel of any smooth-bore gun to which section 1 of the principal Act applies other than one which has a barrel with a bore exceeding 2 inches in diameter; ...

KEYNOTE

The 'principal Act' is the Firearms Act 1968.

Section 6(2) of the Firearms (Amendment) Act 1988 exempts registered firearms dealers from the offence provided the shortening is done *for the sole purpose* of replacing a defective part of the barrel *so as to produce a new barrel having an overall length of at least 24 inches*.

The length of the barrel of a weapon will be measured from its muzzle to the point at which the charge is exploded (s. 57(6)(a) of the 1968 Act).

Once the shortening has taken place, the nature of the firearm will have changed in which case the person will also commit the relevant possession offence unless he/she has the appropriate authorisation.

2.3.5 Shotguns

A shotgun is defined under s. 1(3)(a) of the Firearms Act 1968. Section 1 (amended by the Firearms (Amendment) Act 1988, s. 2) states:

> (3) ...
>> (a) a shotgun within the meaning of this Act, that is to say a smooth-bore gun (not being an airgun) which—
>>> (i) has a barrel not less than 24 inches in length and does not have any barrel with a bore exceeding 2 inches in diameter;
>>> (ii) either has no magazine or has a non-detachable magazine incapable of holding more than two cartridges; and
>>> (iii) is not a revolver gun ...
>> (3A) A gun which has been adapted to have such a magazine as is mentioned in subsection (3)(a)(ii) above shall not be regarded as falling within that provision unless the magazine bears a mark approved by the Secretary of State for denoting that fact and that mark has been made, and the adaptation has been certified in writing as having been carried out in a manner approved by him, either by one of the two companies mentioned in section 58(1) of this Act or by such other person as may be approved by him for that purpose.

KEYNOTE

When considering the above definition, it helps to remember the 'Rule of 2'—a shotgun barrel must be at least 2 feet long (see s. 57(6)(a) in **para. 2.3.4.3**), the bore must not exceed 2 inches in diameter and the non-detachable magazine must hold no more than two cartridges.

For the 'two companies' referred to in s. 1(3A), **see para. 2.3.2.2**.

2.3.5.1 Shotgun Offences

OFFENCE: **Possessing Shotgun without Certificate—*Firearms Act 1968, s. 2(1)***
- Triable either way • Five years' imprisonment and/or a fine on indictment
- Six months' imprisonment and/or a fine summarily

The Firearms Act 1968, s. 2 states:

> (1) Subject to any exemption under this Act, it is an offence for a person to have in his possession, or to purchase or acquire, a shotgun without holding a certificate under this Act authorising him to possess shot guns.

KEYNOTE

A shotgun certificate is granted by a chief officer of police under s. 26B of the 1968 Act and will have certain conditions attached to it. A person failing to comply with those conditions commits the offence below.

OFFENCE: **Failing to Comply with Conditions of Shotgun Certificate—*Firearms Act 1968, s. 2(2)***
- Triable summarily • Six months' imprisonment and/or a fine

The Firearms Act 1968, s. 2 states:

> (2) It is an offence for a person to fail to comply with a condition subject to which a shot gun certificate is held by him.

The conditions and forms used in relation to the grant of shotgun certificates are contained in the Firearms Rules 1998 (SI 1998/1941) and the Firearms (Amendment) Rules 2005 (SI 2005/3344).

2.3.5.2 Shortening a Shotgun Barrel

OFFENCE: **Shortening Barrel of Shotgun to Less Than 24 Inches—*Firearms Act 1968, s. 4(1)***

- Triable either way • Seven years' imprisonment and/or a fine on indictment
- Six months' imprisonment and/or a fine summarily

The Firearms Act 1968, s. 4 states:

(1) Subject to this section, it is an offence to shorten the barrel of a shot gun to a length less than 24 inches.

KEYNOTE

The same exclusions as for the offence of shortening a smooth-bore section 1 firearm apply to this offence, i.e. registered firearms dealers are excluded from the wording of the conversion offence (s. 6(2) of the Firearms (Amendment) Act 1988) provided the shortening is done *for the sole purpose* of replacing a defective part of the barrel so as to produce a new barrel having an overall length of at least 24 inches.

For the length of the barrel, see s. 57(6)(a) in **para. 2.3.4.3**.

Once the shortening or conversion has taken place, the nature of the firearm will have changed (e.g. from a shotgun into a section 1 firearm), in which case the person will also commit the relevant possession offence unless he/she has the appropriate authorisation.

2.3.6 Restrictions on Transfer of Firearms

The Firearms (Amendment) Act 1997 created a number of offences concerned with the transfer, lending, hiring etc. of firearms and ammunition. It is an offence to fail to comply with these requirements (ss. 32 to 35). The mode of trial and punishment depends on whether the weapon is a section 1 firearm or a shotgun.

In brief, a person 'transferring' (i.e. selling, letting on hire, lending or giving) a section 1 firearm or ammunition to another must:

- produce a certificate or permit entitling him/her to do so (s. 32(2)(a));
- comply with all the conditions of that certificate or permit (s. 32(2)(b)); and
- must personally hand the firearm or ammunition over to the receiver (s. 32(2)(c)).

The 1997 Act also requires that any person who is the holder of a certificate or permit who is involved in such a transfer (which includes lending a shotgun for a period of more than 72 hours) shall within seven days of the transfer give notice to the chief officer of police who granted the certificate or permit (s. 33(2)).

Notice is also required of certificate or permit holders where a firearm is lost, deactivated or destroyed or where ammunition is lost, or where firearms are sold outside Great Britain (see ss. 34 and 35).

OFFENCE: **Trade Transactions by Person not Registered as Firearms Dealer—*Firearms Act 1968, s. 3(1)***

- Triable summarily • Six months' imprisonment and/or a fine

The Firearms Act 1968, s. 3 states:

(1) A person commits an offence if, by way of trade or business, he—
    (a) manufactures, sells, transfers, repairs, tests or proves any firearm or ammunition to which section 1 of this Act applies, or a shot gun;
    (b) exposes for sale or transfer, or has in his possession for sale, transfer, repair, test or proof any such firearm or ammunition, or a shot gun, or

(c) sells or transfers an air weapon, exposes such a weapon for sale or transfer or has such a weapon in his possession for sale or transfer,

without being registered under this Act as a firearms dealer.

KEYNOTE

A registered firearms dealer is a person who, by way of trade or business, manufactures, sells, transfers, repairs, tests or proves firearms or ammunition to which s. 1 of this Act applies, or shotguns, or sells or transfers air weapons.

If the person undertakes the repair, proofing etc. of a section 1 firearm or ammunition or a shotgun otherwise than as a trade or business, he/she commits an offence (which is triable either way and is punishable by five years' imprisonment and/or a fine on indictment or by six months' imprisonment and/or a fine summarily) under s. 3(3) unless he/she can point to some authorisation under the Act allowing him/her to do so.

Section 3 goes on to create further either way offences of selling or transferring a firearm or ammunition to someone other than a registered firearms dealer or someone otherwise authorised under the Act to buy or acquire them and of falsifying certificates with a view to acquiring firearms.

Registration is under s. 33 of the 1968 Act.

'Transferring' is also defined under s. 57(4) and includes letting on hire, giving, lending and parting with possession.

Section 9(2) of the 1968 Act exempts auctioneers from the restrictions on selling and possessing for the purposes of sale of firearms and ammunition where the auctioneer has a permit from the chief officer of police. There are further defences provided by s. 9 (for carriers and warehouse staff) and also under s. 8 (transfer to people authorised to possess firearms without a certificate).

2.3.7 Imitation Firearm Offences

OFFENCE: **Converting Imitation Firearm—*Firearms Act 1968, s. 4(3)***
- Triable either way • Five years' imprisonment and/or a fine on indictment
- Six months' imprisonment and/or a fine summarily

The Firearms Act 1968, s. 4 states:

(3) It is an offence for a person other than a registered firearms dealer to convert into a firearm anything which, though having the appearance of being a firearm, is so constructed as to be incapable of discharging any missile through its barrel.

KEYNOTE

This offence involves the conversion of anything which has the appearance of a firearm so that it can be fired. Once the conversion has taken place, the nature of the imitation firearm will have changed, in which case the person will also commit the relevant possession offences unless he/she has the appropriate authorisation.

OFFENCE: **Possession of Articles for Use in Connection with Conversion— *Firearms Act 1968, s. 4A***
- Triable either way • Five years' imprisonment and/or a fine on indictment
- Six months' imprisonment and/or a fine summarily

The Firearms Act 1968, s. 4A states:

(1) A person, other than a registered firearms dealer, commits an offence if—
   (a) the person has in his or her possession or under his or her control an article that is capable of being used (whether by itself or with other articles) to convert an imitation firearm into a firearm, and
   (b) the person intends to use the article (whether by itself or with other articles) to convert an imitation firearm into a firearm.

2.3.7.1 Violent Crime Reduction Act 2006—Imitation Firearm Offences

Sections 36 to 41 of the Violent Crime Reduction Act 2006 created three specific summary offences to deal with the misuse of firearms:

Section 36 makes it an offence to manufacture, import, modify or sell *realistic imitation firearms* as defined in s. 38.

Section 39 makes it an offence to manufacture, modify or import an imitation firearm that does not conform to specifications set out in regulations to be made by the Secretary of State.

Section 40 inserted s. 24A into the 1968 Act and makes it an offence to sell an imitation firearm to a person under 18. It also makes it an offence for a person under 18 to purchase an imitation firearm.

2.3.8 Prohibited Weapon

A prohibited weapon is defined under the Firearms Act 1968, s. 5. The definition covers the more powerful or potentially destructive firearms and their ammunition (such as automatic weapons and specialist ammunition) and also small firearms.

The test as to whether a weapon is a 'prohibited' weapon is a purely objective one and is not affected by the intentions of the defendant. Therefore, where a firearm was capable of successively discharging two or more missiles without repeated pressure on the trigger, that weapon was 'prohibited' irrespective of the intentions of the firearms dealer who was in possession of it (*R v Law* [1999] Crim LR 837).

2.3.8.1 List of Prohibited Weapons and Ammunition

The full list of prohibited weapons and ammunition is contained in s. 5(1) and (1A) of the Firearms Act 1968. This list often (but not always) relates to weapons used in a military context and includes:

- automatic weapons;
- most self-loading or pump-action weapons;
- any firearm which either has a barrel less than 30 cm in length or is less than 60 cm in length overall, other than an air weapon, a muzzle-loading gun or a firearm designed as signalling apparatus;

- most smooth-bore revolvers;
- any weapon, of whatever description, designed or adapted for the discharge of any noxious liquid, gas or other thing;
- any air rifle, air gun or air pistol which uses, or is designed or adapted for use with, a self-contained gas cartridge system;
- any cartridge with a bullet designed to explode on or immediately before impact;
- if capable of being used with a firearm of any description, any grenade or bomb (or other like missile) or rocket or shell designed to explode on or immediately before impact.

KEYNOTE

In relation to weapons designed or adapted for the discharge of any noxious liquid, gas or other thing, taking an empty washing-up bottle and filling it with hydrochloric acid does not amount to adapting it, neither is such a thing a 'weapon' for the purposes of s. 5 (*R* v *Formosa*; *R* v *Upton* [1991] 2 QB 1). This is because to do so does not change the nature of the washing-up bottle itself as the bottle has not been adapted or altered and is therefore not a weapon 'designed or adapted' for the discharge of any noxious liquid etc. The same logic applies to a water pistol filled with ammonia (*R* v *Titus* [1971] Crim LR 279). Any other approach could be problematic to say the least. In the words of Lloyd LJ (in *Formosa*), '[this] would mean that a householder who filled a milk bottle with acid in order to destroy a wasps' nest would be in possession of a weapon adapted for the discharge of a noxious liquid and would therefore be guilty of the offence of possessing a prohibited weapon; until, of course, he had used the acid for the purpose in question when the milk bottle would revert to its pristine innocence. That could not be right.'

An electric 'stun gun' has been held to be a prohibited weapon as it discharges an electric current (*Flack* v *Baldry* [1988] 1 WLR 393) and it continues to be such even if it is not working (*Brown* v *DPP* (1992) *The Times*, 27 March).

2.3.8.2 Possessing or Purchasing Prohibited Weapons or Ammunition

OFFENCE: **Possessing or Purchasing Prohibited Weapons or Ammunition—**
Firearms Act 1968, s. 5
- Triable either way • 10 years' imprisonment and/or a fine on indictment
- Six months' imprisonment and/or a fine summarily

The Firearms Act 1968, s. 5 states:

(1) A person commits an offence if, without the authority of the Secretary of State or the Scottish Ministers, he has in his possession, or purchases, or acquires [a prohibited weapon or ammunition] ...

KEYNOTE

A person may still be in possession of a prohibited weapon even when it is in parts and the accused is in possession of those parts (*R* v *Pannell* (1983) 76 Cr App R 53), or where the weapon is missing an essential part such as the trigger (*R* v *Clarke* [1986] 1 WLR 209).

2.3.8.3 Possession

As an offence contrary to s. 5 of the 1968 Act is a strict liability offence, there is no need to prove that the accused knew the nature of the thing he/she possessed (that it was a firearm or ammunition) in order to prove the offence—it is sufficient to establish that the accused was in possession of the article (*R* v *Deyemi* [2007] EWCA Crim 2060). For example, in *Price* v *DPP* [1996] CLY 1469 an accused was held to have been in possession of the contents of a rucksack (ammunition) notwithstanding that he had no idea of its contents, and was indeed mistaken as to whom it belonged, and as to its nature and quality. If an accused is carrying a rucksack and the rucksack contains ammunition for a section 1 firearm, the accused is in 'possession' of the ammunition irrespective of his/her knowledge or ignorance of its presence in the rucksack (*R* v *Waller* [1991] Crim LR 381; *R* v *Cremin* [2007] EWCA Crim 666).

'Possession' means the firearm or ammunition is in the custody or under the control of the defendant (in *Sullivan* v *Earl of Caithness* [1976] QB 966, it was held that a person can remain in possession of a firearm even if someone else has custody of it).

2.3.8.4 Prohibited Weapons—Exemptions

Section 5A of the Firearms Act 1968 provides for a number of occasions where the authority of the Secretary of State will not be required to possess or deal with certain weapons under certain conditions.

The main areas covered by s. 5A are:

- authorised collectors and firearms dealers possessing or being involved in transactions of weapons and ammunition;
- authorised people being involved in transactions of particular ammunition used for lawful shooting and slaughtering of animals, the management of an estate or the protection of other animals and humans.

Special exemptions

There are a number of special exemptions to the offences under s. 5 of the Firearms Act 1968 involving firearms (under s. 5(1)(aba)).

The exemptions include:

- **Slaughterers**—a slaughterer, if entitled under s. 10 of the 1968 Act, may possess a slaughtering instrument. In addition, persons authorised by certificate to possess, buy, acquire, sell or transfer slaughtering instruments are exempt from the provisions of s. 5 (s. 2 of the Firearms (Amendment) Act 1997).
- **Humane killing of animals**—this exemption allows a person authorised by certificate to possess, buy, acquire or transfer a firearm solely for use in connection with the humane killing of animals (s. 3 of the Firearms (Amendment) Act 1997). When determining whether a firearm falls within the meaning of a 'humane killer', the definition of a 'slaughtering instrument' under s. 57(4) may be referred to (*R* v *Paul (Benjamin)* [1999] Crim LR 79).
- **Shot pistols for vermin**—this exemption allows a person authorised by certificate to possess, buy, acquire or transfer a 'shot pistol' solely for the shooting of vermin (s. 4(1) of the Firearms (Amendment) Act 1997). A 'shot pistol' is a smooth-bored gun chambered for .410 cartridges or 9 mm rim-fire cartridges (s. 4(2)).
- **Treatment of animals**—this exemption allows a person authorised by certificate to possess, buy, acquire or transfer a firearm for use in connection with the treatment of animals or for the purpose of tranquillising or otherwise treating any animal (s. 8 of the Firearms (Amendment) Act 1997). This exemption also applies to offences involving firearms under s. 5(1)(b) and (c).
- **Races at athletic meetings**—a person may possess a firearm at an athletic meeting for the purpose of starting races at that meeting (s. 5(a) of the Firearms (Amendment) Act 1997). Similarly, a person authorised by certificate to possess, buy or acquire a firearm solely for the purposes of starting such races may possess, buy, acquire, sell or transfer

a firearm for such a purpose (s. 5(b)). The use of this exemption is less commonplace as many sporting events use electronic starting systems rather than a starting pistol.

- **Trophies of war**—a person authorised by certificate to do so may possess a firearm which was acquired as a trophy before 1 January 1946 (s. 6 of the Firearms (Amendment) Act 1997).
- **Firearms of historic interest**—some firearms are felt to be of particular historical, aesthetic or technical interest. Section 7(4) of the Firearms (Amendment) Act 1997 makes detailed provision for the exemption of such firearms, exemptions which exist in addition to the general exemptions under s. 58 of the Firearms Act 1968 (**see para. 2.3.10**).
- **Air weapons**—in relation to air weapons with self-contained gas cartridges, owned before 20 January 2004, owners, if they applied for a firearms certificate before 1 April 2004, may retain their weapons.

2.3.9 General Exemptions

The general exemptions apply to the provisions of ss. 1 to 5 of the Firearms Act 1968. They include:

Police Permit Holders

Under s. 7(1) of the 1968 Act, the chief officer of police may grant a permit authorising the possession of firearms or ammunition under the conditions specified in the permit.

Clubs, Athletics and Sporting Purposes

Section 11 of the 1968 Act provides exemptions for a person:

- borrowing the firearm/ammunition from a certificate holder *for sporting purposes only* but where the person carrying the firearm/ammunition is under 18, this applies only if the other person is aged 18 or over (s. 11(1));
- possessing a firearm at an athletic meeting for the purposes of starting races (s. 11(2)) (**see para. 2.3.8.4** for comments on the prevalence of starting pistols);
- in charge of a miniature rifle range buying, acquiring or possessing miniature rifles and ammunition, and using them at such a rifle range (s. 11(4));
- who is a member of an approved rifle club, miniature rifle club or pistol club to possess a firearm or ammunition *when engaged as a club member in target practice* (s. 15(1) of the Firearms (Amendment) Act 1988);
- borrowing a shotgun from the occupier of private premises and using it on those premises *in the occupier's presence* but where the person borrowing the shotgun is under 18; this only applies if the occupier is aged 18 or over (s. 11(5) of the 1968 Act);
- using a shotgun at a time and place approved by the chief officer of police for shooting at artificial targets (s. 11(6)).

Borrowed Rifle on Private Premises

Section 16 of the Firearms (Amendment) Act 1988 states:

(1) A person ('the borrower') may, without holding a certificate under this Act, borrow a rifle or shot gun from another person on private premises ('the lender') and have the rifle or shot gun in his or her possession on those premises if—
(a) the four conditions set out in subsections (2) to (5) are met, and
(b) in the case of a rifle, the borrower is aged 17 or over.
(2) The first condition is that the borrowing and possession of the rifle or shot gun are for either or both of the following purposes—
(a) hunting animals or shooting game or vermin;
(b) shooting at artificial targets.

(3) The second condition is that the lender—

    (a) is aged 18 or over,

    (b) holds a certificate under this Act in respect of the rifle or shot gun, and

    (c) is either—

        (i) a person who has a right to allow others to enter the premises for the purposes of hunting animals or shooting game or vermin, or

        (ii) a person who is authorised in writing by a person mentioned in sub-paragraph (i) to lend the rifle or shot gun on the premises (whether generally or to persons specified in the authorisation who include the borrower).

(4) The third condition is that the borrower's possession and use of the rifle or shot gun complies with any conditions as to those matters specified in the lender's certificate under this Act.

(5) The fourth condition is that, during the period for which the rifle or shot gun is borrowed, the borrower is in the presence of the lender or—

    (a) where a rifle is borrowed, a person who, although not the lender, is aged 18 or over, holds a certificate under this Act in respect of that rifle and is a person described in subsection (3) (c)(i) or (ii);

    (b) where a shot gun is borrowed, a person who, although not the lender, is aged 18 or over, holds a certificate under this Act in respect of that shot gun or another shot gun and is a person described in subsection (3)(c)(i) or (ii).

(6) Where a rifle is borrowed on any premises in reliance on subsection (1), the borrower may, without holding a firearm certificate, purchase or acquire ammunition on the premises, and have the ammunition in his or her possession on those premises for the period for which the firearm is borrowed, if—

    (a) the ammunition is for use with the firearm,

    (b) the lender's firearm certificate authorises the lender to have in his or her possession during that period ammunition of a quantity not less than that purchased or acquired by, and in the possession of, the borrower, and

    (c) the borrower's possession and use of the ammunition complies with any conditions as to those matters specified in the certificate

Visitors' Permits

Section 17 of the Firearms (Amendment) Act 1988 provides for the issuing of a visitor's permit by a chief officer of police and for the possession of firearms and ammunition by the holder of such a permit.

Antiques as Ornaments or Curiosities

Section 58(2) of the 1968 Act allows for the sale, buying, transfer, acquisition or possession of antique firearms *as curiosities or ornaments*. Whether a firearm is such an antique will be a question of fact to be determined by the court in each case. Mere belief in the fact that a firearm is an antique will not be enough (*R v Howells* [1977] QB 614).

Authorised firearms dealers

Section 8(1) of the 1968 Act provides for registered firearms dealers (or their employees) to possess, acquire or buy firearms or ammunition in the ordinary course of their business without a certificate. If the possession etc. is not in the ordinary course of their business, the exemption will not apply.

2.3.10 Air Weapons

Air weapons are defined under s. 1(3)(b) of the Firearms Act 1968. In summary, these are air rifles, air guns or air pistols which are not prohibited weapons under s. 5(1) and which are not of a type declared to be specially dangerous.

Any air rifle, air gun or air pistol that uses or is designed or adapted for use with a self-contained gas cartridge system *does* fall within the definition of a prohibited weapon at s. 5(1).

Carbon dioxide is not air so firearms using compressed carbon dioxide as the power source are treated as air weapons and, if not regarded as 'specially dangerous', are exempt from the firearm certificate procedure (s. 48 of the Firearms (Amendment) Act 1997).

KEYNOTE

'Specially Dangerous' Air Weapons

Some air weapons are deemed to be specially dangerous and therefore subject to stricter control than conventional air weapons. Listed in r. 2 of the Firearms (Dangerous Air Weapons) Rules 1969, as amended, they include:

  (1) [Any] air rifle, air gun or air pistol—
      (a) which is capable of discharging a missile so that the missile has, on being discharged from the muzzle of the weapon, kinetic energy in excess, in the case of an air pistol, of 6ft lb or, in the case of an air weapon other than an air pistol, of 12ft lb, or
      (b) which is disguised as another object.
  (2) Rule 3 of these Rules does not apply to a weapon which only falls within paragraph (1)(a) above and which is designed for use only when submerged in water.
  (3) An air weapon to which this rule applies is hereby declared to be specially dangerous.

An air weapon which is declared 'specially dangerous' under these Rules is considered a section 1 firearm under the Firearms Act 1968 and requires a firearms certificate.

'Harpoon guns' are an example of weapons designed only for use when submerged in water.

2.3.10.1 Air Weapon Offences

Section 32 of the Violent Crime Reduction Act 2006 imposes a 'face to face' requirement on trade transactions by persons selling air weapons.

OFFENCE: **Sales of Air Weapons by Way of Trade or Business to be Face to Face—*Violent Crime Reduction Act 2006, s. 32***
    • Triable summarily • Six months' imprisonment and/or a fine

The Violent Crime Reduction Act 2006, s. 32 states:

  (1) This section applies where a person sells an air weapon by way of trade or business to an individual in Great Britain who is not registered as a firearms dealer.
  (2) A person is guilty of an offence if, for the purposes of the sale, he transfers possession of the air weapon to the buyer otherwise than at a time when both—
      (a) the buyer, and
      (b) either the seller or a representative of his,
      are present in person.

KEYNOTE

A representative of the seller is a reference to a person who is:

- employed by the seller in his/her business as a registered firearms dealer;
- a registered firearms dealer who has been authorised by the seller to act on his/her behalf in relation to the sale; or
- a person who is employed by a person falling within s. 32(3)(b) in his/her business as a registered firearms dealer.

This allows an air weapon to be sent from one registered firearms dealer to another to make the final transfer in person to the buyer. It also enables someone to buy an air weapon from a dealer in a distant part of the country without one or other party to the transaction having to make a long journey, while still preserving the safeguards of a face-to-face handover.

OFFENCE: **Firing an Air Weapon Beyond Premises**—*Firearms Act 1968, s. 21A*

> • Triable summarily • Fine

The Firearms Act 1968, s. 21A states:

(1) A person commits an offence if—
   (a) he has with him an air weapon on any premises; and
   (b) he uses it for firing a missile beyond those premises.
(2) In proceedings against a person for an offence under this section it shall be a defence for him to show that the only premises into or across which the missile was fired were premises the occupier of which had consented to the firing of the missile (whether specifically or by way of a general consent).

KEYNOTE

'Premises' is not defined by the Act other than it 'includes any land'.

This offence makes it an offence for a person of *any* age to fire an air weapon beyond the boundary of premises. A defence is provided to cover the situation where the person shooting has the consent of the occupier of the land over or into which he/she shoots.

OFFENCE: **Failing to Prevent Minors from Having Air Weapons**—*Firearms Act 1968, s. 24ZA*

> • Triable summarily • Fine

The Firearms Act 1968, s. 24ZA states:

(1) It is an offence for a person in possession of an air weapon to fail to take reasonable precautions to prevent any person under the age of eighteen from having the weapon with him.
(2) Subsection (1) does not apply where by virtue of section 23 of this Act, the person under the age of eighteen is not prohibited from having the weapon with him.
(3) In proceedings for an offence under subsection (1) it is a defence that the person charged with the offence—
   (a) believed the other person to be aged eighteen or over; and
   (b) had reasonable ground for that belief.

The offence does not apply to an antique air weapon held as a curiosity or ornament (s. 58(2) of the 1968 Act) or, under s 24ZA(2), apply in circumstances where young persons are permitted to have an air weapon with them under one of the exceptions set out in s. 23 of the Act (**see para. 2.3.15**).

2.3.11 Criminal Use of Firearms

There is a series of firearms offences linked to criminal behaviour. The aggravating factor of the presence of a firearm is evidenced by the fact that the majority carry a life imprisonment sentence; those that do not, still carry 10 years' imprisonment.

2.3.11.1 Possession with Intent to Endanger Life

OFFENCE: **Possession with intent to Endanger Life**—*Firearms Act 1968, s. 16*

> • Triable on indictment • Life imprisonment and/or a fine

The Firearms Act 1968, s. 16 states:

> It is an offence for a person to have in his possession any firearm or ammunition with intent by means thereof to endanger life or to enable another person by means thereof to endanger life, whether any injury has been caused or not.

2.3.11.2 Possession with Intent to Cause Fear of Violence

OFFENCE: **Possession with Intent to Cause Fear of Violence—*Firearms Act 1968, s. 16A***
  • Triable on indictment • 10 years' imprisonment and/or a fine

The Firearms Act 1968, s. 16A states:

> It is an offence for a person to have in his possession any firearm or imitation firearm with intent—
> (a) by means thereof to cause, or
> (b) to enable another person by means thereof to cause,
>
> any person to believe that unlawful violence will be used against him or another person.

2.3.11.3 Using Firearm to Resist Arrest

OFFENCE: **Using Firearm to Resist Arrest—*Firearms Act 1968, s. 17(1)***
  • Triable on indictment • Life imprisonment and/or a fine

The Firearms Act 1968, s. 17 states:

> (1) It is an offence for a person to make or attempt to make any use whatsoever of a firearm or imitation firearm with intent to resist or prevent the lawful arrest or detention of himself or another person.

2.3.11.4 Having Firearm with Intent to Commit Indictable Offence or Resist Arrest

OFFENCE: **Having Firearm with Intent to Commit an Indictable Offence or Resist Arrest—*Firearms Act 1968, s. 18(1)***

- Triable on indictment • Life imprisonment and/or a fine

The Firearms Act 1968, s. 18 states:

(1) It is an offence for a person to have with him a firearm or imitation firearm with intent to commit an indictable offence, or to resist arrest or prevent the arrest of another, in either case while he has the firearm or imitation firearm with him.

KEYNOTE

This offence requires the defendant to 'have with him' a firearm. This is a more restrictive expression than 'possession' and requires that the firearm is 'readily accessible' to the defendant. In *R v Pawlicki* [1992] 1 WLR 827, the Court of Appeal decided that defendants in an auction room had firearms 'with them' which were in a car 50 yards away. Where a defendant left a firearm in his house which was a few miles from the scene of the relevant criminal offence, it was held that this was not enough to meet the requirement of 'having with him' (*R v Bradish* [2004] EWCA Crim 1340). Despite this narrower meaning, the defendant does not have to be shown to have been 'carrying' the firearm (*R v Kelt* [1977] 1 WLR 1365).

In *R v Stoddart* [1998] 2 Cr App R 25, the Court of Appeal made it clear that there are three elements to this offence:

(a) that the accused had with him a firearm or imitation firearm;
(b) that he intended to have it with him; and
(c) that at the same time he had the intention to commit an indictable offence or to resist or prevent arrest.

Proving (b) and (c) is made easier by s. 13(2) of the Act (below).

Intention

In proving the intent for this offence, s. 18 states:

(2) In proceedings for an offence under this section proof that the accused had a firearm or imitation firearm with him and intended to commit an offence, or to resist or prevent arrest, is evidence that he intended to have it with him while doing so.

It is not necessary to show that the defendant intended to use the firearm to commit the indictable offence or to prevent/resist the arrest (*Stoddart*).

The mental element is an essential part of this offence, so if the defendant only formed the intent as a result of duress (as to which, see chapter 1.4), this ingredient will not have been established (*R v Fisher* [2004] EWCA Crim 1190).

Section 18 does not appear to require that any arrest be 'lawful'.

This offence includes imitation firearms in the general sense (see para. 2.3.2.4).

The power of entry and search under s. 47 of the 1968 Act applies to this offence (see para. 2.3.13).

2.3.11.5 Possessing Firearm while Committing a Schedule 1 Offence

OFFENCE: **Possessing Firearm while Committing or Being Arrested for sch. 1 Offence—*Firearms Act 1968, s. 17(2)***

• Triable on indictment • Life imprisonment and/or a fine

The Firearms Act 1968, s. 17 states:

> (2) If a person, at the time of his committing or being arrested for an offence specified in schedule 1 to this Act, has in his possession a firearm or imitation firearm, he shall be guilty of an offence under this subsection unless he shows that he had it in his possession for a lawful object.

KEYNOTE

This offence may be committed in two ways; either by being in possession of the weapon *at the time of committing* the sch. 1 offence or by being in possession of it *at the time of being arrested* for such an offence. In the second case, there may be some time between actually committing the sch. 1 offence and being arrested for it. Nevertheless, if the defendant is in possession of the firearm at the time of his/her arrest, the offence is committed (unless he/she can show that it was for a lawful purpose).

There is no need for the defendant to be subsequently *convicted* of the sch. 1 offence, or even to prove that it has been committed; all that is needed is to show that the defendant, at the time of the commission of the sch. 1 offence and/or of his/her arrest for a sch. 1 offence, had a firearm/imitation firearm in his/her possession (*R* v *Nelson* [2001] QB 55).

It is for the defendant to prove that the firearm was in his/her possession for a lawful purpose.

This offence includes imitation firearms in the general sense (**see para. 2.3.2.4**).

Schedule 1 Offences

There are a number of offences contained in sch. 1 but the *main* offences may be remembered by using the mnemonic ACTOR:

• Abduction—part I of the Child Abduction Act 1984 (child abduction).
• Criminal damage—s. 1 of the Criminal Damage Act 1971.
• Theft, robbery, burglary, blackmail and taking a conveyance—Theft Act 1968.
• Offences against the person—assaults and woundings (ss. 20 and 47 of the Offences Against the Person Act 1861), assault on police (s. 89 of the Police Act 1996) and civilian custody officers (s. 90(1) of the Criminal Justice Act 1991 and s. 13(1) of the Criminal Justice and Public Order Act 1994).
• Rape and other sexual/abduction offences—the following offences under the Sexual Offences Act 2003: s. 1 (rape), s. 2 (assault by penetration), s. 4 (causing a person to engage in sexual activity without consent), where the activity caused involved penetration within subs. (4)(a)–(d) of that section, s. 5 and s. 6 (rape and assault of a child under 13), s. 8 (causing or inciting a child under 13 to engage in sexual activity), where an activity involving penetration within subs. (2)(a)–(d) of that section was caused, s. 30 and s. 31 (sexual activity with/causing or inciting a person with a mental disorder impeding choice), where the touching involved or activity caused penetration within subs. (3)(a)–(d) of that section. Also offences under part I of the Child Abduction Act 1984.

Although covering several types of assault, sch. 1 does not extend to wounding/causing grievous bodily harm with intent (s. 18 of the Offences Against the Person Act 1861). Schedule 1 also covers the aiding, abetting or attempting to commit such offences.

2.3.11.6 Using Someone to Mind a Weapon

OFFENCE: **Using Someone to Mind a Weapon—*Violent Crime Reduction Act 2006, s. 28(1)***

- Triable on indictment • 10 years' imprisonment and/or a fine (firearms etc.)
- Four years' imprisonment and/or a fine (offensive weapons etc.)

The Violent Crime Reduction Act 2006, s. 28 states:

(1) A person is guilty of an offence if—
  (a) he uses another to look after, hide or transport a dangerous weapon for him; and
  (b) he does so under arrangements or in circumstances that facilitate, or are intended to facilitate, the weapon's being available to him for an unlawful purpose.
(2) For the purposes of this section the cases in which a dangerous weapon is to be regarded as available to a person for an unlawful purpose include any case where—
  (a) the weapon is available for him to take possession of it at a time and place; and
  (b) his possession of the weapon at that time and place would constitute, or be likely to involve or to lead to, the commission by him of an offence.

KEYNOTE

The offence was designed to close a perceived loophole in the law where people escaped prosecution by entrusting their weapon to another person, in particular to a child. Using children in this way may risk injury to them and draw them into gun/knife crime as a result of their early association with weapons. Using a minor to mind a firearm is an aggravating factor attracting harsher sentences (s. 29(3)(a)).

A 'dangerous weapon' means a firearm *other than* an air weapon or a component part of, or accessory to, an air weapon; or a weapon to which s. 141 or 141A of the Criminal Justice Act 1988 applies (specified offensive weapons, knives and bladed weapons) (s. 28(3)).

2.3.12 Further Firearms Offences

Alongside offences associated with the criminal use of firearms are several offences dealing with an offender 'having with him' a firearm in a public place and whilst trespassing.

2.3.12.1 Having Firearm or Imitation Firearm in Public Place

OFFENCE: **Having Firearm/Imitation Firearm in Public Place—*Firearms Act 1968, s. 19***

- Triable either way • Seven years' imprisonment and/or a fine on indictment
(if the weapon is an imitation firearm 12 months' imprisonment and/or a fine)
- If the weapon is an air weapon, six months' imprisonment and/or a fine

The Firearms Act 1968, s. 19 states:

A person commits an offence if, without lawful authority or reasonable excuse (the proof whereof lies on him), he has with him in a public place—
(a) a loaded shot gun,
(b) an air weapon (whether loaded or not),
(c) any other firearm (whether loaded or not) together with ammunition suitable for use in that firearm, or
(d) an imitation firearm.

The offence is triable only summarily when the firearm is an air weapon. The s. 19 offence may be committed whether the air weapon is lethal barrelled or not (*Street* v *DPP* [2003] EWHC 86 (Admin)).

A 'public place' includes any highway and any other premises or place to which, at the material time, the public have or are permitted to have access whether on payment or otherwise (s. 57(4) of the Act).

If the weapon is a shotgun, it must be loaded. 'Loaded' means there is ammunition in the chamber or barrel (or in any magazine or other device) whereby the ammunition can be fed into the chamber or barrel by the manual or automatic operation of some part of the weapon (see s. 57(6)(b)). If the weapon is an imitation firearm (see para. 2.3.2.4) or an air weapon, the offence is committed by the defendant having it with him/her. In the case of other firearms, the offence is committed by the defendant having the firearm with him/her together with ammunition suitable for use in it.

For the meaning of 'has with him', see para. 2.3.11.4.

This offence is one of strict liability. If you can show that the defendant knew that he/she had something with him/her and that the 'something' was a loaded shotgun, an air weapon, an imitation firearm or another firearm with ammunition, the offence is complete (*R* v *Vann and Davis* [1996] Crim LR 52). It is for the defendant to show lawful authority or reasonable excuse; possession of a valid certificate does not of itself provide lawful authority for having the firearm/ammunition in a public place (*Ross* v *Collins* [1982] Crim LR 368).

2.3.12.2 Trespassing with Firearms

OFFENCE: **Trespassing with Firearm in Building—*Firearms Act 1968, s. 20(1)***
   • Triable either way (unless imitation firearm or air weapon) • Seven years' imprisonment and/or a fine on indictment • Six months' imprisonment and/or a fine summarily

The Firearms Act 1968, s. 20 states:

(1) A person commits an offence if, while he has a firearm or imitation firearm with him, he enters or is in any building or part of a building as a trespasser and without reasonable excuse (the proof whereof lies on him).

If the relevant firearm is an imitation or an air weapon, the offence is triable summarily.

It is immaterial whether the firearm is loaded or whether the accused has any ammunition with them.

This offence is committed either by entering a building/part of a building or simply by *being* in such a place, in each case as a trespasser while having the firearm. As there is no need for the defendant to have 'entered' the building as a trespasser in every case, the offence might be committed after the occupier has withdrawn any permission for the defendant to be there.

For the interpretation of 'has with him', see para. 2.3.11.4.

It will be for defendants to prove that they had reasonable excuse (on the balance of probabilities).

This offence includes imitation firearms in the general sense (see para. 2.3.2.4).

The power of entry and search under s. 47 of the 1968 Act applies to this offence (see para. 2.3.13).

OFFENCE: **Trespassing with Firearm on Land—*Firearms Act 1968, s. 20(2)***
   • Triable summarily • Three months' imprisonment and/or a fine

The Firearms Act 1968, s. 20 states:

(2) A person commits an offence if, while he has a firearm or imitation firearm with him, he enters or is on any land as a trespasser and without reasonable excuse (the proof whereof lies on him).

2.3.13 Police Powers

The Firearms Act 1968, s. 47 states:

(1) A constable may require any person whom he has reasonable cause to suspect—

    (a) of having a firearm, with or without ammunition, with him in a public place; or

    (b) to be committing or about to commit, elsewhere than in a public place, an offence relevant for the purposes of this section,

to hand over the firearm or any ammunition for examination by the constable.

2.3.13.1 Power to Demand Documentation

The Firearms Act 1968, s. 48 states:

(1) A constable may demand, from any person whom he believes to be in possession of a firearm or ammunition to which section 1 of this Act applies, or of a shot gun, the production of his firearm certificate or, as the case may be, his shot gun certificate.

Failing to produce any of the required documents or to let the officer read them, or failing to show an entitlement to possess the firearm or ammunition, initiates the power of seizure under s. 48(2). It also gives the officer the power to demand the person's name and address.

If the person refuses to give his/her name or address or gives a false name and address, he/she commits a summary offence (s. 48(3)).

2.3.14 Possession or Acquisition of Firearms by Convicted Persons

Section 21 of the Firearms Act 1968 places restrictions on convicted persons in respect of their possession of firearms and/or ammunition.

Any person who has been sentenced to:

- custody for *life*; or
- to preventive detention, imprisonment, corrective training, youth custody or detention in a young offender institution for *three years or more*;

must not, *at any time*, have a firearm or ammunition in his/her possession, i.e. a life-time ban.

Section 21 goes on to provide that any person who has been sentenced to imprisonment, youth custody, detention in a young offender institution or a secure training order for *three months or more, but less than three years*, must not have a firearm or ammunition in his/her possession at any time before the end of a five-year period beginning on the date of his/her release.

Date of release means, for a sentence partly served and partly suspended, the date on which the offender completes the part to be served and, in the case of a person subject to a secure training order, the date on which he/she is released from detention (under the various relevant statutes) or the date halfway through the total specified by the court making the order, whichever is the latest (s. 21(2A)).

Section 110 of the Anti-social Behaviour, Crime and Policing Act 2014 extends the definition of a prohibited person to include persons with suspended sentences of three months or more. The period of five years will begin on the second day after the date on which sentence was passed. A suspended sentence can only be for a maximum of two years so the permanent prohibition will not apply.

A person holding a licence under the Children and Young Persons Act 1933 or a person subject to a recognizance to keep the peace or be of good behaviour with a condition relating to the possession of firearms, must not, *at any time during the licence or the recognizance*, have a firearm or ammunition in his/her possession (s. 21(3)).

Where sentences or court orders are mentioned, their Scottish equivalents will also apply and a person prohibited in Northern Ireland from possessing a firearm/ammunition will also be prohibited in Great Britain (s. 21(3A)).

Section 21 *does not apply to imitation firearms* as there is no express reference to them in the section and because the reference in the Firearms Act 1982 does not apply.

Section 21(6) provides that a person prohibited under this section from having in his/her possession a firearm or ammunition may apply to the Crown Court for a removal of the prohibition and, if the application is granted, that prohibition shall not then apply to him/her.

2.3.14.1 Supplying Firearm to Person Prohibited by s. 21

OFFENCE: **Selling or Transferring Firearm to Person Prohibited by s. 21—*Firearms Act 1968, s. 21(5)***
- Triable either way • Five years' imprisonment and/or a fine on indictment
- Six months' imprisonment and/or a fine summarily

The Firearms Act 1968, s. 21 states:

(5) It is an offence for a person to sell or transfer a firearm or ammunition to, or to repair, test or prove a firearm or ammunition for, a person whom he knows or has reasonable ground for believing to be prohibited by this section from having a firearm or ammunition in his possession.

KEYNOTE

Given that all people are presumed to know the law once it is published, it would seem that the knowledge or belief by the defendant would apply to the *convictions* of the other person, not the fact that possession by that person was an offence.

2.3.15 Other Restrictions on Possession or Acquisition

Sections 22 to 24 of the Firearms Act 1968 create a number of summary offences restricting the involvement of people of various ages in their dealings with certain types of firearm and ammunition.

In summary, the age restrictions are as follows:

- a person under 18:
  - must not purchase or hire any firearm or ammunition (s. 22(1)(a));
  - must not have with him/her an air weapon or ammunition for an air weapon (s. 22(4)). An exception to this is where the person is under the supervision of another who is at least 21 years old. However, if the person under 18 fires the weapon beyond the relevant premises, he/she will commit an offence under s. 21A (**see para. 2.3.10.1**) and the person supervising him/her will be guilty of an offence (allowing the person under 18 they are supervising to use it to fire any missile beyond those premises under s. 23(1)). It is not an offence under this section for a person aged 14 or over to have with him/her an air weapon or ammunition on private premises with the consent of the occupier (s. 23(3));
  - it is an offence to sell or let on hire an air weapon or ammunition for an air weapon to a person under the age of 18 (s. 24(1)(a)), or to make a gift/part with possession of an air weapon or ammunition for an air weapon to such a person (unless under the permitted circumstances above) (s. 24(4));
  - it is an offence to sell an imitation firearm to a person under the age of 18 (s. 24A(2)) or for a person under 18 to purchase one (s. 24A(1)). It is a defence to show that the vendor believed that the purchaser was 18 or over and had reasonable grounds for that belief (s. 24A(3));
- a person under 15:
  - must not have with him/her an assembled shotgun unless supervised by a person aged at least 21 or while the shotgun is securely covered so that it cannot be fired (s. 22(3)); and
  - it is an offence to make a gift of a shotgun/ammunition to such a person (s. 24(3));
- a person under 14:
  - must not have in his/her possession a section 1 firearm or ammunition (s. 22(2));
  - must not part with possession of any firearm or ammunition to which s. 15 of the Firearms (Amendment) Act 1988 applies, except in circumstances where under s. 11(1), (3) or (4) of this Act, he/she is entitled to have possession of it without holding a firearm certificate; and
  - it is an offence to make a gift or lend or part with possession of such a firearm/ammunition to such a person (s. 24(2)) (subject to some exceptions relating to sports and shooting clubs—see s. 11 of the Firearms Act 1968 and s. 15 of the Firearms (Amendment) Act 1988).

There is a further provision creating an offence for a person under 18 who is the holder of a certificate using a firearm for a purpose not authorised by the European Weapons Directive (s. 22(1A)).

KEYNOTE

For the full extent of these restrictions and their exemptions, reference should be made to the 1968 and 1988 Acts. Note that s. 24(5) of the Firearms Act 1968 provides that it is a defence to prove that the person charged with an offence believed that other person to be of or over the age mentioned and had reasonable grounds for the belief.

It is a summary offence (punishable by one months' imprisonment and/or a fine) to be in possession of *any* loaded firearm when drunk (s. 12 of the Licensing Act 1872). There is no requirement that the person be in a public place.

2.4 Terrorism and Associated Offences

2.4.1 Introduction

The law on terrorism contained in this chapter relates to the Terrorism Act 2000, Anti-terrorism, Crime and Security Act 2001, Terrorism Act 2006 and the Counter-Terrorism and Border Act 2019.

2.4.2 Terrorism Defined

Terrorism is defined in the Terrorism Act 2000, s. 1 as:

(1) ... the use or threat of action where—
   (a) the action falls within subsection (2),
   (b) the use or threat is designed to influence the government or an international governmental organisation, or to intimidate the public or a section of the public, and
   (c) the use or threat is made for the purpose of advancing a political, religious, racial or ideological cause.
(2) Action falls within this subsection if it—
   (a) involves serious violence against a person,
   (b) involves serious damage to property,
   (c) endangers a person's life, other than that of the person committing the action,
   (d) creates a serious risk to the health or safety of the public or a section of the public, or
   (e) is designed seriously to interfere with or seriously to disrupt an electronic system.
(3) The use or threat of action falling within subsection (2) which involves the use of firearms or explosives is terrorism whether or not subsection (1)(b) is satisfied.

KEYNOTE

This definition includes domestic terrorism, and should be considered when dealing with other, more familiar offences such as blackmail, contamination of goods and threats to kill.

The definition recognises that terrorist activity may be motivated by religious, racial or fundamental reasons rather than simply political ones. It also encompasses broad activities (including threats) which, though potentially devastating in their impact on society, may not be overtly violent. Examples of such activity might be interference with domestic water and power supplies or serious disruption of computer networks.

The provision at s. 1(3) means that, where the relevant criminal activity involves the use of firearms or explosives, there is no further need to show that the behaviour was designed to influence the government or to intimidate the public or a section of the public. An example of such activity might be the shooting of a senior military or political figure. A 'firearm' for this purpose includes air weapons (s. 121).

The reference to 'action' here includes action outside the United Kingdom. Similarly, references to people, property, the public and governments apply to all those features whether in the United Kingdom or elsewhere (s. 1(4)).

2.4.2.1 Membership of a Proscribed Organisation

OFFENCE: **Membership of a Proscribed Organisation—*Terrorism Act 2000, s. 11***

- Triable either way • 10 years' imprisonment and/or a fine on indictment
- Six months' imprisonment and/or a fine summarily

The Terrorism Act 2000, s. 11 states:

(1) A person commits an offence if he belongs or professes to belong to a proscribed organisation.
(2) It is a defence for a person charged with an offence under subsection (1) to prove—
    (a) that the organisation was not proscribed on the last (or only) occasion on which he became a member or began to profess to be a member, and
    (b) that he has not taken part in the activities of the organisation at any time while it was proscribed.

KEYNOTE

Specific organisations are proscribed by the Secretary of State and include some of the most active and widely known terrorist groups across the world, including Al-Qa'ida (sch. 2 to the Act). What amounts to membership is likely to depend on the nature of an organisation, e.g. membership of a loose and unstructured organisation may not need any formal steps or express process by which a person becomes a member (*R* v *Ahmed* [2011] EWCA Crim 184).

The reverse burden of proof contained in s. 11(2) has been held as imposing an evidential, as opposed to a persuasive, burden of proof (*Attorney-General's Reference (No. 4 of 2002), Sheldrake* v *DPP* [2004] UKHL 43).

Other offences relating to proscribed organisations are provided by s. 12 and include: inviting support; arranging or managing (or assisting in doing so) a meeting of three or more people in public or private, to support, further the activities or be addressed by a person belonging to a proscribed organisation; or addressing a meeting to encourage support or further the activities of the organisation. The Counter-Terrorism and Border Security Act 2019 extends this section by adding that the offence may be committed by expressing an opinion or belief supportive of a proscribed organisation whilst being reckless as to whether a person to whom the expression is directed will be encouraged to support a proscribed organisation (s. 12(1A)).

The Act also created a summary offence of wearing an item of clothing, or wearing, carrying or displaying an article in such a way or in such circumstances as to arouse reasonable suspicion that the defendant is a member or supporter of a proscribed organisation (s. 13). In *Pwr* v *DPP* [2020] EWHC 798 (Admin) it was held that s. 13(1) was a strict liability offence and, although Article 10 of the European Convention on Human Rights (freedom of expression) was engaged, s. 13(1) was a proportionate response. The Counter-Terrorism and Border Security Act 2019 extended this section whereby the offence can be committed by publishing an image of an item of clothing or other article in such a way or in such circumstances as to arouse 'reasonable suspicion' that the writer is a member of or supports a proscribed organisation (s. 13(1A)). Reference to an image is a reference to a still or moving image (produced by any means) (s. 13(1B)).

2.4.3 Terrorism Act 2000: Financial Measures

The main financial measures under the Terrorism Act 2000 relate to terrorist fundraising, possession of property and funding arrangements, and include:

- *inviting* another to provide money or other property (s. 15(1));
- *providing* money or other property (s. 15(3));
- *receiving* money or other property (s. 15(2));
- *possessing* money or other property (s. 16(2));
- *arranging* for money or other property to be made available (s. 17);

in each case intending that, or having reasonable cause to suspect that, it may be used for the purposes of terrorism (ss. 15, 16(2) and 17);

- *using* money or other property for the purposes of terrorism (s. 16(1));
- *concealing, moving or transferring* any terrorist property (s. 18).

Each of these offences is punishable by a maximum of 14 years' imprisonment on indictment (s. 22).

In relation to ss. 15, 16(2) and 17, 'having reasonable cause to suspect' does not mean that the accused must actually suspect that money may be used for the purpose of terrorism but from the information available to the accused, a reasonable person *would* (not might or could) suspect that the money might be used for terrorism (*R* v *Lane* [2018] UKSC 36).

2.4.4 Terrorism Act 2000: Duty of Disclosure and Tipping Off

The 2000 Act creates a number of offences in relation to the unlawful disclosure of information and provides where disclosure is permissible.

2.4.4.1 Disclosure of Information

OFFENCE: **Disclosure of Information—*Terrorism Act 2000, s. 19***
- Triable either way • Five years' imprisonment and/or a fine on indictment
- Six months' imprisonment and/or a fine summarily

The Terrorism Act 2000, s. 19 states:

(1) This section applies where a person—
  (a) believes or suspects that another person has committed an offence under any of sections 15 to 18, and
  (b) bases his belief or suspicion on information which comes to his attention—
    (i) in the course of a trade, profession or business, or
    (ii) in the course of his employment (whether or not in the course of a trade, profession or business).
(1A) But this section does not apply if the information came to the person in the course of a business in the regulated sector.
(2) The person commits an offence if he does not disclose to a constable as soon as is reasonably practicable—
  (a) his belief or suspicion, and
  (b) the information on which it is based.

KEYNOTE

In relation to s. 19(2), a constable includes an authorised member of staff of the National Crime Agency (s. 19(7B)).

This section requires businesses to report any suspicions they may have that someone is laundering terrorist money or committing any of the other terrorist property offences in ss. 15 to 18. Section 19(1)(b) ensures the offence is focused on suspicions which arise at work.

'Employment' means any employment (paid or unpaid) including work under a contract for services or as an office holder, work experience provided pursuant to a training course or programme or in the course of training for employment, and voluntary work (s. 22A).

It is a defence for a person to prove that he/she had a reasonable excuse for not making the disclosure (s. 19(3)), or that the matters specified were disclosed in accordance with an established procedure for the making of disclosures (s. 19(4)). Disclosure by a professional legal adviser is not required if the information was obtained in privileged circumstances (s. 19(5)).

The Act also provides for offences of failure to disclose information by businesses in the 'regulated sector', i.e. accountancy firms, investment companies, etc. (s. 21A) and tipping-off by businesses in the regulated sector (s. 21D). Businesses in the regulated sector are described in sch. 3A to the Act.

2.4.4.2 Disclosure of Information: Permission

The Terrorism Act 2000, s. 20 states:

(1) A person may disclose to a constable—
  (a) a suspicion or belief that any money or other property is terrorist property or is derived from terrorist property;
  (b) any matter on which the suspicion or belief is based.
(2) A person may make a disclosure to a constable in the circumstances mentioned in section 19(1) and (2).
(3) Subsections (1) and (2) shall have effect notwithstanding any restriction on the disclosure of information imposed by statute or otherwise.
(4) Where—
  (a) a person is in employment, and
  (b) his employer has established a procedure for the making of disclosures of the kinds mentioned in subsection (1) and section 19(2),
  subsections (1) and (2) shall have effect in relation to that person as if any reference to disclosure to a constable included a reference to disclosure in accordance with the procedure.

> **KEYNOTE**
>
> References to a constable include references to a National Crime Agency officer authorised for the purposes of this section by the Director General of that Agency (subs. (5)).
>
> Section 20 ensures that businesses can disclose information to the police without fear of breaching legal restrictions.

2.4.4.3 Information about Acts of Terrorism

OFFENCE: **Information about Acts of Terrorism—*Terrorism Act 2000, s. 38B***
  - Triable either way • 10 years' imprisonment and/or a fine on indictment
  - Six months' imprisonment and/or a fine summarily

The Terrorism Act 2000, s. 38B states:

(1) This section applies where a person has information which he knows or believes might be of material assistance—
  (a) in preventing the commission by another person of an act of terrorism, or
  (b) in securing the apprehension, prosecution or conviction of another person, in the United Kingdom, for an offence involving the commission, preparation or instigation of an act of terrorism.
(2) The person commits an offence if he does not disclose the information as soon as reasonably practicable in accordance with subsection (3).
(3) Disclosure is in accordance with this subsection if it is made—
  (a) in England and Wales, to a constable ...

> **KEYNOTE**
>
> This offence relates to any person who has information that he/she knows or believes might help prevent an act of terrorism or help bring terrorists to justice.
>
> A person resident in the United Kingdom could be charged with this offence notwithstanding that he/she was outside the country when he/she became aware of the information (s. 38B(6)).
>
> It is a defence for a person charged to prove that he/she had a reasonable excuse for not making the disclosure (s. 38B(4)).

2.4.4.4 Disclosure of and Interference with Information Offences

OFFENCE: **Disclosure of Information etc.—*Terrorism Act 2000, s. 39***
  - Triable either way • Five years' imprisonment and/or a fine on indictment
  - Six months' imprisonment and/or a fine summarily

The Terrorism Act 2000, s. 39 states:

(1) Subsection (2) applies where a person knows or has reasonable cause to suspect that a constable is conducting or proposes to conduct a terrorist investigation.

(2) The person commits an offence if he—
    (a) discloses to another anything which is likely to prejudice the investigation, or
    (b) interferes with material which is likely to be relevant to the investigation.

(3) Subsection (4) applies where a person knows or has reasonable cause to suspect that a disclosure has been or will be made under any of sections 19 to 21B or 38B.

(4) The person commits an offence if he—
    (a) discloses to another anything which is likely to prejudice an investigation resulting from the disclosure under that section, or
    (b) interferes with material which is likely to be relevant to an investigation resulting from the disclosure under that section.

KEYNOTE

The offences within this section, including that at s. 39(2)(a), which is sometimes called 'tipping off', are essential to the disclosure regime and have a powerful deterrent effect. The defence at s. 39(5)(a) is listed in s. 118(5) and therefore imposes an evidential burden only on the defendant.

It is a defence for a person charged with an offence under s. 39(2) or (4) to prove that he/she did not know and had no reasonable cause to suspect that the disclosure or interference was likely to affect a terrorist investigation, or that he/she had a reasonable excuse for the disclosure or interference. The evidential burden of proof lies on the defendant.

Section 21D of the Act also provides for a similar offence of 'tipping off' in the regulated sector.

2.4.5 Terrorism Act 2006: Offences

For the purposes of the 2006 Act the offences are grouped into three specific areas; encouragement etc. of terrorism; preparation of terrorist acts and terrorist training; offences involving radioactive devices and materials and nuclear facilities and sites. The offences relating to preparation of terrorist acts and offences involving radioactive devices are beyond the scope of this Manual.

2.4.5.1 Encouragement etc. of Terrorism

The offences within this group are:

- publishes a statement to encourage the commission, preparation or instigation of acts of terrorism or Convention offences (s. 1(2));
- engages in the dissemination of terrorist publications (s. 2(1)).

For the purpose of both these sections it is necessary to prove that the published statement(s) glorifies the act of terrorism and that a reasonable person would understand the statement as an encouragement or inducement to them to commit, prepare or instigate an act of terrorism. This 'reasonable person test' was introduced by the Counter-Terrorism and Border Security Act 2019.

'Glorification' includes any form of praise or celebration, and similar expressions are to be construed accordingly (s. 20(2)). The 'Convention offences' mentioned in s. 1(2) are those offences listed in sch. 1 to the Act and include offences in relation to explosives, biological weapons, chemical weapons, nuclear weapons, hostage-taking, hijacking, terrorist funds, etc.

In relation to an offence under s. 2 of the Act it was held that videos uploaded onto the internet of scenes showing attacks on soldiers of the Coalition forces in Iraq and Afghanistan by insurgents were depicting scenes of terrorism within the definition of s. 1

of the 2000 Act (*R v Gul* [2013] UKSC 64). Under this section, although the accused is free to argue that the prosecution constituted an unacceptable interference with the applicant's right to freedom of speech at common law, this defence is always a matter to be determined by the jury (*R v Brown* [2011] EWCA Crim 2751). In *Faraz v R* [2012] EWCA Crim 2820, it was held that evidence of possession of a publication cannot prove by itself that a person was encouraged by it to commit or instigate terrorist offences. This section does not prevent a person from holding offensive views or personally supporting a terrorist cause or communicating the fact that he or she supports such a cause. What this section prohibits is the intentional or reckless dissemination of a terrorist publication where the effect of an offender's conduct is a direct or indirect encouragement to the commission, preparation or instigation of acts of terrorism (*R v Ali (Humza)* [2018] EWCA Crim 547).

Section 3(1) provides that the offences under ss. 1 and 2 can be committed by publishing a statement electronically, i.e. via the internet. In *Iqbal v R* [2014] EWCA Crim 2650 the defendant posted and shared videos, articles and lectures that amounted to the glorification or encouragement of terrorism. 'Statement' includes a communication of any description, including a communication without words consisting of sounds or images or both (s. 20(6)). Section 3(3) provides for a notice to be served by a constable on the person electronically publishing the statement declaring that it is, in the constable's opinion, unlawfully terrorism-related and requiring its removal or modification (s. 3(3)). The methods for giving such a notice are provided in s. 4 of the Act. The offences under ss. 1 and 2 are punishable on indictment by a term of imprisonment not exceeding fifteen years or a fine or both, and summarily by a term of imprisonment not exceeding six months or a fine or both.

2.4.6 Terrorism Act 2000: Police Powers

The Terrorism Act 2000 (Codes of Practice for the Exercise of Stop and Search Powers) Order 2012 (SI 2012/1794) sets out the basic principles for the use of powers by police officers.

2.4.6.1 Arrest without Warrant

The Terrorism Act 2000, s. 41 states:

(1) A constable may arrest without a warrant a person whom he reasonably suspects to be a terrorist.

KEYNOTE

The definition of a terrorist is broadly a person who has committed one of the main terrorism offences under the Act (including ss. 11, 12, 15 to 18, 54 and 56 to 63), or is or has been concerned in the commission, preparation or instigation of acts of terrorism (s. 40).

A magistrates' warrant may be obtained authorising any constable to enter and search the specified premises for the purpose of arresting the person to whom s. 41 applies (s. 42).

2.4.6.2 Search of Persons

The Terrorism Act 2000, s. 43 states:

(1) A constable may stop and search a person whom he reasonably suspects to be a terrorist to discover whether he has in his possession anything which may constitute evidence that he is a terrorist.
(2) A constable may search a person arrested under section 41 to discover whether he has in his possession anything which may constitute evidence that he is a terrorist.
(3) …

(4) A constable may seize and retain anything which he discovers in the course of a search of a person under subsection (1) or (2) and which he reasonably suspects may constitute evidence that the person is a terrorist.

(4A) Subsection (4B) applies if a constable, in exercising the power under subsection (1) to stop a person whom the constable reasonably suspects to be a terrorist, stops a vehicle (see section 116(2)).

KEYNOTE

Where a vehicle is stopped the constable may search the vehicle, and anything in or on it, to discover whether there is anything which may constitute evidence that the person concerned is a terrorist, and may seize and retain anything which the constable discovers in the course of such a search, and reasonably suspects may constitute evidence that the person is a terrorist (s. 43(4B)). Nothing in s. 43(4B) confers a power to search any person but the power to search in that subsection is in addition to the power in subsection (1) to search a person whom the constable reasonably suspects to be a terrorist (s. 43(4C)).

In relation to s. 43(4A), s. 116(2) provides that the power to stop a person includes the power to stop a vehicle (other than an aircraft which is airborne).

2.4.6.3 Search of Vehicles

The Terrorism Act 2000, s. 43A states:

(1) Subsection (2) applies if a constable reasonably suspects that a vehicle is being used for the purposes of terrorism.

(2) The constable may stop and search—
    (a) the vehicle;
    (b) the driver of the vehicle;
    (c) a passenger in the vehicle;
    (d) anything in or on the vehicle or carried by the driver or a passenger;
    to discover whether there is anything which may constitute evidence that the vehicle is being used for the purposes of terrorism.

KEYNOTE

A constable may seize and retain anything which the constable discovers in the course of a search under this section, and reasonably suspects may constitute evidence that the vehicle is being used for the purposes of terrorism (s. 43A(3)).

'Driver' in relation to an aircraft, hovercraft or vessel, means the captain, pilot or other person with control of the aircraft, hovercraft or vessel or any member of its crew and, in relation to a train, includes any member of its crew (s. 43A(5)).

2.4.6.4 Stop and Search in Specified Locations

The Terrorism Act 2000, s. 47A states:

(1) A senior police officer may give an authorisation under subsection (2) or (3) in relation to a specified area or place if the officer—
    (a) reasonably suspects that an act of terrorism will take place; and
    (b) reasonably considers that—
        (i) the authorisation is necessary to prevent such an act;
        (ii) the specified area or place is no greater than is necessary to prevent such an act; and
        (iii) the duration of the authorisation is no longer than is necessary to prevent such an act.

(2) An authorisation under this subsection authorises any constable in uniform to stop a vehicle in the specified area or place and to search—
    (a) the vehicle;
    (b) the driver of the vehicle;

(c) a passenger in the vehicle;

(d) anything in or on the vehicle or carried by the driver or a passenger.

(3) An authorisation under this subsection authorises any constable in uniform to stop a pedestrian in the specified area or place and to search—

(a) the pedestrian;

(b) anything carried by the pedestrian.

KEYNOTE

A constable in uniform may exercise the power conferred by an authorisation only for the purpose of discovering whether there is anything which may constitute evidence that the vehicle concerned is being used for the purposes of terrorism or (as the case may be) that the person concerned is a terrorist within the meaning of s. 40 (s. 47A(4)). However, the power conferred by such an authorisation may be exercised whether or not the constable reasonably suspects that there is such evidence (s. 47A(5)).

A constable may seize and retain anything which the constable discovers in the course of a search if he/she reasonably suspects that it may constitute evidence that the vehicle concerned is being used for the purposes of terrorism or (as the case may be) that the person is a terrorist (s. 47A(6)).

A 'senior police officer' who may give an authorisation is a police officer for the area who is of at least the rank of assistant chief constable (or commander) (sch. 6B).

Authorisation may also be given to prohibit or restrict parking on a specified road where it is considered expedient for the prevention of acts of terrorism (s. 48(1) and (2)). The power may be exercised by a constable placing a traffic sign on the road concerned (s. 49(1)).

2.4.7 Cordons

The 2000 Act gives the police the power, for a limited period, to designate or demarcate a specific area as a cordoned area for the purposes of a terrorist investigation, for instance, in the wake of a bomb.

2.4.7.1 Cordoned Areas

The Terrorism Act 2000, s. 33 states:

(1) An area is a cordoned area for the purposes of this Act if it is designated under this section.

(2) A designation may be made only if the person making it considers it expedient for the purposes of a terrorist investigation.

(3) If a designation is made orally, the person making it shall confirm it in writing as soon as is reasonably practicable.

KEYNOTE

Section 32 provides the meaning of 'terrorist investigation' as an investigation of:

- the commission, preparation or instigation of acts of terrorism;
- an act which appears to have been done for the purposes of terrorism;
- the resources of a proscribed organisation;
- the commission, preparation or instigation of an offence under this Act or under part 1 of the Terrorism Act 2006 other than an offence under s. 1 or 2 of that Act.

The person making a designation shall arrange for the demarcation of the cordoned area, so far as is reasonably practicable, by means of tape marked with the word 'police', or in such other manner as a constable considers appropriate (s. 33(4)).

2.4.7.2 Power to Designate

The Terrorism Act 2000, s. 34 states:

(1) Subject to subsections (1A), (1B) and (2), a designation under section 33 may only be made—

    (a) where the area is outside Northern Ireland and is wholly or partly within a police area, by an officer for the police area who is of at least the rank of superintendent, and

    (b) ...

(1A) ...

(1B) ...

(1C) ...

(2) A constable who is not of the rank required by subsection (1) may make a designation if he considers it necessary by reason of urgency.

(3) Where a constable makes a designation in reliance on subsection (2) he shall as soon as is reasonably practicable—

    (a) make a written record of the time at which the designation was made, and

    (b) ensure that a police officer of at least the rank of superintendent is informed.

(4) An officer who is informed of a designation in accordance with subsection (3)(b)—

    (a) shall confirm the designation or cancel it with effect from such time as he may direct, and

    (b) shall, if he cancels the designation, make a written record of the cancellation and the reason for it.

KEYNOTE

This power is designated to be investigatory in its nature.

Subsections (1A), (1B) and (1C) provide powers to designate to the Ministry of Defence and British Transport Police in relation to specified areas under their jurisdiction.

The period of designation begins at the time the order is made and ends on the date specified in the order. The initial designation cannot extend beyond 14 days (s. 35(2)). However, the period during which a designation has effect may be extended in writing from time to time by the person who made it, or an officer of at least superintendent rank (s. 35(3)). There is a time limit of 28 days on extended designations and this appears to mean an overall time limit of 28 days beginning with the day on which the order is made (s. 35(5)).

2.4.7.3 Police Powers

The Terrorism Act 2000, s. 36 states:

(1) A constable in uniform may—

    (a) order a person in a cordoned area to leave it immediately,

    (b) order a person immediately to leave premises which are wholly or partly in or adjacent to a cordoned area,

    (c) order the driver or person in charge of a vehicle in a cordoned area to move it from the area immediately,

    (d) arrange for the removal of a vehicle from a cordoned area,

    (e) arrange for the movement of a vehicle within a cordoned area,

    (f) prohibit or restrict access to a cordoned area by pedestrians or vehicles.

KEYNOTE

The officer giving the order or making the arrangements and prohibitions set out here must be in uniform. Therefore detectives or other plain clothes officers involved in the terrorist investigation will not have these powers available to them.

The powers under s. 36 are among those that can be conferred on a Police Community Support Officer designated under sch. 4 to the Police Reform Act 2002.

Failing to comply with an order, prohibition or restriction under this section is a summary offence punishable by three months' imprisonment and/or a fine (s. 36(2) and (4)).

This wording will presumably cover refusal. There is a defence if the person can show that he/she had a reasonable excuse for the failure.

A superintendent or above may request passenger, service and crew information from an owner or agent of a ship or aircraft which is arriving, or expected to arrive, at any place in the United Kingdom or is leaving, or expected to leave, from any place in the United Kingdom (Immigration, Asylum and Nationality Act 2006, s. 32(2)). There is a similar power to request freight information from the owners or agents of a ship or aircraft, and in the case of a vehicle, the owner or hirer (s. 33(2) and (3)).

It is an offence if without reasonable excuse a person fails to comply with a requirement imposed under ss. 32(2) or 33(2). The request must be for a police purpose, i.e. the prevention, detection, investigation or prosecution of criminal offences; safeguarding national security; and such other purposes as may be specified (s. 33(5)).

2.4.8 Offences Involving Explosive Substance

OFFENCE: **Causing Explosion Likely to Endanger Life or Property—*Explosive Substances Act 1883, s. 2***
- Triable on indictment • Life imprisonment

The Explosive Substances Act 1883, s. 2 states:

(1) A person who in the United Kingdom or (being a citizen of the United Kingdom and Colonies) in the Republic of Ireland unlawfully and maliciously causes by any explosive substance an explosion of a nature likely to endanger life or to cause serious injury to property shall, whether any injury to person or property has been actually caused or not, be guilty of an offence ...

KEYNOTE

The consent of the Attorney-General (or Solicitor-General) is required before prosecuting this offence (s. 7(1) of the 1883 Act).

'Explosive substance' includes any materials for making any explosive substance; any implement or apparatus used, or intended or adapted to be used for causing or aiding any explosion (s. 9(1)).

The definition of 'explosive' under the Explosives Act 1875 also applies to this offence (*R* v *Wheatley* [1979] 1 WLR 144). Therefore fireworks and petrol bombs will be covered (*R* v *Bouch* [1983] QB 246).

Articles which have been held to amount to 'explosive substances' include:

- shotguns (*R* v *Downey* [1971] NI 224);
- electronic timers (*R* v *Berry (No. 3)* [1995] 1 WLR 7; *R* v *G* [2009] UKHL 13);
- gelignite with a fuse and detonator (*R* v *McCarthy* [1964] 1 WLR 196).

You must prove that the act was carried out 'maliciously'.

Sections 73 to 75 of the Explosives Act 1875 provide powers to search for explosives in connection with the offences under ss. 2, 3 and 4.

OFFENCE: **Attempting to Cause Explosion or Keeping Explosive with Intent— *Explosive Substances Act 1883, s. 3***
- Triable on indictment • Life imprisonment

The Explosive Substances Act 1883, s. 3 states:

(1) A person who in the United Kingdom or a dependency or (being a citizen of the United Kingdom and Colonies) elsewhere unlawfully and maliciously—
  (a) does any act with intent to cause, or conspires to cause, by an explosive substance an explosion of a nature likely to endanger life, or cause serious injury to property, whether in the United Kingdom or elsewhere, or

(b) makes or has in his possession or under his control an explosive substance with intent by means thereof to endanger life, or cause serious injury to property, whether in the United Kingdom or elsewhere, or to enable any other person so to do

shall, whether any explosion does or does not take place, and whether any injury to person or property is actually caused or not, be guilty of (an offence) …

OFFENCE: **Making or Possessing Explosive under Suspicious Circumstances—** ***Explosive Substances Act 1883, s. 4***

- Triable on indictment • 14 years' imprisonment

The Explosive Substances Act 1883, s. 4 states:

(1) Any person who makes or knowingly has in his possession or under his control any explosive substance under such circumstances as to give rise to a reasonable suspicion that he is not making it or does not have it in his possession or under his control for a lawful object, shall, unless he can show that he made it or had it in his possession or under his control for a lawful object, be guilty of [an offence] …

KEYNOTE

The offence under s. 3 is one of specific intent.

Both of the offences under ss. 3 and 4 require the consent of the Attorney-General (or Solicitor-General) before a prosecution can be brought.

In cases of 'possession' the wording of these offences requires the prosecution to prove that a defendant *had* the relevant article in his/her possession and that he/she knew the nature of it (*R v Hallam* [1957] 1 QB 569). This should be contrasted with the usual approach to offences involving 'possession' where the second part (knowledge of the 'quality' of an item) does not need to be shown. However, the concept of 'in your possession' or 'under your control' is a wide one, as illustrated in a case where the defendant had moved out of his property and left homemade bombs and other articles in some boxes with a friend. New tenants in the property had discovered the boxes which later turned up on a rubbish tip. The defendant went to the police station after learning that he was a suspect and he claimed that he had collected the articles many years previously when he was too young to appreciate how dangerous they were. Although he had left the boxes with his friend he was nevertheless convicted of the offence under s. 4(1) as he still had the explosives under his control when he left the property (*R v Campbell* [2004] EWCA Crim 2309).

'Reasonable suspicion' in this case will be assessed *objectively*, that is, you must prove that the circumstances of the possession or making of the explosive substance would give rise to suspicion in a reasonable and objective bystander (*R v Fegan* (1971) 78 Cr App R 189; *R v G* [2009] UKHL 13).

Whether a person's purpose in having the items prohibited by these offences is a 'lawful object' will need to be determined in each case (*Fegan*). In *R v Riding* [2009] EWCA Crim 892, the defendant alleged he had made a pipe bomb out of mere curiosity, using explosives drained from a number of fireworks. The defence contended that 'lawful object' meant the absence of a criminal purpose rather than a positive object that was lawful. However, the court was satisfied it meant the latter and mere curiosity could not be a 'lawful object' in making a lethal pipe bomb. However, in *R v Copeland* [2020] UKSC 8 it was held that personal experimentation or self-education could be regarded as a 'lawful object'. In a further case considering the lawful object defence, it was held that given the obvious risks with using explosive substances, any experimentation involving them which gives rise to a risk of harm to other people or their property, or other unlawfulness such as causing a public nuisance, will not be capable of coming within the scope of the defence (*R v Flint* [2020] EWCA Crim 1266).

There is no need to show any criminal intent or an unlawful purpose on the part of the defendant (see *Campbell*).

2.5 Cybercrime

2.5.1 Introduction

Cybercrime is defined as the use of any computer network for criminal activity. Given the extent to which computers are a part of everyday life for millions of people in the workplace and/or in the home, it becomes clear that the impact of criminal activity via a computer network has huge implications for the government, businesses and for the individual and therefore it is essential that police officers have an understanding of the law that relates to this area of criminality.

There is no single piece of legislation that deals with cybercrime; rather there is the legislation dealing with the end result of the use of a computer network for criminal activity e.g. the Fraud Act 2006 and then a variety of legislation dealing with computer misuse (particularly 'hacking'), data protection and malicious communications (activities dealt with by the Computer Misuse Act 1990, the Data Protection Act 1988 and the Malicious Communications Act 1998).

It is worthwhile noting that s. 20 of the Police and Criminal Evidence Act 1984 specifically deals with powers of seizure in respect of information stored in electronic form.

2.5.2 Offences under the Computer Misuse Act 1990

The Computer Misuse Act 1990 Act ensures the United Kingdom's compliance with the European Union Framework Decision on Attacks Against Information Systems. This compliance requires that penalties relating to 'hacking' into computer systems, unauthorised access to computer material, the intentional serious hindering of a computer system and importing tools for cyber crime, reflect the seriousness of the criminal activities that can be involved in committing these offences.

2.5.2.1 Unauthorised Access to Computer Materials

OFFENCE: **Unauthorised Access to Computer Material ('Hacking')—*Computer Misuse Act 1990, s. 1***
* Triable either way
* Two years' imprisonment and/or a fine on indictment
* Six months' imprisonment and/or a fine summarily

The Computer Misuse Act 1990, s. 1 states:

(1) A person is guilty of an offence if—
   (a) he causes a computer to perform any function with intent to secure access to any program or data held in any computer or to enable any such access to be secured;
   (b) the access he intends to secure, or enable to be secured, is unauthorised; and
   (c) he knows at the time when he causes the computer to perform the function that that is the case.
(2) The intent a person has to have to commit an offence under this section need not be directed at—
   (a) any particular program or data;
   (b) a program or data of any particular kind; or
   (c) a program or data held in any particular computer.

KEYNOTE

'Computer' is not defined and therefore must be given its ordinary meaning. Given the multiple functions of many electronic devices such as mobile phones, this could arguably bring them within the ambit of the Act.

This offence involves 'causing a computer to perform any function', which means more than simply looking at material on a screen or having any physical contact with computer hardware. In the latter case an offence of criminal damage may be appropriate. Any attempt to log on would involve getting the computer to perform a function (even if the function is to deny you access!).

Any access must be 'unauthorised'. If the defendant is authorised to *access* a computer, albeit for restricted purposes, then it was originally held that he/she did not commit this offence if he/she then *used* any information for some other unauthorised purpose (e.g. police officers using data from the Police National Computer (PNC) for private gain (*DPP* v *Bignell* [1993] 1 Cr App R 1)). However, in *R* v *Bow Street Metropolitan Stipendiary Magistrate, ex parte Government of the USA* [2000] 2 AC 216 it was held that where an employee accessed accounts that fell outside his normal scope of work and passed on the information, in this instance to credit card forgers, he was not authorised to access the specific data involved.

Essentially, the purpose of this section is to address unauthorised access as opposed to unauthorised use of data, and behaviour such as looking over a computer operator's shoulder to read what is on the screen would not be covered.

In order to prove the offence under s. 1 you must show that the defendant intended to secure access to the program or data. This is therefore an offence of 'specific intent' and lesser forms of *mens rea* such as recklessness will not do.

You must also show that the defendant knew the access was unauthorised.

The Privacy and Electronic Communications (EC Directive) Regulations 2003 (SI 2003/2426) regulate the use of cookies and internet tracking devices, along with the use of unsolicited email and text messages. Guidance in their extent and practical effect is prepared by the Office of the Information Commissioner.

The powers of entry, search and seizure under the Police and Criminal Evidence Act 1984 apply to this offence.

2.5.2.2   Definition of Terms

The 1990 Act defines a number of its terms at s. 17 which states:

(2)   A person secures access to any program or data held in a computer if by causing a computer to perform any function he—
  (a)   alters or erases the program or data;
  (b)   copies or moves it to any storage medium other than that in which it is held or to a different location in the storage medium in which it is held;
  (c)   uses it; or
  (d)   has it output from the computer in which it is held (whether by having it displayed or in any other manner);
  and references to access to a program or data (and to an intent to secure such access) shall be read accordingly.

(3)   For the purposes of subsection (2)(c) above a person uses a program if the function he causes the computer to perform—
  (a)   causes the program to be executed; or
  (b)   is itself a function of the program.

(4)   For the purposes of subsection (2)(d) above—
  (a)   a program is output if the instructions of which it consists are output; and
  (b)   the form in which any such instructions or any other data is output (and in particular whether or not it represents a form in which, in the case of instructions, they are capable of being executed or, in the case of data, it is capable of being processed by a computer) is immaterial.

(5)   Access of any kind by any person to any program or data held in a computer is unauthorised if—
  (a)   he is not himself entitled to control access of the kind in question to the program or data; and
  (b)   he does not have consent to access by him of the kind in question to the program or data from any person who is so entitled,
  but this subsection is subject to section 10.

(6) References to any program or data held in a computer include references to any program or data held in any removable storage medium which is for the time being in the computer; and a computer is to be regarded as containing any program or data held in any such medium.

...

(8) An act done in relation to a computer is unauthorised if the person doing the act (or causing it to be done)—

    (a) is not himself a person who has responsibility for the computer and is entitled to determine whether the act may be done; and

    (b) does not have consent to the act from any such person.

In this subsection 'act' includes a series of acts.

KEYNOTE

Securing access will therefore include:

- altering or erasing a program or data;
- copying or moving a program or data to a new storage medium;
- using data or having it displayed or 'output' in any form from the computer in which it is held.

Under s. 17(5) access is 'unauthorised' if the person is neither entitled to control that type of access to a program or data, nor does he/she have the consent of any person who is so entitled. The provision under s. 17(5)(a) was the basis for the decision in *Bow Street* (see para. 2.5.2.1). This definition does not affect the powers available to any 'enforcement officers', i.e. police officers or other people charged with a duty of investigating offences (s. 10).

2.5.2.3   Unauthorised Access to Computers with Intent

OFFENCE: **Unauthorised Access with Intent to Commit Further Offences—**
Computer Misuse Act 1990, s. 2

    - Triable either way   • Five years' imprisonment and/or a fine on indictment
    - Six months' imprisonment and/or a fine summarily

The Computer Misuse Act 1990, s. 2 states:

(1) A person is guilty of an offence under this section if he commits an offence under section 1 above ('the unauthorised access offence') with intent—

    (a) to commit an offence to which this section applies; or

    (b) to facilitate the commission of such an offence (whether by himself or by any other person); and the offence he intends to commit or facilitate is referred to below in this section as the further offence.

(2) This section applies to offences—

    (a) for which the sentence is fixed by law; or

    (b) for which a person of twenty-one years of age or over (not previously convicted) may be sentenced to imprisonment for a term of five years (or, in England and Wales, might be so sentenced but for the restrictions imposed by section 33 of the Magistrates' Courts Act 1980).

(3) It is immaterial for the purposes of this section whether the further offence is to be committed on the same occasion as the unauthorised access offence or on any future occasion.

(4) A person may be guilty of an offence under this section even though the facts are such that the commission of the further offence is impossible.

KEYNOTE

The defendant must be shown to have had the required intent at the time of the access or other *actus reus*.

The intended further offence does not have to be committed at the same time, but may be committed in future (e.g. where the data is used to commit an offence of blackmail or to secure the transfer of funds from a bank account).

The provision as to impossibility (s. 2(4)) means that a person would still commit the offence if he/she tried, say, to access the bank account of a person who did not in fact exist.

2.5.2.4 Unauthorised Acts with Intent to Impair Operation of Computer, etc.

OFFENCE: **Unauthorised Acts with Intent to Impair, or with Recklessness as to Impairing, Operation of Computer, etc.—*Computer Misuse Act 1990, s. 3***

- Triable either way • 10 years' imprisonment and/or a fine on indictment
- Six months' imprisonment and/or a fine summarily

The Computer Misuse Act 1990, s. 3 states:

(1) A person is guilty of an offence if—
   (a) he does any unauthorised act in relation to a computer;
   (b) at the time when he does the act he knows that it is unauthorised; and
   (c) either subsection (2) or subsection (3) below applies.
(2) This subsection applies if the person intends by doing the act—
   (a) to impair the operation of any computer;
   (b) to prevent or hinder access to any program or data held in any computer; or
   (c) to impair the operation of any such program or the reliability of any such data.
(3) This subsection applies if the person is reckless as to whether the act will do any of the things mentioned in paragraphs (a) to (c) of subsection (2) above.

KEYNOTE

This section is designed to ensure that adequate provision is made to criminalise all forms of denial of service attacks in which the attacker denies the victim(s) access to a particular resource, typically by preventing legitimate users of a service accessing that service. An example of this is where a former employee, acting on a grudge, impaired the operation of a company's computer by using a program to generate and send 5 million emails to the company (*DPP* v *Lennon* [2006] EWHC 1201 (Admin)).

The intention referred to in s. 3(2), or the recklessness referred to in s. 3(3), need not relate to any particular computer, any particular program or data, or a program or data of any particular kind (s. 3(4)). An 'unauthorised act' can include a series of acts, and a reference to impairing, preventing or hindering something includes a reference to doing so temporarily (s. 3(5)).

The 'hindering' provided by this section is intended to cover programs that generate denial of service attacks, or malicious code such as viruses.

Causing a computer to record that information came from one source when it in fact came from another clearly affects the reliability of that information for the purposes of s. 3(2)(c) (*Zezev* v *USA*; *Yarimaka* v *Governor of HM Prison Brixton* [2002] EWHC 589 (Admin)).

2.5.2.5 Unauthorised Acts Causing, or Creating Risk of, Serious Damage

OFFENCE: **Unauthorised Acts Causing, or Creating Risk of, Serious Damage—*Computer Misuse Act 1990, s. 3ZA***

- Triable on indictment • 14 years' imprisonment and/or a fine

The Computer Misuse Act 1990, s. 3ZA states:

(1) A person is guilty of an offence if—
   (a) the person does any unauthorised act in relation to a computer;
   (b) at the time of doing the act the person knows that it is unauthorised;
   (c) the act causes, or creates a significant risk of, serious damage of a material kind; and
   (d) the person intends by doing the act to cause serious damage of a material kind or is reckless as to whether such damage is caused.
(2) Damage is of a 'material kind' for the purposes of this section if it is—
   (a) damage to human welfare in any place;
   (b) damage to the environment of any place;

(c) damage to the economy of any country; or

(d) damage to the national security of any country.

(3) For the purposes of subsection (2)(a) an act causes damage to human welfare only if it causes—

(a) loss to human life;

(b) human illness or injury;

(c) disruption of a supply of money, food, water, energy or fuel;

(d) disruption of a system of communication;

(e) disruption of facilities for transport; or

(f) disruption of services relating to health.

(4) It is immaterial for the purposes of subsection (2) whether or not an act causing damage—

(a) does so directly;

(b) is the only or main cause of the damage.

KEYNOTE

Reference to doing an act includes a reference to causing an act to be done, and 'act' includes a series of acts. In reference to a country, this includes a reference to a territory, and to any place in, or part or region of, a country or territory (s. 3ZA(5)).

Where an offence under this section is committed as a result of an act causing or creating a significant risk of serious damage to human welfare of the kind mentioned in s. 3ZA(3)(a) or (b), or serious damage to national security, a person guilty of the offence is liable, on conviction on indictment, to imprisonment for life, or to a fine, or to both (s. 3ZA(7)).

Section 3ZA(1) sets out the elements of the offence. The *actus reus* (or conduct element) is that the accused undertakes an unauthorised act in relation to a computer (as in s. 3(1)(a) of the 1990 Act) and that act causes, or creates a significant risk of causing, serious damage of a material kind. The *mens rea* (namely the mental elements of the offence) is that the accused, at the time of committing the act, knows that it is unauthorised (as in s. 3(1)(b) of the 1990 Act) and intends the act to cause serious damage of a material kind or is reckless as to whether such damage is caused. An unauthorised act is defined in s. 17(8) of the 1990 Act as an act where the person doing the act does not have responsibility for the computer in question, which would thereby entitle him or her to determine whether the act is undertaken, and does not have the consent of the person responsible for the computer to commit the act.

2.5.2.6 Making, Supplying or Obtaining Articles for Use in Offences under s. 1, 3 or 3ZA

OFFENCE: **Making, Supplying or Obtaining Articles for Use in Offences under s. 1, 3 or 3ZA—*Computer Misuse Act 1990, s. 3A***

- Triable either way • Two years' imprisonment and/or a fine on indictment
- Six months' imprisonment and/or a fine summarily

The Computer Misuse Act 1990, s. 3A states:

(1) A person is guilty of an offence if he makes, adapts, supplies or offers to supply any article intending it to be used to commit, or to assist in the commission of, an offence under section 1, 3 or 3ZA.

(2) A person is guilty of an offence if he supplies or offers to supply any article believing that it is likely to be used to commit, or to assist in the commission of, an offence under section 1, 3 or 3ZA.

(3) A person is guilty of an offence if he obtains any article—

(a) intending to use it to commit, or to assist in the commission of, an offence under section 1, 3 or 3ZA, or

(b) with a view to its being supplied for use to commit, or to assist in the commission, of, an offence under section 1, 3 or 3ZA.

(4) In this section 'article' includes any program or data held in electronic form.

2.5.3   The Data Protection Act 2018

The Data Protection Act 2018 is intended to provide a comprehensive legal framework for data protection in the UK. It sets standards for protecting personal data, in accordance with the General Data Protection Regulation (EU) 2016/679 ('GDPR'). The GDPR forms part of the data protection regime alongside the 2018 Act.

The four main matters provided for are general data processing, law enforcement data processing, data processing by the intelligence services, and regulatory oversight and enforcement.

The responsibility for compliance with the principles relating to processing of personal data rests on the shoulders of the 'controller', meaning an employer, public authority, agency or any other body which alone or jointly with others determines the purposes and means of the processing of personal data (Article 2(d) of the GDPR). The controller is required to notify the supervisory authority before starting to process data.

The supervisory authority with regulatory oversight of the GDPR in the UK is undertaken by the Information Commissioner who monitors the data protection level, gives advice to the government about administrative measures and regulations, and starts legal proceedings when the data protection regulation has been violated (Article 28). Individuals may lodge complaints about violations to the Information Commissioner.

2.5.3.1   Personal Data

The Data Protection Act 2018, s. 2 states:

(1) The GDPR, the applied GDPR and this Act protect individuals with regard to the processing of personal data, in particular by —
    (a) requiring personal data to be processed lawfully and fairly, on the basis of the data subject's consent or another specified basis,
    (b) conferring rights on the data subject to obtain information about the processing of personal data and to require inaccurate personal data to be rectified, and
    (c) conferring functions on the Commissioner, giving the holder of that office responsibility for monitoring and enforcing their provisions.

KEYNOTE

Personal data shall be processed lawfully, fairly and in a transparent manner in relation to the data subject (Article 6).

'Personal data' means any information relating to an identified or identifiable living individual.

'Identifiable living individual' means a living individual who can be identified, directly or indirectly, in particular by reference to —

(a) an identifier such as a name, an identification number, location data or an online identifier, or

(b) one or more factors specific to the physical, physiological, genetic, mental, economic, cultural or social identity of the individual.

(Article 2a of the GDPR)

Data are 'personal data' when someone is able to link the information to a person, even if the person holding the data cannot make this link. Some examples of 'personal data' are: address, credit card number, bank statements, criminal record etc.

The GDPR covers the processing of personal data in two ways: personal data processed wholly or partly by automated means (i.e. information in electronic form); and personal data processed in a non-automated manner which forms part of, or is intended to form part of, a 'filing system' (i.e. manual information in a filing system). The notion processing means 'any operation or set of operations which is performed upon personal data, whether or not by automatic means, such as collection, recording, organization, storage, adaptation or alteration, retrieval, consultation, use, disclosure by transmission, dissemination or otherwise making available, alignment or combination, blocking, erasure or destruction' (Article 2(b)).

The data subject has the right to be informed when his/her personal data is being processed. The controller must provide his name and address, the purpose of processing, the recipients of the data and all other information required to ensure the processing is fair (Articles 10 and 11).

Data may be processed only if at least one of the following is true:

- when the data subject has given his/her consent (Article 7);
- when the processing is necessary for the performance of or the entering into a contract;
- when processing is necessary for compliance with a legal obligation;
- when processing is necessary in order to protect the vital interests of the data subject;
- processing is necessary for the performance of a task carried out in the public interest or in the exercise of official authority vested in the controller or in a third party to whom the data are disclosed;
- processing is necessary for the purposes of the legitimate interests pursued by the controller or by the third party or parties to whom the data are disclosed, except where such interests are overridden by the interests for fundamental rights and freedoms of the data subject. The data subject has the right to access all data processed about him/her. The data subject even has the right to demand the rectification, deletion or blocking of data that is incomplete, inaccurate or not being processed in compliance with the data protection rules (Article 12).

In relation to Article 7, the data subject has the right to withdraw his or her consent at any time. The withdrawal of consent shall not affect the lawfulness of processing based on consent before its withdrawal.

Personal data may be processed only insofar as it is adequate, relevant and not excessive in relation to the purposes for which they are collected and/or further processed. The data must be accurate and, where necessary, kept up to date; every reasonable step must be taken to ensure that data which are inaccurate or incomplete, having regard to the purposes for which they were collected or for which they are further processed, are erased or rectified; the data should not be kept in a form which permits identification of data subjects for longer than is necessary for the purposes for which the data were collected or for which they are further processed. Appropriate safeguards may be adopted for personal data stored for longer periods for historical, statistical or scientific use (Article 6).

2.5.3.2 Sensitive Personal Data

Some of the personal data that may be processed can be more sensitive in nature and therefore requires a higher level of protection. The GDPR refers to the processing of this data as 'special categories of personal data'. This means personal data about an individual's:

- race;
- ethnic origin;
- political opinions;
- religious or philosophical beliefs;
- trade union membership;
- genetic data;
- biometric data (where this is used for identification purposes);
- health data;
- sex life; or
- sexual orientation.

KEYNOTE

There must still be a lawful basis for processing special category data under Article 6, in exactly the same way as for any other personal data.

This type of data could create more significant risks to a person's fundamental rights and freedoms, for example, by putting them at risk of unlawful discrimination. Additional specific conditions need to be satisfied in relation to this type of data (Article 9(2)).

The processing of the personal data of a child is lawful where the child is at least 16 years old. Where the child is below the age of 16 years, the consent or authorisation of the holder of parental responsibility is required (Article 8).

2.5.3.3 Data Protection Principles

The six data protection principles are central to GDPR compliance and all organisations are required to comply and demonstrate privacy by design.

The GDPR requires organisations to show how they comply with the principles, for example, by documenting the decisions you take about a processing activity.

The principles provided by Article 5 of the GDPR require that personal data shall be:

1. processed lawfully, fairly and in a transparent manner in relation to individuals;
2. collected for specified, explicit and legitimate purposes and not further processed in a manner that is incompatible with those purposes; further processing for archiving purposes in the public interest, scientific or historical research purposes or statistical purposes shall not be considered to be incompatible with the initial purposes;
3. adequate, relevant and limited to what is necessary in relation to the purposes for which they are processed;
4. accurate and, where necessary, kept up to date; every reasonable step must be taken to ensure that personal data that are inaccurate, having regard to the purposes for which they are processed, are erased or rectified without delay;
5. kept in a form which permits identification of data subjects for no longer than is necessary for the purposes for which the personal data are processed; personal data may be stored for longer periods insofar as the personal data will be processed solely for archiving purposes in the public interest, scientific or historical research purposes or statistical purposes subject to implementation of the appropriate technical and organisational measures required by the GDPR in order to safeguard the rights and freedoms of individuals;
6. processed in a manner that ensures appropriate security of the personal data, including protection against unauthorised or unlawful processing and against accidental loss, destruction or damage, using appropriate technical or organisational measures.

2.5.3.4 Offences Relating to Personal Data

The 2018 Act creates a number of offences in relation to personal data, proceedings for which can only be instigated by the Commissioner, or with the consent of the Director of Public Prosecutions.

These offences include:

- Unlawful obtaining etc of personal data (s. 170).
- Re-identification of de-identified personal data (s. 171).
- Alteration etc of personal data to prevent disclosure to data subject (s. 173).

Specific defences are provided in relation to these offences including where it was necessary for the purposes of preventing or detecting crime.

All these offences are triable summarily and punishable by a fine.

2.5.4 Malicious Communications

OFFENCE: **Malicious Communications—*Malicious Communications Act 1988, s. 1(1)***
- Triable either way • Two years' imprisonment and/or a fine
- Six months' imprisonment and/or a fine summarily

The Malicious Communications Act 1988, s. 1 states:

(1) Any person who sends to another person—
    (a) a letter, electronic communication or article of any description which conveys—
        (i) a message which is indecent or grossly offensive;
        (ii) a threat; or
        (iii) information which is false and known or believed to be false by the sender; or
    (b) any article or electronic communication which is, in whole or part, of an indecent or grossly offensive nature,
    is guilty of an offence if his purpose, or one of his purposes, in sending it is that it should, so far as falling within paragraph (a) or (b) above, cause distress or anxiety to the recipient or to any other person to whom he intends that it or its contents or nature should be communicated.

KEYNOTE

'Sending' will include transmitting (note that this offence is complete as soon as the communication is sent).

'Purposes' is simply another way of saying 'intention'.

Section 1(1)(b) covers occasions where the article itself is indecent or grossly offensive (such as putting dog faeces through someone's letter box).

The offence is not restricted to threatening or indecent communications and can include giving false information provided that *one* of the sender's purposes in so doing is to cause distress or anxiety. The relevant distress or anxiety may be intended towards the recipient or any other person.

In addition to letters, the above offence also covers *any* article; it also covers electronic communications which include any oral or other communication by means of an electronic communications network. This will extend to communications in electronic form such as emails, text messages, pager messages, social media, etc. (s. 1(2A)).

It is clear from s. 1(3) that the offence can be committed by using someone else to send, deliver or transmit a message. This would include occasions where a person falsely reports that someone has been a victim of a crime in order to cause anxiety or distress by the arrival of the police.

2.5.4.1 Defence Regarding Malicious Communications

Section 1 of the 1988 Act goes on to state:

> (2) A person is not guilty of an offence by virtue of subsection (1)(a)(ii) above if he shows—
>   (a) that the threat was used to reinforce a demand *made by him on reasonable grounds*; and
>   (b) that he believed, *and had reasonable grounds for believing*, that the use of the threat was a proper means of reinforcing the demand.

KEYNOTE

The italicised words in the offence (author's emphasis) make the relevant test *objective*. It will not be enough that the person claiming the defence under s. 1(2) *subjectively* believed that he/she had reasonable grounds; the defendant will have to show:

- that there were *in fact* reasonable grounds for making the demand;
- that he/she believed that the accompanying threat was a proper means of enforcing the demand; and
- that *reasonable grounds existed* for that belief.

Given the decisions of the courts in similarly worded defences under the Theft Act 1968 (e.g. blackmail; see chapter 3.1), it is unlikely that any demand could be reasonable where agreement to it would amount to a crime.

The defence is intended to cover financial institutions and other commercial concerns which often need to send forceful letters to customers.

<table>
<tr><td>2.6</td><td></td></tr>
</table>

2.6 Racially and Religiously Aggravated Offences

2.6.1 Introduction

The Crime and Disorder Act 1998 sets out circumstances in which certain existing offences become racially or religiously aggravated. The 'aggravated' form of the offence carries a higher maximum penalty than the ordinary form of the offence. Those offences are dealt with in the relevant chapters of the Manuals—the first group is assaults and follows this chapter.

2.6.2 The Offences

The offences that can become racially or religiously aggravated can be grouped in four categories:

- Assaults:
  - wounding or grievous bodily harm—Offences Against the Person Act 1861, s. 20;
  - causing actual bodily harm—Offences Against the Person Act 1861, s. 47;
  - common assault—Criminal Justice Act 1988, s. 39 (**see chapter 2.7**).
- Criminal damage:
  - 'simple' criminal damage—Criminal Damage Act 1971, s. 1(1) (**see chapter 3.10**).
- Public order:
  - causing fear or provocation of violence—Public Order Act 1986, s. 4;
  - intentional harassment, alarm or distress—Public Order Act 1986, s. 4A;
  - causing harassment, alarm or distress—Public Order Act 1986, s. 5.
- Harassment:
  - harassment—Protection from Harassment Act 1997, s. 2;
  - stalking—Protection from Harassment Act 1997, s. 2A;
  - putting people in fear of violence—Protection from Harassment Act 1997, s. 4;
  - stalking involving fear of violence or serious alarm or distress—Protection from Harassment Act 1997, s. 4A (**see para. 2.8.6**).

KEYNOTE

The basic offence must have been committed. Only when that is accomplished should consideration then be given as to whether the offence is aggravated within the meaning of s. 28 of the Act (**see para. 2.6.3**). While the definition of a 'racist' incident is of critical importance to police officers, that definition ('a racist incident is any incident which is perceived to be racist by the victim or any other person') must not be confused with the definition of a 'racially or religiously aggravated' offence under s. 28 of the Act. A 'racist' incident does not automatically become a racially or religiously aggravated offence.

2.6.3 'Racially or Religiously Aggravated'

Section 28 of the Crime and Disorder Act 1998 states:

(1) An offence is racially or religiously aggravated for the purposes of sections 29 to 32 ... if—
   (a) at the time of committing the offence, or immediately before or after doing so, the offender demonstrates towards the victim of the offence hostility based on the victim's membership (or presumed membership) of a racial or religious group; or
   (b) the offence is motivated (wholly or partly) by hostility towards members of a racial or religious group based on their membership of that group.
(2) In subsection (1)(a) above—
   'membership', in relation to a racial or religious group, includes association with members of that group;
   'presumed' means presumed by the offender.
(3) It is immaterial for the purposes of paragraph (a) or (b) of subsection (1) above whether or not the offender's hostility is also based, to any extent, on any other factor not mentioned in that paragraph.
(4) In this section 'racial group' means a group of persons defined by reference to race, colour, nationality (including citizenship) or ethnic or national origins.
(5) In this section 'religious group' means a group of persons defined by reference to religious belief or lack of religious belief.

2.6.4 Timing of the Hostility

A racial insult uttered moments before an assault on a doorman was enough to make the offence racially aggravated for the purposes of s. 29 of the Crime and Disorder Act 1998 (*DPP* v *Woods* [2002] EWHC 85 (Admin)). In *DPP* v *McFarlane* [2002] EWHC 485 (Admin), it was decided that, where the expressions 'jungle bunny', 'black bastard' and 'wog' were used, the offence was made out as the words were used immediately before and at the time of the commission of the offence (contrary to s. 4 of the Public Order Act 1986).

The word 'immediately' in s. 28(1)(a) not only means immediately before but also *immediately after* the commission of the offence.

The need for any such hostility to be demonstrated *immediately* means that it must be shown to have taken place in the immediate context of the basic offence. In *Parry* v *DPP* [2004] EWHC 3112 (Admin), the defendant had caused damage to a neighbour's door by throwing nail polish over it. The police attended 20 minutes after the damage had occurred and spoke to the defendant who was, by that time, sitting in his own house. The defendant made comments demonstrating hostility based on the victim's membership of a racial group. The defendant was convicted of racially aggravated criminal damage but appealed and the conviction was quashed. The court held that the wording of the statute meant that any hostility had to be demonstrated *immediately* before or *immediately* after the substantive offence and that the courts below (magistrates') had not been entitled to consider the retrospective effect of the comments made later by the defendant.

2.6.5 Demonstration of Hostility

Section 28(1)(a) requires that the defendant demonstrate hostility immediately before, during or after committing the offence. This is not to establish the accused's state of mind, but what he/she *did* or *said* so as to demonstrate hostility towards the victim. The demonstration will often be by way of words, shouting, holding up a banner etc. or by adherence to a group that is demonstrating racial hostility.

In the context of criminal damage, the Divisional Court has confirmed that the relevant hostility can be demonstrated even if the victim is no longer present or is not present (*Parry*). However, the need for any such hostility to be demonstrated *immediately* means that it must be shown to have taken place in the immediate context of the offence.

2.6.6 Hostility

Common to both factors under s. 28(1)(a) and (b) is the notion of 'hostility' which is not defined by the Act. The *Oxford English Dictionary* defines 'hostile' as 'of the nature or disposition of an enemy; unfriendly, antagonistic'. It would seem relatively straightforward to show that someone's behaviour in committing the relevant offences was 'unfriendly or antagonistic'.

2.6.7 Victim

The demonstration of hostility will be towards the *victim* based on the *victim's* membership or presumed membership of a racial or religious group (under s. 28(1)(a)). This causes no difficulty where the offence is one of assault, public order or harassment where the victim is a person or where the offence is a criminal damage matter and the property is owned by a person (s. 30(3) of the Act provides that the person to whom the property belongs or is treated as belonging, will be treated as the victim). However, there are problems where the victim of criminal damage is a corporate body, e.g. where a bus shelter belonging to a transport company is damaged by racist graffiti. Of course, the transport company may have a legal personality but it is impossible for it to have a race or a religion. Therefore it cannot be possible to prove the offence under s. 28(1)(a) as it must be based on the victim's membership or presumed membership of a racial or religious group. In these circumstances, the most suitable charge will be under s. 28(1)(b) of the Act (motivation).

Police officers can be victims of these offences and are entitled to the same protection under the legislation as anyone else (*R* v *Jacobs* [2001] 2 Cr App R (S) 38).

KEYNOTE

The victim's perception of the incident (whatever it is) is totally irrelevant.

2.6.8 Motivation by Hostility

Section 28(1)(b) is concerned with the accused's motivation, which does concern his/her subjective state of mind. It will often be the case that the kind of demonstration referred to in **para. 2.6.5** would be evidence of such motivation. In *Taylor* v *DPP* [2006] EWHC 1202 (Admin), it was decided that use of phrases such as 'fucking nigger' and 'fucking coon bitch', patently not used in a jesting manner, must, in the circumstance of the case, have led any judge to find that the offence (in this case, the Public Order Act 1986, s. 5(1)(a)) was motivated, at least in part, by racial hostility as described in s. 28(1)(b). The fact that the offence is motivated only in part by such hostility would not alter the fact that the offence has been committed (motivated wholly or *partly* by such hostility).

2.6.9 Racial Groups

Section 28(4) of the Crime and Disorder Act 1998 states that a 'racial group' means a group of persons defined by reference to race, colour, nationality (including citizenship) or ethnic or national origins.

In determining whether or not a group is defined by *ethnic origins*, the courts will have regard to the judgment in the House of Lords in *Mandla* v *Dowell Lee* [1983] 2 AC 548. In that case, their lordships decided that Sikhs were such a group after considering whether they as a group had:

- a long shared *history*;
- a *cultural tradition* of their own, including family and social customs and manners, often, but not necessarily, associated with religious observance;
- either a *common geographical origin* or descent from a small number of *common ancestors*;
- a *common language*, not necessarily peculiar to that group;
- a *common literature* peculiar to that group;
- a *common religion* different from that of neighbouring groups or the general community surrounding the group; and
- the characteristic of being a *minority* or an *oppressed* or a *dominant* group within a larger community.

Lord Fraser's dictum in *Mandla* suggests that the first two characteristics above are essential in defining an 'ethnic group', while the others are at least relevant. His lordship also approved a decision from New Zealand to the effect that Jews are a group with common ethnic origins (*King-Ansell* v *Police* [1979] 2 NZLR 531).

KEYNOTE

When considering whether an offence was racially motivated under s. 28, hostility demonstrated to people who were foreign nationals simply because they were 'foreign' can be just as objectionable as hostility based on some more limited racial characteristic. In *DPP* v *M* [2004] EWHC 1453 (Admin), a juvenile used the words 'bloody foreigners' immediately before smashing the window of a kebab shop. The Divisional Court held that this was capable of amounting to an expression of hostility based on a person's membership or presumed membership of a racial group for the purposes of s. 28(1)(a) of the Crime and Disorder Act 1998. Although the statutory wording used the expression 'a racial group', the court held that a specific and inclusive definition of such a group had to be used by the defendant (e.g. the defendant did not have to single out a specific nationality) and the size of group referred to by a defendant (such as all 'foreigners') was irrelevant. In *R* v *Rogers* [2005] EWCA Crim 2863, the defendant had called three Spanish women 'bloody foreigners' and told them to 'go back to your own country'. The prosecution case was that the defendant had demonstrated hostility based on the women's membership of a racial group. The court's decision clarifies the position that for an offence to be aggravated under s. 28 the defendant has first to form a view that the victim is a member of a racial group (within the definition in s. 28(4)) and then has to say (or do) something that demonstrates hostility towards the victim based on membership of that group. However, the Court of Appeal noted that the very wide meaning of racial group under s. 28(4) gives rise to a danger of aggravated offences being charged where mere 'vulgar abuse' had included racial descriptions that did not truly indicate hostility to the race in question. Consequently, s. 28 should not be used unless the prosecuting authority is satisfied that the facts truly suggest that the offence was aggravated (rather than simply accompanied) by racism.

The Divisional Court has held that the words 'white man's arse licker' and 'brown Englishman' when used to accompany an assault on an Asian victim did not necessarily make the assault 'racially aggravated' and that the prosecution had not done enough to show that the assailants' behaviour fell under the definition set out in s. 28 of the 1998 Act (*DPP* v *Pal* [2000] Crim LR 756), a case that is hard to reconcile with s. 28(2).

Traditional Romany gypsies are capable of being a racial group on the basis of ethnic origin (*Commission for Racial Equality* v *Dutton* [1989] QB 733). The term 'Travellers' would not be covered, although in *O'Leary* v *Allied Domecq* (2000) 29 August, unreported (Case No. 950275-79) it was held that 'Irish Travellers' were a distinct group for the purposes of the Race Relations Act 1976. However, it should be noted that this decision is only 'persuasive' (as it was a county court decision) and our courts have yet to decide firmly whether 'Irish Travellers' are a 'racial group' for the purposes of the Crime and Disorder Act 1998. It is likely that the 'Irish' element would be covered anyway as English and Scottish people have been held to constitute groups defined by reference to national origins and thus as members of 'racial groups' in the broad sense as defined and protected from discrimination under the Race Relations Act 1976 (now the Equality Act 2010) (*Northern Joint Police Board* v *Power* [1997] IRLR 610). This decision ought logically to extend to Irish and Welsh people. This does not mean that 'travellers' are entirely excluded from the protection the Act offers as, for example, if a 'New-Age' traveller were subject to a trigger offence accompanied by a demonstration of hostility based on his/her skin colour or religion as opposed to being simply a 'New-Age' traveller, the offence would be committed.

In *Attorney-General's Reference (No. 4 of 2004), sub nom Attorney-General v D* [2005] EWCA Crim 889, the use of the word 'immigrant', in its simple implication that a person was 'non-British', was specific enough to denote membership of a 'racial group' within its meaning in s. 28(4) of the Crime and Disorder Act 1998.

2.6.10 Religious Groups

A 'religious group' may, for the purposes of the Act, include a group defined by its lack of religious beliefs. If, for example, D assaults V and at the time of the assault D demonstrates hostility towards V because V is an atheist or humanist who rejects religious beliefs, D must be guilty of a religiously aggravated offence. The same could be said of an assault on an agnostic.

A purely religious group such as Rastafarians (who have been held not to be members of an ethnic group *per se* (*Dawkins* v *Crown Suppliers (Property Services Agency)* [1993] ICR 517) are covered by the aggravated forms of offences as they are a religious group. In reality, a number of racial groups will overlap with religious groups in any event; Rastafarians would be a good example. An attack on a Rastafarian might be a racially aggravated offence under s. 28 because it was based on the defendant's hostility towards a *racial group* (e.g. African-Caribbeans) into which many Rastafarians fall. Alternatively, an attack might be made on a white Rastafarian based on the victim's religious beliefs (or lack of religious beliefs), i.e. his/her 'membership of a religious group'. Muslims have also been held not to be a racial group (*JH Walker* v *Hussain* [1996] ICR 291) but Muslims are clearly members of a religious group and, as such, are covered by the Act.

KEYNOTE

To be guilty of an offence that is racially or religiously aggravated, it is not necessary that the accused be of a different racial, national or ethnic (or religious) group from the victim (*R* v *White* [2001] EWCA Crim 216).

2.6.11 Membership

An important extension of 'racial or religious groups' is the inclusion of people who associate with members of that group. 'Membership' *for the purposes of s. 28(1)(a)* will include *association* with members of that group (s. 28(2)). This means that a white man who has a black female partner would potentially fall within the category of a 'member' of her racial group and vice versa. Moreover, people who work within certain racial or religious groups within the community could also be regarded as members of those groups for these purposes.

For the purposes of s. 28(1)(a), 'membership' will also include anyone *presumed by the defendant* to be a member of a racial or religious group. Therefore, if a defendant wrongly presumed that a person was a member of a racial or religious group, say a Pakistani Muslim, and assaulted that person as a result, the defendant's *presumption* would be enough to make his/her behaviour 'racially or religiously aggravated', even though the victim was in fact an Indian Hindu.

Such a presumption would not extend to the aggravating factors under s. 28(1)(b). The only apparent reason for this would seem to be that the s. 28(1)(a) offence requires hostility to be demonstrated towards a particular person ('the victim'), while the offence under s. 28(1)(b) envisages hostility towards members of a racial or religious group generally and does not require a specific victim.

2.6.12 Other Factors

Section 28(3) goes on to provide that it is immaterial whether the defendant's hostility (in either case under s. 28(1)) is also based to any extent on *any other factor*. This concession in s. 28(3) only prevents the defendant pointing to another *factor* in order to explain his/her behaviour in committing the relevant offence (assault, criminal damage etc.). Although it removes the opportunity for a defendant to argue that his/her behaviour was as a result of other factors (e.g. arising out of a domestic dispute), the subsection does not remove the burden on the prosecution to show that the defendant either demonstrated racial or religious hostility or was motivated by it.

2.7 Non-fatal Offences Against the Person

2.7.1 Introduction

Non-fatal offences against the person are common, so officers need to be able to consider what type of assault they are dealing with. This chapter begins by explaining some of the basic areas of assault law before moving on to deal with more serious assault crimes.

2.7.2 Assault

An assault is any act which intentionally or recklessly causes another to apprehend immediate unlawful violence (*Fagan* v *Metropolitan Police Commissioner* [1969] 1 QB 439). The mental elements involved, i.e. the intention or recklessness on the part of the defendant and the 'apprehension' on the part of the victim, means that *no physical contact* between the offender and victim is required. If X shouts at Y *'I'm going to kick your head in!'*, intending Y to believe the threat and Y does believe it, an assault has been committed by X against Y. Assault can only be committed by carrying out an act; it cannot be committed by an omission.

2.7.2.1 Mental Elements of Assault

On the part of the defendant, the *mens rea* needed to prove assault is either:

- the intention to cause apprehension of immediate unlawful violence; or
- subjective recklessness as to that consequence.

The victim must 'apprehend' (believe) that he/she is going to be subjected to immediate unlawful violence, so the state of mind of the *victim* in an assault is relevant. If X threatened to shoot Y with an imitation pistol, then X could be charged with assault provided Y believed that the pistol was real and that he/she was going to be shot (apprehending unlawful violence). The fact that the pistol was an imitation and could never actually physically harm Y is not important as X has caused Y to apprehend immediate violence being used (*Logdon* v *DPP* [1976] Crim LR 121). If Y knew that the pistol was an imitation and that it could not be fired to hurt him, then Y would not believe the threat and would not 'apprehend' immediate unlawful violence and there would be no assault committed by X. Likewise, if X threw a stone at Y, who has his back to X when the stone is thrown, and the stone sails past Y's head without Y noticing it, there would be no assault as Y did not 'apprehend' unlawful violence.

'Apprehension' does not mean 'fear' so there is no need to show that the victim was actually in fear. So if V is threatened with violence by D and V does apprehend the threat of immediate violence, it does not matter whether he/she is frightened by it. He/she may relish the opportunity to teach D a lesson, and yet still be regarded as the victim of D's assault. The violence apprehended by the victim does not have to be a 'certainty'. Causing a fear of some possible violence can be enough (*R* v *Ireland* [1998] AC 147) provided that the violence feared is about to happen in the *immediate* future (*R* v *Constanza* [1997] 2 Cr App R 492).

2.7.2.2 What is 'Immediate'?

Although the force threatened must be immediate, that immediacy is somewhat elastic. Courts have accepted that where a person makes a threat from outside a victim's house to the victim inside, an assault is committed even though there will be some time lapse before the defendant can carry out the threat.

In *Ireland*, the House of Lords suggested that a threat to cause violence 'in a minute or two' might be enough to qualify as an assault; a threat to provoke some apprehension of violence in the more distant future would not suffice.

The victim must be shown to have feared the use of *force*; it will not be enough to show that a person threatened by words (or silence) feared more words or silence.

2.7.2.3 Words

Words (and silence) can amount to an assault provided they are accompanied by the required *mens rea*. In *Ireland*, it was held that telephone calls to a victim, followed by silences (which led the victims to fear that unlawful force would be used against them), could fulfil the requirements for the *actus reus* of assault if it brought about the desired consequences (e.g. fear of the immediate use of unlawful force). It was accepted that 'a thing said is also a thing done' and the view that words can never amount to an assault was rejected.

Where the words threatening immediate unlawful force come in the form of letters, it has been held that an assault may have been committed (*Constanza* at **para. 2.7.2.1**). It is natural to assume that *any form of communication* can be used as a method for an assault. Thus, it would be possible to assault someone via an email or a text message.

2.7.2.4 Conditional Threats

Words can *negate* an assault if they make a conditional threat, e.g. where you attend an incident and one person says to another '*If these officers weren't here, I'd chin you!*'. In this situation the defendant is making a *hypothetical* threat and is really saying 'if it weren't for the existence of certain circumstances, I would assault you' (*Tuberville* v *Savage* (1669) 1 Mod Rep 3). This should be contrasted with occasions where the defendant makes an immediate threat conditional upon some real circumstance, e.g. '*If you don't cross the road, I'll break your neck*'. Such threats have been held, in a civil case, to amount to an assault (*Read* v *Coker* (1853) 138 ER 1437).

2.7.3 Battery

A battery is committed when a person intentionally or recklessly (subjectively) inflicts unlawful force on another (*Fagan* v *Metropolitan Police Commissioner* [1969] 1 QB 439). Battery *requires physical contact* with the victim, so the offence could not be carried out via the phone (causing psychiatric injury (*R* v *Ireland* [1998] AC 147)). It is sufficient to constitute battery that the defendant attacks the clothing which another is wearing (*R* v *Day* (1845) 1 Cox CC 207).

Battery need not be preceded by an assault. A blow may, for example, be struck from behind, without warning.

A very small degree of physical contact will be enough, not, as many think, an act involving serious violence.

That force can be applied directly or indirectly. For example, where a defendant punched a woman causing her to drop and injure a child she was holding, he was convicted of the offence against that child (*Haystead* v *Chief Constable of Derbyshire* [2000] 3 All ER 890). In *DPP* v *Santa-Bermudez* [2003] EWHC 2908 (Admin), the defendant was held to have committed a battery against a police officer when he falsely assured her that he had no 'sharps' in his possession, and thus caused her to stab herself on a hypodermic needle as she searched him.

2.7.4 Assault or Battery?

Although the terms 'assault' and 'battery' have distinct legal meanings, they are often referred to as simply 'assaults' or 'common assault'. It is, however, important to separate the two expressions when charging or laying an information against a defendant, as to include both may be bad for duplicity (*DPP* v *Taylor* [1992] QB 645). In *Taylor*, the Divisional Court held that all common assaults and batteries are now offences contrary to s. 39 of the Criminal Justice Act 1988 (**see para. 2.7.11**), and that the information must include a reference to that section.

2.7.5 Consent

A key element in proving an assault is the *unlawfulness* of the force used or threatened. Although the courts have accepted consent as a feature which negates any offence, they have been reluctant to accept this feature in a number of cases. The two principal questions that may arise in this context are:

- did the alleged victim in fact consent (expressly or by implication) to what was done; and
- if so, do public policy considerations invalidate that consent?

2.7.6 Legitimate Consent to Risk of Injury

One of the more straightforward policy considerations would include the implied consent to contact with others during the course of everyday activities. We are all 'deemed' to consent to various harmless and unavoidable contact, such as brushing against another on a crowded train. In such a case, it will be a matter of fact to decide whether the behaviour complained of went beyond what was acceptable in those particular circumstances.

There are times when a person may consent to even serious harm, such as during properly conducted sporting events (*Attorney-General's Reference (No. 6 of 1980)* [1981] QB 715), tattooing and medical operations. Participants in contact sports such as football are deemed to consent to the risk of clumsy or mistimed tackles or challenges; but this does not include tackles that are deliberately late or intended to cause harm (e.g. in an off-the-ball incident (*R* v *Lloyd* (1989) 11 Cr App R (S) 36)). Injuries caused in an unauthorised prize fight could not be consented to as this would not be a properly conducted sporting event. In *R* v *Barnes* [2004] EWCA Crim 3246, the defendant appealed against his conviction for inflicting grievous bodily harm after he caused a serious leg injury by way of a tackle during a football match. The tackle took place after the victim had kicked the ball into the goal but, while accepting that the tackle was hard, the defendant maintained that it had been a fair challenge and that the injury caused was accidental. The Court of Appeal held that where injuries were sustained in the course of contact sports, public policy limited the availability of the defence of consent to situations where there had been implicit consent to what had occurred. Whether conduct reached the required threshold to be treated as 'criminal' would depend on all the circumstances. The fact that the actions of the defendant had been within the rules and practice of the game would be a firm indication that what had occurred was not criminal, although in highly competitive sports even conduct *outside the rules* could be expected to occur in the heat of the moment, and such conduct still might not reach the threshold level required for it to be criminal. The court held that the threshold level was an objective one to be determined by the type of sport, the level at which it was played, the nature of the 'act', the degree of force used, the extent of the risk of injury and the state of mind of the defendant.

Teachers who are employed at schools for children with special needs, including behavioural problems, do not impliedly consent to the use of violence against them by pupils (*H* v *CPS* [2010] EWHC 1374 (Admin)).

What of the situation where the consent of the victim has been obtained by fraud? In *R* v *Richardson* [1999] QB 444, a dentist (Diane Richardson) who had been suspended by the General Dental Council continued practising dentistry. The circumstances came to light and charges of assault were brought. Although initially convicted, the Court of Appeal quashed the conviction on the basis that fraud will only negate consent if it relates to the identity of the person or to the nature and quality of the act. Richardson did not lie about her identity (she did not lie about her name) or about the nature and quality of the act (the dentistry carried out). While her behaviour was reprehensible, it did not amount to an offence. This does not mean that persons without appropriate qualifications sneaking into a surgery and putting on a white coat and calling themselves 'Doctor' followed by their true name could avoid liability if they then made physical contact with another in the guise of providing treatment. While there is no fraud as to identity, any treatment carried out would be caught by a fraud in respect of the quality of the act. Consent would also be negated if a genuine doctor indecently touched his patients on the basis that this was part of a routine medical examination when its true purpose was for sexual gratification (*R v Tabassum* [2000] 2 Cr App R 328).

2.7.7 Consent to Sado-masochistic Injuries

Where actual bodily harm (or worse) is deliberately inflicted, consent to it will ordinarily be deemed invalid on the grounds of public policy even if 'victims' know exactly what they are consenting to.

An example of this approach can be seen in the case of *R v Brown* [1994] 1 AC 212. That case involved members of a sado-masochist group who inflicted varying degrees of injuries on one another (under ss. 20 and 47 of the Offences Against the Person Act 1861) for their own gratification. The group claimed that they had consented to the injuries and therefore no assault or battery had taken place. Their lordships followed an earlier policy that *all assaults which result in more than transient harm will be unlawful unless there is good reason for allowing the plea of 'consent'*. Good reason will be determined in the light of a number of considerations:

- the practical consequences of the behaviour;
- the dangerousness of the behaviour;
- the vulnerability of the 'consenting' person.

Sado-masochistic injury may justifiably be made the subject of criminal law on grounds of the 'protection of health'. It was for this reason that the European Court of Human Rights held that there had been no violation of the defendants' right to respect for private and family life (under Article 8) in *Brown*.

Further issues in clarifying what will amount to 'true' or effective consent were added by the decision of the Court of Appeal in *R v Wilson* [1997] QB 47. In that case, the court accepted that a husband might lawfully brand his initials on his wife's buttocks with a hot knife provided she consented (as she appeared to have done). The reasoning behind the judgment seems to be based on the fact that the branding was similar to a form of tattooing, but also on the policy grounds that consensual activity between husband and wife is not a matter for criminal investigation. Therefore, if a situation arose where a husband and wife took part in mutual branding in the privacy of their home, their criminal liability would arguably depend on whether they caused the harm for purposes of sado-masochistic pleasure or out of some affectionate wish to be permanently adorned with the mark of their loved one.

2.7.8 Consent to Serious Harm for Sexual Gratification

Section 71(2) of the Domestic Abuse Act 2021 states that it is *not a defence* that the victim of a 'relevant offence' consented to the infliction of the serious harm for the purposes of obtaining sexual gratification.

KEYNOTE

'Relevant Offence'

A 'relevant offence' means an offence under section 18, 20 or 47 of the Offences Against the Person Act 1861.
  'Serious harm' means:

- grievous bodily harm, within the meaning of s. 18 of the 1861 Act;

- wounding, within the meaning of that section, or
- actual bodily harm, within the meaning of s. 47 of the 1861 Act.

Section 71(2) does not apply in the case of an offence under s. 20 or s. 47 of the 1861 Act where:

- the serious harm consists of, or is as a result of, the infection of the victim with a sexually transmitted infection in the course of sexual activity, and
- the victim consented to the activity in the knowledge or belief that the defendant had the sexually transmitted infection.

It does not matter whether the harm was inflicted for the purposes of obtaining sexual gratification for the defendant, for the victim or for some other person (s. 71(5)).

2.7.9 'Corporal' and 'Reasonable' Punishment

Corporal Punishment

Section 548 of the Education Act 1996 outlaws corporal punishment in *all* British schools, including independent schools. Staff may use reasonable force in restraining violent or disruptive pupils as 'corporal punishment' shall not be taken to be given to a child by virtue of anything done for reasons that include averting an immediate danger of personal injury to or an immediate danger to the property of any person (including the child him/herself (s. 548(5)).

Reasonable Punishment

The Children Act 2004, s. 58 states:

(1) In relation to any offence specified in subsection (2), battery of a child cannot be justified on the ground that it constituted reasonable punishment.
(2) The offences referred to in subsection (1) are—
(a) an offence under section 18 or 20 of the Offences Against the Person Act 1861 (wounding or causing grievous bodily harm);
(b) an offence under s. 47 of that Act (assault occasioning actual bodily harm);
(c) an offence under s. 1 of the Children and Young Persons Act 1933 (cruelty to persons under 16).

Section 58 of the Children Act 2004 prohibits the defence of reasonable punishment for parents or adults acting *in loco parentis* (meaning 'in place of the parent') where the accused person is charged with an offence mentioned in s. 58(2) against a child (a 'child' for the purposes of the Children Act 2004 is a person under the age of 18 (s. 65(9)). However, the reasonable punishment defence remains available for parents and adults acting *in loco parentis* charged with common assault under the Criminal Justice Act 1988, s. 39. Whether the actions of the defendant are 'reasonable' will be important; physical punishment where a child is hit (causing injury reddening to the skin) with an implement such as a cane may well be considered 'unreasonable'. It is important to note that the law does not rule out physical chastisement by a parent etc. but that chastisement should only constitute 'mild smacking' rather than cause injuries subject to assault charges.

2.7.10 Assault Offences

Having considered the key common elements in this area, the specific offences are set out below.

2.7.11 Common Assault and Battery

OFFENCE: **Common Assault/Battery—*Criminal Justice Act 1988, s. 39***
- Triable summarily • Six months' imprisonment

OFFENCE: **Racially or Religiously Aggravated—*Crime and Disorder Act 1998,
s. 29(1)(c)***

- Triable either way • Two years' imprisonment and/or a fine on indictment
- Six months' imprisonment and/or a fine summarily

KEYNOTE

The racially or religiously aggravated offence can be tried on indictment without having to be included alongside another indictable offence as is the case with common assaults generally (Criminal Justice Act 1988, s. 40).

CPS Charging Standards state that a charge under s. 39 of the Act is appropriate where *no injury or injuries which are not serious* occur. In *R v Misalati* [2017] EWCA Crim 2226, the appellant spat towards the complainant. The appeal court confirmed that although there was no actual violence, spitting is an assault whether it makes contact with the victim or causes fear of immediate unlawful physical contact.

The injury sustained by the victim should always be considered first, and in most cases the degree of injury will determine the appropriate charge. The appropriate charge will usually be contrary to s. 39 where injuries amount to *no more* than the following:

- grazes;
- scratches;
- abrasions;
- minor bruising;
- swellings;
- reddening of the skin;
- superficial cuts.

2.7.12 Assaults on Emergency Workers

The Assaults on Emergency Workers (Offences) Act 2018 states that a common assault or battery committed against an emergency worker acting in the exercise of functions as such a worker is punishable:

- on summary conviction, to imprisonment for a term not exceeding 12 months, or to a fine, or to both;
- on conviction on indictment, to imprisonment for a term not exceeding 12 months, or to a fine, or to both.

KEYNOTE

When Does it Apply?

The circumstances in which an offence is to be taken as committed against a person acting in the exercise of functions as an emergency worker include circumstances where the offence takes place at a time when the person is not at work but is carrying out functions which, if done in work time, would have been in the exercise of functions as an emergency worker.

Increased Sentence

Although the Act provides for an increase in sentence to 12 months for common assault/battery on an emergency worker, the reality is that this increased sentence is not at the disposal of the magistrates' court. Section 154 of the Criminal Justice Act 2003 (increase in the maximum term that may be imposed on summary conviction of an offence triable either way) is not in force. Until that is the case, the reference to 12 months above is to be read as six months.

The fact that the victim of the offence is an emergency worker is an aggravating factor when considering other offences under the Offences Against the Person Act 1861. This is the case for a number of offences, such as s. 20 (malicious wounding/GBH), s. 18 (wounding/GBH with intent) and s. 47 (assault occasioning actual bodily harm) (s. 2(3)). Where this is the case, the court must treat the fact that the offence was committed on an emergency worker as an aggravating factor (that is to say, a factor that increases the seriousness of the offence) and must state in open court that the offence is so aggravated (s. 2(2)).

'Emergency Worker'

An 'emergency worker' means:

- a constable;
- a person (other than a constable) who has the powers of a constable or is otherwise employed for police purposes or is engaged to provide services for police purposes;
- a National Crime Agency officer;
- a prison officer;
- a person (other than a prison officer) employed or engaged to carry out functions in a custodial institution of a corresponding kind to those carried out by a prison officer;
- a prisoner custody officer, so far as relating to the exercise of escort functions;
- a custody officer, so far as relating to the exercise of escort functions;
- a person employed for the purposes of providing, or engaged to provide, fire services or fire and rescue services;
- a person employed for the purposes of providing, or engaged to provide, search services or rescue services (or both);
- a person employed for the purposes of providing, or engaged to provide:
  - ◆ NHS health services; or
  - ◆ services in the support of the provision of NHS health services;
  and whose general activities in doing so involve face-to-face interaction with individuals receiving the service or with other members of the public.

It is immaterial whether the employment or engagement is paid or unpaid (s. 3(2)).

Custodial Institution

A 'custodial institution' includes a prison, a young offender institution, a secure training centre, secure college or remand centre. It also includes a removal centre, a short-term holding facility or pre-departure accommodation (as defined by s. 147 of the Immigration and Asylum Act 1999) (s. 3(3)).

Custody Officer

This is not to be confused with the term 'custody officer' at a designated police station. A 'custody officer' means a person in respect of whom a certificate is for the time being in force certifying that he/she has been approved by the Secretary of State for the purpose of performing escort duties and/or custodial duties at secure training centres.

Escort Functions

'Escort functions', in the case of a prisoner custody officer, means the functions specified in s. 80(1) of the Criminal Justice Act 1991. In the case of a custody officer, it means the functions specified in para. 1 of sch. 1 to the Criminal Justice and Public Order Act 1994.

NHS Health Services

'NHS health services' means any kind of health services provided as part of the health service continued under s. 1(1) of the National Health Services Act 2006 and under s. 1(1) of the National Health Service (Wales) Act 2006.

2.7.13 Assault Occasioning Actual Bodily Harm

OFFENCE: **Assault Occasioning Actual Bodily Harm—*Offences Against the Person Act 1861, s. 47***

- Triable either way • Five years' imprisonment on indictment
- Six months' imprisonment and/or a fine summarily

OFFENCE: **Racially or Religiously Aggravated—*Crime and Disorder Act 1998, s. 29(1)(b)***

- Triable either way • Seven years' imprisonment and/or a fine on indictment
- Six months' imprisonment and/or a fine summarily

The Offences Against the Person Act 1861, s. 47 states:

> Whosoever shall be convicted ... of any assault occasioning actual bodily harm shall be liable ... to be kept in penal servitude ...

KEYNOTE

The only difference between an assault committed under s. 39 of the Criminal Justice Act 1988 and an assault under s. 47 of the Offences Against the Person Act 1861 is the degree of harm suffered by the victim and the sentence available. The *mens rea* and *actus reus* of the offence under s. 39 of the Criminal Justice Act 1988 and the offence under s. 47 of the Offences Against the Person Act 1861 are exactly the same.

It must be shown that 'actual bodily harm' was a consequence, directly or indirectly, of the defendant's actions.

So what is 'actual bodily harm'? In *DPP* v *Smith* [1961] AC 290, it was noted that the expression needed 'no explanation' and, in *R* v *Chan-Fook* ([1994] 1 WLR 689), the court advised that the phrase consisted of 'three words of the English language which require no elaboration and in the ordinary course should not receive any'. While the phrase 'bodily harm' has its ordinary meaning, it has been said to include any hurt calculated to interfere with the health or comfort of the victim: such hurt need not be permanent, but must be more than transient and trifling (*R* v *Miller* [1954] 2 QB 282).

CPS Charging Standards state that a charge under s. 47 would be appropriate where the injuries are serious. Whilst CPS charging standards may be considered persuasive and/or influential regarding the appropriate charge, the fact remains that they do not represent the law—consequently, it is useful to consider specific case law decisions where the courts stated that the injuries amounted to a s. 47 offence for more authoritative direction.

Psychological harm that involves more than mere emotions such as fear, distress or panic can amount to a s. 47 offence. This may amount to shock (*Miller*) and mental 'injury' (*Chan-Fook*). Where psychiatric injury is relied upon as the basis for an allegation of assault occasioning actual bodily harm, and the matter is not admitted by the defence, then expert evidence must be called by the prosecution (*Chan-Fook*).

The Administrative Court has accepted that a momentary loss of consciousness caused by a kick but without any physical injury can be 'actual harm' because it involved an injurious impairment of the victim's sensory abilities which did not fall within the 'trifling' category described in *R* v *Miller* (*T* v *DPP* [2003] EWHC 266 (Admin)).

It was held in *DPP* v *Smith (Ross Michael)* [2006] EWHC 94 (Admin) that the *substantial* cutting of a person's hair against his/her will could amount to actual bodily harm even though no pain or other injury may be involved. In *Smith*, the defendant cut off his ex-partner's ponytail, deliberately and without her permission. Even though medically and scientifically speaking, the hair above the surface of the scalp is no more than dead tissue, it remains part of the body and is attached to it. While it is so attached, it falls within the meaning of 'bodily' in the phrase 'actual bodily harm' as it is concerned with the body of the individual victim. Therefore the same would be true of fingernails.

CPS Charging Standards state that ABH should generally be charged where injuries and overall circumstances indicate that the offence clearly merits more than six months' imprisonment and where the prosecution intends to represent that the case is not suitable for summary trial. Examples may include cases where there is a need for a number of stitches (but not superficial application of steri-strips) or a hospital procedure under anaesthetic.

2.7.14 Wounding or Inflicting Grievous Bodily Harm

OFFENCE: **Wounding or Inflicting Grievous Bodily Harm—*Offences Against the Person Act 1861, s. 20***

- Triable either way • Five years' imprisonment on indictment
- Six months' imprisonment and/or a fine summarily

OFFENCE: **Racially or Religiously Aggravated—*Crime and Disorder Act 1998, s. 29(1)(a)***

- Triable either way • Seven years' imprisonment and/or a fine on indictment
- Six months' imprisonment and/or a fine summarily

The Offences Against the Person Act 1861, s. 20 states:

> Whosoever shall unlawfully and maliciously wound or inflict any grievous bodily harm upon any other person, either with or without any weapon or instrument, shall be guilty of a misdemeanor …

KEYNOTE

Maliciously

Although the word maliciously suggests some form of evil premeditation, 'malice' here amounts to *subjective recklessness*. It means that the defendant must realise that there is a risk of *some harm* being caused to the victim but took the risk anyway. The defendant does not need to foresee the degree of harm which is eventually caused, only that his/her behaviour may bring about some harm to the victim.

Wound

Wounding requires the breaking of the continuity of the whole of the skin (dermis and epidermis) or the breaking of the inner skin within the cheek, lip or urethra. A cut which breaks all the layers of a person's skin, whether caused externally (e.g. a knife wound) or internally (e.g. a punch causing a tooth to puncture the cheek), will amount to a wound. It does not include the rupturing of internal blood vessels (bruising).

The definition of wounding may encompass injuries that are relatively minor in nature, e.g. a small cut. CPS Charging Standards state that an assault contrary to s. 20 should be reserved for the type of wounds considered to be *really serious* (thus equating the offence with the infliction of grievous, or serious, bodily harm). For example, a cut on the back of a person's hand requiring two stitches and not resulting in 'really serious harm' is likely to be considered as a s. 39 or perhaps a s. 47 assault. If the same injury were across the surface of the eye causing loss of sight in the eye and thereby resulting in 'really serious harm', a charge of s. 20 or s. 18 assault may be appropriate.

Inflict

In *R v Ireland* [1998] AC 147, it was stated that no 'assault' is needed for this offence and that harm could be 'inflicted' indirectly (in this case, by menacing telephone calls inflicting psychiatric harm). Therefore there is now little, if any, difference between inflicting harm and 'causing' harm. It should be enough to show that the defendant's behaviour brought about the resulting harm to the victim.

Grievous Bodily Harm

CPS Charging Standards are, once again, helpful but it should be noted that there is no definitive list of the kind of injuries that may be considered to be 'really serious'.

A case involving a visible disfigurement is *R v Marsh* [2011] EWCA Crim 3190, where the female offenders became involved in a fight with a 16-year-old girl. One held the girl's arms behind her back while the second cut the girl's face with a key, causing a 4 cm laceration which would leave a permanent scar; the offenders were convicted of a s. 20 offence.

In *R v Birmingham* [2002] EWCA Crim 2608, it was held that a large number of minor wounds were capable of amounting to grievous bodily harm on a charge of aggravated burglary.

Sexually Transmitted Infections (STIs)

The courts have recognised that person-to-person transmission of a sexual infection that will have serious consequences for the infected person's health can amount to grievous bodily harm under the Offences Against the Person Act 1861 (in *R v Dica* [2004] EWCA Crim 1103, there was an acceptance that the *deliberate* infection of another with the HIV virus could amount to grievous bodily harm). This issue was explored further in *R v Konzani* [2005] EWCA Crim 706. In that case, the defendant appealed against convictions for inflicting grievous bodily harm on three women contrary to s. 20. The defendant had unprotected consensual sexual intercourse with the women, but *without having disclosed* that he was HIV-positive. The women subsequently contracted the HIV virus. The Court of Appeal held that there was a critical distinction between taking a risk as to the various potentially adverse (and possibly problematic) consequences of unprotected consensual intercourse, and the giving of informed consent *to the risk of infection with a fatal disease*. Before consent to the risk of contracting HIV could provide a defence, that consent had to be an *informed* consent in this latter sense (*Dica*). Therefore, simply having an honestly held belief that the other person was consenting would only help if that consent would itself have provided a defence to the passing of the infection.

The case of *R v Golding* [2014] EWCA Crim 889 raised the issue of whether genital herpes could be described as 'really serious harm' so as to come within s. 20 of the Act. The defendant did not disclose his diagnosis of genital herpes to the victim which he passed on to her. The court found that Golding understood both that he had the infection and how it is transmitted, and by not preventing transmission—or disclosing his condition thereby allowing the complainant to make an informed decision whether or not she wanted to risk acquiring herpes—he was guilty of reckless grievous bodily harm under s. 20 of the Act.

CPS Charging Standards state that 'informed consent' does not necessarily mean that the suspect must disclose his/her condition to the complainant. A complainant may be regarded as being informed for the purposes of giving consent where a third party informs the complainant of the suspect's condition, and the complainant then engages in unprotected sexual activity with the suspect. Similarly, a complainant may be regarded as being informed if he/she becomes aware of certain circumstances that indicate that the suspect is suffering from a sexually transmitted infection, such as visiting the suspect while he/she is undergoing treatment for the infection in hospital, or the appearance of sores on the suspect's genitalia.

2.7.15 Wounding or Causing Grievous Bodily Harm with Intent

OFFENCE: **Wounding or Causing Grievous Bodily Harm with Intent—*Offences Against the Person Act 1861, s. 18***

> • Triable on indictment only • Life imprisonment

The Offences Against the Person Act 1861, s. 18 states:

> Whosoever shall unlawfully and maliciously by any means whatsoever wound or cause any grievous bodily harm to any person with intent to do some grievous bodily harm to any person, or with intent to resist or prevent the lawful apprehension or detainer of any person, shall be guilty of felony …

KEYNOTE

An offence under s. 18 may take one of four different forms, namely:

(a) wounding with intent to do grievous bodily harm;
(b) causing grievous bodily harm with intent to do so;
(c) maliciously wounding with intent to resist or prevent the lawful apprehension etc. of any person; or
(d) maliciously causing grievous bodily harm with intent to resist or prevent the lawful apprehension etc. of any person.

Although there are similarities with the offence under s. 20 (**see para. 2.7.14**), you must show the appropriate *intent* (e.g. to do grievous bodily harm to *anyone* or to resist/prevent the lawful apprehension/detention of *anyone*). Factors that may indicate such a specific intent include:

• a repeated or planned attack;
• deliberate selection of a weapon or adaptation of an article to cause injury, such as breaking a glass before an attack;
• making prior threats;
• using an offensive weapon against, or kicking a victim's head.

In form (a) or (b), where the intent was to cause grievous bodily harm, the issue of 'malice' will not arise. However, where the intent was to resist or prevent the *lawful* arrest of someone (in form (c) or (d)), the element of maliciousness (subjective recklessness) as set out above (**see para. 2.7.14**) will need to be proved. In addition, where it is alleged that D acted with the intent to avoid or resist the lawful apprehension of any person, it may be his/her own arrest or that of another he/she resisted, but the lawfulness of that arrest or detention must in either event be proved by the prosecution. It does not follow that D must be proved to have known the arrest etc. was lawful, but in a case such as *Kenlin* v *Gardiner* [1967] 2 QB 510, where D mistook the arresting officers for kidnappers, mistaken self-defence may be raised by the defence.

The word 'cause', together with the expression 'by any means whatsoever', seems to give this offence a wider meaning than s. 20. However, the increasingly broad interpretation of the s. 20 offence means that there is little difference in the *actus reus* needed for either offence.

The intentional infliction of a sexually transmitted infection can amount to an offence under s. 18 of the Act. CPS guidance states that for such a prosecution to proceed, there must be scientific and/or medical and factual evidence which proves the contention that the defendant intentionally and actually transmitted the infection to the complainant. The consent of the complainant to sexual activity in the knowledge that the defendant is infectious does not amount to a defence in cases of intentional infection (*R* v *Donovan* [1934] 2 KB 498; *Attorney-General's Reference (No. 6 of 1980)* [1981] QB 715, CA).

In relation to injuries brought about by driving motor vehicles, the Court of Appeal has held that there is nothing wrong in principle in charging a driver with causing grievous bodily harm as well as dangerous driving in appropriate circumstances (*R* v *Bain* [2005] EWCA Crim 7). It follows that bringing about other forms of significant or lasting injury with a motor vehicle could be dealt with under the offences in this part of the chapter. However, in *Bain* it was held that where a driver was charged with both offences (causing grievous bodily harm and dangerous driving), a court could not impose consecutive terms of imprisonment for both offences arising out of the same incident. The specific offence of causing serious injury by dangerous driving (under s. 143 of the Legal Aid, Sentencing and Punishment of Offenders Act 2012) may be a far more appropriate charge when the offence has been brought about by driving a mechanically propelled vehicle.

The provisions of ss. 28 and 29 of the Crime and Disorder Act 1998 in relation to racially or religiously aggravated assaults do not apply to this offence. However, the courts must still take notice of any element of racial or religious aggravation when determining sentence (Criminal Justice Act 2003, s. 145—increase in sentences for racial or religious aggravation).

2.7.16 Assault with Intent to Resist Arrest

OFFENCE: **Assault with Intent to Resist Arrest—** *Offences Against the Person Act 1861, s. 38*

- Triable either way • Two years' imprisonment

The Offences Against the Person Act 1861, s. 38 states:

> Whosoever . . . shall assault any person with intent to resist or prevent the lawful apprehension or detainer of himself or of any other person for any offence, shall be guilty of a misdemeanor . . .

KEYNOTE

It must be shown that the defendant intended to resist or prevent the lawful arrest or detention of a person (his/her own arrest/detention or that of another) and that the arrest was lawful (*R* v *Self* [1992] 1 WLR 657). Provided they were acting within their powers, this offence can apply to arrests made not only by police officers but also by any person who has a power of arrest, i.e. members of the public.

Once the lawfulness of the arrest is established, the state of mind necessary for the above offence is that required for a common assault coupled with an intention to resist/prevent that arrest/detention. It is irrelevant whether or not the person being arrested/detained had actually committed an offence. These principles were set out by the Court of Appeal in a case where the defendant mistakenly believed that the arresting officers had no lawful power to do so. The court held that such a mistaken belief does not provide a defendant with the defence of 'mistake'. Similarly, a belief in one's own innocence, however genuine or honestly held, cannot afford a defence to a charge under s. 38.

2.7.17 Assaults on Police

There is an offence which deals specifically with assaults on police officers and those assisting them.

OFFENCE: **Assault Police—*Police Act 1996, s. 89***
- Triable summarily • Six months' imprisonment and/or a fine

The Police Act 1996, s. 89 states:

(1) Any person who assaults a constable in the execution of his duty, or a person assisting a constable in the execution of his duty, shall be guilty of an offence ...

KEYNOTE

This offence requires that the officer was acting in the execution of his/her duty when assaulted. If this is not proved, then part of the *actus reus* will be missing. Even a minor, technical and inadvertent act of unlawfulness on the part of the officer will mean that he/she cannot have been acting in the lawful execution of his/her duty. While the precise limits of a constable's duty remain undefined, it is clear that a police officer may be acting in the course of his/her duty even when doing more than the minimum the law requires (*R* v *Waterfield* [1964] 1 QB 164). It is also clear that any action amounting to assault, battery, unlawful arrest or trespass to property takes the officer outside the course of his/her duty (*Davis* v *Lisle* [1936] 2 KB 434).

A court may infer from all the circumstances that an officer was in fact acting in the execution of his/her duty (*Plowden* v *DPP* [1991] Crim LR 850).

Where the assault is made in reaction to some form of physical act by the officer, it must be shown that the officer's act was not in itself unlawful.

Other than the powers of arrest and detention, police officers have no general power to take hold of people in order to question them or keep them at a particular place while background inquiries are made about them. Therefore, if an officer does hold someone by the arm for questioning without arrest, there may well be a 'battery' by that officer (*Collins* v *Wilcock* [1984] 1 WLR 1172). The courts have accepted, however, that there may be occasions where a police officer is justified in taking hold of a person to attract his/her attention or to calm him/her down (*Mepstead* v *DPP* [1996] COD 13).

Where a prisoner is arrested and brought before a custody officer, that officer is entitled to assume that the arrest has been lawful. Therefore, if the prisoner goes on to assault the custody officer, that assault will be an offence under s. 89(1) even if the original arrest turns out to have been unlawful (*DPP* v *L* [1999] Crim LR 752).

There is no need to show that the defendant knew, or suspected, that the person was in fact a police officer or that the police officer was acting in the lawful execution of his/her duty (*Blackburn* v *Bowering* [1994] 1 WLR 1324). However, if the defendant claims to have been acting in self-defence under the mistaken and honestly held belief that he/she was being attacked, there may not be sufficient *mens rea* for a charge of assault.

These offences are simply a form of common assault upon someone carrying out a lawful function.

2.7.17.1 Obstructing a Police Officer

OFFENCE: **Obstruct Police—*Police Act 1996, s. 89***
- Triable summarily • One months' imprisonment and/or a fine

The Police Act 1996, s. 89 states:

(2) Any person who resists or wilfully obstructs a constable in the execution of his duty, or a person assisting a constable in the execution of his duty, shall be guilty of an offence ...

No offence under s. 89(2) can be committed unless the officer was acting in the lawful execution of his/her duty.

Resistance suggests some form of physical opposition; obstruction does not and may take many forms, e.g. warning other drivers of a speed check operation (*R (DPP)* v *Glendinning* (2005) EWHC 2333 (Admin)—note that the persons warned about the speed check must be actually committing or about to commit the speeding offence), deliberately providing misleading information (*Ledger* v *DPP* [1991] Crim LR 439), deliberately drinking alcohol before providing a breath specimen (*Ingleton* v *Dibble* [1972] 1 QB 480) or 'tipping off' people who were about to commit an offence (*Green* v *Moore* [1982] QB 1044). Obstruction has been interpreted as making it more difficult for a constable to carry out his/her duty (*Hinchcliffe* v *Sheldon* [1955] 1 WLR 1207). Refusing to answer an officer's questions is not obstruction (*Rice* v *Connolly* [1966] 2 QB 414), neither is advising a person not to answer questions (*Green* v *DPP* (1991) 155 JP 816) unless perhaps the defendant was under some duty to provide information. Any obstruction must be *wilful*, that is the defendant must intend to do it. The obstruction will not be 'wilful' if the defendant was simply trying to help the police, even if that help turned out to be more of a hindrance (*Willmot* v *Atack* [1977] QB 498).

Obstruction can be caused by omission but only where the defendant was already under some duty towards the police or the officer. There is also a common law offence of refusing to go to the aid of a constable when asked to do so in order to prevent or diminish a breach of the peace (*R* v *Waugh* (1986) *The Times*, 1 October).

2.7.18 Threats to Kill

OFFENCE: **Making a Threat to Kill—*Offences Against the Person Act 1861, s. 16***
- Triable either way • 10 years' imprisonment on indictment
- Six months' imprisonment and/or a fine summarily

The Offences Against the Person Act 1861, s. 16 (amended by the Criminal Law Act 1977, s. 65, sch. 12) states:

A person who without lawful excuse makes to another a threat, intending that that other would fear it would be carried out, to kill that other or a third person shall be guilty of an offence …

The proviso that the threat must be made 'without lawful excuse' means that a person acting in self-defence or in the course of his/her duty in protecting life (e.g. an armed police officer) would not commit this offence (provided that his/her behaviour was 'lawful').

A threat can be communicated in any way. In *R* v *Martin* (1993) 14 Cr App R (S) 645, the offender sent two anonymous notes stained with blood to the victim and in *R* v *Patel* [2012] EWCA Crim 2172 the offender threatened his former partner that he would kill their young son and then sent a text message to her that he had done so.

You must show that the threat was made (or implied (*R* v *Solanke* [1970] 1 WLR 1)) with the intention that the person receiving it would fear that it would be carried out. It is the *intention* of the person who makes the threat which is important in this offence. It does not matter whether the person to whom the threat is made *does* fear that the threat will be carried out.

The threat may be to kill another person at some time in the future or it may be an immediate threat, but the threatened action must be directly linked with the defendant. Simply passing on a threat on behalf of a third person *without the necessary intent* would be insufficient for this offence.

A threat to a pregnant woman in respect of her unborn child is not sufficient if the threat is to kill it before its birth (the unborn child is not a 'person'). But if it is a threat to kill the child after its birth, this would appear to be an offence within this section (*R* v *Tait* [1990] 1 QB 290).

2.8 Hatred and Harassment Offences

2.8.1 Introduction

The law in relation to offences involving hatred and harassment has been subject to considerable development in recent times. The result is a wide-ranging set of offences and powers that enable appropriate action to be taken in relation to such activity and, in certain circumstances, to protect against such activity occurring in the first place.

2.8.2 Offences Involving Racial, Religious or Sexual Orientation Hatred

Offences involving racial, religious or sexual orientation hatred are dealt with by the Public Order Act 1986. This section provides a summary of these offences which are aimed at addressing incidents specifically motivated by racial hatred, religious hatred or hatred on the grounds of sexual orientation.

For the purposes of the offences contrary to ss. 18 to 23 of the 1986 Act, 'racial hatred' means hatred against a group of persons defined by reference to colour, race, nationality (including citizenship) or ethnic or national origins (s. 17).

For the purposes of offences contrary to ss. 29B to 29G of the 1986 Act, 'religious hatred' means hatred against a group of persons defined by reference to religious belief or lack of religious belief (s. 29A).

Section 29AB of the 1986 Act defines 'hatred on the grounds of sexual orientation'. The definition covers hatred against a group of persons defined by reference to their sexual orientation, be they heterosexual, homosexual or bi-sexual.

2.8.2.1 Use of Words, Behaviour or Display of Written Material

OFFENCE: **Use of Words or Behaviour or Display of Written Material—*Public Order Act 1986, s. 18***

- Triable either way • Seven years' imprisonment and/or a fine on indictment
- Six months' imprisonment and/or a fine summarily

The Public Order Act 1986, s. 18 states:

(1) A person who uses threatening, abusive or insulting words or behaviour, or displays any written material which is threatening, abusive or insulting, is guilty of an offence if—
  (a) he intends thereby to stir up racial hatred, or
  (b) having regard to all the circumstances racial hatred is likely to be stirred up thereby.
(2) An offence under this section may be committed in a public or a private place, except that no offence is committed where the words or behaviour are used, or the written material is displayed, by a person inside a dwelling and are not heard or seen except by other persons in that or another dwelling.

2.8.2.2 Defence

The Public Order Act 1986, s. 18 states:

> (4) In proceedings for an offence under this section it is a defence for the accused to prove that he was inside a dwelling and had no reason to believe that the words or behaviour used, or the written material displayed, would be heard or seen by a person outside that or any other dwelling.

2.8.2.3 Publishing or Distributing Written Material

OFFENCE: **Publishing or Distributing Written Material—*Public Order Act 1986, s. 19***

  • Triable either way • Seven years' imprisonment and/or a fine on indictment
  • Six months' imprisonment and/or a fine summarily

The Public Order Act 1986, s. 19 states:

> (1) A person who publishes or distributes written material which is threatening, abusive or insulting is guilty of an offence if—
> (a) he intends thereby to stir up racial hatred, or
> (b) having regard to all the circumstances racial hatred is likely to be stirred up thereby.
> (2) ...
> (3) References in this Part to the publication or distribution of written material are to its publication or distribution to the public or a section of the public.

2.8.2.4 Defence

The Public Order Act 1986, s. 19 states:

> (2) In proceedings for an offence under this section it is a defence for an accused who is not shown to have intended to stir up racial hatred to prove that he was not aware of the content of the material and did not suspect, and had no reason to suspect, that it was threatening, abusive or insulting.

2.8.2.5 Use of Words, Behaviour or Display of Written Material

OFFENCE: **Use of Words or Behaviour or Display of Written Material—*Public Order Act 1986, s. 29B***

  • Triable either way • Not exceeding seven years' imprisonment and/or a fine on indictment • Not exceeding six months' imprisonment and/or a fine summarily

The Public Order Act 1986, s. 29B states:

> (1) A person who uses threatening words or behaviour, or displays any written material which is threatening, is guilty of an offence if he intends thereby to stir up religious hatred or hatred on the grounds of sexual orientation.
> (2) An offence under this section is committed in a public or private place, except that no offence is committed where the words or behaviour are used, or the written material is displayed, by a

person inside a dwelling and are not heard or seen except by other persons in that or another dwelling.

KEYNOTE

The defences available to the offence under s. 18 apply to this particular section (no reason to believe the words or behaviour, etc., would be heard or seen outside the dwelling (s. 29B(4)), or where used solely for the purpose of being included in a programming service (s. 29B(5)).

Section 29J of the Act provides that the offences of stirring up religious hatred are not intended to limit or restrict discussion, criticism or expressions of antipathy, dislike, ridicule or insult or abuse of particular religions or belief systems or lack of religion or of the beliefs and practices of those who hold such beliefs or to apply to persons newly converted to a religious faith, evangelism or the seeking to convert people to a particular belief or to cease holding a belief.

In relation to the sexual orientation element of these offences the relevant act (namely, words, behaviour, written material or recordings or programme) must be threatening, and the offender must intend thereby to stir up hatred on the grounds of sexual orientation.

2.8.2.6 Publishing or Distributing Material

OFFENCE: **Publishing or Distributing Written Material—*Public Order Act 1986, s. 29C***

- Triable either way • Not exceeding seven years' imprisonment and/or a fine on indictment • Not exceeding six months' imprisonment and/or a fine summarily

The Public Order Act 1986, s. 29C states:

(1) A person who publishes or distributes written material which is threatening is guilty of an offence if he intends thereby to stir up religious hatred or hatred on the grounds of sexual orientation.

(2) References in this Part to the publication or distribution of written material are to its publication or distribution to the public or a section of the public.

KEYNOTE

The offences under ss. 29B and 29C differ from the offences of stirring up racial hatred in part 3 of the 1986 Act, in two respects. First, the offences apply only to 'threatening' words or behaviour, rather than 'threatening, abusive or insulting' words or behaviour. Secondly, the offences apply only to words or behaviour if the accused 'intends' to stir up religious hatred or hatred on grounds of sexual orientation, rather than if hatred is either intentional or 'likely' to be stirred up.

2.8.3 Harassment and Stalking

There is a significant amount of material to examine in relation to the offences associated with harassment and stalking under the Protection from Harassment Act 1997. To aid understanding, the offences have been broken down into their component parts and follow the below order:

- Harassment contrary to ss. 1 and 2 of the Act (**see para. 2.8.4**). This section includes the law in relation to injunctions and restraining orders
- Putting people in fear of violence contrary to s. 4 of the Act (**see para. 2.8.5**)
- Stalking contrary to s. 2A of the Act and stalking involving fear of violence etc. contrary to s. 4A of the Act (**see para. 2.8.6**).

2.8.4 The Harassment Offences

OFFENCE: **Harassment—*Protection from Harassment Act 1997, ss. 1 and 2***
- Triable summarily • Six months' imprisonment and/or a fine

OFFENCE: **Racially or Religiously Aggravated Harassment—*Crime and Disorder Act 1998, s. 32(1)(a)***
- Triable either way • Two years' imprisonment and/or a fine on indictment
- Six months' imprisonment and/or a fine summarily

The Protection from Harassment Act 1997, ss. 1 and 2 state:

> 1.—(1) A person must not pursue a course of conduct—
>   (a) which amounts to harassment of another, and
>   (b) which he knows or ought to know amounts to harassment of the other.
> (1A) A person must not pursue a course of conduct—
>   (a) which involves harassment of two or more persons, and
>   (b) which he knows or ought to know involves harassment of those persons, and
>   (c) by which he intends to persuade any person (whether or not one of those mentioned above)—
>   (i) not to do something that he is entitled or required to do, or
>   (ii) to do something that he is not under any obligation to do.
>   …
> 2.—(1) A person who pursues a course of conduct in breach of section 1(1) or (1A) is guilty of an offence.

2.8.4.1 'Person' and Companies

'Person' here does not include companies or corporate bodies and therefore they cannot be the victim of harassment or apply for injunctions under this part of the legislation. However, an individual employee or a clearly defined group of individuals could be such a victim (*DPP* v *Dziurzynski* [2002] EWHC 1380 (Admin)) and as such they can apply for injunctions (*Daiichi UK Ltd* v *(1) Stop Huntingdon Cruelty, and (2) Animal Liberation Front* [2003] EWHC 2337 (QB)). For injunctions relating to companies, **see para. 2.8.4.10.**

In *Majrowski* v *Guy's and St Thomas' NHS Trust* [2005] EWCA Civ 251, the Court of Appeal held that a company could be a 'person' capable of harassing 'another' within the meaning of the Act. This ruling could therefore have implications in relation to the self-employed, customers and suppliers of businesses and members of the public in general. Where it can be shown that the conduct was carried out in the course of employment the employer could be held to be vicariously liable for that conduct.

2.8.4.2 'Course of Conduct'

The 'course of conduct' by a person is defined under s. 7 of the Act which states:

> (3) A 'course of conduct' must involve—
>   (a) in the case of conduct in relation to a single person (see s. 1(1)), conduct on at least two occasions in relation to that person, or
>   (b) in the case of conduct in relation to two or more persons (see s. 1(1A)), conduct on at least one occasion in relation to each of those persons.
> (3A) A person's conduct on any occasion shall be taken, if aided, abetted, counselled or procured by another—
>   (a) to be conduct on that occasion of the other (as well as conduct of the person whose conduct it is); and
>   (b) to be conduct in relation to which the other's knowledge and purpose, and what he ought to have known, are the same as they were in relation to what was contemplated or reasonably foreseeable at the time of the aiding, abetting, counselling or procuring.

(4) 'Conduct' includes speech.

(5) References to a person, in the context of the harassment of a person, are references to a person who is an individual.

KEYNOTE

The definition of a 'course of conduct' in s. 7 is an inclusive but not exhaustive list.

It appears that doing something remotely which has the desired effect on the victim, such as deliberately making a dog bark at someone, could form part of a 'course of conduct' for the purposes of an offence under the 1997 Act (*R (On the Application of Taffurelli) v DPP* [2004] EWHC 2791 (Admin)). However, simply *failing* to stop a dog barking is a different matter and one that the Divisional Court in *Taffurelli* did not resolve.

2.8.4.3 'Harassment'

'Harassment' includes alarming the person or causing him/her distress (s. 7(2) of the 1997 Act). The inclusion of harm and distress is significant as it has been held that a person, in this case a police officer, can be alarmed for the safety of another (*Lodge* v *DPP* [1989] COD 179). Although the words used in s. 7 are 'alarm *and* distress', the Divisional Court has held that they should be taken disjunctively and not conjunctively, that is, the court need only be satisfied that the behaviour involved one or the other; alarm *or* distress (*DPP* v *Ramsdale* [2001] EWHC Admin 106).

2.8.4.4 The s. 1(1A) Offence

The s. 1(1A) offence was introduced specifically to protect employees working for certain companies from harassment by animal rights protestors. Because of the courts' strict interpretation of the elements of the s. 1 offence (as discussed above) it was unclear how far such employees could be protected by this provision when they had not previously been harassed *individually* even where fellow employees had been. Section 1(1A) makes it an offence for a person to pursue a course of conduct involving the harassment of two or more people on separate occasions which the defendant knows or ought to know involves harassment. The purpose of such harassment is to persuade *any person* (not necessarily one of the people being harassed) not to do something he/she is entitled to do (such as going to work) or to do something he/she is not under any obligation to do (such as releasing animals or passing on confidential information).

The sort of behaviour envisaged by the offence would be the making of threats and intimidation which forces an individual or individuals to stop doing lawful business with another company or with another person. The subsection is not intended to outlaw peaceful protesting or lobbying. For instance, a person simply distributing leaflets outside a shop would not commit this offence unless they threatened or intimidated the people to whom they were handing their leaflets and that person felt harassed, alarmed or distressed. There would also need to be at least two separate incidents amounting to 'a course of conduct'.

KEYNOTE

Examples of 'course of conduct' in relation to s. 1(1A) are provided in Home Office Circular 34/2005 and include:

- Where an animal rights extremist sends a threatening letter on one occasion to an individual who works for a company and the same extremist sends a threatening email on another occasion to another individual who works for the same company, and his intention is to persuade the individuals that they should not work for that company because of the work that company does, or the contract that it has with other companies, he would commit an offence.

- Where an animal rights extremist sends a threatening letter on one occasion to an individual who works for company A and the same extremist sends a threatening email on another occasion to another individual who works for company B, and his intention is to persuade the individuals that they should not work for these companies because both companies supply company C, or he intends by his actions to persuade companies A and B not to supply company C, he would commit an offence. In both these examples, if the letters or emails were sent by separate extremists, yet it could be proved that they were acting together, they both would be guilty of an offence. Additionally, under the new s. 3A both an individual employee or a company can apply for an injunction (see para. 2.8.4.10).

2.8.4.5 General Points

Not all courses of conduct will satisfy the offence of harassment. *Lau* v *DPP* [2000] 1 FLR 799 involved a battery (slapping across the face) against the complainant on one occasion, followed sometime later by a threat being made to the complainant's boyfriend in her presence. The court held that the evidence of a 'course of conduct' by the defendant was insufficient to convict. It stated that regard should be had to the number of incidents and the relative times when they took place; the fewer the incidents and the further apart in time that they took place, the less likely it was that a court would find that harassment had taken place.

There are some incidents that do not amount to harassment. Where a defendant approached the victim to strike up conversations and had sent her a gift, this was insufficient to constitute harassment. However, such incidents could provide a background to later behaviour that included covertly filming the victim and rummaging through her rubbish (*King* v *DPP* [2001] ACD 7).

On occasions the courts have accepted that two instances of behaviour by the defendant several months apart will suffice. Where a defendant wrote two threatening letters to a member of the Benefits Agency staff, he was convicted of harassment even though there had been four and a half months' interval between the two letters (*Baron* v *CPS* (2000) 13 June, unreported). The opposite course of conduct was found to amount to harassment where a defendant made several calls to the victim's mobile phone in the space of five minutes. In this case several abusive and threatening messages were left on the victim's voicemail facility and later replayed one after the other (*Kelly* v *DPP* [2002] EWHC 1428 (Admin)). The court held that it was enough that the victim was alarmed or distressed by the course of conduct as a whole rather than by each act making up the course of conduct. This is a different requirement from the more serious offence under s. 4 where the victim must be caused to fear violence on at least two occasions. In relation to that more serious offence, a magistrates' court has been allowed to regard a defendant's conduct on the second occasion as almost retrospectively affecting previous conduct on the first occasion.

There is no specific requirement that the activity making up the course of conduct be of the same nature. Therefore two distinctly different types of behaviour by the defendant (e.g. making a telephone call on one occasion and damaging the victim's property on another) may suffice. In a case involving the racially or religiously aggravated offence, the aggravating element will need to be proved in relation to both instances of the defendant's conduct.

Some behaviour will be sufficiently disturbing or alarming for two instances alone to suffice (e.g. the making of overt threats). Other behaviour, however, may not be sufficient to establish 'harassment' after only two occasions (e.g. the sending of flowers and gifts) and may require more than the bare statutory minimum of two occasions.

Although it may be helpful in terms of proving the occurrence of two or more acts amounting to 'a course of conduct', the practice in some police areas of issuing warnings and maintaining a register of the same (particularly in relation to their own officers) is not a specific requirement of the Act and may raise some issues of procedural fairness.

The repeated commission of other offences (say, public order offences or offences against property) involving the same victim may also amount to harassment. In such cases the advice of the CPS should be sought as to which charge(s) to prefer.

To recap the s. 1 offence, you must prove that:

- the 'person' pursued a 'course of conduct' and
- the 'course of conduct' amounted to 'harassment'.

The final element required to prove the offence is that the defendant knew, or ought to have known, that his/her conduct amounted to harassment.

To avoid the practical difficulties of proving the subjective intention of the defendant, the offence focuses on an *objective test*.

2.8.4.6 What a Reasonable Person Would Think Amounts to Harassment

In addition, s. 1 of the 1997 Act states:

(2) For the purposes of this section, the person whose course of conduct is in question ought to know that it amounts to or involves harassment of another if a reasonable person in possession of the same information would think the course of conduct amounted to or involved harassment of the other.

KEYNOTE

Section 1(2) requires the jury/court to consider whether the defendant ought to have known that his/her conduct amounted to or involved harassment by the *objective* test of what a 'reasonable person' would think. Section 1(3)(c) also imposes an objective test as to whether that conduct was reasonable in the judgment of the jury/court. As a result, the Court of Appeal has held that no characteristics of the defendant can be attached to the word 'reasonable' (*R* v *Colohan* [2001] EWCA Crim 1251).

Although the defendant's mental illness may be relevant to sentence, the protective and preventive nature of the Act together with the objective nature of the tests above means that such illness does not provide a defence.

2.8.4.7 Aiding and Abetting

If someone aids, abets, counsels or procures another to commit an offence under the 1997 Act, the conduct of the 'primary' defendant will be taken to be the conduct of the aider, abettor, counsellor or procurer of the offence. This does not prevent the primary defendant's conduct from being relevant; what it does is to make the aider, abettor, etc. of the offence liable for the conduct which he/she has facilitated. The Act also makes provision for determining the knowledge and intention of aiders, abettors, etc. and although this is referred to as 'collective harassment', it overlaps with the concept of incomplete offences (**see chapter 1.3**) and the advice of the CPS should be sought in formulating appropriate charges.

2.8.4.8 Defences

If the person concerned in the course of conduct can show that he/she did so:

- for the purpose of preventing or detecting crime, or
- under any enactment or rule of law to comply with a particular condition or requirement, or
- in circumstances whereby the course of conduct was reasonable,

the offence under s. 1(1) and (1A) will not apply (s. 1(3)).

The burden of proving any of these features or circumstances lies with the defendant (on the balance of probabilities). Examples might be police or DSS surveillance teams, or court officers serving summonses.

Whether a course of conduct is 'reasonable' will be a question of fact for a court to decide in the light of all the circumstances. The wording of s. 1(2) suggests that such a test is an *objective* one (i.e. as a reasonable bystander) and not one based upon the particular belief or perception of the defendant, otherwise the main effect of the 1997 Act would be considerably diluted.

KEYNOTE

In *KD* v *Chief Constable of Hampshire* [2005] EWHC 2550 (QB) a police officer obtained from a female interviewee, over the course of several visits to her home, detailed explicit information about her sexual conduct. The interviewee was the mother of a complainant who had been allegedly raped and assaulted. The court held that the information obtained was not for the purpose of preventing or detecting crime under s. 1(3)(a) but to satisfy the officer's lewd interest.

2.8.4.9 Injunctions and Restraining Orders

The courts have two significant sources of power available to them to deal with harassment under the 1997 Act. These are injunctions and restraining orders. Injunctions are issued in the ordinary way of any civil injunction whereas restraining orders follow a *conviction* for an offence under ss. 2 or 4 (**see para 2.8.5**) of the Act.

2.8.4.10 Injunctions

Under ss. 3 and 3A of the Protection from Harassment Act 1997, the High Court or a county court may issue an injunction in respect of civil proceedings brought in respect of an actual or apprehended breach of s. 1(1) and (1A). The effect of this is that a defendant may be made the subject of an injunction even though his/her behaviour has not amounted to an offence under the 1997 Act.

Section 3 also states:

(3) Where—
   (a) in such proceedings the High Court or a county court grants an injunction for the purpose of restraining the defendant from pursuing any conduct which amounts to harassment, and
   (b) the plaintiff considers that the defendant has done anything which he is prohibited from doing by the injunction, the plaintiff may apply for the issue of a warrant for the arrest of the defendant.

The person who is the victim of the offence under s. 1(1A) or any person at whom the persuasion is aimed, may apply for an injunction. Therefore, where people who work for a life science or fur company are being harassed in order to persuade them not to work for that company, or in order to persuade the company not to supply another company, either the employees themselves or the company in question could apply for an injunction.

Section 3A states:

(1) This section applies where there is an actual or apprehended breach of section 1(1A) by any person ('the relevant person').
(2) In such a case—
   (a) any person who is or may be a victim of the course of conduct in question, or
   (b) any person who is or may be a person falling within section 1(1A)(c),
   may apply to the High Court or the county court for an injunction restraining the relevant person from pursuing any conduct which amounts to harassment in relation to any person or persons mentioned or described in the injunction.
(3) Sections 3(3) to (9) apply in relation to an injunction granted under subsection (2) above as they apply in relation to an injunction granted as mentioned in section 3(3)(a).

Anyone arrested under a warrant issued under s. 3(3)(b) may be dealt with by the court at the time of his/her appearance. Alternatively, the court may adjourn the proceedings and release the defendant, dealing with him/her within 14 days of his/her arrest provided the defendant is given not less than two days' notice of the adjourned hearing (Rules of the Supreme Court (Amendment) 1998 (SI 1998/1898) and the County Court (Amendment) Rules 1998 (SI 1998/1899)).

In a case involving an injunction restraining the actions of an anti-vivisection group, the Divisional Court held that the 1997 Act was not a means of preventing individuals from exercising their right to protest over issues of public interest. Such an extension of the law had clearly not been Parliament's intention and the courts would resist any attempts to interpret the Act widely (*Huntingdon Life Sciences Ltd* v *Curtin* (1997) *The Times*, 11 December).

The application for an injunction is essentially a private matter being pursued by an individual. The point at which the matter becomes of concern to policing is where the injunction is breached without reasonable excuse. The civil standard of proof (balance of probabilities) will apply to injunction applications (*Hipgrave* v *Jones* [2004] EWHC 2901 (QB)).

In harassment cases the High Court can grant a provisional injunction under s. 37(1) of the Senior Courts Act 1981. This injunction can restrain conduct which is not in itself tortious or unlawful but is reasonably necessary to protect the legitimate interests of others. This includes the power to impose an exclusion zone when granting a non-molestation injunction (*Burris* v *Azadani* [1995] 1 WLR 1372). However in *Hall* v *Save Newchurch Guinea Pigs (Campaign)* [2005] EWHC 372 (QB), the court held that a 200 km² exclusion zone was not reasonably necessary for the protection of the protected person's rights.

2.8.4.11 Breach of Injunctions

OFFENCE: **Breach of Injunction—*Protection from Harassment Act 1997, s. 3(6)***

- Triable either way • Five years' imprisonment and/or a fine on indictment
- Six months' imprisonment and/or a fine summarily

The Protection from Harassment Act 1997, s. 3 states:

(6) Where—
   (a) the High Court or a county court grants an injunction for the purpose mentioned in sub-section (3)(a), and
   (b) without reasonable ...
   he is guilty of an offence.

Civil injunctions generally will only involve the police where a power of an arrest has been attached (e.g. under s. 3(3) above). In these cases the role of the police will be to bring the defendant before the court in order that he/she can explain his/her behaviour. There is therefore no investigative or prosecuting function on the part of the officers. Section 3(6), however, creates a specific offence of breaching the terms of an injunction.

If a defendant breaches an injunction and commits the offence under s. 3(6), he/she will be dealt with in the way of any other prisoner brought into police detention and will face a prison sentence of five years.

2.8.4.12 Civil Claims for Harassment

Under s. 3(1) conduct or apprehended conduct falling within s. 1(1) and (1A) may be the subject of a civil claim by the victim/intended victim. This creates a 'statutory tort' of harassment in addition to the criminal offence.

2.8.4.13 Restraining Orders

The Protection from Harassment Act 1997, s. 5 states:

> (2) The order may, for the purpose of protecting the victim or victims of the offence, or any other person mentioned in the order, from conduct which—
> (a) amounts to harassment, or
> (b) will cause a fear of violence,
> prohibit the defendant from doing anything described in the order.

Section 5A of the Act enables the courts in England and Wales to impose a restraining order, when sentencing for any offence, for the purpose of protecting a person from conduct which amounts to harassment or will cause a fear of violence (**see para. 2.8.5**) by the defendant. The court will be able to make a restraining order on acquittal for any offence where it considers it necessary to protect a person from harassment. Any person mentioned in the restraining order has the right to make a representation if an application is made to vary or discharge the restraining order (equivalent powers are available in respect of Northern Ireland).

KEYNOTE

Unlike the injunction under s. 3(3), restraining orders can be made in a criminal court.

The order may be made for the protection of the victim or anyone else mentioned and it may run for a specified period or until a further order. Any order must identify by name the parties it is intended to protect (*R* v *Mann* (2000) 97(14) LSG 41).

In a case arising out of protests against fur retailers, the Divisional Court held that restraining orders under the 1997 Act did not generally breach the right to freedom of speech and association as protected by Articles 10 and 11 of the European Convention on Human Rights (*Silverton* v *Gravett* (2001) LTL 31 October).

The prosecutor, the defendant or anyone else mentioned in the order may apply to the court that made it to have the order varied or discharged (s. 5(4)). The courts have the power to vary an order made for a specified period of time so as to extend the expiry date of the order (*DPP* v *Hall* [2005] EWHC 2612 (Admin)). In *R* v *Debnath* [2005] EWCA Crim 3472 an order prohibiting an offender from publishing information indefinitely was held to be lawful and not in breach of Article 10 (Freedom of Expression) of the European Convention on Human Rights.

An example of how restraining orders can operate can be seen in *R* v *Evans (Dorothy)* [2004] EWCA 3102. In that case the appellant had been convicted of harassing her neighbours and a restraining order under s. 5(5) had been made by the court. Among other things, the order prohibited the appellant from 'using abusive words or actions' towards her neighbours. Some time into the life of the order, the neighbour called a plumber out to their house and he parked his van in the street. It was alleged that the appellant then moved her own car, which was also parked in the street, into such a position that it effectively blocked the plumber's van. The appellant was convicted of the offence of breaching the order and appealed, partly on the basis that her conduct could not properly be said to have amounted to 'abusive action'. The Court of Appeal held that such matters should be approached in the same way as specific legislation which outlaws abusive conduct, and that a jury was entitled to conclude that, as she had been motivated by spite, the appellant's actions could be 'abusive' for this purpose.

2.8.4.14 Breach of Restraining Order

OFFENCE: **Breach of Restraining Order—*Protection from Harassment Act 1997, s. 5(5)***

- Triable either way • Five years' imprisonment and/or a fine on indictment
- Six months' imprisonment and/or a fine summarily

The Protection from Harassment Act 1997, s. 5 states:

(5) If without reasonable excuse the defendant does anything which he is prohibited from doing by an order under this section, he is guilty of an offence.

KEYNOTE

The above offence is one of strict liability and therefore whether the defendant believed that the order was no longer in force is only relevant to the extent that he/she may have a reasonable excuse (*Barber* v *CPS* [2004] EWHC 2605 (Admin)). The prosecution needs simply to prove the existence and terms of the order (which it can do by an admission from the defendant in interview) and the doing of anything prohibited by it. Once that is done the offence is complete.

In the case of *R* v *Evans (Dorothy)* [2004] EWCA Crim 3102, the Court of Appeal held that harassment takes many forms and therefore the courts need to be able to prohibit conduct in fairly wide terms (e.g. in the wording of the order). It is, however, unclear just how far the defendant's subjective understanding of the terms of the order will be relevant. If a defendant honestly believed that his/her conduct did not breach the terms of the order, this would certainly be relevant when considering whether or not he/she had a 'reasonable excuse'.

Substituting or failing to include a charge under ss. 2 or 4 removes the court's powers to make a re-straining order which may be the main remedy sought by a victim. In any cases of doubt the guidance of the CPS should be sought.

2.8.5 Putting People in Fear of Violence

OFFENCE: **Putting People in Fear of Violence—*Protection from Harassment Act 1997, s. 4***
- Triable either way • 10 years' imprisonment and/or a fine on indictment
- Six months' imprisonment and/or a fine summarily

OFFENCE: **Racially or Religiously Aggravated—*Crime and Disorder Act 1998, s. 32(1)(b)***
- Triable either way
- 14 years' imprisonment and/or a fine on indictment
- Six months' imprisonment and/or a fine summarily

The Protection from Harassment Act 1997, s. 4 states:

(1) A person whose course of conduct causes another to fear, on at least two occasions, that violence will be used against him is guilty of an offence if he knows or ought to know that his course of conduct will cause the other so to fear on each of those occasions.

KEYNOTE

'Course of conduct' is discussed above.

The defendant's course of conduct must cause the victim to fear that violence *will* (rather than might) be used against *him or her* (rather than someone else) so:

- showing that the conduct caused the victim to be seriously frightened of what *might happen* in the future is not enough (*R* v *Henley* [2000] Crim LR 582);
- causing a person to fear, on at least two occasions, that violence would be used against a member of their family is not enough (*Mohammed Ali Caurti* v *DPP* [2001] EWHC Admin 867).

The defendant must know, or ought to know that their conduct will cause the other person to fear violence. This may be shown by any previous conversations or communications between the defendant and the victim, together with the victim's response to the defendant's earlier behaviour (e.g. running away, calling the police, etc.).

The fear of violence being used against the victim must be present on both occasions. If it is present on one occasion but not the other, the offence under s. 2 above may be appropriate. This is not necessarily as straightforward as it may seem. What if the defendant's conduct on the first occasion (e.g. a threat to burn the victim's house down) did not cause the victim undue concern, but a second threat some time later to do the same thing *did* put the victim in fear of violence, partly because this was the second time the threat had been made? These were the circumstances in *R (On the Application of A)* v *DPP* [2004] EWHC 2454 (Admin), where the defendant argued that the victim had only been put in fear of violence by his threats to burn her house down on the second occasion and that therefore the offence had not been made out. The Divisional Court disagreed and held that the magistrates were entitled to find as a matter of fact that the two incidents had put the victim in fear of violence, notwithstanding her admission that, on the first occasion, she had not been too concerned.

Unlike some of the other racially or religiously aggravated offences, provisions are specifically made for alternative verdicts in relation to harassment (s. 32(6) of the Crime and Disorder Act 1998). Where the racially or religiously aggravated form of the offence is charged, the aggravating element of the defendant's conduct must be shown in relation to both instances.

As with the s. 2 offence, a single instance of behaviour may be enough to support a charge for another offence.

This offence is not one of *intent* but one which is subject to a test of reasonableness against the standard of an ordinary person in possession of the same information as the defendant.

For the powers of a court to issue a restraining order in relation to this offence, **see para. 2.8.4.13**.

The Protection from Harassment Act 1997, s. 4 goes on to state:

(2) For the purposes of this section, the person whose course of conduct is in question ought to know that it will cause another to fear that violence will be used against him on any occasion if a reasonable person in possession of the same information would think the course of conduct would cause the other so to fear on that occasion.

2.8.5.1 Defence

The Protection from Harassment Act 1997, s. 4 states:

(3) It is a defence for a person charged with an offence under this section to show that—
 (a) his course of conduct was pursued for the purpose of preventing or detecting crime,
 (b) his course of conduct was pursued under any enactment or rule of law or to comply with any condition or requirement imposed by any person under any enactment, or
 (c) the pursuit of his course of conduct was reasonable for the protection of himself or another or for the protection of his or another's property.

KEYNOTE

There is a slight difference in the wording of the defence when compared with that under s. 1(3) above. There, the defendant may show that his/her conduct was reasonable in the particular circumstances. In relation to the offence under s. 4, the defendant must show that his/her conduct was reasonable *for the protection of him/herself, another person or his/her own/another's property*. These are the only grounds on which the defendant may argue reasonableness in answer to a charge under s. 4. He/she could not therefore argue, say, that the pursuit of the course of conduct was 'reasonable' in order to enforce a debt or to communicate with the victim.

In addition, s. 12 allows for the Secretary of State to certify that the conduct was carried out by a 'specified person' on a 'specified occasion' related to:

- national security,
- the economic well-being of the United Kingdom, or
- the prevention or detection of serious crime,

on behalf of the Crown. If such a certification is made, the conduct of the specified person will not be an offence under the 1997 Act.

2.8.6 The Stalking Offences

The Protection of Freedoms Act 2012 created the specific offence of 'stalking' and inserted the below offences into the Protection from Harassment Act 1997.

2.8.6.1 The Offence of Stalking

OFFENCE: **Stalking—*Protection from Harassment Act 1997, s. 2A***
- Triable summarily • Six months' imprisonment and/or a fine

OFFENCE: **Racially or Religiously Aggravated Stalking—*Crime and Disorder Act 1998, s. 32(1)(a)***
- Triable either way • Two years' imprisonment and/or a fine on indictment
- Six months' imprisonment and/or a fine summarily

The Protection from Harassment Act 1997, s. 2A states:

(1) A person is guilty of an offence if—
    (a) the person pursues a course of conduct in breach of s. 1(1), and
    (b) the course of conduct amounts to stalking.

For the purposes of the offence under s. 2A (and also the following offence under s. 4A below), a course of conduct amounts to stalking of another person if:

- it amounts to harassment of that person (under s. 7(2) of the Protection from Harassment Act 1997, references to harassing a person include alarming the person or causing the person distress);
- the acts or omissions involved are ones associated with stalking; and
- the person whose course of conduct it is knows or ought to know that the course of conduct amounts to harassment of the other person.

KEYNOTE

What is 'Stalking'?

Section 2A(3) lists examples of behaviours associated with stalking. The list is not exhaustive but gives an indication of the types of behaviour that may be displayed in a stalking offence. The listed behaviours are:

- following a person;
- contacting, or attempting to contact, a person by any means;
- publishing any statement or other material (i) relating or purporting to relate to a person, or (ii) purporting to originate from a person;
- monitoring the use by a person of the internet, email or any other form of electronic communication;
- loitering in any place (whether public or private);
- interfering with any property in the possession of a person;
- watching or spying on a person.

Section 2A does not include a specific defence for stalking. However, because an offence of stalking can only be established where an offence of harassment has occurred, a person charged with an offence under s. 2A could rely on the defence to harassment under s. 1(3) (see para. 2.8.4.8).

Under s. 2B of the Act the police have a power of entry in relation to the s. 2A stalking offence. A constable can apply to a justice of the peace, who may issue a warrant authorising entry and search of premises providing there are reasonable grounds to believe the conditions in s. 2B are met. A constable may seize and retain anything for which a search was authorised, and may use reasonable force, if necessary, in the exercise of any power conferred by s. 2B.

2.8.6.2 Stalking Involving Fear of Violence or Serious Alarm or Distress

OFFENCE: **Stalking Involving Fear of Violence or Serious Alarm or Distress—** *Protection from Harassment Act 1997, s. 4A*

- Triable either way • 10 years' imprisonment and/or an unlimited fine on indictment • Six months' imprisonment and/or a fine summarily

OFFENCE: **Racially or Religiously Aggravated Stalking Involving Fear of Violence or Serious Alarm or Distress—*Crime and Disorder Act 1998, s. 32(1)(b)***

- Triable either way • 14 years' imprisonment and/or a fine on indictment
- Six months' imprisonment and/or a fine summarily

The Protection from Harassment Act 1997, s. 4A states:

(1) A person ('A') whose course of conduct—
   (a) amounts to stalking, and
   (b) either—
      (i) causes another ('B') to fear, on at least two occasions, that violence will be used against B, or
      (ii) causes B serious alarm or distress which has a substantial adverse effect on B's usual day-to-day activities,

   is guilty of an offence if A knows or ought to know that A's conduct will cause B so to fear on each of those occasions or (as the case may be) will cause such alarm or distress.

KEYNOTE

For the purposes of s. 4A(1)(b)(i) a person (A) ought to know that A's course of conduct will cause another (B) to fear that violence will be used against B on any occasion if a reasonable person in possession of the same information would think the course of conduct would cause B so to fear on that occasion.

The second arm of the offence prohibits a course of conduct which causes 'serious alarm or distress' which has a 'substantial adverse effect on the day-to-day activities of the victim'. It is designed to recognise the serious impact that stalking may have on victims, even where an explicit fear of violence is not created by each incident of stalking behaviour.

The phrase 'substantial adverse effect on the usual day-to-day activities' is not defined in s. 4A, and thus its construction will be a matter for the courts via judicial interpretation. However, the Home Office considers that evidence of a substantial adverse effect caused by the stalker may include:

- victims changing their routes to work, work patterns or employment;
- victims arranging for friends or family to pick up children from school (to avoid contact with the stalker);
- victims putting in place additional security measures in their home;
- victims moving home;
- physical or mental ill-health;
- victims' deterioration in performance at work due to stress;
- victims stopping or changing the way they socialise.

Although some victims try to continue their existing routines in defiance of a stalker, they may still be able to evidence substantial impact on their usual day-to-day activities, depending on the individual case.

For the purposes of s. 4A(1)(b)(ii), A ought to know that A's course of conduct will cause B serious alarm or distress which has a substantial adverse effect on B's usual day-to-day activities if a reasonable person in possession of the same information would think the course of conduct would cause B such alarm or distress.

Under s. 4A(4), there is a defence to the offence of stalking involving fear of violence or serious alarm or distress which is a mirror image of the defence to the offence under s.4 (see para. 2.8.5.1).

2.8.7   Police Direction to Prevent Intimidation or Harassment

In response to a number of campaigns against individuals believed to be involved in animal experiments, the Criminal Justice and Police Act 2001 gives the police specific powers to prevent the intimidation or harassment of people in their own or others' homes. Situations envisaged by the legislation typically arise where protestors gather outside a house where a particular individual is believed to be. Under such circumstances s. 42 provides the most senior ranking police officer at the scene with discretionary powers to give directions to people in the vicinity. The power arises where:

- the person is outside (or in the vicinity of) any premises that are used by any individual as his/her dwelling, and
- the constable *believes*, on reasonable grounds, that the person is there for the purpose of representing or persuading the resident (or anyone else)
- that he/she should not do something he/she is entitled or required to do, or
- that he/she should do something that he/she is under no obligation to do, and
- the constable also believes, on reasonable grounds, that the person's presence amounts to, or is likely to result in, the harassment of the resident or is likely to cause alarm or distress to the resident.

Although the premises involved may be in use by any 'individual' (e.g. *not* a company) and the purpose may be to persuade that or any other 'individual', the officer must believe that the ultimate effect will be harassment, alarm or distress of the *resident*. The requirement for reasonable grounds means that their existence or otherwise will be judged objectively and not simply from the personal standpoint of the officer using the power. Nevertheless, the officer is given a great deal of individual discretion in using this power.

A direction given under s. 42 requires the person(s) to do all such things as the officer specifies as being *necessary* to prevent the harassment, alarm or distress of the resident, including:

- a requirement to leave the vicinity of the premises in question, and
- a requirement to leave that vicinity and not to return to it within such period as the constable may specify, not being longer than three months,

and (in either case) the requirement to leave the vicinity may be to do so immediately or after a specified period of time (s. 42(4)).

The direction may be given orally and, where appropriate, may be given to a group of people together (s. 42(3)). There is no requirement that the officer giving the direction be in uniform.

The power under s. 42 cannot be used to direct someone to refrain from conduct made lawful under s. 220 of the Trade Union and Labour Relations (Consolidation) Act 1992 (Peaceful picketing).

2.8.7.1   Contravening a s. 42 Direction

OFFENCE: **Knowingly Contravening a s. 42 Direction—*Criminal Justice and Police Act 2001, s. 42(7)***

- Triable summarily • Three months' imprisonment and/or a fine

The Criminal Justice and Police Act 2001, s. 42 states:

> (7) Any person who knowingly fails to comply with a requirement in a direction given to him under this section (other than a requirement under subsection (4)(b)) shall be guilty of an offence.

OFFENCE: **Unlawfully Returning to Vicinity—*Criminal Justice and Police Act 2001, s. 42(7A)***

- Triable summarily • Imprisonment for a term not exceeding six months and/or a fine

The Criminal Justice and Police Act 2001, s. 42 states:

(7A) Any person to whom a constable has given a direction including a requirement under subsection (4)(b) commits an offence if he—
    (a) returns to the vicinity of the premises in question within the period specified in the direction beginning with the date on which the direction is given; and
    (b) does so for the purpose described in subsection (1)(b).

2.8.7.2 Harassment etc. of Person in their Home

OFFENCE: **Harassment of a Person in their Home—*Criminal Justice and Police Act 2001, s. 42A***

- Triable summarily • Imprisonment for a term not exceeding six months and/or a fine

The Criminal Justice and Police Act 2001, s. 42A states:

(1) A person commits an offence if—
    (a) that person is present outside or in the vicinity of any premises that are used by any individual ('the resident') as his dwelling;
    (b) that person is present there for the purpose (by his presence or otherwise) of representing to the resident or another individual (whether or not one who uses the premises as his dwelling), or of persuading the resident or such another individual—
        (i) that he should not do something that he is entitled or required to do; or
        (ii) that he should do something that he is not under any obligation to do;
    (c) that person—
        (i) intends his presence to amount to the harassment of, or to cause alarm or distress to, the resident; or
        (ii) knows or ought to know that his presence is likely to result in the harassment of, or to cause alarm or distress to, the resident; and
    (d) the presence of that person—
        (i) amounts to the harassment of, or causes alarm or distress to, any person falling within subsection (2); or
        (ii) is likely to result in the harassment of, or to cause alarm or distress to, any such person.

(2) A person falls within this subsection if he is—

    (a) the resident,

    (b) a person in the resident's dwelling, or

    (c) a person in another dwelling in the vicinity of the resident's dwelling.

KEYNOTE

This offence has a number of elements, each of which must be proved if a successful prosecution is to be brought. The ingredients include:

- Place—the defendant must be shown to have been in the relevant place (outside or in the vicinity of a 'dwelling'). 'Dwelling' means any structure or part of a structure occupied as a person's home or as other living accommodation (whether the occupation is separate or shared with others) but does not include any part not so occupied (s. 42A(7)).
- Purpose—the defendant's purpose in being there must be to represent to, or persuade the resident/another individual that he/she should not do something he/she is entitled/required to do or that he/she should do something that he/she is not under any obligation to do.
- Intention/knowledge—you must prove that the defendant intended his/her presence to amount to harassment of, or to cause alarm or distress to, the resident or that he/she knew/ought to have known that his/her presence was likely to have that result.
- Consequences—you must show that the defendant's presence amounted to/was likely to result in the harassment of, or causing alarm or distress to, any resident, person in the resident's dwelling, or person in another dwelling in the vicinity of the resident's dwelling.

References in s. 42A(1)(c) and (d) to a person's presence are references either to his/her presence alone or together with that of any other people who are also present (s. 42A(3)).

For the purposes of this section a person ought to know that his/her presence is likely to result in the harassment of, or to cause alarm or distress to, a resident if a reasonable person in possession of the same information would think that it was likely to have that effect (s. 42A(4)).

2.9 Child Protection

2.9.1 Introduction

The application of the law and the use of measures to protect children, particularly those relating to 'police protection', are among some of the most contentious issues that any police officer may be involved in.

2.9.2 Child Abduction

There are two offences of abducting children; the first applies to people 'connected with the child', the second to others 'not connected with the child'.

2.9.2.1 Person Connected with Child

OFFENCE: **Child Abduction—Person Connected with Child—*Child Abduction Act 1984, s. 1***
- Triable either way • Seven years' imprisonment on indictment
- Six months' imprisonment and/or a fine summarily

The Child Abduction Act 1984, s. 1 states:

(1) Subject to subsections (5) and (8) below, a person connected with a child under the age of 16 commits an offence if he takes or sends the child out of the United Kingdom without the appropriate consent.

'Connected with a Child'

The Child Abduction Act 1984, s. 1 states:

(2) A person is connected with the child for the purposes of this section if—
    (a) he is a parent of the child; or
    (b) in the case of a child whose parents were not married to, or civil partners of, each other at the time of his birth, there are reasonable grounds for believing that he is the father of the child; or
    (c) he is a guardian of the child; or
    (ca) he is a special guardian of the child; or
    (d) he is a person named in a child arrangements order as a person with whom the child is to live; or
    (e) he has custody of the child.

KEYNOTE

Special Guardian

A 'special guardian' is created by a Special Guardian Order (SGO). A SGO fundamentally secures the child's long-term placement and is an order made by the court appointing one or more individuals to be the child's 'special guardian'. It is a private law order made under the Children Act 1989 and is intended for those children who cannot live with their birth parents and who would benefit from a legally secure placement. The order can enable a child to remain in his/her family as, unlike adoption, it does not end the legal relationship between a child and his/her parents.

A SGO usually lasts until the child is 18.

A parent of a child may not be appointed as a child's special guardian.

'Appropriate Consent'

The Child Abduction Act 1984, s. 1 states:

(3) In this section 'the appropriate consent' in relation to a child, means—
  (a) the consent of each of the following—
    (i) the child's mother;
    (ii) the child's father, if he has parental responsibility for him;
    (iii) any guardian of the child;
    (iiia) any special guardian of the child;
    (iv) any person named in a child arrangements order as a person with whom the child is to live;
    (v) any person who has custody of the child; or
  (b) the leave of the court granted under or by virtue of any provision of Part II of the Children Act 1989; or
  (c) if any person has custody of the child, the leave of the court which awarded custody to him.

2.9.2.2   **'Defence' for Person Connected with a Child**

The Child Abduction Act 1984, s. 1 states:

(4) A person does not commit an offence under this section by taking or sending a child out of the United Kingdom without obtaining the appropriate consent if—
  (a) he is a person named in a child arrangements order as a person with whom the child is to live, and he takes or sends the child out of the United Kingdom for a period of less than one month; or
  (b) he is a special guardian of the child and he takes or sends the child out of the United Kingdom for a period of less than three months.
(4A) Subsection (4) above does not apply if the person taking or sending the child out of the United Kingdom does so in breach of an order under Part II of the Children Act 1989.
(5) A person does not commit an offence under this section by doing anything without the consent of another person whose consent is required under the foregoing provisions if—
  (a) he does it in the belief that the other person—
    (i) has consented; or
    (ii) would consent if he was aware of all the relevant circumstances; or

(b) he has taken all reasonable steps to communicate with the other person but has been unable to communicate with him; or

(c) the other person has unreasonably refused to consent.

KEYNOTE

A further provision (s. 1(5A)) states that the 'defence' at s. 1(5)(c) will not apply if the person who refused to consent is a person:

- named in a child arrangements order as a person with whom the child is to live; or
- who has custody of the child; or
- who is a special guardian of the child; or
- is, by taking or sending the child out of the United Kingdom, acting in breach of a court order in the United Kingdom.

2.9.2.3 Person Not Connected with Child

OFFENCE: **Child Abduction—*Person Not Connected with Child—Child Abduction Act 1984, s. 2***

- Triable either way • Seven years' imprisonment on indictment
- Six months' imprisonment and/or a fine summarily

The Child Abduction Act 1984, s. 2 states:

(1) Subject to subsection (3) below, a person other than one mentioned in subsection (2) below, commits an offence if, without lawful authority or reasonable excuse, he takes or detains a child under the age of 16—

(a) so as to remove him from the lawful control of any person having lawful control of the child: or

(b) so as to keep him out of the lawful control of any person entitled to lawful control of the child.

(2) The persons are—

(a) where the father and mother of the child in question were married to, or civil partners of, each other at the time of his birth, the child's father and mother;

(b) where the father and mother of the child in question were not married to each other at the time of his birth, the child's mother; and

(c) any other person mentioned in section 1(2)(c) to (e) above.

KEYNOTE

This offence will include keeping a child in the place where he/she is found and inducing the child to remain with the defendant or another person.

The consent of the victim is irrelevant.

The word 'remove' for the purpose of s. 2(1)(a) effectively means a substitution of authority by a defendant for that of the person lawfully having it and physical removal from a particular place is not required (*Foster v DPP* [2004] EWHC 2955 (Admin)).

Section 2(1)(a) requires the child *there and then* to be in the lawful control of someone entitled to it when he/she is taken or detained, whereas s. 2(1)(b) requires only that the child be kept out of the lawful control of someone entitled to it when taken or detained. Whether or not a person is under the lawful control of another is a question of fact (*R v Leather* [1993] Crim LR 516). A child can be removed from lawful control without necessarily being taken to another place. It may suffice if the child is deflected into some unauthorised activity induced by the defendant.

2.9.2.4 Defence for Person Not Connected with a Child

The Child Abduction Act 1984, s. 2 states:

(3) … it shall be a defence for [the defendant] to prove—

    (a) where the father and mother of the child in question were not married to, or civil partners of, each other at the time of his birth—

        (i) that he is the child's father; or

        (ii) that, at the time of the alleged offence, he believed, on reasonable grounds, that he was the child's father; or

    (b) that, at the time of the alleged offence, he believed that the child had attained the age of 16.

KEYNOTE

The defence under s. 2(3)(a) of the Child Abduction Act 1984 will not apply where D mistakenly takes the wrong child from a nursery, thinking it to be his daughter, although it is just possible that D may, in such circumstances, be able to advance a defence of reasonable excuse under s. 2(1) (*R v Berry* [1996] 2 Cr App R 226).

2.9.3 Child Cruelty

OFFENCE: **Child Cruelty—*Children and Young Persons Act 1933, s. 1***
- Triable either way • 10 years' imprisonment on indictment
- Six months' imprisonment and/or a fine summarily

The Children and Young Persons Act 1933, s. 1 states:

(1) If any person who has attained the age of 16 years and has responsibility for any child or young person under that age, wilfully assaults, ill-treats (whether physically or otherwise), neglects, abandons, or exposes him, or causes or procures him to be assaulted, ill-treated (whether physically or otherwise), neglected, abandoned, or exposed, in a manner likely to cause him unnecessary suffering or injury to health (whether the suffering or injury is of a physical or a psychological nature), that person shall be guilty of an offence …

KEYNOTE

This offence may be considered to fall into two broad categories:

- instances of violent assault;
- cases of cruelty and neglect.

Instances of violent assault may be more appropriately dealt with by charging with assault offences.

To be convicted of the offence, D must be over 16 at the time of the offence and have 'responsibility' for the child. Responsibility for a child or young person can be shared and whether a person had such responsibility in each case will be a matter of both fact and law (*Liverpool Society for the Prevention of Cruelty to Children* v *Jones* [1914] 3 KB 813). Anyone having parental responsibility or any other legal liability to maintain a child or young person will be presumed to have responsibility for that child and that responsibility does not cease simply because the person ceases to have care of the child. Others such as babysitters may also have 'responsibility' for the child while in their care (see generally s. 17).

The Act makes provisions and presumptions in relation to issues of causation. So, for example, if a parent or other person legally liable to maintain the child or young person, or a guardian, has failed to provide adequate food, clothing, medical aid or lodging for the child or young person, he/she will be deemed to have neglected the child or young person for the above purposes (s. 1(2)).

Similarly, a person will be presumed to have neglected the child where it is proved that the child was an infant under three years old who died as a result of suffocation (other than by disease or blockage of the airways by an object) while in bed with someone of 16 years or over who was under the influence of drink or a prohibited drug when he/she went to bed or at any later time before the suffocation (s. 1(2)(b)).

The reference in s. 1(2)(b) to the infant being 'in bed' with another ('the adult') includes a reference to the infant lying next to the adult in or on any kind of furniture or surface being used by the adult for the purpose of sleeping (and the reference to the time when the adult 'went to bed' is to be read accordingly) (s. 1(2A)). A drug is a prohibited drug for the purpose of s. 1(2)(b) in relation to a person if the person's possession of the drug immediately before taking it constituted an offence under s. 5(2) of the Misuse of Drugs Act 1971.

A defendant may be charged with the above offence even where the child has died (s. 1(3)(b)).

Section 1 creates only one single offence, albeit one that can be committed in many different ways, by both positive acts (assault, ill-treatment, abandonment or exposure) and omission (neglect) (*R* v *Hayles* [1969] 1 QB 364). Although any aspect of neglect must be shown to have occurred in a manner likely to cause unnecessary suffering or injury to health, there is no need to show that any such suffering or injury actually came about.

2.9.4 Police Powers under the Children Act 1989

The police have specific statutory powers to deal with the threat of significant harm posed to children and these are set out below.

Section 46 of the Children Act 1989 states:

(1) Where a constable has reasonable cause to believe that a child would otherwise be likely to suffer significant harm, he may—
   (a) remove the child to suitable accommodation and keep him there; or
   (b) take such steps as are reasonable to ensure the child's removal from any hospital, or other place, in which he is then being accommodated is prevented.
(2) For the purposes of this Act, a child with respect to whom a constable has exercised his powers under this section is referred to as having been taken into police protection.

KEYNOTE

For most purposes of the 1989 Act, someone who is under 18 years old is a 'child' (s. 105).

The wording of s. 46(1) means that an officer may use the powers at s. 46(1)(a) and (b) if he/she has reasonable cause to believe that, if the powers are not used, a child is likely to suffer significant harm. The issues arising from similar wording in relation to powers of arrest have been considered by the courts on a number of occasions. Generally, tests of reasonableness impose an element of objectivity and the courts will consider whether, in the circumstances, a reasonable and sober person might have formed a similar view to that of the officer.

'Harm' is defined under s. 31(9). It covers all forms of ill-treatment including sexual abuse and forms of ill-treatment that are not physical. It also covers the impairment of health (physical or mental) and also physical, intellectual, emotional, social or behavioural development. The definition also extends to impairment suffered from seeing or hearing the ill-treatment *of any other person*.

When determining whether harm to a child's health or development is '*significant*', the child's development will be compared with that which could reasonably be expected of a similar child (s. 31(10)).

The power under s. 46 is split into two parts:

• a power to *remove* a child to suitable accommodation and keep him/her there; and
• a power to take reasonable steps to *prevent* the child's removal from a hospital or other place.

The longest a child can spend in police protection is 72 hours (s. 46(6)). It should be remembered that this is the *maximum* time that a child can be kept in police protection, not the norm.

As soon as is reasonably practicable after using the powers under the Act, the 'Initiating Officer' (the officer who takes the child into police protection and undertakes the initial inquiries) must do a number of things as set out above. These include:

• telling the local authority within whose area the child was found what steps have been, and are proposed to be, taken and why. This aspect of communicating with the local authority is a critical part of the protective powers;

- giving details to the local authority within whose area the child is ordinarily resident of the place at which the child is being kept;
- telling the child (if he/she appears capable of understanding) of what steps have been taken and why, and what further steps may be taken;
- taking such steps as are reasonably practicable to discover the wishes and feelings of the child;
- making sure that the case is inquired into by a 'designated officer' (see para. 2.9.4.1);
- taking such steps as are reasonably practicable to inform:
  - the child's parents;
  - every person who is not the child's parent but who has parental responsibility for the child; and
  - any other person with whom the child was living immediately before being taken into police protection; of the steps that the officer has taken under this section. the reasons for taking them and the further steps that may be taken with respect to the child. This element of informing the child, parent and/or relevant carers of what is happening and why is also a vital part of the protective process.

Where the child was taken into police protection by being removed to accommodation which is not provided by or on behalf of a local authority or as a refuge (under s. 51), the officer must, as soon as is reasonably practicable after taking a child into police protection, make sure that the child is moved to accommodation provided by the local authority. Every local authority must receive and provide accommodation for children in police protection where such a request is made (s. 21).

The 'Initiating Officer' and the 'Designated Officer' must not carry out these two separate roles (Home Office Circular 17/2008). The Circular also states that a police station is not 'suitable accommodation' and children should not be brought to a police station except in exceptional circumstances, such as a lack of immediately available local authority accommodation, and then only for a short period. On no account should a child who has been taken into police protection be taken to the cell block area of a police station.

When considering action under s. 46, it is possible that the child may already be the subject of an Emergency Protection Order (EPO) applied for by a local authority or authorised body under s. 44.

In considering the proper approach under these circumstances, the Court of Appeal has held that:

- There is no express provision in the Act prohibiting the police from invoking s. 46 where an EPO is in place and it is not desirable to imply a restriction which prohibits a constable from removing a child under s. 46 where the constable has reasonable cause to believe that the child would otherwise be likely to suffer significant harm.
- The s. 46 power to remove a child can therefore be exercised even where an EPO is in force in respect of the child.
- Where a police officer knows that an EPO is in force, he/she should not exercise the power of removing a child under s. 46, unless there are compelling reasons to do so.
- The statutory scheme accords primacy to the EPO procedure under s. 44 because removal under that section is sanctioned by the court and involves a more elaborate, sophisticated and complete process of removal than under s. 46.
- Consequently, the removal of children should usually be effected pursuant to an EPO, and s. 46 should only be invoked where it is not reasonably practicable to execute an EPO.
- In deciding whether it is practicable to execute an EPO, the police should always have regard to the paramount need to protect children from significant harm.
- Failure to follow the statutory procedure may amount to the police officer's removal of the child under s. 46 being declared unlawful.

(*Langley* v *Liverpool City Council and Chief Constable of Merseyside* [2005] EWCA Civ 1173.)

2.9.4.1 Designated Officer

The reference at s. 46(3)(e) of the Act to a 'designated officer' is a reference to the appropriate officer designated for that police station for the purposes of this legislation by the relevant chief officer of police. This is a key role in ensuring the effective use of the statutory framework set up for the protection of children in these circumstances. The responsibility for ensuring that the case is inquired into by the designated officer, together with the other responsibilities under s. 46(3) and the responsibility for taking steps to inform people under s. 46(4), clearly rest with the police officer exercising the power under s. 46.

The designated officer must inquire fully and thoroughly into the case; he/she must also do what is reasonable in all the circumstances for the purpose of safeguarding or promoting the child's welfare (having regard in particular to the length of the period during which the child will be so protected) (s. 46(9)(b)).

Where a child has been taken into police protection, the designated officer shall allow:

- the child's parents;
- any person who is not a parent of the child but who has parental responsibility for the child;
- any person with whom the child was living immediately before being taken into police protection;
- any person in whose favour a contact order is in force with respect to the child;
- any person who is allowed to have contact with the child by virtue of an order under s. 34; and
- any person acting on behalf of any of those persons;

to have such contact (if any) with the child as, in the opinion of the designated officer, is both reasonable and in the child's best interests (s. 46(10)).

The designated officer may apply for an 'emergency protection order' under s. 44 (s. 46(7)). Such an order allows the court to order the removal of the child to certain types of accommodation and to prevent the child's removal from any other place (including a hospital) where he/she was being accommodated immediately before the making of the order (s. 44(4)). An emergency protection order gives the applicant 'parental responsibility' for the child while it is in force. It also allows the court to make certain directions in relation to contact with the child and a medical or psychiatric assessment. Section 44A allows the court to make an order excluding certain people from a dwelling house where the child lives and to attach a power of arrest accordingly.

While the designated officer can apply for an emergency protection order without the local authority's knowledge or agreement (see s. 46(8)), there should be no reason why, given proper multi-agency cooperation and a well-planned child protection strategy, this situation would come about.

On completing the inquiry into the case, the designated officer must release the child from police protection *unless he/she considers that there is still reasonable cause for believing that the child would be likely to suffer significant harm if released* (s. 46(5)).

While a child is in police protection, neither the officer concerned nor the designated officer will have parental responsibility for the child (s. 46(9)(a)).

When a local authority is informed that a child is in police protection, they have a duty to make 'such enquiries as they consider necessary to enable them to decide whether they should take any action to safeguard' the child (s. 47(1)(b)). A court may issue a warrant for a constable to assist a relevant person to enter premises in order to enforce an emergency protection order.

2.9.4.2   Contravention of Protection Order or Police Protection

OFFENCE: **Acting in Contravention of Protection Order or Power Exercised under s. 46—*Children Act 1989, s. 49***

> • Triable summarily • Six months' imprisonment

The Children Act 1989, s. 49 states:

(1) A person shall be guilty of an offence if, knowingly and without lawful authority or reasonable excuse, he—
  (a) takes a child to whom this section applies away from the responsible person;
  (b) keeps such a child away from the responsible person; or
  (c) induces, assists or incites such a child to run away or stay away from the responsible person.
(2) This section applies in relation to a child who is—
  (a) in care;
  (b) the subject of an emergency protection order; or
  (c) in police protection,
  and in this section 'the responsible person' means any person who for the time being has care of him by virtue of the care order, the emergency protection order, or section 46, as the case may be.

KEYNOTE

Where a child is taken in contravention of s. 49, the court may issue a 'recovery order' under s. 50. The order, which is also available where a child is missing or has run away, requires certain people to produce the child to an authorised person (which includes a constable (s. 50(7)(b)) or to give certain information about the child's whereabouts to a constable or officer of the court (s. 50(3)). It can authorise a constable to enter any premises and search for the child.

Under s. 102 of the 1989 Act, a court may issue a warrant to enter premises in connection with certain provisions of the Act which regulate children's homes, foster homes, child-minding premises and nursing homes for children. Section 102 allows for constables to assist any person in the exercise of their powers under those provisions. It makes allowances for a constable to be accompanied by a medical practitioner, nurse or health visitor (s. 102(3)).

2.9.4.3   Disclosure of Information Regarding Child

Where a child is reported missing, problems can arise once the child is discovered to be safe and well but one of the parents wants the police to disclose the whereabouts of the child. This situation arose in *S v S (Chief Constable of West Yorkshire Police Intervening)* [1998] 1 WLR 1716 and the Court of Appeal provided some clarification of the issues. In that case, the mother left home with her three-year-old child after a marriage breakdown. The father reported the child's absence to the police who found the child and her mother in a refuge. At the request of the mother, the police advised the father that both she and the child were safe but refused to disclose their whereabouts. The father applied 'without notice' (i.e. without telling the police) to the county court which then made an order under s. 33 of the Family Law Act 1986, requiring the police to disclose the information. The chief constable was granted leave to intervene and, following another order from the court to disclose the child's whereabouts, the chief constable appealed. The Court of Appeal held that it was only in exceptional circumstances that the police should be asked to divulge the whereabouts of a child under a s. 33 order. Their primary role in such cases should continue to be finding missing children and ensuring their safety.

However, the court went on to say that, in such cases:

• The police are *not* in a position to give 'categoric assurances' of confidentiality to those who provide information as to the whereabouts of a child. The most they could say is that, other than by removing the child, it would be *most unlikely* that they would have to disclose the information concerning the child's whereabouts.

- An order under s. 33 provides for the information to be disclosed to the court not to the other party or his/her solicitor.
- An order under s. 33 should not normally be made in respect of the police without their being present (*ex parte*).

Note that the provision of information by police officers in relation to civil proceedings involving children is governed by regulations; specific advice should therefore be sought before disclosing any such information.

2.10 Offences Involving the Deprivation of Liberty

2.10.1 False Imprisonment

OFFENCE: **False Imprisonment—*Common Law***

- Triable on indictment • Unlimited maximum penalty

It is an offence at common law falsely to imprison another person.

> **KEYNOTE**
>
> The elements required for this offence are the unlawful and intentional/reckless restraint of a person's freedom of movement (*R* v *Rahman* (1985) 81 Cr App R 349). Locking someone in a vehicle or keeping him/her in a particular place for however short a time may amount to false imprisonment if done unlawfully. An unlawful arrest may amount to such an offence and it is not uncommon for such an allegation to be levelled at police officers against whom a public complaint has been made. On the other hand, making a *lawful* arrest will mean that the person was lawfully detained and no offence would be committed in such circumstances.
>
> In *R* v *Shwan Faraj* [2007] EWCA Crim 1033, the court stated that there was no reason why a householder should not be entitled to detain someone in his house whom he genuinely believed to be a burglar; he would be acting in defence of his property in doing so (a lawful detention of the person). However, a householder would have to honestly believe he needed to detain the suspect and would have to do so in a way that was reasonable.

2.10.2 Kidnapping

OFFENCE: **Kidnapping—*Common Law***

- Triable on indictment • Unlimited maximum penalty

It is an offence at common law to take or carry away another person without the consent of that person and without lawful excuse.

> **KEYNOTE**
>
> The required elements of this offence are the unlawful taking or carrying away of one person by another by force or fraud (*R* v *D* [1984] AC 778). Force includes the threat of force (*R* v *Archer* [2011] EWCA Crim 2252). These requirements go beyond those of mere restraint needed for false imprisonment. Parents may be acting without lawful excuse, for instance if they are acting in breach of a court order in respect of their children (see chapter 2.9). The 'taking or carrying away' need not involve great distances as a short distance (just a few yards/metres) will suffice (*R* v *Wellard* [1978] 1 WLR 921).
>
> The taking or carrying away of the victim must be without the consent of the victim. If the victim consents to an initial taking but later withdraws that consent, the offence would be complete. If the consent is obtained by fraud, the defendant cannot rely on that consent and the offence will be made out (*R* v *Cort* [2003] EWCA Crim 2149). In *R* v *Hendy-Freegard* [2007] EWCA Crim 1236, the defendant was a confidence trickster who pretended to be an undercover agent working for MI5 or Scotland Yard. He told his victims that he was investigating the activities of the IRA and that his investigations had

revealed that they were in danger. This allowed him to take control of their lives for years and, in doing so, to direct them to move about the country from location to location. The defendant was eventually arrested and convicted of kidnapping on the basis that the offence of kidnapping had occurred as his victims had made journeys around the country which they had been induced to make as a result of the defendant's false story. The defendant successfully appealed against the kidnapping conviction, with the court stating that causing a person to move from place to place when unaccompanied by the *defendant* could not itself constitute either taking or carrying away or deprivation of liberty, which were necessary elements of the offence.

The state of mind required for this offence is the same as that for false imprisonment, indeed the only thing separating the two offences seems to be *actus reus* (*R* v *Hutchins* [1988] Crim LR 379).

2.10.3 Slavery, Servitude and Forced or Compulsory Labour

The Modern Slavery Act 2015 consists of seven parts. Part 1 provides for offences of slavery and human trafficking. Modern slavery includes sexual exploitation, forced criminality and begging, labour exploitation, domestic servitude and organ or tissue harvesting. Victims can be of any age, culture, background or gender. Part 2 of the Act provides for two civil preventative orders, the Slavery and Trafficking Prevention Order and the Slavery and Trafficking Risk Order.

2.10.4 Offence of Slavery, Servitude and Forced or Compulsory Labour

OFFENCE: **Slavery, Servitude and Forced or Compulsory Labour—*Modern Slavery Act 2015, s. 1***
> • Triable either way • Life imprisonment on indictment • Six months' imprisonment and/or a fine summarily

The Modern Slavery Act 2015, s. 1 states:

(1) A person commits an offence if—
   (a) the person holds another person in slavery or servitude and the circumstances are such that the person knows or ought to know that the other person is held in slavery or servitude, or
   (b) the person requires another person to perform forced or compulsory labour and the circumstances are such that the person knows or ought to know that the other person is being required to perform forced or compulsory labour.

KEYNOTE

In s. 1(1), the references to holding a person in slavery or servitude or requiring a person to perform forced or compulsory labour are to be construed in accordance with Article 4 of the European Convention on Human Rights (s. 1(2)).

Article 4 of the European Convention on Human Rights states:

1. No one shall be held in slavery or servitude.
2. No one shall be required to perform forced or compulsory labour.
3. For the purpose of this Article the term 'forced or compulsory labour' shall not include:
   (a) any work required to be done in the ordinary course of detention imposed according to the provisions of Article 5 of this Convention or during conditional release from such detention;
   (b) any service of a military character or, in case of conscientious objectors in countries where they are recognised, service exacted instead of compulsory military service;
   (c) any service exacted in case of an emergency or calamity threatening the life or well-being of the community;
   (d) any work or service which forms part of normal civic obligations.

In determining whether a person is being held in slavery or servitude or required to perform forced or compulsory labour, regard may be had to all the circumstances (s. 1(3)). The list of particular vulnerabilities which may be considered is non-exhaustive but explicitly includes regard being made to any of the person's personal circumstances (such as the person being a child under the age of 18, the person's family relationships and any mental or physical illness) which may make the person more vulnerable than other persons. Regard may also be had to any work or services provided by the person, including work or services provided in circumstances which constitute exploitation within s. 3(3)–(6) (see para. 2.10.5, Keynote for the meaning of 'exploitation'). This makes it clear that the forced and compulsory labour offence can cover a broad range of types of work and services including, for example begging or pick-pocketing, which could amount to exploitation under s. 3(5) or (6).

Section 1(5) states that the consent of a person (whether an adult or a child) to any of the acts alleged to constitute holding the person in slavery or servitude, or requiring the person to perform forced or compulsory labour, does not preclude a determination that the person is being held in slavery or servitude, or required to perform forced or compulsory labour.

2.10.5   Offence of Human Trafficking

OFFENCE: **Human Trafficking—*Modern Slavery Act 2015, s. 2***
> • Triable either way • Life imprisonment on indictment • Six months' imprisonment and/or a fine summarily

The Modern Slavery Act 2015, s. 2 states:

(1) A person commits an offence if the person arranges or facilitates the travel of another person ('V') with a view to V being exploited.

(2) It is irrelevant whether V consents to the travel (whether V is an adult or a child).

(3) A person may in particular arrange or facilitate V's travel by recruiting V, transporting or transferring V, harbouring or receiving V, or transferring or exchanging control over V.

(4) A person arranges or facilitates V's travel with a view to V being exploited only if—
  (a) the person intends to exploit V (in any part of the world) during or after the travel, or
  (b) the person knows or ought to know that another person is likely to exploit V (in any part of the world) during or after the travel.

(5) 'Travel' means—
  (a) arriving in, or entering, any country,
  (b) departing from any country,
  (c) travelling within any country.

(6) A person who is a UK national commits an offence under this section regardless of—
  (a) where the arranging or facilitating takes place, or
  (b) where the travel takes place.

(7) A person who is not a UK national commits an offence under this section if—
  (a) any part of the arranging or facilitating takes place in the United Kingdom, or
  (b) the travel consists of arrival in or entry into, departure from, or travel within, the United Kingdom.

KEYNOTE

Meaning of Exploitation

The s. 2 trafficking offence is committed by arranging or facilitating travel with a view to the victim's exploitation. Section 3 of the Modern Slavery Act 2015 sets out the meaning of exploitation for the purposes of s. 2.

Exploitation includes slavery, servitude and forced or compulsory labour by reference to the offence under s. 1. Equivalent conduct outside England and Wales also comes within this definition (s. 3(2)).

Section 3(3) sets out that exploitation includes sexual exploitation by reference to conduct which would constitute the commission of an offence of taking, or permitting to take, indecent photographs of children or any of the sexual offences provided for in part 1 of the Sexual Offences Act 2003 (these include offences relating to rape, sexual assault, prostitution and child pornography). Section 3(3)(b) ensures that equivalent conduct committed outside England and Wales also comes within the definition even though for jurisdictional reasons it would not be an offence under English law.

Exploitation includes exploitation in the context of trafficking for organ removal or for the sale of human tissue by reference to offences in the Human Tissue Act 2004. Again, equivalent conduct outside England and Wales is within the definition (s. 3(4)).

Section 3(5) states that exploitation also includes all other types of exploitation where a person is subject to force, threats or deception which is designed to induce him/her:

(a) to provide services of any kind;

(b) to provide a person with benefits of any kind; or

(c) to enable another person to acquire benefits of any kind.

The above would include forcing a person to engage in activities such as begging or shop theft. It is not necessary for this conduct to be a criminal offence. Section 3(6) broadens the type of exploitation described in s. 3(5) so that it includes where a person is used (or there is an attempt to use the person) to do something for such a purpose, having been chosen on the grounds that he/she is a child, is ill, disabled or related to a person, in circumstances where a person without the illness, disability or family relationship would be likely to refuse.

Committing an Offence with Intent to Commit an Offence under Section 2

A person commits an offence under s. 4 of the Modern Slavery Act 2015 if the person commits any offence with the intention of committing an offence under s. 2 (including an offence committed by aiding, abetting, counselling or procuring an offence under that section).

A person guilty of an offence under s. 4 is liable, on indictment, to imprisonment for a term not exceeding 10 years and, on summary conviction, to imprisonment for a term of six months or a fine or both (s. 5(2)).

Where the offence under s. 4 is committed by kidnap or false imprisonment, a person guilty of that offence is liable, on conviction on indictment, to imprisonment for life (s. 5(3)).

UK National

'UK national' means:

(a) a British citizen,

(b) a person who is a British subject by virtue of Part 4 of the British Nationality Act 1981 and who has a right of abode in the United Kingdom, or

(c) a person who is a British overseas territories citizen by virtue of a connection with Gibraltar.

2.10.6 Forfeiture and Detention of Land Vehicle, Ship or Aircraft

The Modern Slavery Act 2015 provides powers to courts to order the forfeiture of vehicles involved in offences under s. 2 of the Act. The Act provides powers to the police and immigration service to detain vehicles connected to offences under s. 2 of the Act.

2.10.6.1 Forfeiture of Land Vehicle, Ship or Aircraft

The Modern Slavery Act 2015, s. 11 states:

(1) This section applies if a person is convicted on indictment of an offence under section 2.

(2) The court may order the forfeiture of a land vehicle used or intended to be used in connection with the offence if the convicted person—

(a) owned the vehicle at the time the offence was committed,

(b) was at that time a director, secretary or manager of a company which owned the vehicle,

(c) was at that time in possession of the vehicle under a hire-purchase agreement,

(d) was at that time a director, secretary or manager of a company which was in possession of the vehicle under a hire-purchase agreement, or

(e) was driving the vehicle in the course of the commission of the offence.

(3) The court may order the forfeiture of a ship or aircraft used or intended to be used in connection with the offence if the convicted person—

(a) owned the ship or aircraft at the time the offence was committed,

(b) was at that time a director, secretary or manager of a company which owned the ship or aircraft,

(c) was at that time in possession of the ship or aircraft under a hire-purchase agreement,

(d) was at that time a director, secretary or manager of a company which was in possession of the ship or aircraft under a hire-purchase agreement,

(e) was at that time a charterer of the ship or aircraft, or

(f) committed the offence while acting as captain of the ship or aircraft.

(4) But where subsection (3)(a) or (b) does not apply to the convicted person, forfeiture of a ship or aircraft may be ordered only if subsection (5) applies or—

(a) in the case of a ship other than a hovercraft, its gross tonnage is less than 500 tons;

(b) in the case of an aircraft, the maximum weight at which it may take off in accordance with its certificate of airworthiness is less than 5,700 kilogrammes.

(5) This subsection applies where a person who, at the time the offence was committed—

(a) owned the ship or aircraft, or

(b) was a director, secretary or manager of a company which owned it,

knew or ought to have known of the intention to use it in the course of the commission of an offence under section 2.

(6) Where a person who claims to have an interest in a land vehicle, ship or aircraft applies to a court to make representations about its forfeiture, the court may not order its forfeiture without giving the person an opportunity to make representations.

KEYNOTE

'Captain' means master (of a ship) or commander (of an aircraft).

2.10.6.2 Detention of Land Vehicle, Ship or Aircraft

The Modern Slavery Act 2015, s. 12 states:

(1) If a person ('P') has been arrested for an offence under section 2, a constable or senior immigration officer may detain a relevant land vehicle, ship or aircraft.

(2) A land vehicle, ship or aircraft is relevant if the constable or officer has reasonable grounds to believe that an order for its forfeiture could be made under section 11 if P were convicted of the offence.

(3) The land vehicle, ship or aircraft may be detained—

(a) until a decision is taken as to whether or not to charge P with the offence,

(b) if P has been charged, until P is acquitted, the charge against P is dismissed or the proceedings are discontinued, or

(c) if P has been charged and convicted, until the court decides whether or not to order forfeiture of the vehicle, ship or aircraft.

(4) A person (other than P) may apply to the court for the release of the land vehicle, ship or aircraft on the grounds that the person—

(a) owns the vehicle, ship or aircraft,

(b) was, immediately before the detention of the vehicle, ship or aircraft, in possession of it under a hire-purchase agreement, or

(c) is a charterer of the ship or aircraft.

(5) The court to which an application is made under subsection (4) may, if satisfactory security or surety is tendered, release the land vehicle, ship or aircraft on condition that it is made available to the court if—

(a) P is convicted, and

(b) an order for its forfeiture is made under section 11.

(6) In this section, 'the court' means—

(a) if P has not been charged, or P has been charged but proceedings for the offence have not begun to be heard, a magistrates' court;

(b) if P has been charged and proceedings for the offence have begun to be heard, the court hearing the proceedings.

(7) In this section, 'senior immigration officer' means an immigration officer not below the rank of chief immigration officer.

KEYNOTE

In ss. 11 and 12, a reference to being an owner of a vehicle, ship or aircraft includes a reference to being any of a number of persons who jointly own it.

2.10.7 Prevention Orders

Part 2 of the Modern Slavery Act 2015 makes provision (ss. 14 to 34) for the introduction of civil orders to enable prohibitions to be imposed by the courts on individuals convicted of a slavery or trafficking offence, or those involved in slavery or trafficking but who have not been convicted of a slavery or trafficking offence. The rationale for creating these orders is to enable law enforcement bodies and the courts to take tougher action against those involved in trafficking, and to protect individuals from the harm caused by slavery or trafficking by preventing future offending. The orders complement existing civil orders, enabling the courts to impose necessary prohibitions on individuals where there is evidence of that individual posing a risk of causing another person to be the victim of slavery, or trafficking for exploitation.

2.10.7.1 Slavery and Trafficking Prevention Orders on Sentencing

Section 14 provides for slavery and trafficking prevention orders (STPO) on conviction. Section 14(1) enables a court (e.g. the magistrates' court, youth court, Crown Court or in limited cases the Court of Appeal) to impose a STPO on a person on a conviction or other finding in respect of that person for a slavery or human trafficking offence. A slavery or human trafficking offence is defined in s. 14(3) and s. 34(1) and means an offence listed in sch. 1 to the Act. Schedule 1 includes reference to the offences in part 1 (ss. 1 and 2 of the Act), the preceding offences in England and Wales and equivalent offences in Scotland and Northern Ireland. Section 14(2) provides that the court must be satisfied that there is a risk that the defendant may commit a slavery or human trafficking offence and that it is necessary to make a STPO for the purposes of protecting persons generally, or particular persons, from physical or psychological harm which would be likely to occur if the defendant committed such an offence.

2.10.7.2 Slavery and Trafficking Prevention Orders on Application

Section 15 provides for a STPO in cases other than on conviction etc. An application for a STPO may be made to a magistrates' court by a chief officer of police, an immigration officer or the Director General of the National Crime Agency (NCA) (s. 15(1)). The NCA, established under s. 1 of the Crime and Courts Act 2013, holds the national lead for tackling slavery and human trafficking. Where an application is made by an immigration officer or the Director General of the NCA, the immigration officer or Director General must notify the chief officer of police for the area where the offender resides or is believed to intend to reside (s. 15(7)).

The court, in accordance with s. 16(2), must be satisfied that the defendant is a relevant offender and that, since the defendant became a relevant offender, he/she has acted in a way which demonstrates that there is a risk that the defendant may commit a slavery or human trafficking offence and that it is necessary to make a STPO for the purpose of protecting persons generally, or particular persons, from physical or psychological harm which would be likely to occur if the defendant committed such an offence.

2.10.7.3 Effect of Slavery and Trafficking Orders

Section 17(1) provides that a STPO may prohibit the person in respect of whom the order is made from doing *anything* described in it. The nature of any prohibition is a matter for the court to determine. A prohibition may include preventing a person from participating in a particular type of business, operating as a gangmaster, visiting a particular place, working with children or travelling to a specified country. The court may only include in an order prohibitions which it is satisfied are *necessary* for the purpose of protecting persons generally, or particular persons, from physical or psychological harm which would be likely to occur if the defendant committed a slavery or human trafficking offence (s. 17(2)). A STPO may last for a fixed period of at least five years or until further order (s. 17(4)). The prohibitions specified in it may each have different durations.

2.10.7.4 Prohibitions on Foreign Travel

A STPO may prohibit a person from travelling to any specified country outside the United Kingdom, any country other than a country specified in the order or any country outside the United Kingdom (s. 18(2)). Such a prohibition may be for a fixed period not exceeding five years, but may be renewed at the end of that period (s. 18(1) and (3)). A person prohibited from travelling to any country must surrender all his/her passports to the police (s. 18(4)). The police must return any such passports, unless they have been returned to the relevant national or international issuing authorities, once the all-country prohibition ceases to have effect (s. 18(5) and (6)).

2.10.7.5 Requirement to Provide Name and Address

Section 19 provides that a defendant subject to a STPO may be required by the court to notify to the persons specified in the order, within three days, their name and address (including any subsequent changes to this information). Section 18(2) provides that the court must be satisfied that this requirement is necessary for the purpose of protecting persons generally, or particular persons, from the physical or psychological harm which would be likely to occur if the defendant committed a slavery or human trafficking offence. Section 17(7) sets out that where this information is provided to the NCA, the NCA must provide this information to the chief officer of police for each relevant police area.

2.10.7.6 Variation, Renewal and Discharge

Under s. 20 of the Act, a person in respect of whom a STPO has been made or the police, NCA or an immigration officer (where they applied for the original order) may apply to the court which made the order to vary, renew or discharge the order. An order may not be discharged within five years of it being made without the consent of the person concerned and the relevant chief officer of police (s. 20(6)).

2.10.7.7 Interim Slavery and Trafficking Prevention Orders

Section 21 provides for an interim STPO to be made where an application has been made for a STPO under s. 15 and the court considers that it is just to do so. For example, the court may make an interim order in a case where it is satisfied that this is necessary for the purpose of protecting a person from immediate harm pending the full determination of the application for the order. An interim order must be made for a specified period and ceases to have effect once the main application has been determined (s. 21(7)). An interim order may be varied, renewed or discharged (s. 21(8)).

2.10.7.8 Appeals

A person may appeal against the making of a STPO on conviction in the same manner as an appeal against sentence. A person in respect of whom an order is made may also appeal a decision under s. 20 to vary, renew or discharge an order. Section 22(4) sets out the powers of the Crown Court when determining an appeal. It will be open to the court to revoke the order or to amend its provision (either the duration or the prohibitions contained in it).

2.10.8 Slavery and Trafficking Risk Orders

Section 23 of the Modern Slavery Act 2015 enables a magistrates' court to make a slavery and trafficking risk order (STRO) on an application by a chief officer of police, an immigration officer or the Director General of the NCA. A STRO may be made against either an adult *or* person under 18. Where an application is made by an immigration officer or the Director General of the NCA, the immigration officer or Director General must notify the chief officer of police for the area where the offender resides or is believed to intend to reside (s. 23(6)).

The test for making a STRO is that the court is satisfied that there is a risk that the defendant may commit a slavery or human trafficking offence and that it is necessary to make a STRO for the purpose of protecting persons generally, or particular persons, from physical or psychological harm which would be likely to occur if the defendant committed such an offence. There is no requirement for the person in respect of whom an order is sought to have previously been convicted or cautioned in relation to a criminal offence (s. 23(2)).

An application for a STRO is made by complaint to a magistrates' court (in relation to a person aged under 18, a reference to a magistrates' court is to be taken as referring to a youth court).

KEYNOTE

All of the issues relevant to a STPO apply in exactly the same way to a STRO (e.g. the effect of a STPO, the prohibitions on foreign travel and the requirement of a STPO to provide a name and address are mirrored in the legislation dealing with a STRO).

2.10.9 Offences

Section 30 makes it an offence for a person to do anything which is prohibited by an STPO, interim STPO, STRO or interim STRO, or the Northern Ireland equivalents of an STPO or interim STPO, without reasonable excuse.

Where an order includes a foreign travel prohibition in respect of all countries outside the United Kingdom, s. 30(2) makes it an offence for the person subject to the order to fail, without reasonable excuse, to surrender all his/her passports. It is also an offence for a person to fail to comply with a requirement to provide his/her name and address.

The maximum penalty for either offence is six months' imprisonment or a fine or both on summary conviction, or five years' imprisonment following conviction on indictment (s. 30(3)). Section 30(4) precludes the court from making an order for a conditional discharge following a conviction for an offence in this section.

Property Offences

3.1 | Theft

3.1.1 Theft

OFFENCE: **Theft—*Theft Act 1968, s. 1***
- Triable either way • Seven years' imprisonment on indictment
- Six months' imprisonment and/or a fine summarily

The Theft Act 1968, s. 1 states:

(1) A person is guilty of theft if he dishonestly appropriates property belonging to another with the intention of permanently depriving the other of it; and 'thief' and 'steal' shall be construed accordingly.

KEYNOTE

The final line of s. 1 is important and states that the words ' "thief" and "steal" shall be construed accordingly'. This means that in any Theft Act 1968 offence where the words 'thief' and/or 'steal' are used (such as in the Theft Act 1968 offence of robbery (s. 8) or handling stolen goods (s. 22)), the 'thief' is the person who commits the theft offence and 'steal' means to commit theft. All of the elements of the theft offence must be present to '*steal*'. The definition of robbery (s. 8) tells us that 'A person is guilty of robbery if he steals'. If an element of theft has not been satisfied then the defendant will not commit theft and will not 'steal'. No 'steal' = no robbery.

Where the property in question belonged to D's spouse or civil partner, a prosecution for theft may only be instituted against D by or with the consent of the DPP (s. 30(4)). This restriction must also apply to charges of robbery or of burglary by stealing etc. but does not apply to other persons charged with committing the offence jointly with D; nor does it apply when the parties are separated by judicial decree or order or under no obligation to cohabit (s. 30(4)(a)). Theft from businesses (classed as 'theft from a shop') involving first-time offenders who are not substance misusers and where the value of the goods stolen is less than £100 can be dealt with by way of fixed penalty notice.

3.1.2 Low-value Shoplifting

Section 176 of the Anti-social Behaviour, Crime and Policing Act 2014 inserts s. 22A into the Magistrates' Courts Act 1980, which provides that low-value shoplifting is a *summary offence*. This is subject to one exception: where a person accused of shoplifting is 18 or over, they are to be given the opportunity to elect Crown Court trial, and if the defendant so elects, the offence is no longer summary and will be sent to the Crown Court (s. 22A(2)).

Otherwise, the effect of s. 22A is that offences of low-value shoplifting cannot be sent to the Crown Court for trial or committed there for sentence; they will attract a maximum penalty of six months' custody and they will be brought within the procedure in s. 12 of the Magistrates' Courts Act 1980 that enables defendants in summary cases to be given the opportunity to plead guilty by post.

Shoplifting is not a specific offence as such but constitutes theft under s. 1 of the Theft Act 1968; accordingly, s. 22A(3) defines shoplifting for the purposes of this provision, which applies if the value of the stolen goods does not exceed £200. For these purposes, the value of the goods is to be determined by the price at which they were offered for sale rather than the intrinsic value, and also for the value involved in several shoplifting offences to be aggregated where they are charged at the same time (s. 22A(4)). So, for example, where a person is charged with three counts of shoplifting, having allegedly taken £80 worth of goods from three separate shops (a total of £240), the procedure would not apply in that case as the aggregate sum exceeds the £200 threshold.

Low-value shoplifting will be tried summarily (as it must be unless the defendant elects); the maximum penalty is six months' imprisonment or a fine.

An offence of shoplifting includes secondary offences such as aiding and abetting.

Section 22A(5) amends s. 1 of the Criminal Attempts Act 1981 to provide that it is an offence to attempt to commit low-value shoplifting.

Section 176(6) of the Anti-social Behaviour, Crime and Policing Act 2014 provides that certain powers conferred by the Police and Criminal Evidence Act 1984 on the police and others in respect of indictable offences remain available in respect of low-value shoplifting, notwithstanding that it is reclassified as summary only. The powers concerned include a power of arrest exercisable by a person other than a constable (for example, a store detective), powers enabling police officers to enter and search premises and vehicles in various circumstances for the purposes of searching for evidence in connection with an investigation or arresting individuals suspected of committing offences, and powers enabling a magistrate to authorise such entry and search.

3.1.3 Dishonestly

If a person cannot be shown to have acted 'dishonestly', he/she is not guilty of theft. The decision as to whether or not a defendant was dishonest is a question of fact for the jury or magistrate(s) to decide. Whilst there is no statutory definition of the term 'dishonestly', the 1968 Act does deal with the issue by setting out a number of specific circumstances where the relevant person will *not* be treated as dishonest and one circumstance where a person *may* be dishonest.

The Theft Act 1968, s. 2 states:

(1) A person's appropriation of property belonging to another is not to be regarded as dishonest—
    (a) if he appropriates the property in the belief that he has in law the right to deprive the other of it, on behalf of himself or of a third person; or
    (b) if he appropriates the property in the belief that he would have the other's consent if the other knew of the appropriation and the circumstances of it; or
    (c) (except where the property came to him as trustee or personal representative) if he appropriates the property in the belief that the person to whom the property belongs cannot be discovered by taking reasonable steps.

KEYNOTE

In all three instances, it is the person's *belief* that is important.

Right in Law

- X is owed £100 by Y. Y tells X that he will not give him the money so X, *honestly believing that he has a right in law to do so*, takes £100 cash from Y's wallet as payment for the debt. It does not matter that there is no actual right in law for X to behave in this way; the honestly held belief by X that he does have a right in law means that he is not dishonest. The belief *need not even be reasonable*, only honestly held, and could be based on a 'mistake'. If, in the above example, X took Y's pedal cycle (worth £700) as payment for the debt, *honestly believing* that he had a right in law to do so, then X would not be dishonest if he/she honestly believed he/she had a right in law to take the pedal cycle as payment for the debt. This would also include the situation where the person acts on the basis of belief in the legal right of another. So if X, acting for the benefit of Y, took property from Z (wrongly but honestly believing that Y was entitled to it), X would not be dishonest.

Consent

- Under s. 2(1)(b), the person appropriating the property must believe both elements, i.e. that the other person would have *consented* had he/she known of the appropriation *and the circumstances of it*. For example, a person is about to run out of time on a street parking meter and needs £5 to park for the next hour or risk incurring a fine. Believing that a work colleague would consent in this situation, the person takes £5 belonging to the colleague from a change jar on the colleague's desk. If the person *honestly believes the work colleague would consent to the taking and the circumstances of it*, this would not be dishonest. If the person knew that the work colleague would not approve, this would be dishonest.

Lost

- Under s. 2(1)(c), the belief has to be in relation to the likelihood of *discovering* the 'owner' by taking reasonable steps. The nature and value of the property, together with the attendant circumstances, will be relevant. The chances of finding the owner of a valuable, monogrammed engagement ring found after a theatre performance would be considerably greater than those of discovering the owner of a can of beer found outside a football ground. Again, it is the defendant's *honest belief* at the time of the appropriation that is important here, not that the defendant went on to take reasonable steps to discover the person to whom the property belongs.
- Trustees or personal representatives cannot rely on s. 2(1)(c). This is because a trustee or personal representative can never be personally entitled to the property in question (unless the trust or will states that is the case) as if the beneficiary cannot be found, the person entitled to the property in question (now effectively 'ownerless goods') is the Crown.

The Theft Act 1968, s. 2 states:

(2) A person's appropriation of property belonging to another may be dishonest notwithstanding that he is willing to pay for the property.

KEYNOTE

If a person appropriates another's property, leaving money or details of where he/she can be contacted to make restitution, this will not of itself negate dishonesty (*Boggeln v Williams* [1978] 1 WLR 873). The wording of s. 2(2) gives latitude to a court where the defendant was willing to pay for the property. The subsection says that such an appropriation *may* be dishonest, not that it *will always* be dishonest.

....

EXAMPLE

X wants to buy some milk and sees an unattended milk float displaying a sign, 'Milk—£1 for 2 Litres'. X waits for several minutes but nobody in charge of the milk float appears, so X leaves £1 on the float and takes a 2-litre container of milk. The fact that the milk is for sale and X left payment would be convincing evidence to suggest that X is not dishonest.

The conclusion may be different if Y wants to own a painting that is on display in a museum. Y has made several approaches to buy the painting but has been told that the painting is not for sale. Y knows the painting is worth £10,000 and decides to take the painting from the museum, leaving a cheque for £10,000 in its place. Just because Y is willing to pay the market value for the painting does not mean to say that he is not dishonest.

3.1.4 Dishonesty: Case Law

Where 'dishonesty' needs to be considered but s. 2 of the Theft Act 1968 is of no assistance (s. 2 will not cater for every circumstance), the magistrates/jury will consider 'dishonesty' in the same way that it is considered in civil cases.

The test for dishonesty in civil cases was set out in *Barlow Clowes International (in liq)* v *Eurotrust International Ltd* [2006] 1 All ER 333 and *Royal Brunei Airlines Sdn Bhd* v *Tan* [1995] 3 All ER 97.

KEYNOTE

The Test for Dishonesty

When dishonesty is in question, the magistrates/jury will first have to ascertain the actual state of the individual's knowledge or belief as to the facts (this does not have to be a reasonable belief—the question is whether the belief is genuinely held). Once his/her actual state of mind as to knowledge or belief is established, the question of whether his/her conduct had been honest or dishonest is to be determined by the magistrates/jury by applying the (objective) standards of ordinary decent people. There is no requirement that the defendant had to appreciate that what he/she had done was, by those standards, dishonest.

The test has a role for the state of mind of the defendant (in relation to the facts) but there is no requirement for him/her to appreciate the dishonesty of his/her actions.

Taking this approach means that to prove dishonesty, a prosecutor need only place before a court facts of what the defendant did and thought and then invite the court to hold that he/she was dishonest according to the standards of ordinary decent people.

3.1.5 Appropriates

The Theft Act 1968, s. 3 states:

> Any assumption by a person of the rights of an owner amounts to an appropriation, and this includes, where he has come by the property (innocently or not) without stealing it, any later assumption of a right to it by keeping or dealing with it as owner.

KEYNOTE

The owner of property has many rights in relation to it—the right to sell it, to give it away or to destroy it are just *some* examples. 'Appropriation' does not envisage that a person assumes *all* of those rights, just *one* of them would suffice for 'appropriation' to occur.

While damaging or destroying property is clearly an act of 'appropriation' (*R* v *Graham* [1997] 1 Cr App R 302), it does not follow that an act of destruction of property is also thereby automatically theft of that property. *Dishonestly* causing the destruction of property can itself amount to an offence of theft (*R* v *Kohn* (1979) 69 Cr App R 395) but this does not make theft an appropriate charge where D merely smashes V's car window by throwing a brick through it. Criminal damage would be the appropriate charge on such facts as there is clearly no 'dishonesty' present in such an act.

It is important to note that there can be an 'appropriation' without any criminal liability and appropriation itself does not amount to an offence of theft; it simply describes one of the elements of the criminal conduct that must exist before a charge of theft can be made out. An appropriation requires no mental state on the part of the appropriator. It is an objective act.

Where an appropriation takes place and is accompanied by the other elements of the offence, there will be a theft.

Appropriation under s. 3(1) envisages a *physical* act (*Biggs* v *R* (2003) 12 December, unreported).

When and where the particular act amounting to an appropriation took place is of importance when bringing a charge of theft (and in other offences such as robbery and aggravated burglary).

The decision of the House of Lords in *R v Gomez* [1993] AC 442 significantly developed the meaning of 'appropriation'. Following an earlier case (*Lawrence v Metropolitan Police Commissioner* [1972] AC 626), Lord Keith disagreed with the argument made in *Gomez* that an act expressly or impliedly authorised by the owner of the property in question can never amount to an 'appropriation' and pointed out that the decision in *Lawrence* was a direct contradiction of that proposition. The House of Lords upheld the convictions for theft in *Gomez* and accepted that there are occasions where property can be 'appropriated' for the purposes of the Theft Act 1968, *even though the owner has given his/her consent or authority*.

A number of issues come from this decision:

- *Taking or depriving*. It is not necessary that the property be 'taken' in order for there to be an appropriation, neither need the owner be 'deprived' of the property. Similarly, there is no need for the defendant to 'gain' anything by an appropriation.
- *Consent*. It is irrelevant to the issue of appropriation whether or not the owner consented to that appropriation. This is well illustrated in *Lawrence*, the decision followed by the House of Lords in *Gomez*. In *Lawrence*, a tourist gave his wallet full of unfamiliar English currency to a taxi driver for the latter to remove the correct fare. The driver in fact helped himself to ('appropriated') far more than the amount owed. It was held that the fact that the wallet and its contents were handed over freely (with consent) by the owner did not prevent the taxi driver's actions from amounting to an 'appropriation' of it.
- *Interfering with goods*. Simply swapping the price labels on items displayed for sale in a shop *will* amount to an 'appropriation'. This is because to do so, irrespective of any further intention, involves an assumption of one of the owner's rights in relation to the property (the right to put a price on property). If that appropriation were accompanied by the other elements of the offence, then theft is committed.
- *More than one appropriation*. There may be an appropriation of the same property on more than one occasion. However, once property has been *stolen* (as opposed to merely appropriated), that same property cannot be stolen again by the same thief (*R v Atakpu* [1994] QB 69). Appropriation can also be a continuing act; that is, it can include the whole episode of entering and ransacking a house and the subsequent removal of property (*R v Hale* (1979) 68 Cr App R 415).

In *R v Hinks* [2001] 2 AC 24, the House of Lords was asked to rule on whether a person could 'appropriate' property belonging to another where the other person made her an absolute gift of property, retaining no proprietary interest in the property or any right to resume or recover it. In that case, the defendant had befriended a middle-aged man of limited intelligence who had given her £60,000 over a period of time. The defendant was charged with five counts of theft and, after conviction, eventually appealed to the House of Lords. Their lordships held that:

- in a prosecution for theft, it was unnecessary to prove that the taking was without the owner's consent (as in *Lawrence*);
- it was immaterial whether the act of appropriation was done with the owner's consent or authority (as in *Gomez*); and
- *Gomez* therefore gave effect to s. 3(1) by treating 'appropriation' as a neutral word covering 'any assumption by a person of the rights of an owner'.

The essence of the decision by the House of Lords in *Hinks* is that even though a person obtains good title to property under civil law (the gift), they can still be convicted of theft as the circumstances of the gift-giving are dishonest.

If a person, having come by property, innocently or not, without stealing it, later assumes any rights to it by keeping it or treating it as his/her own, then he/she 'appropriates' that property (s. 3(1)).

KEYNOTE

A later assumption of the rights of an owner amounts to 'appropriation' and could lead to an offence of theft.

X is shopping in a large department store and has placed several items in his shopping basket. Thinking about other things, X absent-mindedly walks out of the store without paying for the goods. Once outside the store, X realises what he has done but as the store alarm has not activated and nobody has noticed X leaving the store without paying, X decides to keep the goods and walks away from the store. X initially came by the goods innocently but his later assumption of the rights of an owner means he has now 'appropriated' the goods and in the circumstances commits theft.

An exception to these circumstances is provided by the Theft Act 1968, s. 3 which states:

> (2) Where property or a right or interest in property is or purports to be transferred for value to a person acting in good faith, no later assumption by him of rights which he believed himself to be acquiring shall, by reason of any defect in the transferor's title, amount to theft of the property.

KEYNOTE

If a person buys a car in good faith and gives value for it (i.e. purchases it from a car dealer believing the car dealer owns the car and has every right to sell it and they purchase it at a reasonable price) but then discovers it has been stolen, a refusal to return it to the original owner would not, without more, *attract liability for theft*. Without s. 3(2), the retention of the vehicle would be caught by s. 3(1). This narrow exemption does not mean, however, that the innocent purchaser gets good title to the car (*National Employers' Mutual Insurance Association Ltd* v *Jones* [1990] 1 AC 24), nor would it provide a defence if the stolen goods are a gift and the 'donee' (recipient) subsequently discovers that they had been stolen (the 'donee' will not have given 'value' for the property).

3.1.6 Property

The Theft Act 1968, s. 4 states:

> (1) 'Property' includes money and all other property, real or personal, including things in action and other intangible property.
> (2) A person cannot steal land, or things forming part of land and severed from it by him or by his directions, except in the following cases, that is to say—
>   (a) when he is a trustee or personal representative, or is authorised by power of attorney, or as liquidator of a company, or otherwise, to sell or dispose of land belonging to another, and he appropriates the land or anything forming part of it by dealing with it in breach of the confidence reposed in him; or
>   (b) when he is not in possession of the land and appropriates anything forming part of the land by severing it or causing it to be severed, or after it has been severed; or
>   (c) when, being in possession of the land under a tenancy, he appropriates the whole or part of any fixture or structure let to be used with the land.
>   For purposes of this subsection 'land' does not include incorporeal hereditaments; 'tenancy' means a tenancy for years or any less period and includes an agreement for such a tenancy, but a person who after the end of a tenancy remains in possession as statutory tenant or otherwise is to be treated as having possession under the tenancy, and 'let' shall be construed accordingly.
> (3) A person who picks mushrooms growing wild on any land, or who picks flowers, fruit or foliage from a plant growing wild on any land, does not (although not in possession of the land) steal what he picks unless he does it for reward or for sale or other commercial purpose. For purposes of this subsection 'mushroom' includes any fungus, and 'plant' includes any shrub or tree.
> (4) Wild creatures, tamed or untamed, shall be regarded as property; but a person cannot steal a wild creature not tamed nor ordinarily kept in captivity, or the carcase of any such creature, unless either it has been reduced into possession by or on behalf of another person and possession of it has not since been lost or abandoned, or another person is in course of reducing it into possession.

Money

Coins and banknotes are property (*R* v *Davis* (1989) 88 Cr App R 347). 'Money' does not include cheques or credit balances held in banks and building societies (but see below).

Personal Property

Personal property includes tangible personal property which might be described as 'things in possession'. The TV in your house, the settee you sit on etc. are all examples of 'personal' property.

Things in Action and Other Intangible Property

Under s. 4(1) 'things in action' would include patents, company shares and trademarks and other things which can only be enforced by legal action as opposed to physical possession. Other intangible property would include software programs and perhaps credits accumulated on store loyalty cards. Confidential information, such as the contents of an examination paper, is not intangible property *per se* (*Oxford* v *Moss* (1979) 68 Cr App R 183). However, if those contents were written on a piece of paper, the paper itself would be 'real' property. It has been accepted by the Court of Appeal that contractual rights obtained by buying a ticket for the London Underground may amount to a 'thing in action' (*R* v *Marshall* [1998] 2 Cr App R 282).

Cheques and Credit Balances

Cheques will be property as they are pieces of paper ('personal' property albeit of very little value). The contents of a bank or building society account, however, are also a 'thing in action' that can be stolen provided the account is in credit or within the limits of an agreed overdraft facility (*R* v *Kohn* (1979) 69 Cr App R 395). Reducing the credit balance in one account and transferring a like sum into your own account amounts to an 'appropriation' of property within the meaning of s. 1. This principle (set out in *Kohn*) was reaffirmed in *R* v *Williams (Roy)* [2001] 1 Cr App R 23 by the Court of Appeal.

Land

Under s. 4(2), you cannot generally steal land. However, there are three exceptions to this general rule:

(1) Trustees or personal representatives or someone in a position of trust to dispose of land belonging to another, can be guilty of stealing it if, in such circumstances, they dishonestly dispose of it.

EXAMPLE

Two company employees are asked by the company directors to sell land belonging to the company. The value of the land is £10,000 an acre. The company employees sell the land to each other for £1,000 an acre. The company employees are in a position of trust and have 'breached the confidence reposed in them' and commit theft of the land.

---

(2) Persons not in possession of the land may commit theft in a variety of ways. This may be accomplished by severing fixtures, plants, topsoil etc. from the land or by appropriating such property after it has been severed. If X decides to take an established and cultivated rosebush from the garden of his neighbour by ripping it out of the ground and then planting it in his own garden, this would be theft as the rosebush has been severed from the land (see below for wild plants). This would not include a person who dishonestly moves a boundary fence so as to appropriate some part of a neighbouring property as the land has not been 'severed'.

(3) Tenants can steal land but only fixtures and structures let to be used with the land. Examples of 'fixtures' would be a fireplace or the kitchen sink; a structure might be a greenhouse or a garden shed which is fixed to the land. A tenant cannot steal land such as topsoil or a rosebush growing in the garden of the rented premises as these things are not 'fixtures or structures'.

Things Growing Wild

Things growing wild on any land are 'property' and could be stolen by a person not in possession of the land if he/she severed and appropriated them. However, s. 4(3) of the Act tells us that a person who picks mushrooms, flowers, fruit and foliage growing wild on any land will not commit theft by so doing, unless

3.1.7   What is not Property?

'Identity theft' is a misleading phrase as adopting another person's characteristics and using his/her administrative data (such as National Insurance number) is not theft of the information as this 'confidential information' is not 'property' for the purposes of the Theft Act 1968.

Human bodies (dead or alive) are not property ('there is no property in a corpse' (*Doodeward* v *Spence* (1908) 6 CLR 406)). However, a body or body parts are capable of being stolen if they have acquired different attributes by virtue of the application of skill (such as dissection or preservation techniques for exhibition or teaching purposes). An Egyptian mummy would be the property of the museum it was kept in. This principle was upheld by the Court of Appeal in *R* v *Kelly* [1999] QB 621, after the conviction of two people involved in the theft of body parts from the Royal College of Surgeons. The court upheld the convictions for theft on the grounds that the process of *alteration* (amputation, dissection and preservation) which the body parts had undergone did make them 'property' for the purposes of the 1968 Act.

Fluids taken from a living body are property, so a motorist has been convicted of stealing a specimen of his own urine provided by him for analysis (*R* v *Welsh* [1971] RTR 478). The same rule would clearly apply to a blood sample.

Electricity is not property and cannot be stolen—it is the subject of a specific offence (abstracting electricity) under s. 13 of the Theft Act 1968.

3.1.8   Belonging to Another

The Theft Act 1968, s. 5 states:

(1) Property shall be regarded as belonging to any person having possession or control of it, or having in it any proprietary right or interest (not being an equitable interest arising only from an agreement to transfer or grant an interest).
(2) Where property is subject to a trust, the persons to whom it belongs shall be regarded as including any person having a right to enforce the trust, and an intention to defeat the trust shall be regarded accordingly as an intention to deprive of the property any person having that right.

to' the garage proprietor who had possession of it (*R v Turner (No. 2)* [1971] 1 WLR 901). In determining whether or not a person had 'possession' of property for the purposes of s. 5(1), the period of possession can be finite (i.e. for a given number of hours, days etc.) or infinite (*R v Kelly* [1999] QB 621).

It is not necessary to show who does own the property, only that it 'belongs to' someone other than the defendant. An example of how this principle operates can be seen in a case where the two defendants went diving in a lake on a golf course, recovering sacks of 'lost' balls which it was believed they were going to sell. This activity was carried out without the permission of the golf club which owned the course. Although the defendants argued that the balls had been abandoned by their owners, the Crown had shown that they were 'property belonging to another' (the golf club) and therefore the convictions were safe (*R v Rostron; R v Collinson* [2003] EWCA Crim 2206).

Where money is given to charity collectors, it becomes the property of the relevant charitable trustees at the moment it goes into the collecting tin (*R v Dyke* [2001] EWCA Crim 2184). If s. 5(2) did not exist, those charitable trustees could take the donation to the charity and do what they wished with it, including placing the charitable funds in their own bank account. Charitable trusts are enforceable by the Attorney-General and an appropriation of the trust property by a charitable trustee will amount to theft from the Attorney-General.

When a cheque is written, it creates a 'thing in action'. That thing in action belongs only to the payee (the 'payee' is the person to whom the cheque is made payable). Therefore a payee of a cheque cannot 'steal' the thing in action which it creates (*R v Davis* (1989) 88 Cr App R 347).

You must show that the property belonged to another *at the time of the appropriation*. Where a defendant decides not to pay for goods *after* property passes to him/her (e.g. people refusing to pay for meals after they have eaten or deciding to drive off having filled their car with petrol), the proper charge is found under the Fraud Act 2006 or by charging with the offence of making off without payment. If ownership of the property had passed to the defendant *before* he/she appropriated it (e.g. by virtue of the Sale of Goods Act 1979; *Edwards v Ddin* [1976] 1 WLR 942), then this element of theft would not be made out and an alternative charge should be considered.

3.1.9 Obligations Regarding Another's Property

The Theft Act 1968, s. 5 states:

(3) Where a person receives property from or on account of another, and is under an obligation to the other to retain and deal with that property or its proceeds in a particular way, the property or proceeds shall be regarded (as against him) as belonging to the other.

KEYNOTE

'Obligation' means a legal obligation not a moral one (*R v Hall* [1973] QB 126). Whether or not such an obligation exists is a matter of law for a trial judge to decide (*R v Dubar* [1994] 1 WLR 1484).

Instances under s. 5(3) most commonly involve receiving money from others to retain and use in a certain way (e.g. travel agents taking deposits, solicitors holding funds for mortgagees or pension fund managers collecting contributions (*R v Clowes (No. 2)* [1994] 2 All ER 316)). The Court of Appeal has held that one effect of s. 5(3) is that property can be regarded as belonging to another even where it does not 'belong' to that person on a strict interpretation of civil law (*R v Klineberg* [1999] 1 Cr App R 427). In that case, the defendants collected money from customers in their timeshare business and told the customers that their deposits would be placed with an independent trustee. Instead, the defendants paid the sums into their company account, thereby breaching the 'obligation' under s. 5(3) to deal with the money in a particular way.

Section 5(3) would also include, say, the owner of a shopping centre who invites shoppers to throw coins into a fountain which will be donated to charity; if the owner did not deal with those coins in the way intended (e.g. keeping the money), the provisions of s. 5(3) may well apply.

3.1.10 Obligation to Restore Another's Property

The Theft Act 1968, s. 5 states:

(4) Where a person gets property by another's mistake, and is under an obligation to make restoration (in whole or in part) of the property or its proceeds or of the value thereof, then to the extent of that obligation the property or proceeds shall be regarded (as against him) as belonging to the person entitled to restoration, and an intention not to make restoration shall be regarded accordingly as an intention to deprive that person of the property or proceeds.

KEYNOTE

Where extra money is mistakenly credited into an employee's bank account, the employee will be liable for stealing the extra money if he/she dishonestly keeps it (*Attorney-General's Reference (No. 1 of 1983)* [1985] QB 182 where a police officer's account was credited with money representing overtime which she had not actually worked).

Section 5(4) only applies where someone *other than the defendant* has made a mistake. Such a mistake can be a mistake as to a material fact; whether or not a mistake as to law would be covered is unclear.

The obligation to make restoration is a *legal* one and an unenforceable or moral obligation will not be covered by s. 5(4). An example of a *moral* obligation can be found in the case of *R v Gilks* [1972] 1 WLR 1341, when a relief manager at a betting shop mistakenly paid out winnings against the wrong horse. The Court of Appeal held that the defendant did not owe a legal obligation to return the money because the bookmaker could not have sued on a gaming transaction and therefore s. 5(4) did not apply—the obligation to return the money in this case was a *moral* one as in 1972 gambling debts were not legally enforceable (they are now—Gambling Act 2005 in force since 1 September 2007).

3.1.11 Intention of Permanently Depriving

If you cannot prove an intention permanently to deprive, you cannot prove theft (*R v Warner* (1970) 55 Cr App R 93).

If there is such an intention at the time of the appropriation, giving the property back later will not alter the fact and the charge will be made out (*R v McHugh* (1993) 97 Cr App R 335).

In certain circumstances, s. 6 may help in determining the presence or absence of such an intention.

The Theft Act 1968, s. 6 states:

(1) A person appropriating property belonging to another without meaning the other permanently to lose the thing itself is nevertheless to be regarded as having the intention of permanently depriving the other of it if his intention is to treat the thing as his own to dispose of regardless of the other's rights; and a borrowing or lending of it may amount to so treating it if, but only if, the borrowing or lending is for a period and in circumstances making it equivalent to an outright taking or disposal.

KEYNOTE

The key feature of s. 6(1) is the intention to treat 'the thing' as one's own to dispose of regardless of the other's rights. An example of such a case would be where property is 'held to ransom' (*R v Coffey* [1987] Crim LR 498). If X kidnaps a dog belonging to Y and tells Y that the dog will be returned in exchange for £500, the conclusion to be drawn is that if the ransom is not paid, the dog will not be returned, i.e. there is an intention to permanently deprive.

The borrowing or lending of another's property is specifically caught within s. 6(1). If a person takes property from his/her employer (e.g. carpet tiles) and uses it in a way which makes restoration unlikely or impossible (e.g. by laying them in his/her living room), s. 6(1) will apply (*R v Velumyl* [1989] Crim LR 299).

If X is given a football season ticket by Y to use for one match but then X holds on to the season ticket for several matches knowing that this was not part of the arrangement and against the wishes of Y, s. 6(1) would help to prove the required intention to permanently deprive because the circumstances of the borrowing make it equivalent to an outright taking.

In a case involving robbery, the defendants took the victim's personal stereo headphones from him and broke them in two, rendering them useless before returning them to him. The Administrative Court held that a person who took something and dealt with it for the purpose of rendering it useless in this way demonstrated the intention of treating that article as his/her own to dispose of. The court did not accept the argument that the property had to be totally exhausted before s. 6 applied and held that the magistrates had been wrong to accept the submission of no case to answer on this point (*DPP* v *J* [2002] EWHC 291 (Admin)). Therefore, the deliberate breaking of an item of property will amount to the 'intention to permanently deprive'; however, unless this action is accompanied by the other theft elements, it will be criminal damage. Note that in this case the offence dealt with was robbery so that the other elements of theft were plainly satisfied when the defendant initially took the property.

The Theft Act 1968, s. 6 states:

(2) Without prejudice to the generality of subsection (1) above, where a person, having possession or control (lawfully or not) of property belonging to another, parts with the property under a condition as to its return which he may not be able to perform, this (if done for purposes of his own and without the other's authority) amounts to treating the property as his own to dispose of regardless of the other's rights.

KEYNOTE

Section 6(2) deals with occasions such as pawning another's property. In pawning the property, the defendant parts with the property on the basis that he/she *might* be able to recover it (there could never be certainty of recovery). So, there is a possibility that the defendant may not be able to do so, i.e. that he/she will be unable to meet the conditions under which he/she parted with another person's property. In such a case, s. 6(2) would help in proving an intention permanently to deprive.

3.2 | Robbery

3.2.1 Robbery

OFFENCE: **Robbery—*Theft Act 1968, s. 8***

> • Triable on indictment • Life imprisonment

The Theft Act 1968, s. 8 states:

> (1) A person is guilty of robbery if he steals, and immediately before or at the time of doing so, and in order to do so, he uses force on any person or puts or seeks to put any person in fear of being then and there subjected to force.

KEYNOTE

The Theft Element of the Offence

For there to be a robbery, there must be a theft; so if there is no theft, then there can be no robbery. The word 'steal' in the offence relates to the offence under s. 1 of the Theft Act 1968 and, therefore, if *any* element of theft cannot be proved, the offence of robbery will not be made out. For example, in *R v Robinson* [1977] Crim LR 173, D, who was owed £7 by P's wife, approached P, brandishing a knife. A fight followed, during which P dropped a £5 note. D picked it up and demanded the remaining £2 owed to him. Allowing D's appeal against a conviction for robbery, the Court of Appeal held that the prosecution had to prove that D was guilty of theft, and that he would not be (under the Theft Act 1968, s. 2(1)(a)) if he believed that he had a right in law to deprive P of the money, even though he knew that he was not entitled to use the knife to get it, i.e. there was no dishonesty (but **see chapter. 3.3** for blackmail).

The Robbery Time Frame

Section 8(1) requires that the force must be used or the threat made 'immediately before or at the time' of the theft. There is no guidance as to what 'immediately before' means. Clearly, if the force used or threatened is *after* the offence of theft has taken place, there will be no robbery; however, theft can be a continuing offence. This was decided in *R v Hale* (1979) 68 Cr App Rep 415, where the Court of Appeal stated that appropriation is a continuing act and whether it has finished or not is a matter for the jury to decide. From the robbery perspective, *Hale* decides that where D had assumed ownership of goods in a house, the 'time' of stealing is a continuing process. It does not end as soon as the property is picked up by the defendant and can be a continuing act so long as he/she is in the course of removing it from the premises. So, if D uses or threatens force to get away with the property (while still in the house, for example), a robbery is committed. This would not be the case if the defendant used force outside the house as there must come a time when the appropriation ends. The issue may be resolved by asking the question, 'Was D still on the job?' (*R v Atakpu* [1994] QB 69).

In Order to Do So

The use or threat of force must be 'in order' to carry out the theft. Force used in any other context means the offence is not committed, for example:

- Two men are fighting outside a pub. One man punches the other in the face and the force of the blow knocks the man out. As the injured man falls to the floor, his wallet drops out of his jacket pocket and onto the pavement. His opponent decides that he will steal the wallet. *No robbery is committed in these circumstances because the force is used for a purpose other than to steal.*

The question to ask in such circumstances is 'Why has the force been used and/or threatened?' If the answer is anything other than 'to enable the defendant to commit theft', then there is no offence of robbery.

Force

A small amount of force used in order to accomplish a theft may change that theft into a robbery. For example, in *R v Dawson* (1977) 64 Cr App R 170 the defendant and two others surrounded their victim. One of the attackers 'nudged' the victim and while he was unbalanced, another stole his wallet. In *Dawson*, the court declined to define 'force' any further than to say that juries would understand it readily enough. In line with general principles of *actus reus* (criminal conduct), the force used by the defendant must be used voluntarily. Therefore, the accidental use of force such as when a pickpocket, in the process of stealing a wallet from his victim on a train, is pushed into his victim by the train jolting on the railway line would not be a robbery.

On Any Person

The force used to accomplish a robbery need not be used against the owner or possessor of the property. For example, a gang of armed criminals use force against a security guard in order to overpower him and steal cash from the bank he is standing outside and guarding.

Use of Force on Property

Force does not actually have to be used 'on' the *person*, i.e. on the actual body of the victim. It may be used indirectly, for example on something that the victim is carrying and thereby transferring the force to the person. This was the case in *R v Clouden* [1987] Crim LR 65, where the Court of Appeal dismissed an appeal against a conviction for robbery when the defendant had wrenched the victim's shopping basket from her hand and ran off with it. However, in *P v DPP* [2012] EWHC 1657 (Admin), it was held that snatching a cigarette from the hand of the victim was incapable of amounting to robbery. Mitting J stated that 'It cannot be said that the minimum use of force required to remove a cigarette from between the fingers suffices to amount to the use of force against that person'. In this case, there was no evidence of direct physical contact between the victim and the thief.

The Fear of Force

Where only the *threat* of force is involved, the intention must be to put a person in fear for *him/herself*; an intention to put someone in fear for *another* is not enough (*R v Taylor* [1996] 10 Archbold News 2). This may seem at odds with the approach to the actual use of force in the offence of robbery (in that force *can* be used against a third party who is unconnected with the property subject to the theft).

....

EXAMPLE

A man enters a betting shop and approaches the cashier. Without saying a word, he passes a note to the cashier that simply says, 'Look to your left'. The cashier looks and sees the man's accomplice standing several feet away and pointing a knife at the back of one of the shop's customers. The customer is oblivious to the actions of the man's accomplice. The man passes a second note to the cashier that says, 'Give me the money in the till or else he gets it!' The cashier, fearing for the customer, hands over the contents of the betting shop till. This is not robbery as the cashier cannot fear force for the betting shop customer. However, whilst there is no robbery there would be an offence of blackmail (Theft Act 1968, s. 21).

Let us say that instead of handing the contents of the betting shop till over to the offender, the cashier shakes her head and refuses to hand over any money. At this point, the man signals to his accomplice who shouts at the customer 'Look here!' The customer turns around and can clearly see the knife in the hand of the accomplice pointing towards him and fears force for himself. The man speaking to the cashier repeats his demand and the cashier hands over the contents of the betting shop till. This is a robbery as the customer fears force for himself.

In a final variation of this example, let us once again say that instead of handing the contents of the betting shop till over to the offender after the note demanding money is passed to her, the cashier shakes her head and refuses to hand over any money. At this point, the man signals to his accomplice who pulls the customer's head backwards and drags the knife across the side of the customer's throat causing a small cut. The customer screams in terror and at this point the cashier concedes to the man's demand and hands over the till contents. At this point in time, a robbery is committed as force is actually being used (albeit on a third party).

General Points

Any threats to use force at some time in the future (even by a matter of minutes) would constitute an offence of blackmail. Threats to use force at some place other than the location of the offence fall into the same category. This effectively excludes threats made via the telephone in all but the most improbable of situations.

3.3 | Blackmail

3.3.1 Blackmail

OFFENCE: **Blackmail—*Theft Act 1968, s. 21***

> • Triable on indictment • 14 years' imprisonment

The Theft Act 1968, s. 21 states:

(1) A person is guilty of blackmail if, with a view to gain for himself or another or with intent to cause loss to another, he makes any unwarranted demand with menaces; and for this purpose a demand with menaces is unwarranted unless the person making it does so in the belief—

    (a) that he has reasonable grounds for making the demand; and

    (b) that the use of the menaces is a proper means of reinforcing the demand.

(2) The nature of the act or omission demanded is immaterial, and it is also immaterial whether the menaces relate to action to be taken by the person making the demand.

KEYNOTE

The phrase 'with a view to' has been held (albeit under a different criminal statute) by the Court of Appeal to be less than 'with intent to' (*R* v *Zaman* [2002] EWCA Crim 1862). In *Zaman*, the court accepted that 'with a view to' meant simply that the defendant had something in his contemplation as *something that realistically might occur*, not that he necessarily intended or even wanted it to happen. Clearly, this is a very different test from 'intent'. In the above offence, then, it appears that the state of mind needed to prove the first element is that the defendant contemplated some gain for him/herself or for another as being realistically likely to flow from his/her actions. The alternative is an 'intent' to cause loss.

There is no requirement for dishonesty or theft and the offence is aimed at the making of the demands rather than the consequences of them.

3.3.2 Meaning of Gain and Loss

Section 34 of the 1968 Act states:

(2) For the purposes of this Act—

    (a) 'gain' and 'loss' are to be construed as extending only to gain or loss in money or other property, but as extending to any such gain or loss whether temporary or permanent; and—

        (i) 'gain' includes a gain by keeping what one has, as well as a gain by getting what one has not; and

        (ii) 'loss' includes a loss by not getting what one might get, as well as a loss by parting with what one has; ...

KEYNOTE

Keeping what you already have can amount to a 'gain'. Similarly, not getting something that you might expect to get can be a 'loss'.

For example, a person makes unwarranted demands with menaces with a view to getting a sports fixture cancelled and avoiding losing money that he/she has bet on the outcome of that fixture. Here the intention of keeping what the defendant already had (the money at risk on the bet) amounts to 'gain' as defined under

---

s. 34(2). Similarly, the intention of preventing others getting what they might have got (their winnings or the club's earnings) could amount to a 'loss'.

A blackmailer need not be seeking any kind of material profit. In *R v Bevans* (1988) 87 Cr App R 64, the defendant, who was crippled with arthritis, went to a doctor, produced a gun and demanded a pain-killing morphine injection, threatening to shoot the doctor if he did not comply; this was held to be blackmail as the drug involved was a form of property.

Note that a demand for sexual favours would not constitute an offence of blackmail as those sexual favours are not 'money or other property'.

3.3.3 Criminal Conduct

The offence of blackmail is complete when the demand with menaces is made. As a result, it is extremely difficult, if not impossible, to have an offence of attempted blackmail as the defendant will either be preparing to make the demand or will have made it. It does not matter whether the demands bring about the desired consequences or not. If a demand is made by letter, the act of making it is complete when the letter is posted. The letter does not have to be received (*Treacy v DPP* [1971] AC 537).

The Court of Appeal has held that words or conduct which would not intimidate or influence anyone to respond to the demand would not be 'menaces'. As such, the term requires threats and conduct of such a nature and extent that a person of normal stability and courage might be influenced or made apprehensive so as to give in to the demands (*R v Clear* [1968] 1 QB 670).

Menaces will therefore include threats but these must be significant *to the victim*. If a threat bears a particular significance for a victim (such as being locked in the boot of a car to someone who is claustrophobic), that will be enough provided the defendant was aware of that fact. If a victim is particularly timid and the defendant knows it, that timidity may be taken into account when assessing whether or not the defendant's conduct was 'menacing' (*R v Garwood* [1987] 1 WLR 319).

In the converse situation, where an apparently serious threat fails to intimidate the victim at all, the offence is still committed. For example, if X approaches Y and threatens to break Y's legs unless Y gives X £50 but Y is unconcerned by the threat, this would still constitute blackmail as a threat to break someone's legs would influence a person of normal stability and courage.

3.3.4 Unwarranted?

If a defendant raises the issue that his/her demand was reasonable and proper, you will have to prove that he/she did not genuinely believe:

- that he/she had reasonable grounds for making the demand; and
- that the use of the particular menaces employed was not a proper means of reinforcing it.

The defendant's *belief* will be subjective and therefore could be entirely unreasonable. Whilst that is the case, such a subjective belief is subject to restriction. In *R v Harvey* (1981) 72 Cr App R 139, the defendant was convicted of kidnapping, malicious wounding, false imprisonment and blackmail. The charges arose out of an incident where he had been sold a substance that he falsely believed to be cannabis and in an attempt to get his money back he had made threats to kill, maim and rape. The defendant appealed on the basis that the judge's summing-up on the blackmail charge in relation to what were 'proper' threats was wrong. The judge had said, 'This is a matter of law. It cannot be a proper means of reinforcing the demand to make threats to commit serious offences.' The appeal was dismissed and the conviction upheld. The question of the defendant's belief should be left to the jury. The word 'proper' in s. 21(1) of the Theft Act 1968 had a wide meaning and *no act which was not believed to be lawful could be described as 'proper'*. In the present case, the judge's direction was not strictly correct, but no jury could hesitate before deciding that the defendant believed his threats to be 'proper'.

3.4 | Burglary

There are two forms of burglary—s. 9(1)(a) and s. 9(1)(b).

3.4.1 Section 9(1)(a)

OFFENCE: **Burglary—*Theft Act 1968, s. 9***

- Triable on indictment if 'ulterior offence' is so triable, or if committed in dwelling and violence used; otherwise triable either way • 14 years' imprisonment if building/part of building is dwelling • Otherwise 10 years' imprisonment on indictment
- Six months' imprisonment and/or a fine summarily

The Theft Act 1968, s. 9 states:

(1) A person is guilty of burglary if—
  (a) he enters any building or part of a building as a trespasser and with intent to commit any such offence as is mentioned in subsection (2) below; or ...
(2) The offences referred to in subsection (1)(a) above are offences of stealing anything in the building or part of a building in question, of inflicting on any person therein any grievous bodily harm and of doing unlawful damage to the building or anything therein.

KEYNOTE

Enters

The Theft Act 1968 does not define the term 'entry' and so we are left to resolve the meaning of this term by reference to case law and the decisions of the courts. The common law rule was that the insertion of any part of the body, *however small*, was sufficient to be considered an 'entry'. So where D pushed in a window pane and the forepart of his finger was observed in the building, that was enough (*R* v *Davis* (1823) Russ & Ry 499). This approach was narrowed considerably in *R* v *Collins* [1973] QB 100, where it was said that entry needed to be 'effective and substantial'. The ruling in *Collins* was rejected by the Court of Appeal in *R* v *Brown* [1985] Crim LR 212, where it was stated that the 'substantial' element was surplus to requirements and that entry need only be 'effective'. Whether an entry was 'effective' or not was for the jury to decide. So the decision of the court in *Brown* appears to be the current accepted approach to defining the term; entry must therefore be 'effective'.

An 'effective' entry does not mean that the defendant has to enter a building or part of a building to such a degree that the ulterior offence, which he/she is entering with the intention to commit (the theft, grievous bodily harm or criminal damage), can be committed (*R* v *Ryan* [1996] Crim LR 320). Nor does it mean that the defendant must get his/her whole body into the building. In *Brown*, the defendant had his feet on the ground outside the building with the upper half of his body inside the building as he searched for goods to steal; this was held to be an entry. In *Ryan*, the defendant, who had become trapped by his neck with only his head and right arm inside the window, was held to have 'entered' the building. In *Brown*, the Court of Appeal stated that it would be astounding if a smash-and-grab raider, who inserted his hand through a shop window to grab goods, was not considered to have 'entered' the building.

At common law, the insertion of an instrument would constitute entry as long as the instrument was inserted to enable the ulterior offence to take place, e.g. a hook inserted into premises to steal property or the muzzle of a gun pushed through a letterbox with a view to cause grievous bodily harm. Insertion of an instrument merely to facilitate entry, e.g. using a coat hanger to open a window lock, *would not* be entry. Although there is no recent authority on the issue, it is likely that this line of reasoning in relation to the use of instruments in burglary is still acceptable.

Entry must be deliberate and not accidental.

Ultimately, whether the defendant has entered a building or not will be a question of fact for the jury or magistrate(s).

Trespasser

To be guilty of the offence of burglary, the defendant must know or be reckless as to the fact that they are entering as a trespasser (i.e. they must know they are entering without a right by law or with express or implied permission to do so) or be reckless as to that fact. Sometimes a defendant may have general permission to enter a building or part of a building for a legitimate purpose; however, the true intention of the defendant when entering is not for that legitimate purpose but in order to steal or commit grievous bodily harm or to cause criminal damage. As these intentions invariably form no part of the permission to enter the building or part of it, any entry in such circumstances means that the defendant becomes a trespasser the moment he/she enters the building or part of the building. In such circumstances, the exceeding of the granted permission places the defendant in a position of being a trespasser from the outset.

EXAMPLE

X has a key to Y's home and has permission from Y to enter Y's home at any time and sleep in one of the bedrooms. Intending to steal from Y's home, X uses the key to get into Y's house. This means that X has committed a burglary under s. 9(1)(a) at Y's house. Y did not give X the keys to the house so that he could steal.

This example is very similar to the circumstances in *R v Jones and Smith* [1976] 1 WLR 672, where the defendant was convicted of burglary when he took two televisions from his father's home. He had a key to the premises and was free to come and go as he liked but when he entered his father's house (using the key) accompanied by a friend at 3 am and stole the television sets, he committed burglary as it was his intention to steal as such an intent voids the general permission to enter.

3.4.2 Building

The Theft Act 1968, s. 9 states:

(4) References in subsections (1) and (2) above to a building ... which is a dwelling, shall apply also to an inhabited vehicle or vessel, and shall apply to any such vehicle or vessel at times when the person having a habitation in it is not there as well as at times when he is.

KEYNOTE

Building

A building is generally considered to be a structure of a permanent nature (*Norfolk Constabulary* v *Seekings and Gould* [1986] Crim LR 167), although a substantial portable structure with most of the attributes of a building can be a 'building' for the purposes of burglary. For example, in *B & S* v *Leathley* [1979] Crim LR 314 a portable container measuring 25 ft by 7 ft by 7 ft and weighing three tons, which had occupied the same position for three years and was connected to mains electricity and which was due to remain in the same position for the foreseeable future, was considered to be a building for the purposes of burglary. An unfinished house can be a building for the purposes of burglary (*R v Manning* (1871) LR 1 CCR 338), although at what precise point a pile of building materials becomes an 'unfinished house' and therefore a building or part of a building would be a question of fact for the jury to decide. Tents and marquees are considered to fall outside the term, even if the tent is someone's home (the Criminal Law Revision Committee intended tents to be outside the protection of burglary).

The effect of s. 9(4) is to include *inhabited* vehicles and vessels (such as house boats or motor homes) within the term. A canal boat that is not inhabited is not a building as, whilst it may be capable of habitation, it is not being lived in.

3.4.3   Intentions at the Time of Entry

The intentions at the time of entry (not before or after) must be as follows:

- Stealing. This means an intention to commit theft under s. 1 (and 'thief' and 'steal' will be construed accordingly). It will not include abstracting electricity because electricity is not 'property' for the purposes of theft (*Low* v *Blease* [1975] Crim LR 513), neither will it include taking a conveyance (no intention to permanently deprive). The property which the defendant intends to steal must be in a building or part of a building.
- Inflicting grievous bodily harm. In proving an intention to commit grievous bodily harm under s. 9(1)(a), it is not necessary to prove that a wounding/grievous bodily harm offence was actually committed (*Metropolitan Police Commissioner* v *Wilson* [1984] AC 242). The offence in question in respect of a burglary under s. 9(1)(a) is of grievous bodily harm contrary to s. 18 of the Offences Against the Person Act 1861.
- Causing unlawful damage. This includes damage not only to the building but to anything in it (**see chapter 3.10**).

3.4.4   Conditional Intent

Provided the required intention can be proved, it is immaterial whether or not there is anything 'worth stealing' within the building (*R* v *Walkington* [1979] 1 WLR 1169). The same will be true if the person to whom the defendant intends to cause serious harm is not in the building or part of the building at the time (**see also para. 1.3.4**).

3.4.5   Section 9(1)(b)

OFFENCE: **Burglary—*Theft Act 1968, s. 9***
   - Triable on indictment if 'ulterior offence' is so triable, or if committed in dwelling and violence used; otherwise triable either way • 14 years' imprisonment if building/part of building is a dwelling • Otherwise 10 years' imprisonment on indictment
   - Six months' imprisonment and/or a fine summarily

The Theft Act 1968, s. 9 states:

(1) A person is guilty of burglary if—

...

    (b) having entered any building or part of a building as a trespasser he steals or attempts to steal anything in the building or that part of it or inflicts or attempts to inflict on any person therein any grievous bodily harm.

KEYNOTE

This type of burglary involves a defendant's behaviour *after* entering a building or part of a building as a trespasser.

The defendant must have entered the building or part of a building as a trespasser; it is not enough that the defendant subsequently became a trespasser in that part of the building by exceeding a condition of entry (e.g. hiding in the public area of a shop during opening hours until the shop closed). However, where a person has entered a particular building (such as a shop) lawfully and without trespassing, if he/she later moves to *another part* of the building as a trespasser, this element of the offence will be made out.

....

EXAMPLE

D enters a public house near closing time with a friend who buys him a drink from the bar. D's entry onto that part of the premises has been authorised by the implied licence extended to members of the adult public by the publican and therefore D is not a trespasser. D then goes into the lavatories to use them as such. At this point, he has entered another part of a building but again his entry is made under the implied licence to customers wishing to use the lavatories. While inside the lavatory area, D decides to hide until after closing time in order to avoid buying his friend a drink.

Once the publican has shut the pub for the night, D becomes a trespasser in the lavatory. This is because he is not supposed to be there, i.e. he has no express or implied permission or lawful right to be in the lavatory after the pub has closed. While D is a trespasser at this point in time, if he went on to steal from the lavatory he would not commit burglary because he did not enter the lavatory as a trespasser, he became one at a later stage by exceeding a condition of entry. It is essential, for an offence of burglary to occur, that the defendant has entered the building or part of a building as a trespasser. D then leaves the lavatory and walks into the lounge area. Now D has entered a part of a building as a trespasser. Having no particular intention at this point, however, D has still not committed an offence of burglary.

On seeing the gaming machines in the lounge, D decides to break into them and steal the money inside. At this point, although he has two of the required intentions for s. 9(1)(a) (an intention to steal and an intention to cause unlawful damage), those intentions were formed after his entry into the lounge. Therefore, D has not committed burglary under s. 9(1)(a). Because he has not stolen/attempted to steal or inflicted/attempted to inflict grievous bodily harm on any person therein, D has not committed burglary under s. 9(1)(b) either.

D then breaks open a gaming machine in order to steal the cash contents. At this point, he commits burglary under s. 9(1)(b). This is because, having entered a part of a building (the lounge) as a trespasser (because the pub is closed and D knows that to be the case), he attempts to steal. If he simply caused criminal damage to the machine without an intention of stealing the contents, D would not commit this offence because causing unlawful damage is only relevant to the offence under s. 9(1)(a).

....

Unlike s. 9(1)(a), there are only two further elements to the offence under s. 9(1)(b): the subsequent attempted theft of anything in the building or part of it, or the subsequent inflicting/attempted inflicting of grievous bodily harm to any person therein. The assault offences in question in respect of a burglary under s. 9(1)(b) are grievous bodily harm contrary to s. 18 or s. 20 of the Offences Against the Person Act 1861.

It has been suggested that if, having entered a building or part of a building as a trespasser, the defendant commits an offence of criminal damage, this will be an offence under s. 9(1)(b) of the Act as to damage or destroy something is also to steal it. *This is not the case.* If a person enters in such circumstances and causes criminal damage, there is little argument that such an activity would satisfy part of the offence of theft, i.e. appropriating property (see para. 3.1.5), but where is the 'dishonesty'? In addition, this would clearly be an unwarranted extension of the burglary offence under s. 9(1)(b) of the Theft Act 1968. If Parliament wanted such activity to be caught by the legislation, it would have included the offence of criminal damage within the definition of burglary under s. 9(1)(b).

3.5.1 Aggravated Burglary

OFFENCE: **Aggravated Burglary—*Theft Act 1968, s. 10***

- Triable on indictment • Life imprisonment

The Theft Act 1968, s. 10 states:

(1) A person is guilty of aggravated burglary if he commits any burglary and at the time has with him any firearm or imitation firearm, any weapon of offence, or any explosive; ...

KEYNOTE

An aggravated burglary is committed when a person commits an offence of burglary (either a s. 9(1)(a) or a s. 9(1)(b)) and at the time he/she has with him/her a WIFE.

W – Weapon of offence
I – Imitation firearm
F – Firearm
E – Explosive

At the Time

These words require consideration of the type of burglary the defendant is charged with. The moment at which a burglary under s. 9(1)(a) is committed is at the point of entry, therefore it is essential that the defendant has the WIFE with him/her when entering a building or part of a building with the intention of committing one of the trigger offences under s. 9(1)(a). If that is the case, the defendant commits aggravated burglary. The moment at which a burglary under s. 9(1)(b) is committed is when the defendant steals, inflicts grievous bodily harm on any person or attempts to do either. If the defendant has the WIFE with him/her when committing or attempting to commit either offence, an aggravated burglary is committed.

· ·

EXAMPLE

A person (X) enters the kitchen of a house as a trespasser intending to steal property. At the point of entry, X does not have any WIFE item with him, so at this point in time X has committed a s. 9(1)(a) burglary. While X is in the kitchen, the occupier of the house enters the kitchen and disturbs him. X picks up a carving knife (not intending to steal it but intending to hurt the occupier with it if necessary) and threatens the occupier with it. At this point, the carving knife becomes a weapon of offence (intended to cause injury and because of the concept of 'instant arming' (see below)) but this is not an aggravated burglary as X has not committed or attempted to commit theft or to inflict GBH. The occupier rushes towards X who stabs the occupier, inflicting GBH in the process. This is a s. 9(1)(b) burglary and at the time of its commission X has a WIFE item with him; as a result, this becomes an aggravated burglary.

· ·

Has with Him

'Has with him' is more restrictive than the term 'possession'. It will require the defendant to have some degree of *immediate control* of the item (*R* v *Pawlicki* [1992] 1 WLR 827) and will normally (but not exclusively) be the same as 'carrying' (*R* v *Klass* [1998] 1 Cr App R 453) although the defendant need not actually have the WIFE

---

item *on his/her person* to be in *immediate control* of it. It is also essential that the individual has knowledge of the presence of the WIFE item. So if a burglary is committed by a single offender who knows he/she has a bayonet in his/her coat pocket when the offence is committed, the issue of aggravated burglary is clear. However, what of the situation where two offenders commit such a burglary? Liability depends on knowledge.

EXAMPLE

X and Y decide to commit a burglary together. X is concerned about being disturbed during the burglary and decides to take a knuckleduster (a weapon of offence *per se* as it is made for causing injury) along with him when the burglary takes place; he does not tell Y about the knuckleduster. When X and Y enter the building, they intend to burgle; both commit a s. 9(1)(a) burglary. As X has a knuckleduster with him at the time, X commits an aggravated burglary. However, Y does not commit the aggravated offence because he has no knowledge of the existence of the WIFE item. If X had told Y about the knuckleduster, then Y would have the required knowledge and would be deemed to have it with him so both would be guilty under s. 10 (*R* v *Jones* [1979] CLY 411).

Therefore, if the defendant has no knowledge of the WIFE item, he/she does not commit the aggravated offence.

If several people are charged with the offence of aggravated burglary, it must be shown that one of the defendants who actually entered the building or part of a building had the weapon with him/her. The offence is not committed if the WIFE item was being carried by a person who *did not* enter the building (*R* v *Klass* [1998] 1 Cr App R 453). In *Klass*, the court considered the example of an armed getaway driver who remains in a car outside the building while his colleagues burgle a nearby house. The fact that the driver has, for example, a weapon of offence with him would not mean that an aggravated burglary, rather than a burglary, has been committed.

It is important to note that the aggravated offence is committed due to the presence of the WIFE when the s. 9(1)(a) or s. 9(1)(b) burglary is carried out. It is irrelevant that the defendant had the item with him/her for some other purpose unconnected with the burglary offence.

Instant Arming

Ordinary items can, instantaneously, change into weapons of offence; it is the intention of the person to use an item in a particular way that allows this to take place. In *R* v *Kelly* (1993) 97 Cr App R 245, the defendant entered a building using a screwdriver to facilitate entry. When he was confronted, he prodded the person confronting him in the stomach with the screwdriver. At that moment, the screwdriver instantly became a weapon of offence and the defendant was later convicted of aggravated burglary.

3.5.2   Firearm/Weapon of Offence/Explosive

The Theft Act 1968, s. 10 goes on to state:

(1) ... and for this purpose—
   (a) 'firearm' includes an airgun or pistol, and 'imitation firearm' means anything which has the appearance of being a firearm, whether capable of being discharged or not, and
   (b) 'weapon of offence' means any article made or adapted for use for causing injury to or incapacitating a person, or intended by the person having it with him for such use; and
   (c) 'explosive' means any article manufactured for the purpose of producing a practical effect by explosion, or intended by the person having it with him for that purpose.

Weapon of Offence

This includes:

- items *made* for causing injury, e.g. a bayonet or a knuckleduster (see para 3.5.1);
- items *adapted* for causing injury, e.g. a screwdriver that has been sharpened at the tip;

- items *intended* for causing injury, e.g. an ordinary cutlery knife. The cutlery knife is certainly inoffensive in everyday use but if the defendant *intends* to use it to injure, it will fall into this category;
- items *made, adapted or intended* to incapacitate a person, e.g. handcuffs, rope, CS spray and chloroform.

The defendant must not only know of the presence of the weapon but also that it is a weapon of offence (this element of the offence does not apply to weapons of offence *per se* (they are what they are) but only to items adapted or intended to cause injury/incapacitate).

Note that the defences of lawful authority or reasonable excuse in relation to the possession of an offensive weapon appear not to apply to the offence of aggravated burglary.

Imitation Firearm

This includes anything which has the appearance of being a firearm, whether capable of being discharged or not (but note that this will not include the defendant's fingers pointed at someone under a coat to resemble a firearm (*R* v *Bentham* [2005] UKHL 18)).

Firearm

This does not relate to the definition under the Firearms Act 1968. Indeed, the term is not defined other than to include airguns and air pistols.

Explosive

This would cover explosives such as TNT and items such as grenades as they are both manufactured to produce a practical effect by explosion. It also covers an item intended by the person having it with him/her for such a purpose, potentially bringing home-made devices or substances into the equation. The issue in relation to fireworks has yet to be firmly resolved by the courts, although they may well be excluded from the definition as fireworks are, by and large, manufactured to produce a pyrotechnic rather than practical effect by explosion and have been described as 'things that are made for amusement' (*Bliss* v *Lilley* (1862) 32 LJMC 3).

3.6 | Taking a Conveyance without Consent

3.6.1 Taking a Conveyance without Consent

OFFENCE: **Taking a Conveyance without the Owner's Consent—*Theft Act 1968, s. 12***

- Triable summarily • Six months' imprisonment and/or a fine

The Theft Act 1968, s. 12 states:

> Subject to subsections (5) and (6) below, a person shall be guilty of an offence if, without having the consent of the owner or other lawful authority, he takes any conveyance for his own or another's use or, knowing that any conveyance has been taken without such authority, drives it or allows himself to be carried in or on it.

KEYNOTE

Taking a conveyance without consent (usually referred to as TWOC) is a summary only offence and as such there can be no 'attempt' (Criminal Attempts Act 1981, s. 1(1) and (4)).

As a summary offence, s. 12(1) proceedings are ordinarily subject to the time limit of six months from the day when the offence was committed (s. 127 of the Magistrates' Courts Act 1980). However, this restriction has caused significant problems in cases where the analysis of forensic evidence has been needed. As a result, the Vehicles (Crime) Act 2001 extended the time limit for s. 12(1) offences. Where there is a certificate setting out the date on which sufficient evidence came to the knowledge of the person responsible for commencing the prosecution, proceedings should be commenced within six months of the date specified. This is subject to the proviso that such proceedings shall not be commenced after the end of the period of three years beginning with the day on which the offence was committed.

Once a conveyance has been 'taken', it cannot be 'taken' again by the same person before it has been recovered (*DPP v Spriggs* [1994] RTR 1). However, where the original taker abandons the conveyance, it may be 'taken' again by a further defendant and the original taker may be responsible for further offences arising out of its use before it is recovered.

The person taking the conveyance must do so intentionally, i.e. not simply by moving it accidentally (*Blayney v Knight* (1974) 60 Cr App R 269).

3.6.2 Consent of the Owner

Any 'consent' given must be true consent if the defendant is to avoid liability.

This area of the law has been subject to some rather unusual decision-making in the courts, one of which relates to consent. Consent, even if obtained by a deception, is still a valid consent. *This will be the case unless the deception is one where identity is an issue.*

....

EXAMPLE

John Smith (who does not possess a driving licence) is walking along the street when he finds a driving licence in the name of Paul Grey. Smith takes the driving licence and visits a car hire company and asks to hire a car for a day. The assistant at the reception of the car hire company asks Smith for a driving licence and Smith produces the licence he found in the street (in the name of Paul Grey). The assistant photocopies the licence and asks for the fee of £100 which Smith pays. The assistant hands over a set of car keys and Smith drives away in the car (intending to return it later that day).

The above scenario *would not* represent an offence of TWOC; this is because the assistant has handed over a set of keys to Smith and consented to Smith taking the car. The relevant deception here relates to the possession of the driving licence, *not to the name on the driving licence*. The assistant would have handed over the keys to the car if the name on the driving licence was 'Bugs Bunny'; identity is not an issue (*Whittaker* v *Campbell* [1984] QB 318).

Where consent is obtained by misrepresentation as to the purpose or destination of the journey, that misrepresentation has been held not to negate the consent given. So where D falsely represented to the owner of a car that he needed to drive it from Bedlington to Alnwick to sign a contract and was given the vehicle by the owner, he did not commit the offence when he drove it to Burnley instead. Once again, identity is not an issue when such consent is given (*R* v *Peart* [1970] 2 QB 672).

If, after a lawful purpose had been fulfilled, the defendant did not return the car but drove it off on his own business, the offence is committed as the defendant is going beyond the limits of the consent that had been given by the owner (*R* v *Phipps* (1970) 54 Cr App R 300).

3.6.3 Lawful Authority

A police officer removing a vehicle which is obstructing traffic after an accident, council workers removing a vehicle parked in contravention of parking restrictions or an agent of a finance company repossessing a vehicle would be examples of such lawful authority.

3.6.4 Takes

You must show that the conveyance was moved. It does not matter by how little the conveyance is moved but simply starting the engine is not enough (*R* v *Bogacki* [1973] QB 832) nor is hiding in a car or doing anything else in it while it is stationary. A conveyance is taken even if it is put onto another vehicle to do so (*R* v *Pearce* [1973] Crim LR 321, where a rubber dinghy was put on the roof rack of a car and taken away).

3.6.5 Conveyance

The Theft Act 1968, s. 12(7) states:

(a) 'conveyance' means any conveyance constructed or adapted for the carriage of a person or persons whether by land, water or air, except that it does not include a conveyance constructed or adapted for use only under the control of a person not carried in or on it, and 'drive' shall be construed accordingly ...

KEYNOTE

This definition includes cars, motor cycles, boats or aircraft.

The definition does not extend to hand carts or animals used as conveyances as neither are constructed or adapted for the carriage of persons.

Pedal cycles are expressly excluded by virtue of s. 12(5) of the Act. It is a separate summary offence (punishable with a fine) for a person, without having the consent of the owner or other lawful authority, to take a pedal cycle for his/her own or another's use, or to ride a pedal cycle knowing it to have been taken without such authority (Theft Act 1968, s. 12(5)). The defence under s. 12(6) also applies to pedal cycles.

3.6.6 For His Own or Another's Use

The conveyance must be taken for the taker's or someone else's ultimate use *as a conveyance*. So standing at the rear of a conveyance and pushing it around a corner to hide it as a practical joke satisfies the first part ('taking') but not the second 'for his own or another's use as a conveyance' (*R v Stokes* [1983] RTR 59). This is because although the defendants may have 'taken' the conveyance, it did not 'convey' them because they were in it or on it and, further, they did not take it so that someone could ultimately use it as such. If the practical joker pushed the car round a corner in order for a friend to then get into it and start it out of earshot and drive it to a further location, the offence would be committed at the time of pushing the car (it is being 'taken' to be used as a conveyance in the future).

When a person got into a Land Rover that was blocking his path and released the handbrake, allowing the vehicle to coast for several metres, it was held that his actions satisfied both elements (*R v Bow* (1977) 64 Cr App R 54). This is because getting into (or onto) a conveyance and moving it necessarily amounts to *taking it for use as a conveyance*, therefore the motives of the defendant in doing so are irrelevant. In the rubber dinghy example (**see para. 3.6.4**), the dinghy was ultimately going to be used as a conveyance by someone in the future.

3.6.7 Allow to be Carried

The person who commits this offence *must know* that the conveyance has been taken without the consent of the owner or other lawful authority; 'suspecting' the conveyance has been taken would not be enough. Further, the conveyance must *actually move* when the person drives it or allows him/herself to be carried in or on it (the same as the 'take' element of the offence).

3.6.8 Defences

The Theft Act 1968, s. 12(6) states:

> (6) A person does not commit an offence under this section by anything done in the belief that he has lawful authority to do it or that he would have had the owner's consent if the owner knew of his doing it and the circumstances of it.

It is essential that this belief exists at the time of the taking. It is not enough if the owner says, later, that he would have consented had he known (*R v Ambler* [1979] RTR 217). The defence is available in answer to all forms of the offence under s. 12 (including allowing to be carried).

3.6.9 Aggravated Vehicle-taking

OFFENCE: **Aggravated Vehicle-taking—*Theft Act 1968, s. 12A***

> • Triable either way • If the accident under s. 12A(2)(b) caused death 14 years' imprisonment, otherwise two years' imprisonment and/or a fine on indictment
> • Six months' imprisonment and/or a fine summarily

The Theft Act 1968, s. 12A states:

(1) Subject to subsection (3) below, a person is guilty of aggravated taking of a vehicle if—
  (a) he commits an offence under section 12(1) above (in this section referred to as a 'basic offence') in relation to a mechanically propelled vehicle; and
  (b) it is proved that, at any time after the vehicle was unlawfully taken (whether by him or another) and before it was recovered, the vehicle was driven, or injury or damage was caused, in one or more of the circumstances set out in paragraphs (a) to (d) of subsection (2) below.
(2) The circumstances referred to in subsection (1)(b) above are—
  (a) that the vehicle was driven dangerously on a road or other public place;
  (b) that, owing to the driving of the vehicle, an accident occurred by which injury was caused to any person;
  (c) that, owing to the driving of the vehicle, an accident occurred by which damage was caused to any property, other than the vehicle;
  (d) that damage was caused to the vehicle.

KEYNOTE

In addition to the above sentences, where a person is convicted of aggravated vehicle-taking, disqualification from driving (for a minimum of 12 months) is obligatory, endorsement of licence is obligatory and the penalty points which may be imposed for the offence are 3 to 11. The fact that the person concerned did not drive the vehicle at any particular time or at all is not a special reason to avoid obligatory disqualification (Road Traffic Offenders Act 1988, s. 34).

Before this offence is made out, there must first of all be an offence under s. 12(1) which includes an offence of 'being carried', and the conveyance involved must be a 'mechanically propelled vehicle'.

You need only prove that *one* of the consequential factors occurred before the vehicle was recovered (*Dawes* v *DPP* [1995] 1 Cr App R 65); namely that, between the vehicle being taken and its being recovered:

- it was driven dangerously on a road/public place;
- owing to the driving of it, an accident occurred by which injury was caused to anyone or damage was caused to any other property; or
- damage was caused to it.

'Dangerous driving' will require the same proof as the substantive offence.

A vehicle will be 'recovered' once it has been restored to its owner or other lawful possession or custody (s. 12A(8)). This would include occasions where a vehicle has come into the possession of the police.

The word 'accident' for the purposes of the offence of aggravated vehicle-taking is not defined by the Theft Act 1968. Therefore a broad interpretation of the word is taken rather than any restricted form (such as that under s. 170 of the Road Traffic Act 1988). So, for example, if a s. 12(1) offence was committed in relation to a mechanically propelled vehicle and, after it was taken and before it was recovered, there was an 'accident' where the only person injured was the driver of the mechanically propelled vehicle, this would amount to an offence of aggravated vehicle-taking.

In *R* v *Hughes* [2013] 2 All ER 613, the Supreme Court held that in cases of causing death by driving when uninsured (s. 3ZB of the Road Traffic Act 1988) the defendant must be proved to have done something more than merely drive his/her vehicle on the road so that it was there to be involved in a fatal accident. It must be proved that the defendant did or omitted to do something else that contributed in a more than minimal way to the death. There must, in other words, be something more than mere 'but for' causation. The same approach is taken in respect of aggravated vehicle-taking. On a charge of aggravated vehicle-taking, the Crown must prove some act or omission in the control of the mechanically propelled vehicle which involves

---

some element of fault on the part of the driver, whether amounting to careless or inconsiderate driving or not, and which contributed in some more than minimal way to the outcome. In *R* v *Taylor* [2016] 1 WLR 500, the defendant was charged with taking a truck without consent, and that 'owing to the driving of the vehicle, an accident occurred by which [death] was caused'. But although the truck was involved in a fatal collision with a scooter while the defendant was driving it, the fault was *entirely that of the scooter rider*, so the defendant could not be said to have 'caused' the latter's death. There must be a direct causal connection between the driving and the death, injury and/or damage.

Damage to the vehicle does not include damage caused by breaking into it in order to commit the 'basic offence'. This is because damage caused at this point will be caused before the vehicle has been 'taken' and so, at that stage, the 'basic offence' will not have been carried out.

3.6.9.1 Defence to Aggravated Vehicle-taking

The Theft Act 1968, s. 12A states:

(3) A person is not guilty of an offence under this section if he proves that, as regards any such proven driving, injury or damage as is referred to in subsection (1)(b) above, either—

    (a) the driving, accident or damage referred to in subsection (2) above occurred before he committed the basic offence; or

    (b) he was neither in nor on nor in the immediate vicinity of the vehicle when that driving, accident or damage occurred.

KEYNOTE

'Immediate vicinity' is not defined but will be a question of fact for the jury/magistrate(s) to determine in each case.

3.7 Handling Stolen Goods

3.7.1 Handling Stolen Goods

OFFENCE: **Handling Stolen Goods—*Theft Act 1968, s. 22***
- Triable either way • 14 years' imprisonment on indictment
- Six months' imprisonment and/or a fine summarily

The Theft Act 1968, s. 22 states:

> (1) A person handles stolen goods if (otherwise than in the course of the stealing) knowing or believing them to be stolen goods he dishonestly receives the goods, or dishonestly undertakes or assists in their retention, removal, disposal or realisation by or for the benefit of another person, or if he arranges to do so.

KEYNOTE

Handling can only be committed otherwise than in the course of stealing. The 'stealing' referred to is the time whereby the original goods became 'stolen' in the first place.

If 'goods' are not 'stolen goods', there is no handling. Whether they are so stolen is a question of fact for a jury or magistrate(s). If the goods have yet to be stolen, s. 22 would not apply and the offence of conspiracy should be considered (*R* v *Park* (1988) 87 Cr App R 164).

It is sensible, before examining the activities associated with this offence, to consider what is being 'handled'—what are 'goods' and 'stolen goods'?

3.7.2 Meaning of 'Goods' and 'Stolen Goods'

Goods

The Theft Act 1968, s. 34(2)(b) states:

> 'Goods', except insofar as the context otherwise requires, includes money and every other description of property except land, and includes things severed from the land by stealing.

KEYNOTE

A 'thing in action' (**see para. 3.1.6**) is 'goods' because it falls within 'every other description of property'.

Stolen Goods

The Theft Act 1968, s. 24 states:

> (1) The provisions of this Act relating to goods which have been stolen shall apply whether the stealing occurred in England or Wales or elsewhere, and whether it occurred before or after the commencement of this Act, provided that the stealing (if not an offence under this Act) amounted to an offence where and at the time when the goods were stolen; and references to stolen goods shall be construed accordingly.

(2) For purposes of those provisions references to stolen goods shall include, in addition to the goods originally stolen and parts of them (whether in their original state or not),—

    (a) any other goods which directly or indirectly represent or have at any time represented the stolen goods in the hands of the thief as being the proceeds of any disposal or realisation of the whole or part of the goods stolen or of goods representing the stolen goods; and

    (b) any other goods which directly or indirectly represent or have at any time represented the stolen goods in the hands of a handler of the stolen goods or any part of them as being the proceeds of any disposal or realisation of the whole or part of the stolen goods handled by him or of goods so representing them.

(3) But no goods shall be regarded as having continued to be stolen goods after they have been restored to the person from whom they were stolen or to other lawful possession or custody, or after that person and any other person claiming through him have otherwise ceased as regards those goods to have any right to restitution in respect of the theft.

(4) For purposes of the provisions of this Act relating to goods which have been stolen (including subsections (1) to (3) above) goods obtained in England or Wales or elsewhere either by blackmail or subject to subsection (5) below, by fraud (within the meaning of the Fraud Act 2006) shall be regarded as stolen; and 'steal', 'theft' and 'thief' shall be construed accordingly.

(5) Subsection (1) above applies in relation to goods obtained by fraud as if—

    (a) the reference to the commencement of this Act were a reference to the commencement of the Fraud Act 2006, and

    (b) the reference to an offence under this Act were a reference to an offence under section 1 of that Act.

The Theft Act 1968, s. 24A states:

(8) References to stolen goods include money which is dishonestly withdrawn from an account to which a wrongful credit has been made, but only to the extent that the money derives from the credit.

KEYNOTE

Goods Stolen Outside England and Wales

Under s. 24(1), a person can still be convicted of handling if the goods were stolen outside England and Wales but only if the goods were taken under circumstances which amounted to an offence in the other country.

Proceeds of Stolen Property

Under s. 24(2), goods will be classed as stolen only if they are the property which was originally stolen or if they had at some time represented the *proceeds* of that property in the hands of the thief or a 'handler'.

Therefore if a mobile phone is stolen by X, and sold to Y (an unsuspecting party who is neither the thief nor a 'handler') who then part-exchanges it for a new one at a high street retailer, the first mobile phone will be 'stolen' goods (the original stolen property is 'stolen goods') but the new mobile phone in the hands of Y will not be 'stolen goods'. If Z (the first person buying the original stolen mobile phone) *knew* or *believed* that it was stolen, the mobile phone will be treated as stolen goods in the hands of Z.

Stolen Goods Ceasing to be 'Stolen'

Under s. 24(3), once goods have been restored to lawful possession they cease to be stolen. This situation does not cause problems when police officers recover stolen property and then wait for it to be collected by a handler (*Houghton* v *Smith* [1975] AC 476) as the Criminal Attempts Act 1981 and the common law rulings on 'impossibility' (see chapter 1.3) mean that a defendant could be dealt with in a variety of ways:

- Theft—collecting the property will be an 'appropriation'.
- Handling—an *arrangement* to come and collect stolen goods will probably have been made while they were still 'stolen'.
- Criminal attempt—the person collecting the goods has gone beyond merely preparing to handle them.

What are Stolen Goods?

Goods gained through offences such as robbery or burglary will be 'stolen' as theft is an intrinsic element of both offences—such goods are 'stolen'.

Section 24(4) states that apart from the goods described in subss. (1) to (3) (stolen goods, proceeds of goods in the hands of the thief and the 'handler' etc.), goods obtained by fraud and blackmail are included in the definition of 'stolen goods'. The reference to fraud is to the general offence of fraud under s. 1 of the Fraud Act 2006 (s. 24(5)).

Section 24A(8) provides that if a wrongful credit has been made to an account and money is dishonestly withdrawn from that account (money which derives from the wrongful credit), then that money is 'stolen goods'.

Property Outside the Scope of s. 21 or s. 24A(8)?

If the property in question appears to represent the proceeds of an offence that falls outside the scope of s. 24 or s. 24A(8), it may be possible to consider charges under the 'money laundering' provisions.

No Conviction Required for the 'Origin' Offence

There is no need to prove that the thief, blackmailer etc. has been convicted of the primary offence before prosecuting the alleged handler, neither is it always necessary to *identify* who that person was.

3.7.3 Handling—*Mens Rea* and *Actus Reus*

Mens Rea

The defendant must *know* or *believe* the goods to be stolen. Turning a blind eye to the facts 'can be capable, depending on the circumstances, of providing evidence going to prove knowledge or belief' (*Martin Edward Pace & Simon Peter Rogers* v *R* [2014] EWCA Crim 186). Suspicion will not be enough (*R* v *Griffiths* (1974) 60 Cr App R 14).

Knowledge or belief that the goods were stolen is not enough; the goods must be handled dishonestly. Here, dishonesty will be determined as per the decision in *Barlow Clowes* and *Royal Brunei Airlines* (**see para. 3.1.4**).

Actus Reus

The offence of handling stolen goods has many facets. Therefore to charge a defendant without specifying a particular form of handling is not bad for duplicity (*R* v *Nicklin* [1977] 1 WLR 403). However, the offence can be divided for practical purposes into two parts:

- *receiving/arranging to receive* stolen goods, in which case the defendant acts for his/her own benefit; and
- *assisting/acting for the benefit of another* person, in which case that assistance to another or benefit of another must be proved.

KEYNOTE

Receiving

This form of the handling offence is committed at the point the 'stolen goods' are received. However, receiving does not require the physical reception of goods and can extend to exercising control over them. Things in action, such as bank credits from a stolen cheque, can be 'received'.

'Arranging to receive' would cover circumstances which do not go far enough to constitute an attempt; that is, actions which *are* merely preparatory to the receiving of stolen goods may satisfy the elements under s. 22 even though they would not meet the criteria under the Criminal Attempts Act 1981.

Assisting/Acting for Another's Benefit

Assisting or acting for the benefit of another can be committed by misleading police officers during a search (*R* v *Kanwar* [1982] 1 WLR 845).

Disposing of the stolen goods or assisting in their disposal or realisation usually involves physically moving them or converting them into a different form (*R* v *Forsyth* [1997] 2 Cr App R 299).

If the only person 'benefiting' from the defendant's actions is the defendant, this element of the offence will not be made out (*R* v *Bloxham* [1983] 1 AC 109). In *Bloxham*, the appellant bought and part-paid for a car which he subsequently discovered to be stolen. He then sold the car at a slight loss and was convicted of handling in respect of this sale, the allegation being that he 'realised' the car for the benefit of the buyer. The House of Lords reversed this decision holding that the mischief at which the Act was aimed was the actions of those who knowingly received from the thief or facilitated the disposal of stolen goods. A purchaser of goods purchased in good faith who sells the goods after discovering they have been stolen *does not come within the ambit of the section*, even if the transaction could be described as a disposal or realisation for the benefit of the person to whom they sell it. The phrase 'by or for the benefit of another' limits the reach of the law to the situation where the handler acts *on another's behalf* in removing, disposing, realising or retaining goods (the possession of the stolen property would now be caught by s. 329 of the Proceeds of Crime Act 2002 (see para. 3.9.6) and the sale of the vehicle by fraud by false representation (s. 2 of the Fraud Act 2006, see para. 3.8.4). Similarly, if the only 'other' person to benefit is a co-accused on the same charge, the offence will not be made out (*R* v *Gingell* [2000] 1 Cr App R 88).

3.7.4 Power to Search for Stolen Goods

The Theft Act 1968, s. 26 states:

(1) If it is made to appear by information on oath before a justice of the peace that there is reasonable cause to believe that any person has in his custody or possession or on his premises any stolen goods, the justice may grant a warrant to search for and seize the same; but no warrant to search for stolen goods shall be addressed to a person other than a constable except under the authority of an enactment expressly so providing.

(2) ...

(3) Where under this section a person is authorised to search premises for stolen goods, he may enter and search the premises accordingly, and may seize any goods he believes to be stolen goods.

(4) ...

(5) This section is to be construed in accordance with section 24 of this Act; and in subsection (2) above the references to handling stolen goods shall include any corresponding offence committed before the commencement of this Act.

KEYNOTE

Section 26 provides a general power to search for and seize stolen goods, whether identified in the search warrant or not, and magistrates are entitled to act on material provided by the police that gives rise to a reasonable belief that stolen goods will be found (*R Cruickshank Ltd* v *Chief Constable of Kent Constabulary* [2002] EWCA Civ 1840).

3.7.5 Evidence and Procedure on a Charge of Handling

Section 27 of the Theft Act 1968 allows for the admissibility of previous misconduct and states:

(3) Where a person is being proceeded against for handling stolen goods (but not for any offence other than handling stolen goods), then at any stage of the proceedings, if evidence has been

given of his having or arranging to have in his possession the goods the subject of the charge, or of his undertaking or assisting in, or arranging to undertake or assist in, their retention, removal, disposal or realisation, the following evidence shall be admissible for the purpose of proving that he knew or believed the goods to be stolen goods—

(a) evidence that he has had in his possession, or has undertaken or assisted in the retention, removal, disposal or realisation of, stolen goods from any theft taking place not earlier than 12 months before the offence charged; and

(b) (provided that seven days' notice in writing has been given to him of the intention to prove the conviction) evidence that he has within the five years preceding the date of the offence charged been convicted of theft or of handling stolen goods.

KEYNOTE

This provision applies to all forms of handling (*R* v *Ball* [1983] 1 WLR 801) but it can only be used where handling is the *only offence* involved in the proceedings.

The evidence is admissible solely for the purpose of proving the defendant knew or believed the goods to be stolen goods and not any other purpose (*R* v *Duffus* (1994) 158 JP 224).

It should be noted that the provisions under s. 27(3)(a) and (b) are *separate*—for example, evidence could be introduced regarding a defendant's conviction for theft three years preceding the offence charged (under s. 27(3)(b)). There is no need for the element under s. 27(3)(a) to be present *as well as* that theft conviction.

3.7.6 Proof that Goods were Stolen

The Theft Act 1968, s. 27 states:

(4) In any proceedings for the theft of anything in the course of transmission (whether by post or otherwise), or for handling stolen goods from such a theft, a statutory declaration made by any person that he dispatched or received or failed to receive any goods or postal packet, or that any goods or postal packet when dispatched or received by him were in a particular state or condition, shall be admissible as evidence of the facts stated in the declaration, subject to the following conditions—

(a) a statutory declaration shall only be admissible where and to the extent to which oral evidence to the like effect would have been admissible in the proceedings; and

(b) a statutory declaration shall only be admissible if at least seven days before the hearing or trial a copy of it has been given to the person charged, and he has not, at least three days before the hearing or trial or within such further time as the court may in special circumstances allow, given the prosecutor written notice requiring the attendance at the hearing or trial of the person making the declaration.

KEYNOTE

Section 27(4) allows for evidence to be admitted proving that goods 'in the course of transmission' have been stolen. They allow for a statutory declaration by the person dispatching or receiving goods or postal packets as to when and where they were dispatched and when or if they arrived and, in each case, their state or condition (e.g. if they had been opened or interfered with). The declaration will only be admissible in circumstances where an oral statement would have been admissible *and* if a copy has been served on the defendant at least seven days before the hearing and he/she has not, within three days of the hearing, served written notice on the prosecutor requiring the attendance of the person making the declaration.

This section is to be construed in accordance with s. 24 generally (s. 27(5)).

3.8 Fraud

3.8.1 Introduction

The Fraud Act 2006 provides a general offence of fraud which can be committed in three ways (by false representation, by failing to disclose information and by abuse of position). It also deals with offences of obtaining services dishonestly and possessing, making and supplying articles for use in fraud. In addition to the offence of fraud, there is a series of closely related offences which deal with the falsification of documents or other 'instruments'.

3.8.2 Fraud

OFFENCE: **Fraud—*Fraud Act 2006, s. 1***
- Triable either way • 10 years' imprisonment and/or a fine on indictment
- Six months' imprisonment and/or a fine summarily

The Fraud Act 2006, s. 1 states:

(1) A person is guilty of fraud if he is in breach of any of the sections listed in subsection (2) (which provide for different ways of committing the offence).
(2) The sections are—
  (a) section 2 (fraud by false representation),
  (b) section 3 (fraud by failing to disclose information), and
  (c) section 4 (fraud by abuse of position).

KEYNOTE

The essence of these fraud offences is in the *conduct and ulterior intent* of the defendant. This means that a defendant's unsuccessful 'attempt' to commit the offence of fraud may amount to the commission of the substantive offence, effectively excluding the possibility of an offence under the Criminal Attempts Act 1981.

3.8.3 Gain and Loss

Fraud offences under ss. 2, 3 and 4 are all committed when the defendant carries out the *actus reus* of the offence intending to 'make a gain for himself or another' and/or 'to cause loss to another'. As the 'gain' and 'loss' elements are essential to these offences, it is useful to examine their meaning before looking at the specific offences.

The Fraud Act 2006, s. 5 states:

(1) The references to gain and loss in sections 2 to 4 are to be read in accordance with this section.
(2) 'Gain' and 'loss'—
  (a) extend only to gain and loss in money or other property;
  (b) include any such gain or loss whether temporary or permanent;
  and 'property' means any property whether real or personal (including things in action and other intangible property).
(3) 'Gain' includes a gain by keeping what one has, as well as getting what one does not have.
(4) 'Loss' includes a loss by not getting what one might get, as well as a loss by parting with what one has.

3.8.4 Fraud by False Representation

The Fraud Act 2006, s. 2 states:

(1) A person is in breach of this section if he—
    (a) dishonestly makes a false representation, and
    (b) intends, by making the representation—
        (i) to make a gain for himself or another, or
        (ii) to cause loss to another or to expose another to the risk of loss.
(2) A representation is false if—
    (a) it is untrue or misleading, and
    (b) the person making it knows that it is, or might be, untrue or misleading.
(3) 'Representation' means any representation as to fact or law, including a representation as to the state of mind of—
    (a) the person making the representation, or
    (b) any other person.
(4) A representation may be express or implied.
(5) For the purposes of this section a representation may be regarded as made if it (or anything implying it) is submitted in any form to any system or device designed to receive, convey or respond to communications (with or without human intervention).

KEYNOTE

Dishonestly

'Dishonestly' in s. 2(1)(a) refers to the test of dishonesty as per the decision in *Barlow Clowes* and *Royal Brunei Airlines* (see para. 3.1.4). The same test applies to ss. 3 and 4 of the Act.

Representation

A representation is false if it is untrue or misleading *and* the person making it knows this is or knows this might be the case; an untrue statement made in the honest belief that it is in fact true, would not suffice. The words 'or might be' involve a subjective belief of the person making the representation. Where a defendant makes a false representation knowing that it is false or might be, the offence of fraud is complete.

The representation may be express or implied and can be communicated in words or conduct. There is no limitation on the way in which the representation must be expressed, so it could be written, spoken or posted on a website.

A representation may be implied by conduct. For example, a person dishonestly misusing a credit card to pay for items hands the card to a cashier without saying a word. By handing the card to the cashier, the person is falsely representing that he/she has the authority to use it for that transaction. It is immaterial whether the cashier accepting the card for payment is deceived by the representation as the cashier's state of mind plays no part in the commission of the offence.

Any representation made must be one as to fact or law, so a broken promise is not in itself a false representation. However, a statement may be false if it misrepresents the current intentions or state of mind of the person making it or anyone else. For example, D visits V's house and tells V that he needs emergency work carried out on his roof. D states that he is in a position to do the work immediately but only if V pays him £1,000 there and then. V gives D the money and D then leaves without carrying out the work; the truth of the matter was that D had never intended to carry out the work. Such a 'promise' by D would amount to an offence as it involved a false representation, i.e. he never intended to keep the promise.

A representation may be *proved* by inference. Where an elderly person has paid D vastly more for a job or product (such as gardening work) than it was worth, it may be open to a court or jury to *infer* that D must dishonestly have misrepresented the value of that job or product, even if there is no direct evidence of any such misrepresentation (*R* v *Greig* [2010] EWCA Crim 1183). When an unidentified imposter presented himself to take a driving theory test in D's name, it could be inferred that D was complicit in any false representations made by that person with a view to gaining a pass certificate in his name (*Idrees* v *DPP* [2011] EWHC 624 (Admin)).

The offence is complete the moment the false representation is made. The representation need never be heard or communicated to the recipient and, if carried out by post, would be complete when the letter is posted (*Treacy* v *DPP* [1971] AC 537).

Phishing

The offence is committed by someone who engages in 'phishing' (the practice of sending out emails in bulk, usually purporting to represent a well-known brand in the hope of sending victims to a bogus website that tricks them into disclosing bank account details).

Machines

The offence of fraud applies to cases where the representation is made to a machine (for example, where a person enters a number into a 'chip and PIN' machine) (s. 2(5)).

3.8.5 Fraud by Failing to Disclose

The Fraud Act 2006, s. 3 states:

A person is in breach of this section if he—

(a) dishonestly fails to disclose to another person information which he is under a legal duty to disclose, and

(b) intends, by failing to disclose the information—

(i) to make a gain for himself or another, or

(ii) to cause loss to another or to expose another to a risk of loss.

KEYNOTE

The term 'legal duty' has not been defined but will include duties under oral contracts as well as written contracts. The Law Commission's *Report on Fraud* dealt with the concept of legal duty and stated that duties might arise:

- from statute;
- where the transaction is one of the utmost good faith;
- from the express or implied terms of a contract;
- from the custom of a particular trade or market; or
- from the existence of a fiduciary relationship between parties.

The legal duty to disclose information will exist if:

- the defendant's actions give the victim a cause in action for damages; or
- if the law gives the victim the right to set aside any change in his/her legal position to which he/she may have consented as a result of the non-disclosure.

A fiduciary relationship is one relating to the responsibility of looking after someone else's money in a correct way. Examples of such behaviour would include solicitors failing to share vital information with a client in the context of their work relationship, in order to carry out a fraud upon that client, or if a person intentionally failed to disclose information relating to a heart condition when making an application for life insurance. Where recipients of benefits dishonestly fail to disclose income etc. that they are legally required to disclose, fraud by failing to disclose is an appropriate charge (*R* v *El-Mashta* [2010] EWCA Crim 2595).

3.8.6 Fraud by Abuse of Position

The Fraud Act 2006, s. 4 states:

(1) A person is in breach of this section if he—
   (a) occupies a position in which he is expected to safeguard, or not to act against, the financial interests of another person,
   (b) dishonestly abuses that position, and
   (c) intends, by means of the abuse of that position—
      (i) to make a gain for himself or another, or
      (ii) to cause loss to another or to expose another to a risk of loss.
(2) A person may be regarded as having abused his position even though his conduct consisted of an omission rather than an act.

KEYNOTE

The 'position' that the defendant occupies may be the result of an assortment of relationships. The Law Commission explained the meaning of 'position' at para. 7.38 of the *Report on Fraud*:

> The necessary relationship will be present between trustee and beneficiary, director and company, professional person and client, agent and principle, employee and employer, or between partners. It may arise otherwise, for example within a family, or in the context of voluntary work, or in any context where the parties are not at arm's length.

The term 'abuse' is not defined by the Act.

Liability for the offence could develop from a wide range of conduct, for example:

- an employee of a software company uses his position to clone software products with the intention of selling the products on;
- an estate agent values a house belonging to an elderly person at an artificially low price and then arranges for the agent's brother to purchase the house;
- a person who is employed to care for a disabled person and has access to that person's bank account, abuses that position by transferring funds to invest in a high-risk business venture of his own.

The offence can also be committed by omission, for example:

- an employee fails to take up the chance of a crucial contract in order that an associate or rival company can take it up instead of and at the expense of the employer.

3.8.7 Possession or Control of Articles for Use in Frauds

OFFENCE: **Possession or Control of Articles for Use in Frauds—*Fraud Act 2006, s. 6***
- Triable either way • Five years' imprisonment and/or a fine on indictment
- Six months' imprisonment and/or a fine summarily

The Fraud Act 2006, s. 6 states:

(1) A person is guilty of an offence if he has in his possession or under his control any article for use in the course of or in connection with any fraud.

KEYNOTE

What is an 'Article'?

The Fraud Act 2006, s. 8 states:

(1) For the purposes of—
   (a) sections 6 and 7, and
   (b) the provisions listed in subsection (2), so far as they relate to articles for use in the course of or in connection with fraud, 'article' includes any program or data held in electronic form.

---

(2) The provisions are—

    (a) section 1(7)(b) of the Police and Criminal Evidence Act 1984 (c 60),

    (b) ...

    (c) ...

An 'article' can be anything whatsoever. For the purposes of ss. 6 and 7 of the Act, an 'article' includes any program or data held in electronic form. Examples of cases where electronic programs or data could be used in fraud are:

- a computer program that generates credit card numbers;
- a computer template that can be used for producing blank utility bills;
- a computer file that contains lists of other people's credit card details.

The offence under s. 6 can be committed *anywhere at all*, including the home of the defendant. It is committed when the defendant has articles in his/her possession and also when the defendant has them in his/her control, so the defendant may be some distance away from the articles and still commit the offence. The s. 6 offence applies to 'any fraud' which will therefore include *all fraud offences* under the 2006 Act. However, the offence is only committed in respect of *future* offences and not offences that have already taken place (*R v Sakalauskas* [2014] 1 All ER 1231). The offence can be committed if possession or control is to enable *another to* commit an offence of fraud.

3.8.8   Making or Supplying Articles for Use in Frauds

OFFENCE: **Making or Supplying Articles for Use in Frauds—*Fraud Act 2006, s. 7***

      • Triable either way • 10 years' imprisonment on indictment and/or a fine

      • Six months' imprisonment and/or a fine summarily

The Fraud Act 2006, s. 7 states:

(1) A person is guilty of an offence if he makes, adapts, supplies or offers to supply any article—

    (a) knowing that it is designed or adapted for use in the course of or in connection with fraud, or

    (b) intending it to be used to commit, or assist in the commission of, fraud.

KEYNOTE

For the definition of an 'article', see para. 3.8.7.

This offence ensures that any activity in respect of the making, supplying etc. of any 'article' for use in fraud offences is an offence. Making an 'offer to supply' would not require the defendant to be in possession of the 'article'. Examples of such behaviour include:

- a person makes a viewing card for a satellite TV system, enabling him/her to view all satellite channels for free;
- the same person then offers to sell similar cards to work colleagues although he/she has only made the one prototype card and does not actually have further cards to sell;
- a number of the person's work colleagues express an interest in buying the cards, so the person makes a dozen more cards and then actually supplies them to those work colleagues.

3.8.9   Obtaining Services Dishonestly

OFFENCE: **Obtaining Services Dishonestly—*Fraud Act 2006, s. 11***

      • Triable either way • Five years' imprisonment and/or a fine on indictment

      • Six months' imprisonment and/or a fine summarily

The Fraud Act 2006, s. 11 states:

(1) A person is guilty of an offence under this section if he obtains services for himself or another—
   (a) by a dishonest act, and
   (b) in breach of subsection (2).
(2) A person obtains services in breach of this subsection if—
   (a) they are made available on the basis that payment has been, is being or will be made for or in respect of them,
   (b) he obtains them without any payment having been made for or in respect of them or without payment having been made in full, and
   (c) when he obtains them, he knows—
      (i) that they are being made available on the basis described in paragraph (a), or
      (ii) that they might be, but intends that payment will not be made, or will not be made in full.

KEYNOTE

Unlike the other Fraud Act 2006 offences, the offence under s. 11 is not a conduct crime; it is a *result crime* and requires the *actual obtaining* of the service. However, the offence does not require a fraudulent representation or deception. Someone would commit this offence if, intending to avoid payment, he/she slipped into a concert hall to watch a concert without paying for the privilege. The offence can be committed where the defendant intends to avoid payment or payment in full but the defendant must know that the services are made available on the basis that they are chargeable, i.e. services provided for free *are not covered* by the offence.

If D sneaks aboard a lorry or a freight train and obtains a free ride, D would commit no offence under s. 11 because the haulage company or freight train operator does not provide such rides, even for payment.

The terms 'service' and 'obtaining' are not defined by the Act. The fact that 'service' is not defined means that in the situation where a person obtains the 'services' of a prostitute (an illegal service) without intending to pay him/her, the s. 11 offence can be committed.

3.8.10   False Accounting

OFFENCE: **False Accounting—*Theft Act 1968, s. 17***
   • Triable either way   • Seven years' imprisonment on indictment
   • Six months' imprisonment and/or a fine summarily

The Theft Act 1968, s. 17 states:

(1) Where a person dishonestly, with a view to gain for himself or another or with intent to cause loss to another,—
   (a) destroys, defaces, conceals or falsifies any account or any record or document made or required for any accounting purpose; or
   (b) in furnishing information for any purpose produces or makes use of any account, or any such record or document as aforesaid, which to his knowledge is or may be misleading, false or deceptive in a material particular;
   he shall [commit an offence].
(2) For purposes of this section a person who makes or concurs in making in an account or other document an entry which is or may be misleading, false or deceptive in a material particular, or who omits or concurs in omitting a material particular from an account or other document, is to be treated as falsifying the account or document.

KEYNOTE

This section creates two offences: destroying, defacing etc. accounts and documents; and using false or misleading accounts or documents in furnishing information. A record or account need not necessarily be a document. In *Edwards* v *Toombs* [1983] Crim LR 43, it was held that a turnstile meter at a soccer stadium was a record and thus within the scope of the section.

An offence under s. 17 can be committed by omission as well as by an act. Failing to make an entry in an accounts book, altering a till receipt or supplying an auditor with records that are incomplete may, if accompanied by the other ingredients, amount to an offence.

There is no requirement to prove an intention permanently to deprive but there is a need to show dishonesty as per the decision in *Barlow Clowes* and *Royal Brunei Airlines* (see para. 3.1.4). The requirement as to gain and loss is the same as for blackmail (see chapter 3.3).

The misleading, false or deceptive nature of the information furnished under s. 17(1)(b) must be 'material' to the defendant's overall purpose, i.e. the ultimate gaining or causing of loss. Such an interpretation means that the defendant's furnishing of information need not relate directly to an accounting process and could be satisfied by lying about the status of a potential finance customer (*R v Mallett* [1978] 1 WLR 820).

Where the documents falsified are not intrinsically 'accounting' forms, such as insurance claim forms filled out by policyholders, you must show that those forms are treated for accounting purposes by the victim (*R v Sundhers* [1998] Crim LR 497). An application for a mortgage or a loan to a commercial institution is a document required for an accounting purpose, the rationale being that applications for a mortgage or a loan to commercial institutions will, if successful, lead to the opening of an account which will show as credits in favour of the borrower, funds received from the borrower and as debits paid out by the lender to, or on behalf of, the borrower (*R v O and H* [2010] EWCA Crim 2233).

3.9 | Proceeds of Crime

3.9.1 Proceeds of Crime Act 2002

The offences and powers under the Proceeds of Crime Act 2002 are connected with day-to-day criminality and are relevant to all police officers. This chapter provides an overview of the three principal offences relating to 'money laundering' created by s. 327 (concealing criminal property), s. 328 (arrangements in relation to criminal property) and s. 329 (acquisition, use and possession of criminal property) of the Act. To begin with, we examine the concepts of 'criminal conduct' and 'criminal property'.

3.9.2 Criminal Conduct

The Proceeds of Crime Act 2002, s. 340 states:

> (2) Criminal conduct is conduct which—
>   (a) constitutes an offence in any part of the United Kingdom, or
>   (b) would constitute an offence in any part of the United Kingdom if it occurred there.

Section 340(4) states that it is immaterial:

- who carried out the criminal conduct;
- who benefited from it;
- whether the conduct occurred before or after the passing of the Act.

So criminal conduct not only includes the behaviour of the defendant but also of any other person. Effectively, this states that *any offence*, committed by *any person*, *anywhere* at all and at *any time* is 'criminal conduct'. As a consequence of s. 340, a conviction can be obtained under the Proceeds of Crime Act even if the prosecution cannot specify the offence or offences that gave rise to the proceeds or identify the person(s) responsible for the offence(s).

3.9.3 Criminal Property

The Proceeds of Crime Act 2002, s. 340 states:

> (3) Property is criminal property if—
>   (a) it constitutes a person's benefit from criminal conduct or it represents such a benefit (in whole or in part and whether directly or indirectly) and,
>   (b) the alleged offender knows or suspects that it constitutes or represents such a benefit.

KEYNOTE

The offences under ss. 327, 328 and 329 are often referred to as 'money laundering'. Note that the definition of 'property' *does not just relate to money*. Section 340(9) of the Act defines property as *all* property *wherever* situated and includes:

- money;
- all forms of property, real or personal, heritable or movable; and
- things in action and other intangible or incorporeal property.

(Incorporeal property relates to property or an asset that does not have value in material form, such as a right or a patent.)

The *mens rea* relating to criminal property and therefore to all three offences is knowing or *suspecting*. Dishonesty is not required. In *R v Da Silva* [2006] EWCA Crim 1654, the Court of Appeal upheld the conviction, concluding that the word 'suspect' meant that the defendant had to think that there was a possibility, which was more than fanciful, that the relevant facts existed. A vague feeling of unease would not suffice. The fact that suspicion alone will suffice means that proving such offences is remarkably less burdensome for the prosecution than the potential alternative to such offences, a charge of handling stolen goods where the defendant must be proved to know or believe that goods are stolen goods.

3.9.4 Concealing Criminal Property

OFFENCE: **Concealing Criminal Property—*Proceeds of Crime Act 2002, s. 327***
- Triable either way • 14 years' imprisonment on indictment and/or a fine
- Six months' imprisonment and/or a fine summarily

The Proceeds of Crime Act 2002, s. 327 states:

(1) A person commits an offence if he—
  (a) conceals criminal property;
  (b) disguises criminal property;
  (c) converts criminal property;
  (d) transfers criminal property;
  (e) removes criminal property from England and Wales and Scotland or from Northern Ireland.
(2) But a person does not commit such an offence if—
  (a) he makes an authorised disclosure under section 338 and (if the disclosure is made before he does the act mentioned in subsection (1)) he has the appropriate consent;
  (b) he intended to make such a disclosure but had a reasonable excuse for not doing so;
  (c) the act he does is done in carrying out a function he has relating to the enforcement of any provision of this Act or of any other enactment relating to criminal conduct or benefit from criminal conduct.
(3) Concealing or disguising criminal property includes concealing or disguising its nature, source, location, disposition, movement or ownership or any rights with respect to it.

KEYNOTE

There is an overlap between offences of concealing criminal property and handling stolen goods. However, whereas handling only occurs 'otherwise than in the course of stealing' and 'by or for the benefit of another', the offence under s. 327 can potentially be committed *during the commission of an offence* and *for the benefit of the thief*. On a literal reading of s. 327, a thief who conceals, disguises or sells property that he/she has just stolen may thereby commit offences under that section because the definition of criminal property applies to the laundering of an offender's own proceeds of crime as well as those of someone else.

The offence can be committed in a variety of ways. In *R v Fazal* [2010] 1 WLR 694, D allowed his bank account to be used by a friend to launder money, and it was held that he was guilty of converting criminal property (contrary to s. 327(1)(c)) whenever such monies were deposited in, retained in or withdrawn from the account.

In *R v Pace* [2014] EWCA Crim 186, the Court of Appeal rejected the argument that on a charge of attempting to commit the offence under s. 327(1)(c), it would be sufficient for the prosecution to prove that D merely suspected the property in question to be criminal property. Suspicion of this kind suffices for the substantive offence (as it does for all such offences under ss. 327 to 329) but it cannot, said the court, suffice for an attempt.

Section 327(2) creates several defences to charges under s. 327.

3.9.5 Arrangements in Relation to Criminal Property

OFFENCE: **Arrangements in relation to Criminal Property—***Proceeds of Crime Act 2002, s. 328*

- Triable either way • 14 years' imprisonment on indictment and/or a fine
- Six months' imprisonment and/or a fine summarily

The Proceeds of Crime Act 2002, s. 328 states:

(1) A person commits an offence if he enters into or becomes concerned in an arrangement which he knows or suspects facilitates (by whatever means) the acquisition, retention, use or control of criminal property by or on behalf of another person.

KEYNOTE

This offence will often be apt for the prosecution of those who launder on behalf of others. This could catch persons who work in financial or credit institutions, accountants etc., who in the course of their work facilitate money laundering by or on behalf of other persons and also family members (husband/wife, partner etc.). The natural and ordinary meaning of s. 328(1) was that the arrangement to which it referred must be one which related to property which was criminal property at the time when the arrangement began to operate on it. To say that it extended to property which was originally legitimate but became criminal only as a result of carrying out the arrangement was to stretch the language of the section beyond its proper limits (*R v Geary (Michael)* [2010] EWCA Crim 1925).

Section 328 includes the same defences against committing the offence as those included in s. 327(2).

3.9.6 Acquisition, Use and Possession of Criminal Property

OFFENCE: **Acquisition, Use and Possession of Criminal Property—***Proceeds of Crime Act 2002, s. 329*

- Triable either way • 14 years' imprisonment on indictment and/or a fine
- Six months' imprisonment and/or a fine summarily

The Proceeds of Crime Act 2002, s. 329 states:

(1) A person commits an offence if he—
    (a) acquires criminal property;
    (b) uses criminal property;
    (c) has possession of criminal property.

KEYNOTE

A thief who uses or retains possession of property that he/she has just stolen (this being criminal property as defined in s. 340) must therefore be guilty of an offence under s. 329(1)(b) or (c), the maximum penalty for which is twice that for basic theft. It does not follow that such a charge would be appropriate.

This offence is committed where a person knows or suspects that the property which is acquired etc., constitutes or represents his/her own or another's benefit from criminal conduct; the same defences against committing the offence apply as in s. 327.

An additional defence exists under s. 329(2)(c) which states that a person will not commit the offence if he/she acquired or used or had possession of the property for adequate consideration (e.g. being paid a proper market price of £3,000 to fix a roof). The effect of the defence in s. 329(2)(c) is that persons, such as trades people, who are paid for ordinary consumable goods and services in money that comes from crime are not under any obligation to question the source of the money. However, the defence is not available to

---

a defendant who provides goods or services knowing or suspecting that those goods or services will help a person *to actually carry out criminal conduct.*

The coincidence between an offence of handling stolen goods and those described from the Proceeds of Crime Act 2002 might provide a dilemma as to which offence to charge. In such a situation, CPS guidance states that if it is possible to charge money laundering or handling stolen goods, then money laundering may be more appropriate if 'either a defendant has possessed criminal proceeds in large amounts or in lesser amounts, but repeatedly and where assets are laundered for profit'. However, a money laundering charge should only be considered where proceeds are more than *de minimis* (about minimal things) in any circumstances where the defendant who is charged with the underlying offence has done more than simply consume the proceeds of crime.

3.10 Criminal Damage

3.10.1 Introduction

The prevalence of offences of criminal damage is well documented and damage in all forms has a harmful effect on the environment, the community and the economy.

3.10.2 Simple Damage

OFFENCE: **Simple Damage—*Criminal Damage Act 1971, s. 1(1)***
- Triable either way • 10 years' imprisonment on indictment
- Six months' imprisonment and/or a fine summarily

OFFENCE: **Racially or Religiously Aggravated—*Crime and Disorder Act 1998, s. 30(1)***
- Triable either way • 14 years' imprisonment and/or a fine on indictment
- Six months' imprisonment and/or a fine summarily

The Criminal Damage Act 1971, s. 1 states:

> (1) A person who without lawful excuse destroys or damages any property belonging to another intending to destroy or damage any such property or being reckless as to whether any such property would be destroyed or damaged shall be guilty of an offence.

KEYNOTE

Although triable either way, if the value of the property destroyed or the damage done is less than £5,000, the offence is to be tried summarily (Magistrates' Courts Act 1980, s. 22). If the damage in such a case was caused by fire (arson), this rule will not apply.

The fact that the substantive offence is, by virtue of the value of the damage caused, triable only summarily does not make simple damage a 'summary offence' for all other purposes. If it did, you could only be found guilty of attempting to commit criminal damage if the value of the intended damage was more than £5,000 (because the Criminal Attempts Act 1981 does not extend to summary offences) (see chapter 1.3). Therefore, where a defendant tried to damage a bus shelter in a way that would have cost far less than £5,000 to repair, his argument that he had only attempted what was in fact a 'summary offence' was dismissed by the Divisional Court (*R* v *Bristol Magistrates' Court, ex parte E* [1999] 1 WLR 390).

The Theft Act 1968 states that where the property in question belonged to D's spouse or civil partner, a prosecution for unlawful damage may only be instituted against D by or with the consent of the DPP (s. 30(4)). This restriction does not apply to other persons charged with committing the offence jointly with D; nor does it apply when the parties are separated by judicial decree or order or under no obligation to cohabit (s. 30(4)(a)).

Where the damage caused is less than £300, the offence can be dealt with by way of fixed penalty notice.

If the offence involves only the painting or writing on, or the soiling, marking or other defacing of, any property by whatever means, the power to issue a graffiti notice may apply (under s. 43 of the Anti-social Behaviour Act 2003).

The racially or religiously aggravated form of this offence is triable either way irrespective of the cost of the damage.

3.10.2.1 Destroy or Damage

The terms 'destroy' or 'damage' are not defined. 'Destroying' property suggests that it has been rendered useless but there is no need to prove that 'damage' to property is in any way permanent or irreparable.

Whether an article has been damaged will be a question of fact for each court to determine on the evidence before it. Defacing of a pavement by an artist using only water-soluble paint (*Hardman* v *Chief Constable of Avon and Somerset* [1986] Crim LR 330) and graffiti smeared in mud can amount to damage, even though it is easily washed off (*Roe* v *Kingerlee* [1986] Crim LR 735). In *R* v *Fiak* [2005] EWCA Crim 2381, the defendant had been arrested and placed in a police cell which he flooded by stuffing a blanket down the cell lavatory and repeatedly flushing. The defendant argued that there was no evidence that the blanket or the cell had been 'damaged'; the water had been clean and both the blanket and the cell could be used again when dry. The Court of Appeal disagreed and held that while the effect of the defendant's actions in relation to the blanket and the cell was remediable, the reality was that the blanket could not be used until it had been dried and the flooded cell was out of action until the water had been cleared. Therefore both had sustained damage for the purposes of the Act. This case illustrates that putting property temporarily out of use, even for a short time and in circumstances where it will revert to its former state of its own accord, may fall within the definition of 'damage'.

3.10.2.2 Property

Property is defined in the 1971 Act by s. 10 which states:

(1) In this Act 'property' means property of a tangible nature, whether real or personal, including money and—
   (a) including wild creatures which have been tamed or are ordinarily kept in captivity and any other wild creatures or their carcasses if, but only if, they have been reduced into possession ... or are in the course of being reduced into possession; but
   (b) not including mushrooms growing wild on any land or flowers, fruit or foliage of a plant growing wild on any land.

KEYNOTE

This definition is similar to the definition of 'property' for the purposes of theft (see chapter 3.1) but there are some differences, e.g. 'real' property (i.e. land and things attached to it) can be damaged even though it cannot be stolen, whereas intangible property (such as copyright) can be stolen but cannot be damaged. Trampling flower beds, digging up cricket pitches, chopping down trees in a private garden and pulling up genetically modified crops could potentially amount to criminal damage.

Pets or farm animals are property for the purposes of this Act. Cases of horses being mutilated would, in addition to the offence of 'cruelty' itself, amount to criminal damage.

3.10.2.3 Belonging to Another

Section 10 states:

(2) Property shall be treated for the purposes of this Act as belonging to any person—
   (a) having the custody or control of it;
   (b) having in it any proprietary right or interest (not being an equitable interest arising only from an agreement to transfer or grant an interest); or
   (c) having a charge on it.

3.10.2.4 Lawful Excuse

Section 5 of the Criminal Damage Act 1971 provides for two occasions where a defendant may have a 'lawful excuse'. These can be remembered as 'permission' (s. 5(2)(a)) and 'protection' (s. 5(2)(b)). Both involve the belief of the defendant.

3.10.2.5 Permission

A person shall be treated as having lawful excuse under s. 5(2):

(a) if at the time of the act or acts alleged to constitute the offence he believed that the person or persons whom he believed to be entitled to consent to the destruction of or damage to the property in question had so consented, or would have so consented to it if he or they had known of the destruction or damage and its circumstances ...

EXAMPLE

An elderly motorist asks you to help him get his keys out of his partner's car as he had locked them inside. You tell the motorist that the car may be damaged as a result of your efforts but the motorist tells you that is alright and to go ahead. Section 5(2)(a) would provide a statutory defence to any later charge of criminal damage by the owner. The main element here would be that you believed you had the consent of the motorist (who is someone you believed to be entitled to consent to that damage) to damage the vehicle in these circumstances.

3.10.2.6 Protection

A person shall be treated as having lawful excuse under s. 5(2):

(b) if he destroyed or damaged or threatened to destroy or damage the property in question or, in the case of a charge of an offence under section 3 above, intended to use or cause or permit the use of something to destroy or damage it, in order to protect property belonging to himself or another or a right or interest in property which was or which he believed to be vested in himself or another, and at the time of the act or acts alleged to constitute the offence he believed—
(i) that the property, right or interest was in immediate need of protection; and
(ii) that the means of protection adopted or proposed to be adopted were or would be reasonable having regard to all the circumstances.

KEYNOTE

A 'right or interest in property' includes any right or privilege in or over land, whether created by grant, licence or otherwise (s. 5(4)).

Key features of this defence are the immediacy of the need to protect the property and the reasonableness of the means of protection adopted. This defence has attracted the most attention of the courts in cases involving demonstrators claiming to be acting in furtherance of their political beliefs. In a case involving 'peace campaigners', it was held that the threat presented by a possible nuclear attack in the future did not excuse the carrying of a hacksaw for cutting through the perimeter fence of an airbase (*R* v *Hill* (1989) 89 Cr App R 74).

This defence also applies to the offence of having articles for causing damage (see para. 3.10.6).

Belief

It is immaterial whether a 'belief' was justified as long as it was honestly held (s. 5(3)). Although this test is supposed to be an *objective* one, the evidence will be based largely on what was going through a defendant's mind at the time. In *Jaggard* v *Dickinson* [1981] QB 527, the defendant had broken a window to get into a house. Being drunk at the time, she had got the wrong house but the court accepted that her belief (that it was the right house and that the owner would have consented) had been honestly held, and that it did not matter whether that belief was brought about by intoxication, stupidity, forgetfulness or inattention. That is not to say however, that *any* honestly held belief will suffice. An example of someone claiming, unsuccessfully, a defence under both s. 5(2)(a) and (b) can be seen in *Blake* v *DPP* [1993] Crim LR 586. There the defendant was a vicar who wished to protest against Great Britain's involvement in the Gulf War. In order to mark his disapproval, the defendant wrote a quotation from the Bible in ink on a pillar in front of the Houses of Parliament. He claimed:

- he was carrying out God's instructions and had a lawful excuse based on his belief that God was the person entitled to consent to such damage and that God had in fact consented or would have done so (s. 5(2)(a)); and
- he had damaged the property as a reasonable means of protecting other property located in the Gulf from being damaged by warfare (s. 5(2)(b)).

The Divisional Court did not accept either proposition, holding that in the first case a belief in God's consent was not a 'lawful excuse' and, in the second case, that the defendant's conduct was too remote from any immediate need to protect property in the Gulf States. The test in relation to the defendant's belief appears then to be largely subjective (i.e. what was/was not going on in the defendant's head at the time) but with an objective element in that the judge/magistrate(s) must decide whether, on the facts as believed by the defendant, his/her acts were capable of protecting property.

Taking a different tack, peace campaigners in *R* v *Jones (Margaret)* [2004] EWCA Crim 1981 argued that their fear of the consequences of war in Iraq, which they claimed to be illegal, prompted them to conspire to cause damage at an airbase and that such fear amounted both to duress (as to which, **see para. 1.4.3**) and lawful excuse under s. 5(2)(b). The Court of Appeal held that a jury would be entitled to consider some of the subjective beliefs of the defendants in determining the reasonableness of their actions.

In *R* v *Kelleher* [2003] EWCA Crim 2846, a demonstrator at the Guildhall Gallery knocked the head off a statue of Baroness Thatcher claiming that he acted in fear for his son's future which had been placed in jeopardy by the joint actions of the US and UK governments, and for which Baroness Thatcher was partly responsible. His appeal against conviction brought under s. 5(2)(b) failed.

Section 5(5) allows for other general defences (**see chapter 1.4**) at criminal law to apply in addition to those listed under s. 5.

It is not an offence to damage your own property unless there are aggravating circumstances. This is the case even if the intention in doing so is to carry out some further offence such as a fraudulent insurance claim (*R* v *Denton* [1981] 1 WLR 1446).

3.10.3 Aggravated Damage

OFFENCE: **Aggravated Damage—*Criminal Damage Act 1971, s. 1(2)***
- Triable on indictment • Life imprisonment

The Criminal Damage Act 1971, s. 1 states:

(2) A person who without lawful excuse destroys or damages any property, whether belonging to himself or another—

(a) intending to destroy or damage any property or being reckless as to whether any property would be destroyed or damaged; and

(b) intending by the destruction or damage to endanger the life of another or being reckless as to whether the life of another would be thereby endangered;

shall be guilty of an offence.

KEYNOTE

The aggravating factor in this offence is the intention of endangering life or recklessness as to whether life is endangered. The life endangered must be that of another (not the life of the defendant).

The reference to 'without lawful excuse' does not refer to the statutory defences under s. 5, which are not applicable here, but to general excuses such as self-defence or the prevention of crime.

You must show that the defendant either intended or was reckless as to the following consequences:

- the damage being caused; and
- the risk of endangering the life of another.

Where a defendant fired a gun through a window pane, he was clearly reckless as to the damage his actions would cause. However, the court felt that even though two people were standing behind the window and they were obviously put in some danger, it was the missile which endangered their lives and not the result of the damage. Therefore the court held that the defendant was not guilty of this particular offence (*R* v *Steer* [1988] AC 111). In *R* v *Webster and Warwick* [1995] 2 All ER 168, damaging the windscreen of a car or ramming a car was held to be capable of endangering life as a result of the damage.

It is the damage which the defendant intended or was reckless about which is relevant, rather than the actual damage that happens to be caused (this could turn out to be minor damage). In *R* v *Dudley* [1989] Crim LR 57, trivial damage was caused but the conviction was upheld since the defendant created a risk of much more serious damage which was capable of endangering life.

3.10.4 Arson

OFFENCE: **Arson—*Criminal Damage Act 1971, s. 1(3)***

- Triable either way • Life imprisonment on indictment • Where life is not endangered six months' imprisonment and/or a fine summarily

The Criminal Damage Act 1971, s. 1 states:

(3) An offence committed under this section by destroying or damaging property by fire shall be charged as arson.

KEYNOTE

When 'simple' or 'aggravated' damage is caused and the destruction or damage is caused by fire, the offence will be charged as 'arson'. The restrictions on the mode of trial for simple damage under s. 1(1) do not apply to cases of arson. Aggravated damage caused by arson is triable only on indictment and carries a maximum penalty of life imprisonment.

Criminal liability for either gross negligence or unlawful act manslaughter may arise from an offence of arson. In *R* v *Willoughby* [2004] EWCA Crim 3365, the defendant enlisted the help of another man in burning down a public house on which the defendant owed money. Having poured petrol around the inside of the building, the defendant set fire to it, killing the other person and injuring himself in the process. The defendant was convicted of both arson and manslaughter. The Court of Appeal held that by convicting the defendant of arson, the jury had showed that they were sure that he (on his own or jointly) had deliberately spread petrol by being reckless or with the intention that the premises would be destroyed. Provided that such conduct had been the cause of the death, the jury were therefore also bound to convict the defendant of manslaughter.

3.10.5 Threats to Destroy or Damage Property

OFFENCE: **Threats to Destroy or Damage Property—*Criminal Damage Act 1971, s. 2***

- Triable either way • 10 years' imprisonment on indictment
- Six months' imprisonment and/or a fine summarily

The Criminal Damage Act 1971, s. 2 states:

A person who without lawful excuse makes to another a threat, intending that that other would fear it would be carried out,—

(a) to destroy or damage any property belonging to that other or a third person; or

(b) to destroy or damage his own property in a way which he knows is likely to endanger the life of that other or a third person;

shall be guilty of an offence.

KEYNOTE

The key element is the defendant's intention that the person receiving the threat fears it will be carried out. So there is no need to show that the other person actually feared or believed that the threat would be carried out or that the defendant intended to carry it out; nor does it matter whether the threat was even capable of being carried out.

....

EXAMPLE

If a person, enraged by a neighbour's inconsiderate parking, shouts over the garden wall, '*When you've gone to bed I'm going to pour paint stripper over your car!*', the offence will be complete, provided you can show that the person making the threat intended the neighbour to fear it would be carried out.

....

Where a group of protestors staged a protest in the pods of the London Eye and threatened to set fire to themselves, their conduct was held to be capable of amounting to a threat to damage the property of another (as a consequence of setting themselves on fire) contrary to s. 2(a) (*R v Cakmak* [2002] EWCA Crim 500).

In *Cakmak*, the court held that the gist of the offence under s. 2(a) was the making of a threat and that any such threat had to be considered objectively.

Whether:

- there has been such a threat to another;
- the threat amounted to 'a threat to damage or destroy property';
- the defendant had the necessary state of mind at the time;

are all questions of fact for the jury to decide (per *Cakmak*).

While not usually enough to amount to the substantive offence under s. 2, a person's conduct which represents a threat to damage property may be relevant in triggering police action. In *Clements v DPP* [2005] EWHC 1279 (Admin), several protestors left a public highway, crossed a ditch and approached the perimeter fence of an RAF base. The defendant ignored a police warning to return to the road and the police attempted to restrain the protestors in order to prevent criminal damage to the fence. After a scuffle, the defendant was subsequently convicted of assaulting a police constable in the execution of his duty (as to which, **see para. 2.7.17**). The key issues at trial were whether the police officer had acted in the course of his duty and the extent to which the officer had reasonable grounds to believe that the defendant would cause criminal damage. The Divisional Court held that the officer had to consider the whole event in context and at the relevant time a political protest was ensuing the defendant had deliberately left the public highway and refused to return to it; he had no legitimate reason to approach the fence; and it was plainly reasonable for the police officer to believe that he could cause criminal damage to the fence.

The defence to criminal damage under s. 5(2) ('permission'—**see para. 3.10.2.5**) *does not* apply where the accused knows that the threatened damage is likely to endanger life.

3.10.6 Having Articles with Intent to Destroy or Damage Property

OFFENCE: **Having Articles with Intent to Destroy or Damage Property—***Criminal Damage Act 1971, s. 3*

- Triable either way • 10 years' imprisonment on indictment
- Six months' imprisonment and/or a fine summarily

The Criminal Damage Act 1971, s. 3 states:

A person who has anything in his custody or under his control intending without lawful excuse to use it or cause or permit another to use it—

(a) to destroy or damage any property belonging to some other person; or

(b) to destroy or damage his own or the user's property in a way which he knows is likely to endanger the life of some other person;

shall be guilty of an offence.

KEYNOTE

This offence covers anything which a defendant has 'in his custody or under his control', a broader term than 'possession'. This offence applies to graffiti 'artists' carrying aerosols and advertisers with adhesives for sticking illicit posters.

The key element is intention. This time the required intention is that the 'thing' be used to cause criminal damage to another's property or to the defendant's own property in a way which the defendant knows is likely to endanger the life of another.

Just as it is not an offence to damage your own property in a way which endangers no one else, neither is it an offence to have something which you intend to use to cause damage under those circumstances.

....

EXAMPLE

If the owner of a 10-metre high conifer decides to trim the top with a chainsaw and a ladder, putting himself, but no one else, at considerable risk, he commits no offence either by causing the damage or by having the chainsaw. If he intends to fell the tree in a way which he realises will endanger the life of his neighbours or passers-by, then he may commit the offence under s. 3(b).

....

Such articles are 'prohibited' articles for the purposes of the power of stop and search under s. 1 of the Police and Criminal Evidence Act 1984.

A conditional intent (an intent to use something to cause criminal damage if the need arises) will be enough (*R* v *Buckingham* (1976) 63 Cr App R 159).

There is a statutory power to apply to a magistrate for a search warrant under s. 6 of the Criminal Damage Act 1971 for anything that could be used or is intended to be used to destroy or damage property.

The Criminal Damage Act 1971, s. 6 states:

(1) If it is made to appear by information on oath before a justice of the peace that there is reasonable cause to believe that any person has in his custody or under his control or on his premises anything which there is reasonable cause to believe has been used or is intended for use without lawful excuse—

  (a) to destroy or damage property belonging to another; or

  (b) to destroy or damage any property in a way likely to endanger the life of another,

  the justice may grant a warrant authorising any constable to search for and seize that thing.

(2) A constable who is authorised under this section to search premises for anything, may enter (if need be by force) and search the premises accordingly and may seize anything which he believes to have been used or to be intended to be used as aforesaid.

3.10.7 Contamination or Interference with Goods

OFFENCE: **Contamination or Interference with Goods—*Public Order Act 1986, s. 38(1)***

- Triable either way • 10 years' imprisonment and/or a fine on indictment
- Six months' imprisonment and/or a fine summarily

The Public Order Act 1986, s. 38 states:

(1) It is an offence for a person, with the intention—
   (a) of causing public alarm or anxiety, or
   (b) of causing injury to members of the public consuming or using the goods, or
   (c) of causing economic loss to any person by reason of the goods being shunned by members of the public, or
   (d) of causing economic loss to any person by reason of steps taken to avoid any such alarm or anxiety, injury or loss,

   to contaminate or interfere with goods, or make it appear that goods have been contaminated or interfered with, or to place goods which have been contaminated or interfered with, or which appear to have been contaminated or interfered with in a place where goods of that description are consumed, used, sold or otherwise supplied.

(2) It is also an offence for a person, with any such intention as is mentioned in paragraph (a), (c) or (d) of subsection (1), to threaten that he or another will do, or to claim that he or another has done, any of the acts mentioned in that subsection.

(3) It is an offence for a person to be in possession of any of the following articles with a view to the commission of an offence under subsection (1)—
   (a) materials to be used for contaminating or interfering with goods or making it appear that goods have been contaminated or interfered with, or
   (b) goods which have been contaminated or interfered with, or which appear to have been contaminated or interfered with.

(4) ...

(5) In this section 'goods' includes substances whether natural or manufactured and whether or not incorporated in or mixed with other goods.

(6) The reference in subsection (2) to a person claiming that certain acts have been committed does not include a person who in good faith reports or warns that such acts have been, or appear to have been, committed.

KEYNOTE

'Goods' includes 'natural' goods (e.g. fruit and vegetables) or 'manufactured' goods (e.g. shampoo or disinfectant).

Section 38 creates two offences. The first involves the contamination of, interference with or placing of goods with the intentions set out at s. 38(1)(a)–(d). An example of this offence is the case of *R v Cruikshank* [2001] EWCA Crim 98, where the offender pleaded guilty to contaminating food in a supermarket by inserting pins, needles and nails into various items. He persisted in this behaviour for three months and some minor injuries were incurred by customers who bought the contaminated products.

Section 38(2) involves the making of threats to do, or the claiming to have done, any of the acts in s. 38(1) with any of the intentions set out at s. 38(1)(a), (c) or (d). It is difficult to see how a threat or claim made with the intention of causing injury to the public (s. 38(1)(b)) would not also amount to an intention to cause them alarm or anxiety but the legislation clearly excludes it.

Section 38(6) allows for people to communicate warnings in good faith where such acts appear to have been committed.

Where threats to contaminate goods are made, there may also be grounds for charging blackmail. A good example of threats to commit this offence and the overlap with blackmail is the case of *R v Witchelo* (1992) 13 Cr App R (S) 371, where the defendant, a police officer, was sentenced to 13 years' imprisonment after obtaining £32,000 from food producers to whom he had sent threatening letters.

PART FOUR

Sexual Offences

4.1 | Sexual Offences

4.1.1 Introduction

The majority of offences in this chapter are dealt with under the Sexual Offences Act 2003. The Act provides measures such as the presumptions about consent that will be made by a court under certain circumstances. Apart from the offence of rape (under ss. 1 and 5 of the Act), the offences are 'gender neutral', i.e. they can be committed by a male or a female.

It is important to note that there is an overlap between many of the offences, for example a mentally disordered person could be raped under s. 1 (because of his/her lack of ability to give true consent) or subjected to sexual activity contrary to s. 30 (due to an inability to refuse). In all circumstances, it is essential that the most appropriate option is chosen.

4.1.2 Anonymity

The Sexual Offences (Amendment) Act 1992, s. 1 states:

(1) Where an allegation has been made that an offence to which this Act applies has been committed against a person, no matter relating to that person shall during that person's lifetime be included in any publication, if it is likely to lead members of the public to identify that person as the person against whom the offence is alleged to have been committed.

(2) Where a person is accused of an offence to which this Act applies, no matter likely to lead members of the public to identify a person as the person against whom the offence is alleged to have been committed ('the complainant') shall during the complainant's lifetime, be included in any publication.

(3) ...

(3A) The matters relating to a person in relation to which the restrictions imposed by subsection (1) or (2) apply (if their inclusion in any publication is likely to have the result mentioned in that subsection) include in particular—

(a) the person's name,

(b) the person's address,

(c) the identity of any school or other educational establishment attended by the person,

(d) the identity of any place of work, and

(e) any still or moving picture of the person.

KEYNOTE

Offences Covered

The Sexual Offences (Amendment) Act 1992 provides anonymity to a victim/complainant of most sexual offences. It applies to almost all sexual offences under part 1 of the Sexual Offences Act 2003 (such as rape, assault by penetration, sexual assault by touching etc.) as well as attempts and conspiracy to commit such acts. It also applies to aiding, abetting, counselling or procuring any of these offences. It *does not* apply to the offences dealing with sex with an adult relative (ss 64 and 65) and sexual activity in a public lavatory (s. 71).

Publication

Includes any speech, writing, relevant programme or other communication in whatever form, which is addressed to the public at large or any section of the public (and for this purpose every relevant programme shall be taken to be so addressed), but does not include an indictment or other document prepared for use in particular legal proceedings (s. 6(1)).

Lifetime Anonymity

The alleged victim/complainant is entitled to anonymity *throughout their lifetime.* Once an allegation of one of the offences in question has been made, nothing may be published which is likely to lead members of the public to identify the alleged victim/complainant. The protection under s. 1(2) applies from the time someone is accused for that person's lifetime even if proceedings are later abandoned.

Lifting Restrictions

Under s. 3 of the Act, the prohibition on publicity may be lifted by order of the court if either:

- publicity is required by the accused so that witnesses will come forward and the conduct of the defence is likely to be seriously prejudiced if the direction is not given; or
- the trial judge is satisfied that imposition of the prohibition imposes a substantial and unreasonable restriction on the reporting of the proceedings and it is in the public interest to relax the restriction.

4.2 | Rape

4.2.1 Rape

OFFENCE: **Rape—*Sexual Offences Act 2003, s. 1***

> • Triable on indictment • Life imprisonment

The Sexual Offences Act 2003, s. 1 states:

(1) A person (A) commits an offence if—
   (a) he intentionally penetrates the vagina, anus or mouth of another person (B) with his penis,
   (b) B does not consent to the penetration, and
   (c) A does not reasonably believe that B consents.
(2) Whether a belief is reasonable is to be determined having regard to all the circumstances, including any steps A has taken to ascertain whether B consents.

KEYNOTE

Rape is an offence that can *only* be committed via the use of the penis. Therefore rape (as a principal offender) can only be committed by a man, although a woman who encourages or assists a man to penetrate another person with his penis, not reasonably believing the other person is consenting, may be convicted of aiding and abetting rape (*R* v *Cogan* [1976] QB 217). It can be committed if the defendant penetrates the vagina, anus or mouth of the victim with the penis. 'Vagina' is taken to include the vulva (s. 79(9)). In respect of penetration of the vagina, it is not necessary to show that the hymen was ruptured.

You must show that the victim did not in fact consent at the time and that the defendant did not reasonably believe that he/she consented. The wording is supported by the further provision that whether or not the defendant's belief is reasonable will be determined having regard to all the circumstances (s. 1(2)). Section 1(2) does not positively require an accused to have taken steps to ascertain whether the complainant consents. However, this is something a jury will consider when considering the reasonableness of his belief. More steps are likely to be expected where there is no established relationship.

4.2.2 Criminal Conduct

To prove rape, you must show that the defendant intentionally penetrated the vagina, mouth or anus of the victim with his penis. Penetration is a continuing act from entry to withdrawal (s. 79(2)). The 'continuing' nature of this act is of importance when considering the issue of consent and the statutory presumptions under ss. 75 and 76. While it is not necessary to prove ejaculation (indeed, it is entirely irrelevant to the offence), the presence of semen or sperm may be important in proving the elements of a sexual offence. References to a part of the body (for example, penis, vagina) will include references to a body part which has been surgically constructed, particularly if it is through gender reassignment (s. 79(3)). The offence thus protects transsexuals. It also means, however, that a person who has a surgically constructed penis can commit the offence of rape.

4.2.3 Consent

The Sexual Offences Act 2003, s. 74 states:

> For the purpose of this Part, a person consents if he agrees by choice, and has the freedom and capacity to make that choice.

The issue of consent is a question of fact although legislation has included some specific situations which allow presumptions and conclusions to be made regarding a lack of consent.

Any consent given must be 'true' consent, not simply a *submission* induced by fear or fraud. Therefore, if the person does not have any real choice in the matter, or the choice is not a genuine exercise of free will, then he/she has not 'consented'.

An example of how 'true' consent operates is the case involving PC Stephen Mitchell who committed a number of sexual offences against vulnerable women over a period of years. On one occasion, Mitchell drove one of his victims to a dirt track and told her that if she did not do as he said, he would ensure her children were taken away from her for good, and then raped her. Any 'consent' given by the victim could not be 'true' because her choice to participate in the act of sexual intercourse would not be by the genuine exercise of free will (a 'gun to the head'-type scenario).

'Capacity' is an integral part of the definition of consent. A valid consent can only be given by a person who has the capacity to give it. The Sexual Offences Act 2003 does not define 'capacity'. Common law principles that developed under the old law suggest that complainants will not have had the capacity to agree by choice where their understanding and knowledge were so limited that they were not in a position to decide whether or not to agree (*R* v *Howard* (1965) 1 WLR 13). Some people are not capable of giving the required consent—these are addressed in further sections of this chapter.

Even if freely given, consent may still be withdrawn at any time. Once the 'passive' party to sexual penetration withdraws consent, any continued activity (for example, penetration in rape: *R* v *Cooper* [1994] Crim LR 531) can amount to a sexual offence provided all the other ingredients are present.

In *R* v *B* [2006] EWCA Crim 2945, the Court of Appeal stated that whether an individual had a sexual disease or condition, such as being HIV-positive, was not an issue as far as consent was concerned. The case related to a man who was alleged to have raped a woman after they had met outside a nightclub. When arrested, the man informed the custody officer that he was HIV-positive, a fact he had not disclosed to the victim prior to sexual intercourse. At the original trial, the judge directed that this non-disclosure was relevant to the issue of consent. On appeal, the court stated that this was not the case and that the consent issue for a jury to consider was whether or not the victim consented to sexual intercourse, not whether she consented to sexual intercourse with a person suffering from a sexually transmitted disease. However, in *R* v *McNally* [2013] EWCA Crim 1051 (**see para. 4.2.4**), the Court of Appeal observed that *B* was not an authority that HIV status *could not* vitiate consent. *B* left the issue open and HIV status *could* vitiate consent if, for example, the complainant had been positively assured that the accused was not HIV-positive.

KEYNOTE

So the situation with a person who is *HIV-positive* and *is aware* of his condition, is as follows:

- if the accused makes no mention of his condition, this will not be rape (*R* v *B*). However, it may constitute an offence under the Offences Against the Person Act 1861 (s. 20 or s. 18) (*R* v *Dica* and *R* v *Konzani*, at **para. 2.7.14**);
- if the accused positively assures the complainant that he is not HIV-positive, this *could* constitute rape (*R* v *McNally*).

4.2.4 Conditional Consent

Section 74 has been considered by the High Court and the Court of Appeal in a series of cases where apparent consent in relation to sexual offences was considered *not to be true consent*, either because a condition upon which consent was given was not complied with or because of a material deception (other than one which falls within s. 76 of the Sexual Offences Act 2003 (**see para. 4.2.6**)). The judgments identified three sets of circumstances in which the consent to sexual activity might be vitiated where the condition was breached.

In *Assange* v *Sweden* [2011] EWHC 2489 (Admin), the Divisional Court considered the situation in which A knew B (the complainant) would only consent to sexual intercourse if he used a condom. The court rejected the view that the conclusive presumption in s. 76 of the Sexual Offences Act 2003 would apply and concluded that the issue of consent could be determined under s. 74 rather than s. 76, and stated that it would be open to a jury to hold that if B had made it clear that she would only consent to sexual intercourse if A used a condom, then there would be no consent if, without B's consent, A did not use a condom or removed or tore the condom. A's conduct in having sexual intercourse without a condom in circumstances where B had made it clear that she would only have sexual intercourse if A did use a condom, would therefore amount to an offence.

In *R (F)* v *DPP* [2013] EWHC 945 (Admin), the High Court examined an application for judicial review of the refusal of the DPP to initiate a prosecution for rape and/or sexual assault on B by A (her former partner). 'Choice' and the 'freedom' to make any particular choice must, the court said, be approached in 'a broad commonsense way'. Against what the court described as the 'essential background' of A's 'sexual dominance' of B and B's 'unenthusiastic acquiescence to his demands', the court considered a specific incident when B consented to sexual intercourse only on the clear understanding that A *would not* ejaculate inside her vagina. B believed that A intended and agreed to withdraw before ejaculation, and A knew and understood that this was the *only basis* on which B was prepared to have sexual intercourse with him. When he deliberately ejaculated inside B, the result, the court said, was B being deprived of choice relating to the crucial feature on which her original consent to sexual intercourse was based and, accordingly, her consent was negated. Contrary to B's wishes, and knowing that she would not have consented and did not consent to penetration or the continuation of penetration, if B had an inkling of A's intention, A deliberately ejaculated within her vagina. This combination of circumstances falls within the statutory definition of rape.

The third case, *McNally* v *R* [2013] EWCA Crim 1051, differs from the other two cases. Unlike *Assange* and *F*, both of which turned on an express condition, *McNally* was concerned with the material deception of B by A. The unusual facts considered by the court involved the relationship between two girls which, over three years, developed from an internet relationship to an 'exclusive romantic relationship' that involved their meeting and engaging in sexual activity. From the start, A presented herself to B as a boy, a deception she maintained throughout their relationship. Examining the nature of 'choice' and 'freedom', the court determined that 'deception as to gender can vitiate consent'. The court's reasoning is that while, in a physical sense, the acts of assault by penetration of the vagina are the same whether perpetrated by a male or a female, the sexual nature of the acts is, on any common-sense view, different where the complainant is deliberately deceived by a defendant into believing the latter is male. Assuming the facts to be proved as alleged, B chose to have sexual encounters with a boy and her preference (her freedom to choose whether or not to have a sexual encounter with a girl) was removed by A's deception. Demonstrating that the circumstances in which consent may be vitiated are not limitless, the court explained that, in reality, some deceptions (such as in relation to wealth) will *obviously not be sufficient* to vitiate consent.

In *R* v *Lawrence* [2020] EWCA Crim 971, the Court of Appeal considered whether a lie about fertility could negate consent. Lawrence had been convicted on two counts of rape on the basis that his false representation to the complainant that he had had a vasectomy vitiated her consent in that she had only agreed to unprotected sex as a result of the representation. Otherwise she would have insisted on him wearing a condom. The appeal was allowed—the court stated that a lie about fertility was different from a lie about whether a condom was being worn during sex, different from engaging in intercourse not intending to withdraw having promised to do so and different from engaging in sexual activity having misrepresented one's gender. The complainant agreed to sexual intercourse with Lawrence without imposing any physical restrictions. She agreed both to penetration of her vagina and to ejaculation without the protection of a condom. In so doing, she was deceived about the nature or quality of the ejaculate and therefore of the risks and possible consequences of unprotected intercourse. The deception was one which related not to the physical performance of the sexual act but to risks or consequences associated with it. It made no difference to the issue of consent whether there was an express deception or a failure to disclose. The issue was whether Lawrence's lie was sufficiently closely connected to the performance of the sexual act, rather than the broad circumstances surrounding it and, in this case, it was not. Lawrence's lie about his fertility was not capable in law of negating consent.

4.2.5 Sections 75 and 76—Applicability

Sections 75 and 76 of the Sexual Offences Act 2003 allow presumptions to be made in relation to the absence of consent. They apply to offences under:

- s. 1 (rape);
- s. 2 (assault by penetration);
- s. 3 (sexual assault);
- s. 4 (causing sexual activity without consent).

4.2.6 Section 75—Evidential Presumptions about Consent

The Sexual Offences Act 2003, s. 75 states:

(1) If in proceedings for an offence to which this section applies it is proved—
   (a) that the defendant did the relevant act,
   (b) that any of the circumstances specified in subsection (2) existed, and
   (c) that the defendant knew that those circumstances existed,
   the complainant is to be taken not to have consented to the relevant act unless sufficient evidence is adduced to raise an issue as to whether he consented, and the defendant is to be taken not to have reasonably believed that the complainant consented unless sufficient evidence is adduced to raise an issue as to whether he reasonably believed it.

KEYNOTE

This means that if the prosecution can show that the defendant carried out the relevant act in relation to certain specified sexual offences (for example, penetration in rape) and that any of the circumstances below existed and the defendant knew they existed, it will be presumed that the victim did not consent. Then the defendant will have to satisfy the court, by reference to evidence, that this presumption should not be made.

Section 75(2) sets out the circumstances in which evidential presumptions *may* apply. They are that:

(a) *any person* was, at the time of the relevant act (or immediately before it began), using violence against *the complainant* or causing *the complainant* to fear that immediate violence would be used against him/her;

(b) *any person* was, at the time of the relevant act or immediately before it began, causing *the complainant* to fear that violence was being used, or that immediate violence would be used, against *another person*;

(c) *the complainant* was, and the defendant was not, unlawfully detained at the time of the relevant act;

(d) *the complainant* was asleep or otherwise unconscious at the time of the relevant act;

(e) because of *the complainant's* physical disability, the complainant would not have been able at the time of the relevant act to communicate to the defendant whether the complainant consented;

(f) *any person* had administered to or caused to be taken by the complainant, without the complainant's consent, a substance which, having regard to when it was administered or taken, was capable of causing or enabling the complainant to be stupefied or overpowered at the time of the relevant act.

The 'relevant act' for each offence covered by s. 75 will generally be obvious but is set out specifically at s. 77.

It is important to note that the circumstances set out in s. 75(2) are not exhaustive in terms of deciding when consent will be absent. There may be circumstances that fall outside the situations described in s. 75(2) where consent does not exist. For example, the case of PC Stephen Mitchell (**see para. 4.2.3**) did not involve any of the circumstances set out in s. 75(2) and yet he was still guilty of rape as his victim's consent was not *true* consent; it was obtained by a threat to take her children away (submission). The fact that this situation does not appear in the sets of circumstances listed in s. 75(2) merely means that a presumption in relation to consent cannot be made in such a case—*it does not mean that the victim consented to the activity.*

4.2.7   Conclusive Presumptions about Consent

Section 76 of the Sexual Offences Act 2003 states:

(1) If in proceedings for an offence to which this section applies it is proved that the defendant did the relevant act and that any of the circumstances specified in subsection (2) existed, it is to be conclusively presumed—

(a) that the complainant did not consent to the relevant act, and

(b) that the defendant did not believe that the complainant consented to the relevant act.

(2) The circumstances are that—

(a) the defendant intentionally deceived the complainant as to the nature or purpose of the relevant act;

(b) the defendant intentionally induced the complainant to consent to the relevant act by impersonating a person known personally to the complainant.

These provisions deal with situations where the defendant either misrepresents the nature or purpose of what he/she is doing (for example, pretending that inserting a finger into the victim's vagina is for medical reasons) or impersonates the victim's partner. Section 76 requires that a misunderstanding was created by the defendant and that it was done deliberately. Once it is proved, beyond a reasonable doubt, that these circumstances existed then it is conclusive and the defendant cannot argue against them.

In *R v Bingham* [2013] 2 Cr App R 307 (seven counts of causing his girlfriend to engage in sexual activity without consent under s. 4 of the Sexual Offences Act 2003 (**see para. 4.3.5**)), B, using pseudonyms, established an online Facebook relationship with his girlfriend so as to persuade and then blackmail her into providing him with photographs of her engaging in sexual activity. The Court of Appeal held that the reliance at trial upon s. 76 was misplaced. The motive behind the conduct was sexual gratification, and there was no deception as to that (i.e. there was no deception as to the purpose of the act). The prosecution would have had forceful arguments under s. 74 on the basis that the victim only complied because she was being blackmailed. In the light of s. 76(2), it would appear that deception as to the identity of the recipient would not be sufficient as it was impersonation of a person unknown to the complainant. This case can be contrasted with *R v Devonald* [2008] EWCA Crim 527 (another s. 4 offence). In this case, the court held that s. 76 did apply; it was open to the jury to conclude that the complainant was deceived into believing he was masturbating for the gratification of a 20-year-old girl via a webcam when in fact he was doing it for the father of a former girlfriend who was teaching him a lesson. Here, 'purpose' has been given a wide meaning in that the deception was not as to sexual gratification, rather it was to the purpose of the masturbation (to teach the victim a lesson).

It is important to emphasise the fact that s. 76 deals with situations where the defendant:

- deceives the victim regarding the nature and purpose of the act; or
- induces the victim to consent to the relevant act by impersonating a person known personally to the complainant.

If the deception/inducement *does not* relate to either of these aims, then s. 76 has no application. For example, in *R* v *Jheeta* [2007] EWCA Crim 1699, the defendant deceived the complainant into having sex more frequently than she would have done otherwise. In these circumstances, the conclusive presumptions under the Sexual Offences Act 2003 had no relevance as the complainant had not been deceived as to the nature or purpose of the sexual intercourse. Likewise, a false promise to marry made by A to B to encourage B to have sexual intercourse would not be covered, nor would a false promise to pay B in exchange for sexual intercourse.

4.3 Sexual Assault

There are several specific offences dealing with types of sexual assault: these are discussed below.

4.3.1 Assault by Penetration

OFFENCE: **Assault by Penetration—*Sexual Offences Act 2003, s. 2***
> • Triable on indictment • Life imprisonment

The Sexual Offences Act 2003, s. 2 states:

(1) A person (A) commits an offence if—
   (a) he intentionally penetrates the vagina or anus of another person (B) with a part of his body or anything else,
   (b) the penetration is sexual,
   (c) B does not consent to the penetration, and
   (d) A does not reasonably believe that B consents.

KEYNOTE

This offence involves penetration by any part of the body or anything else whatsoever. It is therefore a broad offence covering insertion into the vagina or anus (though not the mouth) of *anything* (such as a dildo or even an animal), provided that the penetration is 'sexual'. Whether a belief is reasonable is to be determined having regard to all the circumstances, including any steps the defendant has taken to ascertain whether the victim consents (s. 2(2)).

4.3.2 The Definition of the Term 'Sexual'

Section 78 of the Act defines the term 'sexual' and provides that penetration, touching or any other activity will be sexual if a reasonable person would consider that:

(a) whatever its circumstances or any person's purpose in relation to it, it is sexual by its very nature; or
(b) because of its nature, it *may* be sexual and, because of its circumstances or the purpose of any person in relation to it, it is sexual.

Therefore, activity under (a) covers things that a reasonable person would always consider to be sexual (for example, masturbation), while activity under (b) covers things that may or may not be considered sexual by a reasonable person depending on the circumstances or the intentions of the person carrying it out (or both). For instance, a doctor inserting his/her finger into the vagina of a patient might be considered sexual by its nature, but if done for a purely medical purpose in a hospital (the circumstances and genuine medical purpose of the doctor in examining the patient), it would not be sexual.

If the activity would not appear to a reasonable person to be sexual, then it will not meet either criterion and, irrespective of any sexual gratification the person might derive from it, the activity will not be 'sexual'. Therefore weird or exotic fetishes that no ordinary person would regard as being sexual or potentially sexual will not be covered. This pretty well follows the common law developments in this area (*R* v *Court* [1989] AC 28 and *R* v *Tabassum* [2000] 2 Cr App R 328).

KEYNOTE

The offence of assault by penetration contains the first reference to the term 'sexual'. The term is exceptionally important for a variety of offences contained in the Sexual Offences Act 2003. What has been said above in relation to how this term is interpreted will apply to *all* offences contained in the Sexual Offences Act 2003 where the term 'sexual' is used, apart from the offence under s. 15A (sexual communication with a child) and s. 71 (sexual activity in a public lavatory).

4.3.3 Sexual Assault

OFFENCE: **Sexual Assault—*Sexual Offences Act 2003, s. 3***
- Triable either way • 10 years' imprisonment on indictment
- Six months' imprisonment and/or fine summarily

The Sexual Offences Act 2003, s. 3 states:

(1) A person (A) commits an offence if—
    (a) he intentionally touches another person (B),
    (b) the touching is sexual,
    (c) B does not consent to the touching, and
    (d) A does not reasonably believe that B consents.

KEYNOTE

Touching for the purposes of the above offence includes touching a person's clothing while they are wearing it. Therefore, where a man approached a woman and asked *'Do you fancy a shag?'*, grabbing at a pocket on her tracksuit bottoms as she tried to walk away, he was properly convicted of the s. 3 offence even though he did not touch her person (*R* v *H* [2005] EWCA Crim 732).

The conduct must be intentional (rather than reckless or accidental).

Whether a belief is reasonable is to be determined having regard to all the circumstances, including any steps the defendant has taken to ascertain whether the victim consents (s. 3(2)).

4.3.4 The Definition of the Term 'Touching'

Section 79(8) states that touching includes touching:

- with any part of the body;
- with anything else;
- through anything;

and in particular, touching amounting to penetration (this could include kissing).

The part of the body touched does not have to be a sexual organ or orifice. There is no requirement for force or violence so the lightest touching will suffice. 'Touching' for the purposes of an offence under s. 3 includes the touching of a victim's clothing while they are wearing it even though the person of the victim is not touched through the clothing (*R* v *H* [2005] EWCA Crim 732). In *H*, it was held that it was not Parliament's intention to preclude the touching of a victim's clothing from amounting to a sexual 'assault'. Where touching was not automatically by its nature 'sexual', the test under s. 78(b) applies (**see** para. **4.3.2**). In a case where that section applies, it will be appropriate for a trial judge to ask the jury to determine whether touching was 'sexual' by answering two questions. First, would the jury, as 12 reasonable people, consider that the touching could be sexual and, if so, whether in all the circumstances of the case, they would consider that the purpose of the touching *had in fact been* sexual.

The victim need not be aware of the touching. For example, in the case of *R v Bounekhla* [2006] EWCA Crim 1217 the accused surreptitiously took his penis out of his trousers and ejaculated onto a woman's clothing when pressed up against her dancing at a nightclub.

If touching does not occur, the offence is not completed, although the circumstances may amount to an attempt. Nevertheless, it remains arguable that ejaculation onto a victim's clothing without contact with any part of the accused's body still constitutes a touching.

KEYNOTE

The offence of sexual assault contains the first reference to the term 'touching'. The term is exceptionally important for a variety of offences contained in the Sexual Offences Act 2003. What has been said above in relation to how this term is interpreted will apply to all offences contained in the Sexual Offences Act 2003 where the term 'touching' is used.

4.3.5 Causing Sexual Activity without Consent

OFFENCE: **Causing a Person to Engage in Sexual Activity without Consent—**
Sexual Offences Act 2003, s. 4
• If it involves penetration: of the victim's anus or vagina, of victim's mouth with penis, of any other person's anus or vagina with a part of victim's body or by the victim, or of any person's mouth by victim's penis—triable on indictment; life imprisonment • Otherwise triable either way; 10 years' imprisonment on indictment; six months' imprisonment and/or a fine summarily

The Sexual Offences Act 2003, s. 4 states:

(1) A person (A) commits an offence if—
    (a) he intentionally causes another person (B) to engage in an activity,
    (b) the activity is sexual,
    (c) B does not consent to engaging in the activity, and
    (d) A does not reasonably believe that B consents.

KEYNOTE

The offence is committed when A causes B to engage in sexual activity without B's consent, whether or not A also engages in it and whether or not A is present.

The offence can involve a number of permutations, for example a woman making a man penetrate her, a man forcing someone else to masturbate him, a woman making another woman masturbate a third person or even an animal. The shocking circumstances of *R v H* [2008] EWCA Crim 1202 are an example of where an animal was used in the commission of the offence where the visibly mentally disabled victim was forced, among other things, to be penetrated in the anus by a dog. It would include causing a person to act as a prostitute. Apart from the defendant and the victim, there may be others involved who also consent—they may be liable for aiding and abetting under the right circumstances.

The term 'activity' is not defined and is capable of being given a wide interpretation, although it must have actually taken place. The activity engaged in must be 'sexual' in accordance with s. 78. It can include engaging someone in a conversation of a sexual nature (*R v Grout* [2011] EWCA Crim 299).

This offence overlaps partly with rape in that it deals with vaginal, anal and oral penetration. The offence is wider than rape, in that rape can only be committed by a man, as a principal, and does not involve

---

penetration with an object. The offence can be committed by and against persons of either sex and includes cases of 'female rape', i.e. where A causes B to penetrate her vagina with his penis. Furthermore, the offence makes A criminally liable for causing B to engage in sexual activity where B cannot himself be convicted of any offence because he has a defence such as duress or is under the age of criminal responsibility (**see chapter 1.4**).

Whether a belief is reasonable is to be determined having regard to all the circumstances, including any steps the defendant has taken to ascertain whether the victim consents (s. 4(2)).

4.3.6 Rape and Other Offences Against Children Under 13

Offences under ss. 1 to 4 of the Sexual Offences Act 2003 are 'mirrored' by ss. 5 to 8 of the Act. The common features of the offences under ss. 5 to 8 are that the victim is a child under the age of 13 and that, once the *actus reus* of the offence is proved, no issue of 'consent' to the activity arises—a child under 13 cannot 'consent' to such activity.

OFFENCE		OFFENCE—VICTIM U13		MODE OF TRIAL/SENTENCE
Section 1 Rape	→	Section 5 Rape	→	Triable on Indictment—life imprisonment
Section 2 Assault by Penetration	→	Section 6 Assault by Penetration	→	
Section 3 Sexual Touching	→	Section 7 Sexual Touching	→	Triable Either Way Indictment—14 years' imprisonment
Section 4 Causing Sexual Activity	→	Section 8 Causing or Inciting Activity	→	Summary—six months' imprisonment and/or fine

In *R* v *Walker* [2006] EWCA Crim 1907, the Court of Appeal held that s. 8 of the Act created two offences: (a) intentionally causing; and (b) intentionally inciting a child under 13 to engage in sexual activity. The offence is centred on the concept of incitement and the acts had to be intentional or deliberate, but it was not a necessary ingredient for incitement of sexual activity that the defendant had intended the sexual activity to take place. An individual can commit an offence of incitement even if the activity he/she is encouraging, etc. does not take place.

4.4 Sexual Offences against Children

4.4.1 Introduction

The Sexual Offences Act 2003 contains specific offences relating to sexual activity involving or directed towards children.

The Act makes special exceptions to some offences of aiding, abetting or counselling some offences involving children (an example is provided in **para. 4.4.5** but the full list of offences is set out in s. 73(2); basically, it covers specific offences against children under 13 and offences involving sexual activity with a child under 16).

4.4.2 Sexual Activity with a Child

OFFENCE: **Sexual Activity with a Child—*Sexual Offences Act 2003, s. 9***
- If involves penetration of victim's anus or vagina by a part of defendant's body or anything else, of victim's mouth with defendant's penis, of defendant's anus or vagina by a part of victim's body or of defendant's mouth by victim's penis—triable on indictment; 14 years' imprisonment • Otherwise triable either way; 14 years' imprisonment on indictment; six months' imprisonment summarily

The Sexual Offences Act 2003, s. 9 states:

(1) A person aged 18 or over (A) commits an offence if—
    (a) he intentionally touches another person (B),
    (b) the touching is sexual, and
    (c) either—
        (i) B is under 16 and A does not reasonably believe that B is 16 or over, or
        (ii) B is under 13.

> **KEYNOTE**
>
> You must show that the defendant intentionally touched the victim sexually and either that the victim was under 13 (in which case the offence is complete) or that the victim was under 16 and that the defendant did not reasonably believe he/she was 16 or over. In either case, consent is irrelevant.
>
> The sexual activity caused or envisaged may be with the defendant or with a third person. In the case of incitement, there is no need for the sexual activity itself to take place.

4.4.3 Causing or Inciting a Child to Engage in Sexual Activity

OFFENCE: **Causing or Inciting a Child to Engage in Sexual Activity—*Sexual Offences Act 2003, s. 10***
- If it involves penetration of the victim's anus or vagina, of victim's mouth with penis, of any other person's anus or vagina with a part of victim's body or by victim, or of any person's mouth by victim's penis—triable on indictment; 14 years' imprisonment • Otherwise triable either way; 14 years' imprisonment on indictment; six months' imprisonment and/or fine summarily

The Sexual Offences Act 2003, s. 10 states:

(1) A person aged 18 or over (A) commits an offence if—
    (a) he intentionally causes or incites another person (B) to engage in an activity,
    (b) the activity is sexual, and
    (c) either —
        (i) B is under 16 and A does not reasonably believe that B is 16 or over, or
        (ii) B is under 13.

KEYNOTE

Where the child is aged 13 or over, but under 16, the prosecution must prove that A did not reasonably believe that he/she was 16 or over. The sexual activity which is caused or incited may be activity with A (for example, where A causes or incites the child to have sexual intercourse with him), on the child him/herself (for example, where A causes or incites the child to strip for A's sexual gratification) or with a third person (for example, where A causes or incites the child to have sexual intercourse with A's friend). The incitement constitutes an offence whether or not the activity incited actually takes place. Whether or not the child consented to the activity caused or incited, or to the incitement, is irrelevant.

4.4.4 Sexual Activity in Presence of a Child

OFFENCE: **Engaging in Sexual Activity in the Presence of a Child—*Sexual Offences Act 2003, s. 11***
- Triable either way • 10 years' imprisonment on indictment
- Six months' imprisonment summarily

The Sexual Offences Act 2003, s. 11 states:

(1) A person aged 18 or over (A) commits an offence if—
    (a) he intentionally engages in an activity,
    (b) the activity is sexual,
    (c) for the purpose of obtaining sexual gratification, he engages in it—
        (i) when another person (B) is present or is in a place from which A can be observed, and
        (ii) knowing or believing that B is aware, or intending that B should be aware, that he is engaging in it, and
    (d) either—
        (i) B is under 16 and A does not reasonably believe that B is 16 or over, or
        (ii) B is under 13.

KEYNOTE

The activity in which the offender is engaged must be 'sexual' and intentional and must be in order to obtain sexual gratification (for the defendant).

A person under 16 must be present or in a place from which the defendant can be observed and the defendant must know, believe or intend that the child was aware that he/she was engaging in that activity. Therefore, it is not necessary to show that the child was in fact aware of the activity in every case. Because of the wording in s. 79(7), 'observation' includes direct observation or by looking at any image.

In relation to the child, you must show that either the child was under 13 (in which case the offence is complete) or that he/she was under 16 and that the defendant did not reasonably believe him/her to be 16 or over.

This offence is aimed at, for example, people masturbating in front of children or performing sexual acts with others where they know they can be seen (or they want to be seen) by children directly or via a camera/video phone etc.

4.4.5 Causing a Child to Watch a Sex Act

OFFENCE: **Causing a Child to Watch a Sexual Act—*Sexual Offences Act 2003, s. 12***

- Triable either way • 10 years' imprisonment on indictment
- Six months' imprisonment summarily

The Sexual Offences Act 2003, s. 12 states:

(1) A person aged 18 or over (A) commits an offence if—

(a) for the purpose of obtaining sexual gratification, he intentionally causes another person (B) to watch a third person engaging in an activity, or to look at an image of any person engaging in an activity,

(b) the activity is sexual, and

(c) either—

(i) B is under 16 and A does not reasonably believe that B is 16 or over, or

(ii) B is under 13.

KEYNOTE

This offence is concerned with intentionally causing a child to watch a third person engaging in sexual activity or to look at an image of a person *engaging in sexual activity*. 'Image' includes a moving or still image and includes an image produced by any means and, where the context permits, a three-dimensional image (s. 79(4)); it also includes images of an imaginary person (s. 79(5)).

The display of sexual images or sexual activity might, in certain circumstances, be appropriate, for example for medical or educational reasons, hence the requirement that the offence depended on the corrupt purpose of 'sexual gratification'. The offence under s. 12 of the Act does not require that such gratification has to be taken immediately; i.e. the section does not require that the offence can only be committed if the proposed sexual gratification and the viewed sexual act, or display of images, were simultaneous, contemporaneous or synchronised. For example, the defendant may cause a child to watch a sexual act to put the child in a frame of mind for future sexual abuse, as well as where the defendant does so to obtain enjoyment from seeing the child watch the sexual act (*R* v *Abdullahi* [2006] EWCA Crim 2060). The approach to 'sexual gratification' taken in *Abdullahi* is equally applicable to other offences where this phrase appears (the offences under ss. 11 and 15A of the Act, for example).

You must show that either the child was under 13 (in which case the offence is complete) or that he/she was under 16 and that the defendant did not reasonably believe him/her to be 16 or over.

4.4.6 Child Sex Offences Committed by Children or Young Persons

The offences under ss. 9 to 12 can only be committed by a person aged 18 or over. So what happens if the offender is under 18? This situation is catered for by s. 13(1) of the Sexual Offences Act 2003 which states that a person under 18 commits an offence under this section (s. 13) if he/she does anything which would be an offence under any of ss. 9 to 12 if he/she were aged 18. A person guilty of an offence under s. 13 is liable:

- on conviction on indictment, to imprisonment for a term not exceeding five years; or
- on summary conviction, to imprisonment for a term not exceeding six months and/or a fine.

4.4.7 Arranging or Facilitating the Commission of a Child Sex Offence

OFFENCE: **Arranging or Facilitating Commission of Child Sex Offence—*Sexual Offences Act 2003, s. 14***

> • Triable either way • 14 years' imprisonment on indictment • Six months' imprisonment summarily

The Sexual Offences Act 2003, s. 14 states:

> (1) A person commits an offence if—
>> (a) he intentionally arranges or facilitates something that he intends to do, intends another person to do, or believes that another person will do, in any part of the world, and
>> (b) doing it will involve the commission of an offence under any of sections 9 to 13.

KEYNOTE

The relevant offences are those set out in ss. 9 to 13 of the Act described in the earlier paragraphs of this chapter.

The offence applies to activities by which the defendant intends to commit one of those relevant child sex offences him/herself, or by which the defendant intends or believes another person will do so, in either case in any part of the world. The offence is complete whether or not the sexual activity actually takes place. Examples of the offence would include a defendant approaching a third person to procure a child to take part in sexual activity with him or where the defendant makes travel arrangements for another in the belief that the other person will commit a relevant child sex offence.

This part of the Act specifically excludes the actions of those acting for the child's protection who arrange or facilitate something that they believe another person will do, but that they do not intend to do or intend another person to do. Acting for the child's protection must fall within one of the following:

- protecting the child from sexually transmitted infection;
- protecting the physical safety of the child;
- preventing the child from becoming pregnant; or
- promoting the child's emotional well-being by the giving of advice, and *not* for obtaining sexual gratification or for causing or encouraging the activity constituting the relevant child sex offence or the child's participation in it. This statutory exception (contained in s. 14(2) and (3)) covers activities such as health workers supplying condoms to people under 16 who are intent on having sex in any event and need protection from infection.

4.4.8 Meeting a Child Following Sexual Grooming

OFFENCE: **Meeting a Child Following Sexual Grooming—*Sexual Offences Act 2003, s. 15***

> • Triable either way • 10 years' imprisonment on indictment
> • Six months' imprisonment summarily

The Sexual Offences Act 2003, s. 15 states:

> (1) A person aged 18 or over (A) commits an offence if—
>> (a) A has met or communicated with another person (B) on one or more occasions and subsequently—
>>> (i) A intentionally meets B,
>>> (ii) A travels with the intention of meeting B in any part of the world or arranges to meet B in any part of the world, or
>>> (iii) B travels with the intention of meeting A in any part of the world,

(b) A intends to do anything to or in respect of B, during or after the meeting mentioned in paragraph (a)(i) to (iii) and in any part of the world, which if done will involve the commission by A of a relevant offence,

(c) B is under 16, and

(d) A does not reasonably believe that B is 16 or over.

KEYNOTE

The initial action of the defendant involves either a meeting or a communication with the victim (who must be under 16) on at least *one previous occasion*. Such meetings or communications can be innocuous, such as family occasions or during the course of youth activities and so on. The only requirement prior to an intentional meeting during which an offender intends to do anything to a complainant which, if carried out, would involve the commission by the offender of a relevant offence is a meeting or communication 'on one or more occasions'. There is no requirement that either communication be sexual in nature (*R v G* [2010] EWCA Crim 1693).

The communication can include text messaging or interactions in internet 'chat rooms'. Such contact can have taken place in any part of the world.

Once the earlier meeting or communication has taken place, the offence is triggered by:

- an intentional meeting with the victim;
- a defendant travelling with the intention of meeting the victim;
- a defendant arranging to meet the victim;
- the victim travelling to meet the defendant in any part of the world.

The activity at s. 15(1)(a)(iii) means that an offence will be committed by an adult where a child under 16 travels to meet the adult or the adult arranges to meet the child.

At the time of any of the above activities, the defendant must intend to do anything to or in respect of the victim, during or even after the meeting, that would amount to a relevant offence. A relevant offence here is generally any offence under part I of the Act (all the offences covered in this chapter). Note that the intended offence *does not* have to take place.

You must show that the victim was under 16 and that the defendant did not reasonably believe that he/she was 16 or over.

4.4.9 Sexual Communication with a Child

OFFENCE: **Sexual Communication with a Child—*Sexual Offences Act 2003, s. 15A***

- Triable either way • Two years' imprisonment on indictment
- Six months' imprisonment summarily

The Sexual Offences Act 2003, s. 15A states:

(1) A person aged 18 or over (A) commits an offence if—
  (a) for the purpose of obtaining sexual gratification, A intentionally communicates with another person (B),
  (b) the communication is sexual or is intended to encourage B to make (whether to A or another) a communication that is sexual, and,
  (c) B is under 16, and A does not reasonably believe that B is 16 or over.

KEYNOTE

'Sexual'

The definition of the term 'sexual' under s. 78 of the Act does not apply to this offence.

For the purposes of this section, a communication is sexual if—

- any part of it relates to 'sexual activity'; or

- a reasonable person would, in all the circumstances but regardless of any person's purpose, consider any part of the communication to be sexual.

'Sexual activity' means any activity that a reasonable person would, in all the circumstances but regardless of any person's purpose, consider to be sexual (s. 15A(2)).

The offence criminalises conduct where an adult intentionally communicates (for example, by email, text message, written note or orally) with a child under 16 (whom the adult does not reasonably believe to be aged 16 or over) for the purpose of obtaining sexual gratification if the communication is sexual or intended to encourage the child to make a communication that is sexual. The offence may be committed, for example, by talking sexually to a child via an internet chat room or sending sexually explicit text messages to a child as well as inviting a child to communicate sexually (irrespective of whether the invitation is itself sexual).

The offence is designed to ensure that it does not criminalise, for example, ordinary social or educational interactions between children and adults or communications between young people themselves as the communication must be for the corrupt purpose of obtaining 'sexual gratification'.

The interpretation of the term 'sexual gratification' is the same as that taken in ss. 11 and 12 of the Act so it would not matter if the defendant made a relevant communication in order to obtain immediate sexual gratification or the obtaining of such gratification was part of a longer term plan, or both.

4.4.10 Abuse of Position of Trust

The prohibited behaviour under ss. 16 to 19 is along the same lines as that prohibited by the child sex offences in ss. 9, 10, 11 and 12 (see paras 4.4.2 to 4.4.5), except that they are committed by a person in 'a position of trust' (POT) and can be committed against a 'child' who is 'under 18' (so the victim can be 16 or 17 years old).

The following table illustrates the relationship between the offences:

OFFENCE		OFFENCE Offender in POT POT victim is a 'Child' = under 18 years	MODE OF TRIAL/ SENTENCE
Section 9 Sexual Activity with a Child	→	Section 16 Sexual Activity with a Child	Triable Either Way Indictment—five years' imprisonment Summary—six months' imprisonment and/or fine
Section 10 Causing/Inciting a Child to Engage in Sexual Activity	→	Section 17 Causing/Inciting a Child to Engage in Sexual Activity	
Section 11 Sexual Activity in the Presence of a Child	→	Section 18 Sexual Activity in the Presence of a Child	
Section 12 Causing a Child to Watch a Sexual Act	→	Section 19 Causing a Child to Watch a Sexual Act	

KEYNOTE
Position of Trust

A person commits an offence under ss. 16 to 19 when they are aged 18 or over and are in a 'position of trust' in relation to the victim. A 'position of trust' is defined under s. 21 of the Act which is a lengthy, wide-ranging and detailed provision that is beyond the scope of this Manual; however, several examples are provided below:

- where the child is detained following conviction for a criminal offence, for example in a secure training centre or a young offenders institution (s. 21(2));

4.4.11   Familial Child Sex Offences

Sections 25 and 26 of the Sexual Offences Act 2003 deal with offences where there is a familial relationship between the offender and the victim.

4.4.11.1   Sexual Activity with a Child Family Member

OFFENCE: **Sexual Activity with Child Family Member—*Sexual Offences Act 2003, s. 25***

> • Where defendant is 18 or over at the time of the offence and if involves penetration of victim's anus or vagina by a part of defendant's body or anything else, of victim's mouth with defendant's penis, of defendant's anus or vagina by a part of victim's body or of defendant's mouth by victim's penis—triable on indictment: 14 years' imprisonment • Otherwise triable either way; 14 years' imprisonment on indictment; six months' imprisonment and/or a fine summarily • Or, where defendant is under 18 at the time of the offence; five years' imprisonment on indictment; six months' imprisonment and/or a fine summarily

The Sexual Offences Act 2003, s. 25 states:

(1) A person (A) commits an offence if—
   (a) he intentionally touches another person (B),
   (b) the touching is sexual,
   (c) the relation of A to B is within section 27,
   (d) A knows or could reasonably be expected to know that his relation to B is of a description falling within that section, and
   (e) either—
      (i) B is under 18 and A does not reasonably believe that B is 18 or over, or
      (ii) B is under 13.

KEYNOTE

For the relevant definitions of touching and sexual, see paras 4.3.4 and 4.3.2.

The further elements that must be proved are the existence of the relevant family relationship between the defendant and the victim, and the age of the victim.

Where the relevant family relationship is proved it will be presumed that the defendant knew or could reasonably have been expected to know that he/she was related to the victim in that way. Similarly, where it is proved that the victim was under 18, there will be a presumption that the defendant did not reasonably believe that the victim was 18 or over. In respect of both the relationship and the age of the defendant under these circumstances, the defendant will have an evidential burden to discharge in that regard (s. 25(2) and (3)).

The relevant family relationships are set out in s. 27. These cover all close family relationships along with adoptive relationships. They are where:

- the defendant or the victim is the other's parent, grandparent, brother, sister, half-brother, half-sister, aunt or uncle; or
- the defendant is or has been the victim's foster parent.

Additional categories are where the defendant and victim live or have lived in the same household, or the defendant is or has been regularly involved in caring for, training, supervising or being in sole charge of the victim and:

- one of them is or has been the other's step-parent;
- they are cousins;
- one of them is or has been the other's stepbrother or stepsister; or
- they have the same parent or foster parent.

There are exceptions for situations where the defendant and the victim are lawfully married at the time or where (under certain circumstances) the sexual relationship pre-dates the family one. For example, where two divorcees each have a child of 17 who are engaged in a sexual relationship before their respective parents marry and move all four of them into the same household.

4.4.11.2 Inciting a Child Family Member to Engage in Sexual Activity

OFFENCE: **Inciting Sexual Activity with a Child Family Member—*Sexual Offences Act 2003, s. 26***

- Where defendant is 18 or over at the time of the offence and if involves incitement to penetration: of victim's anus or vagina by a part of defendant's body or anything else, of victim's mouth with defendant's penis, of defendant's anus or vagina by a part of victim's body or of defendant's mouth by victim's penis— triable on indictment: 14 years' imprisonment • Otherwise triable either way; 14 years' imprisonment on indictment; six months' imprisonment and/or a fine summarily • Or, where defendant is under 18 at the time of the offence; five years' imprisonment on indictment; six months' imprisonment and/or a fine summarily

The Sexual Offences Act 2003, s. 26 states:

(1) A person (A) commits an offence if—
  (a) he intentionally incites another person (B) to touch, or allow himself to be touched by, A,
  (b) the touching is sexual,
  (c) the relation of A to B is within section 27,
  (d) A knows or could reasonably be expected to know that his relation to B is of a description falling within that section, and
  (e) either—
    (i) B is under 18 and A does not reasonably believe that B is 18 or over, or
    (ii) B is under 13.

KEYNOTE

An example of this offence would be where A encourages B to masturbate A or cajoles B into agreeing to have sex with him. The offence is committed whether or not the sexual touching takes place. So where in the above example A has encouraged B to masturbate him, but the masturbation does not take place because another person enters the room, the offence is nevertheless complete.

The further elements that must be proved are the existence of the relevant family relationship between the defendant and the victim, and the age of the victim.

Where the relevant family relationship is proved, it will be presumed that the defendant knew or could reasonably have been expected to know that he/she was related to the victim in that way. Similarly, where it is proved that the victim was under 18, there will be a presumption that the defendant did not reasonably believe that the victim was 18 or over. In respect of both the relationship and the age of the defendant under these circumstances, the defendant will have an evidential burden to discharge in that regard (s. 26(2) and (3)).

Whether or not the child consented to the incitement or the activity being incited is irrelevant.

4.4.12 Offences Involving Photographs and Images of Children

There are various offences dealing with prohibited and/or pornographic photographs and images.

4.4.12.1 Indecent Photographs

The Protection of Children Act 1978 and the Criminal Justice Act 1988 detail offences relating to the taking, possession of and distribution of indecent photographs of children. The term 'photograph' is common to both offences and covers far more than the traditional image of what a 'photograph' might be considered to be.

4.4.12.2 What is a Photograph?

Section 7 of the Protection of Children Act 1978 provides a definition of a photograph for the purposes of the Act (the same definition applies to the offence under s. 160 of the Criminal Justice Act 1988) and states:

(1) The following subsections apply for the interpretation of this Act.

(2) References to an indecent photograph include an indecent film, a copy of an indecent film, and an indecent photograph comprised in a film.

(3) Photographs (including those comprised in a film) shall, if they show children and are indecent, be treated for all purposes of this Act as indecent photographs of children and so as respects of pseudo-photographs.

(4) References to a photograph include—
   (a) the negative as well as the positive version; and
   (b) data stored on a computer disc or by other electronic means which is capable of conversion into a photograph.

(4A) References to a photograph also include—
   (a) a tracing or other image, whether made by electronic or other means (of whatever nature)—
      (i) which is not itself a photograph or pseudo-photograph, but
      (ii) which is derived from the whole or part of a photograph or pseudo-photograph (or a combination of either or both); and
   (b) data stored on a computer disc or by other electronic means which is capable of conversion into an image within paragraph (a);
   and subsection (8) applies in relation to such an image as it applies in relation to a pseudo-photograph.

(5) 'Film' includes any form of video-recording.

(6) 'Child', subject to subsection (8), means a person under the age of 18.

(7) 'Pseudo-photograph' means an image, whether made by computer graphics or otherwise howsoever, which appears to be a photograph.

(8) If the impression conveyed by a pseudo-photograph is that the person shown is a child, the pseudo-photograph shall be treated for all purposes of this Act as showing a child and so shall a pseudo-photograph where the predominant impression conveyed is that the person shown is a child notwithstanding that some of the physical characteristics shown are those of an adult.

(9) References to an indecent pseudo-photograph include—
    (a) a copy of an indecent pseudo-photograph; and
    (b) data stored on a computer disc or by other electronic means which is capable of conversion into an indecent pseudo-photograph.

KEYNOTE

'Pseudo-photographs' include computer images and the above offences will cover the situation where part of the photograph is made up of an adult form. The use of the internet to facilitate such offences has led to a great deal of case law on the subject and what follows is a summary of several key decisions by the courts on these issues:

- Downloading images from the internet will amount to 'making' a photograph for the purposes of s. 1(1)(a) of the 1978 Act (*R* v *Bowden* [2001] QB 88).
- 'Making' pseudo-photographs includes voluntary browsing through indecent images of children on and from the internet. Once an image is downloaded, the length of time it remains on the screen is irrelevant (*R* v *Smith and Jayson* [2002] EWCA Crim 683).
- In the same case, the Court of Appeal held that a person receiving an unsolicited email attachment containing an indecent image of a child would not commit the offence under s. 1(1)(a) by opening it if he/she was unaware that it contained or was likely to contain an indecent image. This was because s. 1(1)(a) does not create an absolute offence.
- Copying onto a hard drive and storing 'pop-ups' containing indecent images of children amounts to possessing those images (*R* v *Harrison* [2007] EWCA Crim 2976).
- If images have been deleted from a computer so that their retrieval is impossible and, at the material time, a person cannot gain access to them and the images are beyond a person's control, that person cannot be in possession of them (*R* v *Porter* [2006] EWCA Crim 560).
- Evidence indicating an interest in paedophile material generally along with evidence to show how a computer had been used to access paedophile news groups, chat lines etc. can be relevant to show it was more likely than not that a file containing an indecent image of a child had been created deliberately (*R* v *Toomer* [2001] 2 Cr App R (S) 8).
- An image consisting of two parts of two different photographs taped together (the naked body of a woman taped to the head of a child) is not a 'pseudo-photograph'. If such an image were to be photocopied, it could be (*Atkins* v *DPP* [2000] 1 WLR 1427).
- Where a defendant had knowledge that images were likely to be accessed by others, any images would be downloaded 'with a view to distribute' (*R* v *Dooley* [2005] EWCA Crim 3093).

4.4.12.3   Protection of Children Act 1978

OFFENCE: **Indecent Photographs—*Protection of Children Act 1978, ss. 1, 1A and 1B***

- Triable either way • 10 years' imprisonment on indictment
- Six months' imprisonment and/or a fine summarily

The Protection of Children Act 1978, s. 1 states:

1 Indecent photographs of children
(1) Subject to sections 1A and 1B, it is an offence for a person—
    (a) to take, or permit to be taken or to make, any indecent photograph or pseudo-photograph of a child; or
    (b) to distribute or show such indecent photographs or pseudo-photographs; or
    (c) to have in his possession such indecent photographs or pseudo-photographs, with a view to their being distributed or shown by himself or others; or
    (d) to publish or cause to be published any advertisement likely to be understood as conveying that the advertiser distributes or shows such indecent photographs or pseudo-photographs, or intends to do so.

(2) For purposes of this Act, a person is to be regarded as distributing an indecent photograph or pseudo-photograph if he parts with possession of it to, or exposes or offers it for acquisition by, another person.

(3) ...

(4) Where a person is charged with an offence under subsection (1)(b) or (c), it shall be a defence for him to prove—

    (a) that he had a legitimate reason for distributing or showing the photographs or pseudo-photographs or (as the case may be) having them in his possession; or

    (b) that he had not himself seen the photographs or pseudo-photographs and did not know, nor had any cause to suspect, them to be indecent.

(5) References in the Children and Young Persons Act 1933 (except in sections 15 and 99) to the offences mentioned in Schedule 1 to that Act shall include an offence under subsection (1)(a) above.

KEYNOTE

A person will be a 'child' for the purposes of the Act if it appears from the evidence as a whole that he/she was, at the material time, under the age of 18 (Protection of Children Act 1978, s. 2(3)).

Once the defendant realises, or should realise, that material is indecent, any distribution, showing or retention of the material with a view to its being distributed will result in an offence being committed under the 1978 Act if the person depicted turns out to be a child (R v Land [1999] QB 65).

If the impression conveyed by a pseudo-photograph is that the person shown is a child or where the predominant impression is that the person is a child, that pseudo-photograph will be treated for these purposes as a photograph of a child, notwithstanding that some of the physical characteristics shown are those of an adult (s. 7(8) of the 1978 Act).

'Distributing' will include lending or offering to another.

Although the offences include video recordings, possession of exposed but undeveloped film (i.e. film in the form in which it is taken out of a camera) does not appear to be covered. The offence at s. 1(1)(b) and (c) of the 1978 Act can only be proved if the defendant showed/distributed the photograph etc. or intended to show or distribute the photograph etc. to someone else (R v Fellows [1997] 1 Cr App R 244 and R v T [1999] 163 JP 349). If no such intention can be proved, or if the defendant only had the photographs etc. for his/her own use, the appropriate charge would be under s. 160 of the Criminal Justice Act 1988.

Sections 1 and 2 of the Criminal Evidence (Amendment) Act 1997 apply to an offence under s. 1 of the Protection of Children Act 1978 (and to conspiracies, attempts or incitements in the circumstances set out in the 1997 Act).

A legitimate purpose for possessing such material might be where someone has the material as an exhibits officer or as a training aid for police officers or social workers.

The consent of the DPP is needed before prosecuting an offence under the Protection of Children Act 1978.

The Protection of Children Act 1978, s. 1A states:

1A Marriage and other relationships

(1) This section applies where, in proceedings for an offence under section 1(1)(a) of taking or making an indecent photograph or pseudo-photograph of a child, or for an offence under section 1(1)(b) or (c) relating to an indecent photograph or pseudo-photograph of a child, the defendant proves that the photograph was of the child aged 16 or over, and that at the time of the offence charged the child and he—

    (a) were married, or civil partners of each other or

    (b) lived together as partners in an enduring family relationship.

(2) Subsections (5) and (6) also apply where, in proceedings for an offence under section 1(1)(b) or (c) relating to an indecent photograph or pseudo-photograph of a child, the defendant proves that the photograph was of the child aged 16 or over, and that at the time when he obtained it the child and he—

    (a) were married, or civil partners of each other or

    (b) lived together as partners in an enduring family relationship.

(3) This section applies whether the photograph or pseudo-photograph showed the child alone or with the defendant, but not if it showed any other person.

(4) In the case of an offence under section 1(1)(a), if sufficient evidence is adduced to raise an issue as to whether the child consented to the photograph or pseudo-photograph being taken or made, or as to whether the defendant reasonably believed that the child so consented, the defendant is not guilty of the offence unless it is proved that the child did not so consent and that the defendant did not reasonably believe that the child so consented.

(5) In the case of an offence under section 1(1)(b), the defendant is not guilty of the offence unless it is proved that the showing or distributing was to a person other than the child.

KEYNOTE

There is a specific defence to offences under s. 1(1)(a), (b) and (c) of the Protection of Children Act 1978 (making, distributing or possessing with a view to distributing) where the defendant can prove that the photograph was of a child aged 16 or over, the photograph only showed the defendant and the child and that, at the time of the offence, they were married, in a civil partnership or lived together as partners in an enduring family relationship (s. 1A). If the defendant can show these elements, then the following further conditions of the defence will apply:

- In the case of an offence under s. 1(1)(a) (taking or permitting to be taken etc.), the defendant will have an evidential burden of showing that the child consented or that the defendant reasonably believed that the child consented to the making of the photograph (s. 1A(4)).
- In the case of an offence under s. 1(1)(b) (distributing or showing), you must prove that the distributing or showing was to a person other than the child in the photograph (s. 1A(5)).
- In the case of an offence under s. 1(1)(c) (possession with a view to distribution or showing etc.), the defendant will have an evidential burden of demonstrating that the image was to be shown/distributed to no person other than the child and that the child consented to the defendant's possession of the photograph (s. 1A(6)).

The Protection of Children Act 1978, s. 1B states:

1B Exception for criminal proceedings, investigations etc.

(1) In proceedings for an offence under section 1(1)(a) of making an indecent photograph or pseudo-photograph of a child, the defendant is not guilty of the offence if he proves that—

(a) it was necessary for him to make the photograph or pseudo-photograph for the purposes of the prevention, detection or investigation of crime, or for the purposes of criminal proceedings, in any part of the world,

(b) at the time of the offence charged he was a member of the Security Service or the Secret Intelligence Service, and it was necessary for him to make the photograph or pseudo-photograph for the exercise of any of the functions of that Service, or

(c) at the time of the offence charged he was a member of GCHQ, and it was necessary for him to make the photograph or pseudo-photograph for the exercise of any of the functions of GCHQ.

KEYNOTE

There is a limited defence in relation to the making of an indecent photograph or pseudo-photograph contrary to s. 1(1)(a) of the Protection of Children Act 1978 where the defendant proves that:

- it was necessary for the defendant to make the photograph or pseudo-photograph for the purposes of the prevention, detection or investigation of crime or for criminal proceedings in any part of the world; or
- at the time the defendant was a member of the Security Service, Secret Intelligence Service or GCHQ (Government Communications Headquarters) and it was necessary for the exercise of any of the functions of that Service/GCHQ (s. 1B).

In order to assist police officers and prosecutors, NPCC and the CPS have published a Memorandum of Understanding. It sets out factors that will be taken into account in deciding whether the intention of someone accused of an offence under s. 1(1)(a) attracted criminal liability when 'making' a photograph etc. As the Memorandum points out:

> This reverse burden is intended to allow those people who need to be able to identify and act to deal with such images to do so. It also presents a significant obstacle to would-be abusers and those who exploit the potential of technology to gain access to paedophilic material for unprofessional (or personal) reasons.

The purpose of the Memorandum is to reassure those whose duties properly involve the prevention, detection or investigation of this type of crime and also as a warning to others who might claim this defence having taken it upon themselves to investigate such offences. In summary, the following criteria will be considered:

- How soon after its discovery the image was reported and to whom.
- The circumstances in which it was discovered.
- The way in which the image was stored and dealt with, and whether it was copied.
- Whether the person's actions were reasonable, proportionate and necessary.

4.4.12.4 Criminal Justice Act 1988

OFFENCE: **Indecent Photographs—*Criminal Justice Act 1988, s. 160***

> - Triable either way • Five years' imprisonment on indictment
> - Six months' imprisonment and/or a fine

The Criminal Justice Act 1988, ss. 160 and 160A state:

160 Possession of indecent photograph of child

(1) Subject to section 160A, it is an offence for a person to have any indecent photograph or pseudo-photograph of a child in his possession.

(2) Where a person is charged with an offence under subsection (1) above, it shall be a defence for him to prove—

    (a) that he had a legitimate reason for having the photograph or pseudo-photograph in his possession; or

    (b) that he had not himself seen the photograph or pseudo-photograph and did not know, nor had any cause to suspect, it to be indecent; or

    (c) that the photograph or pseudo-photograph was sent to him without any prior request made by him or on his behalf and that he did not keep it for an unreasonable time.

160A Marriage and other relationships

(1) This section applies where, in proceedings for an offence under section 160 relating to an indecent photograph or pseudo-photograph of a child, the defendant proves that the photograph or pseudo-photograph was of the child aged 16 or over, and that at the time of the offence charged the child and he—

    (a) were married, or civil partners of each other or

    (b) lived together as partners in an enduring family relationship.

(2) This section also applies where, in proceedings for an offence under section 160 relating to an indecent photograph or pseudo-photograph of a child, the defendant proves that the photograph or pseudo-photograph was of the child aged 16 or over, and that at the time when he obtained it the child and he—

    (a) were married, or civil partners of each other or

    (b) lived together as partners in an enduring family relationship.

(3) This section applies whether the photograph or pseudo-photograph showed the child alone or with the defendant, but not if it showed any other person.

(4) If sufficient evidence is adduced to raise an issue as to whether the child consented to the photograph or pseudo-photograph being in the defendant's possession, or as to whether the defendant reasonably believed that the child so consented, the defendant is not guilty of the offence unless it is proved that the child did not so consent and that the defendant did not reasonably believe that the child so consented.

For the meaning of 'photograph' and 'pseudo-photograph', **see para. 4.4.12.2, Keynote.**

A person will be a 'child' for the purposes of the Act if it appears from the evidence as a whole that he/she was, at the material time, under the age of 18 (Criminal Justice Act 1988, s. 160(4)).

The statutory defence under s. 160(2)(b) of the 1988 Act requires that the defendant (1) has not seen the material and (2) did not know or have any cause to suspect it was indecent. The defendant will be acquitted of the offence under s. 160 if he/she proves that (1) he/she had not seen the material and (2) did not know (and had no cause to suspect) that it was an indecent photograph of a child. This was confirmed in *R v Collier* [2004] EWCA Crim 1411 and arose from an argument where the material relating to children had been among other adult material that the defendant did know was indecent—he just did not know that it was an indecent photograph of a child.

4.4.12.5 Coroners and Justice Act 2009

OFFENCE: **Possession of Prohibited Images of Children—*Coroners and Justice Act 2009, s. 62***

- Triable either way • Three years' imprisonment on indictment and/or a fine
- Six months' imprisonment and/or a fine

The Coroners and Justice Act 2009, s. 62 states:

(1) It is an offence for a person to be in possession of a prohibited image of a child.
(2) A prohibited image is an image which—
    (a) is pornographic,
    (b) falls within subsection (6), and
    (c) is grossly offensive, disgusting or otherwise of an obscene character.

KEYNOTE

An image is 'pornographic' if it is of such a nature that it must reasonably be assumed to have been produced solely or principally for the purpose of sexual arousal.

An image falls within subs. (6) if it is an image which focuses solely or principally on a child's genitals or anal region, or portrays any of the acts mentioned below. Those acts are:

- the performance by a person of an act of intercourse or oral sex with or in the presence of a child;
- an act of masturbation by, of, involving or in the presence of a child;
- an act which involves penetration of the vagina or anus of a child with a part of a person's body or with anything else;
- an act of penetration, in the presence of a child, of the vagina or anus of a person with a part of a person's body or with anything else;
- the performance by a child of an act of intercourse or oral sex with an animal (whether dead or alive or imaginary);
- the performance by a person of an act of intercourse or oral sex with an animal (whether dead or alive or imaginary) in the presence of a child.

Penetration is a continuing act from entry to withdrawal.

Section 62(4) of the offence states that where (as found in a person's possession) an individual image forms part of a series of images, the question of whether it is pornographic must be determined by reference both to the image itself and the context in which it appears in the series of images. Where an image is integral to a narrative (for example, a mainstream film) which when it is taken as a whole could not reasonably be assumed to be pornographic, the image itself may not be pornographic, even though if considered in

Meaning of 'Image' and 'Child'

Section 65 states that an 'image' includes a moving or still image (produced by any means) such as a photograph or film, or data (stored by any means) which is capable of conversion into a movable or still image, such as data stored electronically (as on a computer disk), which is capable of conversion into an image. This covers material available on computers, mobile phones or any other electronic device. It should be noted that the term 'image' *does not* include an indecent photograph, or indecent pseudo-photograph, of a child as these are subject to other controls (see s. 160 of the Criminal Justice Act 1988 at **para. 4.4.12.4**).

A 'child' means a person under the age of 18 (s. 65(5)). Where an image shows a person, the image is to be treated as an image of a child if the impression conveyed by the image is that the person shown is a child, or the predominant impression conveyed is that the person shown is a child despite the fact that some of the physical characteristics shown are not those of a child (s. 65(6)).

References to an image of a person include references to an image of an imaginary person. References to an image of a child include references to an image of an imaginary child.

Defence

The Coroners and Justice Act 2009, s. 64 states:

(1) Where a person is charged with an offence under section 62(1), it is a defence for the person to prove any of the following matters—
   (a) that the person had a legitimate reason for being in possession of the image concerned;
   (b) that the person had not seen the image concerned and did not know, nor had any cause to suspect, it to be a prohibited image of a child;
   (c) that the person—
      (i) was sent the image concerned without any prior request having been made by or on behalf of the person, and
      (ii) did not keep it for an unreasonable time.

This section sets out a series of defences to the s. 62 offence of possession of prohibited images of children.

4.4.13 Sexual Exploitation of Children

Offences under ss. 47 to 50 of the Act deal with the sexual exploitation of children

4.4.13.1 Paying for the Sexual Services of a Child

OFFENCE: **Paying for Sexual Services of a Child—*Sexual Offences Act 2003, s. 47***
- If victim is child under 13: triable on indictment; life imprisonment
- Where victim is under 16 at the time of the offence and if involves penetration of victim's anus or vagina by a part of defendant's body or anything else, of victim's mouth with defendant's penis, of defendant's anus or vagina by a part of victim's body or by victim with anything else—triable on indictment: 14 years' imprisonment • Otherwise triable either way: seven years' imprisonment on indictment; six months' imprisonment and/or a fine summarily

The Sexual Offences Act 2003, s. 47 states:

(1) A person (A) commits an offence if—

    (a) he intentionally obtains for himself the sexual services of another person (B),

    (b) before obtaining those services, he has made or promised payment for those services to B or a third person, or knows that another person has made or promised such a payment.

KEYNOTE

If the child is under 13, the offence is complete at this point. If the child is under 18, you must prove that the defendant did not reasonably believe that the child was 18 or over (s. 47(1)(c)).

Payment means any financial advantage, including the discharge of an obligation to pay or the provision of goods or services (including sexual services) gratuitously or at a discount (s. 47(2)). This would include situations where the child victim is given drugs or other goods/services at a cheaper rate in exchange for sexual services from the child.

4.4.13.2 Causing, Inciting, Arranging or Facilitating the Sexual Exploitation of Children

OFFENCE: **Causing, Inciting, Controlling, Arranging or Facilitating the Sexual Exploitation of Children—*Sexual Offences Act 2003, ss. 48 to 50***

- Triable either way • 14 years' imprisonment on indictment
- Six months' imprisonment and/or a fine summarily

The Sexual Offences Act 2003, s. 48 states:

(1) A person (A) commits an offence if—

    (a) he intentionally causes or incites another person (B) to be sexually exploited, in any part of the world ...

The Sexual Offences Act 2003, s. 49 states:

(1) A person (A) commits an offence if—

    (a) he intentionally controls any of the activities of another person (B) relating to B's sexual exploitation in any part of the world ...

The Sexual Offences Act 2003, s. 50 states:

(1) A person (A) commits an offence if—

    (a) he intentionally arranges or facilitates the sexual exploitation in any part of the world of another person (B) ...

KEYNOTE

These offences are aimed at those who seek to recruit children for prostitution or to take part in pornography, or otherwise control these activities and arrangements anywhere in the world. For the accused to be guilty of the incitement offence, it is not necessary that B actually becomes a prostitute or involves him/herself in pornography.

If the child is under 13, the offences are complete once the relevant conduct of the defendant has been proved and any belief the defendant may have had as to the child's age is irrelevant to guilt. If the child is under 18, you must prove that the defendant did not reasonably believe that the child was 18 or over (see subs. (1)(b) of each).

For the purposes of ss. 48 to 50, a person (B) is sexually exploited if:

- on at least one occasion and whether or not compelled to do so, B offers or provides sexual services to another person in return for payment or a promise of payment to B or a third person; or
- an indecent image of B is recorded and sexual exploitation is to be interpreted accordingly (s. 51(2)).

Payment means any financial advantage, including the discharge of an obligation to pay or the provision of goods or services (including sexual services) gratuitously or at a discount (s. 51(3)).

These offences would be committed if the child is recruited on a one-off basis, as well as on those occasions where the child is habitually involved. Unlike the general offence of controlling prostitution (**see para. 4.6.3**), there is no need to show that the causing or inciting was done for gain. The expressions used in the sections are deliberately wide and will, in places, overlap. Controlling the activities of the child would include, for example, setting the relevant price or specifying which room or equipment is to be used. Arranging will include taking an active part in the transport or travel arrangements or organising relevant facilities (such as hotel rooms etc.).

4.4.13.3 Information About Guests at Hotels

Section 116 of the Anti-social Behaviour, Crime and Policing Act 2014 confers a power on a police officer, of at least the rank of inspector, to serve a notice on the owner, operator or manager of a hotel that the officer reasonably believes has been or will be used for the purposes of child sexual exploitation or conduct preparatory to or connected with it.

For the purposes of s. 116, 'child sexual exploitation' is defined at s. 116(8) to include offences under any of the following sections of the Sexual Offences Act 2003:

- ss. 1 to 13 (rape, assault and causing sexual activity without consent, rape and other offences against children under 13 and child sex offences);
- ss. 16 to 19 (abuse of position of trust);
- ss. 25 and 26 (familial child sex offences);
- ss. 30 to 41 (persons with a mental disorder impeding choice, inducements etc. to persons with a mental disorder, and care workers for persons with a mental disorder);
- ss. 47 to 50 (abuse of children through prostitution and pornography);
- s. 61 (administering a substance with intent);
- ss. 66 and 67 (exposure and voyeurism).

An offence under s. 1 of the Protection of Children Act 1978 (indecent photographs of children) is also included under s. 116.

The notice must be in writing and specify the hotel to which it relates, the date on which it comes into effect and the date on which it expires. It must also explain the information that a constable may require the person issued with a notice to provide, avenues of appeal against the notice and the consequences of failure to comply. The notice must also specify the period for which it has effect which, under s. 116(3), must be no more than six months.

The Anti-social Behaviour, Crime and Policing Act 2014, s. 116 states:

(4) A constable may require a person issued with a notice under this section to provide the constable with information about guests at the hotel.
(5) The only information that a constable may require under subsection (4) is—
  (a) guests' names and addresses;
  (b) other information about guests that—
    (i) is specified in regulations made by the Secretary of State, and
    (ii) can be readily obtained from one or more of the guests themselves.
(6) A requirement under subsection (4)—
  (a) must be in writing;
  (b) must specify the period to which the requirement relates;
  (c) must specify the date or dates on or by which the required information is to be provided.

The period specified under paragraph (b) must begin no earlier than the time when the requirement is imposed and must end no later than the expiry of the notice under this section.

4.4.14 Possession of a Paedophile Manual

OFFENCE: **Possession of a Paedophile Manual—*Serious Crime Act 2015, s. 69***
- Triable either way • Three years' imprisonment and/or fine
- Six months' imprisonment and/or fine

The Serious Crime Act 2015, s. 69 states:

(1) It is an offence to be in possession of any item that contains advice or guidance about abusing children sexually.
(2) It is a defence for a person (D) charged with an offence under this section—
  (a) to prove that (D) had a legitimate reason for being in possession of the item, and
  (b) to prove that—
    (i) D had not read, viewed or (as appropriate) listened to the item, and
    (ii) D did not know, and had no reason to suspect, that it contained advice or guidance about abusing children sexually; or
  (c) to prove that—
    (i) the item was sent to D without any request made by D or on D's behalf, and
    (ii) D did not keep it for an unreasonable time.

'Abusing children sexually' means doing anything that constitutes an offence under part 1 of the Sexual Offences Act 2003 against a person under 16 or doing anything that constitutes an offence under s. 1 of the Protection of Children Act 1978 involving indecent photographs (but not pseudo-photographs) (s. 69(8)).

The term 'item' has a wide meaning and includes both physical and electronic documents (e.g. emails or information downloaded to a computer) (s. 69(8)).

Section 69(2) sets out a series of defences to the offence of possession of a paedophile manual. They are the same as for other comparable offences, for example the possession of indecent images of children under s. 160(2) of the Criminal Justice Act 1988. They are:

- that the person had a legitimate reason for being in possession of the item; this would be a question of fact for the jury to decide on the individual circumstances of a case. It could cover, for example, those who can demonstrate that they have a legitimate work reason for possessing the item;
- that the person had not seen (or listened to) the item in his/her possession and therefore neither knew, nor had cause to suspect, that it contained advice or guidance about abusing children sexually; and
- that the person had not asked for the item—it having been sent without request—and that he/she had not kept it for an unreasonable period of time; this will cover those who are sent unsolicited material and who act quickly to delete it or otherwise get rid of it.

The standard of proof in making out the defence is the balance of probabilities.

Proceedings for an offence under s. 69(1) may not be instituted in England and Wales except by or with the consent of the DPP.

4.4.15 Offences Outside the United Kingdom

Section 72 of and sch. 2 to the Sexual Offences Act 2003 allow for the prosecution of British citizens and UK residents for sexual offences against children committed abroad. Section 72(1) makes it an offence for a UK national to commit an act outside the United Kingdom which would constitute a relevant sexual offence if done in England and Wales. This has the effect of removing the requirement that the act committed must have been illegal in the country where it took place, in respect of the prosecution of UK nationals.

Section 72 applies to:

- an offence under any of ss. 5 to 19, 25, 26 and 47 to 50;
- an offence under any of ss. 1 to 4, 30 to 41 and 61 where the victim of the offence was under 18 at the time of the offence;
- an offence under s. 62 or 63 where the intended offence was an offence against a person under 18;
- an offence under—
  (i) s. 1 of the Protection of Children Act 1978 (indecent photographs of children); or
  (ii) s. 160 of the Criminal Justice Act 1988 (possession of indecent photograph of a child).

4.5 Sexual Offences Against People with a Mental Disorder

4.5.1 Introduction

The Sexual Offences Act 2003 is centred largely upon the fact that certain mental disorders deprive the sufferer of the ability to refuse involvement in sexual activity. This is different from, and wider than, a lack of consent at the time and focuses on the victim's inability to refuse.

4.5.2 Definition of 'Mental Disorder'

The relevant definition of a 'mental disorder' is that of s. 1(2) of the Mental Health Act 1983 which defines mental disorder as meaning any disorder or disability of the mind, so a person with learning difficulties finds protection in the Act.

4.5.3 Sexual Activity with Mentally Disordered Person

OFFENCE: **Sexual Activity with a Person with a Mental Disorder—***Sexual Offences Act 2003, s. 30*
• If involves penetration of victim's anus or vagina, of victim's mouth with defendant's penis, or of defendant's mouth by victim's penis—triable on indictment; life imprisonment • Otherwise triable either way; 14 years' imprisonment on indictment; six months' imprisonment and/or a fine summarily

The Sexual Offences Act 2003, s. 30 states:

(1) A person (A) commits an offence if—
    (a) he intentionally touches another person (B),
    (b) the touching is sexual,
    (c) B is unable to refuse because of or for a reason related to a mental disorder, and
    (d) A knows or could reasonably be expected to know that B has a mental disorder and that because of it or for a reason related to it B is likely to be unable to refuse.

KEYNOTE

A person is unable to refuse if:

• he/she lacks the capacity to choose whether to agree to the touching (whether because of a lack of sufficient understanding of the nature or reasonably foreseeable consequences of what is being done, or for any other reason); or
• he/she is unable to communicate such a choice to the defendant (s. 30(2)).

You must show that the defendant knew or could reasonably have been expected to know both that the victim had a mental disorder *and* that because of it (or for a reason related to it) he/she was likely to be unable to refuse. In *Hulme* v *DPP* [2006] EWHC 1347 (Admin), the Divisional Court examined a decision reached by a magistrates' court in relation to a complainant who was a cerebral palsy sufferer

---

with a low IQ (aged 27). The magistrates' court had decided that the complainant was unable to refuse to be touched sexually; the Divisional Court agreed and the conviction against the defendant (who was 73) was upheld.

If the defendant obtains the victim's agreement to sexual touching by means of any inducement (offered or given), or a threat or deception for that purpose, the defendant commits a specific (and similarly punishable) offence under s. 34. An example would be where the defendant promises to give the victim some reward in exchange for allowing sexual touching. If the defendant uses an inducement, threat or deception to cause the victim to engage in or agree to engage in sexual activity, there is a further specific offence (similarly punishable) under s. 35.

In these specific cases of inducements, threats or deception, there is still the need to prove that the defendant knew (or could reasonably have been expected to know) of the victim's mental disorder but *no need to prove that the victim was unable to refuse.*

4.5.4 Causing or Inciting a Person with a Mental Disorder to Engage in Sexual Activity

OFFENCE: **Causing or Inciting a Person with a Mental Disorder to Engage in Sexual Activity—*Sexual Offences Act 2003, s. 31***
> • If the activity involves causing or inciting penetration of victim's anus or vagina, of victim's mouth with defendant's penis. or of defendant's mouth by victim's penis—triable on indictment; life imprisonment • Otherwise triable either way; 14 years' imprisonment on indictment; six months' imprisonment and/or a fine summarily

The Sexual Offences Act 2003, s. 31 states:

(1) A person (A) commits an offence if—
    (a) he intentionally causes or incites another person (B) to engage in an activity,
    (b) the activity is sexual,
    (c) B is unable to refuse because of or for a reason related to a mental disorder, and
    (d) A knows or could reasonably be expected to know that B has a mental disorder and that because of it or for a reason related to it B is likely to be unable to refuse.

KEYNOTE

Section 31 covers the situation where A causes or incites B to engage in sexual activity, for example where A causes B to have sexual intercourse with A's friend or incites him/her to do so, even if the incitement does not result in B engaging in sexual activity. As that is an 'incomplete' or unfinished offence (as to which, **see** chapter 1.3), it is not necessary to prove that the sexual activity took place.

4.5.5 Sexual Activity in Presence of Mentally Disordered Person

OFFENCE: **Sexual Activity in Presence of a Person with a Mental Disorder—*Sexual Offences Act 2003, s. 32***
> • Triable either way • 10 years' imprisonment on indictment
> • Six months' imprisonment and/or a fine summarily

The Sexual Offences Act 2003, s. 32 states:

(1) A person (A) commits an offence if—
    (a) he intentionally engages in an activity,
    (b) the activity is sexual,

(c) for the purpose of obtaining sexual gratification, he engages in it—
  (i) when another person (B) is present or is in a place from which A can be observed, and
  (ii) knowing or believing that B is aware, or intending that B should be aware, that he is engaging in it,
(d) B is unable to refuse because of or for a reason related to a mental disorder, and
(e) A knows or could reasonably be expected to know that B has a mental disorder and that because of it or for a reason related to it B is likely to be unable to refuse.

KEYNOTE

For the requirements in proving the victim's inability to refuse, see the previous offence under s. 30.

'Observation' includes direct observation or by looking at any image (s. 79(7)).

If the victim agrees to be present or in the place referred to in s. 32(1)(c)(i) because of any inducement (offered or given), or a threat or deception practised by the defendant for that purpose, the defendant commits a specific (and similarly punishable) offence under s. 36. For instance, where the defendant pays the mentally disordered person to stay in a particular place while the activity occurs. In these specific cases of inducements, threats or deception, there is still the need to prove that the defendant knew (or could reasonably have been expected to know) of the victim's mental disorder but *no need to prove that the victim was unable to refuse.*

4.5.6 Causing Person with Mental Disorder to Watch Sexual Act

OFFENCE: **Causing a Person with a Mental Disorder to Watch a Sexual Act—*Sexual Offences Act 2003, s. 33***
  • Triable either way • 10 years' imprisonment on indictment
  • Six months' imprisonment summarily

The Sexual Offences Act 2003, s. 33 states:

(1) A person (A) commits an offence if—
  (a) for the purpose of obtaining sexual gratification, he intentionally causes another person (B) to watch a third person engaging in an activity, or to look at an image of any person engaging in an activity,
  (b) the activity is sexual, and
  (c) B is unable to refuse because of or for a reason related to a mental disorder, and
  (d) A knows or could reasonably be expected to know that B has a mental disorder and that because of it or for a reason related to it B is likely to be unable to refuse.

KEYNOTE

The above offence is concerned with intentionally causing a person with a mental disorder to watch a third person engaging in such activity *or* to look at an image of a person engaging in such activity. 'Image' includes a moving or still image and includes an image produced by any means and, where the context permits, a three-dimensional image (s. 79(4); it also includes images of an imaginary person (s. 79(5))).

If the victim agrees to watch or look because of any inducement (offered or given), or a threat or deception practised by the defendant for that purpose, the defendant commits a specific (and similarly punishable) offence under s. 37. For example, where the defendant (with the appropriate motive) deceives the mentally disordered person into watching a film which is actually a live video feed of sexual activity. In these specific cases of inducements, threats or deception, there is still the need to prove that the defendant knew (or could reasonably have been expected to know) of the victim's mental disorder but *no need to prove that the victim was unable to refuse.*

4.6 | Offences Relating to Prostitution

4.6.1 Introduction

There are numerous offences connected with prostitution. This section begins with the definition of a prostitute before examining some of those offences.

4.6.2 Definition of a Prostitute

The Sexual Offences Act 2003 defines prostitution and provides that a prostitute is a person (A) who:

- on at least one occasion; and
- whether or not compelled to do so;
- offers or provides sexual services to another person;
- in return for payment or a promise of payment to A or a third person (s. 51(2)).

This definition applies to both men and women.

4.6.3 Offence of Causing, Inciting or Controlling Prostitution

OFFENCE: **Causing, Inciting or Controlling Prostitution—*Sexual Offences Act 2003, s. 52***
- Triable either way • Seven years' imprisonment on indictment
- Six months' imprisonment and/or a fine summarily

The Sexual Offences Act 2003, s. 52 states:

(1) A person commits an offence if—
  (a) he intentionally causes or incites another person to become a prostitute in any part of the world, and
  (b) he does so for or in the expectation of gain for himself or a third person.

The Sexual Offences Act 2003, s. 53 states:

(1) A person commits an offence if—
  (a) he intentionally controls any of the activities of another person relating to that person's prostitution in any part of the world, and
  (b) he does so for or in the expectation of gain for himself or a third person.

KEYNOTE

Where the victim is under 18, the specific offence under s. 48 should be considered (see para. 4.4.13).

The first offence above is concerned with intentional causing or inciting, the latter being an incomplete offence (see chapter 1.3).

The second offence above addresses those who intentionally control the activities of prostitutes (pimps).

Unlike the offence involving persons under 18, you must show the defendant acted for, or in the expectation of, gain for him/herself or another. Gain means any financial advantage, including the discharge of an obligation to pay or the provision of goods or services (including sexual services) gratuitously or at a discount or the goodwill of any person which is or appears likely, in time, to bring financial advantage (s. 54). This definition covers the actions of someone who hopes to build up a relationship with, say, a drug dealer who will eventually give the defendant cheaper drugs as a result of his/her activities. Although you do not need to show that money, goods or financial advantage actually passed to the defendant, you must show that he/she wanted or at least expected that someone would benefit from the conduct.

4.6.4 Paying for Sexual Services of a Prostitute Subjected to Force

OFFENCE: **Paying for Sexual Services of a Prostitute Subjected to Force—*Sexual Offences Act 2003, s. 53A***
- Triable summarily • Fine

The Sexual Offences Act 2003, s. 53A states:

(1) A person (A) commits an offence if—
  (a) A makes or promises payment for the sexual services of a prostitute (B),
  (b) a third person (C) has engaged in exploitative conduct of a kind likely to induce or encourage B to provide the sexual services for which A has made or promised payment, and
  (c) C engaged in that conduct for or in the expectation of gain for C or another person (apart from A or B).
(2) The following are irrelevant—
  (a) where in the world the sexual services are to be provided and whether those services are provided,
  (b) whether A is, or ought to be, aware that C has engaged in exploitative conduct.
(3) C engages in exploitative conduct if—
  (a) C uses force, threats (whether or not relating to violence) or any other form of coercion, or
  (b) C practises any form of deception.

KEYNOTE

This offence is committed if someone pays or promises payment for the sexual services of a prostitute who has been subject to exploitative conduct of a kind likely to induce or encourage the provision of sexual services for which the payer has made or promised payment. The person responsible for the exploitative conduct must have been acting for or in the expectation of gain for him/herself or another person, other than the payer or the prostitute.

It does not matter where in the world the sexual services are to be provided. An offence is committed regardless of whether the person paying or promising payment for sexual services knows or ought to know or be aware that the prostitute has been subject to exploitative conduct. In other words, the offence is one of *strict liability* and *no mental element* is required in respect of the offender's knowledge that the prostitute was forced, threatened, coerced or deceived.

4.6.5 Brothels and Keeping a Disorderly House

There are several summary offences aimed at landlords, tenants and occupiers of premises used as brothels (ss. 34 to 36 of the Sexual Offences Act 1956) as well as the offence under s. 33A of the Act (below) and the common law offence of keeping a disorderly house.

OFFENCE: **Keeping a Brothel Used for Prostitution—*Sexual Offences Act 1956, s. 33A***
- Triable either way • Seven years' imprisonment on indictment
- Six months' imprisonment and/or a fine summarily

The Sexual Offences Act 1956, s. 33A states:

(1) It is an offence for a person to keep, or to manage, or act or assist in the management of, a brothel to which people resort for practices involving prostitution (whether or not also for other practices).

KEYNOTE

A brothel is a place to which people resort for the purposes of unlawful sexual intercourse with more than one prostitute; it is not necessary that full sexual intercourse takes place or is even offered. Homosexual activity is as capable as heterosexual activity of founding the existence of a brothel. A massage parlour where other acts of lewdness or indecency for sexual gratification are offered may be a brothel.

Prostitution means offering or providing sexual services, whether under compulsion or not, to another in return for payment or a promise of payment to the prostitute or a third person (s. 51(2)).

OFFENCE: **Keeping a Disorderly House—*Common Law***
- Triable on indictment • Unlimited sentence

It is an offence at common law to keep a disorderly house.

KEYNOTE

To prove this offence, you must show that the house is 'open' (i.e. to customers), that it is unregulated by the restraints of morality and that it is run in a way that violates law and good order (*R* v *Tan* [1983] QB 1053).

There must be 'knowledge' on the part of the defendant that a house is being so used (*Moores* v *DPP* [1992] QB 125).

The offence also requires some persistence and will not cover a single instance, for example of an indecent performance.

4.6.6 Soliciting

OFFENCE: **Soliciting by Persons—*Street Offences Act 1959, s. 1***
- Triable summarily • Fine

The Street Offences Act 1959, s. 1 states:

(1) It shall be an offence for a person aged 18 or over whether male or female persistently to loiter or solicit in a street or public place for the purpose of prostitution.

(2) ...

(3) [Repealed]

(4) For the purposes of this section—

(a) conduct is persistent if it takes place on two or more occasions in any period of three months;

(b) any reference to a person loitering or soliciting for the purposes of prostitution is a reference to a person loitering or soliciting for the purposes of offering services as a prostitute.

KEYNOTE

This offence is committed *only by those offering services as a prostitute*, not by those receiving such services (those receiving services may, however, be committing 'soliciting' offences as below).

Instead of a fine, the court may make a rehabilitative order against a person convicted of the soliciting by persons offence (s. 1(2A) of the Street Offences Act 1959, as amended).

A 'street' includes any bridge, road, lane, footway, subway, square, court, alley or passage, whether a thoroughfare or not, which is for the time being open to the public; and the doorways and entrances of premises abutting on a street and any ground adjoining and open to a street.

A prostitute soliciting from the balcony or window of a house adjoining a street or public place is taken to be in the street or public place if the person being solicited is in the street or public place (*Smith* v *Hughes* [1960] 2 All ER 859). The physical presence of the prostitute is necessary (the placing of notices in windows offering the services of a prostitute has been held not to be soliciting (*Weisz* v *Monahan* [1962] 1 All ER 664)).

'Public place' is not defined.

The person 'soliciting' need not be in a public place (provided the solicitation extends into the public place) nor is there any requirement that the soliciting must involve any active form of approach. It has been held that a prostitute sitting on a stool in a window under a light is soliciting (*Behrendt* v *Burridge* [1976] 3 All ER 285).

'Loitering' is simply lingering with no intent to move on either on foot or in a vehicle.

OFFENCE: **Soliciting by 'Kerb-crawling'—*Sexual Offences Act 2003, s. 51A***

- Triable summarily • Fine

The Sexual Offences Act 2003, s. 51A (as amended) states:

(1) It is an offence for a person in a street or public place to solicit another (B) for the purpose of obtaining B's sexual services as a prostitute.
(2) The reference to a person in a street or public place includes a person in a vehicle in a street or public place.

KEYNOTE

Kerb-crawling or soliciting is punishable on the *first occasion* the activity takes place. In the case of kerb-crawling, there is no requirement for the soliciting to be shown to be likely to cause nuisance or annoyance to others.

The term 'street' is as per the definition given in the Keynote above. 'Public place' is not defined.

4.7 Preparatory Offences

There are specific provisions to prevent substantive offences from happening.

4.7.1 Administering Substance with Intent

OFFENCE: **Administering Substance with Intent—*Sexual Offences Act 2003, s. 61***
- Triable either way • 10 years' imprisonment on indictment
- Six months' imprisonment and/or a fine summarily

The Sexual Offences Act 2003, s. 61 states:

(1) A person commits an offence if he intentionally administers a substance to, or causes a substance to be taken by, another person (B)—
   (a) knowing that B does not consent, and
   (b) with the intention of stupefying or overpowering B, so as to enable any person to engage in a sexual activity that involves B.

KEYNOTE

This offence is aimed at the use of 'date rape' drugs administered without the victim's knowledge or consent but would also cover the use of any other substance with the relevant intention. It would cover A spiking B's soft drink with alcohol where B did not know he/she was consuming alcohol, but it would not cover A encouraging B to get drunk so that A could have sex with B, where B knew he/she was consuming alcohol.

The substance could be injected or applied by covering the victim's face with a cloth impregnated with the substance.

This offence applies both when A him/herself administers the substance to B, and where A causes the substance to be taken by B, for example when A persuades a friend (C) to administer a substance to B, so that A can have sex with B, because C knows B socially and can more easily slip the substance into B's drink than A.

However, the intended sexual activity need not involve A. In the example given above, it could be intended that C or any other person would have sex with B.

The term 'sexual' used in this section in the phrase 'sexual activity' is defined in s. 78 of the Act (see para. 4.3.2).

The sexual activity in this offence could involve A having sexual intercourse with or masturbating B, could involve A causing B to commit a sexual act upon him/herself (e.g. masturbation) or could involve B and a third party engaging in sexual activity together, regardless of whether the third party has administered the substance. This is an offence of intent rather than consequence so there is no need for the victim to be stupefied or overpowered or for the sexual activity to take place, for example because a friend of B saw what was happening and intervened to protect B.

4.7.2 Committing Criminal Offence with Intent to Commit a Sexual Offence

OFFENCE: **Committing Criminal Offence with Intent to Commit a Sexual Offence—***Sexual Offences Act 2003, s. 62*

> • Where the offence committed is kidnapping or false imprisonment—triable on indictment only: life imprisonment • Otherwise triable either way: 10 years' imprisonment on indictment; six months' imprisonment and/or a fine summarily

The Sexual Offences Act 2003, s. 62 states:

(1) A person commits an offence under this section if he commits any offence with the intention of committing a relevant sexual offence.

KEYNOTE

'Relevant sexual offence' means an offence under part I of the Act (virtually all regularly occurring sexual offences) including aiding, abetting, counselling or procuring such an offence (s. 62(2)). It *does not extend* to other sexual offences under the Protection of Children Act 1978.

It is designed to deal with the commission of any criminal offence where the defendant's intention is to commit a relevant sexual offence. This would cover an array of possible circumstances where the defendant's ulterior motive in committing the first offence is to carry out the relevant sexual offence. It would apply, for example, where A kidnaps B so that A can rape B but is caught by the police before committing the rape. It would also apply where A detained B in his/her flat with this intention, or assaulted B to subdue him/her so that A could more easily rape B.

There is no express requirement for there to be any immediate link in time between the two offences. It could cover any situation from the theft of drugs or equipment to be used in the course of the sexual offence and going equipped for burglary, to the taking of a vehicle or even dangerous driving with the intention in each case of committing the further relevant sexual offence.

If A does commit the intended offence, he/she could be charged with the substantive sexual offence in addition to this offence.

4.7.3 Trespass with Intent to Commit Sexual Offence

OFFENCE: **Trespass with Intent to Commit a Relevant Sexual Offence—***Sexual Offences Act 2003, s. 63*

> • Triable either way • 10 years' imprisonment on indictment
> • Six months' imprisonment and/or a fine summarily

The Sexual Offences Act 2003, s. 63 states:

(1) A person commits an offence if—
   (a) he is a trespasser on any premises,
   (b) he intends to commit a relevant sexual offence on the premises, and
   (c) he knows that, or is reckless as to whether, he is a trespasser.

KEYNOTE

For 'relevant sexual offence', **see para. 4.7.2**.

A person is a trespasser if they are on the premises without the owner's or occupier's consent, whether express or implied, or they are there without a power at law to be there. Generally, defendants ought to know whether they are trespassing or not and recklessness will be enough in that regard.

Premises here will include a structure or part of a structure (including a tent, vehicle or vessel or other temporary or movable structure (s. 63(2)).

This offence is intended to capture, for example, the situation where A enters a building owned by B, or goes into B's garden or garage without B's consent, and A intends to commit a relevant sexual offence against the occupier or other person on the premises.

The offence applies regardless of whether or not the substantive sexual offence is committed.

A will commit the offence if he/she has the intent to commit a relevant sexual offence at any time while he/she is a trespasser. The intent is likely to be inferred from what the defendant says or does to the intended victim (if there is one) or from items in the possession of the defendant at the time he/she commits the trespass (e.g. condoms, pornographic images, rope etc.).

A separate offence is needed to cover trespass (as opposed to relying on s. 62) because trespass is a civil tort and not a criminal offence.

The defendant must intend to commit the relevant offence *on the premises*.

4.8 | Other Sexual Offences

4.8.1 Sex with an Adult Relative

OFFENCE: **Sex with an Adult Relative: Penetration—*Sexual Offences Act 2003, s. 64***

- Triable either way • Two years' imprisonment on indictment
- Six months' imprisonment and/or a fine summarily

The Sexual Offences Act 2003, s. 64 states:

(1) A person aged 16 or over (A) (subject to subsection (3A)) commits an offence if
 (a) he intentionally penetrates another person's vagina or anus with a part of his body or anything else, or penetrates another person's mouth with his penis,
 (b) the penetration is sexual,
 (c) the other person (B) is aged 18 or over,
 (d) A is related to B in a way mentioned in subsection (2), and
 (e) A knows or could reasonably be expected to know that he is related to B in that way.

OFFENCE: **Sex with an Adult Relative: Consenting to Penetration—*Sexual Offences Act 2003, s. 65***

- Triable either way • Two years' imprisonment on indictment
- Six months' imprisonment and/or a fine summarily

The Sexual Offences Act 2003, s. 65 states:

(1) A person aged 16 or over (A) (subject to subsection 3A)) commits an offence if—
 (a) another person (B) penetrates A's vagina or anus with a part of B's body or anything else, or penetrates A's mouth with B's penis,
 (b) A consents to the penetration,
 (c) the penetration is sexual,
 (d) B is aged 18 or over,
 (e) A is related to B in a way mentioned in subsection (2), and
 (f) A knows or could reasonably be expected to know that he is related to B in that way.

KEYNOTE

For either offence to be committed, the penetration must be 'sexual'. This requirement ensures that a penetration for some other purpose, for example where one sibling helps another to insert a pessary for medical reasons, is not caught by this offence.

A 'relative' for ss. 64 and 65 is a parent, grandparent, child, grandchild, brother, sister, half-brother, half-sister, uncle, aunt, nephew or niece.

The Criminal Justice and Immigration Act 2008 amended ss. 64 and 65 so that the offences of sex with an adult relative are committed where an adoptive parent has consensual sex with their adopted child when he/she is aged 18 or over.

The adopted person does not commit this offence unless he/she is aged 18 or over.

In both offences, where the relevant relationship is proved, it will be taken that the defendant knew or could reasonably have been expected to know that he/she was related in that way unless sufficient evidence is adduced to raise an issue as to whether he/she knew or could reasonably have been expected to know that he/she was so related.

4.8.2 Possession of Extreme Pornographic Images

This offence covers a more limited range of material than the Obscene Publications Act. It creates a possession offence in respect of a sub-text of extreme pornographic material which is defined in s. 63 of the Criminal Justice and Immigration Act 2008.

OFFENCE: **Possession of Extreme Pornographic Images—*Criminal Justice and Immigration Act 2008, s. 63***

> • Triable either way • Three years' imprisonment on indictment and/or a fine (where the images contain life-threatening acts or serious injury) • Two years' imprisonment on indictment and/or a fine (where the images contain acts of necrophilia or bestiality) • Six months' imprisonment and/or a fine summarily

The Criminal Justice and Immigration Act 2008, s. 63 states:

(1) It is an offence for a person to be in possession of an extreme pornographic image.

KEYNOTE

There are three elements to the offence. An image must come within the terms of *all three elements* before it will fall foul of the offence. Those elements are:

- that the image is pornographic;
- that the image is grossly offensive, disgusting or otherwise of an obscene character; and
- that the image portrays in an explicit and realistic way, one of the following extreme acts:

  ◆ an act which threatens a person's life (this could include depictions of hanging, suffocation or sexual assault involving a threat with a weapon);
  ◆ an act which results in or is likely to result in serious injury to a person's anus, breasts or genitals (this could include the insertion of sharp objects or the mutilation of the breasts or genitals);
  ◆ an act involving sexual interference with a human corpse (necrophilia);
  ◆ a person performing an act of intercourse or oral sex with an animal (whether dead or alive) (bestiality);
  ◆ an act which involves the non-consensual penetration of a person's vagina, anus or mouth by another with the other person's penis;
  ◆ an act which involves the non-consensual sexual penetration of a person's vagina or anus by another with a part of the other person's body or anything else;
  ◆ and a reasonable person looking at the image would think that the people and animals portrayed were real.

An 'extreme pornographic image' is an image which is both pornographic and an extreme image. An image is 'pornographic' if it is of such a nature that it must reasonably be assumed to have been produced solely or principally for the purpose of sexual arousal. Section 63(4) and (5) provides that where an image is integral to a narrative (e.g. a documentary film) which taken as a whole could not reasonably be assumed to be pornographic, the image itself may be taken not to be pornographic even though if considered in isolation the contrary conclusion would have been reached.

An 'image' means either still images (such as photographs) or moving images (such as those in a film). The term also incorporates any type of data, including that stored electronically (as on a computer disk), which is capable of conversion into an image. This covers material available on computers, mobile phones or any other electronic device. The scope of the definition of image is also affected by the requirement that the persons or animals portrayed in an image must appear to be real. Therefore animated characters, sketches, paintings and the like are excluded (s. 63(8)). References to parts of the body include body parts that have been surgically constructed (s. 63(9)). Section 64 of the Act provides an exclusion from the scope of the offence under s. 63 for classified films (by the British Board of Film Classification). Proceedings cannot be instituted without the consent of the DPP.

General Defences

Several defences to the offence are set out in s. 65 of the Act. They are:

- that the person had a legitimate reason for being in possession of the image; this will cover those who can demonstrate that their legitimate business means that they have a reason for possessing the image;
- that the person had not seen the image and therefore neither knew, nor had cause to suspect, that the images held were extreme pornographic images; this will cover those who are in possession of offending images but are unaware of the nature of the images; and
- that the person had not asked for the image—it having been sent without request—and that he/she had not kept it for an unreasonable period of time; this will cover those who are sent unsolicited material and who act quickly to delete it or otherwise get rid of it.

Defence: Participation in Consensual Acts

Section 66 of the Act provides an additional defence for those who participate in the creation of extreme pornographic images. The defence is limited and will not cover images relating to bestiality and necrophilia images that depict a real corpse.

To use the defence, a defendant must prove (on the balance of probabilities) that he/she directly participated in the act or acts portrayed in the image and that the act(s) did not involve the infliction of non-consensual harm on any person. Where the image depicts necrophilia, the defendant must also prove that the human corpse portrayed was not in fact a corpse. Non-consensual harm is harm which is of such a nature that, in law, a person cannot consent to it being inflicted on him/herself, or harm to which a person can consent but did not in fact consent.

PART FIVE

Offences in Immigration Enforcement and Asylum (This section is for Immigration Enforcement and National Crime Agency Candidates only)

This Part covers offences under the Immigration Act 1971, the Immigration and Asylum Act 1999, the Asylum and Immigration (Treatment of Claimants, etc.) Act 2004, the Immigration, Asylum and Nationality Act 2006, the UK Borders Act 2007, the Identity Documents Act 2010, as well as the associated powers. It also covers the Police and Criminal Evidence Act 1984 (Application to Immigration Officers and Designated Customs Officials) Order 2013 and offences in relation to marriage.

The information in this Part is fully testable for candidates from Immigration Enforcement and the National Crime Agency *only*. Please see **How to Use** *Blackstone's Police Investigators' Manual 2022* on page xvii for further information.

5.1 | The Immigration Act 1971

This chapter is only for examination candidates from Immigration Enforcement and the National Crime Agency.

5.1.1 Introduction

The Immigration Act 1971 is the main Act of Parliament dealing with immigration issues in the United Kingdom. The Act regulates the entry and stay of individuals in the United Kingdom, creates several offences relating to such behaviour and provides a variety of powers to immigration officers and the police.

When considering *all* immigration-related offences, it should be noted that the United Kingdom is bound by the Council of Europe Treaty ratified by the government on 17 December 2008 (in force 1 April 2009) which places specific and positive obligations upon EU States to prevent and combat trafficking and protect the rights of victims. It provides for the possibility of not imposing penalties on victims for their involvement in unlawful activities to the extent that they have been compelled to do so.

Adults and children arrested by the police and charged with committing criminal offences might be the victims of trafficking. This most frequently arises when they have been trafficked here to commit criminal offences. But trafficked victims may also be apprehended by law enforcement where they are escaping from their trafficking situation. Therefore, officers must be alert to the fact that the suspect may be a victim of trafficking and consider referring the suspect through the national referral mechanism (NRM) to the competent authority for victim identification and referral to appropriate support.

5.1.2 The Immigration Act 1971—Offences

The Immigration Act 1971 provides a number of offences relating to unlawful entry to the United Kingdom.

5.1.2.1 Illegal Entry

OFFENCE: **Illegal Entry—*Immigration Act 1971, s. 24***

• Triable summarily • Six months' imprisonment and/or a fine

The Immigration Act 1971, s. 24 states:

(1) A person who is not a British citizen shall be guilty of an offence . . . in any of the following cases—
    (a) if contrary to this Act he knowingly enters the United Kingdom in breach of a deportation order or without leave;
    (aa) . . .
    (b) if, having only a limited leave to enter or remain in the United Kingdom, he knowingly either—
        (i) remains beyond the time limited by the leave; or
        (ii) fails to observe a condition of the leave;

(c) if, having lawfully entered the United Kingdom without leave by virtue of section 8(1) above, he remains without leave beyond the time allowed by section 8(1);

(d) if, without reasonable excuse, he fails to comply with any requirement imposed on him under Schedule 2 to this Act to report to a medical officer of health or to attend, or submit to a test or examination, as required by such an officer;

(e) if, without reasonable excuse, he fails to observe any restriction imposed on him under Schedule 2 or 3 to this Act as to residence, as to his employment or occupation or as to reporting to the police or to an immigration officer or to the Secretary of State;

(f) if he disembarks in the United Kingdom from a ship or aircraft after being placed on board under Schedule 2 or 3 to this Act with a view to his removal from the United Kingdom;

(g) if he embarks in contravention of a restriction imposed by or under an Order in Council under section 3(7) of this Act.

KEYNOTE

All of the offences in s. 24 can only be committed by a person who is *not* a British citizen.

Section 24 is concerned generally with non-British citizens who enter the United Kingdom illegally or who 'overstay' having been granted limited leave to be here; it also addresses occasions where such people disregard some other lawful requirements placed upon them. The offence requires actual entry and *will* not have been committed if entry has not occurred.

For the offence to be committed, a person must *knowingly* enter in breach of a deportation order or without leave. By contrast, a person is an illegal entrant (for removal purposes) simply if he/she *unlawfully* enters or seeks to enter in breach of a deportation order or of the immigration laws.

A person commits an offence under s. 24(1)(b)(i) on the day when he/she first knows that the time limited by his/her leave has expired and continues to commit it throughout any period during which he/she is in the United Kingdom thereafter, but that person shall not be prosecuted under the provision more than once in respect of the same limited leave.

The reference in s. 24(1)(c) to 'section 8(1)' refers to the special provisions made for seamen, aircrew etc. landing lawfully in the United Kingdom. The provisions of s. 8(1) of the Immigration Act 1971 allow for the crew of a ship or aircraft to enter the United Kingdom without leave for a limited amount of time in certain circumstances. These apply when the seaman is to depart aboard the same ship on which he/she arrived, or the aircrew is leaving on any plane within seven days. In both situations, they must arrive and depart as an officially engaged or employed crew member and not a passenger. When such a person remains in the United Kingdom beyond the time allowed by s. 8(1), he/she commits an offence under s. 24(1)(c). These provisions do not apply when the crew member has a deportation order in force against them or has at any time been refused leave to enter the United Kingdom and has not since then been given leave to enter or remain, or an immigration officer requires them to submit to an examination under sch. 2 to the Act.

Although the burden of proof is normally on the prosecution, an exception is made in relation to the offence under s. 24 if the case is brought within six months of the date of entry. In these cases, the burden is on the accused to show on the balance of probabilities that he/she entered the United Kingdom legally (Immigration Act 1971, s. 24(4)(b)).

Section 28 of the Immigration Act 1971 provides that an extended time limit will apply to the prosecution of the offence under s. 24. An information relating to an offence under s. 24 may, in England and Wales, be tried by a magistrates' court if it is laid within six months of the commission of the offence *or* it is laid within three years of the commission of the offence and not more than two months after the date certified by a police officer *above* the rank of chief superintendent to be the date on which evidence sufficient to justify proceedings came to the notice of an officer of the police force to which he/she belongs. A person charged with such an offence may be tried where the offence was committed or at any place he/she may be.

5.1.2.2   Use of Deception to Enter or Remain

OFFENCE: **Use of Deception—*Immigration Act 1971, s. 24A***

• Triable either way • Two years' imprisonment on indictment • Six months' imprisonment and/or a fine summarily

The Immigration Act 1971, s. 24A states:

(1) A person who is not a British citizen is guilty of an offence if, by means which include deception by him—

   (a) he obtains or seeks to obtain leave to enter or remain in the United Kingdom; or

   (b) he secures or seeks to secure the avoidance, postponement or revocation of enforcement action against him.

KEYNOTE

This offence is aimed at the more calculated actions by non-British citizens to get (or try to get) leave to enter or stay in the United Kingdom, or to evade deportation.

'Deception' here has its ordinary meaning and is not specifically defined within the 1971 Act.

This offence can be committed in a control zone in France or Belgium and powers of arrest (see para. 5.1.3.1) are exercisable there.

The offence can be committed by *seeking to enter* as well as *actually by entering*, and also embraces action taken to remain in the United Kingdom and to prevent and defer removal. It has been used against failed asylum-seekers who have sought asylum again under a false identity (*R v Nagmadeen* [2003] EWCA Crim 2004). The deception must be material (but it does not have to be the sole means of obtaining entry etc.) and must be by the immigrant personally.

It is worth noting that the relevant criminal conduct by the defendant here can be any *means which includes deception by him*. Therefore, although the entire course of conduct by the defendant need not amount to a deception, it will be necessary to show that the defendant him/herself carried out some act of deception (e.g. giving false details, providing misleading information etc.). It will not be enough for this offence to show that someone else practised a deception in order to bring about the consequences at s. 24A(1)(a) and (b) for another person (but see later for further offence of assisting and harbouring).

'Enforcement action' means:

- the giving of removal directions;
- the making of a deportation order; or
- removal.

Section 31 of the Immigration and Asylum Act 1999 sets out defences, based on Article 31 of the Convention Relating to the Status of Refugees ('the Refugee Convention'), to the offence under s. 24A. Section 31 of the Immigration and Asylum Act 1999 states that it is a defence to the deception offence (s. 24A) and certain other offences, including offences under s. 4 or 6 of the Identity Documents Act 2010 (see para. 5.6.2), for a refugee who has come to the United Kingdom directly from another country to show that he/she:

(a) presented him/herself to the UK authorities without delay;

(b) showed good cause for his/her illegal entry or presence in the United Kingdom; and

(c) made a claim for asylum as soon as was reasonably practicable after his/her arrival in the United Kingdom.

The statutory defence under s. 31 does not apply to the offence of illegal entry under s. 24 of the Immigration Act 1971.

The extended time limit discussed in **para. 5.1.2.1** does not apply to this offence.

5.1.2.3 Illegal Working

OFFENCE: **Illegal Working—*Immigration Act 1971, s. 24B***

- Summary only • Six months' imprisonment and/or a fine

The Immigration Act 1971, s. 24B states:

(1) A person ('P') who is subject to immigration control commits an offence if—

   (a) P works at a time when P is disqualified from working by reason of P's immigration status, and

(b) at that time P knows or has reasonable cause to believe that P is disqualified from working by reason of P's immigration status.

(2) For the purposes of subsection (1) a person is disqualified from working by reason of the person's immigration status if—

(a) the person has not been granted leave to enter or remain in the United Kingdom, or

(b) the person's leave to enter or remain in the United Kingdom—

(i) is invalid,

(ii) has ceased to have effect (whether by reason of curtailment, revocation, cancellation, passage of time or otherwise), or

(iii) is subject to a condition preventing the person from doing work of that kind.

KEYNOTE

The reference in s. 24B(1) to a person who is subject to immigration control is to a person who under this Act requires leave to enter or remain in the United Kingdom.

Section 24B(10) states that the reference in subs. (1) to a person working is to that person working—

(a) under a contract of employment,

(b) under a contract of apprenticeship,

(c) under a contract personally to do work,

(d) under or for the purposes of a contract for services,

(e) for a purpose related to a contract to sell goods,

(f) as a constable,

(g) in the course of Crown employment,

(h) as a relevant member of the House of Commons staff, or

(i) as a relevant member of the House of Lords staff.

Section 24B(11) states that a 'contract to sell goods' means a contract by which a person acting in the course of a trade, business, craft or profession transfers or agrees to transfer the property in goods to another person (and for this purpose 'goods' means any tangible movable items).

'Crown employment', in relation to England and Wales and Scotland, has the meaning given by s. 191(3) of the Employment Rights Act 1996 and, in relation to Northern Ireland, has the meaning given by Article 236(3) of the Employment Rights (Northern Ireland) Order 1996 (SI 1996/1919 (NI 16)) (s. 24B(11)).

A 'relevant member of the House of Commons staff' has the meaning given by s. 195(5) of the Employment Rights Act 1996 and a 'relevant member of the House of Lords staff' has the meaning given by s. 194(6) of the Employment Rights Act 1996 (s. 24B(11)).

Section 24B(12) states that s. 24B(1) does not apply to—

(a) service as a member of the naval, military or air forces of the Crown, or

(b) employment by an association established for the purposes of Part 11 of the Reserve Forces Act 1996.

A 'contract' means a contract whether express or implied and, if express, whether oral or in writing (s. 24B(13)).

If a person is convicted of an offence under subs. (1) in England and Wales, the prosecutor must consider whether to ask the court to commit the person to the Crown Court under s. 70 of the Proceeds of Crime Act 2002 (committal with view to confiscation order being considered).

5.1.2.4   Assisting Unlawful Immigration and Asylum-seekers

OFFENCE: **Assisting Unlawful Immigration to Member State—*Immigration Act 1971, s. 25***

• Triable either way • 14 years' imprisonment on indictment • Six months' imprisonment and/or a fine summarily

The Immigration Act 1971, s. 25 states:

(1) A person commits an offence if he—

(a) does an act which facilitates the commission of a breach of immigration law by an individual who is not a citizen of the European Union, and

(b) knows or has reasonable cause for believing that the act facilitates the commission of a breach of immigration law by the individual, and

(c) knows or has reasonable cause for believing that the individual is not a citizen of the European Union.

KEYNOTE

This offence requires that the defendant facilitated the commission of any breach of immigration law by someone who is not an EU citizen.

The offence refers to an act which 'facilitates' a breach of 'immigration law'. Thus, the first element in the offence is complicit dishonesty on the part of the person whose entry or stay is facilitated (e.g. that the visa applicant knew that the documents with which he/she had been provided by the accused and on which he/she relied in making his/her visa application were false); proof of dishonesty on the part of the accused is not sufficient (*R v Kaile* [2009] EWCA Crim 2868).

'Immigration law' means a law in a Member State (which includes Norway and Iceland) and which controls, in respect of some or all people who are not nationals of the State, entitlement to enter, travel across or be in the State (s. 25(2)). This means that the offence covers acts of facilitating entry or stay in *other Member States*. In *R v Kapoor* [2012] EWCA Crim 435, the Court of Appeal held that for the purposes of s. 25(2) an immigration law is a law which determines whether a person is lawfully or unlawfully either entering the UK, or in transit or being in the UK. Thus, if a person, with the necessary knowledge or reasonable cause to believe, facilitates the unlawful entry or unlawful presence in the United Kingdom of a person who is not a citizen of the EU, he/she commits the offence. The court held that s. 2 of the Asylum and Immigration (Treatment of Claimants) Act 2004 (**see para. 5.3.2.1**) was not an 'immigration law' for the purposes of s. 25(2).

The Secretary of State may make an order prescribing additional States which are to be regarded as 'Member States' for the purposes of the section if he/she considers it necessary for the purpose of complying with the United Kingdom's EU obligations (see s. 25(7)).

A document issued by the relevant government of a Member State will be conclusive in certifying any matter of law in this regard (s. 25(3)).

You must show that, in doing so, the defendant *knew* or had *reasonable cause for believing* both that their act facilitated the commission of the breach of immigration law and also that the person was not an EU citizen.

It also includes acts of assisting non-EU citizens who entered the United Kingdom lawfully to remain unlawfully. In *R v Javaherifard* [2005] EWCA Crim 3231, the Court of Appeal held that it is possible to facilitate entry by acts close to but following actual entry (e.g. by making arrangements to get illegal entrants away quickly from the port of disembarkation).

Section 25(1) applies to things done whether inside or outside the United Kingdom (the defendant's nationality is immaterial) (see s. 25(4)).

The accused cannot rely on the protection of Article 31 of the Refugee Convention (**see para. 5.1.2.2**) in relation to facilitating the entry into the United Kingdom of another (*Sternaj v DPP* [2011] EWHC 1094 (Admin)).

It is worth noting the Court of Appeal's observations that drivers and others involved in these types of offences are often of previous good character—in fact that is one of the criteria by which they are selected by the main organisers so as not to arouse suspicion of the authorities (*R v Salem* (2003) LTL 5 February).

5.1.2.5 Helping Asylum-seekers to Enter the United Kingdom

OFFENCE: **Helping Asylum-seeker to Enter United Kingdom—***Immigration Act 1971, s. 25A*

- Triable either way • 14 years' imprisonment on indictment • Six months' imprisonment and/or a fine summarily

The Immigration Act 1971, s. 25A states:

(1) A person commits an offence if—
   (a) he knowingly and for gain facilitates the arrival in or attempted arrival in, or entry or attempted entry into, the United Kingdom of an individual, and
   (b) he knows or has reasonable cause to believe that the individual is an asylum-seeker.

KEYNOTE

In order to prove this particular offence, you must show that the defendant acted in the *knowledge* that they facilitated the arrival/attempted arrival or entry/attempted entry into the United Kingdom of a person whom they *knew* was (or had *reasonable cause to believe* to be) an asylum-seeker and that, in so doing, they acted 'for gain'—the whole essence of this offence is profiteering thus financial gain is an essential element of the offence.

'Asylum-seeker' means a person who *intends* to claim that to remove them from, or require them to leave, the United Kingdom would be contrary to the United Kingdom's obligations under the Refugee Convention or the Human Rights Convention (in each case as defined under s. 167(1) of the Immigration and Asylum Act 1999) (s. 25A(2)). This presumably means that a person could be guilty of this offence even though the immigrant did not make a claim under the Refugee Convention or the European Convention on Human Rights (ECHR), provided it can be established that the immigrant intended to make such a claim.

Section 25A applies in the case of an asylum-seeker who arrives/attempts to arrive in or enters/attempts to enter the United Kingdom without any breach of immigration law being committed by the person gaining entry (*Sternaj*).

The right to claim asylum is protected by the Universal Declaration of Human Rights so the act of assisting asylum-seekers to arrive in the United Kingdom and claim asylum cannot therefore be unlawful *per se*, hence this offence does not apply to anything done by a person acting on behalf of an organisation which aims to assist asylum-seekers and *does not charge for its services* (s. 25A(3)).

A conspiracy to 'assist persons claiming asylum in the UK' is not an offence known to law (*R* v *Hadi* [2001] EWCA Crim 2534).

5.1.2.6 Assisting Entry to United Kingdom in Breach of Deportation Order

OFFENCE: **Assisting Entry to United Kingdom in Breach of Deportation Order— *Immigration Act 1971, s. 25B***

> • Triable either way • 14 years' imprisonment on indictment • Six months' imprisonment and/or a fine summarily

The Immigration Act 1971, s. 25B states:

(1) A person commits an offence if he—
   (a) does an act which facilitates a breach or attempted breach of a deportation order in force against an individual who is a citizen of the European Union, and
   (b) knows or has reasonable cause for believing that the act facilitates a breach or attempted breach of the deportation order.
(2) ...
(3) A person commits an offence if he—
   (a) does an act which assists the individual to arrive in, enter or remain, or attempt to arrive in, enter or remain, in the United Kingdom,
   (b) knows or has reasonable cause for believing that the act assists the individual to arrive in, enter or remain or attempt to arrive in, enter or remain, in the United Kingdom, and
   (c) knows or has reasonable cause for believing that the Secretary of State has made an order excluding the individual from the United Kingdom on the grounds of public policy, public security or public health.

5.1.2.7 Obstructing an Immigration Officer

OFFENCE: **Obstructing an Immigration Officer—*Immigration Act 1971, s. 26(1)(g)***

• Triable summarily • Six months' imprisonment and/or a fine

The Immigration Act 1971, s. 26 states that a person shall be guilty of an offence:

(1)(g) if, without reasonable excuse, he obstructs an immigration officer or other person lawfully acting in the execution of this Act.

5.1.3 The Immigration Act 1971—Powers

Immigration officers are provided with essential powers of arrest and search in order to deal with offences outlined in **para. 5.1.2** and related offences—these powers can be found in ss. 28A to 28H of the Immigration Act 1971.

5.1.3.1 Arrest Without Warrant

There are a number of powers of arrest set out in the Immigration Act 1971.

The Immigration Act 1971, s. 28A states:

(1) An immigration officer may arrest without warrant a person—
 (a) who has committed or attempted to commit an offence under section 24 or 24A; or
 (b) whom he has reasonable grounds for suspecting has committed or attempted to commit such an offence.
(2) But subsection (1) does not apply in relation to an offence under section 24(1)(d).
(3) An immigration officer may arrest without warrant a person—
 (a) who has committed an offence under section 24B, 25, 25A or 25B; or
 (b) whom he has reasonable grounds for suspecting has committed that offence.
(4) …

(5) An immigration officer may arrest without warrant a person ('the suspect') who, or whom he has reasonable grounds for suspecting—

    (a) has committed or attempted to commit an offence under section 26(1)(g); or

    (b) is committing or attempting to commit that offence.

(6) The power conferred by subsection (5) is exercisable only if either the first or the second condition is satisfied.

(7) The first condition is that it appears to the officer that service of a summons (or, in Scotland, a copy complaint) is impracticable or inappropriate because—

    (a) he does not know, and cannot readily discover, the suspect's name;

    (b) he has reasonable grounds for doubting whether a name given by the suspect as his name is his real name;

    (c) the suspect has failed to give him a satisfactory address for service; or

    (d) he has reasonable grounds for doubting whether an address given by the suspect is a satisfactory address for service.

(8) The second condition is that the officer has reasonable grounds for believing that arrest is necessary to prevent the suspect—

    (a) causing physical injury to himself or another person;

    (b) suffering physical injury; or

    (c) causing loss of or damage to property.

(9) For the purposes of subsection (7), an address is a satisfactory address for service if it appears to the officer—

    (a) that the suspect will be at that address for a sufficiently long period for it to be possible to serve him with a summons (or copy complaint); or

    (b) that some other person specified by the suspect will accept service of a summons (or copy complaint) for the suspect at that address.

(9A) An immigration officer may arrest without a warrant a person—

    (a) who has committed an offence under section 26A or 26B; or

    (b) whom he has reasonable grounds for suspecting has committed an offence under section 26A or 26B

(9B) An immigration officer may arrest without warrant a person who, or whom the immigration officer has reasonable grounds of suspecting—

    (a) has committed or attempted to commit an offence under s. 21(1) or (1A) of the Immigration, Asylum and Nationality Act 2006 (employment of illegal worker etc.), or

    (b) is committing or attempting to commit that offence.

KEYNOTE

The power of arrest under s. 28A(5) relates to the offence under s. 26(1)(g) (obstructing an immigration officer).

In relation to the exercise of the power conferred by subs. (5), it is immaterial that no offence has been committed (s. 28A(10)).

In Scotland, the powers conferred by s. 28A(3) and (5) may also be exercised by a constable (s. 28(11)).

The power of arrest under s. 28A(9A) relates to the offences relating to registration cards (s. 26A) and possession of immigration stamps (26B).

5.1.3.2 Arrest with Warrant

The Immigration Act 1971, s. 28AA states:

(1) This section applies if on an application by an immigration officer a justice of the peace is satisfied that there are reasonable grounds for suspecting that a person has committed an offence under s. 24(1)(d).

(2) The justice of the peace may grant a warrant authorising any immigration officer to arrest the person.

(3) In the application of this section to Scotland a reference to a justice of the peace shall be treated as a reference to the sheriff or a justice of the peace.

5.1.3.3 Search and Arrest by Warrant

The Immigration Act 1971, s. 28B states:

(1) Subsection (2) applies if a justice of the peace is, by written information on oath, satisfied that there are reasonable grounds for suspecting that a person ('the suspect') who is liable to be arrested for a relevant offence is to be found on any premises.

(2) The justice may grant a warrant authorising any immigration officer or constable to enter, if need be by force, the premises named in the warrant for the purpose of searching for and arresting the suspect.

(3) Subsection (4) applies if in Scotland the sheriff or a justice of the peace is by evidence on oath satisfied as mentioned in subsection (1).

(4) The sheriff or justice may grant a warrant authorising any immigration officer or constable to enter, if need be by force, the premises named in the warrant for the purpose of searching for and arresting the suspect.

KEYNOTE

A 'relevant offence' means an offence under s. 24(1)(a) to (f) (illegal entry), s. 24A (use of deception) and 24B (illegal working). It also applies to the offences under ss. 2 and 35(3) of the Asylum and Immigration (Treatment of Claimants, etc) Act 2004 (see chapter 5.3) and to the offence under s. 21 of the Immigration, Asylum and Nationality Act 2006 (see chapter 5.4).

'Premises' includes any vehicle, vessel, aircraft or hovercraft, any offshore installation, any renewable energy installation and any tent or movable structure.

5.1.3.4 Search and Arrest Without Warrant

The Immigration Act 1971, s. 28C states:

(1) An immigration officer may enter and search any premises for the purpose of arresting a person for an offence under section 25, 25A or 25B.

KEYNOTE

The power may be exercised only to the extent that it is reasonably required for that purpose and only if the officer has reasonable grounds for believing that the person whom he/she is seeking is on the premises (s. 28C(2)).

In relation to premises consisting of two or more separate dwellings, the power is limited to entering and searching any parts of the premises which the occupiers of any dwelling comprised in the premises use in common with the occupiers of any such other dwelling and any such dwelling in which the officer has reasonable grounds for believing that the person whom he/she is seeking may be (s. 28C(3)).

The power may be exercised only if the officer produces identification showing that they are an immigration officer (whether or not they are asked to do so) (s. 28C(4)).

5.1.3.5 Business Premises—Entry to Arrest

The Immigration Act 1971, s. 28CA states:

(1) A constable or immigration officer may enter and search any business premises for the purpose of arresting a person—

    (a) for an offence under s. 24,

    (ba) for an offence under s. 24B

    (b) for an offence under s. 24A, or

    (c) under paragraph 17 of Schedule 2.

5.1.3.6   Entry and Search of Premises

The Immigration Act 1971, s. 28D states:

(1) If, on the application made by an immigration officer, a justice of the peace is satisfied that there are reasonable grounds for believing that—
  (a) a relevant offence has been committed,
  (b) there is material on the premises specified in the application which is likely to be of substantial value (whether by itself or together with other material) to the investigation of the offence,
  (c) the material is likely to be relevant evidence,
  (d) the material does not consist of or include items subject to legal privilege, excluded material or special procedure material, and
  (e) any of the conditions specified in subsection (2) applies,
  (f) he may issue a warrant authorising an immigration officer to enter and search the premises.
(2) The conditions are that—
  (a) it is not practicable to communicate with any person entitled to grant entry to the premises;
  (b) it is practicable to communicate with a person entitled to grant entry to the premises but it is not practicable to communicate with any person entitled to grant access to the evidence;
  (c) entry to the premises will not be granted unless a warrant is produced;
  (d) the purpose of a search may be frustrated or seriously prejudiced unless an immigration officer arriving at the premises can secure immediate entry to them.

5.1.3.7 Entry and Search of Premises following Arrest

The Immigration Act 1971, s. 28E states:

(1) This section applies if a person is arrested for an offence under this Part at a place other than a police station.

(2) An immigration officer may enter and search any premises—

    (a) in which the person was when arrested, or

    (b) in which he was immediately before he was arrested,

    for evidence relating to the offence for which the arrest was made ('relevant offence').

(3) The power may be exercised—

    (a) only if the officer has reasonable grounds for believing that there is evidence on the premises; and

    (b) only to the extent that it is reasonably required for the purpose of discovering relevant evidence.

KEYNOTE

'Offence under this Part' means the same as 'relevant offence' in **para. 5.1.3.6**.

In relation to premises consisting of two or more separate dwellings, the power is limited to entering and searching any dwelling in which the arrest took place or in which the arrested person was immediately before his/her arrest and any parts of the premises which the occupier of any such dwelling uses in common with the occupiers of any such dwellings comprised in the premises (s. 28E(4)).

An officer may seize and retain anything he/she finds during the search which he/she has reasonable grounds for believing is relevant evidence (s. 28E(5)), except items subject to 'legal privilege' (s. 28E(6)) (see **para. 1.6.3.8**).

5.1.3.8 Entry and Search of Premises following Arrest under Section 25, 25A or 25B

The Immigration Act 1971, s. 28F states:

(1) An immigration officer may enter and search any premises occupied or controlled by a person arrested for an offence under section 25, 25A, 25B.

(2) The power may be exercised—

    (a) only if the officer has reasonable grounds for suspecting that there is relevant evidence on the premises;

    (b) only to the extent that it is reasonably required for the purpose of discovering relevant evidence; and

    (c) subject to subsection (3), only if a senior officer has authorised it in writing.

(3) The power may be exercised—

    (a) before taking the arrested person to a place where he is to be detained; and

    (b) without obtaining an authorisation under subsection (2)(c),

    if the presence of that person at a place other than one where he is to be detained is necessary for the effective investigation of the offence.

KEYNOTE

The specified offences are s. 25 (assisting unlawful immigration), s. 25A (helping an asylum-seeker to enter the United Kingdom) and s. 25B (assisting entry to the United Kingdom in breach of a deportation/exclusion order).

An officer who has relied on subs. (3) must inform a senior officer as soon as is practicable (s. 28F(4)).

The officer authorising a search, or who is informed of one under subs. (4), must make a record in writing of the grounds for the search and the nature of the evidence that was sought (s. 28F(5)).

An officer searching premises under this section may seize and retain anything he/she finds which he/she has reasonable grounds for suspecting is relevant evidence (s. 28F(6)). 'Relevant evidence' means evidence, other than items subject to legal privilege, that relates to the offence in question (s. 28F(7)).

'Senior officer' means an immigration officer not below the rank of chief immigration officer (s. 28F(8)).

5.1.3.9   Search for Personnel Records—Warrant Unnecessary

The Immigration Act 1971, s. 28FA states:

    (1) This section applies where—
        (a) a person has been arrested for an offence under section 24(1), 24A(1) or 24B(1),
        (b) a person has been arrested under paragraph 17 of Schedule 2,
        (c) a constable or immigration officer reasonably believes that a person is liable to arrest for an offence under section 24(1) or 24A(1), or
        (d) a constable or immigration officer reasonably believes that a person is liable to arrest under paragraph 17 of Schedule 2.
    (2) A constable or immigration officer may search business premises where the arrest was made or where the person liable to arrest is if the constable or immigration officer reasonably believes—
        (a) that a person has committed an immigration employment offence in relation to the person arrested or liable to arrest, and
        (b) that employee records, other than items subject to legal privilege, will be found on the premises and will be of substantial value (whether on their own or together with other material) in the investigation of the immigration employment offence.
    (3) A constable or officer searching premises under subsection (2) may seize and retain employee records, other than items subject to legal privilege, which he reasonably suspects will be of substantial value (whether on their own or together with other material) in the investigation of—
        (a) an immigration employment offence, or
        (b) an offence under section 105 or 106 of the Immigration and Asylum Act 1999 (c. 33) (support for asylum-seeker: fraud).

KEYNOTE

Section 28FA(4) states that the power under subs. (2) may be exercised only to the extent that it is reasonably required for the purpose of discovering employee records other than items subject to legal privilege. The constable or immigration officer must produce identification showing his/her status (only when the premises are occupied) and the constable or immigration officer must reasonably believe that at least one of the following conditions applies.

Those conditions are—

- that it is not practicable to communicate with a person entitled to grant access to the records;
- that permission to search has been refused;
- that permission to search would be refused if requested; and
- that the purpose of a search may be frustrated or seriously prejudiced if it is not carried out in reliance on subs. (2) (s. 28FA(5)).

In this section, 'immigration employment offence' means an offence under s. 21 of the Immigration, Asylum and Nationality Act 2006 (employment) (s. 28FA(7)).

'Business premises' means premises (or any part of premises) not used as a dwelling (Immigration Act 1971, s. 28L(2)).

'Employee records' means records which show an employee's name, date of birth, address, length of service, rate of pay, nationality or citizenship (Immigration Act 1971, s. 28L(3)).

For 'items subject to legal privilege', **see para. 1.6.3.8.**

5.1.3.10   Search for Personnel Records—With Warrant

The Immigration Act 1971, s. 28FB states:

    (1) This section applies where on an application made by an immigration officer in respect of business premises a justice of the peace is satisfied that there are reasonable grounds for believing—
        (a) that an employer has provided inaccurate or incomplete information under section 134 of the Nationality, Immigration and Asylum Act 2002 (compulsory disclosure by employer),

(b) that employee records, other than items subject to legal privilege, will be found on the premises and will enable deduction of some or all of the information which the employer was required to provide, and

(c) that at least one of the conditions in subsection (2) is satisfied.

(2) Those conditions are—

(a) that it is not practicable to communicate with a person entitled to grant access to the premises,

(b) that it is not practicable to communicate with a person entitled to grant access to the records,

(c) that entry to the premises or access to the records will not be granted unless a warrant is produced, and

(d) that the purpose of a search may be frustrated or seriously prejudiced unless an immigration officer arriving at the premises can secure immediate entry.

(3) The justice of the peace may issue a warrant authorising an immigration officer to enter and search the premises.

KEYNOTE

For the meaning of 'business premises' and 'employee records', **see para. 5.1.3.9.**

An immigration officer searching premises under a warrant issued under this section may seize and retain employee records, other than items subject to legal privilege, which he/she reasonably suspects will be of substantial value (whether on their own or together with other material) in the investigation of an offence under s. 137 of the Nationality, Immigration and Asylum Act 2002 (disclosure of information: offences) in respect of a requirement under s. 134 of that Act or an offence under s. 105 or 106 of the Immigration and Asylum Act 1999 (support for asylum-seeker: fraud) (s. 28FB(5)).

5.1.3.11   Searching Arrested Persons

The Immigration Act 1971, s. 28G states:

(1) This section applies if a person is arrested for an offence under this Part at a place other than a police station.

(2) An immigration officer may search the arrested person if he has reasonable grounds for believing that the arrested person may present a danger to himself or others.

(3) The officer may search the arrested person for—

(a) anything which he might use to assist his escape from lawful custody; or

(b) anything which might be evidence relating to the offence for which he has been arrested.

KEYNOTE

'An offence under this Part' is a reference to part 3 of the Immigration Act 1971 (Criminal Proceedings). This covers a whole series of offences including offences under s. 24(1)(a) to (f) (illegal entry), s. 24A (use of deception), s. 24B (illegal working), s. 25 (assisting unlawful immigration to a Member State), s. 25A (helping an asylum-seeker) and s. 25B (assisting entry in breach of a deportation/exclusion order).

The power under subs. (3) may only be exercised if the officer has reasonable grounds for believing that the arrested person may have concealed on him/her anything of a kind mentioned in that subsection and only to the extent that it is reasonably required for the purpose of discovering such a thing (s. 28G(4)).

The power does not authorise an officer to demand the removal of any of the person's clothing in public other than an outer coat, jacket and gloves, *but it does* authorise the search of a person's mouth (s. 28G(5)).

An officer searching a person under subs. (2) may seize and retain anything he/she finds, if he/she has reasonable grounds for believing that the person might use it to cause physical injury to themselves or another person (s. 28G(6)).

An officer searching a person under subs. (3) may seize and retain anything he/she finds if he/she has reasonable grounds for believing that the person may use it to assist their escape from lawful custody or that it is evidence which relates to the offence in question as long as it is not an item subject to legal privilege (see para. 1.6.3.8) (s. 28G(7)).

5.1.3.12 Searching Persons in Police Custody

The Immigration Act 1971, s. 28H states:

(1) This section applies if a person—
    (a) has been arrested for an offence under this Part; and
    (b) is in custody at a police station or in police detention at a place other than a police station.
(2) An immigration officer may, at any time, search the arrested person in order to see whether he has anything—
    (a) which he might use to—
        (i) cause physical injury to himself or others;
        (ii) damage property;
        (iii) interfere with evidence; or
        (iv) assist his escape; or
    (b) which the officer has reasonable grounds for believing is evidence relating to the offence in question.

KEYNOTE

'An offence under this Part' is a reference to part 3 of the Immigration Act 1971 (Criminal Proceedings). This covers a whole series of offences including offences under s. 24(1)(a) to (f) (illegal entry), s. 24A (use of deception), s. 24B (illegal working), s. 25 (assisting unlawful immigration to a Member State), s. 25A (helping an asylum-seeker) and s. 25B (assisting entry in breach of a deportation/exclusion order).

For the meaning of 'police detention', **see para. 1.6.5.2.**

For the meaning of 'custody officer', **see para. 1.6.2.**

The power may be exercised only to the extent that the custody officer concerned considers it to be necessary for the purpose of discovering anything of a kind mentioned in subs. (2) (s. 28H(3)).

The officer searching a person under this section may seize and retain anything he/she finds, if he/she has reasonable grounds for believing that that person might use it for one or more of the purposes mentioned in subs. (2)(a), in which case it may be retained by the police or, if it is evidence relating to the offence in question, in which case it may be retained by an immigration officer (s. 28H(4) to (6)).

The person from whom something is seized must be told the reason for the seizure unless he/she is:

- violent or appears likely to become violent; or
- is incapable of understanding what is said to him/her (s. 28H(7)).

An intimate search *may not* be conducted under this section (s. 28H(8)). For the meaning of an 'intimate search, **see para. 1.7.19.**

The person carrying out the search under this section must be the same sex as the person searched (s. 28H(9)).

5.2 The Immigration and Asylum Act 1999

5.2.1 Introduction

The Immigration and Asylum Act 1999 provides legislation to deal with individuals who possess and/or use false documents in relation to immigration matters. The Act provides several offences to deal with false and dishonest representations made in respect of part VI of the Act. Part VI of the Act acknowledges that an asylum-seeker and his/her dependants may need support from the State in the form of accommodation or provision for essential living needs (including meals and personal care items) or both.

5.2.2 Offences under the Immigration and Asylum Act 1999

False or dishonest representations in support of an asylum-seeker are dealt with by the Immigration and Asylum Act 1999.

5.2.2.1 False Representations in Respect of Support for an Asylum-seeker

OFFENCE: **False Representations—*Immigration and Asylum Act 1999, s. 105***
- Triable summarily • Three months' imprisonment and/or a fine

The Immigration and Asylum Act 1999, s. 105 states:

(1) A person is guilty of an offence if, with a view to obtaining support for himself or any other person under any provision made by or under this Part, he—
   (a) makes a statement or representation which he knows is false in a material particular;
   (b) produces or gives to a person exercising functions under this Part, or knowingly causes or allows to be produced or given to such a person, any document or information which he knows is false in a material particular;
   (c) fails, without reasonable excuse, to notify a change of circumstances when required to do so in accordance with any provision made by or under this Part; or
   (d) without reasonable excuse, knowingly causes another person to fail to notify a change of circumstances which that other person was required to notify in accordance with any provision made by or under this Part.

5.2.2.2 Dishonest Representations in Respect of Support for an Asylum-seeker

OFFENCE: **Dishonest Representations—*Immigration and Asylum Act 1999, s. 106***
- Triable either way • Seven years' imprisonment and/or a fine on indictment • Six months' imprisonment and/or a fine summarily

The Immigration and Asylum Act 1999, s. 106 states:

(1) A person is guilty of an offence if, with a view to obtaining any benefit or other payment or advantage under this Part for himself or any other person, he dishonestly—
   (a) makes a statement or representation which is false in a material particular;
   (b) produces or gives to a person exercising functions under this Part, or causes or allows to be produced or given to such a person, any document or information which is false in a material particular;

(c) fails to notify a change of circumstances when required to do so in accordance with any provision made by or under this Part; or

(d) causes another person to fail to notify a change of circumstances which that other person was required to notify in accordance with any provision made by or under this Part.

(2) ...

(3) In the application of this section to Scotland, in subsection (1) for 'dishonestly' substitute 'knowingly'.

KEYNOTE

The power to enter and search (under s. 28E of the Immigration Act 1971) applies to these offences (**see para. 5.1.3.7**).

The power to search a person (under s. 28G of the Immigration Act 1971) applies to a person arrested for these offences (**see para. 5.1.3.11**).

5.3 The Asylum and Immigration (Treatment of Claimants, etc.) Act 2004

> This chapter is only for examination candidates from Immigration Enforcement and the National Crime Agency.

5.3.1 Introduction

In addition to the more general immigration offences and provisions discussed in **chapter 5.1**, there are specific statutory measures designed to deal with other immigration offences. These are dealt with by the Asylum and Immigration (Treatment of Claimants, etc.) Act 2004.

5.3.2 Offences

There has been a steady flow of offences covered by s. 2 of the Act (failing to produce an immigration document) and the offence under s. 35 (fail to comply with a requirement) is high on the agenda across Immigration Enforcement. In addition, the offence relating to trafficking people into, within or out of the United Kingdom for the purpose of exploitation is constantly in the media spotlight due to its increasing occurrence.

5.3.2.1 Entering the United Kingdom without a Passport etc.

OFFENCE: **Entering the United Kingdom without a Passport etc.—*Asylum and Immigration (Treatment of Claimants, etc.) Act 2004, s. 2***

- Triable either way • Two years' imprisonment and/or a fine on indictment • Six months' imprisonment and/or a fine summarily

The Asylum and Immigration (Treatment of Claimants) Act 2004, s. 2 states:

(1) A person commits an offence if at a leave or asylum interview he does not have with him an immigration document which—
 (a) is in force, and
 (b) satisfactorily establishes his identity and nationality or citizenship.
(2) A person commits an offence if at a leave or asylum interview he does not have with him, in respect of any dependent child with whom he claims to be travelling or living, an immigration document which—
 (a) is in force, and
 (b) satisfactorily establishes the child's identity and nationality or citizenship.
(3) But a person does not commit an offence under subsection (1) or (2) if—
 (a) the interview referred to in that subsection takes place after the person has entered the United Kingdom, and

(b) within the period of three days beginning with the date of the interview the person provides to an immigration officer or to the Secretary of State a document of the kind referred to in that subsection.

(4) It is a defence for a person charged with an offence under subsection (1)—

    (a) to prove that he is an EEA national,

    (b) to prove that he is a member of the family of an EEA national and that he is exercising a right under the Community Treaties in respect of entry to or residence in the United Kingdom,

    (c) to prove that he has a reasonable excuse for not being in possession of a document of the kind specified in subsection (1),

    (d) to produce a false immigration document and to prove that he used that document as an immigration document for all purposes in connection with his journey to the United Kingdom, or

    (e) to prove that he travelled to the United Kingdom without, at any stage since he set out on the journey, having possession of an immigration document.

(5) It is a defence for a person charged with an offence under subsection (2) in respect of a child—

    (a) to prove that the child is an EEA national,

    (b) to prove that the child is a member of the family of an EEA national and that the child is exercising a right under the Community Treaties in respect of entry to or residence in the United Kingdom,

    (c) to prove that the person has a reasonable excuse for not being in possession of a document of the kind specified in subsection (2),

    (d) to produce a false immigration document and to prove that it was used as an immigration document for all purposes in connection with the child's journey to the United Kingdom, or

    (e) to prove that he travelled to the United Kingdom with the child without, at any stage since he set out on the journey, having possession of an immigration document in respect of the child.

(6) Where the charge for an offence under subsection (1) or (2) relates to an interview which takes place after the defendant has entered the United Kingdom—

    (a) subsections (4)(c) and (5)(c) shall not apply, but

    (b) it is a defence for the defendant to prove that he has a reasonable excuse for not providing a document in accordance with subsection (3).

(7) For the purposes of subsections (4) to (6)—

    (a) the fact that a document was deliberately destroyed or disposed of is not a reasonable excuse for not being in possession of it or for not providing it in accordance with subsection (3), unless it is shown that the destruction or disposal was—

        (i) for a reasonable cause, or

        (ii) beyond the control of the person charged with the offence, and

    (b) in paragraph (a)(i) 'reasonable cause' does not include the purpose of—

        (i) delaying the handling or resolution of a claim or application or the taking of a decision,

        (ii) increasing the chances of success of a claim or application, or

        (iii) complying with instructions or advice given by a person who offers advice about, or facilitates, immigration into the United Kingdom, unless in the circumstances of the case it is unreasonable to expect non-compliance with the instructions or advice.

(8) A person shall be presumed for the purposes of this section not to have a document with him if he fails to produce it to an immigration officer or official of the Secretary of State on request.

KEYNOTE

If a person is unable to produce an immigration document at a leave or asylum interview in respect of either themselves or a child with whom they claim to be living or travelling then they will commit an offence. A person does not commit the offence if the interview takes place after the person has entered the United Kingdom and within the period of three days beginning with the date of the interview the person provides an immigration document to an immigration officer or to the Secretary of State.

There are various defences to the charges. In respect of a person's failure to produce their own document it will be a defence for them to prove that:

(a) they are an EEA national;

(b) they are a member of the family of an EEA national and they are exercising a right under the Community Treaties in respect of entry to or residence in the United Kingdom;

(c) they have a reasonable excuse for not being in possession of an immigration document; or

(d) they travelled to the United Kingdom without, at any stage since they set out on that journey, having possession of an immigration document.

The term reasonable excuse is not defined under the Act. This will ultimately be a matter for the courts to decide. However, certain factors are specifically excluded from amounting to a reasonable excuse under s. 2(7) of the Act which states:

For the purposes of subsections (4) to (6):

(a) the fact that a document was deliberately destroyed or disposed of is not a reasonable excuse for not being in possession of it or for not providing it in accordance with subsection (3), unless it is shown that the destruction or disposal was—

   i. for a reasonable cause, or

   ii. beyond the control of the person charged with the offence, and

(b) in paragraph (a)(i) 'reasonable cause' does not include the purpose of—

   i. delaying the handling or resolution of a claim or application or the taking of a decision,

   ii. increasing the chances of success of a claim or application, or

   iii. complying with instructions or advice given by a person who offers advice about, or facilitates, immigration into the United Kingdom, unless in the circumstances of the case it is unreasonable to expect non-compliance with the instructions or advice.

In *Soe Thet* v *Director of Public Prosecutions* [2006] EWHC 2701 (Admin), the appellant asserted that he had never been in possession of a genuine travel document and relied on s. 2(4)(c) on the basis that he could not commit an offence if he could provide a reasonable excuse for not being in possession of a genuine passport in the first place. In this case, the High Court concluded that Thet was unable to obtain a passport in his country of origin, Burma, because he had been a political prisoner. He therefore had a 'reasonable excuse' for not providing a genuine passport as the Burmese authorities would not have provided him with one. The defendant must satisfy the tribunal as to where he/she is from. The defences arising under ss. 2(4)(c) and 2(6)(b) refer to genuine documents only.

The position was further clarified in *Mohammed and Osman* [2007] EWCA Crim 2332. If an applicant states that he/she has travelled on a genuine travel document but does not have a reasonable excuse for not providing it at interview, he/she will be caught by the Act. In the case of *Mohammed*, she was unable to obtain a genuine travel document because of lack of issuing facilities. Neither could she produce false travel documents as they were removed by an agent.

The following excuses *might be considered reasonable* following the effects of the decisions in *Thet* and *Mohammed and Osman*.

The applicant who states that he/she has travelled on a genuine document:

- they are unable to obtain a genuine travel document because of the political situation in the country of origin (as in *Thet*);
- they are unable to obtain a genuine travel document because of lack of issuing facilities (as in *Mohammed* who did not know where to go to obtain a genuine passport—the Court of Appeal indicated that this could amount to a defence);
- their genuine travel document has been stolen en route, or in the UK, through no fault of the applicant;
- their genuine travel document has been destroyed en route, or in the UK, through no fault of the applicant.

The applicant who states that he/she has travelled on a false document:

- they are able to produce that false document and prove he/she has used it to enter the UK;
- they can establish a reasonable excuse for not being in possession of a genuine passport (i.e. the *Thet* reason referred to above).

The applicant who says that he/she never had any documents:

- they must show that at no stage in their journey to the UK, did they have any travel documents at all (e.g. if they can prove that they were smuggled for the entire journey in a lorry).

Section 2(8) of the Act creates a statutory presumption that a person does not have a document with them if they fail to produce it to an immigration officer or official of the Secretary of State on request.

The available defences therefore (following the cases referred to earlier) can be summarised as follows:

- Defence 1—s. 2(4)(c): does the applicant have a reasonable excuse for not being in possession of a genuine document? If yes, they have a defence, even if they travelled on false documents.
- Defence 2—s. 2(4)(d): if they travelled on false documents, can they produce them? If yes, they have a defence.
- Defence 3—s. 2(4)(e): can they prove that at no stage did they travel to the UK without documents at all (either genuine or false)? If yes, they will have a defence.

An example of the defence under s. 2(4)(c) being used was in *Soe Thet* v *Director of Public Prosecutions* [2006] EWHC 2701 (Admin).

It is also a defence for a person to produce a false immigration document and to prove that he/she used that document as an immigration document for all purposes in connection with his/her journey to the United Kingdom.

In respect of a person's failure to produce a document for a child with whom he/she claims to be living or travelling, it will be a defence for him/her to prove that:

(a) the child is an EEA national;
(b) the child is a member of the family of an EEA national and that they are exercising a right under Community Treaties in respect of entry to or residence in the United Kingdom;
(c) the person has a reasonable excuse for not being in possession of an immigration document in respect of the child; or
(d) that he/she travelled to the United Kingdom with the child without, at any stage since he/she set out on the journey, having possession of an immigration document in respect of the child.

It is also a defence for a person to produce a false immigration document and to prove that it was used as an immigration document for all purposes in connection with the child's journey to the United Kingdom.

An immigration officer or a police constable who has a reasonable suspicion that an offence under the section has been committed may arrest the person without a warrant (s. 2(10)).

'EEA national' means a national of a State which is a contracting party to the Agreement on the European Economic Area signed at Oporto on 2 May 1992 (as it has effect from time to time).

An 'immigration document' means:

(a) a passport; and
(b) a document which relates to a national of a State other than the United Kingdom and which is designed to serve the same purpose as a passport.

The phrase 'leave or asylum interview' means an interview with an immigration officer or an official of the Secretary of State at which a person:

(a) seeks leave to enter or remain in the United Kingdom; or
(b) claims that to remove them from or require them to leave the United Kingdom would breach the United Kingdom's obligations under the Refugee Convention or would be unlawful under s. 6 of the Human Rights Act 1998 as being incompatible with their Convention rights.

For the purposes of this section, a document which purports to be, or is designed to look like, an immigration document, is a false immigration document, and an immigration document is a false immigration document if and insofar as it is used:

(a) outside the period for which it is expressed to be valid;
(b) contrary to provision for its use made by the person issuing it; or
(c) by or in respect of a person other than the person to or for whom it was issued.

5.3.2.2 Deportation or Removal—Co-operation

The Asylum and Immigration (Treatment of Claimants, etc.) Act 2004, s. 35 states:

(1) The Secretary of State may require a person to take specified action if the Secretary of State thinks that—
  (a) the action will or may enable a travel document to be obtained by or for the person, and

(b) possession of the travel document will facilitate the person's deportation or removal from the United Kingdom.

(2) In particular, the Secretary of State may require a person to—

(a) provide information or documents to the Secretary of State or to any other person;

(b) obtain information or documents;

(c) provide fingerprints, submit to the taking of a photograph or provide information, or submit to a process for the recording of information, about external physical characteristics (including, in particular, features of the iris or any other part of the eye);

(d) make, or consent to or co-operate with the making of, an application to a person acting for the government of a State other than the United Kingdom;

(e) co-operate with a process designed to enable determination of an application;

(f) complete a form accurately and completely;

(g) attend an interview and answer questions accurately and completely;

(h) make an appointment.

KEYNOTE

Under s. 35(3), a person commits an offence if he/she fails without *reasonable excuse* to comply with a requirement of the Secretary of State under s. 35(1). Fear of persecution in the home country was held *not* to constitute a reasonable excuse for non-compliance with a requirement to attend for interview by officials of that country's embassy in *R v Tabnak* [2007] EWCA Crim 380. Reasonable excuse should relate to *ability*, not willingness, to comply. Home Office guidance on the Act indicates that travel difficulties and health emergencies might constitute reasonable excuses.

The offence is triable either way and punishable with two years' imprisonment and/or a fine on indictment or, on summary conviction, to imprisonment for six months and/or a fine.

If a constable or immigration officer reasonably suspects that a person has committed an offence under s. 35(3) then he/she may arrest the person without warrant (s. 35(5)).

A 'travel document' means a passport or other document which is issued by or for Her Majesty's Government or the government of another State and which enables or facilitates travel from the United Kingdom to another State.

The term 'removal from the United Kingdom' means removal under:

(a) sch. 2 to the Immigration Act 1971 (control on entry) (including a provision of that schedule as applied by another provision of the Immigration Acts);

(b) s. 10 of the Immigration and Asylum Act 1999 (removal of person unlawfully in United Kingdom); or

(c) sch. 3 to the Act.

Section 35 of the Act was examined in *The Queen (Babbage) v Secretary of State for the Home Department* [2016] EWHC 148 (Admin). The ruling in the case stated that the continued detention of a Zimbabwean national who had been administratively detained by the Secretary of State for the Home Department for more than two years was unlawful. The judgment raises questions about the legality of the practice of detaining Zimbabwean nationals who do not have a current Zimbabwean passport and who are unwilling to return voluntarily. It also raises questions about the practice of pursuing prosecutions of such individuals under s. 35 of the Asylum and Immigration (Treatment of Claimants, etc.) Act 2004 for, essentially, declining to accept voluntary return. The circumstances of the case are too detailed to set out in full although two points from the judgment are relevant to s. 35 of the Act.

- In all immigration detention challenges, detention cannot be justified by reference to expeditious steps to prosecute the claimant under s. 35 because he continues to decline voluntary return (or to prosecute on any other ground). The power of detention can be exercised only for the purpose of effecting deportation where there remains a realistic prospect of doing so. This applies regardless of the strength of the prosecution case.

- Someone should not in any event be referred for prosecution under s. 35 of the 2004 Act (or threatened with prosecution) for declining to complete a voluntary return disclaimer or state an intention to return, or for declining to say at a travel document interview with their national authorities that they are willing to return voluntarily if that does not correspond to their true intention. The judgment means that it is exceptionally unlikely that someone could be convicted on this basis.

5.4 The Immigration, Asylum and Nationality Act 2006

> This chapter is only for examination candidates from Immigration Enforcement and the National Crime Agency.

5.4.1 Introduction

In the same way that a 'handler' of stolen property may be seen to encourage offences of theft, those who employ persons who are subject to immigration control may be seen to encourage immigration offences.

5.4.2 Offences

Sections 21 and 22 of the Immigration, Asylum and Nationality Act 2006 create offences dealing with individuals and bodies corporate who employ persons subject to immigration control. The offence under s. 21 has been amended by s. 35 of the Immigration Act 2016.

5.4.2.1 Employing Persons Known to be Not Entitled to Work in the United Kingdom

OFFENCE: **Employing Persons—*Immigration, Asylum and Nationality Act 2006, s. 21***

- Triable either way • Five years' imprisonment and/or a fine on indictment
- Six months' imprisonment and/or a fine summarily

The Immigration, Asylum and Nationality Act 2006, s. 21 states:

(1) A person commits an offence if he employs another ('the employee') knowing that the employee is disqualified from employment by reason of the employee's immigration status.

(1A) A person commits an offence if the person—
   (a) employs another person ('the employee') who is disqualified from employment by reason of the employee's immigration status, and
   (b) has reasonable cause to believe that the employee is disqualified from employment by reason of the employee's immigration status.

(1B) For the purposes of subsections (1) and (1A) a person is disqualified from employment by reason of the person's immigration status if the person is an adult subject to immigration control and—
   (a) the person has not been granted leave to enter or remain in the United Kingdom, or
   (b) the person's leave to enter or remain in the United Kingdom—
      (i) is invalid,
      (ii) has ceased to have effect (whether by reason of curtailment, revocation, cancellation, passage of time or otherwise), or
      (iii) is subject to a condition preventing the person from accepting the employment.

The Immigration, Asylum and Nationality Act 2006, s. 22 states:

(1) For the purposes of section 21(1) a body (whether corporate or not) shall be treated as knowing a fact about an employee if a person who has responsibility within the body for an aspect of the employment knows the fact.

(1A) For the purposes of section 21(1A) a body (whether corporate or not) shall be treated as having reasonable cause to believe a fact about an employee if a person who has responsibility within the body for an aspect of the employment has reasonable cause to believe that fact.

(2) If an offence under section 21(1) or (1A) is committed by a body corporate with the consent or connivance of an officer of the body, the officer, as well as the body, shall be treated as having committed the offence.

(3) In subsection (2) a reference to an officer of a body includes a reference to—
   (a) a director, manager or secretary,
   (b) a person purporting to act as a director, manager or secretary, and
   (c) if the affairs of the body are managed by its members, a member.

(4) Where an offence under section 21(1) or (1A) is committed by a partnership (whether or not a limited partnership) subsection (2) above shall have effect, but as if a reference to an officer of the body were a reference to—
   (a) a partner, and
   (b) a person purporting to act as a partner.

The UK Borders Act 2007

This chapter is only for examination candidates from Immigration Enforcement and the National Crime Agency.

5.5.1 Introduction

This is a large piece of legislation but only one offence is dealt with in this chapter—assaulting an immigration officer.

5.5.2 Assaulting an Immigration Officer

The UK Borders Act 2007, s. 22 states:

> (1) A person who assaults an immigration officer commits an offence.

5.6 The Identity Documents Act 2010

> This chapter is only for examination candidates from Immigration Enforcement and the National Crime Agency.

5.6.1 Introduction

You may have noticed that in the section dealing with 'Fraud' (**see chapter 3.8**) there was no mention of false passports or immigration documents in the offence dealing with custody or control of specific instruments and materials (Forgery and Counterfeiting Act 1981, s. 5(2) and (4)). This is because the Identity Cards Act 2006 specifically dealt with these documents under s. 25. The Identity Cards Act 2006 was, in turn, repealed on 21 January 2011 by the Identity Documents Act 2010, s. 1(1). Offences and definitions that appeared in the Identity Cards Act 2006 now appear as offences and definitions in the 2010 Act.

5.6.2 Offences under the Identity Documents Act 2010

The main offences associated with false identity documents are provided for under ss. 4 to 6 of the Act.

5.6.2.1 Possession of False Identity Documents etc. with Improper Intention

OFFENCE: **Possession of False Identity Documents etc. with Improper Intention—*Identity Documents Act 2010, s. 4***
- Triable on indictment • Ten years' imprisonment and/or a fine

The Identity Documents Act 2010, s. 4 states:

(1) It is an offence for a person ('P') with an improper intention to have in P's possession or under P's control—
  (a) an identity document that is false and that P knows or believes to be false,
  (b) an identity document that was improperly obtained and that P knows or believes to have been improperly obtained, or
  (c) an identity document that relates to someone else.
(2) Each of the following is an improper intention—
  (a) the intention of using the document for establishing personal information about P;
  (b) the intention of allowing or inducing another to use it for establishing, ascertaining or verifying personal information about P or anyone else.
(3) In subsection (2)(b) the reference to P or anyone else does not include, in the case of a document within subsection (1)(c), the individual to whom it relates.

OFFENCE: **Apparatus Designed or Adapted for the Making of False Identity Documents etc.—*Identity Documents Act 2010, s. 5***
- Triable on indictment • Ten years' imprisonment and/or a fine

The Identity Documents Act 2010, s. 5 states:

(1) It is an offence for a person ('P') with the prohibited intention to make or to have in P's possession or under P's control—
   (a) any apparatus which, to P's knowledge, is or has been specially designed or adapted for the making of false identity documents, or
   (b) any article or material which, to P's knowledge, is or has been specially designed or adapted to be used in the making of such documents.
(2) The prohibited intention is the intention—
   (a) that P or another will make a false identity document, and
   (b) that the document will be used by somebody for establishing, ascertaining or verifying personal information about a person.

OFFENCE: **Possession of False Identity Documents etc. without Reasonable Excuse—*Identity Documents Act 2010, s. 6***
   • Triable either way • Two years' imprisonment and/or a fine on indictment
   • Six months' imprisonment and/or a fine summarily

The Identity Documents Act 2010, s. 6 states:

(1) It is an offence for a person ('P'), without reasonable excuse, to have in P's possession or under P's control—
   (a) an identity document that is false,
   (b) an identity document that was improperly obtained,
   (c) an identity document that relates to someone else,
   (d) any apparatus which, to P's knowledge, is or has been specially designed or adapted for the making of false identity documents, or
   (e) any article or material which, to P's knowledge, is or has been specially designed or adapted to be used in the making of such documents.

5.6.2.2 Meaning of 'Identity Document'

The Identity Documents Act 2010, s. 7 states:

(1) For the purposes of sections 4 to 6 'identity document' means any document that is or purports to be—
   (a) an immigration document,
   (b) a United Kingdom passport (within the meaning of the Immigration Act 1971),
   (c) a passport issued by or on behalf of the authorities of a country or territory outside the United Kingdom or by or on behalf of an international organisation,
   (d) a document that can be used (in some or all circumstances) instead of a passport,
   (e) a licence to drive a motor vehicle granted under Part 3 of the Road Traffic Act 1988 or under Part 2 of the Road Traffic (Northern Ireland) Order 1981, or
   (f) a driving licence issued by or on behalf of the authorities of a country or territory outside the United Kingdom.
(2) In subsection (1)(a) 'immigration document' means—
   (a) a document used for confirming the right of a person under the EU Treaties in respect of entry or residence in the United Kingdom,
   (b) a document that is given in exercise of immigration functions and records information about leave granted to a person to enter or to remain in the United Kingdom, or
   (c) a registration card (within the meaning of section 26A of the Immigration Act 1971).
(3) In subsection (2)(b) 'immigration functions' means functions under the Immigration Acts (within the meaning of the Asylum and Immigration (Treatment of Claimants, etc.) Act 2004).
(4) References in subsection (1) to the issue of a document include its renewal, replacement or re-issue (with or without modifications).
(5) In this section 'document' includes a stamp or label.
(6) The Secretary of State may by order amend the definition of 'identity document'.

5.6.2.3 Meaning of 'Personal Information'

The Identity Documents Act 2010, s. 8 states:

(1) For the purposes of sections 4 and 5 'personal information', in relation to an individual ('A'), means—
    (a) A's full name,
    (b) other names by which A is or has previously been known,
    (c) A's gender,
    (d) A's date and place of birth,
    (e) external characteristics of A that are capable of being used for identifying A,
    (f) the address of A's principal place of residence in the United Kingdom,
    (g) the address of every other place in the United Kingdom or elsewhere where A has a place of residence,
    (h) where in the United Kingdom and elsewhere A has previously been resident,
    (i) the times at which A was resident at different places in the United Kingdom or elsewhere,
    (j) A's current residential status,
    (k) residential statuses previously held by A, and
    (l) information about numbers allocated to A for identification purposes and about the documents (including stamps or labels) to which they relate.
(2) In subsection (1) 'residential status' means—
    (a) A's nationality,
    (b) A's entitlement to remain in the United Kingdom, and
    (c) if that entitlement derives from a grant of leave to enter or remain in the United Kingdom, the terms and conditions of that leave.

5.6.2.4 Other Definitions

The Identity Documents Act 2010, s. 9 states:

(1) 'Apparatus' includes any equipment, machinery or device and any wire or cable, together with any software used with it.
(2) In relation to England and Wales and Northern Ireland, an identity document is 'false' only if it is false within the meaning of Part 1 of the Forgery and Counterfeiting Act 1981 (see section 9(1)).
(3) An identity document was 'improperly obtained' if—
    (a) false information was provided in, or in connection with, the application for its issue to the person who issued it, or
    (b) false information was provided in, or in connection with, an application for its modification to a person entitled to modify it.
(4) In subsection (3)—
    (a) 'false' information includes information containing any inaccuracy or omission that results in a tendency to mislead,
    (b) 'information' includes documents (including stamps and labels) and records, and
    (c) the 'issue' of a document includes its renewal, replacement or re-issue (with or without modifications).
(5) References to the making of a false identity document include the modification of an identity document so that it becomes false.
(6) This section applies for the purposes of sections 4 to 6.

KEYNOTE

The three offences at ss. 4, 5 and 6 are effectively the same as the older offence under s. 25 of the Identity Cards Act 2006. The s. 25(5) offence was considered in *R v Unah* [2011] All ER (D) 97 (Jul), in which it was held that whether the defendant's ignorance of a document's falsity would amount to a 'reasonable excuse' for possessing must be a question of fact. The same must be true for the offence under s. 6.

Section 31 of the Immigration and Asylum Act 1999 sets out defences, based on Article 31 of the Convention Relating to the Status of Refugees (the 'Refugee Convention'), to the offences under s. 4 or 6 of the Identity Documents Act 2010, for a refugee who has come to the United Kingdom directly from another country to show that he/she:

(a) presented him/herself to the UK authorities without delay;

(b) showed good cause for his/her illegal entry or presence in the United Kingdom; and

(c) made a claim for asylum as soon as was reasonably practicable after his/her arrival in the United Kingdom.

The Police and Criminal Evidence Act 1984—Powers

The Police and Criminal Evidence Act 1984 (Application to Immigration Officers and Designated Customs Officials) Order 2013

> This chapter is only for examination candidates from Immigration Enforcement and the National Crime Agency.

5.7.1 The Order

The purpose of the 2013 Order is to apply certain provisions of the Police and Criminal Evidence Act 1984 (PACE) to criminal investigations conducted by immigration officers and designated customs officials and to persons designated by customs officials. This includes powers of arrest, search of premises and seizure of evidence as well as obligations in respect of persons detained on suspicion of having committed customs offences.

Immigration officers have not previously had access to the PACE powers. Customs officials currently have access to certain PACE powers relating to the criminal investigation and detention of suspects by virtue of the Police and Criminal Evidence Act 1984 (Application to Revenue and Customs) Order 2007 ('the 2007 PACE Order'). These powers were provided via application of s. 22 of the Borders, Citizenship and Immigration Act 2009. This Order extends certain PACE powers (such as arrest, search and seizure) to immigration officers carrying out criminal investigations and effectively replicates the PACE powers already available to customs officials under the 2007 PACE Order with the addition of some extra PACE provisions. It also repeals some of the provisions of the Borders, Citizenship and Immigration Act 2009.

Schedules 1 and 2 detail the provisions of PACE that are now applied to investigations conducted by immigration officers (sch. 1) and to investigations conducted, and to persons detained, by designated customs officials (sch. 2).

In relation to PACE, the following provisions apply to an investigation conducted by an immigration officer:

Section 8(1) to (6) (power of justice of the peace to authorise entry and search of premises) (subject to the modification in art. 8) (**see chapter 1.6**).

Section 9(1) (special provisions as to access) and sch. 1 (special procedure) (**see chapter 1.6**).

Section 15 (search warrants: safeguards) (**see chapter 1.6**).

Section 16 (execution of warrants) (**see chapter 1.6**).

Section 17(1)(a)(i), (1)(b), (1)(cb)(i), (1)(d), (2) and (4) (entry for purpose of arrest etc.) (**see chapter 1.6**).

Section 18 (entry and search after arrest) (subject to the modification in art. 10) (**see chapter 1.6**).

Section 19 (general power of seizure etc.) (subject to the modification in art. 9(1)) (**see chapter 1.6**).

Section 20 (extension of powers of seizure to computerised information) (**see chapter 1.6**).

Section 21 (access and copying) (subject to the modification in art. 9(3)) (**see chapter 1.6**).

Section 22(1) to (4) and (7) (retention) (subject to the modification in art. 11) (**see chapter 1.6**).

Section 24(1) to (5)(c)(iii) and (5)(d) to (5)(f) (arrest without warrant: constables) (subject to the modification in art. 7).

Section 28 (information to be given on arrest).

Section 29 (voluntary attendance at police station etc.).

Section 30(1) to (4)(a) and (5) to (13) (arrest elsewhere than at police station).

Section 31 (arrest for further offence).

Section 32(1) to (9) (search upon arrest).

Section 46A(1) and (1A) to (3) (power of arrest for failure to answer to police bail) (**see chapter 1.10**).

Section 51(b) (savings).

Section 107(2) (police officers performing duties of higher rank).

The Police and Criminal Evidence Act 1984 should be consulted for a full explanation of the above sections.

Offences in Relation to Marriage

> This chapter is only for examination candidates from Immigration Enforcement and the National Crime Agency.

5.8.1 Introduction

'Sham' marriages are becoming a more common occurrence; some as an individual incident and others facilitated on a large scale. Although there may be a variety of immigration-related offences that individuals may be prosecuted for when involved in such behaviour, it is also worth considering certain offences relating to marriage that have been on the statute books for a little longer.

5.8.2 Bigamy

OFFENCE: **Bigamy—*Offences Against the Person Act 1861, s. 57***

- Triable either way • On indictment seven years' imprisonment and/or a fine
- Six months' imprisonment and/or a fine summarily

The Offences Against the Person Act 1861, s. 57 states:

> Whosoever, being married, shall marry any other person during the life of the former husband or wife, whether the second marriage shall have taken place in England or Ireland or elsewhere, shall be guilty of [an offence], and being convicted thereof shall be liable to [imprisonment] for any term not exceeding seven years....: Provided, that nothing in this section contained shall extend to any second marriage contracted elsewhere than in England and Ireland by any other than a subject of Her Majesty, or to any person marrying a second time whose husband or wife shall have been continually absent from such person for the space of seven years then last past, and shall not have been known by such person to be living within that time, or shall extend to any person who, at the time of such second marriage, shall have been divorced from the bond of the first marriage, or to any person whose former marriage shall have been declared void by the sentence of any court of competent jurisdiction.

KEYNOTE

The *actus reus* of bigamy is committed where the defendant 'marries' another person whilst still lawfully married to a surviving spouse. No offence is committed, however, where the defendant's original spouse has been missing for seven years or more; nor is any offence committed under English law where a foreigner commits bigamy abroad, even if their original marriage was registered in England. If, however, the defendant is a British (or British overseas etc.) citizen, it is irrelevant where the bigamous marriage takes place, because bigamy is punishable in England and Wales (or in Northern Ireland) if committed by a person anywhere in the world (*R v Earl Russell* [1901] AC 446).

The defendant must go through a ceremony of marriage that purports to be legally binding. The defendant does not commit bigamy where, for example, he/she contracts an unregistered Islamic marriage

---

in England without disclosing the existence of a subsisting marriage (*Al-Mudaris* v *Al-Mudaris* [2001] All ER (D) 288 (Feb)).

The burden is on the prosecution to prove that the defendant was validly married on an earlier occasion and that this marriage was still subsisting at the time of the second ceremony.

To establish the defence (continually absent for seven years), the defendant must adduce evidence of continual absence for that period. The prosecution must then prove either that there was no such continual absence or that the defendant knew his/her spouse to be alive at some time during that period.

5.8.3 False Statements with Reference to Marriage

OFFENCE: **False Statements with Reference to Marriage—*Perjury Act 1911, s. 3***
* Triable either way • On indictment seven years' imprisonment and/or a fine
* Six months' imprisonment and/or a fine summarily

The Perjury Act 1911, s. 3 states:

(1) If any person—
    (a) for the purpose of procuring a marriage, or a certificate or licence for marriage, knowingly and wilfully makes a false oath, or makes or signs a false declaration, notice or certificate required under any Act of Parliament for the time being in force relating to marriage; or
    (b) knowingly and wilfully makes, or knowingly and wilfully causes to be made, for the purpose of being inserted in any register of marriage, a false statement as to any particular required by law to be known and registered relating to any marriage; or
    (c) forbids the issue of any certificate or licence for marriage by falsely representing himself to be a person whose consent to the marriage is required by law knowing such representation to be false, or
    (d) with respect to a declaration made under section 16(1A) or 27B(2) of the Marriage Act 1949—
        (i) enters a caveat under subsection (2) of the said section 16, or
        (ii) makes a statement mentioned in subsection (4) of the said section 27B, which he knows to be false in a material particular.
he shall be guilty of [an offence].

KEYNOTE

An offence under s. 3 is committed *only* by a person who acts for the purposes of procuring a marriage or licence etc. but whether or not he/she succeeds in this purpose is irrelevant. A false statement cannot, however, give rise to liability under s. 3(1)(a) or (b) unless it concerns something which must be by law stated correctly (*R* v *Frickey* [1956] Crim LR 421).

A similar offence in respect of civil partnerships exists (see Civil Partnership Act 2004, s. 80).

Section 13 of the Perjury Act 1911 (corroboration is required in perjury cases) will apply to this offence

Every person who aids, abets, counsels, procures or suborns another person to commit an offence against this Act [Perjury Act 1911] shall be liable to be proceeded against, indicted, tried and punished as if he/she were a principal offender (Perjury Act 1911, s. 7(1)).

Every person who incites another person to commit an offence against this Act shall be guilty of [an offence], and, on conviction thereof on indictment, shall be liable to imprisonment, or to a fine, or to both such imprisonment and fine (Perjury Act 1911, s. 7(2)).

5.8.4 Forced Marriage

Forced marriage has been described as 'little more than slavery' and an 'indefensible abuse of human rights'. The Anti-social Behaviour, Crime and Policing Act 2014 outlaws the practice.

5.8.4.1 Offence of Forced Marriage

OFFENCE: **Offence of Forced Marriage: England and Wales**

> • Triable either way • On indictment seven years' imprisonment • Six months' imprisonment and/or a fine summarily

The Anti-social Behaviour, Crime and Policing Act 2014, s. 121 states:

(1) A person commits an offence under the law of England and Wales if he or she—
  (a) uses violence, threats or any other form of coercion for the purpose of causing another person to enter into a marriage, and
  (b) believes, or ought reasonably to believe, that the conduct may cause the other person to enter into the marriage without free and full consent.

(2) In relation to a victim who lacks capacity to consent to marriage, the offence under subsection (1) is capable of being committed by any conduct carried out for the purpose of causing the victim to enter into a marriage (whether or not the conduct amounts to violence, threats or any other form coercion).

(3) A person commits an offence under the law of England and Wales if he or she—
  (a) practises any form of deception with the intention of causing another person to leave the United Kingdom, and
  (b) intends the other person to be subjected to conduct outside the United Kingdom that is an offence under subsection (1) or would be an offence under that subsection if the victim were in England or Wales.

KEYNOTE

The offence of forced marriage catches a person who intentionally forces a person to enter into marriage, believing the person does not consent (s. 1), or a person who deceives someone into going abroad for the specific purpose of forcing them to marry (s. 3).

An offence is committed *whether or not* the forced marriage goes ahead, meaning that the offence is a *conduct* crime rather than a result crime.

The term 'marriage' is to be widely interpreted. A 'marriage' means any religious or civil ceremony of marriage recognised by the customs of the parties to it or the laws of any country in which it is carried out, as constituting a binding agreement, whether or not it would be legally binding according to the law of England and Wales (s. 121(4)).

It is irrelevant whether the conduct mentioned in subs. (1)(a) is directed at the victim of the offence under that subsection or another person. So, for example, the offence could be committed by a father threatening his daughter that if she does not marry a certain person, he will injure one of her friends (s. 121(6)).

The meaning of 'lacks the capacity to consent' is connected to the Mental Capacity Act 2005. Simply put, the 'capacity test' (under the Mental Capacity Act 2005) is the question, 'Does this person have the capacity to make this decision at this time?' If the decision is that the person lacks capacity, the offence under s. 1 would be committed by *any conduct* carried out for the purpose of causing the victim to marry, whether or not it amounts to violence, threats or any other form of coercion (s. 121(2)).

The word 'deception' in s. 121(3) is not defined. What s. 121(3) does is to additionally capture as a criminal offence any form of deception practised with the intention both of causing another person to leave the United Kingdom to travel to another country and that the other person be subjected to conduct that is an offence under subs. (1) or would be an offence if the victim were in England and Wales.

It is important to note that subss. (7) and (8) of s. 121 make provision to take extra-territorial jurisdiction over both the coercion and deception elements.

---

(7) A person commits an offence under subsection (1) or (3) only if, at the time of the conduct or deception—
  (a) the person or the victim or both of them are in England or Wales,
  (b) neither the person nor the victim is in England or Wales but at least one of them is habitually resident in England and Wales, or
  (c) neither the person nor the victim is in the United Kingdom but at least one of them is a UK national.

(8) 'UK national' means an individual who is—
  (a) a British citizen, a British overseas territories citizen, a British National (Overseas) or a British Overseas citizen;
  (b) a person who under the British Nationality Act 1981 is a British subject; or
  (c) a British protected person within the meaning of that Act.

Any of the prohibited acts in subss. (1) and (2) carried out outside the United Kingdom by a UK national or person habitually resident in England or Wales, or to a UK national or person habitually resident in England or Wales, will be an offence under domestic law and triable in the courts of England and Wales. It will also be an offence under domestic law if the prohibited acts in s. 121(1) or (2) are conducted by or against a person habitually resident in England and Wales, but take place in Scotland or Northern Ireland.

Section 122 of the Act creates an offence of forced marriage in Scotland. The provisions of this section broadly mirror those in s. 121.

5.8.4.2 Breaching a Forced Marriage Protection Order

Part 4A of the Family Law Act 1996 empowers a court to make an order for the purpose of protecting:

- a person from being forced into a marriage or from any attempt to be forced into a marriage; or
- a person who has been forced into a marriage.

A forced marriage protection order may contain such prohibitions, restrictions or requirements and any other such terms as the court considers appropriate for the purposes of the order.

Breaching a forced marriage protection order is a criminal offence with a maximum penalty of five years' imprisonment. This means that designated persons and/or the police will always be able to arrest for breach of a forced marriage protection order, without the need for the courts to attach a power of arrest, or for the victim to apply to the civil court for an arrest warrant. A person will only be guilty of a criminal offence if aware of the existence of the order at the time of the breach. For a victim who does not want to pursue criminal proceedings, the option will still remain of applying for an arrest warrant for breach of a forced marriage protection order in the civil court.

PART SIX

Offences in Customs and Excise Management and Serious Organised Crime (This section is for National Crime Agency Candidates only)

This Part covers offences under the Customs and Excise Management Act 1979 and the Serious Organised Crime and Police Act 2005, as well as the associated powers. There is also coverage of offenders assisting investigations and prosecutions.

The information in this Part is fully testable for candidates from the National Crime Agency *only*. Please see **How to Use** *Blackstone's Police Investigators' Manual 2022* on page xvii for further information.

6.1 The Customs and Excise Management Act 1979

> This chapter is only for examination candidates from the National Crime Agency.

6.1.1 Introduction

Until 2005 the Inland Revenue and Customs and Excise were separate government departments. As a consequence of this historical separation, the legislation creating offences against the public revenue and the powers associated with them are contained in different Acts of Parliament, although the major piece of legislation dealing with this area of the law is the Customs and Excise Management Act 1979.

6.1.2 Powers under the Customs and Excise Management Act 1979

As you might expect, there are a large number of powers available to an authorised officer under the Act; this section examines powers under parts III, IV, XI and XII of the Act.

6.1.2.1 Officers' Powers of Boarding

The Customs and Excise Management Act 1979, s. 27 states:

(1) At any time while a ship is within the limits of a port, or an aircraft is at an aerodrome, or a vehicle is—
   (a) entering, leaving or about to leave the United Kingdom,
   (b) within the prescribed area,
   (c) within the limits of or entering or leaving a port or any land adjacent to a port and occupied wholly or mainly for the purpose of activities carried on at the port,
   (d) at, entering or leaving an aerodrome,
   (e) at, entering or leaving an approved wharf, transit shed, customs warehouse or free zone, or
   (f) at, entering or leaving any such premises as are mentioned in subsection (1) of section 112 below,
   any officer and any other person duly engaged in the prevention of smuggling may board the ship, aircraft or vehicle and remain therein and rummage and search any part thereof.

KEYNOTE

A 'ship' includes any boat or other vessel whatsoever (and, to the extent provided in s. 2, any hovercraft). All other provisions of the customs and excise Acts shall apply as if references (however expressed) to goods or passengers carried in or moved by ships or vessels included references to goods or passengers carried in or moved by hovercraft (Customs and Excise Management Act 1979, s. 1).

A 'port' means a port appointed by the Commissioners under s. 19 of the Customs and Excise Management Act 1979.

The term 'aircraft' is not defined by the Act.

An 'aerodrome' means any area of land or water designed, equipped, set apart or commonly used for affording facilities for the landing and departure of aircraft (Customs and Excise Management Act 1979, s. 1).

The term 'vehicle' is not defined other than to state that it includes a railway vehicle (Customs and Excise Management Act 1979, s. 1).

The Commissioners may approve, for such periods and subject to such conditions and restrictions as they think fit, places for the loading or unloading of goods or of any class or description of goods. These are classed as 'approved wharfs' (Customs and Excise Management Act 1979, s. 20).

The Commissioners may approve, for such periods and subject to such conditions and restrictions as they think fit, places for the deposit of goods imported and not yet cleared out of charge, including goods not yet reported and entered under reg. 5 of the Customs Controls on Importation of Goods Regulations 1991. These are classed as 'transit sheds' (Customs and Excise Management Act 1979, s. 25).

For the purposes of subs. (1), 'customs warehouse' means a victualling warehouse or a place approved by the Commissioners under Article 98 of Council Regulation (EEC) No. 2913/92 or Article 505 of Commission Regulation (EEC) No. 2454/93 (s. 27(1A)).

The Treasury may, by order, designate any area in the United Kingdom as a special area for customs purposes. An area so designated shall be known as a 'free zone' (Customs and Excise Management Act 1979, s. 1).

Subsection (1) of s. 112 states:

> An officer may, subject to subsection (2) below, at any time enter upon any premises of which entry is made, or is required by or under the revenue trade provisions of the customs and excise Acts to be made, or any other premises owned or used by a revenue trader for the purposes of his trade and may inspect the premises and search for, examine and take account of any machinery, vehicles, vessels, utensils, goods or materials belonging to or in any way connected with that trade.

A further power and associated offence is provided for at s. 27(2):

> The Commissioners may station officers in any ship at any time while it is within the limits of a port, and if the master of any ship neglects or refuses to provide—
> (a) reasonable accommodation below decks for any officer stationed therein; or
> (b) means of safe access to and egress from the ship in accordance with the requirements of any such officer,
>   the master shall be liable on summary conviction to a penalty of level 2 on the standard scale.

6.1.2.2   Officers' Powers of Access

The Customs and Excise Management Act 1979, s. 28 states:

(1) Without prejudice to section 27 above, the proper officer shall have free access to every part of any ship or aircraft at a port or aerodrome and of any vehicle which falls within paragraphs (a) to (f) of subsection (1) of section 27 above or is brought to a customs and excise station, and may—
   (a) cause any goods to be marked before they are unloaded from that ship, aircraft or vehicle;
   (b) lock up, seal, mark or otherwise secure any goods carried in the ship, aircraft or vehicle or any place or container in which they are so carried; and
   (c) break open any place or container which is locked and of which the keys are withheld.

KEYNOTE

'Proper' in relation to the person by, with or whom, or the place at which, anything is to be done, means the person or place appointed or authorised in that behalf by the Commissioners (Customs and Excise Management Act 1979, s. 1).

For 'ship', 'aircraft', 'port', 'aerodrome' and 'vehicle', see **para. 6.1.2.1**.

'Goods' are not defined other than to include storage and baggage (Customs and Excise Management Act 1979, s. 1).

A 'container' is defined as including any bundle or package and any box, cask or other receptacle whatsoever (Customs and Excise Management Act 1979, s. 1).

Any goods found concealed on board any such ship, aircraft or vehicle shall be liable to forfeiture (s. 28(2)).

6.1.2.3 Power to Inspect Aircraft, Aerodromes, Records etc.

The Customs and Excise Management Act 1979 s. 33 states:

(1) The commander of an aircraft shall permit an officer at any time to board the aircraft and inspect—
   (a) the aircraft and any goods loaded therein; and
   (b) all documents relating to the aircraft or to goods or persons carried therein;
   and an officer shall have the right of access at any time to any place to which access is required for the purpose of any such inspection.

(2) The person in control of any aerodrome shall permit an officer at any time to enter upon and inspect the aerodrome and all buildings and goods thereon.

(3) The person in control of an aerodrome licensed under any enactment relating to air navigation or authorised by a certificate under the Aerodromes Regulation and, if so required by the Commissioners, the person in control of any other aerodrome shall—
   (a) keep a record in such form and manner as the Commissioners may approve of all aircraft arriving at or departing from the aerodrome;
   (b) keep that record available and produce it on demand to any officer, together with all other documents kept on the aerodrome which relate to the movement of aircraft; and
   (c) permit any officer to make copies of and take extracts from any such record or document.

KEYNOTE

'Commander' in relation to aircraft, includes any person having or taking the charge or command of the aircraft (Customs and Excise Management Act 1979, s 1).

For 'goods', see para. 6.1.2.2.

For 'aerodrome', see para. 6.1.2.1.

The 'Aerodromes Regulation' means Commission Regulation (EU) No. 139/2014 of 12 February 2014 laying down requirements and administrative procedures related to aerodromes pursuant to Regulation (EC) No. 216/2008 of the European Parliament and of the Council.

If any person contravenes or fails to comply with any of the provisions of this section he/she shall be liable on summary conviction to a penalty of level 4 on the standard scale or to imprisonment for a term not exceeding three months, or to both (s. 33(4)).

6.1.2.4 Power to Prevent Flight of Aircraft

The Customs and Excise Management Act 1979, s. 34 states:

(1) If it appears to any officer or constable that an aircraft is intended or likely to depart for a destination outside the United Kingdom and the Isle of Man from—
   (a) any place other than a customs and excise airport; or
   (b) a customs and excise airport before clearance outwards is given,
   he may give such instructions and take such steps by way of detention of the aircraft or otherwise as appear to him necessary in order to prevent the flight.

KEYNOTE

A 'customs and excise airport' means an aerodrome for the time being designated as a place for the landing or departure of aircraft for the purposes of the customs and excise Acts by an order made by the Secretary of State with the concurrence of the Commissioners which is in force under an Order in Council made in pursuance of s. 60 of the Civil Aviation Act 1982 (Customs and Excise Management Act 1979, s. 1).

Any person who contravenes any instructions given under subs. (1) shall be liable on summary conviction to a penalty of level 4 on the standard scale, or to imprisonment for a term not exceeding three months, or to both (s. 34(2)).

If an aircraft flies in contravention of any instruction given under subs. (1) or notwithstanding any steps taken to prevent the flight, the owner and the commander thereof shall, without prejudice to the liability of

---

any other person under subs. (2), each be liable on summary conviction to a penalty of level 4 on the standard scale, or to imprisonment for a term not exceeding three months, or to both, unless he/she proves that the flight took place without his/her consent or connivance (s. 34(3)).

6.1.2.5 Forfeiture of Goods Improperly Imported

The Customs and Excise Management Act 1979, s. 49 states:

(1) Where—
    (a) except as provided by or under the Customs and Excise Acts 1979, any imported goods, being goods chargeable on their importation with customs or excise duty, are, without payment of that duty—
        (i)   unshipped in any port,
        (ii) unloaded from any aircraft in the United Kingdom,
        (iii) unloaded from any vehicle in, or otherwise brought across the boundary into, Northern Ireland, or
        (iv) removed from their place of importation or from any approved wharf, examination station or transit shed; or
    (b) any goods are imported, landed or unloaded contrary to any prohibition or restriction for the time being in force with respect thereto under or by virtue of any enactment; or
    (c) any goods, being goods chargeable with any duty or goods the importation of which is for the time being prohibited or restricted by or under any enactment, are found, whether before or after the unloading thereof, to have been concealed in any manner on board any ship or aircraft or, while in Northern Ireland, in any vehicle; or
    (d) any goods are imported concealed in a container holding goods of a different description; or
    (e) any imported goods are found, whether before or after delivery, not to correspond with the entry made thereof; or
    (f) any imported goods are concealed or packed in any manner appearing to be intended to deceive an officer,
    those goods shall, subject to subsection (2) below, be liable to forfeiture.
(2) Where any goods, the importation of which is for the time being prohibited or restricted by or under any enactment, are on their importation either—
    (a) reported as intended for exportation in the same ship, aircraft or vehicle; or
    (b) entered for transit or transhipment; or
    (c) entered to be warehoused for exportation or for use as stores,
    the Commissioners may, if they see fit, permit the goods to be dealt with accordingly.

KEYNOTE

For 'goods', see para. 6.1.2.2.

For 'vehicle', 'approved wharf' and 'transit shed', see para. 6.1.2.1.

The Commissioners may approve, for such periods and subject to such conditions and restrictions as they think fit, a part of, or a place at, any customs and excise airport for the loading and unloading of goods and the embarkation and disembarkation of passengers. These are classed as 'examination stations' (Customs and Excise Management Act 1979, s. 22).

'Lands', in relation to aircraft, includes alighting on water (Customs and Excise Management Act 1979, s. 1).

6.1.2.6 Provisions as to Arrest of Persons

The Customs and Excise Management Act 1979, s. 138 states:

(1) Any person who has committed, or whom there are reasonable grounds to suspect of having committed, any offence for which he is liable to be arrested under the customs and excise Acts may be arrested by any officer or any member of Her Majesty's armed forces or coastguard at any time within 20 years from the date of the commission of the offence.

6.1.2.7   Provisions as to Detention, Seizure and Condemnation of Goods etc.

The Customs and Excise Management Act 1979, s. 139 states:

(1)   Any thing liable to forfeiture under the customs and excise Acts may be seized or detained by any officer or constable or any member of Her Majesty's armed forces or coastguard.

(1A)   A person mentioned in subsection (1) who reasonably suspects that any thing may be liable to forfeiture under the customs and excise Acts may detain that thing.

(1B)   References in this section and Schedule 2A to a thing detained as liable to forfeiture under the customs and excise Acts include a thing detained under subsection (1A).

(2)   Where any thing is seized or detained as liable to forfeiture under the customs and excise Acts by a person other than an officer, that person shall, subject to subsection (3) below, deliver that thing to an officer.

(3)   Where the person seizing or detaining any thing as liable to forfeiture under the customs and excise Acts is a constable and that thing is or may be required for use in connection with any proceedings to be brought otherwise than under those Acts it may, subject to subsection (4) below, be retained in the custody of the police until either those proceedings are completed or it is decided that no such proceedings shall be brought.

(4)   The following provisions apply in relation to things retained in the custody of the police by virtue of subsection (3) above, that is to say—

   (a)   notice in writing of the seizure or detention and of the intention to retain the thing in question in the custody of the police, together with full particulars as to that thing, shall be given to an officer;

   (b)   any officer shall be permitted to examine that thing and take account thereof at any time while it remains in the custody of the police;

   (c)   nothing in section 31 of the Police (Northern Ireland) Act 1998 shall apply in relation to that thing.

(5)   Subject to subsections (3) and (4) above and to Schedules 2A and 3 to this Act, any thing seized or detained under the customs and excise Acts shall, pending the determination as to

its forfeiture or disposal, be dealt with, and, if condemned or deemed to have been condemned or forfeited, shall be disposed of in such manner as the Commissioners may direct.

(5A) Schedule 2A contains supplementary provisions relating to the detention of things as liable to forfeiture under the customs and excise Acts.

(6) Schedule 3 to this Act shall have effect for the purpose of forfeitures, and of proceedings for the condemnation of any thing as being forfeited, under the customs and excise Acts.

(7) If any person, not being an officer, by whom any thing is seized or detained or who has custody thereof after its seizure or detention, fails to comply with any requirement of this section or with any direction of the Commissioners given thereunder, he shall be liable on summary conviction to a penalty of level 2 on the standard scale.

(8) Subsections (2) to (7) above shall apply in relation to any dutiable goods seized or detained by any person other than an officer notwithstanding that they were not so seized as liable to forfeiture under the customs and excise Acts.

6.1.2.8 Forfeiture of Ships etc. used in Connection with Goods Liable to Forfeiture

The Customs and Excise Management Act 1979, s. 141 states:

(1) Without prejudice to any other provision of the Customs and Excise Acts 1979, where any thing has become liable to forfeiture under the customs and excise Acts—

(a) any ship, aircraft, vehicle, animal, container (including any article of passengers' baggage) or other thing whatsoever which has been used for the carriage, handling, deposit or concealment of the thing so liable to forfeiture, either at a time when it was so liable or for the purposes of the commission of the offence for which it later became so liable; and

(b) any other thing mixed, packed or found with the thing so liable,

shall also be liable to forfeiture.

(2) Where any ship, aircraft, vehicle or animal has become liable to forfeiture under the customs and excise Acts, whether by virtue of subsection (1) above or otherwise, all tackle, apparel or furniture thereof shall also be liable to forfeiture.

(3) Where any of the following, that is to say—

(a) any ship not exceeding 100 tons register;

(b) any aircraft; or

(c) any hovercraft,

becomes liable to forfeiture under this section by reason of having been used in the importation, exportation or carriage of goods contrary to or for the purpose of contravening any prohibition or restriction for the time being in force with respect to those goods, or without payment having been made of, or security given for, any duty payable thereon, the owner and the master or commander shall each be liable on summary conviction to a fine not exceeding £20,000 or a penalty equal to the value of the ship, aircraft or hovercraft, whichever is the less.

6.1.2.9 Power to Search Premises—Search Warrant

The Customs and Excise Management Act 1979, s. 161A states:

(1) If a justice of the peace is satisfied by information upon oath given by an officer that there are reasonable grounds to suspect that anything liable to forfeiture under the customs and excise Acts is kept or concealed in any building or place, he may by warrant under his hand authorise any officer, and any person accompanying an officer, to enter and search the building or place named in the warrant.

KEYNOTE

Section 161A(2) states that an officer or other person so authorised has power:

(a) to enter the building or place at any time, whether by day or night, on any day, and search for, seize, and detain or remove any such thing, and

(b) so far as is necessary for the purpose of such entry, search, seizure, detention or removal, to break open any door, window or container and force and remove any other impediment or obstruction.

Section 161A(2A) states that the power in subs. (2)(a) includes power to search for and remove documents relating to any such thing (including documents about title, storage and movement).

Where there are reasonable grounds to suspect that any still, vessel, utensil, spirits or materials for the manufacture of spirits is or are unlawfully kept or deposited in any building or place, subss. (1), (2) and (2A) apply in relation to any constable as they would apply in relation to an officer (s. 161A(3)).

The powers conferred by a warrant under this section are exercisable until the end of the period of one month beginning with the day on which the warrant is issued (s. 161A(4)).

A person other than a constable shall not exercise the power of entry conferred by this section by night unless accompanied by a constable (s. 161A(5)).

6.1.2.10 Power to Search Vehicles or Vessels

The Customs and Excise Management Act 1979, s. 163 states:

(1) Without prejudice to any other power conferred by the Customs and Excise Acts 1979, where there are reasonable grounds to suspect that any vehicle or vessel is or may be carrying any goods which are—
   (a) chargeable with any duty which has not been paid or secured; or
   (b) in the course of being unlawfully removed from or to any place; or
   (c) otherwise liable to forfeiture under the customs and excise Acts,
   any officer or constable or member of Her Majesty's armed forces or coastguard may stop and search that vehicle or vessel.

(2) If when so required by any such officer, constable or member the person in charge of any such vehicle or vessel refuses to stop or to permit the vehicle or vessel to be searched, he shall be liable on summary conviction to a penalty of level 3 on the standard scale.

KEYNOTE

For 'vehicle', see para. 6.1.2.1.

This section shall apply in relation to aircraft as it applies in relation to vehicles or vessels but the power to stop and search in subs. (1) shall not be available in respect of aircraft which are airborne (s. 163(3)).

6.1.2.11 Power to Search—Articles

The Customs and Excise Management Act 1979, s. 163A states:

(1) Without prejudice to any other power conferred by the Customs and Excise Acts 1979, where there are reasonable grounds to suspect that a person in the United Kingdom (referred to in this section as 'the suspect') has with him, or at the place where he is, any goods to which this section applies, an officer may—
   (a) require the suspect to permit a search of any article that he has with him or at that place, and
   (b) if the suspect is not under arrest, detain him (and any such article) for so long as may be necessary to carry out the search.

KEYNOTE

The goods to which this section applies are dutiable alcoholic liquor, or tobacco products, which are:

(a) chargeable with any duty of excise; and
(b) liable to forfeiture under the customs and excise Acts.

6.1.2.12 Power to Search Persons

The Customs and Excise Management Act 1979, s. 164 states:

(1) Where there are reasonable grounds to suspect that any person to whom this section applies (referred to in this section as 'the suspect') is carrying any article—
   (a) which is chargeable with any duty which has not been paid or secured; or

(b) with respect to the importation or exportation of which any prohibition or restriction is for the time being in force under or by virtue of any enactment,

an officer may exercise the powers conferred by subsection (2) below and, if the suspect is not under arrest, may detain him for so long as may be necessary for the exercise of those powers and (where applicable) the exercise of the rights conferred by subsection (3) below.

(2) The officer may require the suspect—
   (a) to permit such a search of any article which he has with him; and
   (b) subject to subsection (3) below, to submit to such searches of his person, whether rub-down, strip or intimate,

as the officer may consider necessary or expedient; but no such requirement may be imposed under paragraph (b) above without the officer informing the suspect of the effect of subsection (3) below.

KEYNOTE

A rub-down or strip search shall not be carried out except by a person of the same sex as the suspect; and an intimate search shall not be carried out except by a suitably qualified person (s. 164(3A)). A 'rub-down search' means any search which is neither an intimate search nor a strip search (Customs and Excise Management Act 1979, s. 1).

A 'strip search' means any search which is not an intimate search but which involves the removal of an article of clothing which:

(a) is being worn (wholly or partly) on the trunk; and

(b) is being so worn either next to the skin or next to an article of underwear (Customs and Excise Management Act 1979, s. 164(5)).

An intimate search means any search which involves a physical examination (i.e. an examination which is more than simply a visual examination) of a person's body orifices (Customs and Excise Management Act 1979, s. 164(5)).

If the suspect is required to submit to a search of his/her person, he/she may require to be taken:

(a) except in the case of a rub-down search, before a justice of the peace or a superior of the officer concerned; and

(b) in the excepted case, before such a superior;

and the justice or superior shall consider the grounds for suspicion and direct accordingly whether the suspect is to submit to the search (s. 164(3)).

This section applies to the following persons, namely:

- any person who is on board or has landed from any ship or aircraft;
- any person entering or about to leave the United Kingdom;
- any person within the dock area of a port;
- any person at a customs and excise airport;
- any person in, entering or leaving any approved wharf or transit shed which is not in a port;
- any person in, entering or leaving a free zone;
- in Northern Ireland, any person travelling from or to any place which is on or beyond the boundary.

6.1.2.13 Penalty for Fraudulent Evasion of Duty etc.

The Customs and Excise Management Act 1979, s. 170 states:

(1) Without prejudice to any other provision of the Customs and Excise Acts 1979, if any person—
   (a) knowingly acquires possession of any of the following goods, that is to say—
      (i) goods which have been unlawfully removed from a warehouse or Queen's warehouse;
      (ii) goods which are chargeable with a duty which has not been paid;
      (iii) goods with respect to the importation or exportation of which any prohibition or restriction is for the time being in force under or by virtue of any enactment; or

(b) is in any way knowingly concerned in carrying, removing, depositing, harbouring, keeping or concealing or in any manner dealing with any such goods,

and does so with intent to defraud Her Majesty of any duty payable on the goods or to evade any such prohibition or restriction with respect to the goods he shall be guilty of an offence under this section and may be arrested.

(2) Without prejudice to any other provision of the Customs and Excise Acts 1979, if any person is, in relation to any goods, in any way knowingly concerned in any fraudulent evasion or attempt at evasion—

(a) of any duty chargeable on the goods;

(b) of any prohibition or restriction for the time being in force with respect to the goods under or by virtue of any enactment; or

(c) of any provision of the Customs and Excise Acts 1979 applicable to the goods,

he shall be guilty of an offence under this section and may be arrested.

KEYNOTE

A person found guilty of this offence is liable, on summary conviction, to a fine of a prescribed sum or a fine amounting to three times the value of the prescribed goods (whichever is the greater) and/or to a term of imprisonment for six months. On indictment, the punishment is a penalty of any amount and/or a maximum of seven years' imprisonment (s. 170(3)).

Penalties may be enhanced in a wide variety of situations (for offences involving drugs, firearms, forgery and counterfeiting, sealskins and nuclear material) For specific sentencing provisions, reference should be made to the Act.

Where any person is guilty of an offence under this section, the goods in respect of which the offence was committed shall be liable to forfeiture (s. 170(6)).

6.2 The Serious Organised Crime and Police Act 2005

This chapter is only for examination candidates from the National Crime Agency.

6.2.1 Introduction

Part 2 of the Serious Organised Crime and Police Act 2005 is divided into six chapters. This chapter of the Manual examines elements of chapters 1 and 2 of part 2.

6.2.2 Chapter 1—Investigatory Powers of the DPP

Chapter 1 enables designated members of staff of the NCA, police constables or officers of Revenue and Customs, acting under the supervision of the DPP, the Director of Revenue and Customs Prosecutions or the Lord Advocate, to compel people to cooperate with an investigation by producing documents and answering questions.

6.2.2.1 Disclosure Notices

The Serious Organised Crime and Police Act 2005, s. 62 states:

(1) If it appears to the Investigating Authority—
   (a) that there are reasonable grounds for suspecting that an offence to which this Chapter applies has been committed,
   (b) that any person has information (whether or not contained in a document) which relates to a matter relevant to the investigation of that offence, and
   (c) that there are reasonable grounds for believing that information which may be provided by that person in compliance with a disclosure notice is likely to be of substantial value (whether or not by itself) to that investigation,
   he may give, or authorise an appropriate person to give, a disclosure notice to that person.
(2) In this Chapter 'appropriate person' means—
   (a) a constable,
   (b) a National Crime Agency officer who is for the time being designated under section 9 or 10 of the Crime and Courts Act 2013, or
   (c) an officer of Revenue and Customs.
(3) In this Chapter 'disclosure notice' means a notice in writing requiring the person to whom it is given to do all or any of the following things in accordance with the specified requirements, namely—
   (a) answer questions with respect to any matter relevant to the investigation;
   (b) provide information with respect to any such matter as is specified in the notice;
   (c) produce such documents, or documents of such descriptions, relevant to the investigation as are specified in the notice.
(4) In subsection (3) 'the specified requirements' means such requirements specified in the disclosure notice as relate to—
   (a) the time at or by which,
   (b) the place at which, or
   (c) the manner in which,

the person to whom the notice is given is to do any of the things mentioned in paragraphs (a) to (c) of that subsection; and those requirements may include a requirement to do any of those things at once.

(5) A disclosure notice must be signed or counter-signed by the Investigating Authority.

(6) This section has effect subject to section 64 (restrictions on requiring information etc.) [**see para. 6.2.2.3**].

6.2.2.2 Production of Documents

The Serious Organised Crime and Police Act 2005, s. 63 states:

(1) This section applies where a disclosure notice has been given under section 62.

(2) An authorised person may—
(a) take copies of or extracts from any documents produced in compliance with the notice, and
(b) require the person producing them to provide an explanation of any of them.

(3) Documents so produced may be retained for so long as the Investigating Authority considers that it is necessary to retain them (rather than copies of them) in connection with the investigation for the purposes of which the disclosure notice was given.

(4) If the Investigating Authority has reasonable grounds for believing—
(a) that any such documents may have to be produced for the purposes of any legal proceedings, and
(b) that they might otherwise be unavailable for those purposes,
they may be retained until the proceedings are concluded.

(5) If a person who is required by a disclosure notice to produce any documents does not produce the documents in compliance with the notice, an authorised person may require that person to state, to the best of his knowledge and belief, where they are.

(6) In this section 'authorised person' means any appropriate person who either—
(a) is the person by whom the notice was given, or
(b) is authorised by the Investigating Authority for the purposes of this section.

(7) This section has effect subject to section 64 (restrictions on requiring information etc.) [**see para. 6.2.2.3**].

6.2.2.3 Restrictions on Requiring Information

The Serious Organised Crime and Police Act 2005, s. 64 states:

(1) A person may not be required under section 62 or 63—
(a) to answer any privileged question,
(b) to provide any privileged information, or
(c) to produce any privileged document,
except that a lawyer may be required to provide the name and address of a client of his.

KEYNOTE

A 'privileged question' is a question which the person would be entitled to refuse to answer on grounds of legal professional privilege in proceedings in the High Court (s. 64(2)).

'Privileged information' is information which the person would be entitled to refuse to provide on grounds of legal professional privilege in such proceedings (s. 64(3)).

A 'privileged document' is a document which the person would be entitled to refuse to produce on grounds of legal professional privilege in such proceedings (s. 64(4)).

Section 64(5) states that a person may not be required under s. 62 to produce any excluded material (as defined by s. 11 of the Police and Criminal Evidence Act 1984).

In the application of this section to Scotland, subss. (1) to (5) do not have effect, but a person may not be required under s. 62 or 63 to answer any question, provide any information or produce any document which he/she would be entitled, on grounds of legal privilege, to refuse to answer or (as the case may be) provide or produce.

In subs. (6)(b), 'legal privilege' has the meaning given by s. 412 of the Proceeds of Crime Act 2002. That means 'protection in legal proceedings from disclosure, by virtue of any rule of law relating to the confidentiality of communications'; and 'items subject to legal privilege' are communications between a professional legal adviser and his/her client or communications made in connection with or in contemplation of legal proceedings and for the purpose of those proceedings.

Section 64(8) states that a person may not be required under s. 62 or 63 to disclose any information or produce any document in respect of which he/she owes an obligation of confidence by virtue of carrying on any banking business, unless:

(a) the person to whom the obligation of confidence is owed consents to the disclosure or production; or

(b) the requirement is made by, or in accordance with a specific authorisation given by, the Investigating Authority.

Subject to the preceding provisions, any requirement under s. 62 or 63 has effect despite any restriction on disclosure (however imposed) (s. 64(9)).

6.2.2.4 Restrictions on Use of Statements

The Serious Organised Crime and Police Act 2005, s. 65 states:

(1) A statement made by a person in response to a requirement imposed under section 62 or 63 ('the relevant statement') may not be used in evidence against him in any criminal proceedings unless subsection (2) or (3) applies.

(2) This subsection applies where the person is being prosecuted—
   (a) for an offence under section 67 of this Act, or
   (b) for an offence under section 5 of the Perjury Act 1911 (c. 6) (false statements made on oath otherwise than in judicial proceedings or made otherwise than on oath), or
   (c) for an offence under section 2 of the False Oaths (Scotland) Act 1933 (c. 20) (false statutory declarations and other false statements without oath) or at common law for an offence of attempting to pervert the course, or defeat the ends, of justice.

(3) This subsection applies where the person is being prosecuted for some other offence and—
   (a) the person, when giving evidence in the proceedings, makes a statement inconsistent with the relevant statement, and
   (b) in the proceedings evidence relating to the relevant statement is adduced, or a question about it is asked, by or on behalf of the person.

KEYNOTE

This section provides that a statement made by a person in response to a requirement imposed under this chapter cannot be used in evidence in criminal proceedings against them, other than proceedings for an offence under s. 67 or for an offence of giving a false statutory declaration or statement. The only exception is where the person seeks in other criminal proceedings to use another statement which is inconsistent with the statement made in response to the requirement under this chapter.

6.2.2.5 Power to Enter and Seize Documents

The Serious Organised Crime and Police Act 2005, s. 66 states:

(1) A justice of the peace may issue a warrant under this section if, on an information on oath laid by the Investigating Authority, he is satisfied—
   (a) that any of the conditions mentioned in subsection (2) is met in relation to any documents of a description specified in the information, and
   (b) that the documents are on premises so specified.

(2) The conditions are—
   (a) that a person has been required by a disclosure notice to produce the documents but has not done so;
   (b) that it is not practicable to give a disclosure notice requiring their production;

(c) that giving such a notice might seriously prejudice the investigation of an offence to which this Chapter applies.

(3) A warrant under this section is a warrant authorising an appropriate person named in it—

    (a) to enter and search the premises, using such force as is reasonably necessary;

    (b) to take possession of any documents appearing to be documents of a description specified in the information, or to take any other steps which appear to be necessary for preserving, or preventing interference with, any such documents;

    (c) in the case of any such documents consisting of information recorded otherwise than in legible form, to take possession of any computer disk or other electronic storage device which appears to contain the information in question, or to take any other steps which appear to be necessary for preserving, or preventing interference with, that information;

    (d) to take copies of or extracts from any documents or information falling within paragraph (b) or (c);

    (e) to require any person on the premises to provide an explanation of any such documents or information or to state where any such documents or information may be found;

    (f) to require any such person to give the appropriate person such assistance as he may reasonably require for the taking of copies or extracts as mentioned in paragraph (d).

(4) A person executing a warrant under this section may take other persons with him, if it appears to him to be necessary to do so.

(5) A warrant under this section must, if so required, be produced for inspection by the owner or occupier of the premises or anyone acting on his behalf.

(6) If the premises are unoccupied or the occupier is temporarily absent, a person entering the premises under the authority of a warrant under this section must leave the premises as effectively secured against trespassers as he found them.

(7) Where possession of any document or device is taken under this section—

    (a) the document may be retained for so long as the Investigating Authority considers that it is necessary to retain it (rather than a copy of it) in connection with the investigation for the purposes of which the warrant was sought, or

    (b) the device may be retained for so long as he considers that it is necessary to retain it in connection with that investigation,

as the case may be.

(8) If the Investigating Authority has reasonable grounds for believing—

    (a) that any such document or device may have to be produced for the purposes of any legal proceedings, and

    (b) that it might otherwise be unavailable for those purposes,

it may be retained until the proceedings are concluded.

(9) Nothing in this section authorises a person to take possession of, or make copies of or take extracts from, any document or information which, by virtue of section 64, could not be required to be produced or disclosed under section 62 or 63.

KEYNOTE

This section provides for a magistrate, or sheriff in Scotland, to issue a warrant to enter and seize documents where someone has failed to provide documents specified in a disclosure notice or it is not practicable to give a disclosure notice or doing so might seriously prejudice an investigation. The warrant would authorise a constable, a designated officer of the NCA or an officer of HMRC to enter, using force if necessary, and search the premises and seize and retain any specified documents. The constable or other person authorised by the warrant may take other people with him/her on the search, but must show the warrant to the occupier of the premises on request.

6.2.2.6 Offences in Connection with Disclosure Notices or Search Warrants

OFFENCE: **Fail to Comply/Make False Statement/Wilful Obstruction—*Serious Organised Crime and Police Act 2005, s. 67***

    • Triable either way • Two years' imprisonment and/or a fine • Six months' imprisonment and/or a fine

The Serious Organised Crime and Police Act 2005, s. 67 states:

(1) A person commits an offence if, without reasonable excuse, he fails to comply with any requirement imposed on him under section 62 or 63.
(2) A person commits an offence if, in purported compliance with any requirement imposed on him under section 62 or 63—
    (a) he makes a statement which is false or misleading, and
    (b) he either knows that it is false or misleading or is reckless as to whether it is false or misleading.
    'False or misleading' means false or misleading in a material particular.
(3) A person commits an offence if he wilfully obstructs any person in the exercise of any rights conferred by a warrant under section 66.

6.2.2.7 Manner in Which Disclosure Notice May Be Given

The Serious Organised Crime and Police Act 2005, s. 69 states:

(1) This section provides for the manner in which a disclosure notice may be given under section 62.
(2) The notice may be given to a person by—
    (a) delivering it to him,
    (b) leaving it at his proper address,
    (c) sending it by post to him at that address.
(3) The notice may be given—
    (a) in the case of a body corporate, to the secretary or clerk of that body;
    (b) in the case of a partnership, to a partner or a person having the control or management of the partnership business;
    (c) in the case of an unincorporated association (other than a partnership), to an officer of the association.
(4) For the purposes of this section and section 7 of the Interpretation Act 1978 (c. 30) (service of documents by post) in its application to this section, the proper address of a person is his usual or last-known address (whether residential or otherwise), except that—
    (a) in the case of a body corporate or its secretary or clerk, it is the address of the registered office of that body or its principal office in the United Kingdom,
    (b) in the case of a partnership, a partner or a person having the control or management of the partnership business, it is that of the principal office of the partnership in the United Kingdom, and
    (c) in the case of an unincorporated association (other than a partnership) or an officer of the association, it is that of the principal office of the association in the United Kingdom.
(5) This section does not apply to Scotland.

KEYNOTE

This section provides that a disclosure notice may be given to a person by delivering it to them, leaving it at their proper address or sending it by post to them at that address. The definition of a person's 'proper address' is his/her usual or last-known address.

6.2.3 Chapter 2—Offenders Assisting Investigations and Prosecutions

Chapter 2 places the mechanism by which a defendant can plead guilty and offer Queen's Evidence in return for a discounted sentence on a statutory footing.

6.2.3.1 Assistance by Offender—Immunity from Prosecution

The Serious Organised Crime and Police Act 2005, s. 71 states:

(1) If a specified prosecutor thinks that for the purposes of the investigation or prosecution of any offence it is appropriate to offer any person immunity from prosecution he may give the person a written notice under this subsection (an 'immunity notice').

(2) If a person is given an immunity notice, no proceedings for an offence of a description specified in the notice may be brought against that person in England and Wales or Northern Ireland except in circumstances specified in the notice.

(3) An immunity notice ceases to have effect in relation to the person to whom it is given if the person fails to comply with any conditions specified in the notice.

(4) Each of the following is a specified prosecutor—

(a) the Director of Public Prosecutions;

(b) the Director of Revenue and Customs Prosecutions;

(c) the Director of the Serious Fraud Office;

(d) the Director of Public Prosecutions for Northern Ireland;

(e) a prosecutor designated for the purposes of this section by a prosecutor mentioned in paragraphs (a) to (d).

(5) The Director of Public Prosecutions or a person designated by him under subsection (4)(e) may not give an immunity notice in relation to proceedings in Northern Ireland.

(6) The Director of Public Prosecutions for Northern Ireland or a person designated by him under subsection (4)(e) may not give an immunity notice in relation to proceedings in England and Wales.

(7) An immunity notice must not be given in relation to an offence under section 188 of the Enterprise Act 2002 (c. 40) (cartel offences).

KEYNOTE

This section provides for a designated prosecutor from the CPS, the Revenue and Customs Prosecutions Office, the Serious Fraud Office or the Northern Ireland Director of Public Prosecutions Office to grant a person conditional immunity from prosecution. The immunity notice itself must be written and specify the offences for which the person will be immune from prosecution in England and Wales or Northern Ireland. The notice will normally include conditions, breach of which would lead to the immunity being revoked.

6.2.3.2 Assistance by Offender—Undertakings as to Use of Evidence

The Serious Organised Crime and Police Act 2005, s. 72 states:

(1) If a specified prosecutor thinks that for the purposes of the investigation or prosecution of any offence it is appropriate to offer any person an undertaking that information of any description will not be used against the person in any proceedings to which this section applies he may give the person a written notice under this subsection (a 'restricted use undertaking').

(2) This section applies to—

(a) criminal proceedings;

(b) proceedings under Part 5 of the Proceeds of Crime Act 2002 (c. 29).

(3) If a person is given a restricted use undertaking the information described in the undertaking must not be used against that person in any proceedings to which this section applies brought in England and Wales or Northern Ireland except in the circumstances specified in the undertaking.

(4) A restricted use undertaking ceases to have effect in relation to the person to whom it is given if the person fails to comply with any conditions specified in the undertaking.

(5) The Director of Public Prosecutions for Northern Ireland or a person designated by him under section 71(4)(e) may not give a restricted use undertaking in relation to proceedings in England and Wales.

(6) The Director of Public Prosecutions or a person designated by him under section 71(4)(e) may not give a restricted use undertaking in relation to proceedings in Northern Ireland.

(7) Specified prosecutor must be construed in accordance with section 71(4).

KEYNOTE

This section provides for a designated prosecutor (as specified in subs. (4) of s. 71) to grant a person a conditional undertaking that any information that individual provides will not be used in any criminal proceedings, or proceedings under part 5 of the Proceeds of Crime Act 2002, against that person in England and Wales or

---

Northern Ireland. The notice containing the undertaking must be in writing and specify the circumstances in which the information provided will not be used against that person. The notice will normally include conditions, breach of which would lead to the undertaking being revoked.

6.2.3.3 Assistance by Defendant—Reduction in Sentence

The Serious Organised Crime and Police Act 2005, s. 73 states:

(1) This section applies if a defendant—
    (a) following a plea of guilty is either convicted of an offence in proceedings in the Crown Court or is committed to the Crown Court for sentence, and
    (b) has, pursuant to a written agreement made with a specified prosecutor, assisted or offered to assist the investigator or prosecutor in relation to that or any other offence.

(2) In determining what sentence to pass on the defendant the court may take into account the extent and nature of the assistance given or offered.

(3) If the court passes a sentence which is less than it would have passed but for the assistance given or offered, it must state in open court—
    (a) that it has passed a lesser sentence than it would otherwise have passed, and
    (b) what the greater sentence would have been.

(4) Subsection (3) does not apply if the court thinks that it would not be in the public interest to disclose that the sentence has been discounted; but in such a case the court must give written notice of the matters specified in paragraphs (a) and (b) of subsection (3) to both the prosecutor and the defendant.

(5) Nothing in any enactment which—
    (a) requires that a minimum sentence is passed in respect of any offence or an offence of any description or by reference to the circumstances of any offender (whether or not the enactment also permits the court to pass a lesser sentence in particular circumstances), or
    (b) in the case of a sentence which is fixed by law, requires the court to take into account certain matters for the purposes of making an order which determines or has the effect of determining the minimum period of imprisonment which the offender must serve (whether or not the enactment also permits the court to fix a lesser period in particular circumstances),
affects the power of a court to act under subsection (2).

(6) If, in determining what sentence to pass on the defendant, the court takes into account the extent and nature of the assistance given or offered as mentioned in subsection (2), that does not prevent the court from also taking account of any other matter which it is entitled by virtue of any other enactment to take account of for the purposes of determining—
    (a) the sentence, or
    (b) in the case of a sentence which is fixed by law, any minimum period of imprisonment which an offender must serve.

(7) If subsection (3) above does not apply by virtue of subsection (4) above, sections 174(1)(a) and 270 of the Criminal Justice Act 2003 (c. 44) (requirement to explain reasons for sentence or other order) do not apply to the extent that the explanation will disclose that a sentence has been discounted in pursuance of this section.

(8) In this section—
    (a) a reference to a sentence includes, in the case of a sentence which is fixed by law, a reference to the minimum period an offender is required to serve, and a reference to a lesser sentence must be construed accordingly;
    (b) a reference to imprisonment includes a reference to any other custodial sentence within the meaning of section 76 of the Powers of Criminal Courts (Sentencing) Act 2000 (c. 6) or Article 2 of the Criminal Justice (Northern Ireland) Order 1996 (S.I. 1996/ 3160).

(9) An agreement with a specified prosecutor may provide for assistance to be given to that prosecutor or to any other prosecutor.

(10) References to a specified prosecutor must be construed in accordance with section 71.

This section provides that the Crown Court, when sentencing defendants who plead guilty in proceedings before that court and who have entered into a written agreement to provide assistance in any investigation or prosecution, can take account of the nature and extent of that assistance. Section 73(3) requires the court in passing a lower sentence to set out what the sentence would otherwise have been, unless it is in the public interest not to do so (in which case the court must provide a written notice of what the sentence would have been to the prosecutor and the defendant). This section applies to offences for which there is a minimum sentence and also to sentences fixed by law in determining the minimum period of imprisonment that a person must serve.

The intention is that the court can in exceptional circumstances exercise its power under s. 73(2) to reduce a person's sentence or minimum period of imprisonment, as the case may be, to reflect the assistance provided or offered.

Section 73(6) provides that the court's decision (or not) to take into account the assistance provided or offered by a person does not affect any other power it may have when determining that person's sentence or minimum term for imprisonment.

Section 73(7) disapplies the specified provisions, which would otherwise require the court to explain the reasons for passing its sentence on a person, where the court has decided (under s. 73(4)) that it is not in the public interest to make such an explanation.

6.2.3.4 Assistance by Defendant—Review of Sentence

The Serious Organised Crime and Police Act 2005, s. 74 states:

(1) This section applies if—
    (a) the Crown Court has passed a sentence on a person in respect of an offence, and
    (b) the person falls within subsection (2).

(2) A person falls within this subsection if—
    (a) he receives a discounted sentence in consequence of his having offered in pursuance of a written agreement to give assistance to the prosecutor or investigator of an offence but he knowingly fails to any extent to give assistance in accordance with the agreement;
    (b) he receives a discounted sentence in consequence of his having offered in pursuance of a written agreement to give assistance to the prosecutor or investigator of an offence and, having given the assistance in accordance with the agreement, in pursuance of another written agreement gives or offers to give further assistance;
    (c) he receives a sentence which is not discounted but in pursuance of a written agreement he subsequently gives or offers to give assistance to the prosecutor or investigator of an offence.

(3) A specified prosecutor may at any time refer the case back to the court by which the sentence was passed if—
    (a) the person is still serving his sentence, and
    (b) the specified prosecutor thinks it is in the interests of justice to do so.

(4) A case so referred must, if possible, be heard by the judge who passed the sentence to which the referral relates.

(5) If the court is satisfied that a person who falls within subsection (2)(a) knowingly failed to give the assistance it may substitute for the sentence to which the referral relates such greater sentence (not exceeding that which it would have passed but for the agreement to give assistance) as it thinks appropriate.

(6) In a case of a person who falls within subsection (2)(b) or (c) the court may—
    (a) take into account the extent and nature of the assistance given or offered;
    (b) substitute for the sentence to which the referral relates such lesser sentence as it thinks appropriate.

(7) Any part of the sentence to which the referral relates which the person has already served must be taken into account in determining when a greater or lesser sentence imposed by subsection (5) or (6) has been served.

(8) A person in respect of whom a reference is made under this section and the specified prosecutor may with the leave of the Court of Appeal appeal to the Court of Appeal against the decision of the Crown Court.

(9) Section 33(3) of the Criminal Appeal Act 1968 (c. 19) (limitation on appeal from the criminal division of the Court of Appeal) does not prevent an appeal to the Supreme Court under this section.

(10) A discounted sentence is a sentence passed in pursuance of section 73 or subsection (6) above.

(11) References—

(a) to a written agreement are to an agreement made in writing with a specified prosecutor;

(b) to a specified prosecutor must be construed in accordance with section 71.

(12) In relation to any proceedings under this section, the Secretary of State may make an order containing provision corresponding to any provision in—

(a) the Criminal Appeal Act 1968 (subject to any specified modifications), or

(b) the Criminal Appeal (Northern Ireland) Act 1980 (c. 47) (subject to any specified modifications).

(13) A person does not fall within subsection (2) if—

(a) he was convicted of an offence for which the sentence is fixed by law, and

(b) he did not plead guilty to the offence for which he was sentenced.

(14) Section 174(1)(a) or 270 of the Criminal Justice Act 2003 (c. 44) (as the case may be) applies to a sentence substituted under subsection (5) above unless the court thinks that it is not in the public interest to disclose that the person falls within subsection (2)(a) above.

(15) Subsections (3) to (9) of section 73 apply for the purposes of this section as they apply for the purposes of that section and any reference in those subsections to subsection (2) of that section must be construed as a reference to subsection (6) of this section.

KEYNOTE

This section provides that where a person is still serving a sentence imposed by the Crown Court and one of the conditions in s. 74(2) applies, a specified prosecutor may refer the person's sentence back to the court for review (where possible to the original sentencing judge), where he/she considers it is in the interests of justice to do so. The conditions are that the defendant received a reduced sentence on the basis of an agreement to assist, but then knowingly failed to give that assistance; or the defendant gives or agrees to give assistance after they have been sentenced.

Section 74(5) gives the court a power to substitute a greater sentence where it considers the person has failed to assist (not exceeding the sentence it could have passed but for the agreement). However, where a person has provided assistance or offered to assist, s. 74(6) gives the court a power to take that into account and to reduce the individual's sentence accordingly.

Section 78(8) and (9) provide that normal avenues of appeal against sentence apply.

6.2.3.5 Proceedings under Section 74—Exclusion of the Public

The Serious Organised Crime and Police Act 2005, s. 75 states:

(1) This section applies to—

(a) any proceedings relating to a reference made under section 74(3), and

(b) any other proceedings arising in consequence of such proceedings.

(2) The court in which the proceedings will be or are being heard may make such order as it thinks appropriate—

(a) to exclude from the proceedings any person who does not fall within subsection (4);

(b) to give such directions as it thinks appropriate prohibiting the publication of any matter relating to the proceedings (including the fact that the reference has been made).

(3) An order under subsection (2) may be made only to the extent that the court thinks—

(a) that it is necessary to do so to protect the safety of any person, and

(b) that it is in the interests of justice.

(4) The following persons fall within this subsection—

(a) a member or officer of the court;

(b) a party to the proceedings;

(c) counsel or a solicitor for a party to the proceedings;

(d) a person otherwise directly concerned with the proceedings.

(5) This section does not affect any other power which the court has by virtue of any rule of law or other enactment—

    (a) to exclude any person from proceedings, or

    (b) to restrict the publication of any matter relating to proceedings.

KEYNOTE

This section provides that a court in dealing with a defendant under s. 74 can exclude people from the court or impose reporting restrictions, but only to the extent that it is necessary to protect the safety of any person and it is in the interests of justice. The court cannot exclude court staff, parties to the proceedings (or their legal representatives) or others directly concerned with the proceedings.

6.2.4 Chapter 4—Protection of Witnesses and Other Persons

Chapter 4 of the Serious Organised Crime and Police Act 2005 contains provisions relating to protection arrangements for persons at risk. This legislation relates not just to witnesses, but covers any person whose safety may be at risk as a result of the threat of the criminal actions of another person. This includes witnesses, law enforcement officers, jurors, judges, magistrates, prosecutors and their staff. It also covers informants or sources and those convicted of criminal offences.

6.2.4.1 Protection Arrangements for Persons at Risk

This is dealt with by s. 82 of the Serious Organised Crime and Police Act 2005 which was amended by the Anti-social Behaviour, Crime and Policing Act 2014. The Serious Organised Crime and Police Act 2005, s. 82 states:

(1) A protection provider may make such arrangements as he considers appropriate for the purpose of protecting any person if he reasonably believes that the person's safety is at risk in view of the criminal conduct or possible criminal conduct of another person.

(2) A protection provider may vary or cancel any arrangements made by him under subsection (1) if he considers it appropriate to do so.

(3) If a protection provider makes arrangements under subsection (1) or cancels arrangements made under that subsection, he must record that he has done so.

(4) In determining whether to make arrangements under subsection (1), or to vary or cancel arrangements made under that subsection, a protection provider must, in particular, have regard to—

    (a) the nature and extent of the risk to the person's safety,

    (b) the cost of the arrangements,

    (c) the likelihood that the person, and any person associated with him, will be able to adjust to any change in their circumstances which may arise from the making of the arrangements or from their variation or cancellation (as the case may be), and

    (d) if the person is or might be a witness in legal proceedings (whether or not in the United Kingdom), the nature of the proceedings and the importance of his being a witness in those proceedings.

(5) A protection provider is—

    (a) a chief officer of a police force in England and Wales;

    (b) the chief constable of the Police Service of Scotland;

    (c) the Chief Constable of the Police Service of Northern Ireland;

    (d) the Director General of the National Crime Agency;

    (e) any of the Commissioners for Her Majesty's Revenue and Customs;

    (f) [repealed]

    (g) a person designated by a person mentioned in any of the preceding paragraphs to exercise his functions under this section.

(5A) In subsection (1), criminal conduct means conduct which constitutes an offence in England and Wales or Scotland, or would do if it occurred there.

(5B) Nothing in this section prevents a protection provider from making arrangements under this section for the protection of a person where non-statutory arrangements have already been made in respect of that person.

(6) [Repealed]

(7) Nothing in this section affects any power which a person has (otherwise than by virtue of this section) to make arrangements for the protection of another person.

KEYNOTE

Section 82 places arrangements for protecting witnesses and other persons who are involved in investigations or proceedings where the risk to their safety is so serious and life threatening that specialist protection measures, which might include a change of identity and/or relocation, are necessary on a statutory footing. Where UK law enforcement agencies refer a person to a designated protection provider and following assessment they are provided with protection arrangements under s. 82(1), the duty of care under Article 2 of the ECHR passes from the referring agency to the designated protection provider. The provisions of s. 82 only apply to those who are ordinarily resident in the United Kingdom. Protection arrangements may be varied or cancelled by the protection provider. Where a UK law enforcement agency is satisfied that it can provide suitable and sustainable risk management measures to mitigate any threat to life, it is not obliged to refer the matter to one of the designated protection providers under s. 82 and it may continue to provide protection outside those provisions (s. 82(7) refers). This means that police officers, for example, can continue to provide lesser levels of protection, e.g. security locks, panic alarms etc. and agencies which prefer to may continue to make arrangements outside those provisions.

Protected Person

Section 94(3) states that a person is a protected person if:

- arrangements have been made for his/her protection under subs. (1) of s. 82; and
- the arrangements have not been cancelled under subs. (2) of that section.

The reference to a person being 'associated' with a protected person refers to a person who is:

- a member of the same family as the protected person; or
- they live in the same household as the protected person; or
- they have lived in the same household as the protected person.

(See s. 94(4).)

Witness in Legal Proceedings

Section 94(6) states that a reference to a person who is a witness in legal proceedings includes a reference to a person who provides any information or any document or other thing which might be used in evidence in those proceedings or which (whether or not admissible as evidence in those proceedings):

- might tend to confirm evidence which will or might be admitted in those proceedings;
- might be referred to in evidence given in those proceedings by another witness; or
- might be used as the basis for any cross-examination in the course of those proceedings;

and a reference to a person who might be, or to a person who has been, a witness in legal proceedings is to be construed accordingly.

Section 94(7) states that a reference to a person who is a witness in legal proceedings *does not include* a reference to a person who is *an accused person* in criminal proceedings unless he/she is a witness for the prosecution and a reference to a person who might be, or to a person who has been, a witness in legal proceedings is to be construed accordingly.

Those that are eligible for protection under s. 82 of these provisions include:

- witnesses;
- those who have complied with a disclosure notice;
- those who have been given an immunity notice (not Scotland);
- those who have been given a restricted use undertaking if the undertaking continues to have effect in relation to them (not Scotland);
- jurors;
- judges and magistrates;
- prosecutors and their staff (including secondees and employees of the Civil Recovery Unit and the Financial Crime Unit in Scotland);

- law enforcement officers;
- sources; and
- family members of or those living or who have lived in the same household or have or have had a close personal relationship with the person specified.

The term 'witness' includes those in both civil and criminal proceedings and covers those whose testimony may not be admissible in court but could provide the basis for cross-examination during the proceedings, or corroborates or confirms evidence submitted to the proceedings. An accused person will not be eligible for protection as a witness under these provisions unless he/she is giving evidence against a co-accused (or acting as an informant). The term includes witnesses in proceedings which take place outside the United Kingdom, including before international tribunals.

The provisions apply to judges and magistrates and justices of the peace who are normally resident in the United Kingdom and sit on international tribunals that have criminal jurisdiction. Prosecutors will include those who are normally resident in the United Kingdom, irrespective of where the proceedings take place. Domestic tribunals are not included in these provisions since it seems highly unlikely that it will be necessary to provide protection for any domestic tribunal member or witness.

The provisions apply to law enforcement officers and cover anyone who is or has been a constable, customs, immigration or prison officer or a member of the Serious Organised Crime Agency (SOCA) (abolished and replaced by the National Crime Agency (NCA) on 7 October 2013) as well as those working in the area of financial crime, proceeds of crime seizure, assets recovery etc. It also covers anyone who exercises or has exercised functions on behalf of the National Crime Intelligence Service (NCIS) or the National Crime Squad (NCS). This will ensure that retired officers from those organisations remain eligible for protection after the provisions of the Act setting up SOCA come into force.

6.2.4.2 Joint Arrangements

The Serious Organised Crime and Police Act 2005, s. 83 states:

(1) Arrangements may be made under section 82(1) by two or more protection providers acting jointly.
(2) If arrangements are made jointly by virtue of subsection (1), any powers conferred on a protection provider by this Chapter are exercisable in relation to the arrangements by—
    (a) all of the protection providers acting together, or
    (b) one of the protection providers, or some of the protection providers acting together, with the agreement of the others.
(3) Nothing in this section or in section 84 affects any power which a protection provider has to request or obtain assistance from another protection provider.

KEYNOTE

Section 83 aims to facilitate cooperation between protection providers to help to ensure that protection arrangements are delivered as effectively as possible. It allows several protection providers to provide protection to the same person concurrently or to agree between them who should provide protection. Joint arrangements are normally temporary and usually occur in cases where a witness has been relocated.

6.2.4.3 Transfer of Responsibility to Other Protection Provider

The Serious Organised Crime and Police Act 2005, s. 84 states:

(1) A protection provider who makes arrangements under section 82(1) may agree with another protection provider that, as from a date specified in the agreement—
    (a) the protection provider will cease to discharge any responsibilities which he has in relation to the arrangements, and
    (b) the other protection provider will discharge those responsibilities instead.

(2) Any such agreement may include provision for the making of payments in respect of any costs incurred or likely to be incurred in consequence of the agreement.

(3) If an agreement is made under subsection (1), any powers conferred on a protection provider by this Chapter (including the power conferred by subsection (1)) are, as from the date specified in the agreement, exercisable by the other protection provider as if he had made the arrangements under section 82(1).

(4) Each protection provider who makes an agreement under subsection (1) must record that he has done so.

KEYNOTE

This section recognises that protection providers may wish to transfer responsibility for someone who has been granted protected status under s. 82(1) to another protection provider. The section aims to ensure that witness protection is provided in the most efficient way so that a relocated witness can, if requested, be protected by the police force or other protection provider in whose area he/she now resides, resulting in a more responsive and cost-effective service.

The section allows protection providers to permanently transfer responsibility for providing protection to another protection provider. This must be properly recorded. Such arrangements normally occur where it is deemed more appropriate for protection to be provided by the force or protection provider in whose area a protected person has been relocated.

Any arrangement entered into under these provisions can include reimbursement for the costs of the transfer. The new provider is granted the same powers as the original protection provider had when first authorising protection. This will ensure that the new protection provider can provide appropriate protection and can also vary or cancel that protection, or transfer responsibility for that protection to a third provider if appropriate.

6.2.4.4 Duty to Assist Protection Providers

The Serious Organised Crime and Police Act 2005, s. 85 states:

(1) This section applies if a protection provider requests assistance from a public authority in connection with the making of arrangements under section 82(1) or the implementation, variation or cancellation of such arrangements.

(2) The public authority must take reasonable steps to provide the assistance requested.

(3) Public authority includes any person certain of whose functions are of a public nature but does not include—

(a) a court or tribunal,

(b) either House of Parliament or a person exercising functions in connection with proceedings in Parliament, or

(c) the Scottish Parliament or a person exercising functions in connection with proceedings in the Scottish Parliament.

KEYNOTE

This section refers to cases where the protection provider may need assistance from public authorities to set up and implement effective protection arrangements. A person who is under assessment for, or has been granted protected status, and their family will often have to be relocated and receive assistance from a number of different agencies. For example, the cooperation of housing, education and health authorities etc. is often essential if a person is to begin a new life.

The aim of this provision is to secure more cooperation and understanding from such organisations in their dealings with protected persons who are faced with extremely difficult and sometimes life-threatening circumstances. Because of their circumstances, the normal channels for such individuals to request assistance are not generally available. Requests for assistance come via designated protection providers and are unusual because agencies will often be asked to provide services to persons with either anonymised

---

documentation or no previous documentation at all. This is bound to be contrary to the standard procedures of most public authorities and may place their employees in a very difficult position.

The majority of cooperative relationships between protection providers and service providers in the field of protection services have been fostered over the years by individual law enforcement agencies. They may have been instigated on an ad hoc basis as needs arose. This section provides a statutory basis for such arrangements.

Section 85 places a duty on all public authorities to take 'reasonable steps' to provide assistance to protection providers when requested to do so. It will be for those agencies to which requests are made to decide what is and what is not 'reasonable'.

The term 'public body' includes any person or organisation whose functions are of a public nature, although it does not include a court or tribunal, either House of Parliament, or the Scottish Parliament or those connected with parliamentary proceedings. This is intended to cover two main types of organisation: those involved in the provision of documentation, such as identity documents, and those concerned with the provision of services, such as housing, education, employment, welfare etc.

6.2.4.5 Disclosing Information about Protection Arrangements

OFFENCE: **Disclosing Information about Protection Arrangements—*Serious Organised Crime and Police Act 2005, s. 86***

- Triable either way • Two years' imprisonment, a fine or both on indictment
- Imprisonment not exceeding 12 months (six months in Scotland and Northern Ireland) and/or a fine not exceeding the statutory maximum summarily

The Serious Organised Crime and Police Act 2005, s. 86 states:

(1) A person commits an offence if—
   (a) he discloses information which relates to the making of arrangements under section 82(1) or to the implementation, variation or cancellation of such arrangements, and
   (b) he knows or suspects that the information relates to the making of such arrangements or to their implementation, variation or cancellation.

KEYNOTE

In making protection arrangements, it is necessary to both disclose the fact that a person is protected and to engage assistance from a diverse range of people. Such people are often privy to the procedures used in making those arrangements and this section seeks to ensure that such information is not disclosed. It would also apply where another person who was not involved in the arrangements disclosed information (unless they did not know or suspect the information related to protection arrangements).

Section 86 creates an offence which may be committed if any person discloses information which relates to the making of protection arrangements under s. 82(1) or to the implementation, variation or cancellation of such arrangements. The purpose of this clause is to deter individuals from disclosing information which could be harmful to protected persons or those involved in the provision of their protection measures.

The offence only applies to disclosures. If the information in question is already in the public domain by virtue of an earlier disclosure, subsequent references to that information are unlikely to be considered disclosures for the purpose of this offence. The person disclosing the information must know or suspect that the information relates to protection arrangements. It *will not* constitute an offence where a person who discloses information is unaware that it relates to protection arrangements.

In order for disclosure to take place, the information disclosed would need to have become known to a third party and the person disclosing must have intended the information to become known to a third party. The form of the disclosure is therefore relevant—if the information is, for example, published in a newspaper or put on the internet, then the presumption is that the information would become known to someone. If the information was contained in a private email which was not opened then this would be very likely to only constitute attempt.

Defence to Liability under Section 86

The Serious Organised Crime and Police Act 2005, s. 87 states:

(1) A person (P) is not guilty of an offence under section 86 if—

    (a) at the time when P disclosed the information, he was or had been a protected person,

    (b) the information related only to arrangements made for the protection of P or for the protection of P and a person associated with him, and

    (c) at the time when P disclosed the information, it was not likely that its disclosure would endanger the safety of any person.

(2) A person (D) is not guilty of an offence under section 86 if—

    (a) D disclosed the information with the agreement of a person (P) who, at the time the information was disclosed, was or had been a protected person,

    (b) the information related only to arrangements made for the protection of P or for the protection of P and a person associated with him, and

    (c) at the time when D disclosed the information, it was not likely that its disclosure would endanger the safety of any person.

(3) A person is not guilty of an offence under section 86 if he disclosed the information for the purposes of safeguarding national security or for the purposes of the prevention, detection or investigation of crime.

(4) A person is not guilty of an offence under section 86 if—

    (a) at the time when he disclosed the information, he was a protection provider or involved in the making of arrangements under section 82(1) or in the implementation, variation or cancellation of such arrangements, and

    (b) he disclosed the information for the purposes of the making, implementation, variation or cancellation of such arrangements.

(5) The Secretary of State may by order make provision prescribing circumstances in which a person who discloses information as mentioned in section 82(1) is not guilty in England and Wales of an offence under that section.

(6) The Scottish Ministers may by order make provision prescribing circumstances in which a person who discloses information as mentioned in section 86(1) is not guilty in Scotland of an offence under that section.

(6A) The Department of Justice in Northern Ireland may by order make provision prescribing circumstances in which a person who discloses information as mentioned in section 86(1) is not guilty in Northern Ireland of an offence under that section.

(7) If sufficient evidence is adduced to raise an issue with respect to a defence under or by virtue of this section, the court or jury must assume that the defence is satisfied unless the prosecution proves beyond reasonable doubt that it is not.

KEYNOTE

There will be occasions when information is disclosed by protected persons which does not endanger anyone's safety. In such cases, an offence would not be committed under s. 86. Similarly, such occasions will occur where another person discloses information with the consent of the protected person and again, providing no one's safety is endangered, an offence will not be committed.

Section 87 sets out defences to the offence of knowingly disclosing information about protection arrangements. It limits liability in that it exempts acts of disclosure which will not result in harm. It also provides exemptions where the circumstances are such that disclosure is made for the prevention, detection or investigation of crime.

The test for the purposes of these defences is whether it is likely at the time of disclosure that such disclosure would endanger anyone's safety. It does not matter if it turns out that no one's safety is in fact endangered. A person's fear and stress may be relevant to establishing whether, at the time of the disclosure, their safety is endangered but it does not necessarily follow that the fact that a protected person suffers fear and distress means that their safety is endangered.

6.2.4.7 Disclosing Information Relating to Persons Assuming New Identity

OFFENCE: **Disclosing Information Relating to Persons Assuming New Identity—** *Serious Organised Crime and Police Act 2005, s. 88*

> • Triable either way • Two years' imprisonment on indictment • Six months' imprisonment and/or fine summarily

The Serious Organised Crime and Police Act 2005, s. 88 states:

(1) A person (P) commits an offence if—

    (a) P is or has been a protected person,

    (b) P assumed a new identity in pursuance of arrangements made under section 82(1),

    (c) P discloses information which indicates that he assumed, or might have assumed, a new identity, and

    (d) P knows or suspects that the information disclosed by him indicates that he assumed, or might have assumed, a new identity.

(2) A person (D) commits an offence if—

    (a) D discloses information which relates to a person (P) who is or has been a protected person,

    (b) P assumed a new identity in pursuance of arrangements made under section 82(1),

    (c) the information disclosed by D indicates that P assumed, or might have assumed, a new identity, and

    (d) D knows or suspects—

        (i) that P is or has been a protected person, and

        (ii) that the information disclosed by D indicates that P assumed, or might have assumed, a new identity.

KEYNOTE

Disclosing information relating to an identity change will only constitute an offence where it is likely that another's safety is endangered. The most likely circumstances where this offence will be committed are where relationships involving protected witnesses have broken down. A situation may also arise where someone who has assisted with protection arrangements either knowingly or inadvertently discloses information relating to an identity change.

The purpose of the offence is to deter individuals and organisations with access to a person's original identity from disclosing information which could be harmful. It will also apply to protected persons themselves in cases where they reveal their true identities in order to cause harm to another protected person, such as an ex-partner.

A person commits an offence under this section if he/she knowingly discloses information relating to a protected person's new identity (s. 94(5) states that a new identity is assumed by a person if they either become known by a different name or they make representations about their personal history or circumstances which are false or misleading). The offence only applies to disclosures. If the original identity of a protected person is already in the public domain by virtue of an earlier disclosure, subsequent references to the original identity are unlikely to be considered disclosures for the purpose of this offence. The person disclosing the identity of a protected person must know or suspect that the person is receiving or has received protection. It will not constitute an offence where a person discloses the true identity of a protected person but is unaware that that person is or has been protected.

The offence applies to private individuals and also to employees of institutions which have access to a protected person's original identity.

6.2.4.8 Defence to Liability under Section 88

The Serious Organised Crime and Police Act 2005, s. 89 states:

(1) P is not guilty of an offence under section 88(1) if, at the time when he disclosed the information, it was not likely that its disclosure would endanger the safety of any person.

(2) D is not guilty of an offence under section 88(2) if—
  (a) D disclosed the information with the agreement of P, and
  (b) at the time when D disclosed the information, it was not likely that its disclosure would endanger the safety of any person.
(3) D is not guilty of an offence under section 88(2) if he disclosed the information for the purposes of safeguarding national security or for the purposes of the prevention, detection or investigation of crime.
(4) D is not guilty of an offence under section 88(2) if—
  (a) at the time when he disclosed the information, he was a protection provider or involved in the making of arrangements under section 82(1) or in the implementation, variation or cancellation of such arrangements, and
  (b) he disclosed the information for the purposes of the making, implementation, variation or cancellation of such arrangements.
(5) The Secretary of State may by order make provision prescribing circumstances in which a person who discloses information as mentioned in subsection (1) or (2) of section 88 is not guilty in England and Wales of an offence under that subsection.
(6) The Scottish Ministers may by order make provision prescribing circumstances in which a person who discloses information as mentioned in subsection (1) or (2) of section 88 is not guilty in Scotland of an offence under that subsection.
(6A) The Department of Justice in Northern Ireland may by order make provision prescribing circumstances in which a person who discloses information as mentioned in subsection (1) or (2) of section 88 is not guilty in Northern Ireland of an offence under that subsection.
(7) If sufficient evidence is adduced to raise an issue with respect to a defence under or by virtue of this section, the court or jury must assume that the defence is satisfied unless the prosecution proves beyond reasonable doubt that it is not.

KEYNOTE

There are circumstances where, in dealing with protected persons, law enforcement agencies, out of necessity, have to disclose the fact that an identity change has taken place, e.g. for medical or educational purposes. There may also be occasions when a protected person discloses their real identity in a medical emergency.

Section 89 sets out defences to the offence of knowingly disclosing the identity of protected persons. It limits liability in that it exempts acts of disclosure which are likely not to result in harm. It also provides exemptions where the circumstances are such that disclosure by a protection provider is necessary.

6.2.4.9 Protection from Liability

The Serious Organised Crime and Police Act 2005, s. 90 states:

(1) This section applies if—
  (a) arrangements are made for the protection of a person under section 82(1) and
  (b) the protected person assumes a new identity in pursuance of the arrangements.
(2) No proceedings (whether civil or criminal) may be brought against a person to whom this section applies in respect of the making by him of a false or misleading representation if the representation—
  (a) relates to the protected person, and
  (b) is made solely for the purpose of ensuring that the arrangements made for him to assume a new identity are, or continue to be, effective.
(3) The persons to whom this section applies are—
  (a) the protected person;
  (b) a person who is associated with the protected person;
  (c) a protection provider;
  (d) a person involved in the making of arrangements under section 82(1) or in the implementation, variation or cancellation of such arrangements.

6.2.4.10 Provision of Information

The Serious Organised Crime and Police Act 2005, s. 93 states:

(1) This section applies if—
   (a) a protection provider makes arrangements under section 82(1).
   (b) [repealed]
(2) The protection provider must inform the person to whom the arrangements relate of the provisions of this Chapter as they apply in relation to the arrangements.
(3) If the protection provider considers that the person would be unable to understand the information, by reason of his age or of any incapacity, the information must instead be given to a person who appears to the protection provider—
   (a) to be interested in the welfare of the person to whom the arrangements relate, and
   (b) to be the appropriate person to whom to give the information.
(4) If arrangements are made jointly under section 82(1) (by virtue of section 83), the protection providers involved in the arrangements must nominate one of those protection providers to perform the duties imposed by this section.

The Crime and Courts Act 2013

> This chapter is only for examination candidates from the National Crime Agency.

6.3.1 Introduction

Part 1 of the Crime and Courts Act 2013 abolishes the Serious Organised Crime Agency (SOCA) and replaces it with the National Crime Agency (NCA).

The Crime and Courts Act 2013, s. 1 states:

(1) A National Crime Agency, consisting of the NCA officers, is to be formed.

(2) The NCA is to be under the direction and control of one of the NCA officers, who is to be known as the Director General of the National Crime Agency.

(3) The NCA is to have—
   (a) the functions conferred by this section;
   (b) the functions conferred by the Proceeds of Crime Act 2002; and
   (c) the other functions conferred by this Act and by other enactments.

(4) The NCA is to have the function (the 'crime-reduction function') of securing that efficient and effective activities to combat organised crime and serious crime are carried out (whether by the NCA, other law enforcement agencies, or other persons).

(5) The NCA is to have the function (the 'criminal intelligence function') of gathering, storing, processing, analysing, and disseminating information that is relevant to any of the following—
   (a) activities to combat organised crime or serious crime;
   (b) activities to combat any other kind of crime;
   (c) exploitation proceeds investigations (within the meaning of section 341(5) of the Proceeds of Crime Act 2002), exploitation proceeds orders (within the meaning of Part 7 of the Coroners and Justice Act 2009), and applications for such orders.

KEYNOTE

The NCA became fully operational on 7 October 2013. The NCA is headed by a Director General who will also be an NCA officer. The principal functions of the NCA will be the crime-reduction function (s. 1(4)) and the criminal intelligence function (s. 1(5)).

The crime-reduction function relates to securing that efficient and effective activities to combat organised crime and serious crime are carried out (whether by the NCA, other law enforcement agencies or other persons). In discharging this function, the NCA may itself undertake activities to combat serious crime and organised crime, including by preventing, detecting or investigating such crime, or otherwise. When discharging functions relating to organised or serious crime, the NCA may carry out activities in relation to *any kind of crime* (whether or not that crime is serious or organised). For example, in circumstances where an NCA officer reasonably suspects that an offence is about to be, or is being, committed, that officer *is not* prevented from exercising powers merely because the offence does not relate to organised or serious crime (s. 1(11) and para. 5 of sch. 1). This reflects the role of the NCA in the reduction of crime in other ways and mitigating the consequences of crime and acknowledges that the investigation and prosecution of organised criminals is only one of the strategies that may be deployed to tackle organised criminality and that there are a range of disruption tactics that will need to be deployed by the NCA in order to reduce the harm and impact caused by organised criminal groups.

In addition to undertaking activities of its own, the NCA may discharge its crime-reduction function in other ways:

- by ensuring that other law enforcement agencies and others also carry out activities to combat serious and organised crime (s. 1(8)); and

- by improving cooperation between law enforcement and other agencies to combat serious crime and organised crime and by improving coordination of their collective efforts to combat serious crime and organised crime (s. 1(9)).

It is important to note that the role of the NCA in tackling serious crime and organised crime does not include the function of the NCA itself prosecuting offences—in England and Wales the prosecutorial function will be undertaken by the CPS and the Serious Fraud Office and in Northern Ireland the prosecutorial function will be undertaken by the Public Prosecution Service.

6.3.2 Powers of NCA Officers

The Crime and Courts Act 2013, s. 10 states:

(1) The Director General may designate any other NCA officer as a person having one or more of the following—
   (a) the powers and privileges of a constable;
   (b) the powers of an officer of Revenue and Customs;
   (ba) the powers of a general customs official;
   (c) the powers of an immigration officer.
(2) The Director General may not designate an NCA officer under this section as having particular operational powers unless the Director General is satisfied that the officer—
   (a) is capable of effectively exercising those powers;
   (b) has received adequate training in respect of the exercise of those powers; and
   (c) is otherwise a suitable person to exercise those powers.
(3) The Director General may modify or withdraw a designation of an NCA officer by giving notice of the modification or withdrawal to the officer.
(4) For further provision about designations under this section, see Schedule 5.

KEYNOTE

Section 10 is an exceptionally important section of the Act as it provides the Director General of the NCA with the ability to designate NCA officers with operational powers. These include:

- the powers and privileges of a constable;
- the powers of an officer of Revenue and Customs; and
- the powers of an immigration officer.

Paragraph 5 of sch. 1 is of particular note as it provides:

- for the purposes of the discharge of NCA functions which relate to organised crime or serious crime, an NCA officer may, in particular, carry on activities in relation to any kind of crime (whether or not serious or organised);
- in circumstances in which an NCA officer reasonably suspects that an offence is about to be, or is being, committed, that officer is not prevented from exercising powers merely because the offence does not relate to organised crime or serious crime.

Section 10(4) provides further information about such designations which is contained in sch. 5 to the Act.

Paragraph 6 of sch. 5 provides that a designation of an officer as having operational powers may be subject to limitations specified in the designation. This may include limitations on which operational powers the designated officer has or limitations on the purposes for which an NCA officer may exercise legal powers.

Paragraph 7 of sch. 5 provides that the designation of an officer as having operational powers does not have any limitation of time unless the designation specifies a period for which it is to have effect. Any designation, however, remains subject to any subsequent modification or withdrawal and only has effect while a person remains an NCA officer.

Paragraph 8 of sch. 5 provides that the Director General or other NCA officer may be designated with operational powers whether or not that person already has, or previously had, any such powers. Sub-paragraph (3) provides that if a person is both an NCA officer designated with operational powers and a special constable or a member of the PSNI Reserve, none of the powers that a person has as an NCA officer are exercisable at any time when the person is exercising any power or privilege of a special constable or a constable of the PSNI Reserve.

Paragraph 9 of sch. 5 provides that an NCA officer must produce evidence of his/her designation if they exercise or purport to exercise any operational power in relation to another person and the other person requests the officer to produce such evidence (sub-para. (1)). This paragraph does not specify the form which such evidence should take. A failure to produce evidence of designation does not make the exercise of the power invalid (sub-para. (2)).

6.3.2.1 Designation—Powers of a Constable

If an NCA officer (other than the Director General) is designated as a person having the powers and privileges of a constable, the NCA officer has—

(a) in England and Wales and the adjacent UK waters, all the powers and privileges of an English and Welsh constable;
(b) in Scotland and the adjacent UK waters, all the powers and privileges of a Scottish constable;
(c) in Northern Ireland and the adjacent UK waters, all the powers and privileges of a Northern Ireland constable; and
(d) outside the United Kingdom and UK waters, all the powers and privileges of a constable that are exercisable overseas.

This is subject to any limitations regarding the designation as a constable and applies to enactments providing for the issuing of warrants (part 4 of sch. 5)

6.3.2.2 Designation—Powers of Officers of Revenue and Customs

If an NCA officer is designated as a person having the powers of an officer of Revenue and Customs, the NCA officer has, in relation to any customs matter, the same powers as an officer of Revenue and Customs would have. This is subject to any limitations regarding designation and applies to enactments providing for the issue of warrants (part 5 of sch. 5)

6.3.2.3 Designation—Powers of Immigration Officers

If an NCA officer is designated as a person having the powers of an immigration officer, the NCA officer has, in relation to any relevant matter, the same powers as an immigration officer would have. This is subject to any limitations regarding designation and applies to enactments providing for the issue of warrants (part 6 of sch. 5)

6.3.2.4 Designation—Powers of General Customs Officials

If an NCA officer is designated as a person having the powers of a general customs official, the NCA officer has, in relation to any customs matter, the same powers as a general customs official would have. This is subject to any limitations regarding designation and applies to enactments providing for the issue of warrants (part 5A of sch. 5)

KEYNOTE

Section 158 of the Policing and Crime Act 2017, which came into force on 1 April 2017, amended ss. 9 and 10 of and sch. 5 to the Crime and Courts Act 2013 to enable the Director General of the NCA to designate an NCA officer with the powers of a General Customs Official (GCO).

Designation as a GCO does not confer certain anti-money laundering or anti-terrorist financing powers so an NCA officer carrying out financial investigations into such matters will need to continue to rely on the relevant powers conferred in the Proceeds of Crime Act 2002 and the Terrorism Act 2000 on a constable or an officer of HMRC, as appropriate NCA officers designated as a GCO will be able to access:

- the Police and Criminal Evidence Act 1984 (PACE) powers available to a GCO in England and Wales under the PACE 1984 (Application to immigration officers and designated customs officials in England and Wales) Order 2013;
- the Criminal Law (Consolidation) (Scotland) Act 1995 as it applies to NCA officers in Scotland designated as GCOs;
- the Police and Criminal Evidence (Northern Ireland) Order 1989 as it applies to NCA officers in Northern Ireland designated as GCOs;
- powers of seizure and forfeiture of drug-cutting agents in the Serious Crime Act 2015;
- powers of entry, search and seizure in connection with the production, supply etc. of a psychoactive substance in the Psychoactive Substances Act 2016;
- the maritime enforcement and cross-border powers in the Policing and Crime Act 2017.

6.3.3 Offences Relating to Designations

Part 7 of sch. 5 to the Crime and Courts Act 2013 creates a series of offences (resistance/ assault/impersonation) which are very similar to offences contained in the Police Act 1996 (ss. 89 and 90).

6.3.3.1 Obstructing a Designated Officer

OFFENCE: **Obstruct a Designated Officer—*Crime and Courts Act 2013, sch. 5, para. 21***

> • Triable summarily • One month's imprisonment and/or fine

The Crime and Courts Act 2013, sch. 5, para. 21 states:

(1) A person commits an offence if the person resists or wilfully obstructs—
   (a) a designated officer acting in the exercise of an operational power, or
   (b) a person who is assisting a designated officer in the exercise of such a power.

6.3.3.2 Assault a Designated Officer

OFFENCE: **Assault a Designated Officer—*Crime and Courts Act 2013, sch. 5, para. 22***

> • Triable summarily • Six months' imprisonment and/or fine

The Crime and Courts Act 2013, sch. 5, para. 22 states:

(1) A person commits an offence if the person assaults—
   (a) a designated officer acting in the exercise of an operational power, or
   (b) a person who is assisting a designated officer in the exercise of such a power.

6.3.3.3 Impersonate a Designated Officer

OFFENCE: **Impersonating a Designated Officer—*Crime and Courts Act 2013, sch. 5, para. 23***

> • Triable summarily • Six months' imprisonment and/or fine

The Crime and Courts Act 2013, sch. 5, para. 23 states:

(1) A person commits an offence if, with intent to deceive—
   (a) the person impersonates a designated officer,
   (b) the person makes any statement or does any act calculated falsely to suggest that the person is a designated officer, or

(c) the person makes any statement or does any act calculated falsely to suggest that the person has powers as a designated officer that exceed the powers the person actually has.

KEYNOTE

The offences of obstruct and assault a designated person will only apply if the designated person is acting in the exercise of an operational power. So (as with the offences under the Police Act 1996 where police officers not acting in the lawful execution of their duty are not protected by the legislation), an NCA officer who is not acting in the exercise of an operational power will not be protected by the offences under paras 21 and 22. Also note that the offences under paras 21 and 22 can be committed against a person who is assisting the designated officer in the exercise of an operational power.

6.3.4 Restrictions on Disclosures

Part 2 of sch. 7 to the Act places restrictions on NCA officers regarding the disclosure of particular types of information.

The Crime and Courts Act 2013, sch. 7, para. 2 states:

HMRC & customs information
(1) An NCA officer must not disclose—
   (a) HMRC information,
   (b) personal customs information, or
   (c) personal customs revenue information,
   unless the relevant authority consents to the disclosure.
(2) If an NCA officer has disclosed—
   (a) HMRC information,
   (b) personal customs information, or
   (c) personal customs revenue information,
   to a person, that person must not further disclose that information unless the relevant authority consents to the disclosure.
(3) In this paragraph—
   'HMRC information' means information obtained by the NCA from the Commissioners or a person acting on behalf of the Commissioners;
   'personal customs information' and 'personal customs revenue information' have the same meanings as in the Borders, Citizenship and Immigration Act 2009 (see section 15(4) of that Act);
   'relevant authority' means—
   (a) the Commissioners or an officer of Revenue and Customs (in the case of a disclosure or further disclosure of HMRC information);
   (b) the Secretary of State or a designated general customs official (in the case of a disclosure or further disclosure of personal customs information);
   (c) the Director of Border Revenue or a designated customs revenue official (in the case of a disclosure or further disclosure of personal customs revenue information).

The Crime and Courts Act 2013, sch. 7, para. 3 states:

Social security information
(1) An NCA officer must not disclose social security information unless the relevant authority consents to the disclosure.
(2) If an NCA officer has disclosed social security information to a person, that person must not further disclose that information unless the relevant authority consents to the disclosure.
(3) In this paragraph—
   'relevant authority' means—
   (a) the Secretary of State (in the case of a disclosure or further disclosure of information held, when disclosed to the NCA, for the purposes of the functions of the Secretary of State);
   (b) the Department for Social Development in Northern Ireland (in the case of a disclosure or further disclosure of information held, when disclosed to the NCA, for the purposes of the functions of a Northern Ireland department);

'social security information' means information which, when disclosed to the NCA, was information held for the purposes of any of the following functions of the Secretary of State or a Northern Ireland Department—

(a) functions relating to social security, including functions relating to—

    (i) statutory payments as defined in section 4C(11) of the Social Security Contributions and Benefits Act 1992;

    (ii) maternity allowance under section 35 of that Act;

    (iii) statutory payments as defined in section 4C(11) of the Social Security Contributions and Benefits (Northern Ireland) Act 1992;

    (iv) maternity allowance under section 35 of that Act;

    (v) schemes and arrangements under section 2 of the Employment and Training Act 1973;

(b) functions relating to the investigation and prosecution of offences relating to tax credits.

The Crime and Courts Act 2013, sch. 7, para. 4 states:

Intelligence service information

(1) An NCA officer must not disclose intelligence service information unless the relevant authority consents to the disclosure.

(2) If an NCA officer has disclosed intelligence service information to a person, that person must not further disclose that information unless the relevant authority consents to the disclosure.

(3) In this paragraph—

'intelligence service' means—

(a) the Security Service,

(b) the Secret Intelligence Service, or

(c) GCHQ (which has the same meaning as in the Intelligence Services Act 1994);

'intelligence service information' means information obtained from an intelligence service or a person acting on behalf of an intelligence service;

'relevant authority' means—

(a) the Director-General of the Security Service (in the case of information obtained by the NCA from that Service or a person acting on its behalf);

(b) the Chief of the Secret Intelligence Service (in the case of information obtained by the NCA from that Service or a person acting on its behalf);

(c) the Director of GCHQ (in the case of information obtained from GCHQ or a person acting on its behalf).

The Crime and Courts Act 2013, sch. 7, para. 5 states:

Arrangements for publishing information

The Director General must not disclose information if the disclosure would be in breach of a requirement that is imposed on the Director General by the framework document in accordance with section 6(2).

KEYNOTE

Section 6(2) of the Act imposes a duty on the Director General of the NCA to publish information about the exercise of NCA functions and other matters relating to the NCA and to publish information in accordance with those arrangements (set out in the Framework Document). Paragraph 5 of sch. 7 imposes limits on the information that can be published. For example, information obtained from HM Revenue and Customs can only be published with the consent of the Commissioners for Revenue and Customs.

Appendix

Summary of PACE Code of Practice for the Detention, Treatment and Questioning of Persons under s. 41 of, and sch. 8 to, the Terrorism Act 2000 (Code H)

A thick grey line down the margin denotes text that is an extract of the PACE Code itself (i.e. the actual wording of the legislation). This material is examinable for both Sergeants and Inspectors.

As stated at the start of **chapter 1.9**, Code H has been introduced and applies to people in police detention following their arrest under the Terrorism Act 2000, s. 41; the latest revision applies after midnight on 21 August 2019, notwithstanding that the person has been arrested before that time. In the main, Code H mirrors Code C. The latest revisions to Codes C and H enable the use of live-link electronic communication systems to provide interpretation services for suspects which would not require the interpreter to be physically present at the police station. The revisions incorporate detailed conditions and safeguards to ensure that live-link interpretation does not adversely impact on the suspect.

Code H is not reproduced within the Manual but should be available in custody suites and at police stations. Generally, the provisions to Code H are mirrored (with modifications as necessary) in the current version of PACE Code C and *vice versa* in order to ensure consistency; however, in relation to reviews and extensions of detention there are significant differences from the equivalent provisions in PACE Code C owing to the changes made to maximum detention times by the Terrorism Act 2006.

Code H has been expanded in scope to incorporate provisions relating to the post-charge questioning of terrorist suspects. Part 2 of the Counter-Terrorism Act 2008 provides that a judge may authorise the questioning of a person by a constable after that person has been charged with a terrorism offence or an offence with a terrorist connection. The post-charge questioning provisions of the 2008 Act also introduce a new mandatory Code for the video recording with sound of such questioning.

Section 1—General

This section covers the scope and applicability of the Code (which are, by definition, different from the equivalent provisions of Code C); it also covers the availability of the Code, definitions, applicability to the deaf, blind and speech impaired, and the use of reasonable force, and in these respects follows Code C.

> 1N The powers under Part IV of PACE to detain and release on bail (before or after charge) a person arrested under section 24 of PACE for any offence (see PACE Code G (Arrest)) do not apply to persons whilst they are detained under the terrorism powers following their arrest/detention under section 41 of, or Schedule 7 to, TACT. If when the grounds for detention under these powers cease the person is arrested under section 24 of PACE for a specific offence, the detention and bail provisions of PACE will apply and must be considered from the time of that arrest.

Section 2—Custody Records

This section follows Code C. It covers general requirements for making custody records, including the exemption for counter-terrorism officers from disclosing their identities on custody records and provisions as to access to custody records by detainees' solicitors and disclosure of those records to them.

Section 3—Initial Action in Respect of Arrested Individuals

Code H broadly follows Code C in respect of detainees' rights and arrangements for exercising them but differs in a number of respects:

- the record will indicate that the arrest was under s. 41 as opposed to indicating the offence in respect of which the arrest was made—Note 3G indicates that, where an arrest is made on grounds of sensitive information which cannot be disclosed, the recorded grounds 'may be given in terms of the interpretation of "terrorist" set out in . . . s. 40(1)(a) or (b)';
- there is a specific provision to the effect that risk assessments do not form part of the custody record and should not be shown to the detainee or his/her legal representative;
- there are provisions relating to the initial steps that may be taken in connection with the identification of suspects;
- the custody officer is allowed to direct custody staff to carry out certain actions in relation to a detainee's rights and entitlements, need for medical treatment and the risk assessment process.

Section 4—Detainees' Property

This section of Code H includes a simplification of the circumstances in which a custody officer should search a detainee to ascertain what he/she has in his/her possession but there is no material change in comparison with Code C.

Section 5—Right not to be Held Incommunicado

This section allows a detainee to be visited by those in whose welfare the detainee has an interest. The detainee's right to have someone informed of his/her whereabouts closely follows the equivalent section of Code C but there is much more detailed guidance on visiting rights. A requirement is imposed for custody officers to liaise with the investigation team to ascertain the risks presented by visits. Where visits from relatives etc. present a risk, consideration of more frequent visits from independent visitor schemes is suggested. Visits from official visitors ('official visitors' may include accredited faith representatives and MPs) may be allowed subject to consultation with the officer in charge of the investigation. Note 5B indicates that custody officers should bear in mind the effects of prolonged detention under the Act and consider the health and welfare benefits that visits bring to the health and welfare of detainees who are held for extended periods. However, Note 5G reminds officers that the nature of terrorist investigations means that they need to have 'particular regard to the possibility of suspects attempting to pass information which may be detrimental to public safety, or to an investigation'.

Section 6—Right to Legal Advice

The principal difference from Code C is that there is provision for an authorisation to be given whereby a detainee may only consult a solicitor within sight and hearing of a qualified officer (a uniformed officer of at least the rank of inspector who has no connection with the investigation). This section also introduces additional safeguards for detainees who change their mind about wanting advice.

Section 7—Citizens of Independent Commonwealth Countries or Foreign Nationals

Section 7 shows no material change from the equivalent Code C provisions.

Section 8—Conditions of Detention

The main differences from Code C are that there is specific reference to allowing detainees to practise religious observance and to the provision of reading material, including religious texts. Police should consult with representatives of religious communities on provision of facilities for religious observance and handling of religious texts and other articles. The benefits of exercise for detainees, particularly in the cases of prolonged detention, are emphasised. If facilities exist, indoor exercise is to be offered if requested or if outdoor exercise is not practicable. Although the same restrictions on putting a juvenile in a cell apply as under Code C, there is no requirement to include occasions when a juvenile is so confined on the custody record.

Section 9—Care and Treatment of Detained Persons

Section 9 of Code H begins by requiring that, notwithstanding other requirements for medical attention, 'detainees who are held for more than 96 hours must be visited by a healthcare professional at least once every 24 hours'. In all other material respects, the provisions are the same as under Code C.

Section 10—Cautions

Insofar as relevant, the provisions on cautions closely follow those of Code C.

Section 11—Interviews (General)

There are no material differences from Code C under this section. The Code H equivalent is, however, much shorter, reflecting the fact that not all instances covered by the Code C equivalent are relevant to detention of terrorist suspects.

Section 12—Interviews in Police Stations

The only material difference here is set out at para. 12.9:

> 12.9 During extended periods where no interviews take place, because of the need to gather further evidence or analyse existing evidence, detainees and their legal representative shall be informed that the investigation into the relevant offence remains ongoing. If practicable, the detainee and legal representative should also be made aware in general terms of any reasons for long gaps between interviews. Consideration should be given to allowing visits, more frequent exercise, or for reading or writing materials to be offered. *See paragraph 5.4, section 8 and Note 12C.*

Note 12C indicates that consideration should be given to the matters referred to in para. 12.9 after a period of over 24 hours without questioning.

Section 13—Interpreters

Section 13 shows no material change from the equivalent Code C provisions.

Section 14—Reviews and Extensions of Detention

This section contains significant changes from the equivalent provisions in Code C, s. 15, owing to the changes made to maximum detention times by the Terrorism Act 2006. It is set out in full below.

14 Reviews and Extensions of Detention under the Terrorism Act 2000

(a) General

14.0 The requirement in *paragraph 3.4(b)* that documents and materials essential to challenging the lawfulness the detainee's arrest and detention must be made available to the detainee or their solicitor, applies for the purposes of this section.

14.1 The powers and duties of the review officer are in the Terrorism Act 2000, Schedule 8, Part II. See *Notes 14A and 14B*. A review officer should carry out their duties at the police station where the detainee is held and be allowed such access to the detainee as is necessary to exercise those duties.

14.2 For the purposes of reviewing a person's detention, no officer shall put specific questions to the detainee:
- regarding their involvement in any offence; or
- in respect of any comments they may make:
  - when given the opportunity to make representations; or
  - in response to a decision to keep them in detention or extend the maximum period of detention.

Such an exchange could constitute an interview as in *paragraph 11.1* and would be subject to the associated safeguards in *section 11*.

14.3 If detention is necessary for longer than 48 hours from the time of arrest or, if a person was being detained under TACT Schedule 7, from the time at which the examination under Schedule 7 began, a police officer of at least superintendent rank, or a Crown Prosecutor may apply for a warrant of further detention or for an extension or further extension of such a warrant under *paragraph 29* or (as the case may be) 36 of Part III of Schedule 8 to the Terrorism Act 2000. See *Note 14C*.

14.4 When an application is made for a warrant as described in *paragraph 14.3*, the detained person and their representative must be informed of their rights in respect of the application. These include:
- (i) the right to a written notice of the application (*see paragraph 14.4*);
- (ii) the right to make oral or written representations to the judicial authority/High Court judge about the application;
- (iii) the right to be present and legally represented at the hearing of the application, unless specifically excluded by the judicial authority/High Court judge;
- (iv) their right to free legal advice (see *section 6* of this Code).

14.4A TACT *Schedule 8 paragraph 31* requires the notice of the application for a warrant of further detention to be provided before the judicial hearing of the application for that warrant and that the notice must include:
- (a) notification that the application for a warrant has been made;
- (b) the time at which the application was made;
- (c) the time at which the application is to be heard;
- (d) the grounds on which further detention is sought.

A notice must also be provided each time an application is made to extend or further extend an existing warrant.

(b) Transfer of persons detained for more than 14 days to prison

14.5 *Not used.*
14.6 *Not used.*
14.7 *Not used.*
14.8 *Not used.*
14.9 *Not used.*
14.10 *Not used.*

(c) Documentation

14.11 It is the responsibility of the officer who gives any reminders as at *paragraph 14.4*, to ensure that these are noted in the custody record, as well any comments made by the detained person upon being told of those rights.

14.12 The grounds for, and extent of, any delay in conducting a review shall be recorded.

14.13 Any written representations shall be retained.

14.14 A record shall be made as soon as practicable about the outcome of each review and, if applicable, the grounds on which the review officer authorises continued detention. A record shall also be made as soon as practicable about the outcome of an application for a warrant of further detention or its extension.

14.15 *Not used.*

Notes for Guidance

14A *TACT Schedule 8 Part II sets out the procedures for review of detention up to 48 hours from the time of arrest under TACT section 41 (or if a person was being detained under TACT Schedule 7, from the time at which the examination under Schedule 7 began). These include provisions for the requirement to review detention, postponing a review, grounds for continued detention, designating a review officer, representations, rights of the detained person and keeping a record. The review officer's role ends after a warrant has been issued for extension of detention under Part III of Schedule 8.*

14B *A review officer may authorise a person's continued detention if satisfied that detention is necessary:*
   (a) *to obtain relevant evidence whether by questioning the person or otherwise;*
   (b) *to preserve relevant evidence;*
   (c) *while awaiting the result of an examination or analysis of relevant evidence;*
   (d) *for the examination or analysis of anything with a view to obtaining relevant evidence;*
   (e) *pending a decision to apply to the Secretary of State for a deportation notice to be served on the detainee, the making of any such application, or the consideration of any such application by the Secretary of State;*
   (f) *pending a decision to charge the detainee with an offence.*

14C *Applications for warrants to extend detention beyond 48 hours, may be made for periods of 7 days at a time (initially under TACT Schedule 8 paragraph 29, and extensions thereafter under TACT Schedule 8, paragraph 36), up to a maximum period of 14 days (or 28 days if the Detention of Terrorists Suspects (Temporary Extension) Bill) is enacted and in force) from the time of their arrest (or if they were being detained under TACT Schedule 7, from the time at which their examination under Schedule 7 began). Applications may be made for shorter periods than 7 days, which must be specified. The judicial authority or High Court judge may also substitute a shorter period if they feel a period of 7 days is inappropriate.*

14D *Unless Note 14F applies, applications for warrants that would take the total period of detention up to 14 days or less should be made to a judicial authority, meaning a District Judge (Magistrates' Court) designated by the Lord Chief Justice to hear such applications.*

14E *If by virtue of the relevant provisions described in Note 14C being enacted the maximum period of detention is extended to 28 days, any application for a warrant which would take the period of detention beyond 14 days from the time of arrest (or if a person was being detained under TACT Schedule 7, from the time at which the examination under Schedule 7 began), must be made to a High Court Judge.*

14F *If, when the Detention of Terrorists Suspects (Temporary Extension) Bill is enacted and in force, an application is made to a High Court judge for a warrant which would take detention beyond 14 days and the High Court judge instead issues a warrant for a period of time which would not take detention beyond 14 days, further applications for extension of detention must also be made to a High Court judge, regardless of the period of time to which they refer.*

14G *Not used.*

14H *An officer applying for an order under TACT Schedule 8 paragraph 34 to withhold specified information on which they intend to rely when applying for a warrant of further detention or the extension or further extension of such a warrant, may make the application for the order orally or in writing. The most appropriate method of application will depend on the circumstances of the case and the need to ensure fairness to the detainee.*

14I *After hearing any representations by or on behalf of the detainee and the applicant, the judicial authority or High Court judge may direct that the hearing relating to the extension of detention under Part III of Schedule 8 is to take place using video conferencing facilities. However, if the judicial authority requires the detained person to be physically present at any hearing, this should be complied with as soon as practicable. Paragraph 33(4) to (9) of TACT Schedule 8 govern the hearing of applications via video-link or other means.*

14J *Not used.*

14K *Not used.*

15 Charging and post-charge questioning in terrorism cases

(a) Charging

15.1 Charging of detained persons is covered by PACE and guidance issued under PACE by the Director of Public Prosecutions. Decisions to charge persons to whom this Code (H) applies, the charging process and related matters are subject to section 16 of PACE Code C.

(b) Post-charge questioning

15.2 Under section 22 of the Counter-Terrorism Act 2008, a judge of the Crown Court may authorise the questioning of a person about an offence for which they have been charged, informed that they may be prosecuted or sent for trial, if the offence:
   - is a terrorism offence as set out in section 27 of the Counter-Terrorism Act 2008; or
   - is an offence which appears to the judge to have a terrorist connection. See *Note 15C*.

The decision on whether to apply for such questioning will be based on the needs of the investigation. There is no power to detain a person solely for the purposes of post-charge questioning. A person can only be detained whilst being so questioned (whether at a police station or in prison) if they are already there in lawful custody under some existing power. If at a police station the contents of *sections 8* and *9* of this Code must be considered the minimum standards of treatment for such detainees.

15.3 The Crown Court judge may authorise the questioning if they are satisfied that:
   - further questioning is necessary in the interests of justice;
   - the investigation for the purposes of which the further questioning is being proposed is being conducted diligently and expeditiously; and
   - the questioning would not interfere unduly with the preparation of the person's defence to the charge or any other criminal charge that they may be facing.

See Note 15E

15.4 The judge authorising questioning may specify the location of the questioning.

15.5 The judge may only authorise a period up to a maximum of 48 hours before further authorisation must be sought. The 48 hour period would run continuously from the commencement of questioning. This period must include breaks in questioning in accordance with *paragraphs 8.6* and *12.2* of this Code (see *Note 15B*).

15.6 Nothing in this Code shall be taken to prevent a suspect seeking a voluntary interview with the police at any time.

15.7 For the purposes of this section, any reference in *sections 6, 10, 11, 12* and *13* of this Code to:
   - 'suspect' means the person in respect of whom an authorisation has been given under section 22 of the Counter-Terrorism Act 2008 (post-charge questioning of terrorist suspects) to interview them;
   - 'interview' means post-charge questioning authorised under section 22 of the Counter-Terrorism Act 2008;
   - 'offence' means an offence for which the person has been charged, informed that they may be prosecuted or sent for trial and about which the person is being questioned; and
   - 'place of detention' means the location of the questioning specified by the judge (see *paragraph 15.4*), and the provisions of those sections apply (as appropriate), to such questioning (whether at a police station or in prison) subject to the further modifications in the following paragraphs:

Right to legal advice

15.8 In *section 6* of this Code, for the purposes of post-charge questioning:
   - access to a solicitor may not be delayed under *Annex B*; and
   - *paragraph 6.5* (direction that a detainee may only consult a solicitor within the sight and hearing of a qualified officer) does not apply.

Cautions

15.9 In *section 10* of this Code, unless the restriction on drawing adverse inferences from silence applies (see paragraph 15.10), for the purposes of post-charge questioning, the caution must be given in the following terms before any such questions are asked:

'You do not have to say anything. But it may harm your defence if you do not mention when questioned something which you later rely on in Court. Anything you do say may be given in evidence.'

Where the use of the Welsh Language is appropriate, a constable may provide the caution directly in Welsh in the following terms:

'Does dim rhaid i chi ddweud dim byd. Ond gall niweidio eich amddiffyniad os na fyddwch chi'n sôn, wrth gael eich holi, am rywbeth y byddwch chi'n dibynnu arno nes ymlaen yn y Llys. Gall unrhyw beth yr ydych yn ei ddweud gael ei roi fel tystiolaeth.'

15.10 The only restriction on drawing adverse inferences from silence, see *Annex C*, applies in those situations where a person has asked for legal advice and is questioned before receiving such advice in accordance with *paragraph 6.7(b)*.

Interviews

15.11 In *section 11*, for the purposes of post-charge questioning, whenever a person is questioned, they must be informed of the offence for which they have been charged or informed that they may be prosecuted, or that they have been sent for trial and about which they are being questioned.

15.12 *Paragraph 11.2* (place where questioning may take place) does not apply to post-charge questioning.

Recording post-charge questioning

15.13 All interviews must be video recorded with sound in accordance with the separate Code of Practice issued under section 25 of the Counter-Terrorism Act 2008 for the video recording with sound of post-charge questioning authorised under section 22 of the Counter-Terrorism Act 2008 (see *paragraph 11.8*).

Notes for Guidance

15A *If a person is detained at a police station for the purposes of post-charge questioning, a custody record must be opened in accordance with section 2 of this Code. The custody record must note the power under which the person is being detained, the time at which the person was transferred into police custody, their time of arrival at the police station and their time of being presented to the custody officer.*

15B *The custody record must note the time at which the interview process commences. This shall be regarded as the relevant time for any period of questioning in accordance with paragraph 15.5 of this Code.*

15C *Where reference is made to 'terrorist connection' in paragraph 15.2, this is determined in accordance with section 30 of the Counter-Terrorism Act 2008. Under section 30 of that Act a court must in certain circumstances determine whether an offence has a terrorist connection. These are offences under general criminal law which may be prosecuted in terrorism cases (for example explosives-related offences and conspiracy to murder). An offence has a terrorist connection if the offence is, or takes place in the course of, an act of terrorism or is committed for the purposes of terrorism (section 98 of the Act). Normally the court will make the determination during the sentencing process, however for the purposes of post-charge questioning, a Crown Court Judge must determine whether the offence could have a terrorist connection.*

15D *The powers under section 22 of the Counter-Terrorism Act 2008 are separate from and additional to the normal questioning procedures within this code. Their overall purpose is to enable the further questioning of a terrorist suspect after charge. They should not therefore be used to replace or circumvent the normal powers for dealing with routine questioning.*

15E *Post-charge questioning has been created because it is acknowledged that terrorist investigations can be large and complex and that a great deal of evidence can come to light following the charge of a terrorism suspect. This can occur, for instance, from the translation of material or as the result of additional investigation. When considering an application for post-charge questioning, the police must 'satisfy' the judge on all three points under paragraph 15.3. This means that the judge will either authorise or refuse an application on the balance of whether the conditions in paragraph 15.3 are all met. It is important therefore, that when making the application, to consider the following questions:*
- *What further evidence is the questioning expected to provide?*
- *Why was it not possible to obtain this evidence before charge?*
- *How and why was the need to question after charge first recognised?*

- *How is the questioning expected to contribute further to the case?*
- *To what extent could the time and place for further questioning interfere with the preparation of the person's defence (for example if authorisation is sought close to the time of a trial)?*
- *What steps will be taken to minimise any risk that questioning might interfere with the preparation of the person's defence?*

This list is not exhaustive but outlines the type of questions that could be relevant to any asked by a judge in considering an application.

16 Testing persons for the presence of specified Class A drugs

16.1 The provisions for drug testing under section 63B of PACE (as amended by section 5 of the Criminal Justice Act 2003 and section 7 of the Drugs Act 2005), do not apply to persons to whom this Code applies. Guidance on these provisions can be found in section 17 of PACE Code C.

Annex A Intimate and Strip Searches

A Intimate search

1. An intimate search consists of the physical examination of a person's body orifices other than the mouth. The intrusive nature of such searches means the actual and potential risks associated with intimate searches must never be underestimated.

(a) Action

2. Body orifices other than the mouth may be searched if authorised by an officer of inspector rank or above who has reasonable grounds for believing that the person may have concealed on themselves anything which they could and might use to cause physical injury to themselves or others at the station and the officer has reasonable grounds for believing that an intimate search is the only means of removing those items.
3. Before the search begins, a police officer or designated detention officer, must tell the detainee:
    (a) that the authority to carry out the search has been given;
    (b) the grounds for giving the authorisation and for believing that the article cannot be removed without an intimate search.
4. An intimate search may only be carried out by a registered medical practitioner or registered nurse, unless an officer of at least inspector rank considers this is not practicable, in which case a police officer may carry out the search. See Notes A1 to A5.
5. Any proposal for a search under paragraph 2 to be carried out by someone other than a registered medical practitioner or registered nurse must only be considered as a last resort and when the authorising officer is satisfied the risks associated with allowing the item to remain with the detainee outweigh the risks associated with removing it. See Notes A1 to A5.
6. An intimate search at a police station of a juvenile or a vulnerable person may take place only in the presence of an appropriate adult of the same sex (see Annex L), unless the detainee specifically requests a particular adult of the opposite sex who is readily available. In the case of a juvenile the search may take place in the absence of the appropriate adult only if the juvenile signifies in the presence of the appropriate adult they do not want the adult present during the search and the adult agrees. A record shall be made of the juvenile's decision and signed by the appropriate adult.
7. When an intimate search under paragraph 2 is carried out by a police officer, the officer must be of the same sex as the detainee (see Annex L). A minimum of two people, other than the detainee, must be present during the search. Subject to paragraph 6, no person of the opposite sex who is not a medical practitioner or nurse shall be present, nor shall anyone whose presence is unnecessary. The search shall be conducted with proper regard to the dignity, sensitivity and vulnerability of the detainee including in particular, their health, hygiene and welfare needs to which paragraphs 9.4A and 9.4B apply.

(b) Documentation

8. In the case of an intimate search under paragraph 2, the following shall be recorded as soon as practicable, in the detainee's custody record:

- the authorisation to carry out the search;
- the grounds for giving the authorisation;
- the grounds for believing the article could not be removed without an intimate search;
- which parts of the detainee's body were searched;
- who carried out the search;
- who was present;
- the result.

9.   If an intimate search is carried out by a police officer, the reason why it was impracticable for a registered medical practitioner or registered nurse to conduct it must be recorded.

B Strip search

10.   A strip search is a search involving the removal of more than outer clothing. In this Code, outer clothing includes shoes and socks.

(a) Action

11.   A strip search may take place only if it is considered necessary to remove an article which a detainee would not be allowed to keep, and the officer reasonably considers the detainee might have concealed such an article. Strip searches shall not be routinely carried out if there is no reason to consider that articles are concealed. The conduct of strip searches.

12.   When strip searches are conducted:
   (a)   a police officer carrying out a strip search must be the same sex as the detainee (see Annex I);
   (b)   the search shall take place in an area where the detainee cannot be seen by anyone who does not need to be present, nor by a member of the opposite sex (see Annex I) except an appropriate adult who has been specifically requested by the detainee;
   (c)   except in cases of urgency, where there is risk of serious harm to the detainee or to others, whenever a strip search involves exposure of intimate body parts, there must be at least two people present other than the detainee, and if the search is of a juvenile or a vulnerable person, one of the people must be the appropriate adult. Except in urgent cases as above, a search of a juvenile may take place in the absence of the appropriate adult only if the juvenile signifies in the presence of the appropriate adult that they do not want the adult to be present during the search and the adult agrees. A record shall be made of the juvenile's decision and signed by the appropriate adult. The presence of more than two people, other than an appropriate adult, shall be permitted only in the most exceptional circumstances;
   (d)   the search shall be conducted with proper regard to the dignity, sensitivity and vulnerability of the detainee in these circumstances including in particular, their health, hygiene and welfare needs to which paragraphs 9.4A and 9.4B apply. Every reasonable effort shall be made to secure the detainee's co-operation, maintain their dignity and minimise embarrassment. Detainees who are searched shall not normally be required to remove all their clothes at the same time, e.g. a person should be allowed to remove clothing above the waist and redress before removing further clothing;
   (e)   if necessary to assist the search, the detainee may be required to hold their arms in the air or to stand with their legs apart and bend forward so a visual examination may be made of the genital and anal areas provided no physical contact is made with any body orifice;
   (f)   if articles are found, the detainee shall be asked to hand them over. If articles are found within any body orifice other than the mouth, and the detainee refuses to hand them over, their removal would constitute an intimate search, which must be carried out as in Part A;
   (g)   a strip search shall be conducted as quickly as possible, and the detainee allowed to dress as soon as the procedure is complete.

(b) Documentation

13.   A record shall be made on the custody record of a strip search including the reason it was considered necessary, those present and any result.

Notes for Guidance

A1   Before authorising any intimate search, the authorising officer must make every reasonable effort to persuade the detainee to hand the article over without a search. If the detainee agrees, a registered medical practitioner or registered nurse should whenever possible be asked to assess the risks involved and, if necessary, attend to assist the detainee.

A2   If the detainee does not agree to hand the article over without a search, the authorising officer must carefully review all the relevant factors before authorising an intimate search. In particular, the officer must consider whether the grounds for believing an article may be concealed are reasonable.

A3   If authority is given for a search under paragraph 2, a registered medical practitioner or registered nurse shall be consulted whenever possible. The presumption should be that the search will be conducted by the registered medical practitioner or registered nurse and the authorising officer must make every reasonable effort to persuade the detainee to allow the medical practitioner or nurse to conduct the search.

A4   A constable should only be authorised to carry out a search as a last resort and when all other approaches have failed. In these circumstances, the authorising officer must be satisfied the detainee might use the article for one or more of the purposes in paragraph 2 and the physical injury likely to be caused is sufficiently severe to justify authorising a constable to carry out the search.

A5   If an officer has any doubts whether to authorise an intimate search by a constable, the officer should seek advice from an officer of superintendent rank or above.

Annex B—Delay in Notifying Arrest or Allowing Access to Legal Advice for Persons Detained under the Terrorism Act 2000

A DELAYS under TACT Schedule 8

1.   The rights as in *sections 5* or *6*, may be delayed if the person is detained under the Terrorism Act 2000, section 41, has not yet been charged with an offence and an officer of superintendent rank or above has reasonable grounds for believing the exercise of either right will have one of the following consequences:
      (a)   interference with or harm to evidence of a serious offence,
      (b)   interference with or physical injury to any person,
      (c)   the alerting of persons who are suspected of having committed a serious offence but who have not been arrested for it,
      (d)   the hindering of the recovery of property obtained as a result of a serious offence or in respect of which a forfeiture order could be made under section 23,
      (e)   interference with the gathering of information about the commission, preparation or instigation of acts of terrorism,
      (f)   the alerting of a person and thereby making it more difficult to prevent an act of terrorism, or
      (g)   the alerting of a person and thereby making it more difficult to secure a person's apprehension, prosecution or conviction in connection with the commission, preparation or instigation of an act of terrorism.

2.   These rights may also be delayed if the officer has reasonable grounds for believing that:
      (a)   the detained person has benefited from his criminal conduct (to be decided in accordance with Part 2 of the Proceeds of Crime Act 2002), and
      (b)   the recovery of the value of the property constituting the benefit will be hindered by—
            (i)   informing the named person of the detained person's detention (in the case of an authorisation under paragraph 8(1)(a) of Schedule 8 to TACT), or
            (ii)   the exercise of the right under paragraph 7 (in the case of an authorisation under paragraph 8(1)(b) of Schedule 8 to TACT).

3.   Authority to delay a detainee's right to consult privately with a solicitor may be given only if the authorising officer has reasonable grounds to believe the solicitor the detainee wants to consult will, inadvertently or otherwise, pass on a message from the detainee or act in some other way which will have any of the consequences specified under paragraph 8 of Schedule 8 to the Terrorism Act 2000. In these circumstances, the detainee must be allowed to choose another solicitor. See *Note B3*.

4.   If the detainee wishes to see a solicitor, access to that solicitor may not be delayed on the grounds they might advise the detainee not to answer questions or the solicitor was initially asked to attend the police station by someone else. In the latter case the detainee must be told the solicitor has come to the police station at another person's request, and must be asked to sign the custody record to signify whether they want to see the solicitor.

5.   The fact the grounds for delaying notification of arrest may be satisfied does not automatically mean the grounds for delaying access to legal advice will also be satisfied.

6.   These rights may be delayed only for as long as is necessary but not beyond 48 hours from the time of arrest (or if a person was being detained under TACT Schedule 7, from the time at which the examination under Schedule 7 began). If the above grounds cease to apply within this time the detainee must as soon

as practicable be asked if they wish to exercise either right, the custody record noted accordingly, and action taken in accordance with the relevant section of this Code.

7. A person must be allowed to consult a solicitor for a reasonable time before any court hearing.

B Documentation

8. The grounds for action under this Annex shall be recorded and the detainee informed of them as soon as practicable.

9. Any reply given by a detainee under *paragraph 6* must be recorded and the detainee asked to endorse the record in relation to whether they want to receive legal advice at this point.

C Cautions and special warnings

10. When a suspect detained at a police station is interviewed during any period for which access to legal advice has been delayed under this Annex, the court or jury may not draw adverse inferences from their silence.

Notes for Guidance

B1 *Even if Annex B applies in the case of a juvenile, or a vulnerable person, action to inform the appropriate adult and the person responsible for a juvenile's welfare, if that is a different person, must nevertheless be taken as in paragraph 3.15 and 3.17.*

B2 *In the case of Commonwealth citizens and foreign nationals, see Note 7A.*

B3 *A decision to delay access to a specific solicitor is likely to be a rare occurrence and only when it can be shown the suspect is capable of misleading that particular solicitor and there is more than a substantial risk that the suspect will succeed in causing information to be conveyed which will lead to one or more of the specified consequences.*

Annex J—Transfer of Persons Detained for more than 14 Days to Prison

1. When a warrant of further detention is extended or further extended by a High Court judge to authorise a person's detention beyond a period of 14 days from the time of their arrest (or if they were being detained under TACT Schedule 7, from the time at which their examination under Schedule 7 began), the person must be transferred from detention in a police station to detention in a designated prison as soon as is practicable after the warrant is issued, unless:
    (a) the detainee specifically requests to remain in detention at a police station and that request can be accommodated, or
    (b) there are reasonable grounds to believe that transferring the detainee to a prison would:
        (i) significantly hinder a terrorism investigation;
        (ii) delay charging of the detainee or their release from custody, or
        (iii) otherwise prevent the investigation from being conducted diligently and expeditiously.
    Any grounds in (b)(i) to (iii) above which are relied upon for not transferring the detainee to prison must be presented to the senior judge as part of the application for the extension or further extension of the warrant. See *Note J1*.

2. If at any time during which a person remains in detention at a police station under the warrant, the grounds at (b)(i) to (iii) cease to apply, the person must be transferred to a prison as soon as practicable.

3. Police should maintain an agreement with the National Offender Management Service (NOMS) that stipulates named prisons to which individuals may be transferred under this paragraph. This should be made with regard to ensuring detainees are moved to the most suitable prison for the purposes of the investigation and their welfare, and should include provision for the transfer of male, female and juvenile detainees. Police should ensure that the Governor of a prison to which they intend to transfer a detainee is given reasonable notice of this. Where practicable, this should be no later than the point at which a warrant is applied for that would take the period of detention beyond 14 days.

4. Following a detainee's transfer to a designated prison, their detention will be governed by the terms of Schedule 8 to TACT 2000 and the Prison Rules and this Code of Practice will not apply during any period that the person remains in prison detention. The Code will once more apply if the person is transferred back from prison detention to police detention. In order to enable the Governor to arrange for the production of the detainee back into police custody, police should give notice to the Governor of the relevant prison as soon as possible of any decision to transfer a detainee from prison back to a police station. Any transfer between a prison and a police station should be conducted by police and this Code will be applicable during the period of transit. *See Note 2J.* A detainee should only remain in police custody having been transferred back from a prison, for as long as is necessary for the purpose of the investigation.

5. The investigating team and custody officer should provide as much information as necessary to enable the relevant prison authorities to provide appropriate facilities to detain an individual. This should include, but not be limited to:

    (i)   medical assessments
    (ii) security and risk assessments
    (iii) details of the detained person's legal representatives
    (iv) details of any individuals from whom the detained person has requested visits, or who have requested to visit the detained person.

6. Where a detainee is to be transferred to prison, the custody officer should inform the detainee's legal adviser beforehand that the transfer is to take place (including the name of the prison). The custody officer should also make all reasonable attempts to inform:

    • family or friends who have been informed previously of the detainee's detention; and
    • the person who was initially informed of the detainee's detention in accordance with *paragraph 5.1.*

7. Any decision not to transfer a detained person to a designated prison under paragraph 1, must be recorded, along with the reasons for this decision. If a request under paragraph *1(a)* is not accommodated, the reasons for this should also be recorded.

Notes for Guidance

J1   *Transfer to prison is intended to ensure that individuals who are detained for extended periods of time are held in a place designed for longer periods of detention than police stations. Prison will provide detainees with a greater range of facilities more appropriate to longer detention periods.*

J2   *This Code will only apply as is appropriate to the conditions of detention during the period of transit. There is obviously no requirement to provide such things as bed linen or reading materials for the journey between prison and police station.*

Annex K

The documents considered essential for the purposes of this Code and for which (subject to paragraphs 3 to 7) written translations must be created are the records made in accordance with this Code of the grounds and reasons for any authorisation of a suspects detention under the provisions of the Terrorism Act 2000 or the Counter Terrorism Act 2008 (post charge questioning) to which this Code applies as they are described and referred to in the suspect's custody record. Translations should be created as soon as practicable after the authorisation has been recorded and provided as soon as practicable thereafter, whilst the person is detained or after they have been released.

Index

A

abduction of children 2.9.2–2.9.2.4
  child arrangements orders (CAOs) 2.9.2.1
  connected with child, persons who
    are 2.9.2.1–2.9.2.2
  consent 2.9.2.1–2.9.2.2
  defences 2.9.2.2, 2.9.2.4
  kidnapping 2.9.2.1
  not connected with child, persons who
    are 2.9.2.3–2.9.2.4
  special guardians 2.9.2.1, 2.9.2.2
  UK, taking or sending child out
    of 2.9.2.1–2.9.2.2
absconding 1.10.9–1.10.10
abuse of position
  fraud, by 3.8.1–3.8.2
  trust, of 4.4.10
accessories 1.2.8–1.2.8.2
  actus reus 1.2.8–1.2.8.2
  aiding, abetting, counselling or
    procuring 1.2.8, 1.2.9
  causal links 1.2.8
  definition 2.3.2.1
  encouragement 1.2.8, 1.2.8.2
  firearms and gun crime 2.3.2.1
  foreseeability 1.2.8.2
  joint enterprise 1.2.8.2
  mens rea 1.1.11, 1.2.8–1.2.8.2
  parasitic accessory liability 1.2.8.2
  principals 1.2.8–1.2.8.1
  withdrawal 1.2.8
actual bodily harm (ABH), assault
  occasioning 2.7.13
actus reus **(criminal conduct)** 1.2.1–1.2.10
  accessories 1.2.8–1.2.8.2
  automatism 1.2.2, 1.2.3
  coincidence with *mens rea* 1.2.4
  corporate liability 1.2.9
  facts in issue 1.5.3
  handling stolen goods 3.7.3
  intervening acts 1.2.7
  omissions 1.2.5
  vicarious liability 1.2.10
  voluntary acts 1.2.2, 1.2.3
administering a substance with
  intent 4.7.1
adverse inferences from
  silence 1.9.5–1.9.5.1
  audio recordings of interviews 1.9.7
  cautions 1.9.2.3
  failure to mention facts 1.9.2.3
  interviews 1.9.2.4–1.9.2.6, 1.9.4.3, 1.9.5–
    1.9.5.1, 1.9.6–1.9.6.1
  restrictions 1.9.5–1.9.5.1
  special warnings 1.9.2.4–1.9.2.6
  terrorism offences 1.9.2.3
aggravated offences *see also* **racially and**
  religiously aggravated offences
  assault 2.7.12
  burglary 3.5–3.5.2
  criminal damage 3.10.3–3.10.7
  drugs, supply of 2.2.4.2
  firearms and gun crime 2.3.4.2
  vehicle-taking 3.6.9–3.6.9.1

aiding, abetting, counselling or
  procuring 1.2.8, 1.2.9, 1.3.3.1,
    2.8.4.7, 4.2.1, 4.4.1
air weapons 2.3.8.4 2.3.10–2.3.10.1
  airsoft guns 2.3.2.1
  antiques 2.3.10.1
  beyond premises, firing 2.3.10.1
  definition 2.3.10
  minors from having weapons, failing to
    prevent 2.3.10.1
  sales face to face 2.3.10.1
  specially dangerous weapons 2.3.10
aircraft *see* **ships and aircraft**
alibis 1.11.11.2
ammunition
  definition 2.3.2.3
  list 2.3.8.1
  possession 2.3.4.2, 2.3.8.2, 2.3.14
  section 1 firearms 2.3.4.3
animals
  criminal damage 3.10.2.2
  firearms and gun crime 2.3.8.4
  harassment by animal rights
    protestors 2.8.4.4, 2.8.4.10 2.8.4.13,
    2.8.7
  humane killing 2.3.8.4
  slaughterers 2.3.8.4
  treatment or tranquilising, use of weapons
    for 2.3.8.4
  vermin, shot pistols for 2.3.8.4
  wild creatures 3.1.6, 3.10.2.2
anonymity 4.1.2
appropriate adult
  absence of appropriate adult, commencing
    interviews in 1.9.3.1
  audio recordings of
    interviews 1.9.8–1.9.9.1
  charges 1.7.17–1.7.17.1
  conditions of detention 1.7.12.1
  custody records 1.7.13.2
  delays 1.7.5.1
  drink or drugs, persons under influence
    of 1.7.5.3
  drug tests 1.7.18.1
  identification procedures 1.8.3–1.8.3.1,
    1.8.9–1.8.10
  independence 1.7.5.4
  interpreters 1.7.28
  intimate searches 1.7.19
  juveniles 1.7.5.4–1.7.5.5, 1.7.7, 1.7.17–
    1.7.17.1, 1.7.19–1.7.21.1, 1.8.3.1,
    1.9.3.2
  leave the room, requirement
    to 1.9.3.2–1.9.3.3
  legal advice, right to 1.7.10–1.7.10.1,
    1.7.21
  live links 1.7.28–1.7.28.1, 1.9.4, 1.9.4.4
  mental health conditions/mental
    disabilities, persons with 1.7.5.3,
    1.7.7
  MHA patients 1.7.7
  notice 1.7.7
  reviews of detention 1.7.16.13
  samples 1.8.7.3–1.8.7.4
  special groups 1.7.5.5

  visual recording of
    interviews 1.9.13–1.9.13.1
  vulnerable persons 1.7.5.3–1.7.5.5, 1.7.7,
    1.7.21–1.7.21.1
  welfare of appropriate adult 1.7.5.4
arrest
  assault with intent to resist arrest 2.7.16
  bail 1.7.7.1, 1.10.2.6, 1.10.3.3
  cross-border powers 1.7.16.12
  custody officers 1.7.7.1
  customs and excise management 6.1.2.6
  defence of lawful arrest 1.4.5–1.4.5.2
  delays in notification 1.7.20–1.7.20.1
  deportation/removal, failure to cooperate
    with 5.3.2.2
  detention of people under arrest 1.7.7.1
  entry and search, powers of 1.6.5–1.6.5.2,
    5.1.3.7–5.1.3.8
  false imprisonment 2.10.1
  fingerprints 1.8.5–1.8.5.1
  firearms to resist arrest, use
    of 2.3.11.3–2.3.11.4
  forced marriages 5.8.4.2
  grounds 1.7.7.1
  harassment 2.8.4.11
  immigration enforcement 5.1.3.1–5.1.3.3,
    5.1.3.7–5.1.3.8, 5.1.3.11, 5.3.2.2
  indictable offences 1.6.5.1, 1.6.5.3
  injunctions 2.8.4.11
  life, right to 1.4.5–1.4.5.2
  Northern Ireland, offences committed
    in 1.7.16.12
  photographs, identification
    through 1.8.6.1
  public, by members of the 2.7.16
  re-arrest 1.7.16.12, 1.10.2.3
  release of persons arrested 1.10.1–1.10.11
  resisting arrest 1.4.2, 2.3.11.3–2.3.11.4,
    2.7.16
  Scotland 1.7.16.12, 1.9.14
  searches 5.1.3.3, 5.1.3.7–5.1.3.8, 5.1.3.11
  terrorism 2.4.6.1
  voluntary attendance at the police
    station 1.7.7
  warrants 1.7.7.1, 2.4.6.1, 5.1.3.1–5.1.3.3,
    5.3.2.2
arson 3.10.4
artist's composites 1.8.4.2, 1.8.4.7, 1.8.12
assault 2.7.2–2.7.13, 2.7.17
  actual bodily harm (ABH),
    occasioning 2.7.13
  aggravated assault 2.7.12
  arrest, with intent to 2.7.16
  battery or assault 2.7.4
  child protection 2.9.3
  common assault 2.7.4, 2.7.9, 2.7.11,
    2.7.16
  conditional threats 2.7.2.4
  designated officers 6.3.3, 6.3.3.2, 6.3.3.3
  emails or text messages 2.7.2.3
  emergency workers, assaults on 2.7.12
  fear 2.7.2.1
  immediate unlawful violence,
    apprehension of 2.7.2–2.7.2.2
  immigration enforcement 5.5.2